⟶ *American Foreign Policy in the Nuclear Age*

AMERICAN FOREIGN POLICY

IN THE NUCLEAR AGE →

second edition

CECIL V. CRABB, Jr.   *Vassar College*

Harper & Row, Publishers   *New York, Evanston, and London*

LIBRARY OF CONGRESS CATALOG CARD NUMBER: 65–11132

B-P

CONTENTS ➡

Preface   vii
Acknowledgments   ix

1. FOUNDATIONS OF AMERICAN FOREIGN POLICY   1

The Nature of Foreign Policy Goals   1
The Means of Foreign Policy   5
The Ingredients of American Power   7

2. AMERICA LOOKS AT THE WORLD —A Study in National Character   21

American Attitudes Toward Power   23
Moralism: The Shadow   27
Morality: The Substance   30
Isolationism in Word and Deed   34
The Theme of Progress and Hope   37

3. THE PRESIDENT, THE DEPARTMENT OF STATE, AND AMERICAN FOREIGN POLICY   42

The President's Constitutional Powers   43
Historical-Traditional Techniques of Presidential Leadership   48
The President's Emergency Powers   51
The Department of State: Its Function and Organization   53
The Foreign Service   57

4. THE MILITARY ESTABLISHMENT AND OTHER EXECUTIVE AGENCIES   66

The Military and American Foreign Policy   66
The National Defense Establishment   68
Continuing Problems in National Security Policy   72
Other Executive Agencies and Foreign Affairs   80

5. THE ROLE OF CONGRESS IN FOREIGN RELATIONS   91

Constitutional Powers of Congress over Foreign Relations   92
Extraconstitutional and Informal Techniques   104

6. EXECUTIVE-LEGISLATIVE RELATIONS AND BIPARTISANSHIP   112

Bipartisan Techniques and Procedures   114
Barriers to Unity   118

7. PUBLIC OPINION AND DECISION-MAKING   129

The Anatomy of Public Opinion   129
Public Opinion and Public Policy: Action and Reaction   132
Minorities, Interest Groups, and Sectionalism   137

8. THE COLD WAR IN HISTORICAL PERSPECTIVE   152

Enduring Goals of Russian Foreign Policy   152
Russian-American Relations Before World War II   158

9. ELEMENTS OF THE COLD WAR   166

The Ideological Front   166
The Strategic-Geopolitical Front   178
The Economic-Military Front   182

10. WESTERN EUROPE—The New World and the Old   194

Containment, Recovery, and Rearmament   197
European Economic Integration   201
NATO: Soviet Challenge and Western Response   209

Political Unification in the North
Atlantic Area   220

11. THE MIDDLE EAST AND AFRICA
—The Diplomacy of Emerging
Societies   227
The Arab-Israeli Conflict   227
Strategic-Military Problems in the
Middle East   232
The West and Arab Nationalism   236
The Awakening of Africa   245
Major Issues in Afro-American
Relations   247

12. THE WESTERN HEMISPHERE
—Vicissitudes of the Good
Neighbor Policy   264
Hemispheric Security and Solidarity   265
Problems of Hemispheric Trade
and Aid   279
Communism in Latin America   287

13. ASIA—New Nations and Ancient
Problems   299
The United States and Communist
China   302
The Challenge of Asian National-
ism and Neutralism   314
Defense and Security in the Pacific   327

14. PSYCHOLOGICAL WARFARE
—Logomachy at Midcentury   338
Psychological Warfare: Its
Nature and Uses   338
The Communist Ideological
Offensive   342

The American "Campaign of
Truth"   346

15. FOREIGN ECONOMIC POLICY
—The World's Creditor on Trial   358
American Tariff and Trade Policies   360
The Future of Foreign Aid   371
The Balance-of-Payments Deficit
and Other Foreign Economic
Problems   385

16. THE QUEST FOR WORLD PEACE
AND SECURITY   393
International Organization Before
World War II   393
The UN and the Postwar World   399
The U.S. and the UN: Some
Persistent Issues   409

17. DISARMAMENT—Turning Swords
into Plowshares   422
Disarmament in Historical
Perspective   422
Persistent Issues in Disarmament
Negotiations   430
"Atoms for Peace"   443

18. THE GUIDING PRINCIPLES OF
AMERICAN FOREIGN POLICY   449
The Postwar Re-examination of
American Policy   450
Toward a Philosophy of Foreign
Affairs   457

Bibliography   471
Index   483

PREFACE →

Many significant events have occurred—both in the domestic and international setting of American foreign policy—since the first edition of this study appeared in 1960. Any attempt to evaluate the principles, problems, and prospects of America's relations with the outside world must always take into account the recent internal and external shifts in power and policy. We must seek to relate them to the broad stream of national diplomatic history and to the context within which decision making in foreign affairs occurs.

This text does not endeavor to focus upon "current events" or to provide simply an up-to-the-minute catalogue of issues affecting American interests in Western Europe, in the Arab world, or in Southeast Asia. Instead, it seeks to make contemporary events intelligible by providing a framework within which the formulation and execution of American foreign policy may be understood, and within which emergent trends in global affairs may be assessed in terms of their implications for the United States. As a teacher, one finds that any discussion of principles and problems is often more interesting and more relevant to students if it can focus upon fairly contemporary examples. Frequently, working backward from current issues to an examination of the historical evolution of policy, or an appraisal of its domestic setting, provides the most illuminating and engaging approach to the subject-matter.

The response of those who used this textbook in its first edition has encouraged me to believe that its basic structure and approach were sound. Accordingly, the emphasis in revision has been upon (1) deleting dated material to incorporate a discussion of important events and trends in national and international affairs since 1960; and (2) making the relationship between both old and new material in the field of American foreign policy more specifically pointed and relevant.

The following are a few of the changes embodied in this edition. Factual and statistical data on the sinews of American national power has been brought up-to-date with economic and other projections into the 1970s. In the discussion of the roles of the President, the State Department, military establishment, and other executive agencies, extensive reference was made to developments during the late Eisenhower, and the Kennedy-Johnson periods. The section on the State Department was completely rewritten utilizing heavily the findings of several recent studies focusing upon executive decision making. The role of the National Security Council and other executive "committees" in foreign relations has been examined extensively and critically. More current examples of Congress' role in foreign policy have been cited relying upon the results of several recent appraisals of legislative influence upon foreign policy. The chapter on the role of public opinion in foreign policy was substantially revised with the intention of taking into account recent studies of public opinion as a force in foreign relations. A significant addition is the discussion of the role and influence of lobbies representing foreign countries and interests.

In the latter part of the book—Chapters 8 through 18—even more extensive changes were made. The chapter dealing with ideological, strategic-geopolitical, and economic elements in the cold war was completely revised and brought up-to-date. Here considerable attention was given the Kremlin's concept of "peaceful co-existence" and its meaning for the United States. In the chapter on American relations with Western Europe the discussion centered around the evolution of the European Economic Community and other regional organizations, the Gaullist challenge to American foreign policy, and the disputes within NATO. The portion dealing with the Middle East and Africa was rewritten. Innovations include appraisals of Arab and African "neutralism" and their implications for the United States, a discussion of the meaning and significance of "African socialism," and an evaluation of the waning of colonialism on the African scene. The discussion of Latin America in Chapter 12 focuses attention upon the evolution of the Alliance for Progress and the problems besetting that organization. The impact of "Castroism" upon relations between the United States and its southern neighbors is also taken up. The appraisal of America's relations with Asia (Chapter 13) was reorganized around three central themes; the problem of Red China, "Asian neutralism" and its meaning for America, and the issue of defense and security in Asia as exemplified by the conflict in South Vietnam.

The remaining chapters have been changed to include: an analysis of the new techniques in psychological warfare and propaganda, like the U.S. Information Agency and the Peace Corps; an evaluation of the Trade Expansion Act, American economic relations with the European Common Market, and the recurrent balance of payments problem; an assessment of the changing character of the United Nations, with particular reference to the role of the Afro-Asian countries in that organization; and an analysis of the developing prospects in great power negotiations over disarmament.

The Berlin and Southeast Asian crises, the internecine warfare on Cyprus, the rebellion in the Congo, the continuing Arab-Israeli dispute, the Gaullist challenge to American diplomatic leadership—these are but a few of the issues reminding us that American awareness of external events, the ability to think dispassionately about them, and the capacity to evolve effective responses are constantly being seriously tested. It has always been basic to the philosophy underlying our democracy that an informed and interested citizenry is indispensable to the successful pursuit of American global objectives and this fact has lost none of its pertinence with the passage of time. It has become incontestably clear during the period since World War II, when the United States finally shouldered its rightful position of global leadership, that foreign policy is an extraordinarily complex matter, requiring thorough and continuing study of the nature and implications of problems encountered in a rapidly changing external environment. America's rise to world power has entailed new responsibilities, not only for officials, but for citizens as well.

If the reader gains a better grasp of the factual material necessary for an understanding of America's relations with the international community, if he finds that his own thinking about the subject has been stimulated, and if, above all, he receives some incentive to delve more deeply into what are the transcendent problems of the age in which he lives, then this book will have largely fulfilled its purpose.

CECIL V. CRABB, JR.

Vassar College
February, 1965

ACKNOWLEDGMENTS ➞

The second edition of this book, fully as much as the first, is a product of my teaching and my continuing research in the field of American foreign policy and international relations at Vassar College.

The Faculty Committee on Research and the administration of Vassar College have generously provided financial assistance for research on portions of the book. Both the Ford Foundation (program of research on public affairs) and the Rockefeller Foundation granted me assistance for research on parts of the study, for which I am most grateful.

The comments, suggestions, and criticism of many friends and colleagues have been invaluable. Faculty members in other institutions have been kind enough to communicate their reactions to me. My own students at Vassar, along with students in other colleges and universities, have given me their candid reactions. All such comments have been carefully considered and utilized in planning revisions.

The staff of the Joint University Library on the campus of Vanderbilt University was generous and ingenious in assisting me in my research needs. As always, the staff of the Vassar College Library was most cooperative in providing all manner of aid.

The contribution of Mrs. Lester F. Tubby in providing professional typing assistance was indispensable in meeting publication deadlines.

Here, as in all my writing ventures, I owe an enormous debt to my extremely versatile wife, Harriet. Somehow, she was able to find time from her own full schedule to serve as editor and critic for portions of the manuscript. In addition, with exemplary grace and good humor, she endured the inconveniences and disruptions caused by a husband who "writes book." In all respects, she continues fully to merit the title of co-author.

My indebtedness to friends, colleagues, and family of course in no way diminishes my full and sole responsibility for the contents, including any errors of fact and judgment that may have found their way into this study.

I am most deeply indebted to my parents, to whom this book is fondly dedicated.

American Foreign Policy in the Nuclear Age

1 ➤ FOUNDATIONS OF

AMERICAN FOREIGN POLICY ➤

Reduced to its most fundamental ingredients, foreign policy consists of two elements: national objectives to be achieved and means for achieving them. The interaction between national goals and the resources for attaining them is the perennial subject of statecraft. In its ingredients the foreign policy of all nations, great and small, is the same.

To say that foreign policy consists essentially of ends and means, however, is a statement that misleads by its very simplicity. Its breadth does not reveal the obvious differences in national goals and the methods used by various countries for attaining them. No one can doubt, for instance, that the foreign policies of the United States and the Soviet Union today are at antipodes in many respects. Similarly, in recent history sharp divergencies have existed between the policies of Israel and the Arab states, India and Pakistan, China and Japan, Germany and France. Let us begin by looking at the goals of American foreign policy.

THE NATURE OF FOREIGN POLICY GOALS

The Pre-eminence of National Security

If self-preservation is the first law of nature, it is also the first law of foreign policy. Safeguarding the security of the nation is the foremost obligation of the statesman. As Nicholas J. Spykman phrased it:

Because territory is an inherent part of a state, self-preservation means defending its control over territory; and, because independence is of the essence of the state, self-

preservation also means fighting for independent status. This explains why the basic objective of the foreign policy of all states is the preservation of territorial integrity and political independence.[1]

Admittedly, this pre-eminent goal is seldom stated so baldly. For instance, Secretary of State Dean G. Acheson phrased it this way: "To build our strength so that the things we believe in can survive is the practical and vitally necessary expression in times of our moral dedication."[2] Secretary of State John Foster Dulles declared that "The broad goal of our foreign policy is to enable the people of the United States to enjoy, in peace, the blessings of liberty."[3] President John F. Kennedy believed that America's "basic goal" was to seek "a peaceful world community of free and independent states, free to choose their own future and their own system so long as it does not threaten the freedom of others."[4] However articulated, it is the same goal: preservation of the identity of the nation, which is a basic premise underlying the attainment of other foreign policy goals.

The reader needs to be cautioned that preservation of national security is by no means the *only* goal of statecraft. Nations may and do pursue a variety of goals of greater or lesser urgency. Often other goals may eclipse the centrality of the security issue in a nation's relations with the outside world. Moreover the term "national security" is not defined here, and no very satisfying definition of it can be given that would apply alike to all countries. Few concepts are at once so fundamental, and

1

yet so elusive, as this one. In common with many other ideas that must be dealt with in the study of foreign affairs, it is a relative concept. Its meaning for individual nations will be determined by numerous variables: history, geography, cultural traditions, strategy and tactics in war, the nature of the economic system, and public opinion, to list but a few of the major influences. Nations may be, and frequently in history have been, mistaken in their estimate of what constitutes security. Hitler, no doubt, believed that attacking Poland and France, and later Russia, would promote German security. His miscalculation had disastrous consequences for the German nation.

Security is one of those elastic terms like justice or equality or democracy. Almost every nation is in favor of it in the abstract, both for itself and generally for other nations. But nations disagree violently over what it means in concrete circumstances. So great may be the different conceptions of it that security for one country can mean disaster for another. For the Kremlin security might, and possibly does, mean nothing less than a communized world, directed from Moscow. For the United States it conceivably entails the eventual extinction of communism as a militant ideology and of Russia as a great power. Such examples suggest that attempts to achieve security can lead to a strange paradox: while security is the underlying foreign policy goal of every state, concrete efforts to achieve it are productive of endless *insecurity* throughout the international community as a whole.

Still another attribute of the security concept requires emphasis. A nation's conception of security is never static. It changes over the years—imperceptibly perhaps, even monthly and daily. The explosion of the first Soviet atomic bomb in 1949, for instance, revolutionized official American thinking about national security. By 1957 another major change in American ideas about security was necessitated by the success of the Soviet Union in launching its Sputnik by means of a powerful long-range guided missile. Security then is closely linked with technological progress. New inventions like the aircraft carrier and giant stratospheric bombers loaded with nuclear weapons contributed to the security of great sea and air powers like the United States and Britain. After their adversaries had gotten these weapons too, and an extensive sub-marine fleet and guided missiles besides, the balance of military power became more favorable to the sprawling land mass of the communist empire.

Pre-eminent as is the role played by security in foreign policy, it can be overstressed. Nations can and have manifested an almost pathological fixation with this goal, to the exclusion of other goals. The fate of Hitler's Third Reich, and the consequences of certain steps in Soviet foreign policy under Stalin and his successors, illustrate a kind of inverse law about national security: the more a narrowly conceived concept of security comes to actuate foreign policy, usurping other national goals, the more *insecure* the nation may ultimately become, after other nations also begin to take steps to safeguard their own well-being in the face of ominous threats by hostile neighbors.

For nations, as for individuals within nations, there is no such thing as absolute security. A measure of insecurity is inherent in life itself and may well be one basic force that spurs human progress. The eminent historian and one-time State Department official, George Kennan, notes that in international affairs "there is no security in a search for the absolute defense. Security lies in accepting the moderate risks in order that the immoderate ones may be avoided."[5]

Suppose it were possible for us to specify those conditions that would best promote the security of the United States, that would eliminate every possible threat to our national existence. What would those conditions be? Several ideas might occur to us. We might think that if only the threat of international communism were removed, the United States would achieve security. But upon reflection, we would remember that threats to our national existence arose long before communism became a powerful international force. We would conclude that our security would not automatically be guaranteed by eliminating the existing enemy.

Perhaps we might specify the triumph of democracy throughout the world. Wilsonian idealists believed that this would promote—some thought it would guarantee—international peace and justice. Yet we know that democratic countries, our own among them, can and do fight wars, and not always defensive wars. We think of the Mexican and Spanish-American wars in our own history. We recall the numerous colonial wars of Britain and France. We remember that Britain, France, and Israel invaded Egypt in 1956, that France carried out what amounted to a war of extermination against rebel groups in Algeria, and that India relied upon force to absorb the Portuguese colony of Goa. These examples should make us highly skeptical of the view that international peace will prevail after all countries have adopted democratic philosophies or forms of government.

Perhaps we might reluctantly propose a *Pax Americana*. If the entire world could be put under American hegemony, or if other countries could be persuaded to accept American "leadership" in world affairs, surely that would eliminate all threats to American security. Such a view would also most likely prove false. It is a commonplace of history that world empires generate their own internal tensions and ultimately disintegrate from within. The historian Arnold Toynbee has identified the "universal state" as one of the stages of a civilization in decay. Internal conflicts—we may conveniently call them civil wars or revolutions—can tear an empire to pieces. Conflicts are in fact generated by the very effort of a nation to extend its hegemony beyond a certain optimum point. No one knows exactly what this point is. It is reached when the nation can no longer effectively integrate and communicate with the territories under its jursidiction.

The American people have always had a peculiar propensity for believing that perfect or near-perfect security could be achieved. Yet it is difficult, if not impossible, for us even to imagine circumstances that are not productive of some insecurity for the nation. The concept of security thus reminds us of certain doctrines of the world's great religions, such as the obligation of Christian believers to strive for the sinless life. Statesmen know that perfect security is not possible, yet they must constantly strive to attain it by all the means at their command.

Lesser Goals of Foreign Policy

While security is the most fundamental goal of foreign policy, other goals may be more evident in the day-to-day conduct of international affairs. The relationship between a nation's contemporary foreign policy goals and security may not always be evident and direct.

Take the history of American postwar foreign relations. Both the Democratic and Republican parties have supported reciprocal trade with other countries. Technical assistance to underdeveloped countries has also received bipartisan support. So has economic aid, cultural interchange, the United Nations, disarmament, political independence for colonial peoples, and peaceful development of atomic energy. These goals have formed important elements in American foreign policy since 1945. All of these goals are related in some degree to the promotion of national security. Choose any of the goals listed—from the reduction of world trade barriers to the peaceful use of nuclear power—and their connection with security is not difficult to establish. Efforts to reduce trade barriers, for example, are based in some measure upon the belief that economic tensions are productive of international tensions and war. One of the reasons for technical assistance to other countries is the belief that it will help underdeveloped nations promote their own security from Communist domination and, in the process, aid the defense of the free world. A similar relationship could be established for the other goals. Almost never is a foreign policy goal totally divorced from security considerations.

For some policies the relationship to national security is much more direct than for others. This leads to the thought that a nation's foreign policy will emphasize security aspects in direct ratio to the degree the nation believes itself threatened by other countries. No lengthy documentation is needed to prove that the policies of the United States toward Soviet Russia in the postwar era have been more concerned with security objectives than have its policies toward Canada and India. Russia poses a visible and ominous threat to the United States and its allies; Canada and India do not. The United States will naturally be less motivated by security considerations in dealing with its friends and with neutralist countries than with its avowed diplomatic enemies.

Besides preserving its independence as a nation, what else is the United States seeking to achieve in world affairs? What other objectives does it believe important in its external relations? Answers to these questions are likely to vary greatly, depending upon circumstances prevailing at home and abroad in any given period. Moreover, they are likely to differ according to the vantage point of the individual answering the questions. Several lists of the goals of American foreign policy, ranging from broad principles to enumeration of detailed objectives toward particular problems, are published periodically in the volumes of the Department of State *Bulletin* and are contained in the testimony of executive officials before congressional committees. Almost never are these lists identical. Their differences hinge upon such considerations as the specific problems facing the nation at any time, the viewpoint of the official compiling the list, and perhaps the purpose for which the list was drawn up. In an age of growing specialization, the broad area of foreign relations, no less than other areas of national life, has become progressively divided and subdivided among an ever-larger circle of governmental agencies. Agencies specializing in narrow segments of foreign policy find it difficult to relate their work to the nation's over-all objectives in world affairs. Too often the nation's foreign policy is merely the sum of the goals of particular agencies, some of which are more skilled than others in generating support among private groups and high-ranking governmental officials for their point of view.

Below the level of preserving national security, the selection of lesser foreign policy goals and the assignment of different priorities to them is usually a process that goes on subconsciously, continuously, and often accidentally. Rather than attempting to list the lesser goals of American foreign policy, therefore, it seems more profitable to think in terms of categories of goals, proceeding from those of highest to lowest order of priority. First on the list is national security and its corollaries: provision for adequate defense, together with any other steps—extension of military and economic assistance to other countries, propaganda warfare, maintenance of strong military alliances, collaboration with the allies, preservation of a strong economic base at home—that directly or indirectly enhance the nation's security. Next on the list would be secondary goals: those objectives, pursuance of which is desirable as long as there is no significant impairment of national security. In the recent period, the following objectives could be included in this list: peace, nonintervention in the internal affairs of other countries, respect for international law and treaties, support for collective security, worldwide economic progress and human welfare, respect for human rights, and reciprocal trade. Last, there exists a category of objectives that might be labeled variously "desires, hopes, inclinations, and aspirations." These enjoy very low priority—so low that they will be sacrificed altogether when they conflict with the attainment of higher goals. Recent

diplomatic experience indicates that the following might properly be included in this category: friendship with all countries, including Russia and Red China; liberation of the Eastern European satellite countries, Tibet, Cuba, and other nations embraced within the communist empire; universal peace; propagation of the democratic ideology and support for politically free governmental institutions; disarmament, significant reductions in the American defense budget, and withdrawal of the nation's armed forces from overseas; unimpeded cultural exchange, freedom of information, and termination of propaganda warfare; imposition of an enforceable system or world law, at least over selected areas of international intercourse; inculcation of ethical principles in the conduct of world affairs. It is debatable whether objectives in this category can meaningfully be called "foreign policies" of the United States at all. For example, liberation of the communist satellites is no doubt a widely-held hope, a profound national desire; but it is not a foreign policy goal to which the United States is prepared to commit its energies and resources, since active pursuit of it would entail serious risks to national security.

Quite clearly then, all the foreign policy goals of the United States or any other country are not of equal importance and urgency. Choices must continually be made among them. Many of the goals included in the three categories outlined above are mutually exclusive. The United States could not, for instance, simultaneously seek friendship with Russia and Red China and arouse their apprehension by ringing the communist zone with military bases; nor could it at one and the same time commit itself to promote worldwide economic advancement and slash its economic assistance programs to other countries.

What factors will determine the order of priority a nation establishes among its lesser goals of foreign policy? Completely satisfactory answers to this question would require volumes devoted to individual countries, for the answers involve nothing less than the history and cultural heritage of a nation, its basic philosophic tenets, its experiences, its religious, social, and political institutions, its hopes and aspirations as a society. America's foreign policies, Secretary of State Dean Acheson once said, "grow out of, and are expressive of, our entire national life. They reflect our total culture."[6]

At root, the question goes back to what kind

of conception a society holds of the universe and man's place within it. From this underlying unity—for every organized society has a certain basic consensus on this question, else it would not be a society—many corollary beliefs are derived, relating to man's destiny, his potentialities and limitations, his tendencies for good and for evil. All these play their part in determining the order in which a nation will rank its subordinate foreign policy goals. In Chapter 2 we shall examine the effect of American national character on historic American foreign policy goals. In like manner, many scholars have identified important elements in the Russian historical experience and in communist ideology which have had far-reaching implications for Soviet foreign policy. The same point could be made about the importance of Hinduism and of Gandhi in shaping India's viewpoints toward the outside world, or the importance of emperor worship in convincing the Japanese before World War II that they had a mandate from heaven to dominate weaker countries.

These examples suffice to show that the hierarchy of lesser foreign policy goals is an exceedingly complex matter, a product of almost every influence making a nation what it is.

THE MEANS OF FOREIGN POLICY

Earlier we suggested that there were two elements in the foreign policy of any nation: objectives and means for reaching them. Let us now look at the means by which nations try to reach their goals in foreign affairs. This leads us directly to one of the most important and complex subjects basic to interstate relations: national power. *Power is the ability of a nation to influence the actions of other countries in a manner favorable to itself.* Its most fundamental aim is preservation of national security. Americans are not accustomed to discussing international questions in the language of "power politics." Indeed, they have tended to believe that power politics could be eliminated altogether. But Americans are very accustomed to discussing the *reality* of power. They devote considerable time and energy to learning "how to win friends and influence people," how to get a promotion, how to put across a sales contract, and how to pass or defeat legislation in which they are interested. These are all efforts to exercise power. On a limited scale, such efforts resemble in many ways power politics on the international level.

The Manifestations of Power

One significant difference between power as exercised by individuals within the state and by nations within the world community resides in the role of force and coercion. Normally within a state, especially within a democratic state, force plays a relatively insignificant role in interpersonal and intergroup relationships. The government monopolizes force, using it to prevent violations of its laws when all other methods of restraint have failed. But in international affairs, force and coercion are used (or the threat of their use is invoked) frequently by all members of the world community. In its most extreme manifestation, the use of force takes the form of war. On its most primitive level, national power is the capacity to preserve the identity of the nation by military force, construed broadly to include propaganda, economic, and other modern methods of warfare. That is why the power of a nation is often judged solely—and when solely, then erroneously—by the strength of its armed forces. Every other goal of foreign policy—the ability of the United States, let us say, to preserve advantageous trade relations with the outside world, or to contribute to the advancement of economically backward countries, or to propagate democratic ideology—presupposes the continued existence of the nation. This is the *sine qua non* of all national policy, foreign or domestic.

Though military strength is a central element in a nation's power, it is by no means the only element, nor is it always the most important one in the day-to-day conduct of international affairs. The free world alliance against the communist bloc, for example, is not held together because of the overwhelming military superiority of the United States over its members. The cement of this alliance is to be found much more in recognition of a common danger, geographical proximity, ideological affinity, and a sense of common purpose. Decisions emerging from the alliance are a result more of persuasion than of coercion by the dominant nations within it.

Manifestly, there are limits to the usefulness of military power. It cannot be used to compel other nations, such as Burma in the postwar period, to accept American economic and technical assistance, even for their own good. Respect for American military strength has not always forced other nations, such as India, Egypt, or Ghana, to accept the American position on issues dividing the communist and noncommunist worlds. Nor does the mere existence of great military power prevent the growth of Communist influence in areas like Southeast Asia or Latin America. In other words, *force is not always relevant to certain kinds of foreign policy situations.* Remembering the definition—that power is *influence*—the improper use of force may in fact result in lessened, rather than in increased, influence over the actions of other countries.

Power thus has many manifestations. Some of the more important of these are: persuasion and friendship; propaganda; economic aid (leading sometimes to economic coercion); ideological penetration; moral suasion; and public opinion. There is no necessity to examine these manifestations of power here. That can better be done in future chapters, when we discuss American foreign policy toward specific international problems. At this stage, we must take note of some of the general characteristics of power.

The Relativity of Power

A basic fact to be grasped about the concept is that *power is always relative.* We observed earlier that national security is a dynamic, not a static, concept. This largely stems from the relativity of power. When we ask, "What is the power of the United States in world affairs?" we are trying to solve an equation containing an almost infinite number of variables. No two experts from the State Department, the Pentagon, or other governmental agencies would answer this question in exactly the same way, because no final and completely authoritative answer is ever possible. The variables in the problem derive from the four important respects in which power is relative.

Power is relative with respect to time. The power of the United States has undergone a profound transformation within the past fifty years. This change has resulted principally from two facts: proven ability to wage war successfully, and the decision to play a more active role in world affairs, which has demanded that the United States develop and use some of its tremendous potential power during time of peace. Furthermore, America's power today is far vaster than it was immediately after World War II, when its armed forces had been stripped to skeleton strength, and before it had begun to develop nuclear weapons in large quantities.

The fact that power is relative to time is highlighted by the distinction between *potential* power and power *in being.* If it is asked, "What is the power of the United States and the NATO community to defend Western Europe from a possible Communist attack?" a major consideration would be the amount of time available to the free world to bring its military forces to bear in defense. Throughout the postwar period the United States has possessed great power in being. Yet the existing power of the United States is only a fraction of its potential power. And, as Winston Churchill noted time and again, the great power potential of the United States, more than any other single factor, has been instrumental in deterring further Communist military intrusions into the free world.

Power is relative to the problem toward which it is directed. When we evaluate national power, we must always think in terms of power to reach certain specified objectives, to achieve concrete goals. America's power to defend its shores from aggression may be entirely different from its capacity to deal with communist influences in Asia, to maintain friendly relations with Egypt, to raise living standards in Iran, or to prevent excessive use of the veto in the United Nations. Success in foreign affairs demands skill in using appropriate weapons and skill in dealing with diverse global problems.

The power of one country is relative to that of other countries. The ability of the United States to influence the course of world events will almost invariably require comparative judgments about power. Knowing that the United States at any given time possessed 5 or 25 or 50 hydrogen bombs would tell us little or nothing of significance about American power. Such weapons might have little relevance to the problem under consideration. But even if they did, we could still not settle the issue until we asked: "What is the power of the United States *relative to the power of other countries* that are actively concerned with the problem at hand?" The issue of relative power has come into clear focus in recent years because of the steady accretion in Soviet nuclear and missile technology. In the immediate postwar period, the United States had a monopoly on nuclear weapons. In this one category its power was therefore infinitely greater than the Soviet Union's. Gradually, the USSR began to acquire such weapons, along with effective methods of delivery. The Kremlin's rate of production for such weapons grew much faster than the American rate. If we assume that, by the mid-1960s, the free world coalition had a two-to-one lead over the communist bloc in nuclear striking power, its relative position vis-à-vis the Communist bloc had deteriorated greatly—so much so in fact that "nuclear parity" had been largely reached between the two camps. Both sides were equal, or nearly so, in the capacity to achieve objectives requiring reliance upon nuclear weapons.

The same principle of course holds for non-military types of power, although differentials of strength are much more difficult, if not virtually impossible, to measure with precision. What is the relative power of the United States and India to persuade masses throughout Asia to support a given course of action in foreign affairs? What is the respective influence of countries such as Britain and Egypt in determining Arab attitudes toward the free world coalition? How much power does the United States possess to gain widespread acceptance of its policies within the NATO alliance? In international affairs, there is power and countervailing power, American push and Soviet or Indian or Egyptian pull. To decide what the power of a nation is, it is necessary to identify all the forces that are operative in any given international issue.

Power is relative to the country by which it is applied. Suppose, for purposes of illustration, that we measure the relative power of countries by looking *only* at their military forces. What kind of evaluation is possible? No matter what the statistics show, the effective military power of two countries is never exactly comparable. This is true, even if it could be shown—and in reality of course it could not—that the military strengths of two nations were exactly equal. Why is it not possible to think that "ten divisions are ten divisions," irrespective of the country to which they belong?

Ignoring for the moment the fact that the divisions of two countries will differ markedly in firepower, number of troops, leadership, and many other respects, we may note that ten Russian divisions would be more easily available to the Kremlin for crushing the Hungarian Revolt than would ten American divisions to Washington for dealing with anti-American demonstrations in Egypt or South Vietnam. Few limitations exist on the Kremlin's ability to use troops for such purposes. Governmental leaders of the United States, on the other hand, must operate within a con-

stitutional framework of civilian control over the military establishment and within a historical tradition which emphasizes nonintervention in the internal affairs of other countries.

Merely possessing power, along with even greater potential power, is no guarantee that a nation will exert strong influence in world affairs. Totalitarian regimes are often free to use all the powers at their command for diplomatic ends. Democratic nations, however, usually limit, sometimes severely, the ends for which certain kinds of power may be utilized.

THE INGREDIENTS OF AMERICAN POWER

The major elements that combine to make up the power of a nation are: geography, economic and technological resources, population, military forces, ideology, and national character. We shall treat the last three of these elements in separate chapters.

Geographical Determinants of American Power

Because they are the most permanent elements in a nation's power, and because they underlie other kinds of power, geographical attributes have been held by leading scholars to be the most fundamental in determining a nation's role in world affairs. "Power," the noted geographer Nicholas J. Spykman once wrote, "is in the last instance the ability to wage successful war, and in geography lie the clues to the problems of military and political strategy." He concludes that geography "is the most fundamental factor in the foreign policy of states because it is the most permanent."[7] Such statements cannot be accepted without qualification. Geographical factors may have the greatest degree of permanence. But even they change with the passage of time. Canals have been dug to connect important waterways; deserts have been made arable; swamps have been drained and converted into usable land; airplanes have conquered the obstacle of distances and overcome impassable land barriers; expeditions by the United States and other countries within recent years have shown that even the polar regions of the world can be made habitable. Consequently, it would be a mistake to regard geographical factors as fixed and unyielding before the efforts of man.

Another warning about trying to prove too much from geography is in order at the outset. There is the danger of falling into a kind of geographical determinism, popularly called "geopolitics." During the 1920s and 1930s, German geopoliticians especially were responsible for propagating the view that geographical pressures determine foreign policy; that German expansionism, such as the *Drang Nach Osten* (drive to the east), was dictated by certain natural and immutable geographical urges that gave Germany and its partners a special mandate to conquer Europe and eventually the world. Geopolitics thus became the tool of aggressive dictators. Such geopolitical thinking has been thoroughly discredited by reputable scholars. The prevailing view is that man's actions are not determined irrevocably by a supposed geographic destiny.

Keeping these qualifications in mind, let us examine the salient geographical facts about American power, starting with climate. The United States is in the temperate zone, the zone in which great nations have invariably been situated. Scholars since antiquity have sought to establish a correlation between national greatness and climate.[8] That no precise correlation is possible is now conceded. Nevertheless, it seems that climatic extremes militate against a nation's becoming a great power in world affairs. Most of the United States escapes both extreme tropical heat and Arctic cold. Another climatic factor conducive to energetic life is moderate variation in temperature, rainfall, humidity, and wind velocities. The United States escapes the stultifying effect of uniform climatic conditions for long periods. These facts are of cardinal importance for American economic pursuits, especially agriculture, and undoubtedly have some significance in shaping the character and outlook of the American people.[9]

No one ingredient in the power of a nation is likely to be so basic as its geographical location. Location determines the pattern of relations between a nation and other countries. It is crucial in national defense. The presence or absence of "natural frontiers," as Poland has discovered throughout its history, can decide whether or not national security can be preserved. Location is crucial in trade and commerce. Britain and Japan—small islands off the coasts of Europe and Asia—became great nations because of their ability to use the oceans as highways of commerce. Even the cultural and ideological influence exerted by a nation may depend on its location. Greek and Roman thought infused the European world because of the proximity of these nations to the European hinterland and the consequent ease of communication.

Long imbued with the idea of Western "hemispheric solidarity," Americans have difficulty appreciating the objective facts about their geographical relationship with the rest of the world. Having expanded over a continent which contains few natural land barriers, the people of the United States have traditionally thought in continental terms. They have tended to believe that land connects and that water divides. They have overlooked the fact that land can present formidable barriers, and that oceans may cease to be obstacles to contact between nations. In the twentieth century travel is often easier by sea or air than by land. Freight can be hauled much more cheaply by water than by land. Military forces can often be transported more conveniently by sea or air than by land.

Widespread reliance by Americans upon the Mercator map projection is also responsible for distorted notions about geographic relationships. Every map distorts global relationships to some degree. The peculiarity of the Mercator projection is that it suggests that the United States *is* geographically isolated, except from Canada and Latin America. Vast ocean distances seem to divide the United States from Europe and Asia. The accessibility of polar routes, first by airplanes and now by submarine, does not emerge. The Western Hemisphere appears to be a geographically compact unit, with the other great land areas of the earth scattered along its fringes. Such "ship thoughts," as George T. Renner has labeled them, have largely dominated American thinking about foreign affairs throughout the nation's history.[10]

The only realistic perspective from which the salient facts about America's relationships with the rest of the world become apparent is to visualize them in global dimensions. More than at any other stage in history, the globe, not the map, needs to be the constant source of reference for every student of foreign policy. Once Americans adopt the perspective of the globe—thereby comprehending relationships that are obscured by flat map projections—they will understand several basic facts about their country's geographical location. One is that America is not isolated, nor has it ever been isolated to the degree imagined in the nation's folklore. The United States is not safely protected by two expansive oceans and by Arctic wastelands to the north. Arbitrary divisions of the globe into hemispheres by lines running north and south possess virtually no military or strategic validity. An almost infinite number of hemispheres can be projected on the globe, including of course those dividing the world along an east-west axis, or those created by lines running at an acute angle to the equator. And, as S. W. Boggs has observed, if hemispheres were projected embracing the United States, they could be drawn in such a way that there would be "no human being anywhere on earth" who did not "live in some hemisphere that includes *all* of the United States." Every major area of culture in the world is part of some imaginable "American hemisphere."[11]

Global thinking facilitates a proper understanding of distances between the United States and other countries. Americans are inclined to view the Western Hemisphere as the immediate backyard of the United States. A not untypical expression of this misconception was Wisconsin Governor Philip LaFollette's warning to Americans during World War II to beware lest they fight "not in this hemisphere where we can be supreme, but . . . with expeditionary forces four thousand miles away in Europe and six thousand miles away in Asia."[12]

Few Americans are psychologically prepared to believe that Europe is the closest neighbor of the United States, excluding Canada, Mexico, and the Caribbean countries. Few Americans today would look upon a trip from Washington, D.C., to San Francisco (about 2300 miles) as a particularly lengthy journey, especially if it were made by a transcontinental jet airplane. Yet this is approximately the distance by air from Chicago to the southern tip of Greenland, to the Arctic Circle, or the Beaufort Sea north of Alaska and east of Soviet Siberia; from San Francisco to the Bering Sea adjacent to Siberia; from Denver to the Beaufort Sea and Baffin Island in the northeastern Arctic Ocean; from Cleveland to the Arctic Circle and the North Atlantic west of Greenland; and from Boston to Iceland. In the Western Hemisphere, this is also about the distance from New York to the Panama Canal—a distance farther than the mileage by plane or ship from the "bulge" of Africa at Dakar to the closest point in South America.

The erroneous assumptions underlying Governor LaFollette's statement quoted earlier are highlighted by the fact that from Madison, Wisconsin, it is farther to Brazil than to Benghazi in North Africa; about equidistant to

Ankara, Turkey, and Buenos Aires, Argentina; closer to every major European capital than to Buenos Aires (and only one, Athens, is as far as Rio de Janeiro); closer to Gibraltar than to Bolivia, Argentina, Chile, Paraguay, and Uruguay (and it is closer by sea to Gibraltar from the nearest American port than from Miami to the nearest point in South America); closer to Manchuria than to Buenos Aires.[13] New York City is 3700 miles from Gibraltar, about 3000 miles less than the distance to Buenos Aires and nearly 1800 miles less than the distance to Rio de Janeiro. Washington, D.C., is closer to Berlin than to Rio de Janeiro; Chicago closer to many points in Russia than to many Latin American countries; Boston closer to Moscow than to half the countries in Latin America.[14]

These facts possess added significance in an age of supersonic, long-range aircraft and guided missiles capable of being launched from remote sites and of traversing the shortest distances to selected targets. Ocean expanses, Arctic wastelands, deserts, and the like, present no obstacles to airplanes and missiles. To appreciate the impact these technological advances have had upon America's relation with the outside world, let us imagine that an enemy wished to attack this country. Both the United States and the Soviet Union possess intermediate-range (1500-mile) guided missiles. Utilizing missile sites in Eastern Germany, Soviet Russia could bring the whole of Western Europe, including Iceland and Spain, plus the coastal fringe areas of North Africa, within its range. Using bases in Bulgaria, an intermediate-range missile attack could be launched against practically any point in the Mediterranean Sea, including about half of Algeria, most of Libya, all of Egypt, and about one-third of Iran. An arc drawn with a 1500-mile radius centered upon New York City would extend into waters north of Newfoundland, into the central Atlantic, southward through Haiti and the Dominican Republic. An enemy submarine firing a 1500-mile missile, submerged 500 miles in the Atlantic east of New York City, could bring most of the United States east of the Mississippi River within its range. The same submarine submerged 500 miles off the coast of California would command a field of fire embraced by an arc extending from the northern tip of Idaho, east to Colorado, and southeast to the Arizona–New Mexico boundary. Similarly, a submarine submerged in the Gulf of Mexico 500 miles south of New Orleans could fire an intermedi-ate-range missile at Philadelphia in the north-east, Detroit in the north, Omaha in the northwest, and Pueblo, Colorado, in the west.

The United States and Soviet Russia also possess long-range, 5000-mile, guided mis-siles. These weapons nullify any remaining vestige of protection afforded the United States by its geographical location. The arc formed by a radius of 5000 miles centered on Moscow includes Alaska, sweeps through north-ern Oregon, passes through the north-central and midwestern portions of the United States and embraces most of the eastern and Atlantic seaboard area, excluding only the extreme southern portions of the country. This means that the industrial heartland of the United States would be within range of missiles launched from behind the Iron Curtain.

Translating these data into general strategic terms, we may say that today almost every point in the United States is within range of an enemy armed with submarine- or ship-launched intermediate-range missiles or of air-craft with round-trip range of 3000 to 4000 miles. When missiles with a 5000-mile range are envisioned, no point in the United States or the Western Hemisphere remains outside the field of fire of enemy missiles. These facts demonstrate forcefully that any thought of hemispheric isolation or noninvolvement by the United States in global affairs is a dangerous fiction.

If the concept of hemispheres must be re-tained in the study of international affairs, a much more meaningful term would be "North-ern Hemisphere." America's presence in the "North Atlantic quarter-sphere" Hartshorne has written, "is the most important aspect of our location, now as in the past."[15] This zone includes Europe, North America, the greater portion of the Soviet Union, and the connect-ing and intervening oceans. It contains about one-third of the world's population and ap-proximately nine-tenths of its industrial com-plex. With the exception of Japan, it embraces all the great military powers known to modern history.[16]

Geographical facts and concepts have a vital bearing upon every goal of American foreign policy. They have, for example, largely deter-mined the nation's response to the communist challenge since World War II. The American concept of containment has rested upon the premise that enemy control over the great land mass of Europe and Asia—roughly coterminous with what the eminent geographer Sir Halford Mackinder called the "world island"—would give an adversary a well-nigh impregnable po-sition from which to extend its influence to other nations and regions. From Eurasia, an aggressor could soon overrun the Near and Middle East, the fringe lands of the Far East, and Africa. If an enemy succeeded in con-solidating its hold upon these areas, it would then be able to isolate the United States from its major allies by cutting sea communication-transportation routes at key points, by imposing an economic blockade, and perhaps by pene-trating South America politically and mili-tarily. The huge Eurasian land mass contains two-thirds of the land area of the earth, five-sixths of its population, and a large proportion of its natural resources. Its possession in enemy hands would place the United States in a mili-tarily and economically vulnerable position, such that it could not, in all likelihood, con-tinue to maintain its independence.[17]

The United States consequently has no choice about playing an active role in global affairs. That decision has been foreordained by the facts of geography and the economic-strategic corollaries deriving from those facts. The only real alternatives relate to the kind of role it will play. Will its policies be based upon realities? Or will they be based upon stereotypes and misconceptions concerning the nation's relationships with other important countries? The first alternative is, of course, no guarantee to success in the diplomatic field, but it is clearly a *sine qua non* of successful policy. The second, on the other hand, could jeopardize the continued existence of the United States as a great and independent power.

Economic and Technological Determinants of American Power

Since World War I it has become apparent that a nation's power—especially its capacity to wage war—is largely determined by its eco-nomic base. Without the ability to equip mili-tary forces, and to keep them supplied with materials of war for long periods, a nation can-not protect its security or its vital interests. Creation of a firm economic foundation to sup-port its foreign policy, therefore, demands that a nation possess or have unimpeded access to important industrial raw materials.

In over-all terms, the United States has been

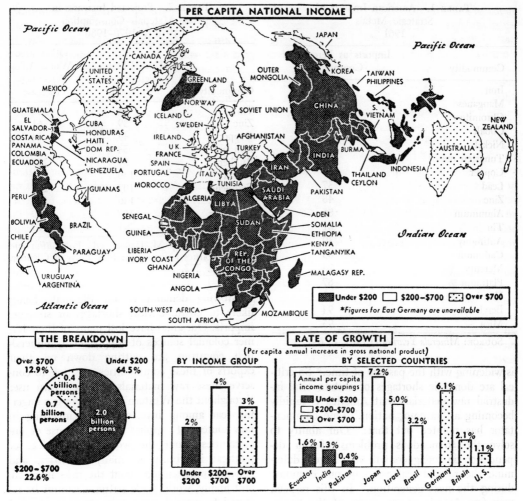

The Uneven Distribution of the World's Income. (Source: *The New York Times*, April 21, 1963. © 1963 by The New York Times Company. Reprinted by permission.)

the most richly endowed nation on earth in the broad range of strategic raw materials needed to sustain an industrial economy. America is the leading producer of steel. Of a total world output of 355 million tons annually, approximately one-fourth comes from the United States. Even then, American steel mills operate at something like two-thirds of their normal capacity. When the steel-making potential of the United States and its cold war allies (chiefly Western Germany, Japan, the United Kingdom, and France) is considered, then five out of the six largest steel-producing countries in the world are in the free world coalition, accounting for well over half of the world's total production of this vital commodity.[18]

However, American reserves of high-grade iron ore are being exhausted at a rapid rate. By the mid-1960s, the United States depended upon imports for over 20 percent of its iron ore supply, chiefly from fields in Labrador and Venezuela.[19] The situation in regard to other metals is even more discouraging from the standpoint of industrial self-sufficiency. Domestic supplies of many strategic metals are either totally exhausted or very near the point of exhaustion. Especially critical are shortages of copper, high-grade bauxite ore from which aluminum is derived, lead, zinc, manganese, and tin. The following chart shows the extent to which the United States is dependent upon imported supplies of strategic metals.

The most significant fact about these domestic shortages is perhaps the fact that the disparity between domestic supply and demand

TABLE 1. American Imports of
Strategic Metals
1961

Commodity	Imports as Percent of Consumption
Iron	20
Manganese	96
Chromite	95
Cobalt	98
Nickel	87
Tungsten ore	24
Copper	23
Lead	37
Zinc	48
Aluminum	86
Tin	81
Antimony	39
Cadmium	63
Mercury	24
Platinum	87
Uranium concentrate	42
Beryl ore	94
Mica	95

SOURCE: *Minerals Yearbook: 1961, I.,* 6–7.

TABLE 2. Projected Increases in
Raw Materials Consumption
1950 to 1970–1980

Commodity	United States Percentage Increase	Other Free World Allies Percentage Increase
Tin	18	50
Zinc	39	61
Copper	43	54
Iron ore	54	73
Rubber	89	203
Nickel	100	100
Petroleum	109	275
Tungsten	150	150
Fluorspar	187	260
Aluminum	291	415

SOURCE: Philip M. Hauser, ed., *Population and World Politics* (New York: Free Press of Glencoe, 1958), p. 272.

Growing demand is not the only factor likely to create critical shortages of strategic imports. Our allies have lost many of their former colonial sources of supply; many mineral-rich countries are cutting down on their exports of these commodities, wishing to conserve these raw materials for their own use; throughout the Western world there is a lingering fear among investors about investing in new sources of supplies abroad because of uncertainties about the world market, fear of political instability in many countries, and general apprehension about the risks involved; and finally, world trade patterns cannot be restored to normal, cannot be divested of what are often dominant military-strategic motivations, so long as the cold war persists.[21]

These facts have an obvious and far-reaching bearing upon national security. Writing during World War II, Nicholas Spykman observed that in the event of Axis penetration of South America, the United States would be "surrounded by enemy territory and submitted to economic strangulation by the simple process of blockade through embargo."[22] Today, such a prospect, growing out of enemy control of Latin America, would be even more alarming, since the United States relies much more heavily than during the era of World War II upon imports of strategic raw materials. Communist domination of the Eurasian land mass, followed by Communist control over Latin America, would thus cut hemispheric lines of trade and threaten the American economy, and ultimately the national military establishment, with paralysis.

is widening with the passage of time.* So critical are domestic shortages of certain vital industrial raw materials that America is rapidly becoming a "have-not nation." One commentator has pointed out that: "Our ability to solve the tremendous problems of our dependence on foreigners will very largely determine the rate of expansion of our economy during the next generation." In this respect, very few Americans are aware of the "painful truth" that "our basic long-range position in the international economy is not one of strength, but one of great potential weakness."[20] Another authoritative study reported that the United States and its free world allies could expect the following percentage increases in the consumption of strategic raw materials between 1950 and the period 1970–1980:

* Thus, a high American policy-maker pointed out in mid-1962 that "World demand for minerals and metals, which more than doubled in the 1950s over what it had been in the 1930s, is likely to double again by the 1970s." The decade of the 1960s was expected to witness a 45–50 percent increase in free world consumption of aluminum and a 50 percent increase in consumption of petroleum. Such data dictate that the United States "develop, and maintain the availability of, a wide variety of resource materials." George C. McGhee, "Mineral Resources and the World of the 1960s," *Department of State Bulletin,* 46 (April 30, 1962), 724–725.

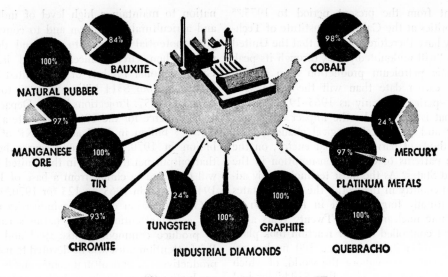

100% NATURAL RUBBER
84% BAUXITE
98% COBALT
97% MANGANESE ORE
100% TIN
24% MERCURY
97% PLATINUM METALS
93% CHROMITE
24% TUNGSTEN
100% INDUSTRIAL DIAMONDS
100% GRAPHITE
100% QUEBRACHO

*Natural graphite, strategic grade   DOMESTIC PRODUCTION   IMPORTS

The United States Must Import Strategic Materials for Major Industries. (Source: Chart from the U.S. Department of State, *Mutual Security Program, 1959*, p. 8; data from the U.S. Department of Interior, *Minerals Yearbook: 1961, 1*, 6–7 and Philip H. Trezise, "Are Imports Necessary?" *Department of State Bulletin, 46* [May 28, 1962], 884–886.)

Turning to another important area of American economic and military power—fuels and energy sources—we find a more promising picture. The United States produces approximately one-third of the global output of energy; it has almost six times the per capita world average of energy production. America produces almost three times the energy produced by the Soviet Union. Its output of this element of economic power is approximately equal to the combined output of Soviet Russia, the Middle East, the Far East, and Africa.[23]

By the early 1960s, the principal sources of energy for the American economy were crude petroleum, natural gas, and coal, in that order. Historically, the United States has been richly endowed with primary fuels, and for at least two of them present supplies remain adequate for anticipated demand. Thus, the estimated natural gas reserves of the nation are placed at 263 trillion cubic feet—enough (at a withdrawal rate of nearly 16 trillion cubic feet annually) to last more than a decade and a half, even if no new reserves are discovered.[24] Coal reserves are much more impressive. Out of an original estimated total of 1.7 trillion tons in the United States, more than 1.6 trillion tons remain, of which half are currently regarded as recoverable for industrial use.[25] These reserves

could supply the global demand for coal for nearly seven centuries. New technological processes (like "hydrogenation"—or addition of hydrogen to coal) are putting a greater premium than ever upon the value of coal deposits. In time, coal, along with new processes such as peacetime nuclear energy and solar energy, may very largely displace petroleum and natural gas as major sources of industrial energy.[26]

Vast petroleum reserves have also made possible the spectacular economic growth of the United States during the past century. In the early 1960s, petroleum continued to supply approximately one-third of the energy consumed by the nation. In that same period, America produced nearly one-third of the global output of crude petroleum, or nearly 300 million barrels annually. Yet, national petroleum supplies were rapidly approaching the point of exhaustion. Estimates of proved reserves were placed at 32 billion barrels, or slightly over a ten years' supply at current consumption levels.[27] An indication of this tendency was that, from 1930 to 1960, American imports of oil rose by more than 500 percent. That domestic petroleum supplies might be exhausted at an even more rapid rate than anticipated was suggested by the fact that the consumption rate of mineral energy fuels is expected to grow by 2.13

percent from the present period to 1975.[28] Authorities at the California Institute of Technology have therefore predicted that the United States "will undoubtedly pass through its peak domestic petroleum production at a considerably earlier date than will the world as a whole—perhaps as early as 1965–1970."[29]

What is likely to be the impact of nuclear power and other technological changes, such as methods of harnessing solar energy, on the future patterns of energy consumption in the United States? As the most technologically advanced country in the world, the United States has naturally forged ahead in fields such as peacetime nuclear energy. Twenty years after the first controlled nuclear reaction took place on December 2, 1942, some 500 nuclear reactors existed throughout the world, of which half were in America. More than $30 billion had been appropriated by Congress for the peaceful development of the atom, and the Atomic Energy Commission operated upon a budget of around $3 billion annually. The world's first useful nuclear reactor went into operation in 1951; a decade later, a nuclear-powered battery weighing merely 5 pounds furnished the energy to send a radio signal from the Transit-IV A satellite back to earth. Moreover, by the early 1960s, the Atomic Energy Commission was widely disseminating information about peacetime nuclear development in overseas exhibits.[30]

Nevertheless, several factors indicated that it would be many years before nuclear power significantly displaced more traditional sources of fuel. A major inhibiting factor was cost. Modern steam plants can produce electric power, for example, almost one-half as expensively as nuclear power stations. That is one reason why other countries (such as Great Britain) may well utilize nuclear energy for industrial power sooner and more extensively than the United States, since cost differentials may be far less significant for such countries than for America.[31] Other limiting influences are likely to be the location of traditional sources of fuel close to industrial complexes, and the usual inertia encountered to technological changes of this magnitude. Governments which are able to introduce or speed up the use of nuclear power by fiat, or societies that find traditional fuels expensive, may thus rely more heavily upon this source of power than the American society.[32]

Fundamental to the maintenance of American power in global affairs is the ability of the nation to maintain a high level of industrial and agricultural production and to convert its great potential capacity to war and defense needs when circumstances demand it. The Gross National Product of the United States increased from $314 billion in 1947 to $453 billion in 1957. Projections by the Department of Commerce for the 1960s anticipate a GNP of $615 billion in 1965 and a GNP of $750 billion in 1970.* This same source believes that output per man-hour in the United States will continue to climb, from a base of 100 in 1947, to 116 in 1965, to 125 for 1970.[33]

Our discussion of specific industries earlier has called attention to the nation's capacity to produce commodities like steel and fuels. Brief attention must also be devoted to national productivity in agricultural commodities, since productive capacities in agriculture often surpass those in industry as a whole. The United States, for example, produces almost 50 percent of the world's total supply of corn, over 30 percent of its supply of cotton, over 28 percent of its supply of edible vegetable oils and of oats, and over 15 percent of its wheat supply.[34] America, as its political leaders are continually aware, must deal with the perennial problem of large agricultural surpluses. Not only does the nation currently produce oversupplies of major agricultural commodities, but its capacity to produce even larger supplies is far from utilized fully. In the decade 1950–1960, for example, agricultural productivity in the United States rose more than 25 percent—at a time when efforts were being made to *reduce* the production of certain crops and when the farm population of the United States was declining.[35] The capacity of the United States to produce agricultural commodities in such abundance is clearly a vital element in its ability to maintain an extensive foreign aid program, to carry out programs like "Food for

---

* Although the subject is discussed at greater length in Chapter 9, here it may be illuminating to note that the American economic growth rate, in the opinion of most competent economists, has lagged considerably behind the Soviet rate in recent years. Admittedly, this is a problem on which calculations can differ widely; the selection of different periods of time for measuring the growth rate, for example, can yield significantly different results. Nevertheless, the Soviet growth rate of 9–10 percent annually is more than double the economic growth rate experienced since World War II by the United States. See Klaus Knorr and William J. Baumol, *What Price Economic Growth?* (Englewood Cliffs, N.J.: Prentice-Hall, 1961), pp. 4–5.

Peace," and, in time of war, to sustain the military efforts of itself and its allies.

These considerations also apply for industrial production in the United States. During World War II, when America was the "arsenal of democracy," experience demonstrated convincingly that considerably unutilized industrial potential existed in the United States. Without resorting to manpower drafts or touching the bottom of the labor barrel, American industry turned out vast quantities of arms for its own military machine and that of its principal allies. As much as any other factor, this ability was perhaps crucial in tipping the scales of military power decisively in favor of the Allies. This ability remains in the nuclear age. As we have noted, in certain segments of the economy, a considerable potential capacity exists for greater production if the need arises. In specific industries such as coal mining and railroad transportation, the output per man-hour rose more than 40 percent in the decade 1950–1960. It rose over 20 percent in steel production, over 35 percent in cement production, and almost 50 percent in petroleum refining.[36] Similarly, the labor force of the nation could be augmented by as much as 60–70 percent if this were required for national security.[37] Still another index of America's productive might lies in projections of electric energy output. The Federal Power Commission, for example, has predicted that in the period 1960–1980, the output of electric energy in the United States will increase by 275 percent.[38] The over-all index of industrial production is expected to hit 178 by 1975 (using the year 1957 as a base). This reflects an economic growth rate of 3.38 percent annually.[39] These data suggest that America's tremendous economic base remains strong and that, if national security required it, national productive capacity could be vastly increased to support military or diplomatic objectives.

Population as a Determinant of National Power

Throughout history, students of international affairs have been aware of the intimate connection between population and national power. This relationship is as complex as it is far-reaching in its implications. Military strength, economic productivity, scientific and technological know-how, national morale, the long-range goals of a society—all of these are functions of the size and character of the nation's population. Size of population is crucial

in determining national power. Yet mere size alone cannot guarantee a nation great-power status. If this were the case, global affairs would be controlled by heavily populated countries like India and China, which between them possess nearly 40 percent of the total population of the world. Lacking another key ingredient in national power—adequate land and other resources requisite for a fairly high standard of living and a broad industrial base —the hundreds of millions of people living in these countries may constitute more of a drain upon the power of the nation than an addition to it. The equation of national power contains many variables, and it is the relationship among these variables that largely determines whether nations will be weak or strong. Consequently, to decide whether a nation is "overpopulated," "underpopulated," or possesses an "optimum" population, consideration must be given to the capacity of the nation to support its people. Nevertheless, in recent history nations have been powerful only when they have possessed reasonably large populations. Perhaps the figure fifty million people could be taken as an approximate lower limit for nations that aspire to become great powers.

By the beginning of the 1960s, the United States had a population of more than 175 million—considerably larger than Britain, France, or Germany, somewhat less than the Soviet Union, and much less than China or India. Throughout American history the rate of population growth has been phenomenal. The population quadrupled in the first half of the nineteenth century; trebled during the last half; and has more than doubled since 1900. There has been an uneven growth during each decade, but the trend of the population curve has been steadily upward. The large population expansion during World War II and throughout the postwar era surprised many demographers. Many had come to regard the United States as a country possessing a relatively stable population, compared with the rapid growth witnessed in regions like Africa, Asia, and Latin America. The census of 1950 revealed that they had underestimated the total population of the country by 5 percent, which entailed an error of 41 percent in predicting the *growth* of the population over the preceding decade. Consequently, in recent years demographers have become more cautious in predicting population trends. Now they normally make several predictions, utilizing different sets of assumptions concerning possible changes in the birth rate, death rate, median marriage age of the population, immigration, and related factors.

The census of 1960 showed a total American population of over 180 million people. Population projections for the decade 1960–1970 anticipated the following population increases, depending upon assumptions utilized in making the prediction:

TABLE 3.   Estimates of Total American Population 1960–1970

Year	Estimated Total Population
1960	180,677,000
1965	
Series II[a]	196,200,000
Series III	194,500,000
1970	
Series II	214,200,000
Series III	208,931,000

[a] Series II is based upon the assumption that American fertility rates for the period 1956–1957 continue to 1965–1970. Series III is based upon the assumption that fertility rates for the 1955–1957 period decline to levels reached in 1949–1951, by 1965–1970.

SOURCE: *Statistical Abstract of the United States: 1962*, p. 6.

The extent to which differing assumptions about fertility levels and other influences upon population growth can yield significantly different results is highlighted by projections of the American population for the year 2000. For example, at current population growth rates, if 98 percent of American women marry and have 3.35 children each, then the total American population in 2000 will reach almost 400 million people. A slightly lower (or "medium") set of assumptions yields a total of about 330 million; and a still lower set of assumptions yields a population of about 280 million people by that date.[40]

In spite of unanticipated wartime and post-war high population growth rates, the rate of population increase in the United States (calculated at 1.7 percent annually, on the basis of the 1960 census) remains considerably less than the growth rate in many other countries, notably those in Asia, Africa, and Latin America. The rate of American population increase is almost exactly equal to that for North America as a whole (1.8 percent annually). Among the world's major regions this is among the lowest growth rates prevailing, with only Western Europe (whose population is growing

only at 0.8 percent annually) having a significantly lower rate. On the other hand, Africa's population is expanding at the rate of 2.1 percent yearly, South America's at 2.7 percent, and Asia's at 2.0 percent.[41] Within these overall totals, certain countries have growth rates significantly exceeding the American rate or the world average. For example, Costa Rica's population is expanding by 4.4 percent annually, Brazil's by 3.6 percent, Syria's by 4.8 percent, South Vietnam's by 3.9 percent, Red China's by 2.4 percent, and Cambodia's by 3.8 percent. The population growth rate of the Soviet Union (1.8 percent annually) is almost exactly the same as America's, although *Asian* population groups in the USSR are growing at a rate of 3.0 per cent annually. By contrast, the lowest population growth rates are found in countries like Japan (0.9 percent annually), France (1.0 percent), Italy (0.5 percent), United Kingdom (0.7 percent), and Belgium (0.5 percent).[42] All of this means that *relatively* the population of the United States is falling behind those of underdeveloped countries in Latin America, Africa, the Middle East, and Asia.

Ever since 1798, when the English clergyman Thomas Malthus published his classic *Essay on the Principle of Population*, students of politics have been conscious of the influence of population stimuli in determining national policies and global economic-political relationships. Modern scholarship has found many faults with Malthusian concepts, principally because they do not accord sufficient weight to man's ingenuity in overcoming adverse environmental factors and because Malthus tended to elevate observed population trends into inexorable "laws" purporting to govern the behavior of societies.[43] Yet one need not succumb to a simple demographic determinism to anticipate the steady evolution of population problems as pivotal global and regional issues. One authority has written that the "most salient demographic change" in recent history is "the astonishing rise in the rate of growth of the world's total population."[44] The crude birth rate for selected countries like Burma, Ceylon, Colombia, Egypt, Iran, Mexico, and Venezuela, for example, is from 50 to almost 100 percent higher than the rate for the United States, and almost three times that of countries in Western Europe.[45]

Americans—many of whom are aware that the United States has contributed approximately $100 billion since World War II to bolster the military and economic strength of nations in the free world—are perhaps not psychologically prepared to believe that the gap in the standard of living and production between richer industrialized nations and poorer developing nations is steadily *widening*, and that this tendency is expected to continue for many years, perhaps decades, to come. A UN study, for example, showed that countries with a $200 per capita annual income have expanded their economic output by a rate of only 2 percent per year; the growth rate of more advanced countries was 3–4 percent, with Japan and West Germany achieving rates of 7.2 percent and 6.1 percent, respectively. While newly developing countries have sometimes achieved real gains in productivity and standards of living, their relative positions vis-à-vis more economically advanced countries in the North Atlantic Community and Europe has declined.[46] In some cases, industrialized nations have made even more rapid productive gains. In other cases, the population explosion in poorer countries continues to outstrip productive increases. In almost all cases throughout the underdeveloped world, governmental leaders are hard-pressed to prevent consumption levels from rising faster than productive levels, thereby preventing the society from accumulating the savings required to make a decisive economic "breakthrough" into the age of modernization.*

Attempts to calculate the human absorptive capacity of the earth encounter innumerable obstacles, so many in fact as to render such calculations of questionable value.[47] Nevertheless, it is crucial to know that reserves of many of the earth's resources are finite, and to observe that so far in history there has appeared no limit to the capacity of the human race to expand its numbers. Scientists will doubtless continue to ponder the theoretical capacity of the earth to sustain human life; the world's statesmen, however, will be much more vitally interested in such questions as: On what basis will the available resources of the globe be divided among the countries of the world? What countries will make this determination? And by what criteria will it be made? Admittedly, such questions have always been present in some degree in international politics, and in some eras they have been uppermost. In the second half of the twentieth century, however, they may well transcend other issues, such as the cold war. As members of the richer industrial society of the West—a society that will be hard-pressed to maintain its privileged position in a world of mushrooming population and of vocal demands for a greater share of the earth's resources by underdeveloped countries—both Russia and America may conceivably discover in that kinship a common bond that transcends prevailing national and ideological differences, just as they were driven to at least a minimum degree of unity to protect their vital interests during World War II.

Size alone is not the only important aspect of a nation's population. The character of the population is no less significant in determining the magnitude and nature of a country's power. For example, the ratio of younger people to middle-aged and elderly people within the society bears an intimate relationship to such elements in national power as the nature of the labor force and the size or strength of the armed services. In recent years, the United States has experienced an aging process within its population.

Census data for 1960 indicated that the life expectancy of the American population had been pushed ahead to 66.5 years for males and 73.0 years for females.** As life expectancy continues to climb, perhaps at slower rates, demographers expect a further aging in the American

* One student of the problem has emphasized that Americans are addicted to the myth that "economic development cannot fail." Yet he believes realism demands recognition that "for the majority of nations now attempting the long climb" toward economic advancement, "the outcome in our time will be defeat." After one or two decades of sustained effort to raise economic levels, a few notable successes may be achieved, but "a far greater number of the mass of the population will conclude their initial stage of the march very little, if any, higher than their starting elevation." Robert L. Heilbroner, *The Great Ascent: The Struggle for Economic Development in Our Time* (New York: Harper & Row, 1963), pp. 19–20. These were major considerations in prompting the Kennedy Administration to accept a plan that had previously been turned down by the Eisenhower Administration, to make information and assistance on population control available to countries that requested it from the United States. *The New York Times*, May 12, 1963.

** *Demographic Yearbook: 1961*, pp. 121–125. Here again, data for the United States become more meaningful when they are compared with those of other countries. The following figures provide a selective comparison with the *male* life expectancy in countries throughout the underdeveloped world: Congo Republic (Leopoldville), 37.6 years; Guinea (rural population), 30.5 years; Guatemala, 43.8 years; Mexico, 37.9 years; Burma, 30.6 years; India, 32.4 years; Thailand, 48.6 years.

population. Projections of population estimates for 1980, on the basis of assumed "high" fertility rates, indicate that by that year, approximately 9 percent of the American people will be over 65 years of age. Recent demographic experience has also revealed an increased percentage in the number of children among the total population. By 1980, projections indicate that the proportion of the population under 5 years of age will rise to more than 13 percent.

These facts have manifold implications for American foreign policy and for closely related domestic issues. They mean that the "working population" between the ages of 21 and 65 years must support a larger percentage of dependents than formerly. In 1955, the employed labor force was 41 percent of the total population; for 1975, Bureau of the Census estimates place this figure at 38 percent of the total population.[48] Moreover, there will be a smaller percentage of the total population available for military service. A higher allocation of governmental expenditures will have to be directed toward providing services for the very young and the very old. And the aged as a group—to whom many political commentators ascribe a much more conservative point of view about many national issues—will have a greater voice in shaping national decisions.

Another highly significant population trend has been the gravitation of masses of Americans to the cities and the suburbs. As late as 1920, the American population was almost exactly evenly divided between rural and urban elements. By 1930, the balance had begun to swing sharply in favor of the urban (72 million) versus the rural (53 million) dwellers in the United States. The census of 1960 classified 115 million Americans as urban, while 65 million were classified as rural. The ratio of urban to rural population had thus come close to a proportion of 2 to 1.[49] Within this broad movement, a noteworthy trend has been the phenomenal growth of what the Bureau of the Census defines as "metropolitan areas": a county or parts of contiguous counties containing at least one city of 50,000 inhabitants or more or with "twin cities" having a combined population of at least 500,000 people. The census of 1960 showed that the United States contained 212 such areas, having a total population of 113 million people. This category of population in the United States showed a 26.4 percent increase in the decade 1950–1960![50] The gravitation of the American people to the suburbs was a population trend of cardinal importance, vitally affecting problems like national defense or the ability of policymakers to make "creditable" the nation's willingness to use its nuclear arsenal for the protection of the free world. In an age of nuclear weapons, delivered by supersonic aircraft for guided missiles, the increasing population concentration of Americans in such areas created a progressively formidable problem of defense. The American people have only dimly sensed the degree to which prevailing and projected population trends affect traditional concepts of national security and dictate military strategy for defense and offense. Discussion of these manifold ramifications at this point would carry us far afield.* Suffice it to say that the increasing vulnerability of the civilian population and of industrial sites to attack by enemy aircraft or guided missiles more and more calls into question the degree to which the United States can realistically rely upon a policy of "massive retaliation" against the communist empire's expansive tendencies. At the present time, and for an indefinite period in the future, the United States is much more vulnerable to such attacks than its possible adversaries. Proposals designed to reduce the nation's vulnerability—an adequate civil defense program and dispersal of key industrial sites—have encountered widespread resistance and apathy among the population and have thus far had little impact.[51]

Other characteristics of the American population may be alluded to briefly. As the population gets older, an increase in chronic disease levels may be anticipated. Even today, population authorities refer to inadequate medical and dental care for the nation; to the prevalence of malnutrition among certain population groups; to poor housing and sanitation in the larger cities; to the inordinately high incidence of accidents, especially from automobiles—an incidence level so high as almost to qualify as a chronic epidemic in our highly industrialized-urbanized society; and to an alarming growth in mental illness over recent decades.

Of great importance too is the existing and future need for greatly expanded educational facilities to accommodate the growing

---

* Discussion of the factors underlying American military and defense strategy vis-à-vis the Communist bloc is presented in Chapter 9, dealing with elements of the cold war, and in Chapter 10, dealing with the strategy of NATO.

2 → AMERICA LOOKS AT THE WORLD → a study in national character

Objective factors—land, natural resources, economic capacities, population, military forces, and other elements—comprise the basic ingredients of national power. They do not, however, determine what nations will do with their power or decide how a society visualizes its relationships with the outside world. Nations may be strong enough to influence the course of world events in a manner favorable to themselves; yet whether they will do so cannot be determined merely by studying statistics relating to military forces, capacity to produce steel, or national income. For three-quarters of a century before World War II—omitting the interlude of World War I—the United States was a slumbering giant who did not know his own strength and was indifferent to the strength of other countries. It had some power in being and far greater potential power. But its citizens were captivated by the illusion that power was unimportant, that other countries were as indifferent to America's power as America was indifferent to theirs, and that national security could somehow be preserved irrespective of developments on the international scene. That illusion nearly brought the nation to the brink of disaster.

The Role of National Character

What factors determine how the power of nations is utilized? In seeking the answers to this question we must examine what has been called "national character." The question that

Winston Churchill defiantly addressed to the Nazi Government early in World War II—"What kind of people do they think we are?"—is at once a necessary inquiry in any study of foreign policy and an inordinately complex one. As the historian Henry Steele Commager observed, it was because Hitler failed so completely to comprehend the importance of national character that the Nazi bid for world domination ended in catastrophe. His failure was

> fundamental and pervasive. . . . He failed to realize, as throughout history tyrants have failed to realize, that a people's character is, in the last analysis, the most important thing about them. . . . For material things cannot in themselves achieve something. They count only where there is a will to use them, and whether they count for weal or for woe depends upon the way that they are used.[1]

When we ask: "What is the national character of the American people?" we shall focus upon the characteristics they exhibit as they look out upon the world. We want to establish the psychological perspective or frame of reference within which they approach foreign policy. We are searching for what an eminent English scholar, Sir Ernest Barker, called the "sum of acquired tendencies" and the "expectable action" of a nation. He elaborated this idea by saying:

> Each nation lives in a set of ideas (and of emotions associated with the ideas and even

with the very words used to express the ideas), which is peculiar to itself. . . . Any man who has to act between nations . . . is bound to understand, to the best of his power, the peculiarities of each national fund of ideas. He must realize that there are as many atmospheres, and as many characters, as there are nations. . . . Nations are realities; and their characters—the set of their minds, and the atmosphere of their ideas—are as real as they are.[2]

Put more simply, we are asking: Are there certain habits of mind that we can identify as distinctive elements in the American approach to foreign relations? Many authorities agree that there are. Before we attempt to delineate them, however, certain reservations should be considered.

Pitfalls in the Study of National Character

In the first place, some authorities deny the existence of national character altogether. They believe that attempts to discuss it entail nothing more than impressionism and hasty generalization which scientific methodology cannot support.[3] While their admonitions have some validity, most students agree that the subject is important, that it permits investigation and that we can learn something about it, however tentative and qualified our conclusions must sometimes be.

Second, it is imperative that we avoid stereotyped thinking in dealing with the concept of national character. All of us are familiar with stereotypes in this field. "The Germans are inherently militaristic and expansionist." The inference follows that peace with Germany is an illusion. "The French are decadent, immoral, and unreliable." Hence, they make very poor allies. "The Italians are opportunistic and cowardly." Hence, they are easily defeated in war and they, too, make poor allies. "The Latin Americans are ignorant and proud, politically immature, mercurial, and easily misled." Hence, they need guidance by the United States in solving their problems. Such sweeping characterizations are largely false, and the inferences drawn from them are equally false. Sometimes there is a germ of truth in such stereotypes—enough to make them widely accepted. Similarly, by choosing certain episodes in American diplomatic history one could also find enough evidence to make credulous people believe that the United States is imperialistic, money-loving, war-mongering, fickle, and xenophobic. These examples illustrate an important point in the study of national character: nations should be characterized by traits which are in accord with the over-all pattern of the nation's history and ethos and which represent, as nearly as possible, typical behavior of the people described.

A third warning concerns the breadth of the field of study. Scholars in every branch of knowledge have something to contribute here. The physiologist and chemist tell us how our bodies perform; the geneticist enlightens us about the influences of heredity; the psychologist discusses the human personality in its complex ramifications; the social scientist informs us concerning the impact of political, social, economic, and cultural institutions upon man's behavior; and the historian supplies knowledge and interpretations of man's past. This list of course is not complete, for it must be re-emphasized that every discipline has something to offer. The study of national character resembles the creation of a mosaic. To complete the picture, pieces of different sizes, shapes, and importance must be taken from diverse sources. Only then will a recognizable image emerge.

In the fourth place, it must be recognized that many of the traits of national character delineated in this chapter constitute subconscious premises growing out of historical experience, rather than explicit and clearly thought-out popular attitudes on matters of public policy. For this reason, inconsistencies persist among diverse traits of national character. To cite an example dealt with at length at a later stage: Americans in the past have exhibited a dogmatic attachment to "principle" in international affairs, while at the same time remaining devoted to expediency and trial-and-error methods in coping with many of their domestic problems. Yet such inconsistencies are seldom perceived by the average American, chiefly perhaps because he infrequently questions the basic values and beliefs that shape his attitudes toward problems at home and abroad.

A final warning concerns the danger of regarding national character as something fixed and unalterable. The character of neither individuals nor nations is cast in a permanent mold. Sir Ernest Barker wrote: ". . . There is no such thing as a given and ineluctable national character, which stamps and makes the members of a nation, and is their individual and collective destiny. Character is not a destiny to each nation. Each nation makes its character and its destiny."[4] The proper analogy to illustrate national character is an organism —evolving, adapting to influences about it, learning from mistakes, ever-changing.

With these admonitions in mind, let us examine more closely the leading attributes of American national character.

AMERICAN ATTITUDES TOWARD POWER

No feature of the approach of the American people to foreign relations is more pronounced and has had more important consequences for their foreign policy than their attitude toward power conflicts and, specifically, toward war. Throughout most of their history, the American people have deprecated the role of power in international affairs. They have looked upon conflict as abnormal, transitory, and avoidable. Hostilities have existed among nations, not because their vital interests sometimes clashed, but because of "misunderstandings." These, it was believed, could be eliminated by a variety of means: agreements to denounce war "as an instrument of national policy," as in the Kellogg-Briand Pact of 1928; pledges to reduce armaments; solemn oaths to respect the territorial integrity of small countries; ratification of the charter of an international organization; resounding declarations of high principle, such as the Fourteen Points or the Four Freedoms; faith in the "moral opinion of mankind" to deter aggressors; and belief that international student exchange programs and "good will missions" will reduce tensions, as the nations "get to know each other better."

Few writers have stressed the American misunderstanding of the fundamental role of power as frequently, and as pointedly, as Walter Lippmann. Our approach to foreign relations has ever been filled with "stereotyped prejudices and sacred cows and wishful conceptions," to the extent that we are often incapable of formulating workable policies. Our basic weakness is a failure to recognize, "to admit, to take as the premise of our thinking, the fact that rivalry and strife and conflict among states, communities, and factions are the normal condition of mankind."[5]

Such habits of thought stem from a variety of influences in the nation's history. From America's own internal experience, the people have taken the view that fundamental human conflicts did not exist, or if they did, that they could be quickly resolved, because within its own borders remarkably few such conflicts

have in fact persisted. Marxist ideology notwithstanding, the United States perhaps approximates more nearly than any other country the "classless society."[6] In America, conflicts of all kinds—economic, religious, ethnic, racial —have produced relatively little enduring strife, compared with the Old World and the newer nations of Asia and Africa. America has never experienced prolonged and irreconcilable divisions among its people. We have not pitted the Old Regime against the New, the proletariat against the owners of the means of production, religious dissenters against the orthodox, the inheritors of great wealth against the middle class. Somehow, America has learned to channel existing differences into nonviolent avenues, to smooth them out, to make them seem secondary to the task of creating upon a continent the "American way of life." This has been done by providing unparalleled opportunities for material advancement; by steadily trying to offer equal opportunities for all in ever-widening spheres of national life; by de-emphasizing doctrinal and ideological differences in favor of immediate and attainable goals for human betterment; by listening to the demands of dissatisfied groups and, in time, meeting most of them; by insisting upon fair play in economic, social, and political life. Our experience has built in us the conviction that perseverance and will power can solve all problems.

Except for the Civil War, the United States has avoided these societal conflicts that have periodically torn older nations asunder and that, in many of them, have become endemic in their national life. Americans believe that conflict among peoples can be eliminated because they have to a remarkable degree proved it by their own experience.

Then too, the New World came to deprecate power because of the break it made, or thought it made, with the Old World after the Revolution. Throughout the seventeenth and eighteenth centuries, settlers had come to America to escape the tribulations of the old order. Tyrannous monarchs and ministers of state, censors, religious persecutors, entrenched aristocracies, dynastic rivalries, diplomatic intrigues—these they were leaving behind when they came to America. There they were carving out a "new society" where liberty, democracy, equality, freedom, and security for all would prevail. Power politics might be the keynote of the Old World; the dignity of the human spirit, progress, democracy—these came in the course of time to be the themes of the New World. Time and again after the Revolution, America's leaders asserted that Europe and America had separate interests. The United States had no stake in the quarrels of Europe. America wanted nothing so much as for Europe to mind its own business and, if Europe must continue to indulge in power struggles, to keep them away from the American shores.

Consequences for American Security

The consequences of America's attitude toward the role of power conflicts have been far-reaching and decisive. Such an attitude has heavily colored the nation's appraisal of the basis of its security. From superficial examinations of their own history, Americans have believed that their security could be explained by a variety of factors, none of which had anything to do with power. There was first the evident fact of geographical separation from Europe and Asia which, before the air age, did provide a substantial amount of military protection. Then there was the fact that the United States had repeatedly warned other countries to stay out of the Western Hemisphere—and, with few exceptions, the warning had been heeded. There was also the belief that if America chose to ignore the Old World, the Old World would respond by ignoring America. The illusion persisted that no vital interests connected the Old and New Worlds, that America could be secure no matter what transpired in Europe. From the time of the Monroe Doctrine in 1823 to World War II, the United States acted as though its security were a natural right; as though changes in the European balance of power could not affect it; and as though power played an inconsequential, if not altogether negligible, role in international relations. Walter Lippmann has written that for over a hundred years

> The idealistic objections to preparedness, to strategic precautions, and to alliances came to dominate American thinking. . . . The objections flourished, and became a national ideology, owing to the historical accident that in that period Asia was dormant, Europe divided, and Britain's command of the sea unchallenged. As a result, we never had to meet our obligations in this hemisphere and in the Pacific, and we enjoyed a security which in fact we took almost no measures to sustain.[7]

Because the American mythology has traditionally de-emphasized power, historically the United States lived off an unrecognized and unacknowledged inheritance: the British fleet ruled the seas, and the quarrels of Europe kept aggressors otherwise occupied.

A corollary of the American failure to accept the role of power has been the failure to understand that, in the successful management of foreign affairs, assets must equal or exceed liabilities. While it is true that power cannot be calculated with great precision, a rough kind of equilibrium must be maintained between a nation's foreign commitments and its ability to protect them. Bankruptcy, Walter Lippmann has argued, is the only word to describe American foreign policy at crucial intervals in history. American foreign policy was bankrupt for the same reason that we speak of a bankrupt business: obligations were assumed greater than the nation's resources, at least greater than the resources available to the nation's leaders at any given time. The art of conducting foreign policy successfully, Lippmann has contended, "consists in bringing into balance, with a comfortable surplus of power in reserve, the nation's commitments and the nation's power."[8]

In almost any period in American history since 1900, evidence of bankruptcy can be found. The American acquisition of the Philippines after the war with Spain was, in the words of the diplomatic historian Samuel F. Bemis, "The Great Aberration." It was an aberration because annexation of these islands entailed responsibilities which the United States did not begin to appreciate. After some of the implications of extending America's boundaries thousands of miles into the Pacific —to the very doorstep of Japan—finally became apparent, the United States was still unwilling to take the necessary steps to protect its commitments there.

From World War I to World War II this pattern of bankruptcy was repeated on an even broader and more ominous scale. At the very time when threats to its commitments were growing, especially in the Orient, America was *reducing* its military power. Not until 1941 did the American people begin to understand that America's refusal to use its power in behalf of its vital interests was in itself a policy. No nation, especially a powerful nation, can escape having an influence in world affairs. America's unwitting vote in this period was cast on the side of destroying the military security of the Atlantic Community, of turning over the military approaches of the Western Hemisphere to would-be conquerors, of giving Japan a free hand in the Pacific, in summary, of doing every-thing possible to insure bankruptcy in foreign affairs.

Wars Are Aberrations

Another corollary of America's failure to understand the role of power can be found in its attitude toward the causes and consequences of war. Clausewitz taught that war is but the continuation of policy by other means. Hence the cliché that America has never lost a war nor won a peace means that the American people have not had a clear grasp of the political issues leading to and growing out of war, and therefore their policies for dealing with such issues have often been feeble and ineffective.

American history has been characterized by a recurrent failure on the part of public opinion to visualize the connection between foreign policy and national power, especially military aspects of national power. Viewing wars as essentially aberrations, instead of alternative methods of settling international disputes, the American people have evinced minimum historic awareness of the long-term political implications of military decisions. Following both world wars in which the United States has participated, the public failed to assess the implications of the changes wrought by war, either for their own country or for the international community as a whole. Instead, large segments of the population have tended to believe that the nation could return to the *status quo ante bellum*, apparently on the premise that the distribution of global power had not altered in any way that would impair their country's security.

This mentality is well illustrated by the revisionism that has characterized historical writing and literature following virtually every war in which the United States has been engaged. Recurrent themes in revisionist writings have been that responsibility for hostilities rested on both sides, and often more on the American side than on the enemy's; that the United States had no vital interests at stake and hence was under no necessity to fight; and that the American people had been deluded by a variety of influences—propaganda, munitions makers, Wall Street, political leaders—into believing that their security demanded recourse to arms.[9] Revisionism, writes Dexter Perkins, has tried to convince the citizenry that "every war in which this country has been engaged was really quite unnecessary or immoral or both; and that it behooves us in the future to pursue policies very different from those pursued in the past." Behind such thinking, he continues, often lies "the assumption that the will to avoid war is sufficient to prevent war."[10] Walter Lippmann has made this point even more forcefully. Writing in 1940, he explained the blindness of Americans toward the Axis dictators by referring to "a falsification of American history." The American people had been "miseducated by a swarm of innocent but ignorant historians, by reckless demagogues, and by foreign interests, into believing that America entered the other war because of British propaganda, loans of the bankers, the machinations of President Wilson's advisers, and drummed-up patriotic ecstasy. The people have been told to believe that anyone who challenges this explanation of 1917 and insists that America was defending American vital interests is himself a victim or an agent of British propaganda."[11]

In the more recent era, an illustration of American inability to comprehend the connection between military power and diplomatic success was provided by the Indochinese crisis of 1954, leading to the partition of that country between Communist North Vietnam and the pro-Western Republic of Vietnam in the south. This settlement was reached after a prolonged and bitter military contest between pro-Western and pro-Communist forces, in which the tide of battle turned decisively in favor of the latter. The partition of Indochina (along with the "neutralization" of Laos and Cambodia as part of the same agreement) was thus a step taken most reluctantly by Western, particularly American, policy-makers. Yet, as one American negotiator explained: "It will be well to remember that diplomacy has rarely been able to gain at the conference table what cannot be gained or held on the battlefield."[12]

America Reacts to Power

The unwillingness of many Americans to recognize the reality of power in world affairs, in the face of the persistence of conflicts on the world scene among competing powerful states, has resulted in several behavior patterns characteristic of the American approach to foreign relations. One of these patterns has been periodic retreat into an illusory isolationism. When it became clear after World War I that power rivalries were as deeply embedded in international relationships as before, America's reaction was to retire from the field and "let Europe stew in its own juice." Similarly after World War II, with apparently little thought concerning the consequences of its actions, the United States brought its troops home from overseas and demobilized its armed forces. Reluctantly, it began to rebuild its military strength only after unmistakable evidence had convinced the nation that its continued security permitted no other course.

Paradoxically, widespread public misapprehension about the centrality of power in global relationships has also led to popular viewpoints and national policies that are diametrically opposed to isolationism. For example, Americans have shown an affinity for policies whose evident purpose was to make a frontal assault upon the problem of international conflicts in the hope of eliminating them altogether, much as medical science would concentrate its energies and skill to eliminate an epidemic. This pattern of behavior is illustrated by the eagerness many Americans display in embracing slogans and in participating in verbal crusades. Significant numbers of Americans expected that World War I was "the war to end wars" and that victory would "make the world safe for democracy." Two decades later, the conviction prevailed widely that once the Axis was defeated, the goal of "One World" would be achieved, perhaps by establishing the United Nations or by instituting the "Four Freedoms," one of which was freedom from fear. As cooperation among the wartime Allies withered in the face of rising cold war tensions, basically the same mentality was displayed by the tendency of many Americans to think that reiteration of the determination to "stand firm" in the face of communist threats and intonation of militant phrases like "massive retaliation" would go far toward preserving national security.

Still another behavior characteristic that stems from misconceptions about the role of power in global affairs has been the tendency throughout much of American history to identify threats to national security with specific countries and to think that, once this threat was eliminated, international conduct would thenceforth be conducted within an atmosphere of harmony and good will. A logical corollary of this view is that a foreign policy aimed at the total elimination of the existing threat offers the greatest—some Americans might argue, the only—promise of ultimate security. This thinking has been widely exhibited by groups advocating an "interventionist" foreign policy in dealing with the Communist bloc. Such groups have urged the na-

tion to "strike at the root of the problem, once and for all" by "settling accounts" decisively with Moscow and Peiping. Specific policies supported by such groups have included "liberating" the Iron Curtain countries from the communist grip, expanding the Korean War to the Asiatic mainland, and countering the latest communist diplomatic maneuver with the threat of all-out nuclear war. From time to time, a small but occasionally highly vocal minority of Americans has advocated preventive war against the Communist bloc.

Disillusionment must inevitably follow in the wake of utopian expectations. Expecting too much, the American people have ever been reluctant to settle for the attainable; and when they would not take the attainable, they frequently have preferred to absolve themselves of further responsibility for international peace and security. From apathy, to fervent involvement, to disenchantment, to apathy once more —this has been an all-too familiar cycle in American foreign relations. The marked oscillation in moods in American foreign policy has engaged the attention of many writers.[13] That a regular frequency exists for such cycles, or that American public reactions can be predicted by a kind of mathematical projection of historical moods, can be doubted. But the fact of often violent swings in the American public temper toward foreign relations is a phenomenon no historian can deny. It is considered by informed commentators a serious obstacle to sustained and successful efforts in the foreign policy field.

People Are Good; Rulers Are Bad

America's failure to appreciate the role of power is also reflected in the contrast it often draws between peoples and their rulers. Throughout its history the United States has had a profound suspicion of political authority.[14] It has embraced Jefferson's dictum that "that government is best which governs least," and it has clung to this credo over the past half-century, even while the powers of government on all levels were being expanded to unprecedented magnitudes.

Americans have periodically sought to explain the presence of conflict in global affairs by distinguishing between the unfriendly acts of governmental leaders and the supposedly peaceful inclinations of ordinary citizens.[15] Admittedly, this distinction can be used advantageously as a diplomatic technique to encourage a rift between an unfriendly government and its people, in the hope that the leaders can thereby be overthrown or induced to modify their policies. President Wilson undoubtedly was motivated by this hope when he repeatedly distinguished between the leaders and citizens of Imperial Germany. The Allies, he said, had no quarrel with the "German people" but only with their misguided rulers. During World War II, President Roosevelt took the same position toward the political hierarchies of Germany and Italy and, to a lesser degree, Japan. The people of these two countries, it was widely believed, had been seduced by their rulers into paths of military conquest. After World War II, much the same attitude could be discerned in America's relationships with Soviet Russia and Red China. Political orators proclaimed that the common people throughout the communist empire were essentially peace-loving and that they yearned for deliverance from their communist masters. Diverse motivations of course prompted these utterances: hope that public opinion behind the Iron Curtain would compel a softening of the totalitarian regimes prevailing, that it would induce a withdrawal of Russian power eastward, and that it would perhaps evoke a more receptive response to Western views on unresolved diplomatic issues than had been experienced through official diplomatic channels.

Distinctions between peoples and their leaders, nevertheless, rest upon questionable assumptions. For one thing, they often naïvely presuppose that rulers can govern without reference to the wishes of their subjects. For another thing, they fail to account for the continuity between a nation's foreign policy goals and its historic goals and needs as a society. Third, citizens of other countries often actively share the goals of their leaders or, at a minimum, are relatively indifferent to foreign policy questions. Finally, even if the rulers of a country have advanced beyond the point of receiving explicit public approval for their policies, public opinion will oftentimes support such policies once the issue of patriotism infuses disputes with foreign nations. It is open to serious question, for example, whether many of the issues dividing Russia and the West today would melt away if Russia adopted democratic political institutions. Similarly, it is doubtful whether a liberalization of the communist regime in China would appreciably alter that country's determination to become the dominant power in the Orient. Optimistic

hopes of this kind, widely held by groups within the United States, are but another evidence that Americans consistently underestimate the role of national power in world affairs and do not sufficiently grasp the connection between it and foreign policy goals.

MORALISM: THE SHADOW

A second discernible trait in American national character is the emphasis placed upon moralism in relations with other countries. Moralism is not the same as morality, although both derive from a common etymological root. Morality has to do with the substance of behavior. It is conduct in accordance with a predetermined code of behavior, and throughout Christendom this refers to behavior sanctioned by the Christian faith. Moralism, as used here, is concerned with appearances, with the concepts and language employed in foreign relations, with the symbols used, and with the way that ends and means are visualized and expressed publicly. Moralism is not so much moral behavior but public recognition that such behavior is expected and is being carried out by one's own country. Thus it is possible for a nation devoted to moralism to be in fact moral, immoral, or amoral, however the case may be, in its actual conduct. Later in the chapter we shall have more to say about morality in American foreign relations. Now we are interested in the questions: What forms has moralism taken in American foreign policy? What are its tangible evidences?

American Conceptions of "Manifest Destiny"

Americans have always drawn a significant contrast between their own territorial expansion and expansion by other countries. They have deprecated expansionism as a goal of foreign policy—even while in the midst of expanding. Denouncing the British Empire and applauding its dissolution; condemning Germany's territorial ambitions; castigating Soviet Russia's aggrandizements; and, as late as 1950, going to war to vindicate the principle that aggression cannot be condoned—these ideas have formed dominant themes in successive periods of American diplomatic history.

Toward their own experience of expansionism, Americans have taken a somewhat different view. Seemingly irresistible pressure—Americans called it "Manifest Destiny"—propelled American dominion westward to the Pacific and, after that, outward to the Caribbean and

Pacific islands. Believing that this process had nothing in common with ordinary expansionism—soon forgetting that many great Indian tribes were almost exterminated in the process and the remainder confined to almost barren reservations—America looked upon westward expansion as a God-given right. As Ray A. Billington, a historian of westward expansion, observed concerning the Mexican War:

> Every patriot who clamored for Mexico's provinces would indignantly deny any desire to exploit a neighbor's territory. The righteous but ill-informed people of that day sincerely believed their democratic institutions were of such magnificent perfection that no boundaries could contain them. Surely a benevolent Creator did not intend such blessing for the few—expansion was a divinely ordered means of extending enlightenment to despot-ridden masses in near-by countries. This was not imperialism, but enforced salvation. So the average American reasoned in the 1840s when the spirit of manifest destiny was in the air.[16]

Or as a Congressman from Massachusetts sardonically observed in the 1840s: Manifest Destiny was opening "a new chapter in the law of nations or rather, in the special laws of our own country, for I suppose the right of a manifest destiny to spread will not be admitted to exist in any other nation except the universal Yankee nation."[17]

"No Compromise with Principle"

No nation in history has placed so much emphasis upon "principle" in dealing with other countries as the United States. "No compromise with principle!" is a perennial slogan of the American people. Before virtually every international conference in recent history, America's leaders have devoted an inordinate amount of time and energy to giving public assurances that principle would not be abandoned. During the 1950s and 1960s, for example, a major barrier to high-level diplomatic conferences between leaders of the communist and the free world has been deepseated public apprehension that such conferences inherently favored the enemy, that diplomatic "sellouts" and "secret deals" would prove unavoidable. In their attitudes toward such negotiations, certain groups within the United States came dangerously close to equating the very process of negotiation and diplomacy with "appeasement" and abandonment of principle in international affairs. The

tendency of vocal groups and individuals within the United States to make such an identification placed formidable obstacles in the path of a flexible and imaginative American foreign policy and compelled officials often to spend as much time reassuring critics as endeavoring to achieve the nation's goals in the outside world.*

This emphasis, one might even say fixation, upon principle has its roots deep in the nation's past. The diplomatic historian Dexter Perkins has shown that it underlay America's failure to reach an accord with Great Britain after the Revolution and, against its own true diplomatic interests, America's affinity for the French cause during the Napoleonic period.[18] The Monroe Doctrine in 1823 literally resounded with principles. In this period and in later ones, America identified itself with revolutionary causes abroad. In the mid-nineteenth century, for example, American enthusiasm for European revolutionary causes threatened to precipitate several diplomatic incidents between the United States and European governments.

We have already alluded to the skillful manner in which many Americans justified expansionism upon moralistic grounds. Our attitude toward Spain late in the nineteenth century was shaped by the view that the Cuban rebellion accorded with our ideas of justice and morality. At no time did our insistence upon principle emerge so clearly as during World War I, when it lay at the root of our

---

* Sir Anthony Eden, a British statesman who openly opposed Chamberlain's appeasement policies in the late 1930s, has stated that it was the fault of those policies that they cherished "the illusion that to buy a little time, even at the expense of the security of an ally . . . was to contribute to peace, whereas it was in truth a surrender to the threat of force, laying the paving stones to war." The test of whether a proposal in international affairs constitutes appeasement, he has emphasized, is whether it will "serve only to relax tension for a while, or whether it is in the true interests of lasting peace." A government must, therefore, "consider whether its decision gives peace, not just for an hour or a day or two, but in its children's time. That is the difference between appeasement and peace." *The New York Times*, September 29, 1963. Admittedly, the difference between legitimate peace proposals and appeasement remains cloudy and involves judgments that will not always command universal agreement. Synonyms for appeasement listed by Webster—to pacify, quiet, calm, sooth, allay—suggest that the idea is basic to human relationships and is central to efforts aimed at resolving differences among nations by peaceful means.

quarrel with Germany and, by contrast, our long-suffering endurance of repeated British provocations. The Allies were fighting for freedom and democracy; for freedom of the seas (even while they denied it to us); for self-determination and independence from monarchial and totalitarian rule; for the rights of small nations; and for international integrity. What did the Central Powers, especially Germany, stand for? They represented militarism and authoritarian rule within, expansionism and calloused opportunism without. They were breakers of treaties, violators of innocent nations, and, perhaps most heinous of all, contemptuous of the ordinary standards of decency and morality expected of nations in the Western community. American principles and German behavior (at least America's image of it) were at antipodes. It was this fact which more than any other finally drew the United States into World War I.

Principle again pervaded the American attitude toward dictators in the interwar period. In the eyes of many Americans, the most serious indictment of, and great cause for concern about, Japanese or German or Italian diplomatic conduct was that these countries were frequently violating openly international agreements like the Kellogg-Briand Pact, the Covenant of the League of Nations, or that their conduct was at variance with the conventions, understandings, and rules of comity that normally governed relations among civilized societies. Americans often tended to condemn the Axis dictators much more because they regarded treaties as "scraps of paper" or because their pledged word was contradicted with impunity than because the Axis powers posed a growing military and economic threat to the security of the North Atlantic community. Strong aversion to the behavior of international gangsters, rather than a rational understanding of America's own vital interests in the mounting conflict, steadily drew the American people closer to the Allies.[19]

Turning to the postwar period, we find evidences of moralism toward a number of important international issues. Soviet Russia's exploitation of the Eastern European satellites, for instance, was viewed as a calculated and willful violation of the agreements reached at Yalta and Potsdam concerning the treatment to be accorded conquered and liberated nations. So great was America's aversion to Soviet machinations in this area that the United States sometimes took a keener interest in

events there—in an area where it had in fact very few vital interests—than in many other areas, such as Southeast Asia or the Middle East, where its own diplomatic interests were more direct and fundamental. Similarly, moral principle has been invoked repeatedly in defense of America's attitude toward Red China. The vast majority of Americans has felt that Red China cannot be permitted to "shoot its way into the United Nations" and that it must prove "by deeds and not words" that it is ready to become a peace-loving member of the family of nations before American recognition of the communist regime can even be contemplated.

Some Consequences of Moralism

America's affinity for moralism has had both positive and negative aspects. On the positive side it may be said that no other course accords with American experience and ideology. If Americans invoke principle more than most countries, it may be because the American people are conscious of how often principle is lacking in international affairs. If they insist upon a "decent respect for the opinions of mankind," it is because of a deep conviction that mankind is tired of Machiavellianism, that it yearns for an international order in which justice, enforced by law, prevails. In common with all reformers, Americans tend to concentrate upon the ultimate goal without gazing down at the pitfalls in the path of its attainment. If they are forever exhorting other nations and calling them to repentance, it is because they are so impressed with the need for charting new paths. Americans are asking other countries to pattern their conduct according to standards which, for the most part, Americans are willing to accept for themselves.

To foreigners, Americans must resemble nothing so much as the Puritan: motivated by high ideals, austere, unshakable in his conviction that goodness will triumph in the end —but at the same time impatient with wrongdoing, sanctimonious, and at times insufferably self-righteous.

An uncritical attachment to principle also has its negative side. It can cause the nation to dispense with all colors on the political spectrum, leaving only black and white. When significant numbers of Americans evaluate prevailing global issues in terms of consummate righteousness versus consummate wickedness, habits of mind and practices are inculcated that seriously interfere with success in the foreign policy field. In the late 1950s and early 1960s, for example, a notable characteristic of American attitudes in foreign affairs was the obvious impatience and lack of sympathy displayed by Americans in dealing with "neutralist" or "nonaligned" countries. Although their leaders usually displayed deeper insight into the phenomenon of neutralism, masses of Americans tended to evaluate the movement according to the simple axiom: countries that are not incontestably with us are against us. To the American mind, when nonaligned governments like India or Indonesia or Egypt did not take an unequivocal stand against communism, or when they did not accept American strategies in the cold war, they were widely accused of voluntarily or involuntarily siding with the enemy. Since Americans have believed that there could be no compromise with principle in their relations with the Communist bloc, and since they have systematically identified their own policy positions with "principle," they have expected other countries to support the American diplomatic position, at the risk of being considered a member or satellite of the communist cause.

Informed commentators have likewise stressed the tendency of Americans to postulate total extremes and mutually exclusive alternatives in their approach to vexatious and often highly complex global issues. For example, in wartime, goals are delineated sharply: unconditional surrender or complete defeat; appeasement or victory; universal democracy or absolutism. International conflicts thus become, or are constantly in danger of becoming, Armageddons.[20] Firmly convinced of the goodness of their cause, Americans often find it difficult to understand why it does not triumph and triumph speedily. "The illusion of American omnipotence," the perceptive British observer D. W. Brogan has written, resides in the belief that "any situation which distresses or endangers the United States can only exist because some Americans have been fools or knaves." Large numbers of Americans, he feels, have yet to learn that "the world cannot be altered overnight by a speech or a platform."[21]

In practice, the American propensity to believe that principle must not be compromised frequently resolves itself into the view that there can be no compromise at all. As a society, Americans have shown minimum preparedness to live with vexatious problems in the international community for extended periods of time. Their expectation is that problems will be "solved" and that tensions can be "eliminated." Frequently, they assume that threats to world peace and stability can be "removed," much as a housewife would summon an exterminator to deal with pests. So prominently does principle infuse their approach to such issues that the American people have often overlooked a lesson they have learned, or are still in the process of learning, in their own internal affairs. This is that very few problems in human relations are ever solved in a final sense. They are ameliorated, softened, mitigated, outlived, tempered, adjusted to—but seldom solved. This lesson emerges with striking force from any study of such diverse problems as divorce, delinquency, alcoholism, traffic accidents, crime, and a host of others. Nevertheless, sizable numbers of Americans confidently look forward to the elimination of the "communist problem" and, more generally, conflicts arising from clashing national interests. Their own experience could also teach them another pertinent lesson: few human problems yield before a dogged insistence upon principle, accompanied by short-lived and passionate crusades to eliminate the problem. More often, they yield instead to persistent and understanding efforts to deal with them and to an awareness that, if principle is present at all, it is likely to be present in some degree on both sides.

MORALITY: THE SUBSTANCE

The American people have been outstandingly moralistic in their foreign affairs. Have they at the same time been more than ordinarily moral? What is their record in practicing the ideals they have professed and have tried to impose on others? In broad outline, the answer is that throughout their diplomatic history American citizens have placed a high value on moral behavior for themselves and for other countries as well.

The American Attitude Toward War

If we are to judge by the number of wars, both major and minor, in which the United Stated has engaged, the record does not indicate that the nation has been conspicuously peace-loving. From the Revolution to the Korean War, there have been eight major wars and in between a host of small-scale ones. Reviewing this record, Dexter Perkins comments that "it does not seem to be a strikingly pacific one, at least not utterly out of line with the history of other nations." He adds also that we must keep in mind that territorial acquisitions —for which many other countries are forced to wage war—came to Americans primarily through purchase and negotiation.[22]

But the number of wars in which the United States has been engaged proves little or nothing about the extent of morality in its foreign policy. America has fought only one, the Mexican War, which could even remotely be construed as a war for territorial aggrandizement, and even then it compensated Mexico for the territory taken. America has traditionally been slow to anger. It has never gone to war over a "diplomatic incident." In its two greatest wars it has endured repeated provocations and has devoted months to seeking peaceful solutions before finally and reluctantly drawing the sword. This fact alone, of course, does not prove superior morality on the part of the American society; in part, the explanation derives from an overwhelming preoccupation with domestic pursuits and from a widespread inability to perceive the connection between events in Europe and national security. Nevertheless, the United States has probably been as unwarlike as any great power in history. In the vast majority of instances, only repeated provocations have forced the nation to enter military conflicts.

Moreover, the terms imposed upon vanquished nations have not, in the main, been severe. After both World War I and II, it was the United States that tried to mitigate the severity of the terms which the Allies wished to inflict upon the enemy. With rare exceptions, vindictiveness has not been a characteristic of the American mind. This may occasionally have been a passing phase, but it soon gave way to a sincere desire to help rehabilitate conquered nations, to aid them in re-entering the family of nations.

We have already alluded to America's reluctance to take foreign territories as a result of war. The United States has of course done so, but usually because, as in the Spanish-American War, there appeared no other alternative. Moreover, it has repeatedly refused to take reparations and indemnities. A classic case was the Boxer Rebellion (1900), when indemnities paid to the United States were set aside for the future education of Chinese students in America. Following all its wars in recent history, it has given generously through governmental and private agencies for the relief

of suffering following in the wake of hostilities.

We conclude that America has never been a warlike country and that in victory it has been magnanimous.

Is America "Imperialistic"?

America's territorial expansion raises the question: Can the United States fairly be accused of being imperialistic? The answer depends in large part upon how imperialism is defined. If it signifies the acquisition of foreign territory primarily for the exploitation and advantage of the mother country, only one judgment on American foreign policy is possible. It has been remarkably nonimperialistic.

As Dexter Perkins insists, a fundamental distinction must be maintained between expansionism and imperialism.[23] The United States —beginning as a weak country along the fringes of the Atlantic Ocean and becoming within 150 years one of two superpowers—has expanded more than any country in recent history, with the possible exception of Russia under tsarist and communist rule. Most of America's territory was acquired by purchase or negotiation. That taken by conquest—by some interpretations, Florida, the territory acquired after the Mexican War, the Philippines, and the Panama Canal region—was later compensated for by the United States. Admittedly, this account ignores the fact that most of the continental United States was in fact taken by conquest from its original inhabitants, the Indian tribes. And, parenthetically, it also ignores the fact that in dealing with the Indians the United States was guilty of violating practically every moral precept it has tried to follow toward other countries.

American domination over foreign territories, Perkins holds, has "always been rule with an uneasy conscience."[24] Toward the vast continental land mass at home, one principle was consistently followed throughout American history: whenever the frontier lands were ready for statehood, they were admitted to the Union on an equal plane with the older states. Toward colonial societies a somewhat different but closely related principle has prevailed: they were to be tutored in the art of self-government and prepared for ultimate independence. Two overseas possessions—Alaska and Hawaii—were groomed for admittance into the Union, and were admitted in 1958 and 1959, respectively.

American administration of possessions and

dependencies overseas has almost invariably led to marked improvement in their national life. Living standards were pushed up; modern sanitary practices were introduced; education was fostered and made available to ever-growing numbers; democratic political processes were encouraged among the inhabitants. After reviewing the broad stream of America's colonial record, Perkins concludes that "in the moderation which ought to go with strength, the United States has played and is playing a creditable role."[25]

What America has done with its territories, however, may not be as significant as what it has not done. For, as Herbert Feis has emphasized, few countries in history have voluntarily foregone as many opportunities to acquire additional territory and to impose their will on weaker countries as the United States. Historically, the United States has refused to join with other strong countries in parceling out colonies and spheres of influence. Much of the tension developing between Japan and the United States during the 1930s, finally leading to Pearl Harbor, could be traced to America's refusal to join with Japan in staking out spheres of influence in the Orient; the Roosevelt Administration's refusal to acquiesce in unilateral Japanese expansionism further widened the gulf between the two countries. After World War II successive administrations in Washington steadfastly refused any *rapprochement* with the Soviet Union based upon a division of the world between the two power giants.[26]

America and Militarism

Another manifestation of the American national character is the attitude of its people toward the military establishment. We shall have more to say about this in Chapter 4, when we shall examine the constitutional and ideological restrictions which the American people have imposed upon their armed forces. Throughout history, the American people have opposed a large standing army. They have preferred to raise troops by voluntary recruitment rather than by conscription. A fundamental principle of the American constitutional pattern has always been civilian control over the military. So firmly have precedent and public opinion supported this doctrine that not even during time of war has there appeared significant danger of military domination of the government. President Truman's unceremonious dismissal of General Douglas MacArthur in 1951 caused a temporary public furor; but sober reflection convinced most citizens that Truman's action vindicated a principle that must be preserved. Even popular generals must be required to accept the strategy of the nation's elected political leaders on pain of instant dismissal.

The aversion of Americans to military service may also be seen in the rapidity with which the United States has demobilized conscripted forces at the end of major wars. After World War II it would be charitable to say that the army was demobilized; it would be more accurate to say that it disintegrated. America's historic bent for frenzied demobilization has had fateful consequences for national security and the security of the North Atlantic community. Following World War II, two years at least were required before public opinion accepted the fact that, at a number of crucial points around the globe, power vacuums had developed. The alternatives finally came to be seen as simple and painful: either the United States rebuilt its military machine to the level required for discharging its diplomatic responsibilities, or else many strategic areas—Greece, Iran, Western Europe, North Africa, Japan, Korea—might well pass into the communist orbit.

Though America has been antimilitaristic, it has not been antimilitary. The distinction here is fundamental. Americans have feared and distrusted the substance of military power, but they have applauded and glorified many of its trappings and incidentals. "I Love a Parade" describes America's attitude toward military pomp and ceremony. No other country in the world has so many military academies for the training of its youth—schools, it must be emphasized, which stress the building of disciplined minds, strong bodies, and courtly behavior, rather than trying to produce a military elite dedicated to bringing the nation glory through conquest. Few national holidays and athletic occasions are complete without an impressive parade, often including precision marching units from some military post or, if not that, then at least several civilian bands carefully trained in close-order drill. America has found a substitute for militarism: it lies, in large part, in glorifying many of the superficial aspects of military life, while at the same time rejecting its substance.[27]

"A Moral Equivalent for War"

The great American philosopher William James urged the nation to find a moral equivalent for war—some concept or activity that would elicit the same sense of dedication to a higher cause, the same spirit of sacrifice, the same passionate ardor that Americans had demonstrated during time of war. James's idea has lost none of its pertinency with the passage of time. In the post-World War II era, Americans sometimes showed considerably more reluctance about supporting activities designed to assure peace and to attack the long-range causes of war than about making sacrifices once the nation entered into hostilities.

Nevertheless, from the time of the Jay Treaty with England in 1794, the United States has been in the forefront of nations seeking alternatives to force for settling international disputes. For example, it has time and again favored the arbitration of boundary and territorial disputes.[28] It has followed the same course toward controversies over neutral rights, such as occurred with Britain over the "Alabama claims" during 1866–1872, and over violations of American neutral rights during World War I and II.[29] It has sponsored and joined efforts to institutionalize arbitration, as when it accepted the Hague conventions of 1899 and 1907, and when it sponsored the Bryan arbitration treaties in the early 1900s.[30]

In seeking a moral equivalent to war, it has taken the lead in establishing international organizations for dealing with threats to the peace. True, it refused to join the League of Nations. Nevertheless, it supported the League in a number of ways during the years that followed; and during the 1930s it cast its moral, though never its military, influence behind efforts of the League to deal with repeated aggressions by the Axis states. During World War II it very early took the initiative in planning for a new international security organization to preserve world peace. Since the war, few countries have been more conscious of the necessity for strengthening the United Nations than the United States. Not that its record in the UN has been free from blame. America has ignored the UN in a number of important instances and to that extent has contributed to weakening its prestige. Still, it has worked diligently to establish the UN upon a firm foundation and to endow it with enough power to deal effectively with international threats. In the case of major international and regional crises in the recent period —the Korean War, the Middle Eastern conflict in 1956, the Congo crisis in 1960, and the Cuban crisis in 1962—the United States has been in the forefront of states calling for collective action to prevent or curb military hostilities. In the Middle Eastern and Congo crises, American influence was highly instrumental in preserving the authority of the United Nations in the face of attempts by the Soviet Union and other states to undermine it. Toward the Cuban crisis, if Washington did not lean initially upon the United Nations to deal with the threat of a communist intrusion into the Western Hemisphere, it at least was willing to accept subsequent attempts by the United Nations to mitigate the crisis and to avert a head-on American-Soviet military confrontation.

Since World War II, America's traditional sponsorship of arbitration and the conference method for settling international disputes has also been tempered by the popular disillusionment growing out of postwar negotiations with the Communist bloc. The great emphasis accorded to "principle" in approaching cold war issues, along with the widespread popular equation of compromise with appeasement, has notably reduced America's traditional enthusiasm for conference diplomacy and arbitration techniques. Nevertheless, Americans have traditionally placed great faith in their ability to persuade other countries to settle differences rationally and without recourse to violence.

This, along with a number of other aspects of their national character discussed in this chapter, is at once one of the virtues as well as one of the weaknesses of American foreign policy. It is a virtue, because as long as diplomats are talking—even when their talk sometimes degenerates into propaganda and irresponsible accusations—there is still hope that armies will not march. If war is to be avoided, a rational discussion of the issues that give rise to tensions would appear to be the only conceivable preventive.

But interminable talk, conferences, meetings "at the summit," and the like, can also be detrimental. Unmindful of the limitations inherent in diplomatic conferences and high-level negotiations, Americans often tend to entertain unrealistic expectations about the results that can be achieved. Productive negotiations require a will to peaceful and mutually acceptable solutions on the part of all participants. Fair and reasonable offers, as Chamberlain discovered in dealing with Hitler, and Roosevelt and Truman found out in dealings with Stalin, can furnish the basis for lasting accords only when the other side is also interested in reaching an equitable agreement. When it is not—when, instead, it views concessions as but the prelude to further, and perhaps greater, concessions—then negotiations may not only be unproductive; in some instances, they can create the appearance of progress in resolving outstanding diplomatic issues, thereby encouraging the public to believe that prevailing controversies have in fact been settled. In turn, this may easily result in public unwillingness to support national defense efforts and other programs vital to the achievement of national policy objectives. This is not to suggest that all diplomatic conferences, even those between ideological antagonists, are futile and ought to be discontinued. Barren as they sometimes prove, diplomatic exchanges are obviously to be preferred to military showdowns. But public opinion should not expect too much from such conferences. When spectacular results are not forthcoming, the public should not despair of reaching agreements in the future and should not condemn diplomatic techniques as a whole. Such disillusionment, growing out of unreasonable expectations, places an additional barrier in the path of sustained attempts to achieve a *modus vivendi* among nations with competing ideologies and rival national goals.

ISOLATIONISM IN WORD AND DEED

Isolationism has pervaded the American approach to foreign relations since the earliest days of the Republic. America's pattern of isolationist thought is well illustrated by its foreign policies during the 1920s and 1930s. What is not so widely recognized is that isolationism goes much deeper than merely the desire to avoid foreign entanglements. It is above all a habit of mind, a cluster of national attitudes, a feeling of spiritual separation from other countries, especially Europe, with roots penetrating deeply into the nation's heritage and experience.

Isolationism, as Albert K. Weinberg has aptly put it, is "not a theory of American foreign policy. Isolationism is a theory about a theory of American foreign policy."[31] It is more than a doctrine advanced to explain the objective facts of America's geographical relationship with the rest of the world. Instead, it is supposed to explain *what the American people believe to be the proper relationship between themselves and other countries*. Isolationist thinking permeates the American cultural experience, its philosophy, and what may be called more generally "the American way of life." It is basically a conviction that Americans are different from other people; that they do not look to foreigners for guidance but that

foreigners should look to them; that their national destiny is to serve as a beacon to pilot all mankind into new paths of greatness—but that all this should be done primarily by precept and example.

The Roots of American Isolationism

The influences that have contributed to isolationist thinking are many and complex. Here we can do no more than allude to some of the more important ones.[32] The desire for separation from the vicissitudes of Europe brought settlers to the New World. The wish to begin life anew, to leave behind the turmoil, the hopelessness, the bigotry of the Old World —these ambitions brought the religious dissenter, the peasant, the adventuresome aristocrat, the skilled artisan, the speculator, and the felon to American shores. From all walks of life they came, and with one objective: to find a new birth, as it were, in a far-off continent.

The Revolution cut the political ties with England, and as the years passed, Americans came to believe more firmly than ever in their uniqueness. Washington and Jefferson both cautioned their countrymen that America and Europe had different interests and advised that America's best course was to concentrate on keeping these interests distinct. Very early in the nation's history, isolationism became the underlying principle of foreign policy. One pretext after another, for example, was found to justify America's refusal to honor the French alliance during the Napoleonic wars. Against the wishes of many citizens, especially those in New England, the nation was finally drawn into a war against England in 1812. But within a little over a decade, President Monroe in 1823 asserted that the United States had but one objective in its relations with the Old World: it wanted the European countries to mind their own business and, if they must persist in power struggles, to keep them out of the Western Hemisphere. Owing to an underlying identity of interests between the United States and Great Britain—an identity that did not become widely recognized until the post-World War II period—America, shielded by the British navy, experienced remarkably few challenges to the Monroe Doctrine during the course of almost a century.

America Looks Inward

From the Monroe Doctrine until World War II the American people were profoundly isolationist. We must regard participation in

World War I as an interlude. Its politico-strategic significance generally passed unnoticed within the United States. Historically, the energies, thoughts, and ambitions of the American people have been directed inward. Americans possessed a continent to populate and to incorporate within the boundaries of their country. They were feverishly creating out of their seemingly unlimited resources vast wealth and expanding opportunities for all. The ceaseless intrigues and struggles witnessed on the continent of Europe held no appeal compared with the challenge of creating the "American way of life." Passionately dedicated to the belief that human progress was limitless, the American people were tackling many of the formidable problems older civilizations had been unable to solve and, in most instances at least, they were solving them reasonably well: problems of unemployment, of unequal distribution of land, of racial and national minorities, of religious liberty, of illiteracy, of political oppression, of the pressure of population upon food supply, of the equitable distribution of wealth, and of hereditary rights. And if America's solutions to these and other problems left some groups unsatisfied, the solutions were at least good enough to force acknowledgment even from foreigners that the "new society" was becoming a reality across the Atlantic.

Isolationism derived then as much from the dominant concern of the American society with domestic affairs as it did from a deliberate rejection of foreign entanglements. The achievement of virtually every goal associated with the "American dream" demanded that internal interests receive primary attention. This fact prompted one of the nation's leading historians, Charles A. Beard, to prefer the term "continentalism," instead of isolationism, to characterize the nation's historic orientation in foreign policy. Elaborating Beard's idea, a contemporary American observer, Max Lerner, has written: "It was not so much a question of cutting America off from the world as it was of rounding out and fully exploiting the part of the world that was America."[33]*

* Lerner's comprehensive study, *America as a Civilization*, affords many insights into the American mind. His discussion of isolationism is particularly illuminating. Lerner calls attention to the kinship existing between two seemingly antithetical schools of thought in foreign affairs, isolationism and interventionism. The isolationist wants to reduce the nation's foreign commitments and follow a go-it-alone philosophy in foreign relations. By

America Is the "New Society"

What then were the elements in this new society, this "American way of life"? We shall leave its dominant theme—belief in the perfectibility of man and his institutions—for consideration later in the chapter. There was intense pride in the accomplishments of the American people. A perceptive observer, D. W. Brogan, has written admiringly: "To have created a free government, over a continental area, without making a sacrifice of adequate efficiency or of liberty is the American achievement. It is a unique achievement in world history."[34] A recent American writer credits the United States with two phenomenal accomplishments: it has succeeded in preserving, in an age of centralization and autocracy, the self-reliance of the individual and the autonomy of the local unit of government; and it has come closer than any nation in effecting a separation between the holders of economic and political power.[35]

Then too there was the theme of cultural separation that pervaded American literature during the nineteenth century. Listen to James Russell Lowell in "A Fable for Critics":

Forget Europe wholly, your veins throb
    with blood,
To which the dull current in hers is but
    mud; . . .
O my friends, thank your god if you have
    one, that he
Twixt the Old World and you sets a gulf
    of a sea; . . .
To your own New-World instincts contrive
    to be true, . . .[36]

This was a dominant strain of New World literature throughout the greater part of the nineteenth and twentieth centuries. Not that American writers did not acknowledge their great dependence upon a common English and

contrast, the interventionist advocates greater reliance upon military power in dealing with threats to security, and urges the nation to undertake diplomatic offensives to achieve goals like the liberation of the communist satellite countries or the overthrow of the communist regime in China. Despite the marked dissimilarities in their methods, Lerner contends, their underlying goal is basically the same: to create conditions throughout the world that will permit the United States once again to focus its energies on domestic affairs, with minimum involvement in foreign affairs. Both schools operate upon the assumpton that the nation's destiny continues to be, as in the past, preoccupation with the American way of life, see *ibid.*, pp. 881-907, *passim.*

European literary heritage. But now they wanted a literature distinctly American, one that would express the nation's hopes and ideals in a way that European writers never could. This uniquely American flavor made Walt Whitman America's outstanding poet. "I Hear America Singing" may not have been his greatest poem, but it expressed better than most his abiding ambition: to chronicle in song the American way of life, to point to both its achievements and its unsolved problems, and to show the world that America was well on the way toward building a society based upon the principle of the brotherhood of man.

> Thou, too, sail on, O Ship of State!
> Sail on, O Union, strong and great!
> Humanity with all its fears,
> With all the hopes of future years,
> Is hanging breathless on thy fate!

These familiar lines from Henry Wadsworth Longfellow ("The Building of the Ship," 1849) point to another consequence of the belief that America was the new society. America's example, it was thought, would be sufficient for other nations to take hope and, by tugging at their own bootstraps, as the American people had done, to raise themselves to new levels of human attainment. The United States, as Hans Kohn put it, has been the "universal nation" in two senses. First, American institutions, philosophies, and accomplishments have mirrored the hopes of mankind. Second, for over a century, America's doors were open to receive the stranger and to provide him every opportunity for making the American dream come true.[37] This part of the American dream had been expressed by Jefferson in 1817, when he wrote that America's mission was

> to consecrate a sanctuary for those whom the misrule of Europe may compel to seek happiness in other climes. This refuge once known will produce reaction on the happiness even of those who remain there, by warning their taskmasters that when the evils of Egyptian oppression become heavier than those of the abandonment of country, another Canaan is open where their subjects will be received as brothers. . . .[38]

Emerson was convinced that "Our whole history appears like a last effort of the Divine Providence in behalf of the human race. . . ."[39] And in 1839, John Louis O'Sullivan wrote an article entitled "The Great Nation of Futurity," the theme of which was that

> Our national birth was the beginning of a new history, the formation and progress of an untried political system, which separates us from the past and connects us with the future only; so far as regards the entire development of the rights of man, in moral, political and national life, we may confidently assume that our country is destined to be the great nation of futurity.

The writer concluded that America

> is destined to manifest to mankind the excellence of divine principles. . . . For this blessed mission to the nations of the world, which are shut out from the life-giving light of truth, has America been chosen. . . .[40]

By the twentieth century, the belief that America was ordained by Providence to redeem the world by example had, like the early Christian expectation of the coming of the Kingdom, been modified in the light of realities. But such thinking persisted as late as the post-World War II period. Many Americans apparently saw no reason why underdeveloped countries all over the world could not repeat America's experience by evolving slowly from a "frontier" society to become in the course of time, and with American assistance, a mature, democratic, industrial-urban nation. That many countries were having difficulty doing so was interpreted widely in the United States as a sign that they were variously indolent, politically misled, or willfully ignorant.[41]

Some Consequences of Isolationist Thought

The way in which isolationist thinking has shaped American foreign relations is a subject too vast to engage our attention here. It must be left for future chapters, when we examine American foreign policy toward major questions. But we can at least point to several specific corollaries of America's isolationist mentality.

A well-known maxim of American foreign relations, down to the post-World War II period, has been the desire to avoid "entangling alliances" in order to preserve freedom of action in world affairs. If America was to regenerate the world by example, it must remain free to save itself.[42] Closely related to this idea is that of "nonintervention." America demanded that the Old World keep out of the New, and, in turn, was willing to forego intervention in the affairs of other countries. Moreover, until the recent period, America usually refused joint action with other countries. The Monroe Doctrine was proclaimed unilaterally even though Britain had initially suggested it. The United States refused to join the League of Nations. Toward the dictators in the 1930s it usually preferred to play a lone hand. Not until the postwar years has the United States been willing to engage in joint action for long periods of time.

Isolationism has been manifested also in America's reluctance to assume foreign territorial commitments. When they were assumed, every effort was made to reduce them as soon as possible. Territorial acquisitions in the wake of the Spanish-American War furnish a good example of this attitude.[43] Even in the postwar period, this desire to shun foreign ties has been evident. Required to spend billions of dollars annually for defense and foreign aid, and to keep large military establishments in other countries, America has not yet become reconciled to foreign involvement as a permanent feature of its foreign policy. Every year Congress, invoking the pressure of public opinion, reduces the foreign aid budget below executive requests.

The great awakening which came in American national consciousness only after World War II was the realization that the United States was not isolated from the world and never had been. The United States might pretend that it was; it might delude itself into thinking that by will power alone the nation could avoid entanglement in the destiny of the world. But this mythology, the nation discovered through painful experience, courted national disaster. Other nations did not regard the United States as isolated. Other nations were very much interested in what America would do with its massive power. Other nations would not accept the view that America could remain aloof from political developments around the globe. After World War II the American people had at last come to see, if at times only dimly, that disengagement was possible only for a minor power, a decadent power, or a country that deliberately chose to imperil its own future security. What kind of involvement was it to be? What ought to be its objectives? What were the proper means to attain them? These were the questions that Americans in the mid-twentieth century were accepting as the overriding foreign policy questions of their age.

THE THEME OF PROGRESS AND HOPE

We have reserved the theme of progress and hope for consideration last, because it is per-

haps the most distinctively identified with the American national character. This theme pervades every aspect of the American way of life and has been a dominant note in American foreign relations.

Distinguished foreign visitors to America have agreed that America "was the land of perfectionism. The American knew that nothing was impossible, in his brave new world, and history confirmed his intuition. Progress was not, to him, a mere philosophical ideal but a commonplace of experience, and he could not understand why foreigners should see vulgar realities where he saw visions."[44] Lord Bryce found that, in America, "Men seem to live in the future rather than in the present. Not that they fail to work while it is called today, but that they see the country not merely as it *is* but as it *will be,* twenty, thirty, fifty, a hundred years hence, when the seedlings they have planted shall have grown to forest trees."[45] A more recent writer has stated that when he looked at America he saw "a people who, by everlastingly tugging at their own bootstraps, have raised themselves to a new peak of economic welfare."[46] Contrasting the attitude of Americans toward world affairs in the postwar period with that exhibited by Europeans, Brogan writes: "Probably the only people in the world who now have the historical sense of inevitable victory are the Americans."[47] And an American has written of his own country:

America pulses with life. It may, like a tree, have its rotten branches, its dead wood; but when those branches are cut away—as happens again and again—the tree goes on flourishing. This is something which cannot be said for any blueprint society, of the Left or Right, bureaucratic or theocratic. Contrary to what was taught by the Fascists 20 years ago, it is the democratic society that is dynamic and the doctrinaire society that is static.[48]

The Wellsprings of Optimism

What explains this undeniable optimism, this belief in the limitless possibilities for the advancement of mankind? We have already touched many of the explanations, so that we shall treat them here only briefly. Let us answer the question by asking another: What *other* credo could possibly accord with America's philosophical and religious heritage, its material advancement, and the total pattern of its history? Optimism and hope have ever pervaded American thought, because in no other country in the world has there been so much ground for optimism and hope. If it was believed that the lot of mankind could be infinitely improved, that was because America had demonstrated it. When the Seabees chose their motto during World War II— "The difficult we do at once, the impossible takes a little longer"—they were expressing a great national creed.

The eminent American historian Frederick Jackson Turner believed that no influence was more important in instilling optimism than the frontier. As Ray A. Billington has phrased the Turner thesis: ". . . No one force did more to Americanize the nation's people and institutions than the repeated rebirth of civilization around the western edge of settlement during the three centuries required to occupy the continent."[49] An American orator in the nineteenth century, Edward Everett, commented that "the wheel of fortune is in constant revolution, and the poor, in one generation, furnish the rich of the next."[50] When Horace Greeley advised "Go West, young man!" he was in effect expressing the national conviction that a new start was always possible, that by will power alone an individual could leave his past behind and carve out a new future for himself and his posterity.

The closing of the frontier was a milestone in the nation's history, but not as important as sometimes supposed. After 1900, new frontiers beckoned: disease must be wiped out; corruption must be eradicated from American political life; industry must be compelled to operate within a context of the public interest; depressions must be prevented and protection afforded against unemployment; wealth must be distributed more equitably; religious, racial, ethnic, and social barriers must be torn down; education must be made available to all; and new paths must be blazed in the one area which seemed most persistently to defy man's best efforts—the conduct of international affairs.

Underneath the conviction that mankind could and must improve itself lay firm philosophical and theological foundations. One was the religious heritage of Calvinism, with its emphasis upon predestination. An important part of this belief was that material blessings were an outward symbol of salvation. As the American dream unfolded, it was easy for this belief to become corrupted into the view that material blessings *were* salvation. If faith could

move mountains, then the moving of mountains, must surely be a sign of superior faith! Material progress and the view that America had been predestined by Divine Providence to lead in the spiritual regeneration of the world were the warp and woof of the New World's credo.[51]

From Enlightenment philosophy America took a belief in the perfectibility of man and his institutions. The Enlightenment philosophers had believed passionately in the inherent goodness of man as he was led by reason. Two political upheavals—the French and the American Revolutions—had tried to prove them right. Both tried to create the "new society." One failed and the other succeeded; but somehow, Americans fixed their attention only on their own success. Scornful of religious dogmas emphasizing natural depravity and "the fall" of man, fiercely devoted to the scientific study of nature, clinging doggedly to the conviction that "all men are created equal" and that they possess equal rights, Enlightenment philosophers and their intellectual descendants never doubted that good would conquer evil, if man would make the necessary effort.*

America, says the anthropologist Geoffrey Gorer, has always been a materialistic nation —not merely in the narrow sense of wishing to possess material goods and judging success by their acquisition, but in a much deeper sense. It has been materialistic because it has believed profoundly that personality, character, human qualities, and actions can all be manipulated

* That such habits of mind have diminished little throughout the course of American history is indicated by a UN-sponsored study of public opinion in various countries. Findings based upon surveys of public opinion within the United States are especially illumining. The "security index"—a device to measure over-all satisfaction with a society's status—was very high for the United States. A high percentage of Americans (50 percent) thought that human nature could be changed, although only half this number thought it was likely. Significantly, Americans scored higher than any other group polled in placing environment at the head of the list of factors determining national character, further suggesting the American people's belief in beneficial change. Slightly more Americans believed that world peace could be achieved than believed that it could not be achieved. All groups in the American society, even the most dissatisfied ones, characterized the United States still as the "land of opportunity." The adjectives Americans relied upon heavily to characterize themselves were: peace-loving, generous, intelligent, progressive, hard-working, and brave. See: William Buchanan and Hadley Cantril, *How Nations See Each Other* (Urbana, Ill.: University of Illinois Press, 1953), pp. 32, 83–84.

in the same way that man manipulates machines to create better products and achieve a higher standard of living. If matter is subordinate to the will, so is human character and personality.[52] "The power of positive thinking" can remove problems and eliminate barriers to human progress. As D. W. Brogan has phrased it: "Many, very many Americans . . . find it inconceivable that an American policy, announced and carried out by the American government, acting with the support of the American people, does not immediately succeed."[53] Their history, he feels, does not prepare them to accept the fact that "great as is American power, it is not so great as to quell, by its mere existence, all opposition."[54]

Some Consequences of the American Dream

Optimism and almost boundless confidence in man's ability—and possibly even more important, his desire—to improve his lot is reflected in a variety of attitudes and actions characteristic of the American people. We have already referred to the historically naïve belief that military force and "power politics" can and must be eliminated from the sphere of international relations. Until recent years it was difficult for many Americans to believe that other countries might plan and carry out aggression, exploit weaker countries, willfully violate treaties, and embark upon programs of aggrandizement. America has ever thought that good intentions could prevent war, especially if they were committed to paper, and statesmen pledged the sacred honor of the nation to abide by them. The main thing, America has traditionally believed, is agreement on broad principles—justice, democracy, freedom, self-determination, peace—and trust that the good will of reasonable men will translate these into specific courses of action beneficial to all.[55] There is a close parallel, D. W. Brogan has observed, "between the optimism that led to the enactment of prohibition and the optimism which welcomed that international Volstead Act, the Kellogg Pact. In that optimism there was a strong element of the old-time religion, of belief in the old evangelical mass conversion. Hundreds and thousands had renounced the world, the flesh, and the devil . . . why should not the nations renounce mutual murder?"[56]

Not infrequently, the ingrained optimism, characteristic of the American approach to foreign relations, has infused a new breath of hope into seemingly fruitless international nego-

tiations. In many instances, like disarmament negotiations or reliance upon the United Nations, American diplomatic initiative has been largely responsible for maintaining the quest for global peace and security. Despite many setbacks in achieving their foreign policy goals, Americans as a whole have never been prone to accept the view that mankind was fated forever to witness violent clashes of rival national ambitions, which in the nuclear age might imperil future civilization itself.

Yet America's buoyant optimism has also tended to breed utopian expectations about the nation's role in the global scene. Projecting their own domestic experiences into this realm, Americans have traditionally had bright visions and idealistic goals for the world community. When these had little immediate effect upon an often unreceptive and intractable international environment, in time large segments of the American society were prone to retreat into a kind of crestfallen and disillusioned isolationism. Such habits of mind, for example, have long been conspicuous in connection with the foreign aid program. Distressed by the meager results sometimes achieved with such aid, and chagrined that it did not always guarantee a pro-Western orientation on the part of the recipient countries, individuals and groups within the American society tended to oppose foreign aid *per se* or to urge that it be reduced drastically. That such habits of mind continued to pose great difficulties for policy-makers was indicated by President Kennedy late in 1963. The President urged his fellow citizens to "acknowledge the realities" confronting the United States in external affairs. Americans, he emphasized, must "recognize that we cannot remake the world simply by our command. We cannot remake [other nations] in our own image, nor can we enact their laws, nor can we operate their government, nor can we dictate their policies."[57] President Kennedy thus sought to counteract the American disposition to believe that progress in international affairs was as feasible, or could be made as rapidly, as progress on the American continent itself. When events proved otherwise, Americans were too often psychologically unprepared to accept the inherent differences between domestic and foreign affairs, and then to revise their expectations in the light of prevailing global realities.

Optimism is closely tied up with another American trait: affinity for expediency and pragmatism, and rejection of doctrinaire blue-prints for remaking society. America's acknowl-edged material prosperity is an eloquent testimonial to ingenuity, improvisation, and experimentation. The quest for wealth at home has been accompanied by an easy tolerance of differing opinions, so long as these did not interfere with material progress.[58] Few Ameri-cans have been struck by the contradiction between pragmatism at home and great em-phasis upon "principle" often manifested in the nation's relationships with foreign coun-tries. Lewis Galantière has written: "We are not doctrinaire, we have no dogmas to exalt; we are empiricists, and our defects are revealed when we are compelled to shift rapidly from the short to the long view. We leave ourselves free to act as seems rationally requisite or emotionally satisfying in any present situa-tion."[59]

Such habits of mind can and do place difficult barriers in the way of successful foreign policy, all the more so when the nation has emerged as the leader of a great coalition. Post-war experience has highlighted many of these limitations upon effective policy when sus-tained foreign commitments are demanded. Maintaining the long-run military effort re-quired to implement the doctrine of contain-ment, providing economic and technical assistance to other countries on a basis that will permit long-term planning and material progress, preserving continuous and effective liaison with the allies, following consistent policies toward problems in international trade —in these instances evolving effective foreign policies has been hampered from time to time by the pragmatic tendencies of the American people and has challenged them as never before to formulate and to pursue predictable and consistent courses of action in their foreign relations.

NOTES

1. Henry S. Commager, ed. *America in Per-spective* (New York: Random House, 1947), p. xi.
2. Ernest Barker, *National Character* (Lon-don: Methuen and Co.), 1948, p. xi.
3. Boyd C. Shafer, *Nationalism: Myth and Reality* (New York: Harcourt, Brace, & World, 1955). Boyd contends that there is no such thing as national character, and he cites the views of other commentators to support his thesis.
4. Barker, *op. cit.*, p. 7.
5. Quoted in D. W. Brogan, *The American Problem* (London: Hamish Hamilton, 1944), p. 18.
6. Hans Kohn, *American Nationalism: An In-terpretive Essay* (New York: Macmillan, 1957), pp. 140–150. This is one of the most illuminating treatments of American nationalism available.
7. Walter Lippmann, *U.S. Foreign Policy: Shield of the Republic* (Boston: Little, Brown and Co., 1943), p. 49.
8. *Ibid.*, p. 9.
9. Cushing Stout, "The Twentieth Cen-tury Enlightment," *American Political Science Review*, **XLIX** (June, 1955), 335–337.
10. Dexter Perkins, "American Wars and Critical Historians," *Yale Review*, **40** (Summer, 1951), 686, 695.
11. Kohn, *op. cit.*, p. 219.
12. Quoted in Royal Institute of International Affairs, *Survey of International Affairs: 1954* (London: Oxford University Press, 1957), pp. 68–69.
13. Dexter Perkins, *The American Approach to Foreign Policy* (Cambridge, Mass.: Har-vard University Press, 1952), pp. 114–128; F. L. Klingberg, "The Historical Alterna-tion of Moods in American Foreign Policy," *World Politics*, **4** (January, 1952), 239–273.
14. Geoffrey Gorer, *The American People* (New York: Norton, 1948), pp. 30–39. A provocative study of American character by a cultural anthropologist, even if the explanations offered sometimes seem highly oversimplified.
15. *Ibid.*, pp. 227–229.
16. Quoted in Kohn, *op. cit.*, p. 181.
17. Quoted in *ibid.*, p. 183.
18. Perkins, *The American Approach to For-eign Policy*, *op. cit.*, pp. 68–70.
19. *Ibid.*, pp. 69–75.
20. Walter Lippmann, "The Rivalry of Nations," *The Atlantic Monthly*, **181** (February, 1948), 19–20. A cogent essay dealing with certain deeply embedded American ideas about the outside world.
21. D. W. Brogan, "The Illusion of American Omnipotence," *Harper's Magazine*, **205** (December, 1952), 21, 28. The intervening years have done little to change the force of Brogan's perceptive observations about American attitudes in global affairs.
22. Perkins, *The American Approach to For-eign Policy*, *op. cit.*, p. 84.
23. *Ibid.*, pp. 30–31.
24. *Ibid.*, p. 32.
25. *Ibid.*, p. 45.

26. Herbert Feis, "Is the United States Imperialistic?" *Yale Review*, **41** (Autumn, 1951), 13–24.

27. Brogan, *The American Problem, op. cit.*, pp. 62–65; Gorer, *op. cit.*, pp. 30–39.

28. Julius W. Pratt, *A History of United States Foreign Policy* (Englewood Cliffs, N.J.: Prentice-Hall, 1955), pp. 143–154, 201–218, 247–352, 458–460. An interestingly written and scholarly one-volume account of American foreign relations.

29. *Ibid.*, pp. 315–319; 466–482; 634–645.

30. *Ibid.*, pp. 451–456.

31. Albert K. Weinberg, "The Historical Meaning of the American Doctrine of Isolation," *American Political Science Review*, **34** (April, 1940), 539.

32. For more detailed discussion of the sources of isolationist thought, see: Max Beloff, "The Foundations of American Policy," *The Spectator* (London), **194** (February 25 and March 4, 1955), 210–211 and 247–249, respectively; Gorer, *op. cit.*, pp. 224–237; Lippmann, *U. S. Foreign Policy: Shield of the Republic, op. cit.*, and Weinberg, *op. cit.*

33. Max Lerner, *America as a Civilization* (New York: Simon and Schuster, 1957), p. 888.

34. Brogan, *The American Problem, op. cit.*, p. 101.

35. Lewis Galantière, "America Today: A Free-Hand Sketch," *Foreign Affairs*, **28** (July, 1950), 532.

36. Cited in Kohn, *op. cit.*, p. 69.

37. *Ibid.*, p. 139.

38. *Ibid.*, p. 138.

39. Quoted in *ibid.*, p. 140.

40. Quoted in *ibid.*, pp. 152–153.

41. Gorer, *op. cit.*, pp. 223–224.

42. Weinberg, *op. cit.*, pp. 539–541.

43. *Ibid.*, pp. 542–544.

44. Commager, *op. cit.*, p. xix.

45. Quoted in Ernest L. Klein, *Our Appointment with Destiny* (New York: Farrar, Straus & Co., 1952), p. 97.

46. Quoted in *ibid.*, pp. 8–9.

47. Brogan, "The Illusion of American Omnipotence," *op. cit.*, p. 22.

48. Galantière, *op. cit.*, p. 547.

49. Kohn, *op. cit.*, p. 21.

50. Quoted in *ibid.*, p. 18.

51. Ralph Barton Perry, *Characteristically American* (New York: Knopf, 1949), pp. 93–105. In this volume a distinguished American philosopher examines his society's character, with particular attention to its philosophical and religious roots.

52. Gorer, *op. cit.*, pp. 137–224.

53. Brogan, "The Illusion of American Omnipotence," *op. cit.*, pp. 25–26.

54. *Ibid.*, p. 23.

55. Perkins, *The American Approach to Foreign Policy, op. cit.*, p. 111.

56. Brogan, *The American Problem, op. cit.*, pp. 62–63.

57. *The New York Times*, September 27, 1963.

58. Gerald W. Johnson, *Our English Heritage* (Philadelphia: Lippincott, 1949), pp. 44–45.

59. Galantière, *op. cit.*, p. 535.

3 ➡ THE PRESIDENT, THE
DEPARTMENT OF STATE, AND
AMERICAN FOREIGN POLICY ➡

Constitutional Appearance and Reality

In any discussion of American foreign relations, one must grasp at the outset the distinction between constitutional *appearance* and *reality*. Constitutional myth holds that the American government is divided into three co-equal branches and that each has certain clearly defined duties and prerogatives. Constitutional reality proclaims that—at least in foreign affairs, and very largely in domestic affairs also—this belief is sharply at variance with American historical experience.

We may dispose of the Supreme Court's role in American foreign relations by saying that its function is mainly confined to prescribing the spheres of the other two branches and to keeping each within its proper orbit. Yet it is possible to exaggerate the importance of even this modest role. Time and again in American diplomatic history the Supreme Court has refused to mediate between the President and Congress, on the ground that disputes between them were "political" in nature and hence outside the jurisdiction of the Court. In foreign affairs its mediating role has been reluctant, limited, and tardy. The Court has chosen to leave twilight zones. One commentator writes that the Court "has fixed neither the outer boundaries nor the inner divisions of the President's martial authority, and has failed completely to draw the line between his powers and those of Congress. . . ."[1] Typical of the cautious attitude of the Court was the verdict of Justice Swayne in 1870 that "The measures to be taken in carrying on war and to suppress insurrection are not defined. The decision of all questions rests wholly in the discretion of those to whom the substantial powers involved are confided by the Constitution."*

The Constitution divides the bulk of power in the foreign policy field between the executive and legislative departments. Yet, as we shall see more fully below, historical experience has greatly modified certain provisions of the Constitution and has added traditions and precedents to the American governmental system. The total impact of these changes is to magnify greatly the powers of the President and to reduce those of Congress over foreign relations. Admitting that today legislative influence in foreign affairs has increased significantly over the prewar period—reaching perhaps the highest plane in American history

* *Stewart* v. *Kahn*, 11 Wallace 493 (1871). Examples of questions the Supreme Court has held to be political, and hence subject to executive or legislative treatment alone, are: the determination of boundaries between countries; the determination of the country that possesses sovereignty over particular areas; whether a country ought to be classified as a belligerent under international law; whether a country has properly ratified a treaty; whether a person is properly accredited to the United States; whether the terms of a treaty are still in effect. For these and other examples, see Edward S. Corwin, ed., *The Constitution of the United States of America* (Washington, D.C.: Legislative Reference Service, Library of Congress, 1953), pp. 471–475.

—the President is still the dominant influence in world affairs. Throughout history, writes a leading student of the Constitution, "the greatest single force in setting the course of American foreign policy has been Presidential initiative. . . ."[2] We now turn to a detailed investigation of the President's powers in foreign affairs.

These powers may be conveniently grouped into three categories: those specifically set forth in the Constitution; those which have evolved through usage and tradition; and—a special category of both—war or emergency powers giving the President authority to deal with national crises. Recognizing that these categories are often closely entwined, that no arbitrary and rigid compartmentalization is possible, let us look at each of them more fully.

THE PRESIDENT'S CONSTITUTIONAL POWERS

The Treaty-Making Process

The Constitution provides that the President "shall have power, by and with the advice and consent of the Senate, to make treaties, provided two-thirds of the Senators present concur . . ." (Art. II, Sec. 2). Responsibility for treaties—formal and usually long-range agreements in the international field—is thus divided between the President and Senate. The treaty process embodies two stages: negotiating agreements and ratifying them. The constitutional requirement for ratification is clearly set forth. Treaties become law only when two-thirds of the members of the Senate present approve them. However, controversy has always surrounded the provision that the President makes treaties with the "advice" of the Senate. Specifically, what does this mean? How does the Senate give its advice? To what degree is this advice binding upon the President? Such questions have been productive of endless argument.* Various answers are possible. They may be grouped broadly into two schools of thought. The theory most frequently voiced by the Senate itself is that this clause compels the President

to consult with the upper chamber from the *earliest stages* of negotiation, that it requires him to regard the Senate as an advisory council in reaching agreements with other countries. The second school—the view expressed by successive Presidents—is that "advice and consent" are in fact tantamount to the same thing. The President seeks the "advice" of the Senate when he requests its "consent" to a treaty already prepared and signed by executive officials.

Whatever the merits of the argument—the Founding Fathers probably held the first theory—there can be no doubt about which view has predominated. Throughout the entire process of treaty-making the President retains the initiative. Tradition and precedent have reduced the Senate's role largely to deciding whether treaties shall or shall not be ratified. The executive branch negotiates them, signs them in the name of the United States, presents them to the Senate for approval, and, after they are ratified, proclaims them as law. The Senate may refuse to ratify them, in which case the President has other means of achieving agreements with other nations. Moreover, the chief executive may refuse to accept amendments affixed by the Senate; he may withdraw the treaty from consideration by the Senate at an time; and he may even refuse to proclaim a treaty after it has been ratified, if he feels its terms no longer accord with the national interest.

So passive has the Senate's role become in the treaty-making process that even senators themselves have cautioned that body against attempts to intrude into the President's direction of foreign affairs by construing the "advice and consent" clause broadly. Thus the highly respected Senator Arthur H. Vandenberg (Republican of Michigan) told his colleagues in 1948:

I think the Senate is entitled, at any time it pleases, to use the advice clause of the Constitution to tell the Executive what it thinks concerning foreign affairs. But I think it would be a tragic and unfortunate thing if the habit ever became general or too contagious because I respectfully submit, . . . only in those instances in which the Senate can be sure of a complete command of all the essential information prerequisite to an intelligent decision, should it take the terrific chance of muddying the international waters by some sort of premature and ill-advised expression of its advice to the Executive.[3]

* For examples, consult: Cecil V. Crabb, Jr., *Bipartisan Foreign Policy: Myth or Reality* (New York: Harper & Row, 1957), chap. 1; D. F. Fleming, *The Treaty Veto of the American Senate* (New York: Putnam, 1930); W. Stull Holt, *Treaties Defeated by the Senate* (Baltimore: Johns Hopkins University Press, 1933).

Treaties are the traditional and most formal kind of international agreement, but they are by no means the only type. With increasing regularity, Presidents have come to rely upon "executive agreements"—understandings between heads of state—rather than upon more formal treaties to carry out foreign policy goals. George Washington negotiated such an agreement in 1792, providing for reciprocal mail delivery. Although other Presidents utilized executive agreements over the years that followed, Franklin D. Roosevelt raised them to a new pinnacle of importance as a technique of executive control over foreign relations. A well-known example is the "Destroyer Deal" made between FDR and Prime Minister Churchill in 1940, exchanging fifty obsolete destroyers for British bases in the Western Hemisphere. The following year FDR was granted authority by Congress to enter into agreements with the nation's allies for the provision of lend-lease assistance. During the war, allied conferences at Casablanca, Tehran, Yalta, and Potsdam resulted in a host of agreements concerning military strategy and postwar political settlements. None of these was submitted to the Senate for approval. Surveying diplomatic experience during the first half of the twentieth century, one commentator found that almost half of the international commitments made by the United States were in the form of executive agreements. In more recent years they "have outnumbered treaties by perhaps ten to one."[4]

Executive agreements are of two types: those reached by the President alone, and those that receive prior or subsequent legislative sanction. The former are exemplified by the Yalta and Potsdam agreements referred to above. Increasingly, however, Congress has participated in giving effect to executive agreements. Congress empowered FDR to enter into the lend-lease agreements alluded to earlier. The United Nations Participation Act of December 20, 1945, authorized the President "to negotiate a special agreement or agreements with the Security Council which shall be subject to the approval of the Congress by appropriate Act or joint resolution" providing for the allocation of American military forces for the use of the Council in maintaining international peace.[5] Congress has also given the President authority to enter into agreements with other countries to reduce tariffs on a reciprocal basis.

Wherein do executive agreements differ from treaties? The Constitution designates treaties as the "supreme law of the land," whereas executive agreements are not so designated, unless they become the supreme law of the land by virtue of legislative sanction. The terms "treaties," "agreements," and "compacts" are used in the Constitution, but constitutional authorities do not feel that the courts have ever provided a clear differentiation among them.* And in Edward S. Corwin's view, "what difference there once may have been has been seriously blurred in practice within recent decades."[6] Nevertheless, some differences are suggested by historical experience. Congress can change the terms of certain types of executive agreements, or repeal them by subsequent legislation, as exemplified by Congress' action in 1924 in superseding Theodore Roosevelt's 1904 "Gentleman's Agreement" with Japan on Japanese immigration to the United States. Asked in 1918 how long a particular executive agreement remained valid, Secretary of State Robert Lansing told the Senate Foreign Relations Committee that the agreement in question remained in force only so long as the President and his principal subordinates chose to abide by it.[7] This may be contrasted with treaty agreements, which customarily carry a stipulated time limit. Presumably, those executive agreements that have received congressional approval would be terminated if Congress withdrew its approval, although it must be admitted that for certain categories of problems the President might continue to accept the existence of an understanding with foreign governments.

The Supreme Court has been most reluctant to intrude into the field of foreign relations. It expressed a typical view in *United States* v. *Pink* in 1942. This case involved FDR's agreement recognizing Soviet Russia. The court ruled that the President had recognized Russia following Russia's adherence to certain conditions and that the Court "would usurp the executive function if we held that that decision was not final and conclusive on the courts."** We must conclude that there are very few effective limitations upon the President's power to arrive at understandings with other heads of state by means of executive agreements and that such agreements consti-

* For an extended treatment of the meaning of these terms, see the Supreme Court's opinion in *Holmes* v. *Jennison*, 14 Peters 540 (1840).

** 315 U.S. 203 (1942).

tute an important executive tool in the management of foreign relations.

Authority over the Military Establishment

Few clauses in the Constitution have been more productive of disagreements between the President and Congress than Article II, Section 2, providing that "The President shall be Commander-in-Chief of the Army and Navy. . . ." As with the treaty power, Congress also possesses important prerogatives over the military establishment, such as the duty to provide for the army and navy, to regulate its size, to equip and support it, and to declare war. Theoretically, this fact places substantial limits upon the President's control of foreign relations, because success in foreign affairs is heavily dependent upon military strength.

Assuming then that Congress has provided for adequate military force, what agency of the government shall determine its use for foreign policy ends? By virtue of its powers in this field, and especially its power to declare war, can Congress instruct the President in the use of the military establishment in times of peace or war? Is the President limited in the use he can make of armed forces to the extent that he must not risk war without the consent of Congress?

The answer to all these questions is negative.[8] Once the armed forces have come into being and their character (e.g., their size, the proportion of ground, naval, and air forces to the whole) has been determined by Congress, the President alone utilizes them in behalf of national policy. It is difficult to unravel the exact intention of the founding fathers when they gave Congress the power to "declare war." In their era, wars usually were "declared" formally, often weeks or months before hostilities actually began. Legislators could therefore safely debate the wisdom of going to war. Quite obviously this luxury is not afforded the nation today. In an age of nuclear weapons and blitzkrieg tactics, the nation could be destroyed while its leaders deliberated. Speed in committing the armed forces for defense has thus come to be vital to national survival.

The facts of military life have largely rendered the right of Congress to declare war a dead letter, at least as far as this clause limits the power of the President to utilize the armed forces for foreign policy ends. The President, says Charles Fairman, is clearly "vested with power adequate to directing the defense of the United States."[9] The controlling legal decision

here, as with so many bearing upon the scope of the President's authority, goes back to Lincoln's era. During the Civil War he blockaded Southern ports without legislative approval. In *The Prize Cases* the Supreme Court held that the President could not legally "initiate war," but he was "bound to accept the challenge without waiting for any special legislative authority."[*] This principle—that the chief executive is required to meet any threat arising to the security of the country—has stood for over a century.

Stated differently, war has come to be regarded as a state of reality rather than a condition specified by legislative decree. The President must react to it, and react swiftly. A senator observed over a century ago that "another country can commence a war against us without the cooperation of Congress."[10] Richard Henry Dana, in arguing *The Prize Cases* before the Supreme Court, contended that war "is a state of things, and not an act of legislative will."[**] President Eisenhower made essentially the same point when he said in 1954 that "hanging ought to be the fate of any President who failed to act instantly to protect the American people against a sudden attack in this atomic age."[11]

In the postwar period, controversy over executive and legislative prerogatives relating to military affairs has taken place on three occasions: over President Truman's handling of the Korean War, over his proposal to send American ground forces to participate in NATO's defense efforts in Europe in 1951, and over President Eisenhower's request for congressional support of the Eisenhower Doctrine in 1957. President Truman did not wait to receive legislative sanction before committing American troops to halt communist aggression in Korea in 1950. Truman's action elicited scattered and altogether ineffectual protests on Capitol Hill.

Controversy also surrounded President Truman's plan in 1951 to station American troops on the European continent—the first time in history that American troops were to be stationed in friendly countries during peacetime for an indefinite period. Throughout the troops-to-Europe debate, the President and his advisers insisted that the White House did not "need" legislation authorizing this step, but that the administration would welcome it in the interest of demonstrating bipartisan unity.

[*] 2 Black 635 (1863).
[**] 2 Black 659–660 (1863).

Ultimately, Congress voted to approve substantially the steps decided upon by executive policy-makers.[12] Again in 1957 the issue of control over the military establishment arose when the Eisenhower Administration submitted a detailed program to Congress for dealing with recurrent crises in the turbulent Middle East. Secretary of State Dulles affirmed the traditional view when he declared that "under our constitutional system the President . . . is Commander in Chief of the Armed Forces . . . and, as such, has the right to determine their disposition. That is a right which cannot be impaired by action of Congress."[13] Similarly, when President Eisenhower in 1955 requested stand-by authority from Congress to use military forces if necessary to protect Formosa from threatened communist attack, he believed that, desirable as a legislative resolution would be, this power was already largely "inherent in the authority of the Commander in Chief" to safeguard national security.[14]

Maintenance of Diplomatic Relations with Other Governments

From Washington's Administration onward, it has been a settled constitutional principle that, as the chief of state, the President alone maintains relations between the United States and foreign governments. The Constitution, said President Grant in 1877, "has indicated the President as the agency to represent the national sovereignty, and to receive all official communications" from other governments.[15]

Foreign diplomats are accredited to the President of the United States. Official communications from other governments are addressed to him or his subordinates. Longstanding diplomatic protocol prohibits foreign governments from having any official contact with other leaders or institutions within the American government or from appealing to public groups over the head of the President, upon pain of having diplomats violating this rule declared *persona non grata*, thereby requiring them to leave the country. On occasion, flagrant departure from this rule has led to strained diplomatic relations between the United States and foreign countries, as exemplified by tensions growing out of Imperial Germany's propaganda activities in the United States prior to the country's entry into World War I.

The severance of diplomatic relations often is the prelude to war between countries. When a nation has deliberately chosen to embark upon war or when it feels that war is unavoidable, it will recall its own diplomats and revoke the credentials of the diplomats of its enemies. The power to sever diplomatic relations belongs exclusively to the President, stemming from his position as the sole channel of communication with foreign governments.

Conversely, the principle that the President is the official spokesman for the United States in its dealings with foreign countries prohibits unauthorized *official* contacts between citizens of the United States and other governments. Citizens who violate this rule will almost certainly have their passport privileges revoked and may even be liable to criminal prosecution. In view of widespread foreign travel by congressmen and the general public, however, this rule is not likely to be enforced stringently unless such individuals embarrass executive policy-makers by working against established American policy.

Quite clearly the power of the President in controlling relations with other governments greatly enhances his already dominant position in the management of foreign relations. By such methods as cables and personal interviews, the chief executive and his subordinates are in constant communication with other countries. A steady stream of information about developments in the international community pours into the State Department, the Defense Department, the CIA, the Commerce Department, and many other executive departments. Such information, together with data gathered by the President's agents from other sources, gives the chief executive data requisite for sound decisions in the foreign policy field.

Intimately related to the problem of maintaining relations with other countries is the issue of recognition. Recognition of another government normally is followed by an exchange of diplomatic representatives with that government, entailing the twofold process of sending American diplomatic officials abroad and receiving diplomatic officials accredited to the United States. Concerning the first of these acts, both the President and the Senate have certain prerogatives. The Constitution (Article II, Section 2) stipulates that high-level diplomatic appointments, along with all other major presidential appointments, must receive the confirmation of the Senate. Inasmuch as our principal interest here is examination of the President's powers, we shall reserve fuller treatment of the Senate's role for Chapter 5. At this point it is enough to emphasize that Presidents possess many ways of circumventing effective Senate control over their actions. They may rely upon "personal representatives" who may or may not already hold governmental positions. The chief spokesman for American foreign policy during the Wilson Administration was Colonel Edward M. House, who performed many diplomatic functions at home and abroad, with minimum liaison with the State Department. Franklin D. Roosevelt leaned heavily upon Harry Hopkins, so much so that ultimately Hopkins was referred to in the press as "Roosevelt's personal foreign office." In the early months of World War II, Hopkins played a decisive role in cementing closer Anglo-American relations, a process made possible in part by his prolonged residence at Prime Minister Churchill's home.[16] Then, too, Presidents may make "interim appointments" in the diplomatic field when the Senate is not in session. Even if the Senate ultimately refuses to confirm the individual so appointed, he may have already performed important duties, as was the case with Philip Jessup, President Truman's appointee to the American delegation to the United Nations in 1951.[17]

Vigorous claims have been asserted periodically throughout American history that the Senate's power of confirmation gives that body the right to determine the substance of American foreign policy by specifying the duties that appointees are to carry out. Yet after more than 150 years, the Senate's power in this sphere is clearly peripheral. Determined and imaginative Presidents are seldom deterred from carrying out policies they believe to be in the national interest, even when they encounter opposition in the Senate.

The second stage in recognition involves the reception of accredited diplomatic officials from other countries. Here the President has a completely free hand. The Constitution stipulates that the President "shall receive Ambassadors and other public ministers" (Article II, Section 3), leaving the chief executive free to exercise his discretion in the reception of foreign diplomats. He may receive them or refuse to receive them, as his conception of the national interest dictates. It is not unusual for foreign countries to inquire whether certain individuals are acceptable, before sending them abroad. Moreover, having initially received a diplomat from abroad, the President may declare him *persona non grata*, whereupon he will be forced to leave the country. Although a wise President will always take account of opinion prevailing on Capitol Hill and throughout the country generally, he is under no constitutional obligation to heed congressional resolutions or other indications of public sentiment dealing with the question of recognition.*

Recognition involves much more than the mere formality of who shall represent the United States abroad and who shall be accredited to this country by other governments. Normally, the recognition of one country by another implies a willingness to conduct harmonious relations with that country. A government's refusal to recognize another government, on the other hand, usually signifies misunderstandings and tensions between them, as illustrated by America's refusal for many years to recognize the communist regime in Soviet Russia and its continuing unwillingness in the recent period to accord recognition to Red China.** Recognition then is an important tool of diplomacy available to the President. Its use in specific circumstances will be governed by the nation's objectives in foreign policy. Quite often, considerations of national security enter into the issue of recognition. During World War II, for instance, FDR and Secretary of State Hull succeeded in acquiring rights to Greenland—a vital base protecting the northeastern approaches to the continent—by refusing to recognize the existing Danish Government, which had capitulated to Hitler, and by dealing instead with the Danish Government-in-Exile, which was amenable to the agreement.[18] After the war, relations with Soviet Russia were strained over a number of recognition questions. Presidents Truman, Eis-

* In spite of this fact, Congress has not been reluctant in recent years to express itself vigorously on matters like the recognition of Red China. Thus, Section 105 of the Mutual Security Appropriations Act for fiscal year 1959 states: "The Congress hereby reiterates its opposition to the seating in the United Nations of the Communist China regime . . . the President is *requested* to inform the Congress insofar as is compatible with the requirements of national security, of the implications upon the foreign policy of the United States" if Red China is seated in the UN. See House Resolution 13192, 85th Congress, 2nd Session, August 23, 1958 (italics inserted).

** Nonrecognition is not synonymous with a severance of diplomatic relations. Nonrecognition usually implies coolness in the relations between two countries but does not usually lead to war. Conversely, nations—Russia and America are examples—may continue to recognize each other, although a considerable amount of tension prevails in relations between them.

enhower, Kennedy, and Johnson refused to recognize Soviet incorporation of the Baltic States into the USSR; creation of the "East German People's Republic"; and Russian hegemony over formerly independent countries in Eastern Europe. In the Far East, the overriding question involving recognition has concerned Red China. Ever since the communist regime came into power in 1949, the United States has consistently refused to accord recognition to it or to support its admission into the United Nations. As explained more fully in Chapter 13, events since 1949 have tended to call into question many of the assumptions underlying this policy. If and when recognition is eventually extended, the decision will be taken by the President and will be based upon his estimate of how such a step accords with the over-all objectives of the United States in world affairs.

HISTORICAL-TRADITIONAL TECHNIQUES OF PRESIDENTIAL LEADERSHIP

Let us look next at certain important techniques of presidential diplomatic leadership that are largely an outgrowth of history and tradition. Some of these techniques are not mentioned, except perhaps by indirection, in the Constitution. Yet many of them have become well-nigh permanent features of the American constitutional system.

The President's Control over Information

Wise decisions in foreign policy, as in any field, require the continuous collection and evaluation of information pertinent to the problems at hand. It follows, therefore, that executive leadership in foreign relations flows naturally from the ability of the executive branch to gather such information and, when national security demands it, to preserve its confidential character. Through the intelligence activities of the State Department, the Central Intelligence Agency, the military establishment, and other agencies, the President is in a unique position to know more about external developments than any other individual or group within the government.

Very early in American history, Congress recognized the necessity to give the chief executive and his advisers wide discretionary powers to gather information and to keep it confidential. Alone among the executive departments, the Department of State has always been regarded by Congress as solely accountable to

the President. This principle also governs legislative relations with the Central Intelligence Agency and the National Security Council. Other executive agencies may from time to time be *required* to furnish records and data for the guidance of Congress. In regard to the State Department and other agencies concerned with national security problems, however, Congress can only *request* the President to supply desired information when such a step is "not incompatible with the public interest."[19] The right—even the constitutional duty—of the chief executive to withhold confidential information bearing upon national security has been affirmed again and again throughout American history, not alone by the President but by the Supreme Court as well.* And much as individual congressmen from time to time complain about the "wall of secrecy" surrounding deliberations of the executive branch, Congress itself has done much to perpetuate this state of affairs by enacting legislation that provides severe penalties for the release of classified information dealing with such matters as the operations of the Department of Defense or information related to national defense, the activities of the Central Intelligence Agency, and unauthorized possession of any classified information.[20] When the National Security Council, the highest interdepartmental committee in the government, was created in 1947, Congress deliberately ordered that it report solely to the President. Reporting to Congress, said one legislator, would be like "reporting to the entire world."[21]

In recent years, successive Presidents have staunchly resisted efforts by congressional investigating committees to obtain confidential information from the executive departments. During a controversial Senate investigation of the army in 1954, instigated by Senator Joseph McCarthy (Republican of Wisconsin), President Eisenhower instructed Secretary of De-

---

* The case of *United States ex. rel. Touhy v. Ragen*, 95 L. Ed. 417, illustrates the Supreme Court's historic viewpoints on the matter of executive secrecy. This case also contains a lengthy annotation on court decisions dealing with this issue.

Reviewing prevailing legal opinion on this matter, one authoritative study concludes that unauthorized citizens have "no enforceable legal right to inspect any federal non-judicial records." Its over-all finding is that "the opportunity of the people to know depends upon the favorable exercise of official grace or indulgence of 'discretion.'" Harold L. Cross, *The People's Right To Know* (New York: Columbia University Press, 1953), p. 197.

fense Charles E. Wilson to refuse McCarthy's demands for executive records. Wilson was directed to instruct his subordinates "not to testify to . . . conversations or communications or to produce any . . . documents or reproductions."*

In these and similar situations, neither elected officials in Congress nor the general public have independent sources of information that can rival those available to the President and his chief advisers. As foreign policy decisions more and more depend upon accurate knowledge about complex questions, the problem arising from inadequacy of information available to the rank and file of citizens becomes magnified. Successful democracy presupposes citizen competence to judge public issues and to vote intelligently—capacities which will be severely limited by inability to secure, and perhaps understand, requisite information. Yet so long as the country is confronted by a ruthless and resourceful diplomatic opponent, a high premium must exist upon preserving the confidential character of information that, were it disclosed, might impair national security. The problem facing the President is thus a delicate one. The survival of democracy itself demands that as much information as possible be made public; yet the security of the nation may require that vast quantities of such information remain classified. If the citizen and his representatives in Congress must accord the President considerable latitude in the disclosure of information, an equal obligation exists for the President and his advisers to make public as much information as national security permits, even when such information reveals incompetence among executive officials or widespread failures within the executive branch to deal with national policy questions successfully.

Congress of course has not always admitted the right of Presidents to withhold information. As a rule, however, legislators understand that the proper conduct of foreign affairs demands

* The student is urged to read the letter from President Eisenhower to Secretary of Defense Charles E. Wilson on May 17, 1954. Here the President affirms, and gives his reasons for upholding, the principle that the President must withhold "information whenever he found that what was sought was confidential or its disclosure would be incompatible with the public interest or jeopardize the safety of the Nation." Text in Dwight D. Eisenhower, *Mandate for Change: 1953–1956* (Garden City, N.Y.: Doubleday, 1963), pp. 597–598.

a wide area of secrecy, even from them; for most of them are aware that untimely "leaks" of information to the press can create embarrassing diplomatic incidents and, in extreme cases, can even prejudice national security. This realization in large measure underlies their acceptance of the fact that Congress can seldom command as comprehensive and accurate information about foreign affairs as the executive; it explains in no small part too why few congressmen are willing at critical junctures to pit their judgments of external events against the judgments of the President and his chief subordinates.

The President and Public Opinion

Although the role of the President as a molder of public opinion first came into clear prominence with Theodore Roosevelt, successive Presidents have sharpened public relations tools into powerful weapons for dealing with Congress, pressure groups, or dissident members of their own party. No President used this weapon with such telling effect as Franklin D. Roosevelt. He was the first to systematize the collection of data about public opinion, relying upon opinion polls, newspaper surveys, White House mail, and grass roots reports. And no President in American history has been so successful in generating grass-roots support for his programs, with which to overcome legislative opposition. Binkley observes that FDR "had only to glance toward a microphone or suggest that he might go on the air again and a congressional delegation would surrender. They had no relish for the flood of mail and telegrams they knew would swamp them after another fireside talk to the nation."[22] It was Roosevelt, too, who first encouraged reporters to *give him information* about how his policies were being received throughout the country. Today, Presidents regularly rely upon their press conferences to learn about currents in public opinion and to uncover problems within the government that require their attention.[23]

President Truman utilized his numerous appointments—often as many as 95 a week—to familiarize him with public thinking. Eisenhower leaned more heavily upon television appearances and "stag dinners," at which 15–20 guests were usually invited for an informal conference. Another significant development under Eisenhower was the use of the Vice-President as a roving good-will ambassador who tried to interpret the President's program to the nation and to receive the public reaction to it. Vice-President Richard Nixon traveled many thousands of miles in this capacity.[24]

When the President desires to address the nation, the facilities of every radio and television network are available to him. In the day-to-day conduct of government, his words and decisions are carried almost instantaneously by the wire services from the White House to every major capital of the world. No other governmental leader is provided with such extensive coverage, and none therefore has the opportunity, if he has both the desire and the ability to use it, to rally public opinion to his cause.

The President as Legislative Leader

According to the principle of separation of powers, the President should not have anything to do with legislation. It is doubtful that even the Founding Fathers believed in rigid adherence to this principle, and it certainly has never been strictly observed in American governmental practice. In many ways, the President is the foremost legislator in the government. Preparation of needed legislation, followed by efforts to secure its passage through Congress, is now recognized as one of the executive department's most time-consuming and compelling duties. Lawrence H. Chamberlain found that almost half of the major federal statutes enacted during the past 75 years emanated from the executive departments. About half the bills introduced into Congress annually originate in the executive branch.[25] So firmly ingrained has this practice become that congressmen have been known to protest when the executive was derelict in preparing measures for their consideration. Thus, Senator Homer Ferguson (Republican of Michigan) complained about President Truman: "If the President wants to tell the people he stands for a certain thing, he ought to come out with his proposal. He ought to come to the House and Senate with a message. And he ought to provide a bill that is exactly what he wants."[26]

All of the great legislative enactments affecting American foreign relations in the postwar period—the Greek-Turkish Aid Program, the Marshall Plan, the China Aid Bill, the Point Four Program, the Mutual Security Program, reduction of tariffs, programs for developing peacetime nuclear energy, research and development programs—have had their origin in the executive branch. And after their initiation, executive officials have, at critical junctures,

pressed for their adoption by Congress. The scope of the present-day global commitments of the United States has drawn Congress more and more into the foreign policy process. But it has also drawn the executive more and more into the *legislative* process, requiring him, as in foreign affairs generally, to provide the direction and initiative needed for framing legislation bearing upon external affairs. In fact, the success or failure of an incumbent administration is judged to a large extent by the degree to which it can claim a *legislative* record of successfully dealing with existing foreign and internal problems.

The President as a Political Leader

Adequate discussion of the political role of the President would require a volume. The most we can do here is take for granted his pre-eminent political position and suggest some of the consequences of this position for foreign affairs. Historically, one of the President's most effective means for influencing the actions of legislators has been the patronage he has had to distribute to the party faithful, in the form of appointments to the federal service. No President in recent history has surpassed FDR in the skillful way he utilized this weapon.[27] Since the New Deal, the importance of patronage has declined, because more jobs have been placed under civil service regulations.

In addition, the President plays an influential role in national elections. Every national candidate who is a member of the President's party desires to have his "endorsement" in a political campaign. The regularity with which candidates seek to "ride the President's coattails" is a well-known phenomenon in American political history, as illustrated by President Eisenhower's success in carrying a number of Republican candidates into office with him by his victories in 1952 and 1956.

Members of Congress do not follow a party line slavishly in their legislative actions. Still, they prefer, when possible, to work in close harmony with their party leaders, because such a course pays tangible political benefits. The party in power tries to establish a record which will generate wide voter appeal. Such a record can only be created if the party, led by the President, works in close harmony to produce it.

Power To Commit the Nation

Following the disastrous Bay of Pigs invasion of Cuba in 1961, President Kennedy observed that he had listened fully to the advice of his advisers in this instance—and that the advice he received had been wrong. Nevertheless, as President, he alone assumed full responsibility for this ill-fated undertaking.[28] This event thus illustrated a power that has more and more come to be exercised decisively by the chief executive in his response to rapidly changing circumstances abroad: the ability *to commit the nation* to a specified course of action which Congress or other agencies of government are all but powerless to change. Virtually every major undertaking in foreign affairs at some stage requires legislative support, thereby giving Congress an influence in foreign relations today transcending its influence in earlier eras. Yet the power of the President to commit the nation to particular policies and diplomatic moves can, at least in the short run, largely negate Congress's newly found power in the foreign policy field.

Postwar diplomatic experience is replete with examples. Take the Greek-Turkish Aid Program of 1947. After President Truman announced dramatically on March 12 that "it must be the policy of the United States to support free people who are resisting subjection by armed minorities or outside pressures, . . ."[*] what choice did Congress have but to agree—and subsequently to vote the funds required to translate these words into effective policy for saving Greece from communist domination? The answer was provided by a *St. Louis Post Dispatch* editorial on the President's speech: "Congress may ponder and debate but the President's address has committed the nation to all-out diplomatic action just as a declaration of a shooting war must necessarily follow when the President asks for it."[29]

A similar result could be anticipated when President Eisenhower requested standby authority early in 1955 to protect Formosa and other Chinese off-shore islands from a threatened attack by Red China.[**] Once the request was made of Congress, no realistic alternative to its approval existed. Congress, as prominent Democrats were heard to complain, could not turn the President down without implying to the world that it was indifferent to the fate of Formosa and without conveying a strong impression abroad that it had repudi-

ated executive leadership. To decline the request was to invite almost certain communist expansionism in the Orient.[30] Under such circumstances, Congress is not prepared to deal with the grave international consequences that would flow from a repudiation of the President's leadership.

THE PRESIDENT'S EMERGENCY POWERS

Immediately after the Civil War, the Supreme Court declared that "the government, within the Constitution, has all the powers granted to it which are necessary to preserve its existence. . . ."[†] This doctrine has been repeatedly affirmed, as in 1934 when the Court held that "the war power of the Federal Government . . . *is a power to wage war successfully.* . . ."[‡] From the Civil War onward, national crises have called for the exercise of sweeping governmental powers, powers which many students have thought were unknown to the original Constitution. The point of principal concern to us is that exercise of these powers has entailed a vast expansion in executive authority to deal with national crises.

The emergency powers of the President derive primarily from two constitutional sources: his designation as commander in chief (Art. II, Sec. 2); and his obligation to "take care that the laws be faithfully executed" (Art. II, Sec. 3). Together these two clauses constitute the so-called "war powers" of the executive. Besides this constitutional source, Congress within the last half-century has added to the President's power to deal with national emergencies. Relying both upon his authority as commander in chief and legislative authority given him for coping with emergency conditions, Franklin D. Roosevelt created numerous new governmental agencies during World War II and made them responsible solely to himself, often bypassing established executive departments. In an executive order issued on February 19, 1942, Roosevelt directed his military commanders to bar American citizens of Japanese ancestry from occupying designated areas on the West Coast; this order was subsequently incorporated into an act of Congress.[31] When President Truman, on December 16, 1950, proclaimed "the existence of a national emergency," according to the noted constitutional commentator Edward S. Corwin,

---

[*] See President Truman's message to a joint session of Congress on March 12, 1947: *Congressional Record*, **93**, 1980–1981.

[**] Text in *Congressional Record* (daily edition), January 24, 1955, p. 497–499.

[†] *Ex parte Milligan*, 4 Wallace 2 (1866).

[‡] *Home Building and Loan Association* v. *Blaisdell*, 290 U. S. 398 (1934). Italics inserted.

he activated over sixty statutes or portions of statutes that become applicable during periods characterized as "a condition of emergency" or "in time of war or national emergency." In most cases, the President determines when such conditions prevail. His determination will, in turn, greatly enlarge his own powers, in part by removing limitations existing upon them during normal times.[32]

Lincoln was the first President to claim broad executive powers for dealing with a national crisis. During the spring and summer of 1861, Lincoln took many steps which, up to that time, had been thought to lie largely or exclusively within the domain of Congress. He ordered a blockade of Southern ports in the absence of a "declaration of war" and directed that ships violating the blockade be confiscated. He increased the size of the army and navy; called out the militia; closed the post office to treasonable correspondence; expended funds from the treasury without legislative authorization; and suspended the writ of habeas corpus. During the course of the Civil War, Lincoln also freed the slaves on his own authority and drew up plans for the "reconstruction" of the South that contemplated little, if any, active participation by Congress. Collectively, these actions asserted "for the President, for the first time in our history, an initiative of indefinite scope in meeting the domestic aspects of a war emergency."[33]

Lincoln's dynamic conception of presidential emergency power has become firmly incorporated into the nation's constitutional fabric. Speaking for the Supreme Court in the Neagle case,[*] Justice Miller in 1890 asked whether the President was limited "to the enforcement of acts of Congress or of treaties of the United States according to their *express terms*. . . ." He answered in the negative, holding that in the discharge of his constitutional obligation to take care that the laws be faithfully executed, the President also was required to include "the rights, duties and obligations growing out of the Constitution itself, our international relations, and all the protection implied by the nature of the government under the Constitution." In the spirit of this idea, President Wilson armed American merchant shipping, in spite of the fact that Congress refused to pass a law giving him such authority.[34] The power of Presidents to take such steps was justified by Solicitor General John W. Davis in 1914

by his assertion that "in ways short of making laws or disobeying them, the Executive may be under a grave constitutional duty to act for the national protection in situations not covered by the acts of Congress, and in which, even, it may not be said that his action is the direct expression of any particular one of the independent powers which are granted to him specifically by the Constitution."[35]

In the 1950s the scope of the President's emergency powers came to the fore sharply in the steel seizure case,[**] growing out of President Truman's seizure of a steel company to avert a strike in a vital defense industry. At first glance, the Supreme Court's opinion declaring Truman's seizure of the steel mills unconstitutional might seem a decisive setback for the concept of residual executive power for dealing with emergencies. Unquestionably, the Court's opinion was a landmark in attempting to set limits to that power. Nonetheless, the Court's decision turned on the fact that Congress had already provided methods by which the President could deal with conditions like those prevailing in this case, but that the President did not avail himself of these methods before ordering seizure. The Court's opinion did not deny the existence of a vast reservoir of executive emergency power. On the contrary, according to one commentator the justices were in wide agreement that "the President does possess a residual of resultant power above, or in consequence of, his granted powers to deal with emergencies in the absence of restrictive legislation. . . ." The court's opinion underscored the fact, however, that "any action of the President touching the internal economy of the country for which the justification of emergency is pleaded is always subject to revision and disallowance by the legislative power."[36]

What then are the limitations upon the emergency powers of the President? One stems from the limitations imposed upon President Truman by the Supreme Court in the steel seizure case, in which the Court was reiterating long-standing precedent: when Congress has specified the means by which the President is to cope with emergencies, then the President is obligated to follow the procedure prescribed by law. Moreover, the President cannot take action that is plainly denied him by constitutional prohibitions, although admittedly Presi-

---

[*] 135 U. S. 1 (1890).

[**] *Youngstown Company v. Sawyer*, 343 U. S. 579 (1952).

dents in recent years have sometimes taken an extremely elastic view of constitutional provisions designed to keep governmental power within clearly defined boundaries.* In the long run, the dikes that will confine presidential power within its proper channels are to be found, as Clinton Rossiter suggests, in deeply ingrained principles, such as the concept of separation of powers and federalism, the determination of Congress to resist usurpation of power by the President, the threat of impeachment, the operation of a healthy two-party system, and public opinion.[37] In the final analysis, these constitute the most effective barriers against presidential "dictatorship." Yet it must be confessed that these limitations are in almost every case *long-range* checks upon the President, and that in the short run—especially when the security of the country may hang in the balance—very few restraints, beyond his own devotion to the American Constitution and prescribed courses of action under it, are likely to bind a forceful President. We must therefore conclude with Abbot Smith that

> The President's activities in foreign affairs are such as almost to give him the power of war and peace; certainly the effective limitations on his power are political in nature and not constitutional; he would be ill-advised to move faster than the sentiment of the country will allow, but his constitutional disabilities alone will never actually prevent him from getting the nation practically into a state of war.[38]

THE DEPARTMENT OF STATE: ITS FUNCTION AND ORGANIZATION

A few months after President Kennedy took office in 1961, a White House assistant wrote to a legislator that President Kennedy

> . . . has made it very clear that he does not want a large separate organization between him and his Secretary of State. Neither does he wish any question to arise as to the clear authority and responsibility of the Secretary of State . . . as the agent of coordination in all our major policies toward other nations.[39]

Former Secretary of State Dean Acheson once defined the Secretary of State's duty as seeing "that the President is kept fully and timely informed so that he may perform his constitutional duty of conducting the nation's foreign relations with all the freedom of decision which each situation permits."[40] Acheson's conception was exemplified by the intimate relationship prevailing between President Eisenhower and Secretary of State John Foster Dulles. Although Eisenhower accorded Dulles perhaps as much freedom to manage foreign affairs as any President has ever given a subordinate, Dulles was continually aware that his role was advisory, and that the President ultimately determined the foreign policy of the United States.** Nevertheless, within broad policy guidelines, Dulles possessed wide latitude to formulate and carry out specific policies, designed to achieve national objectives. Chief executives before and after Eisenhower have perforce relied upon the Department of State, and its top official, the Secretary of State, to conduct the day-by-day diplomatic business of the United States and to advise the White House about significant developments and problems in the external sphere.

The Challenge of New Obligations

The expanding global obligations incurred by the United States over the past quarter-century have been mirrored in the phenomenal growth in the size and activities of the Department of State. In the infancy of the Republic, the State Department, headed by Secretary of State Thomas Jefferson, had five clerks in Washington, three ministers, and sixteen consular officials. And even in Jefferson's day there existed some feeling in Congress that the State Department was overstaffed![41]

By the mid-1960s, the State Department had a total of almost 25,000 employees, of which some 70 percent served overseas and 30 percent served in Washington.† Its officials manned nearly 300 foreign posts, located in approximately 110 countries. An average of 2,000 cables poured in and out of the State Department daily, as officials in Washington

* See, for example, the case of *Korematsu* v. *United States*, 323 U. S. 214 (1944).

** The relationship between Eisenhower and Dulles is described in Sherman Adams, *First-Hand Report: The Story of the Eisenhower Administration* (New York: Harper & Row, 1961), pp. 87–89. In a number of important instances, Dulles evidently did not agree with policies ultimately decided by the President. For examples, see *ibid.*, pp. 87–88, 112–114; Emmet Hughes, *Ordeal of Power* (New York: Atheneum, 1963), p. 105; Roscoe Drummond and Gaston Coblens, *Duel at the Brink* (Garden City, N.Y.: Doubleday, 1960), p. 28.

† It must be noted here, as Chapter 4 emphasizes in detail, that this is by no means the total of *all* governmental employees involved in various phases of foreign relations.

endeavored to keep abreast of often rapidly changing developments abroad and relayed instructions to the field.[42] Indicative of the mushrooming in State Department personnel is one observer's facetious remark that today, there are more *children* attached to the American embassy in Moscow than there were officials several years ago![43]

As long as isolationism remained the keynote of America's foreign relations, State Department duties consisted chiefly of routine consular business, furnishing information about and promoting foreign trade, protecting American lives and property in other countries, and performing ceremonial functions. Since World War II, the United States has become actively involved in an expanding range of global activities; the organizational structure of the State Department, together with the attendant involvement of numerous other executive agencies in foreign affairs, reflects the nation's new role. During the 1930s, for instance, national defense and foreign policy took approximately 35–40 percent of the federal budget; today, they take 75–80 percent. Along with a quantitative increase in State Department business has gone a fundamental change in its *character*. A noteworthy trend since World War II has been the extent to which economic, social, cultural, and informational aspects of foreign policy have assumed unprecedented importance. Judged by the number of employees involved in these activities, they appear in some instances to eclipse *political* aspects of America's relations with the outside world.*

Basic Organizational Structure

In common with other executive departments, since World War II the State Department has experienced a great proliferation among its internal units. The Hoover Commission in 1948 found that the department contained 94 separate units, with 25 officials reporting directly to the Secretary of State. After thorough study, a basic reorganization plan

was proposed which, if it did not cut down drastically on the size of the department, at least brought some semblance of order out of the administrative jungle previously prevailing.[44]

The basic organizational pattern of the State Department conforms to the same hierarchical system prevailing in most governmental agencies. Lines of authority radiate down from the Secretary of State, through his immediate subordinates, to a variety of operating units at the bottom. But there are a number of special organizational features tending to disguise the pyramidal structure of the department. Three semiautonomous agencies—the Arms Control and Disarmament Agency, the Agency for International Development, and the Peace Corps—enjoy a significant degree of independence in their operations, although they remain responsible to the Secretary of State for over-all policy guidance. Within the State Department itself, two somewhat contradictory administrative principles are reflected in the prevailing organizational pattern. One is the attempt to organize foreign affairs according to the major *regions*, and within each region by country, with which the United States maintains relations. Thus the Bureau of African Affairs contains a "Ghanaian desk," a "Nigerian desk," and similar desks for each important country in Africa with which the United States maintains relations. The second principle is *functional* organization. Certain international responsibilities of the State Department cut across regional and national lines. For example, the Bureau of Economic Affairs may be concerned with implications of the emergence of the European Common Market for the United States, or it may be required to appraise American policy toward the efforts of economically emerging countries to stabilize prices of their primary exports. Similarly, the Office of International Scientific Affairs may be concerned with peacetime applications of nuclear energy, the exchange of scientific information across national frontiers, or some aspect of space technology.

The Secretary of State, as we have indicated, is the chief foreign policy adviser to the President. Below him in the administrative hierarchy is the Under Secretary, who often serves as Acting Secretary during the former's numerous absences from Washington. Next is the Under Secretary for Political Affairs, under whose supervision the major operating bureaus of the State Department function. In turn, he

---

* Estimating the total number of employees engaged in each aspect of foreign policy would be extremely difficult, if not impossible, because the involvement of a number of governmental agencies in foreign relations is often peripheral and sporadic. State Department data indicate the following breakdown about its employees: 43 percent are engaged in political aspects of policy, 23 percent in economic aspects, 19 percent in consular affairs, 6 percent in intelligence and research, 6 percent in cultural affairs, and 3 percent in public affairs. Department of State, "Manpower Profile," Chart XI.

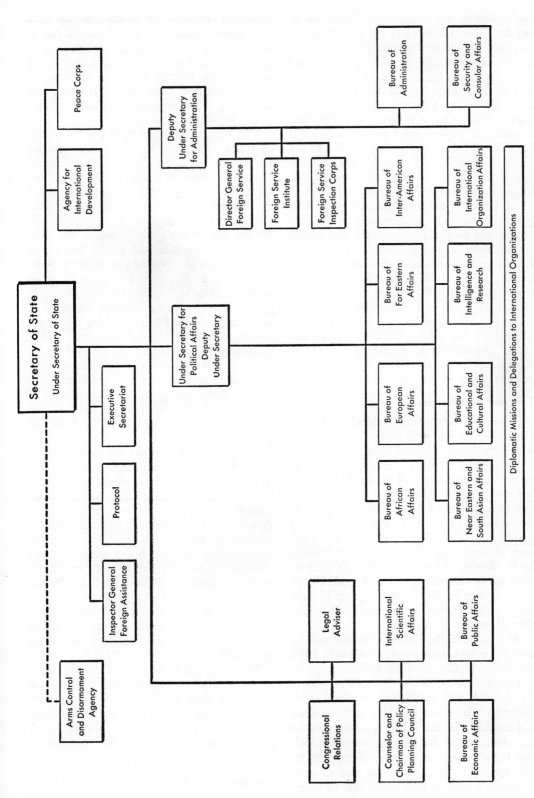

Organization of the Department of State. (Source: *U.S. Government Organization Manual, 1964–1965,* p. 586.)

has assistants, like the Deputy Under Secretary for Political Affairs and the Deputy Under Secretary for Administration. The latter's responsibility extends to supervising the internal operation of the department, including operation of the Foreign Service, the Foreign Service Institute, and the consular services of the United States. One other position in the State Department requires brief comment. This is the office of Counselor, initially created in the period 1907–1919 and re-established in 1937. Under the present administrative system, the Counselor heads the Policy Planning Council, whose activities we shall describe more fully below. Normally, the Counselor is an able and experienced Foreign Service officer who advises his superiors in the department on important foreign policy issues and who undertakes selected assignments from time to time. In the recent period, the best-known Counselor was George F. Kennan, a distinguished historian and recognized authority on the Soviet Union. More than any other official in the government, Kennan was responsible for providing the theoretical foundations for America's postwar policy of containment.

The Functional Bureaus

"More and more of the problems facing the Government," one authoritative study has observed, "transcend national boundaries. . . ."[45] Consequently, a striking phenomenon in recent years has been the extent to which the number and size of the functional bureaus within the Department of State have expanded to take account of this fact. The collection and preparation of intelligence data for the guidance of State Department officials is handled by the Bureau of Intelligence Research. As we shall see in Chapter 4, this unit works closely with the Central Intelligence Agency in gathering and collating intelligence information throughout the government.

As a result of the Hoover Commission's investigation into executive organization in 1949, the Office of Congressional Relations was established to facilitate the State Department's harmonious and continuous relations with Congress. This office (working with presidential assistants in the White House) provides the focal point for liaison activities seeking both to generate legislative support for the President's foreign policies and to communicate sentiment on Capitol Hill to executive officials. The services of this office are available for diverse undertakings, such as answering routine constituent inquiries to congressmen about various aspects of American foreign policy, arranging the itineraries of legislators and legislative committees planning foreign trips, briefing members of Congress about some new crisis in world affairs, and scheduling testimony by diplomatic officials before legislative inquiries.

The Bureau of Public Affairs has a variety of duties, which may be conveniently grouped under two headings: disseminating information about American foreign policy and collecting and appraising public reactions to American foreign policy for the guidance of State Department officials. This office is responsible for the department's relations with the press and other communications media. From time to time, as in the case of the Japanese Peace Conference in San Francisco in 1951, it arranges nationwide radio and television programs. It also devotes considerable time to evaluating public opinion by relying upon such diverse sources as editorial comments, public opinion polls, the resolutions adopted by interest groups and other organizations, statements of prominent citizens, and departmental mail to gauge public attitudes. Summaries of findings made by officers in this unit are circulated periodically throughout the State Department.

Closely related activities are carried on by the Bureau of Educational and Cultural Affairs, one of the newer offices in the State Department. Reflecting the unprecedented attention now given to cultural aspects of diplomacy, this office administers overseas educational and cultural exchange programs with an expanding number of countries. Such activities entail supervision of continuing programs, such as student and faculty exchanges under the Fulbright Program, sponsorship of musical, dance, and other artistic tours to other countries, and promotion of occasional tours by educators or other specialized groups.

The Bureau of Security and Consular Affairs is principally concerned with carrying on traditional State Department functions, such as issuing passports and visas, handling refugee programs, and protecting the security of American diplomatic and consular installations abroad.

The Geographic Bureaus

The operating heart of the State Department is to be found among those agencies—

the geographical bureaus—that have responsibility for the *political* relationships of the United States with other countries and with certain international and regional organizations. For many years, political relations with these areas were organized under four geographic headings: Inter-American affairs, European affairs, Far Eastern affairs, and Near East and South Asian affairs. The addition of two new bureaus in the postwar era—International Organization affairs and African affairs—testifies eloquently to increasing American involvement in the manifold developments in the outside world. The bureaus conduct the ordinary day-by-day diplomatic business of the United States with the countries or organizations under their jurisdiction. Moreover, they provide the link between the State Department in Washington and the embassies or other installations in the field.* Since the early 1960s, this has meant that the country desks must supervise the activities of a large number of non-State Department officials and agencies abroad, since in theory (if not always in fact) the American ambassador in Lebanon or India or Korea is in charge of the "country team" including *all* American officials within the country. The ambassador, in turn, reports to the appropriate country desk in the Department of State.

Positions on the country desks are filled by experts on the country in question, generally Foreign Service officers or other officials who have spent a number of years in, and often considerable time studying about, the country; some of these officials at least are fluent in the language of the country. Their superiors, not excluding the Secretary of State or even the President himself, are heavily dependent upon these officers for advice in dealing with the broad range of questions that arise in America's relations with that country. It is not unusual, particularly during times of crisis within the country, for one or more desk officers to be summoned to the White House for a conference with the President.

The Bureau of International Organization Affairs calls for special comment. It supervises the relationships between the United States and international or regional organizations—chiefly, of course, the United Nations. The United States Mission to the UN, headed by an ambassador, reports directly to this office and, in turn, receives its instructions from it. This bureau also coordinates American policy toward regional bodies such as NATO and the Organization of American States. A mounting burden in recent years has been the necessity for this office to handle the arrangements for an increasing number of international conferences. The number of such conferences has grown from approximately 75 annually during the 1930s to around 300 annually in the early 1960s.

THE FOREIGN SERVICE

Its Role and Duties

Out of a total of nearly 25,000 employees in the Department of State in the United States and overseas, more than 9000 are members of the Foreign Service, from whose ranks comes the core of diplomatic officials that administers the State Department's global responsibilities.[46] Several classifications exist in the Foreign Service, ranging from career ambassador and career minister (the highest and next-highest appointments, respectively) to the Foreign Service staff, whose duties consist chiefly in providing stenographic services, clerical personnel, technicians, and custodial workers. In between, there is the classification of Foreign Service Officer. This group, numbering about 2500 permanent officials and nearly 1000 members of the Foreign Service Reserve in 1963, provides the corps of officers comprising the career diplomatic service of the United States. Both the State Department in Washington and the overseas posts depend heavily upon the Foreign Service to conduct foreign relations. The President and his chief advisers rely upon officers of the Foreign Service to report and appraise events in the outside world. In addition, these officers perform consular functions, carry on ceremonial functions, and endeavor to promote better understanding of the United States abroad.

Organization and Reorganization

Throughout the greater part of the nation's history, the selection of diplomatic personnel was haphazard. Very few guiding principles prevailed in the establishment of a professional corps of diplomats or in formulating clearly

---

* For a detailed treatment of the internal organization and operation of one of the principal geographic bureaus in the State Department, see the discussion of the Bureau of Inter-American Affairs in Senate Foreign Relations Committee, *The Formulation and Administration of United States Foreign Policy*, pp. 181–189.

defined organizational precepts for its operation. For nearly a century and a half, political considerations more often than not governed the making of appointments; almost always, low salaries compelled diplomats to subsidize their activities in foreign countries out of their own private funds.

The Foreign Service as it exists today owes its origin to the Rogers Act of 1924, when Congress spelled out requirements for entry into the service and set up a basic organizational structure. For the first time, the principle was accepted that appointments to the Foreign Service ought to be on the basis of merit.[47]

Since that year, successful applicants for the diplomatic service have been required to pass a battery of difficult written and oral examinations. The high standards applied to entrance into the Foreign Service are illustrated by the results of the examination for the year 1961. Some 8000 candidates took the written portion of the examination, of whom 1000 passed. Among that number, 300 subsequently passed the oral examinations and were eligible for appointment to the diplomatic service.[48] Once accepted as a Foreign Service officer, an official's performance is evaluated periodically; his future in the service is governed by the principle of "up—or out." That is, he must be promoted regularly or is discharged from the service. Foreign Service officers may ultimately reach Class 1, and in a few cases, career ambassador or career minister, entitling them to the highest diplomatic positions in the State Department and in its overseas posts.

The postwar era has witnessed a number of major and minor reorganizations of the Foreign Service to correct long-standing deficiencies and to enable the service to respond to the new responsibilities facing the United States in global affairs. Immediately after World War II, several considerations—the shift in the State Department's duties, evident organizational duplication throughout the executive branch, a decline in enlistments in the diplomatic career service—dictated a sweeping modification in existing organizational patterns. Guided chiefly by the State Department's own recommendations, Congress in 1946 enacted the Foreign Service Act.

The Act did not contemplate sweeping changes in the Foreign Service. In the language of Congress, it attempted merely to "improve, strengthen, and expand" the existing corps. Salary scales for each officer grade were raised

sharply, the number of grades was reduced, allowances, promotions, leaves, and retirement benefits were liberalized. The objective was to make the service a more attractive career, and give it a better competitive position among other governmental agencies and with private industry. As we have noted, the principle of "promotion—up, or selection—out" governed an officer's continuance in the service. A Foreign Service Institute was also established in Washington to train successful applicants for the service and to provide periodic in-service and language training for officers already on the job. Moreover, the Act of 1946 set up a "career service" (called the Foreign Service Staff) for clerical and secretarial employees. Primarily designed to grant this group attractive salaries and job security rights, it also served to overcome their feeling of inferiority in traditionally being excluded from the Foreign Service.

While these reforms did much to strengthen the Foreign Service, new problems appeared after 1946. In the late Truman and early Eisenhower periods, for example, diplomatic officials became prime targets for legislative and private investigations aimed at disclosing alleged communist influence upon policy-making. Subjected to frequent irresponsible attacks, and uncertain about the viewpoints of even high-level executive officials toward them, the Foreign Service suffered declining morale and administrative efficiency.* So critical had this problem become by the mid-1950s that one observer declared it "no exaggeration to say that the experiment of professional diplomacy, as undertaken by the United States in 1925, had failed."[49] Although such verdicts were extreme, declining recruitment rates for the Foreign Service, along with statements by officers themselves, indicated beyond question that serious difficulties impeded the effective operation of the diplomatic corps.[50]

At length, the Eisenhower Administration appointed a Public Committee on Personnel, headed by Dr. Henry M. Wriston of Brown

---

* Shortly after the beginning of the Eisenhower Administration, Secretary of State Dulles made a talk to State Department officials in which he pointedly demanded their "positive loyalty" to the Dulles-Eisenhower program. Whether intended or not, this speech was widely construed as implying that such officials were not already loyal or that there was at least some doubt about their loyalty in the minds of leaders of the new administration. See Hughes, *Ordeal of Power, op. cit.*, pp. 85, 254.

University, to investigate problems prevailing in the Foreign Service and to make recommendations for its improvement. The Wriston Committee's recommendations were designed to repair some of the damage to morale sustained by the service within recent years, by making it possible to attract and hold well-qualified individuals and by eliminating practices that had interfered with this goal. One key recommendation was integration of State Department personnel into the Foreign Service. Many State Department employees had heretofore been under civil service. This move, coupled with periodic rotation among officers serving in Washington and those serving overseas, was designed to improve morale and to broaden the experience of the nation's diplomats. To make the recruitment program more dynamic, entrance requirements into the Foreign Service were to be liberalized, and prolonged delays in processing applications eliminated. Other recommendations entailed introduction of a program of scholarships for prospective Foreign Service officers who had passed the requisite examinations and introduction of a system of congressional appointments similar to that prevailing in the military officer schools.*

Another reorganization followed the Wriston Report. Over 1440 State Department officials and 1200 members of its "staff corps" —administrative specialists who had never taken the Foreign Service examination—were brought into the service. More frequent rotation of officers between Washington and overseas

* These, along with another long-standing proposal for training American diplomats—establishment of a Foreign Service Academy similar to the military academies—have run into persistent opposition on Capitol Hill. Not untypical of congressional sentiment about such an academy was the viewpoint expressed by Senator Claiborne Pell (Democrat of Rhode Island), a former Foreign Service officer. He was convinced that in preparing promising young people for entrance into the diplomatic service, a better course was "utilizing the existing facilities in our great universities and . . . utilizing and expanding the facilities of the Foreign Service Institute" in Washington. Senator Pell, along with other members of Congress, has been deeply troubled, for example, by a possible conflict between adherence to the principle of academic freedom at such an educational institution and the possibility that the viewpoints of faculty members might oftentimes conflict with the viewpoints and policies of the government about major foreign policy issues. Accordingly, he doubts that it would really be possible to inculcate and maintain a spirit of freedom of inquiry in an official institution of this kind. *The New York Times*, June 3, 1963.

posts became accepted practice. Foreign Service examinations were made somewhat less difficult, and recruitment was intensified. The Foreign Service Institute's program was expanded to provide more frequent in-service training for experienced officers. Throughout the years that followed, greater emphasis was placed upon acquisition of language skills by members of the diplomatic corps. On the whole, these changes were unquestionably beneficial. After 1954, morale in the Foreign Service improved, and a sharp upsurge took place in the number of applicants for entry into the diplomatic service.[51]

Continuing Problems

Despite intensive concern about State Department organization and operation throughout the postwar period, several recurrent problems hamper its effective operation. These will demand continuing attention on the part of officials and students of government alike in the years ahead. A dominant one relates to the appointment of, and to the authority exercised by, the ambassador or minister, who is theoretically the highest American official resident in foreign countries. Take first the matter of how such officials are initially appointed. Traditionally, candidates for ambassadorships have had above all to meet two criteria: they must be wealthy, and they must be members of—and frequently substantial contributors to—the President's political party. For the larger and more important diplomatic posts abroad, particularly in Western Europe, an outside income has been indispensable, since the operating budget available to the embassy was almost never adequate to cover all necessary expenses. The following case illustrates the problem created when such considerations govern the appointment of high-ranking diplomatic personnel. On July 2, 1957, the Senate Foreign Relations Committee met in executive session to consider President Eisenhower's nomination of Mr. Maxwell H. Gluck for the position of ambassador to Ceylon. Some significant highlights from this hearing are presented below.

Mr. Gluck: My qualifications generally are a varied business background. Ever since boyhood, I have had experience in industry, commerce, business, finance, and so forth.

I have never been in the diplomatic service before.

. . . . . .

Senator Fulbright: How much did you contribute to the Republican Party in the 1956 election?

Mr. Gluck: Well, I wouldn't know offhand, but I made a contribution.

Senator Fulbright: Well, how much?

Mr. Gluck: Let's see; I would say, all in all, twenty or thirty thousand dollars.

. . . . . .

Senator Fulbright: You don't think that is a pertinent reason for the appointment.

Mr. Gluck: I don't think it is the only reason.

Senator Fulbright: It is the principal reason, is it not?

Mr. Gluck: I don't think I want to admit that is the principal reason.

. . . . . .

Senator Fulbright: Why are you interested in Ceylon?

Mr. Gluck: I am not particularly interested only in Ceylon, but I am interested in a Government post where I can do some work and do some good at it.

Senator Fulbright: What makes you think you could do that in Ceylon?

Mr. Gluck: Unless I run into something that I am not aware of I think I ought to do a fairly good job in the job I have been nominated for.

Senator Fulbright: What are the problems in Ceylon you think you can deal with?

Mr. Gluck: One of the problems are the people there, not necessarily a problem, but the relationship of the United States with the people in Ceylon. I believe I can—I think I can establish, unless we—again, unless I run into something that I have not run into before—a good relationship and good feeling toward the United States.

. . . . . .

Senator Fulbright: Do you consider we are on friendly relations with India?

Mr. Gluck: Well, I think it is more—I think a lot depends on who is there, and what they do. I don't think we are on the friendliest relations with them, but I believe it can be strengthened a little more in one direction, or a little more in another direction, depending on what is done in that country.

. . . . . .

Senator Fulbright: Do you know who the Prime Minister in India is?

Mr. Gluck: Yes; but I can't pronounce his name.

Senator Fulbright: Do you know who the Prime Minister of Ceylon is?

Mr. Gluck: I have a list—

Senator Fulbright: Who is it?

Mr. Gluck: His name is a bit unfamiliar now. I cannot call it off, but I have obtained from Ambassador Crowe a list of all the important people there and I went over them with him.

I have a synopsis of all the people, both Americans, ambassadors, and officials from other countries, and I have from him also a sort of little biography or history of them, with what his opinion of them is; and so—

Senator Fulbright: That's all, Mr. Chairman.

Alone among the committee members, Senator Fulbright voted against this nomination, although he confessed philosophically that "it is ridiculous to send [a] man with so little preparation to an area where these people are a sensitive and strange people, and I think it will do us no good. However, I am not going to raise Cain. I know it is an old and evil custom that afflicts us."* In fairness to Mr. Gluck, it must be noted that his record in Ceylon was much more creditable than might have been expected on the basis of his apparent lack of preparation for the appointment. As with many other ambassadors so appointed, the staff of experienced Foreign Service officers in the field enabled him to carry out his duties satisfactorily and without untoward incident.

However, appointments on this basis have increasingly been criticized by officials in government and by observers outside it. By the 1960s, considerable progress had been made toward the goal of a more professionalized diplomatic corps, including the positions of ambassadors and ministers. Thus in 1962, President Kennedy announced that "We have a higher percentage of ambassadorial posts occupied by career men, 68 percent, than at most any time in this century. . . ."[52] There seemed every reason to suppose that this tendency would continue, however slowly. Ultimately, Congress would be compelled to face realistically one of the most bewildering anomalies in the administration of American foreign policy: the unwillingness of the legislative branch of the richest country in the world to appropriate sufficient funds for the solvent operation of its foreign embassies.

A second problem involving the ambassador or minister lies in the obstacles such officials

* These extracts are taken from: Senate Foreign Relations Committee, *The Nomination of Maxwell H. Gluck*, Hearings, 85th Congress, 1st Session, July 2, 1957, pp. 1–4.

have encountered in effectively coordinating American policy abroad, among a proliferating circle of governmental agencies involved in overseas activities. As we shall see more fully in Chapter 4, contemporary emphasis upon informational, cultural, military, and foreign assistance aspects of foreign policy has engendered an increasingly acute problem of blending the efforts of many governmental agencies into a single, cohesive foreign policy that achieves American goals abroad. By the late 1950s and early 1960s, diffuse and disunified efforts by governmental agencies in certain foreign countries occasioned deep concern. Accordingly, on May 29, 1961, President Kennedy explicitly directed that the ambassador in each country was to coordinate all governmental activities collectively carried out by what came to be called the American "country team." The President's directive stipulated that the ambassador was to supervise "not only the personnel of the Department of State and the Foreign Service, but also the representatives of all other U.S. agencies which have programs or activities" in that particular country.[53] In the ensuing months, a congressional committee found that the concept of the "country team" had done much to correct earlier organizational deficiencies and that "the field is refreshingly free of inter-agency strife. In general the deep jurisdictional clashes evident in Washington are absent."[54] Yet events revealed that this verdict was perhaps premature and altogether too sanguine. The next chapter will call attention to enough examples of interagency conflict in key countries to indicate that sometimes serious problems remain and that, at best, the concept of the ambassador as head of the "country team" has had only partial success.*

A second continuing problem is illustrated by a comment made by President Eisenhower

* The testimony of Dr. Robert W. Tufts to the Senate Committee on Government Operations on March 25, 1963, called attention forcefully to the persistence of the problem. Reporting on results found by a staff study carried out by this committee, Dr. Tufts reaffirmed an earlier finding that "To a degree the primacy of the Ambassador is a polite fiction, especially where budgetary and programming decisions are concerned. Most elements of the country team do not, in other words, regard themselves as parts of the Ambassador's staff. . . ." He also found that in some instances, the ambassador himself was reluctant to provide forceful direction of the country team. See Senate Government Operations Committee, *Administration of National Security*, Hearings, 88th Congress, 1st Session, 1963, Part 1, 104–109.

on March 6, 1953, during a meeting of the Cabinet:

Ever since 1946, I know that all the so-called experts have been yapping about what would happen when Stalin dies and what we, as a nation, should do about it. Well, he's dead. And you can turn the files of our government inside out—in vain—for any plans laid. We have no plan. We are not even sure what difference his death makes.[55]

This lament— "We have no plan"—has been heard frequently throughout the postwar period, as the United States has been required to grapple with a host of issues in a global environment characterized by numerous, often sudden, and sometimes decisive changes calling for drastic modifications in American policies. Many of the deficiencies of American policy in recent years unquestionably stem from inadequate "policy planning." State Department officials have found themselves perennially occupied with what former Secretary of State Dean Acheson has labeled "the thundering present." Insufficient attention has been devoted to "determining the emerging future and the policy appropriate to it."[56]

Recognition of the need for better policy planning has existed for many years. As part of the early postwar reorganization of the State Department, a Policy Planning Staff, later renamed the Policy Planning Council, was created to remedy this organizational defect. Its assigned function was to question the adequacy of existing policies and the validity of their basic assumption, to study significant trends in international affairs affecting America's interests, and to prepare appraisals of alternative responses, along with their recommendations, for consideration by high-level officials in the State Department, the White House, and other executive agencies. Experienced diplomatic officials are basically agreed about two points concerning policy planning. One is that as never before it is a vital segment of foreign policy, particularly in permitting the United States to "take the initiative" in dealing intelligently with emerging issues rather than merely reacting to them with little preparation when a crisis looms. The second point is that even now policy planning is being carried out with only limited success. The apparently overwhelming temptation—inevitable perhaps when almost every day brings some new crisis abroad —is for officials supposedly engaged in policy planning to become immersed in the day-to-day details of foreign policy, instead of devoting their time and energy to analyzing problems that lie in the future and that, in some cases at least, may remain largely hypothetical. Policy planners themselves encourage this tendency to the extent that they sometimes *want* to become more immersed in dealing with immediate, concrete issues confronting the United States abroad. Furthermore, the members of the Policy Planning Council are extremely able individuals; it has therefore proved difficult to prevent their being "drafted" for special assignments with other units within the State Department.* In some measure, the history of the Policy Planning Council reflects a deeply ingrained tendency in the American approach to foreign relations, about which we have commented at length in Chapter 2. This is the propensity to be concerned almost exclusively with tangible, here-and-now questions that are handled pragmatically. Historically, the American people themselves have been little inclined to think seriously about global trends and future developments affecting their national interests. If State Department officials have difficulty, in Townsend Hoopes's words, in treating "future trends as serious realities," they are reflecting an innate characteristic of the pragmatic American society.[57]

Still other persistent problems affecting the State Department relate to the role and authority of the Secretary of State as the President's chief foreign affairs adviser. With the increasing complexity of America's involvement in global affairs have inescapably come new duties and minutiae of administration that must be borne by the Secretary of State. By the mid-1960s, a widespread conviction existed among informed students of American government that the position required careful and ongoing study, leading perhaps to major administrative changes. Something of the nature of the problem involved was suggested in 1962 by Secretary of State Dean Rusk, who compared the responsibilities of his office to a four-motored aircraft. One motor was his relations with the President; another, his relations with the State Department; another, his relations with Congress; and still another, his rela-

tions with the public. All four engines had to synchronize if the secretary were, in turn, to perform his assigned duties successfully.[58] Increasingly, the domestic and foreign responsibilities devolving upon the secretary have proved massive and inordinately time-consuming. The schedule of negotiations and meetings abroad, for example, had mounted sharply in recent years, requiring that the secretary spend an excessive amount of time outside Washington. Other demands, like ceremonial functions, have tended more and more to infringe upon the secretary's time. The amount of time this official has been obliged to devote to legislative consultations has also tended to expand appreciably in recent years.

These facts have given rise to a number of suggestions, designed to relieve the Secretary of State (and sometimes his principal advisers) of many peripheral duties in order that he may devote more time to the formulation and appraisal of policy and to the supervision of important areas of policy. The Brookings Institution, a private and highly respected research organization in Washington, D.C., in the early 1960s recommended sweeping organizational modifications within the State Department, entailing the creation of a new Cabinet official—Secretary of Foreign Affairs—who would have over-all responsibility for the political, economic, and informational aspects of foreign policy. Under him, three principal subordinates—a Secretary of State to manage political affairs, a secretary for foreign economic operations, and a secretary for informational and cultural aspects of foreign policy—would deal with the major segments of American foreign relations, thereby relieving this official of many of the more time-consuming and marginal duties of administration presently interfering with his effective operation.[59] A somewhat comparable proposal for the creation of a "First Secretary" of the Cabinet, outranking other departmental heads in the government, was endorsed by President Eisenhower.[60] Thus far, however, Eisenhower has been the only prominent official of government to support this measure enthusiastically. Most other incumbent and former officials have strongly criticized both the idea of a new super-Secretary of State and the further subdivision of the State Department into more sharply delineated operating units. One study criticizes such proposals as embodying "serious shortcomings and limitations." They would both "fail to solve the problems" they seek to

---

* For appraisals of the operations of the Policy Planning Council in recent years, see the testimony of former Secretary of State Acheson in Senate Government Operations Committee, *Administration of National Security: Selected Papers*, pp. 99–100; and *Administration of National Security: Basic Issues*, pp. 5–6.

solve; at the same time, they would "introduce grave new difficulties into the working of our national policy machinery."[61] This study underscores such obstacles as the lack of real *power* over other departments, increasingly involved in foreign affairs, that a super-secretary might actually exercise; concern that creation of this position would derogate from other Cabinet posts and induce only "submissive" individuals to accept appointment to them; fear that the historically varied relationship prevailing between a President and his Secretary of State, in which sometimes the President himself largely directs foreign affairs, would be impaired; apprehension that a super-secretary might even become a rival to the President himself, and a contestant with him for leadership over the executive branch; and belief that this move might render difficult the maintenance of harmonious and cooperative executive-legislative relations, especially in cases of conflict between the super-secretary and other Cabinet officers.[62] Secretary of State Christian Herter rejected the proposals for a variety of reasons, in part because he doubted

> . . . the assumption of equivalence for areas such as diplomacy, information, and foreign economic matters. I do not believe the areas are, in fact, equivalent. If these three principal areas are to be equated, it will then become necessary to establish what I fear would be an excessively large coordinating mechanism at the level of the super Secretary of State. Instead of being relieved of burdens, he might find his load increased.[63]

The kind of bureaucratic "layering" envisioned in this proposal was also poignantly criticized by former Secretary of State Acheson when he said: "The result of this reorganization would give the President and the [proposed new] Secretary plenty of time to think and talk, but not much to think or talk about."[64]

We may conclude our discussion of organizational and other continuing problems in State Department operation by citing an observation of Mr. Roger Hilsman, who served as Assistant Secretary of State for Far Eastern Affairs, in the Kennedy and Johnson Administrations:

> It is almost traditional in America to view foreign affairs as a problem in public administration. When our minds turn to the business of relating ourselves to the outside world, we tend to think of reorganization, of rearranging the parts of the gov-

ernment. Yet all this organizational tinkering hardly seems rewarding. Many of our failures in foreign policy are probably not failures at all, but lack of power to shape the events we deplore. No nation is so strong that it can dictate the course of history. . . . one suspects that even our true failures in foreign policy would not have yielded to better organization. . . . few of our true failures are attributable to bad administration in carrying policy out. Our true failures probably lie more often in failing to recognize emerging problems in time to evolve effective policies or in meeting big, bold, demanding problems with half-measures, timorous and cramped.[65]

Our discussion of the role of the President and State Department has focused attention upon a trend of considerable importance for the foreign policy process, to which we turn in the next chapter: the growing involvement of military and other executive agencies in the formulation and administration of foreign relations.

NOTES

1. Clinton Rossiter, *The Supreme Court and the Commander in Chief* (Ithaca: Cornell University Press, 1951), p. 5. A capable treatment of legal and constitutional aspects of executive power.
2. Edward S. Corwin, *Total War and the Constitution* (New York: Knopf, 1947), p. 12, italics omitted. Discusses the President's emergency powers.
3. Quoted in Cecil V. Crabb, Jr., *Bipartisan Foreign Policy: Myth or Reality?* (New York: Harper & Row, 1957), p. 16.
4. William L. Langer, "The Mechanism of American Foreign Policy," *International Affairs*, 24 (July, 1948), 322.
5. Edward S. Corwin, ed., *The Constitution of the United States of America* (Washington, D.C.: Legislative Reference Service, Library of Congress, 1953), p. 445.
6. *Ibid.*, p. 443.
7. *Ibid.*, p. 436.
8. For detailed documentation, see: Charles Fairman, "The President as Commander-in-Chief," in *The Presidency in Transition* (a symposium) (Gainesville, Fla.: University of Florida Press, 1949); Rossiter, *op. cit.*, pp. 11–25; Corwin, *Total War and the Constitution, op. cit.*, pp. 7–33.
9. Fairman, *op. cit.*, p. 145.
10. Quoted in Edward S. Corwin, *The President's Control of Foreign Relations* (Princeton, N.J.: Princeton University Press,

1917), p. 137. Though lacking contemporary examples, this is still a classic work analyzing the President's powers.

11. Quoted in Edward S. Corwin and Louis W. Koenig, *The President Today* (New York: New York University Press, 1956), p. 48.

12. Crabb, *op. cit.*, pp. 87–96.

13. Quoted in the *Congressional Record*, 103, 1870.

14. Dwight D. Eisenhower, *Mandate for Change: 1953–1956* (Garden City, N.Y.: Doubleday, 1963), p. 468.

15. Corwin, *The President's Control of Foreign Relations, op. cit.*, p. 44.

16. Hopkins's diplomatic activities are described in Robert E. Sherwood, *Roosevelt and Hopkins*, I (New York: Bantam Books, 1948), 283, 285, 305, 328, 536.

17. *The New York Times*, October 23, 1951.

18. Julius W. Pratt, *A History of United States Foreign Policy* (Englewood Cliffs, N.J.: Prentice-Hall, 1955), p. 642. A scholarly and readable account of American foreign relations.

19. Corwin, *The President's Control of Foreign Relations, op. cit.*, p. 177.

20. Harold L. Cross, *The People's Right To Know* (New York: Columbia University Press, 1953), pp. 231–233. A thorough appraisal of the problem of access to governmental information.

21. Elias Huzar, "Reorganization for National Security," *Journal of Politics*, 12 (February, 1950), 149.

22. Wilfred E. Binkley, *President and Congress* (New York: Knopf, 1947), p. 250. Provides valuable historical insight into executive-legislative relations.

23. Anthony Leviero, "The Press and the President," *New York Times Magazine*, August 21, 1949, pp. 10–11, 51–52.

24. Corwin and Koenig, *op. cit.*, p. 70.

25. Wilfred E. Binkley, "The President and Congress," in *The Presidency in Transition, op. cit.*, p. 73.

26. Quoted in *ibid.*, p. 74.

27. Binkley, *President and Congress, op. cit.*, p. 246.

28. *Documents on American Foreign Relations: 1962* (New York: Harper & Row, 1963), pp. 47–48.

29. Quoted in *The New York Times*, March 13, 1947.

30. For fuller discussion, see Crabb, *op. cit.*, pp. 251–254.

31. Corwin, *The Constitution of the United States of America, op. cit.*, pp. 393–395.

32. *Ibid.*, pp. 81–82.

33. Corwin, *Total War and the Constitution, op. cit.*, p. 19.

34. Corwin, *The Constitution of the United States of America, op. cit.*, p. 493.

35. *Ibid.*, p. 496.

36. *Ibid.*, p. 499.

37. Clinton Rossiter, *The American Presidency* (New York: New American Library, 1956), pp. 31–53.

38. Abbot Smith, "Mr. Madison's War," *Political Science Quarterly*, 57 (June, 1942), 229.

39. Quoted in Senate Government Operations Committee, *Administration of National Security: Basic Issues*, 88th Congress, 1st Session (Washington, D.C.: 1963), p. 6.

40. Quoted in Senate Government Operations Committee, *Administration of National Security: Selected Papers*, 87th Congress, 2nd Session (Washington, D.C.: 1962), p. 88.

41. Bertram D. Hulen, *Inside the Department of State* (New York: Whittlesley House, 1939), p. 15.

42. See Department of State, "Summary of Employment," August 31, 1963; and "Manpower Profile, Departmental and Foreign Service," July, 1963 (mimeographed documents).

43. This fact is cited by George F. Kennan in his detailed appraisal of State Department organization included in Senate Government Operations Committee, *Organizing for National Security—Selected Materials*, 86th Congress, 2nd Session (Washington, D.C.: 1960), pp. 107–121.

44. James L. McCamy, *The Administration of American Foreign Affairs* (New York: Knopf, 1950), pp. 70–73. Although dated, this remains a valuable treatment of State Department organization and operation.

45. Senate Foreign Relations Committee, *The Formulation and Administration of United States Foreign Policy*, 86th Congress, 2nd Session (Washington, D.C.: 1960), p. 59. This study by the Brookings Institution provides an admirable, succinct account of policy formulation.

46. Department of State, "Summary of Employment," *op. cit.*, p. 1.

47. The principles guiding the operation of the Foreign Service down to the postwar era are described and appraised in Alona E. Evans, "The Re-Organization of the American Foreign Service," *International Affairs*, 24 (April, 1948), 206–217; and James L. McCamy and Alesandro Corradini, "The People of the State Department and Foreign Service," *American Political Science Review*, 48 (December, 1954), 1067–1082.

48. Senate Government Operations Committee, *Organizing for National Security*, Hear-

ings, 86th Congress, 2nd Session, I (Washington, D.C.: 1960), 1293.

49. George F. Kennan, "The Future of Our Professional Diplomacy," *Foreign Affairs*, **33** (July, 1955), 98.

50. Henry M. Wriston, *Diplomacy in a Democracy* (New York: Harper & Row, 1956), p. 7. An able analysis, based upon the author's findings as chairman of the Public Committee on Personnel to investigate the Foreign Service.

51. *Documents on American Foreign Relations: 1954, op. cit.,* pp. 58–61.

52. Senate Government Operations Committee, *Administration of National Security: Selected Papers, op. cit.,* p. 22.

53. Cited in Senate Government Operations Committee, *Administration of National Security: Basic Issues, op. cit.,* pp. 9–10.

54. *Ibid.,* p. 11.

55. Emmet Hughes, *Ordeal of Power* (New York: Atheneum, 1963), p. 101.

56. Quoted in Senate Government Operations Committee, *The Secretary of State and the National Security Policy Process,* 87th Congress, 1st Session (Washington, D.C.: 1961), p. 8.

57. Senate Government Operations Committee, *Administration of National Security: Selected Papers, op. cit.,* p. 90.

58. *Documents on American Foreign Relations: 1962, op. cit.,* p. 31.

59. Senate Government Operations Committee, *The Formulation and Administration of United States Foreign Policy, op. cit.,* pp. 3–4.

60. Sherman Adams, *First-Hand Report: The Story of the Eisenhower Administration* (New York: Harper & Row, 1961), pp. 460–461.

61. Senate Government Operations Committee, *Super-Cabinet Officers and Superstaffs,* 86th Congress, 2nd Session (Washington, D.C.: 1960), p. 122.

62. *Ibid.,* pp. 122–123.

63. Senate Government Operations Committee, *Organizing for National Security, op. cit.,* I, 699.

64. Quoted in Senate Government Operations Committee, *Administration of National Security: Selected Papers, op. cit.,* p. 92.

65. Quoted in *ibid.,* pp. 99–100.

4 → THE MILITARY

ESTABLISHMENT AND OTHER

EXECUTIVE AGENCIES →

THE MILITARY AND AMERICAN FOREIGN POLICY

Addressing graduation exercises at the U.S. Military Academy in 1962, President John F. Kennedy told the newly commissioned graduates:

> . . . the period just ahead in the next decade will offer more opportunities for service to the graduates of this Academy than ever before in the history of the United States, because all around the world, in countries which are heavily engaged in the maintenance of their freedom, graduates of this Academy are heavily involved; whether it is in Viet Nam or in Laos or in Thailand, whether it is a military advisory group in Iran, whether it is a military attaché in some Latin American country during a difficult and challenging period, whether it is the commander of our troops in South Korea —the burdens that will be placed upon you when you fill those positions . . . will require more from you than ever before in our history. The graduates of West Point, the Naval Academy and the Air Academy in the next ten years will have the greatest opportunity for the defense of freedom that this Academy's graduates have ever had. . . .

At another point in his speech, the President said: "Our forces . . . must fulfill a broader role as a complement to our diplomacy, as an arm of our diplomacy, as a deterrent to our adversaries, and as a symbol to our Allies of our determination to support them."[1]

The essential idea being emphasized by President Kennedy originated during the 1930s when Secretary of State Cordell Hull observed, in discussing America's relations with the Axis Powers:

> Soon after I came into the State Department, when I would be talking with the representatives of the thugs at the head of governments abroad . . . they would look at me in the face but I soon discovered that they were looking over my shoulder at our Navy and our Army and that our diplomatic strength . . . goes up or down with their estimate of what that amounts to.[2]

And in 1951, General Omar N. Bradley, commander of army ground forces in Europe during World War II and later chairman of the Joint Chiefs of Staff, wrote in his memoirs:

> The American army has . . . acquired a political maturity it sorely lacked at the outbreak of World War II. At times during that war we forgot that wars are fought for the resolution of political conflicts, and in the ground campaign for Europe we sometimes overlooked political considerations of vast importance. Today, after several years of cold war, we are intensely aware that a military effort cannot be separated from political objectives.[3]

All of these statements are variations on Clausewitz's famous aphorism that war is merely the continuation of politics by other means. In the postwar period, as Americans have confronted a determined and expansive diplomatic opponent, citizens and officials have become perhaps even more conscious that the converse of Clausewitz's dictum is no less true: politics is a form of war by other means. In its simplest terms, the relationship between national policies and military force has been described by General Matthew B. Ridgway as follows:

> The statesman, the senior civilian authority, says to the soldier . . . : This is our national policy. This is what we wish to accomplish or would like to do. What military means are required to support it?

> The soldier studies this problem in detail.

> "Very well," he says to the statesman. "Here is what your policy will require in men and guns, in ships and planes."[4]

Admittedly, as we shall see, this is a highly simplified version of how civilian-military coordination of national policy goals is actually achieved. Yet it calls attention to a fact that was understood most imperfectly down to the postwar era: the military establishment plays an indispensable role in protecting the nation's diplomatic vital interests. Effective diplomacy and sound national security policies are opposite sides of the coin of national survival and of the achievement of American goals at home and abroad. Although military officers have occasionally assumed diplomatic responsibilities in the past, as when Commodore Perry "opened up" Japan in 1854, or when they often performed diplomatic functions during the era of "gunboat diplomacy" in Latin America in the early 1900s, formal and continuing military participation in national policy decisions remained haphazard and expediential before World War II. After an intensive search of the evidence during the McKinley-Roosevelt-Taft period, for example, one writer has stated: "I have yet to find a letter from a Secretary of State, asking for a military cost accounting before some diplomatic stroke." He found that before the 1930s, liaison among the Secretaries of State, War, and Navy was usually indirect, by letter only.[5]

Down to World War II, various makeshift arrangements were relied upon to provide coordination between civilian and military policy-makers.[6] That the integration of military and civilian aspects of national policy was still imperfect was indicated by a number of diplomatically far-reaching decisions taken during World War II. Conspicuous examples were the decisions to permit the Russians to occupy Berlin, to divide Korea at the 38th Parallel, and to insist upon Soviet participation in the war against Japan. In these instances, military considerations predominated in reaching decisions that had profound diplomatic implications. Little thought was given at the time to the ultimate political, economic, or strategic consequences of such decisions, or to their over-all influence upon the diplomatic position of the United States.[7] The prevailing mentality in approaching wartime decisions of this kind was revealed by General Omar N. Bradley, who wrote in connection with conflicting British and American views toward Germany: "As soldiers we looked naïvely on this British inclination to complicate the war with political foresight and nonmilitary objectives."[8] Military leaders were not alone in forgetting Clausewitz's dictum. After World War II, for example, the State Department showed considerable reluctance to relieve the army of the responsibility for occupation affairs in conquered Germany.[9]

Except in the rare case when militarism *per se* actuates a nation's policies, military action is always undertaken in behalf of *political* objectives.* Awareness of this fact is doubtless more widespread now than in any previous era of American history. Yet there is still a perennial danger that it will be forgotten especially in time of war—general or limited. General Douglas MacArthur's celebrated remark during the Korean conflict— "In war there is no substitute for victory"—reflects this tendency, as does Senator William Jenner's (Republican of Indiana) criticism in the same period: "If our military are not permitted to develop a defense or to fight a war [victoriously] . . . but their strategy is diluted by political considerations of the State Department, what chance . . . do we have to defend this country . . . ?"[10] By contrast, Robert Lovett, former Secretary of Defense, stated in 1960: "The military professionals should be contributors to and not makers of national political policies. They are trained to carry out such policy, not to originate it."[11] Or, as Admiral Sidney W. Souers said in the same year: ". . . it is not the responsibility of the military to determine foreign policy."[12] How

---

* As the term is used here, "political objectives" refers to the larger goals of American foreign relations, as discussed in Chapter 1, and not in the more limited sense to issues that are prominent in domestic politics.

well are such realizations understood by those involved in policy determination and execution? How well is the military establishment organized to perform its functions? Has the desirable level of military-civilian coordination been achieved in the American government? Such questions are fundamental and require more detailed examination.

THE NATIONAL DEFENSE ESTABLISHMENT

The Military Services Before World War II

Increasingly in the period before World War II, experience showed the futility of trying to preserve national security when civilian leaders ignored military factors. By World War I, two problems of civilian-military coordination had already come to the forefront. First, internal reorganization of the military establishment was indicated in order to make it a more effective instrument of national policy. Second, new machinery was needed for coordinating military efforts with those of civilian agencies.

World War I revealed the desirability of unification of the armed services. The emergence of air power as a major component of American military strength, and the dramatization of its effects by General Billy Mitchell during the 1920s and 1930s, provided new impetus to the unification movement. In the 1924–1945 period over fifty bills were introduced into Congress calling for the merger of the armed services and the establishment of a joint military command. Although studies of military unification continued throughout the war, little was done to make unification a reality. A consensus prevailed throughout all the agencies of government that so radical a change must await the end of hostilities. Before and during the war, when coordination was required among the military services it was usually reached by a process of "mutual agreement." The disaster at Pearl Harbor revealed forcefully how inadequate such agreements were for preserving national security. Yet until the postwar period, high-ranking military officials clung to the idea that successful prosecution of six major wars in a century and a quarter demonstrated the feasibility of continued separation of the services.[13]

Within the military establishment, disagreements arose over such issues as the proper roles of the army, navy, and air force in safeguarding national defense; over the best combination of the services to assure maximum coordination among them; over the establishment and operation of a joint command; and over the proper relationships to be set up between the nation's chief military commanders and their civilian superiors.[14] Studies of these and equally complex problems continued during the war and into the immediate postwar era. In addition to the purely military aspects of modifications in the prevailing defense organization, there were urgent problems arising from rapid demobilization after the war and from conversion to a peacetime footing. Finally, on December 19, 1945, President Truman asked Congress to unify the armed services. His recommendations were patterned closely after a report prepared for the navy by Ferdinand Eberstadt. Extended legislative hearings and more detailed studies ensued, so that it was not until the spring of 1947 that Congress passed the National Security Act. This act, together with its later modifications, provides the basis for the present defense establishment.

Reorganization of the Pentagon

The cardinal fact about the defense reorganization in 1947 that substantially governed changes made in subsequent years was that the plan which finally emerged represented a compromise between two extreme positions, and as a compromise it satisfied no interested group completely. One extreme position favored little significant change in American defense organization. Deep fears existed about the emergence of anything resembling the German General Staff; apprehension prevailed lest the separate services lose their identities. Powerful vested interests like the Navy League, the Air Force Association, and the Associations of the United States Army opposed sweeping changes. These groups often had influential supporters on Capitol Hill. Ranged against this group were advocates of radical changes in the existing defense pattern. Advocates of sweeping reorganization pointed to innumerable instances in the nation's history—the most disastrous being Pearl Harbor—to support the view that America could no longer afford the luxury of three powerful services operating virtually autonomously. Critics lamented that recurrent disputes over "service jurisdictions" and ineffectual efforts to secure "voluntary cooperation" among rival services had too long impaired national security.

The Act of 1947 tried to steer a middle

course between these two positions, leaning perhaps more toward the former than toward the latter. It united the military branches, but not too closely. It placed the Department of Defense under the Secretary of Defense, but took pains to prevent his becoming a "military tsar." It provided for a Joint Chiefs of Staff, but carefully circumscribed the group's powers and left its members as the *operating* commanders of their respective services. These compromises, and others, are explicable only if it is grasped that the plan of defense reorganization itself was above all a compromise and that, at least in some instances, it represented an attempt to synthesize viewpoints that tended in the final analysis to be irreconcilable. With these general ideas in mind, let us examine specific changes introduced into the national defense establishment.

The apex of the organizational hierarchy in the Pentagon is the Office of Secretary of Defense, headed by a civilian Secretary of Defense. This officer represents the Defense Department in the Cabinet and in the National Security Council. Legally, the Secretary of Defense is the channel by which orders are transmitted from the President to the military services. Although the secretary enjoys broad powers, such as preparation of the overall military budget, he is nevertheless restricted in his control over the direct operations of the separate military branches. Orders to the services which, by law, should be transmitted from the President to the Secretary of Defense, and thence to the services, have gone directly to the civilian secretaries at the head of each branch, thereby effectively bypassing the Office of Secretary of Defense. In 1949, Congress added to the authority of the Secretary of Defense, but with the clear stipulation that the military services were to be kept separate and that no "general staff" was to be imposed over them.

The second major innovation introduced by the defense reorganization of 1947 was establishment of the Joint Chiefs of Staff. This organ was to impart needed coordination in over-all defense planning, while avoiding creation of a totally unified military command system. The Joint Chiefs comprise the military commanders from each of the three principal services, plus the Commandant of the Marine Corps, when decisions affect its interests. A voting chairman presides, with the chairmanship rotating among the services. The Joint Chiefs of Staff serve as the principal military

advisers to the President, the National Security Council and the Secretary of Defense. Hanson Baldwin has summarized its duties by saying that:

> They are charged as a body with the preparation of strategic and logistic plans and the provision of "strategic direction" for the armed forces, with the establishment of unified commands, the formulation of policies for joint training and education of the armed forces, and the "review" of the services' manpower and equipment requirements. A grab-bag provision of the law also requires them to perform "such other duties" as are directed.[15]

Thus to avoid the extreme of overcentralization, the nation's highest military commanders are utilized in two rather contradictory capacities: *individually*, as operating heads of their respective branches, they are charged with carrying out assignments given to their service arms and with maintaining them as an effective fighting force; *collectively*, as the nation's highest military staff, they are responsible for formulating over-all interservice policies and programs designed to utilize *all* military branches in the way best calculated to promote national security. This kind of built-in ambiguity has well-nigh guaranteed that as an institution the Joint Chiefs would suffer from schizophrenic tendencies.*

The third category of changes brought about in 1947 and in subsequent years concerned the military departments. A major innovation in

---

* Problems arising from the operations of the Joint Chiefs are brought out clearly in General James M. Gavin's book, *War and Peace in the Space Age* (New York: Harper & Row, 1958). General Gavin emphasizes how the individual service chiefs are required simultaneously to think in terms of the interests of their own services and in the larger terms of the best conceivable coordinated plan for national security. More often than not, in such a contest, the interests of the individual services prevail. The system encourages "reciprocity" and "horse trading" among the service heads; not infrequently, decisions are made on a two-against-one basis. Gavin, whose views of course favor the army side, believes this occurred in limiting army missile development to weapons of no more than 250-mile range and in spending vast sums for "supercarriers." This condition in turn promotes, if it does not make virtually inevitable, attempts by the individual services to cultivate "sympathetic" viewpoints on Capitol Hill, largely breaking down the concept that the viewpoints of the Pentagon are coordinated through the Secretary of Defense. Whatever the motives of individual commanders, in Gavin's opinion *the system* perpetuates such phenomena. *Ibid.*, pp. 166–179, 257–265.

1947 was elevation of the air force to a separate department, putting it on a plane of equality with the army and navy. Each of the services was now headed by a civilian secretary who, together with the senior military commander in each arm—who also served on the Joint Chiefs of Staff—administered the affairs of the department. Various provisions of the law of 1947 and later modifications tried to assure at least the semblance of coordination and liaison among the military departments in meeting common problems like procurement, manpower needs, and research and development.

After an extended period of adjustment during the late 1940s and early 1950s, when competition among the services in programs such as missile development made many commentators wonder how much actual "unification" was being achieved, genuine interservice cooperation gradually infused many spheres of national defense. In time, five new agencies were set up within the Defense Department to perform services common to all military arms: the Defense Atomic Support Agency, the National Security Agency, the Defense Communications Agency, the Defense Intelligence Agency, and the Defense Supply Agency. The existence of these agencies indicated growing willingness by the separate military branches to subordinate their differences in behalf of a common defense effort.[16] Moreover, the trend toward military unification—toward bringing the defense organization more into harmony with the actual functions performed by military units in the modern era—was exemplified by the creation of unified "commands," prepared to carry out diverse assignments under widely differing conditions. Thus President Eisenhower described the Strategic Air Command as "designed primarily for instant destruction of the enemy by large-scale nuclear attack." For many years, the air force provided the bulk of SAC's forces, but with the navy's acquisition of missile-firing submarines and attack carriers, its forces were also integrated into SAC.[17] Similarly, in the Kennedy Administration the ability of the United States to fight limited, "brush-fire" wars and guerilla conflicts was greatly augmented by the creation of the Strike Command, composed chiefly of army and air force units. Late in 1963 the Strike Command was assigned responsibility for the defense of the Middle East, South Asia, and much of Africa, relieving the navy of that responsibility. Created

in 1961, two years later the Strike Command had 200,000 men (8 army divisions, 50 tactical air squadrons, and a small naval squadron) at its disposal. Yet this step, as expected, was accompanied by evident apprehension in some Pentagon circles about the implications of continued military unification.[18]

The National Security Council

In addition to reorganizing the military services, the National Security Act of 1947 also established a new high-level agency to facilitate coordination throughout the government for policies affecting national security. NSC has been called the "most important high-policy committee in the national government today . . ."[19] In the words of the act establishing the agency, the National Security Council was set up to "advise the President with respect to the integration of domestic, foreign and military policies relating to the national security so as to enable the military services and other departments . . . to cooperate more effectively in matters involving the national security. . . ."[20] During its existence, the council has had several different types of members. The statutory members are currently the President, as chairman, the Vice-President, the Secretary of State, the Secretary of Defense, the director of the Agency for International Development, and the director of the Office of Civil and Defense Mobilization. In addition, the President can and does "invite" other officials to attend NSC meetings. Certain officials—like the director of the Bureau of the Budget, the chairman of the Atomic Energy Commission, and the Secretary of the Treasury—have had in some periods what amounted to a standing invitation to attend meetings of NSC. Other officials—like the Attorney General, the director of the U.S. Information Agency, and the chairman of the Council of Economic Advisers—have attended NSC meetings occasionally, when problems directly related to their agencies were under discussion.[21]

The National Security Council is the highest agency within the executive branch for coordinating national security policy. A former member of the council under the Eisenhower Administration has observed that five guidelines govern the council's deliberations. (1) The council's principal function is "to advise the President" and not to "serve as a planning or operational mechanism." (2) The council must "integrate all germane views" throughout the executive branch in formulating its recommendations. (3) The council is charged with appraising "the objectives, risks, and commitments of the United States in relation to our actual and potential military power" in carrying out national policies. (4) While the council is for the President's "personal use," it is not the *only* mechanism the President possesses for securing advice on national security problems. (5) The ultimate role of the council is "advisory only. It recommends; the President decides."[22]

Implicit in this conception of the National Security Council's role are three points requiring further emphasis. First, NSC and other mechanisms set up to advise the President are used at the chief executive's discretion. It follows that each President is likely to conceive their roles somewhat differently and to rely upon them in differing degrees. Postwar experience has demonstrated the validity of this expectation. President Eisenhower, for instance, utilized the National Security Council more than any President since its establishment. With a background of military service —in which reliance upon "staff" agencies is heavily emphasized—President Eisenhower quite naturally perhaps transferred this conception of decision-making to the realm of national security policy.* Presidents Truman and Kennedy, on the other hand, did not use the NSC mechanism as frequently or fully as Eisenhower did. As we shall see, in President Kennedy's case, a characteristic of his administration's approach to national security policy was the frequency with which the White House relied upon *ad hoc* committees and other extraordinary devices to advise the President and to provide needed coordination in national security policies.

Second, it must be emphasized that, constitutionally and actually, the President ultimately formulates national policy and arrives at major decisions affecting the nation's security in the world community. Policy decisions

are not made by majority vote of the President's principal advisers; nor do they emerge finally by an informal "sense of the meeting" among this group. After listening to the viewpoints of his chief subordinates, who bring to bear information and ideas from many different vantage points bearing upon national security, the President alone resolves issues in question and commits the United States Government to a given policy.** The point was expressed forcefully on one occasion by President Eisenhower: "The National Security Council is set up to do one thing—advise the President. I make the decisions, and there is no use trying to put any responsibility on the National Security Council—it's mine."[23]

Third, although the National Security Council is the highest governmental agency for advising the President about national security policy, it is by no means the *only* source of information available to the chief executive, nor is it always the most influential one. General Robert A. Cutler has stated that

> . . . the Council is only one way a President makes up his mind. He may make it up in any way that he determines, and Presidents do. He may make up his mind at the Cabinet, and he may make up his mind with some other people, and he may make up his mind when he is alone. He is not compelled to make up his mind in any particular way.

Since "no law can compel the executive branch to come to a policy decision in a particular way," General Cutler contended that a great virtue of the National Security Council arrangement is its *flexibility*. It permits different Presidents to utilize it differently and does not (in the words of Senator Mike Mansfield, Democrat of Montana) attempt to get executive policy-making "embedded in legislative concrete."[24]

---

* See discussion of Eisenhower's reliance on staff agencies in Dwight D. Eisenhower, *Mandate for Change: 1952–1956* (Garden City, N.Y.: Doubleday, 1963), pp. 114–119, 132–135, 447–448, and Robert Cutler, "The Development of the National Security Council," *Foreign Affairs,* 34 (April, 1956), 441–458. Cutler points out, for example, that under Eisenhower a fairly clear division of labor emerged, whereby NSC considered all matters directly affecting national security, while the Cabinet confined its discussion to other issues requiring decisions. *Ibid.,* p. 441.

** Although formal "votes" are seldom taken within the National Security Council, the decision of the President, according to General Cutler, might emerge in one of two ways. After extended discussion, it might often appear that there was no objection to a specified course of action, in which case the President's lack of objection would be tantamount to approval. In other cases, the President would review the written record of NSC meetings, including proposals for action; when he initialed these records, this signified his approval of the proposals in question. Senate Government Operations Committee, *Organizing for National Security,* Hearings, 87th Congress, 1st Session, I (Washington: 1961), 601–602.

CONTINUING PROBLEMS IN NATIONAL SECURITY POLICY

Establishment of the National Security Council, together with other changes made in administrative machinery to deal with national security problems, has done a great deal to supply needed coordination within the executive branch in approaching major external problems. Postwar experience has made abundantly clear, however, that the formulation and execution of national security poses a *continuing* challenge to policy-makers. Major aspects of the problem require ongoing study and attention, both by officials and intelligent citizens.

Coordinating Effective Security Policy

While some informed commentators believe that, on balance, the National Security Council has been eminently successful in carrying out its assigned functions,* other, and no less well-informed, commentators believe NSC has never functioned altogether according to intentions, and that several major difficulties are *inherent* in its very conception and structure. In this view, the problem of coordinating government-wide activities in national security affairs requires continuing investigation and perhaps radical curative measures.

Among the critics of NSC, a representative viewpoint has been expressed by the experienced public servant George F. Kennan. Kennan is unconvinced that organizational changes introduced since World War II have corrected the "fragmentation and diffusion of power" prevailing in the field of national security policy. Even now, "the system of diffused authority spreads downward into a thousand branches and twigs of the governmental tree." In Kennan's view, agencies like NSC have in reality compounded the problem. In his judgment, the National Security Council is a

. . . body capable only of sporadic, solemn decisions, laboriously prepared and negotiated among the various Government offices prior to their submission to the President. . . . What the foreign affairs segment of the Government needs is not primarily an occasional National Security Council paper but intimate day-by-day, hour-by-hour direc-

* For generally favorable verdicts on the operations of NSC in the recent period, see the testimony of Admiral Sidney W. Souers and of General Robert Cutler in: Senate Government Operations Committee, *op. cit.*, I, 559–576, 587–608.

tion, sensitive to the smallest significant change in the world situation. It needs, in the language of the day, to be ridden herd on; and this is precisely what the National Security Council cannot do for it.

In support of his contentions, Kennan calls attention to a curious phenomenon about policy formulation and execution within recent years. This is the extent to which the President, and sometimes his principal advisers such as the Secretary of State, have been inclined to operate outside established bureaucratic "channels" in formulating key policies, especially when crises exist abroad. Kennan has commented:

On countless occasions subordinates have been surprised and disappointed—sometimes even personally hurt—to find that the Secretary [of State] or the President has been more decisively influenced by some chance outside contact or experience than by the information and advice offered to him through the regular channels. . . . In short, the busy senior executive frequently finds more useful and meaningful to him the product of the individual mind than the product of a tortured collective effort; and it is only the latter that he gets from his assistants.[25]

Experience under the Kennedy Administration—particularly the White House's response to the Soviet missile buildup in Cuba in 1962 —suggested that there was considerable validity in Kennan's observations.** For a number of

** An outstanding characteristic of President Kennedy's handling of the Cuban crisis was his reliance upon a special "team" or task force— individuals who, one observer has stated, were "handpicked by Kennedy" and who "represented the men in whom he put his reliance for conducting this country's security affairs" during that crisis. Conspicuous members were Vice-President Lyndon Johnson, Secretary of Defense Robert McNamara, Secretary of State Dean Rusk and Under Secretary Robert Ball, the President's brother, Attorney-General Robert Kennedy, General Maxwell Taylor, chairman of the Joint Chiefs of Staff, and White House Assistants Ted Sorensen and McGeorge Bundy; other officials also participated in decision-making during the crisis. In part, creation of this special team may have come about because the Soviet experts in the State Department had previously assured the President that no Soviet missile buildup in Cuba was likely. *After* the Administration's policies to deal with the Soviet threat in Cuba had been decided upon, this advisory group was given a formal title—"Executive Committee of the National Security Council"! See Hugh Sidey, *John F. Kennedy: President* (New York: Atheneum, 1963), pp. 325–342.

years after its establishment in 1947, the National Security Council was periodically criticized as a device whose principal virtue lay in promoting compromises among diverse agency viewpoints within the executive branch. Officials involved in the deliberations of NSC have frequently denied such charges.[26] Nevertheless, criticism persists. George F. Kennan is not alone in continuing to insist that, as a high-level committee, NSC unavoidably drafts, and the President ultimately accepts, policy directives so vaguely worded that eventually they must be "renegotiated" by executive agencies when the time comes to translate them into specific steps and programs designed to achieve national purposes.[27] Another experienced government official, Paul Nitze, has echoed such criticism. Nitze divides the policy process into three distinct, if closely interrelated, stages: the *formulation* of policy, the making of *decisions,* after alternative courses of action have been carefully evaluated, and the *execution* of policy. Devices like NSC are especially useful in the first stage. It is when they endeavor to intrude into the second and third stages—particularly the stage of decision —that they often impede, rather than facilitate, the making of sound policies.[28] The point that these and other critics emphasize relates to a problem to which we shall return presently: the inherent weakness of committees as devices for formulating imaginative proposals enabling the United States to meet its responsibilities within a rapidly changing global environment.

Below the level of the National Security Council, other efforts are made to assure harmonious integration of civilian and military components of national policy. An important example is the continuing activity carried on to assure smooth cooperation between the Defense and State Departments. Secretary of State Herter has stated that: "The two Departments naturally have very extensive relationships on a multitude of subjects, which enable the Department of State to inject foreign policy considerations into military affairs at all stages." He noted that he and the Secretary of Defense "confer with each other frequently" and that they participated in the formal meetings of the National Security Council and of the Joint Chiefs of Staff. On a lower level, under secretaries and assistant secretaries from both departments regularly conferred with each other and with spokesmen for the Joint Chiefs. Within the Department of Defense, the incumbent of a position created in 1953—

Assistant Secretary of Defense for International Security Affairs (ISA)—was specifically charged with meshing defense efforts with the activities of the Department of State. ISA is thus the focal point for continuing liaison with the State Department. According to Secretary of Defense Thomas S. Gates, "In an average day there will be several hundred separate contacts between individuals in the two organizations—by meeting, phone call, or exchange of correspondence. Similiar contacts are made daily between the State Department and the military services and the Joint Chiefs of Staff."[29] Besides these activities, efforts have been made to surmount departmental vested interests and to promote coordinated national policies, by exchange of personnel between the Defense and State Departments and by use of institutions like the National War College for in-service training of officials involved in all phases of national security policy.[30] For the future, it has been proposed that a "joint career service" for these two departments might go far toward imparting greater continuity to governmental efforts affecting national security and toward generating more mutual understanding between civilian and military policy-makers. Thus far, this suggestion has met with little enthusiasm by high-ranking executive officials.[31]

Financial Aspects of National Security Policy

Throughout most of the postwar period, somewhere between one-half and two-thirds of the national budget has been devoted to the broad field of national security. In general terms, these funds are used to pay for past wars, to deal with present crises, and to finance projects designed to promote future security. Budgetary aspects of national security have thus become all-important. Nearly every step taken by the President and his principal advisers to safeguard the vital interests of the United States—from providing military aid to the NATO allies, to sending military forces to the Middle East, to training the armed forces of South Vietnam, to maintaining an expensive and continuing program of missile development—requires large financial outlays, sometimes totaling billions of dollars in the aggregate.

President Kennedy's Budget Director, David E. Bell, once stated that

. . . the essential idea of the budget process is to permit a systematic consideration of our Government's program requirements in the light of available resources; to identify marginal choices and the judgment factors that bear upon them; to balance competing requirements against each other; and, finally, to enable the President to decide upon priorities and present them to the Congress in the form of a coherent work program and financial plan.[32]

Mr. Bell's statement is a variation upon a theme emphasized in Chapter 1. America's resources are finite. Resources that can be utilized for the promotion of national security must be allocated in turn among a number of governmental agencies concerned with particular sectors of the problem; all such agencies are prone to believe, as a matter of course, that their particular contribution to the collective security effort ought to be expanded. How are the aggregate resources available to the President then to be divided among the programs upon which the security of the nation depends? The answer to this question is ultimately embodied in the White House budget submitted to Congress. At intervals in recent years, competent observers have charged that budgetary considerations played too prominent a role in formulating national security policy, to the point of dominating the policy process. Thus early in the 1960s, the distinguished public servant Averell Harriman contended that the Bureau of the Budget and the Treasury Department "exert too strong an influence upon policy decisions in the national security and foreign policy field." Harriman recommended strongly that "their wings be clipped."[33] High-ranking military and civilian officials in the Pentagon have been even more outspokenly critical of the intrusion of budgetary agencies into the field of national security policy. In the late Eisenhower period, for example, military leaders complained openly that the so-called "New Look" in national defense—stressing massive nuclear retaliation against a potential enemy, and deemphasizing the importance of traditional land and sea forces—derived primarily from the imposition of stringent financial limitations imposed upon the military services. A not untypical criticism was expressed by Army Chief of Staff, General Matthew B. Ridgway, who complained that "pressure was brought on me, in the name of economy, to keep the semblance, but not the reality, of a fighting force overseas." In this commander's view, the imposition of arbitrary budgetary ceilings upon the military branches seriously impaired their

ability to safeguard the nation's security and its diplomatic vital interests. Particularly jeopardized was the ability of the United States to engage in local limited wars in which the enemy relied upon other means than outright aggression to achieve its objectives.[34] In that period, and later, most governmental officials accepted the verdict of Admiral Sidney W. Souers that, even though agencies such as the National Security Council were always required "to measure the cost of national security policies in terms of necessary manpower, resources, and money," nevertheless "budgetary considerations should not themselves be the determinants of policy."[35] Few official or unofficial commentators would disagree with President Kennedy's assertion that the United States could and must "afford" whatever defense program was required to preserve its security at home and abroad.

Yet such general propositions do not dispose of the problem involved in integrating budgetary considerations into the formulation of national security policies. Once it is realized that the resources available to policy-makers are limited—and that they are (except perhaps in time of actual warfare) almost always *less* than governmental agencies feel they need—efforts must always be made to allocate them in a manner best achieving national purposes. No matter if policy-makers had available double or triple or any other multiple of the funds they currently expend, the essential problem would remain. In reality, it is two problems. The President must first determine the *total* amount of money he can reasonably ask Congress to appropriate for all governmental operations. After that, he must make allocations from this total to finance the separate programs his administration proposes. In other words, having decided how much money is available, the White House must establish some system of *priorities* among agencies and programs demanding money. This priority must then be expressed in budgetary terms.

This process in turn may take place essentially in one of two ways. Either the President and his chief financial advisers can first agree upon an over-all budgetary ceiling for all federal expenditures; and after that, upon ceilings for defense aspects of the budget, requiring in turn that each of the armed services operate within prescribed financial limitations. Or, the defense requirements of the nation can first be formulated by officials charged with this responsibility; after that, these requirements can be reduced to budgetary terms. Each of these methods has advantages and disadvantages. Since no President can be indifferent to the level of governmental spending (of which defense expenditures are a major part), the former method permits the White House to keep a tight rein upon over-all governmental expenses and to assure that an approximate balance will be maintained between income and expenditures. Yet, as military officials have often been heard to complain, this method also entails arbitrarily imposed financial ceilings and "directed verdicts," within which defense officials must operate in arriving at policies designed to promote national security. Officials in the Pentagon perhaps inevitably believe that this is a perversion of the normal process of policy formulation—and, under some conditions, an invitation to national disaster. The proper course, they are inclined to believe, is to determine precisely the security needs of the country and then to give them budgetary expression. Yet, as successive Presidents in recent years have become aware, this procedure has the distinct drawback of imposing few effective limitations upon spiraling defense expenditures and of coping with the general problem of bringing federal revenues and outlays into at least rough equilibrium.

Awareness of the merits and drawbacks inherent in each approach persuaded officials in the late Eisenhower and the Kennedy periods that the best procedure lay in striving for a kind of middle way between the two extremes. The basic idea in this new procedure was that from the earliest stages of budget planning, and at all important intermediate stages prior to the time the President's budget requests were put in final form for presentation to Congress, officials and agencies involved with national security planning were actively consulted about the nation's defense requirements. Thus President Eisenhower's Secretary of Defense, Thomas S. Gates, noted that the Joint Chiefs of Staff and the Assistant Secretary of Defense for International Security Affairs were brought into budget discussions at an early date.[36] Defense Secretary McNamara observed that officials in the Pentagon "start with the political objective," presented by the State Department. Subsequently, the Defense Department endeavors to "develop a military program that will support the political objective." President Kennedy, he affirmed, informed the Pentagon that "the defense budget is to be established without regard to arbitrary [budget] ceilings." The general directive, given to Defense Department officials by the White House, was "to attain the specific force levels necessary to support the political objective at the lowest cost."[37]

The nature of the problem of reconciling available resources, as expressed ultimately in the President's budget, with the security requirements of the country is such that no totally satisfactory or final administrative solution is likely to be found. The dilemma described by Robert A. Lovett will pose a continuing challenge to policy-makers. In Lovett's view, when budgetary considerations predominate, to the point of virtually "dictating" national security programs, then certain budgetary agencies of government will be exercising "authority without responsibility." Yet, if budgetary considerations are totally disregarded or given insufficient attention, then defense agencies will be exercising "responsibility without authority." Avoiding the dilemma will unquestionably demand careful study and intelligent efforts by policy-makers throughout the years ahead.

Military Influence upon American Society

The Founding Fathers were intensely suspicious of military power.* James Madison, for instance, believed that a standing army was "one of the greatest mischiefs that can possibly happen. . . ."[38] Accordingly, the founders placed many obstacles in the Constitution against military influence upon the government. The Constitution designates the President as the commander in chief of the military establishment, thereby assuring civilian dominance over the armed forces. It provides that Congress shall raise and support the armed forces and make appropriations for their operations no longer than two years. In practice, Congress votes upon the national defense budget annually. Congress also formulates rules and regulations for governing the conduct of the military services. As part of its power of confirmation, the Senate must concur in the appointment and promotion of high-ranking military commanders. Two levels of armed forces were envisioned under the Constitution:

* For detailed treatments of civilian-military relations in the United States, see: Samuel P. Huntington, *The Soldier and the State* (Cambridge, Mass.: Harvard University Press, 1957); Jerome G. Kerwin, ed., *Civil-Military Relationships in American Life* (Chicago: University of Chicago Press, 1948); Walter Millis, *Arms and the State* (New York: Twentieth Century Fund, 1958).

the national forces, which the founders expected would be kept to a minimum level, and the state militia. The latter was left under the control of the states until it was called into the service of the United States by the President. Summarizing the various constitutional limitations upon the military, Huzar wrote that "Congress was to provide the sword which the President was to wield."[39]

Throughout the greater part of American history, so long as the United States had minimum international responsibilities, no significant danger arose that the military would dominate the national government or otherwise usurp civilian functions. Not once in American history has the serious threat of a military-led *coup d'état* existed, even during time of war. Former military commanders like President Eisenhower have often been outstanding in their determination to resist military encroachment upon civilian authority. Eisenhower was outspoken in cautioning his countrymen against the potential dangers of expanded military influence in American life. Viewing the broad stream of American experience, Quincy Wright believes that the proper criticism to be made is not that there has been too much military influence in national councils but that, if anything, there has often tended to be too little.[40]

Are such observations still applicable—when national security efforts have penetrated almost every aspect of American life? In an age when more than half the tax revenues are expended by the Pentagon, when millions of American families are conscious that their sons must enter military service, when educations and careers can be disrupted by an untimely "call-up" of military reserve forces, when a high state of military preparedness must be constantly maintained for dealing with crises in Cuba or South Vietnam or possibly the NATO area, when civilian employment in some regions is heavily geared to defense contracts —under these conditions can it still be said that the influence of the military establishment is being kept within constitutional bounds and that it poses no threat to the American democracy? Knowledgeable commentators admit the vastly expanded role of the military in all spheres of American life and fully concede that the *potential* risk of undue military influence is perhaps greater today than ever in American history. Some commentators are convinced that very few Americans are sufficiently aware of the extent to which military influence has grown in all major segments of society, culture, the economy, and government, thereby posing the risk that with the passage of time such influence will become more and more dominant.[41]

In spite of such facts, most commentators are in fairly wide agreement that Quincy Wright's verdict remains basically as sound today as 25 or 50 years ago. In the vast preponderance of cases, military officers trained in the American constitutional and philosophical tradition remain fully conscious that their role in policy determination is important but always *subordinate*; they accept the principle of civilian control over the military as one of the cornerstones of the democratic system. Informed observers, including former public officials who have had wide contact with the military hierarchy, are convinced that the rule of civilian supremacy infuses the approach of the armed forces to the formulation of defense policies and programs.[42]

This is not to say civilian policy-makers or intelligent citizens can be complacent about the problem of growing military influence in American society. The price of liberty in this field, as in all the others, remains eternal vigilance in resisting intentional or unintentional encroachments upon basic constitutional doctrines. Nor do we suggest that, from time to time, developments occasioning genuine public concern about the problem do not and will not arise. A perennial challenge, for example, is safeguarding the deliberations of government from undue influence by the "military mind." This concept, admittedly difficult to define with precision and objectivity, refers to certain distinctively military ways of appraising national issues and of formulating responses to them, to habits of mind (often as much unconscious as conscious) which are sometimes characteristic of the military hierarchy because of its training, experience, and the heavy obligations imposed upon it by civilian policy-makers.[43] Conspicuous features of the military mind have been a reluctance to change outmoded weapons systems and tactics—fighting the next war with the weapons of the last; an addiction to essentially military soluitons to crises in external affairs, accompanied by an inability to recognize the limitations inherent in such an approach; a predictable readiness to believe that the nation's military defenses are inadequate, irrespective of the current level of defense spending; and manifestation of a super-patriotic, ultranationalistic approach to relations with other countries. Above all, military leaders are too often tempted to reduce complex diplomatic issues into contests of power and force and, in the process, to gloss over political, economic, cultural, and ideological dimensions of foreign policy. The risk always exists that they will forget that military force is but *one element* in the formula of national power, and that power itself is the *means* available to the nation's leaders for the achievement of major national goals.[44]

Ironically, one of the most serious dangers of undue military influence in governmental deliberations in recent years has stemmed not so much from the ambitions of military leaders *per se* as from a different and somewhat unexpected source. This has been the tendency of *civilian* groups inside and outside the government to assign to military officials themselves certain responsibilities they neither want nor are well prepared to carry out. This problem arises chiefly when military figures are expected to discuss, in public speeches or before legislative committees, aspects of national policy that lie outside their fields of competence and training, but are instead the direct responsibility of the President and his top civilian advisers. In some instances, and despite White House or Defense Department directives to the contrary, military leaders willfully talk about dimensions of public policy within their province, such as the level of defense spending, the allocation of funds among the major military services, or decisions to rely (or not to rely) upon military force in dealing with particular global crises. Periodically, committees of Congress endeavor to elicit military opinions about all manner of policy decisions and encourage military commanders to discuss publicly any differences between the President's civilian and military advisers on selected policy questions. Efforts seeking to air fundamental differences among officials and agencies concerned with national security policy are often partisan-inspired attempts to embarrass the President politically. In other instances, they may derive from a belief on Capitol Hill that the public is entitled to know how decisions affecting national security were arrived at, even if this means exposing disagreements within the executive branch to full public view. In still other instances, legislators and private organizations seek to have prominent military leaders "legitimatize" a proposed policy or program, by suggesting that such action is demanded by military leaders to protect the security of the country. Whatever its motivations, willful or unconscious persistence in this practice erodes the principle of military subordination to civilian policy-makers and leads to confusion about the legitimate function of each group in the policy-making process. Some military leaders (who are often reluctant to discuss policy questions outside their area of special competence) have themselves been more prone recently to recognize and accept this fact than have members of Congress and private organizations.[45]

Attaining and preserving the proper balance between a necessary and legitimate military role in national security policy and a firm adherence to the constitutional principle of civilian dominance is clearly a two-way street. Military officials are more than ever required to be unceasingly mindful of constitutional limitations upon their role and of the companion necessity to *keep* their role subordinate in an age of recurrent international crises. For their part, civilian policy-makers and enlightened citizens are obliged to safeguard the precept of civilian supremacy by steadfastly resisting deliberate or indeliberate military usurpations of civilian functions, by devising new safeguards for keeping growing military influence within its proper bounds, and by refraining from the temptation to encourage greater military participation in various stages of decision-making than is actually required by national security. Concluding their study of the influence of the military within the American government, Sapin and Snyder urge that

> . . . civilians must decide precisely what meaningful civilian supremacy is . . . and must be prepared to check the expansion of the military functions beyond proper limits. If it is true that greater self-awareness and nonmilitary training are increasingly necessary for military leaders, it is equally true that civilians must be willing to exercise vigilance and to learn to evaluate military views.[46]

Or, as General Ridgway has maintained, if military leaders need to be reminded perpetually of their subordinate role, it is no less indispensable that civilians recognize the integrity of the military component by permitting military officials to be free from a "party line" imposed from above, in order that they can offer their best qualified judgment about the measures required to protect the security of the United States and to carry out its diplomatic objectives.[47]

Unfinished Business in Defense Organization

In the late Eisenhower period, General James M. Gavin, former Army Chief of Research and Development, evaluated recent attempts to evolve an effective defense organization by saying:

Unity of purpose is fundamental to survival. However, purpose is one thing and accomplishment is another. . . . The devisive forces that bear upon decision-making in the Department of Defense are many: industrial interests, political pressures, professional competence or lack of it in committees, personal prejudices, and service interests. All work against unity of purpose. . . . Some of the most able and most intelligent Americans in public life have sought to bring order out of the decision-making maze of the Department of Defense, only to fail. It has been the organization that has defeated them.[48]

Echoing General Gavin's assessment, Robert A. Lovett, Secretary of Defense under Truman, wrote that the National Security Act of 1947 and its subsequent modifications possessed "the fault of all compromises . . . contradictions and straddles. . . ."[49] And in the same period the able *New York Times* reporter James Reston lampooned postwar attempts to achieve workable defense arrangements, by saying that the Joint Chiefs of Staff were "The most expensive organization in America today, composed of three equally powerful officers who preside over the military budget and govern a loose confederation of warring tribes." He characterized the role of the chairman of the Joint Chiefs as one "who passes along the grievances and differences of 'the chiefs' to the Secretaries of the Army, Navy and Air Force, who in turn pass them to the Secretary of Defense, who sends them to the President, who returns them to the Pentagon for review."[50]

Such viewpoints underscore the fact that, throughout the postwar period, despite intensive official and unofficial concern with defense organization, culminating in organizational changes in the defense establishment, considerable unfinished business confronts officials concerned with this problem. It is clear, for example that the traditional division of the armed services into land, sea, and air components is increasingly obsolete, in the light of modern military technology and the actual responsibilities the defense establishment must assume at home and abroad. Dr. James Perkins has obsolete.**

Modern weapons and derived modern strategy have made largely obsolete existing organizations in the Pentagon. If anything is clear, it is that modern warfare does not divide itself into problems of land, sea, and air.

In the contemporary era, Dr. Perkins and others have emphasized, "Functional tasks now divide along the lines of strategic deterrence, limited warfare, continental military defense, civil defense, [and] military assistance to allies." In the light of these facts, this observer has concluded, "The hard unvarnished truth is that it has been impossible to assign tasks on a functional basis along existing lines."[51]

In the same vein, General Maxwell D. Taylor, former Army Chief of Staff, has declared that the institution of the Joint Chiefs of Staff remains "defective in its failure to provide clear guidance for the formulation of military strategy and for the generation of the military forces to implement that strategy." To a significant degree, he has atributed this failure to perpetuation of the traditional division of military forces into land, sea, and air components—even though if such forces are used, they will be committed as "combinations of Army, Navy, and Air Force" units to carry out atomic retaliation against an enemy, participation in limited war or maintenance of continental air defense. Existing budgeting procedures for national defense, utilized in allocating resources to the armed forces, however, continued to follow outdated concepts.* General Taylor has also described the Joint Chiefs as a defective mechanism in another respect. This institution has "the strength and weakness of any committee." It is ill-equipped to deal with threats to national security where speed of decision is mandatory, when events do not permit the luxury of a slow resolution of interservice differences on the proper policy to adopt. Speaking generally, this spokesman has concluded that "you cannot fight wars by committees," however adequately the Joint Chiefs may serve as planners of defense policy.[52]

---

* Under Kennedy, budgetary procedures underwent a number of changes to take into account General Taylor's criticisms. See *The New York Times*, September 16, 1962.

If postwar experience is a reliable guide, part of the continuing problem of creating successful administrative machinery for national security policy derives from the persistent opposition to sweeping changes among officials in, and supporters of, the separate military services. During his tenure in the White House, President Eisenhower continually felt the pressure brought by groups opposing modifications in traditional patterns of defense organization, particularly when one of the military arms such as the army or navy found its budgetary requests substantially reduced.[53] President Kennedy also encountered inertia among vested military interests, in his attempt to modernize the armed forces and to equip the United States more adequately for coping with guerrilla warfare, insurrections, and communist-instigated subversion. Even more than Eisenhower, he was convinced that new measures were long overdue for coping successfully with a variety of paramilitary conflicts and harassments, such as the conflicts in Laos, South Vietnam, and Berlin.* In facing such challenges, he was not always sure that some of the nation's military commanders understood the issues involved or were prepared to evolve new approaches for resolving them.[54]

Deeply ingrained interservice rivalries and diffuse governmental efforts also attended American missile and space satellite programs in the late 1950s and early months of 1960. News dispatches reported at one stage that 61 different agencies had a part in missile programs! For a time, it appeared that a serious "missile gap" had appeared, that threatened to give a commanding lead to the Soviet Union in military technology. Subsequent events revealed that this gap had been greatly exaggerated and that, in some vital respects, American military technology was significantly more advanced than the Soviet Union's. American ingenuity also succeeded in reducing the distressingly slow "lead time" required to bring advanced weapons from the planning to the production stage. Thus, weapons like the nuclear missile-firing submarine, advanced long-range missiles like the hard-site Minuteman, and highly sophisticated reconnaisance

space satellites were developed and integrated into the nation's military effort much more rapidly than many critics had anticipated. These developments suggested that by the mid-1960s considerably more support for unified efforts among the armed services existed than was the case a decade earlier. Progress was being made in attacking the citadel of entrenched service provincialism, and the evidence suggested that greater progress would be made with the passage of time. Yet it had to be recognized that the process would not always proceed smoothly and evenly. Attachment to traditional concepts and to established organizational norms was often encouraged by powerful vested interests inside and outside the government. Sometimes, industries engaged in particular segments of defense production encouraged maintenance of the *status quo*, particularly when they faced the loss of valuable defense contracts because of decisions that certain categories of weapons were obsolete.**

Moreover, Congress has also exhibited schizophrenic tendencies in dealing with the problem of defense organization in the recent period. Much as legislators have been prone to criticize military leaders for their attachment to traditional modes of thought and their lack of wholehearted acceptance of "unified" defense efforts, certain congressional groups and influential legislators have themselves contributed to the inertia often evident in the Pentagon. As General Gavin suggests, legislators are keenly sensitive to constituency pressures growing out of executive decisions to close down superfluous military installations or to cancel defense contracts, upon which the prosperity of a legislator's district may depend heavily. While members of Congress endorse

---

* Some of the problems encountered by President Kennedy and his vigorous Secretary of Defense, Robert A. McNamara, in this matter are discussed in detail in Sidey, *op. cit.*, pp. 22–27; Joseph Kraft, "McNamara and His Enemies," *Harpers Magazine*, **223** (August, 1961), 41–48; and Jack Raymond, "Mr. McNamara Remodels the Pentagon," *The Reporter*, **26** (January 18, 1962), 31–35.

** While General James M. Gavin makes no effort to minimize interservice rivalries, he nevertheless points out that powerful business and industrial interests often keep such conflicts alive in order to prevent the cancellations of defense contracts. He has concluded that "the amount of money that is spent on nationwide advertising, by industry, for hardware that is obsolete is sizable, and the pressure that industry can place through lobbies in terms of employment, payrolls, and effect upon constituents is impressive in Congress." Too many industries, he believes, "still insist that . . . products be used long after they become obsolete." This tendency is therefore an important contributory force in the maintenance and exploitation of interservice disputes and in the consequent time lag in the production of new weapons. Gavin, *op. cit.*, pp. 255–257.

the principle of military "unification" or defense "modernization," they are often loath to support it in practice when the result is economic dislocation for their constituents. Moreover, partisans of the army, navy, or air force often find sympathetic supporters on Capitol Hill, especially among legislative committees that deal with the separate military services.* A classic case in the recent period has been the chairman of the House Armed Services Committee, Representative Carl Vinson (Democrat of Georgia). For years, Congressman Vinson was an outspoken champion of naval power. He viewed with ingrained disfavor any proposals that tended to weaken the navy, and he frequently used his strategic position in Congress to block such proposals.[55] That Vinson's power had to be reckoned with by proponents of greater military integration would be an understatement. One episode illustrates both the scope of his power and his own conception of his role. The story is told that Congressman Vinson was once informed he was being considered for appointment as Secretary of Defense. His reply was that he had rather run the Pentagon from Capitol Hill! However exceptional this case might be, experienced legislators like Vinson believed that over the years they had acquired a vast backlog of information and insight into national defense problems. They had seen a parade of Secretaries of Defense and secretaries of the separate services come and go—perhaps after spending no more than two or three years as senior officers in the defense establishment. Accordingly, they entertained strong ideas about how national security problems ought to be approached and about the ideal pattern of defense organization. They were, therefore, congenitally unprepared to give the President or the Secretary of Defense as much power to make sweeping changes as the executive branch periodically requested, or otherwise to relinquish Congress's traditional authority to regulate the over-all pattern of national defense organization.

* An illustrative episode took place late in 1963, when Secretary of Defense McNamara overrode the navy's plans to build a new nuclear-powered aircraft carrier. This decision evoked heated opposition from the Joint Committee on Atomic Energy, which favored the navy's viewpoint. In the words of one reporter, the committee's view was that it "had long experience on atomic matters and that it had a record of being right regarding military applications of atomic energy." *The New York Times*, November 4, 1963, dispatch by John W. Finney.

OTHER EXECUTIVE AGENCIES AND FOREIGN AFFAIRS

Our discussion thus far of the roles of the President, the State Department, and the military establishment has revealed that coordination of the activities of governmental agencies is a central problem in formulating and executing effective American foreign policy. The problem exists on three levels. First, the efforts of the President, the State Department, and the military services—the agencies most *directly* concerned with foreign policy—must be merged to assure sound policies at the top. Then other executive agencies must be included whose activities in foreign affairs may normally be tangential, but whose role may be highly important in selected phases of American foreign relations. Third, to unite all governmental efforts still further, executive activities must be coordinated with those of Congress. The remainder of this chapter is concerned with the second of these problems. The two chapters that follow will discuss the role of Congress and the problem of executive-legislative relations.

The nature and implications of the problem with which we are concerned came into clear focus toward the end of 1963, at a time when the Kennedy Administration was seeking to check communist expansion in South Vietnam. For a period of several weeks, it was feared that the President had "lost control" of American policy in that situation. News dispatches from South Vietnam were filled with reports of diplomatic cross purposes produced by the conflicting activities of several influential agencies involved in dealing with the communist threat. A writer for United Press International described American policy in South Vietnam as a "five-headed monstrosity" of rival and self-defeating maneuvers among American governmental agencies. For a time, the tug of war among them threatened to rival the conflict between communist and anti-communist forces within the country. The five agencies involved were the United States embassy in Saigon, the arm of the State Department, which supposedly "coordinated" *all* American diplomatic and military activities within the country; the Military Assistance Command, the arm of the Pentagon, which was responsible for carrying out the military campaign against communist elements; the Central Intelligence Agency (CIA), which collected intelligence data and which, in addition, had for a long time sup-

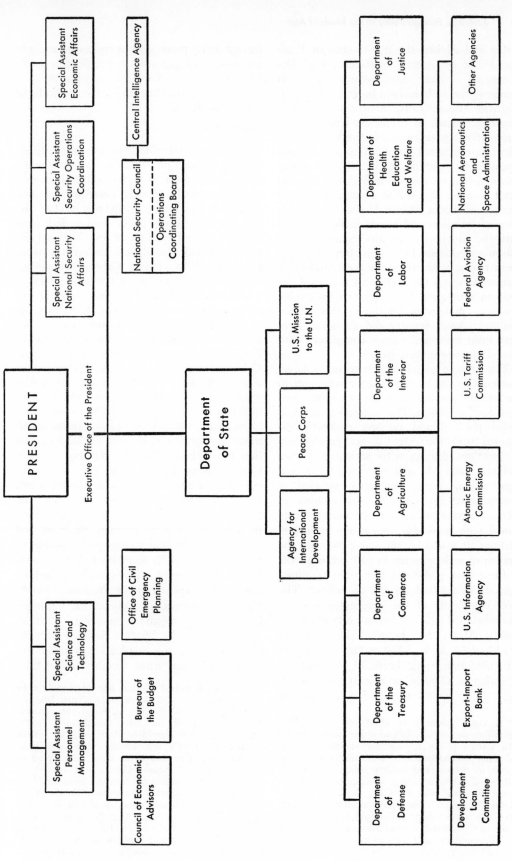

Foreign Affairs Responsibilities in the Executive Branch. (Source: Adapted from the Senatorial Foreign Relations Committee, *United States Foreign Policy: The Formulation and Administration of United States Policy*, 86th Congress, 2nd Session, Brookings Institute, 1960, p. 44.)

ported and advised the government of President Diem; the Agency for International Development, which administered American economic and technical aid programs to South Vietnam (theoretically, always under State Department guidance); and the United States Information Agency, which in this country and elsewhere conducted American propaganda and psychological warfare activities. All these groups were, of course, under the ultimate supervision of the White House. Yet for a number of weeks, White House control was obviously minimal and largely ineffectual. Not until the situation in South Vietnam evoked outspoken criticism from legislators, from the Diem regime itself, from the press, and other nongovernmental observers—and not until the problem ultimately threatened to undermine American diplomatic efforts in this pivotal Southeast Asian country—did President Kennedy insist upon full agency compliance with State Department directives.[56]

This episode merely symptomized a larger problem that has become progressively acute in the formulation and execution of recent American foreign policy. The nation's expanding global political and military commitments, coupled with the extraordinary proliferation of programs dealing with social, economic, cultural, and informational aspects of foreign policy, have necessarily entailed a corresponding expansion in the number of governmental agencies and committees concerned with particular dimensions of foreign relations. It would be impossible to count the number of such agencies, in part because some of these have peripheral and often transitory interests in selected aspects of policy.* The sheer complexity of the governmental structure concerned with national security prompted Senator Henry M. Jackson (Democrat of Washington) to brand it a "modern Hydra with nine times nine heads."[57] Without endeavoring to identify, or discuss the role of, every governmental agency involved in the foreign policy process, let us endeavor merely to get some conception of their collective activities and to understand the resulting problem posed in coordinating department efforts in foreign relations.

The Cabinet

Before the establishment of the National Security Council in 1947, the Cabinet was the chief mechanism for providing high-level executive coordination of governmental policies. Since 1947, however, the role of the Cabinet in the foreign policy sphere has been heavily eclipsed by that of the National Security Council. President Eisenhower particularly tended to confine Cabinet discussions chiefly to considerations of domestic policy.**

While the Cabinet has been the principal advisory body to the President throughout the greater part of American history, its role has varied considerably under different Presidents. Forceful executives have often bypassed the Cabinet and even the State Department altogether. To achieve their foreign policy objectives, they have worked directly with diplomatic missions or agents abroad, with high-ranking military advisers, or through personal representatives. It must not be forgotten that the Cabinet, like the National Security Council, is an *advisory* body only. Final decisions must always be made by the President. How influential the Cabinet's views will be therefore depends upon a variety of factors: the competence of its members, the kinds and urgency of prevailing foreign policy problems, the willingness of its members to become well informed on complex issues, and the inclinations and viewpoints of the President himself. Under Eisenhower the Cabinet was improved immensely by sound organizational changes developed initially by the National Security Council, where the emphasis was upon full background preparation, members doing their

* A chart prepared in 1960 for a legislative committee showed the following executive agencies with foreign policy responsibilities: the President had seven "special assistants" concerned with various aspects of defense and foreign policy. Besides the State and Defense Departments, the National Security Council, and the CIA, the chart showed a total of 24 agencies or interdepartmental committees active in the foreign policy field. Senate Foreign Relations Committee, *United States Foreign Policy: The Formulation and Administration of United States Policy*, p. 44.

** General Robert Cutler, one of Eisenhower's chief advisers for national security affairs, has said that the National Security Council was created "to carve out of the total Government sphere certain areas that should be dealt with by certain of the President's top advisers, leaving in the Cabinet areas that had to be dealt with by all of his top advisers." Senate Government Operations Committee, *Organizing for National Security*, Hearings, **I**, 585. Presidential discretion in deciding how he shall utilize his staff agencies is well illustrated by one observer's comment that President Kennedy "nearly put the Cabinet on the shelf as far as being a force in policy matters" during the early weeks of his administration. Sidey, *op. cit.*, p. 383.

"homework" before meetings, and relevant and frank discussion. Other Presidents before and after Eisenhower have utilized the Cabinet quite differently. FDR and Truman tended to regard it chiefly as a body for expressing divergent opinions within the executive branch, for permitting the President to assess public reactions to existing and anticipated policy developments, and for sensing the political implications of proposed governmental programs.[58]

Economic Agencies and Foreign Affairs

In the economic field, there has been a tremendous proliferation of agencies whose activities impinge upon foreign affairs. This growth can be attributed chiefly to two factors: the vastly expanded activities of the national government in the economic realm generally since the New Deal, and the ever-growing attention devoted to economic aspects of international affairs since World War II. It is no exaggeration to say that today the operations of almost every executive agency have some major economic consequences. And the activities of a great many of these agencies bear directly upon foreign affairs.

The Treasury Department has obvious interests in selected aspects of foreign policy. Besides its obligation to assure sound national fiscal policy, the department has other interests impinging more directly upon foreign relations. It is heavily involved, for example, in the suppression of traffic in illegal drugs and narcotics, requiring it to work intimately with agencies of the UN and with other countries to carry out this objective. Even more fundamentally, the Treasury has been deeply concerned about a problem that has plagued American foreign economic policy in the recent era—America's adverse balance of international payments, occasioning in some periods an appreciable outflow of gold reserves. The manifold complexities of the problem, together with its intimate relationship to diplomatic questions, such as relations with the NATO allies or the underdeveloped countries, has given the Treasury Department a persistent stake in foreign affairs.*

Another agency whose impact upon foreign relations can sometimes be highly significant is the Council of Economic Advisers, a staff organ

for advising the President on over-all economic trends and for recommending long-range economic policies. CEA prepares the President's Economic Report to Congress, submitted to Capitol Hill early each year; in addition, it submits regular reports and recommendations on major economic developments. Unlike agencies such as the Treasury Department, CEA has no *operating* responsibilities—a fact that sometimes brings it into conflict with agencies that do have responsibility for actually carrying out economic programs at home and abroad.[59]

The Japanese attack on Pearl Harbor in 1941 highlighted many organizational deficiencies in the American government, one of which was the absence of long-range, sustained planning for the allocation of civilian and industrial mobilization when global crises arise. After World War II, therefore, a bewildering succession of alphabetical agencies in Washington assumed this function. At length, the Office of Defense Mobilization was established by executive order of President Truman after the Korean War emergency; it was later renamed the Office of Civil and Defense Mobilization. This agency prepares studies and estimates of civilian and military manpower requirements, raw material availability, industrial and agricultural production, economic stabilization, and related problems.[60]

Our earlier discussion called attention to another executive agency that sometimes plays a decisive role in national security and foreign policy. This is the Bureau of the Budget, part of the Executive Office of the President. BuBud (as it is called in Washington) is the focal point for coordinating all budgetary matters within the executive branch and is responsible, under ultimate White House direction, for drawing up a unified executive budget for submission to Congress. From the earliest stages of budget preparation, therefore, its officials work intimately with other agencies in preparing budget estimates. As the sequence of stages in budget preparation proceeds, BuBud carefully screens all agency requests for funds. As in other sectors of government, it therefore exercises considerable power in the determination of programs and projects designed to promote national security.[61] Congress counts heavily upon the Bureau of the Budget to eliminate unnecessary and duplicating executive programs and to keep governmental costs within bounds. Since Congress is often prone to rely upon this agency's appraisal of

* The nature and implications of the balance of payments problem facing the United States within the past several years is discussed in detail in Chapter 15.

existing programs, and of adding new ones, the Bureau of the Budget is in a key position to determine the financial limits within which foreign and related domestic policies are formulated and carried out. So pervasive is its influence in budgetary matters that vocal complaints from time to time are heard about the danger of its usurping the State Department or Defense Department functions.[62]

A number of independent regulatory commissions also have duties touching the sphere of foreign relations. The Tariff Commission is concerned with tariffs and reciprocal trade. Its recommendations to the President are often decisive in determining tariff rates; these rates have at times become sources of considerable international controversy. The Federal Aviation Agency controls air transportation within the United States, and between it and foreign countries. The Maritime Commission supervises the American merchant marine fleet. Charged with overseeing all aspects of the development of nuclear power for military and civilian purposes, the Atomic Energy Commission has come to play a key role in the relations between the United States and other countries. The two largest deposits of uranium ore available to the free world are located in Canada and the Congo Republic. AEC has also been actively concerned with such foreign policy issues as disarmament negotiations between the West and Russia, UN proposals for peacetime use and control of nuclear power, and analysis of radioactive fall-out from the testing of nuclear weapons. Under Eisenhower, officials of the AEC were conspicuous in voicing their belief that levels of radioactive fall-out from nuclear testing did not exceed safe tolerances—estimates that agencies and other scientific groups were prone to challenge as entirely too optimistic. Moreover, American officials involved in propaganda activities were concerned about the impact of policies upon Asian, African, and other foreign societies, where deep apprehension about radioactive fall-out existed.

Brief mention must also be made of two other executive departments that have come to be drawn more and more into the national security and foreign policy process. One of these is the Department of Commerce, established to promote business enterprise at home and abroad. Like the Treasury Department, this agency is keenly interested in foreign trade, particularly in promoting American business enterprises abroad. By the late Eisenhower period, both the White House and influential legislative groups subscribed to the philosophy of "Trade, Not Aid," meaning that in its economic relations with some foreign countries at least, the United States ought to depend more upon private business investments and trade to encourage the economic advancement of underdeveloped societies. Emergence of the European Economic Community (or Common Market) has also posed an enduring challenge to the Commerce Department in its attempts to encourage overseas business expansion and to maintain America's competitive position in the world market.

The other agency is the Department of Agriculture. Saddled with mounting agricultural surpluses at home—and faced with deeply embedded legislative opposition to significant reduction in agricultural price supports that perpetuate such surpluses—this agency has come to look with favor upon proposals designed to dispose of commodity surpluses overseas. Agriculture Department officials have sometimes clashed openly with State Department official on the issue of surplus disposal programs.[63] Moreover, this department has assumed growing responsibilities for agricultural aspects of foreign aid programs. Next to the State and Defense Departments, the Department of Agriculture (along with the Post Office) has the largest representation overseas among executive agencies.[64] Officials from this agency are trying to teach more advanced scientific methods of agricultural production to economically primitive societies.

Agencies Concerned with Foreign Assistance

Since the inauguration of the Greek-Turkish Aid Program in 1947 and the Marshall Plan in 1948, the provision of economic, military, and technical assistance to other countries has been a consistent feature of American foreign policy. A great deal of organizational change within the national government has attended the administration of these programs. Providing liaison between the State Department and the agencies that have operating responsibilities for various aspects of foreign aid has been a recurrent problem.

Although massive foreign aid programs did not become a permanent feature of American foreign policy until after 1947, a number of *ad hoc* and emergency programs existed before that date. During World War II, for example, the Lend-Lease Administration extended billions of dollars' worth of military equipment and other aid to the Allies. After the war, such agencies were abolished and their functions transferred helter-skelter to the State Department and other agencies of government.[65] The program of Marshall Plan aid to Europe in 1948 witnessed the creation of the first of a series of semi-autonomous agencies responsible for administering foreign assistance program.* This means that the organization administering foreign assistance—currently, the Agency for International Development (AID)—is under direct supervision of the Department of State and acts "as an arm of that department" in carrying out aid projects in some 70 different foreign countries.[66] AID's function, in other words, is to administer foreign assistance within over-all policy guidelines established by the State Department and, ultimately, by the President.

Agencies Concerned with Informational Aspects of Foreign Policy

As with foreign aid administration, the organizational pattern of governmental agencies involved in propaganda and informational aspects of foreign policy since World War II has been quite complex. Propaganda and informational dimensions of foreign relations received little or no continuing attention in the United States before World War II. After that conflict erupted, the Office of War Information was set up to direct American propaganda campaigns against the Axis Powers. Like many other such agencies, OWI was abolished after

the war; its functions (on a greatly reduced scale) were transferred to the State Department. Not until after the inauguration of the Truman Doctrine in 1947 did the American government seriously concern itself again with propaganda as an instrument of diplomacy. In 1948, the Voice of America was created within the State Department. In the years that followed, VOA led a checkered existence; in some periods it came under the sharp attack of legislative committees and public groups who questioned its purpose, effectiveness, and the loyalty of many of its employees. Almost every year, the appropriations granted by Congress for its operations were substantially below levels requested by the White House. Organizational changes continued,** and in 1953, at the request of President Eisenhower, Congress enacted a major reorganizational plan, the intention of which was to eliminate duplicating activities in this field and to place psychological warfare activities upon a sound continuing basis. Accordingly, the United States Information Agency was established. USIA incorporated the Voice of America as its broadcasting arm; in addition, it undertook a variety of other activities designed, in the words of USIA Director Edward R. Murrow, to "emphasize the ways in which U.S. policies harmonize with those of other peoples . . . and underline those aspects of American life and culture which facilitate sympathetic understanding of our policies."[67] By 1963, USIA had approximately 1300 officers stationed in the United States and in some 239 foreign posts in 106 countries.[68] Like the Agency for International Development, USIA is an administrative agency that takes policy guidance from the State Department.†

Agencies Engaged in Intelligence Activities

A noteworthy innovation introduced by the National Security Act of 1947 was the establishment of the Central Intelligence Agency as a separate organ accountable to the National Security Council. CIA grew out of a widely prevailing conviction that American intelligence activities were inadequate for successful

---

* The European Cooperation Administration (ECA) was set up to administer the Marshall Plan. After the Korean War, when economic and military aspects of aid were merged into one program, ECA was superseded by the Mutual Security Agency, created in 1951. In turn, foreign aid administration was reorganized again in 1953, when the Foreign Operations Administration was set up; this agency was abolished in 1955, when the International Cooperation Administration (ICA) was established to administer *economic* aid programs, while *military* assistance was turned over to the Department of Defense. Again, in 1961, President Kennedy altered the pattern of aid administration by abolishing ICA and establishing the Agency for International Development (AID). AID continued to administer economic and technical foreign assistance and to coordinate military aid programs to other countries; in addition, it was given responsibility for the economic aspects of the Food for Peace program, involving the use of American surplus agricultural commodities. The organizational history of foreign aid administration is discussed in Agency for International Development, *Report to the Congress on the Foreign Assistance Program for Fiscal Year 1962* (Washington, D.C.: Government Printing Office, 1963), pp. 1–5.

** From 1951 to 1953, psychological and informational aspects of foreign policy were administered by a new agency, the Psychological Strategy Board, created by President Truman.

† The psychological dimension of the cold war and of America's relationships with other countries in the free world is discussed in detail in Chapter 14.

diplomacy and out of a long-standing realization that more effective high-level coordination in the intelligence field was indispensable for sound policy determination. Pearl Harbor was still vividly remembered as the price that might be paid for inadequate and poorly coordinated intelligence operations within the government. CIA's duty is to "plan, develop, and coordinate all Federal foreign intelligence activity."[69] It is the principal advisory body to NSC on intelligence matters. Although by law he is not a member of NSC, the director of CIA is regularly invited by the President to attend its meetings. Under President Eisenhower, every meeting of the National Security Council included "an oral briefing by the Director of Central Intelligence summarizing important developments that are occurring throughout the world." This official devoted "particular attention to those areas which are on the Council agenda that day."[70] Officials from the CIA also work intimately with State Department officers in preparing papers on major foreign policy issues and trends that are later discussed fully at NSC meetings.[71]

Intelligence activities may be grouped broadly into two categories: the collection and evaluation of information required to formulate national policies, and covert operations involving such cloak-and-dagger functions as espionage, sabotage, arranging for refugees to escape from other countries, breaking foreign codes, and related activities. According to a former naval intelligence officer, the task of the intelligence expert in over-all terms is to "winnow the extraneous data from the vital facts and to set these facts in proper perspective, thereby providing the factual basis for high-level policy decisions. . . ."[72] By this definition, a number of governmental agencies—from the Bureau of Intelligence Research in the State Department, to the Defense Intelligence Agency in the Pentagon, to the FBI, and units within other agencies like the Treasury Department and the Atomic Energy Commission—routinely carry on intelligence operations of central importance for foreign affairs.[73] The CIA is distinctive in two major respects. First, it *coordinates* the intelligence operations of the entire "intelligence community" within the American government, drawing upon the resources of all agencies within the community in preparing its reports for the National Security Council and the President. Second, it conducts the *covert* intelligence operations of the United States at

home and abroad, as we have described them above.

How well has CIA carried out its assigned functions since 1947? "The golden word of intelligence is silence," one source has emphasized. The same source is convinced that "Public revelation of sensitive intelligence is never a harmless act. It both jeopardizes the normal conduct of foreign relations and compromises the sources of vital intelligence."[74] For these reasons, it is extremely difficult for outsiders to gain reliable information about the scope and effectiveness of CIA's activities. Press reports and exposés are more than ordinarily suspect because of the difficulty of verifying requisite information and conclusions. Nevertheless, it seems clear that several fundamental problems remain in the matter of integrating intelligence operations into the broad stream of national security and foreign policy. If it is true, for instance, that "Intelligence is a source of information for diplomacy—not a part of it," this is a principle which the CIA itself has not always apparently accepted.[75] Late in 1963, for example, as we have noted, it seemed clear that CIA agents were deeply implicated in carrying out essentially diplomatic functions in South Vietnam, where their efforts threatened for a time to usurp the role of the State Department and to perpetuate widespread confusion in the country and outside it about (1) the goals of American policy in Asia, and (2) the methods needed to carry it out successfully. State Department officials on the scene complained openly about the "independence" of CIA agents and the inability of the American embassy in Saigon to control their activities. Similarly, in the U-2 incident arising in 1960, the CIA carried out a high-level photographic reconnaissance operation that had far-reaching diplomatic repercussions. Although President Eisenhower ultimately assumed personal responsibility for the U-2 flights, it was evident that the timing of such flights, theoretically involving careful assessments of their diplomatic implications, was decided by the CIA.[76]

In these and other cases, the CIA almost never defends its record publicly and cannot do so without seriously compromising its sources of information or endangering its current activities. Yet such examples indicate that effective White House or State Department control over CIA operations is sometimes lacking and that the nature of CIA's duties inherently poses a persistent challenge to the President and his principal subordinates directly concerned with foreign policy.

Interdepartmental Committees and Agencies

While the National Security Council is the highest governmental agency concerned with unifying policies in the broad field of national security, there are a number of lower-level committees and agencies which also attempt coordination of selected aspects of American foreign policy. The Hoover Commission in 1948 found that, in addition to NSC, there were 32 interagency committees in the field of foreign affairs. Examples of interagency committees are the National Advisory Council on International Monetary and Financial Problems, the Trade Policy Committee, and the Interagency Committee on Agricultural Surplus Disposal. Among the 3000 or so committees existing within the Department of Defense in the early 1960s were the Human Factors Engineering Committee and the Interdepartmental Screw Thread Committee.[77] Although the totality of intra- and interagency committees by the 1960s was probably unknown even to policy-makers themselves, there was good reason to suppose that the process of committee proliferation had gone on apace since the time of the Hoover Commission, thereby enhancing what Robert A. Lovett called the "foulup factor" in decision-making.[78] An urgent public need, according to the experienced public servant Averell Harriman, was a "committee-killing committee," set up to eliminate bureaucratic layers seriously impeding defense and foreign policy.[79] George F. Kennan has added that an increasingly intricate and cumbersome committee structure has compelled high-ranking policy-makers to bypass formal organization structures altogether in reaching major policy decisions.[80]

The tendency of governmental committees to multiply must, of course, be explained by reference to something other than Mr. Parkinson's now familiar "laws" explaining the behavior of bureaucracies. Defenders of the committee system contend with considerable justification that foreign policy issues "have achieved a degree of complexity which renders them no longer fit subjects for individual judgment and insight. . . ." Decision-making therefore doubtless requires "organized collective study" and "funds of specialized knowledge," in order that diverse "governmental interests can be brought to bear" in any successful approach to global problems.[81] In brief,

the growth of such committees within the decision-making process reflects the complexity of the modern world and of America's manifold relations with it. Without efforts to coordinate policy formulation and execution by reliance upon committees and other devices, the American approach to defense and foreign policy would become highly fragmented, confusing, and often self-defeating.

Nevertheless, it remains true that the proliferation of intradepartmental and interdepartmental committees has come to pose serious obstacles to the foreign policy process. Committees often require inordinate amounts of time to reach decisions. Frequently, agency representatives on them have little power to negotiate agreements, only to discuss issues with their colleagues from other departments. Before decisions can be arrived at, "clearances" must be obtained from senior officers in the agencies concerned—the likelihood of which tends to vary inversely with the novelty of the proposal under discussion by the committee. This leads to what is surely the most crucial weakness of decision-making by committees, as reflected in William H. Kinter's observation about the National Security Council. Because this agency is

> . . . composed of personnel associated with operating agencies, there is a tendency for decisions to reflect the minimum upon which all agencies can agree rather than the cohesive total which may be required to advance United States interests. The recommendations finally agreed upon and presented to higher authority are often so vague and general that each agency can, at least with minor changes, fit them to its own self-endorsed policy.[82]

And a Brookings Institution study has likewise emphasized a long-standing criticism that a committee like NSC "dilutes its policy recommendations so that all its members may agree to something that can be presented to the President for approval." This leads to "damage to program and policy objectives."[83] George F. Kennan has similarly criticized the tendency, engendered in his view by overreliance upon committees, of senior policy officials to say: "Anything you fellows can agree on is all right with me." More often than not, committees are apt to "agree on" maintenance of the *status quo*, by eliminating the more radical or novel features of policy proposals because they are unacceptable to some agency involved in policy deliberations.

That committees are unavoidable, and often useful, governmental devices cannot be denied. Yet they cannot rival, nor must they become a substitute for, the imaginative, penetrating, and above all creative thinking that can only be done by capable *individuals*, who are not afraid to challenge long-accepted doctrines and to propose measures designed to move the country off diplomatic dead-center.[84] Even President Eisenhower, who was prone to rely heavily upon "staff" agencies, has observed that "Organization cannot make a genius out of an incompetent; even less can it, of itself, make the decisions which are required to trigger necessary action."[85] Recognizing the strengths and weaknesses of committee systems, and maintaining the proper balance in policy-making that this recognition entails, will require diligence and continuing study among officials in Washington for an indefinite period in the future.

NOTES

1. Cited in Senate Government Operations Committee, *Administration of National Security: Selected Papers*, 87th Congress, 2nd Session (Washington, D.C.: 1962), pp. 17, 19.
2. Quoted in Ernest R. May, "The Development of Political-Military Consultation in the United States," *Political Science Quarterly*, 70 (June, 1955), 171. A valuable background study in the evolving problem of coordinating civilian and military efforts.
3. General Omar N. Bradley, *A Soldier's Story* (New York: Holt, Rinehart & Winston, 1951), p. xi.
4. General Matthew B. Ridgway, *Soldier: The Memoirs of Matthew B. Ridgway* (New York: Harper & Row, 1956), p. 271.
5. May, *op. cit.*, pp. 163–164.
6. These are described in *ibid.*, pp. 167–168, 172, 173–174.
7. For more detailed discussion of these wartime decisions, see John L. Snell, ed. *The Meaning of Yalta* (Baton Rouge, La.: Louisiana State University Press, 1956), pp. 133–157; Senate Armed Service and Foreign Relations Committees, *The Military Situation in the Far East*, Hearings, 82nd Congress, 1st Session (Washington, D.C.: 1951), pp. 3328–3342; Dwight D. Eisenhower, *Crusade in Europe* (Garden City, N.Y.: Doubleday, 1948), pp. 398–403.
8. Bradley, *op. cit.*, p. 536.
9. Eisenhower, *op. cit.*, pp. 441–442.
10. Quoted in Timothy W. Stanley, *American Defense and National Security* (Washington, D.C.: Public Affairs Press, 1956), p. 5. Very useful for background on the problem of defense reorganization in the modern period.
11. Senate Government Operations Committee, *Organizing for National Security*, Hearings, 87th Congress, 1st Session, I (Washington, D.C.: 1961), 16. The volumes in this series, together with studies published by the committee, provide a wealth of information on national security organization in the 1960s.
12. *Ibid.*, I, 561.
13. Ray S. Cline, and Maurice Matloff, "Development of War Department News on Unification," *Military Affairs*, 13 (Summer, 1949), 65.
14. Stanley, *op. cit.*, pp. 68–69.
15. *The New York Times*, January 12, 1958.
16. Senate Government Operations Committee, *Administration of National Security: Selected Papers*, *op. cit.*, p. 36.
17. Dwight D. Eisenhower, *Mandate for Change: 1953–1956* (Garden City, N.Y.: Doubleday, 1963), pp. 449–450.
18. *The New York Times*, October 8 and November 6, 1963.
19. Edward H. Hobbs, *Behind the President* (Washington, D.C.: Public Affairs Press, 1954), p. 136.
20. Cited in Senate Government Operations Committee, *Organizing for National Security—Selected Materials*, 86th Congress, 2nd Session (Washington, D.C.: 1960), p. 76.
21. *Ibid.*, p. 78.
22. See the statement by General Robert A. Cutler in Senate Government Operations Committee, *Organizing for National Security*, *op. cit.*, I, p. 579.
23. Quoted in Senate Government Operations Committee, *Organizing for National Security—Selected Materials*, *op. cit.*, p. 88.
24. Senate Government Operations Committee, *Organizing for National Security*, *op. cit.*, I, 584.
25. Kennan's viewpoints are included in Senate Government Operations Committee, *Organizing for National Security—Selected Materials*, *op. cit.*, pp. 107–121.
26. See the views of General Cutler in Senate Government Operations Committee, *Organizing for National Security*, *op. cit.*, I, 575, 582, 589; and of Admiral Souers in *ibid.*, 561–552, 567, 574–575.
27. The phrase is Senator Henry M. Jackson's, as used in his speech to the National War College on April 16, 1959, cited in Senate

Government Operations Committee, *Organizing for National Security—Selected Materials*, op. cit., p. 154.

28. For Nitze's views, see *ibid.*, p. 165 and 164–172 *passim*.

29. Senate Government Operations Committee, *Organizing for National Security*, op. cit., I, 731. For other examples of such liaison, see *ibid.*, pp. 1184–1185.

30. Senate Foreign Relations Committee, *United States Foreign Policy: The Formulation and Administration of United States Foreign Policy*, 86th Congress, 2nd Session (Washington, D.C.: 1960), p. 87. This study prepared by the Brookings Institution provides a useful, succinct treatment of organizational machinery in foreign affairs.

31. See the views of Secretary of State Christian A. Herter in Senate Government Operations Committee, *Organizing for National Security*, op. cit., I, 701.

32. *Ibid.*, pp. 1134–1135.

33. *Ibid.*, p. 631.

34. Ridgway, op. cit., p. 286. For other discussions of the "New Look" in defense policy under Eisenhower, see Robert J. Donovan, *Eisenhower: The Inside Story* (New York: Harper & Row, 1956), pp. 51–64. A journalistic account, based, however, on Cabinet records of Eisenhower's first term.

35. Senate Government Operations Committee, *Organizing for National Security*, op. cit., I, 561.

36. *Ibid.*, p. 755.

37. *Ibid.*, p. 1194.

38. Quoted in Elias Huzar, *The Purse and the Sword* (Ithaca, N.Y.: Cornell University Press, 1950), p. 9. This volume provides a comprehensive discussion of the control of the military through appropriations.

39. *Ibid.*, p. 21.

40. Kerwin, op. cit., p. 126.

41. See Fred J. Cook, *The Warfare State* (New York: Macmillan, 1962); and Waldemar A. Nielson, "Huge, Hidden Impact of the Pentagon," *New York Times Magazine*, July 25, 1961, pp. 9, 31–36.

42. See the views of former Secretary of Defense Robert A. Lovett in Senate Government Operations Committee, *Administration of National Security—Selected Papers*, op. cit., pp. 142–143; and of former Secretary of Defense Thomas S. Gates, in *ibid.*, pp. 143–146.

43. For further analysis of the "military mind," consult Hanson Baldwin, "The Military Move In," *Harper's Magazine*, 195 (December, 1947), 481–489; John P. Marquand, "Inquiry into the Military Mind," *New York Times Magazine*, March 30, 1952, p. 53 *ff.*; Walter Mills, "Puzzle of the 'Military Mind,'" *New York Times Magazine*, November 18, 1962, p. 33 *ff.*

44. Kerwin, op. cit., pp. 118–119; Burton M. Sapin and Richard C. Snyder, *The Role of the Military in American Foreign Policy* (Garden City, N.Y.: Doubleday, 1954), p. 19.

45. For a further analysis of the problem discussed here, see the memorandum submitted by former Secretary of Defense Robert Lovett, in Senate Government Operations Committee, *Administration of National Security—Selected Papers*, op. cit., pp. 137–143.

46. Sapin and Snyder, op. cit., pp. 76–77.

47. Ridgway, op. cit., p. 270.

48. General James M. Gavin, *War and Peace in the Space Age* (New York: Harper & Row, 1958), pp. 257–258. An illuminating treatment of defense problems and organization by an experienced military commander.

49. *The New York Times*, January 5, 1958.

50. *Ibid.*, November 10, 1957.

51. Senate Government Operations Committee, *Organizing for National Security*, op. cit., I, 773.

52. *Ibid.*, pp. 769–770, 774.

53. Dwight D. Eisenhower, *Mandate for Change: 1953–1956*, op. cit., p. 133; Sherman Adams, *First-Hand Report: The Story of the Eisenhower Administration* (New York: Harper & Row, 1961), pp. 398–399, 402–403, 418–421.

54. Sidey, op. cit., pp. 72–77.

55. Russell Baker, "Again Vinson Mounts the Ramparts," *New York Times Magazine*, May 4, 1958, pp. 13, 78.

56. CIA activities in South Vietnam are described in *The New York Times*, June 23, September 9, and September 22, 1963; and in the dispatch by United Press International reporter Lyle C. Wilson, in the *Poughkeepsie Journal*, September 18, 1963.

57. Senate Government Operations Committee, *Organizing for National Security—Selected Materials*, op. cit., p. 152.

58. Arthur W. MacMahon, *Administration and Foreign Affairs* (University, Ala.: University of Alabama Press, 1953), pp. 41–44; Sidey, op. cit., pp. 218, 341, 382.

59. Hobbs, op. cit., pp. 99–100.

60. Stanley, op. cit., p. 23.

61. For an account highlighting the intrusion of budgetary agencies into defense policy, see Edward L. Katzenbach, "Bubud's Defense Policy," *The Reporter*, 22 (June 23, 1960), 25–30.

62. Senate Government Operations Committee, *Organizing for National Security*, op. cit., I, 34–35, 37, 631–632.

63. Adams, *op. cit.*, pp. 207–208.
64. Senate Committee on Government Operations, *Organization of Federal Executive Departments and Agencies*, 87th Congress, 2nd Session (Washington, D.C.: 1962), p. 5.
65. Stanley, *op. cit.*, pp. 40–41.
66. Agency for International Development, *The Story of A.I.D.* (Washington, D.C.: no date), p. 2.
67. United States Information Agency, *Foreign Service—USIA* (Washington, D.C.: no date), p. 2.
68. United States Information Agency, *Facts About USIA* (Washington, D.C.: 1963), p. 1.
69. James L. McCamy, *The Administration of American Foreign Affairs* (New York: Knopf, 1950), p. 289.
70. Senate Government Operations Committee, *Organizational History of the National Security Council*, 86th Congress, 2nd Session (Washington, D.C.: 1960), p. 36.
71. *Ibid.*, pp. 33–34.
72. Roger Hilsman, "Intelligence and Policy-Making in Foreign Affairs," *World Politics*, **5** (October, 1952), 3.
73. The over-all pattern of governmental intelligence activity is described in Hanson W. Baldwin, "The Growing Risk of Bureaucratic Intelligence," *The Reporter*, **29** (August 15, 1963), 46–52.
74. Senate Government Operations Committee, *Organizing for National Security, op. cit.*, **II**, 483–484.

75. *Ibid.*, p. 483.
76. See the report of the Senate Foreign Relations Committee on the U-2 incident, in *The New York Times*, June 26, 1960.
77. Senate Government Operations Committee, *Organizing for National Security, op. cit.*, **I**, 745, 1190.
78. *Ibid.*, p. 14.
79. Senate Government Operations Committee, *Organizing for National Security—The Secretary of State and National Security Policy Process*, 87th Congress, 1st Session (Washington, D.C.: 1961), p. 5.
80. *Ibid.*, p. 809.
81. See the viewpoints expressed in Senate Government Operations Committee, *Organizing for National Security—Selected Materials, op. cit.*, pp. 108–110, and *Organizing for National Security, op. cit.*, **I**, 855, 858–859.
82. William R. Kintner, *Forging a New Sword* (New York: Harper & Row, 1958), p. 52.
83. Brookings Institution, *Administrative Aspects of United States Foreign Assistance Programs* (Washington, D.C.: 1957), pp. 99–100.
84. Trenchant criticisms of the "layering" and other problems associated with an elaborate committee system are set forth in Senate Government Operations Committee, *Organizing for National Security, op. cit.*, **I**, 13–20, 30–31, 623–625, 669–670, 745–746, 1190–1191.
85. Eisenhower, *Mandate for Change: 1953–1956, op. cit.*, p. 114.

5 ➡ THE ROLE OF CONGRESS

IN FOREIGN RELATIONS ➡

A striking phenomenon associated with the control of foreign relations in recent American history is the expanded role of Congress in virtually all phases of external affairs. As Representative Chester E. Merrow (Republican of New Hampshire) declared, perhaps somewhat prematurely: "In practice the Congress has become a coequal partner with the Executive in giving substance to United States leadership."[1]

The new role of Congress springs from a variety of factors. One of these is the greater involvement of the United States in world affairs since World War II. Another is the nature of contemporary foreign policy problems and programs accompanying America's new responsibilities. The underpinnings of American foreign policy today are vast and continuing programs of economic, military, and technical assistance; efforts to reduce world trade barriers; programs of cultural exchange and information dissemination; participation in the varied activities of the United Nations and regional associations such as the Organization of American States and NATO; and peacetime development of atomic power. New domestic policies too have been necessary to support national security. To maintain its position as leader of the free world coalition, the United States has had to preserve a strong and viable economic system at home. In the face of rapid technological progress by its diplomatic enemies, it has been compelled to give increasing attention to the development of new weapons, to scientific research and to space technology. The pressure of world events has compelled the United States to maintain a high degree of internal and external readiness to safeguard its security.

Expansion of congressional influence upon foreign relations has been an inevitable byproduct, directly, by injecting Congress into the foreign policy process as never before, and, indirectly, by heightening its role in closely related domestic policies. In some foreign policies, such as assisting with the economic growth of underdeveloped nations, promoting world trade, or contributing equipment and manpower to NATO, Congress has played a major role. In other policies, such as formulating American policy toward summit conferences or responding to the latest Soviet disarmament proposal, its role has been tangential. But in the second half of the twentieth century, very few congressional activities are totally divorced from foreign relations or have implications solely for domestic affairs.

Legislative Activities in Foreign Affairs —A Case Study

To illustrate the point, let us consider a case study of legislative activity in the foreign policy field by examining the work of the House Foreign Affairs Committee in 1957 and contrasting its activities with those of House committees in an earlier period.[2] In the first session of the 85th Congress, the House Foreign Affairs Committee consisted of 32 members— 17 Democrats and 15 Republicans—with a staff of 12 employees. Internally, the committee was organized into eight standing subcommittees for the following important areas: Near East and Africa, International Organizations and Movements, Far East and the Pacific, National Security, Foreign Economic Policy, Europe, State Department Organization and Foreign Operations, and Inter-American Affairs. There were, in addition, two *ad hoc* subcommittees: one to study the creation of a commission for protecting American foreign investments and the prevention of claims against the United States; the other to study two bills seeking to curb foreign travel by "certain unaccompanied minors not possessing valid passports." Two conference committees were also established to reconcile conflicting House and Senate versions of a resolution on the Hungarian crisis of 1956 and differing House and Senate bills on the Mutual Security Program for 1958.

A detailed statistical breakdown of its activities for the year indicates that the committee had 126 bills (including 61 duplicates) referred to it; that it considered 33 of these; that it reported 12 favorably to the House; that of these, the House passed 10 and these 10 were eventually enacted into law. It also considered 18 resolutions, of which 7 were reported favorably to the House and eventually passed. The committee held a total of 161 hearings, both public and executive, and accumulated 3176 pages of testimony from 338 witnesses. Its reports on measures touching foreign affairs ran to 796 pages. The full committee met 79 times, and its subcommittees met 82 times, for a total of 161 meetings in all. The full committee devoted a total of 257 hours to its work —finally authorizing aproximately $3.3 billion to be spent in the sphere of foreign relations. These data take on added significance when compared with the committee's activities before World War II. Prior to the war, the House Foreign Affairs Committee was largely ornamental.[3] It ranked far down on the list of desirable committee assignments in Congress, and it possessed little influence over American foreign policy. During 1933–1934, for example, it held only 37 full committee and 9 subcommittee meetings. In that same period it recommended legislation requiring expenditures of approximately $200,000. By 1951, financial authorization voted by the committee had increased 70,000 per cent to roughly $14 billion.[4]

The statistical summary of activities of the House Foreign Affairs Committee for 1957 indicates both the cost and scope of congressional participation in foreign affairs. There remain, however, many other important aspects of legislative participation which must be examined, especially Congress's role in certain selected aspects of foreign relations.

CONSTITUTIONAL POWERS OF CONGRESS OVER FOREIGN RELATIONS

Profoundly suspicious of executive power, and believing generally that too much power should not be conferred upon any one branch of the government, the Founding Fathers divided control over foreign relations. It is not surprising, therefore, that conflict between the two branches has characterized the management of foreign relations throughout the greater part of American history. With most important powers shared and—what may be more troublesome—with a twilight zone sometimes left between the executive and legislative branches, institutional conflicts are well-nigh inevitable under the American system of government. The Constitution provides a standing invitation for both branches to struggle for leadership, to jockey for position, and to dominate the management of internal and foreign affairs.

Senate Ratification of Treaties

Nowhere has conflict shown up more forcefully than in the treaty-making process. In Chapter 3 we discussed this process from the point of view of the President's powers to reach agreements with other countries. We shall not retrace the ground covered there, except to recall that the President has many methods of circumventing Senate control over his actions, the most important being the executive agreement.

What then is the real significance of the constitutional requirement that the President may make treaties with the advice and consent of the Senate? Before World War II, this provision was cited from time to time by the Senate in its efforts to influence the *substance* of American foreign policy. Periodically, the Senate has insisted upon the right to determine whether negotiations ought to take place with other countries and upon the conditions to be complied with before they might take place.[5] In the face of increasing executive control over treaty-making, dating from George Washington's determination to ignore the Senate until after agreements had already been reached with other countries, the Senate at intervals has tried to re-establish what it believed to be its rightful role.[6] That such efforts have done little to reverse the steady accretion of executive power to reach agreements, unhindered by senatorial supervision, is illustrated by events during the World War I era. Certain Republican senators proposed sending eight of their number to France to acquaint themselves first-hand with Wilson's peace negotiations at Paris while these negotiations were still in progress. They believed this step amply justified under the advice and consent clause of the Constitution. It is significant that in the end they did not carry through with this intention. Wilson completed the negotiations leading to the Treaty of Versailles without any prior consultation with the Senate. He did take a nominal Republican with him to Paris, the former diplomat Henry White, but White in no sense spoke for Senate Republicans, nor did he have any power to reach agreements later binding upon them.[7]

The later consequences of this episode drive home the point that although the Senate's role in treaty-making has declined, it was neither then, nor is it now, a mere formality. The Treaty of Versailles, for instance, was so emasculated with Senate modifications and amendments that Wilson would not accept it. When the Senate refused to yield, the resulting deadlock prevented American entry into the League of Nations. Until 1901, the Senate altered or amended 80 to 90 treaties placed before it. About one-third of these either failed of ratification or were later abandoned by the President as unsatisfactory. During the next quarter-century, 58 proposed treaties were changed by the Senate; 40 percent of them were abandoned or discarded by the President as no longer in the national interest.[8]

These facts suggest that the contemporary importance of the advice and consent clause of the Constitution lies not primarily in giving the Senate a *veto* over agreements between the United States and other countries, since the Senate can hardly prevent the President from reaching some kind of *de facto* agreement. Rather, the clause gives the Senate an opportunity to affect policy by attaching amendments and conditions and affords it an occasion to express its viewpoints. Because a minimum degree of executive-legislative harmony is indispensable to consistent and sustained efforts in foreign affairs, the chief executive is likely to take expressions of senatorial opinion seriously and, if possible, to arrive at agreements acceptable to both branches.

To promote closer executive-legislative liaison, executive officials have sought the co-operation of the Senate Foreign Relations Committee in concluding most of the important treaties agreed to between the United States and other countries in recent years. Thus, Senators Arthur H. Vandenberg (Republican of Michigan) and Tom Connally (Democrat of Texas) played a prominent part immediately after the war in negotiating the minor Axis peace treaties. Considerable dissatisfaction was voiced with these treaties when they were put before the Senate, most notably about the treaty with Italy. But these two senators were able to convince their colleagues that the agreements were the best attainable under the circumstances. Similarly, the North Atlantic Treaty, signed on April 4, 1949, grew out of the "Vandenberg Resolution," expressing the sense of the Senate that a closer military association ought to be established among the nations of the North Atlantic community. Early drafts of the treaty were discussed continually with the Foreign Relations Committee, and the committee was kept informed as negotiations proceeded with other countries.[9] A sustained effort to foster close collaboration between the executive branch and the Senate in treaty-making also occurred in 1951, when John Foster Dulles, then a special assistant to the Secretary of State, worked for a period of several months to generate unity throughout the government on the terms of a peace treaty with Japan.[10]

Recent emphasis upon bipartisanship in foreign affairs and the evident need for more effective executive-legislative liaison when critical foreign policy issues are at stake have given the Senate, along with the House, a more dynamic role in the foreign policy process. Executive officials have consulted the Senate during the formation of important foreign policies more than at any other stage in American history. Even so, the Senate's role in treaty-making continues to be subordinate. It cannot initiate treaties, nor can it effectively prevent agreements the President believes to be in the national interest. It can reject treaties submitted to it or substantially modify them by amendments. It can express its opinions in a variety of ways. But in a showdown the President may still ignore the Senate, especially if he finds senators obdurate and if agreements must be made speedily and decisively.

Senate Confirmation of Appointments

Along with its power to ratify treaties, the Senate also enjoys a unique prerogative in foreign affairs through its power to confirm executive appointments. In Chapter 3, we evaluated the President's ability to nullify this power, too, by utilizing personal representatives, executive officers, and by making interim appointments while the Senate is not in session. Nevertheless, as with the treaty power, the President normally prefers to work with the Senate by having his appointments confirmed in the prescribed constitutional manner.

In the early period of American history, the Senate was prone to use its powers of confirmation to pass upon the establishment of diplomatic missions abroad. This occurred for example in 1809, when the Senate refused to approve an exchange of ministers between the United States and Russia.[11] The confirmation power has also been used to influence the treaty-making process, as when the Senate refused for some time to confirm negotiators who were to settle outstanding differences with Great Britain in Washington's Administration. Bitter and prolonged wrangling ensued between the President and Senate before the highly controversial Jay Treaty, signed in 1794, could even be negotiated. Under Cleveland, the upper chamber rejected a fisheries agreement with England, because the President had sent negotiators who had not received Senate confirmation. The dispute over confirmation, however, may have been a pretext for defeating a treaty which many senators, particularly those from New England, opposed anyway.[12]

McKinley was the first President to utilize a personal diplomatic agent who had not been confirmed in his assignment by the Senate. Then and in the years that followed, the Senate has protested against this practice. One significant expression of disapproval was an amendment affixed to the Treaty of Versailles, providing that no diplomatic representatives could be sent to the League of Nations without prior senatorial confirmation. This was a clear rebuke to Wilson, who had ignored the Senate in negotiating the treaty. More generally, it was a firm enunciation of the Senate's right to pass on diplomatic appointments.[13]

In the postwar period, along with other legislative prerogatives in the foreign policy field, the power of confirmation has received renewed emphasis. Two examples may be cited to illustrate the point. First, when the United States joined the United Nations, the Senate successfully insisted upon the right to confirm the appointments of high-ranking diplomatic personnel assigned both to existing and future UN agencies. Second, when Congress approved the Greek-Turkish aid bill in 1947, it added a proviso that the Senate must confirm the appointments of any high officials sent to oversee the administration of foreign aid in other countries. The following year, Congress also specified that the roving ambassador to supervise administration of the Marshall Plan should be confirmed by the Senate.[14]

On a number of occasions, conflict has prevailed over diplomatic appointments. A highly controversial episode was President Truman's appointment of Philip Jessup as a member of the U.S. delegation to the United Nations in 1951. This appointment was made in the face of well-nigh unanimous Senate opposition, based upon the belief that Jessup had been too closely identified with left-wing causes. Although the Senate refused to confirm Jessup's appointment, President Truman gave him an "interim appointment" after the Senate adjourned, so that he joined the United States delegation anyway.

Senate influence upon foreign affairs through the power of confirmation, on the whole, affords very little direct opportunity to determine the substance of American foreign policy. Forceful Presidents are not likely to be deterred for long by Senate opposition. Wilson's use of Colonel House as his personal representative to carry out important missions and FDR's use of Harry Hopkins for similar purposes show that the confirmation hurdle can be circumvented.

Congressional Control over Appropriations

Commenting upon the difficulties encountered by the Eisenhower Administration in winning legislative acceptance of its foreign aid programs, former Presidential Assistant Sherman Adams has observed that:

> . . . Eisenhower was not able to induce Congress to appropriate funds to cover the bare bones of a program that always seemed [to Congress] more concerned with putting out fires than it did with a soundly planned project to get the countries involved onto their economic feet.

In his efforts to gain legislative support for foreign aid projects, Adams has commented,

President Eisenhower "carried the battle . . . to Capitol Hill and fought it every step of the way." In spite of Eisenhower's great popularity and his varied attempts to generate support for foreign aid, Adams concluded, the program "was doomed for a slashing no matter how hard the President fought for it."[15] On another occasion in the early Eisenhower period, the Senate Appropriations Committee reported a bill to the Senate prohibiting any American contribution to the United Nations if Red China were admitted to that organization. In the face of President Eisenhower's conviction that the bill "could seriously hamper me in the conduct of foreign affairs," the move was defended by its sponsors as a legitimate attempt to convey the Senate's viewpoints on an important and controversial issue. Eventually, President Eisenhower was able to get this portion of the bill withdrawn, but only after he pledged to communicate legislative viewpoints on the matter forcefully to other governments.[16]

Although President Kennedy possessed solid Democratic majorities in the House and Senate, he often fared little better than his predecessor in his requests to Congress for foreign aid and certain other appropriations. Thus, for fiscal year 1964, the House of Representatives slashed the Kennedy Administration's foreign aid budget request by nearly $1 billion (or 25 percent), a move President Kennedy publicly condemned as "the sharpest cut . . . ever made in a foreign authorization bill." In the President's view, the House had taken a "shortsighted, irresponsible and dangerously partisan action." Congress's persistent hostility toward certain aspects of the foreign aid program—reflecting deep-seated and continuing public skepticism and opposition—was described by the President as risking a "repudiation of the foreign policy which this country has pursued since the end of the Second World War."[17]

Chief executives in the contemporary period have thus been brought face to face with the reality, as expressed by Senator Robert M. LaFollette (Republican of Wisconsin) in 1943, that: "The great power which the legislative arm of the Government has is the power over the purse strings."[18] Mindful that the English Parliament had finally established its supremacy because of the monarchy's dependence upon it for funds, and recalling too that colonial legislatures had used this power effectively against colonial governors, the Founding Fathers counted heavily upon the power of the purse to assure congressional supervision over all phases of governmental activity. Important programs and policies almost invariably require funds for their implementation—all the more so in our age of recurrent international crises. One-half to two-thirds of the national budget approximately is now devoted to foreign policy and national defense.

Congress can use its power of the purse to affect foreign, and related domestic policies, in many different ways. It can of course simply refuse to appropriate funds for measures proposed by the executive branch. That is its prerogative. But such drastic action seldom occurs, chiefly because Congress is as aware as executive officials of the gravity of conditions prevailing in the international community. It has no desire to risk diplomatic defeat for the United States by ill-advised refusals to cooperate with the White House in formulating measures pertaining to national security. Moreover, the President may, and normally does, exert pressure upon Congress in a variety of ways to assure sympathetic consideration of his budgetary requests. These ways may involve personal appeals to Congress and to public opinion, close liaison with party leaders, testimony by his high-level advisers upon the necessity of proposed measures, and promises of support in forthcoming political campaigns.*

Yet in practice, Congress' ability to influence the course of foreign relations does not arise so much from its power to withhold funds altogether for needed programs. In undertakings like foreign aid, defense spending, and other projects requiring appropriations, the White House can normally count upon receiving most of the funds it has requested to carry on activities at home and abroad deemed vital by the President, even if frequently the executive branch must ultimately settle for less money than it believes ideally desirable for such programs. Rather the appropriations process affords Congress numerous and varied opportunities to express its opinions, to inquire into the necessity for proposed programs, to investigate the administration of existing programs, to introduce changes in projects suggested by

---

* For an illuminating treatment of President Eisenhower's tactics in generating support for his foreign aid requests, see Sherman Adams, *First-Hand Report: The Story of the Eisenhower Administration* (New York: Harper & Row, 1961), pp. 375–380.

executive policy-makers, and occasionally to redraft executive proposals extensively.* Once funds have been provided, Congress exercises continuing supervision over such programs in an attempt to see that expenditures are being made in accordance with the law, that widespread waste and duplication do not exist, that programs authorized earlier are still in the national interest, and that governmental activities are taking account of altered circumstances in the external arena. Like legislative activity in other aspects of foreign relations, the power of the purse chiefly affords Congress opportunity to modify and amend proposals initiated by the executive branch. Virtually all of the great legislative enactments that have been foundations of postwar American foreign policy—the Greek-Turkish aid bill, the China aid program, the Marshall Plan, the Point Four (or technical assistance) program, the Mutual Security program, the Peace Corps, and other measures—originated within the executive branch. In most cases, they were modified partially or heavily by Congress, either initially by the foreign affairs committees or, in some cases, other committees that might have jurisdiction, or later by the appropriations committees. The latter nearly always cut budgetary requests submitted by the White House, even when these had been approved in whole or in substantial part by the policy committees.

Postwar experience has called attention to a number of major problems arising from legislative control of appropriations for foreign policy. Legislation entailing expenditures in both domestic and foreign affairs must in effect go through Congress twice. A measure is considered first by a standing committee. If the committee approves it, it then goes to the full house, and if it is authorized there, then the appropriations committee of that chamber will consider it with a view to recommending funds

* A not untypical example of legislative initiative in foreign policy by reliance upon the appropriations process is afforded by the State Department appropriation for 1959. Section 104 provided, "None of the funds appropriated in this title shall be used (1) to pay the United States contribution to any international organization which engages in the direct or indirect promotion of the principle or doctrine of one world government or one world citizenship; (2) for the promotion, direct or indirect, of the principle or doctrine of one world government or one world citizenship." See: Senate Appropriations Committee, H.R. 12428 (Report No. 1683), 85th Congress, 2nd Session, 1958, p. 13.

for its implementation. Again assuming a favorable committee recommendation, the measure returns to the full house for passage as an appropriations bill. After the bill is approved by both houses, it is sent to the President for signature, after which it becomes law.

This complicated process is perhaps made clearer by focusing briefly upon Congress's treatment of President Eisenhower's foreign aid budget request for fiscal year 1959. The President's total budget request for military, economic, and technical assistance to other countries was $3.9 billion. After consideration by the Foreign Affairs Committee, the House "authorized" approximately $3 billion; and after study by the Senate Foreign Relations Committee, the Senate "authorized" nearly $2.1 billion. The total agreed-upon authorization by the House and Senate was $3.7 billion, which included funds permitted to be "carried over" from the previous year. After consideration by the Appropriations Committee, the House (as usual) cut the actual appropriation to $3.1 billion; and after the same process in the Senate, the upper chamber (as expected) agreed upon a higher appropriation of $3.5 billion. Ultimately, the House and Senate compromised on a total appropriation of $3.3 billion, arrived at by "splitting the difference" between the House and Senate bills. Thus, the President finally got $3.3 billion out of his original request for $3.9 billion to support foreign aid programs.[19]

Now, aside from the fact that this is a most cumbersome and time-consuming procedure, a number of other fundamental criticisms can be made of it, especially when foreign policy measures are involved. First, there is the inability of the appropriations committee, not to speak of Congress as a whole, to examine the executive budget *in its totality*. Not until the last stages of the appropriations process have been reached are the items within the separate budgetary requests, like the pieces in a jigsaw puzzle, reassembled to form a meaningful picture of expenditures as a whole. When the appropriations committee in each chamber receives the budget, it parcels out the separate items to its subcommittees—for agriculture, military affairs, foreign affairs, and other areas—for detailed study. These subcommittees in turn maintain little effective liaison with the full committee and almost none with the standing committees of Congress which earlier authorized the program demanding an appropriation. Moreover, full appropriations committee review of subcommittee actions is hasty and superficial. The consequence is that the parent committee often does not have a clear conception of the actions its subcommittees have taken and the reasons for these actions. Not until all subcommittee reports have come in, usually just before the adjournment of Congress, is it possible to know the total appropriations Congress is making in any given year. Senator Harry F. Byrd (Democrat of Virginia), influential chairman of the Senate Finance Committee, once complained that "the budget picture is never seen again as a whole until after it has become the law of the

Getting in Condition. (Source: Alexander in *The Philadelphia Evening Bulletin*, reproduced in *The New York Times*, August 11, 1963.)

land . . . There is no way of telling what total appropriations or expenditures are, and there is no way of comparing the effect of action on the bills with the revenue situation. . . . The bills are passed as separate and unrelated pieces."[20]

Another problem endemic in the organization of Congress is the difficulty of coordinating the efforts of the appropriations committees with those of the standing committees. With reference to national defense, one legislator defined their different roles by saying that it was the responsibility of the standing committee on armed services, for instance

to recommend measures that will provide us with a defense establishment . . . adequate to the assurance of our national security. . . . It is the responsibility of the Appropriations Committee to recommend appropriations to effectuate such measures, and to see, as best it can, that the Nation will get value received in the expenditure of the funds made available.[21]

The same distinction holds for the appropriations committees and all other standing committees. That the line between their jurisdictions is difficult to draw precisely, however, has been illustrated many times by events in the postwar period. The history of legislative action on the Marshall Plan in the 1947–1948 period is a case in point. This undertaking had been preceded by what was most likely the most intensive joint executive-legislative stock-taking in American diplomatic history. Standing and select committees of Congress, executive agencies, and private study groups pooled their efforts to assure as thorough a study as time permitted of Europe's economic needs and of America's resources for meeting them. Finally, in the spring of 1948, Congress authorized a long-range program of economic assistance to Europe that contemplated an ultimate expenditure of approximately $12 billion in American funds.[22]

Yet in the face of this unprecedented executive-legislative collaboration by a Republican Congress and a Democratic President, the House Appropriations Committee threatened to emasculate the Marshall Plan later in the summer by cutting the first year authorization 25 percent. In the words of its chairman, John Taber (Republican of New York): "the architects of this worldwide relief program have no definite plan and no definite program. . . ."[23] The committee's position prompted Senator Arthur H. Vandenberg, chairman of the powerful Foreign Relations Committee, to denounce Taber's committee on the floor of the Senate —a highly irregular procedure—and to urge Congress vigorously to restore the reduction in funds. Not even Vandenberg's great influence, however, was able to undo the damage completely. In the end, both houses had to agree to a cut in the earlier authorization.[24]

This episode exemplifies a tendency that has become a major barrier to intelligent formulation of basic foreign policy programs: the inclination of individual legislators and committees of Congress to apply across-the-board percentage reductions in requested appropriations or, alternatively, to vote lump sum reductions in even figures, like 50 or 100 or 500 million dollars. Most infrequently is such an approach dictated by logic or concern for sound policy decisions. More often it stems from the inability of the average legislator to establish a priority among separate items in a complex budget, a prevailing feeling on Capitol Hill that economies must be effected somewhere, and a determination on the part of Congress to resist any intimation that it has become merely a rubber stamp in considering executive budget requests.*

Assignments to appropriations committees are highly prized by Congressmen. Perhaps even more than other committees of Congress, appropriations committees are fiercely independent. They resent any intrusion upon their prerogatives, and routinely they show little inclination to be bound by the actions of other committees. Their hearings are almost always held in secret. Much of the testimony taken is "off the record" and is hence not even available to other legislators. Their members know that very few legislators have the time or the expert knowledge to assimilate thousands of pages of the executive budget requests and "justifications" submitted along with the budget, to read hundreds of pages of testimony by expert witnesses, and to acquire detailed knowledge about a host of large and small executive expenditures. Committee recom-

mendations are, therefore, usually accepted with little change by the entire house. Floor debate on their reports tends to be desultory and superficial. Almost never are amendments to their recommendations successfully made on the floor. *For all practical purposes the appropriations committees are Congress itself when dealing with expenditures.*

These generalizations have been illustrated many times in the recent period by legislators whose roles in the appropriations process give them ample power to influence the formulation and administration of American foreign policy. Among the examples that might be cited,** an outstanding one has been the case of Congressman John J. Rooney (Democrat of New York), chairman of the House Appropriations subcommittee that deals with the Department of State's annual operating budget.

Something of Rooney's orientation in foreign affairs and his imperiousness in dealing with State Department budget requests is conveyed by the following excerpts from the hearing on the State Department appropriation for 1960.[25] The individuals questioned by Rooney were State Department officials, attempting to justify portions of the department's budget. At the outset, the Department of State requested an item involving $2.7 million to cover expanded intelligence activities:

---

* Political motivations are also unquestionably present sometimes when Congress votes percentage or lump sum reductions, as indicated by the following incident related to the author by a former high-ranking official in the Truman Administration. This officer was approached by a legislator who had consistently supported the administration's foreign policy programs. Now, however, the legislator said that he would be unable to support large foreign aid appropriations in the future, lamenting that: "My political opponent is waging a very effective campaign against me by attacking my support of 'foreign give-away programs,' huge defense budgets, and high taxes. I must somehow convince my constituents that I am zealously looking after their economic welfare, else I am in danger of being defeated in the next election." The following strategy was accordingly agreed upon: the administration would deliberately ask Congress for 20 percent more funds than it needed in certain categories of foreign aid; then the legislator could dramatically demand reductions in the "padded" executive budget by moving to pare it 20 percent, "cutting the fat" from the budget. This strategy was carried out. The administration eventually got the funds it really needed. The legislator demonstrated to his constituents that he was a trustworthy guardian of their pocketbooks, thereby aiding him in his successful campaign for re-election!

** A parallel case to the one discussed above is to be found in the decisive influence exercised for years by Congressman Otto E. Passman (Democrat of Louisiana), chairman of the Foreign Operations Subcommittee of the House Appropriations Committee. Representative Passman has not disguised his adamant opposition to foreign aid programs—characterizing them as among "the greatest foreign-policy failures in history." He has defined his purpose in dealing with foreign aid as not so much to "end the program at one stroke but rather to help 'contain' it, to encourage common sense in its policies and operations and to curb its waste and mismanagement." He has described foreign aid as a "political fact of life" that must be terminated gradually. Yet he blames foreign aid for undermining the value of the dollar, for becoming a symbol of "international charity," for subsidizing foreign competitors, and for failing to win friends abroad by a policy of "dollar diplomacy." In view of his attitude, it is small wonder that the phrase "to Passmanize" has become a well-known expression in Washington for making deep cuts in the President's foreign aid requests despite the most vigorous White House objections. For a candid statement of Passman's views, see: Otto E. Passman, "Why I Am Opposed to Foreign Aid," *New York Times Magazine*, July 7, 1963, pp. 16–17; and *The New York Times*, October 15, 1963.

Congressman Rooney: I must be fair and say this: This proposal being presented to us seems to me, for one, to be unwarranted. You are going to have a job justifying this. If you can do so, go right ahead.

After the State Department requested funds to create 47 new diplomatic posts and to expand other posts, this exchange took place:

Congressman Rooney: That means this would be a beef-up of practically 330 positions?
Mr. Henderson: That is right.
Congressman Rooney: Go ahead and see if you can justify it.

Further along, this exchange occurred:

Congressman Rooney: Let me try to summarize it this way . . . is it a fair conclusion to say that there are no real [staff] reductions of any kind?
Mr. Hall: No, sir; because there is a—
Congressman Rooney: Do not elaborate. 'No, sir' is enough.

At a later point, this dialogue occurred:

Mr. Henderson: . . . We are asking for 17 additional people . . . who are to observe carefully all the maneuvers of international communism in its efforts to penetrate economically the various countries of the world, and are to try to devise methods of frustrating these efforts of international communism.
Congressman Rooney: You mean this has not been done for the last 4 or 5 years?
Mr. Henderson: It has not been done in the way it should be done. . . . There has not been . . . a world approach to this problem . . . we should have a global approach. . . .
Congressman Rooney: . . . You have had more Assistant Secretaries in the last few years than you can shake a stick at. What do those people do? Do you mean to say they have been sitting around and not considering this on a global approach basis? . . . Are they not capable, competent, and able?
Mr. Henderson: Some of the people would be if they——
Congressman Rooney: They are not capable, competent, and able to attack this on a worldwide basis?
Mr. Henderson: If they could be freed from their other duties. . . .

After Mr. Henderson had completed his statement, Rooney retorted: "So far we have proceeded two pages, and you have not as yet pointed out anything a youngster in high school in the United States is not familiar with." Pressing this official on the matter of the 17 additional appointments requested, Rooney continued:

Congressman Rooney: Let me explore this. Are you saying you have not been doing anything with respect to combating communism on a global scale up to now?
Mr. Henderson: No, sir.
Congressman Rooney: It would appear so from your statement.
Mr. Henderson: Mr. Chairman, we are not doing as much as we should do.
Congressman Rooney: Every time the Department has come here in the last 14 or 15 years that I have been on this committee, it has gotten additional money because it was fighting global communism.
Mr. Henderson: We are fighting global communism, but we have been fighting it on a continent-by-continent scale, or a country-by-country scale.
Congressman Rooney: You used to do it on a country scale, and then you got into it on a regional scale. What is this? . . . It is now 'global.' . . . Each year you add more and more people, and the world picture becomes sicker. The picture we listen to today is certainly the worst I have listened to in 15 years.

Further on, Rooney shifted his attention to another budgetary allotment:

Congressman Rooney: What is the representation and liaison activity with public groups. Is that in order to get bigger and better appropriations?
Mr. Henderson: No, sir. . . .
Congressman Rooney: [Speaking of personnel in the Office of Congressional Relations] These are the people you want to get interested in bigger and better appropriations for the State Department; are they not?
Mr. Hall: No, sir. . . .
Congressman Rooney: Would they not primarily be lobbying in behalf of more money for foreign aid?

And another State Department official who confronted Rooney by saying, "Mr. Chairman, we are keeping our shop the same size as last year," was greeted with the retort:

Congressman Rooney: Why could you not cut it in half?
Mr. Macomber: It is a pretty busy operation, Mr. Chairman.

These excerpts are sufficient to indicate the nature of Rooney's power over the operations of the State Department, and to suggest why one observer who studied his activities in detail felt justified in writing an article on "The Foreign Policy of John J. Rooney." The gist of it was that the concurrence of this key legislator was indispensable before the State Department could undertake new functions, add personnel, or significantly increase budgetary allocations for its manifold activities. Although technically under the supervision of the full House Appropriations Committee, Rooney's subcommittee enjoyed *de facto* autonomy. The full committee "endorses the recommendations of the subcommittee in minutes, rarely taking more than an hour." As for the House itself, only once in several years did it significantly alter State Department appropriations as drawn up by Rooney's subcommittee—and only then with respect to a $15,000 item, out of a total budget of $223 million.[26]

Congress and the National Defense Budget

The President, Elias Huzar observed, was designated commander in chief of the military forces, but he "was to command only those forces which Congress put at his disposal. . . ."[27] And General Omar Bradley stated before a congressional committee in 1949 that: "Under our form of government, the military policy of the United States is shaped by the Congress not by the armed forces . . . because . . . Congress controls the appropriations which in the final analysis . . . control the military policy. . . ."[28]

The founders counted heavily upon the power of the purse to guard against military usurpation and to assure that the armed forces would always be utilized in the public interest. Thus the Constitution gives Congress the power to raise and support the military forces of the nation and specifies that Congress may not make any military appropriation for longer than two years. In practice, Congress makes annual appropriations, thereby assuring itself an opportunity to review national defense policy at frequent intervals.*

Many items in the military budget tend to be recurrent and relatively fixed, such as military pay scales, and long-range research and development contracts. They are not subject to drastic alteration by Congress without interfering with a sustained defense effort. Still,

* Some items in the military budget must be "carried over" from year to year to assure needed continuity. This is true, for example, of long-range defense contracts, research and development costs, and commercial leases.

opportunities exist every year for Congress to change the direction of national defense policy by amending budget requests to reflect the legislative will. These opportunities have been utilized repeatedly throughout the postwar period. Spurred by the recommendations of its Appropriations Committee, the House in 1949 was adamant in support of a 55-group air force—in 1948, it had approved a 70-group force—despite the fact that President Truman had recommended only 48 groups. Even though the Senate was inclined to support the President, in the end it, too, was forced to accede to insistent House demands for increased air power. Here was a forceful legislative attempt to determine an important phase of national security policy—a phase that had profound repercussions for foreign affairs —even over the opposition of the chief executive.

The denouement of this issue brought into clear focus some aspects of executive and legislative prerogatives in this field. Although President Truman eventually signed the military appropriations bill for 1950 expanding the air force, he announced publicly that he did not intend to be bound by the action of Congress. Defense needs, he stated, had to be judged "in the light of total national policies and . . . in the light of our foreign policy and the economic and fiscal problems facing us domestically. . . . I am, therefore, directing the Secretary of Defense to place in reserve the amount provided by the Congress . . . for increasing the structure of the Air Force." Almost the identical situation arose late in the Eisenhower Administration, when legislators were deeply concerned about an alleged "missile gap" in America's defenses. Congress again voted additional funds for defense spending which the President did not use.[29] Highly disturbed by prevailing reports of a grave disparity between American and Soviet missile strength—in the face of the President's repeated statements that a "missile gap" did not exist—majorities in both houses of Congress expanded certain aspects of the defense budget beyond the totals requested by the White House. Critics of his defense budget, the President wrote, "in 1957 and 1958, saw disastrous bomber gaps in our defense establishment, and though that illusionary gap never existed, spent useless millions to fill it."[30]

Congress's role in dealing with the defense budget raises several other major questions about the implications of legislative power in defense and, more broadly, foreign policy. One of these, as we have already suggested, is the legal and theoretical distinction between the roles of the standing committees of Congress and the appropriations committees. Under the rules of Congress itself, appropriations bills are not supposed to contain substantive legislation; their function is to provide funds for the implementation of programs already approved (or "authorized") by Congress. Postwar experience has amply indicated that this distinction is far easier to draw in theory than in practice—and that, in fact, Congress seldom makes an effort to adhere to the rule rigidly. In a field like national defense, for example, how is it actually possible to differentiate between the question of whether the defense needs of the country *require* a 70-group or 55-group air force—a determination which the standing committees on armed services are supposed to make—and the question of whether the United States can *afford* an air force of 70 or 55 groups —a determination that the appropriations committees are supposed to make? Huzar wrote in 1950 that all the military appropriations measures "since 1933 have contained provisions bearing on military policy and administration. . . ."[31] A close scrutiny of appropriations bills since 1950 would unquestionably reveal a continuation of this tendency.

Various pretexts are invoked to justify intrusion by appropriations committees into the field of substantive policy. Supposedly the need to "correct the mistakes" of the standing committees or to "clarify the legislative intent" explains such actions. In reality, policy provisions inserted by one or both appropriations committees more often than not reflect the views of their members on foreign or closely related domestic policy. Sometimes such provisions are deliberately inserted into appropriations bills to forestall a presidential veto. The President cannot veto the policy provision without vetoing a needed appropriation! Even legislators who disapprove "policy-making by appropriations committees" are sometimes powerless to prevent it, since the rules of floor debate often effectively prevent such members from raising points of order when the entire House or Senate considers appropriations measures.[32] Whatever their motivation, the tendency of appropriations committees to intrude themselves into legislative policy raises an increasingly serious problem that we shall examine at length in the next chapter: dis-unified and poorly coordinated efforts *within* Congress itself in dealing with important aspects of foreign relations.

If unified action among committees is not easy to maintain, it is also hard to coordinate activities *within* and *between* the two appropriations committees. We have already referred to the fact that the military subcommittees have considerable working autonomy. Members of the House Appropriations Committee traditionally serve on no other congressional committee. This practice cannot be followed in the much smaller Senate, where legislators must serve on numerous committees and subcommittees. The result is that a *de facto* division of labor has emerged between the House and Senate: the House committee—in practice, its military subcommittee—examines the defense budget in great detail and makes its recommendations; then the Senate committee acts as a kind of financial supreme court, permitting the military services to "appeal" House cuts and to request restoration of needed funds. House and Senate conferees later reconcile higher Senate and lower House expenditures, and merge them into a unified appropriations measure.[33]

The dominant role of the House in the appropriations process is exemplified by legislative treatment of the national defense budget. The average member of Congress has little effective influence upon the defense budget. The really effective force, in this and other aspects of major appropriations, tends to be the subcommittee of the House Appropriations Committee that has jurisdiction, and to a much lesser extent, its counterpart in the Senate.* How well are these subcommittees,

* The dominant position of the House of Representatives in the appropriations process has long been under attack in the Senate, where the feeling has existed for many years that the upper chamber too often plays merely a nominal role in the provision of funds. The House, by contrast, clings to its traditional prerogatives in this area, in some measure as a counterbalance against the Senate's preferential role in treaty ratification and in the confirmation of executive appointments. The point of view prevailing in the two chambers was brought into clear focus in mid-1962, when the appropriations process came to a complete standstill, after the chairmen of the House and Senate Appropriations Committees were unable to agree upon procedures for resolving differences between the two chambers. The Senate (quite unsuccessfully) insisted upon its constitutional right to "originate" appropriations measures and not in effect to "review" important budgetary decisions already taken by the House. See *The New York Times*, July 15, 1962.

consisting of approximately 5 Representatives and 20 senators, prepared to do their job of scrutinizing defense appropriations? Even for the House subcommittee, whose members devote full time to this one committee assignment, careful examination of the national defense budget is a well-nigh impossible task. Committee studies tend to be highly selective and often bog down into a discussion of petty details, frequently those relating to a member's constituency. Especially in time of war or cold war, committee members must lean heavily upon the judgments of military commanders. One legislator commented that during World War II, "The War Department, or . . . General Marshall . . . virtually dictated the budget."[34] Legislators concede that they are not skilled military strategists and that they must often accept the word of military spokesmen that certain expenditures are necessary. A member of the House subcommittee told military officials in 1950 that " . . . we are not kidding ourselves. We know we cannot go into every dollar of expenditure. We can do our best, but we have to trust you gentlemen to wisely spend, under the policies which we approve, funds which we appropriate."[35]

This dependence is reflected too in the tendency of the two appropriations committees to grant the military departments considerable discretion in spending, especially in time of national crises. Flexibility is assured through a variety of bookkeeping devices, such as transfer of funds from one budget item to another, carry-overs from year to year, provision of funds under very broad titles, and emergency and contingent funds. A classic case was development of the atomic bomb during World War II. Over $800 million was spent by the military before even the members of the appropriations committees knew that the Manhattan Project was well under way. Normally the President and the Secretary of Defense have sizable contingent funds, which they may use in whatever manner they think necessary to protect national security.[36]

We have devoted considerable space in this chapter to the importance of Congress's control over the purse strings as a means of influencing foreign relations, because this is a subject that has not yet received the attention its importance deserves. What then are we to conclude about this power? It is apparent that Congress today relies upon it perhaps more than upon any other technique to affect defense and foreign policy. Yet many significant obstacles remain in the path of intelligent and effective use of this power. Congress has come to see that great discretion must often be given to executive policy-makers if national security is to be preserved. While Congress has ultimate power of the purse, it understands today, perhaps more than at any time in American history, that the entire nation is dependent upon enlightened executive leadership.

The Congressional Power to "Declare War"

Another constitutional provision intended to give Congress substantial control over military and foreign policy is its right to "declare war." This power, as we noted in Chapter 3, has largely lost its original significance. No longer do nations give advance notice of their intention to go to war. Pearl Harbor and the communist attack on South Korea in 1950 must be regarded as typical of the way enemies are likely to begin conquests today.

The congressional power to declare war "has never prevented war when the President wanted one."[37] Historical evidence abounds to support this contention—from Polk's belligerent position toward Mexico in the 1840s, to Cleveland's militant stand during the Venezuelan boundary dispute with Britain in 1897, to FDR's "shoot on sight" order to the navy in dealing with Nazi U-boats before World War II, to Truman's intervention in the Korean War in 1950, to President Kennedy's military intervention in South Vietnam and his proclamation of a naval blockade against Castro's Cuba in 1962. Presidents have thus not hesitated to protect national security whenever it was threatened and in whatever manner was required under the circumstances.* While it is expected that, in most major military conflicts at least, the President will get Congress

---

* An interesting illustration of the chief executive's power in this regard was afforded by President Kennedy's response to the increasingly grave communist challenge to South Vietnam in the early 1960s. As the Kennedy Administration expanded the American military involvement in this strategic country, its critics asserted that the United States was engaged in a de facto war, without the consent of Congress. Kennedy justified the American buildup in Southeast Asia by saying (1) that forces of the United States were chiefly for purposes of "training and transportation" in assisting native troops to meet the communist challenge, and (2) that American troops were authorized to fire upon Communists when necessary for their self-defense. See Richard P. Stebbins, *The United States in World Affairs: 1962* (New York: Harper & Row, 1963), p. 195.

to declare war, its declaration merely confirms the self-evident: that military hostilities actually exist between the United States and other countries.

The right of Congress to declare war is less important as a legislative permit to engage in hostilities than in two other particulars. One of these relates to public opinion. Nothing perhaps so dramatically conveys the unified determination of the American people to protect their interests as the spectacle of both houses of Congress overwhelmingly approving the President's resort to armed force in a crisis.* This gesture both unites the home front and serves notice to the enemy that all agencies of the government are whole-heartedly behind the national effort required to safeguard the nation's interests. Second, a congressional declaration of war has important legal consequences. Numerous legislative grants of authority to the President take effect during periods of war and national emergency; these give the chief executive vast powers he does not ordinarily have in peacetime.

General Legislative Authority in Foreign Affairs

Along with its control over appropriations, Congress has general legislative authority over foreign policy or related domestic policy measures. Congress, for example, decides the legal framework within which executive departments operate. This power may range from establishing an agency like the National Security Council, specifying its powers and personnel, and maintaining supervision over its operations by means of its investigative power, to giving the President wide discretion in the realm of reciprocal tariff reductions with other nations. Eventually, almost all continuing governmental activities at home and abroad require legislative support. Yet, as Robert Dahl has

written, "Perhaps the single most important fact about Congress and its role in foreign policy . . . is that it rarely provides the initiative. . . . in foreign policy the President proposes, the Congress disposes—and in a very large number of highly important decisions . . . the Congress does not even have the opportunity to dispose."[38] Chapter 3 called attention to a number of techniques by which a forceful President may virtually compel favorable congressional action. Congress can pass upon executive proposals by accepting them, modifying them, or rejecting them; but it does not usually formulate them without considerable assistance from the executive branch. It realizes that intimate executive-legislative collaboration is required in the foreign policy field, because Congress possesses neither the requisite information nor the expert judgment nor the time to arrive at sound decisions unilaterally.

An illustrative episode occurred in 1948, when Congress was considering the Marshall Plan. The staff director of the Republican Policy Committee** showed GOP senators a stack of material 18 inches high, consisting of documentary material already assembled on the Marshall Plan, exclusive of appropriations committee reports since these were not yet ready. Asked by a senator how long it would take to assimilate this material, the director replied that it would require him two months of reading, providing he had no other duties. The senator then estimated that it would take the average member of Congress from four to five months to go through the material.[39] The Marshall Plan, of course, was but one among many important measures considered by Congress in 1948. Subsequent years did not make this problem any less acute. As an illustration, the hearings conducted by the House Appropriations Committee on the Department of Defense appropriation for fiscal year 1960 totaled more than 4000 printed pages! This voluminous record did not include separate hearings held on the provision of American military assistance to foreign countries. Added to the difficulty of assimilating such a tremendous volume of information is the often chaotic organization of material within the printed record of hearings, and the tendency of committees to have statistics, charts, and other data scattered helter-skelter throughout several volumes of testimony. Moreover, the

---

* This aspect of Congress's power to declare war was fully understood by President Eisenhower in dealing with Communist Chinese threats in the Formosa Straits in 1955. Early in that year, the President asked Congress to pass the "Formosa Resolution," giving him stand-by authority to use armed force if necessary to repulse a Communist attack on the Nationalist Chinese regime on Formosa. In requesting this authority, the President publicly stated that authority "for some of the actions which might be required would be inherent in the authority of the Commander-in-Chief"; yet a "suitable congressional resolution" would "clearly and publicly establish the authority of the President" and make clear "the unified and serious intentions" of the United States. Dwight D. Eisenhower, *Mandate for Change: 1953–1956* (New York: Doubleday, 1963), pp. 467–468.

** This is a party, as distinct from a legislative, committee in the Senate.

indexes to such hearings often are so sketchy as to make it nearly impossible to pinpoint information on selected subjects.

While Congress normally concedes the primacy of the President in foreign relations, this is not to say that the legislative branch never takes the initiative or fails to insist upon its own point of view, even in the face of evident White House opposition. For instance, in 1948, the House Foreign Affairs Committee initiated a bill to provide military assistance to Western Europe, but the bill was abandoned when it failed to receive White House endorsement. A year later, however, the Mutual Defense Assistance Program substantially embodied the committee's recommendations.[40] In the more recent period, Congress has not been reluctant about insisting upon its own viewpoints in certain areas of foreign policy, especially those in which it could safely defy presidential wishes without jeopardy to national security. A recurrent theme, for example, has been legislative insistence that a fixed percentage of American foreign assistance be used to promote private enterprise abroad. Despite the opposition of the Kennedy Administration, the House in 1963 added an amendment to the Mutual Security Program requiring that at least 50 percent of the funds be expended for this purpose.[41] Another area of acute legislative sensitivity and intensity of feeling has been America's relations with "neutralist" countries such as Indonesia, India, Egypt, and Yugoslavia. Since the emergence of neutralism as an influential global force around 1955, congressional attitudes have often been openly hostile to the movement. On innumerable occasions, Congress has taken steps designed to convey widespread American skepticism about the neutralist outlook. A dramatic and possibly far-reaching case occurred in the summer of 1962, when the House Ways and Means Committee reported a bill denying neutralist Yugoslavia "most-favored-nation" tariff preferences, granted to most countries friendly with the United States. This move reflected deep congressional and perhaps national disillusionment with "Titoism." Congress was not deterred from pursuing this course by the conviction of American Ambassador to Yugoslavia George F. Kennan; it was "the greatest windfall Soviet diplomacy could encounter in this area."[42] Similarly, Congress has from time to time expressed its undisguised opposition to Arab belligerency toward Israel, toward the policies of nationalist regimes such as President Nasser's in Egypt,

and toward traditional Arab monarchies such as the one in the tiny Arabian principality of Yemen. During the Eisenhower Administration, Sherman Adams has stated, "the members of Congress were acutely aware of the strong popular sentiment in this country for Israel." Executive efforts to work out more harmonious relations with Nasser, and to bring about Israeli withdrawal from Egyptian territory following the Suez crisis of 1956, met recurrent opposition on Capitol Hill.[43] An indication of congressional attitudes came in August, 1963, when the House Foreign Affairs Committee threatened to cut off all American foreign assistance to Egypt unless Nasser's government withdrew its military forces from Yemen and modified its long-standing hostility to Israel.[44] Deep misgivings about the foreign policy of India have also periodically been voiced in Congress in the recent period. Legislators have been especially chagrined by the failure of India to come to an agreement with Pakistan in the long-smoldering Kashmir issue. In the summer of 1963, the House Foreign Affairs Committee frankly warned India and Pakistan that American economic assistance would be drastically curtailed if progress were not forthcoming in resolving the Kashmir question.[45]

Although it concedes wide latitude to the executive to manage foreign relations, Congress nevertheless has come to expect prolonged executive-legislative consultation before important policies are announced and before international commitments are assumed that require implementing funds. Congress, said a subcommittee of the House Foreign Affairs Committee in 1948, can

. . . no longer be confronted with agreements involving commitments requiring Congressional appropriations without prior consultation. Repeated attempts by the Executive to force Congressional action by this technique may result in embarrassing the Executive rather than the Congress.[46]

The problem, then, in the face of recurrent external crises requiring forceful American leadership, is that of coordinating executive and legislative efforts.

EXTRACONSTITUTIONAL AND INFORMAL TECHNIQUES

Legislative Investigations and Foreign Affairs

During the year 1961, the Senate alone conducted the following investigations touching national security and foreign policy: the Aeronautical and Space Science Committee investigated the National Aeronautical and Space Administration; the Armed Services Committee carried on three investigations—into problems in the Defense Department, strategic weapons and delivery systems, and secret hearings on the Central Intelligence Agency; the Commerce Committee looked into the problem of foreign competition in textile manufacturing; the Foreign Relations Committee held eight different investigations into various aspects of foreign policy; the Government Operations Committee evaluated national policy machinery; and the Judiciary Committee held seven hearings having ramifications for foreign affairs.[47]

These examples call attention to the extent to which a highly effective instrument for asserting legislative influence in foreign relations is Congress's powers of investigation. Legislative investigations had comparatively little influence upon foreign policy before World War II. The only significant exception was the Nye Committee investigation during the 1930s into the influence of the munitions makers on American foreign policy before and during World War I. Its findings were highly instrumental in creating an isolationist climate of opinion within the United States by supporting the view that America had been drawn into the war by the intrigues of profit-hungry industrialists.[48]

During and after World War II, legislative investigations probed virtually every phase of American foreign policy. Conducted by several important committees of Congress, whose members differed widely in knowledge about foreign policy and in attachment to traditional democratic principles of fair procedure, the results of these investigations were decidedly mixed. Some committees unquestionably injured the prestige of the United States at home and abroad and jeopardized the stability of its foreign relations. Other investigations have resulted in needed clarifications of national policy and in improved administration.

One of the most far-reaching clashes in American history between executive and legislative prerogatives over national defense policy occurred when the Committee on the Conduct of the War tried to compel President Lincoln to follow congressional advice during the Civil War. The Committee on the Conduct of the War

was encouraged . . . by the public impatience at the slowness with which military operations against the Confederacy were proceeding. . . . They consistently urged a more vigorous prosecution of the war and less lenience toward the institution of slavery. . . . So far did the committee depart from its legitimate purpose that it became a veritable thorn in the flesh of the President. The members took over partial control of military operations. Their investigating missions to the front undermined army discipline and discouraged the more capable commanders. . . . Interrogating generals as if they were schoolboys and advising the President like military experts, they sought to intimidate Lincoln by threatening to arouse Congress against him.[49]

With certain modifications, this description might also apply to postwar investigations of American foreign policy in the Far East, of the problem of East-West trade, and of the operations of the Voice of America.

Yet legislative investigations have also made important positive contributions to American foreign and closely related domestic policies. A model constructive investigation was that carried on by the Truman Committee during World War II.* Binkley believes that the Truman Committee represented the "highest development of the congressional investigating committee," and that Senator Truman perhaps contributed more than any other civilian except the President to the winning of the war.[50] The committee grew out of Senator Truman's conviction that Congress ought to carry on investigations while waste could still be eliminated from the war effort and unsound practices could be corrected, instead of waiting until after the war when it could do no more than try to assess the blame for failures. By contrast, after World War I there had been over a hundred congressional investigations, most of them "motivated by partisan desires to fix blame on the opposition"; they had "raked over the coals for more than fifteen years after the war."[51]

The model afforded by the Truman Committee was forgotten by many investigating committees after World War II. The relationship between their activities and legislation was often ill-defined, if not altogether nonexistent. This was especially true of committees whose primary jurisdictions lay outside the field of foreign relations or national security

* This committee, known as the Special Senate Committee Investigating the National Defense Program, was established in March, 1941, and was named for its chairman, Senator Harry S Truman (Democrat of Missouri).

and whose members had little first-hand knowledge of these areas. During the 1940s and 1950s, subcommittees of the House Un-American Activities Committee, the Senate Judiciary Committee, or the Senate Committee on Government Operations roamed afield looking for officials who were responsible for the "loss" of China to communism, for Soviet control over Eastern Europe, or for subversive groups that supposedly led national policymakers astray at critical junctures throughout recent diplomatic history. If such investigations were noteworthy for their barren results, a fundamental long-range consequence indirectly stemming from them was to inculcate an utterly false—one might say, potentially disastrous—illusion in the public mind, which often compounded the problem of formulating and carrying out effective policies in the recent period. This was a new devil theory of diplomacy, comparable to the one gripping the American mind after World War I. If the foreign policy of the United States during and after World War II sometimes left much to be desired in an area like the Far East, for example, the assumption guiding such investigations was that the nation's diplomatic interests had been "betrayed" by Democratic officials in high places. Such assumptions typified the "illusion of American omnipotence," a corollary of which was the widespread belief that events in the outside world could be altered at the will of the United States. When experience sometimes proved otherwise, then betrayal—not pervasive ignorance and indifference about complex developments abroad, not lack of sound diplomatic judgments, not failure to appraise global political currents correctly, not realization that America's great power is finite—was advanced as the only possible explanation. If even intensive legislative investigations frequently had difficulty identifying the subversive influences operating upon American policies, in many cases this was because they were such obvious and fundamental, if unspectacular, forces as widespread public apathy about international events, unrealistic public and official expectations, and unwillingness to pay the price that a successful policy exacted—failures often as evident on Capitol Hill as anywhere else in the nation.

Nevertheless, with all their apparent faults—many of which can be, and some of which have been, corrected—congressional investigations can make a useful contribution to American foreign policy. A most valuable investigation in the postwar era was the joint Senate Foreign Relations–Armed Services Committee investigation into President Truman's dismissal of General Douglas MacArthur in 1951. MacArthur was a distinguished national hero. During the Korean War, he seemed to many citizens to stand unflinchingly against certain unwholesome tendencies: appeasement of the Communists, kow-towing to the allies, and undue surrender of sovereignty to the United Nations. His dismissal precipitated what William S. White has called "the gravest and most emotional Constitutional crisis that the United States has known since the Great Depression."[52] Seldom in American history has the principle of civilian control over the military been in such great jeopardy as when President Truman, after repeated provocations, finally ordered MacArthur home from Korea.

Under the strong leadership of Senator Richard Russell (Democrat of Georgia), the joint committee conducted a prolonged investigation into MacArthur's dismissal, and in the process probed into recent American policies in the Far East. As the facts came to light, the congressional and national furor subsided. Not even Republicans cared to challenge the President's *right* to dismiss the General. Throughout its investigation, the committee sought unity among its members. Its final "Message to the American People," says White "dissolved a national emotionalism the exact like of which had not heretofore been seen. . . ." The committee "protected not only the American tradition of the pre-eminent civil authority; [it] halted what was then an almost runaway movement toward rejection of the United Nations."[53]

The verdict, then, on legislative investigations in foreign affairs is that sometimes they have been instruments for legislative mischief. If they followed the lead of several distinguished committees within recent American history, they could be instruments for good and make a beneficial contribution to public policy and administration.

Congressional Resolutions

Legislative resolutions expressing the opinion of Congress on questions of public policy are not law and have no binding force on the executive. Nevertheless, they can be important techniques by which Congress influences the course of foreign relations. We have already mentioned the Vandenberg Resolution, which initiated negotiations leading to the North

Atlantic Treaty in 1949. Similarly, American relations with Red China have been heavily influenced by two legislative resolutions adopted in 1951. At that time, both houses of Congress branded Red China an "aggressor" for intervening in the Korean War late in 1950. The Senate resolution went further by expressing the conviction that Red China should not be admitted to the United Nations. These resolutions unquestionably expressed the dominant sentiment of the American people. Presidents Truman, Eisenhower, Kennedy, and Johnson have been unprepared to override legislative and public opinion on this issue.*

Neither the White House nor Congress operates in a vacuum. Each is highly sensitive to public opinion and to deep convictions held by officials in the other branch. Whenever possible, the President and Congress prefer to adopt policies that can command wide public support. Congressional resolutions on foreign policy issues are thus important barometers of opinion for the executive. They may reflect deep public concern about contemporary policy issues; they may call attention forcefully to widespread dissatisfaction with existing policies; and they may strengthen the President's hand in dealing with other countries by conveying the impression abroad of unanimity within the American government.

Speeches and Activities of Individual Legislators

Closely related to formal legislative resolutions as a means for affecting foreign policy are the speeches and activities of individual members of Congress. The lack of strict party discipline in the legislature, along with the tradition

of legislative freedom of speech, most notably in the Senate, gives members wide latitude to comment publicly on outstanding international issues. They may do this by delivering formal speeches or impromptu remarks; by introducing bills and amendments to bills; by inserting material into the *Congressional Record*; by holding press conferences; by making speeches outside Congress, especially over radio and television channels; by "leaking" information to the press; by traveling abroad; and in a variety of other ways. Expressions of opinion on Capitol Hill are studied carefully by other governments.

A few examples from American diplomatic history must suffice to highlight the importance of this phenomenon. Adverse Senate reaction to the Treaty of Versailles, resulting in ultimate Senate rejection of that document, colored the American approach to international organization for the next two decades. Then in the 1920s, Japanese-American relations were substantially influenced by the opposition of legislators (notably those from the West Coast) to continued Japanese immigration to the United States. Anti-Japanese sentiment on Capitol Hill, in the words of one study, became a "sore point in relations with Japan, to the discomfiture of the Department of State."[54]

In the years after World War II, individual legislators time and again affected the course of American foreign relations. Thus until his death, Senator Pat McCarran (Democrat of Nevada) almost single-handedly shaped Congress's attitude on questions of immigration and refugee relief. He and President Truman were constantly at odds over the admittance of displaced persons from Europe. McCarran remained a determined foe of any proposed liberalization of immigration quotas.[55] Conversely, under President Truman, two senators —Arthur H. Vandenberg (Republican of Michigan) and Tom Connally (Democrat of Texas) —alternated as chairman of the Foreign Relations Committee when their party controlled Congress. Both were individuals of strong opinions about foreign affairs; their voices carried considerable weight in the deliberations of their party; and both maintained firm control over committee proceedings, so that ill-considered and hasty legislation, or measures the chairman did not support, were usually killed in committee. On one occasion, for example, Senator Connally admitted frankly what he intended to do with a measure introduced by

---

* Other legislative resolutions in the postwar era have requested the President to use his efforts to promote the economic and political unification of Europe; to bring Spain into the NATO defense system; to investigate—with a view to curtailing—trade between America's cold war allies and the Communist bloc; to take the lead in condemning Soviet suppression of the Hungarian revolt in 1956; to sponsor various proposals aimed at strengthening the United Nations; and to authorize the President to use military force, if necessary, for the achievement of national policy goals in areas like the Far East, the Middle East, and the Caribbean. See: Cecil V. Crabb, Jr., *Bipartisan Foreign Policy: Myth or Reality?* (New York: Harper & Row, 1957), p. 252; Guy M. Gillette, "The Senate in Foreign Relations," *Annals of the American Academy of Political and Social Science*, **289** (September, 1953), 57; Carl Marcy and Francis O. Wilcox, "Congress and the United Nations," *Foreign Policy Reports*, **27** (May 15, 1951), 50–55.

Senator William Knowland (Republican of California), a staunch and persistent advocate of militant American policies against communism in Asia. Pressed by Knowland for favorable committee action, Connally stated: "I assure the Senator from California that this matter will have in the Foreign Relations Committee exactly the consideration that it so richly deserves . . . "—whereupon Connally looked up at the press gallery and drew his finger dramatically across his throat.[56]

In William S. White's expressive phraseology:

A senate committee is an imperious force; its chairman, unless he be a weak and irresolute man, is emperor. It makes in its field in ninety-nine cases out of a hundred the real decisions of the Institution itself. What bills it approves are approved by the Senate; what bills it rejects are rejected, with rare exceptions. . . . To override, say, the Committee on Foreign Relations or the Committee on Finance involves a parliamentary convulsion scarcely less severe, as the Senate sees it, than that accompanying the overturn, say, of a British government. And in fact the one crisis . . . will hardly occur so frequently as will the other.[57]

Under the rules of each chamber the chairman is in a position virtually to dictate what measures will be considered by his committee and hence by Congress as a whole. Only he can call the committee into session, and many chairmen have been dilatory about doing this to delay consideration of measures they did not support. Senator Pat McCarran, for instance, was able to delay legislative consideration of a displaced persons act recommended by President Truman in 1948–1949, through prolonged and deliberate absence on an "inspection trip" to Europe. The committee could do little during his absence.

Yet the ability to influence foreign policy, sometimes decisively, is by no means limited to chairmen of important legislative committees or to members of the committees concerned with foreign relations. Two noteworthy cases occurred in President Kennedy's administration. In 1962, Senator Henry M. Jackson, a member of the Government Operations Committee, made a widely publicized speech urging the United States not to count too heavily upon the United Nations to protect its security or to achieve its diplomatic objectives. His speech, as the Kennedy Administration was aware, unquestionably reflected the

viewpoints of other legislators and of millions of American citizens. For that reason, and because he was a member of Kennedy's own party, it had wide repercussions both within the United States and outside it.[58] At the end of the same year, Senator Allen J. Ellender (Democrat of Louisiana) caused great consternation among executive officials because of his uninhibited remarks during and after a tour of the African continent. During his tour, Senator Ellender stated candidly that "I have yet to see any part of Africa where Africans are ready for self-government." The senator implied (although he later denied the implication) that indigenous African governments would require "help" from white countries for the next half-century. Subsequently, Senator Ellender accused State Department officials of "tiptoe diplomacy," in their refusal to accept such unpleasant truths out of fear of offending "thin-skinned politicians" in Africa.[59] Not unexpectedly, such remarks deeply affronted African sensibilities and seriously complicated the task of forging more harmonious African-American relations. In this and comparable cases, the State Department was obliged to remind other countries that Congress was an equal and coordinate branch of the American government, that legislators were free to voice their individual opinions on global issues, but that the senator's views did not represent the foreign policy of the nation as formulated by the President and his subordinates.

Congressional Travel

During the first six months of 1957, study missions from the House Foreign Affairs Committee visited the following countries:

Austria	Guatemala	Norway
Belgium	Luxembourg	Poland
France	Mexico	Spain
Germany	Netherlands	United Kingdom
Greece	Nicaragua	Yugoslavia

In this period, members of the committee also attended the NATO Parliamentary Conference, the autumn meeting of the 12th session of the United Nations General Assembly, and the inauguration of the President of Nicaragua.[60]

Extensive congressional travel is a comparatively recent phenomenon. The first year in which legislators traveled abroad to inspect the operations of an overseas diplomatic mission was in 1936. Since that time, individual legislators and study missions have traveled widely. For example, a total of two hundred legislators went abroad in 1947–1948 to study conditions in Europe that necessitated the Marshall Plan. Today it is a rare congressman who cannot find one reason or another to go abroad every year or two on an investigation tour—whether it be studying the administration of technical assistance in India, conditions in American military posts in the NATO area, conflict along the Israeli-Egyptian border, or communist activities in Latin America.

Information gained by legislative travel now gives Congress a competence in foreign affairs it did not possess in an earlier period, when it had to depend almost entirely upon the judgments of executive officials. In certain cases, investigations abroad can have highly significant consequences for foreign policy. Thus the Herter Committee which devoted weeks to collecting data abroad about Europe's economic condition in the 1947–1948 period was extremely influential in generating legislative support for the Marshall Plan.

That foreign travel provides legislators opportunities to develop greater expertise and deeper insight in the realm of foreign affairs can hardly be doubted. The State Department, in fact, has on occasion even suggested to committees that some of their members go abroad to inspect overseas operations, such as administration of the Mutual Security Program. In such cases, and even when the initiative comes from the committee, the State Department works closely with legislative groups to plan itineraries, furnish liaison officers and guides, arrange interviews and entertainment, and make other necessary arrangements.

Within recent years the cost of these trips has largely been borne out of "counterpart funds"—that is, foreign balances accruing to the credit of the United States. Such balances are built up as foreign governments repay the United States for various economic and technical assistance programs. These funds must usually be spent within the foreign country itself. Even after counterpart funds are used to defray administrative expenses of foreign aid programs and the costs of American defense efforts within the country, large accruals remain that can be used to finance legislative travel within the country. In a literal sense, therefore, trips by legislative groups abroad do not cost the American taxpayer anything, particularly if they point to ways of eliminating duplication or unnecessary expenditures in overseas military

and economic aid programs. Even so, by the early 1960s, the growing number of legislative "junkets" abroad had fallen under increasing public criticism in the United States, where the feeling existed that in many cases more constructive uses of counterpart funds could be found and that the results achieved from extensive legislative travel were sometimes not commensurate with the cost involved.

Congress and Foreign Policy—the Continuing Problem

The numerous and varied opportunities available to legislators to influence American foreign relations sometimes create serious obstacles in the formulation and execution of clear and sustained foreign policies. The public views and activities of 100 senators and 435 representatives can on occasion create a veritable cacophony in the foreign policy field. Other countries, unaccustomed to the vagaries of a government whose constitutional cornerstone is the doctrine of separation of powers, often have difficulty disentangling what they see and hear in the executive branch and in Congress, and arriving at a true expression of American foreign policy. They fail to consider that speeches made by legislators may be calculated to assure and edify local constituents and to aid in re-election.

Within the United States, the governmental orchestra suffers from a superfluity of soloists. Players chronically tend to ignore the conductor—occasionally domestic and foreign observers may even wonder if all are playing the same music. In such cases the United States is at a grave disadvantage in the management of its foreign relations. Techniques have evolved throughout American history, particularly in the postwar period, designed to assure a reasonable degree of harmonious orchestration. We shall examine these techniques in Chapter 6.

NOTES

1. Chester E. Merrow, "United States Leadership in a Divided World," *Annals of the American Academy of Political and Social Science*, 289 (September, 1952), 8.
2. The activities of the committee in 1957 are described in detail in House Foreign Affairs Committee, *Survey of Activities of the Committee on Foreign Affairs*, 85th Congress, 1st Session, January 3–August 30, 1957, *passim*. This series provides a useful

source for illustrating Congress's expanding role in foreign policy.

3. Albert C. F. Westphal, *The House Committee on Foreign Affairs* (New York: Columbia University Press, 1942), pp. 13–26. This volume provides useful information on the committee's role down to the period of World War II.

4. James P. Richards, "The House of Representatives in Foreign Affairs," *Annals of the American Academy of Political and Social Science*, **289** (September, 1953), 67.

5. Cecil V. Crabb, Jr., *Bipartisan Foreign Policy: Myth or Reality?* (New York: Harper & Row, 1957), pp. 14–15.

6. Mike Mansfield, "The Meaning of the Term 'Advice and Consent,' " *Annals of the American Academy of Political and Social Science*, **289** (September, 1953), 127–133.

7. Allan Nevins, *Henry White* (New York: Harper & Row, 1930, pp. 397–404.

8. Guy M. Gillette, "The Senate in Foreign Relations," *Annals of the American Academy of Political and Social Science*, **289** (September, 1953), 52–53.

9. Arthur H. Vandenberg, Jr., ed., *The Private Papers of Senator Vandenberg* (Boston: Houghton Mifflin, 1952), pp. 403–408. An indispensable primary source dealing with the career of perhaps the most influential legislator in recent American foreign relations.

10. John Foster Dulles, *A Peace Treaty in the Making* (San Francisco: Japanese Peace Conference, September 4–8, 1951). Describes Dulles's extensive efforts to draft an acceptable treaty with Japan.

11. Felix Nigro, "Senate Confirmation and Foreign Policy," *Journal of Politics*, **14** (May, 1952), 281–283.

12. *Ibid.*, pp. 290–291.

13. *Ibid.*, pp. 292–293.

14. *Ibid.*, pp. 294–298.

15. Sherman Adams, *First-Hand Report: The Story of the Eisenhower Administration* (New York: Harper & Row, 1961), pp. 376, 379. An account, by an intimate adviser of President Eisenhower, that provides a valuable primary source for the period 1952–1960.

16. Dwight D. Eisenhower, *Mandate for Change: 1953–1956* (Garden City, N.Y.: Doubleday, 1963), pp. 214–215. President Eisenhower's memoirs afford an indispensable source on American foreign relations during his administration.

17. *The New York Times*, August 21 and 24, 1963.

18. Quoted in Elias Huzar, *The Purse and the Sword* (Ithaca, N.Y.: Cornell University Press, 1950), p. 26. A definitive study of congressional control over the military, through the power of the purse.

19. *Congressional Quarterly Almanac: 1958*, **14**, 59–60.

20. Quoted in Huzar, *op. cit.*, pp. 396–397.

21. Quoted in *ibid.*, p. 40.

22. Congress's investigations of the Marshall Plan are described in Crabb, *op. cit.*, pp. 62–64.

23. *Congressional Record*, **94**, 7168.

24. Vandenberg, *op. cit.*, pp. 397–398.

25. See House Appropriations Committee, *The Departments of State and Justice, the Judiciary and Related Agencies—Appropriations for 1960*, 86th Congress, 1st Session, Washington; 1959, pp. 1–20, 24–41, 105–109. This series affords an illuminating source for illustrating legislative attitudes toward the State Department.

26. William L. Rivers, "The Foreign Policy of John J. Rooney," *The Reporter*, **24** (June 22, 1961), 36–38.

27. Huzar, *op. cit.*, p. 19.

28. Quoted in *ibid.*, p. 132.

29. For the Truman Administration's views on national defense, see Stephen K. Bailey and Howard D. Samuel, *Congress at Work* (New York: Holt, Rinehart & Winston, 1952), p. 381. For a similar situation under Eisenhower, see Eisenhower, *op. cit.*, pp. 445–458.

30. Eisenhower, *op. cit.*, p. 454.

31. Huzar, *op. cit.*, p. 45.

32. Arthur W. MacMahon, "Congressional Oversight of Administration: The Power of the Purse," *Political Science Quarterly*, **58** (June, 1943), 174. Despite the fact that it was written more than 20 years ago, this article (and its continuation in *ibid.*, September, 1943, pp. 380–414) still affords illuminating insight into Congress's use of the appropriations power.

33. Huzar, *op. cit.*, pp. 29–34.

34. Quoted in *ibid.*, p. 58.

35. Quoted in *ibid.*, p. 62.

36. See *ibid.*, p. 320; 336–341.

37. Quincy Wright, "International Law in Relation to Constitutional Law," *American Journal of International Law*, **17** (April, 1923), 235.

38. Robert A. Dahl, *Congress and Foreign Policy* (New York: Harcourt, Brace & World, 1950), p. 58. Calls attention forcefully to obstacles impeding effective legislative participation in foreign affairs.

39. *Ibid.*, pp. 129–130.

40. Robert B. Chiperfield. "The Committee on Foreign Affairs," *Annals of the American Academy of Political and Social Science*, **289** (September, 1953), 80–81.

41. *The New York Times*, August 22, 1963.
42. *The New York Times*, June 17, 1962.
43. Adams, *op. cit.*, pp. 247–248, 279–280.
44. *The New York Times*, August 10, 1963.
45. *Ibid.*
46. Quoted in William L. Langer, "The Mechanism of American Foreign Policy," *International Affairs*, 24 (July, 1948), 327.
47. *Congressional Quarterly Almanac: 1961*, 17, 996–998.
48. James A. Perkins, "Congressional Investigations of Matters of International Import," *American Political Science Review*, 34 (April, 1940), 285. Perkins's article furnishes a succinct treatment of the evolution of legislative investigating power in foreign affairs.
49. Wilfred E. Binkley, *President and Congress* (New York: Knopf, 1947), p. 115.
50. *Ibid.*, pp. 268–269.
51. Bailey and Samuel, *op. cit.*, p. 296.
52. William S. White, *Citadel: The Story of the U.S. Senate* (New York: Harper & Row, 1957), p. 242. Written by an experienced journalist, this is a provocative, though sometimes highly impressionistic, account.
53. *Ibid.*, p. 250.
54. Bertram D. Hulen, *Inside the Department of State* (New York: Whittlesley House, 1939), p. 246.
55. Bailey and Samuel, *op. cit.*, pp. 256–257.
56. Quoted in White, *op. cit.*, p. 190.
57. *Ibid.*, p. 181.
58. See the *New York Herald Tribune*, March 21, 1962, and the *Congressional Quarterly Almanac: 1962*, 18, 326.
59. *Washington Post*, March 8, 1963.
60. House Foreign Affairs Committee, *Survey of Activities of the Committee on Foreign Affairs*, *op. cit.*, p. 6.

6 ➡ EXECUTIVE-LEGISLATIVE RELATIONS AND BIPARTISANSHIP ➡

The astute Frenchman Alexis de Tocqueville once observed that a democracy

> is unable to regulate the details of an important undertaking [in foreign affairs], to persevere in a design, and to work out its execution in the presence of serious obstacles. It cannot combine its measures with secrecy, and it will not await their consequences with patience.[1]

That de Tocqueville's perceptiveness has stood the test of experience is plainly indicated by American diplomatic history. The eminent historian and former State Department official George F. Kennan has likened the American democracy to "one of those prehistoric monsters with a body as long as this room and a brain the size of a pin. . . ." He lies in the mud inert for long periods, but when aroused "he lays about him with such blind determination that he not only destroys his adversary but largely wrecks his native habitat." Like the monster, the American approach to foreign relations has often oscillated between "an undiscriminating indifference" and "a holy wrath equally undiscriminating."[2]

These comments—separated by over a century of American diplomatic history and by innumerable instances of public turmoil at home over important international issues—point to a problem that has increasingly engaged the attention of scholars and commentators. Some have even wondered whether the American democracy is congenitally incapable of carrying out sustained and effective foreign policies in the midst of recurrent international crises, within a domestic environment of chronic citizen apathy and lack of understanding of complex external problems. The gravity of international problems in the nuclear age, coupled with the well-nigh infinite possibilities prevailing within the United States for disrupting the continuity and stability of foreign policy, create formidable difficulties for American policy-makers. Communist officials are largely unhampered by such potentially divisive forces as a constitutional doctrine of separation of powers, an outspoken opposition party, active and resourceful pressure groups, or vocal public opinion. They therefore possess an enormous advantage over the United States and other democratic governments, with respect to ability to formulate long-range diplomatic objectives and to carry them out with a minimum of opposition and disruption within the government and throughout the nation as a whole.

Events since World War II have given unrivaled urgency to the problem of government-wide coordination of efforts in the diplomatic field and of finding means to reduce to a minimum the public turbulence that has characterized American foreign relations at intervals in the past. Yet, if the necessity for greater unity has become apparent, so has the difficulty of securing it. Opportunities for internal contention over foreign policy and for intragovernmental conflict have multiplied with the grow-ing complexity of international problems and with the greater American involvement in world affairs. The close entanglement of inter-nal and external policy measures has com-pounded the problem, with the result that no clear delineation between them is now pos-sible.

Disunity in American Diplomatic History

As a generalization, it may be said that im-portant foreign policy questions in American history have always engendered varying degrees of dissension within the national government and throughout the country at large. The only significant exceptions are the major wars in which the nation was engaged—and even then internal disagreement ultimately prevailed over the causes of the war, the degree to which American vital interests were directly involved, postwar political and economic settlements, and related questions. Internal dissension over foreign policy questions can be traced from the earliest days of the Republic over such major issues as the Jay Treaty, the Louisiana Purchase, and the War of 1812, on through the course of the nineteenth century over the Texas controversy and Mexican War, the many ramifications of the slavery issue, and Manifest Destiny, down to the mid-twentieth century.* As an example of disunity in the modern pe-riod, the student of American foreign relations has but to examine closely the fierce partisan and intragovernmental wrangle that character-ized the Roosevelt Administration's efforts to deal with the rising Axis threat during the 1930s, and especially its efforts to secure repeal of American neutrality legislation.[3]

Of all the examples of such disunity that might be cited, one stands out—both because it precipitated an unusually intense domestic controversy over a diplomatic issue and because its ultimate consequences were of singular im-portance. This was President Wilson's bitter fight with Senate Republicans over United States membership in the League of Nations. Wilson's opponents, led by Senator Henry Cabot Lodge of Massachusetts, protested vigorously against his failure to consult the Senate in the early stages of planning for the League of Nations and to include one or more

of their number among his official negotiating party in Europe. Wilson had attempted a rudi-mentary kind of bipartisan collaboration when he took the former diplomat and nominal Re-publican Henry White with him to Paris to provide liaison with the Republican opposition at home. Republicans, however, had little con-fidence in White, and he proved completely in-capable of providing the expected liaison. Meanwhile, Republicans left no doubt about their intentions regarding the Treaty of Ver-sailles; they proposed to emasculate the League of Nations proposal with crippling amend-ments and reservations which would be com-pletely unacceptable to Wilson.[4]

For his part, Wilson evinced little awareness of the strength of his Republican foes and of the isolationist bloc in the Senate. Nor did he demonstrate any inclination to reach agree-ments with it. He adamantly refused to accept even minor modifications of the treaty, and the Senate proved equally unyielding. This deadlock—resulting in America's refusal to join the League of Nations—colored the American approach to international relations for two de-cades thereafter. While it does not constitute a particularly praiseworthy chapter in American diplomatic experience, it at least taught valu-able lessons for future policy-makers. This epi-sode, for example, was the chief impetus in shaping the determination of President Roose-velt and Secretary of State Cordell Hull to avoid a partisan battle during and after World War II, and to work for integrated govern-mental support for the new international or-ganization growing out of the war.

Sources of Conflict in Foreign Relations

The League of Nations controversy high-lighted three potential sources of conflict over foreign policy issues: *institutional discord* be-tween the President and Congress, or the Sen-ate alone; *partisan controversy* over diplomatic questions; and *personal animosity* among key individuals involved in the foreign policy proc-ess. Two additional sources of disunity have become especially pronounced since World War II: *controversy and poorly integrated efforts within Congress and within the execu-tive branch.* In the postwar period, these last two sources of disunity have sometimes proved more troublesome than the more traditional sources.

Internal disunity over foreign affairs as a rule has its origins in a number of tributaries that often converge and re-enforce each other to

* The examples cited here are dealt with at length in Julius W. Pratt, *A History of United States Foreign Policy* (Englewood Cliffs, N.J.: Pren-tice-Hall, 1955), pp. 77–80, 86–104, 125–140, 201–219, 220–236, 237–262, 367–394.

form a floodcrest of controversy and factionalism. Institutional or personal discord may
generate partisan disputes, and vice versa. Dis-
harmony within the executive branch may
produce confusion and diffuse efforts within
Congress. A number of techniques, most of
them evolved during the postwar period, have
been used for the prevention of internal instability when major foreign policy decisions confront
the nation. Collectively, these techniques for
generating unity comprise what has come to be
called a bipartisan approach to foreign relations.*

BIPARTISAN TECHNIQUES AND PROCEDURES

Before analyzing the specific practices associated with bipartisan collaboration in foreign
affairs, a word of caution is in order. From its
inception, the concept of bipartisanship was,
and remains, exceedingly fluid and elastic. Admittedly, widespread agreement has existed
since World War II that governmental unity
was desirable—sometimes, imperative—in dealing with major external problems. Members of
both great political parties have customarily
agreed upon the necessity for unity. Yet
substantial controversy has continued to surround the question of the precise techniques
and procedures best calculated to achieve it.
Certain practices associated with bipartisan
foreign policy have commanded almost universal support. Others have met with various
degrees of opposition. In practice, the executive branch has come to advocate some practices strongly, while members of Congress
prefer other procedures for generating bipartisan support for foreign policy decisions.
New bipartisan techniques are continually
evolving in the light of experience. Meanwhile,
disagreement among individuals and agencies
concerned with the foreign policy process
periodically breaks out over the exact scope and
meaning of bipartisanship in foreign affairs.
The precise connotations of the concept, and
many of its implications, have not been, and
for reasons that will become apparent presently,
perhaps cannot be, defined with exactitude.

* Occasionally, other terms like "nonpartisan" or
"unpartisan" are used to designate the approach desired. Bipartisanship is employed throughout this
chapter, however, because it conveys more forcefully
the idea of *collaboration* in formulating important
foreign policy measures. Such collaboration has come
to be regarded as the principal prerequisite of a
bipartisan approach.

Prior Consultations on Foreign Policy Measures

Among the practices associated with bipartisan foreign policy, none is more fundamental
than the requirement of prior consultation in
the initial stages of policy formulation. Senator
Arthur H. Vandenberg (Republican of Michigan), the foremost advocate of bipartisan cooperation in the postwar period, once defined
the goal as a "meeting of the minds" toward
problems prevailing in the international field.[5]
Legislative action on important foreign policy
measures since World War II has almost invariably been preceded by a greater or lesser
amount of prior consultation between officials
in the executive and legislative branches. A
notable example was the United Nations
Charter. State Department officials worked
closely with the Senate Foreign Relations Committee over a period of almost three years to
assure Senate acceptance of the nascent United
Nations.[6] Similarly, the Marshall Plan was
finally approved by Congress in 1948 after what
was probably the most intensive collaborative
stocktaking in American diplomatic history.**
Significant bipartisan consultation also preceded the China Aid bill of 1948, the North
Atlantic Treaty, the Mutual Defense Assistance Program, and later programs of American
economic, technical, and military aid to foreign
countries.[7] President Eisenhower's requests in
1955 and 1957 for legislative authority to use
troops, if necessary, for preserving the security
of Formosa and the Middle East from threatened communist attack were eventually granted
by Congress, but only after legislative and
executive officials had discussed conditions
existing in these areas and had agreed that
communist threats against them were imminent.[8] Similarly, President Kennedy kept congressional leaders informed about the buildup
of Soviet missile strength in Cuba; as the
crisis deepened, he informed them of his
intention to blockade Cuba before he told
the country of his action on a nationwide
television appearance.[9]

Although prior consultation is widely regarded as the *sine qua non* of bipartisan cooperation, no clear consensus exists concerning
the nature of these consultations. Much de-

** Preliminary studies of the Marshall Plan are
described in Senate Foreign Relations Committee–
House Foreign Affairs Committee, *The European
Recovery Program*, Senate Document No. 111, 80th
Congress, 1st Session, 1947.

pends on such diverse influences as the external problem under consideration, the time available for decision, the personalities of the individuals involved in the decision, and the extent to which unity is believed to be a paramount goal. Quite clearly, consultations cannot be tailor-made in advance to fit all conceivable kinds of international situations. Considerable improvisation is therefore inevitable. Yet certain basic patterns of consultation have emerged. Liaison is provided on the highest level by the President, the Secretary of State, and their principal advisers, when basic policy measures are under consideration in the government. When legislation like foreign aid or the State Department budget is being considered by Congress, the Secretary of State usually appears personally before the appropriate legislative committees. The President himself may meet with legislative leaders at a White House conference to explain proposed programs and to review existing policies.

At a lower level, continuous consultation is provided by the Office of Congressional Relations in the State Department and those officials on the White House staff, and in other executive agencies, charged with cultivating harmonious relations with Congress. Liaison on this level may range from legislative requests to the executive branch for information, to briefings for legislators conducted by the State Department, to informal get-togethers attended by legislative and executive officials, to formal appearances by subordinate executive officials before legislative committees.

The establishment of a subcommittee system in the Foreign Affairs and Foreign Relations Committees, to correspond with the major geographical and functional divisions of the State Department, has facilitated exchange of information between the legislative and executive branches. A former chairman of the House committee observed that:

One of the most helpful signs in collaboration between the executive and legislative branches has been a greater use of the subcommittees. Today the Assistant Secretaries [of State] invariably seek out Members of the appropriate subcommittee and arrange a meeting to impart the latest developments in their particular fields of responsibility. This approach has provided a tremendous sense of participation even though Congressmen may be listeners. It builds up a mutual confidence on the part of both branches.[10]

A corresponding change took place in the executive branch, as a result of the findings of the Hoover Commission, when the State Department established the Office of Congressional Relations, whose function it was to promote more intimate collaboration with Congress on foreign policy measures.

Yet in spite of considerable progress in establishing liaison procedures capable of assuring widespread consultation about certain kinds of foreign policy problems, there remains room for much improvement. For instance, many congressmen were dissatisfied with the way the White House presented the Eisenhower Doctrine for legislative approval, early in 1957. The Eisenhower Doctrine was labeled a "bipartisan" measure by the Administration. Yet, according to Senator J. William Fulbright (Democrat of Arkansas, and influential member of the Foreign Relations Committee), bipartisanship in actuality had consisted of "leaks to the press, speeches to specially summoned Saturday joint sessions (of legislative committees), and dramatic secret meetings of the Committee on Foreign Relations after dark one evening before the Congress was even organized, in an atmosphere of suspense and urgency. . . ." In Fulbright's opinion, "All of this was designed to manage the Congress, to coerce it into signing this blank check."[11] Fulbright's opinions were echoed by a number of other Democrats. Senator Hubert Humphrey (Democrat of Minnesota), for example, criticized the way in which the doctrine was presented to Congress. The Administration had not consulted the *recognized leaders*—"namely, the majority leader and minority leader and the heads of committees." Instead, it had engaged in a kind of high-pressure publicity campaign to convince Congress that the Eisenhower Doctrine ought to be adopted as a bipartisan measure. In dealing with the opposition party, the doctrine "was handled with a kind of Hollywood public relations treatment."[12] Similar complaints came from Republicans during the Kennedy Administration. When Congress significantly reduced the foreign aid bill for fiscal year 1964, for example, President Kennedy strongly criticized Republicans for abandoning a "bipartisan" approach to foreign relations. Republican legislators tended to retort, however, that true bipartisanship required presidential consultation with the leaders of both political parties and that "we have not had the consultation that was necessary."[13]

Legislators as Negotiators and Observers

A bipartisan practice rich with historical tradition is the use of legislators and members of the opposition party as negotiators and observers at international conferences. This custom dates back to the War of 1812, when two legislators participated in negotiating the peace treaty.[14] McKinley followed the same practice at the end of the Spanish-American War; the treaty of peace with Spain might have been rejected by the Senate except for this fact.[15] Henry White's inability to provide liaison between President Wilson and Senate Republicans to assure acceptance of the Treaty of Versailles constituted a lesson which executive officials in later years were careful to observe: bipartisan support for policy is not likely to emerge unless care is taken to work through the *acknowledged leaders* of the opposition party.

The individual most closely identified with bipartisanship in the modern period was Senator Arthur H. Vandenberg. Vandenberg once wrote of "wearing three hats."[16] He was, first of all, the chairman of the Foreign Relations Committee in the 80th Congress (1947–1948); then he was the acknowledged Republican spokesman on foreign policy questions; finally, he served as president of the Senate and consequently came in close touch with that body's opinions and activities. Because of his great prestige and influence with reference to foreign policy issues, Vandenberg could provide invaluable assistance to the Truman Administration in the immediate postwar period, especially in negotiating with the Soviet Union. His presence at the right hand of Secretary of State James Byrnes, during negotiations over the minor Axis peace treaties for instance, provided a forceful demonstration of American unity. On one significant occasion in 1946, when the Truman Administration's diplomatic efforts were severely challenged by the speeches of Secretary of Commerce Henry A. Wallace, Vandenberg's firm statement that the "authority of American foreign policy is dependent upon the degree of American unity behind it . . . " and that "most Republicans have been glad to join Democrats, thus presenting a united American front to the world," served blunt notice to the Soviet Union that the Administration's increasingly firm policies had solid bipartisan support.[17]

Much the same purpose was served under the Kennedy Administration, when the President asked a bipartisan delegation of legislators to attend the signing ceremonies of the nuclear test-ban agreement in Moscow. Fearing that a delegation consisting solely of the Administration's supporters might give the pact a "partisan flavor," President Kennedy therefore counteracted this impression by including spokesmen for the Republican Party. For reasons that we shall discuss presently, several GOP leaders were reluctant to serve in this capacity, since they were known to be opposed to the nuclear test-ban and did not wish to be identified with the agreement.[18] As a rule, however, as D. F. Fleming has written:

> When powerful Senate leaders act as negotiators of a treaty they acquire a paternal interest in the document and are likely to defend it vigorously. . . . Other Senators, too, are likely to look upon the treaty as made by capable, friendly hands and therefore to be attacked with much more restraint.[19]

"Politics Stops at the Water's Edge"

"I ask Congress for unity in these crucial days," said President Truman on January 8, 1951. "I do not ask for unanimity. I do not ask for an end to debate. . . . Let us debate the issues, but let every man among us weigh his words and deeds. There is a sharp difference between harmful criticism and constructive criticism."[20] This theme was echoed by Senator John F. Kennedy, when he accepted the nomination of the Democratic Party for the presidency in 1960. "The times are too grave," he admonished, "the challenge too urgent, the stakes too high to permit the customary passions of political debate."[21] Candidates and political leaders alike have endorsed the ideal stated by Senator Vandenberg in 1947 of "an unpartisan American foreign policy—not Republican, not Democratic, but American—which substantially unites our people at the water's edge in behalf of peace."[22]

As with other aspects of the concept, it is easier to accept this principle of bipartisanship than to translate it into specific practices and rules of behavior designed to facilitate the goal of unity. Nevertheless, several corollary ideas seem implicit in the principle. First, when criticism of existing policy is necessary— and advocates of bipartisanship have repeatedly insisted that there must be no moratorium on criticism—it should be constructive and not destructive. Obviously, this requirement is susceptible to highly subjective interpretations. Whether criticisms are constructive or destructive is a question that will be decided largely by whether a supporter or a critic of current American policy is asked to evaluate it, or possibly by the circumstances under which it is advanced, as in the midst of a political campaign.

A large area of independent judgment must always exist concerning the permissible limits of criticism. Former President Eisenhower, for example, enunciated a principle long endorsed by the opposition party when he declared in 1962 that even though Americans were obliged to support the President during critical periods like the recent Cuban crisis, still "a foreign crisis must not become an excuse for silence or submission by us Republicans." Eisenhower pointed out that silence about public policy was equated with loyalty only under a dictatorship.[23] A leading Democratic spokesman, Mr. Adlai Stevenson, has concurred that

> . . . in politics, criticism divorced from honest and constructive purpose ceases to be a proper instrument of democracy. Criticism, as an instrument not of inquiry and reform, but of power, quickly degenerates into the techniques of deceit and smear. . . . If criticism is distorted into calumny, mudslinging, and doubletalk . . . it is not simply this or that party or this or that political figure that must suffer. It is the Republic itself.[24]

Second, genuine bipartisanship presupposes that those individuals who join in bipartisan endeavors do so in good faith and with a sincere desire to achieve great national purposes. This requirement, in turn, demands the existence of a high degree of mutual confidence among the major participants. Such an ingredient was lacking, for example, between officials of the Truman Administration and Senator Taft. Besides being a leading political candidate, Senator Taft had more than once expressed reservations about bipartisan collaboration. Similarly, Democrats during the Eisenhower Administration did not fully "trust" Secretary of State John Foster Dulles and were often alienated by his imperious manner. Under such circumstances, efforts to achieve constructive bipartisan cooperation yielded minimum results.

Third, bipartisanship contemplates that neither political party will seek to exploit foreign policy issues for partisan ends, particularly during political campaigns. Implicit in the theory of bipartisanship is the idea that each party shares *equally* in the gains and losses

registered in the foreign policy field. Although this may be the theory, for reasons that we shall examine in greater detail presently, it has proved well-nigh impossible in practice to adhere to it. Here it is enough to suggest that the explanation must be sought in something other than the tendency of bipartisanship's proponents to disregard their own preachments. The evident disparity between theory and practice is rooted in the political system itself and in the very nature of democratic government.

Admittedly, the *appearance* of bipartisan unity sometimes has immense value, diplomatically. It may convey the impression abroad of unified governmental public support for basic policy measures. It may go far toward making policies more publicly acceptable. It may communicate the gravity with which the incumbent administration views developments in the outside world. It may instill a feeling of confidence in the government's policies. Many of these advantages are realized, for example, in the kind of meeting held between President Kennedy and former President Eisenhower following the disastrous Bay of Pigs invasion attempt of Cuba. This bipartisan gesture unquestionably contributed to preventing a national partisan discord over this aspect of Cuban policy.[25]

Before examining certain perennial and troublesome problems encountered in the attempt to conduct foreign policy upon a bipartisan basis, it is appropriate to ask how effectively the bipartisan approach has operated throughout the postwar era. As a generalization, it may be said that greater unity has prevailed over foreign relations since World War II than might have been expected on the basis of diplomatic experience. Both branches of the government and both major political parties stand united today behind the essentials of American foreign policy, particularly those intimately related to national security. Despite occasional lapses, communist policymakers and the nation's diplomatic allies alike have been able to count with reasonable assurance upon the continuity of American diplomatic leadership under successive administrations and upon the fulfillment of America's overseas commitments.

Yet if impressive unity has prevailed, so has substantial disunity. Not even Wilson's bitter wrangle with Senate Republicans surpassed the level of partisan strife and public controversy witnessed toward selected aspects of postwar American foreign relations. Illustrative episodes include intense disputes over the Roosevelt and Truman Administrations' Far Eastern policies, and vituperative criticisms directed at such executive officials as Secretaries of State Dean G. Acheson and, to a lesser extent, John Foster Dulles. The House of Representatives even tried in 1951 to compel Acheson's retirement by an unsuccessful move to terminate his salary. Since World War II, no national election has failed to include widespread public controversy over certain aspects of America's relations with the outside world. In presidential years particularly, such as 1952, Republicans have discovered issues in this field that promised to be powerful vote-getting devices; both then and in 1956 such issues were of unquestioned importance in ending their 20-year tenure as the opposition party.

Why has the unprecedented emphasis on bipartisan cooperation often failed to prevent schisms over certain aspects of foreign policy, even though an underlying consensus has prevailed over its fundamentals? What are the limitations inherent in, or frequently encountered in, a bipartisan approach?

BARRIERS TO UNITY

Constitutional Obstacles

Formidable barriers to bipartisan collaboration in foreign affairs are inherent in the American constitutional system. Following the concept of separation of powers, the founders deliberately divided control of foreign relations between the President and Congress. Whatever may have been the original intention of the Founding Fathers, American diplomatic experience has clearly elevated the President into a position of leadership in this realm. The role of Congress is important, and has become increasingly so in the modern period, but it is nevertheless a *subordinate* role. Congress may modify proposals made by executive officials; and, for short periods at least, it can block at least certain steps contemplated by the White House. Yet the initiative in foreign affairs rests with the President and his chief advisers. Efforts to achieve bipartisan cooperation, therefore, must always be carried on within a framework of executive supremacy in foreign relations.

This fact has profound significance for bipartisanship. It means, first, that the President must always remain at the helm of the ship of state. Under the Constitution, it is his responsibility to preserve national security, and he cannot abdicate this responsibility merely because greater unity within the government might be ideally desirable. Obviously, attempts to create unity may contribute to the broad goal of national security. At times, however, as when President Truman decided upon American assistance to Greece in 1947 and intervened with troops in Korea in 1950, a chief executive must take steps demanded by the diplomatic interests of the country, regardless of whether such steps have received widespread initial bipartisan support. However useful bipartisan collaboration may be, there are times when it will have to be sacrificed to the paramount constitutional obligation of the President to manage foreign relations in the manner best calculated to assure national security.*

Second, under the American Constitution, Congress bears little or no direct responsibility for certain kinds of activities in the sphere of foreign relations. This is true, for instance, of the recognition of other governments, which is purely an executive function. It is difficult to see how completely satisfactory bipartisan procedures can be worked out within the existing constitutional framework to cover such problems.** For if, on the one hand, the President permits Congress to share in making

** A striking example of the President's dominant role, even within a context of attempted bipartisan cooperation, in foreign affairs was provided by the Cuban crisis of 1962. After President Kennedy and his advisers had decided upon a blockade as the most effective response to the Soviet missile buildup in Cuba, and only two hours before he made his memorable speech to the American people announcing this decision, the President had a conference with a group of high-ranking congressional officials. Some legislators contended strongly that a blockade of Cuba was not sufficiently strong action; they favored outright military invasion. One report stated that "The President listened without anger, but was not to be dissuaded." In short, as in most crises, the President was informing legislative leaders about the course he *intended to take* to preserve national security. See the lengthy recapitulation of events during the Cuban crisis in *The New York Times*, November 3, 1962; reprinted in David L. Larson, ed., *The 'Cuban Crisis' of 1962* (Boston: Houghton Mifflin, 1963), pp. 220–243.

** It is clear that, in some instances, Congress does not *want* to share the responsibility for decisions in foreign affairs, particularly those that might prove domestically unpopular. See Sherman Adams's discussion of legislative unwillingness to "share" in Eisenhower's contemplated use of sanctions against Israel in 1956 or in possible American intervention in Jordan, in *First-Hand Report: The Story of the Eisenhower Administration* (New York: Harper & Row, 1961), pp. 285, 291.

policies in these instances, then he is allowing the legislature to make decisions for which he is constitutionally responsible. If, on the other hand, he excludes such questions from the area of bipartisan cooperation, then he invites the charge that he has arbitrarily limited the bipartisan process, that he really does not want unity on the issue in question, and that he has freed the opposition party to criticize policy openly. No example from postwar experience better illustrates the complexities of this kind of problem for the bipartisan approach than the Truman Administration's diplomacy toward Nationalist China.[26]

In the third place, a constitutional no man's land exists in regard to the control of domestic aspects of foreign relations, notably the use of troops in behalf of diplomatic objectives. After a century and a half of constitutional history, the exact boundaries between legislative and executive prerogatives remain shadowy. This virtually invites the two branches to struggle for supremacy, to maximize their own power, and to resist expansion in the powers of the other branch. Such considerations were undoubtedly behind the so-called Great Debate on American defense policy late in 1950 and early in 1951. Although the ostensible issues involved the commitment of American ground troops to Europe, this debate must be at least partially explained as a recurrence of a constitutional struggle that has erupted many times in American history over the exact scope of legislative and executive prerogatives in the military and defense field. Genuine bipartisan cooperation is predicated upon some kind of understanding as to the jurisdictions of the President and Congress, in order that a profitable division of labor in foreign affairs may result.

To summarize: under the American Constitution relations between the President and Congress are almost always in a state of actual or potential turbulence. This condition is not accidental. To avoid the extremes of dictatorship and of mass rule, the Founding Fathers deliberately sought to make unified governmental policy difficult and to place many obstacles in the way of coordinating activities among the branches. The founders, in other words, deliberately sought to prevent too much unity within the American government. The theory was that divided responsibilities—bringing, as they must, inevitable disunity, perhaps even deadlock—would go far to preserve the Republic from domination by any one branch.

While the founders obviously could not foresee the later consequences of such disunity, especially in the realm of foreign relations, it is difficult even today to overcome altogether the constitutional doctrine of separation of powers. As long as each branch continues to possess independent powers in foreign affairs, a certain amount of conflict and contention between them will likely remain a permanent feature of the American government.

Disunity Within the Executive Branch

The postwar emphasis upon bipartisanship might suggest that internal divisions over foreign relations have their origins primarily in hostile executive-legislative relations or partisan controversies. Yet it has become progressively apparent that considerable disunity may originate within the executive branch alone. A prerequisite for bipartisan agreements is agreement among executive officials themselves over basic policies and programs. In the absence of such agreement, bipartisan procedures can accomplish little. Senator Vandenberg pointed out when Truman's Secretary of Commerce, Henry A. Wallace, publicly disagreed with the government's foreign policies that there can be only one Secretary of State at a time.[27] Republicans wanted to collaborate with Democratic policy-makers, Vandenberg stated, but they had great difficulty doing so when doubt existed at home and abroad over the individuals who spoke for the administration and over the fundamentals of American policy at any given time.

This problem became especially acute, almost endemic, in the early Eisenhower Administration—so much so that *The New York Times* correspondent Cabell Phillips was led to observe that a kind of "tripartisanship" was needed: the Administration had first to unify the speeches and activities of those within its official family before it could solicit the cooperation of the Democratic opposition.[28] Similarly, a veritable babel of voices within the Eisenhower Administration was heard during 1957 over the question of disarmament. The Defense Department, the State Department, the Atomic Energy Commission, and the President's special assistant in charge of disarmament studies tended to take contradictory positions on the prospects of reaching agreements with the USSR on arms control and on the implications for American security in doing so. In the midst of the confusion, it was not always clear just where President Eisenhower himself stood on the disarmament problem.[29] Nor did this problem disappear with the Kennedy Administration. The prolonged crisis in South Vietnam (where the United States was obliged both to press a guerrilla war against the Communists and to demand liberalization of President Diem's oppressive regime) called attention to proliferation of executive agencies involved in foreign affairs and to the tendency of efforts within the executive branch itself sometimes to become confused and self-defeating.[30]

Disunity Within Congress

For reasons to be discussed elsewhere in this chapter, party leadership seldom can be counted on to provide effective coordination of policy in Congress. The result is that collaboration between the President and Congress is sometimes considerably easier to bring about than integration of legislative activities alone.

It cannot be too strongly emphasized that congressional organization and procedure are not conducive to unified governmental efforts in foreign affairs. In spite of reforms inaugurated by the Legislative Reorganization Act of 1946, congressional committees have tended to proliferate. By the early 1960s, there were no less than a total of 290 standing or special committees and subcommittees in Congress.[31] When this fact is coupled with the growing interdependence of domestic and foreign policies and programs, and the traditional independence exercised by legislative committees, the opportunities for disjointed and self-defeating efforts within Congress alone are almost without limit. As we noted at length in Chapter 3, some of the more serious sources of disunity within Congress are: conflicting jurisdictions among standing policy committees; disagreements between policy committees and appropriations committees; the extremely fragmentary treatment that Congress accords the national defense and foreign aid budgets; and the virtually inseparable relationship prevailing today between internal and external policy measures.*

* A conspicuous example of legislative disunity in foreign affairs was provided in 1951 in connection with President Truman's request for authority to send surplus American wheat to India during a period of acute famine in that country. Dilatory tactics by the House Rules Committee (many of whose members were highly critical of Prime Minister Nehru's policies) created the impression abroad that the United States was niggardly and was unwilling to use its own great agricultural surpluses for

These illustrations highlight the fact that disunity within the government over foreign affairs is not exclusively a product of executive-legislative conflict or of partisan controversies. In view of the great complexity of foreign policy issues and the vast expansion in the size of the executive branch in recent years, it has become increasingly difficult to unify even executive efforts so that a reasonably clear understanding of American diplomatic goals is possible and, after that, so that bipartisan collaboration may take place on the basis of carefully worked out executive proposals.

After reviewing the mechanism for controlling foreign relations within the United States, one commentator concluded that:

> The Congress of the United States still remains without any very clear method of integrating the control of foreign policy in either house and certainly lacks any machinery for coordination in both houses, except in so far as party leadership may afford it.[32]

A second factor militating heavily against unified efforts within Congress is the weakness of party organization and the substantial freedom legislators possess to follow their own independent judgments on questions of national policy. Party lines within Congress** are seldom rigid. Party leaders have few weapons at their disposal for coercing errant members into following a predetermined party line. National party platforms are not drafted by the party membership in Congress at all, but by delegates elected on the state and local level. It is not unknown for the presidential candidate himself to repudiate at least parts of the platform altogether; and legislative candidates on the state and local level are even less

humanitarian purposes. Even though Congress eventually approved Truman's request, much of the good will that might have accrued to the United States was lost when Soviet Russia (whose donation was much smaller than America's) sent wheat to Nehru's government before America. The Rules Committee—consisting primarily of conservative legislators with little or no experience in foreign relations and little awareness of the consequences of their action—thus frustrated what might have been a significant diplomatic achievement. See *Congressional Quarterly Almanac: 1951*, **7**, 233–237.

** D. W. Brogan, *Politics in America* (New York: Harper & Row, 1954); V. O. Key, *Politics, Parties, and Pressure Groups* (New York: Crowell, 1952); Angus Campbell et al., *The American Voter* (New York: Wiley, 1960); and E. E. Schattschneider, *Party Government* (New York: Holt, Rinehart & Winston, 1942).

inclined to be bound by platform declarations. In political campaigns, especially for the House, candidates for Congress are primarily concerned with issues specifically affecting their states or districts. They do not hesitate to challenge positions taken by their national party leaders or even to oppose certain aspects of their own party's record in office.

The President and his chief political advisers have consequently come to depend far more on persuasion and conciliation to win support for their program among members of their own party than upon stern disciplinary measures. There are very few effective disciplinary measures that can be utilized against party defectors. Presidential interference in local elections is strongly resented and can often backfire to the detriment of the President's own prestige. Candidates for national office, of course, usually want the endorsement of the White House in forthcoming campaigns. But the President and the national party organization no less need the support of state and local party leaders. The result is that the President usually endorses the candidacy of even those members of his party who have opposed him on important domestic and foreign issues. Presidents customarily follow the principle that the election of *any* candidate from their own party is preferable to the election of a member of the opposition.

Given the extremely decentralized party organization within the United States, and the near impossibility of enforcing acceptance of a party line upon members, a major obstacle to bipartisan agreements in foreign relations lies in the difficulty of translating bipartisan understandings into agreements that are *binding upon Congress as a whole*. There is no guarantee that proposals carefully worked out between the two Foreign Affairs Committees and the State Department will be accepted by other committees, such as the Rules or the Appropriations Committees, or by rank-and-file party members. The two individuals who were conspicuously successful in bringing about bipartisan collaboration in the postwar era—Senators Vandenberg and Walter F. George (Democrat of Georgia)—were singularly effective in surmounting this obstacle. Both served as chairman of the Foreign Relations Committee, and both were also highly influential in the deliberations of their party organizations. Both were consequently in a position to reach agreements with reasonable assurance that they would be accepted by their colleagues in

Congress. William S. White explained Senator George's role under the Eisenhower Administration in the following terms:

> He spoke, and speaks, on world affairs for the entire Democratic party in the Senate as few men can have done in history. In effect, he pledged, and indeed committed, the whole power of the Democratic party in this field to the President. And while he was at it he flung about the President the capacious cloak of the immense, incontestably conservative prestige of the Southern Democrats.
> . . . Thus, when Mr. George began to make it plain that he saw no reason whatever why the Administration should not negotiate with the Communists, or move a bit away from the China Nationalists, it was impossible even for the most implacable Senate Republican right-wingers to cry out "soft on communism."[33]

The combination of talents called for is so exceptional that there is no mystery why the Truman Administration had difficulty locating a successor to Vandenberg, why the Eisenhower Administration experienced the same difficulty in finding a legislator who could replace Senator George, and why the Kennedy and Johnson Administrations found no comparable Republican legislator with whom they could arrive at similar bipartisan agreements. The combination of talents and prerogatives possessed by figures like Senators Vandenberg and George—chairmanship of the powerful Foreign Relations Committee, deep insight into foreign policy issues, greater than average influence within their own political parties, and the great respect accorded them both by members of Congress and officials in the executive branch—appears infrequently. This fact alone places pitfalls in the path of a successful bipartisan approach to foreign relations.

No treatment of the sources of disunity within Congress would be complete without reference to the influence of constituency pressures upon the activities of legislators. Among all the factors that may shape legislative behavior and viewpoints on both domestic and foreign issues, none is more fundamental at times than grass-roots opinion in state or local constituencies. Such pressures have been reflected most noticeably in the over-all voting records of legislators from states containing large foreign-born populations, such as New York, Illinois, or Wisconsin. People in these states are more than ordinarily concerned with American relations with those countries from which local minority groups have come. Legislators from these states were especially vocal during the postwar period in demanding lenient Allied treatment of Italy, in questioning the Nuremberg war crimes trials, and in urging vigorous American protests against Soviet machinations in Eastern Europe.[34]

William S. White has observed that in the Senate there is a "great pluralism of winds and cross-winds. There is in the Senate no possibility of finding and fixing a single economic interest, for this is a deliberately and unchangeably disparate place where unity in such an area of life is not only unacceptable but is consciously fought."[35] When foreign policy issues like the tariff arise that tend to fragment an already loose party alignment into sectional and local interest groups, than the difficulty of achieving enduring bipartisan agreements is greatly compounded. Grass-roots constituency pressures are often much more decisive in influencing legislative behavior in regard to these questions than appeals to party loyalty or to the principle of bipartisanship.

Confusion over Bipartisan Procedures

Some of the procedures engendering unity have come to be accepted as normally integral features of bipartisan collaboration. In regard to others, however, there has existed, and continues to exist, a substantial degree of controversy. Consider first the requirement that prior consultation ought to precede major decisions in the foreign policy field.

What exactly should be the nature of these consultations? Who ought to be included in them? To what extent should consultations permit the legislative branch to make significant modifications in proposals submitted by executive officials? To what degree does prior consultation bind the members of the opposition party to support resultant decisions? Should consultations take place solely on foreign policy issues, or should they be extended to cover closely related domestic issues as well? These question have fomented misunderstandings throughout the postwar years. To date no answers satisfactory to both branches of the government and to both political parties have emerged.

As to the nature of consultations, Republicans complained on a number of occasions under Truman and Kennedy, and Democrats complained under Eisenhower, that many so-called "consultations" were in actuality only briefing sessions at which executive officials *informed* legislators of steps they intended to take to deal with major external problems. As early as 1946, the GOP presidential aspirant Harold Stassen told the Truman Administration that "Republicans would like to be co-pilots in the foreign policy take-offs as well as in the crash landings . . . ," a view reaffirmed several times also by Senator Vandenberg.[36] There are, however, substantial limitations to this co-pilot conception of bipartisanship. External crises sometimes make decisive executive action mandatory. In these circumstances, Congress may be presented with a *fait accompli* it can either approve or disapprove, when it has any power to affect the decision at all. On other occasions, Congress may actually bear no responsibility for contemplated actions. Following a co-pilot conception of bipartisanship in these instances might result in substantial modifications of historic constitutional principles governing the scope of executive and legislative prerogatives in foreign affairs. Then again, the President, who must make the ultimate decision, may become convinced that certain steps are required in the diplomatic field, even though many legislators oppose these steps. Much as he might ideally desire unity, the President has a greater constitutional obligation to conduct foreign relations in the manner best calculated to protect national security.

The selection of individuals to be included in bipartisan consultations is also an extremely complex and controversial issue. Obviously, officials from the State Department and the White House staff, along with representatives of other departments concerned with specific decisions, should participate. The two Foreign Affairs Committees or their appropriate subcommittees in Congress should be consulted. What other groups should be drawn in? We have already noted that a significant trend has been the extent to which the activities of many other congressional committees increasingly bear directly or indirectly upon external affairs. A given foreign policy decision might conceivably be within the province of the Armed Services Committees, the Interstate and Foreign Commerce Committee, the Agriculture Committees, to list but a few—and it will almost certainly be considered sooner or later by the Appropriations Committees. Furthermore, to assure bridging the gulf between the legislative committees and the party organization, the *political leadership* in Congress must sometimes be included.

It is apparent that a law of diminishing returns governs the degree to which consultations can profitably be extended to include all groups within the government, directly or indirectly concerned with specific diplomatic decisions. Very often such decisions must be made quickly. Frequently, too, constructive consultations require that confidential information be made available. The chances are great that such information will eventually become public if it is given to several committees and to individual party leaders. Moreover, there is the distinct probability that ever broadening consultations will make the foreign policy process within the United States diffuse, discursive, and inordinately time-consuming.

Just what obligations are assumed by participants in the bipartisan process? Once they have agreed to join in bipartisan endeavors, how much are the participants obligated to support the policies that emerge? If the President seeks bipartisan support, is he required to accept changes proposed by legislators? After bipartisan consultations have begun, is either side free to withdraw from them because it disagrees with decisions taken? Postwar experience affords no very clear guidance on these questions.*

An additional difficulty in devising satisfactory bipartisan consultations relates to the

* Not only is it a question of the degree to which the President and his chief advisers ought actually to accept modifications in policies and programs suggested by the opposition party. There is also the question of how much executive policy-makers ought to *appear* to accept such modifications, in order that members of the opposite party can psychologically feel, and perhaps claim, that bipartisan cooperation is not a one-way street. This problem arose, for example, in the difficulties experienced by Secretary of State Dulles in trying to arrive at bipartisan policies toward Asia. On this issue, one commentator differentiated between Dulles's "declaratory policy" and his "operational policy" with respect to Red China. The former—often highly belligerent and ultranationalistic—was designed to win the support of many of Dulles's congressional critics, who favored a "hard" line in dealing with communism in that region; the latter, however, seemed to be aimed at actually *reducing* American commitments to Chiang Kai-shek and of avoiding an open military confrontation with Peiping. To whatever extent this behavior might have contributed to winning bipartisan support in Congress, it gave the impression of a highly contradictory and confused American policy to observers at home and abroad. See Joseph C. Harsch, "John Foster Dulles: A Very Complicated Man," *Harper's Magazine*, **213** (September, 1956), 27–34.

range of subject matter that ought to be included in them. If a prevailing conception of bipartisanship is that "politics stops at the water's edge," a necessary inquiry is: in questions involving national security in the mid-twentieth century, just where does the water's edge begin? Policies and programs promoting national security touch such seemingly disparate questions as whether the level of governmental taxation is too high; whether the domestic economy is sound; and whether levels of education and scientific research are adequate. Should these and other closely related "domestic" questions be included in the scope of bipartisan consultations? If so, there would appear to be few important questions of governmental policy which could safely be omitted.

The lack of a clear dividing line between foreign and domestic questions leaves two basic alternatives for advocates of bipartisanship: either executive and legislative officials can conceive of foreign policy issues narrowly and confine consultations to these issues alone; or they can recognize the almost inextricable ties between internal and external questions, and extend liaison techniques to include the broad range of domestic issues affecting national security. The former course well-nigh guarantees that disunity will appear within the government on closely related domestic questions and will almost certainly spread eventually to the realm of foreign relations. The latter course risks making a bipartisan approach cumbersome and time-consuming, if indeed it does not almost foreordain governmental paralysis and indecision in the face of recurrent and ominous external threats. To date, in the vast majority of cases, both Democratic and Republican administrations have preferred the former course. For instance, after initially suggesting that bipartisan cooperation should include relevant domestic questions, the Eisenhower Administration dropped this proposal because of opposition from Republicans and Democrats alike.[37]

Still another problem associated with bipartisan consultation centers on the question: Who is entitled to speak for the opposition party and to reach agreements in its name? Factionalism, always present to some degree in American politics, afflicts the opposition party uniquely, because it lacks both a designated party leader and a clear-cut program. One reason that bipartisan collaboration over the Treaty of Versailles foundered was because there was no individual who enjoyed the confidence of both President Wilson and Senate Republicans. Similarly, under the Truman Administration, influential members of the GOP complained that the two Republican "advisers" to the State Department, John Foster Dulles and John Sherman Cooper, prominent Republican from Kentucky, had no official position, could not speak for them, and could not, therefore, bind Congress to approve understandings arrived at with Democratic policy-makers.

The identical problem arose again in 1957, when President Eisenhower requested the former Democratic presidential candidate Adlai Stevenson to serve in his administration as a Democratic consultant on foreign affairs. Stevenson accepted this assignment, even though a substantial question existed even in his own mind concerning just whom he actually represented. Stevenson was sometimes referred to as the "titular head" of the Democratic Party. But exactly what did this title signify? He held no official or political position, nor could it be said with any assurance that he was the opposition party's designated spokesman on foreign policy issues, a role much more likely to be performed in fact by legislators like Senators Mike Mansfield of Montana or J. William Fulbright of Arkansas.[38] Moreover, at the very time Stevenson was presumably seeking bipartisan unity, another organization of the Democratic Party, in which former President Truman, Eleanor Roosevelt, Dean G. Acheson—and even sometimes Adlai Stevenson himself—played a prominent part, was severely criticizing the Republican record in the field of missile development and scientific research generally. Stevenson therefore served with the administration for a few weeks only. Stevenson resigned his post because of fear that his position was, in his words, "without authority and necessarily identified with decisions I might not always agree with and could not publicly oppose."[39] This view was echoed by former President Eisenhower in the midst of the Cuban crisis late in 1962, when he declared that all Americans must, of course, support the President as commander in chief, but that this did not imply silence by Republicans on the "issues" of the current political campaign or willingness to accept Kennedy's domestic politics or his desire to elect "a virtually one-party Congress."[40] Comparable reservations about participation in bipartisan endeavors had

been voiced by Wendell Willkie during the Roosevelt Administration. Asked by the administration to help convince Republicans to support preparedness measures in Congress, Willkie refused to do so. He stated on August 9, 1940: "I do not think it appropriate for me to enter into advance commitments and understandings. If the National Administration . . . publicly takes any given position with reference to our foreign policy, I may on appropriate occasion comment thereon."[41]

Individuals who assume leading roles in providing bipartisan liaison must, so to speak, have one foot in each camp. The incumbent administration must thoroughly trust and respect them as straightforward and capable of giving their independent judgment about major foreign policy issues. An individual who is *persona non grata* to the party in power, such as Senator Taft was with the Truman Administration, can provide very little useful bipartisan liaison. Similarly, individuals so selected must always enjoy the confidence of their own party and be trusted by it not to become so closely identified with the administration in power that they ignore their own party's historic and current viewpoints on important international questions. A peculiar combination of talents and qualifications is demanded, so much so that remarkably few individuals in the postwar period have been conspicuously successful in bringing about enduring bipartisan accords.*

Finally, even if satisfactory consultations can be arranged, their cumulative burden upon executive policy-makers can become extremely onerous and time-consuming. The number and variety of bipartisan consultations has grown impressively throughout the postwar period, as efforts to achieve unity in national policy have been put on a more systematic and sustained basis. For example, during one six-month period in 1954, Secretary of State John Foster Dulles held more than 90 meetings with legislative leaders. From 1953 to 1957, he met on 214 different occasions with legislative groups. His predecessor, Secretary of State Dean G. Acheson, has stated that it was not unusual for him

---

* Out of his experiences as Secretary of State, Dean Acheson has given a detailed analysis of the personal qualities that are important for individuals prominent in the bipartisan process. See Dean G. Acheson, *A Citizen Looks at Congress* (New York: Harper & Row, 1957), pp. 72–75. The subject is also discussed further in Cecil V. Crabb, Jr., *Bipartisan Foreign Policy: Myth or Reality?* (New York: Harper & Row, 1957), pp. 217–220.

to devote half of his working day to bipartisan consultations![42]

That the problem has become no less acute in the intervening years is indicated by the following schedule of legislative conferences held by Secretary of Defense McNamara, under the Kennedy Administration:

"related to the relief of General MacArthur." On the basis of this and other experiences with bipartisan consultations, Acheson has concluded sardonically that: "The understanding of relevance continues to elude the gentlemen of Capitol Hill."[43] When major policy issues are at stake, important legislative committees

TABLE 4.   Congressional Appearances of Secretary of Defense McNamara, January 20 to August 1, 1961

Date	Number of Hours	Congressional Committees
Feb. 16	1.5	Department of Defense Subcommittee, House Appropriations Committee.
Feb. 23	5.0	House Armed Services Committee.
Feb. 27	1.5	Space Committee.
Apr. 4	6.0	Senate Armed Services Committee.
Apr. 5	6.0	Do.
Apr. 6	4.0	Department of Defense Subcommittee, House Appropriations Committee.
Apr. 7	4.0	Do.
Apr. 10	1.5	Do.
Apr. 11	5.0	House Armed Services Committee.
Apr. 18	5.0	Department of Defense Subcommittee, Senate Appropriations Committee.
Apr. 25	1.0	Government Procurement Subcommittee, Senate Small Business Committee.
May 31	4.5	Department of Defense Subcommittee, House Appropriations Committee.
June 8	3.0	House Foreign Affairs Committee.
June 14	6.0	Senate Foreign Relations Committee.
June 29	2.0	Foreign Operations Subcommittee, House Appropriations Committee.
July 26	4.0	Department of Defense Subcommittee, Senate Appropriations Committee.
July 27	3.0	Senate Armed Services Committee.
July 28	3.0	House Armed Services Committee.
July 31	6.0	Department of Defense Subcommittee, House Appropriations Committee.
Aug. 1	2.5	House Government Operations Committee (Civil Defense).
Total 20 (days)	74.5	

SOURCE: Senate Government Operations Committee, *Organizing for National Security*, Hearings, 87th Congress, 1st Session, **I** (Washington: 1961), 1213.

It is open to serious question whether the total burden of consultations represents the most effective utilization of the time and talents of high-ranking executive officials, granting that some consultation is both desirable and unavoidable. Former Secretary of State Acheson is inclined to doubt it. He cites his own frequent, lengthy, and in many respects, fruitless appearances before the Senate Armed Services-Foreign Relations Committees at the time of the investigation into General Douglas MacArthur's dismissal in 1951. This joint hearing entailed an extended, wide-ranging inquiry into recent decades of American Far Eastern policy. With some legislators participating in the investigation, partisan motivations abounded, as members of the Democratic and Republican parties sought to justify earlier positions of their parties. In Acheson's words, "Not more than an hour" of his interrogation

are seldom content to question officials less exalted than the Secretary of State himself, or his highest assistants. And it is exceedingly difficult for executive officials to limit either the number or the scope of their appearances on Capitol Hill without inviting the charge that they are withholding information from Congress or that they do not really want bipartisan collaboration on particular issues.

Political Repercussions of Bipartisanship

Discussing the Republican party's prospects in the presidential election of 1960, Vice-President Nixon, the GOP candidate for President, declared: "If you ever let them [the Democrats] campaign only on domestic issues, they'll beat us—our only hope is to keep it on foreign policy." Finding a majority of their political advisers in agreement, Republican strategists settled upon the choice of Henry Cabot Lodge of Massachusetts for vice-presidential candidate, since "Lodge was the best man to lift Americans' imagination to the problems of foreign policy. . . ."[44] That Democratic political leaders were not unmindful of the importance of foreign policy issues in the campaign was borne out by such indications as Adlai Stevenson's view that American foreign policy had become "a thing of wonder and mirth" to other countries, and the polls conducted by the Kennedy camp showing that America's declining prestige in international affairs was the dominant issue of the political campaign.[45]

These examples focus attention upon what is perhaps the most durable obstacle to implementation of a bipartisan approach to foreign relations: those inherent in the American political system. At the time of his confirmation as Secretary of State in 1953, John Foster Dulles explained the seeming contradiction between his support for the bipartisan principle and his often sharp attacks upon the policies of Democratic policy-makers, by saying:

> . . . under our Constitutional system we have a general election every four years . . . one side presents his case, and the other side presents the other case, as two lawyers do when they go into court. At that stage the two parties are not judges and they are not judicial. In my opinion they should not be . . . but when that time is past, then I believe we should try to work together on a bipartisan basis. . . .[46]

Dulles's statement calls attention to two contrary and powerful forces that tend to pull any discussion of foreign policy questions in opposite directions: the widely admitted need for maximum unity when important international issues are at stake, and the equally compelling necessity for full and periodic debate on paramount questions of public policy.

Let us consider first an assumption implicit in the process of a bipartisan approach to foreign policy questions: the principle that under this approach both parties share equally in the credit or blame for developments in external affairs. This principle collides head-on with another deeply ingrained precept of the American democratic system. This is that the party in power is held responsible by the electorate for the successful management of domestic and foreign affairs. Postwar experience suggests that it is virtually impossible to reconcile these two principles and that, in practice, leaders and adherents of both political parties are prone (especially during national elections) to abandon the former in favor of the latter. Such a result is almost guaranteed by two other tendencies that have emerged on the basis of experience with the bipartisan principle. One is that the party in power almost invariably claims credit for *successful* policies. The other is that the opposition party no less invariably divorces itself from responsibility for *unsuccessful* policies. Thus, since World War II, Republicans have campaigned repeatedly on issues such as the Roosevelt Administration's "appeasement" of the Soviet Union at the Yalta Conference, the loss of China to communism, and the communist efforts to infiltrate the Western Hemisphere. Democrats periodically attack the Republican party's historic "isolationism," the U-2 affair under Eisenhower, and the general decline in American influence and prestige under Republican leadership.

While recognizing the all too familiar fact that self-seeking politicians can and do exploit foreign policy problems in elections to the detriment of the national interest, it remains true that gains and losses in foreign affairs cannot be shared equally by the two major parties without radical innovations in the American political system and perhaps in the process of democracy itself. If the incumbent party has governed well, it is natural—in a democracy, perhaps desirable and inevitable—that it should seek to be returned to office on the basis of its record. Conversely, an opposition party cannot voluntarily forego opportunities to inject international questions—especially those involving alleged *failures* in American policy—into the political arena without inviting the charge that it "lacks alternatives" of its own or that it can do no better than acquiesce in ineffectual efforts by incumbent officials. In brief, the opposition party cannot accept a theory of bipartisanship that entails a moratorium on criticism. If it did so, it would largely forfeit any claim it may make to being an effective opposition. As we have already observed, in the last analysis the administration in power must decide upon the foreign policies the national interest requires. The opposite side of this coin is that the opposition party must likewise decide when policies have proved unsuccessful and must assume the responsibility of calling these policies to the attention of the electorate.

All of this suggests that bipartisanship in foreign policy may place the opposition party in a peculiarly vulnerable position. Advocates of the bipartisan principle have proclaimed, almost as a matter of ritual, there must be no moratorium on public debate, but criticism of delicate foreign policy questions ought always to be "constructive." Aside from the difficulty of interpreting this stipulation objectively, this idea means that the opposition party is always in danger of being compromised. Either it attacks policies that, in its judgment, need criticizing—thereby risking the accusation that it has abandoned the concept of bipartisanship and is indifferent to the need for unity in critical times. Or it withholds its criticisms for the sake of unity or the *appearance* of unity—and risks the no less damaging charge that it is no longer an effective opposition party and that it is equally to blame for ineffectual efforts in foreign relations. Either way, it can be penalized. For its leaders know full well that, however much participants in the process of foreign policy may agree that credit and blame ought theoretically to be shared equally, this is the view neither of the electorate as a whole nor of rank-and-file party members, whose principal concern is winning elections.*

It cannot perhaps be too often emphasized that a cardinal distinction between totalitarian and democratic governments lies in the degree to which each believes the creation of unity to be a pre-eminent goal of policy-makers. Democracies operate upon the basis of consent, which

inevitably implies a certain amount of dissent and dissension over important public issues. Totalitarian governments eliminate dissent openly and forcibly, but democracies may accomplish the same purpose, consciously or unconsciously, by more indirect and subtle means. Adlai Stevenson has observed that

> . . . in many minds "criticism" has today become an ugly word. It has become almost *lèse-majesté*. It conjures up pictures of insidious radicals hacking away at the very foundations of the American way of life. It suggests nonconformity and nonconformity suggests disloyalty and disloyalty suggests treason, and before we know where we are, this process has all but identified the critic with the saboteur and turned political criticism into an un-American activity instead of democracy's greatest safeguard.[47]

Under a bipartisan approach to foreign relations, there is not only the problem of *whether* criticism will emerge, but also the problem of *when* it emerges. Surely one purpose of enlightened criticism is to bring about needed changes in policy while there is yet time to prevent major policy failures. *Ex post facto* criticism whose purpose is merely to identify the individuals responsible for diplomatic ineptitude often serves little constructive purpose. This kind of criticism has been all too common in recent American experience.

One final point requires emphasis. "History," to quote Republican members of the House Foreign Affairs Committee, "is strewn with wreckage of countries that were united but on the wrong course." The paramount goal shared by both branches of the government and by both political parties is successful foreign policy. Unquestionably, bipartisan procedures sometimes contribute to reaching that goal. But sometimes too, other techniques and practices —firm executive leadership, clear public delineation of the issues by party spokesmen, replacement of incapable officials by more capable ones—can advance the nation's diplomatic interests better than an uncritical attachment to the bipartisan principle. In the last analysis, one condition above all others is likely to prove the most durable incentive for national unity in foreign affairs: a conviction that the incumbent officials are aware of crucial problems in the international community and that they are working conscientiously to formulate intelligent and realistic policies for dealing with these problems.

---

* This dilemma was highlighted in 1963 by the interest displayed by the Kennedy Administration in permitting American grain dealers to sell wheat to the Soviet Union. Such a move represented a reversal of American policy of many years' standing. The President and his advisers were, therefore, highly desirous of gaining assurance of widespread bipartisan support before undertaking it. Thus one news dispatch pointed out that officials of the administration had been consulting Republican leaders in Congress "in an attempt to gain an advance and public endorsement of the move that would make it impossible for Republican candidates to make a campaign issue out of the sale if it were made—and if United States-Soviet relations then took a turn for the worse." In other words, in the Republican view, the President was seeking GOP concurrence with the move, which would emerge as an "achievement" of the Democratic Administration if successful, and GOP silence on the move if it failed! *The New York Times*, October 1, 1963. Ironically, Democrats made virtually the same objection in 1957, when President Eisenhower asked for legislative authority to deal with a deteriorating situation in the Middle East. See *The Christian Science Monitor*, January 25, 1957.

NOTES

1. Quoted in William L. Langer, "The Mechanism of American Foreign Policy," *International Affairs*, 24 (July, 1948), 321.
2. George F. Kennan, *American Diplomacy: 1900–1950* (Chicago: University of Chicago Press, 1951), pp. 66–67.
3. William L. Langer and S. Everett Gleason, *The Challenge to Isolation* (New York: Harper & Row, 1952), pp. 136–147, 280–291.
4. George H. Haynes, *The Senate of the United States*, II (Boston: Houghton Mifflin, 1938), 700; W. Stull Holt, *Treaties Defeated by the Senate* (Baltimore: Johns Hopkins University Press, 1933), pp. 264–265; Allan Nevins, *Henry White* (New York: Harper & Row, 1930), pp. 397–404. These sources supply background on the problem of governmental conflict in foreign relations.
5. Arthur H. Vandenberg, Jr., ed., *The Private Papers of Senator Vandenberg* (Boston: Houghton Mifflin, 1952), p. 550. An indispensable primary source on the origins of postwar bipartisanship.
6. *Ibid.*, pp. 90–171.
7. Cecil V. Crabb, Jr., *Bipartisan Foreign Policy: Myth or Reality?* (New York: Harper & Row, 1957), pp. 74–116. Discusses the nature of, and obstacles to, bipartisan collaboration in foreign affairs.
8. *Ibid.*, pp. 251–254.
9. Hugh Sidey, *John F. Kennedy: President* (New York: Atheneum, 1963), pp. 324, 341.
10. James P. Richards, "The House of Representatives in Foreign Affairs," *Annals of the American Academy of Political and Social Science*, 289 (September, 1953), 71. This article and others in this symposium provide a helpful treatment of Congress's role in foreign relations.
11. *Congressional Record*, 103 (1957), 1856. Other references to the nature of bipartisan procedures appear in Fulbright's speech on the Middle East, pp. 1855–1869.
12. *Ibid.*, pp. 1877–1878.
13. *The New York Times*, August 27, 1963.
14. Haynes, *op. cit.*, pp. 596–597.
15. *Ibid.*, p. 598.
16. Vandenberg, *op. cit.*, p. 318.
17. *The New York Times*, September 15, 1946.
18. *The New York Times*, July 29, 1963.
19. D. F. Fleming, *The Treaty Veto of the American Senate* (New York: G. P. Putnam's Sons, 1930), p. 169. Appraises the Senate's historic role in treaty-making.
20. *Congressional Record*, 97 (1951), 101.
21. Theodore White, *The Making of the President: 1960* (New York: Atheneum, 1961), p. 177. Cites innumerable examples of the role of foreign policy issues in political campaigns.
22. *The New York Times*, November 4, 1947.
23. *The New York Times*, October 28, 1962.
24. Adlai E. Stevenson, "Party of the Second Part," *Harper's Magazine*, 212 (February, 1956), 33. A cogent discussion of an opposition party's role in the United States.
25. Sidey, *op. cit.*, p. 143.
26. Crabb, *op. cit.*, pp. 93–116.
27. *The New York Times*, September 15, 1946.
28. *The New York Times*, October 21, 1954.
29. *The New York Times*, July 2, 1957.
30. *The New York Times*, September 22, 1963.
31. *Congressional Quarterly Almanac: 1962*, 18, 40–60.
32. W. Y. Elliott, "The Control of Foreign Policy in the United States," *Political Quarterly*, 201 (October–December, 1949), 349.
33. William S. White, "Two Parties and One Foreign Policy," *New York Times Magazine*, August 7, 1955, p. 34.
34. "Power of Minorities in '46 Vote," *United States News and World Report*, 21 (October 18, 1946), 22–23.
35. William S. White, *Citadel: The Story of the U.S. Senate* (New York: Harper & Row, 1957), pp. 136–137.
36. *The New York Times*, April 15, 1955.
37. See the dispatches by William S. White in *The New York Times*, November 24, 1954, and January 9, 1955.
38. Douglas Cater, "Who Will Speak for the Democrats?" *The Reporter*, 15 (November 29, 1956), 22–23.
39. *The New York Times*, December 8, 1957.
40. *The New York Times*, October 28, 1962.
41. Quoted in Langer and Gleason, *op. cit.*, p. 754.
42. Sherman Adams, *First-Hand Report: The Story of the Eisenhower Administration* (New York: Harper & Row, 1961), p. 134; Acheson, *op. cit.*, p. 65.
43. Acheson, *op. cit.*, pp. 65, 80–82.
44. White, *op. cit.*, pp. 206–207.
45. *Ibid.*, pp. 120, 319–320.
46. Quoted in Joseph C. Harsch, "John Foster Dulles: A Very Complicated Man," *Harpers Magazine*, 213 (September, 1956), p. 29.
47. Stevenson, *op. cit.*, p. 32.

7 ➝ PUBLIC OPINION AND

DECISION-MAKING ➝

THE ANATOMY OF PUBLIC OPINION

In democratic societies it is axiomatic that governmental policies are heavily conditioned by public opinion. Authoritarian governments, to be sure, cannot totally disregard public sentiment. But they are not as strongly compelled as democracies to take it into account in the day-to-day conduct of public affairs or to feel that it has fixed the outer limits beyond which officials dare not go for fear that their actions will later be repudiated by the citizenry.

At every stage in the foreign policy process—from the consideration of measures to be recommended to Congress, to the exchange of notes between governments, to speeches by representatives to the United Nations—public opinion must always be considered by policymakers within the United States. Sometimes this opinion is clear and determinative, as illustrated by the almost unanimous public clamor demanding speedy demobilization after World War II or the rising national demand that the Kennedy Administration take a firm stand in dealing with Soviet machinations in Cuba. In other instances, like American relations with the European Common Market or policy toward revolutionary ferment in Latin America, public opinion is nebulous, conflicting, and sometimes almost impossible to evaluate clearly.

"Public Opinion"—A Many-Faceted Concept

Although the term public opinion did not come into wide currency until late in the eighteenth century,[1] philosophers and political sages have long been aware of the concept's

pertinence to the study of government. Montesquieu referred to the *esprit général*, Rousseau to the *volonté général*, and German philosophers of the romantic school to the *Volksgeist*. Today popular usage has robbed the term public opinion of many of the incisive and specific qualities associated with it in earlier periods, so that prevailing definitions often cannot include all its nuances and subtleties of meaning. Definitions of the concept are legion. The great authority on British government, A. V. Dicey, called it a "body of beliefs, convictions, sentiments, accepted principles, or firmly-rooted prejudices, which, taken together, make up the public opinion of a particular era. . . ."[2] The sociologist Kimball Young conceived of it as the "beliefs, convictions, or views of individuals on matters or issues of widespread or public interest and concern."[3] Cottrell and Eberhart have contended that the term ought to be applied only to viewpoints of "the 'informed' public" instead of the general, often disinterested and poorly informed, public at large.[4] These and other definitions that might be cited* make it apparent that public opinion is an extremely variegated concept that admits of no brief and altogether satisfactory complete definition. How it is defined will depend heavily upon the facets of public opinion that are being investigated or upon the aspects of its influence that are being stressed.

* For additional definitions, see Emory S. Bogardus, *The Making of Public Opinion* (New York: Association Press, 1951), pp. 5–7; Kimball Young, *Social Psychology* (New York: Appleton-Century-Crofts, 1956), pp. 330–332; Daniel Katz *et al.*, eds., *Public Opinion and Propaganda* (New York: Dryden Press, 1954), pp. 50–51.

Students of public opinion are in fairly general agreement that several elements are central to the concept. First, the term implies a greater or lesser degree of *public agreement* on important socioeconomic-political questions. Second, the term presupposes a certain amount of *public discussion and awareness of contemporary issues.* Some issues provoke immediate and heated public debate and may lead to considerable group action for or against specified policies. In such cases, public opinion may become a dynamic force. In other cases, public consciousness of issues may be hazy or even nonexistent. Or, public opinion may be latent: when events arouse the population to a realization of the importance of public questions, then the citizenry may take an active part in debate over them. Third, the concept of public opinion implies a *rational process* of "arriving at" decisions over a period of time, after the influences that eventually formulate prevailing viewpoints have become operative. Yet it is also clear that public opinion can be—and often is—an *irrational process*. Sometimes irrational elements—personal and group antagonisms, prejudices, emotional reactions, snap judgments, and the like—predominate in shaping popular attitudes.

We shall better understand the complexities of public opinion after we have examined two questions about its basic nature and importance. What is the character of the *public* to which the term alludes? And what is meant by the *opinion* which the public supposedly reflects?

The "Public" and Its Components

Often the term public suggests the connotation of *the people as a unified entity*, as implied by the idea that "the public will not accept" a given course of action, or as suggested by the familiar phrase "We, the people of the United States. . . ." It is indeed possible to cite instances from American diplomatic experience to support the idea that occasionally the great body of the citizenry speaks with a clear and compelling voice in demanding or opposing certain policy measures. As illustrations, in the postwar era a broad national consensus has unquestionably prevailed that the United States must oppose expansionist tendencies by the Communist bloc; similarly, for many years, national sentiment has been overwhelmingly opposed to recognition of Red China. Despite such exceptions, the general rule, as V. O. Key has phrased it, is that on

"a great many issues no majority will can be said to exist save by a strained interpretation of that concept."[5]

This leads to one of the most fundamental facts about the relationship of public opinion to the political process in the American society. In the vast majority of cases, there are *many publics and many opinions*. At any stage, and toward almost any issue in American diplomatic experience, a veritable cacophony of voices is likely to be heard advocating diverse, and sometimes totally contradictory, courses of action. Public officials and informed observers are likely to be impressed by the dissimilarity of public viewpoints encountered, by the different levels of enlightenment reflected by various individuals and groups, by the varying degrees of intensity with which views are espoused, and by the diverse techniques utilized by segments of the public to exert their opinions. The fanatical cries of xenophobic agitators, the "resolutions" passed with machinelike efficiency by highly organized pressure groups, the comments of national TV and press commentators, the behind-the-scenes activities of the lobbies in Washington, the temporary flurries in general public attitudes in the midst of diplomatic crises—all of these and more are ingredients in that complex and elusive, but powerful, force known as public opinion.

Once it is recognized that, on most major national issues, no clear majority sentiment exists among the American people, the question arises: what group expresses "public opinion"? The loudest one? The most influential one? The wealthiest and most resourceful one? Those that can claim the largest memberships? Interest-group lobbies who purport to speak in behalf of public opinion? When pollsters find that 51 percent of the population expresses itself for or against a given proposal, have they at last uncovered what "public opinion" demands?

Such questions make it apparent that even today the term public opinion possesses no clearly defined content. Subjective judgments infuse the concept and are unavoidable in the process of investigating its influence upon policy-making. If the "public" is interpreted to mean (and most definitions directly or tacitly assume this) a majority of the adult population which has devoted serious thought to contemporary domestic and international questions and has arrived at a clearly thought-out verdict about them, then it is questionable whether "public opinion" so defined actually exists.

Public Prejudices, Attitudes, and Opinions

Turning next to the question "What constitutes an opinion?" equally difficult problems arise. If by an opinion we mean *a reasonably enlightened and rational judgment* on any given issue, presupposing, in turn, some background knowledge of the issue, it is evident that in practice "opinions" often are rare. The great body of American citizens is poorly informed about public policy questions, especially those having to do with international affairs. After reviewing the evidence, one study has concluded that a majority of Americans is "not interested in foreign affairs as such," and that citizens "take an interest only when those problems clearly affect their own interests."[6] This verdict is corroborated by the extent to which studies have shown that a voter's awareness of, and interest in, foreign policy issues is related to the degree that his own economic welfare is viewed as directly affected by developments in the global arena.[7]

Public opinion polls and other indexes have repeatedly called attention to the passivity of the ordinary citizen about foreign affairs, and to the primitive level of his knowledge about developments in this sphere. Routinely, between 15 and 25 percent of the public expresses "no opinion" on foreign policy issues—and this proportion sometimes runs as high as 80 percent of the individuals polled.[8] As an illustration, a study of opinions by six different occupation groups in the late 1950s showed the following: on the question of whether America would be better off to "stay at home" rather than assume global responsibilities—6 to 23 percent had no opinion; whether the United States ought to extend economic assistance to countries unable to pay for such aid—7 to 26 percent had no opinion; whether the United States should be as "tough" in world affairs as Soviet Russia or Red China—10 to 26 percent had no opinion; whether the United States ought to aid "neutralist" countries—15 to 40 percent had no opinion.[9]

At the same time, there is a significant and often highly influential minority of citizens at the opposite end of the scale that is both extremely interested in external developments and well informed about them. Study and research organizations like the Council on Foreign Relations, the Foreign Policy Association, the American Association for the United Nations, the Arden House Study Group, and other less publicized professional and journalistic societies are at the forefront of organizations providing detailed information and enlightened judgments about global affairs.

There are thus great *qualitative* differences in public opinion. All opinions are not of equal merit, nor are all entitled to equal respect by policy-makers. Indeed, one may question whether certain kinds of viewpoints expressed by the public should be called "opinions" at all. Perhaps "attitudes" or "sentiments" or "prejudices" would be more accurate designations for viewpoints that are often largely intuitive, based upon hunch or emotionalism, and reflect no very clear appreciation of the complexities and subtleties surrounding major global issues.[10] Dexter Perkins has made the point as follows:

> We speak of "public opinion." The phrase suggests what the eighteenth century faith with regard to democratic government prescribed, that the average man makes up his mind by a purely rational process, by a study of the facts as they are laid before him. But is it not an illusion to assume that . . . is actually what takes place? The *facts*, if ascertainable at all . . . are often extremely complicated and are, for that matter, even when known, likely to be weighed subjectively. In the case of large groups of people, it might be better to speak of "public sentiment" rather than of "public opinion." For precise and detailed knowledge is not in the possession of the average citizen. His mood and prejudices are as important as his considered judgments. Indeed, they may influence policy more deeply.[11]

The Public Opinion Process

"The fact is," a recent study of public opinion affirms, "that we have little reliable knowledge about the role of public opinion in shaping foreign policy." Many, if not most, aspects of the process by which public opinion is formulated, by which it is transmitted to policy-makers, and by which it ultimately influences national policy remain shrouded in uncertainty.[12] While great strides in the scientific study of public opinion have been made in recent years, many aspects of the phenomenon remain, and perhaps will always remain, difficult to assess with desired objectivity and predictability. It is clear, for instance, that there are several fairly distinct, although intimately related, "stages" from the initial formulation and crystallization of public attitudes to their eventual impact upon governmental policy. This process may be thought of as embodying three reasonably distinct movements: the *formulation* of public opinion, the *expression* of public opinion, and the ultimate *incorporation* of public opinion into policy decisions. Any one of these movements, in turn, might be further broken down into its components. The stage of opinion formulation, for example, could involve everything from the prolonged and often unconscious (or subconscious) absorption of impressions and rudimentary ideas, to the intensive and careful study of national issues. This stage could also be viewed as entailing the continual *reformulation* of ideas and impressions, leading to an ultimate "crystallization" of opinion, perhaps in the form of a voter's letter to his congressman, an organization's "resolutions" on national policy questions, or an individual's answer to a pollster's questions about prevailing policy issues.

To conceive of public opinion in terms of a process requires that we view it as a phenomenon in a state of constant flux and modification. It is axiomatic that, in a democratic system, public opinion is often crucial in determining policies and events. What is often not so apparent is that public opinion is being continually *influenced by* policies and events. A sudden and unexpected development in the outside world—like the death of Stalin in Russia, or the Chinese invasion of India, or the introduction of Soviet missiles into Cuba—can very quickly and radically transform public attitudes, if in no other way than by converting feelings that had been largely "latent" into passionate convictions, upon which millions of citizens are finally willing to act. In addition, the number of individuals and groups interested in a given foreign policy issue is constantly changing; the internal composition of groups is changing; their resources for expressing their opinions are changing; their ability to gain "access" to governmental officials is changing; their influence upon such officials is changing; and, over long periods of time at least, often their own viewpoints toward national policy questions are undergoing slow, but perceptible, change. Accordingly, policy officials who want to find out what policies public opinion demands and will support are obliged to observe it continuously, to evaluate it from many vantage points, and to test the validity of their findings at frequent intervals.

In our consideration of the interaction between public opinion and public policy, we begin with a case study that will give our discussion concreteness—the Roosevelt Administration's efforts to safeguard national security in the face of ominous outside threats during the neutrality era of the 1930s.

PUBLIC OPINION AND PUBLIC POLICY: ACTION AND REACTION

The Neutrality Era—Case Study in Public Myopia

The drama of New Deal diplomacy toward the European and Asian dictators before World War II contained two underlying and contradictory themes: the isolationist mentality gripped the American people and compelled the Roosevelt Administration to follow policies of noninvolvement in world affairs, while events in Europe and Asia at the same time tended to draw the United States more and more into the vortex of global crises. If isolationist thinking drugged the American population into a kind of apathetic stupor, the actions of Germany, Italy, and Japan ultimately made new departures in foreign policy mandatory. Caught between the forces of isolationism at home and the progressively greater danger from abroad, the Roosevelt Administration was required to formulate and carry out policies capable of preserving at least the barest essentials of national safety without precipitating a violent isolationist reaction among the citizenry.

Roosevelt had taken office in 1933 under circumstances that well-nigh guaranteed the existence of profound isolationist attitudes throughout the country. First, there was the overriding national preoccupation with domestic problems growing out of the Great Depression. Then, there was the historic heritage of isolationism, re-enforced by international events during the 1920s and early 1930s. Except for the interlude of World War I, the United States had consistently maintained a policy of noninvolvement in European affairs and only limited involvement in Asian affairs. And by the 1930s many Americans had come to regard World War I as an unfortunate and unnecessary departure from traditional American policy. These attitudes were powerfully re-enforced after 1934 by the investigation carried out by the Nye Committee of Congress into the reasons for American participation in World War I. The committee purported to have discovered these reasons in the sinister machinations of armaments manufacturers and profit-hungry industrialists. Ready to believe that

American participation in World War I had been a tragic mistake, the American public as a whole accepted these findings enthusiastically.

The committee's revelations spawned a great outpouring of "revisionist" writing, both factual and fictional, which buttressed the prevailing mythology that the American people had been duped by a combination of Allied propaganda, credulous political leaders, and Wall Street into entering a conflict that was none of its business. Poll surveys on the question of American participation in World War I indicate both the intensity of public feeling on the subject and the way that public feeling came to be modified in time by the impact of crises abroad. That almost half the population could, by early 1941, see no connection between the security of the United States and the security of England and France is an eloquent testimonial to the extent of isolationist thinking.* As Secretary of State Hull pointed out later, it was tragic that the country "was thrown into deepest isolationism at the very moment when our influence was so vitally needed to help ward off the approaching threats of war abroad."[13]

Except for brief flurries of popular resentment against the latest reported outrages of Hitler and Mussolini during the 1930s, American public opinion "remained virtually unaffected by international developments from the fall of 1935 until after the Munich crisis in September, 1938."[14] The polls consistently showed an overwhelming majority, running often as high as 95 percent, opposed to American military intervention in Europe on the side of Britain and France.[15] Public opinion was staunchly opposed also to any suggestion, such as that contained in FDR's "Quarantine Speech" of October 5, 1937, that the United States sever diplomatic relations with any country committing aggression.[16]

After the Munich Conference in the fall of 1938, when it became abundantly clear that wholesale concessions would not satisfy Hitler's insatiable demands for territory, American public opinion began to turn imperceptibly but steadily toward the cause of the Allies. Isolationism was still firmly entrenched on Capitol Hill, so much so that

* For this and other poll surveys on World War I, see Hadley Cantril, *Public Opinion, 1935–1946* (Princeton, N.J.: Princeton University Press, 1951), pp. 201–202. This is a voluminous compendium of polls on various subjects during the period covered.

FDR and Secretary Hull had no success during the first half of 1939 in having Congress repeal or modify existing neutrality legislation in order to permit the shipment of arms to countries threatened by the Axis powers.[17] Public sentiment, however, was clearly moving ahead of congressional opinion. A Gallup poll taken in February, 1939, showed 69 percent of the American people willing to take steps short of war to aid England and France. After Hitler invaded Poland in September, interventionist sentiment within the United States reached a new plane: 21 percent of the people favored outright American intervention on the side of the Allies, and 46 percent approved such a course if it appeared that the Allies would be defeated.[18] Yet during the "phony war" in Europe from September, 1939, to April, 1940, interventionist sentiment within the United States began to wane. Roosevelt's speeches advocating preparedness and aid to England and France met with widespread public disapproval. Prominent isolationists toured the country to warn against any American involvement in European and Asian crises and to discount public apprehensions that Axis victories might eventually endanger American security.

Isolationism receded somewhat after Hitler's attack against the Low Countries and France in the spring of 1940. With the collapse of France and the British military evacuation at Dunkirk, a revolution occurred in American thinking about the European conflict. Suddenly the citizenry believed the nation to be in mortal peril! A great crescendo of public feeling demanding preparedness and large-scale aid to the Allies swept the country. One newsman wrote that "the millions are crying havoc with almost a single voice."[19] Sensing, if not fully comprehending, the historic relationship between American security and British seapower, the American people forged ahead of the Roosevelt Administration in calling for an end to neutrality. The near-hysteria that erupted within the United States after the defeat of France prompted Roosevelt to resort to a "fireside chat" to calm the popular agitation.[20]

Although there were ups and downs in popular sentiment throughout successive months, by the end of 1940, isolationism was rapidly losing its hold upon the minds of most Americans. Powerful congressional isolationists continued to oppose measures recommended by the administration. But from late 1940 onward,

Roosevelt won victory after victory against his opponents at home.* To illustrate, in October, 1940, Roosevelt asked Congress to provide for "total defense." Congress responded by granting nearly $18 billion—almost as much money as the United States had expended during World War I. Similarly, in this period, Congress voted conscription, a measure that the Administration had been most reluctant to propose earlier, for fear that it would arouse formidable isolationist opposition.[21] Before the end of the year the United States and Britain had consummated the destroyer deal, whereby 50 over-age American destroyers were exchanged for British hemispheric bases. The polls showed that the public substantially approved this move, which well-nigh eliminated any lingering doubts about whether the United States was genuinely neutral.[22] Isolationism flared up again early in 1941, when Congress debated and eventually passed the historic Lend-Lease bill. Again, the polls showed that popular sentiment was solidly with Roosevelt in providing "aid short of war" to England and France.[23] Henceforth, as relations deteriorated with Germany over American neutral rights, and as Japan prepared for its treacherous attack at Pearl Harbor, the United States was drawn relentlessly into the storm center of international crises.

Public Opinion and the Outer Limits of Policy

The most striking fact that emerges from the case study of Roosevelt's New Deal diplomacy is the degree to which public opinion within the United States established the boundaries within which the administration was required to operate in its foreign relations. Until the Munich crisis of 1938, the administration could do little more than accept this isolationist frame of mind as an unalterable national conviction that set rigid limits upon the foreign policies of the American government. After the Nye Committee's investigation especially, the administration, according to Secretary of State Cordell Hull, took the position that: "There was no hope of success and nothing to be gained in combating the isolationist wave at that moment. To have done so would

only have brought a calamitous defeat and precipitated a still more disastrous conflict on the whole basic question of isolation itself."[24] As late as 1937, when Roosevelt delivered his forceful "Quarantine Speech"** against Axis aggressions, Hull characterized public thinking by saying: "The reaction against the quarantine idea was quick and violent. As I saw it, this had the effect of setting back for at least six months our constant educational campaign intended to create and strengthen public opinion toward international cooperation."[25]

During periods of isolationist ascendancy, Roosevelt and his advisers could do no more than hope international events would prod the American consciousness into at least a rudimentary understanding of the problem of national security. To have done more would almost certainly have risked sacrificing the limited gains already made in undermining isolationism and would have encouraged the rise of demagogues who were ready to capitalize upon existing isolationist yearnings. In few periods of American history has public opinion shaped American diplomacy as markedly as in the Roosevelt Administration from 1933 to roughly mid-1938.

Should policy-makers follow public sentiment or should they seek to mold it to support policies the national interest demands? We have already answered this question partially by saying that, during certain intervals of the neutrality period, policy-makers could follow no other course than to accept the overwhelming national sentiment in favor of isolationism. Yet Roosevelt's foreign policy activities during the 1930s suggest that the relationship between public opinion and policy-makers is reciprocal. Policy-makers are influenced by public opinion and, in turn, seek to create a favorable environment of national sentiment in behalf of needed policies. This leads us to consider the strength of public opinion in the short run and in the long run. As Roosevelt and Hull found out, for instance, during the period of the Nye Committee investigations, public sentiment over

* One indication of this change is the public opinion polls on the subject of conscription. In September, 1939, 39 percent of the public supported it; by May, 1940, 50 percent were in favor of it; and by October, 1940, 76 percent believed it necessary. See Cantril, op. cit., p. 458.

** The "Quarantine Speech" was prompted by renewed Japanese aggressions in China. The key idea was that the "epidemic of world lawlessness is spreading." To meet this epidemic, Roosevelt urged that the international community "quarantine" aggressor nations. For further commentary on the international implications of the speech, see Julius W. Pratt, A History of United States Foreign Policy (Englewood Cliffs, N.J.: Prentice-Hall, 1955), pp. 624–625.

short periods of time may be nearly irresistible. Over the long run, policy-makers can try to educate the public to domestic and international realities and to raise the level of citizen enlightenment on complex public government problems. Cordell Hull wrote in his *Memoirs*:

> One of the basic principles I set myself for the conduct of foreign affairs was to stimulate an informed American public opinion on international events. . . . I intended to be as liberal as possible in making the workings of our foreign affairs visible to the people. I wanted them to see what was going on so that they could realize the nature of the new forces rising abroad and the vital stake their nation had in the peace of the world.[26]

As the relationship between American security and international events became gradually more apparent to the American people, the administration grew bolder in forging ahead of popular thinking. Writing of the late 1930s, Hull stated: "In our policies toward Europe, as in our policy toward Japan we sought to keep reasonably ahead of public opinion, even while seeking to educate public opinion to the importance of our position in the world and to the fatal fallacy of isolating ourselves."[27]

Maintaining an equilibrium between opinion and policy required then, as always, a delicate touch, an acute sense of timing, and an ability to assess the currents of public sentiment with a high level of accuracy. Masterful as Roosevelt was in discerning what the popular temper demanded at any time, nevertheless there were periods when even Roosevelt failed to maintain this hairline balance. In early New Deal days, for example, he tended to overemphasize the nation's indifference to international affairs and to underemphasize his own ability to provide leadership in awakening the country to the significance of events abroad. Moreover, in the early New Deal particularly, Roosevelt failed sometimes to differentiate between temporary flurries in public opinion and long-range fundamental tendencies.[28] In the months immediately preceding the outbreak of war in Europe, and in the weeks that followed, public thinking forged ahead of the Roosevelt Administration in demanding preparedness and aid to the Allies.[29] Still, Roosevelt excelled in his ability to fathom popular thinking and to formulate policies acceptable to it. He perhaps appreciated the mutual influence of policy-makers and public opinion as well as any man who ever occupied the White House.

Moods and Cycles in Public Opinion

Popular sentiment is subject to changing moods and sometimes the changes are sudden and drastic. Thus, in the 1930s, many Americans moved all the way from a deeply entrenched isolationism to an "interventionist" mentality evident at the time of the collapse of France. Between these extremes, the number of Americans favoring "aid short of war" for England and France varied considerably, depending largely upon international developments and their apparent relevance for American security.

Public opinion polls taken on the subject of American-Japanese relations during the 1930s are a good illustration of the cyclical nature of public opinion. The question was asked repeatedly: Should the United States risk war with Japan rather than let Japan continue its aggressions in Asia? When the question was asked in July, 1940, after events had reached a critical turn in Europe following France's collapse, only 12 percent of the people polled favored firm American resistance to Japanese aggression. By March, 1941, this number had risen to 60 percent, only to fall back to 52 percent by July. By August, 1941, the number had reached a new high of 70 percent.[30] Public responses to the question of whether the Allies or the Axis powers would win the European war showed this same cyclical propensity. In the postwar period, American opinion about the Korean War, within less than a year, showed the following changes on the question: Did the United States make a mistake in intervening in the Korean War?

Poll Date	Yes	No	No Opinion
August, 1950	20%	65%	15%
January, 1951	49%	38%	13%
March, 1951	50%	39%	11%

SOURCE: "The Quarter's Polls," *Public Opinion Quarterly*, **15** (Spring, 1951), 387.

On the question of providing American *military* assistance to foreign countries, a significant variation in public opinion during the period 1948–1956 was also evident. Favorable replies ranged from a low of 43 percent to a high of 75 percent in January, 1951, just after Communist Chinese intervention in the Korean War, when it appeared that the United Nations forces might be driven from the peninsula. From that date until June, 1956, the per-

centage favoring military over economic assistance declined steadily.[31]

In a totally different area, Indian sources for
years have complained about the extreme variability of American opinion about Indian policies. One prominent Indian journal noted that:
"Winged exultations have followed fits of depression and vice versa" in American viewpoints toward India's policies and programs.[32]

Generalizing about such examples, analysts
of public opinion have accounted for them by
pointing to the circumstances under which the
public becomes keenly "aware" of issues and is
motivated politically by them. Thus, with respect to how voters view political parties and
candidates in terms of public issues, one study
has pointed to three criteria that must be satisfied before national policy questions become
important in the public mind: (1) The issue
must be recognized as such by the public; it
must be a question about which the public has
become actively conscious. (2) It must also
arouse some intensity of feeling on the part of
the public, as a question that concerns them
deeply. (3) And it must be also accompanied
by the belief that one political party, rather
than the other, represents the voter's own position. In short, some extraordinary event is
usually required to make the ordinary citizen
cognizant of national issues, especially foreign
policy issues; and when that occurs, his opinions sometimes change radically and quickly.[33]

Some students of public opinion also attribute the variability in public attitudes to the
recurrence of "cycles" in the public tempera-
ment.[34] That such cycles have sometimes
existed may be granted. Considerable doubt remains, however, that there is anything automatic or inevitable about them; nor is it clear
that they occur with predictable frequencies.
A number of short-term causes may well explain their presence, some of which we have
already identified. Besides these, mention
might be made of new developments in the
international scene, the extent to which citizens believe the nation's security and welfare
to be connected with such developments, the
influence of presidential or other official efforts
in informing the public about foreign affairs,
and even domestic events and trends which can
shape public viewpoints about the importance
and meaning of diplomatic developments.
Whatever its causes, the mercurial nature of
public opinion in the United States is a reality
that American policy-makers must constantly
bear in mind in shaping the nation's response

to external problems. If it sometimes poses
great difficulties for officials, at the same time
it also presents an opportunity for them to
inform the public in the hope that long-
standing viewpoints will ultimately change and
be brought more into line with realities confronting the nation in the outside world.

Public Apathy and Ignorance About World Affairs

The isolationist era of the 1930s also calls
attention to another characteristic of public
opinion within the United States that presents
a continuing problem for American foreign relations. James M. Burns has evaluated the influence of public opinion on New Deal diplomacy:

> Outside Washington were the millions of
> voters who held the destinies of foreign
> policy makers in their hands. And here was
> the most unstable foundation of all on which
> to build a consistent program of foreign re-
> lations. Great numbers of these voters were
> colossally ignorant of affairs beyond the
> three-mile limit. . . . the American people,
> lacking stable attitudes built on long experi-
> ence in foreign policy making, swung fitfully
> from one foreign policy mood to another,
> from isolation to neutralism to participation
> in world politics.[35]

"Dark areas of ignorance" characterize the
approach of the American people to foreign
affairs. After analyzing numerous public opinion polls and intensive studies of public opinion
in local communities, one reporter concluded
that, in general:

> 30% of the electorate is *totally unaware* of
>   any given international event;
> 45% is aware of the event but cannot in any
>   sense be considered "informed" about it;
> 25% shows a reasonably high level of en-
>   lightenment about foreign policy issues.[36]

These findings are borne out by other studies
and by an examination of the poll results when
questions were asked about important global
problems in the postwar period. A little over
one-third of the people interviewed in 1947
knew what the Greek-Turkish Aid Program
was all about. Later in the year, only 14 percent could give even an elementary explanation
of the purposes and nature of the Marshall
Plan.[37] Similarly, a poll conducted in Cincin-
nati in this period showed that 30 percent of
the people interviewed had no conception
whatever of the purposes for which the United
Nations existed! Another 27 percent had an

inkling of its purposes, but were classified as "poorly informed" on the subject. Some 42 percent could be called "better informed." But only 1 percent of the total number could answer correctly six simple questions about the functions of the United Nations.[38] Even more distressing, a poll conducted later in the same city showed that a six-month educational campaign about the United Nations had little discernible effect in raising the level of widespread disinterest and ignorance about this organization.[39] These and many other studies have led students of public opinion to agree that, as a general rule, voters are much more interested in, and much better informed about, *domestic* questions than about foreign affairs.[40]

What factors explain the ignorance of the public about contemporary global issues and its manifest lack of interest in them? Some writers emphasize the inability of the public at large to inform itself, stressing the lack of information available to masses of the people about complex international questions. Such commentators are prone to believe that citizen enlightenment will be raised as additional and more "objective" information is put at the disposal of the public.* Yet, McCamy has pointed out that the American people "have available to them much more information about foreign affairs than they ever absorb. . . . If the information beats upon their eyes and ears, it is not taken in and retained."[41] Such conclusions are confirmed by other commentators. One study, for example, points out that: "Very few people seem motivated strongly enough to obtain the information needed to develop a sensitive understanding of decision-making in government."[42] The explanation must therefore be found primarily in other factors, such as the intricacy of national issues,

* This theme is especially pronounced in the writings of sociologists who deal with public opinion. Thus Bogardus argues that the public requires more "unbiased" information upon which to base its judgments. He advocates the issuance of "factual reports," so that the public can make up its mind on the basis of the latest research in the social science field. If a "social science digest" were made available in mass quantities, he contends, then "millions will read and be influenced." Overlooking the objection that writings in social science can never be completely "impartial" (or the objection that they even ought not to be so), American diplomatic experience affords little ground for believing that the average citizen would take the trouble to read and reflect upon such reports, even if they were easily available to him. See Emory S. Bogardus, *The Making of Public Opinion* (New York: Association Press, 1951), pp. 59, 144.

particularly external issues. Probably a majority of citizens simply does not understand complex problems in foreign affairs and is not sufficiently motivated to acquire the requisite background to form an intelligent opinion. Moreover, in most instances, there is little "intensity" of belief about international questions. Such questions seem altogether remote and unconnected with the day-to-day problems facing the ordinary citizen. A widespread belief also exists that the average citizen possesses no real power to influence decisions, especially in foreign affairs. Thus, innumerable polls have called attention to a feeling that problems in these spheres must be left to the "experts" and that the citizen can do very little to make his opinions count in the formulation of national policy.[43] The average citizen's overriding concern with the affairs of everyday life, intellectual laziness, a willingness to substitute prejudice for informed judgment and to take his viewpoints second- and third-hand, frustration growing out of the inability to comprehend complex policy problems, apathy stemming from a feeling that his viewpoints count for little anyhow—these largely explain public disinterest in, and a primitive knowledge of, foreign relations.

MINORITIES, INTEREST GROUPS, AND SECTIONALISM

American society is distinguished by the number of group associations that abound and the decisive part these groups often play in the political life of the nation. That America is a "nation of joiners" is a commonplace fact of unequalled significance for any understanding of American politics. Every American belongs to a number of groups: the family, the neighborhood, religious organizations, business associations and service clubs, labor unions, trade associations, political parties, and fraternal organizations. Besides these, he may be a member of a racial or national minority; his section of the country has distinctive viewpoints on at least some questions of public policy.

The central fact about the American, however, is not so much that he is a joiner, but that he belongs to a number of groups at once and that these create within him what the sociologists call "cross-pressures" in molding his opinions on contemporary issues. Kimball Young has defined a cross-pressure "as the operation of two or more determinants of opinion on the same individual or group."[44] Such cross-pressures are key factors in explaining an important and often bewildering characteristic of public opinion about foreign policy issues. This is the presence of fundamental *incongruities* in public attitudes. Polls have shown repeatedly, for example, that public viewpoints on foreign and related domestic problems are highly inconsistent and often contradictory.* Although there may be a number of significant explanations for this phenomenon, one surely is the fact of multigroup membership in American society. In arriving at his viewpoints about public policy issues, an individual often finds himself torn by forces tending to pull or push his thinking in several different directions and to produce contradictions and anomalies in his attitudes toward a range of important questions. With the realization then that multigroup membership is a distinctive feature of American life, let us examine its effect on public opinion within the United States. Specifically, let us look at the effects of interest-group activity, racial and minority group membership, and sectionalism.

Economic and Other Interest Groups

The distinguishing feature of American life, writes the sociologist Bradford Smith, is the "enormous proliferation of special-interest associations. . . ."[45] Political scientists have long regarded such groups as providing a useful complement to the nonideological two-party system within the United States. If special economic, regional, racial, religious, professional and other interests are unable to get the two major parties to take strong and unambiguous positions on policy issues, they are able to express and agitate for their peculiar viewpoints through the thousands of pressure groups active within the nation. The role of interest groups

in the American politico-governmental system is a vast and fascinating subject. Here, we shall look briefly at some of the principal interest groups active in foreign affairs, and identify certain problems that have special pertinence for the study of foreign relations.

It would be well-nigh impossible to enumerate or perhaps even to estimate the total number of pressure groups within the United States. Even if we could, highly subjective judgments would have to be made about the extent to which hundreds and perhaps thousands of organizations that might be interested in a narrow range of public issues really qualified as "pressure groups."** We may, however, get some idea of their multiplicity and variety by looking at a sampling of the groups that testified before the House Ways and Means Committee on the Trade Expansion Act of 1962, since trade bills are among those generating intense pressure-group interest and activity. The following represents only a small sampling among the groups represented:

> *For the Bill* (sometimes with amendments)
> Small Business Administration
> International Telephone and Telegraph Company
> American Association of University Women
> United Automobile Workers
> American Veterans Committee
> Committee for a National Trade Policy
> Cooperative League of the USA
> American Bankers Association
> Tobacco Institute of America
> League of Women Voters
> *Against the Bill* (in whole or in part)
> National Machine Tool Builders Association
> Nationwide Committee on Import-Export Policy
> Hatters' Fur Cutters Association
> Fine Hardwoods Association
> Optical Manufacturers Association
> International Brotherhood of Operative Potters
> Synthetic Organic Chemical Manufacturers Association
> National Board of Fur Farm Organizations
> Rolled Zinc Manufacturers Association
> National Piano Tuners Association

SOURCE: *Congressional Quarterly Almanac,* **18** (1962), pp. 266–270.

* Such anomalies show up strikingly, for instance, with reference to public opinion about support for the domestic measures (such as higher governmental spending and increased taxes) needed to expand activities in foreign affairs. Conversely, studies have also shown that a substantial number of Americans would be classified as "isolationist-liberal," in that they believe in a comparatively high level of governmental welfare programs at home and will support them, but concurrently they are opposed to foreign aid programs abroad and other measures identified with an "internationalist" foreign policy. After surveying evidence available from polls, Key believed that an often crucial factor in shaping public viewpoints toward global affairs is the state of the domestic economy at any given time. Such incongruities are discussed at length in V. O. Key, Jr., *Public Opinion and American Democracy* (New York: Knopf, 1961), pp. 155–163.

** One helpful study admits that "No one knows how many groups there are in America." Yet it cites various calculations that have been made—showing the range of groups in American life. Such estimates range from only 60 groups that possess real political

This list, as is apparent, does not include some of the best-known and most influential pressure groups within the American society. These are, in the first place, the "big three"— the clusters representing agriculture, labor, and business. Within the agricultural community, three major pressure groups exist, along with a host of regional and commodity organizations. The American Farm Bureau Federation (claiming a membership of 1.6 million farm families) was established during World War I with the help of the government. It has the largest membership and is usually regarded as the most influential agricultural pressure group. Its strength is located chiefly in the middle Corn Belt and the central Cotton Belt. In general, the Farm Bureau represents middle-of-the-road viewpoints on internal and external issues. The National Grange (860,000 members) is the next-largest and the most conservative. Its membership includes many prosperous farmers, mainly dairy farmers; the principal center of its strength is the Northeast. The Grange has tended to take right-of-center positions on such issues as agricultural price supports and tariffs. On the matter of trade, for example, it has long advocated a moderately protectionist position. The National Farmers Union (300,000 members)—the left wing among agricultural pressure groups—is the smallest of the national farmers' organizations. Drawing its strength from many of the Midwestern communities that gave rise to the Populist party and Bryanism, the Union consistently champions the cause of the "underprivileged" at home and abroad. As a rule, its foreign policy position is strongly "internationalist," with firm support for an increase in American foreign-aid spending for other countries.[46]

The merger of the two great American labor unions in 1955 has given labor the advantage of being able to speak for 16 million members —11 million from the older and more conservative American Federation of Labor and 5 million from the younger CIO. Recent events, however, indicate that organized labor is far from being completely unified. Powerful groups within the AFL-CIO, such as the auto workers, the steel workers, the teamsters, the machinists, and carpenters compete for leadership and for influence in policy-making.

In the business community, two major and literally hundreds of smaller interest groups can be discerned. The two most influential on the national level are the United States Chamber of Commerce and the National Association of Manufacturers; the former has a membership of some 3400 local and state chambers, while the latter represents more than 20,000 business firms and regards itself as the "voice of industry" in American society. Besides these two large and well-known organizations, there are a host of trade associations and groups, covering every segment of business activity on a local or regional or national basis. A small sampling of this group includes the National Cheese Institute, the Independent Petroleum Association of America, the American Newspaper Publishers Association, the National Retail Merchants Association, the Retail Druggists Association, and many others. In most instances, these smaller groups are concerned chiefly with safeguarding the economic interests of their own members rather than taking clear positions on broad national policy questions.

In addition to economic interest groups, there are a host of others that represent the viewpoints of veterans, religious denominations, reformers, study groups, racial and national minorities, and educational and professional associations. One of the most influential of these in the field of internal security legislation and veterans' benefits is the American Legion. With over 3 million members and 15,000 local posts, the Legion is in a strong position to generate grass-roots pressure upon legislators and executive officials. The Legion has been especially concerned with the patriotism of governmental officials, teachers, and others in positions of public leadership. Its preoccupation with "Americanism" has been as constant as it has sometimes been undiscriminating. The Legion has come close to relegating to itself a monopolistic position in defining Americanism and in differentiating the true patriot from the subversive. "To question the motive or ideals of the Legion's combined thinking is to question the fundamental principles of America," a Legion publication wrote in the recent past.[47]

Among the more influential religious organizations are the Roman Catholic Church, the National Council of Churches of Christ

---

influence, to an upper limit of well over 50 million "spending units" in the population, as revealed by the census. One study showed that there existed 40,000 to 50,000 local labor groups and some 5,000 local and national business groups. For more detailed discussion, see Donald C. Blaisdell, *American Democracy under Pressure* (New York: Ronald, 1957), pp. 58–60.

in America, various Jewish organizations such as the American Jewish Committee, and other groups such as the Friends Committee on National Legislation. Professional and reform groups often prominent in the field of foreign relations are the United World Federalists, the American Association for the United Nations, the Foreign Policy Association, the Council on Foreign Relations, the League of Women Voters, the American Association of University Women, the National Bar Association, the National Congress of Parents and Teachers, the National Education Association, and the General Federation of Women's Clubs.

This brief delineation of some of the more important interest groups active in foreign affairs illustrates the extent of pressure group activity. It is of cardinal importance in understanding their significant role to remember that *economic, religious, professional, and other groups are subject to the same cross-pressures that beset the individual citizen and that affect other manifestations of public sentiment.* For instance, one writer refers to the "big economic, regional, and commodity group cleavages" that are characteristic of American agriculture. These "make a united front very difficult to attain, except occasionally on a single issue."[48] We have already mentioned that the American labor union movement has deep internal stresses within it, so much so that the merger appears sometimes in danger of disintegrating. Business is not excepted from this rule. Within the business community it is not at all unusual for small and specialized business organizations to oppose the positions taken by the larger national bodies like the Chamber of Commerce and the NAM. The result is that agriculture, labor, business, and other segments of the American society are seldom unified in their approach to public issues. Even comparatively small groups that take positions on limited problems, like the United World Federalists, are frequently torn by internal differences of opinion.* That governmental officials are not unaware of such facts is indicated by President Kennedy's view that many of the most active lobbies in the nation's capital are often not attuned to the viewpoints of their own members, and that the policy positions of these organizations are frequently formulated

* The controversy is fully treated in Bernard Hennessy, "Case Study of Intra-Pressure Group Conflicts: The United World Federalists," *Journal of Politics,* **16** (February, 1954), pp. 76–95.

by the leaders of the group and "handed down" to its members.[49]

In view of the multiplicity of divergent opinions held and expressed by interest groups within the United States, how are governmental officials to arrive at accurate assessments of "public opinion" and to take it into account in the formulation of national policy? An almost infinite number of opinions, of varying degrees of intensity, enlightenment, and objectivity, are directed at Washington. In their efforts to appraise the validity of such opinions, policy-makers are thus confronted with an extremely difficult task. One principle, at any rate, would be accepted as fundamental by a majority of officials and students of public opinion alike: however difficult it might be to define, the "national interest" of the United States is something different from the sum total of competing group opinions. Policy-makers cannot, and should not, endeavor to arrive at a conception of what the public interest demands merely by accepting the most clamorous or momentarily influential pressure groups as representative of "public opinion." Governmental officials are among the first to concede that pressure groups often perform a valuable function within the American democracy. Yet, like administrative experts, pressure groups should be on tap, never on top; their demands should always be considered, but never followed blindly and indiscriminately. They are, and must always be recognized as comprising, merely *one segment* of that elusive entity known as "public opinion." Policy-makers are thus required to balance competing group viewpoints against each other, realizing even as they do so that they are often dealing with a small segment of the total population and that on some issues *no* pressure group or coalition of groups in reality advocates the "public interest."

Racial and National Minorities

Throughout the greater part of its history, the United States opened its shores to mass waves of immigrants from the Old World. President Tyler's message to Congress in 1841 sounded the keynote of the nation's policy toward the immigrant:

> We hold out to the people of other countries an invitation to come and settle among us as members of our rapidly growing family; and for the blessings which we offer them, we require them to look upon our country as their country, and unite with us in the great

task of preserving our institutions and thereby perpetuating our liberties.[50]

The census of 1960 showed that over 34 million Americans were either foreign-born or had parents who were foreign-born.* This figure does not include nearly 19 million Negroes, nor does it count some 5.5 million Jewish persons living in the United States.[51]

Yet, mere size alone cannot account entirely for the decisive influence minority group viewpoints sometimes play in formulating national policy. Since many of the same cross-pressures operate upon these groups as upon all citizens, and since different racial and national minorities seldom see eye to eye on public issues, factors other than size usually account for their decisive role. One such factor is the pattern of their distribution throughout the population as a whole. While a few racial and national minorities, for example the Germans, the Scotch-Irish, and the Negroes, tend to be concentrated in the rural areas, most minority groups have gravitated toward the cities, especially cities along the Eastern seaboard, in the Middle Western hinterland and, more recently, on the Pacific coast. In New York State, for example, almost one-fifth of the total population is classified as foreign-born; over one-tenth of California's population is so classified; and states like Massachusetts, New Jersey, Pennsylvania, Illinois, Minnesota, Wisconsin, Michigan, and Ohio have foreign populations that are considerably above the national average.[52]

While it is neither necessary nor possible to discuss in detail the influence which each important ethnic minority has exercised upon the course of American diplomatic experience, we may briefly note several leading examples. During and after World War II, the German-Americans and Italian-Americans frequently played a significant role in influencing American foreign policy toward the Axis nations.

During the 1920s and 1930s, Italian-Americans were far more sympathetic to Mussolini's regime in Italy than most Americans. After Italy finally deserted the Axis camp in World War II, this group was vocal in demanding

that the American government support relatively lenient peace terms for Italy.[53] Similarly, during earlier periods of American history, the influence of the German-American population upon national policy, and upon the larger environment of public opinion within which public officials must operate, was considerable. Some political analysts believe that this group, whose numbers are heavily concentrated in states like Ohio, Iowa, Missouri, and the Dakotas, was an extremely influential force in shaping the traditional isolationist outlook identified with the Middle West. Between World Wars I and II, it exhibited strongly pro-German and anti-British viewpoints; political officials elected from areas having large German-American constituencies were often prone to oppose any American policy contemplating interventionism against the Axis powers during the 1930s. Another group in this same region—the Russian-Americans, who came to the United States in large numbers during late nineteenth and early twentieth centuries—have perhaps been even more staunchly isolationist in their foreign policy orientation. Studies of attitudes held by this group have revealed an extremely low educational level and a primitive understanding of forces operating upon America's external role. An over-all "cultural isolation" characterizes this group that is conspicuous even for often tightly knit foreign-born segments of the population.[54] Now such data must not of course be construed as an all-sufficient explanation of the traditional isolationist viewpoints of the Midwest. Yet the attitudes of ethnic minorities coalesced with other forces tending to engender an isolationist outlook. A policy of intervention was particularly objectionable when it implied American opposition against the homeland of foreign-born groups. In the more contemporary period, vestiges of this historic outlook have emerged in the strong opposition such groups have evinced toward negotiations with the Soviet Union (especially if they entailed possible diplomatic "deals" to the detriment of the old homeland in Europe), and support for measures designed to promote more harmonious German-American or Italian-American relations.[55]

The Irish-Americans constitute another group whose influence upon American politics generally, and upon foreign relations, has frequently been out of all proportion to the numerical size of the group. Perhaps no other foreign-born group has consistently had such

---

* The census of 1960 showed the following ranking of the homelands among ethnic minorities in the United States, as a percentage of the total foreign-born population in the United States: Italy (13.3 percent), Germany (12.7 percent), Canada (9.3 percent), British Isles (8.5 percent), Poland (8.2 percent), Soviet Union (6.7 percent), and Ireland (5.2 percent). *Statistical Abstract of the United States: 1962*, p. 34.

a decisive impact upon American foreign policy down to World War II. The census of 1960 showed 1.8 million citizens still classified as Irish-Americans, a much lower percentage than certain other groups such as the German-Americans or the Italian-Americans. During the period 1820–1947, some 4.6 million Irish immigrants came to the United States. Settling initially in cities like Boston and New York along the Atlantic seacoast, the Irish gradually pushed inland to inhabit Midwestern cities as well. By 1950, Chicago had an even larger concentration of Irish-Americans than Boston. Over 90 percent of the Irish-American population are city dwellers.[56]

On innumerable occasions throughout American history, this group has both held strong opinions and expressed them vigorously. The Irish-Americans, one commentator has observed, "developed many of the shoulder-hitting methods of American politics characteristic of the 19th century. There were many Irish

Who think that freedom must consist In proving points, with sticks and fists."[57]

An outstanding characteristic of Irish-American opinion historically has been its advocacy of liberal, often revolutionary, political causes and its anticolonialist outlook, particularly its opposition to British influence in world affairs. Throughout the nineteenth century the Irish-Americans were at the forefront of American groups expressing enthusiastic support for the European revolutions of 1848 and other uprisings against established authority. In the late 1860s and early 1870s, the Irish-sponsored Fenian movement even led to abortive expeditions seeking to "liberate" Canada from alleged British dominance—thereby perhaps terminating forever any lingering desire in Canada for eventual union with the United States.[58] The "wrongs of Ireland" was a recurrent theme in the viewpoints of the Irish-American population toward almost every diplomatic issue involving Great Britain or British-American relations. The Anglophobia of these and other groups was conspicuous immediately before, during, and after World War I, when the Irish-Americans vocally opposed the League of Nations, in part because of alleged British dominance over its affairs.[59] Irish-American animosity against Britain also expressed itself during the 1930s in opposition to President Roosevelt's increasingly open support for Britain and France against the Axis powers

and, during the early phases of World War II, against his policies of "aid short of war" to nations confronting Axis expansionism.[60] Even as late as 1946, demonstrations against Britain, during a visit to America by former Prime Minister Winston Churchill, were carried out by Irish-American elements in several cities.[61]

Another ethnic minority whose influence upon American foreign policy, particularly since World War II, has been considerable is the Jewish group. This minority has always been acutely sensitive to global development affecting the rights or interests of Jews. In the early 1900s, for example, it was instrumental in bringing pressure to bear upon the American government to protest repeatedly against tsarist persecution of Jewish elements within Russia. Ill will between the United States and Russia over this question finally led in 1911 to the cancellation of a Russian-American commercial agreement.[62] Jewish influence was likewise conspicuous during the 1930s in persuading the Roosevelt Administration to protest against Hitler's barbarous anti-Semitic policies. The classic case, however, of Jewish influence upon American foreign policy—and perhaps the most outstanding example of successful pressure-group activity in recent American foreign relations—involved the American position toward the issue of Palestine after World War II. Zionist groups and their supporters were both vocal and ingenious in bringing pressure to bear upon all levels and organs of government in behalf of Israel.* Even President Truman, who favored the Zionist cause, acknowledged that this pressure was the strongest he encountered on any foreign policy question during his administration. Ultimately, he was compelled to deny access to the White House altogether to spokesmen for the Zionist cause.[63]

These examples suggest that the size of ethnic minorities may be a less important fac-

---

* The policies of the Truman and later administrations toward Palestine are discussed at length in Chapter 11. It is, of course, almost impossible to prove that any specific policy of the United States in foreign affairs has been "dictated" by pressure groups or other segments of public opinion. Frequently, pressure groups are successful because of a pre-existing disposition on the part of officials, or the general public, to accept their policies. For a vigorous dissent from the view that American policy was substantially influenced by Jewish groups during the 1930s and in other periods, see Leo L. Honor, "American Intercession in Behalf of the Jews," *Journal of Modern History*, **22** (March, 1950), 48–51.

tor in accounting for their influence upon national policy than two other factors that sometimes heighten their role. One of these is the fact that in many states having large ethnic minorities, such groups (which often form political coalitions) frequently hold the political balance of power. Public officials, especially *elective* officials, are thus required to take their viewpoints into consideration in shaping governmental policies and programs. Another fact is the *intensity* with which such groups hold and express their viewpoints. Certain policies may arouse deep feelings among foreign-born elements and may arouse them to concerted action in making known their views to policy-makers.

Lobbying by Foreign Countries

By the early 1960s, an increasingly widespread phenomenon involving public opinion and foreign policy was the extensive lobbying activities carried out within the United States by foreign countries or political groups. By 1963, these activities had become so widespread that they prompted a detailed investigation by the Senate Foreign Relations Committee.[64] Its inquiry divulged wholesale evidence of efforts by foreign interests to influence American public opinion and official viewpoints in a manner favorable to the cause advocated by such lobbies.[*] The problem, as defined by the chairman of the committee, Senator J. William Fulbright (Democrat of Arkansas), is that:

> . . . in recent years there have been increasing numbers of incidents involving attempts by agents of foreign principals to influence the conduct of U.S. foreign policy using techniques outside normal diplomatic channels. Various members of this committee have become disturbed by this trend which has been paralleled by an upsurge in the hiring within this country of public relations men, economic advisers, lawyers, and consultants in miscellaneous areas by foreign governments or groups acting in the interest of foreign governments. The tempo

* The evidence gathered by the Senate Foreign Relations Committee is voluminous. The interested student will find this a rich source of information on the problem, since the committee utilized its power to subpoena records not ordinarily available to other observers. Two secondary accounts are: Douglas Cater, and Walter Pincus, "The Foreign Legion of U.S. Public Relations," *The Reporter*, **23** (December 22, 1960), 15–22; and "Foreign Lobbyists: The Hidden Pressures To Sway U.S. Policy," *Newsweek* (July 30, 1962), 18–22.

of this nondiplomatic activity has picked up in almost direct proportion to our Government's growing political, military, and economic commitments abroad.

Senator Fulbright, along with many other members of Congress, did not believe that such activities were necessarily wrong or that they were always opposed to the interests of the United States. In some instances (as in hearings before the U.S. Tariff Commission) opportunities were accorded foreign interests to be represented.[**] Yet, in general, the senator believed that the United States

> . . . should have only one foreign policy, and that policy must . . . reflect our own interests. We should, however, be given the facilities necessary to distinguish between those activities which arise from genuine domestic interest in foreign policy and those which are inspired by foreign governments acting through paid U.S. citizens.[65]

Earlier investigations of the same problem had led Congress in 1938 to enact the Foreign Agents Registration Act, according to which paid agents of foreign principals were required to register with the Department of Justice and to disclose information about the nature of their interests and their finances. By 1960, some 500 such agents had registered as required. Even so, congressional and executive officials alike were convinced that many such agents active in prompting the cause of foreign interests had *not* registered; and, among those who did, some disclosed little useful information about the scope and nature of their activities in behalf of their clients.[66] The chief cause of legislative concern about lobbying by foreign principals therefore was that frequently the activities of such groups remained shrouded in

** That the activities of individuals representing foreign interests are by no means always detrimental to the United States was indicated by Under Secretary of State George W. Ball, who told the committee on February 4, 1963, that foreign agents "can often serve as an interpreter of systems and habits of thought—as a medium for bridging the gulf of disparate national experiences, traditions, institutions, and customs." Sometimes, such individuals can be of "great use to the Department of State in explaining its own views" to other governments and foreign groups. Inherently, there is no reason why individuals representing other countries "should present any dangers to the integrity of American foreign policy." Senate Foreign Relations Committee, *Activities of Nondiplomatic Representatives of Foreign Principals in the United States*, Hearings, 88th Congress, 1st Session (Washington, D.C.: Government Printing Office, 1963), p. 11.

secrecy. In company with their counterparts in domestic affairs, pressure groups representing outside interests have cultivated the art of "indirect lobbying" into a highly ingenious, intricate, and surreptitious process. Primary reliance is placed upon "educational campaigns" to influence public opinion and prominent news media, in which the role of the lobbyist is often studiously concealed from the general public and from governmental officials. Occasionally, selected foreign policy issues elicit open and direct lobbying activities by individuals and organizations representing foreign interests. This occurred, for example, in 1962, with respect to congressional consideration of a bill proposing to eliminate the premium the United States has traditionally paid on foreign sugar imports. The records of the Senate Foreign Relations Committee reveal that

. . . foreign governments and foreign sugar interests hired more than 20 lobbyists, to our knowledge, some of them on straight salary, some with contingent fees [i.e., the lobbyist's fee depended upon the success of his efforts in defeating the bill]. The final legislation contained both the global concept [i.e., elements of the Kennedy Administration's proposals] and the lobbyists' premium concept.[67]

Citing this as an illustration of the success sometimes achieved by such groups, Senator Fulbright was concerned that foreign governments and interests would come to believe that such lobbying campaigns are "an essential procedure if you are going to succeed in Washington. . . ." Other recent instances in which foreign lobbying has been more than ordinarily successful in creating a public or official atmosphere favorable to foreign clients include the generation of widespread support for interests supporting secessionist Katanga Province during the Congo crisis in the early 1960s, and sympathetic treatment by the American government of the claimants to ownership of alien property confiscated by the American government during World War II.[68]

What are some of the major techniques employed in the "indirect" lobbying activities utilized by foreign-sponsored pressure groups? We may allude briefly to some of the more commonly used techniques. Certain lobbying organizations, like one representing the Republic of China on Formosa (formerly Nationalist China) mounted an extensive public relations campaign involving stories, pictures,

films, and other devices to foster a sympathetic American and, more broadly, global understanding of conditions on Formosa under the regime of Chiang Kai-shek. One lobbyist told the committee that "American editors will publish stories and pictures free of charge if they are interesting for their readers."[69] A letter subpoenaed by the committee revealed the purpose of this campaign explicitly. It was ". . . to make the American people aware of the tremendous uphill fight the 10 million Chinese have won on Taiwan [Formosa]. . . ." The letter continued:

The entire effort behind this campaign would be to arouse public opinion in the United States, Canada, South America, and Europe and to create a sympathetic understanding of Free China that would have dramatic impact on members of the United Nations and prevent the seating of Red China in the United Nations and the lifting of trade sanctions against Red China. Too, this campaign will bring vociferous support from the American people when the day comes for a "return to the mainland."

The lobbying firm engaged for this assignment agreed to carry it out for the sum of $300,000. Some 28 different steps were proposed by this firm for promoting the campaign—including dispatching an agent to Latin America, to make societies in this area "free China conscious"; the widest possible circulation of a film entitled "The Face of Free China"; efforts to get a large Hollywood movie studio to distribute a color film entitled "Taiwan—Asian Showcase"; distribution of pictures and articles to leading news media and magazines; on the principle that "grass-roots publicity is priceless," intensive efforts to place materials in leading newspapers, television and radio stations throughout the United States; authorship of articles to be nominally written by members of Congress; and placement of full-page picture advertisements in leading American newspapers. In proposing these and other steps, the lobbyist confessed to its potential client, the Government Information Office in Taipei, Taiwan, that "Money is the 'oil' that will make it [the campaign] work smoothly."[70]

Other organizations have relied upon different techniques, one of which has been to carry on, contribute to, and otherwise sponsor various "educational" activities in the United States in behalf of foreign interests. Such techniques, for example, have been relied upon extensively by the Jewish Agency's American Section, representing the Jewish Agency in Jerusalem, Israel. American Jewish contributors and their sympathizers contributed over $1 billion to the Jewish Agency down to 1963, indicating in some measure the support for Zionist causes existing in the United States.[71] In turn, from 1955 to 1962, the Jewish Agency extended over $5 million to the American Zionist Council to carry out lobbying and educational activities within the United States.[72] Broadly speaking, the American section of the Jewish Agency promoted Zionist goals in regard to the creation and support of Israel. More specifically, it sought to cooperate with, and assist, other groups "in providing information about Israel, its people, their problems, their progress"; to encourage cultural and educational activities favorable to Zionism; and to promote travel in Israel.[73] An outstanding characteristic of this organization's lobbying activities, in the view of the Foreign Relation Committee, was the extent to which the Jewish Agency's funds were expended by an "indirect" process, in which the ultimate source of such funds was concealed from the final recipient and the general public. For example, an organization known as the Council on Middle Eastern Affairs was supported by the Jewish Agency's American Section; yet some of this organization's own officers were unaware that financial support came ultimately from the Jewish Agency in Israel.[74] Money was also contributed from time to time to sponsor conferences on topics (like the status of Jewish minorities in Russia) that were of interest to Zionist groups. The Jewish Agency also subsidized the costs of trips to Israel by American scholars and writers. Public speakers and lecturers were also subsidized, and copies of publications favorable to Israel's point of view were distributed widely to groups and individuals within the United States. In addition, the Jewish Agency's American Section supported meetings by the presidents of some 19 leading Jewish organizations in the United States "to discuss questions of common interest relating to Israel." This organization also contributed funds to educational programs focusing upon studies of the Hebrew language and related subjects in leading universities. Financial grants were also made to organizations like the Synagogue Council of America; in turn, this organization conducted a "program concentration" relating to proposals in Congress affecting Israel and Zionist interests generally. The Synagogue

Council, for example, cooperated with clergymen of other faiths in testifying before Congress against proposed reductions in foreign aid for Israel—testimony which council spokesmen later believed was instrumental in preventing Congress from reducing the foreign aid allocations to Israel.* Evidence also revealed efforts by the Jewish Agency to promote a "Negro project," in which information about Israel would be disseminated among Negro groups in the United States.[75]

As with lobbying domestically, it is always difficult, if not almost impossible, to "control" such pressure group activities, or even to achieve the more limited objective of requiring such groups to disclose their activities so that citizens and officials alike are aware of the efforts by foreign interests to influence American opinion. Constitutional guarantees of free speech and the right of petition preclude stringent regulatory measures; and the line between "lobbying" and "public relations" or "education" remains so indistinct as to make it virtually impossible to discriminate meaningfully and legally between them. It could therefore be safely predicted that such lobbying activities will remain much like an iceberg: those activities that became visible would constitute only a small proportion of those that remained clandestine and largely unknown to the American people and their officials.

Sectionalism and Foreign Policy

Historically, one of the most influential forces shaping American attitudes and policies in the field of foreign relations was sectionalism. From the period of the Napoleonic Wars around 1800 to the interval between World Wars I and II, regional and sectional viewpoints on external issues were pronounced and often sharply divided. During this era, in some instances strong sectional viewpoints became a dominant characteristic of public attitudes toward the outside world.

What constitutes a "section" or "region"? The sociologist John Gillin has identified them

* In evaluating these and comparable claims by lobbyists, however, the reader must be cautioned that one outstanding result of the committee's investigation was evidence that foreign lobbyists consistently exaggerated their effectiveness in the United States. This practice (known as "puffing") was found to be almost endemic among such organizations and is perhaps well-nigh unavoidable when lobbyists are hired on a "contingent fee" basis—that is, when their compensation varies directly with their "success" in lobbying. See *The New York Times*, October 6, 1963.

as areas that "subscribe to the general list of values of the national culture, but with certain additions, emendations, or special emphases more or less peculiar to themselves."[76] The concept of sectionalism is never static. As one commentator has put it: sectional attitudes "change in area and intensity as issues change and as time passes."[77] Inherently, therefore, arbitrary judgments are always involved in delineating sections during any given period of time. The dilemma is illustrated by the problem confronting governmental agencies. As one commentator has phrased it, the Bureau of the Census "has seen fit to make a sectional breakdown, which is ignored in turn by other organs of the government."[78] Any particular scheme for classifying the sections existing within the United States is thus very largely a function of (1) the *purpose* for which the scheme is employed, and (2) the somewhat arbitrary resolution of questions involving borderline cases. We shall not depart unduly from prevailing usage if we envision six major sections in the United States: the Northeast, the Middle Atlantic states, the Southeast, the Southwest, the Northwest, and the Far West.* Nearly every major section, in turn, is divided into subsections. Thus, for the Southeast, Gillin has identified four subsections: the coastal fringe area, the low country, the Piedmont, and the mountains.[79]

While sectional discords have tended to be characteristic of much of American history, a significant trend in the recent period is the growing *unimportance* of sectional differences in public viewpoints toward foreign affairs. As V. O. Key has expressed it: "The impact of World War II in large degree erased regional differences in mass opinion on broad foreign-policy problems."[80] Today, regional attitudes toward global issues differ almost entirely in the matter of degree and emphasis, rather than of fundamental principle.[81] Forces like the high mobility of the American population, the assimilation of immigrant groups, the growth of mass communications media, the continuing involvement of the United States

in global affairs, the "nationalizing" influence of business and labor organizations (as illustrated by the growing industrialization of the South), expanding educational opportunities —these are but some of the major currents that have largely eroded sectional differences and relegated them to a subordinate place in molding national attitudes toward external affairs. This is not to say that distinctly sectional viewpoints have altogether disappeared or that, occasionally, they will not become dominant themes in the chorus of national opinion about selected foreign policy questions. Perhaps more than any other issue, tariff and trade problems frequently evoke evident regional and sectional viewpoints. Yet even here, as with other questions of national policy, the underlying forces shaping national attitudes may not be sectionalism *per se* as much as other forces we have already discussed, like economic interest or ethnic-racial background. Throughout American history it has always been true, and is perhaps even more true today, that sectional attitudes are heavily overlaid with other influences that may be more significant than geographical location or distinctive regional attitudes in producing sectional variations in national opinion. A recent study has underscored the importance of this point, for example, with respect to the South. If, as Lerche contends, there is a discernible tendency among Southern members of Congress away from the region's traditional "internationalist" outlook, the explanation may be found not so much in the fact that Southerners now have changed their minds about the merits of an internationalist foreign policy; rather, it is probably attributable to the fact that waning Southern advocacy of internationalism is a by-product of Southern opposition to forceful civil rights measures, which in turn fosters a disinclination to support costly and unpopular foreign policy programs.[82]

Public Opinion and Policy-Making in Perspective

An experienced public official has written that 25 years ago, a study of foreign policy formulation in the United States "would have taken little, if any notice of the public relationships" of the State Department. Today,

when our policies involve the positive commitment of national resources and manpower or changing the rules governing our domestic life (e.g., tariff rates), and when these policies must be carried out through

---

* Our usage largely follows John Gillin, "National and Regional Cultural Values in the United States," *Social Forces*, 34 (December, 1955), 111. By contrast, Grassmuck conceives of a sevenfold classification: New England and the North Atlantic States, the Great Lake States, the Border States, the Great Plains, the South, the Rocky Mountain States, and the Pacific Coast. George L. Grassmuck, *Sectional Biases in Congress on Foreign Policy* (Baltimore: Johns Hopkins University Press, 1951), p. 37.

international negotiation and agreement—at such times the dependence of a Secretary of State upon the public approaches the absolute.[83]

If it is axiomatic to assert that, in a democracy, governmental policy must always be founded upon a broad base of public opinion, two other facts about the role of public opinion are not perhaps always evident. One is that informed commentators and officials believe the role of public opinion has become more influential in recent years. The other is that the relationship between public opinion and national policy is a two-way street, with policy-makers both *influencing* and being *influenced* by the viewpoints of the citizenry.

These two developments are illustrated by the growth of State Department organizational machinery concerned with public opinion. President Taft in 1909 introduced a "Division of Information" into the State Department; after that time, formal State Department activities centering upon public attitudes grew apace—until in the recent period the State Department's Bureau of Public Affairs employed almost 150 people and expended a salary budget of around $1 million annually for its work.[84] Within this bureau, the Office of News, the Office of Public Services, the Public Opinion Studies Staff, and other units were concerned directly or indirectly with domestic and overseas opinion about American foreign policy.* To adapt the terminology of trade, we may envision the work of such agencies as falling into two categories: the *exportation* of news and background information about American foreign policy to groups within the United States and abroad, and the *importation* or channeling of public attitudes about foreign affairs to policy officials. In the former realm, the activities of the State Department are extensive and highly organized. Routine and continuing responsibilities include the issuance of press releases; the scheduling of press conferences for the Secretary of State and lesser officials; the sponsoring of "briefing sessions" for newsmen, private organizations,

* The reader is cautioned not to confuse these agencies of the State Department with the United States Information Agency (or one of its prominent divisions, the Voice of America). The latter has primary responsibility for carrying on "informational activities" classified as propaganda or psychological warfare toward other countries, especially those behind the iron curtain. These activities are discussed at length in Chapter 14.

and other groups; the publication and release of historical materials about American foreign policy; and the distribution of a great variety of pamphlets, reports, and data about current American policies. In the latter process—the *importation* of data about public attitudes for the guidance of policy-makers—this division systematically samples press opinion, keeps abreast of public opinion polls, takes note of viewpoints expressed by private organizations, and relies upon other indexes in presenting its findings about public attitudes to policy officials. Since 1943, a small staff of specialists has published brief daily opinion summaries; longer and more complete summaries are distributed monthly. The Department of State has sometimes sponsored public opinion polls to test American sentiment on selected foreign policy issues.

Above the level of the State Department, the President and his immediate advisers rely upon other techniques to supplement findings made available from these sources. Analyses of White House mail, for example, provide an indication of public sentiment. From time to time, Presidents have sent their advisers—who often traveled incognito—to "take the pulse of the country" on outstanding public questions. Presidents have also relied upon interviews and press conferences to highlight tendencies in public thinking. President Eisenhower utilized frequent "stag dinners" for this purpose. A variety of devices—ranging from elaborate, scientifically prepared studies to highly personal and impressionistic reactions—familiarize officials with public attitudes about prevailing national issues.

Yet, there is considerable evidence that, thus far, executive departments and officials have concentrated much more heavily upon the *exportation* of information *to* the public than they have upon the *importation* of information *from* the public. Within the State Department, the scope of organizational activity concerned with the dissemination of information is much more extensive, and (by implication at least) deemed to be more important, than the evaluation of public viewpoints. Moreover, there remains a question about the latter activity that also supports this conclusion. To what extent are studies of public opinion actually *used* by policy-makers? Even if officials are now systematically provided with information about public attitudes, do they utilize such information regularly in the stage of policy formulation and administration? Considerable evidence exists for doubting that this is the case. Writing in 1960, one former official said that there was "little evidence that nongovernmental groups have had an extensive, discernible impact on the formulation, as contrasted with the implementation, of American foreign policies."[85] This judgment agrees with earlier assessments by commentators like McCamy and with recent studies tracing out the detailed formulation of policy within the Department of State. An analysis of the flow of policy-making in the department, for example, accords little or no discernible role to public opinion evaluation in the process of policy formulation.[86] This is but another way of saying that the thrust of State Department concern with public opinion since World War II has been concentrated much more heavily upon *informing* the public than it has been upon being *informed by* the public or in taking public viewpoints into systematic account in the formulation of national policy.

Part of the explanation for this tendency must be found in a fact that has been a major theme in our discussion: a large measure of inevitable subjectivism surrounds the study of "public opinion," to such an extent that, even today, policy-makers are compelled to rely upon highly arbitrary, impressionistic, and unsatisfactory methods of determining what the public demands or opposes in the area of foreign affairs. An interesting case illustrating the complexity of the problem involved the difference between executive and legislative viewpoints concerning legitimate methods of measuring public sentiment. In 1957, legislators on Capitol Hill were outspokenly critical of the results obtained by public opinion polls sponsored by the State Department on the matter of American foreign aid programs. These polls showed a much higher proportion of public sentiment in favor of foreign aid than did congressional mail, which tended in general to be extremely critical of foreign aid. Congressional reactions to such polls were so adverse that the department was compelled to discontinue them.[87] This is but one manifestation of the more general phenomenon whereby executive and legislative officials tend to differ in their estimates of the reliability of one method of assessing public opinion over another. One study showed that executive and legislative officials ranked various methods of testing public opinion as follows:[88]

Method of Discovering Public Opinion	Administrators	Legislators
Public opinion polls	1	5
Visits to the public	2	2
Newspapers	3	3
Personal mail to officials	4	1
Visits from the public	5	4

Since each of these methods has limitations as an accurate index of public opinion, undue reliance upon any one of them inescapably distorts the results obtained. For instance, it is axiomatic that personal mail to officials—the first preference on the list of legislators—is sometimes notoriously unreliable as a guide to popular thinking. Skillful lobbyists can and do generate grass-roots "mail campaigns" to influence Congress. Moreover, legislators have found that citizens who oppose a measure are more likely to be heard from than those who favor it. The mere act of writing to an official usually indicates that the writer feels more strongly about the issue than the silent majority. Similarly, there are many well-known drawbacks to public opinion polls, the first choice of executive officials. Pollsters concede that their findings must always allow for a certain margin of error; and on some issues, this may be a fairly wide margin. A long-standing limitation, which pollsters have had only limited success in overcoming, is the difficulty of measuring *qualitative* differences in opinion and degrees of intensity with which views are held. Other methods for appraising public sentiment encounter comparable difficulties. No single method is completely reliable; nor is there any guarantee that all prevailing methods used collectively will yield a clear and unambiguous result, since the limitations inherent in each separate method are bound to show up in the final result. Such shortcomings of course do not argue in favor of abandoning any or all of these methods. But they reaffirm the intricacy of evaluating public opinion, the necessity for continuing progress in the refinement of techniques for doing so, and the recognition that, for an indefinite period, public officials will be obliged to rely upon a variety of more or less accurate methods of measuring public attitudes.

Basically, the role of public opinion in the American democracy hinges on the question: To what extent ought public officials to be guided by popular thinking and to what extent should they attempt to create public support for policies they believe the national interest demands? One authoritative study asserts that, theoretically, "the electorate does not vote on what government shall do." It reminds us that: "The public's explicit task is to decide not what government shall do but rather *who shall decide* what government shall do."[89] Government "by the people" neither philosophically nor practically contemplates that officials must be guided by every passing whim of the public or that they indiscriminately equate public prejudice and emotionalism with reasoned judgment about important policy questions. On the other hand, our study of Roosevelt's diplomacy during the 1930s indicates that there is, and must be, a continuing interaction between public opinion and public policy. If democratic government demands that officials continually take account of public attitudes, this does not mean that they must follow them blindly, irrespective of international or domestic events. An observer of the Kennedy Administration has written that: "It was a deep Kennedy belief that only the voters could really arouse the government. When their concern was genuine, there was no trouble getting what was needed from the Congress, from the Pentagon, from the State Department and from the White House."[90] Assuming this to be true, public officials surely have as much of an obligation to inform and lead public opinion as to follow it. A President's record in office—and ultimately his place in history—is likely to be determined by the extent to which he can maintain a successful equilibrium between policies the citizenry will support and policies the nation's interests in world affairs demand. While seeking to maintain this balance, he and his subordinates must carry on an unceasing effort to raise the level of public enlightenment and to encourage more active and intelligent participation in the politico-governmental process.

NOTES

1. Wilhelm Bauer, "Public Opinion," *Encyclopedia of the Social Sciences*, 12 (New York: Macmillan, 1934), 669–673.
2. Daniel Katz, *et al.*, eds., *Public Opinion and Propaganda* (New York: Dryden Press, 1954), p. 51. A comprehensive collection of readings on public opinion.
3. *Ibid.*, p. 63.
4. Leonard S. Cottrell, Jr., and Sylvia Eberhart, *American Opinion on World Affairs* (Princeton: Princeton University Press, 1948), pp. 9–10.
5. V. O. Key, Jr., *Public Opinion and American Democracy* (New York: Knopf, 1961), p. 90. An illuminating analysis of public opinion in the United States.
6. Katz, *op. cit.*, p. 35.
7. Key, *op. cit.*, pp. 160–161.
8. Katz, *op. cit.*, pp. 36–37.
9. See the studies cited in *ibid.*, pp. 134, 560–561.
10. Kimball Young, *Social Psychology* (New York: Appleton–Century–Crofts, 1956), p. 332.
11. Dexter Perkins, *The American Approach to Foreign Policy* (Cambridge, Mass.: Harvard University Press, 1952), p. 173. This study supplies valuable historical insight into American propensities in foreign relations.
12. James N. Rosenau, *Public Opinion and Foreign Policy* (New York: Random House, 1961), pp. 4, 98. A theoretical appraisal of the role of public opinion in American foreign relations.
13. Cordell Hull, *The Memoirs of Cordell Hull*, I (New York: Macmillan, 1948), 399.
14. Philip E. Jacob, "Influences of World Events on U.S. 'Neutrality' Opinion," *Public Opinion Quarterly*, 4 (March, 1940), 48.
15. *Ibid.*, p. 58.
16. Julius W. Pratt, A *History of United States Foreign Policy* (Englewood Cliffs, N.J.: Prentice-Hall, 1955), pp. 624–625.
17. *Ibid.*, pp. 631–632.
18. Jacob, *op. cit.*, p. 59.
19. William L. Langer, and S. Everett Gleason, *The Challenge to Isolationism* (New York: Harper & Row, 1952), p. 505. This is one of the best studies of American foreign policy during the New Deal.
20. *Ibid.*, p. 479.
21. *Ibid.*, pp. 680–681.
22. Henry Cantril, *Public Opinion, 1935–1946* (Princeton: Princeton University Press, 1951), p. 1160.
23. Jacob, *op. cit.*, p. 54.
24. Hull, *op. cit.*, p. 400.
25. *Ibid.*, p. 575.
26. *Ibid.*, p. 218.
27. *Ibid.*, p. 575.
28. James M. Burns, *Roosevelt: The Lion and the Fox* (New York: Harcourt, Brace & World, 1956), pp. 262–263.
29. Langer and Gleason, *op. cit.*, p. 505.
30. Cantril, *op. cit.*, p. 352.
31. National Opinion Research Center, University of Chicago, *Occasional Reports*, Series FA–No. 4, pp. 13, 15.
32. *The Statesman*, May 15, 1962.

33. Angus Campbell, *et al.*, *The American Voter* (New York: Wiley & Sons, 1960), pp. 169–170. A scholarly and comprehensive analysis of influences on voting behavior.

34. F. L. Klingberg, "The Historical Alternation of Moods in American Foreign Policy," *World Politics*, 4 (January, 1952), 239–273; Perkins, *op. cit.*, pp. 114–128.

35. Burns, *op. cit.*, p. 248.

36. Lester Markel, ed., *Public Opinion and Foreign Policy* (New York: Harper & Row, 1949), p. 51.

37. James L. McCamy, *The Administration of American Foreign Affairs* (New York: Knopf, 1950), p. 313.

38. *Ibid.*, p. 315.

39. Katz, *op. cit.*, p. 38.

40. See *ibid.*, p. 36; Campbell, *op. cit.*, pp. 50, 53.

41. McCamy, *op. cit.*, p. 316.

42. Campbell, *op. cit.*, pp. 543–544.

43. *Ibid.*, pp. 543–544; Key, *op. cit.*, pp. 213–214; Katz, *op. cit.*, p. 39.

44. Young, *op. cit.*, p. 340.

45. Bradford Smith, *A Dangerous Freedom* (Philadelphia: Lippincott, 1954), p. 253.

46. Theodore W. Schultz, "Which Way Will Farmers Turn?" *Foreign Affairs*, 23 (July, 1945), 627–630.

47. Sam Stavisky, "Where Does the Veteran Stand Today?" *Annals of the American Academy of Political and Social Science*, 259 (September, 1948), 131.

48. Ernest A. Engelbert, "Political Strategy of Agriculture," *Journal of Farm Economics*, 36 (August, 1954), 379.

49. Hugh Sidey, *John F. Kennedy: President* (New York: Atheneum, 1963), p. 352.

50. Quoted in Senate Judiciary Committee, *The Immigration and Naturalization System of the United States*, Hearings, 81st Congress, 2nd Session (Washington, D.C.: Government Printing Office, 1950), p. 47.

51. U.S. Bureau of the Census, *Statistical Abstract of the United States: 1962* (Washington, D.C.: Government Printing Office, 1962), p. 34; *The World Almanac: 1962* (New York: *New York World Telegram and the Sun*, 1963), p. 259.

52. *Statistical Abstract: 1962*, *op. cit.*, p. 33.

53. R. M. MacIver, *Group Relations and Group Antagonisms* (New York: Harper & Row, 1944), p. 37. See Particularly the chapter by Max Ascoli dealing with Italian-American viewpoints on national policy. See also William H. McNeill, *America, Britain, and Russia, 1941–1946* (London: Oxford University Press, 1953), pp. 21, 31 n, and 404. This study ascribes considerable influence to foreign-born elements in shaping American policy during this period.

54. Samuel Lubell, *The Future of American Politics* (New York: Harper & Row, 1952), pp. 132–148. For a discussion of the role of ethnic minorities in the election of 1960, see Theodore H. White, *The Making of the President: 1960* (New York: Atheneum, 1961), pp. 222–230.

55. Lubell, *op. cit.*, pp. 150–152.

56. *Statistical Abstract: 1962*, *op. cit.*, p. 34; Senate Judiciary Committee, *op. cit.*, p. 110.

57. Carl Wittke, *The Irish in America* (Baton Rouge: Louisiana State University Press, 1956), p. 105.

58 Thomas A. Bailey, *A Diplomatic History of the American People* (New York: Appleton-Century-Crofts, 1950), pp. 408–409.

59. Thomas A. Bailey, *Woodrow Wilson and the Great Betrayal* (New York: Macmillan, 1945), pp. 24–27; Wittke, *op. cit.*, pp. 288–291.

60. Hull, *op. cit.*, p. 718.

61. Wittke, *op. cit.*, p. 163.

62. Bailey, *op. cit.*, pp. 560n.

63. Harry S Truman, *Memoirs*, **II** (Garden City, N.Y.: Doubleday, 1955), 156–162.

64. Senate Foreign Relations Committee, *Activities of Nondiplomatic Representatives of Foreign Principals in the United States*, Hearings, 88th Congress, 1st Session (Washington, D.C.: Government Printing Office, 1963). This series provides fascinating data about lobbying by foreign governments and interests in the United States.

65. *Ibid.*, pp. 2–3.

66. *Ibid.*, pp. 3–4, 10, 55–57.

67. *Ibid.*, p. 17.

68. *Ibid.*, pp. 17, 122.

69. *Ibid.*, p. 685.

70. *Ibid.*, pp. 685, 693–696.

71. *Ibid.*, p. 1695.

72. *Ibid.*, p. 1696.

73. *Ibid.*, pp. 1698–1700.

74. *Ibid.*, p. 1710.

75. *Ibid.*, pp. 1722, 1726, 1737–1738, 1756–1767, 1774–1775.

76. John Gillin, "National and Regional Cultural Values in the United States," *Social Forces*, 34 (December, 1955), 111.

77. George L. Grassmuck, *Sectional Biases in Congress on Foreign Policy* (Baltimore: Johns Hopkins University Press, 1951), p. 14.

78. *Ibid.*, p. 35.

79. Gillin, *op. cit.*, p. 111.

80. Key, *op. cit.*, p. 106.

81. *Ibid.,* p. 101.
82. See Charles O. Lerche, Jr., "Southern Congressmen and the 'New Isolationism,'" *Political Science Quarterly,* 75 (September, 1960), 321–337. Appraises changing attitudes among Southern legislators toward world affairs.
83. John S. Dickey, "The Secretary and the American Public," in Don K. Price, ed., *The Secretary of State* (Englewood Cliffs, N.J.: Prentice-Hall, 1960), pp. 139, 142.
84. *Ibid.,* pp. 142, 148–149.
85. *Ibid.,* p. 157.
86. See McCamy, *op. cit.,* p. 331, and the case study of policy formulation by Charlton Ogburn, Jr., in Brookings Institution, *The Formulation and Administration of United States Foreign Policy* (Washington: Brookings Institution, 1960), pp. 172–177.
87. Dickey, *op. cit.,* p. 160.
88. Martin Kriesberg, "What Congressmen and Administrators Think of the Polls," *Public Opinion Quarterly,* 9 (Fall, 1945), 334.
89. Campbell, *op. cit.,* p. 541.
90. Sidey, *op. cit.,* p. 142.

8 → THE COLD WAR IN
HISTORICAL PERSPECTIVE →

Thus far, we have studied the formulation of American foreign policy and evaluated the major influences and institutions that have an important role in it. We now begin a consideration of the substance of American foreign policy in the contemporary era.

In this and subsequent chapters we shall follow a similar approach: first, a brief historical background dealing with the past relations between the United States and other countries or with America's attempt to cope with important international questions is established; then, utilizing this background as a perspective within which to view contemporary problems, the basic issues that have given rise to such problems are analyzed. This chapter and the next examine relations between the United States and Soviet Russia. The sequence of topics covered is indicative of the approach to be followed in the remainder of our study: enduring elements in Russian foreign policy; Russian-American relations to World War II; ideological conflict in the postwar period; strategic-territorial conflict in the postwar period; and economic-military conflict in the postwar period. This approach provides a more helpful frame of reference within which to evaluate current American foreign policy than would a chronological recital of major developments in Soviet-American relations since 1917.

Let us then look initially at certain influences in Russian foreign policy which must be properly understood in order to comprehend the issues that divide Russia and the United States in the contemporary era.

ENDURING GOALS OF RUSSIAN FOREIGN POLICY

The Centrality of Historical Insights

Engraved upon the National Archives Building in Washington are the words: "What Is Past Is Prologue." It is a central thesis of this first chapter dealing with substantive problems in American foreign relations that Americans seldom pay enough attention to the lessons of history in their attempt to understand the issues stemming from the dominant international problem of their age—the cold war. It may appear unnecessary to remind a society as history-minded as the American that the past has much to teach the student of present-day world affairs. Yet Americans seem often more inclined to venerate the past than to learn from it. Applying this idea specifically to Russian-American relations, what we are suggesting is this: history shows a remarkable continuity in Russian foreign policy, whether that foreign policy is practiced by the tsars or the Communists. Continuity can be discerned in both the *goals* of Russian foreign policy and in the *methods* utilized for achieving them.

Two examples must suffice at this stage. Is world domination generally believed to be a cardinal diplomatic ambition of the USSR? "A strange superstition prevails among the Russians, that they are destined to conquer the world . . . ," said a State Department dispatch in the mid-nineteenth century.[1] And is the Kremlin thought by the West to be utterly unprincipled in its dealings with other countries, so much so that its promises are looked upon as worthless? A Russian historian once described tsarist diplomacy as follows:

> The diplomatic methods of the Muscovite boyars often threw the foreign envoys into desperation, particularly those who wanted to carry on their business forthrightly and conscientiously. . . . in order not to fall into their nets it was not enough to make certain that they were lying; it was also necessary to decide what the purpose of the lie was; and what was one to do then? If someone caught them lying, they did not blush and they answered all reproaches with a laugh.[2]

At the time of the Russo-Japanese War in 1905, Theodore Roosevelt declared that "Russia is so corrupt, so treacherous and shifty . . . that I am utterly unable to say whether or not it will make peace, or break off negotiations at any moment."[3] Western diplomats in the modern period would likely find these descriptions remarkably apropos in characterizing the difficulty of maintaining harmonious relations with the USSR.

These examples are cited at the beginning of our study of Russian-American relations to stress the importance of setting contemporary cold war problems within the requisite historical context. Americans are prone to think of the cold war as a conflict between Soviet communism and Western democracy. Ideological elements are unquestionably present. Yet such an oversimplified approach gives rise to many dangers and misapprehensions. Americans are likely to fall into the error of thinking that the Bolshevik Revolution of 1917 ushered in a *totally* new era in the relations between Russia and the outside world, and in international politics generally. This of course is the viewpoint assiduously cultivated by the Kremlin itself. Students of foreign policy, however, must not jump to the conclusion that Russian diplomacy before 1917 is unrelated to present-day Soviet diplomatic behavior. They must be skeptical of the viewpoint—a cardinal article of faith in the communist creed—that Marxist-Leninist-Stalinist ideological compulsions furnish the most useful keys to understanding Russia's activities in the international community since 1917. They must not try to arrive at a guide to Soviet diplomatic conduct merely by piecing together utterances and writings by high-ranking Communist spokesmen.*

* A number of studies of Soviet foreign policy in the recent period implicitly foster such a view. One

What is basic for understanding Soviet diplomatic goals and methods at any stage is not so much what Lenin or Stalin or lesser Communist luminaries *said* Soviet Russia was doing or going to do in world affairs, but rather what Russia has in fact *done* both in the tsarist and in the communist periods. Creation of "People's Democracies" by the bayonets of the Red Army in Eastern Europe does not differ from old-style tsarist imperialism in the same area merely because Stalin baptized his hegemony with quotations from Marx and Lenin. The tsars could invoke a variety of slogans too, such as "legitimacy" and Pan-Slavism, to justify what was in essence *Machtpolitik*.

Age-old Russian foreign policy goals and methods, blended and overlaid with communist ideological compulsions, provide the key to the foreign policies of the Kremlin. More and more since 1917, Soviet Russia has given evidence of diplomatic atavism, a characteristic which is not, of course, peculiar with Russia. One of the most fascinating aspects of Soviet diplomacy is the degree to which Stalin and his successors have ingeniously fused the historic diplomatic ambitions of Old Russia with the communist faith. As much as any other single factor, it is this union that confronts the free world coalition, led by the United States, with a formidable and continuing challenge. Because Americans generally give insufficient attention to the historical elements of Russian foreign policy, we shall devote considerable space here to analyzing them.

Expansionism—The Keynote of Historic Russian Policy

A newspaper reporter during the Crimean War in the mid-1850s wrote of Russia:

> The Russian frontier has advanced: towards Berlin, Dresden and Vienna . . . towards

outstanding example is Nathan Leites's work, *A Study of Bolshevism* (New York: Free Press of Glencoe, 1953). This is a thorough and valuable compendium of communist doctrinal statements on a variety of subjects. Leites attempts, as it were, to provide a kind of "code" to the behavior of the Kremlin in world affairs. Yet, by focusing his inquiry almost entirely upon ideological influences, this study inherently suggests that motivations arising from historical, geographical, strategic factors—not to mention the Soviet Union's day-by-day response to developments in the outside world—are relatively unimportant in explaining the USSR's diplomacy. As we shall see in this chapter and the next, this seems at best a highly questionable assumption.

Constantinople . . . towards Stockholm . . . towards Teheran. . . . The total acquisitions of Russia during the last 60 years are equal in extent and importance to the whole Empire she had in Europe before that time.

And in another dispatch the same reporter declared that:

And as sure as conquest follows conquest, and annexation follows annexation, so sure would the conquest of Turkey by Russia be only the prelude for the annexation of Hungary, Prussia, Galicia, and for the ultimate realization of the Slavonic Empire. . . . The arrest of the Russian scheme of annexation is a matter of the highest moment.

So wrote a German correspondent—Karl Marx—who was to have no little influence on the future course of Russian history.[4] The word that best characterizes Russian foreign policy throughout history and furnishes the most evident and important link between Russia's past and present policies in the international community is the word *expansionism*. Beginning as an insignificant twelfth-century city in the valley of the Dnieper, by the post-World War II period Moscow was the center of an empire that embraced one-fourth of the human race and 13 million square miles, excluding countries like China and Yugoslavia that are ideologically affiliated with the Kremlin.[5]

The saga of Imperial Russia was a story of almost uninterrupted territorial expansion, initially over the great Eurasian plain that stretches from Poland and European Russia to the borders of Persia, India, and China; and then, after the plain had been occupied and consolidated, of continual pressure against the natural boundaries that surround Russia, such as the Dardanelles, the Himalayas, the deserts of Central Asia and the river systems of Manchuria.

Patiently, bit by bit, successive tsars pushed back the boundaries of Russia, and in doing so they sometimes created troublesome international problems. Peter the Great finally won the long-coveted "window on the West" when he wrested much of the Baltic region from Sweden; Catherine the Great participated in Poland's three partitions, in 1772, 1793, and 1795, and pushed Russian frontiers steadily southward to encroach upon the Turkish Empire. Her successors continued the march southward and eastward by maintaining pressure against the frontiers of Turkey, Persia,

Afghanistan, and India—thereby generating one of the most persistent diplomatic problems of the nineteenth century. At Tilsit in 1807, Alexander I and Napoleon attempted to divide most of Europe between them. And after Napoleon's defeat, Alexander annexed Poland, Finland, and Bessarabia, and engaged in intrigues in virtually every country in Europe. Nicholas I and Alexander II sponsored explorations and colonization movements eastward into Central Asia and Siberia, bringing Russia ultimately into conflict with Japanese and, to a lesser extent, British and American diplomatic ambitions in the Orient.

It is instructive to recall tsarist territorial ambitions at the beginning of World War I. Had Imperial Russia been victorious, it expected to push its territory westward to incorporate what was the Poland of 1919–1939; annex East Prussia and all of the area west of the Vistula; annex Eastern Galicia; overthrow the defunct Turkish Government and realize Russia's ancient ambition to control the Straits; and annex Turkish territories bordering Transcaucasia.[6]

Tsarist expansionism derived from several impulses. First of all, Russia pushed inexorably across the Eurasian plain in much the same way as Americans trekked across their continent. Prince Michael Gorchakov wrote of his country's history that Russia, in common with all countries, was "forced to take the road of expansion dictated by necessity rather than by ambitions, a road on which the chief difficulty is to know where to stop."[7] The tendency to expand into territorial vacuums is neither a peculiarly Soviet, nor even tsarist, trait.

Second, the expansionist tendencies of the tsarist state sprang in part from politico-strategic necessities. The vast, frontierless Eurasian plain facilitated Russian internal expansionism, but it also greatly aided foreign incursions into the interior of Russia. Historically, the response of the tsarist state was to provide for defence in depth by creating an extensive buffer zone around its vulnerable geographic heartland. Safeguarding the military approaches to the interior has been a cardinal principle of Russian diplomacy since the time of Peter the Great, as it would have to be a diplomatic principle of any great power faced with a comparable threat.

Third, expansionism by the nineteenth century came to have an economic rationale. Russia, along with the other great powers, wanted a stake in foreign markets, both to increase the treasury and Russian prestige. The search for colonies led primarily to Manchuria, where Russian imperialism clashed with the territorial and economic ambitions of Japan, England, and the United States. As in American and British imperialism, economic concessions necessitated protection by Russian diplomats and soldiers. From 1904 to 1905, the Manchurian venture drew Russia into the most humiliating war in its history when it was humbled by the small island kingdom of Japan.

Fourth, a recurrent motif in Russian expansionism was the "historic mission" of Russia to deliver lesser people from their cultural and spiritual backwardness and to usher in the earthly millennium. Since we shall examine Russian Messianic thought in a later portion of the chapter, we shall merely observe here that the Messianic aspirations of certain secular and religious thinkers within Russia coincided perfectly at points with the diplomatic ambitions of the tsarist state. The foreign policies of Alexander I (1801–1825) illustrate the point. Alexander exhibited a calculating Machiavellianism, combined with a fervent and mystic idealism. He was capable of both the Treaty of Tilsit (1807), whereby he and Napoleon divided Europe between them; and of the high-minded, if totally impractical Holy Alliance (1815), whereby Christian principles were to be made the basis of international conduct. Europeans, writes a contemporary British historian, must have wondered whether Alexander was not "just a cunning hypocrite, cultivating liberal sympathies and evangelical piety as a cloak to hide vast plans of aggressive ambitions. . . ." He was apt to "identify his own interest, or whims, with the good of humanity." Professing that all men ought to be free—at the very time he was annexing Poland, Finland, and Bessarabia —Alexander, "desired all men to be free on condition they did what he wanted them to do."[8]

The Search for Warm Water Ports

Closely related to expansionism is Russia's age-old search for warm water ports. Landlocked around most of its borders, Russia has always needed accessible and usable outlets to the sea. The ports of Murmansk, Archangel, and Leningrad are icebound a considerable portion of the year. To the south, Russian traffic on the Black Sea has always been at the mercy of Turkey, which controls the Darda-

nelles, or Turkey's protectors, such as Great Britain and, to a lesser degree, France during the eighteenth and nineteenth century. Since 1947, the United States has filled the vacuum created by the decline of British power in the Straits area and throughout the Near and Middle East as a whole.

South and eastward, Russian diplomacy has sought to force a breakthrough to the sea by intermittent pressure upon Persia, Afghanistan, and India. In addition to furnishing rich prizes to incorporate into the Russian empire, acquisition of passageways through these countries would give Russia access to the trade routes of the world. The modern American policy of containment had its origins along the Persian-Russian border and in the bleak hills of the Northwest Frontier in India during the nineteenth century. A dominant objective of British diplomacy during the age of *Pax Britannica* was to prevent Russian penetration of the Middle East. Throughout British colonial history, Russia was continually probing soft spots in the British defense perimeter and endeavoring to enlist other people, such as the Afghan tribesmen along the Indian frontiers, to further Russia's diplomatic ambitions.

Still further eastward, Russia advanced over Siberia and Central Asia toward the shores of the Pacific. The tsars at last acquired outlets to the sea when they obtained or leased ports in Siberia and Manchuria late in the nineteenth century. With the completion of the Trans-Siberian Railroad by 1900, these ports became useful, even though they were icebound a goodly part of the year, were extremely vulnerable to foreign attack, as the Russo-Japanese War proved, and even though they were some 6000 miles from European Russia. Russia's search for eastern seaports, coupled with the necessity to assure their accessibility over the railroads of north China, inevitably drew it into the maelstrom of great-power imperialistic rivalry in the Far East.[9]

Are Soviet policy-makers today still seeking outlets to the sea? The question hardly requires an answer. Soviet incorporation of the Baltic States, intermittent pressure on Turkey to give the USSR a larger voice in safeguarding the Turkish Straits and determining policy toward them; Communist intrigue in the northern provinces of Iran in 1946, support for the Greek rebels in 1946–1947, more recent economic blandishments to Afghanistan, India, and Burma, Communist machinations in Syria, Egypt and other Middle Eastern countries—

all of these indicate that there has been little diminution in the traditional Russian urge to the sea.

The "Iron Curtain Complex"

When Winston Churchill stated in 1946 that an iron curtain had descended over Europe, he was coining a phrase that applied equally well to earlier stages in the history of Russia's relations with Europe. An "iron curtain complex" has been characteristic of the Russian attitude toward the outside world for centuries. When a *cordon sanitaire* or formidable geographical barriers did not effectively seal Russia off from contact with its neighbors, then a spiritual iron curtain has done so during most periods of Russian history. Estrangement and hostility took many forms: rigorous government censorship of ideas and communications from abroad; limited contacts between Russian citizens and foreigners; official coolness, amounting often to outright discrimination, toward foreign diplomats in Russia; belief in the inherent superiority of Russian customs and institutions; and unwillingness to cultivate sincere and lasting ties of friendship with other countries. With some significant exceptions, almost every period of Russian history has exhibited a deep-seated xenophobia.*

In pre-Soviet history many factors engendered suspicion and hostility toward the outside world. In some periods, like the late nineteenth and early twentieth century, Russia was militarily much weaker than other countries suspected. The Russo-Japanese War and World War I showed this. Furthermore, Russia was economically backward. The contrast between its rate of industrialization and standard of living and that of its advanced western neighbors was a source of constant embarrassment and insecurity. Moreover, under both the tsars and the Communists, Russia

* While xenophobia has been characteristic of the Russian *government*, there existed a considerable interchange of cultural and political ideas between Russian citizens and the outside world under the tsars. Barghoorn in fact maintains that the Russian population as a whole has traditionally been highly receptive to ideas from abroad and that even under the Communists, Soviet citizens have shown keen interest in the viewpoints of foreigners. See Frederick C. Barghoorn, *Soviet Russian Nationalism* (New York: Oxford University Press, 1956), pp. 162–164. For an illuminating treatment of the impact of American political ideas upon the tsarist state in the eighteenth and nineteenth centuries, consult Max M. Laserson, *The American Impact on Russia* (New York: Macmillan, 1950).

has feared the impact of western political ideals upon a population restive under despotism. Then, too, neither the tsarist nor Communist regime has relished having the whole apparatus of state oppression—the ubiquitous secret police, the massive bureaucracy, the Siberian prison camps, the policies of censorship and suppression of designated minorities—exposed to the gaze and ridicule of the world. Lurid accounts of these aspects of Russian life have always fostered tension between Russia and other countries. To avoid unfavorable reports in foreign countries, Russia has preferred to close the door to foreigners entirely or to permit them to see only a few selected showplaces.

Intense suspicion and fear of the outside world has been engendered also by Russia's historical experiences under both the tsars and the Bolsheviks. The motif of cataclysm, perennial danger from abroad, and impending doom is a recurrent theme in Russian literature and political writing. In large measure it is a product of Russian geography and of history dictated by geographical conditions. The eminent British scholar Sir Bernard Pares has written: "The Great Russian people were hammered out of peaceful, silent pacific elements by constant and cruel blows from enemies on all sides, which implanted into the least intelligent of Russians an instinct of national defense. . . ."[10] And Mazour adds that "The motivating background of Russia's foreign policy is predominantly the need for security. . . ." He continues:

> The Napoleonic Wars culminating with the occupation of Moscow, the Crimean War ending with the disaster at Sevastopol, the Russo-Turkish War . . . , World War I ending with Allied intervention, and above all World War II with its appalling devastation—these are experiences which no nation can forgive or forget.

Whether justified or not, he feels that, inevitably, Russia will seek "a *cordon sanitaire* in reverse, with its bayonets turned westward. . . . it is the ABC of national strategy."[11]

Fostered by countless invasions throughout history, the Russian legacy of suspicion and fear of the outside world is exemplified in the attitude of the reactionary Pobedonostsev, adviser to Alexander III (1881–1894). Pobedonostsev was convinced that "it is impossible to rely upon any of our so-called 'friends' and 'allies,' that all of them are ready to hurl themselves upon us at that very minute when our weakness or errors become apparent."[12]

The "Third Rome" Idea and Russian Messianism

The communist hope of redeeming mankind through the "world revolution" and achieving utopia is a variant of a theme that pervades historic Russian theological and philosophical thought. In a penetrating study of Russian national character, Nicolas Berdyaev states that: "Messianic consciousness is more characteristic of the Russians than of any other people except the Jews. It runs all through Russian history right down to its communist period."[13] Its earliest origins are to be found in the conception of Moscow as the "Third Rome." After the fall of Rome in the fifth century and the collapse of the Byzantine Empire in the fifteenth, the center of Orthodox Christianity shifted to Moscow. To Russian theologians this signified a profound and God-ordained change in the direction of history. Thus the monk Philotheus informed Basil III, Grand Duke of Moscow:

> The first Rome collapsed owing to its heresies, the second Rome fell victim to the Turks, but a new third Rome has sprung up in the north, illuminating the whole universe like the sun. . . . The first and second Rome have fallen, but the third will stand till the end of history, for it is the last Rome. Moscow has no successor; a fourth Rome is inconceivable.[14]

"The Mission of Russia," comments Berdyaev, "was to be the vehicle of the true Christianity. . . . There enters into the messianic consciousness the alluring temptation of imperialism."[15] Strongly reinforcing the theological designation of Moscow as the Third Rome were the viewpoints of the Slavophils, and their nineteenth-century successors, the Pan-Slavists. Compounded of Russian nationalism, mystic ties of race, German idealism, and Hegelian philosophy, Slavophilism predicted the inevitable decay of Europe and the redemption of mankind by the Slavs. "Western Europe is on the high road to ruin," Prince Odoevsky wrote. Advancing the theme of *ex Oriente lux* that permeates Russian philosophic and religious thought, he believed that:

> We Russians, on the contrary, are young and fresh and have taken no part in the crimes of Europe. We have a great mission to fulfill. Our name is already inscribed on the tablets of victory: the victories of science, art and faith await us on the ruins of tottering Europe.[16]

And the Russian mystic Peter Chaadaev believed that "we have a vocation to solve a great many of the problems of the social order . . . to give an answer to questions of great importance with which mankind is concerned."[17] Describing man's quest for spirituality and holiness, the immortal Dostoevsky stated in 1880: "I speak only of the brotherhood of man, not of triumphs of the sword. . . . For I am convinced that the heart of Russia, more than any other nation, is dedicated to this universal union of all mankind. . . ."[18]

The Pan-Slav movement late in the nineteenth century also contained Messianic elements. According to its leading spokesmen, Russian cultural-historical affinity with the Slavs gave the Russian state a special responsibility as protector and defender of their interests. The Pan-Slavs, writes Florinsky, "were in general agreement that it was the historic mission of Russia to liberate the Slavs from a foreign and religious and political yoke. . . ."[19]

Other influences evident in certain periods of Russian thought also supported Messianism and assigned to Moscow a dominant role in achieving the salvation of mankind. One of these was nihilism. Another was anarchism. Berdyaev summarizes the viewpoint of the most famous Russian anarchist, Michael Bakunin, as follows:

> What is needed is to set fire to a world-wide blaze; it is necessary to destroy the old world; upon the ashes of the old world, on its ruins, there will spring up a new and better world of its own accord. . . . Collectivism or communism will not be an affair of organization; it will spring out of the freedom which will arrive after the destruction of the old world.[20]

Also important is the attention given in Russian Orthodox theological thought to the coming of the Kingdom of God. In contrast to Roman Catholic and Protestant thought, Russian Orthodox theology has always emphasized the early apocalyptic message of the Church. The coming of the Kingdom of God will mean the "transfiguration of the world, not only the transfiguration of the individual man." Salvation is conceived of as total and corporate for society.[21]

Russian Messianism, concludes Berdyaev, is perfectly compatible with the mission of Marxism-Leninism-Stalinism to redeem mankind and recreate society anew upon the ruins of the old order. "Russian communism is a distortion of the Russian messianic idea; it proclaims light from the East which is destined to enlighten the bourgeois darkness of the West."[22] Analyzing the Messianic elements in contemporary Soviet policy, Barghoorn observes that the Kremlin "holds out to mankind the vision and prophecy of the earthly paradise, the harmonious society without coercion and inequality. This is the utopian aspect of Soviet Russia's message to the world. . . ."[23] The point is well exemplified by an article in *Izvestia* on February 22, 1948, which discusses Russia's contribution to humanity in World War II:

> The Soviet Army . . . stretched out a brotherly, helping hand to the peoples of Europe languishing in Fascist Slavery. The European peoples have to thank the Soviet Army for their liberation. . . . The Soviet Army saved European civilization from the Fascist barbarians, honorably and worthily performed its historic liberating mission. . . . As always, the Soviet Army stands on guard to protect the peaceful labor and tranquility of the peoples. Always, it stands on guard for peace throughout the world.[24]

RUSSIAN-AMERICAN RELATIONS BEFORE WORLD WAR II

The Nineteenth-Century Pattern

Relations between Russia and the United States in the late eighteenth and throughout most of the nineteenth century were governed by influences that were to shape many of their relationships in the more recent period. At first, Russia and America had relatively few direct contacts and hence few common problems. Geographically separated, their interests touched directly in only one part of the globe —the Far East—and even this occurred only toward the end of the nineteenth century, when the United States emerged as a Pacific power.

A second characteristic of their relations was official coolness, interspersed with periods of ideological hostility and suspicion. The leading democracy in the world and the tsarist autocracy had few ideas and institutions in common. To successive tsars, the American democracy was a fertile seedbed for spawning revolutionary ferment; its very existence encouraged rebellion against established authority within Russia and throughout Europe as a whole. The policy of welcoming political exiles

added to prevailing ideological tensions. To the United States, tsarist Russia was the quintessence of despotism and political backwardness—in short, the antithesis of every American Revolutionary ideal. Informed Americans were aware that it was Alexander I, in concert with the arch-reactionary of the age, Prince Metternich of Austria, who was invoking the principle of "legitimacy" to exterminate all vestiges of political liberalism in post-Napoleonic Europe. And, it was a common American misapprehension that President Monroe's blunt warning to the European powers in the famous Monroe Doctrine of 1823 had kept the Holy Alliance from extending its noxious activities to the American continent.

Given the incompatibility of American and Russian political ideals and institutions, it is understandable why relations between the two countries did not begin auspiciously. The first American Minister to Russia, Francis Dana, was kept cooling his heels in St. Petersburg for two years; even then he left Russia in frustration, without being able to gain audience with Catherine the Great.[25] Alexander I finally extended Russian recognition to America in 1809, long after other countries had done so. It was not until 1824 that treaty relations were established between the two governments.[26]

During the years that followed, ideological hostility colored relations between Russia and the United States on many occasions. Americans were vocally anti-Russian during the Polish Revolt of 1830, which the tsar suppressed with characteristic ruthlessness.[27] Again, in 1863, American public opinion was strongly anti-Russian during the tsar's intervention in Poland, even though the American Civil War marked the high tide of Russian-American friendship.[28]

As the nineteenth century waned, ideological estrangement between Russia and America intensified. Tsarist oppressions, both within Russia and in surrounding countries, drove ever larger groups of refugees to American shores. The program of "Russification" inaugurated by Alexander III (1881–1894), resulting in oppressive measures against minorities within Russia and harsh pogroms against the Jews, aroused heated opposition within the United States, especially on the part of the foreign-born population. On top of this, in the same period there were a number of sensational exposés about Russia by American citizens who had traveled in that country. Especially significant in arousing anti-tsarist sentiment within the United States were the revelations of George Kennan,* whose graphic descriptions of life in the prison camps of Siberia stirred the American consciousness about Russia as perhaps no other influence had done in the tsarist period.[29]

The American people entertained high hopes for the Russian Revolution of 1905. But its perversion by reactionary forces within Russia, coupled with continued persecution of the Jews and other minorities, finally led to a breach in Russian-American relations in 1911, when the United States abrogated the commercial treaty of 1832. Commercial relations between the two countries were not re-established until the period of the New Deal.[30]

While geographical separation and ideological estrangement were important factors in relations between Russia and the United States before World War II, there was a third and much more basic factor. Until the emergence of both countries as superpowers in the contemporary period, the controlling principle in their relations, as DeWitt Poole has phrased it, was that in critical times each nation was "for the other a potential friend in the rear of potential enemies."[31] Until around 1900, for both Russia and the United States the potential enemy was in almost every case Great Britain. After 1900, it came more and more to be Japan; and during the period of the 1930s and World War II it was the Axis powers. During the era of *Pax Britannica*, when it was a dominant goal of British foreign policy to check Russian expansionism, Russian policy sought to undermine British power. For it was Great Britain alone or as the leader of the European coalition that frustrated such Russian objectives as penetration of the Dardanelles and the Middle East. In the same period the United States was also intensely suspicious of British diplomacy. It suspected Downing Street of seeking to exploit American domestic controversies, such as the Civil War, to advance Britain's imperial ambitions.

Until the Anglo-American *rapprochement* at the end of the century, mutual hostility and suspicion of Great Britain often bound Russia and America into concerted diplomatic activity. Russian and American Anglophobia explain every example that might be cited of Russian-American friendship during this period—Alexander's recognition of America in 1809, with-

* The George Kennan alluded to here was a distant relative of the contemporary historian and expert on the Soviet Union, George F. Kennan.

drawal of tsarist claims to the American Northwest in the early 1820s, American sympathy for Russia during the Crimean War (1854–1856), the visit of the Russian fleet to America in 1863, the sale of Russian Alaska to the United States in 1867, the naval mission sent by the United States to Russia in 1866 to congratulate Alexander II upon escape from attempted assassination. Let us look at only one of these instances as illustrative of the point.

The period of the American Civil War witnessed the zenith of Russian-American friendship before World War II. In marked contrast with the other European powers, tsarist Russia openly proclaimed its sympathy for the Union. The appearance of the Russian fleet in New York harbor in 1863 seemed to Americans to signify both that Russia was prepared to give tangible aid to the North and that it was serving blunt notice on other countries to keep out of American affairs. Historical research, however, has convincingly shown that this view was entirely erroneous. The tsar's pro-Union policies were dictated chiefly by fear that the European powers, led by Great Britain, were planning to intervene against Russian suppression of the Polish Revolt of 1863. To keep the Royal Navy from sweeping the small Russian fleet from the seas, the Russian fleet used New York harbor as a haven. If war broke out, this haven might become a base for attacking British commerce. More generally, the tsar wanted to preserve the United States as a strong power in the rear of Britain, because this obviously fitted in with the Russian aim of undermining British influence in world affairs.[32]

Essentially the same considerations shaped Russian-American relationships nearly a half-century later at the end of the Russo-Japanese War (1904–1905). In this instance, however, the common interests between the United States and Russia derived from their mutual desire to check Japanese expansionism in the Orient. Throughout the war, American public opinion was solidly pro-Japanese. Opened for contact with the Western world by Commodore Perry in 1853, Japan was regarded as America's protégé. Moreover, the island kingdom was the underdog, fighting against one of the most corrupt and oppressive despotisms known to history. Besides, it was widely and erroneously believed that Japan was America's ally in the Far East and was prepared to accept the principle of the Open Door in China in good faith. While public sentiment within the United States favored the Japanese cause throughout the war and during the peace negotiations that followed,[33] Theodore Roosevelt's pro-Japanese position changed somewhat as a result of the spectacular Japanese victories over the tsar's forces. In time, Roosevelt appointed himself "honest broker" and sought to mediate between Russia and Japan in arriving at a peace settlement. The negotiations resulting in the Treaty of Portsmouth (1905) constitute a fascinating study in international affairs. They illustrate graphically many important characteristics of tsarist and Japanese diplomacy, and show that strategic-political realities often motivate ideologically unfriendly nations like Russia and America to pursue common diplomatic goals. Thanks largely to Roosevelt's mediation, the peace terms were much more favorable to Russia than might have been expected on the basis of its ignominious defeat by Japan.

Roosevelt's mediation sprang from a desire to create a balance of power in the Orient to thwart what he had come to suspect were the ultimate imperialistic ambitions of Japan. While he had as little regard as ever for the tsarist autocracy, a stable balance of power required that he seek to preserve Russia as a reasonably strong power in Asia.[34] As in the earlier period when both Russia and America were motivated by Anglophobia, and 35 years later when the two countries were united against the Axis powers, relations between them were founded on the familiar and often indispensable diplomatic principle of cultivating the enemy of one's enemies. Of cordiality and genuine friendship between the two nations—not to mention ideological compatibility—there was virtually none. Even so, their diplomatic policies could sometimes be concerted on the basis of compatible national interests.

From 1905 to 1917

Powerful currents were at work after the dawn of the twentieth century to destroy the fundamental identity of diplomatic interests that had provided the foundation for Russian-American relations in the past. One of these was the diplomatic revolution implicit in the long overdue *rapprochement* between Great Britain and the United States. The Hay-

* These treaties cleared the way for American construction of the Panama Canal, superseding the older Clayton-Bulwer Treaty (1850) which had given Britain preferential rights in potential canal routes in Central America.

Pauncefote Treaties (1900–1901)* and, in the same period, British support for the American policy of the Open Door in China, signified the end of diplomatic hostilities between the two countries. Instead of cooperating with Russia to check Britain's imperial ambitions, as time passed, American officials were prepared to join with countries like Britain and Japan to block tsarist diplomatic aspirations in the Far East. The second force operating to alter the earlier pattern of Russian-American relations was the emergence of the United States as a great power and, more significantly, as a Pacific power. Following the victory over Spain, the United States acquired the Philippines as a strategic base in the Far East. This development, along with expanding American economic penetration of China under the mantle of the Open Door, foreordained eventual conflict between American and Russian policy goals in Asia.

Symptomatic of America's new diplomatic strategy in the Far East was the entente between the United States and Japan with respect to Asian affairs, beginning with the Root-Takahira agreement (1908). This understanding, which historians today are inclined to regard as an American diplomatic blunder, demarcated spheres of influence between the United States and Japan in the Orient. In effect, Japan received a free hand to challenge Russia for control over Manchuria. In return, Japan pledged a hands-off policy toward American territorial possessions in the Pacific. For approximately 30 years, the United States followed the policy of largely ignoring—and, by its failure to act, encouraging—Japanese expansionism in Asia. And coincidentally, it was not until the early 1930s, when communist Russia and the United States were confronted with powerful Japanese threats to their interests in Asia, that Moscow and Washington endeavored to heal the breach that had divided them since the Communist Revolution of 1917.

America and the Russian Revolution

When the tsarist autocracy disintegrated because of disastrous Russian defeats during World War I and long-smoldering revolutionary ferment on the home front, what was the policy of the United States toward this epoch-making development? Initially, the United States welcomed the revolutionary movement within Russia, in the hope that at long last a moderate political order would emerge.[35] From

February to October, 1917, however, the United States did nothing tangible to sustain the Kerensky Government or to help it overcome its radical opponents. Beset by increasingly grave internal problems, and by the collapse of the Russian western front against Germany, the Kerensky Government was doomed. It was overthrown in October by the Bolsheviks led by Lenin. With the dissolution of the Constituent Assembly—the designated constitutional convention—early in 1918, all hope for the emergence of a moderate political order shaped along Western parliamentary lines disappeared. From the beginning, American policy toward the Bolshevik regime was compounded of an extreme dislike for communism, a belief that the Communist government would not last, and a profound disillusionment that Russia was willing to desert its allies and to make a separate peace with Germany.[36]

Russia's withdrawal from the war in 1918* imperiled vast stores of war matériel furnished to the tsarist government by the Allies. If these supplies fell into the hands of the Central Powers, the strength of the enemy's war machine would be greatly enhanced. Safeguarding these supplies was therefore the ostensible reason for Allied intervention in Russia during 1918–1920. At the same time, the Allies made no secret of their profound hostility toward the new communist order. Their later action in giving significant aid to the anti-Bolshevik White forces during the Russian civil war, testified to the fact that Allied intervention had political as well as purely military motivations. With the tangible and moral support of the Allies, White armies attacked the Communists from all directions. Before they were finally driven back by the Red Army in the latter stages of the civil war, they had reduced the

* By the treaty of Brest-Litovsk, Russia in 1918 ceded to Germany over 1.3 million miles of territory occupied by 62 million people. This was 25 percent of Russia's area and 44 percent of its population. It included 35 percent of Russia's agricultural land, 89 percent of its coal mines, 73 percent of its iron ore, and 54 percent of its industry. E. Day Carman, *Soviet Imperialism* (Washington, D.C.: Public Affairs Press, 1950), p. 12.

Communist rulers were only partially successful in getting this Carthaginian peace modified after Germany's defeat. Russia was not invited to the Paris Peace Conference. Invoking the principle of "self-determination," the peacemakers created a number of independent states (e.g., the Baltic States and Poland) out of former Russian territory. Russia, in other words, had substantial grounds for feeling that it had been among the defeated powers.

borders of Communist-controlled Russia to roughly those of medieval Muscovy.[37]

Compared with the part played by England and France in the Allied interventions, America's role was never particularly significant. Officially, the United States was committed to nonintervention in Russian internal affairs. American military units did land at Archangel and in Siberia. In Siberia their mission was, as much as anything, to prevent wholesale Japanese annexations of Russian territory. To that extent, as Roosevelt and Hull pointed out to Moscow during the 1930s, American intervention may have helped the Communist regime in this period more than it weakened it.

Nevertheless, besieged on all sides by hostile forces and with its very existence at stake, the new Soviet state "was in no mood to draw careful distinctions between the motives of its respective invaders."[38] The Allies as a whole did not conceal their avowed hostility toward Bolshevism and their sincere hope that it would be overthrown in favor of a more moderate political order. Consequently, Allied intervention seemed at the very inception of the Communist regime to bear out Marxist-Leninist pronouncements about the ever-present "capitalist encirclement," as well as to confirm the fears of earlier tsarist officials that powerful countries would exploit every opportunity available to crush and dismember Russia.

Foreign intervention in Russia could be and was utilized by the Bolsheviks to justify an utterly ruthless policy at home. It furnished a powerful appeal—defense of the Russian Motherland against foreign invaders—to rally the Russian masses, millions of whom were initially hostile to communism, behind the Red Army's attempt to drive out the hated foreigners. The legacy of the civil war in determining future relations between Russia and the outside world can hardly be exaggerated. Allied antagonism to communism "led to intervention, which enabled the Bolsheviks to use nationalism as their rallying cry. The consolidation of Bolshevik power, an event considerably abetted by intervention, only deepened the enmity of American policy makers and heightened their determination to outlast the Soviet state."[39]

Thus, the Soviet Union was conceived in revolution at home and in conflict with the outside world. Having experienced the reality of being "an island of communism in a capitalist sea," Communist leaders could be counted on to believe firmly that the outside world was unalterably hostile to Soviet Russia and that the policies of non-communist countries must be viewed with extreme suspicion.

From the Revolution to the New Deal

For nearly 15 years after the Bolshevik Revolution, the policy of the United States toward Soviet Russia underwent little significant change. After it became apparent that the Soviet regime was not going to be overthrown, American policy under Wilson and successive Republican Presidents was shaped by three fundamental considerations: extreme ideological hostility between American democracy and Soviet communism; disagreements between the two countries over communist repudiation of tsarist war debts and confiscation of foreign-owned property; and communist intrigue in the internal affairs of other countries through the instrumentalities of the Third International and local Communist parties directed from Moscow. As late as 1933, an official State Department memorandum cited these three reasons in support of continuing American refusal to recognize the Soviet government.[40]

By the early 1930s certain influences growing out of internal affairs within the two countries and out of the international community were reshaping relations between them. One of these was the desire of both countries to expand their foreign trade. By the late 1920s Russia had embarked upon the ambitious First Five-Year Plan, by which she hoped substantially to raise agricultural and, to a lesser extent, industrial output. Imports from America would greatly assist in this goal. Meantime, vocal groups throughout the United States were calling for an extension of American markets to Russia, and were bringing pressure to bear upon Congress and the White House to achieve that end.[41]

On the international scene, the imperialistic designs of Japan, Germany, and Italy signaled the end of traditional American-Japanese friendship and drove both the United States and Russia to take steps to promote their own security. Once again, a common enemy was forcing the two nations to collaborate. The first step was the resumption of diplomatic relations. They were renewed between the two nations, after the Kremlin pledged noninterference in the internal affairs of the United States through communist groups directed from Moscow, and agreed to make a satisfactory settle-

ment on repudiated tsarist debts and confiscated foreign property.*

Throughout the "appeasement era" preceding 1939, both Russia and the United States from time to time called for collective efforts by the League of Nations to halt Axis aggression and violations of solemn treaty commitments. At Geneva, Soviet Foreign Minister Litvinov was especially active in trying to arouse a reluctant League to deal with Hitler and Mussolini while there was yet time; and across the Atlantic, Roosevelt and Hull added their voices, though not their armies, in support of the hoped-for coalition against the dictators. Alone among the great powers, Russia and America counseled a united front against the Axis, though such appeals were almost never made jointly.

Were Soviet Foreign Minister Litvinov's impassioned appeals for collective action to preserve European security nothing more than communist propaganda? Were his pledges of Russian assistance—unilaterally if necessary—to countries threatened with incorporation into the Axis empire nothing more than empty promises? No definitive answer can be given. Whatever Russia's response might have been had its offers been accepted, it seems unarguable that the Kremlin in this period was less myopic to the long-range global implications of the Rome-Berlin-Tokyo Axis than other foreign office of the world. The other great powers were insensitive to Litvinov's pleas. Believing, in the words of Winston Churchill, that the rulers of Russia were a "band of cosmopolitan conspirators gathered from the underground world," and thinking that the Red Army, seriously weakened by the Great Purges of the mid-1930s, was no military asset, England and France were unwilling to put Litvinov to the test.

Instead, in their diplomatic moves against the Axis, and in their deliberations with Hitler and Mussolini, they ignored Moscow altogether. And in the crowning act of appease-

---

* Neither of these conditions was fulfilled to the satisfaction of the State Department. Tension characterized relations between the two countries from 1933 to World War II over such questions as the activities of the Comintern and the harassment of State Department officials in Moscow. Department of State, *Foreign Relations of the United States, The Soviet Union: 1933–1939* (Washington, D.C.: 1952), pp. 132–134; 224–225; 446–451. The debt question dragged on for years before it was settled, with the State Department convinced that Russia had never intended to settle the issue fairly.

ment—the Munich Conference of 1938 at which Russia was not present—they exhibited no reluctance about handing over the strategic gateway to western Russia to Hitler. To the Kremlin, the "peace with honor" achieved at Munich must have had all the earmarks of an understanding between the West and Berlin, giving Hitler a free hand for his announced *Drang Nach Osten* (drive to the east), provided he did not jeopardize the security of the West. The sacrifice of Czechoslovakia at Munich could not fail to revive Russian memories of countless invasions through the southeastern gate of Central Europe and convince rulers, already steeped in Marxist-Leninist-Stalinist visions of "capitalist encirclement," of the undying enmity the capitalist world bore the USSR.

Then came the reckoning of August 31, 1939—the black day of the Nazi-Soviet Pact.* Never did Stalin appear so treacherous and so unprincipled as the day he and Hitler, after the fashion of Alexander I and Napoleon at Tilsit in 1807, agreed to divide the major part of Europe between them. At Munich the appeasers had sowed the wind. Now—confronted with an ever more belligerent Axis and a neutralized Russia—they were reaping the whirlwind. Stalin was prepared, as he was prepared many times before and after, to lay aside communist ideological preachments for the sake of Russian strategic territorial gains and traditional diplomatic ambitions. Nothing could have been more at variance with Marxist-Leninist-Stalinist dogma than the spectacle of the great Socialist Motherland allied with that personification of capitalist degeneracy and avarice, Nazi Germany. Yet no other action fitted in so well with diplomatic necessity and with the enduring goals of Russian foreign policy. Reflect upon what Stalin got as a result of this pact: a breathing spell in which to prepare the Red Army for a possible showdown with Hitler; a large part of central and eastern

* The most thorough compilation of documents bearing upon the Nazi-Soviet Pact is the State Department Publication, *Nazi-Soviet Relations, 1939–1941*, edited by Raymond J. Sontag and James S. Beddie, Washington, D.C., 1948. This documentary approach has the disadvantage, however, of treating the pact outside the context of European diplomacy, thereby conveying the impression that the pact bore no relation to the dynamics of international events during the 1930s. For an excellent background study of this period, see Max Beloff, *The Foreign Policy of Soviet Russia, 1929–1941* (New York: Oxford University Press, 1949), two vols.

Poland; most of the Baltic area, paving the way for reincorporation of Finland; a base from which to put increasing pressure on Turkey and to force a way through the Straits; and a broad security zone to protect Russia's ever-vulnerable western frontier—all the while advancing the communist aim of world revolution directed from Moscow. The Nazi-Soviet Pact was a disaster for the West and a master stroke of Soviet diplomacy. It revealed what the world had to confront when it faced traditional Russian foreign policy goals overlaid with communist ideology.

The Uses of History

Mr. Walter Lippmann, a perceptive observer of international affairs, once wrote that:

> . . . the behavior of nations over a long period of time is the most reliable, though not the only index of their national interest. For though their interests are not eternal, they are remarkably persistent. We can most nearly judge what a nation will probably want by seeing what over a fairly long period of time it has wanted; we can most nearly predict what it will do by knowing what it has usually done. . . . Even when they adapt themselves to a new situation, their new behavior is likely to be a modification rather than a transformation of their old behavior.[42]

In stressing the often neglected goals of historic Russian foreign policy, we must of course be mindful of the same admonition that applies to ideological impulses shaping Soviet foreign policy: no *single* causation is likely to prove a satisfactory guide to the Kremlin's diplomatic behavior. Yet Americans have seldom been sufficiently mindful of the distinctive historical context within which Communist policy operates within the USSR or of the basic insights afforded by knowledge of pre-Communist history in Russia.

As far as Russian-American relations before World War II are concerned, several insights are afforded by reflecting upon the historical record. First, until both countries emerged as superpowers in world politics as a result of the defeat of the Axis and the decline of British and French influence, relations between them were essentially episodic. America had no real foreign policy toward Russia until events compelled it in 1947 to formulate one. In the tsarist and early Soviet periods, the foreign policy of the United States toward Russia was determined chiefly by American policies toward other great powers and important international issues. When Russia and America found themselves on the same side of an issue, this was more by accident than design. After the events that had forged a temporary bond were modified, the chances were great that the bond would sooner or later dissolve.

Thus the pattern of Russian-American relations before World War II emerged chiefly as a result of the responses of each country to the actions and policies of other countries, usually common enemies. In this relationship, Great Britain played a key role. Two tendencies in British foreign policy tended to be crucial in gradually modifying Russian-American relations. One was the *rapprochement* between the United States and Britain that came around 1900. The other was the decline of British imperial power that began with World War I; this did not become painfully evident to Americans until after World War II. America's "rise to world power" after World War II thus entailed in substantial measure assumption of diplomatic and military responsibilities that Great Britain had long discharged in checking the expansionist tendencies of the Russian state. When Britain and its allies possessed insufficient power to preserve the security of the West, as in World Wars I and II, the power of the United States provided the increment necessary to assure an Allied victory. With the gradual erosion of British power, there came a time when these roles were reversed. In the postwar period, the United States was the principal source of Western strength; in turn, it relied upon Britain and its other allies to resist threats to global peace and security.

Throughout the course of recent history, nations that had stood as historic buffers between an increasingly stronger America and Russia disappeared, one by one, from the ranks of the great powers. For the first time in history, the Russian and American states confronted each other directly and continuously. No longer could their relations remain episodic, nor could their policies toward each other emerge merely as diplomatic by-products of their policies toward other countries. For many years after World War II, there was no common enemy to induce temporary collaboration between the superpowers. By the 1960s, there were some grounds for thinking that this condition, too, was changing. If Red China could not perhaps be designated a "common enemy," this role was being performed by another de-

velopment: the growing concern in Washington, Moscow, and other capitals for the poverty and economic backwardness existing throughout Latin America, Africa, the Arab world, and Asia. Within the Soviet Union itself, the Khrushchev era had witnessed an unprecedented emphasis upon economic advancement, aimed as never before at satisfying the demands of the Russian society for a higher standard of living. In other settings, long-depressed societies demanded of Russia, America, and other industrialized nations massive assistance in achieving the economic "breakthrough" needed to launch these societies on the path of modernization. The conception of "peaceful coexistence" held by Khrushchev—and by the regime under the new party leader, L. I. Brezhnev, that took power from him at the end of 1964—postulated continuing competition with capitalism. A basic tactic was to demonstrate the superiority of communism in meeting the needs of societies throughout the underdeveloped world. Moscow's strategy appeared to be dictated by recognition, shared with Western societies, that the most formidable common enemy threatening human civilization—the omnipresent specter of thermonuclear war—required both East and West to renounce recourse to military conflict in achieving their diplomatic goals and to engage in at least limited cooperative endeavors designed to promote human betterment. Did this new era actually change the nature of the cold war? Did it give the advantage to the Communist bloc or to the free world? Did it signify any basic change in Soviet goals and methods in dealing with the outside world? We shall examine these questions more fully in the chapters that follow, as we appraise ideological, strategic, and economic aspects of the cold war, and as we deal with cold war issues toward a variety of diplomatic questions.

NOTES

1. Thomas A. Bailey, *America Faces Russia* (Ithaca, N.Y.: Cornell University Press, 1950), p. 62. A history of Russian-American relations, focusing on the role of public opinion.
2. Frederick C. Barghoorn, *Soviet Russian Nationalism* (New York: Oxford University Press, 1956), p. 163. An analysis of nationalism and Soviet communism since 1917.

3. Quoted in Bailey, *op. cit.*, p. 198.
4. Marx's views were paralleled by those of his colleague, Friedrich Engels. See the essay by Engels, from his *The Russian Menace to Europe*, included in Robert A. Goldwin, *et al.*, eds., *Readings in Russian Foreign Policy* (New York: Oxford University Press, 1959), pp. 74–92.
5. George B. Huszar, *et al.*, *Soviet Power and Policy* (New York: Crowell, 1955), pp. 22–23. A helpful symposium, covering various aspects of historic and more recent Soviet policy.
6. E. Day Carman, *Soviet Imperialism* (Washington, D.C.: Public Affairs Press, 1950), p. 11.
7. Michael T. Florinsky, *Russia: A History and An Interpretation*, **II** (New York: Macmillan, 1953), 982. A thorough and scholarly account that is rich in detail and short on interpretation.
8. K. W. B. Middleton, *Britain and Russia*, **II** (London: Hutchinson, no date), pp. 33–34.
9. Florinsky, *op. cit.*, 1262, 1270–1271.
10. Anatole G. Mazour, *Russia: Past and Present* (New York: Nostrand, 1951), p. 114. A succinct and readable textbook on Russian history, with many illuminating insights.
11. *Ibid.*, p. 116.
12. Melvin C. Wren, "Pobedonostsev and Russian Influence in the Balkans, 1881–1888," *Journal of Modern History*, **19** (June, 1947), 132.
13. Nicolas Berdyaev, *The Russian Idea* (New York: Macmillan, 1948), pp. 8–9. A highly original, provocative study of Russian character and viewpoints.
14. Quoted in Mazour, *op. cit.*, pp. 51–52.
15. Berdyaev, *op. cit.*, pp. 8–9.
16. Quoted in Mazour, *op. cit.*, p. 31.
17. Quoted in Berdyaev, *op. cit.*, p. 37.
18. Quoted in Mazour, *op. cit.*, p. 19.
19. Florinsky, *op. cit.*, **II**, 987.
20. Quoted in Berdyaev, *op. cit.*, p. 148.
21. *Ibid.*, p. 195.
22. *Ibid.*, pp. 249–250.
23. Ernest J. Simmons, ed., *Continuity and Change in Russian and Soviet Thought* (Cambridge, Mass.: Harvard University Press, 1955), p. 531. A symposium containing several thought-provoking essays on Russian policy.
24. Quoted in Department of State, *Communist Perspective* (Washington, D.C.: Division of Research for USSR and Eastern Europe, Office of Intelligence Research, 1955), p. 512. An immensely valuable compendium (in Russian and English) of communist doctrinal statements.
25. Bailey, *op. cit.*, pp. 6–7.
26. Malbone W. Graham, "Russian-American Relations, 1917–1933: An Interpretation," *American Political Science Review*, **28** (June, 1934), 388. Argues that Americans have always been ideologically alienated from Russia, even under the tsars.
27. Bailey, *op. cit.*, pp. 39–44.
28. Harold E. Blinn, "Seward and the Polish Rebellion of 1863," *American Historical Review*, **45** (July, 1940), 828–833, *passim*. Discusses a little-known chapter in American diplomatic history.
29. Laserson, *op. cit.*, pp. 293–320.
30. Bailey, *op. cit.*, p. 49
31. Walter Lippmann, *U.S. Foreign Policy: Shield of the Republic* (Boston: Little, Brown & Co., 1943), p. 141.
32. Bailey, *op. cit.*, pp. 81–94.
33. Winston B. Thorson, "American Public Opinion and the Portsmouth Peace Conference," *American Historical Review*, **53** (April, 1948), 439–464, *passim*. Treats an important illustrative episode in changing American attitudes toward Russia.
34. *Ibid.*, p. 449.
35. William A. Williams, *American-Russian Relations: 1781–1947* (New York: Holt, Rinehart & Winston, 1952), pp. 91–92. Although some of its conclusions may be questioned, this book relates the cold war to the broad stream of Russian-American relations.
36. Robert P. Browder, *The Origins of Soviet-American Diplomacy* (Princeton, N.J.: Princeton University Press, 1953), pp. 3–4; Williams, *op. cit.*, p. 109.
37. Bailey, *op. cit.*, p. 241.
38. Browder, *op. cit.*, p. 9.
39. Williams, *op. cit.*, p. 107.
40. Department of State, *Foreign Relations of the United States, The Soviet Union: 1933–1939* (Washington, D.C.: 1952), pp. 6–9. An invaluable documentary source on Soviet-American relations. This series is added to periodically.
41. Williams, *op. cit.*, pp. 236–237.
42. Lippmann, *op. cit.*, p. 138.

9 → ELEMENTS OF
THE COLD WAR →

The cold war infuses almost every problem in contemporary American foreign policy. It affects such diverse issues as American relations with Western Europe and Southeast Asia; tariff questions, reciprocal trade, and foreign aid; American participation in the United Nations and other international efforts directed at reducing world tensions. Because the cold war is all-pervasive, we begin our study of concrete problems in American foreign relations with that subject.

Our purpose here is to establish a frame of reference within which to evaluate more limited issues, such as Soviet-American conflict in the Middle East or disarmament disputes. While the cold war many be aggravated by such specific disagreements, it has its origins in much more fundamental factors. Analysis of these factors will be our task in this chapter.

For convenience, we have divided them into three *fronts* of the cold war: ideological, strategic-geopolitical, and economic-military.

THE IDEOLOGICAL FRONT

Save perhaps for a profession that communist and Western democratic ideologies seek to achieve the best interests of humanity and strive to bring about a more just political-economic-social order, the two philosophies are antithetical on almost every concrete issue that confronts society. Their disagreement over most goals and, more crucially, over the means for reaching them, is so deep and all-pervasive that common agreement on seeking the welfare of society affords practically no real affinity between the two ideologies. Their differences

necessarily color relations between Communist and non-Communist nations in international affairs. Our interest here centers on the limited topic of the relationship between communism as an ideology and Russian behavior in the sphere of foreign relations.* We shall explore

* The literature on communist ideology is voluminous. Among the many helpful summaries and critical commentaries are: Sidney Hook, *Marx and the Marxists* (Princeton, N.J.: Nostrand, 1955); R. N. Carew Hunt, *A Guide to Communist Jargon* (New York: Macmillan, 1957) and *The Theory and Practice of Communism* (London: Geoffrey, Bles, 1957); Barrington Moore, Jr., *Soviet Politics —The Dilemma of Power* (Cambridge, Mass.: Harvard University Press, 1950); George F. Kennan, "The Sources of Soviet Conduct," *Foreign Affairs*, 25 (July, 1947), 566–583, and *Russia and the West Under Lenin and Stalin* (Boston: Little, Brown & Co., 1960); Ernest J. Simmons, ed., *Continuity and Change in Russian and Soviet Thought* (Cambridge, Mass.: Harvard University Press, 1955); Alvin Z. Rubinstein, *The Foreign Policy of the Soviet Union* (New York: Random House, 1960); Philip E. Mosely, ed., *The Soviet Union: 1922–1962* (New York: Praeger, 1963) and *The Kremlin in World Politics* (New York: Vintage Books, 1960); Abraham Brumberg, ed., *Russia Under Khrushchev* (New York: Praeger, 1962); Robert V. Daniels, *A Documentary History of Communism* (New York: Random House, 1960); and Richard C. Gripp, *Patterns of Soviet Politics* (Homewood, Ill.: Dorsey Press, 1963).

In any discussion of ideology it must be kept in mind that the term communism itself is subject to differing interpretations. There are many varieties of communism: the type practiced by the early Christian community and by the "Brook Farm" experiment in early American history; the type advocated by the Mensheviks in Russian history from the early 1900s to 1917, that emphasized an evolutionary development into a communistic society and that was antithetical in many points to the philoso-

that question first by examining the main tenets of communist thought and then relating this credo to the diplomatic behavior of the Soviet Union.

Communist Ideology—An Overview

Communism is a materialistic creed. This means not so much that it is concerned with material advancement—which of course it is —as that it rejects supranatural phenomena, and confines what is known and can be known about human nature and behavior solely to historical experience. This fact at once places it outside the Judeo-Christian tradition. Rejecting such ideas as that man is a creation of the Almighty, that he is constantly tainted with sin, and that consequently no perfect social order can be established on earth, communism claims to "be able, through science and social action, to create an ideal order in which the needs and desires of mankind will be fully satisfied. . . ."[1]

Through the insights afforded by the processes of "dialectical materialism,"[*] communism purports to have found the key to social organization in the "mode of production." At any stage in history, whether in the feudal, capitalist, socialist, or communist era, the prevailing mode of production determines the nature of a society's laws, institutions, ethical and moral codes, class relationships, political systems—in short, every aspect of the societal order. But there is one feature common to all societies, until the communist utopia has been reached.

---

phy espoused by Lenin and his followers; the Marxism advocated today by many groups (particularly Socialist Democratic parties in Europe) who disagree sharply with the Kremlin's brand of communism and who often violently oppose the USSR's policies; and most recently, the communism advocated by Peking, which is at variance in many respects with the Kremlin's conception.

As used in this and later chapters, the term communism is meant to describe the ideology identified with Soviet Russia. This philosophy can perhaps most accurately be described as Marxism-Leninism-Stalinism-Khrushchevism, or more simply as Bolshevism, to differentiate it from other movements purportedly derived from the teachings of Karl Marx.

[*] Marxist thought took from Hegel the idea of the "dialectic"—that is, arriving at truth by the synthesis of opposites. One stage of human history (the thesis) gives rise to tendencies (the antithesis) that ultimately bring in a new stage (synthesis), which is formed by a combination of the old and new. Thus, in Marxist thought, feudalism engendered antifeudal forces. The synthesis of these two stages ushered in the new stage, capitalism.

This is the class conflict. In every precommunist society a struggle takes place between the owners of the means of production —under capitalism, the bourgeoisie—and the workers, or proletariat. The latter are denied their rightful share of the fruits of industry by the entrenched bourgeoisie. Until the prevailing system of production is overturned by revolution, this situation continues. Nothing short of a revolution can usher in a new socialist[**] order, since the entrenched owners will never relinquish control voluntarily. Ostensible improvements in the standard of living of the working class, through such techniques as higher wages and better working conditions, extensions of governmental regulation over economic enterprise, or democratic political reforms, merely constitute efforts on the part of the bourgeoisie to consolidate its power by beguiling the proletariat into believing that its condition is improving, when in fact the exploiting class remains firmly in control. Hence, Bolsheviks reserve some of their sharpest invective for labor union movements, Socialist parties, the British Labor party, and other groups—collectively condemned for the sin of "bourgeois reformism"—that divert the masses from a revolutionary course. Down to the 1960s, it remained a fixed canon of communist belief that "the ruling classes do not yield power of their own free will." Although, under Khrushchev, communist ideology emphasized "peaceful coexistence" and proclaimed that violent revolution was not *required* for the overthrow of capitalism, the equivocal qualification was added that the necessity for violence would depend upon "the strength of the reactionary

---

[**] Despite a widespread misconception in the United States, from the point of view of strict ideological correctness it must be emphasized that the USSR is not now, and has not regarded itself, as a *communist* state, even by its own philosophical criteria. Down to 1961, it was engaged in creating a *socialist* order within Russia—the stage *prior* to the achievement of communism. In that year, Communist leaders announced that the creation of socialism had been completed and that the USSR had now embarked upon the next course—the building of a communist society, a task which was in turn intimately related to successful achievement of the ambitious economic goals Communist leaders had postulated for the USSR. Harrison E. Salisbury, *Khrushchev's "Mein Kampf"* (New York: Belmont, 1961), pp. 27–29. Despite its misleading title, this is an exceedingly valuable reference work, containing the text of the Communist party program adopted in Moscow in 1961, the first sweeping revision of the Soviet ideological program since the days of Lenin.

groups' resistance" to the demands of the proletariat.[2]

Inevitable Conflict and "World Revolution"

No aspect of Marxist thought perhaps has engendered such chagrin and bewilderment outside the Communist world as the nature of the relationship of the USSR and its ideological supporters with other countries. On this point communist ideology abounds with deliberate and indeliberate ambiguities. On this issue, the student of communist ideology is offered a highly varied and often conflicting menu of doctrinal pronouncements. A celebrated one is this one from Lenin in 1919:

> . . . We are living not merely in a state but in a system of states and the existence of the Soviet Republic side by side with imperialist states for a long time is unthinkable. One or the other must triumph in the end. And before that end supervenes, a series of frightful collisions between the Soviet Republic and the bourgeois states will be inevitable.[3]

The following year, Lenin wrote that: ". . . As long as capitalism and socialism exist, we cannot live in peace; in the end, one or the other will triumph—a funeral dirge will be sung over the Soviet Republic or over world capitalism."[4]

Such prophecies of doom for capitalism were echoed even by the advocate of "peaceful coexistence," Nikita Khrushchev, in 1963, when the Central Committee of the Communist party affirmed that:

> We are wholeheartedly for the destruction of imperialism and capitalism. We not only believe in the inevitable downfall of capitalism, but we do everything to ensure this will be achieved by means of the class struggle and as quickly as possible.[5]

At the same time, under Khrushchev the Soviet Union was no less convinced that: "Possibilities are arising to establish essentially new relations between states"; the chief aim of Soviet policy thus became to "provide peaceful conditions" for the construction of a communist order within the USSR and the development of the "world socialist system"; it must also manifest a firm resolution "together with other peace-loving peoples" throughout the world "to deliver mankind from a world war of extermination."[6]

If the emphasis and tone of contemporary Communist statements differ fundamentally from Lenin's regarding relations with capitalist countries, it remains true that communist ideology has consistently assumed an unalterable hostility between the Communist and non-Communist worlds.* Whether this animosity must, or may, take the form of *military* clashes between the two, as Lenin seemed to imply, or whether it can be confined to the level of nonmilitary rivalry and competition, as Khrushchev advocated, their relations were governed by the historically ordained "class struggle." According to communist ideology, as the "general crisis" of world capitalism becomes more intense—as capitalism, so to speak, enters its death throes—non-Communist nations will be tempted to undertake a final Armageddon against the source of their tribulations, the Soviet Union. A familiar theme is thus the view expressed by the Soviet journal *Red Fleet* in 1946, which warned that "so long as the capitalist world exists, the possibility of a new war and of bandit attacks on the USSR are not excluded."[7] Similarly, the Communist party of the USSR decreed in 1961 that modern-day capitalism "stimulates militarism to an unheard-of degree" and cautioned the party faithful that the "new war being hatched by the imperialists threatens mankind with unprecedented human losses and destruction."[8]

The danger of global war, according to the communist conception, thus arises more from the animosity of the capitalist world toward communism than from the reverse. Consistently, the Kremlin has said that communism did not "need" war to achieve its global purposes. Yet if communist ideology itself now concedes that world capitalism has entered a stage in which "its development is not tied to a world war," mutual suspicion and distrust, animosity, bad faith, conflict, and competition remain the major characteristics of relations between the Communist and non-Communist worlds.[9]

* This fact, for example, is highlighted by the frequency with which Communist theoreticians in recent years have reiterated the idea that peaceful coexistence did not apply to *ideological* relations with non-Communist countries. Thus, a high Communist spokesman said in 1962 that "any reconciliation or compromise, even temporarily, with bourgeois ideology either in internal or external spheres is impossible." This was held not to exclude "reasonable compromises" in diplomatic or political affairs. This same construction was put on peaceful coexistence by Khrushchev when he interpreted his celebrated remark—"We will bury you"—to mean not "the physical burial of any people, but the question of historical force of development"; communism would "take the place of capitalism, and capitalism thereby would, so to speak, be buried." *New York Herald Tribune*, February 5, 1962.

It follows that the global political environment is characterized by endless crises and tensions, deriving from the conflicts inherent in the "class struggle" gripping non-Communist countries. In his authoritative work *Problems of Leninism* (1924), Stalin identified three primary sources of such crises: (1) the continuing struggle between the workers and the owners of production within capitalist countries; (2) the increasingly fierce contest between capitalist states for raw materials, markets, and territory, leading to wars among them; and (3) the conflict between imperialist states and their territorial dependencies, leading to a global "anticolonial" movement that was destined to undermine the position of world capitalism.[10] This conception of the multiple crises gripping capitalist societies and fomenting international instability formed a basic principle of Stalin's ideological approach and apparently underlay his diplomacy. Stalin visualized capitalism, according to Robert C. Tucker, as "gravely weakened by the war, shot through with domestic strife in every country, beset by insoluble economic problems, and wallowing in intercapitalist contradictions. . . ."[11] The logical corollary of this belief was that communist strategy dictated a militant and continuing campaign to weaken capitalism further, to exploit differences among capitalist states, and generally to hasten the inevitable demise of communism's implacable enemy.

Consequently, the contemporary rulers of Russia believe that "We will bury you" and that "Capitalism is digging its own grave." There is no change in the long-standing communist conviction that capitalism is incapable of "saving itself" from eventual historical oblivion. Thus, in 1961, Moscow declared that the "general crisis of capitalism" remains grave and irreversible. It was asserted that the center of world capitalism has shifted from Europe to the United States; Washington had appointed itself a "world gendarme" and was "supporting reactionary dictatorial regimes and decayed monarchies, opposing democratic, revolutionary changes and launching aggressions against peoples fighting for independence." The United States, furthermore, was found to have "passed its zenith" and to have "entered the stage of decline" as a great power. If war was no longer necessary to assure capitalism's collapse, it would nonetheless decline, because: "Mankind does not want to, and will not, tolerate the historically outdated capitalist system."[12] Like the more overtly militant Stalinist

regime before it, the Soviet government was prepared to assist the forces of history in relegating capitalism to oblivion.

Communist "Morality"

The moral-humanitarian basis of communist ideology has always formed a conspicuous element in the movement's rationale and programs. If communism rejects "the class morality of the exploiters," it affirms "communist morality," identified as encompassing "the fundamental norms of human morality which the masses . . . evolved in the course of millenniums. . . ." Among the specific items enumerated in the communist moral code are the obligation to assume an "uncompromising attitude to the enemies of Communism, peace and the freedom of nations" and devotion to the "fraternal solidarity with the working people of all countries, and with all peoples."[13] In practice, as Westerners are painfully aware, it is usually almost impossible to distinguish this code of "communist morality" from outright expediency and opportunism in advancing the interests of the Soviet Union in world affairs. Communist "morality," said an official Soviet publication in 1941, is "that which facilitates the destruction of the old world, and which strengthens the new, communist regime." Invoking an unidentified quotation from Lenin, the article continued that: " 'At the foundation of Communist morality lies the struggle for the strengthening and perfecting of Communism.' "[14]

Any policy, any move or maneuver that advances the aims of world communism is *ipso facto* moral; and conversely, immorality is the failure, by commission or omission, to work in behalf of the communist cause. Accordingly, the methods by which communism is to be achieved are exceedingly flexible. Whatever opportunism demands is acceptable.* Said Stalin

---

* Some recent writers on communist thought have differentiated rather sharply between strategy and tactics (the former being the long-range plan of action, the latter the short-run techniques utilized for carrying out that plan). It is by no means certain, however, that Communist spokesmen themselves make such a clear delineation. It is true that Stalin declared: "Strategy deals with the main forces of the revolution" and that it "remains essentially unchanged throughout a given stage. . . ." Yet he also said that: "The strategy of the Party is not something permanent, fixed once and for all. It changes to meet historical turns and shifts. These changes are expressed in the fact that for each separate historical turn there is worked out a separate strategic plan appropriate to it and operating

in 1923: "The strategy of the Party is not something permanent, fixed once and for all. It changes to meet historical shifts. . . ."[15] Or, as Lenin had phrased it earlier in 1920: ". . . the strictest loyalty to the ideas of Communism must be combined with the ability to make all the necessary practical compromises, to 'tack' to make agreements, zigzags, retreats and so on."[16]

The extreme flexibility of communist methods has significant implications for Russia's relations with the outside world. It means that there is no predetermined timetable for ushering in the world revolution. As George Kennan has put it: the Kremlin "is under no ideological compulsion to accomplish its purposes in a hurry." Realization of the ultimate goals of world communism is made contingent upon the development of favorable circumstances in the external environment. Time and again after 1917, Lenin and Stalin cautioned the party faithful against rashness and precipitate action that could only bring injury to the communist cause. They warned, in effect, that "enemies aim at the annihilation of the Party. . . . An all-out attack may come at any time. . . . Until final victory, the very survival of the Party is always uncertain; when the enemy is already severely wounded, he lashes out with unprecedented reckless ferocity."[17] If the final victory of communism depends upon propitious developments in the non-Communist world, then the "inevitable victory" of communism may be postponed indefinitely.

Failure to heed these admonitions—pursuit instead of a "reckless" and "adventurist" policy at the risk of triggering an atomic holocaust—

---

for the whole period. . . . For every historical turn there is a strategic plan which corresponds to its needs and is adapted to its tasks."

This problem highlights the underlying ambiguity of Marxist thought and the impact of exigencies at home and abroad upon the viewpoints advocated by the Kremlin in any period. Whether or not the Kremlin does differentiate between strategy and tactics may be of interest chiefly as a matter of philosophic speculation. For our purposes, a more significant point may be the keynote that has recurred frequently in communist ideology. As expressed by Lenin in 1900, the theme urged loyal Communists to utilize "all methods of political struggle, as long as they correspond to the forces at the disposal of the Party and facilitate the achievement of the greatest results possible under the given conditions!" For additional quotations on this subject, see Department of State, *Communist Perspectives* (Washington, D.C.: Division of Research for USSR and Eastern Europe, Office of Intelligence Research, 1955), pp. 440–455.

was one of the indictments Moscow has brought against Peiping's brand of communism in the recent period. Branding Red China's ideological and diplomatic militancy as "anti-Marxist," and as a species of "Trotskyism," the Kremlin condemned it for indifference to the realities confronting Communist policy-makers and for failure to adapt its ideological precepts to conditions in the external environment— particularly the nuclear balance of terror. In a scathing denunciation of Red China's ideological errors, the Soviet Communist party in 1963 expressed great surprise that the "Chinese comrades . . . who have themselves accomplished a revolution" had not understood the main thing that

> . . . the world revolution today comes both through consolidation of the world system of Socialism and through the revolutionary class struggle of the workers in capitalist countries, and through struggle for national liberation, the strengthening of political and economic independence of newly liberated countries of Asia and Africa, and through struggle for peace, against the wars of aggression and through the antimonopoly struggle of the masses, and by many other ways . . . to overthrow the rule of imperialism.[18]

From this ideological verbiage, several principles could be extracted. The Kremlin believed that the "world revolution" proceeded on many fronts and had to be pursued by a variety of techniques; its successful prosecution did not require global war; no specified timetable governed its achievement and hence, inferentially at least, the Communist world had to accommodate itself to numerous setbacks; more might be lost than gained if Communist groups pressed the revolutionary struggle vigorously under adverse circumstances. Implicit in the Soviet conception was the idea that ideological militancy risked a nuclear confrontation with the West, in which the position of the Communist world itself would be jeopardized. The USSR was saying, in short, to its erstwhile Chinese comrades that the surest path to successful "world revolution" lay in following the USSR's programs at home and abroad!

The USSR—Bastion of World Communism

In the previous chapter we remarked upon the threat posed by the merger of traditional Russian foreign policy goals with the imperatives of communist ideology. At this point, let us examine this identity more closely.

Time and again since 1917, Communist

leaders have called upon all who accepted the Marxist-Leninist-Stalinist faith to work unceasingly for the support of the diplomatic ambitions of the Soviet Union in world affairs. Following the diplomatic line laid down by the Kremlin is tantamount to advancing the interests of world communism. True believers in communism, said Stalin in 1925, will "support Soviet power and foil the interventionist machinations of the imperialists against the Soviet Union . . . mainstay of the revolutionary movement in all countries."[19] And a Communist journal stated in 1948 that

> . . . the only determining criterion of revolutionary proletarian internationalism is: are you for or against the USSR, the motherland of the world proletariat? . . . A real internationalist is one who brings his sympathy and recognition up to the point of practical and maximal help to the USSR in support and defense . . . by every means and in every possible form. . . . The defense of the USSR . . . is the holy duty of every honest man everywhere. . . .[20]

Again, in the new Communist manifesto announced in 1961, it was affirmed that: "The existence of the Soviet Union greatly facilitates and accelerates the building of Socialism in the peoples' democracies," that "isolation from the Socialist camp" impedes the development of countries not already under communism, and that true devotion to the communist cause requires "love of the Socialist motherland. . . ."[21] Equation of the national interests of the Soviet Union with the professed ideological goals of the world communist movement had become, by the 1960s, both a highly controversial and prominent element in communist ideology. It constituted a crucial point of disagreement between Moscow and Peiping, since Mao Tse-tung's regime increasingly challenged the Soviet Union's traditional "leadership" of the world Communist movement. The Communist elite in the USSR, on the other hand, was not inclined to relinquish its position as ultimate expositor of the Marxist creed. The Sino-Soviet dispute aside, belief that Soviet Russia's interests as a state were equivalent to the interests of true Communists everywhere was an ideological tour de force that had proved immensely valuable to the Kremlin. First, it enlisted Communist groups anywhere in the world as agents of the Kremlin and required them to take any steps—treason and espionage not excepted—to carry out the interests of the Communist movement,

as defined in Moscow. Second, it arrogated to the Kremlin the prerogative of interpreting both the *meaning* of contemporary Marxist doctrine and the *methods* required to carry it out, thereby giving the USSR a preferential position over all other claimants in the Communist community. Third, it baptized the goals of Russian foreign policy—expansionism, Messianism, the search for warm water ports, the fixation with national security, and the rest—with a mystique and ideological rationalization that made them appealing to dedicated Communists, fellow travelers, and even certain groups of non-Communists throughout the world. For, once the Kremlin's claim was conceded, advancement of Soviet Russia's goals in world affairs was equivalent to the uplift and progress of humanity at large! Fourth, it eliminated any contradiction that might arise between the ideological aims of communism and the diplomatic ambitions of the Soviet Union and its supporters, by declaring (1) that those were identical to begin with, and (2) that the Soviet Union was the final and authoritative interpreter of both, leaving the Kremlin free to adjust its ideological concepts to its diplomatic interests, or vice versa, while equating its goals with the purpose of humanity at large. That non-Communists regard such pretensions with incredulity does not prevent the USSR from realizing considerable diplomatic and propaganda advantage from them.

Ideological Conflicts and International Tensions

What conclusions can we draw about the effects of ideological conflicts on Russian-American relationships in the contemporary era?

In the first place, the evident antithesis between Western and communist political ideals affects the very language employed in diplomacy. A good illustration is the long-standing controversy between Russia and the United States over interpretation of the Yalta and Potsdam agreements pertaining to Soviet occupation of former Axis territory in Eastern Europe. When the West and Russia talked in terms of establishing "democratic governments" and holding "free elections" in the Axis satellite territories overrun by the Red Army, they were talking a different language. The West obviously thought this agreement demanded free elections by secret ballot, as practiced in America, Britain, or France. It soon discovered that "free elections" according to the Kremlin's interpretation meant elections preceded by the elimination of all "fascist elements" and disfranchisement of "enemies of the people"—or in effect disfranchisement of all groups that could not be faithfully counted on to follow the line dictated by Moscow. The point here is not whether Moscow really intended to abide by the letter and spirit of the Yalta and Potsdam agreements; the point is that these agreements were couched in language bound to foment misunderstanding and ill will in later interpretations. So fundamental is the divergence between Western political ideology and Marxism-Leninism-Stalinism that ordinary terms which formerly had a widely accepted meaning in diplomatic parlance no longer possess a clearly defined content. Ideological conflict means, in other words, that the two most powerful nations on earth sometimes *cannot even communicate* with assurance that their positions are being completely understood by the other side.

In the second place, injection of ideological conflict into international affairs on a scale seldom experienced in recent history has intensified existing sources of disagreement and made problems, which were already inordinately difficult, well-nigh insoluble. Select any problem that has engaged the attention of foreign policy-makers throughout recent history—maintaining the balance of power, establishing a system of collective security and international law, seeking disarmament agreements, trying to achieve solutions of colonial conflicts. All of these and more have served as focal points for intense ideological discord. It is difficult enough under optimum conditions to make a system of collective security operate, without having the United Nations perverted into a propaganda forum which resounds with Soviet vituperations against "capitalist warmongers" and "Wall Street imperialists" *ad nauseum*, and in which the West in turn and largely in self-defense excoriates Moscow's record in internal and external affairs. Over the course of time, in such bodies as the United Nations, both sides have given evidence of being more interested in proving the soundness of their ideological positions than in negotiating settlements of existing cold war tensions.

Third, many students of communist philosophy believe that the ideological conflict foredooms any genuine or lasting settlement between the United States and the USSR or between the Communist bloc and the free world. Pointing to doctrinal assertions by Lenin

and Stalin, they argue that conflict between the two worlds is inescapable as long as "world revolution" remains the Kremlin's announced goal. According to this view, communist advocacy of "peaceful coexistence" is merely a siren song calculated to lull the West into complacency, to paralyze its defense efforts, and in the end to yield the world by default to communism. The only realistic course for the United States, therefore, is to accept communist pronouncements about the coming world revolution at face value and to prepare for continuing conflict, perhaps ultimately a third world war.

Fourth, Marxist-Leninist-Stalinist philosophy gives the Kremlin a powerful advantage over its diplomatic opponents: belief in the inevitable victory of its ideological cause. Besides inculcating in Communist groups a fanaticism and earnestness seldom seen outside religious groups in non-Communist countries, conviction that communism is the "wave of the future," that it is being swept forward by the irresistible tides of history, serves as a powerful tonic to sustain the Kremlin and its supporters during lean years. It gives them a vision that, regardless of day-to-day adversities, remains undimmed; and it evokes loyalties to a cause worthy of their best and untiring efforts. In some degree this advantage partially accounts for the fact that the United States—in spite of its economic advancement, idealism, and remarkable lack of imperialistic motives—sometimes experiences great difficulties in countering communist propaganda and diplomatic maneuvers.

Ideology and Soviet Foreign Policy

. . . There will develop two centers on a world scale: the socialist center drawing together to itself the countries gravitating toward socialism, and the capitalist center drawing together to itself the countries gravitating toward capitalism. The struggle between these two camps will determine the fate of capitalism and socialism throughout the world.[22]

Statements such as this, made by Stalin in 1927, focus attention upon a crucial question for the present age. The answer to it is likely to determine the course of international affairs for generations to come. To what extent generally can the communist credo as declared and interpreted by the Kremlin be taken as a reliable guide to the foreign policy of the Soviet Union? More specifically, does the Communist world's professed belief in the inevitability of "world revolution" foreclose any possibility of averting a new global holocaust? Does the presence of deeply ingrained and irreconcilable ideological disagreements rule out the possibility of an over-all "settlement" of diplomatic issues between East and West, or even limited and specific settlements of outstanding problems such as Berlin or Soviet domination over Eastern Europe?

The question is both fundamental and inordinately difficult—perhaps the most difficult that has faced statesmen and students of global affairs in recent history. At the outset, two simple answers must be rejected as inadequate. The first is that because the ultimate triumph of communism remains a fixed tenet of the Marxist faith, inevitable collision—climaxed perhaps by a nuclear war—is foreordained between the Communist and non-Communist worlds. There is no reason to suppose that history is moving inexorably toward a *Götterdämmerung* climax merely because communist oracles have decreed it, any more than we accept the notion that capitalist countries are doomed to eventual collapse because Marx and his followers have decreed it. A second and opposite error is to dismiss communism's prophesy about its ultimate global triumph as "mere propaganda," on the grounds that every pronouncement emanating from the Kremlin ought to be received with extreme skepticism, if not downright disbelief. Bewilderment engendered by the perpetual "revisions" of communist ideology, and by zigzags of Soviet foreign policy, must not lead us to discount ideology completely as an element animating Soviet Russia's relations with the outside world.

The relationship between communist ideology and Soviet foreign policy is much less direct, far more subtle and involved, than either of these approaches suggests. As a generalization, it may be said that Americans are prone to *overemphasize* the role of ideology as a guiding principle of Soviet diplomacy, to the detriment of other major influences. They are inclined to establish a direct cause-and-effect connection between a Soviet move in Germany, the Middle East, or Southeast Asia and the advancement of "world revolution" or some other communist ideological goal. They are inclined to attribute nearly every Soviet move to the machinations of "international communism," thereby suggesting that the major clues to Soviet diplomatic behavior are to be found in the ideological realm. If Western societies are familiar with many of the major tenets of

the communist faith that re-enforce this tendency, they are less familiar with other tenets that admonish against it. Repeatedly, Communist leaders have cautioned their own followers against "dogmatism" and "Talmudism," which an authoritative Communist source has defined as "the uncritical acceptance of dogma without considering the conditions of its application. . . ." Instead, Russia's ruling elite has, time and again, demanded devotion to "creative Marxism," as a "progressive science which does not stand still but moves forward with life itself and moves life forward." Shortly before his death in 1953, Stalin admonished the party not to regard formulas from Marx, Lenin, and other Communist spokesmen as immutable principles which "will serve for every period and country, for every possible contingency."[23] Ironically, some of the most militant anti-Communist groups in the West are sometimes more inclined than Communists themselves to regard the latters' goals as fixed and unalterable, regardless of circumstances!

In common with every other nation in world affairs, the Soviet Union is obliged to achieve some kind of a crude balance between what it *desires* (for ideological or other reasons) to achieve and what it is *able* to achieve. If one valid generalization can be made about the Soviet diplomatic record since 1917, it is that those in power in Russia have always proven highly perceptive in understanding and accepting the extent to which conditions in the outside world limited their policy choices at home and abroad. In virtually every case—and the Cuban crisis of 1962 affords a recent example —ideological goals were shelved (or "re-interpreted") when pursuit of them endangered the very basis of Soviet security. From Lenin's consent to the humiliating Treaty of Brest-Litovsk with Germany in 1918, to Stalin's acceptance of "socialism in one country" at the end of the 1920s (when it had become apparent that only one country, Soviet Russia, had embraced Marxist socialism), to Khrushchev's recognition of the dangers to humanity of a nuclear war, the Kremlin has demonstrated its appreciation of the realities of global power. Almost never, of course, was communist ideology repudiated or abandoned outright when adjustments had to be made; by various means, it was "re-interpreted" or "brought up to date" or otherwise modified to fit the realities confronting the Soviet Union in internal and external affairs. In the process, Soviet communism was turned into a philosophical credo that would, in many vital respects, be unrecognizable to Karl Marx or even, in the more recent period, to Lenin and Stalin.

This is but another way of saying that one of the valid, if self-evident, ideas emphasized by Marxist thought—that creeds, philosophies, thought patterns, and the like, spring from the broad cultural milieu (or the "mode of production") within which they operate—has been illustrated by the Soviet Union's own history. Soviet experience is, in some undeterminable measure, unquestionably *conditioned* by communist ideology; but communist ideology, in common with every belief system, is also conditioned by the Russian society's experience at home and abroad. Ideology may, in some degree, motivate Soviet diplomatic conduct; but ideology is no less useful as, and has repeatedly been invoked for, a *rationalization of* Soviet conduct in global affairs. It thus conveniently serves both as an end in itself and a means to other ends, that have nothing intrinsically to do with "world revolution" or any other avowed Communist goal. Thus, Stalin's military occupation of Eastern Europe during and after World War II may have contributed to reaching the announced Communist goal of "world revolution." The chances are, however, that it was no more motivated by the desire to foment world revolution than was Julius Caesar's conquest of Gaul or India's absorption of the Portuguese colony of Goa, despite the extent to which Stalin's propaganda machine subsequently rationalized Russia's historic ambitions, and its exploitation of an opportunity for aggrandizement in Europe, by reference to Communist objectives.

For a number of reasons, non-Communist observers often find it extremely difficult to decide when communist ideology is serving as a goal or a means of Soviet policy, or possibly as both. First, there is the problem of differentiating between ideological pronouncements as *propaganda* and as authentic expressions of the Soviet Union's diplomatic purposes. Take the Kremlin's advocacy of "peaceful co-existence" during the 1960s. Does this represent merely a "tactical" shift in the Communist party line, signifying no basic change in underlying ideological goals, or does the Soviet Union sincerely believe that nuclear war must be avoided, that it would be ruinous not only for capitalist countries but for the Soviet state as well, and hence inimical to the interests of global communism? Inferentially, does this indicate Communist reluctance to rely upon

military strength to achieve its objectives? Without access to the Kremlin's archives, it is perhaps impossible to answer such questions with assurance.* Yet, the most significant criterion by which to test the importance of ideological precepts in motivating Soviet foreign policy may not lie so much in the compatibility of recent doctrinal statements with earlier pronouncements, as in the extent to which the Soviet Union bases its policies and behavior upon them over a long period of time. That the Kremlin apparently believes that nuclear war can be, and must be, avoided—and more fundamentally, that its policies toward the West reflect this conviction—is a far more relevant fact than how the USSR rationalizes its conduct by reference to Marx and Lenin.

Second, as we have become fully aware, communist ideology is highly ambiguous. Despite Communist claims of an unbroken philosophical continuum from the period of Marx, many vast areas of uncertainty remain—about such questions as the nature of society under communism, or the role of the state and the party after communism has been achieved—that give successive regimes in the USSR ample scope to improvise and to fill doctrinal gaps in the light of experience.

Third, communist ideology has always been and remains highly inconsistent, containing innumerable ambiguities and contradictory ideas. Nathan Leites finds it significant that

---

* In recent years, the Communist party's viewpoints about reliance upon force to achieve its goals has been equivocal. Military force is sanctioned (or, at least, not ruled out) in supporting "the sacred struggle of the oppressed peoples and their just anti-imperialist wars of liberation." At the same time, peaceful coexistence "implies renunciation of war as a means of settling international disputes"; if the imperialists start a war, they will be resoundingly defeated. Imperialism is thus held to be "the only source of war danger." Salisbury, *op. cit.,* pp. 93, 90, and 88, respectively.

The Communist concept of peaceful coexistence and its implications are set forth fully in Salisbury, *op. cit.,* pp. 87–93, and Nikita S. Khrushchev, "On Peaceful Coexistence," *Foreign Affairs,* **38,** No. 1 (October, 1959), pp. 1–18, reproduced in Mosely, *The Soviet Union: 1922–1962, op. cit.,* pp. 399–417. For appraisals of the doctrine see: Philip E. Mosely, "The Meanings of Coexistence," *Foreign Affairs,* **41,** No. 1 (October, 1962), pp. 36–46, reproduced in Mosely, *The Soviet Union: 1922–1962, op. cit.,* pp. 478–489; the several essays reproduced in Brumberg, *op. cit.,* pp. 46–69, 114–153, 531–657; Louis J. Halle, "The Struggle Called 'Coexistence,'" *New York Times Magazine,* November 15, 1959, pp. 14, 110–118.

the Party "has never allowed a detached analysis, or even an attempt at codification, of its ideology. . . ."[24] Undoubtedly it would be detrimental to the Soviet state to attempt a "codification" of communist dogma, if by that is meant a tightly knit, logically consistent philosophy, constructed on the basis of a careful search of the literature. Such a development would deprive the Communist hierarchy of one of its greatest assets—the extreme flexibility of its ideology, permitting frequent and rapid adaptations to prevailing realities. There are few instances in Soviet history when the Kremlin was bothered for long by discrepancies between communist doctrine and internal and external conditions. Whatever policies were demanded, sooner or later quotations from Marx, Lenin, Stalin or lesser luminaries were available to rationalize Soviet conduct. And when the discrepancy between avowed doctrine and reality could no longer be ignored, then the Kremlin was not above rewriting history to eliminate such contradictions. Far from being a drawback, doctrinal inconsistencies in communist philosophy endow the rulers of Russia with an inexhaustible supply of varied ideological garments in which to clothe their necessary policies.

Fourth, many writers have called attention to the fact that Bolshevism is an ever growing, dynamic faith. As early as 1920, Stalin cautioned against relying on "quotations and maxims," instead of "practical experience," as a guide to correct behavior. Again in 1950, he sternly warned certain party members against the erroneous view that Marxism was a

> collection of dogmas, which "never" change, despite changes in the conditions of the development of society. They think that if they learn these conclusions and formulae by heart and begin to cite them without rhyme or reason, they will be able to solve all problems. . . . But this can be the conviction only of people who see the letter of Marxism, but not its essence. . . .[25]

Recognition of these characteristics of communist ideology—enabling it to serve equally well as a goal and as a means of Soviet foreign policy—must be coupled with awareness of another fact about communism as identified with the USSR. A crucial element in the ideological division between East and West is that *communism, as espoused and practiced by a powerful Russian state*, foments global tensions and creates insecurity in non-Communist countries. Throughout the greater part of the postwar era it has been *Russian* communism that has threatened the West; in more recent years, *Chinese* communism has similarly jeopardized the free world's diplomatic position in Asia. The United States, its allies, and many neutralist countries would not be unduly alarmed about their security if Portugal or Honduras were the citadel of international communism and declared that its ultimate goal was to foment "world revolution." Here we confront again the centrality of an issue discussed in the previous chapter: the blending of Russia's traditional goals as a powerful state with the aims of communist ideology, to produce a diplomatic philosophy in which the nationalistic and ideological elements have proved mutually self-supporting. Outside of Red China's orbit, dedicated Communists can and must support Soviet Russia's national goals in global affairs; conversely, the true Russian patriot embraces and supports the announced goals of international communism, for which Moscow is held to be the final interpreter. It is thus an *intermingling* of national and ideological influences that gives rise to and perpetuates the cold war and creates the risk of outright nuclear war.

If these two influences are basic and no longer separable, we are still left with the inquiry: Which is the most important in animating the Kremlin's foreign policies, ideological compulsions or pursuit of Russia's historic goals as a state? Perhaps the only way the question can be meaningfully answered is to examine what the Soviet Union has done, when it has been compelled to choose between its ideological and its nationalistic purposes. When it has been obliged, as every nation is sometimes required, to sacrifice one goal for the other, how has it resolved the problem? Soviet diplomatic experience since 1917 leaves little doubt about the answer. In the overwhelming majority of instances, the Kremlin has not hesitated to find its ideological goals expendable, to defer them to some unspecified future, to reformulate them, or otherwise to indicate convincingly that the Soviet Union's interests as a state were uppermost. Lenin made this plain when he agreed to the harsh peace treaty with Germany during World War I. Stalin left no doubt about it when he embraced the idea of "socialism in one country," thereby saying in effect that dogged adherence to the goal of "world revolution" might imperil the security of the Soviet Union itself. Again, Stalin was keenly mindful of his nation's security in collaborating with the West against the Axis powers in the early 1930s, during the era of "collective security." After the League of Nations failed to deter aggressive moves of the Axis powers—and after the Munich Conference indicated that the West was indifferent to the Soviet Union's military security—Stalin signed the Nazi-Soviet Pact, in an attempt to come to terms with Hitler, thereby hoping to forestall a long-threatened Nazi attack of Soviet Russia. Similarly, other leaders have made it abundantly clear that there is no compunction about modifying, reinterpreting, or in some instances abandoning stated communist objectives when these interfere with the preservation of the USSR's position as a great power in the nuclear age. In every case, suitable excerpts or interpretations from the literature of communist ideology have been offered to justify these policy shifts.

By various means, communist ideology is adapted in a way that enables the ruling hierarchy in the Kremlin to preserve its own, or Soviet Russia's, existence in the face of adverse conditions at home and abroad. Reviewing the record of Soviet diplomacy, Barrington Moore, Jr., has concluded that:

> The evidence seems to indicate that Marxist doctrine has not made the Soviet Union join any coalition or abandon any alliance that it would not have joined, or abandoned, on grounds of simple national self-interest. . . . Russian expansion can be explained very largely without reference to Marxist ideological factors. For the most part, each step in Soviet expansion can be considered a logical move to counter a specific actual or potential enemy.[26]

Ironically, Louis J. Halle has written, it is thus communist doctrine itself that "has tended to become the 'opium of the people.'" It has come to serve essentially the same purpose that Communists have traditionally identified with religion in non-Communist societies. It legitimatizes, sanctions, rationalizes, and endeavors to make morally and ethically acceptable whatever the ruling hierarchy of Soviet Russia wishes to accomplish. Thus, Halle has stated, "world revolution" is perhaps "still 'on the books' as much as ever" as a theoretical goal of the Communist elite; as a practical matter, "the men in the Kremlin . . . find themselves extended to the utmost in dealing with the immediate, practical politics of power. And in the politics of power the prime element is survival of the fittest through competition."[27]

The question of whether communist ideology serves principally as a goal or a means of Soviet foreign policy is far more crucial than a mere semantical or philosophical exercise. For the answer to the question involves nothing less than the course of East-West relations for decades or generations to come. We may profitably again cite the view of Louis J. Halle that "the contradiction of ends and means pervades the Communist movement and is basic to it." Halle continues:

> We may take it as a practical fact . . . that where ends and means contradict each other the latter will prevail. In other words, the ends will be determined by the means rather than by the intentions of those who avow them. . . . For ends are only what we think about, while means are what we do. . . . Means, therefore, are determinative as ends are not. The man who marches northward from New York City may intend to reach Washington, but the direction he actually takes will determine his destination.[28]

And Barrington Moore, Jr., asserts that "under the impact of political responsibility, goals and tactics, means and ends, have become jumbled up with one another and have often tended to change places. The familiar thesis that the Soviets have pursued a single aim through flexible tactics will not withstand the test of comparison with the historical record."[29]

In his *Inquiry into Soviet Mentality*, Gerhart Niemeyer deals incisively with the relation of ideology to Soviet behavior. He finds that it is precisely in the realm of the more altruistic and eschatological aspects of communist thought that "revisions" have most frequently taken place. Marxist and early Leninist expectations to the contrary, the repressive features of the regime have steadily increased. "In other words, the Soviet rulers wield dictatorial power but do not wield it for the sake of a practically realizable goal. What else then is this dictatorial power but an end unto itself?" Since "the Soviet system does not set up an authority or a principle which its rulers are required to respect and obey," and since "the ruling elite holds the key to everything, including the only authentic version of the dialectic of history," then "must we not say . . . that Soviet power . . . is its own end, and is hence might without service?"[30]

Defectors from behind the iron curtain and from the ranks of communism almost invariably concur in this assessment. Thus the former high-ranking Yugoslav Communist, Milovan

Djilas, has spoken of the "strengthening of the new class and the sovereignty not only of a single ideology, but the sovereignty of thought of a single man or group of individuals" as the force animating the Kremlin's policies. The result has been an "intellectual decline and impoverishment of the ideology itself. . . . The ideology's progress, its elements of truth, have declined in proportion to the increase of physical power of its disciples." Lamenting that, at first, communist ideology in Russia "was guided by the most beautiful, primordial human ideas of equality and brotherhood," Djilas ultimately discovered that "only later did it conceal behind these ideas the establishment of its domination by whatever means." As time passed, experience revealed that: "Power is an end in itself and the essence of contemporary Communism."[31]

Many of these judgments were perhaps more applicable to the oppressive dictatorship imposed upon the Soviet society by Stalin than to the more liberalized regime led by Khrushchev. Yet the basic point remains valid. As the chairman of the Senate Foreign Relations Committee, Senator J. William Fulbright declared in 1963, "means have a way in human affairs of consuming their ends"; Fulbright was convinced that Khrushchev's means were far less inimical to the security of the West, and to the future of human civilization itself, than Stalin's. Conceivably, Khrushchev was a no less dedicated Communist than Stalin or Lenin. He stated, and he may well have believed, that communism will ultimately supersede capitalism. Admittedly, the Soviet Communist party program adopted in 1961 continues to reflect many traditional Marxist goals with reference to the eventual triumph of communism and the decline of capitalism and all other non-communist systems. In this sense, it might be contended that communist doctrine remains unaltered from the time of Lenin, and that subsequent modifications in it represent familiar "tactical" shifts in the face of contemporary realities.

Sooner or later, however, advocates of this view have to face the question: When does a series of "tactical" shifts amount to a *de facto* modification in communist doctrine itself? If the pattern of tactical shifts in the face of internal and external realities persists, then does not the most outstanding feature of Soviet foreign policy become the Kremlin's ability to accept these realities and to base its policies upon them? Taking the Khrushchev era as an

illustration, let us assume that Khrushchev and his supporters in the USSR were as genuinely dedicated to achieving the goals of international communism as were the regimes of Lenin and Stalin. We might, therefore, conclude that the modifications introduced into the Communist party program announced in 1961 represented merely familiar zigzags in pursuit of declared communist objectives. Yet, if Khrushchev were really devoted to raising the Soviet standard of living, if he experienced acute disagreements with his erstwhile Chinese allies, if he was fully mindful of the destructive power of nuclear and hydrogen weapons, if he had become persuaded (after the Cuban episode) that the United States and its allies are prepared to defend the free world's interests at the risk of war, if he had to cope with a permanent undercurrent of disaffection throughout the Soviet satellite zone, if he had found many of the neutralist nations highly critical of militaristic Communist ventures— if these factors required him to change many of Stalin's formerly militant, overtly hostile policies toward non-Communist countries, then irrespective of the Kremlin's ideological convictions, the cold war poses less of a risk for civilization than it did under Stalin. For the *methods* employed in pursuit of Soviet foreign policy—not the philosophical beliefs of its ruling elite—are what threaten the West. What the Communist hierarchy does, infinitely more than what it thinks, foments tension between East and West. The *means* employed by Khrushchev—propoganda attacks, forging ahead with Soviet economic growth, economic and trade competition with the West, identification with the newly emerging countries throughout Africa, the Arab world, and Asia, emphasis upon cultural and informational exchange— could still unquestionably prove effective instruments of global communism under certain circumstances. Yet, in general, they neither risk the future of the Soviet state itself, nor do they threaten worldwide nuclear devastation. In effect, the militant goals of "world revolution" and the demise of capitalism emerged as even more *contingent and conditional* goals under Khrushchev than under previous Soviet leaders. There is no inherent reason why this process of further postponement of ultimate goals cannot and will not continue, assuming that the West maintains its vigilance, evolves effective responses to new Communist stratagems, and convinces the Kremlin that neither Khrushchev's methods, nor those of Lenin and

Stalin earlier, can assure the imposition of communism over unwilling societies without grave risks to the Soviet Union itself. Confronted with that continuing reality, the rulers of the USSR may be expected to react as they have reacted to unpleasant truths in the outside world since 1917: they will push their ultimate ends further into the future; they will concern themselves with attainable internal and external goals; they will remain conscious that the methods they rely upon to carry out their objectives will have to be those that do not bring the security of the Soviet society itself into jeopardy; and they will no doubt continue to forecast ominously the historical "demise" of capitalism, the "inevitable" victory of communism, and the achievement of the ultimate communist millennium. So far as the outside world is concerned, it will matter far less that "world revolution" is still listed high on the Communist agenda than that the methods involved to achieve it are those that can at least be tolerated in an increasingly interdependent world, where international relations must be conducted under an omnipresent nuclear cloud. There is thus no reason to suppose that communism will prove immune to the rule that has applied to many other revolutionary philosophies in history: time and experience are likely to blunt the edges of its more militant, eschatalogical, and utopian features, as its advocates are confronted with the continuing challenge of striking and maintaining a balance between the ideologically desirable and the attainable.* The history of the Soviet Union affords every reason to suppose that, faced with this challenge, Soviet policy-makers will settle for the attainable.

* In this respect, as several commentators have observed, there is a parallel between the "revisionism" characteristic of communist ideology and the early history of Christianity. In its early stages, the latter movement also expected an early realization of the Kingdom of God—an idea that infuses the writings of St. Paul. This expectation unquestionably shaped Christian theology and doctrine for many generations. Gradually, it was abandoned, in the sense that the *imminent* coming of the Kingdom was pushed ahead to an indefinite future; Christian theology, in turn, was also modified to take account of this new conception. Similarly, for many years after the time of Mohammed, the jihad, or "Holy War," loomed large in Islamic thought. It was invoked repeatedly in the period of the Crusades. But after the Crusades, the idea receded and, even among Moslems today, it plays a relatively insignificant role in their relations with Christians and other non-Moslems. Pursuit of jihad, it became apparent, threatened the future of Islamic civilization itself.

THE STRATEGIC—GEOPOLITICAL FRONT

Speaking to the National Press Club in 1950, Secretary of State Dean G. Acheson discussed the problem of East-West relations by saying:

. . . I hear almost every day someone say that the real interest of the United States is to stop the spread of communism. Nothing seems to me to put the cart before the horse more completely than that. Of course we are interested in stopping the spread of communism. . . . Communism is the most subtle instrument of Soviet foreign policy that has ever been devised, and it is really the spearhead of Russian imperialism which would, if it could, take from these people [of Asia] what they have won, what we want them to keep and develop, which is their own national independence, their own individual independence, their own development of their own resources for their own good and not as mere tributary states to this great Soviet Union.[32]

Acheson was calling attention to a facet of the cold war that is often neglected by Americans. The United States obviously dislikes communism and all other totalitarian ideologies wherever they are found. Yet, abstract fear of "world revolution" causes no great perturbation in Washington, London, and Paris. What does occasion grave concern is the fear of Soviet or Chinese expansionism and the consequent imposition of alien, totalitarian political orders, directed from Moscow or Peiping. Communism has confronted the West at least as far back as the publication of the *Communist Manifesto* in 1848. The novel element in international affairs is not, therefore, that Russia is communistic, or even that the communist movement has gained adherents in other countries; it is rather that, since World War II, Russia, and more recently Red China, has gained a new geopolitical base from which to expand and to infiltrate other countries. So formidable is the threat created by this fact that the cold war might have ensued, in many respects unchanged, even if the Communist Revolution of 1917 had never occurred. By the same logic, modifications in the internal character or the ideology of the Soviet or Chinese systems might do little to diminish the strategic threat posed to free world security.

The origins of the cold war late in World War II and in the immediate postwar period can be traced to the strategic-geopolitical conflict. When the military tide turned in the east after the Battle of Stalingrad (1943), the Red Army began to drive the Germans out of Russia, across the Eurasian plain to the north and toward Czechoslovakia in the south, and finally to the very gates of Berlin. In the process, Russia overran and occupied the belt of small countries separating Germany from the USSR. Rounding out occupation of these countries with the Czechoslovak coup in 1948, Russia has remained in direct or indirect control of this territory to the present day.*

Why did Soviet annexation and control over the Eastern European satellite belt precipitate the cold war? There are many reasons. In the first place, Russia's action constituted eloquent testimony to Western policy-makers of Soviet duplicity and of the Kremlin's apparently insatiable appetite for territory. Secondly, the communization of Eastern Europe was at variance with many wartime pledges, such as those given at Yalta, and in opposition to almost every principle of the United Nations Charter. Furthermore, by annexing these territories, Russia was engaging in undisguised imperialism, after the fashion of Japan in Manchuria or Germany in Austria before World War II.

The Postwar Geopolitical Revolution

Yet beyond these reasons there was another which by itself would have necessarily foreordained the cold war. This was that World War II ushered in a geopolitical revolution which profoundly altered the world balance of power. Militarily, as one observer has put it, Communist-dominated Eastern Europe was

a deployment area of great strategic importance, by building up the satellite armies to over one million men . . . to the point where Soviet and satellite forces together cast their shadow over all of Europe and stand as a threat to the security of the free nations beyond their borders. Nothing brings home to free Europeans the reality of the Soviet threat more than to see the Russians encamped on the Elbe and the Danube, and to hear the ancient European capitals of Prague and Budapest speaking with the voice of Moscow.[33]

* The Soviet European satellite empire includes the following countries that were annexed and incorporated into the USSR: Latvia, Lithuania, and Estonia, together with parts of Poland, eastern Germany, Rumania, Czechoslovakia, and Finland. Nominally independent Soviet satellites include: Albania, Poland, Rumania, Bulgaria, Hungary, and Czechoslovakia. Finland preserves its autonomy, but it must be regarded as a part of the Soviet military security system.

From a strategic point of view, Soviet occupation of East-Central Europe came close to what one observer described as the "fulfillment of the Western geopoliticians' bad dreams."[34] For Soviet hegemony over this zone gave the Kremlin control over an area that the famous geographer Sir Halford Mackinder described as the "world island," from which he feared that any would-be conqueror would be in a well-nigh impregnable position to control the destiny of the world."** It is not necessary to accept Mackinder's views literally to recognize that Soviet military dominance over the greater part of the Eurasian land mass presents the United States and its free world allies with a strategic problem of unparalleled magnitude. This fact per se is sufficient to generate continuing apprehension about the security of Western Europe and about the gravity of the Soviet threat to countries along the periphery of its Eurasian empire.

American Policy and the Strategic Imbalance in Europe

The ability of the Red Army to overrun Western Europe in the event of a new war prompted the United States initially to formulate the Marshall Plan for rehabilitating Western Europe's war-devastated economies and, after that, to create the NATO defense system as the sheet anchor of the free world's military efforts. Even in the mid-1960s, the specter of Russian military supremacy hangs like the sword of Damocles over the heads of Western policy-makers. For it is extremely doubtful, even in the nuclear-missile age, whether

** Mackinder's ideas were developed during World War I and reiterated, in modified form, during World War II. His most famous dictum was: "Who rules East Europe commands the Heartland; Who rules the Heartland commands the World Island; Who rules the World Island commands the World." East Europe was the area between the Volga and the Elbe rivers. The Heartland, never precisely defined, was the great Eurasian hinterland, roughly conterminous with the USSR. The World Island was the land mass of the European-Asian-African continents. Thus Mackinder, in opposition to advocates of sea power like Captain Alfred Mahan, believed that ultimate victory belonged to a firmly entrenched, militarily impregnable land mass. For commentary on Mackinder's views, see George B. Huszar, et al., Soviet Power and Policy (New York: Crowell, 1955), pp. 567–586; T. Hammer, "The Geopolitical Basis of Modern War," Military Review, 35 (October, 1956), 75–82; and General Paul M. Robinett, "Survey of the Land Routes into the Soviet Union," Military Review, 35 (August, 1955), 6–12.

Europe could be successfully defended against the Red Army. The threatened military collapse of Western Europe would present the United States with the painful alternatives of raining atomic destruction upon the Soviet Union and upon its friends, to "liberate" them from the communist yoke, or of reconciling itself permanently to the incorporation of Western Europe into the Communist empire.

Soviet evacuation of that part of Europe overrun by the Red Army toward the end of World War II has remained a fixed goal of American foreign policy ever since 1945. Few diplomatic objectives in the postwar era have met with so little success. At the same time, the problem of Soviet control over Eastern Europe remains a root cause of conflict between the Communist and non-Communist worlds.

Settlement of issues growing out of Soviet military occupation of Eastern Europe was a major item on the agenda of the Yalta Conference (February, 1945). At Yalta, the United States and Britain thought they had secured Soviet agreement to proposals guaranteeing the establishment of freely elected, democratic political regimes in Eastern Europe, even while the West conceded that such regimes must remain "friendly" to Russia. Stalin, for example, had agreed to a four-part memorandum on Allied policy toward occupied countries in Eastern Europe, the key phrase of which was that the Big Three *jointly* would assist these countries to "form interim governmental authorities broadly representative of all democratic elements in the population and pledged to the earliest possible establishment through free elections of governments responsive to the will of the people."

Agreements reached at the Yalta Conference thus bound the USSR (1) to establish democratic political orders in the liberated and occupied countries of Eastern Europe and (2) to carry out such steps in concert with the other major Allied powers.* Since 1945,

---

* For reasons that are not altogether clear, the American people have tended to equate the Yalta Conference with the Munich Conference of 1938 by referring to wholesale American "appeasement" of Stalin and to officials of the Roosevelt Administration who allegedly "handed Eastern Europe" to the USSR. Such judgments can derive from only two possible sources: gross ignorance of the context of events within which the conference took place and the agreement ultimately reached or unbridled partisanship.

As regards the Eastern European features of the agreement, the "concessions" made at Yalta were

the United States and its Western allies have protested in vain against the Kremlin's domination over the nations of Eastern Europe. American initiative, for example, has been conspicuous in endeavoring to persuade the UN General Assembly each year to take official notice of the Soviet suppression of the Hungarian Revolt of 1956 and of the ensuing tight-reined Soviet control exercised in this country. Repeatedly, the United States has cited the Soviet presence in this zone as one of the most prominent barriers to a lasting *détente* in the cold war and has indicated that the United States would never "accept" the imposition of an alien regime over the peoples of Eastern Europe.

For its part, the USSR has held steadfastly to the position it assumed in the closing months of World War II: developments in Eastern Europe are no concern of the United States. The Kremlin therefore refuses to acknowledge any legitimate American interest in this area or to permit even United Nations involvement in Hungary or the other satellite states. For nearly 20 years, the impasse has remained. What are the prospects that it may eventually be broken? Has the era of "peaceful coexistence" offered any new hope that this obdurate problem can be resolved to the satisfaction of both Washington and Moscow?

Prospects for a Strategic Realignment

Memories of invasion from the west—by Napoleon, by Germany and the Allies during World War I, by Hitler during World War II—are too deeply woven into the fabric of Rus-

---

chiefly *Soviet* concessions—in the sense that the West had nothing to "concede" in this area. At the time of Yalta, the area was rapidly falling under Soviet military domination. Therefore, Britain and the United States had essentially two choices: they could leave the USSR in unilateral control of the area, or they could seek an agreement specifying *joint* control and the establishment of freely elected governments. The latter course was followed. The USSR obviously did not abide by the agreement reached. In the years ahead, this fact also posed two choices: either the Western governments could protest violations of the Yalta agreement (which they did unceasingly) or they could resort to military force to *compel* Soviet adherence to it, a course which would undoubtedly have triggered World War Three. For further commentary on the Yalta agreement and its later implications, see: Richard F. Fenno, *The Yalta Conference* (Boston: Heath, 1955); John L. Snell, *The Meaning of Yalta* (Baton Rouge: Louisiana University Press, 1956); Edward R. Stettinius, *Roosevelt and the Russians—The Yalta Conference* (Garden City, N.Y.: Doubleday, 1949).

sian national consciousness to be removed by mere promises from the West that Russia has no reason to fear for the security of its borders or by assurances that its security is safeguarded by the United Nations. For basically the same arguments were heard before World War II, when Russian security was presumably guaranteed by the French system of alliances in Eastern Europe and by the League of Nations. Both of these supports ultimately collapsed, permitting Hitler's war machine to penetrate to the gates of Moscow and, in the process, to inflict millions of casualties and billions of dollars' worth of property damage on the USSR.

In whatever degree Western observers may believe Soviet fears about the security of Russia's western frontiers to be irrational, it cannot be denied that they are *real* and that they enter heavily into Soviet diplomatic calculations. Events since World War II—particularly the Soviet suppression of revolts and lesser indications of restiveness in East Germany, Poland, and Hungary—indicate conclusively that *de facto* Russian control over the military and political destiny of Eastern Europe is a fixed principle of the Kremlin's foreign policy. The legitimacy of the principle appears no more debatable than whether the Western Hemisphere ought to be included within the American security zone. Russian willingness to countenance no Western "interference" in the Hungarian revolt of 1956, in fact, had its counterpart in the American unwillingness early in the 1960s to permit the USSR to establish missile sites in Cuba. In both instances, each side regarded its vital interests at stake and would not tolerate the prospect of hostile control over a zone deemed vital to its security.

These considerations suggest that the prospects for an *unconditional* Soviet withdrawal from Eastern Europe, as demanded unceasingly by the United States since 1945, remain as remote as ever. At a minimum, two conditions would almost certainly have to be fulfilled before such a withdrawal would become a reality, or even a subject of serious East-West negotiation. The first is that there would almost assuredly have to be some kind of equivalent American concessions, entailing reductions in American military strength in Western Europe. Anything short of this, George F. Kennan has declared, would "create the general impression of a defeat for Soviet policy in Eastern and Central Europe" and might entail a substantial psychological set-

back for the Kremlin in other areas. Under no conceivable circumstances is the Kremlin likely to be induced to relinquish its military-strategic position in this area unilaterally.* The second condition is that there would also most likely have to be some genuine relaxation in international tensions, perhaps by the successful implementation of a disarmament agreement or some other mutually acceptable endeavor, that would have the effect of dispelling Soviet apprehensions about security, assuming that these can be affected by logic and by events. Postwar experience has indicated that verbal assurances to the Soviet Union do little or nothing to mitigate these fears. An extended period of relatively harmonious "coexistence" with the West, on the other hand, might gradually allay them sufficiently to induce the Soviet Union to test the good intentions of the West by a settlement. This prospect, in turn, might be enhanced by the extent to which modern military technology de-emphasizes the importance of military bases and territorial defense in depth.

For the United States the problem of Soviet hegemony over Eastern Europe remains as baffling as it is crucial. Despite widespread political slogans in the United States about "liberation" of the iron curtain countries and a rollback of Soviet power, that was particularly conspicuous during the Eisenhower Administration, the simple truth was and remains that the future of Eastern Europe lies in Soviet, not American, hands. As the Hungarian Revolt of 1956 drove home painfully to Americans, there is no way short of an all-out nuclear war to compel Soviet evacuation from this zone. This reality has confronted American policy-makers since World War II. And this fact—rather than any imagined "sell-out" of Eastern Europe by officials of the Roosevelt Administration—explains the strategic revolution in Europe ushered in by World War II. As one commentator has explained:

* The question of Soviet occupation of Eastern Europe was highlighted at the end of the 1950s by a series of public lectures and articles by Kennan, Dean G. Acheson, and others, who explored possibilities for a territorial settlement in Europe. Kennan took the view that a *détente* with the USSR was possible and that the United States ought to consider seriously trying to reach it. Acheson rejected this view altogether, holding that Russia neither desired such a settlement, nor could the West seek to achieve it without serious detriment to NATO and Western security. See *The New York Times*, December 8, 1957, and January 19, 1958.

Soviet successes . . . have been our failures, or rather our losses, in terms of the world balance. These are losses that were perhaps inevitable, given the postwar situation with which the United States found itself. We may regret instances of our lack of foresight, of misplaced hope and confidence, or of less than realistic negotiation. But the United States is not the arbiter of the world, least of all in areas which the Red Army overran in our common war against Hitler.[35]

THE ECONOMIC-MILITARY FRONT

As Harrison Salisbury comments, ". . . the USSR will possess productive forces of unparalleled might, it will surpass the technical level of the most developed countries and occupy first place in the world in per capita production."[36] Steadily accelerating economic productivity, said Premier Khrushchev, will be the "battering ram" with which the walls of world "capitalism" will be breached as the "new order" of global communism is finally achieved. Relying on methods of "peaceful coexistence," the Soviet Union proposed to "build communism" by demonstrating a "better life . . . more good things for man, better food, housing, clothes, shoes, new schools, institutions of science and culture, hospitals, in a word, all the life of society and of the cultured man."[37] In the light of this challenge, the economic capabilities of the West and of the Communist world—and more specifically, of its two leaders, the United States and the Soviet Union—became more than ordinarily significant in shaping diplomatic developments.*

Economic Postures and Potentialities

In sheer territorial size, the Communist bloc has a substantial advantage over the non-Communist world. Stretching from Central Europe to the shores of the Pacific, the bloc encompasses one-fourth of the land area of the globe and occupies a strategic position which, as we have seen, gives it many geopolitical advantages. Counting Red China, the

* Since the economic capacities and potentialities of the United States were discussed at length in Chapter 2, primary attention is devoted here to the Soviet Union and its satellites. The Sino-Soviet dispute, coupled with the relative scarcity of reliable data about Red China's economic progress, accounts for minimum emphasis upon that country's contribution to the economic strength of the Communist world. Peking's internal and external policies are dealt with in Chapter 13.

bloc contains slightly less than one billion people, while the free world, including the neutralist nations, contains something over one billion.

When we consider Communist industrial capacities, a striking fact is the extent to which the Soviet Union has forged ahead since 1917, to become one of the leading industrial nations of the world. Competent authorities outside the Communist bloc are widely agreed that Soviet Russia has achieved a very high level of economic growth and that throughout most of the postwar era the USSR and its satellites advanced economically at a faster rate than the United States and its European allies.** Now this fact per se is neither sur-

** Considerable confusion, both deliberate and indeliberate, often surrounds discussion of what might be termed "the battle of the growth rates" as a cold war phenomenon. Economists are prone to believe that concentration upon a single indicator such as the Gross National Product (the total of all goods and services produced within a country) is, at best, likely to yield a distorted conclusion about economic progress. Besides such inherent difficulties, the Westerner always encounters the problem of the discrepancy between official Communist statistics about economic growth and reality. Even Communist economists have from time to time conceded that official figures, for example, were willfully or inadvertently padded to yield a much higher growth rate than has actually been the case in the USSR. Thus the Soviet economist S. G. Strumilin has accused the government of claiming that from 1928 to 1956, industrial output grew by 23-fold, whereas it actually grew 15-fold. Similarly, for 1956, his data showed an 8 percent growth in industrial output, versus 11 percent claimed by the government. *The New York Times,* September 11, 1960. For a detailed discussion of the statistical problem involved in comparing American and Soviet production, see George Bookman, "The Split-Level Soviet Economy," *Fortune,* 63 (October, 1961), 107–110, 257–268.

Nevertheless, a basic consensus exists that Soviet and Communist bloc growth rates since World War II have been impressive and, in most instances, have tended to exceed those of the United States and its free world allies. One estimate for the 1950s gives the United States an average annual growth rate of 3.25 percent; during the same decade, the USSR achieved a 7 percent growth rate. In this decade, *industrial* production expanded 4 percent annually in the United States and 7.5 percent annually in the USSR. Klaus Knorr and William J. Baumol, eds., *What Price Economic Growth* (Englewood Cliffs, N.J.: Prentice-Hall, 1961), p. 4.

More recent data indicate that there was a sharp decline in productivity growth rates in the Communist bloc during the late 1950s and early 1960s. In 1962, for example, productive growth levels were only half those recorded for 1958. See *The New York Times,* June 10, 1962, and August 19, 1963.

prising, nor need it be alarming to Americans, given the primitive state of the Russian economy before the Communist Revolution and the great emphasis subsequently accorded to economic advancement by Lenin, Stalin, and Khrushchev. Ever since the inauguration of the first Soviet Five Year Plan in 1928, an announced goal of Communist planners has been to catch up with and ultimately outstrip the United States economically. This goal was interrupted by World War II, when the bitter contest between the Nazi *Wehrmacht* and the Red Army destroyed some 31,000 mines and factories in the USSR, devastating nearly one-third of Russia's industrial facilities. Not until the early 1950s did the Soviet Union complete the staggering task of rehabilitation; after that, it resumed its earlier goal of endeavoring to surpass the United States as an industrial power. By demonstrating the economic "superiority" of the communist system, Khrushchev declared in 1959, the USSR would "attract millions of new adherents to socialism." By 1970, he affirmed, achievement of the Kremlin's projected goals would alter the global balance of power decisively in favor of the communist cause.[38]

A new Soviet Seven Year Plan, initiated in 1959, translated this strategy into an ambitious program of specific objectives.[39] In vital goods and commodities like steel, oil, electricity, and even in certain categories of consumer goods, the Kremlin committed the resources of the state to a massive program of economic advancement designed to put the Soviet Union at the forefront of industrial nations. Russia and its satellites, for example, possess 25 percent of the steel-making capacity of the world, 36 percent of the world's coal reserves, and 18 percent of its electric power installations.[40] If the extent of its petroleum reserves are unknown, they are vast—enough to enable the Soviet Union to take care of its own and its satellites' needs, and to flood the world market with cheap oil that threatened to disrupt the economy of oil-producing Arab states. The Communist bloc also possesses impressive reserves of strategic raw materials such as iron ore, gold, potassium, salt, ferroalloys, and phosphate. These resources are extensive enough to prompt a well-known Western geographer to say that the "major picture is one of exceptional abundance. . . ."[41]

The heart of the new Seven Year Plan was a projected Soviet economic growth rate of 8.6 percent annually—proclaimed as an "objective law of socialism" that ordained communist superiority over capitalism in the near future, since Soviet planners postulated a growth rate for the United States of only 2 percent annually! Assuming that the Soviet Union achieves and maintains its 8.6 percent annual growth rate, and that the American economy continues to grow at a rate of 3.25 percent annually (the average rate for 1950–1958), successful completion of the Seven Year Plan, together with comparable economic progress in the years that followed, would bring the Soviet Union up to economic parity with the United States by 1980. Upon completion of the plan, the USSR expected to more or less equal American steel production of around 90 million tons of steel annually, to produce 230–240 million tons of oil annually (a 100 percent increase over 1958 production), and to generate 500–520 billion kilowatt hours of electricity (again, a 100 percent increase over 1958). Even in the one area in which the Kremlin had long conceded American economic supremacy —consumer goods—the USSR expected to expand significantly the production of selected commodities such as meat, butter, shoes and hosiery, automobiles and trucks. Moreover, the Soviet Seven Year Plan called for an over-all increase in agricultural production of 70 percent—perhaps the most ambitious aspect of the plan, in the light of communist experience since 1917.[42]

Communist Economic Prospects

If the political elite ruling Soviet Russia is relying upon the economic progress achieved by the Communist bloc to give it a commanding lead over the non-Communist world, what are the prospects that this goal can be reached? In general terms, the answer is that this communist strategy faces a number of formidable obstacles, sufficient not only to cast considerable doubt upon the bloc's ability to surpass the West economically but also to raise the real prospect that in some segments the bloc will not be able to hold its own economically against the United States and its increasingly prosperous European allies. This over-all verdict seems justified, in spite of the USSR's impressive economic progress in the past, its obvious technological ability as demonstrated by the Soviet sputniks and other space exploits that have exceeded American achievements, and its unquestioned ability to lead the Communist bloc to higher productive levels throughout the years ahead. Moreover, in appraising the diplomatic implications of the economic contest between East and West, full recognition must be accorded the fact that on this front, as on all others in the cold war, what is objectively true may not be so important as what is widely *believed* to be true, especially by societies that have adopted a neutralist position toward the great powers. Soviet Russia's record of economic and scientific advancement has incontestably elicited widespread global admiration; in many societies, considerable credence is given to the Communist claim of ultimate economic superiority over the West.

Nevertheless, several considerations dictate caution in accepting Communist claims at face value or in conceding the "inevitability" of the bloc's economic superiority over the United States and its allies. Informed Western observers see little basis in reality for the Communist expectation that the USSR will forge ahead of the United States economically in the near future; on the contrary, there is considerable evidence for believing that, in some respects, the traditional economic disparity between the United States and the Soviet Union may well *widen* with the passage of time. At the outset, care must be exercised in relying upon over-all economic or industrial growth rates, or even productive rates for specific commodities such as steel or electricity, as reliable guides to economic aspects of the cold war. For the *rate* of economic production in any given year, as compared with productive levels in the past, may be far less important than the *actual quantity* of goods and services produced at any given time. For the present, and for a number of years to come, the overriding reality—of which Communist leaders themselves seem amply aware—is that the West has a commanding lead over the Communist bloc in output and is likely to retain it. The Gross National Product of the United States for 1963, for example, was close to $600 billion; it was around $300 billion for the USSR. In that same period, the United States produced (at around 80 percent operating capacity) some 90 million tons of steel, while the USSR (at full operating capacity) produced over 75 million tons; the United States produced more than 360 million metric tons of crude oil, while the Soviet Union produced close to 190 million metric tons; the United States generated almost 950 billion kilowatt hours of electricity, while the Soviet Union generated close to 370 billion kilowatt hours.[43]

Now, this comparison overlooks a factor in the equation of economic capacities which, by the 1960s, threatened to tilt the balance decisively in favor of the West. This was the spectacular economic progress achieved by Western Europe, particularly by the members of the European Economic Community, or Common Market. The next chapter will analyze this phenomenon in detail. Here it is sufficient merely to observe briefly that the Common Market has achieved a level of economic growth that surpasses both the American and Soviet growth rates. Assuming eventual membership (or "association") for Britain and the "Outer Seven" in EEC, its members would then collectively embrace 250 million people, turn out a Gross National Product nearly double that of the Soviet Union, produce more than 100 million tons of steel annually, and hold gold and dollar reserves twice as large as those held by the United States.[44] With this thriving economic region linked militarily with the United States, the Communist world is confronted with an economic capacity and potential that it could not possibly rival in the foreseeable future.

Trends on the European continent aside, it is also apparent that by the 1960s, communist economic strategies were encountering a number of severe difficulties. This was indicated by the fact that by 1962, communist nations accounted for some 37 percent of the world's total industrial output. Fulfillment of the Soviet Seven Year Plan, together with projected economic advancement in the European satellite countries, was expected to give the Communist zone 50 percent of the world industrial production by 1966—a goal which could not possibly be reached on the basis of current productive levels. Indeed, the early 1960s witnessed a dip in Communist productivity levels below those achieved in the late 1950s. By contrast, the West (particularly the Common Market) was achieving a new record of industrial output.[45] The economic tribulations experienced by the Communist bloc had their origins in a number of factors. While it possessed many industrial raw materials in abundance, it was encountering shortages in others that compelled it to rely increasingly upon imports. Some of the satellite countries, like East Germany, were encountering difficulty in maintaining a high level of industrial employment. Within the Soviet Union, on the other hand, an acute shortage in certain categories of skilled labor prevailed; the traditional source of industrial labor—the agricultural sector—was itself suffering chronic productive setbacks.

Even more basically, by the 1960s Russia's Communist regime found itself in a dilemma from which there appeared to be no satisfactory escape. On the one hand the regime put unprecedented emphasis upon expanding consumer goods production, in response to the long-standing and pervasive demands of the Soviet society. The Soviet society enjoyed the highest standard of living experienced since 1917. On the other hand, this very tendency threatened to divert national resources away from heavy industry and to jeopardize fulfillment of the Seven Year Plan. Moreover, the 1960s witnessed keen competition between the Soviet Union and the United States in space technology. As space programs became more ambitious and sophisticated, they also became infinitely more expensive—so expensive in fact that the USSR was hard-pressed to compete successfully without altogether abandoning its visibly higher standard of living at home and its goal of building a superior industrial base. These realities no doubt explained the Kremlin's obvious reluctance to challenge the United States to a "race to the moon"—an undertaking which even many Americans believed prohibitively expensive.[46]

Under tsars and commissars alike, Russia has also found its economic advancement impeded by another crucial deficiency: a primitive internal transportation system. Although the USSR possesses 75,000 miles of railroad—the United States has three times as much—supplemented by an intricate network of internal waterways, Russia altogether lacks a modern highway system. Western military strategists have long regarded the USSR's poorly developed transportation network as one of the most vulnerable points in its military position and as possibly a decisive liability in any military contest between the Communist and non-Communist worlds.[47]

Thus far, we have made little reference to the Achilles' heel of the Soviet economic system—agriculture.* Even during tsarist days,

this was always the weakest segment in the economy, despite the fact that Russia was predominantly an agricultural country. Famines and other agricultural crises have been endemic in Russia. By the 1960s, it appeared that conditions had improved very little after almost a half-century of Communist efforts to intensify agricultural production. Forced collectivization of agriculture, beginning at the end of the 1920s, ultimately resulted in the destruction of millions of head of livestock and in the virtual elimination of the country's most productive peasant class—the kulaks. From the inception, collectivization encountered the unrelenting hostility of the Russian peasants, ushering in a state of incipient conflict between them and the government that has endured to the present day. Collectivization thus witnessed a *decline* in many segments of agricultural production. This tendency was, of course, greatly accelerated by World War II, when widespread devastation took place in the agricultural heartland of the Soviet Union. Before and after the war, recurrent droughts and other adverse weather conditions, severe erosion, and primitive farming techniques added their toll. The result has been a Soviet record in agricultural output that is in some ways inferior to the record achieved under the tsarist regime!

During the late 1950s and the early 1960s, for example, Soviet industrial production rose by nearly 33 percent; in the same interval, agricultural production rose only 5 percent.[48] Although the Kremlin regards "a flourishing, versatile and highly productive agriculture" as "an imperative condition for the building of communism," the record of Soviet agricultural production suggested that communism was being built on uncertain foundations.[49] Khrushchev, for instance, boasted in 1957 that, by the early 1960s, the USSR would equal the United States in meat production, requiring the former to produce around 20 million tons of meat annually. In fact, Russia produced 8.7 million tons of meat in 1960, less than the output in 1959.[50] Recent statistics of Soviet grain production have revealed the same pattern. A dramatic development late in 1963 underscored this aspect of the USSR's agricultural problem, when the Kremlin bought 6 million tons of Canadian wheat to meet

* Our discussion of Soviet and Communist bloc agricultural problems relies heavily upon the following sources: Allen B. Ballard, "A Barnyard View of Soviet Agriculture," *The Reporter*, **28** (May 23, 1963), 38–40; Edward Crankshaw, "Deep Dilemma of Mr. Khrushchev," *New York Times Magazine*, July 22, 1962, pp. 9, 60–62; Thomas P. Whitney, "The Kremlin's Big Problem—The Peasant," *ibid.*, April 24, 1955, pp. 9, 28–34; Ellsworth Raymond,

Soviet Economic Progress (New York: Holt, Rinehart & Winston, 1960), pp. 29–35; and *The New York Times*, January 22, 1961, February 18 and March 11, 1962, and August 17, September 22, and September 29, 1963.

its growing domestic and foreign needs. In the months that followed, overtures were made by Moscow for additional purchases from mounting American surpluses. These moves called attention graphically to the failure of Khrushchev's widely heralded "virgin lands" program for extending grain production into Soviet Asia and Siberia. Initially, these new lands had yielded abundant crops—approximately doubling the USSR's total annual grain harvests and going far toward the goal announced in 1961 of increasing agricultural production by 150 percent within 10 years and by 250 percent within 20 years. Yet within a brief time, agricultural productivity declined again, as a combination of adverse weather, lack of fertilizer and equipment (along with a lack of trained technicians to use the equipment), bureaucratic mismanagement, the continuing hostility of the peasantry, a shortage of skilled agricultural workers, and an increase in demand at home and abroad compounded the agricultural problem.[51]

Attempts to significantly expand Soviet farm output encounter certain hard and highly adverse geographical realities. Nature has not been kind to the Soviet Union. Most of the country lies in the same latitude as Canada; much of the land is like that found around Hudson Bay. Only one million, out of eight and one-half million, square miles can be utilized for agricultural purposes; food can only be grown on 500,000 acres, or about 6 percent of the total land area. While this is approximately the same acreage of cultivable land available to the United States, two factors alone perhaps largely account for the difference between massive American agricultural surpluses, grown on *restricted* acreage, and chronic Soviet agricultural shortages, in spite of intensive efforts to *expand* production. One is the difference in population. Russia's limited agricultural region is required to support a growing population, expected by 1970 to approximate 250 million people, that demands a constantly rising standard of living. Another is the climate and over-all geographical environment affecting agricultural enterprise. Historically, agriculture throughout most of Russia has always been a precarious undertaking. A combination of poor soil throughout much of the country; sparse and uncertain rainfall, 8 to 10 inches a year; extremely short growing seasons; limitations upon the diversity of crops capable of being grown successfully; a rebellious peasantry that has rejected all Communist

inducements to expand over-all agricultural productivity; a declining farm labor force, coupled with the difficulty of persuading well-educated young people to make a career in agriculture; mounting internal and foreign demands—these add up to an enduring and staggering agricultural problem for Soviet economic planners.*

That advanced Soviet science and technology would sooner or later succeed in overcoming some of these difficulties could hardly be doubted. Moreover, the Communist elite had revealed itself to be keenly sensitive to the demands of the peasantry for concessions and

A Poor Harvesting Tool. (Source: Jensen in *The Chicago Daily News,* reproduced in *The New York Times,* September 29, 1963.)

to their inbred hostility to collectivization schemes. Indeed, one of the principal sources of ideological discord between Moscow and Peiping involved the former's *de facto* willingness to admit that collectivized agriculture had failed to meet Communist bloc economic requirements. More than any of his predeces-

* Not the least element in the problem is the sharp increase in Soviet trade commitments. By 1963–1964, for example, the Kremlin had assumed trade obligations calling for a total of 5 to 6 million tons of grain deliveries abroad, chiefly to East Germany, Czechoslovakia, Poland, and Cuba. This was almost exactly equal to the wheat purchased from Canada in that year. *The New York Times,* September 29, 1963.

sors, Khrushchev had come to terms with a reality that not even a totalitarian political order can indefinitely ignore: sooner or later public opinion must be taken into account, if for no other reason than that failure to do so can generate serious economic dislocations, engendering a crippling imbalance between Communist and Western levels of production. Even so, Soviet Russia's agricultural problems remained chronic and momentous. For an indefinite period, agricultural output was likely to lag significantly behind industrial gains and, in the light of rising consumption levels at home and growing foreign commitments, would constitute a serious drain upon Soviet economic resources.*

The Military Balance Sheet

The military historian Samuel L. A. Marshall warns us that:

> War, and the risks of war, are never a matter of counting the chips on both sides of the table, and then coming forth with a plus or minus answer. The wisest man . . . could not forecast the true capability of the United States for a war with limits yet undefined, fought with weapons the effects of which remain unmeasured, engaging peoples whose moral strength in the face of unfathomed danger is unknown and unknowable.[52]

Recognizing that comparisons of military capabilities can never be too precise, that much depends upon the exact circumstances under which forces are utilized, and that rapid changes in military technology sometimes quickly alter existing power configurations, let us examine more closely dominant factors in the equation of East-West military power.

Looking first at total men in uniform, we note that by 1964, the West had a slight edge over the Communist bloc: the former had approximately 8 million men under arms, while the latter had around 7.5 million. While Communist forces had an advantage of "interior lines" (that is, their over-all military

effort was less dispersed, and their supply and communications lines were shorter), nevertheless they were required to deploy over a far-flung area, from East Berlin to Southeast Asia, and from the Sakhalin Islands north of Japan to Bulgaria.[53] Lacking the advantage of interior lines, the United States and its cold war allies were obliged to maintain an even more scattered military effort, that demanded military installations from Greenland in the north to Southeast Asia and the Philippines in the south, and from the NATO area in the West to Korea, Japan, and Okinawa in the east.[54]

Historically, Russia's principal military strength has been concentrated in ground forces; this pattern continues to characterize the military effort of the USSR and its allies in the contemporary era. The Red Army, with 2.5 million men, contains approximately 250 front-line and supporting divisions. Moreover, in the event of all-out global war, and in spite of the Sino-Soviet dispute, Western military strategists would have to take into account the Chinese Communist army, numbering some 2.2 million men. Communist ground strength in Europe was variously estimated as numbering between 90 and 175 combat-ready divisions; over 500 Communist divisions could be mustered in time of war.[55] In land forces, the Communist world possessed an overwhelming military advantage vis-à-vis the United States and its military allies.**

---

* One observer has noted that basically the Kremlin has two alternatives in endeavoring to deal with its critical agricultural problems. It can simply admit failure—and rely upon growing industrial exports to purchase needed food supplies. Or, it can divert massive resources from other sectors in order to raise agricultural output appreciably—at the risk of jeopardizing progress in industry. Neither of these alternatives appeals to Soviet planners. Madelein G. Kalb, "Khrushchev's Economic Problem," *The Reporter*, **27** (December 20, 1962), p. 22.

** By the mid-1960s, considerable disagreement existed among the NATO partners about the exact strength of Communist forces in Europe and about the relative advantage which the Kremlin possessed in this sphere. For a number of years, NATO planners assumed that the Soviet Union could call upon 175 combat-ready divisions in case of war in Europe. Assuming that the NATO allies reached their contribution of 30-odd divisions (which they have not done), and that America could contribute 16 divisions, this disparity decisively favored the Communist world, so much so that NATO strategy throughout the postwar period assumed that Europe could not be successfully defended on the ground. By 1963–1964, however, this assumption was being widely challenged in Washington and in NATO headquarters; the West German government, for example, accepted Washington's view that the number of combat-ready Soviet divisions had been overestimated for many years and that, instead of 175 such divisions, the Kremlin could likely call on only half this number. In part, this explained the tendency of French President de Gaulle and others to de-emphasize the danger of a Communist attack against Europe. See *The New York Times*, November 17, 22, and December 5, 1963.

In air and missile power, the military balance was much more favorable to the West. Despite a prevalent belief in the late 1950s that a serious "missile gap" gave the Communist bloc a growing advantage, as time passed it became clear that Western air and missile strength was equal to, if it did not surpass, Communist strength in such weapons. The American Strategic Air Command—including 1300 strategic bombers—provided the foundation stone of free world defense. American air power, added to the air power of the allies, gave the West almost 3000 long- and medium-range bombers, versus approximately 1300 possessed by the Communist bloc. At all times, the West maintained a force of 500 SAC bombers, armed with nuclear warheads, on "quick reaction alert" to safeguard free world security. These could be refueled in the air by nearly 1000 tankers, thereby bringing Western striking power within range of almost any conceivable target. In addition, the West possessed more than 500 operational Atlas, Titan, and Minuteman long-range missiles; more than 1700 such missiles were scheduled to become operational by 1966. Greatly augmenting Western missile strength also were 10 Polaris-type nuclear submarines, each armed with 16 medium-range missiles, providing submersible missile sites around the periphery of the Communist world. By 1968, the United States expected to have well over 40 Polaris submarines, mounting a total of nearly 700 medium-range missiles.[56] While the Soviet Union possessed advanced missiles (some, according to the Kremlin's claim, capable of an 8000-mile range), American sources estimated total Soviet missile strength as between one-fourth and one-fifth of Western strength. With more than 1000 bombers, the Communist world was believed to possess only 100 to 200 comparable to the SAC's long-range B-52's and B-58's. Somewhat counterbalancing this Western advantage are three facts about the Soviet missile arsenal: Communist missiles have more powerful thrust, hence they are capable of carrying larger warheads, and the arsenal of Soviet intermediate-range missiles is superior.[57] Yet, Western (especially American) bomber and missile strength is expanding at a faster rate than Communist strength. American officials are therefore convinced that, both absolutely and relatively, the air-power disparity will become even more favorable to the West with the passage of time.[58]

By the mid-1960s, a crucial military component was the stockpile of nuclear weapons available to both sides. In 1963, Secretary of Defense Robert S. McNamara declared that "the United States nuclear force is manifestly superior to the Soviet Union's."[59] In McNamara's view, in only one area of nuclear technology did the Soviet Union enjoy a clear lead over the United States: the ability to produce very "high-yield" warheads, with an explosive force measuring tens of megatons. Militarily, such weapons had very limited utility. Below the level of giant nuclear and hydrogen bombs, the Western nuclear arsenal was superior. More specifically, this meant that the United States was ahead of its opponent in the ability to construct nuclear warheads for a wide variety of bombs and missiles. It had a clear advantage in the number and diversity of "tactical" nuclear weapons that would be employed on the battlefield against relatively small targets. Moreover, as we have noted, its methods for delivering nuclear warheads were quantitatively superior to the Soviet Union.

Naval strength is another category in which the West has traditionally excelled and, by the 1960s, Western naval superiority remained decisive. Traditionally, the Soviet Union's naval power has been concentrated in submarines and in coastal shipping. Throughout the postwar period, the USSR—having acquired useful ports by its occupation of the Baltic countries, and having declared the Baltic Sea virtually a Soviet lake—has forged ahead in submarine production. By the 1960s, a fleet of almost 500 modern submarines gave the Communist world a clear quantitative lead over the West in this aspect of naval strength. Although the United States and its allies could muster, all told, around 400 submarines, Western supply and communications routes remained highly vulnerable to a Soviet submarine attack. The magnitude of this danger can be gauged by recalling that Hitler almost defeated Great Britain, and came dangerously close to severing the Atlantic lifelines with America, with a total of only 75 submarines at the start of World War II. Although no Communist country was believed to have any appreciable number of nuclear submarines by the mid-1960s, the Soviet Union was known to be developing a prototype and would undoubtedly acquire this weapon in time. Meanwhile its missile-launching submarines could only fire short-range missiles from the surface.

In other categories of naval power, the balance clearly favored the United States and its allies. The West, for example, possessed close to 70 cruisers, while the Communist bloc had approximately 30. The West also had nearly 60 aircraft carriers capable of launching long-range bombers armed with nuclear weapons, while the Communist bloc apparently had none.* In auxiliary naval vessels, like transport craft, the combined navies of the United States, Great Britain, and the other allies greatly exceeded the tonnage available to the Communist world.[60]

In summary, calculations of military strengths and weaknesses on both sides revealed overwhelming Communist superiority on the ground, certain or possible superiority in tactical aircraft, in the size of the submarine fleet, in the size and thrust of long-range missiles, and in the megaton force of large nuclear warheads. The West enjoyed a superior position in long-range air power, in the quantity and variety of missiles, in nearly all components of seapower, and in the size and diversity of its nuclear stockpile. In general terms, the picture possessed all the earmarks of a military stand-off, with each side enjoying a preponderant advantage in certain categories of weapons and an inferiority in others. We shall have more to say at a later stage about the implications of what has been called "the nuclear balance of terror."

Variables in the Military Equation

Our discussion of military strengths and weaknesses on both sides began with an admonition about the extreme difficulty of computing elements in the military power of nations and in comparing the power of one nation against another. This is a theme to which we must now return, since many imponderables and variables must be kept in mind in any assessment of Western or Communist strength. What weight ought to be attached to such intangible, but absolutely fundamental, considerations as civilian and military morale on both sides? How important in the military equation is the degree of unity prevailing among populations in the Communist and Western worlds? Are the Soviet

* By 1963–1964, the role of attack aircraft carriers in general or limited war was under continuing discussion in the Pentagon and on Capitol Hill. The Defense Department favored a cutback in carrier construction and a de-emphasis upon its value, particularly in general war. Spokesmen for the Navy Department conceded that American carrier strength might be safely reduced. *The New York Times*, September 29, 1963.

satellite armies reliable, or is the Russian population itself prepared to support the Communist hierarchy in the event of war against the West? While it would be foolish to count confidently upon widespread defections behind the iron curtain in the event of war, it is nevertheless profitable to recall that this did occur when the German *Wehrmacht* invaded Russia in World War II. Large numbers of Soviet citizens, particularly ethnic minorities, defected to Germany, only to be repulsed by Hitler's barbarous policies toward "inferior races."

For that matter, the West of course is not free of civilian morale problems. Ever since inauguration of the containment policy in 1947, there has existed a real question—highlighted by the Korean War and later American efforts to check communist expansionism in South Vietnam and Laos—whether Western societies were prepared to make the sacrifices that successful containment of communist expansionist moves demanded, or whether they were prepared indefinitely to maintain programs like foreign aid that were highly instrumental in preventing the germination of communism in societies throughout Latin America, Africa, the Arab world, and Asia. Moreover, the West has been plagued for many years by the fragility of alliances like CENTO and SEATO which often threatened to disintegrate, or become irrelevant, when put to the test. Within the NATO area, continuing disagreement has occurred between the United States and its principal allies over the proper strategy for protecting the security of Western Europe. European societies have been conspicuously less than enthusiastic about an American strategy that depends ultimately upon an ability to rain nuclear devastation upon the Communist bloc and, in the event of an attack upon NATO, perhaps upon the Western allies as well.

It is axiomatic that the effectiveness of a nation's power is a function, among other things, of the circumstances under which it is used. Secretary of Defense McNamara may well have been correct in asserting, late in 1963: "I would not trade our strategic posture for that of the Soviets at any point during the coming decade."[61] Yet the Pentagon would be the first to agree that overwhelming Western superiority in nuclear weapons and methods of delivery did little per se to check communist encroachments in Southeast Asia; nor did a preponderant Western advantage in seapower

effectively prevent extensive communist contacts with newly independent countries in
Africa. Moreover, Western military strategy
rests upon realization of a fact that is inherent
in the confrontation between two antagonistic
and antithetical ideological systems: the
initiative in the use of military power to achieve
diplomatic objectives at the expense of the
free world rests with the Communist bloc.
Western strategists are therefore compelled in
the nature of the case to respond to communist moves and, in most instances, for
ideological and humanitarian reasons, to leave
the decision as to the employment of nuclear
weapons largely to Communist policy-makers.*
This in turn means that the Communist policy-
makers have the advantage both of surprise
and of the ability to choose the circumstances
under which Communist military, and collateral economic, political, and propaganda
forces, would be invoked to best advantage.
Not knowing when and where the next communist push will come, Western nations must
be prepared for any eventuality and must
possess a well-stocked and effective arsenal for
coping with communist maneuvers.

The Nuclear Balance of Terror

Speaking to the Senate Foreign Relations
Committee on August 13, 1963, Secretary of
Defense Robert S. McNamara declared:

. . . I cannot allege that the vast increase
in our nuclear forces, accompanied as it was
by large increases in Soviet nuclear stockpiles, has produced a comparable enhancement in our security. . . . as the President
stated, "A full-scale nuclear exchange lasting
less than 60 minutes, with the weapons now
in existence, could wipe out more than

* Admittedly, at intervals throughout the postwar period, Western policy-makers have threatened
to utilize nuclear weapons; or, at any rate, they have
raised the possibility that they *might* be employed
by the West, even if the Communists did not employ them. President Eisenhower quite clearly inti-
mated as much during the interminable peace negotiations following the Korean War; he, at least,
believes this threat did much to hasten agreement
between Communist and free-world negotiators.
See Dwight D. Eisenhower, *Mandate for Change:
1953–1956* (Garden City, N.Y.: Doubleday, 1963),
pp. 179–181. Similarly, one commentator records
that, in conversations with President de Gaulle,
President Kennedy said that if NATO forces stood
in danger of an imminent Soviet attack, or if Europe itself (but not the United States) were attacked, then he would not hesitate to launch an
atomic strike against Soviet Russia. Hugh Sidey,
John F. Kennedy: President (New York: Atheneum,
1963), p. 184.

300,000,000 Americans, Europeans and Russians. . . ." It is clear that absolute growth
of Soviet capability to inflict damage on the
United States has narrowed the range of
contingencies in which our nuclear deterrent
is credible.[62]

By the 1960s, the West and the Communist
bloc had achieved a "nuclear balance of terror."
Although the atomic arsenal of the West was
superior to that possessed by the Communist
world, each side had enough nuclear weapons
to devastate the other and to imperil the
foundations of civilization itself. In that sense,
the nuclear superiority of the West became
largely superfluous; the capacity for "overkill"
did little to enhance its military or diplomatic
position vis-à-vis its Communist opponents.
Statesmen on both sides of the iron curtain
were fully conscious that an approximate
nuclear stalemate had been reached and that,
whatever the precise number and nature of
nuclear weapons on each side, they were sufficient to wreak widespread global devastation
in the event of war.

What were the military and diplomatic
implications of the nuclear balance of terror,
especially for the United States? We may
analyze the problem by focusing upon two
possible conditions. First, what does relative
nuclear parity mean in case of all-out nuclear
war? Several years ago, British Field Marshal
Viscount Montgomery declared that in a war
of this kind, after the initial blow, "the
advantage will go to that side which has the
greater defensive strength, which can protect
itself against attack, and can survive to strike
back."[63] America's ability to "protect itself
against attack" has remained sharply impaired
because of a highly inadequate civilian defense
and shelter program and the lack of a concerted
effort to "disperse" key industrial installations
as protection against nuclear devastation. Yet
by the 1960s its ability to "strike back" after
sustaining a massive nuclear blow remained impressive and probably exceeded by a wide
margin the ability of the Communist world
to launch a "second strike" nuclear attack.
Secretary of Defense McNamara declared in
1963 that the United States was superior to
the Soviet Union in the "design, diversity, and
numbers" of nuclear weapons; its strategic air
and missile force was "designed to survive" a
nuclear onslaught, and "it will survive." Normally, operating from 55 land bases, SAC
forces could be dispersed to 100 fields in time
of emergency.[64] Widely scattered land, sea,

and air bomber and missile sites thus made it virtually impossible for the Soviet Union to eliminate Western nuclear power. Or, as the military analyst Hanson W. Baldwin put it: "Moscow could hurt, but not destroy us."[65] Even after a surprise Communist attack, sufficient power would remain to destroy enemy military and economic installations. This Western "second strike" capacity both deterred the Communist world from initiating general war and well-nigh guaranteed that, if it came, military victory would accrue to the free world.

Second, what are the major implications of the nuclear balance of terror under conditions short of all-out nuclear conflict? If an approximate nuclear equilibrium has been reached, how do the military and diplomatic positions of each side compare when nuclear weapons are left out? At the outset, we may note that by the 1960s, political leaders in the Communist and non-Communist worlds appeared fully cognizant that nuclear parity existed, and their diplomatic moves tended to reflect this realization. Two events could be cited to illustrate this awareness. In 1956 the West exercised notable restraint in its response to the Hungarian uprising against Soviet dominance. In whatever degree Westerners sympathized with the Hungarians, and however much their governments advocated the ultimate liberation of Eastern Europe from Soviet control, statesmen in Western capitals were not prepared to assist the Hungarians at the risk of precipitating a nuclear holocaust. The USSR manifested similar restraint in 1962 in the Cuban crisis. Despite his obvious desire to establish a Communist missile base in Cuba, and despite his unqualified pledges to support Castro's regime against "American imperialists," Premier Khrushchev also demonstrated that achieving his goal was not worth the risk of a head-on nuclear collision with the West. Both sides, that is to say, had made it clear that they were extremely reluctant to take any diplomatic step that risked mutual destruction. It was notable that even the leaders of Red China—with all their seeming indifference toward the consequences of nuclear war—did not press their demands for the "liberation" of Taiwan (Formosa) to the point of precipitating a nuclear conflict.

All of this meant that the contest between East and West continued unabated—but with primary reliance upon "conventional" (i.e., non-nuclear) weapons, propaganda campaigns, economic rivalry, trade programs, subversive and countersubversive movements, and diplomatic maneuvering. From Laos to Guinea, and from the Himalayas to the Caribbean, each side eschewed the use of nuclear weapons and endeavored to achieve its objectives by use of other techniques—a condition that more or less fulfilled what Premier Khrushchev meant by "peaceful coexistence" or more accurately, "peaceful competition" between East and West.

Under these conditions of the cold war, the West found itself at a number of genuine disadvantages, creating unpalatable policy choices. With nuclear arsenals immobilized by common consent between East and West, the free world faced a relentless opponent that possessed military superiority on the ground and a relatively favorable military position because of advantage of "interior lines." Moreover, the enemy held the initiative in deciding where, when, and under what conditions it would make its next expansive move. This meant that in the 1960s the West continued to confront the same painful choices that had been presented graphically during the Korean War: (1) it could seek to meet localized manifestations of communist aggression and subversion where they occurred, thereby often conceding a clear military superiority in ground and guerrilla forces to the Communist bloc; (2) or, it could bring its overwhelming strategic air and missile superiority into play to counter communist incursions, at the risk of precipitating a third world war. Diplomatically, the first alternative reduced itself to settling for a negotiated peace following a "limited" war, producing perhaps a *status quo ante bellum*, as in Korea; or possibly accepting a disadvantageous political settlement, as in Indochina; or possibly engaging in an interminable and indecisive contest, as in Laos. Psychologically, none of these prospects was satisfying to the American people. The second alternative entailed relying upon nuclear devastation to seek the complete elimination of the Soviet Union, along perhaps with Red China, as centers of global communism, thereby jeopardizing the future of human civilization and, in the process, alienating hundreds of millions of people in societies not actively engaged in the cold war.

By the late 1950s, successive administrations in Washington were fully mindful of the diplomatic dilemma created by the nuclear balance of terror. They sought to mitigate (if they could not altogether eliminate) the dilemma by significantly increasing the ability of the United States to fight "limited" wars. In turn, this required a considerable buildup in military forces capable of engaging in "brush-fire" conflicts. Thus, in 1963, a new American Army–Air Force Strike Command was created and given primary responsibility for free world defense throughout the Middle East, South Asia, and much of Africa, where the most probable forms of attempted communist penetration were limited military thrusts, communist-inspired subversion, propaganda campaigns, and economic activities. Similarly, the Strike Command was charged with responsibility for airlifting American troops quickly to trouble spots such as West Germany, where emergencies could require a rapid buildup of Western forces.[66] While these moves unquestionably bolstered the ability of the West to counter communist moves, the bloc nevertheless continued to hold considerable advantage under conditions of nuclear parity. The West continued to face basically the same choice it had confronted for over a decade: it could confine its military response to hostile communist moves to reliance upon non-nuclear weapons, thereby permitting the communist cause to exploit its military advantages in ground and guerrilla warfare—an advantage that would almost certainly be reflected in ensuing peace negotiations; or it could initiate a global nuclear war, with all of its attendant devastation and its social, economic, and military chaos. The alternatives remained both unavoidable and unappealing. The evidence indicated that, short of massive and undisguised communist military aggression against the free world, the West would confine its response to the former alternative. Yet, successfully following this strategy presupposed another condition that, even by the 1960s, was far from being satisfied: the ability of the public to understand the choices open to policymakers, accompanied by a public willingness to accept the diplomatic results that these choices inescapably produced.

NOTES

1. R. N. Carew Hunt, *The Theory and Practice of Communism* (London: Geoffrey, Bles, 1957), p. 264.
2. Harrison E. Salisbury, *Khrushchev's "Mein Kampf"* (New York: Belmont, 1961), p. 69.
3. Department of State, *Communist Perspective* (Washington, D.C.: Division of Research for USSR and Eastern Europe, Office of Intelligence Research, 1955), pp. 383–384. A valuable compendium of communist doctrinal statements on a variety of subjects.
4. *Ibid.*, p. 384.
5. Quoted in Jerry A. Hough, "The Stalin-Trotsky Split: A Lesson for Kremlinologists," *The Reporter*, 29 (December 5, 1963), 39.
6. Salisbury, *op. cit.*, p. 87.
7. Department of State, *op. cit.*, p. 18.
8. Salisbury, *op. cit.*, p. 56.
9. *Ibid.*, p. 52.
10. Department of State, *op. cit.*, p. 253.
11. Arthur E. Adams, *Readings in Soviet Foreign Policy* (Boston: Heath, 1961), p. 293. A useful collection of primary and secondary source materials.
12. Salisbury, *op. cit.*, pp. 52–62 *passim*.
13. *Ibid.*, pp. 155–156.
14. Department of State, *op. cit.*, p. 238.
15. *Ibid.*, p. 442.
16. *Ibid.*, p. 443.
17. Quoted in Nathan Leites, *A Study of Bolshevism* (New York: Free Press of Glencoe, 1953), p. 416.
18. Text in *The New York Times*, July 15, 1963.
19. Department of State, *op. cit.*, p. 177.
20. *Ibid.*, p. 273.
21. Salisbury, *op. cit.*, pp. 45–49, 156.
22. Hunt, *op. cit.*, p. 100.
23. R. N. Carew Hunt, *A Guide to Communist Jargon* (New York: Macmillan, 1957), pp. 67–69.
24. Leites, *op. cit.*, p. 17.
25. *Ibid.*, p. 245.
26. Barrington Moore, Jr., *Soviet Politics—The Dilemma of Power* (Cambridge, Mass.: Harvard University Press, 1950), pp. 391–392.
27. Louis J. Halle, *Civilization and Foreign Policy* (New York: Harper & Row, 1955), pp. 137–140.
28. *Ibid.*, p. 125.
29. Moore, *op. cit.*, p. 393.
30. Gerhart Niemeyer, *Inquiry into Soviet Mentality* (New York: Praeger, 1956), pp. 14–15.
31. Milovan Djilas, *The New Class: An Analysis of the Communist System* (New York: Praeger, 1957), pp. 129, 163, 169. A revealing account by one who experienced communism.
32. *Documents on American Foreign Relations: 1950* (Boston: World Peace Foundation, 1951), p. 429.

33. C. Grove Haines, ed., *The Threat of Soviet Imperialism* (Baltimore: Johns Hopkins University Press, 1954), p. 209.

34. T. Hammer, "The Geopolitical Basis of Modern War," *Military Review*, 35 (October, 1956), 77. Analyzes the Cold War in the light of geopolitical ideas.

35. Haines, *op. cit.*, p. 217.

36. Salisbury, *op. cit.*, p. 99.

37. Quoted in Madelein G. Kalb, "Khrushchev's Economic Problems," *The Reporter*, 27 (December 20, 1962), 21.

38. *The New York Times*, February 1, 1959.

39. For details on the Soviet Seven Year Plan, see Salisbury, *op. cit.*, 94–174; Ellsworth Raymond, *Soviet Economic Progress* (New York: Holt, Rinehart & Winston, 1960). The latter provides a succinct discussion of the problem facing the West in Soviet economic growth.

40. *The New York Times*, March 20, 1958.

41. George B. Cressey, cited in Raymond, *op. cit.*, p. 7.

42. *The New York Times*, November 16, 1958, and February 1, 1959; *Christian Science Monitor*, January 19, January 28, and February 5, 1959.

43. *The New York Times*, July 14, 1963.

44. *Newsweek*, 61 (January 7, 1963), 26.

45. *The New York Times*, June 10, 1962.

46. *New York Herald Tribune*, May 7, 1962.

47. Otto Wein, "Transportation as a Strategic and Economic Problem of the Soviet Union," *Military Review*, 36 (April, 1956), 75–89; Raymond, *op. cit.*, pp. 26–27.

48. *The New York Times*, March 11, 1962.

49. Salisbury, *op. cit.*, p. 108.

50. *The New York Times*, June 4, 1961.

51. *The New York Times*, September 29, 1963.

52. Quoted in Haines, *op. cit.*, p. 200.

53. *New York Herald Tribune*, November 21, 1961. This dispatch summarizes the findings of the British Institute for strategic studies on free world and Communist bloc military capabilities.

54. *The New York Times*, February 25, 1962, and November 6, 1963.

55. Varying estimates of the size of active and reserve Communist ground forces are cited in: *World Almanac: 1963* (New York: The New York World-Telegram and the Sun, 1963), p. 384; *New York Herald Tribune*, November 21, 1961; *The New York Times*, November 17 and 19, 1963.

56. *Time*, 82 (August 23, 1963), 1; *The New York Times*, November 6, 1963.

57. *New York Herald Tribune*, November 21, 1961; *The New York Times*, November 21, 1963, dispatch by Hanson W. Baldwin.

58. *Time*, *op. cit.*, p. 12.

59. See the text of McNamara's statement on American missile potentialities in *The New York Times*, August 14, 1963.

60. Data on Western and Communist naval strength are contained in: *The New York Times*, August 14, and November 6, 1963; *Time*, *op. cit.*, p. 1.

61. *The New York Times*, November 19, 1963.

62. *The New York Times*, August 14, 1963.

63. Field Marshal Viscount B. Montgomery, "A Look at World War III," *Military Review*, 35 (June, 1955), 105.

64. *The New York Times*, November 21, 1963.

65. *The New York Times*, November 7, 1962.

66. *The New York Times*, November 6, 1963.

10 → WESTERN EUROPE → the

new world and the old

A Century of the Monroe Doctrine

No better illustration can be found of the revolution in American foreign policy brought about by World War II than the relationships that evolved between the United States and Western Europe in the postwar era. With the signing of the North Atlantic Treaty in 1949, the United States intertwined its own security inextricably with that of its Western European allies—thereby finally reversing the principles that had governed American relationships with Europe for nearly a century and a quarter.

From the earliest days of the Republic, the United States has conceived of itself as a new and unique nation whose appointed mission required it to stand aloof from the quarrels and vicissitudes of the Old World. Geography separated the two worlds by thousands of miles of ocean; the American Revolution signified a spiritual-ideological breach. For well over a century thereafter, Americans were primarily concerned with domestic problems and challenges, especially expansion across the continent. George Washington had sounded the keynote of the American outlook in his Farewell Address in 1796, when he declared that "Europe has a set of primary interests, which to us have none or a very remote relation." This view was also supported by Thomas Jefferson, who stated in 1813 that: "The European nations constitute a separate division of the globe; their localities make them a part of a distinct system; they have a set of interests of their own in which it is our business never to engage ourselves." America, on the other hand, "has a hemisphere to itself. It must have its separate system of interests; which must not be subordinated to those of Europe. . . ."[1]

Thus, when President Monroe delivered his classic message to Congress in 1823, he was adding very little to the position already taken by the United States in regard to European affairs since independence. The key thought expressed by the Monroe Doctrine with respect to Europe,* was that: "In the wars of European powers in matters relating to themselves we have never taken any part, nor does it comport with our policy so to do. It is only when our rights are invaded or seriously menaced that we resent injuries or make preparation for our defense." Warning the Holy Alliance to stay out of American affairs, Monroe stated "that we should consider any attempt on their part to extend their system to any portion of this hemisphere as dangerous to our peace and safety. With the existing colonies or dependencies of any European power we have not interfered and shall not interfere."[2]

At the time neither the United States nor Europe was conscious that Monroe was enunciating a principle of American foreign policy that would apply for over a hundred years thereafter. The influences that prompted Monroe's speech were twofold: threatened intervention by the Holy Alliance to return the

* The Monroe Doctrine had two aspects, one governing America's relations with Europe, the other, Europe's relations with the Western Hemisphere. While the first aspect remained relatively unchanged for over a century, except of course for World War I, the other was subject to numerous amendments and modifications in the years that followed 1823. The Western hemispheric applications of the Monroe Doctrine are discussed in Chapter 12.

newly independent states of Latin America to Spain, and machinations of tsarist Russia in the Northwest, climaxed by the Imperial ukase of 1821 which virtually proclaimed the Pacific Northwest a Russian sphere of influence.[3] The Monroe Doctrine had been America's response to these two threats. Over the course of time it became the most famous principle of American foreign policy.

However, the self-abnegation pledge that the United States would not interfere in European affairs was not nearly so sweeping as is sometimes supposed. Monroe pledged only non-interference in "the wars of the European powers in matters relating to themselves. . . ." Thus, the Monroe Doctrine from its inception applied only (1) to Europe's *wars* and (2) to those wars that were *exclusively of European concern*.

Although President Monroe was not conscious of laying down a precept that would bind American foreign policy-makers through successive decades, the Monroe Doctrine's stipulations relating to America's relationships with Europe became the guiding principles of American foreign policy until the Truman Doctrine was proclaimed in 1947. There were, of course, a number of exceptions to noninterference in Europe, notably America's participation in World Wars I and II. But even these examples can be deemed compatible with the Monroe Doctrine, since in both cases American vital interests were very much involved in these European conflicts. German submarines forced the United States into World War I. The Japanese attack on Pearl Harbor, followed by the German declaration of war against the United States, compelled our entry into World War II. It is significant that all through World War II the United States believed that the greatest threat to its own security emanated *from Europe*; hence American policy-makers consistently gave a higher priority to the European theater of war than they did to the Pacific theater.

For nearly a hundred years after 1823, American involvement in the politics of Europe was episodic and transitory. Woodrow Wilson's ill-fated attempt to reorient American foreign policy around the principle of "collective security" is too well-known to require elaboration here. Senate rejection of the League of Nations graphically reaffirmed American isolationist attitudes toward Europe. America did not officially participate in the League's activities, although it sent unofficial "observers" to attend League deliberations, and cooperated on a limited scale with a number of the League's social and humanitarian activities.[4] Prolonged vacillation by the Senate in considering American membership in the World Court constituted further evidence of isolationist tendencies, with the World Court proposal being finally rejected by the Senate in 1935.[5] Then during the 1930s, isolationism made the population insensitive to the most elementary facts concerning the nation's security and the security of the North Atlantic region with which America's destiny was increasingly linked. "Aid short of war" was the most that the American people would support—and sometimes there was very little public support even for this—prior to the Japanese attack of Pearl Harbor in 1941.

Prerequisites of an Isolationist Policy

For almost a hundred years, isolationism accorded both with the desires of the American people and with existing geographic-diplomatic realities, although by the turn of the century many of these realities were beginning to change. At first, few Americans were aware of these changes, preferring as late as the 1930s to cling to old ways long after conditions had passed that had made traditional habits of thought and policies possible. Isolationism was finally abandoned as the policy of the United States, not willfully, but as an inescapable reaction to the facts of international life in the postwar nuclear age, and more specifically a reaction to the inescapable challenge posed by the Soviet threat. Yet, even in the postwar period, many Americans fail to understand why isolationism has been possible historically and why it is an untenable policy today.

Three conditions made possible America's historic withdrawal from the political affairs of the old world. These conditions have either disappeared altogether today or else they have so changed as to make an isolationist course by the United States nothing short of suicidal.

1. *America was geographically isolated from the world.* This fact, as much as any other, explains America's ability for over a hundred years to stay out of great-power conflicts in Europe and to a lesser degree in Asia. America could follow isolationism as a policy because the United States was separated from the storm centers of diplomatic controversy by formidable geographical barriers. Thousands of miles of ocean cut America off from Europe and Asia; the polar icecap and northern Cana-

dian wastelands posed an impenetrable obstacle to the north; no threat could come from the weak, unstable governments that existed in Latin America. In the modern period, annihilation of distance by the fast ocean liner, the submarine, radio and telephone, and finally the jet airplane and supersonic missile has eliminated the geographical fact of isolation from the outside world. Within minutes, destruction could be rained on American cities by a potential aggressor; and, conversely, American retaliatory power could be launched speedily against an enemy. Isolationism will not suffice as a policy, therefore, because isolation is no longer a reality.

2. *Europe's diplomatic troubles were America's well-being.* The United States was also fortunate that suspicion and rivalry among the great powers of Europe prevented them from uniting behind an anti-American policy. As a rule, the United States had only one thing to fear from the Old World: a new grand coalition that might arise to despoil the young nation and to jeopardize its continued independence. Occasionally this danger appeared imminent, as illustrated by the Holy Alliance's threatened intervention in Latin America in the early 1820s. In the main, however, European countries could never subordinate their differences sufficiently to collaborate against the United States. Repeated diplomatic conflicts on the Continent during the nineteenth century—occasioned by Russia's several attempts to penetrate the Near East, France's efforts to re-establish its former position of greatness, countless nationalistic rebellions against entrenched autocracies, Bismarck's determination to make Germany a great power —kept the great powers in an almost constant state of diplomatic ferment and intensified existing hostilities. Europe's infrequent incursions into Western hemispheric affairs—such as French intervention in Mexico during the Civil War—produced controversies among the European states themselves, out of fear that one country would increase its power over the others. Meantime, on the Continent age-old jealousies and antagonisms made European countries reluctant to embark upon expansionist policies in the Western Hemisphere, so long as the fear existed that the first danger to their security lay in Europe.

Continuance of this state of affairs in turn depended on several factors: the existence of a number of European states, roughly equal in power; determination by these states to fight wars for limited ends, in contrast to the doctrine of "total wars," followed by the principle of "unconditional surrender," that has been one factor making a balance of power inoperative in more recent years; recognition by the states of Europe that preservation of the balance-of-power system was in the best interests of all concerned. These conditions do not obtain in the contemporary age. They were destroyed by a combination of World War I, the imperialistic ambitions of Hitler and Mussolini, World War II, the wartime and post-World War II policies of the USSR, independence movements in former colonial areas, the injection of ideological considerations into world politics on a far greater scale than in the nineteenth century—all contributing to the decline of Britain, Germany, France, and Italy as great powers on the European scene and militating against reinstitution of a balance-of-power system comparable to that prevailing earlier.

3. *American security was protected by the Pax Britannica and the subsequent Anglo-American entente.* The nineteenth century was the age of *Pax Brittanica*—unquestionably one of the most stable and benign eras known to the history of international relations. Britain ruled the seas. Utilizing strategic bases in its scattered colonies, it intervened repeatedly to put down threats to international peace and order, whether they came from the diplomatic intrigues of Russia in the Near East, or Germany in Persia, or the Holy Alliance in Latin America. For more than a century after independence, the American people were suspicious of Great Britain, believing firmly that Downing Street harbored territorial ambitions on the American continent and, in more general terms, that it sought to frustrate American diplomatic goals. This frame of mind persisted until around 1900.

Actually, in spite of this prevailing antagonism toward Britain, a fundamental identity of interest lay beneath the surface of Anglo-American relations throughout most of the nineteenth century. Historians are agreed that British acceptance of the principles of the Monroe Doctrine—at least those parts relating to European activities in the Western Hemisphere—largely explains whatever success the doctrine achieved for several decades after 1823 in realizing American diplomatic objectives. Britain was perhaps even more concerned than America about the possibility of other great powers' establishing a strong position in Latin America, thereby enhancing their capacity to jeopardize British sea communications and trade routes. Britain could accept the idea, therefore, that this hemisphere was a special preserve of the United States—a country that possessed no navy worth mentioning and that harbored no expansive tendencies that would be at British expense.

Until about 1900, Americans rarely perceived the relationship between their own security and British power. After that date, however, both countries began openly to acknowledge their mutual interests. Britain feared the growing naval might and imperialist ambitions of Germany and Japan. The age-old imperialistic objectives of tsarist Russia threatened more than ever to infringe upon British colonial and trade interests in the Far East. America, although beginning to expand its navy, had few imperialistic designs that clashed with those of Great Britain. As maritime and trading countries, both nations shared a desire to preserve freedom of the seas and unimpeded access to world markets. Ideological affinity provided another link in the chain of Anglo-American cooperation. British support of the Open Door policy in China at the turn of the century and negotiation of the Hay-Pauncefote Treaty in 1901, preparing the way for American construction of the Panama Canal, signified the new official harmony that now characterized Anglo-American relations.

Nevertheless, it could not be said that American citizens as a whole understood the crucial role of this entente in preserving their security. Periodically, vocal citizens groups "twisted the lion's tail" and railed against the alleged evils of the British Empire. Anglophobia abated during World War I, but in the era of "normalcy" and isolation that followed the war, a majority of Americans appeared to be ignorant of the part played by Anglo-American cooperation in defending the vital interests of the United States. The "inarticulate major premise" of American foreign policy after 1900 has been the assumption that Great Britain and the United States are friends and that in an overwhelming majority of cases their diplomatic objectives are complementary, rather than antagonistic. Britain's dramatic decline as a great power after World War II, a process that actually began with World War I, drove home to Americans as never before how vital for international peace and stability had been Britain's former role as protector of the balance of power in Western Europe and chief defender against Russian expansion across the frontiers

of Europe, the Middle East, and Asia. Moreover, as America discovered painfully in the turbulent postwar period, in its colonial affairs Britain had contributed to international stability through its policies of preparing dependent peoples for orderly and enlightened self-government.

For nearly a century the United States enjoyed the benefits of *Pax Brittanica*. In the postwar years the roles became reversed. Now it was Great Britain that was protected by a *Pax Americana* whose aims differed in few material respects from Britain's efforts to enforce the peace during the nineteenth century.

CONTAINMENT, RECOVERY, AND REARMAMENT

The Origins of Containment

By 1947 the Monroe Doctrine had been superseded by the Truman Doctrine's principle of containment as the guiding rule of America's relationship to Europe. Reduced to its essentials, the new policy anticipated firm and sustained American resistance to Soviet expansionist tendencies. Containment received its most persuasive justification at the hands of George F. Kennan, a high-ranking State Department official and recognized authority on Soviet Russia. In a widely circulated article on "The Sources of Soviet Conduct,"[6] Kennan enunciated the containment idea as America's response to the challenge of Soviet expansionism and hostility toward non-Communist countries. The immediate postwar period had witnessed Soviet hegemony over Eastern Europe, communist intrigue in such countries as Iran, Turkey, Greece, Indochina, and China, as well as Soviet intransigence on such questions as disarmament and control of nuclear weapons. By 1947 it had become apparent on all sides that the wartime policy of great-power collaboration had collapsed.

It was Kennan's belief, sharply challenged by other leading students of international politics,[7] that successful implementation of the containment idea would not only prevent further Soviet incursions into the non-Communist world but would also in time bring about a "mellowing" in the Kremlin's attitudes and policies toward the outside world, possibly aiding the emergence of a less despotic, less xenophobic political order within the USSR.

Containment received its first application in the Greek-Turkish Aid Program of 1947. After that came the Marshall Plan, the North Atlantic Pact, the Mutual Defense Assistance Program, and the Mutual Security Program. Hand in hand with these developments went efforts by the United States to encourage greater economic, military, and political integration on the continent of Europe. All of these were manifestations of the containment idea, because a major impetus in each case was the threat to the security of the North Atlantic community posed by the expansionist policies and impressive military power of the Communist bloc. Whatever specific forms America's relations with Western Europe in the postwar period might take, one goal remained uppermost: to make the North Atlantic area as impregnable as possible against threats to its security emanating from behind the iron curtain, irrespective of whether they came from a threatened Soviet military attack or communist intrigue in the political affairs of Western Europe.

European officials in the main shared Washington's assessment of the communist threat; but to their minds there were perhaps even more compelling reasons for cooperating with the United States to rebuild Europe's devastated economies, strengthen its defenses, and initiate movements aimed at transcending deeply entrenched nationalistic tendencies on the Continent. One was to impart a feeling of greater security among Europe's citizens. Another was to lessen dependence upon the United States, a dependence which, in Europe's weakened position, was both inevitable and widely resented. Still another was ultimately to recreate Western Europe as a powerful independent force in world affairs. Throughout the postwar era the viewpoint has gained adherence among leaders on the Continent that the countries of Europe must forsake ancient nationalistic bickerings and pool their energies and resources, if Western Europe is ever again to play the decisive role in international politics witnessed in earlier eras of modern history.

In examining these developments, our study will focus on four dominant problems in postwar American foreign policy toward Europe. These are: European economic recovery and rearmament; economic unification movements; defense and military collaboration within the North Atlantic region; and movements directed at the political unification of Europe.

The Greek-Turkish Aid Program

In an historic foreign policy address on March 12, 1947, President Truman declared that "it must be the policy of the United States to support free people who are resisting subjection by armed minorities or outside pressures."[8] Truman's address was prompted by the crisis in Greece, where Communist-led rebels were seeking to overthrow the legitimate government. For almost two years, British troops had supported the Greek government's effort to restore stability. But Britain was near bankruptcy. Some liquidation of British overseas commitments therefore became imperative, leaving the United States the alternative of either assuming many of these commitments or accepting further communist intrusions into the free world. The situation in Greece took on added urgency because, at long last, Russia appeared on the verge of achieving its age-old desire to break through into the Mediterranean area.

President Truman consequently asked Congress for an appropriation of $400 million to resist communist expansionism in Greece and to bolster the defenses of nearby Turkey, which had also experienced intermittent Soviet pressures during and since World War II. After prolonged study, Congress granted this request in May, thereby establishing the pattern of economic-military aid to countries struggling against communist aggression. Such aid was to become a permanent feature of American foreign policy in the contemporary period. Along with Yugoslavia's later defection from the Soviet bloc, American economic and military aid proved to be of crucial importance in preserving the political independence of Greece and assuring its continued adherence to the free world alliance.

The European Recovery Program

Even before Congress had approved the Greek-Turkish Aid bill, the Truman Administration had begun studies of Western Europe's progressively critical economic plight. Wartime and early postwar relief programs like the United Nations Relief and Rehabilitation Administration (UNRRA) had done little or nothing to eliminate the causes of economic instability in Europe. By mid-1947, widespread economic distress, bringing in its wake political turbulence, impended in Europe. In a major foreign policy speech on June 5, 1947, Secretary of State George C. Marshall took note of Europe's crisis and suggested that America would be prepared to extend long-range economic assistance, provided Europe took the lead in presenting a carefully worked-out plan for utilizing American assistance to promote lasting regional recovery. Europe was quick to respond. Even Soviet Russia and its satellites expressed an interest in participating in the Marshall Plan. By midsummer, however, communist propaganda organs had begun to denounce the Marshall Plan as an instrument of American imperialism. Neither Russia nor its satellites participated in the discussions that finally resulted in the presentation of a concrete program to the State Department. Lacking access to the Kremlin's archives, no Westerner can be certain of the reason behind Moscow's refusal to participate in the Marshall Plan. No bars originally existed against Russia's association with the plan, although as time passed, the program came more and more to be presented to Congress and the American public as an anti-communist measure. Several hypotheses may be suggested. Russia was apparently unwilling to accept any "conditions" for the use of American aid, particularly any that would involve extensive American "supervision" of its administration. Moreover, in the light of an increasingly anti-Soviet attitude within the United States and especially in Congress, Russia may have actually feared an expansion in American influence in the sensitive Eastern European satellite zone. Several countries in this area had expressed keen interest in participating in the Marshall Plan. Czechoslovakia, for instance, appeared highly enthusiastic about the prospect of American assistance. If extensive American aid to Eastern European countries led to significant progress in rehabilitating these countries, American prestige would be greatly enhanced to the detriment of Soviet influence. Ideological considerations may also have colored Russia's decision. The Kremlin may have thought that long-awaited revolutionary forces could work more successfully in economically debilitated countries.

Whatever the reasons for the Kremlin's obduracy, it is apparent that Soviet refusal to join in the plan was a major blunder in Russia's postwar foreign policy. Perhaps more than any other factor, the Marshall Plan was responsible for the decline of communist influence in Western Europe after 1948. Initially there had appeared considerable opposition within the United States to so costly a measure. This opposition was largely overcome by presenting the plan to Congress as part of the "containment" strategy, a maneuver that would hardly have been possible had Soviet Russia been a participating country. Soviet participation, therefore, probably would have killed the Marshall Plan

outright, or, at a minimum, sharply reduced its scope.

In accordance with American demands, the nations of Western Europe formed a regional association, ultimately called the Organization for European Economic Cooperation (OEEC), to make exhaustive studies of the region's long-term needs and to draw up plans for using American assistance in the most effective way.* By mid-August, OEEC had submitted a proposal calling for nearly $30 billion in American funds, an estimate that was eventually scaled down to $17 billion over a four-year period. By the end of the program, $12.5 billion had actually been appropriated by Congress for European recovery.[9]

The Marshall Plan officially came to an end in 1951. At the time of its expiration, there was no question but that it had largely achieved its basic purpose of rehabilitating the economic systems of the OEEC countries. By 1951, European production had either reached or exceeded prewar levels. Figuring 1947 as 100, the index of industrial output for major Western European countries and for the OEEC area as a whole showed the following prewar and postwar levels:

Country	1938	1947	May, 1951
Western Germany	295	100	334
France	105	100	148
United Kingdom	91	100	135
Western Europe	115	100	162

Progress was also impressive in the revival of European trade. By 1950, international trade had expanded 11 percent over prewar levels, with intra-European trade rising 25 percent over the previous year.[10] This progress made it possible for the nations of Western Europe to contribute to their own defense on an expanded basis. In 1949, these countries were spending 5 percent of their Gross National Product, or $4.5 billion, on defense; by 1951–1952 this had risen to 8 percent of their GNP, or $9 billion.[11]

* OEEC remained in existence until 1961, when it was superseded by the Organization for Economic Cooperation and Development (OEED). While OEEC had been concerned primarily with fostering regional economic cooperation to achieve the goals of the Marshall Plan, as we shall see, OEED was responsible chiefly for coordinating economic policies among its European members and for integrating their foreign aid activities.

The Shift to Military Aid

The change to military aid, for reasons to be discussed later, began in 1950 with the Mutual Defense Assistance Program. In 1952, economic, military, and technical assistance for underdeveloped countries were combined into a single program, known as the Mutual Security Program. In the years that followed, military-defense foreign aid was administered by the Defense Department. Economic and technical assistance was administered by the International Cooperation Administration (ICA), a semiautonomous organ under the policy control of the State Department. MDAP and MSP, in conjunction with influence exerted by the United States through NATO, formal diplomatic channels, and public opinion, resulted in a vast increase in Western Europe's defense efforts. By 1957, Europe was spending $13 billion on its own defense.[12]

By the late 1950s and early 1960s, it had become apparent that Europe's military-defense position was infinitely stronger than it had been ten years earlier. This did not mean that no problems beset NATO's efforts to strengthen Western security; we shall examine many of these later in the chapter. Western Europe, nevertheless, was no longer considered one of the most inviting areas for communist expansionism. This realization underlay the reduction in American military assistance to Europe. Thus, a report to the Senate Foreign Relations Committee observed late in 1963 that: "Present [military assistance] programs in Europe consist entirely of the discharge of past commitments and cost-sharing arrangements [between the United States and its NATO allies], with the exception of programs in Spain and Portugal." For 1964, the United States provided a mere $77 million in military assistance to Europe to defray part of the cost of maintaining NATO's "infrastructure," such as airfields, communications networks, and training installations.[13] In submitting his foreign aid budget for 1965, President Johnson could report to Congress that: "The Western European nations in the North Atlantic Treaty Organization now supply almost all the financial support for their own military forces and also provide military assistance to others."[14]

American Assistance in Perspective

The change in geographic direction, and in underlying purpose, of American foreign assistance programs throughout the postwar era is highlighted by noting the status of Europe in these programs. In the period 1946 to 1954, Europe was by all odds the largest beneficiary of American assistance. Out of a total of some $50 billion in American aid, Europe's share was $33 billion, divided into $26 billion for economic aid and $7 billion for military aid. For the period 1955 to 1962, on the other hand, the United States provided some $47 billion in foreign aid, of which Europe's share was $12.3 billion, divided into $9 billion for military assistance and $3.3 billion for economic assistance.[15] By the mid-1960s, as we have noted, Europe's share of American foreign aid had declined to an insignificant amount.

Responding to growing official and public demands in the United States by the early 1960s, Western European nations had themselves begun to extend larger quantities of assistance to other countries. For the year 1960, for example, European nations, joined by other free world countries, contributed some $1.9 billion to promote the economic progress of underdeveloped countries; in the same year, the United States contributed $2.9 billion.[16] The Development Assistance Committee (DAC) of the Organization for Economic Cooperation and Development, composed of aid-giving nations in Western Europe, the United States, Canada, and Japan, was increasing its allocations to underdeveloped countries and facilitating the flow of private capital from industrialized to needy countries. By 1963, OECD had agreed to the establishment of a development center to be operated under its auspices.[17] In overall terms, European cooperation in the foreign aid activities of the free world was impressive. Expressed as a percentage of the Gross National Products of contributing countries, France, Belgium, and the United Kingdom made a higher proportionate budgetary contribution to foreign aid than did the United States.[18]

By 1963, President Kennedy observed that the flow of funds from other industrialized nations within the free world (chiefly in Western Europe), amounted to about $2 billion annually for overseas assistance.[19] Even so, both Presidents Kennedy and Johnson were convinced that the European allies were able (in President Kennedy's words) to "increase their assistance efforts and to extend assistance on terms less burdensome to the developing countries." Achieving this goal would unquestionably remain an objective of American foreign policy throughout the years ahead.

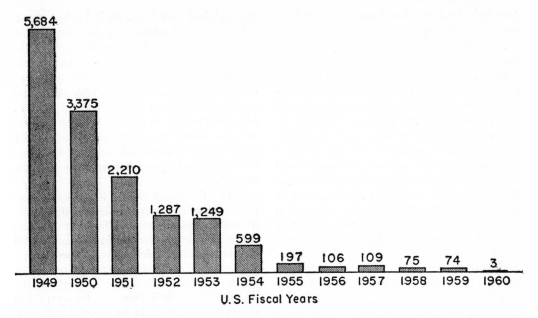

American Economic Assistance to Europe; in millions of U.S. dollars. (Source: Adapted from the U.S. Department of State, *Mutual Security Program, 1959*, p. 67.)

EUROPEAN ECONOMIC INTEGRATION

The American Objective

As early as 1942, John Foster Dulles expressed the thoughts of many leading Americans when he stated that:

Continental Europe has been the world's greatest fire hazard. This has long been recognized, but it has seemed impractical to do anything about it. Now the whole structure is consumed in flames. We condemn those who started and spread the fire. But this does not mean that, when the time comes to rebuild, we should reproduce a demonstrated firetrap.[20]

When the Senate was considering interim aid to Europe in 1947, Dulles told the Senate Foreign Relations Committee that the "basic idea should be, not the rebuilding of the pre-war Europe, but the building of a new Europe, which, more unified, will be a better Europe."[21]

Consistently throughout the postwar period, the United States has encouraged the movements looking toward European unity or European integration. Congress in particular has been keenly interested in the progress of European integration and has not hesitated to express its viewpoints in legislation providing American assistance to Western Europe. Thus the Mutual Security Act of 1954 contained the following expression of congressional sentiment:

The Congress welcomes the recent progress in European cooperation and re-affirms the belief in the necessity of further efforts toward political federation, military integration, and economic unification as a means of building strength, establishing security, and preserving peace in the North Atlantic area. . . . the Congress believes it essential that this Act should be so administered as to support concrete measures to promote greater political federation, military integration, and economic unification in Europe.[22]

Throughout the postwar period, America's support for the *idea* of European economic integration has remained more consistent than its conception of the precise forms such integration was expected to take and of the relationships that were to prevail among economic unification movements on the Continent.*

* The term European unification or integration possesses no very clearly defined context. Even the more specific term *economic unification* is sometimes also imprecise and ambiguous. Robert Marjolin conceives it to envision "free circulation of goods, persons, and capital between the European countries," in turn requiring a "single tariff" for its members, a "single currency with a single bank of issue, and a common budget. In a word, it would mean practically the creation of a single state." The more limited concept of *economic integration* is "any process which brings about a greater degree of unity." Quoted in Michael T. Florinsky, *Integrated Europe?* (New York: Macmillan, 1955), p. 28.

Walter Hallstein, a high official of the European Common Market, has defined the goal of eco-

America's tendency has been to support *all* economic unification movements indiscriminately. Europe's response, deriving from the efforts of many of her own leaders to encourage unification throughout history and, in the more recent period, from insistent American demands, have produced supranational economic institutions which are a curious amalgam of high idealism, opportunism, and sweeping compromises. The consequence is that today a crazy-quilt pattern of regional and supranational organizations has been imposed upon the national boundaries of postwar Europe. Most of these organizations have complex administrative structures. Collectively, they are often interlocked and mutually dependent. Comprehensive treatment of these organizations, or analysis of the often intricate relationships prevailing among them, must be left for other writers.*

Forms of Economic Integration

Throughout modern history, Europe has been plagued by the existence of excessive customs duties and numerous national trade barriers impeding the movement of goods and services across frontiers. In the midst of World War II, the Netherlands, Luxembourg, and Belgium took the first steps to overcome this traditional problem when they established a customs union. For several years, this union

---

nomic unification by saying more simply that "it may be regarded as a means of establishing throughout the territory of its member states as much as possible of the uniformity of economic conditions that normally obtains within a single country." Walter Hallstein, *United Europe: Challenge and Opportunity* (Cambridge, Mass.: Harvard University Press, 1962), p. 40.

* The literature on integration and unification movements in postwar Europe is voluminous. The following provide detailed and illuminating coverage: Florinsky, *op. cit.*; Arthur W. MacMahon, ed., *Federalism: Mature and Emergent* (Garden City, N.Y.: Doubleday, 1955); H. A. Schmitt, *The Path to European Union* (Baton Rouge, La.: Louisiana University Press, 1962); Isaiah Frank, *The European Common Market* (New York: Praeger, 1961); Ernest B. Haas, *The Uniting of Europe* (Stanford, Calif.: Stanford University Press, 1958); Emil Benoit, *Europe at Sixes and Sevens: The Common Market, the Free Trade Association and the United States* (New York: Columbia University Press, 1961); George Lichteim, *The New Europe* (New York: Praeger, 1963); Hallstein, *op. cit.*; Kurt Birrenbach, *The Future of the Atlantic Community* (New York: Praeger, 1963); Richard Mayne, *The Community of Europe: Past, Present, and Future* (New York: Norton, 1962).

accomplished very little. As it became apparent in the early postwar era that only limited steps toward economic cooperation among the nations of Europe had any chance of success, the Benelux countries revived their wartime customs union. A comparable agreement was reached between France and Italy in 1949. Many of the goals implicit in the idea of these customs unions were incorporated into the much more ambitious and successful European Common Market, which came into existence in 1959.

When the Marshall Plan to promote European economic recovery was launched in 1948, its stated objective was to facilitate "the recovery of Western Europe in the form of an integrated unity, which, it was hoped, would be capable of maintaining itself economically, politically, and militarily."[23] Throughout the life of the Marshall Plan, the theory (if not always the practice) in the administration of the program was to foster *regional* economic collaboration among the European recipients, in order to transcend long-standing economic rivalries and to make the best possible use of Europe's collective resources. Consequently, the Organization for European Economic Cooperation (OEEC), established by the Marshall Plan recipients to plan effective use of Marshall Plan aid, continually emphasized the necessity for mutual planning to achieve the program's goals. Yet, OEEC possessed very little actual power to compel adherence to this ideal. Almost always, it had to depend upon voluntary compliance with its directives. Several times it had to reduce its goals sharply, in the face of entrenched nationalistic opposition. In spite of these limitations, OEEC succeeded in overcoming some obstacles facing European economic collaboration. Owing largely to OEEC's efforts, intra-European trade was 70 percent higher at the end of the Marshall Plan period than it had been before the war.[24]

That OEEC had proved its worth as an instrument of regional cooperation on the European continent was indicated by the fact that it remained in existence until 1961, long after the Marshall Plan was terminated. Gradually, its compass was broadened to deal with economic problems and tendencies throughout the North Atlantic area. In 1961, as a result of American initiative, the organization was transformed into the Organization for Economic Cooperation and Development (OECD); its membership was broadened to include the United States and Canada. By the mid-1960s,

Japan (which had cooperated with OECD's activities from the beginning) had applied for membership, which was expected to be offered in the near future.

OECD was concerned with several regional economic problems. A major one was coordinating the foreign aid activities of increasingly prosperous Western nations, in order to eliminate duplication of effort and to plan effective allocations of aid on the basis of shared efforts. The British leader Sir Oliver Franks has emphasized that, in the years ahead, international political relations are likely to turn more than ever upon a "right relationship" between the industrialized Northern and underdeveloped Southern Hemispheres. Accordingly, nations in the Atlantic community must pursue a policy of encouraging and supporting "the largest possible free world, so that in Latin America, Africa, and Asia most nations will wish to live and grow and prosper outside the Communist system, maintaining friendly relations with the Atlantic group so that there increasingly comes into being a great company of peoples not separated by man-made barriers but freely exchanging ideas and goods. Otherwise, nations in the North Atlantic sphere might find themselves cut off and alone in a world indifferent and probably hostile to us."[25] in the light of these considerations, OECD's foreign aid activities could be expected to expand throughout the years ahead. Another major concern of OECD was international financial and monetary problems, particularly those affecting national trade balances. America's trade deficit was a dominant influence acounting for its interest in reorganizing this regional body. Moreover, the decision to transform OEEC into OECD had to be understood against the nascent rivalry emerging between the French-led European Economic Community and the British-oriented Free Trade Area. A transformed OECD might both mitigate some of this rivalry and, simultaneously, strengthen America's own role in the economic deliberations of its European partners. America's "original motive" in supporting OECD, according to Beloff, stemmed from a "feeling that the marginal position of the United States" in European policy formulation "was no longer appropriate."[26] Another observer has formulated the American goal by saying that OECD had to be "made into a force for economic integration, as NATO is already to a certain degree in military affairs."[27]

Economic integration and unification in Western Europe was also being achieved by various "sector" schemes designed to accomplish this result within a specific, and often quite limited, sphere of economic enterprise. A leading example of this approach was the European Coal and Steel Community (ECSC), an outgrowth of the Schuman Plan, set up by the Benelux countries, France, Germany, and Italy on April 18, 1951. As a prominent advocate of European economic integration, Walter Hallstein, has described ECSC: "Its essential characteristics were that it was 'supranational,' that it was practical, and that it was partial [in its scope]."[28] Unlike OEEC or OECD, the Coal and Steel Community possessed supranational authority to formulate regulations and directives binding upon its members in coal and steel production. Moreover, as Hallstein has emphasized, a singular characteristic of ECSC was its *evolutionary* character. From the beginning, its instigators conceived of ECSC as an undertaking that would gradually, and on the basis of experience, chart a course toward expanded supranational collaboration in other phases of European economic life.[29] As an ultimate goal (whose realization would take years and would encounter many obstacles), ECSC envisioned creating what Robert Schuman had called "the European federation which is indispensable to the maintenance of peace."[30]

ECSC was a significant step down the path of European economic unity, therefore, not alone because it represented a successful venture in supranational collaboration in one industrial segment. It was perhaps even more significant for what it foreshadowed. This was the far more ambitious European Common Market, whose goals, organizational pattern, and implications for America we shall examine below.

Another sector approach to economic collaboration among European nations was Euratom, which began operating in 1958. Its members were the Benelux nations, France, Germany, and Italy. Unlike ECSC, which it resembled in many respects, Euratom dealt with an area—the peaceful application of atomic energy—in which there was no backlog of competing national traditions to be overcome. As Europe forges ahead along the path of industrialization and rising standards of living, it is expected that nuclear energy will comprise a growing component of economic power, in a region lacking major petroleum deposits. For its first five-year period (1958–

1962), Euratom expended a total of $215 million in its research programs, covering a wide variety of fields from the development of peacetime nuclear reactors to the applications of nuclear technology in fields such as agriculture and medicine. For the period 1964–1979, Euratom was expected to expend approximately $7 billion on a vast program to develop 80 to 90 nuclear power plants. At that, Euratom will be hard-pressed to keep pace with Europe's accelerating energy requirements; these are expected to quadruple between 1960 and 1980. Unlike the Atomic Energy Commission in the United States, Euratom possesses no responsibility for the development or application of military aspects of nuclear science. Potentially, however, Euratom's vast nuclear resources could be utilized for military purposes.[31]

The European Economic Community

The European Economic Community (EEC), popularly known as the Common Market, is the culmination of the movement toward European economic union, and the most promising step toward political union in the postwar era. EEC is far more comprehensive than Benelux, ECSC, and other predecessors on the European scene. It visualizes the substantial economic merger of the participating countries. What is more, the ultimate goal of EEC is *political* unification. So far as the United States is concerned, few developments in postwar Europe have posed as many far-reaching implications for American foreign policy as the emergence of the European Common Market.

EEC came into existence on January 1, 1958, as the result of a 378-page treaty among its signatories, France, the Federal Republic of Germany, Italy, and the Benelux nations (widely referred to as "the six"). It began operations a year later. The appearance of EEC marked the emergence of a new "trading area," in which internal tariff and other barriers to trade were to be removed, so that within 12 years, trade among its members would be completely free. Concurrently, EEC would move toward the goal of a common tariff toward the outside world, based upon an average of tariff rates applied earlier by its members. For this reason, the Trade Expansion Act of 1962, a matter of highest priority among officials of the Kennedy Administration, was passed by Congress in full realization that executive officials had to be given new powers to negotiate favorable trade agreements with the increasingly

prosperous European Economic Community.*

The appearance of the European Economic Community on the global scene was at once both a cause and a symbol of the "new era" in Western Europe's relations with the outside world. In many respects, EEC rivaled the economic potential of the United States and of the Soviet bloc. If Western Europe increasingly conducted itself like a "third force" on the international scene, the explanation lay in the fact that the members of EEC had achieved a measure of economic independence unimagined 15 years earlier.** Thus, by the early 1960s, EEC had achieved an over-all economic growth rate that outstripped the rate achieved by the United States and the Soviet Union. The following chart highlights this phenomenon.

TABLE 5.   Rate of Industrial Production
1958 = 100

	1959	1963
Italy	112	195
Soviet Union	112	160
West Germany	108	145
United States	114	138
France	102	138
Britain	105	120

SOURCE: *The New York Times,* January 10, 1964.

Measured by the volume of its trade, EEC had also evolved into the largest importing area in the world, purchasing some $37 billion in goods and services from the outside world and

---

* This act, together with other developments in American foreign economic policy related to the emergence of the European Economic Community, is treated in detail in Chapter 15.

** Yet, as data presented by Benoit suggests, the revival of economic productivity in the Common Market area antedated the appearance of EEC. Thus, in the period 1953–1959, the Common Market countries increased their Gross National Products by a total of 35 percent within six years; in the same period, the United States increased its GNP by 16 percent. Industrial production in this same period grew 57 percent for the members of EEC, while it increased 12 percent for the United States. See the table in Benoit, *op. cit.,* p. 189.

Will EEC be capable of maintaining such growth rates as it attained in 1953–1959, or those indicated by the more recent data cited above? Some observers, like Benoit, believe that it is possible, primarily because a dominant goal of EEC is "the possibility of accelerating the diffusion to a larger part of European industry of the high standards of productive efficiency which already prevails in the best plants in Europe itself." *Ibid.,* p. 190, and pp. 189–193, *passim.*

exporting just under $37 billion to other countries. EEC countries purchased over $5 billion in American goods and services and, in turn, sold $2.5 billion worth of goods and services to the United States. Intra-Common Market trade alone reached a volume of more than $15 billion worth of goods and services in 1963. Another indication of EEC's economic strength lay in the rising monetary reserves of its member states. In the decade 1953–1963, for example, French monetary reserves rose from under $1 billion to more than $5 billion; West Germany's climbed from under $2 billion to over $7 billion; Italy's grew from $0.8 billion to $3 billion.[32] These data gave meaning to the dictum of Raymond Aron, one of France's leading political commentators: "Western Europe cannot resign itself to the permanent status of a protected country."

The phenomenal success achieved by "the six" in concerting their economic policies also brought about an acceleration in the timetable initially adopted for more sweeping economic and political merger.[33] Thus, the "second stage" in EEC's evolution contemplated an effective economic union, involving the agricultural, manufacturing, banking, and financial activities of its members. Results attained by the early 1960s enabled EEC planners to visualize achievement of this goal by 1967. The next stage—"political unification"—would follow after economic merger had been successfully accomplished. As a case study in supranational institutions, EEC had evolved midway between limited "sector" approaches, like ECSC, and a true "United States of Europe." One commentator has noted that EEC "already has produced a sort of 'whole' that is greater than the separate parts. The Common Market is still 'them' but the world, with justice, uses the term 'it.' "[34] Decisions within EEC are normally reached by a "qualified majority" of five-sixths or two-thirds of the countries represented. There is a widespread belief among its members that, within a short time, decisions will be arrived at by consensus and unanimity.

With the establishment of EEC, as we observed earlier, organizational changes were made in the relationship between it and earlier agencies, such as the Coal and Steel Community and Euratom. EEC now coordinates the operations of these two organizations. In addition, it exercises supervision over a European Investment Bank, a European Social Fund (that carries on activities such as re-training and employment compensation programs), and an Overseas Development Fund that is especially active in providing assistance to the former overseas dependencies (particularly in Africa) of Common Market members.[35]

Each of the three major subsidiary bodies within the European Economic Community—The Common Market, ECSC, and Euratom—is administered separately by a commission, a plural executive agency, whose members are sworn to place the interests of Europe as a whole ahead of the interests of their own country. A Council of Ministers, containing one representative from each of "the six," serves as a cabinet to review executive decisions. Above the Council of Ministers are two higher bodies: the European Parliament, which (though possessing no actual legislative power) serves as a kind of legislature for over-all policy formulation, and a Court of Justice, established to interpret legal aspects of treaty obligations assumed under the multinational agreement establishing EEC.[36]

The European Free Trade Area

From its inception, the European Economic Community was a "continental" organization, anchored in the two strongest powers of Western Europe—France and West Germany. Given the disparity in national power between these two countries and the other members, it was inevitable that EEC would come to be identified chiefly with France and West Germany, particularly with the former, so long as the Bonn government remained heavily dependent upon NATO for its security and was denied nuclear weapons. From an initial reaction of strong misgivings about the economic and political implications of EEC, the government of Great Britain quickly moved to support a counterforce of European countries, traditionally linked closely in economic and financial affairs with London. This organization was called the European Free Trade Area (or "the outer seven"). It consisted of Britain, Sweden, Denmark, Norway, Austria, Portugal, and Switzerland (Finland is an "associate member"), sometimes called simply "the seven." From the start, EFTA neither possessed the cultural unity inherent in the rival EEC, nor did it postulate sweeping goals, like the ultimate political merger of its members. Moreover, the expectation prevailed, and was strongly nourished by many advocates of European unity, that Britain and the other members of EFTA would eventually join, or at a minimum asso-

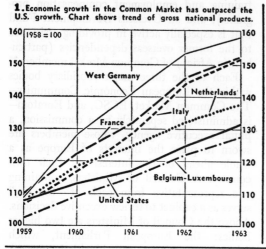

1. Economic growth in the Common Market has outpaced the U.S. growth. Chart shows trend of gross national products.

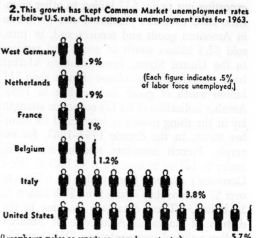

2. This growth has kept Common Market unemployment rates far below U.S. rate. Chart compares unemployment rates for 1963.

(Each figure indicates .5% of labor force unemployed.)

West Germany .9%

Netherlands .9%

France 1%

Belgium 1.2%

Italy 3.8%

United States 5.7%

(Luxembourg makes no reports on unemployment rates)

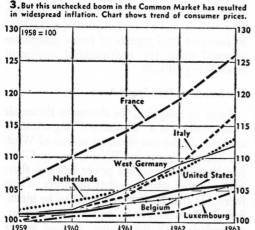

3. But this unchecked boom in the Common Market has resulted in widespread inflation. Chart shows trend of consumer prices.

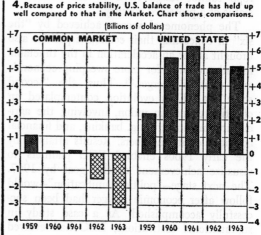

4. Because of price stability, U.S. balance of trade has held up well compared to that in the Market. Chart shows comparisons.

(Billions of dollars)

COMMON MARKET   UNITED STATES

Economic Growth and Inflation—The Pattern in the Common Market and in the United States. (Source: *The New York Times*, March 22, 1964. © 1964 by The New York Times Company. Reprinted by permission.)

ciate with, the Common Market. Indeed, after months of political debate, late in 1962 Britain took the momentous step of requesting membership in the organization, only to be confronted by the obdurate opposition of President de Gaulle of France, who was steadfastly against widening the compass of EEC to include the "Anglo-Saxons."

Meanwhile, EFTA also expanded its trade, both among its own members and with the outside world. By the end of 1963, for example, EFTA's total imports were $27 billion and its exports $23 billion. The United States sold EFTA countries goods and services valued at $2.5 billion and, in return, bought imports valued at $1.8 billion from this trading group. Moreover, EFTA's tariff-cutting activities matched those of its rival, the EEC. After a

series of steps reducing tariff barriers among its members, EFTA was scheduled to eliminate *all* tariff restrictions on trade within its area by 1967. No less than EEC, the members of EFTA were manifesting a remarkable degree of unity in trade affairs. As a result, the United States would be increasingly required throughout the years ahead to arrive at trade agreements with EFTA, as well as EEC, on the basis of mutual concessions and reciprocity.[37]

In the formative stages of both EEC and EFTA, the United States tended to favor both organizations indiscriminately. Both, in Beloff's words, "were welcomed on an equal footing provided that they showed a liberal attitude to the outside world. . . ."[38] At the same time, American officials were always aware that EFTA had a cloud over its future, as a result of Britain's deliberations over membership in the Common Market. Washington never concealed its desire for British affiliation with EEC, provided of course that its members offered acceptable terms. American policymakers have also been aware that EFTA lacked EEC's ultimate political goals. In spite of a declared official "impartiality" toward these rival organizations, therefore, the United States at least implicitly favored EEC over EFTA. This was illustrated in 1960, when American officials publicly endorsed significant tariff reductions by EEC members as applied to their own trade, even if this meant sometimes severe economic dislocations for "the seven."[39] Nor have American officials concealed their evident chagrin at de Gaulle's subsequent veto of British membership in EEC or their expectation that EEC will not accept this verdict as the "last word" on the matter of British membership. If, and when, Gaullist opposition on this controversy is overcome, EFTA's *raison d'être* will have largely disappeared.

Britain and the Common Market

A dominant problem in relations among nations in the Atlantic region is thus the affiliation of Britain, and of smaller countries that follow its lead in economic affairs, to a continental organization postulating eventual *political* merger among its members. After a prolonged period of skepticism about EEC, the British government gradually changed its view. By the early 1960s, it had decided to ask for membership in the organization, a request that was vetoed by French President de Gaulle on January 14, 1963. Among advocates of broader European integration on both sides of the Atlantic, there was no disposition to regard de Gaulle's adamant stand as forever unalterable. American officials continued to seek ways and means of overcoming French objections, while proponents of broader European merger, like Paul-Henri Spaak, counseled Britain to "hold fast" in its determination to resolve existing differences with France.[40] Britain, meanwhile, proceeded to strengthen EFTA and continued the search for a formula that would meet French objections to its membership in (or "association" with) EEC. As time passed, however, French opposition remained as deeply rooted as ever, as indicated in 1964 when Paris once more rejected a British bid for ministerial talks about the thorny issue of Britain's future relationship with the Common Market.[41]

Admittedly, the problem of British membership in EEC, involving the dissolution of EFTA and the subsequent membership of at least some of its members in the Common Market, posed formidable difficulties, some of which involved nothing less than the ultimate future and guiding philosophy of the Common Market. Among the issues at stake, five were perhaps crucial. The first involved Britain's traditional links with its Commonwealth partners, and the remaining overseas dependencies. What would happen to the Commonwealth if Britain joined the Common Market? The answer to this question, of course, chiefly depended upon the conditions under which British membership was made possible. In reality, what was at stake were two fundamentally different conceptions of the kind of economic community EEC ought to be or ought to become. Britain, joined by the members of EFTA, the members of the Commonwealth, and other countries throughout Africa and Asia, sought a broadly based, outward-directed organization, willing to make numerous concessions to accommodate the economic needs of an expanding circle of members. Above all, Britain did not want to be compelled to choose *between* the Commonwealth and the Common Market. And if this choice were finally demanded, nations throughout the Afro-Arab-Asian world would likely interpret this fact as proof of Western indifference toward their economic needs.*

* Reactions throughout the "neutralist" world to developments within the Common Market, as an indication of Western policies toward these areas, are conveyed by the following examples. A spokesman for Nasser's regime in Egypt feared that EEC might "become a great danger to the struggling young African economies," forcing these states to do business on extremely disadvantageous terms. *Egyptian Gazette*, August 4, 1961. An influential Indian journal expressed a similar apprehension that EEC tariff rates would discriminate heavily against, and pose formidable economic problems for, underdeveloped countries. *Times of India*, December 2, 1961. Indonesian, Burmese, Indian, and officials in other countries have called for increasing economic cooperation among underdeveloped nations to counter the adverse effects of the European Common Market. *Hindustan Times*, March 23, 1961; *Egyptian Gazette*, September 27, 1962. Nkrumah of Ghana has been especially vocal in cautioning his African colleagues against the danger of "neo-colonialism," a form of which is economic vassalage perpetuated by the colonial powers of Europe against their former African dependencies. The inclusion of former French possessions in Africa within EEC, he and other African spokesmen have cautioned, would facilitate this new brand of colonialism and severely impede Africa's economic development.

As the acknowledged spokesman for the "continental" powers, French President de Gaulle does not accept this new conception of EEC. To de Gaulle, the Common Market is the symbol and instrument of the "European revival" that has transformed nations on that continent into a bloc of economically viable, culturally related, and geographically cohesive states, determined, under French leadership, to assert their "identity" in global affairs. Such a goal would become impossible—and, indeed, the original members of EEC might become altogether submerged—in an "expanded" Common Market that might conceivably stretch from West Africa to the southeastern Pacific.*

Closely related to this problem is a second stumbling block to agreement about British participation in EEC. This relates to the Common Market's long-range *political* goals. As-

---

Africa Digest, **9** (June, 1960), 218; *Asian Recorder*, **7** (October 8–14, 1961), 4208. A Burmese source has urged Southeast Asian countries to endeavor to terminate their economic dependence upon Western Europe by setting up a Southeast Asian common market of their own. *New Times of Burma*, May 15, 1960.

* Among the features of French President de Gaulle's foreign policy that have "surprised" and often irritated Americans, none perhaps surpasses his sharp differentiation between the unity binding societies on the Continent and those outside it. Thus, at the end of World War II, de Gaulle called for some kind of "association between Slavs, Germans, Gauls, and Latins" to restore stability to war-devastated Europe. Even at this early date, his plans did not include participation by Britain or America. Mayne, *op. cit.*, p. 69.

Much the same mentality was displayed early in 1958, when the French government began to press for the adoption of a plan for a free trade area in Western Europe that was highly "protectionist." In the American view, this conception would collide with French obligations assumed under the General Agreement for Tariff and Trade (GATT) and would discriminate heavily toward the United States and other nonmembers. Consequently, Washington found the French plan unacceptable. The episode again illustrated insistence upon a tightly knit, inward-looking economic union, as distinguished from the kind of expanded union Britain, supported by the United States, advocated. Max Beloff, *The United States and the Unity of Europe* (New York: Random House, 1963), p. 131.

M. Maurice Schumann, Foreign Minister of France for 1951–1954, has contended that "in order that Europe shall be able to make its voice heard and defend its interests in every domain, it must not sacrifice its cohesion merely for the sake of enlarging its scope." He contends that the proponents of EEC would now "be condemning ourselves never to create a political Europe, or to create it too late, if we waited for Britain to lead instead of showing her the way." Maurice Schumann, "France and Germany," *Foreign Affairs*, **41** (October, 1962), 75.

suming that an agreement could be reached to accommodate Britain's economic ties with the Commonwealth, would Britain ever accede to an agreement leading to the *political* merger of countries belonging to EEC? Again, the parliamentary governments, usually resting upon multiparty systems prevailing in Western Europe, have a basic similarity. Could a political formula ever be found that would satisfy both British and European (chiefly perhaps, French) conceptions of desirable supranational political institutions to which the members of EEC would be prepared to surrender a substantial portion of their sovereignty? And if so, what then would become of Britain's links to the Commonwealth, assuming that it still existed?

Behind these questions lay a third issue which, as in so many controversies involving political decision-making, might well be paramount. If Britain entered the European Economic Community, where would the true locus of political power then reside? Would it move to Britain, which presumably maintained (in the Gaullist view, at any rate) its "special" and intimate ties with the United States? Would EEC in effect become dominated by the Anglo-Saxons? Or (a no less unacceptable possibility for France and certain other EEC members) might it lie in a new Anglo-German axis, that would both encourage German military "equality" in NATO and, perhaps in time, eclipse French power on the European scene? Without Britain, the Common Market rested upon the twin pillars of French and German power. As matters stood, Paris's voice was clearly dominant in most decisions taken by EEC. And de Gaulle had made it clear that a leading element in his foreign policy was the forging of a durable Franco-German bond that would inhibit the kind of military "equality" Bonn might eventually get, involving perhaps its acquisition of nuclear weapons, under a more benevolent Anglo-Saxon directorate in EEC.

A fourth and closely related issue involves a problem we have already suggested: Britain's long and intimate ties with the dominant power of the Western alliance, the United States. President de Gaulle's long-standing complaint about "Anglo-Saxon dominance" in the management of NATO finds its parallel in his overt apprehensions about Anglo-Saxon influence upon the Common Market. British membership, in his view, would jeopardize the special and unique relationship that exists among Franks, Latins, Germans, and Slavs and that, in his view, is largely responsible for the renaissance of "European" influence on the global scene. If Britain desires to continue its special relationship with the United States, in the Gaullist view it is welcome to do so; it is not welcome to place that relationship at the center of the Common Market—and thereby convert it into what de Gaulle fears will prove an instrument for achieving objectives largely formulated in London and Washington. This possibility runs exactly counter to de Gaulle's own emphasis upon the necessity for France and its European partners to recover and to assert their own "identity" in a world in which vital diplomatic decisions have tended to be made by American, British, and Soviet policy-makers.

Finally, there is the dilemma posed for other members of EFTA by Britain's decision. The two most extreme cases perhaps are those of Switzerland and Austria. Again, membership in a purely economic union is not the principal stumbling block. Rather it is the obligation of ultimate *political* union with a group of countries belonging to the NATO defense system and plainly identified diplomatically with the "Western bloc." For Switzerland, this prospect would unquestionably violate its long-cherished "neutrality" toward international controversies. For Austria, the prospect would possibly be ruled out altogether, because it violated its state treaty of 1955, whereby the country's wartime occupation was ended, upon the condition that Austria would enter no military alliance system. Vienna therefore would be placed in the excruciating dilemma of either having to stand on the sidelines and passively watch the formation of a new and powerful economic-political European organization or of violating the terms of its state treaty, at the risk of inciting a Soviet move to reoccupy the country. For other countries in EFTA (Finland is a comparable example) choices would be involved that would often demand sweeping modifications in their postwar foreign policies, at the risk of being left in an economically and politically disadvantageous position. For their part, the members of EEC have not been enthusiastic about proposals by the smaller members of EFTA that a special "arrangement" (involving perhaps an "associate" status) be made to permit them to have the tariff concessions available to EEC members, without requiring them to join in steps leading to further political unification.[42]

NATO: SOVIET CHALLENGE AND WESTERN RESPONSE

Origins of NATO

A significant landmark in American postwar foreign policy toward Europe was the creation of the NATO defense community.* Just as economic assistance to Greece and Turkey in 1947 had led to the much more comprehensive and prolonged European Recovery Program, so too was sustained economic assistance to Europe followed by efforts to bolster the military strength of the free world. Initially, these efforts took the form of a military alliance among the nations of Western Europe, which became the nucleus of the North Atlantic Treaty. Within a short time this was supplemented by substantial American military assistance to NATO and to other regional defense organizations.

Several developments in the 1947–1949 period spurred efforts within both the United States and Europe to establish a unified defense system for the North Atlantic area. European Communist parties had agitated militantly against the Marshall Plan. During the late 1940s Communist groups in such countries as France and Italy appeared to be gaining in strength. Moscow's propaganda organs meanwhile were carrying on a virulent anti-American campaign. In China, the Nationalist Government was collapsing before the Communist rebel forces. Then in the spring of 1948 had come the Soviet-engineered *coup* in Czechoslovakia, an event that hastened favorable congressional action on the Marshall Plan. There followed the Berlin blockade of 1948–1949. Here an avowed objective of Soviet foreign policy was to drive the West—and above all, the United States—out of Germany. Had the Kremlin succeeded in this goal, Western Europe would have been left in a highly precarious military-economic position.

Increasingly, Europe's leaders were aware of the need for closer military cooperation among members of the North Atlantic area. With the active encouragement of the United States, five of them on March 17, 1948, signed the

* The text of the North Atlantic Treaty is reproduced in Department of State, *American Foreign Policy: 1950–1955*, I, 812–815. Original signatories of the treaty were the United States, Canada, the United Kingdom, Belgium, Luxembourg, Norway, Iceland, the Netherlands, Denmark, France, Italy, and Portugal. Countries that later joined NATO were: Greece and Turkey (1952) and the Federal Republic of Germany (1955).

Brussels Treaty.* This pact, formed a "collective defense arrangement within the framework of the United Nations Charter . . ." Concurrently, the Senate Foreign Relations Committee, working in close conjunction with the State Department, was attempting to draft a legislative resolution paving the way for American association with a European security system. This resolution, known as the Vandenberg Resolution in honor of its instigator, Senator Arthur H. Vandenberg, was approved by the Senate on June 11, 1948, by a vote of 64–6. It called for "Association of the United States, by constitutional process, with such regional and other collective arrangements as are based on continuous and effective self-help and mutual aid, and as affect its national security."[43] The Senate, in other words, was overwhelmingly in favor of a closer military union between the United States and Western Europe. Europe had created the embryo of such a union under the Brussels Pact; it remained for the United States to join in this effort and for the pact to be extended to other countries. This was done under the North Atlantic Treaty, which the United States ratified on July 21, 1949.

The American Military Commitment Under NATO

By making explicit what had been implicit in the Greek-Turkish Aid Program, the Marshall Plan, and in the firm resistance to Soviet pressure during the Berlin blockade earlier, the North Atlantic Treaty signified that the United States had accepted the principle that its own security was inextricably linked with that of its North Atlantic neighbors. The North Atlantic Treaty is a short document, containing only 14 articles. The key article, expressive of the philosophy behind this military union, was Article 5 by which: "The parties agree that an armed attack against one or more of them in Europe or North America shall be considered an attack against them all. . . . " In the event of an attack, each signatory will exercise the "right of individual or collective self-defense" and will "individually and in concert with the other Parties" take "such actions as it deems necessary, including

---

* The text of the treaty is reprinted in Department of State, *op. cit.*, pp. 968–971. Original signatories were Belgium, France, Luxembourg, the Netherlands, and the United Kingdom. Italy and the Federal Republic of Germany joined the Brussels defense system in 1954.

---

the use of armed force, to restore and maintain international peace and security."

In assessing the nature of the commitment assumed by the United States under NATO, it is profitable to think in terms of the *de jure* and the *de facto* obligation. Widespread fears existed in Congress in this period that American membership in NATO might jeopardize the constitutional right of Congress to declare war. Numerous legislators were apprehensive lest "automatic war" follow an attack against one of the NATO signatories. Therefore, the Vandenberg Resolution had carefully conditioned American participation in NATO upon observance of the "constitutional process" of the United States, which prescribes that only Congress can declare war.[44] Legally then, the obligation assumed by the United States was limited to regarding an attack against one NATO country as an attack against all. Exactly how the United States or any other signatory would react to such an attack was left unspecified. Article 5 of the treaty, said Secretary of State Acheson in 1949, "does not mean that the United States would automatically be at war if one of the other signatory nations were the victim of an armed attack."[45]

The *de facto* commitment assumed by the United States under NATO, however, is another matter. The nature of warfare in the modern period has tended to render the right of Congress to declare war virtually a dead letter. Secretary Acheson suggested as much when he told the Senate Foreign Relations committee in 1949: "If we should be confronted again with an all out armed attack such as has twice occurred in this century and caused world wars, I do not believe that any other action than the use of armed force could be effective." And in recommending ratification of the treaty to the Senate, the committee itself observed that, as far as the United States was concerned, Article 5 reflects a "realization brought about by its experience in two world wars that an armed attack in the North Atlantic area is in effect an attack on itself." Widespread realization of this fact, said the committee, "should have a powerful deterring effect on any would-be aggressor by making clear to him in advance that his attack would be met by the combined resistance of all the nations in the North Atlantic Pact."[46]

As the years passed, the question of automatic war came to be largely academic. Virtually every precept of American defense strategy presupposed intimate collaboration between

European and American military forces and rested upon the doctrine of instant and massive retaliation against an aggressor. The development of guided missiles carrying nuclear warheads gave the Soviet bloc the ability to devastate NATO bases within a matter of minutes. More than ever this fact put a premium upon the ability of the free world to retaliate speedily in the event of war. By late 1957, even Secretary of State John Foster Dulles admitted publicly that in case of a Soviet-instigated attack on Western Europe, the NATO commander would "almost certainly fight back" without waiting for a declaration of war. The NATO forces, of which American forces were an integral part, would return the fire of any aggressor.[47] And by 1961, one observer reported that in conversations with French President de Gaulle, President Kennedy stated that under some circumstances the United States might be compelled to strike the *first* blow in nuclear war. This would conceivably occur if NATO forces were in danger, if the Communist enemy were known to be preparing to strike, or if Europe were attacked by nonnuclear forces.[48]

In summary then, NATO entailed a profound change in American foreign policy by making clear the determination of the United States to fight beyond its own shores to protect the security of the Atlantic system. And it signified a *de facto,* if not *de jure,* alteration in the American constitutional system by notifying potential aggressors that the United States would retaliate instantly, without waiting for a declaration of war, if an attack occurred against its friends in the North Atlantic sphere.

Strategic Implications of NATO

American participation in NATO constituted a milestone in the history of the nation's foreign policy by proclaiming to the world that the American security zone in Europe extended in a belt from Norway to Turkey. Yet the nation's membership in NATO had even wider strategic connotations than this.

The accession of Greece and Turkey to membership in 1952, coupled with the establishment of regional defense systems in other parts of the world subsequently, both strengthened NATO by the addition of more armed forces and by forging links joining these regional defense organizations. Now the NATO alliance extended into the eastern Mediterranean-Near East area, a tinder box of conflict between Russia and Western countries

throughout history. Greek and Turkish accession therefore gave the free world bastions for the protection of the military approaches to the Mediterranean, the Black Sea, the oil fields of the Midle East, the Suez Canal, and North Africa. Equally important, Turkey furnished a strategic bridge to the east by virtue of the fact that the Turks were at the same time members of NATO and of CENTO (Central Treaty Organization), the latter being a security system of anti-Communist countries of the Middle East. By the close of the 1950s, CENTO—the former Baghdad Pact—had been seriously weakened by the defection of Iraq. But Turkey, Iran, and Pakistan, the other members, remained pro-Western. Pakistan's membership simultaneously in CENTO and the Southeast Asia Treaty Organization (SEATO) extended the defense nexus further eastward. And, because the United States is in addition a member of several other military alliances in the Pacific, such as those based on the Korean Treaty, the Japanese Treaty, the Republic of China Treaty, the Philippine Treaty, and the Anzus Treaty, the defense chain, with its western anchor in NATO, reaches as far east as Korea and the Philippines. Finally, American membership in the Rio Treaty, binding the nations of the Western Hemisphere, brings the chain full circle.

In theory, at any rate, the United States had succeeded in surrounding the Communist heartland with a network of military alliances stretching from the Atlantic Ocean to the Sea of Japan. The security of the free world was thus safeguarded by a defense cordon around the perimeter of the Communist zone, thereby deterring Moscow and Peiping from relying upon overt military aggression to achieve their diplomatic goals. How strong is this containment fence, anchored in NATO, in reality? Other chapters deal with problems of free world defense and security in the Arab world, in Asia, and in the Western Hemisphere.* At

---

* See, respectively, Chapters 11, 13, and 12. The defense treaties to which the United States is a party are reproduced in House Foreign Affairs Committee, *Treaty Provisions Relating to the Use of United States Forces for Mutual Defense,* 84th Congress, 2nd Session (Washington, D.C.: 1956). This source also contains maps illustrating these treaty relationships.

It should be kept in mind that, although there is a parallel between defense agreements such as NATO and CENTO (in the Middle East) or SEATO (in South Asia), the nature of the American obligation under each treaty varies somewhat. Thus, the military commitment under SEATO is

a later point in this chapter, we shall examine problems within the NATO community that often militate against its functioning under all circumstances as an effective instrument of free world defense.

Administrative Machinery and Principles

NATO presents a complex organizational pattern which has undergone several major administrative changes since 1949. From the beginning, NATO's constitutional framework was left flexible so that its structure could be modified in the light of experience. Consequently, its growth has been highly pragmatic. The highest policy-making body, the Council, is composed of the foreign ministers of the member countries. The Council is empowered to create whatever subsidiary organs are necessary to advance NATO's purposes, such as a Defense Committee (consisting of the defense ministers of each country) and a Military Committee (consisting of the military chiefs of staff of the member states). The Standing Group, composed of the military commanders from Britain, France, and the United States, serves as the executive agency, meeting in Washington. Increasingly, NATO has been required to forge links also with various regional and supranational organizations in the North Atlantic area. These activities sometimes are directly related to the problem of defense, as with questions of industrialization or manpower; others are more peripherally related to NATO's central concern, such as educational and cultural pursuits.

Following the Korean War, an important organizational change took place within NATO, when an effort was made to "integrate" what were formerly national military contingents that formed NATO's military forces. A joint command called SHAPE (Supreme Headquarters Allied Powers in Europe) was established in Paris and was given control over NATO's ground and air forces. Subsequently, SACLANT (Supreme Allied Command Atlantic) was set up to provide naval defense for the North Atlantic region. An American-Canadian Regional Planning Group also ultimately assumed responsibilty for defending North America against air attack.

Inescapably, NATO's organizational structure and effectiveness are intimately related to (1) the goals of the NATO defense system; (2) differences among the members (especially the more powerful members) of NATO in interpreting the underlying goals, establishing priorities among competing goals, and devising methods for achieving them; (3) regional and global developments in diverse fields, such as military and nuclear technology or trends in East-West relations, that both require continuing study and modification in NATO's objectives and dictate new departures in strategies and tactics for attaining them. Soviet acquisition of atomic and hydrogen weapons, for example, rendered obsolete many of NATO's earlier assumptions about the nature of the threat its members faced and about effective methods for countering it. Similarly, France's resolute determination to acquire its own nuclear *force de frappe* likewise introduces fundamental changes in NATO planning, which may well require future organizational modifications. We shall discuss other significant developments affecting NATO's operations at a later stage. Here it is sufficient to observe merely that, from its inception, NATO has been hard-pressed to evolve an organizational pattern that achieves its purposes satisfactorily, and successfully blends the diverse national viewpoints of its members into a unified regional defense strategy.

Something of the nature of the ongoing challenge NATO faces is suggested by the verdict of a qualified British observer, who noted that the Standing Group in Washington "has become a somewhat shadowy organization with little influence either in the Pentagon or in the alliance as a whole." He also pointed out that SHAPE, as a military planning headquarters, was always in danger of falling "between two stools. It is directed by an American, but as an international commander his views do not necessarily represent those of the U.S. Government." The result was that "new ideas emanating from the NATO military staff may be suspect in Europe as looking like American dictation, and equally suspect in Washington because they have not been through the American policy-making process." Moreover, NATO's organizational structure has revealed a continuing weakness, in the view of this commentator, because of the gulf between military and civilian policy-makers. Organizational patterns thus far have failed to take account of the fact that, with the passage of time, "the diplomatic, arms control, or economic aspects

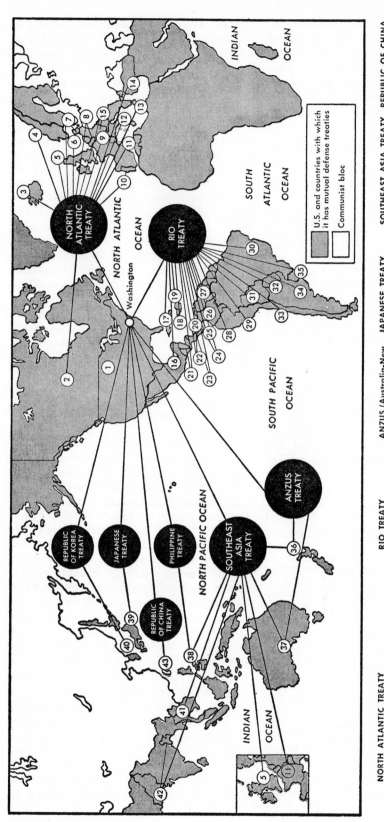

NORTH ATLANTIC TREATY
(15 NATIONS)

1. UNITED STATES
2. CANADA
3. ICELAND
4. NORWAY
5. UNITED KINGDOM
6. NETHERLANDS
7. DENMARK
8. BELGIUM
9. LUXEMBOURG
10. PORTUGAL
11. FRANCE
12. ITALY
13. GREECE
14. TURKEY
15. FEDERAL REPUBLIC
    OF GERMANY

RIO TREATY
(21 NATIONS)

1. UNITED STATES
16. MEXICO
17. CUBA
18. HAITI
19. DOMINICAN
    REPUBLIC
20. HONDURAS
21. GUATEMALA
22. EL SALVADOR
23. NICARAGUA
24. COSTA RICA
25. PANAMA
26. COLOMBIA
27. VENEZUELA
28. ECUADOR
29. PERU
30. BRAZIL
31. BOLIVIA
32. PARAGUAY
33. CHILE
34. ARGENTINA
35. URUGUAY

ANZUS (Australia-New Zealand-United States) TREATY (3 NATIONS)

1. UNITED STATES
36. NEW ZEALAND
37. AUSTRALIA

PHILIPPINE TREATY (BILATERAL)

1. UNITED STATES
38. PHILIPPINES

SOUTHEAST ASIA TREATY (8 NATIONS)

1. UNITED STATES
5. UNITED KINGDOM
11. FRANCE
36. NEW ZEALAND
37. AUSTRALIA
38. PHILIPPINES
41. THAILAND
42. PAKISTAN

JAPANESE TREATY (BILATERAL)

1. UNITED STATES
39. JAPAN

REPUBLIC OF KOREA (South Korea) TREATY (BILATERAL)

1. UNITED STATES
40. REPUBLIC OF KOREA

REPUBLIC OF CHINA (Formosa) TREATY (BILATERAL)

1. UNITED STATES
43. REPUBLIC OF
    CHINA (FORMOSA)

U.S. and countries with which it has mutual defense treaties

Communist bloc

United States Collective Defense Arrangements. (Source: *Report to Congress on the Mutual Security Program*, Chart No. 4.)

of military choices become more important."[49] Such judgments suggest that the problem of NATO's organizational and administrative machinery will require continuing attention, and that evolving diplomatic, economic, and political relationships among its members will raise new questions about the adequacy of NATO's structure.*

Strains and Stresses in the NATO Alliance

Testifying before the House Foreign Affairs Committee in 1957, a high State Department official declared:

> NATO today is a proven and successful alliance. The Communist western advance has been halted and not one inch of territory has been lost since the alliance was founded. Behind the security of the NATO shield the Western European peoples have regained their economic health and are taking new initiative toward economic integration. In most of the NATO countries the . . . alliance is the core and foundation of international security policy. . . .[50]

Nothing has happened in the intervening years to invalidate this verdict. In some respects, the military security of the North Atlantic region was perhaps much stronger by the mid-1960s than it was in the late 1950s. If Americans and Europeans alike were less overtly concerned with the threat of outright communist aggression in the NATO area, or even with communist subversive activities, much of the credit was due to NATO's success in maintaining a "shield" against threatened aggression and in maintaining its nuclear

"sword" in a state of constant readiness for use against possible enemies. Even in its uninterrupted goal of dislodging the allies from Berlin, Moscow had repeatedly indicated its reluctance to achieve its objective at the cost of a military test of strength against the Western allies.

At the same time, events have no less called attention to a number of continuing issues within the NATO community that raise complex and troublesome questions about the organization's effectiveness—if not, indeed, about its very future. By the early 1960s, news media referred repeatedly to "the NATO crisis." Public commentators and serious students of global affairs alike were concerned about whether a succession of such crises was not altogether undermining NATO usefulness as an instrument of Western security. Such pessimistic conclusions were perhaps unwarranted. Yet it was incontestably true that the NATO alliance was being subjected to severe internal pressures and dissensions among its members. Nor could it be denied that continuing and often profound disagreements about its goals, military strategy, and relations with other regional organizations in the North Atlantic area might well impair its future effectiveness.

NATO's internal controversies were almost always interrelated. A disagreement between the United States and France, for example, about de Gaulle's determination to develop a nuclear *force de frappe* had direct implications for the military strategy to be followed by NATO commanders or the question of relative French influence in shaping NATO policies. Similarly, the presence or absence of "consultations" among leading NATO members toward developments, such as the Cuban crisis of 1962 or Paris's decision to recognize Red China, clearly affected the way the European allies (or even the United States itself) assessed the "credibility" of NATO's nuclear deterrent power. By the same token, the special relationship that existed from the beginning between Britain and the United States was both a cause and a result of de Gaulle's growing alienation from the Anglo-Saxons and his determination to exert French independence in world affairs. Recognizing the mutual interdependence of such problems, we may conveniently examine three major issues that have generated continuing controversy within the Western alliance.

1. *Western Defense Strategy in the Nuclear*

---

* The assessment of an American observer, Ernst B. Haas, parallels that of Buchan cited above. Haas believes that "the history of the organization has been a series of crises with clashing viewpoints among the member governments . . ." He notes that NATO has been characterized by "the mushrooming of central institutions, in response to newly felt common needs." Yet in military, economic, and political affairs, most notably in the last, decision-making is extremely slow, cumbersome, diffuse, and often uncertain. Thus, it required the NATO allies four years to agree upon the relationship of West Germany to the organization! It has been unable to override national differences on matters like standardization of armaments and uniform periods of conscription. See the excerpt from his study, cited in Senate Foreign Relations Committee, *Strengthening Free World Security: NATO and Atlantic Cooperation, the United Nations and World Government*, 86th Congress, 2nd Session (Washington, D.C.: 1960), pp. 2–9. This document affords a convenient compendium of appraisals centering on problems in NATO and the Atlantic community.

Age. At the center of the NATO alliance, a discussion and controversy has been taking place among the Western partners about basic defense strategy that has, in turn, colored the views of the allies toward many related issues. One transcendent reality has governed NATO's response to the communist threat. This is the overwhelming disparity between NATO's ground forces and those available to the Communist bloc. Depending upon the particular estimate used (and there were often wide disparities in such figures), for many years NATO was thought to be confronted with massive Communist superiority in ground forces, capable of overrunning Western Europe if the Kremlin launched an aggressive move.* Although recent estimates have tended to upgrade NATO's strength *vis-à-vis* the Communist world, even now Communist superiority in "conventional" forces remains impressive, particularly in the light of NATO's difficulty in fulfilling its military quotas and in preventing France from withdrawing naval and air units from NATO control.

This grim reality in turn dictated the basic strategy which, from the beginning, governed NATO's military planning. This was the twofold idea of utilizing its limited ground forces as a "trip wire" or a "plate glass window" to check aggression, to defend continental Europe as long as possible, and to cause enemy forces to "mass" into inviting targets; concurrently, the NATO "sword"—overwhelming (chiefly

* Throughout the 1950s and early 1960s, the number of combat-ready Communist forces was estimated at between 160 to 175 divisions, totaling between 2 and 2.5 million men. At full strength, by contrast, NATO's contemplated force of 30 divisions constituted a force of 40,000 to 50,000 men. Yet this was an optimistic estimate, since certain NATO countries had never fulfilled their military quota. For many years, French troops were heavily committed in Indochina and Algeria; even after these crises were settled, however, Paris did not contribute its assigned troop quota to the NATO command.

By 1963–1964, Western military planners were convinced that intelligence estimates of Communist forces in Europe had always been too high—perhaps as much as 50 percent in error! Thus Pentagon officials late in 1963 believed that the Communist world had only 50 to 60 fully equipped divisions, maintained at full strength; moreover, equipment and supplies for reserve troops were thought to be inadequate. American divisions, on the other hand, were considered stronger than their Soviet counterparts. This led American defense planners, joined by German officials, to believe that NATO's military position was far stronger than had been supposed. *The New York Times*, November 17, 22, and December 5, 1963.

American) strategic air and missile power—would strike at the industrial heartland of any aggressor, while strategic and tactical nuclear weapons would be used against heavy concentrations of enemy ground forces. Known as the concept of "massive retaliation," this strategy was intended both to "deter" communist aggression and ultimately to defeat the enemy if it occurred.[51]

Now this strategy rested upon two basic assumptions. One was that, in its application, the enemy would suffer more than the free world. The other was that, if a threat should develop against the NATO area, NATO's retaliatory power would in fact *be used* against the enemy, that it was militarily credible. The Soviet acquisition of the atomic bomb in 1949, and of the hydrogen bomb in 1953, coupled with impressive Soviet progress in perfecting missile delivery systems, tended to cast substantial doubt upon the validity of both assumptions. For in an era of "nuclear stalemate" and "balance of terror," it had become clear that massive retaliation against the Soviet heartland would be followed, if not preceded, by the nuclear devastation of the United States and other Western nations by Soviet nuclear-armed missile and bomber attacks. No longer could the West threaten the Communist bloc with nuclear devastation without risking a similar fate for itself. If both sides abjured the use of nuclear weapons, this left the basic Communist superiority in conventional forces unaltered and placed the West at a severe military disadvantage.

These facts have been well-known among political leaders and informed observers within the NATO area, who have become increasingly skeptical about the credibility of NATO's nuclear deterrent. Not only was there the question of whether NATO's nuclear arsenal would in fact *be* used; there was the no less vital question of whether Communist military planners *believed* it would be used and whether in fact many of the NATO allies themselves shared this belief. If the Kremlin doubted the credibility of the West's nuclear deterrent, it might be led to miscalculate the Western response to a hostile move against the free world. If the European allies doubted its credibility, they might be led to support, and perhaps even themselves plan, the kind of independent nuclear force that General de Gaulle believed vitally necessary to protect French, and more broadly European, security.

Persistent doubts about the credibility of

NATO's deterrent power have also arisen from another source. This is a dilemma that has plagued Western defense strategy since NATO's creation. Given the disparity in ground forces between East and West, could Europe in reality be "defended" from a communist onslaught, or would it merely be "liberated" by American nuclear power—and in the process be subjected to the incineration of European society, along with the Communist aggressors? This problem became especially acute when the possibility of a "limited" communist incursion into Western Europe was contemplated. On the basis of experience in Korea, South Vietnam, and Laos, Europeans were not reassured that nuclear retaliatory power afforded a meaningful defense, when great reluctance to use it prevailed among American officials.*

Closely related to this concern has been the conflict between the earlier "trip wire" conception of NATO's limited ground forces and the "forward strategy" advocated increasingly by a progressively stronger Germany, which desires to see NATO's defense perimeter extended as far eastward as possible, to protect all of free Germany from a communist threat. In turn, implementation of this idea involves de-emphasis upon nuclear retaliation and a buildup of Western conventional forces capable of offering effective resistance to the Red Army or Communist satellite forces.[52]

Further complicating the issue of NATO's military strategy is the durability of the American troop commitment to the European continent. Repeatedly, high-ranking American officials, from the President down, have reassured the Western allies that the United

States had no intention of withdrawing its forces from the Continent and thereby further weakening NATO's strength and raising the specter of a choice for the West between nuclear annihilation or surrender in the face of overwhelming Communist ground power. Thus, on June 25, 1963, President Kennedy reiterated in Frankfurt, Germany, that America's military commitments to its cold war allies "are assured, in the future as in the past, by one great fundamental fact—that they are deeply rooted in America's own self-interest. Our commitment to Europe is indispensable— in our interest as well as yours." President Kennedy pledged that "The United States will risk its cities to defend yours, because we need your freedom to protect ours." In Bonn, Kennedy repeated that 400,000 American troops were in Europe, because their presence "meets a very vital need of the United States. The security of Western Europe, the freedom of Western Europe is essential to the security of the United States."[53]

In spite of such assurances, doubts have multiplied on the European scene, especially in France, about the durability of America's military commitment to NATO. Thus, one European commentator has cited a remark of former Secretary of State Christian A. Herter, who is reported to have said: "I can't conceive of the President involving us in an all-out nuclear war unless the facts showed clearly that we are in danger of devastation ourselves. . . ."[54] Prominent Americans like former Presidents Eisenhower and Herbert Hoover have called for a reduction in American troop commitments to Europe—a plea supported in the early 1960s by leading Democrats like Senator J. William Fulbright, chairman of the Foreign Relations Committee. Vocal groups within Congress have also called for a scaling down of American armed forces in Europe and other overseas sites, as a measure to correct the balance of payments deficit or, in other cases, to protest against alleged Common Market "discrimination" against American goods. Official reassurances notwithstanding, supporters of French President de Gaulle's policies continue to exhibit extreme skepticism about the American commitment in Europe. President de Gaulle and his principal advisers have expressed open doubt that Kennedy's pledges would be binding upon future administrations; that, in a military crisis, the United States would react to an attack upon Paris or Amsterdam as it would react to an attack upon

---

* One commentator has described the "big question mark in the mind of many Europeans" on this point by saying: "Knowing as they do that they are threatened by hundreds of medium-range Soviet missiles stationed a few hundred miles from the Iron Curtain, they wonder how the counterforce blows delivered by rockets several thousand miles away would come in time. They are also inclined to believe that the longer the range of a rocket the higher the explosive yield that is required to offset greater inaccuracies in aim." Many Americans might believe that successful thwarting of Soviet missile bases in Cuba "proved" the validity of defending Europe by relying ultimately upon massive retaliation. Yet, this observer feels that it might in fact "work exactly in the opposite direction from that in the Russian attempt to establish bases in Cuba"— by making Europe *more*, not less, vulnerable to nuclear devastation by one side or the other, or both. Francois de Rose, "Atlantic Relationships and Nuclear Problems," *Foreign Affairs*, 41 (April, 1963), 484.

Detroit or Boston; and that the United States has altogether abandoned its practice (exemplified by events in World Wars I and II) of delaying entrance into a European conflict until its own vital interests were clearly at stake.[55]

Finally, strong misgivings among the European allies grew out of a prevalent conviction that reliance upon the American nuclear arsenal offered little protection against the most imminent and real threat facing Europe: the progressively ominous prospect of communist *political* gains in the Mediterranean region, particularly in Greece and Italy. Here, Communist parties and their sympathizers had

Well, That's a Switch. (Source: Mauldin in *The St. Louis Post-Dispatch*, November 16, 1959.)

strengthened their positions as political movements. If not in France or the Low Countries, in the region bordering the Mediterranean, communism was thriving by the mid-1960s. America's armed nuclear might seemed irrelevant to the problem of inhibiting its growth and of removing the danger.[56]

2. *The Anglo-Saxons Versus de Gaulle.* A second problem causing disagreements among the Western allies during the 1960s was the controversy that had developed between the United States and Britain, on the one hand, and France, on the other, concerning decision-making within NATO councils. This problem, like all the others, had ramifications for other issues, such as the credibility of NATO's

nuclear deterrent and the problem of "sharing" nuclear technology among the allies. Yet it had peculiar pertinency for the issue of relative Anglo-Saxon versus French influence in the management of NATO affairs. Very shortly after he was invested as President of the Fifth French Republic in 1958, General de Gaulle proposed to London and Washington that henceforth NATO policies be formulated by an Anglo-American-French "directorate." The demand was rejected by the United States and Britain and was heavily criticized by other NATO members, notably West Germany. Rebuffed in this effort to assert France's growing power, de Gaulle countered by underscoring the "fragility" of the NATO agreement (which became more fragile when he subsequently withdrew French naval units from its control) and, in ensuing weeks, by rejecting American proposals to construct missile launching sites on French soil. Subsequently, de Gaulle also demanded that the United States and Britain recognize France's special "responsibilities" in Africa and the Middle East, by supporting French military intervention in Algeria and in Tunisia in 1961. Yet de Gaulle steadfastly refused to allow the NATO partners to influence France's policies in these areas.[57]

These episodes were but tangible indications of a growing divergence among the Western allies. Ever since World War II, de Gaulle had been convinced that Britain and the United States had forged a "partnership" and a "special relationship" from which France was excluded. The fact that Britain (which had participated with the United States in developing the atomic bomb during World War II) was permitted to "share" many American nuclear secrets re-enforced de Gaulle's conviction. Down to inauguration of the Fifth French Republic in 1958, de Gaulle believed that the Anglo-Saxons largely controlled NATO policy-making, often to the detriment of French interests, as American opposition to French policies in Indochina, the Suez Crisis of 1956, the Algerian conflict, and in other contexts seemed to make amply clear.[58]

For all of his emphasis upon asserting French "independence" and restoring *le grandeur* to France's international role, de Gaulle nevertheless did not believe that the United States could be alienated from France or Western Europe permanently. Repeatedly, officials of the Fifth Republic reiterated their over-all support of NATO and emphasized its indispensability. If America was vital for NATO, NATO was no less vital for America —and for France.[59] Yet, de Gaulle's basic contention was that policy-makers in London and Paris must finally accept, and accommodate themselves to, a reality that had become apparent by the 1960s. This was that France always had been, and was determined to remain, the center of NATO. This being the case, the French voice in NATO policy-making must be enhanced to reflect this basic truth.

Gaullism thus presented the United States and Britain with a choice which, by the mid-1960s, involved painful alternatives. Either the Anglo-Saxons could agree to greater French influence within NATO—to the point of acceding to de Gaulle's wishes on many issues —or else they would be compelled to accept growing French diplomatic independence. The latter course was illustrated late in 1963 by de Gaulle's initiative, in the face of strong American misgivings, in calling for the "neutralization" of South Vietnam and an offer of French assistance in achieving this goal. A few weeks later, the *Quai d'Orsay* extended its proposal to include the whole of Southeast Asia! Early in 1964, Paris also announced its intention to recognize Red China, and to expand its trade with the Communist bloc—both moves clashing head-on with long-standing American policies. Typically, these French decisions were made without any notable effort to concert policies with Washington or to map a common NATO approach.[60]

3. *Nuclear "Sharing" and the Force de Frappe*. Intimately related to the two central problems we have already identified as fostering dissension within NATO is a third major issue: the problem of "sharing" nuclear technology throughout the Western community and the intimately related question of the French nuclear *force de frappe*. Since World War II, as we have noted, French officials have been keenly sensitive to the special relationship existing between the United States and Britain, whereby the latter, alone among the NATO allies, has had access to American nuclear secrets. Toward the other allies, and other countries in the free world generally, the United States has followed a policy since 1945 of prohibiting the disseminating of information about nuclear processes, especially those that had military applications. America's policy of atomic secrecy has been designed to prevent the proliferation of nuclear

weapons, since such proliferation would both vastly compound the problem of negotiating a global disarmament agreement and increase the risk of nuclear conflagrations. Down to the mid-1960s, officials of the Johnson Administration remained convinced that Western security was best served by continuing this policy. Yet European opinion broadly tended to resent this policy, in part because, as one European commentator has expressed it, the first results obtained by the United States in nuclear technology "came mostly from European laboratories."[61]

Heavy Schedule. (Source: Peb in *The Philadelphia Inquirer*, reproduced in *The New York Times*, March 8, 1964.)

The Gaullist view rested upon the conviction that no fully independent and industrialized nation could be expected to forego development of its own nuclear striking force. Militarily, lack of such a force would detract from its security and make it dependent upon other countries. Diplomatically, it would perpetuate a status of political inferiority that collided with *le dignité* of the French society and prevented France from resuming its rightful place in world affairs. Besides, French military planners believed that development of national (as distinct from NATO, or in reality, American) nuclear forces *reduced* the risk of general war. Over against the American view that the French *force de frappe* proliferated nuclear weapons and magnified the risk of war, de Gaulle's government took the position that in fact it would *enhance* the striking power of the NATO system and increase the "deterrent" power of the alliance.* Accordingly, France forged resolutely ahead with its own nuclear weapons program, in the face of vocal American opposition; and it refused to join in the East-West nuclear test-ban accord negotiated in 1963. By 1964, the French government announced its intention of creating a 200-plane nuclear force under its own military control.[62]

America's countermove to this French policy was to propose the creation of a "multinational" NATO nuclear force, that in effect represented a compromise between its earlier refusal to share nuclear technology, and France's insistence upon national nuclear forces. Under this plan, the United States, supported by Britain, proposed the creation of a NATO "mixed force," consisting of nuclear-armed Polaris submarines, manned by crews drawn from all the NATO partners. Control over the nuclear missiles, however, would remain in American hands. This scheme, American officials believed, also had the virtue of according West Germany full nuclear parity with the other NATO allies, without putting atomic and hydrogen weapons in German hands.[63] Actually, the idea of a multinational nuclear force for NATO evolved out of a less sophisticated scheme which the United States and Britain had accepted earlier, known as the "two keys" concept, under which a British and American officer each held a key required to fire nuclear weapons stationed on British soil. A high-ranking French official has described this system as "nothing but a polite fiction designed to soothe the increasingly tender susceptibilities of the Europeans" about

the American monopoly of nuclear weapons.[64] Understandably, therefore, the multinational force idea did not pacify France or in any way deter de Gaulle's government from moving ahead with the creation of its nuclear *force de frappe*.[65] Indeed, de Gaulle countered the American plan with his own suggestion that when the French *force de frappe* became operational, it should become the nucleus for a truly "European" nuclear deterrent, available to any European supranational political authority that might eventually be established.[66]

In concluding our discussion of the intricate and interrelated issues that generated discord within the Western alliance, we may underscore two ideas briefly. The first is that, despite its growing concern with related political, economic, and cultural activities, NATO was, and remains, essentially a *military alliance*. As such, it may be expected to exhibit the characteristics of other military alliances throughout history, a dominant one being periodic ups and downs in the degree of cohesiveness among its members. Internal controversies are likely to appear in direct ratio to the perceived military threat confronting the alliance at any given time. Second, NATO has been, and inescapably will be, influenced decisively by events and developments outside its own borders. Thus, what has evolved as a kind of permanent "crisis of NATO" is directly related to a wider global phenomenon—affecting the Western, Communist, and nonaligned world alike. This is the tendency toward "polycentricity," or the breaking up of the bipolar world into several centers of global power and influence, often exercised by coalitions of nations. A leading characteristic of this movement is insistence upon national "identity" and "self-assertion" by peoples throughout the Afro-Asian-Arab world, leading governments in this area to embrace a foreign policy of diplomatic nonalignment. Psychologically, this diplomatic stance parallels de Gaulle's determination to "be ourselves" in diplomatic affairs. A British spokesman may well be correct when he describes de Gaulle's *force de frappe* as "a political stage in his conception of the rearmament of the soul of France and of her world influence."[67] And de Gaulle himself has asserted categorically that "as much as ever, we lay store on independence . . . We think we are the best judges of what we ought to do" in world affairs. Consequently, Frenchmen are determined "to play our own role" and "to allow

---

* It should not be imagined that such thinking was limited to French viewpoints. Other influential groups on the European continent and in Britain shared the underlying rationale supporting the idea of a national nuclear force. Thus, the British Conservative party, one observer has stated, likewise believed that Britain must develop its own national deterrent "to allow Britain to resist Soviet threats on issues where American support might be in doubt." Such a force would also give "Britain influence within the alliance and a special position in the world at large on nuclear matters." Laurence W. Martin, " 'Honest Brokers' in the Nuclear Muddle," *The Reporter*, 30 (January 2, 1964), 21.

nobody the right to act and to speak for us" on the world scene.[68] In the impulses motivating its external relations, de Gaulle's regime was thus *en rapport* with an expanding group of countries embracing nonalignment as a diplomatic credo. Realization of this fact in turn required new American policies and outlooks that took full account of the psychological, emotional, and ideological foundations upon which de Gaulle's foreign policy was based.*

POLITICAL UNIFICATION IN THE NORTH ATLANTIC AREA

Speaking of movements on the European scene leading to economic cooperation among nations in the North Atlantic area, Mr. Walter Hallstein, president of the Commission of the Common Market, has cautioned against the tendency to differentiate too sharply between "economic" and "political" integration. Supranational economic cooperation ultimately implies "a political phenomenon," he has observed; and "politics is the continuing theme of all these efforts" witnessed in postwar Europe to transcend national rivalries and vested interests.[69] And we may add that the same admonitions apply to military-defense cooperation among Western countries. Ultimately, these efforts also demand a high degree of political collaboration among members of the NATO alliance. This realization has been amply understood by advocates of European union since World War II. In 1948, a committee of the Hague Congress on European unity observed that:

> Judged from any standpoint—political, economic or cultural—it is only by uniting herself that Europe can overcome her immediate difficulties and go forward to fulfill her mission for the future. . . . It is impossible to keep problems of economic collaboration and defense separate from those of general political policy.

Successful implementation of joint economic or military policies, the committee was convinced, required sooner or later "the renunciation or, to be more accurate, the joint exercise of certain sovereign powers."[70]

The dream of a politically unified Europe is

* The writer has discussed this point at greater length in "The Gaullist Revolt Against the Anglo-Saxons," *The Annals of the American Academy of Political and Social Science*, **351** (January, 1964), 15–24. See also Henry A. Kissinger, "Strains on the Alliance," *Foreign Affairs*, **41** (January, 1963), 261–286.

as old as history. The list of illustrious personages advocating this ideal—Dante, Pope Leo X, Erasmus, Grotius, Thomas More, Sully, Fichte, Kant, Mazzini, Churchill, to list but a few—testifies to the importance and durability of the idea.** Yet down to World War II, the idea of European political unification was a dream espoused chiefly by intellectuals. The same historical forces that engendered extensive economic and military collaboration among nations in the North Atlantic community—Soviet hegemony over the heartland of Eurasia; the decline of England, France, and Germany as great powers; Europe's early postwar economic debilitation and military vulnerability; the continuing challenge posed by expansive communism—convinced Western policy-makers that political unification must at least be postulated as an ultimate goal, if indeed in some spheres it was not an urgent necessity.

Such convictions have spawned a profusion of often highly varied plans, institutions, and approaches whose professed goal is political unification. More often than not, several movements and organizations simultaneously embraced this goal; frequently, there was little coordination among their efforts. The results were that, paradoxically, proponents of European "unity" were in danger of jointly creating highly disunified and competing efforts, that in some ways vastly complicated the task of finding common ground among advocates of the same goal. In the space available, we may focus only upon the more important tendencies and developments in the recent period.

The Council of Europe

In March, 1948, the French National Assembly called for the creation of a European constituent assembly to lay the basis for a European federation. Accordingly, on May 5,

** More extended treatment of the historical antecedents of European unity may be found in C. Grove Haines, ed., *European Integration* (Baltimore: Johns Hopkins University Press, 1957), pp. 11–37, 80–97; Florinsky, *op. cit.*, pp. 1–27; Mayne, *op. cit.*, pp. 29–52.

The terms European political integration or unification are often used in a variety of senses. In practice, three concrete proposals, singly or in combination, are encompassed within the terms: a European *federation*, with a central government whose power is limited to certain specified spheres; an *organic union* of states, with a central government possessing broad powers; and *functional unity* among two or more countries, as in the European Coal and Steel Community. Florinsky, *op. cit.*, p. 19.

1949, the Council of Europe came into existence, as a result of agreement among ten nations. Eventually, the Council of Europe included all the members of NATO, plus Ireland, Austria, and Sweden. With its headquarters at Strasbourg, the council has served as a valuable forum for discussion of regional problems and the manifold issues that hampered the achievement of genuine political unity. It has also focused public opinion upon the ideal and generated public support for its ultimate attainment. Yet the council has done little more than this and cannot be regarded as among the more promising avenues for eventual political unification on the European continent.[71]

The Rise and Fall of EDC

The urgency of the communist threat, and the implementation of the American "containment" policy to counter it in the late 1940s, induced American policy-makers to modify early postwar policy toward defeated Germany. NATO, American defense planners became convinced, could never defend Europe from communist aggression without substantial contributions from West Germany; and this contribution could only be made if the Allied occupation of Germany were terminated. Yet, American officials were keenly aware of the existence of deep-seated apprehensions among the European allies to this step. The minimum necessity was a new agreement on Germany rendering it impossible for a revived, rearmed Germany to embark upon the path of *revanche*. The lessons of history and geographical proximity understandably made France more apprehensive about the dangers involved than was generally true of other European societies. Many Frenchmen, in fact, feared a rearmed Germany infinitely more than an expansive Communist bloc.[72]

Efforts to reconcile American insistence upon German rearmament with European misgivings about the move led to the signing on May 27, 1952, of an agreement to establish a European Defense Community (EDC). Although its immediate goal was to terminate the Allied occupation of Germany and to provide for German participation in NATO, EDC was widely regarded as the forerunner of an emergent European political union.

Except in one sense, EDC is now of historic interest only. As, one by one, its signatories ratified the agreement, with the strong encouragement of the United States, its fate finally rested with the French National Assembly. Ironically, it had been to mollify French misgivings that EDC had sought to restrict West Germany's future military power and to assure that it could never again threaten the peace of Europe or the world. Yet after a long and acrimonious debate—in the course of which Secretary of State Dulles was led to threaten Europe with an "agonizing reappraisal" of American relations with Europe if EDC failed—on August 30, 1954, the French Assembly rejected the agreement.* This act brought American-European relations to perhaps their lowest point in the postwar era.[73] The defeat of EDC, it had become apparent by the 1960s, did however highlight certain fundamental divergencies among the Western allies concerning the scope and nature of any agreement contemplating ultimate surrender of national sovereignty to a supranational political institution. As we shall see, many of the issues that explained the demise of EDC reappeared several years later when the United States and its European partners debated other approaches designed to impart greater political unity to the North Atlantic community.

The Western European Union

French rejection of EDC, said Secretary of State Dulles in language seldom used among allies, was a "saddening event" and a "tragedy," in which "nationalism, abetted by communism," endangered the future of Europe. Referring to a "great wave of disillusionment which has swept over the United States," in unmistakable language Dulles observed that American aid to Europe in the future would be conditioned upon steps taken to find an acceptable substitute for EDC.[74] Meanwhile, the United States remained irrevocably committed to German rearmament and German participation in NATO. On October 23, 1954, the Western occupation of Germany was terminated. Concurrently, the signatories of the Brussels Treaty of 1948 (France, Belgium, Luxembourg, the Netherlands, and the United

* A variety of influences apparently motivated the French Assembly to reject the agreement that France itself had insisted upon before consenting to German rearmament. These ranged from lessened fear of the Soviet threat after the death of Stalin, to French unwillingness to surrender its military forces (heavily committed in North Africa) to a unified European command, to persistent fears about Germany's future role. For detailed treatment, see Coral Bell, ed., *Survey of International Affairs, 1954* (New York: Oxford University Press, 1957), pp. 129–130.

Kingdom), invited Italy and Germany to join this European defense agreement, to which were appended protocols specifying limitations upon German rearmament. These prohibited Bonn from manufacturing chemical, biological, or nuclear weapons, long-range bombers and missiles, or large naval vessels. A separate body —the Agency for the Control of Armaments— was set up to supervise compliance with this new treaty.[75] This agreement, creating the Western European Union, was made possible by an offer that might have allayed earlier French misgivings about EDC: a British commitment to station its military forces *permanently* on the European continent, marking a radical departure from Britain's historic policy of "splendid isolation."

While WEU evolved as an alternative for EDC, it was far from a replica of the latter. In Mayne's words, it was "institutionally a pale shadow of EDC, with a much less powerful Assembly and no serious pooling of sovereignty." Ironically, as Mayne points out, those groups in France and elsewhere in Europe who opposed EDC now found themselves confronted with a revival of German military power but without most of the sweeping safeguards that the EDC proposal had contained.[76] Rather than a nascent supranational political institution, WEU might more properly be regarded as an auxiliary body of NATO. Within a few months after its appearance, the spotlight on the stage of European political movements shifted to the much more promising European Economic Community.

The Political Future of EEC

From the beginning, the European Economic Community anticipated the ultimate political merger of its members, at least respecting those matters affecting the economic well-being of the Common Market area. As one commentator has observed: "What lifts the Community far above the importance of a common economic effort—great as that is—is the basic political aim of many influential statesmen of the constituent nations." EEC thus must be viewed as "the first stage in the building of a genuine United States of Europe."[77] An impressive step in this direction was creation of the European Assembly, to supervise EEC's three "communities" (the Common Market, the Coal and Steel Community, and Euratom); its 142 members sat as representatives of broad political viewpoints prevailing in Europe, rather than as representa-

tives of individual countries. Moreover, the Treaty of Rome (in essence, EEC's constitution) calls for the elimination of the right of veto in the Council of Ministers after January 1, 1966—thereby permitting the council to function on the basis of majority vote among its members.[78]

As originally constituted, EEC possessed wide powers to make economic policies binding upon its members. It was expected that, as time passed, the foreign ministers of "the six" would be able to lay the foundations for genuine political union throughout the months and years that followed. Negotiations toward this goal proceeded during the early 1960s, with minimum success. In 1962, for example, a French official said, after a recent EEC foreign ministers' conference, that "it has been impossible to agree on the principle of a European political union."[79] Time did not apparently remove existing roadblocks in the path of success. Thus, early in 1964, Chancellor Ludwig Erhard of West Germany urged his associates in EEC to cure the "political malaise" that had apparently engulfed negotiations on political unity among "the six." Bonn announced its intention of undertaking a new round of negotiations to break the prevailing deadlock.[80] Other officials among the members of the EEC were reported in the same period as "closing ranks" to demand progress in converting the organization into a supranational political organ, capable of imposing its collective will upon individual members.[81]

What was holding up the political evolution of EEC? We have identified a number of the factors in our earlier discussion. While it would be too simple to explain the phenomenon purely in terms of Gaullist viewpoints versus the rest of EEC, or more broadly, in terms of France versus other members in the Atlantic community, this was the over-all explanation. The difficulties plaguing EEC's efforts to find common ground in political unification consisted of at least four specific elements: (1) basic differences in principle, both among EEC members and nations outside EEC, about the form such merger should take; (2) France's militant opposition to any scheme involving a significant diminution of French sovereignty; (3) the lingering question of possible British membership in EEC, with all the political complications this issue posed; and (4) the still remote, but not insignificant, question of future political relationships among all the members of the Atlantic community, in which the viewpoints and policies of the United States were dominant considerations.

If these issues constituted the underlying sources of controversy, the most dramatic obstacle to greater progress was Gaullist insistence upon France's own version of European "political unity." A basic ambivalence has characterized French viewpoints on the issue since World War II. In 1949, for example, French Foreign Minister Robert Schuman submitted the historic "Schuman Plan," out of which the EEC ultimately evolved. The ill-fated EDC was also formulated largely at the instigation of the French government. Early in 1964, French officials once more endorsed the principle of European political unity, urging countries like Italy, the Netherlands, and Belgium to support the idea. A few months later, General de Gaulle himself stated that he did not see how EEC "could live and, . . . develop without political cooperation."[82]

Yet, informed students of French political developments have doubted that de Gaulle and many of his supporters have ever been enthusiastic about the principle of a supranational political organization in Europe, at least one that is acceptable to advocates of genuine political merger among sovereign governments. High French sources have called concepts like European federation "words, just words"; other French officials have stated their belief that no genuine political unity can exist in Europe for at least a decade.[83] In any case, less doubt exists about de Gaulle's conception of the kind of European political unification France supports: it is a *union des patries* ("union of fatherlands"), in which each government largely retains its own "identity" and freedom of action.[84] As one observer has summarized the key idea in this conception, de Gaulle believes in

the nation as the fundamental unit in world affairs. Nations, he believes, can combine for specific objectives, but the difference in size and weight between say, West Germany and Belgium, is too great to allow for confederation.[85]

General de Gaulle himself has deplored the tendency among his European colleagues to engage in meaningless public oratory about "European union." He has stated candidly that "no European people would want to deliver its destiny to a tribunal composed mostly of foreigners. This is true of France." He remains convinced that

to plan to incorporate the policy of Europe in a multilateral Atlantic policy would be acting so that it itself would have none, but then why would it wish to confederate?[86]

On two points particularly, the Gaullist conception remains adamant: British membership in EEC would destroy the political cohesiveness of "the six"; and broader schemes contemplating "North Atlantic union" would inevitably ordain American domination of such a bloc. De Gaulle has thus categorically rejected any plan which, deliberately or indirectly, would, in his words, "deliver Europe under the thumb of America." At the same time, French officials doubt that the United States is ready to accept wholeheartedly the kind of European union they favor—one which, whatever its particular institutional pattern, would increasingly function as a diplomatically independent force on the European and, more broadly, global scene.[87] In the light of these considerations, France's influence—and on questions like the British application to join EEC, it has proved decisive—has been cast in favor of confining European "unity" to the economic realm. Paris has simultaneously moved ahead with steps like development of the nuclear *force de frappe*, the forging of close links with West Germany, and independent French diplomatic initiative on the global scene—the result of which is to leave the French-dominated (or perhaps Franco-German dominated) EEC largely unaltered.

The United States and "Atlantic Partnership"

Early in 1964, Secretary of State Dean Rusk observed that: "Until Western Europe attains a substantial degree of political unity, it is unlikely to make a contribution to world leadership commensurate with its resources." Rusk went on to add that, thus far, policy coordination is much further advanced in the spheres of economics and defense than in that of political action; he urged "all of the Atlantic nations—including the United States" to "improve their performance in seeking common lines of policy and action." Otherwise, the Western partners would "frustrate one another's efforts all over the world."[88]

These remarks reflected growing official American preoccupation with a theme that had come to the fore in relations with Europe in the 1960s: the concept of "Atlantic partnership," encompassing the United States (possibly Canada), Britain, and all the nations of Western Europe. As one high State Department official stated in 1962: "We have regarded a united Europe as a condition to the development of an effective Atlantic partnership." Economic unification among European nations was viewed as a step fostering "substantial internal cohesion in order to complete the foundation upon which the structure of an Atlantic partnership can be erected." In mid-1962, President Kennedy observed that the United States visualized a united Europe as "a partner with whom we could deal on a basis of full equality in all the great and burdensome tasks of building and defending a community of free nations." He added: "The first order of business is for our European friends to go forward in forming the more perfect union which will some day make this partnership possible." Some day, Kennedy pledged, the United States would be ready for a "Declaration of Interdependence," that would afford the basis for discussion of "ways and means of forming a concrete Atlantic partnership . . . between the new union now emerging in Europe and the old American Union. . . . let the world know it is our goal."[89]

Throughout the months that followed, American officials did not amplify these general ideas into specific proposals spelling out the form and nature of the kind of "partnership" they envisaged for the Atlantic community. This fact, coupled with several others, prevented the idea of Atlantic partnership from capturing the imagination of citizens, either in the United States or in Europe. The concept, one observer commented, "has never been accepted enthusiastically or even understood by peoples or governments of Europe."[90] Before progress could be made in implementing the idea, several bedrock problems had to be overcome. To the minds of many European observers, American statements suggested neither that Washington had satisfactory answers to the problems, nor even that it always understood the issues fully.

Did Atlantic partnership, for example, envision an *organic* political unity, with common political institutions having power to bind the governments represented? Or did it contemplate a much looser *federation* (or confederation), in which substantial power, except perhaps in economic and defense matters, would be reserved to the member states? Even more fundamentally, since this was perhaps the basic issue that concerned countries like Britain, France, and West Germany, where would be the real epicenter of power in such a proposed "partnership"? Even the British were apparently concerned that America's conception of "partnership" in practice would mean that some nations are, and would likely remain, "more equal than others" in the process of decision-making.[91] As for France, de Gaulle's reservations about the political amalgamation of countries outside "the six" have already been cited. On several occasions, Paris had made clear its desire to escape American "domination" in policy formulation. Moreover, as a perceptive student of *Realpolitik*, de Gaulle is under no misapprehension that in any political union embracing the United States, the French position of dominance in EEC would likely be jeopardized. An Anglo-American axis, perhaps augmented by the power of West Germany, would largely control policy formulation. Such a course would almost certainly risk loss of France's cherished "identity" and undermine its increasingly independent international role.

No less basic to the future of Atlantic partnership is the question of America's willingness to accept the implications inherent in its own concept. To Europeans (not alone in France), the idea of partnership coincides with the achievement of certain American foreign policy objectives, such as more widespread cost-sharing among the Western allies in providing foreign aid, or imparting greater unity among NATO members in policy toward Red China and Southeast Asia, or in generally inhibiting the emergence of a diplomatic "third force" in Europe. To this extent, Atlantic partnership promotes American interests. Yet the larger question remains, whether the United States itself is willing to be governed by the principles inherent in true partnership—when these demand more frequent acceptance of European viewpoints on a variety of international issues. Is the United States willing to submit questions of public policy, like domestic agricultural price supports, to determination by an Atlantic parliament in which the United States might have only one vote? When the State Department calls for greater "policy coordination" among members of the Atlantic community, does this mean greater willingness than in the past to modify some of its own policies in the light of allied viewpoints?

These were central issues that had to be transcended before the concept of Atlantic partnership would likely emerge as anything more than an ideal or, in some cases, than a diplomatic gambit employed to counter tendencies on the European scene with which the United States disagreed.

NOTES

1. Quoted in Julius W. Pratt, *A History of United States Foreign Policy* (Englewood Cliffs, N.J.: Prentice-Hall, 1955), p. 168.
2. *Ibid.*, p. 169.
3. *Ibid.*, pp. 169–173.
4. *Ibid.*, pp. 527–528.
5. D. F. Fleming, *The United States and the World Court* (Garden City, N.Y.: Doubleday, 1945).
6. George F. Kennan, "The Sources of Soviet Conduct," *Foreign Affairs*, 25 (July, 1947), 556–583. In this article, Kennan sets forth the basic strategy of "containment" the United States has followed toward the Communist world in the postwar era.
7. For a dissenting view, see Walter Lippmann, *The Cold War* (New York: Harper & Row, 1957).
8. *Congressional Record*, 93, 1980–1981.
9. William A. Brown and Redvers Opie, *American Foreign Assistance* (Washington, D.C.: Brookings Institution, 1953), p. 175. Evaluates American aid programs to Europe in the late 1940s and early 1950s.
10. *United States in World Affairs: 1951* (New York: Harper & Row, 1952), p. 219.
11. *Ibid.*, p. 353.
12. House Foreign Affairs Committee, *The Mutual Security Act of 1957*, Hearings, 88th Congress, 1st Session (Washington, D.C.: 1963), p. 24.
13. Senate Foreign Relations Committee, *Foreign Assistance Act of 1963*. Hearings, 88th Congress, 1st Session (Washington, D.C.: 1963), p. 24.
14. Text of the President's budget message in *The New York Times*, January 22, 1964.
15. *The New York Times*, August 25, 1963.
16. Agency for International Development, *The Story of A.I.D.* (Washington, D. C.: no date and unfolioed).
17. Agency for International Development, *Report to the Congress on the Foreign Aid Program for Fiscal Year 1962* (Washington, D.C.: 1963), p. 41.
18. Agency for International Development, *The Story of A.I.D.*, *op. cit.*
19. *The New York Times*, April 3, 1963.
20. Department of State, *American Foreign Policy, 1950–55* (Publication No. 6446, "General Foreign Policy Series," 117), I (Washington, D.C.: 1957), 1442. An invaluable collection of documentary materials on American foreign relations.
21. *Idem.*
22. Senate Foreign Relations Committee, *Legislation on Foreign Relations*, 85th Congress, 1st Session (Washington, D.C.: 1957), p. 5.

23. *United States in World Affairs: 1951, op. cit.*, p. 215.
24. *United States in World Affairs: 1955* (New York: Harper & Row, 1956), p. 79.
25. Lord Frank, "Cooperation Is Not Enough," *Foreign Affairs*, 41 (October, 1962), 27.
26. Max Beloff, *The United States and the Unity of Europe* (New York: Random House, 1963), p. 135. This Brookings Institution study affords valuable insight into American foreign policy toward postwar Europe.
27. Kurt Birrenback, *The Future of the Atlantic Community* (New York: Praeger, 1963), p. 31. A perceptive analysis of issues confronting the Western allies.
28. Walter Hallstein, *United Europe* (Cambridge, Mass.: Harvard University Press, 1963), p. 12. A high official of EEC presents his appraisal of the challenge of European unity.
29. *Ibid.*, p. 13.
30. Quoted in *ibid.*, p. 17.
31. *The New York Times*, January 10 and 26, 1964.
32. *The New York Times*, January 10, 1964.
33. EEC's "timetable" for the transition from one stage to the next is included in Emile Benoit, *Europe at Sixes and Sevens: The Common Market, the Free Trade Association and the United States* (New York: Columbia University Press, 1961), pp. 277–283.
34. *The New York Times*, March 11, 1962, dispatch by Edwin L. Dale, Jr.
35. George Lichtheim, *The New Europe— Today and Tomorrow* (New York: Praeger, 1963), p. 59. A comprehensive analysis of European unification movements and interallied relations.
36. *Idem.*
37. *The New York Times*, January 10, 1964.
38. Beloff, *op. cit.*, p. 131.
39. *The New York Times*, March 20, 1960.
40. Paul-Henri Spaak, "Hold Fast," *Foreign Affairs*, 41 (July, 1963), 611–620.
41. *The New York Times*, January 24, 1964.
42. The problems surrounding British membership in EEC are discussed at length in: Richard Mayne, *The Community of Europe: Past, Present, and Future* (New York: Norton, 1962), pp. 132–154; Warren J. Nystrom and Peter Malof, *The Common Market* (Princeton, N.J.: Van Nostrand, 1962), pp. 109–110, 114–115; Hallstein, *op. cit.*, pp. 80–82, 84; Beloff, *op. cit.*, pp. 139–143, 145–154; Benoit, *op. cit.*, pp. 72–77, 103–107.
43. Department of State, *op. cit.*, pp. 819–820.
44. For the Senate's view on the issue, see Arthur H. Vandenberg, Jr., ed., *The Private Papers of Senator Vandenberg*

(Boston: Houghton Mifflin, 1952), pp. 399–421.

45. Department of State, *op. cit.*, pp. 822.

46. *Ibid.*, pp. 822, 835.

47. *Nashville Tennessean*, November 21, 1957.

48. Hugh Sidey, *John F. Kennedy: President* (New York: Atheneum, 1963), p. 184.

49. See the excerpt from the analysis by Alistair Buchan, director of the British Institute for Strategic Studies, in Senate Foreign Relations Committee, *Problems and Trends in Atlantic Partnership*, 87th Congress, 2nd Session, **I** (Washington, D.C.: 1962), p. 42.

50. House Foreign Affairs Committee, *op. cit.*, Part V, pp. 860–861.

51. *Ibid.*, pp. 539–550.

52. *The New York Times*, June 8, 1963.

53. Text of Kennedy's addresses in *The New York Times*, June 25 and 26, 1963.

54. Francois de Rose, "Atlantic Relationships and Nuclear Problems," *Foreign Affairs*, **41** (April, 1963), 481.

55. *The New York Times*, June 28, 1963.

56. Our discussion of NATO defense strategy draws heavily from: Sir John Slessor, "Control of Nuclear Strategy," *Foreign Affairs*, **42** (October, 1963), pp. 96–106; Senate Foreign Relations Committee. *Problems and Trends in Atlantic Partnership*, *op. cit.*, pp. 32–40; Robert Osgood, NATO: *The Entangling Alliance* (Chicago: University of Chicago Press, 1962), pp. 57–172; Alistair Buchan, "Partners and Allies," *Foreign Affairs*, **41** (July, 1963), 621–638; General Paul Stehlin, "The Evolution of Western Defense," *Foreign Affairs*, **42** (October, 1963), 70–84.

57. Roy C. Macridis and Bernard E. Brown, *The de Gaulle Republic: Quest for Unity* (Homewood, Ill.: The Dorsey Press, 1960), p. 326, and E. Drexel Godfrey, Jr., *The Government of France* (New York: Crowell, 1963), p. 126.

58. General de Gaulle's views toward the Anglo-Saxons are discussed in Macridis and Brown, *op. cit.*, p. 326; Philip M. Williams and Martin Harrison, *De Gaulle's Republic* (London: Longmans, Green, 1960), p. 177.

59. *The New York Times*, October 31, 1963.

60. *The New York Times*, January 28 and February 1, 1964.

61. de Rose, *op. cit.*, p. 480.

62. French views on the necessity for the *force de frappe* are discussed in *The New York Times*, May 18 and 27, and December 4, 1963; *Washington Post*, March 14, 1963.

63. *The New York Times*, January 24, 1964.

64. Stehlin, *op. cit.*, p. 74.

65. *The New York Times*, April 17, 1963, and January 29, 1964.

66. *The New York Times*, September 29, 1963.

67. Slessor, *op. cit.*, p. 97.

68. *The New York Times*, September 29, 1963.

69. Hallstein, *op. cit.*, pp. 38, 63.

70. Quoted in F. C. S. Northrop, *European Union and United States Foreign Policy* (New York: Macmillan, 1954), pp. 6–7. A sociological (sometimes almost mystical) appraisal of the subject.

71. Arnold Zurcher, *The Struggle To Unite Europe, 1940–1958* (New York: New York University Press, 1958), p. 46. An illuminating treatment of problems and implications of European unification.

72. Northrop, *op. cit.*, p. 163.

73. The viewpoints of the Eisenhower Administration on EDC are presented in Dwight D. Eisenhower, *Mandate for Change: 1953–1956* (Garden City, N.Y.: Doubleday, 1963), pp. 395–409.

74. Department of State, *op. cit.*, pp. 1471–1473, 1486.

75. *Ibid.*, pp. 978–984.

76. Mayne, *op. cit.*, pp. 105–106.

77. Robert Heilbroner, "Forging a United Europe: The Story of the European Economic Community," *Public Affairs Pamphlets*, No. 308 (New York: Public Affairs Press, 1961), pp. 3–5.

78. Mayne, *op. cit.*, p. 125; Heilbroner, *op. cit.*, p. 5.

79. *New York Herald Tribune*, April 18, 1962.

80. *The New York Times*, January 11, 1964.

81. *The New York Times*, January 31, 1964.

82. *The New York Times*, January 27 and February 1, 1964.

83. Edmond Taylor, "De Gaulle's Design for Europe," *The Reporter*, **26** (June 7, 1962), pp. 15–16; Godfrey, *op. cit.*, p. 123; *The New York Times*, May 27 and June 17, 1963.

84. Christian A. Herter, "Atlantica," *Foreign Affairs*, **41** (January, 1963), 299–310.

85. *The New York Times*, June 17, 1963, dispatch by Drew Middleton.

86. *The New York Times*, February 1, 1964.

87. *The New York Times*, May 27, 1963.

88. Text of Rusk's address in *The New York Times*, February 1, 1964.

89. *Documents on American Foreign Relations: 1962* (New York: Harper & Row, 1963), pp. 215–216, 226.

90. *The New York Times*, June 15, 1963, dispatch by Drew Middleton.

91. Taylor, *op. cit.*, p. 16.

11 → THE MIDDLE EAST AND AFRICA → the diplomacy of emerging societies

Among the far-reaching changes in the international community brought about by World War II, few surpass in importance the emergence of the Middle East as a maelstrom of great-power conflict. And for the future, few problems will have higher priority for American policy-makers than evolving successful policies toward the continent of Africa.

In recent years, the Middle East has exhibited many of the characteristics associated with the Balkans of the pre-World War I era.* Turmoil and ferment, engendering manifold controversies and antagonisms among great and small powers, appear endemic to the region. While the United States at an early stage in its history developed a fairly well-understood body of principles that governed American diplomatic behavior toward Europe and Asia, it

* Contemporary usage varies widely concerning the territory formerly called the Near East and now usually designated the Middle East. Definitions tend to be arbitrary and to be shaped by the criteria employed to explain the cohesiveness of the region. A recent study uses the phrase Middle East to include Turkey, Iran, Egypt, Libya, Saudi Arabia, Iraq, Syria, Lebanon, Jordan, and Israel. See Robert C. Kingsbury and Norman J. G. Pounds, *An Atlas of Middle Eastern Affairs* (New York: Praeger, 1963), p. 2. A noted geographer prefers the term Southwest Asia to include the area from Turkey to the Arabian peninsula and from Egypt through Afghanistan. George B. Cressey, *Crossroads: Land and Life in Southwest Asia* (New York: Lippincott, 1960), pp. 8–9. In our discussion, the focus will be upon Egypt, the Arabian peninsula, Lebanon, Jordan, Israel, Syria, and Iraq.

had no foreign policy at all for the Middle East before World War II.[1] This fact furnishes one key to American diplomatic efforts in the Middle East in the postwar period. Foreign policy officials in the United States have been required to formulate and carry out policies and programs toward an area with which they have had little or no historical experience and for which lessons from their domestic history afforded minimum guidance—and to do this at a time when turbulence within the area necessitated quick and difficult judgments. Time and again, the urgency of crises has only been matched by their importance, both within the immediate context of the Middle East and within the larger context of the international community.

How has the United States responded to the challenge of events in the contemporary Middle East? We may conveniently seek the answers to this question by centering attention upon three basic problems in the region: the Arab-Israeli dispute; strategic-military issues in the Middle East; and the Western response to Arab nationalism and neutralism.

THE ARAB-ISRAELI CONFLICT

The United States had no foreign policy toward the Middle East prior to World War II, because it thought it had no vital interests in this far-away and backward region. Until the 1930s, American activities in the region were limited chiefly to those carried on by educators, missionaries, and philanthropic groups. These groups won the friendship of the Arab populations, that lasted until it was dissipated by the partition of Palestine in the 1947–1948 period. During the 1930s, American oil companies began to acquire a stake in Middle East fields. By the postwar period, American oil concessions surpassed those of any other country.

During World War II, the United States became conscious as never before of the strategic-military role of the Middle East. Iran provided an indispensable base from which to send war matériel into Russia. Middle East oil was essential to the Allied war machine.

Nevertheless, during World War II, the United States was content to play a subordinate role in Middle Eastern diplomatic and political affairs. Still, it was not beyond giving gratuitous advice to Britain and France concerning their colonial interests in the Middle East.[2] Immediately after the war, the Middle East became a focal point of international discord. During 1946, for example, the nascent United Nations was compelled to deal with a succession of crises involving the Middle East, including Soviet intrigues in northern Iran, complaints by Syria and Lebanon against France, and Soviet efforts to gain control of nearby Greece. In these crises, especially those involving liquidation of colonial empires, the United States often gained the good will of Arab societies, as a country that opposed colonialism.[3]

The Partition of Palestine

Whatever good will existed toward the United States throughout the Arab world was soon dissipated by the inflamed passions accompanying the dispute between Arabs and Jews (or more correctly, Zionists*) over the partition of Palestine in 1947, followed by creation of the State of Israel. Partition was the culmination of a long and progressively bitter controversy between Zionist and Arab groups,

each of which had its partisans among great and small powers on the world scene. The long sequence of events leading to the partition of Palestine is too complex to be traced out here.** Our purpose is served by taking note of one transcendent fact which, perhaps more than any other in the postwar era, colored American relations with Arab states. This was that after World War II, the United States came to be identified by Arabs as the chief backer and defender of Israel. Conversely, Arabs came to look upon America as a country that was insensitive to their demands and interests in the dispute with Israel and was prepared, in nearly every case, to give Israel the benefit of the doubt in the continuing controversy. The result was an alienation of American and Arab opinion that has continued to the present day and has, in turn, affected almost every other significant aspect of Arab-American relations.

This alienation grew out of the fact that, during World War II, influential Zionist organizations in the United States and their supporters carried on an intensive and often highly succesful campaign to generate American support for their goal of a separate Jewish state in Palestine. Millions of dollars were raised in the United States to support the Zionist cause; state legislatures passed resolutions calling upon officials in Washington to accede to Zionist demands; politicians in both major political parties widely endorsed Zionist goals; pressure groups in Washington and throughout the country at large conducted a highly organized drive to win supporters for the Zionist program. As a result, the United States supplanted Great Britain as the center of Zionist agitation and, at least so far as this issue was concerned, largely displaced Britain and France as an object of Arab enmity and suspicion.

Arab apprehensions about the course of American policies became evident immediately after World War II, when Washington began to exert pressure upon Great Britain (as the

---

* While Zionism has roots in the Hebrew religious faith, it is predominantly a *political* movement. Its objective has been the creation of a "national home" for the Jews in Palestine. Many Jews are Zionists, others are not; some are in fact vigorously anti-Zionist. Similarly, many non-Jewish groups and individuals support the Zionist cause. The writer has heard spokesmen for the Arab countries make the distinction between being anti-Semitic and being anti-Zionist. To Arab minds, the key fact about Zionism is that it is a Western-sponsored political movement, detrimental to their interests.

** For the pre-World War II background on events leading to the partition of Palestine in 1947, the student is referred to the following sources: J. C. Hurewitz, *Diplomacy in the Near and Middle East* (Princeton, N.J.: Nostrand, 1956); Vol. II deals with developments after World War I; L. Larry Leonard, "The United Nations and Palestine," *International Conciliation*, **454** (October, 1949), an objective and illuminating discussion of the issue; Charles D. Cremeans, *The Arabs and the World* (New York: Praeger, 1963), pp. 180–213, a perceptive analysis of problems in the Arab world.

League of Nations mandate power in Palestine) to relax barriers against massive Jewish immigration into Palestine, a move which, both in this period and earlier, London steadfastly opposed.[4] Chiefly upon American instigation, an Anglo-American Committee of Inquiry visited Palestine early in 1946. It endorsed increased Jewish immigration to the country; but it also emphasized that any solution to the Palestine problem must protect both Arab and Jewish rights in the country.[5] Within a few months, the United States and Britain formulated a plan for a federal government in Palestine, upon which the later UN partition plan was largely based.[6] As time passed, however, Great Britain made known its coolness toward partition, and its unwillingness to support the plan in the face of rising Arab hostility. For this reason, and because Britain was liquidating many of its overseas commitments, London notified the nascent United Nations that it was relinquishing its mandate authority in Palestine. From April to November, 1947, the UN General Assembly debated the future of the country. It finally voted to accept the partition scheme, although Arab spokesmen expressed their unanimous opposition to the idea and voiced their determination to resist it by force if necessary. The United States played a central role in these events. It emerged as Israel's foremost advocate in the UN and used its influence to rally global support for Israel's cause among disinterested states, such as those in Latin America.[7]

Three dominant influences shaped American policy. One was humanitarianism. Many Americans supported Presidents Roosevelt and Truman in believing that Hitler's barbarous policies toward the Jews created an obligation for Western societies to alleviate somehow the still desperate plight of European Jewry, in part by permitting those who desired to emigrate to Palestine. This would both contribute to a solution of the difficult "refugee problem" prevailing in Europe and provide tangible evidence of Western concern about Jewish privations.[8]

A second influence shaping American policy was historical ignorance of the Arab world and, as an important contributory factor, ingrained suspicion of British colonial policies. In brief, Americans were disposed to believe that the British were emotionally and blindly pro-Arab, an attitude thought to be engendered by Britain's own interests in the Middle East.

Only in the State Department and among military officials did awareness exist of the long-range repercussions of trying to implement the partition scheme in the face of adamant Arab opposition. Toward this issue, the White House not only disregarded State Department warnings, but it also ignored President Roosevelt's earlier wartime pledges that nothing would be done in Palestine inimical to Arab rights. Similarly, the Truman Administration chose to disregard FDR's earlier admonition that partition could only be carried out in Palestine by military force.[9]

Third, and perhaps most galling to Arabs, there was no question that American foreign policy toward the Arab-Israeli dispute was substantially shaped by domestic political considerations. In Chapter 7, we examined the influence of pressure groups on American foreign policy, of which the activities of Zionist groups in this period afford an outstanding example.* Moreover, in political contests during the 1940s, politicians in both the Democratic and Republican parties widely supported the Zionist position. In local elections (particularly in states like New York, New Jersey, Pennsylvania, and Illinois), the Zionist viewpoint received widespread endorsement by candidates.[10]

It would be difficult to cite an example from the record of postwar American diplomacy in which national policy-makers were more insensitive to the long-range diplomatic interests of the nation, and less prepared to evaluate policy alternatives in the light of their implications for American objectives in a vital region such as the Middle East, than in the Palestine controversy.

Conflict After 1947

Hardly had the United Nations adopted the partition plan before open warfare erupted in the Middle East between Jewish and Arab forces. Displaying resourcefulness and a brilliant command of military tactics, and materially aided by internal divisions prevailing among their Arab enemies, Jewish forces successfully defeated or held at bay three Arab armies. On February 24, 1949, both sides finally accepted a UN-sponsored armistice. Meanwhile, on May 14, 1948, the Jewish

* For more detailed discussion of Zionist lobbying activities during and after World War II, see Harry S Truman, *Memoirs* (Garden City, N.Y.: Doubleday, 1955), **II**, 132–169, *passim*; and *The New York Times*, October 5, 1946.

National Council in Tel Aviv had proclaimed the existence of the State of Israel. Within minutes after the event, the Truman Administration extended American recognition to the new Jewish state. Contrasting this haste with the reluctance displayed by the United States in recognizing Communist states like Soviet Russia and Red China, or even new political regimes in Arab countries, Arab spokesmen interpreted Truman's act as another indication of Washington's pro-Israeli bias.

The truce negotiated in 1949, it was expected, would bring an end to military hostilities between the antagonists and open the way for a durable peace between them. In reality, it did nothing of the kind. After 1949, guerrilla warfare, propaganda exchanges and boycotts, border incursions, commando raids and counterraids, noncooperation in fields such as economic planning and water resource development, intense suspicion, and continuing efforts to rally outside support for their respective viewpoints characterized Arab-Israeli relations. The evidence was no more encouraging in the mid-1960s than in the late 1940s that Israel and its Arab neighbors were on the verge of resolving their differences and of arriving at a modus vivendi that would herald a new era of regional peace and stability.[11]

Obstacles to an Arab-Israeli Settlement

Irrespective of the specific issues that must be resolved—and they are many—a pall hangs over the Middle East, and any genuine progress toward an Arab-Israeli *détente* has been rendered all but impossible thus far. One reason is that neither side shows any real disposition to compromise or recognize any merit in the claims of the other side. Positions have thus become frozen and antithetical. Each side reiterates its case with the predictability of a phonograph record, while evincing no willingness to acknowledge the existence of justice in the other side's contentions. As one well-informed student of the problem has put it, "for a decade and a half a state of armed hostility has been fortified by a communications relationship that permits the strident voices . . . to be heard . . . with shattering clarity, while cutting off all possibility of the kind of quiet, direct, face-to-face communication that is essential to the beginning of mutual comprehension."[12]

Within this general atmosphere of continuing ill will, five specific issues have generated persistent tensions between Israel and the Arab states. Beginning with the Arab invasion of Israel in 1948 and continuing thereafter, thousands of Arab refugees left Palestine. By the 1960s, the number of such refugees (and census data about them were sometimes highly unreliable) numbered well over one million persons. No more pathetic conditions can perhaps be imagined than those under which some of these refugees have been compelled to live. Required to spend their lives in UN-supervised "refugee camps" in the Gaza Strip, Lebanon, Jordan, and Syria, the refugees have contributed to, and been the object of, lingering ill will between Israel and the Arab states. Cared for by UNRWA (UN Relief and Works Agency for Palestine Refugees), for whose operations the United States pays most of the bill, the refugees have been especially vocal in their hostility toward Israel and active in inflaming Arab passions against it. Arab governments, on the other hand, have been highly successful in recruiting refugees for their *fedayeen* (or commando) raids across the Israeli frontier and in exploiting their grievances to maintain a crescendo of Arab animosity toward Israel and its Western supporters.[13]

Where does justice lie in this highly controversial and intricate problem? The answer will depend very largely upon how far back one traces the origins of the problem and the decision one reaches concerning the most crucial influences in creating the refugee controversy. Spokesmen for Israel maintain that the Arab refugee problem is entirely the responsibility of the Arab governments. In its view, the problem arose directly out of the warfare which Arab states waged against Israel after its creation in 1947. Israeli officials contend that the vast majority of Arab refugees left Palestine "voluntarily," expecting to return in the wake of victorious Arab armies. Already faced with a burgeoning population that creates pressure upon scarce land resources, Israel is not inclined to assimilate large numbers of Arab refugees, most of whom it regards as hostile to its existence and prepared to assist Arab states in undermining it.[14]

The Arab view, as might be expected, is diametrically opposite. Arab spokesmen contend that their compatriots in Palestine were "driven out" of Israel and dispossessed by the Zionists. Accordingly, they demand that Israel repatriate the refugees by restoring their rightful possessions to them, before progress can be made toward genuine peace negotiations.

Meanwhile, the Arab governments are content for the refugees to be cared for by UNRWA and for the United States—as the country held chiefly responsible by Arabs for the creation of Israel—to continue paying UNRWA's bills.[15]

Second, there is the problem of Israel's borders, with which is tied up the matter of Israel's "expansionist" tendencies. The original partition plan approved by the United Nations in 1947 has, of course, been abandoned. In the course of the warfare that followed partition, Israel expanded its boundaries significantly beyond those specified by this plan; much of what was to become "Arab Palestine" was largely annexed by Jordan, which accounts for the fact that today Jordan perhaps has the most severe refugee problem of any Arab state. The boundaries of Israel thus remain those drawn as a result of the truce in 1949. In Arab eyes this fact (1) violates the earlier partition proposal, and (2) proves Israel's inherently "expansionist" impulses. The latter tendency was reenforced by Israel's military foray into the Sinai region in 1956, when it moved against the nest of *fedayeen* raiders that had repeatedly harassed Israeli villages. In the course of this move, Israel also acquired a part on the Gulf of 'Aqaba, opening into the Red Sea.

Third, there is the matter of the Arab-imposed economic boycott against Israel, receiving its most dramatic expression in Egypt's refusal to permit Israeli-bound shipping to use the Suez Canal, in spite of repeated UN resolutions against this act. In effect, the Arab states take the position that a condition of war still prevails between themselves and Israel, and that the imposition of an economic boycott against their enemy is both legally permissible and militarily mandatory.*

A fourth problem dividing Israel and the Arab states relates to use of scarce water resources of the Middle East for national and regional economic development. The Eisenhower Administration in 1953 endeavored to bring about collaboration among all nations utilizing water from the Jordan river, by encouraging them to establish a kind of Jordan TVA that would allocate water resources, permit more extensive irrigation, provide new sources of electric power generation, and foster industrialization. It was hoped that these steps would create new employment opportunities, thereby offering promise that many Arab refugees could be economically assimilated.[16] This proposal, however, proved unacceptable to the Arabs, since acceptance of it would entail *de facto* recognition of Israel's existence. The Jordan Valley project thus languished as an unfulfilled dream. As the years passed, Israel proceeded unilaterally to divert the waters of the Jordan for use in the arid Negev region to the south. By the mid-1960s, a new crisis impended because of this move. Arab states charged Israel with violating international law and threatened that, if necessary, they would resort to military force to resist Israel's plan.[17]

Finally, there remains the issue that embraces and transcends all other subsidiary questions: Israel's right to exist as a sovereign nation, whose citizens can engage in their pursuits without the continuing threat of Arab harassment and possible future annihilation. The deadlock is illustrated by the contrast between Egyptian President Nasser's conviction that negotiations with Israel were impossible, since "the Israeli aggressions against the Arab lands and Arab rights still continue, while the leaders of Israel have shown no signs of repentance." Arabs, Nasser declared, "do not trust the leaders of Israel."[18] The Israeli view, on the other hand, is that: "The world [has] become accustomed to Arab threats against Israel" and that Israel had successfully "withstood Arab anti-Israel pressure and threats with determination and evident resolve"; in following this policy, it found that "the pressure collapsed, the threats have proved hollow." Meanwhile, Israel has reiterated its desire to meet with Arab leaders to discuss the issues that continue to foment tension in the Middle East.[19]

In its approach to the seething cauldron of Arab-Israeli relations, the United States has followed policies that have been ambivalent, confused, and more often than not, ineffectual. From the period of World War II down to the creation of Israel in 1947, official and unofficial American attitudes were overwhelmingly pro-Israeli. After warfare broke out in Palestine—and after it became apparent that the Arab governments were not prepared to "accept" Israel and arrive at a modus vivendi with it—

* "Boycott," according to an official Arab source, "is an accepted and legitimate weapon which does not violate international law. As long as a state of war exists between the Arabs and Israel, the Arab states have every right to take any safeguard to protect their security and economy." It is justified as being "aimed at the State of Israel and all those who work to bolster its aggressive policies, economically or militarily. . . ." "Boycott Rules," *Arab News and Views*, **10** (New York: Arab Information Center, January, 1964), 2.

American policy began to lose some of its pronounced pro-Zionist cast. This was illustrated in 1954, when a high State Department official spoke bluntly to both sides in the controversy. He urged Israel to "drop the attitude of a conqueror" in its relations with Arab countries. And he called upon Arab states to "accept this State of Israel as an accomplished fact" and to cease "attempting to maintain a state of affairs delicately suspended between peace and war, while . . . desiring neither."[20] Such remarks foreshadowed the next stage in American policy toward the controversy, in which the United States proclaimed its "neutrality" and endeavored to serve the role of "honest broker" between Israel and Arab governments in resolving specific issues dividing them. Thus, in the midst of a threatened outbreak of hostilities over Israel's diversion of Jordan river water for irrigation early in 1964, President Johnson stated that the United States was "neutral" in the dispute. At the same time, he added that America would not stand idly by if the Arab states resorted to arms against Israel—a statement that was widely resented throughout the Arab world and led to vocal anti-American statements in many Arab journals.[21] Arab sources remained convinced in the mid-1960s, no less than in the 1940s, that "Israel was born on the doorstep of the White House" and that continued American protection of Israel would lead to "grave results" in the Middle East.[22] In the Arab view, America's bias in favor of Israel was a "bipartisan" matter; a change of administrations in Washington could not be expected to alter the fact appreciably.[*] Arab animosity toward Israel and its alleged Western supporters heavily conditioned Arab attitudes toward other issues in relations with Western governments. Toward NATO, for example, Arab attitudes were extremely hostile. The

North Atlantic pact, said Nasser of Egypt, "becomes our Number One enemy because it is this pact which . . . supplies Israel with arms."[23]

The United States thus found itself in a cross fire in the Middle East, from which there was no apparent or easy escape. It could not "abandon" Israel, in the face of intense Arab animosity and determination to eliminate Israel as a sovereign state.[**] On the other hand, it could not support Israel unconditionally without jeopardizing its position in the Middle East and perhaps risking Western control over the area's vital oil reserves. Nor was it experiencing any conspicuous success with its declared "neutral" policy. The Arab states did not regard the United States as neutral. In addition, they pointed to a fundamental contradiction between America's attempt to embrace neutrality in this dispute and its earlier strictures against comparable Arab attitudes toward the cold war. We shall examine this point at greater length later.

STRATEGIC–MILITARY PROBLEMS IN THE MIDDLE EAST

The strategic significance of the Middle East makes it one of the central arenas of world politics. This strategic importance arises chiefly from three factors. First, the Middle East is a bridge connecting three continents. Land, sea, and air routes crisscross the area, linking Europe, Asia, and Africa. Second, the Middle East possesses vast reserves of natural resources—chiefly oil. The Middle East contains two-thirds of the proved oil reserves of the world and nearly three-fourths of the oil presently available to the free world. Some 60 percent of the oil concessions in the Arab world are held by the United States; another 30 percent are

---

* This came out clearly during the election of 1960, when Arab spokesmen were asked whether a change in American foreign policy toward the Arab-Israeli contest could be expected. The Foreign Minister of Iraq replied that "there is no difference between the two [major political parties], and we do not care whether the Democrats or the Republicans come into office." Both parties, he believed, "are under Zionist influence in the United States. . . ." *The Iraq Times* (Baghdad), January 5, 1961. The Cairo newspaper *Al Akhbar* agreed that, so far as the Arabs were concerned, it made no difference which party won the election. As in the past, American relations with the Arab world would hinge upon the new Kennedy Administration's policies toward Israel. Cited in "Arab Press Discusses Kennedy's Victory," *Mideast Mirror*, 12 (November 12, 1960), 9.

** While there is no outward diminution in Arab hostility toward Israel, this fact should not be construed to mean that Arab policy toward Israel is monolithic. In reality, divisions have existed since 1947–1948 among Arab countries concerning the proper course to be followed; moreover, certain Arab leaders have revealed great skill in harnessing anti-Israeli sentiment to achieve other goals in the Middle East. This fact became evident late in 1963, following an Arab heads-of-state meeting in Cairo. Arab states like Jordan, Syria, and Saudi Arabia were unquestionably opposed to Israel. Yet they were not inclined to follow Nasser's lead in relying upon military force to prevent Israel from diverting Jordan river water for its use. Cairo, on the other hand, feared attempts by other Arab states deliberately to embroil Egypt in a war with Israel. See *The New York Times*, December 30, 1963.

held by Britain; and most of the remainder are held by French and Dutch companies. American concessions on the Arabian peninsula are particularly rich. Oil fields in the tiny Arabian kingdom of Kuwait, for example, produce over one million barrels of oil daily! Elsewhere, American companies hold substantial concessions in the oil fields of Iran, Iraq, and the small Persian Gulf island of Qatar. By the 1960s, vast new oil fields had been discovered and were being developed in the Saharan regions of Algeria and Libya; the eastern desert region of Egypt also gave promise of containing oil reserves. There was thus every indication that the importance of the Midle East as a major oil-producing region would increase in the years ahead.

A third respect in which the Middle East is of immeasurable strategic importance to the United States lies in the area's role in free-world defense. The Middle East safeguards the southern flank of NATO and is a vital security zone for protecting the sea and air approaches across the South Atlantic to the Western Hemisphere. Today, even more than when Hitler's forces invaded North Africa, enemy control of the Middle East might in the end prove disastrous for the maintenance of Western security.

The Baghdad Pact and CENTO

These considerations induced American officials to strengthen the system of defense against communism in the Middle East. American aid had been extended to Greece and Turkey in 1947. These two countries were brought into NATO in 1951. Yet, before the Khrushchev era of "peaceful coexistence," Washington believed that further steps were needed to formalize defense ties and obligations in the Middle East. Western officials were aware that for generations, the Russian state has sought to penetrate Persia, Afghanistan, and India. Immediately after World War II, the USSR sought to perpetuate its military occupation in northern Iran, thereby threatening to gain control over the country's oil fields and to achieve its ancient dream of acquiring an outlet to the Persian Gulf. In the early postwar period, Soviet pressures against Turkey were also ominous.

In the face of such threats, the United States sought to establish a regional defense system similar to NATO. Yet the anti-Western sentiment sweeping the Arab world as a result of the Palestine controversy, coupled with the

Arab states' desire to terminate Western colonialism in the Middle East, soon revealed that a comprehensive regional defense system was unattainable. The most that could be accomplished was a defense network based upon the "northern tier" countries of Greece, Turkey, Iraq, Iran, and Pakistan. The Baghdad Pact of 1955 thus forged a northern tier defense chain that bound Iraq, Iran, and Pakistan with Britain and, by virtue of British membership in NATO, with Greece and Turkey.[24]

Owing to the vocal opposition of other Arab states, the United States did not join the Baghdad Pact. Throughout most of the Arab world, American sponsorship of the Baghdad Pact was denounced as a new species of "Western imperialism" and as an attempt, after independence had been won by Arab societies, to exercise outside control over Middle Eastern affairs under the guise of protecting the region from communism. Moreover, Israel was highly apprehensive about the implications of the Baghdad Pact, especially as Western arms aid began to flow to pact members. Western arms, in the Israeli view, might well be used in a new Arab attempt to drive Israel into the sea. Having instigated the Baghdad Pact, therefore, the United States held aloof from it, although in the ensuing months it did participate "informally" in the deliberations of its members.

From the beginning, the Baghdad Pact suffered from grave weaknesses that kept it from functioning as the sheet anchor of Western defense in the Middle East, in the same way that NATO served this function on the European continent. It was confined to the northern tier countries of the region—countries which were in the main non-Arab and which frequently clashed in their policies with Arab governments to the south and west. This meant that the dominant ethnic group of the Middle East—the Arabs—was largely unrepresented in the pact. Moreover, the pact never received formal American ratification. While American support for any country theatened with communist aggression might well be taken for granted, on the basis of the Greek-Turkish program earlier and the Eisenhower Doctrine later, the United States nevertheless refrained from committing its own military forces to the Baghdad Pact or offering any "guarantee" of the security of its members. In addition, time revealed that the Baghdad Pact system had another fundamental weakness: it was questionable how long even its Middle Eastern members

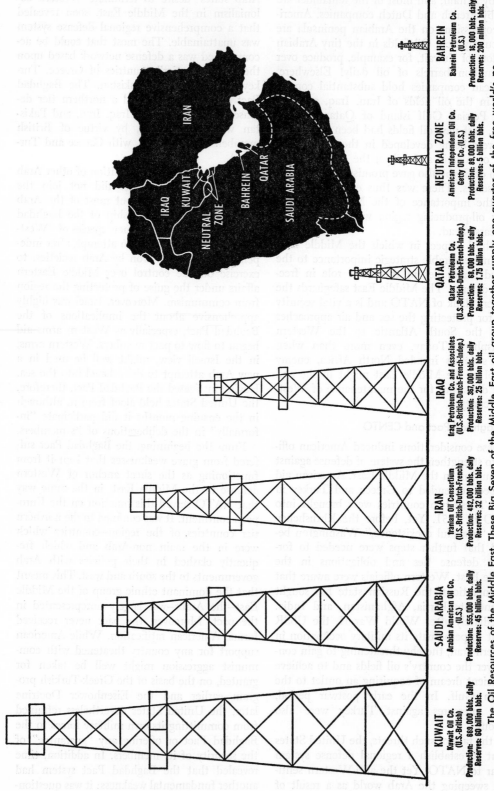

KUWAIT
Kuwait Oil Co.
(U.S.-British)
Production: 689,000 bbls. daily
Reserves: 60 billion bbls.

SAUDI ARABIA
Arabian American Oil Co.
(U.S.)
Production: 555,000 bbls. daily
Reserves: 45 billion bbls.

IRAN
Iranian Oil Consortium
(U.S.-British-Dutch-French)
Production: 482,000 bbls. daily
Reserves: 32 billion bbls.

IRAQ
Iraq Petroleum Co. and Associates
(U.S.-British-Dutch-French-Indep.)
Production: 367,000 bbls. daily
Reserves: 25 billion bbls.

QATAR
Qatar Petroleum Co.
(U.S.-British-Dutch-French-Indep.)
Production: 68,000 bbls. daily
Reserves: 1.75 billion bbls.

NEUTRAL ZONE
American Independent Oil Co.
Getty Oil Co. (U.S.)
Production: 89,000 bbls. daily
Reserves: 5 billion bbls.

BAHREIN
Bahrein Petroleum Co.
(U.S.)
Production: 16,000 bbls. daily
Reserves: 200 million bbls.

The Oil Resources of the Middle East. These Big Seven of the Middle East oil group together supply one quarter of the free world's petroleum needs. Of the Big Seven's output, 60 percent goes to oil-hungry Western Europe, the rest to Asia and Africa, the Middle East for-home consumption, the United States, and other Western Hemisphere nations (Source: Adapted from Don Mackay, Newsweek, July 28, 1958. Production figures, World Almanac: 1964, p. 720.)

could withstand the tide of Arab nationalism sweeping the area and whether, once this tide enveloped them, their ties with the Western-sponsored Baghdad Pact would remain durable.

The gravity of this problem was highlighted by events in Iraq during the late 1950s. In 1958, the government of Feisal II was overthrown, and the King, together with his extremely pro-Western Premier Nuri es-Said, was killed by the revolutionary forces that put Abdel Karim Kassim at the head of the Iraqi government. For the first time since its formal independence in 1930, in the view of Arab nationalists, Iraq had a government whose affairs (or, at any rate, whose *foreign* affairs) were not controlled by a foreign country, in this case Britain. Observers predicted that the *coup d'état* signaled the end of Iraq's membership in the Baghdad Pact; and on March 24, 1959, Kassim's regime repudiated the pact as a Western-conceived scheme foisted upon a pliable and Western-manipulated Iraqi government. With neighboring Syria, Lebanon, Egypt, Tunisia, and other Arab states, Iraq under Kassim embraced a "neutralist" foreign policy, a central precept of which was military noninvolvement with either cold war camp. From that point, the Baghdad Pact—seriously weakened by Iraq's defection—was known as the Central Treaty Organization (CENTO).[25]

The "Eisenhower Doctrine"

The next stage in America's efforts to bolster Middle Eastern defenses occurred as a response to growing communist influence in the area. Egypt and Syria were receiving large stockpiles of arms from behind the iron curtain. During the Suez Crisis of 1956–1957, when British-French-Israeli troops attacked Egypt, there arose the possibility that "Soviet volunteers" might enter the Middle East, ostensibly to rescue Egypt from British-French-Israeli domination. These threats prompted the Eisenhower Administration to ask Congress to approve what came to be designated the "Eisenhower Doctrine," making more explicit Washington's concern with Middle Eastern security. Congress gave the President substantially the authority he requested. A joint resolution passed on March 9, 1957, declared that "preservation of the independence and integrity of the nations of the Middle East" was vital to the American national interest. The key phrase in the resolution granted the President authority "to use armed forces to assist any such nation or group of such nations requesting assistance against

armed aggression from any country controlled by international communism."[26]

The Eisenhower Doctrine was in no sense a blanket guarantee of peace in the Middle East; initially it was directed solely at the danger of communist penetration. Even then, the guarantee was operative only under certain conditions: a request had to be made by one of the Middle Eastern countries before American forces could be used; the threat had to be identified as "armed aggression" as distinct, for example, from a purely internal *coup d'état*; and finally the threat must emanate from a country "controlled by international communism."

As the months passed, however, the Eisenhower Doctrine was broadened in scope, particularly by giving an elastic definition to the concept of "armed aggression." Washington began to invoke the doctrine to deal with cases of "indirect aggression," citing a UN General Assembly resolution of 1949 calling on all states "to refrain from any threats or acts, direct or indirect, aimed at impairing the freedom, independence, or integrity of any state."[27] On July 1, 1958, Secretary of State Dulles stated that "we do not think that the words 'armed attack' preclude treating as such an armed revolution which is fomented abroad, aided and assisted from abroad."[28]

The immediate occasion for this expanded interpretation of the Eisenhower Doctrine was the threat of internal subversion in pro-Western Lebanon. A rebellion against the regime of President Chamoun was being morally and materially aided by pro-communist Syria and Egypt, then joined as the United Arab Republic. A revolution in nearby Iraq had also greatly enhanced communist influence in that country and had given anti-Western elements a new base of operations from which to threaten Lebanon. King Hussein in neighboring Jordan was able to maintain his authority only with the help of British troops. As the crisis mounted in Lebanon, local authorities requested the United States to render assistance. Accordingly, on July 15, 1958, President Eisenhower ordered American marines to enter Lebanon to preserve order in that internally divided country. American intervention was of vital importance in enabling President Chamoun to maintain his authority throughout the country. For the time being, Lebanon was successfully held in the Western camp.

Pointing out that the United States had endeavored to limit and contain "hostile Soviet influence" in the Middle East since the mid-

1950s, a State Department official declared in 1964 that communist influence in this vital region had declined markedly during recent years.[29] Middle Eastern members of CENTO —Pakistan, Iran, and Turkey—retained their independence. Moreover, no Middle Eastern state had a communist regime, nor was any seriously threatened with a communist take-over. Communist parties in key countries such as Iraq, Egypt, and Algeria had either been outlawed or reduced to a relatively ineffectual political minority. To what extent could these results be directly attributed to the efforts of the United States to bolster the defenses of the Middle East by reliance upon the Baghdad Pact and the Eisenhower Doctrine?

In the view of many competent observers, the results of such efforts were, at best, marginal, and, at worst, positively deleterious to the Western position in this vital zone. If the Baghdad Pact afforded unmistakable evidence of the Western determination to preserve the security of strategically located countries such as Iran and Turkey, this gain was largely counterbalanced by certain diplomatic liabilities of the pact. The Baghdad Pact further alienated the most influential Arab state—Nasser's Egypt —from the West and fostered inter-Arab tensions, as Egypt vied with Iraq for the leadership of the Arab masses, prior to the latter's withdrawal from the pact. The pact and the Eisenhower Doctrine provided Egypt and other Arab countries a convenient pretext for acquiring Communist arms to "counterbalance" Western influence in the region. They also fomented new tensions between Western-oriented Turkey and Syria, leading the latter in the late 1950s to gravitate closer to the Communist orbit in economic and military affairs. They clashed head-on with a dominant concept in contemporary Arab nationalism: the determination of Arab states to remain militarily nonaligned from great-power groupings and to avoid permanent diplomatic identification with either East or West.

Perhaps most basically, the principal weakness of the American approach was not so much what it did as what it *failed* to do. Its underlying assumption was that the chief threat to Middle Eastern security arose from the danger of an overt communist *military thrust* into the region. Consequently, it diverted Western attention from what was surely a far more likely danger. This was the risk that communist and pro-communist elements throughout the Arab world would successfully exploit conditions of poverty, social unrest, political turbulence, animosity against Israel and the West, and the pervasive Arab feeling of deep grievance engendered by centuries of foreign domination. If the Middle East offered possibilities for communist intrigue, this was far more likely to stem from these conditions than from the danger that the Kremlin might resort to outright military force to gain its objectives. The Baghdad Pact and Eisenhower Doctrine, in short, did little or nothing to supply the ingredient that has been lacking in postwar Western relations with Middle Eastern countries; and it did a number of things to impede the search for that ingredient. This was a Western approach that somehow blended the interests of newly independent Middle Eastern countries with those of Western countries to form an approach to regional problems which would successfully serve Western and Arab interests. Success in this venture in turn depended upon the ability of the West to understand, and to come to terms with, the psychology of Arab nationalism, a leading ingredient of which was the Arab determination to remain "nonaligned" between the cold war contestants.

THE WEST AND ARAB NATIONALISM

The Sources and Nature of Nationalist Ferment

Since the end of World War II, Arab nationalism has become a mighty stream fed by numerous tributaries. It has threatened to sweep away Western influence throughout the Middle East and to inundate that area in wave after wave of fanaticism and xenophobia, spawning numerous intraregional tensions and inviting great-power antagonisms.

Nationalism has infused virtually every issue troubling the Middle East in the contemporary era. The complaints in 1946 of Syria and Lebanon to the United Nations against French colonialism were anchored in nationalism. Part of the Arab states' opposition to the creation of Israel lay in their historical resentment of Western dictation. Nationalism was a key factor in the Iranian oil dispute which began in 1951 and was not settled until 1953, when Iran successfully nationalized the holdings of the Anglo-Iranian oil company.[30]

Not since the time of the Crusades have the Arab states been politically united.* Their in-

* Once again it is necessary to remind the reader that the term "Middle East" and "Arab world" are not coterminous; the former is much broader than the latter. In earlier portions of the

ternal weaknesses have greatly facilitated the imposition of colonial domination over them. Pan-Arabism is a natural reaction against former colonial subjection and, in the minds of many Arab leaders, the necessary preliminary to restoration of the greatness that once belonged to Islam. Pan-Arabism is sustained by many forces, of which three have been of lasting historical significance: a common language—Arabic; a common religion—Islam; and common racial ties—Semitic. Since World War I, other forces have fostered Arab unity. Most of the Arab states received their independence after World War I from either Britain or France, their colonial masters. Economic backwardness and widespread poverty have given the Arab masses a sense of unity and feeling of separateness from the more advanced Western countries. To a greater or lesser degree, all the Arab states resent involvement in the cold war and desire to retain their independence of action from both the communist bloc and the Western alliance. Finally, since 1947, there has been a powerful new bond of Arab unity: intense hostility to Israel.

Middle Eastern nationalism differs from other nationalist movements with which the student of history is familiar, such as those in nineteenth-century Europe or in India under the leadership of Gandhi and Nehru. In Europe, nationalism meant predominantly "self-determination," a goal that grew out of the philosophy of the French Revolution. But the Middle East "received nationalism in isolation, without liberalism, democracy, and the humanitarian aims. . . ."[31] That is why nationalism in the Middle East has so often "taken . . . the form of chauvinism, of emotional aggression, and of opposition to everything foreign rather than of genuine patriotism." In its over-all manifestations, Middle Eastern nationalism is

. . . distinguished by the over-estimation of one's own nation and the denigration of

others, the lack of the spirit of self-criticism and responsibility, an ambivalent appraisal of the destiny of one's nation based on a feeling of inferiority, and a general tendency to attribute anything wrong with one's nation to the evil-doing of others.[32]

A perceptive student of the Islamic religion has made much the same point about Arab nationalism:

To resist aliens, to work against their domination, even to hate or despise them, is one thing. To respect all members of one's own nation, to envisage its welfare, to evolve an effective loyalty to that welfare, and to work constructively so as to bring it about, is quite another. It is easier to see what one is or should be fighting against, than to imagine what one is or should be fighting for . . . it is sometimes not appreciated how negative until now have been the nationalisms of the Islamic world.[33]

Another conspicuous theme in Arab nationalism has been its defensiveness and its massive sense of insecurity. "The modern Arab," Wilfred C. Smith has observed, "is first and foremost a person defending himself and his society against onslaught." Contemporary Arabs believe themselves to be "still under attack, still reacting to an insecurity almost greater than they can bear."[34] This aspect of Arab nationalism has many sources, too numerous and complex to discuss here.[35] Suffice it to say that it imparts to the Arab nationalist movement an emotional fervor, a hypersensitivity, and deeply ingrained suspicion toward the outside world, that is distinctive. Arabs are quick to discern affronts to their honor and dignity or plots against their newly gained freedoms by foreigners, especially by Western societies. Arab leaders caution the masses continually against the alleged attempts of "imperialists" (meaning principally Western imperialists) to reimpose colonial control over their affairs or to dominate their policies by economic and military means.

For many years, including much of the postwar era, Arab nationalism was outstanding chiefly for its negative qualities. It obviously opposed colonial domination, Israel and the Zionist movement, and any attempt by outside countries to control Arab affairs. It tended to be negative, fanatical, heavily opportunistic and pragmatic, and advocated with a fierce passion that has been graphically demonstrated by the actions of street mobs in Cairo or Baghdad.

Gradually, certain positive goals have emerged,

chapter, we have construed it to include countries like Turkey and Iran which, by most interpretations, are geographically a part of the Middle East. Yet these countries are not usually regarded (certainly not by *Arabs*) as part of the "Arab world." Many criteria might be used to define this concept, but the most common perhaps is use of the Arabic language. By this definition, the Arab world extends from Morocco through Iraq and from Syria through Egypt and the Arabian peninsula. Admittedly, even by this criterion, borderline cases (like northern Sudan and much of the eastern "horn" of Africa) remain.

as nationalist leaders throughout the Arab world have come to realize that the problems of the region cannot be solved merely by tirades against foreigners or by romanticizing the Arab past. Many of the positive goals of Arab nationalism are embraced in the concept of "Arab socialism," as identified with President Nasser of Egypt. Arab socialism is an extremely pragmatic and flexible concept, incorporating a range of diverse elements—from the historic Islamic emphasis upon the welfare of the community and the subordination of individual rights to it, to the American New Deal and Fair Deal programs, to the humanitarian goals espoused by European Socialist and Communist parties. Nasser's goal of creating a "democratic, socialist, cooperative society" and his conviction that democracy "must be social as well as political," has translated itself into a variety of programs designed to promote the welfare of the Arab masses and to establish a political order that has solid mass support. Specific goals of socialism—and in this respect his program enjoys widespread support from Morocco to Iraq—are land reform, industrialization and enhanced agricultural production, the promotion of cooperative societies, expanding educational opportunities, improved sanitation and health facilities, a rising standard of living for the Egyptian masses, creation of new areas of arable land, the emancipation of women, and other steps designed to modernize one of the most primitive and economically backward societies found anywhere on the globe.* The stated goals of Nasser's regime, in the Egyptian President's own words, are

> . . . to end the exploitation of people, to realize national aspirations and to develop the mature political consciousness that is an indispensable preliminary for a sound democracy. . . . Our ultimate aim is to provide Egypt with a truly democratic and representative government, not the type of parliamentary dictatorship which the Palace and a corrupt "Pasha" class imposed on the people.[36]

* More detailed treatment of the positive ingredients in Arab nationalism, particularly in their Egyptian setting, may be found in: J. S. F. Parker, "The United Arab Republic," *International Affairs,* **38** (January, 1962), 15–29; Gamal Abdel Nasser, "The Egyptian Revolution," *Foreign Affairs,* **33** (January, 1955), 199–212; Kingsley Martin, "Conversation with Nasser," *The New Statesman,* **63** (January 5, 1962), 6, and "Arab Socialism," *The New Statesman,* **63** (February 16, 1962), 218–220; Curtis F. Jones, "The New Egyptian Constitution," *Middle East Journal,* **10** (Summer, 1956), 300–307.

Arab "Neutralism" and "Nonalignment"

Our interest in contemporary Arab nationalism centers more upon its foreign than domestic implications. A central corollary of Arab nationalist ideology has been the acceptance and advocacy of foreign policy of "neutralism" or "nonalignment" by the overwhelming majority of Arab countries from Morocco to Iraq. Nonalignment in foreign affairs is regarded by Arab leaders and masses as both a visible symbol, and a necessary consequence, of the gaining and maintenance of Arab independence, as indicated by Nasser's remark in an interview with American newsmen: "We want, above all and everything, to feel that we are free."[37] The connection between the goal of Arab independence and a neutralist position in foreign affairs was further suggested by a speech by Nasser on March 5, 1958, upon the establishment of the United Arab Republic (the union between Syria and Egypt, which was dissolved in 1961). After recounting the Arab effort to achieve independence, Nasser noted:

> You won as a result of a long and bitter struggle. You won in the battle of freedom. You won in the battle of independence. You won in the battle of alignments and alliance. . . . You won when you decided to have an independent policy for yourselves emanating from your own country, land, and conscience. . . . Today, brethren, we must fight and be on the alert in order to preserve this independent policy.[38]

A variation of the same view was expressed by an official Iraqi source under the regime of General Kassim. In foreign affairs, Kassim had committed his government to the goal of "removing the state of dependence and alignment under which the country was labouring and asserting that the Iraqi Republic adheres to the policy of positive neutrality. . . ." Such a policy, it contended, "has contributed appreciably towards winning for Iraq the respect of the countries of the world."[39] Or, as Premier Khalil succinctly defined the foreign policy of the Sudan: "Our foreign policy can be summarized in one word, 'nonalignment,' and at the same time we shall try to promote friendly relations with all countries."[40]

In whatever terms it is expressed by individual Arab leaders—and in whatever degree it had to be recognized that a foreign policy of "neutralism" or "nonalignment" often encompassed highly diverse national policies toward regional and global issues*—the Arab states were agreed on certain essentials of their neutralist credo. One common denominator, as Nasser expressed the idea, was that the voice of Arab states "in international forums is not counted as an automatic one attached to a particular bloc . . . which can be added to or discounted in accordance with the position of a certain great power. . . ."[41] This in turn implied Arab unwillingness to join in foreign-sponsored military pacts or to become *permanently* identified with either cold war power bloc. Nonalignment also implied diplomatic freedom of action. Arab states, along with other neutralist countries in Africa and Asia, were free to evolve policies according to the merits of diplomatic issues confronting them, in accordance with their own interests as their governments perceived them. A neutralist policy, on the other hand, did not preclude *temporary* diplomatic, economic, or military association with either the East or West, or with both concurrently. Yet toward some issues (the dispute with Israel is an example) it meant formulating distinctively Arab policies, which not even other neutralist states outside the Arab zone could support.

Another element in a neutralist or non-aligned policy commanded widespread support throughout the Arab world. This was that such a policy in no way implied traditional "neutrality" toward global controversies, non-involvement in international political discussions and negotiations, or a lack of deep concern about global problems and tendencies. Nor did it signify lack of moral or ethical standards in approaching cold war developments, particularly in evaluating issues involving the risk of a global nuclear conflagration.**

Still another idea deemed incompatible with the Arab conception of a neutralist or non-aligned foreign policy was the theory invoked to justify Western efforts to establish a Middle Eastern defense organization during the 1950s. With the emergence of the cold war, coupled with the withdrawal of French and British military power from the Middle East, American officials become convinced that a "power vacuum" existed in the Arab world that would invite communist expansionism.[42] The "power vacuum" conception deeply offended Arab sensibilities and violated their neutralist credo. "We have no need for the protection of either the Eastern or the Western blocs," Nasser said in 1958. "We have no need for instructions to us by either the East or the West."[43] And the President of Syria, Shukry al-Kuwatly, spoke for Arab nationalists generally when he urged: ". . . let America abandon the thory of 'vacuum of power' in the Middle East. If there is a vacuum of power in any land or region, only the people of that land or region can fill it."[44] Arabs thus agreed with an Indian observer that, in the Western view, "any rich area without some Western power or other occupying it, or dominating the spot, is a vacuum."[45] In whatever degree Americans believed such Arab viewpoints to be exaggerated or naïve, events revealed that such statements correctly described prevailing Arab attitudes.

Eisenhower-Dulles Policies Toward Arab Neutralism

The American response to Arab neutralism may be divided into two stages: the Dulles-Eisenhower period and the late Eisenhower-Kennedy-Johnson period. In each stage, American officials entertained fundamentally differing conceptions both of the origins and nature of Arab neutralism and of its diplomatic implications for the United States. We may highlight official American attitudes in the former period by focusing upon the Dulles-Eisenhower

---

* Even Arab commentators acknowledged that "neutralist" policies in the Arab world often yielded diverse results. Thus, one Arab writer has identified four classifications of Arab neutralist policies, utilizing the extent to which identification with the policies of India (assumed to be the symbol of a truly "nonaligned" nation) could be detected: (1) Iraq and the United Arab Republic (at that time, Syria and Egypt) evinced a high correlation in policies with India; (2) Saudi Arabia, Morocco, and Yemen revealed a fair correlation—but were sometimes more outspokenly anti-communist; (3) Lebanon and Libya gravitated between a "neutralist" and a pro-Western position; and (4) Tunisia and Jordan were usually pro-Western, but sometimes sided with neutralist states. This appraisal is based upon an analysis of voting patterns in the 13th session of the UN General Assembly. See Khalid I. Babaa, "Arab Positive Neutralism" (New York: Arab Information Center, mimeo., no date), p. 43.

** The Arab mentality on this point—widely misunderstood in the West—is illustrated by the viewpoint of an Egyptian publication: "Neutralism does not imply retirement within one's self. Such an attitude would constitute a negative and niggardly stand towards world society and a betrayal of the human ideal. . . . Nonaligned states are in reality committed in the sense that they must exert their efforts for the preservation of peace and the defense of the intangible principles without which the world would be ruled by the law of the jungle." "A Decisive Action for Peace," *The Scribe* (Cairo), 2 (May–June, 1961), 11.

policy toward Egypt's Aswan High Dam and the ensuing Suez Crisis of 1956.

In November, 1954, Abdel Nasser became President of Egypt, following an earlier revolution in 1952 that overthrew the monarchy headed by King Farouk. Nasser soon emerged as the leader of Arab opposition to the Western-sponsored Baghdad pact. In addition, he fanned the flames of Arab animosity toward Israel and openly supported the Algerian revolution against France. Then, in the summer of 1955, Nasser took a step that caused deep concern in Washington: he purchased arms from Communist Czechoslovakia. For the first time, in spite of American efforts to bolster regional defense, communism appeared to be getting a foothold in the Middle East. The Czech-Egyptian arms deal was followed by a significant increase in trade between Egyptian and iron curtain countries and by Cairo's recognition of Red China.

In the same period, negotiations were proceeding between Egypt and the West, chiefly Britain and the United States, for the construction of the Aswan High Dam—an ambitious engineering project in upper Egypt that was to cost $1.5 billion and was to require 10–15 years for completion. After numerous studies, the United States and Britain, along with the World Bank, agreed to extend a substantial loan to Egypt for this project, in the apparent hope that this step would contribute to reversing the tide of suspicion and animosity currently characterizing Arab-Western relations.

But Nasser's policy of spurning military association with the West, and of cultivating military and economic ties with the Communist bloc, led to second thoughts in the State Department about assisting with the Aswan Dam. On July 19, 1956, Secretary of State John Foster Dulles dramatically and abruptly withdrew the American offer, citing numerous technical and financial difficulties why the Aswan Dam project was no longer feasible. Later, however, Dulles candidly admitted that the American offer had been withdrawn because of Egypt's neutralist policies. In justifying the revocation of American funds for the Aswan High Dam, Secretary of State Dulles referred to Egypt's "ever-closer relations with the Soviet bloc countries." He contended: "the Egyptians, in a sense, forced upon us an issue to which I think there was only one proper response: that issue was, do nations which play both sides get better treatment than

nations which are stalwart and work with us? . . ."[46]

Nasser's retort on July 26, 1956, was to nationalize the Suez Canal—thereby plunging the Middle East into the most serious crisis it had experienced since World War II. Prolonged negotiations, both among the Western allies and between them and Egypt, followed. In October, the Suez Canal issue was presented to the UN Security Council. And it was during UN debate on the question that Israeli forces invaded the Sinai region. This was followed on October 5 by a joint Anglo-French invasion of the Suez region, supposedly to "protect" the canal from the two belligerents. In reality, this move had been triggered by a growing Western disenchantment with Nasser in London and Paris and by an undisguised hope that a resort to military force would bring about his overthrow.

These events compelled the United States to take a position it by no means relished. The Anglo-French-Israeli invasion of Egypt occurred during the same period as the ruthless Soviet suppression of the Hungarian revolt. In the American view, the free world could not condone resort to military force against a weak country in one instance and condemn it in the other. Whatever the provocations, the United States could not defend the conduct of its allies or of Israel in attacking Egypt. Aside from being morally reprehensible, such action risked totally alienating opinion throughout Africa, the Arab world, and Asia. In the United Nations, the United States was therefore largely responsible for resolutions condemning Britain, France, and Israel and for compelling them to evacuate Egyptian territory. In a rare exhibition of *mea culpa*, Secretary of State Dulles admitted that the United States and other western countries had never sufficiently understood basic causes of tension and instability throughout the Arab world.[47] Nevertheless, neither during this crisis nor throughout the months that followed was there sufficient realization among American officials and citizens that, to a significant degree, the Suez Crisis of 1956 had been caused initially by American hostility toward the Arab policy of "neutralism."* Such understanding began to

---

* Thus, when former Vice-President Richard M. Nixon visited the site of the Aswan High Dam in 1963, he conceded in effect that the Eisenhower Administration had made a mistake in abruptly terminating aid for the project, thereby compelling Egypt to rely upon Soviet aid. He labeled the dam

emerge in the late Eisenhower period and afforded the basis for fundamental changes in prevailing official assessments of neutralism as a diplomatic credo.

Kennedy-Johnson Policies Toward Arab Neutralism

By the late 1950s, a combination of factors induced American officials to reappraise the neutralist movement, not only in the Arab world but in Asia and Africa as well. One impetus for this new approach came from the retirement and death of Secretary of State Dulles, whose celebrated strictures against a position of diplomatic nonalignment were well-known. Another came from growing realization among State Department officials that forceful and undisguised opposition to neutralism, however it might be urged by American public opinion, seldom paid diplomatic dividends. Still another influence was growing American insight into the origins, ideology, and implications of neutralism—leading to an over-all realization that prevailing popular judgments (e. g., that "neutralism is the next thing to communism" or that "the neutralists are playing the communist game") were often unwarranted and detrimental to American diplomatic interests.

Finally, throughout the months that followed the Suez Crisis, the activities and policies of neutralist nations in the Arab world and elsewhere made abundantly clear that the overwhelming majority of countries holding to a nonaligned diplomatic position were determined to preserve their freedom from *Communist*, as well as from Western, domination and control. As Senator Frank Church (Democrat of Idaho), a member of the Senate Foreign Relations Committee, observed in 1961:

> We have for a long time been terribly concerned about the United Arab Republic being a satellite of the Communist bloc by virtue of this arms supply, which is bigger than any [Communist] arms supply elsewhere in Africa. We are beginning to wake up to the fact that the United Arab Republic may not be a satellite at all, despite the extent of Soviet involvement there. It is one African country where all the Communists are in jail.[48]

"one of the wonders of the modern world" and observed that although Egypt was relying heavily upon foreign technicians to build it, there was "no possibility of infiltration" of the Egyptian government by communism because of this fact. See *The New York Times*, June 24, 1963.

Or, as a State Department official stated the following year, although the USSR had maintained "unrelenting pressure" on the Arab countries for many years, it had not achieved "any noticeable new gains" in this region. He continued:

> The fact that the Sino-Soviet bloc has been held at bay may be attributed mainly to the resolute determination of the countries in the area to maintain their independence. . . .

Although the USSR had evidently sought to gain a dominant position in countries like Egypt, Cairo "has maintained an independent foreign policy posture and its firm opposition to internal Communist subversion."[49] In 1963, Secretary of State Dean Rusk observed about Iraq: "Iraq has a new and stoutly independent government. Other countries in the Middle East and Africa which seemed to be flirting dangerously with the Soviet bloc have been moving toward a warier independence and better relations with the West."[50] The State Department had reached basically the same conclusion about neutralist Morocco, which had required the United States to close down its strategic air bases in the country by 1963. In spite of this fact, one State Department official stated, King Hassan did not want "to be aligned with the Soviet bloc. . . . what he really wants is being able to make up his own mind on individual issues without being involved in any particular bloc. . . . over a period of time he is going to develop sound views on most of the major issues wherever he can."[51]

The new American evaluation of Arab neutralism deirved in no small measure from the increasing tension that, by the late 1950s, surrounded relations between the Communist bloc and many Arab countries. Communist policymakers had unquestionably hoped to capitalize upon deep-seated Arab animosity toward the West, growing out of the period of Western colonialism in the Middle East, Arab hostility toward Israel, and misgivings about Western attempts to draw Arab countries into the Baghdad Pact defense system. Accordingly, the Khrushchev era of "peaceful coexistence" witnessed intensified Soviet efforts to penetrate the Middle East by reliance upon generous trade and economic assistance programs, cultural exchange, military aid, vocal communist support for the Arab case against Israel, and other techniques intended to ingratiate the Communist world with Arab societies. Premier Khrushchev's offer of Soviet "volunteers" to assist Egypt during the conflict with Britain, France, and Israel in the Suez affair of 1956 provided a visible and dramatic symbol of the Communist bloc's apparent solicitude for the Arab world. The period of the mid-1950s marked the nadir of Western-Arab relations in the postwar era; and the Communist bloc displayed great skill in exploiting Arab grievances for its own diplomatic advantage.

That the Kremlin achieved some success by its policies is indicated by the rapport it was able to establish in this period with countries like Syria, whose Minister of State, Khalid al-Azm, publicly reported after a trip behind the iron curtain:

> The USSR . . . does not want to interfere in our affairs nor does it want to interfere with our political or social systems. It wants Syria to have a strong economy to support Syria's political independence. . . . The USSR has given us political support and supplied us with arms, which we were completely unable to obtain from countries other than the USSR.[52]

Again, in the midst of Tunisia's conflict with France in 1961 over French occupancy of the port of Bizerte, a high Tunisian official stated that Russia was ready "to give us all forms of aid which we judge necessary" to assure a Tunisian victory; friendly relations between Tunisia and the USSR were "strengthening and developing day by day," chiefly because of Soviet support for the Tunisian cause.[53]

However disconcerting such evidence of an Arab "neutralist" affinity for the Communist bloc might be for the West, in time the State Department began to credit Arab nationalists with greater acumen in judging the Soviet Union's purposes in the Middle East, than had been the case in the Dulles-Eisenhower period. Arab governments in no way disguised, or apologized for, their readiness to accept Communist economic and military assistance or the support of Communist states in their struggle against Western colonialism and Zionism. Yet, as an Egyptian source explained: Arab states were determined not "to be ruled by others, either directly or indirectly through unrepresentative governments which owe allegiance to and are obliged to carry out the policies of foreign powers."[54] Or, as Nasser phrased it: "They [Americans] say Nasser is turning to the East and wants to put his country under Eastern domination, but dealing commercially with Russia is not the same thing as turning communist. We aim at equal relations with

all nations. To say we are encouraging communism is completely untrue. We have our own philosophy."[55] In 1958, a leading American authority on Middle Eastern affairs, Harold B. Minor, told the Senate Foreign Relations Committee: "We should avoid the erroneous and easy assumption that there is a deliberate trend in any Middle Eastern country toward communism. There is an ideological gulf between Islamic and other Middle Eastern cultures . . . and communism. . . ."[56]

Events by the late 1950s and early 1960s indicated ample Arab awareness of communist intentions in the Middle East. Informed Arabs had become aware that, irrespective of the particular tactics it employed, the Communist world was in reality utilizing Lenin's approach of "supporting nationalism on the false belief that it is the first step toward the ultimate goal of communism."[57]

Continuing conflict between Communist elements in Iraq and the central government in Baghdad, for example, produced rising tensions between the Soviet Union and this key Arab country. Baghdad had become increasingly apprehensive about long-standing Soviet endorsement of a separate state for the large Kurdish minority living in Iraq's northern provinces. The demands of the Kurdish nationalists more often than not received a sympathetic hearing in the Kremlin. After Iraqi Premier Kassim launched military operations against Kurdish separatists, he was vigorously denounced in Communist circles inside and outside the country for his "reactionary measures" and his "persecution of Communists and democrats." Ironically, Kassim utilized Soviet-supplied arms and aircraft in his moves against Kurds and Communists in Iraq![58] By the early 1960s, Iraqi sources were denouncing Communists and their foreign supporters for "brutalities, atrocities, and high-handedness" and for their overt opposition to organizations like the Arab League.[59] Finally, the climax in Iraq's deteriorating relations with the Communist bloc was reached early in 1963. What an official American source described as "made-to-order demonstrations against the Iraqi Embassy in Moscow —the first such demonstration against a neutral, non-Western embassy in Soviet history"—signified the presence of grave tensions in Soviet-Iraqi relations. American officials interpreted this event as symbolizing "Soviet anger against the frustration of its designs for the Communist subversion of Iraq, as part of its long-planned penetration of the Middle East."[60]

Comparable tendencies had become evident in Soviet-Egyptian relations. That Arab leaders like Nasser had no illusions about Soviet intentions in the Middle East was indicated by his observation in 1961 that, when the USSR supported Egypt during the Suez Crisis of 1956, the Kremlin had made an expediential decision in the hope of gaining "an opportunity of having a legitimate place in the Arab community."[61] By the early 1960s, Egyptian sources complained vocally about "a violent campaign . . . launched by communist propaganda organs" against Egypt. One Egyptian source bluntly warned the Kremlin:

Contrary to what was then given wide currency, this policy [of expelling Western colonialism from the Arab world] was not meant to open the doors of the Middle East to Soviet communism. . . .

It strongly condemned the Soviet Union for its twofold policy of "weakening and breaking western influence in the region in order to install itself there and assure freedom of action for the local communist parties." It continued that "the Middle East and the Afro-Asian world will be closed to all alien principles, be they communist or otherwise," and it castigated communism because it "combats Arab Nationalism in the same way that it struggles against other concepts of this kind. . . ."[62]

Nasser himself condemned the Soviet Union for seeking to establish "an all-Arab Communist underground for purposes of subversion and sabotage against neighboring Arab countries"; he pointedly warned Soviet Premier Khrushchev against assuming "responsibility for the protection of Arab Communists" and for "supporting the Communist party in our country." Whatever friendship Arabs might evince for Russia, Nasser stated, "did not exist because of the Communist party but in spite of them [sic]." He warned the Kremlin against attempts to impose a "new type of colonialism" in the Arab world and added that it was in danger of losing whatever good will it had accumulated among Arabs if it persisted in this policy.[63] In a later exchange between Egyptian and Russian officials, an Egyptian legislator wrote to Khrushchev that his country's rejection of capitalism did not mean "that Communism, which proved successful in conditions prevailing in other countries, is suitable for successful application in our country. Our people refuse to be limited to this choice and believe that the ideological scope in the world is bigger than this closed circle." Following these events, Pravda lamented that Arab socialism was as alike "as two peas to capitalism which is doomed by history. . . ."[64]

Nor was the Soviet Union endearing itself to the Arab world by its policy of "dumping" cut-rate oil on the world market, thereby imperiling the price structure of Middle East oil and creating the impression that, for all its avowed solicitude for Arab welfare, the Kremlin was insensitive to Arab economic problems.[65]

Witnessing the growing suspicion between Arab nationalists and Communist forces inside and outside the Middle East, American policymakers concluded that a foreign policy of neutralism or nonalignment was not inherently detrimental to American interests; in fact, it sometimes coincided with them. American acceptance of Arab determination to remain nonaligned was fully compatible with the free world's ideological goals. "We Americans need to realize," a State Department official said in 1960, "that there can be no monolithic dogma in the free world such as is imposed in the Communist bloc. The free world is more diversified than the Communist bloc. It shares no consensus on the best way to maintain independence from communism or on the approaches to the internal problem of modernization and industrialization." Another official added in 1962: "We wish to see the nations in the Near East and South Asia develop, economically and politically, with institutions so strong that they need not fear loss of independence by either Communist subversion or external attack."[66]

Secretary of State Dean Rusk summarized the Kennedy Administration's views toward neutralism in the Arab world and elsewhere by saying: ". . . if we see the underlying issue of our time as that between a world of coercion and a world of choice, the difference between ally and neutral becomes somewhat less important." It was largely with this distinction in mind that, during his presidential campaign, John F. Kennedy identified the strongest force aiding the free world throughout African, Arab, and Asian countries as "the desire of people to be free. . . . they don't want to give their freedom up to become Communists. They want to stay free, independent, perhaps, of us, but certainly independent of the Communists. And I believe that if we identify ourselves with that force . . . we can strengthen freedom. We can make it move. We can put the Communists on the defensive."[67]

Arab-American Relations in Perspective

Even Arab sources conceded by the early 1960s that there was now "a better American appreciation of the neutralist world and its efforts toward reconstruction and world peace."[68] Growing economic and cultural ties between American and Arab countries testified to the improvement in relations. Yet the *rapprochement* in Arab-American relations did not, of course, mean that relations between Washington and Arab capitals were always harmonious and cooperative. Sources of tension and controversy remained. As we suggested earlier in the chapter, there was little improvement in the climate of Arab-Israeli relations and little diminution in Arab animosity toward the United States for its role in championing Israel's cause. By the early 1960s, furthermore, the Arab world was in the grip of a contest between the forces of Arab nationalism, personified in Nasser of Egypt, and the forces of traditionalism, symbolized by the monarchies of Saudi Arabia and Jordan. These forces collided in the tiny Arabian kingdom of Yemen, where pro-Nasser groups fought against pro-Saudi groups in a conflict that had ramifications far beyond Yemen's borders.[69] Moreover, one of the West's staunchest allies in the Middle East—King Hussein of Jordan—found himself under periodic attack by Arab nationalists, often instigated and aided by Cairo. If the United States desired to maintain friendly relations with nationalist leaders like Nasser of Egypt, it was no less determined to support Hussein's regime and assist it in its efforts to modernize the country. Nor did American and Arab interests always coincide in developments outside the Middle East such as the Congo Crisis, the question of disarmament, or appraisals of "Castroism" in Cuba. As the leader of the Western alliance, the United States could count on remaining the target of deep-seated anti-Western animosity, growing out of the era of Western colonialism in the Middle East, for decades and perhaps generations to come. If for no other reason, periodic and heated Arab denunciations of "Western imperialism" were requirements for political candidates and leaders who sought to hold the allegiance of the masses throughout the Middle East. Above all, there remained the chronically tense situation along the Arab-Israeli frontier. No more than in 1947–1948 were the Arabs prepared to "accept" Israel or to arrive at a settlement of outstanding issues with it. The stated American policy of "neutrality" and "impartiality" toward the Arab-Israeli dispute did nothing whatever to convince Arabs that the United States was truly disinterested or that it was finally prepared to concede the justice of many Arab claims.

Even so, the climate of American-Arab relations in the mid-1960s was much improved over that prevailing a decade earlier. If anti-Western sentiments still pervaded the Arab world, they were much less overtly at the center of Arab governmental policies than ten years before. Nationalist leaders in the Middle East were less hesitant (as events like the Cuban Crisis of 1962 indicated) to offend the United States openly. They, fully as much as officials in Washington, were mindful of many real

Seems to Have a Mind of Its Own. (Source: Ray in *The Kansas City Star,* reproduced in *The New York Times,* October 14, 1962.)

advantages in reasonably cordial relations with America and were determined, within the limitations set by their own diplomatic vital interests, to cultivate and preserve them. For its part, the United States had come to see much clearer than it had in the Dulles era that anti-Westernism was not necessarily synonymous with pro-communism. It had largely accepted the idea that the Arab states were determined to base their foreign policy upon a precept which had long been deemed legitimate in the West: pursuit of their own interests, as their own national leaders defined these interests. Far more than during the 1950s, officials in the United States and the Arab world were discovering areas in which their mutual interests coincided.

THE AWAKENING OF AFRICA

A Continent in Transition

By the second half of the twentieth century, Africa was awakening to play a prominent role in international politics after centuries of political and economic hibernation. Prior to World War II, only four countries in the whole of Africa were independent. By 1964, 35 African countries had attained independence; this total would unquestionably increase as dependencies such as Angola and Southern Rhodesia moved toward self-government.

If the march toward political freedom on the African continent commanded global attention, Africa had come to the center of the world stage because of another fact: the *political turbulence* that gripped the continent. Within a brief period of a few weeks during the mid-1960s, one source counted 17 separate crises on the African scene, ranging from an anti-Arab uprising on Zanzibar, to racial discord in Northern Rhodesia, to an army mutiny in Tanganyika.[70] These were all signs of Africa's "coming of age." For American policy-makers, they posed a set of problems for which choices were often difficult and painful.

Even more than in the case of the Arab world, American officials were often ill-prepared to deal successfully with events in Africa. American contact with Africa down to World War II had been fragmentary. Very early, Yankee traders had participated in the lucrative slave trade. In its infancy, the American Republic had continuing quarrels with the rulers of the Barbary Coast. The United States was instrumental in establishing Liberia as an independent country in 1822. Moreover, American delegates participated in the Berlin Conference of 1884–1885, from which the European colonial "scramble" for Africa is dated. The boundaries of many African countries were agreed upon at this conference. During World War II, American military planners became acutely conscious of the strategic significance of Africa and the adjacent Arab world. One of the most decisive battles of this conflict was fought along the desert strip of North Africa. For many decades, American missionaries and educators have also been active on the African continent.[71] Beyond these developments, American contact with Africa has been minimal, leaving the United States little experience upon which to draw in dealing with contemporary African societies.

Profile of the "Dark Continent"

Encompassing an area four times that of the United States, the continent of Africa contains more than 11 million square miles, most of which is in the tropics. Africa is a region of infinite variety and contrasts. The northern portion of the continent is divided from east to west by the greatest desert on the globe, the Sahara; that portion lying athwart the equator includes a dense, at some points an almost impenetrable, tropical rain forest. Elsewhere there is "small bush" country, isolated barren wastes, grasslands, and mountain ranges. Most of the interior of Africa is a great plateau. Africa has the shortest coastline, proportionate to its area, of any continent; with few exceptions, the coastline is unsuitable for the construction of harbors. Climate and geography have conspired to make transportation and communication arduous among African countries and between them and the outside world. Today, the only dependable method of transportation for much of Africa is the airplane.

In Africa's inhospitable environment, there dwell approximately 240 million people, of whom about 5 million are of European stock, with half the latter total living in the Republic of South Africa. Leading ethnic groups are the Arabs, who inhabit much of North Africa; the Semitic-Hamitic peoples of Ethiopia and North-Central Africa, who do not regard themselves as colored; and Negroes or Bantu peoples, who comprise the overwhelming majority of the native population. Over 700 languages and dialects are spoken throughout Africa. Major groups by religion show some 80 million Moslems, 21 million Christians, and the remainder pagan. Illiteracy has been estimated to run between 80 and 90 percent of the *total* population; in 25 countries and dependencies, between 90 and 99 percent of the population is illiterate.*

Africa is classified among the "underdeveloped" regions of the world. The designation is accurate in the sense that cultural-eco-

---

* Data on the leading geographic, economic, and demographic characteristics of Africa are presented in: Andrew Boyd and Patrick van Rensburg, *An Atlas of African Affairs* (New York: Praeger, 1962), pp. 1–22; Walter Goldschmidt, ed., *The United States and Africa* (New York: Praeger, 1963), pp. 3–39, 74–115; and George T. Kimble, *Tropical Africa*, I (New York: Twentieth Century Fund, 1960, 2 vols.), *passim*. Kimble's book is perhaps the most authoritative treatment of the subject available.

nomic levels there are in general primitive, and that insufficient use has been made to date of the continent's resources.* Africa is the source of many important minerals, a number of them vital for the defense program of the United States. Thus, Africa produces virtually all the world's industrial diamonds. Expressed as a percentage of total world production, Africa supplies 94 percent of the columbite, and 84 percent of the cobalt, both vital ingredients in the making of high-grade steel products; 41 percent of the beryllium, 33 percent of the manganese, 29 percent of the chrome, 21 percent of the copper, 13 percent of the tin, 50 percent of the gold, and—perhaps most crucial of all for the free world's defense efforts—a substantial part of the uranium ore used in nuclear processes.[72] Besides Africa's proven reserves in these minerals, some authorities predict vast new discoveries, after the continent's resources are adequately surveyed. Chester Bowles has optimistically labeled Africa "the richest untapped source of mineral wealth still available to a world that is rapidly devouring its resources. . . ."[73] Among the richest potential resources of Africa are numerous sites for the generation of hydroelectric power. Possessing vast river systems, whose courses are severely impeded by rapids and waterfalls, Africa in fact has the greatest hydroelectric potential of any continent in the world. A recent French estimate placed its potential at 200 million *kwh*, which compares with a potential of 75 million *kwh* for the United States and 50 million *kwh* for Western Europe.[74]

Yet it is a temptation to exaggerate the extent or usability of Africa's resources. Measured by the value of its mineral *output*, Africa ranks last among all the continents. It is short on fuels to support massive industrialization. Africa has vast forest reserves, but only about one-third of them are classified as

*"Underdevelopment" is an ambiguous concept. If by underdevelopment is meant *a nation's capacity to raise its economic levels significantly*, then perhaps the United States is the most "underdeveloped" nation on the globe; and in this same sense, Soviet Russia also is high on the list. Yet there is a tendency in the United States and the West generally to use the term "underdeveloped" as a synonym for poor or economically backward. Every country that could be called the latter is not necessarily underdeveloped. A leading authority has said with respect to Africa that "many observers doubt the capacity of the region as a whole to support a larger number of people at present," not to mention Africa's ability to achieve *higher* living standards. Kimble, *op. cit.*, I, 121–122.

"productive"; the remainder are "inaccessible" in the light of modern technology.[75] Similarly, Africa's luxuriant tropical flora do *not*, as is widely supposed, indicate great expanses of fertile soil. In reality, Africa's soil tends to be highly infertile, seriously damaged by extensive erosion and leaching from tropical rains, devoid of key minerals, and lacking adequate water supplies to support greatly expanded agriculture. Chronic diseases and scourges—like malaria, bilharzia (a debilitating intestinal parasite), the tsetse fly, and locust plagues— create an inhospitable environment for humans and livestock. Towering above all other problems besetting Africa's internal development is the absence of an internal transportation system that can knit diverse parts of the continent together, assist in overcoming ingrained provincialism, and facilitate the exchange of goods and services.[76]

For centuries, Africa's chief economic pursuit has been, and is likely to remain, agriculture. Nomadic herding, forestry, and primitive agriculture constitute the way of life for most of the continent's population. It is to agriculture, rather than to industry, that most Africans must look for any improvement in their standard of living. Yet agricultural techniques remain extremely primitive and unproductive. Thus, one African farmer can tend 2–3 acres only, while an American farmer is cultivating 50–200 acres. Put differently, in Africa it takes from 2 to 10 people to raise enough food to supply their own needs along with that of one other person; an American farmer can normally grow enough food for about 25 people.[77] The African farmer must contend with a combination of adverse factors that presents a far more formidable challenge than that confronting the agricultural peasant in Asia or Latin America. Kimble, for example, has observed:

> Take the matter of water. Where water is abundant, as it is in the forest belt, the settler faces the problem of protecting his crops from waterlogging and flooding. . . . Where it is scarce . . . the problem is how to protect his animals from seasonal thirst and starvation, and how to make the most of what water he has with the technical and financial means at his disposal.

Such considerations convince qualified observers that attempts to raise African agricultural productivity face a long uphill struggle.[78] Another authority has said that many African states likely will never have "viable" economies, if by that conception is meant the "capacity of an economy to maintain a customary or expected level of income, or to increase it. . . ."[79]

African economic prospects are rendered even more dubious by projected population statistics. With a present population of around 240 million—and with a declining death rate achieved by expanded health services—Africa is expected to *double* its population within the next half-century.[80] These data suggest why one of the most important dimensions of American foreign policy, and of Western relations generally with Africa, has become the matter of economic and technical assistance to assist the Africans in overcoming some of the most challenging economic problems faced by any region on the globe.

The American "Discovery" of Africa

"As Africa was the last continent to be opened to the world at large," writes Rupert Emerson, "so it was the last to be discovered by the United States. . . ."[81] Africa perhaps remained "the dark continent" more for Americans than for any other group in Western society. Indicative of America's lack of interest in, and knowledge about, Africa is the fact that as late as 1958 the United States had more Foreign Service officials in West Germany alone than in the whole of Africa. If official recognition of the importance of Africa has been slow, within recent years it has been almost frenziedly rapid. For many years, African affairs tended to be dealt with by officials whose primary concern was Western Europe or the Middle East. Finally, in 1958, the State Department set up a Bureau of African Affairs. Besides this new agency, other State Department and governmental agencies became heavily involved with African affairs—like the Bureau of International Organization Affairs in the State Department, that was keenly aware of the greatly enhanced role of African states in the United Nations.[82] In addition, educational exchange programs with Africa have expanded significantly. For the academic year 1961–1962, almost 4000 African students from some 41 different countries were studying in the United States—an increase of 39 percent over the previous year. A similar pattern can be discerned in American propaganda activities in Africa. In 1953, there was only one officer in the United States Information Agency assigned exclusively to Africa! By 1962, USIA planned to operate 43 information centers in Africa,

with 133 officers and almost 500 local employees. The Peace Corps, from its inception in 1961, has been strongly oriented toward Africa. Out of almost 4400 members, nearly a third served in Africa in 1963.[83]

MAJOR ISSUES IN AFRO-AMERICAN RELATIONS

Afro-American relations in the contemporary period have tended to pivot around four central issues. We shall examine each of these issues in some detail, noting its implications for American foreign policy.

American Economic Aid Programs in Africa

From 1946 through mid-1963, the United States provided a total of $2.25 billion in economic assistance to 33 African countries. The largest source has come from the International Cooperation Administration (ICA) and its successor, the Agency for International Development (AID), for technical assistance, development loans, and other forms of aid. Additional aid has come from the Food for Peace Program, that distributes agricultural surpluses abroad, from Export-Import Bank loans, and the Peace Corps. These figures do not take account of the fact that the United States paid approximately one-third of the cost of some $1 billion in United Nations assistance extended to Africa in roughly this same period.[84]

Yet, among all regional recipients of American foreign assistance, Africa's share has been the smallest. Thus for 17 years down to 1964, Africa received only about 3 percent of the total of nearly $72 billion, while Europe received about 40 percent and the Far East about 20 percent. Moreover, American assistance has tended to be heavily *concentrated* in a few African countries. Particularly in the 1950s, a preponderant share of American loans and grants went to South Africa and Northern and Southern Rhodesia. By the early 1960s, the bulk of American economic assistance went to Algeria, the Congo (Leopoldville), Morocco, Tunisia, Liberia, and Nigeria.[85] Justifying this pattern of aid, an American official declared in 1962 that in Africa south of the Sahara "most of our development assistance is concentrated in . . . countries that have real development potential and give promise of promoting moderation and responsibility in African politics."[86]

The limited quantity of over-all American

assistance to Africa throughout the postwar period is not surprising. As we emphasized earlier, the United States had little direct contact with Africa down to the postwar era. Moreover, while much of Africa remained in a colonial status, the United States and other countries were normally required to channel their activities on the African scene through Britain, France, and other colonial powers. Down to the 1950s, the United States also found itself hard-pressed to provide needed assistance to areas, such as Greece and Turkey or Southeast Asia, that were prime targets for communist expansionism and subversion. Consequently, in recent years the percentage of American aid earmarked for Africa has grown more rapidly than for any other region, in contrast with areas like Europe, where American assistance has been steadily declining. Economic aid to Africa, for example, in 1963 was some $526 million, as against $350 million in 1962. In the light of Africa's pressing needs, it is logical to expect that its share of American economic assistance will continue to grow throughout the years ahead.

By the 1960s another factor engendered this expectation. The Communist bloc also had "discovered" Africa and was making a concerted effort to win friends on this continent. It was estimated that the USSR and its satellites had, within a very few years, extended close to $1 billion in economic assistance to needy African countries, chiefly Algeria, Ethiopia, Ghana, Guinea, Mali, Morocco, the Somali Republic, the Sudan, and Tunisia. The Kremlin's cultivation of close economic ties with leftist regimes that governed Ghana, Guinea, and Mali was not surprising. That the USSR and its satellites should extend assistance to monarchies, like those prevailing in Morocco and Ethiopia, or to an avowedly pro-Western government, like Tunisia, however, was designed to "prove" the absence of "strings" in Communist aid programs and to challenge the West even in those countries of Africa most closely identified with its policies.

What goals motivated American assistance programs to the newly independent countries of Africa? Certain objectives—like raising living standards, improving health conditions, expanding educational opportunities, and strengthening governmental administration—were more or less common to all programs. The United States had an obvious interest in fostering stability and in encouraging economic programs, both because these were legitimate

goals in their own right and because they were intimately related to the maintenance of *political* stability on the African scene. Many factors would no doubt influence the future course of "African democracy," but one of these surely would be the success achieved by newly-created governments in solving chronic and formidable economic problems.

America was also developing an expanding stake in Africa's economic future. An economically developing Africa provided an expanding market for American goods. In 1961, for example, the United States exported over $800 million in goods and services to Africa; it bought close to $600 million in African imports. While many imports from Africa were consumer commodities like coffee and cocoa, increasingly the United States depended upon access to uranium, ferroalloys and other ores, crude rubber, nonferrous metals, and precious stones (especially industrial diamonds) from the African continent. American private investment was also finding promising opportunities in Africa. In the decade 1950–1960, such investments tripled in value, reaching close to $1 billion by the end of the period.[87]

Besides such general objectives, the goals of the United States were often heavily conditioned by the context within individual African countries. Thus an executive agency defined American interests in Africa on a country-by-country basis. The document justified aid for Ethiopia on the grounds that it "occupies an important geographical position in Africa"; that it maintains friendly relations with most of the Afro-Asian nations and has made important contributions to the over-all western position" in world affairs; and that it provided troops for the UN operation in South Korea, thereby providing "a symbol of resistance to aggression." Aid to Ghana was justified by essentially different criteria. Ghana was the "newest independent nation in Africa and a member of the British Commonwealth"; as the first African country to gain independence in the recent period, it became "the focus of attention of peoples all over the world who have an interest in the ability of Africans to govern themselves and to create a viable, politically stable state." Most significantly, American policies toward Ghana are held to be "an indicator of American intentions toward new African states." Aid to Somalia, on the other hand, was justified on the grounds that the country "is currently oriented toward the West and it is hoped the new state will continue to support western ideals after independence [in 1960]." Maintaining "economic viability" was deemed an overriding problem confronting this new state.[88]

Recognizing that the goals of American foreign assistance must be adapted to local and regional influences prevailing throughout Africa, we may nevertheless note certain other objectives that have motivated these programs, particularly in the era of "peaceful coexistence" between East and West. American foreign aid has been motivated by an aim that we shall discuss in more detail at a later stage: exclusion of cold-war antagonisms from African soil. America, said Assistant Secretary of State for African Affairs G. Mennen Williams in 1963, had "a fundamental interest in the development of a free and independent Africa." American officials were convinced that "good government and internal stability are principal bulwarks of freedom and independence"; "economic and social progress is the only real security for a free world order." Along with Africans themselves, Washington desired that "the cold war not be introduced into the continent. . . . Thus, in the area of strategic self-preservation, our interests and those of the African states coincide."[89]

The United States has also been interested, since the beginning of Africa's independence period, in fostering harmonious relations between African states and their former colonial masters. American aid "makes continued major reliance on the former metropoles politically feasible, and therefore helps to maintain moderate pro-Western regimes in power" on the African scene. Much as such countries require outside assistance, *too much* dependence by African governments upon former colonial powers might generate internal political tensions. As one American foreign aid official expressed it: "Many African leaders find it politically imperative to diversify their sources of assistance in order to counter charges of submitting to neo-colonial dependence."*

* The nature of African economic dependence upon Europe is underscored by the aid provided to African states by the members of the European Economic Community (EEC). From 1958–1962, EEC countries extended a total of $580 million in aid to African states associated with them; they have committed themselves to extend $730 million to these countries in the period 1963–1967. In addition, certain countries provide "bilateral" aid to Africa. In 1962, for example, France extended $675 million in aid and the United Kingdom, $152 million. EEC also offers a kind of "aid" to African countries in the form of price supports for African commodities. Cited in Goldschmidt, *op. cit.*, p. 154.

American aid to Africa within recent years has also been governed by a realization among policy officials that has not always been shared by the American public at large. This is the extent to which many regimes in Africa—particularly those led by Western-trained elites—are *inherently suspect* by the African masses because of their orientation toward the West. Such regimes are, so to speak, "on trial" with the masses. If they fail, they are likely to be superseded either by movements that are "traditionalist" and highly suspicious of *any* foreign government, or by regimes that favor more intimate economic, military, and political ties with the Communist bloc. This fact has dictated two basic premises of American foreign aid. One is that the United States must continually "identify" with the aspirations of the African masses for social and economic progress, and must provide tangible assistance to make this possible. If moderate regimes are to survive in Africa, one official has said, they must constantly "demonstrate to their peoples, in concrete and understandable terms, the advantages of cooperation with the West and of middle-of-the-road approaches to the solution of their current pressing problems."[90]

The other premise requires somewhat more detailed attention. It grows out of intensified Communist bloc economic activities in Africa. A cardinal tenet of Soviet Russia's and Red China's approach to the underdeveloped world is the idea that Communist countries "understand" the problems inherent in the quest for economic modernization, that Communist experience is far more applicable to the problems confronting Morocco or Guinea or Tanganyika than is Western experience, and that Moscow and Peiping stand ready to supply the needs of countries which request their assistance. Concurrently, the Communist bloc has unceasingly denounced Western aid activities in Africa as "neo-colonialism" that seeks merely to perpetuate African economic bondage to the West and to control African political and diplomatic destinies. Throughout a region that has experienced Western domination but has

One new African country, the Republic of Chad, has used EEC funds to construct 50 bush schools, 38 hospitals of different kinds, 5 social centers, 81 dispensaries, and 185 wells. In 1963, 18 African states signed a new five-year aid pact with EEC. *The New York Times*, January 20, 1964. Europe has been, and in the view of American officials will likely remain, the principal supplier of development funds for Africa.

never experienced—and perhaps does not believe there is even the danger it can experience—Communist domination, such allegations often fall upon receptive ears.

Many of these considerations were highlighted by developments in the Republic of Guinea. Alone among the former French dependencies in West Africa, on September 28, 1958, Guinea chose complete independence from France. Its decision generated extremely tense relations between Conakry and Paris throughout the months that followed. In an obvious desire not to offend its French ally, the United States delayed recognizing this new African state; when the State Department finally did open its embassy, it sent only two officials to Conakry. Meanwhile, Guinea—cut off entirely and abruptly from French assistance, and faced with severe economic dislocations—initially requested the United States to supply military aid and other forms of assistance. Washington evinced little interest in this request and delayed replying to it. At length, President Touré turned to the Communist bloc for assistance. Predictably, the response from this quarter was dramatically enthusiastic. Swarms of Communist technicians entered Guinea, and a total of $127 million in aid was channeled to this new African state.

These developments aroused deep apprehension in the United States—leading official and public sources to conclude that Guinea was on the verge of passing behind the iron curtain. Communism, it was widely believed, had now established a "bridgehead" in West Africa; Touré was depicted as an "African Castro." Guinea's large supplies of bauxite (uranium ore) made the communist penetration of Guinea more than ordinarily alarming to Western observers.

Subsequent events revealed that such Western judgments were premature and ill-founded, reflecting a basic lack of understanding of African nationalism and of the derivative concept, African neutralism. Discerning a Communist-instigated plot against his regime, at the end of 1961 President Touré drastically curtailed Communist activities in his country. Eventually, he expelled the Soviet ambassador from the country. The period that followed, as one commentator put it, witnessed "the growth of warm relations between radical Guinea and the capitalist United States."[91] While Guinea continued to accept Communist aid, the amount tapered off; at the same time Conakry made known its desire to receive

expanded Western assistance. Faced with massive economic problems, Guinea early in 1964 asked the United States to supply $45 million worth of assistance. If it might not be able to count on this entire sum, Guinea was aware that some American assistance was almost certainly forthcoming. In the American view, Touré's regime had demonstrated itself to be an "experiment in complete independence"— a verdict that had been reenforced by Touré's refusal during the Cuban crisis of 1962 to permit Soviet aircraft to land in Guinea, thereby indirectly assisting the American naval blockade of Castro's government.[92]

The Guinean experience provided a sobering test of official and public American conceptions about African nationalism. Two conclusions seemed incontestable. One was that even leftist regimes like Touré's Guinea, along with most other African countries, *preferred* harmonious relations, including economic and military ties, with the West, although such ties might not be *exclusively* with the West. The second was that African states like Guinea were determined to raise their foreign assistance requirements where they could; when their requests were ignored or rebuffed by the West, African countries would turn to the Communist bloc. By 1963, an American official could therefore justify continued assistance to Guinea, because this path "offered a significant alternative to aid from the Communist bloc" and because it contributed to the American goal of encouraging certain African countries "to reestablish its ties with France and the free world." The American refusal to provide aid, on the other hand, could only facilitate the Kremlin's goal of making Guinea "succumb to Communist subversive efforts" and would deny this key African state an "adequate basis . . . to compare the disadvantages of bloc aid with the advantages of a more extensive U.S. aid."*

---

* For the views of executive officials, see: Senate Appropriations Committee, *Mutual Security Appropriations for 1961*, Hearings, 86th Congress, 2nd Session (Washington: 1961), p. 322; and House Foreign Affairs Committee, *Foreign Assistance Act of 1963*, Hearings, 87th Congress, 1st Session (Washington: 1963), p. 190.

More detailed treatments of developments in Guinea since 1958 are provided in David Hapgood, "Guinea's First Five Years," *Current History*, **45** (December, 1963), 355–361; Peter Judd, *African Independence* (New York: Dell, 1962), pp. 286–326; George W. Shepherd, Jr., *The Politics of African Nationalism* (New York: Praeger, 1962), 98–106; James Cameron, *The African Revolution* (New York: Random House, 1961), pp. 143–154.

Varieties of "African Socialism"

"These aims," Dr. Nkrumah of Ghana has said in describing the goals of his regime, "embrace the creation of a welfare state based upon African socialist principles, adapted to suit Ghanaian conditions. . . ."[93] Support for "African socialism" has come to be regarded as an indispensable feature of belief in nationalism by many contemporary African leaders. African socialism, one commentator has written, in "one variety or another is indeed the dominant post-independence ideology" of the African continent.[94] It is widely believed to be an integral part of the broader idea of "African democracy," espoused by the political elites governing contemporary Africa. "If I thought Africans could not produce a democracy," Leopold Senghor of Senegal has declared, "I would leave politics."[95]

If concepts like African socialism and African democracy are prominent features of the current African political landscape, there is widespread agreement among exponents of these ideas that they differ fundamentally both from comparable Western concepts and from those advocated behind the iron curtain. Thus, Spiro is only one among many students of African affairs to insist that "there is something unique about the political *process* in the new African systems" and to emphasize that the very terminology of political discourse has connotations that are peculiar to Africa. Western, particularly American, failure to understand this fact often leads to distorted conceptions about the political evolution of Africa and the ideological character of many of its governments.[96]

Let us focus upon the term "African socialism." Several key facts about this concept must be kept in mind. Socialism on the African scene, in the first place, is (by Western criteria) an *heretical* doctrine, fitting none of the usual categories Westerners are prone to associate with it. The "socialism" of Senghor of Senegal, for example, is a mixture of Marxism, Christian humanitarianism, and Negritude—the last emphasizing race-consciousness (not *racism*) and calling upon Negroes to take pride in their past."* Dr. Nkrumah of Ghana calls himself a "Christian Marxist." For President

* Negritude is discussed more fully in: Vernon McKay, *Africa in World Politics* (New York: Harper & Row, 1963), pp. 124–131; Ezekiel Mphahlele, *The African Image* (New York: Praeger, 1962), pp. 25–41. McKay's recent study is one of the most able discussions of Africa available.

Touré of Guinea, socialism has equally diverse sources. He, along with many other African leaders, differentiates "African socialism" from Marxism (particularly Soviet Marxism). Thus, Touré rejects the key Marxist idea of the "class struggle." The only struggle that Africans feel is applicable to their continent is the struggle against colonialism and its frequent handmaiden, racial discrimination. Touré, like other African spokesmen who are attracted by the idealism and egalitarianism they identify as goals of Marxism, nevertheless severely criticizes communism because it is a "Western" ideology, relying almost entirely upon Western experience in its attempt to evolve universally applicable "laws" of human society.[97] Thus, however much Marxism may be a tributary of "African socialism," Segal has cautioned, "It would be difficult to imagine a more calamitous response to contemporary Guinea than the assumption, made in some Western capitals, that Sekou Touré himself is a Communist and that Guinea emerged . . . as a Soviet satellite."[98] The admonition applies broadly throughout the contemporary African scene.

For the concept of African socialism is an often illogical amalgam of diverse, sometimes contradictory, elements. If it incorporates certain features of Marxism, it also draws heavily from movements like the American New Deal, the programs of the British Labour party, European Socialist parties, Christian idealism and ethical precepts, and (in many parts of Africa) Islamic religious and political thought, and—perhaps above all—*traditional and indigenous* ideas in African society. For the Islamic regions of Africa, the concept of socialism derives from belief in the "Islamic community," in which the Moslem's rights are always related to, and dependent upon, the community's rights.

For many proponents of the doctrine, however, the dominant element in African socialism is the body of African traditions upon which political elites are drawing for their contemporary ideologies. Thus the Tanganyikan head of state, Julius Nyerere, has emphasized the fact that: "The traditional African community was a small one, and the African could not think of himself apart from his community . . . he saw no struggle between his own interests and those of the community. . . ." In Nyerere's view, pre-colonial African society exemplified three key ideas advocated by contemporary African socialists: communalism, egalitarianism, and classlessness. This fact might lead Westerners to conclude that the

African is therefore a "natural Communist." To the contrary, Nyerere and other African leaders have insisted, an altogether fundamental distinction must be drawn between being "communistic" and being "communitary," between favoring the "commune" and the "community." Africans broadly advocate what we may call *community-ism*, while rejecting much of the Marxist analysis of, and program for, human society.[99]

In practice, African socialism has meant, and undoubtedly will continue to mean, that *governments* on the continent will take primary responsibility for economic planning and development. This is guaranteed by another fact which, as much as any other, dictates acceptance of an African socialistic approach: the sheer *magnitude* of Africa's economic problems. On no continent are income levels or standards of living as low as in much of Africa. Few other regions can match Africa in the gravity of problems that must be overcome in the quest for "modernization." Moreover, extensive governmental participation in economic affairs is no innovation for Africa; this was almost invariably the practice during the colonial period. In continuing this approach, Africans are largely carrying on a practice European colonial administrations followed in an earlier era. In addition, throughout Africa, as in the Middle East, Asia, and Latin America, "capitalism" has often become an opprobrious term—suggesting absentee landlords and moneylenders, economic elites who amass great wealth in the midst of grinding poverty, or foreign corporations who exercise vast political power. The relative absence of private capital virtually precludes a belief in *capitalism* in Africa as a viable approach to economic and social problems.[100]

Americans, perhaps more than other Westerners, have failed to understand the nature and roots of "African socialism"; they have often tended to equate it with communism or other movements with which it bears a superficial resemblance. Until their understanding of such concepts becomes more discriminating, the American approach to African problems will rest upon misconceptions and will often yield highly unsatisfactory results.

Colonialism in Africa

Addressing the United Nations in 1959, President Touré of Guinea stated that the fundamental principle which would determine African relations with East and West could be stated simply: "Yes or No—are you for the liberation of Africa?"[101] If all African leaders would not agree fully with an Egyptian view that "colonialism is the basic cause for war,"[102] there is a basic unanimity for the belief that colonialism is at, or near, the top of the list of African diplomatic priority. The first step in improving Western relations with African countries, one commentator has written, is that

> . . . the Western powers must realize that in most of Africa "colonialism," with its connotation of a ruling European group and subordinate African masses, is widely held to be *the* worst enemy. Communism is a secondary peril, and *apartheid* is to most Africans a greater danger than the dictatorship of the proletariat.[103]

Having largely gained their independence from Western control in the postwar era, African societies remain committed to two goals: the rapid achievement of independence for those African dependencies, like Angola and Northern Rhodesia, that have not yet become free; and militant opposition to the *reimposition* of direct or indirect colonial domination over African affairs. The latter goal is aimed at preventing "neocolonialism"—described by a Libyan official as "more dangerous and of much stronger effect" than colonialism, since "it embodies all the disadvantages of colossal colonialism, and, in addition, intellectual slavery."[104] Dr. Nkrumah of Ghana, at the forefront of the African fight against "neocolonialism," has defined it by saying:

> The Imperialists of today endeavour to achieve their ends not merely by military means, but by economic penetration, cultural assimilation, and subversive activities even to the point of inspiring and promoting assassinations and civil strife.[105]

An apparent strategy of the neocolonialists, in this view, is to encourage the Balkanization of Africa into a multitude of small, weak African states who can easily be manipulated by outside powers, and whose economic and military destinies can be controlled by forging tight links with Western organizations like the European Common Market.[106] Another technique used by neocolonialists is the inclusion of certain African countries (like some of the former states in French West Africa) in military alliances, that perpetuate a condition of military and diplomatic "dependence."*

---

* Admittedly, Nkrumah's views are not universally shared by African leaders—particularly not by those West African states that maintain close

Almost all African leaders are mindful of the traditional American opposition to colonialism, as symbolized by Presidents Wilson and Franklin D. Roosevelt. The United States has no "colonial record" in Africa; African governments also know that Washington has often encouraged the prompt liquidation of the British, French, and other empires on the African continent. Yet such facts do not prevent African governments, like the revolutionary regime that gained control of Zanzibar in 1964, from labeling the United States as the "leader of world imperialism and colonialism."[107] Frequently, Americans have succumbed to the temptation to dismiss such judgments as untypical of prevalent African opinion or as merely another tiresome instance of Communist-inspired propaganda. Admittedly, the American position on colonialism is seldom condemned so harshly by most responsible African governments. Yet, when even Emperor Haile Selassie in Ethiopia has called for the use of force to remove colonialism from the African scene, we may be sure that African opposition to colonialism is endemic and that America's policies on this issue are subjected to very close scrutiny by *all* African countries.[108] An American official has called attention to a widespread tendency in Africa and elsewhere to believe that the Americans "are lined up with the Western European powers" and that the United States will "always support . . . any European country when it has a colonial problem."[109] Whether such a conclusion is fully warranted is not our concern. But that Africans widely *believe* it is a justified conclusion can hardly be contested.

To the African mind, this verdict is supported by a number of facts. One is that America's NATO partners, particularly France and Portugal, have unquestionably used arms supplied by the United States against nationalist movements and regimes in Africa. A corollary of this claim is that the United States has done little or nothing to restrain its NATO allies from using arms aid for this purpose. Justified or not, the African assumption has been that Washington had the power

to stop this practice, but has refused to use its power. This failure, in turn, has been interpreted as signifying American indifference toward colonial contests in Africa, in spite of ideological professions favoring independence for political dependencies. Thus, even normally pro-Western African leaders, like Sir Abubakar T. Balewa, the Prime Minister of Nigeria, have urged African countries to bring pressure to bear upon the United States to restrain its European allies.[110]

African states also believe that American support in their present fight against colonialism has been feeble, qualified, and generally ineffectual. In African eyes, America has assumed a *de facto* position on colonialism closely resembling the condition of "neutralism" toward the cold war which (at least in the Eisenhower-Dulles era) was roundly condemned in Washington! Irrespective of its intentions and professions, the United States is seen as having tacitly aided colonialism by failing to denounce it unequivocally, to vote consistently in the United Nations against it, and to insist that its allies cease using American arms aid against African nationalist movements. Citing the fact that the North Atlantic Treaty proclaims the attachment of its members to "safeguard freedom" and to uphold the "principles of democracy, individual liberty and the rule of law," African nationalists have called upon its signatories to apply these principles to the colonial contest in Africa.[111]

Recent American statements explaining the nation's viewpoints toward colonialism in the modern period also generate little enthusiasm among Africans. The following provides an example: "The United States has consistently sought to promote the orderly evolution of dependent peoples to self-government. At the same time, we have been aware that premature independence and irresponsible nationalism may present grave dangers to the independent peoples themselves, as well as to the whole free world."[112] Africans tend to view such statements as equivocal, hedged, innocuous, and generally in marked contrast with the ringing declarations directed against the communist menace to freedom throughout the world. Occasionally, as when the United States voted in the UN in 1961 against Portuguese colonialism in Angola, Africans have vocally applauded America's position and have commended the United States for adhering to its own highest traditions in global affairs. To date, however, such instances of wholehearted

---

links with France. Thus, the President of the Ivory Coast Assembly, Phillippe Yace, said in 1961: "Europe cannot be without Africa, and Africa is aware of the necessity of allying itself with Europe." Quoted in the *Morning News* (Khartoum, Sudan), June 23, 1961. Early in 1964, even so outstanding an African nationalist as Julius Nyerere of Tanganyika was compelled to call in British troops to deal with an army mutiny in his country.

American support have been regarded by Africans as exceptional, even if they are seen as promising indications of the over-all direction of American policies.[113]

The African assessment, it is necessary to reiterate, is not presented here as necessarily reflecting a fair or accurate appraisal of American policy. For their part, Africans no doubt are insensitive to the many diverse strands that must be woven into American policy, such as the need to preserve maximum Western unity. Nor can it be denied that Americans often take a different position from Africans concerning the "evils" of colonialism; frequently, Africans are unwilling to concede *any* beneficial consequences from the colonial era. In that respect, colonialism is to Africans what communism is to Americans! Africans are also prone (in company with many other societies) to exaggerate the scope and effectiveness of American power and to forget that America can no more "dictate" to its increasingly strong European allies than it can to African countries themselves. The main point, however, is that the African mentality about colonialism is intense and real. An understanding of it is, therefore, the first step in evolving an American approach that lays the groundwork for more intimate cooperation between the United States and African countries.

African "Positive Neutralism" and Nonalignment

As with the newly independent Arab states, African countries that have recently won their freedom tend to regard a foreign policy of noninvolvement with cold-war blocs—variously defined as a position of "neutralism," "positive neutralism" or "nonalignment"—as an integral feature of true national sovereignty. Expressing a viewpoint pervasive throughout Africa, one observer has said of Guinea:

> Guinea desires to be friends with East and West, to seek help from anyone who will give it, and to avoid embroilment in a worldwide ideological conflict while at the same time creating a revolutionary one-party socialist state.

Guinea's animating impulse in foreign affairs, President Touré has explained, can be expressed simply: "We want to be ourselves—not drawn to either bloc."[114] President Keita in nearby Mali echoed this idea when he declared that Mali refused to become "a pawn of this or that bloc" in diplomatic affairs; citizens of his country "realize that to make our country a satellite is against our traditions of honour and dignity."[115] Lest it be imagined that such ideas are dominant only in regimes that are conspicuous for their anti-Westernism, it must be emphasized that openly pro-Western African governments, like those in Nigeria and Tanganyika, along with governments that have not yet experienced sweeping nationalist revolutions, like Morocco and Ethiopia, espouse a basically identical foreign policy credo. Emperor Haile Selassie of Ethiopia, for example, has repeatedly voiced his "independence" of either the West or the Communist bloc; he has underscored this determination by accepting aid from both camps.[116] Similarly, pro-Western Nigeria very early committed itself to a policy of nonalignment and of "independence" in foreign policy formulation. Premier Balewa has said: "We consider it wrong for the Nigerian Federal Government to associate itself as a matter of routine with any of the power blocs. . . . This freedom of action will be an essential feature of our policy."[117] Following this policy, Nigeria broke diplomatic relations with France in 1961, after Paris persisted, in the face of widespread African protests, to carry out nuclear tests in the Sahara.

African neutralist viewpoints thus closely parallel those prevailing throughout the Arab world and Asia. With Nasser of Egypt, Nehru of India, and Sukarno of Indonesia, African leaders contend that a policy of neutralism or nonalignment has often been misconstrued by the West. Such a policy does *not* entail or contemplate "neutrality"—either in its traditional international law meaning or in the sense of moral-ethical indifference about global issues. Thus, a leading Nigerian political figure has publicly said that his country follows an "independent" and "not a neutral attitude" in approaching international problems. President Keita of Mali is but one African spokesman to differentiate repeatedly between "neutralism" and "neutrality," the latter suggesting a kind of diplomatic *equilibrisme* or "balancing act" by which African states try to maintain a delicately poised "middle" position between East and West. Not only would any African state stand to "lose its entire personality" by attempting such "neutrality"; tactically, this course would be disastrous since such a state "can be blackmailed by both blocs. . . ." In the same vein, Nkrumah of Ghana has insisted that nonalignment must not be equated with "negative neutralism" by which a nation "withdraws itself entirely from the international problems of peace and war and avoids taking a definitive stand on issues which affect the balance of power in the world today." The King of Morocco has likewise contended that: "Our neutralism is dynamic and alive; its sole concern is to save human values and to promote the peace and progress of the human race."[118] Such considerations induce African leaders to prefer terms like "positive neutralism" or (if the philosophy must be expressed negatively) "nonalignment" to describe the diplomatic stance they have adopted. However it is designated, it does not involve withdrawal from international politics, noninvolvement in attempts to resolve important global issues, lack of concern about events affecting world peace and security, or willingness to leave the settlement of outstanding diplomatic questions solely to the two cold-war coalitions. Even outspoken friends of the West, like Sir Abubakar Balewa of Nigeria, have insisted that although Nigeria knows its "true friends" in the world community, his nation "refused to inherit the prejudices of anyone" and had opened its "hands of friendship to all those who respect our sovereignty."[119]

A diplomatic credo of nonalignment, no less in Africa than in the Arab world and Asia, is a highly variegated concept, often accommodating a wide range of policies and attitudes toward specific international issues. If a majority of African states adheres to nonalignment, these states can and do differ among themselves—and with other neutralist governments outside Africa—on particular questions demanding policy decisions. Ghana and Guinea differed radically upon the correct strategy to be followed toward the Congo Crisis in the early 1960s, especially after the death of the extreme African nationalist Patrice Lumumba. Morocco and West African states to the south have disagreed sharply respecting the former's claims to Mauritania (formerly Spanish Morocco). In like manner, Nigeria and Ghana have taken different positions on Pan-Africanism and on the steps best designed to achieve "African unity." Former members of the French Community, like the Ivory Coast, have advocated the retention of close economic links with France and with the European Common Market; members of the "Casablanca group" (principally Ghana, Guinea, and Mali) have denounced EEC as a neocolonialist plot to perpetuate African economic subjugation. In East Africa, Ethiopia and Somalia have resorted to open warfare in the assertion of their rival border claims. Tanganyika has insisted that an "East African Federation" ought to be the first step toward achievement of African unity, in the face of Guinea's and Ghana's claims to lead that movement. In brief, there is no convincing evidence that common espousal of nonalignment in foreign affairs has led to the creation of anything resembling a strongly united "African bloc" or over-all African unanimity in approaching many local and regional problems, or has inhibited African states from being guided by their own national interests.

That African adherents to nonalignment do not comprise a homogeneous diplomatic bloc is neither surprising nor incompatible with their neutralist professions. For the doctrine of nonalignment is intended principally to define African attitudes and policy toward *cold-war antagonists*. On the East-West conflict, there is substantial agreement among African countries, however much they may differ on local and regional questions. Nonalignment, for example, permits all African countries to maintain contacts with the Western or Communist blocs, or with both concurrently, in cultural affairs, economic aid, trade, and other activities in which African states are keenly interested. It permits voting with either the East or the West, or with neither, in the United Nations as African states are guided by their own conception of their diplomatic interests. Widespread unanimity also exists throughout Africa upon another tenet of nonalignment: the cold war must not be "extended" to the African continent. This means that African states have manifested considerable unity in opposing intervention in episodes like the Congo crisis by either Western or Communist forces and in opposing French nuclear testing in the Sahara region. It means that, as a rule, they oppose military links with cold-war antagonists. It means that their views toward East and West alike are likely to be shaped by how vigorously each cold-war bloc champions African causes, such as the termination of colonialism on the continent or support for a militant stand against the *apartheid* policies of South Africa.

Yet if African states agree broadly on these principles, they nevertheless find ample scope within the concept of nonalignment to permit differences, at least in degree and emphasis, upon how the concept is to be applied in specific cases. Early in 1964, for example, the west African state of Gabon called upon French troops to put down an attempted coup seeking to overthrow the government of President Leon Mba. Paris immediately supplied the necessary forces, and they were successful in restoring Mba to power. Similarly, in this period Nyerere's government in Tanganyika was compelled to call upon London to furnish troops to suppress an army mutiny. The newly independent government of Zanzibar likewise permitted an American space radar station to be operated upon its soil.* And Liberia has similarly been a large recipient of American military aid. Conversely, other African states interpreted nonalignment as permitting heavy reliance upon the Communist bloc in the sphere of military supplies and assistance. Thus, Guinea, Ghana, Morocco, and Mali have been conspicuous as recipients of Communist bloc military assistance.

Differences in the neutralist orientations of African countries were highlighted by the appearance in the early 1960s of three important groupings among newly independent African governments. In December, 1960, twelve of the former French dependencies in West Africa met to form the "Brazzaville group.** Led by the Ivory Coast, this group favored close relations with France and generally followed a pro-Western (or at least, not vocally anti-Western) position in global affairs. The Brazzaville group was in turn expanded the following year into the "Monrovia group," in which Nigeria became the dominant voice.† From its inception, this group impressed Western observers by its "moderate" approach toward global and regional problems.

At the opposite pole was the more radical, more militantly anti-Western "Casablanca bloc" led by Ghana, Guinea, and Egypt (the United Arab Republic). This bloc evolved out of an earlier Ghana-Guinea-Mali Union in 1960; the following year, in a meeting in Casablanca, this union became the nucleus for a new group embracing these countries, along with Egypt, Morocco, and Libya. Subsequently, Libya removed itself from this constellation and joined the "Monrovia" grouping. Formed as a counterpoise to the pro-Western "Brazzaville" group, the Casablanca bloc quickly became conspicuous for its militant anticolonialism, its dedication to "African socialism," and in the Western view, for its over-all reputation as harboring the principal troublemakers on the African scene.‡

These different and often competitive regional groupings were destined to disappear in the face of the widespread African demand that they "melt gradually" into a new Organization of African Unity. Thus, in the summer of 1963, 32 foreign ministers from African countries endorsed this goal; Addis Ababa, the capital of Ethiopia, was selected as the permanent headquarters of the movement.[120] Yet it would be safe to predict that many of the diverse viewpoints that had divided the Casablanca from the Monrovia group would persist and that African "neutralism" would continue to be characterized by wide divergencies in the national policies of its adherents.

The American response to African neutralist tendencies has been part of its over-all response to neutralism globally. As we discovered in our discussion of the Arab world, during the Dulles-Eisenhower era, neutralism was in strong disfavor among American officials, as well as among the general public. Secretary of State Dulles branded a neutralist position "immoral"; the public tended to scorn it as merely diplomatic "fence-sitting," or as an "attempt to get the best of both worlds," or as reflecting a lack of "realism" in the foreign policy of its adherents. Since African states did not begin the march toward independence until the late 1950s, American misgivings about neutralism were directed less at African govern-

---

* African nationalists deplored such "neocolonialist" dependence as Gabon and Tanganyika tended to illustrate. Thus in Gabon, after Mba had been restored, a member of the political opposition asked: How "free is a country when a foreign power is the sole arbiter of when a coup is popular and when it is not?" He pointed out that, in similar circumstances in other former French dependencies (Congo Republic, Dahomey, and Togo), French forces had remained "neutral" in internal political contests. Such comments were not untypical reactions, particularly when the issue at stake in the political wrangling in Gabon was the degree of the country's continued dependence upon France. *The New York Times*, February 23, 1964.

** Its members were: Cameroon, Central African Republic, Chad, Congo Republic (Brazzaville), Dahomey, Gabon, Ivory Coast, Malagasy Republic, Mauritania, Niger, Senegal, and Upper Volta.

† Besides the original Brazzaville group, this new bloc also included Liberia, Nigeria, Sierra Leone, Somalia, and Togo; Tunisia, the Central African Republic, Gabon, Ethiopia, and Libya were also represented at the Monrovia gathering.

‡ The evolution and policies of the major regional groups on the African scene are discussed in detail in Erasmus H. Kloman, "African Unification Movements," in Norman Padelford and Rupert Emerson, *Africa and World Order* (New York: Praeger, 1963), pp. 119–136. This is a valuable series of essays, largely focusing upon Africa's external relations. See also Collin Legum, *Pan-Africanism* (New York: Praeger, 1962), pp. 65–81.

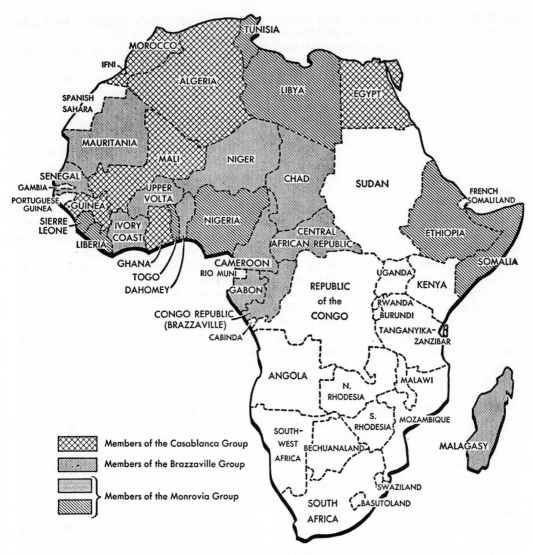

Regional Groupings in Africa.

ments than at those in Asia and the Middle East.

Our analysis of the same phenomenon in the Arab world indicated, however, that by the end of the 1950s, American policies toward neutralism began to change significantly. Thus, in 1960, a State Department official could declare:

> Because we share with the Africans their opposition to making their continent a pawn in the cold war struggle, we should welcome the African neutralist position, based as it is on neither pro-communism nor anti-Americanism.

In its relations with African countries, this official declared, the United States did not "wish to engage in a superficial popularity contest or merely react to Communist initiative, and assistance [for Africa] predicated on such motives would be distasteful to Africans as well."[121] Earlier, another State Department spokesman told the House Foreign Affairs Committee:

> In the long run, the orientation of Africa will depend on where the leaders and peoples feel their best interests lie. The ability of the West to secure the pro-Western orientation of Africa will, therefore, depend less on our ability to convince Africans of the dangers of communism than on our demonstrating to them in positive terms the advantages of cooperation with the West.[122]

The United States government, a high American official declared during a tour of Africa in 1961, was aware that newly independent African countries "will not become mere rubber stamps of any other people."[123] In marked contrast to the Dulles-Eisenhower period, even Defense Department officials now conceded that the United States had no wish to involve African states in cold-war military alliances. American arms aid to Africa was thus "directed at maintaining . . . internal security . . . from which will flower the economic and political developments those nations require."[124]

A test case of American policy toward African neutralist countries—particularly those African states that also maintained close ties with the Communist bloc—was provided by Ghana's Volta river project, involving construction of a large dam, electric power generating facilities, and an aluminum factory. Many parallels could be drawn between this undertaking and the Aswan High Dam project in Egypt. Economically, the Volta river scheme would become the symbol of Ghana's attempt to industrialize; diplomatically, the Western response to Accra's request for assistance would furnish eloquent testimony concerning the extent to which Washington was prepared to translate its new appraisal of neutralism into tangible programs benefitting leading neutralist countries.

For many months after Accra's request for $133 million in American assistance, it was apparent that the State Department found the Volta river project in many respects highly embarrassing. On the one hand, Dr. Nkrumah was at the forefront of the militant "Casablanca group" of African neutralists, that was widely regarded by American public opinion as epitomizing "pro-Communist neutralism." As an avowed "African socialist," Nkrumah was zealous in denouncing Western "imperialism" and "neo-colonialism," in castigating Western (particularly French) nuclear tests, in condemning the European Common Market, and in generally leading the van of African states that were highly critical of Western policies. At home, Nkrumah's Convention People's party steadily tightened its grip upon Ghana, reducing it to a one-party regime resembling those behind the iron curtain. On the other hand, such activities were seldom matched by equally vocal denunciations of Communist "imperialism" in Eastern Europe, outcries when the Soviet Union violated nuclear test-ban agreements, or apparent concern about

the Communist bloc's expansive tendencies in Germany or South Vietnam.

Yet these considerations were balanced, and eventually outweighed, by others which finally induced the State Department at the end of 1961 to grant Accra's request for aid. In the first place, the experience of the earlier Aswan Dam crisis in Egypt remained painfully vivid in the minds of American officials. Suppose the United States turned down Nkrumah's request. What would be the consequences of that decision? Based upon the experience of the Aswan Dam episode, they did not appear attractive. Nkrumah would almost certainly turn dramatically to the Communist bloc; the Kremlin would no doubt be willing and able to assist this now "rejected" African country. Moreover, American refusal would seem to confirm the worst Communist allegations about Western aid, to the effect that it carried "political strings" and that it required close adherence to Western policies by its recipients. Then there was a more long-range consideration that applied not only to Ghana, but to many other African countries as well. If one of America's ultimate goals in Africa was to prevent the spread of communism or other types of political extremism, and to prepare the ground for the emergence of democracy, would these goals be achieved by *refusing* Ghana's request for assistance? No well-informed student of African affairs would contend that Western apathy toward the African quest for higher economic productivity and improved standards of living facilitated attainment of this objective or in any significant way promoted American interests in Africa.

There was the additional fact that, by the early 1960s, American officials were more prepared than before to accept at face value assertions by African leaders that they had no desire to become the pawns of any great-power bloc. Whatever Americans might think of his internal and external policies, the evidence tended to support Nkrumah's claim:

> I and my party are well aware of the realities of our time. As we would not have British masters, so we would not have Russian masters, or any masters for that matter. It is not our intention to substitute one imperialism for another.[125]

Such viewpoints were echoed by the influential African publication *Drum*, which said that in accepting Communist aid, African countries had no intention of "making themselves pawns of communism." *Drum* unabashedly declared that African countries were "prepared to milk the communist cow as long as it makes no demand on them." In support of such claims, *Drum* and other African sources could assert with substantial correctness that African nationalism had never "been in alliance with communism" but had in fact "been its most deadly enemy. Wherever communist influence has made itself felt, African leaders have won the people away by offering them African Nationalism instead."*

Still another fact had become sometimes painfully evident to American officials in their assessment of the diplomatic orientation of African states. This was the extent to which visibly and unequivocally "pro-Western neutralist" governments in Africa often encountered sharp opposition precisely *because of their pro-Western inclination.* Ethiopia, for example, encountered widespread criticism throughout Africa because of its acceptance of the "Eisenhower Doctrine" in 1957, implying a readiness to depend upon the United States for its military security.[126] In West Africa, the government of Sir Abubakar T. Balewa in Nigeria faced much the same opposition. Its political critics claimed that "Nigeria cannot afford to cling to sterile policies [in foreign affairs] and expect to win the respect and confidence of Pan-African nationalism." Political opponents castigated Balewa's policies, because the Nigerian leader "behaves like one who is under the tutelage of Britain and subservient

to America"; the result was that "Nigeria cuts a sorry figure in the outside world and a detestable one in the eyes of all African nationalists."[127] The criticism continually directed at overtly pro-Western reigmes in Africa thus led to a paradoxical conclusion, expressed by an offiicial of Nyasaland: "the safest way of aligning with the West is not to align with the West."[128] Even in its relations with its admitted friends in Africa (not to speak of members of the Casablanca group), the West had to be extremely careful not to undercut the position of such governments at home or to make them vulnerable to the charge that they had lost their independence by associating themselves too conspicuously with the Western bloc—no surer course could be found for undermining the Western position in Africa and for opening the way to expanded communist penetration.

Thus, the American decision to assist with Ghana's Volta river scheme emerged in part as the result of a process that, more often than not, produces major foreign policy decisions. The State Department was confronted with a situation to which there was no ideal policy solution. If it did *not* aid Ghana, this move would unquestionably damage American relations with Africa and with neutralist countries generally. If it *did* aid Ghana, it would be assisting a regime about whose conduct Americans broadly had many reservations. It chose the latter course because, on balance, it risked the fewest deleterious consequences and at least held out the possibility of a gradual improvement in Ghanaian-American relations. Ideologically, the choice grew out of growing realization among executive officials that the contest with communism globally could be reduced to an elementary principle applying to such cases as Ghana. In President Kennedy's words: "We can welcome diversity—the Communists cannot. For we offer a world of choice —they offer the world of coercion and the way of the past shows clearly that freedom, not coercion, is the way of the future."[129]

* These considerations applied no less to Ghana than to so-called "pro-Western" African states. Thus, one American who spent two and one-half years in Ghana replied to widespread charges that Ghana had become "the first Soviet satellite in Africa" by noting: there is no Communist party in Ghana, and the dominant CPP does not belong to the worldwide Communist movement; Ghana had no strong economic ties with the USSR or Red China, with less than 10 percent of its trade carried on with Communist countries; most investment capital in Ghana was Western capital; most technical advisers to Ghana were from the West, chiefly from Canada, America, and Britain; at the UN, Ghana vocally opposed the Soviet "troika" proposal; toward the Cuban Crisis of 1962, Ghana expressed "sympathetic understanding of United States fears"; over-all, "Pan-Africanism is not a communistic movement and is no menace to the United States." See the letter of St. Clair Drake in *The New York Times,* July 30, 1963.

A thorough appraisal of the broader issue of communist influence in Africa is contained in McKay, *op. cit.,* pp. 204–221. McKay's conclusions tend to bear out Drake's assessment of communist influence in Ghana.

NOTES

1. George Lenczowski, *The Middle East in World Affairs* (Ithaca, N.Y.: Cornell University Press, 1952), pp. 422–423. This is a useful survey of the emergence of the Middle East.
2. Cordell Hull, *The Memoirs of Cordell Hull,* **II** (New York: Macmillan, 1948), 1540–1547.

3. Harry N. Howard, "The Arab-Asian States in the United Nations," *Middle East Journal*, 7 (Summer, 1953), 279–292.

4. Harry S Truman, *Memoirs*, II (Garden City, N.Y.: Doubleday, 1955), 136–150. An invaluable primary source on American views toward Palestine.

5. *Ibid.*, pp. 145–146.

6. *Ibid.*, p. 151.

7. Edward B. Glick, "Latin America and the Establishment of Israel," *Middle Eastern Affairs*, 9 (January, 1958), 11–16.

8. Truman, *op. cit.*, pp. 132–138.

9. *Ibid.*, pp. 133, 136, 140.

10. *Ibid.*, p. 154; *The New York Times*, October 5 and 7, 1946.

11. *The New York Times*, October 21, 1963, and January 21, 1964.

12. Joseph E. Johnson, "Arab *vs.* Israeli: A Persistent Challenge to Americans," Address to the 24th American Assembly (Harriman, N.Y.: Arden House, October 24, 1963).

13. An excellent recent study of the refugee question is Don Peretz, "The Arab Refugees: A Changing Problem," *Foreign Affairs*, 41 (April, 1963), 558–571. For more detailed background, see the same author's *Israel and the Palestine Arabs* (Washington: Middle East Institute, 1958).

14. Israel's case on the refugee issue was presented to the UN on December 14, 1962, by Israeli Foreign Minister Mrs. Golda Meir. See the text of her speech in *Israel Digest*, 5 (December 21, 1962), 1–2. For "documentary proof" of Israel's case that the refugees left at the behest of Arab leaders, see *ibid.* (August 17, 1962), p. 3.

15. Arab views on the refugee controversy are contained in the following publications, distributed by the Arab Information Center in New York: Sami Hadawi, "Palestine: Questions and Answers" (September, 1961), pp. 35–46; Fayez A. Sayegh, "The Arab-Israeli Conflict" (November, 1956), pp. 47–55. Another Arab source claims that 75 percent of all land in Israel belongs rightfully to Arab refugees. See "Arab Views on Neutralism, Zionism" (Washington, D.C.: Embassy of the United Arab Republic, Press Section, 1961), p. 1.

16. Don Peretz, "Development of the Jordan Valley Waters," *Middle East Journal*, 9 (Autumn, 1955), 397–412, *passim*. Traces out the development of the Jordan Valley project.

17. *The New York Times*, October 21, 1963, and January 13, 1964.

18. Quoted in Hadawi, *op. cit.*, p. 77.

19. Ivor Bavelle, "Arab Threats," *Israel Digest*, 5 (June 6, 1962), 5; "Premier Ends Scandinavian Tour," *ibid.* (September 28, 1963), 2.

20. Department of State, *The Middle East*, Publication No. 5469, "Near and Middle Eastern Series," 16 (Washington: 1954).

21. *The New York Times*, January 24, 1964.

22. *The New York Times*, January 23, 1964.

23. "Hard-Hitting Speech by President Nasser on Victory Day," *The Scribe* (Cairo), 3 (January, 1961), 13.

24. J. C. Hurewitz, *Diplomacy in the Near and Middle East*, II (Princeton, N.J.: Van Nostrand, 1956), 390–391.

25. The negotiations leading up to the Baghdad Pact and its subsequent history are discussed fully in John C. Campbell, *Defense of the Middle East* (New York: Praeger, 1960), pp. 39–161. This is a comprehensive treatment of developments in the Middle East to the late 1950s.

26. Department of State, *United States Policy in the Middle East*, Publication No. 6505, "Near and Middle Eastern Series," 25 (Washington: 1957), p. 45.

27. *Documents on American Foreign Relations: 1957* (New York: Harper & Row, 1958), p. 237.

28. *Documents on American Foreign Relations: 1958* (New York: Harper & Row, 1959), p. 300.

29. See the views of U. Alexis Johnson, in *The New York Times*, January 21, 1964.

30. Department of State, *The Development of United States Policy in the Near East, South Asia, and Africa, 1951–52*, Publication No. 4851, "Near and Middle Eastern Series," 9 (Washington: 1953), pp. 892–895.

31. Walter Z. Laqueur, *Communism and Nationalism in the Middle East* (New York: Praeger, 1956), p. 7. This is a perceptive treatment of the Arab nationalist movement and of communist activities in the Middle East.

32. *Ibid.*, p. 8.

33. Wilfred C. Smith, *Islam in Modern History* (New York: Mentor Books, 1957), p. 82.

34. *Ibid.*, pp. 117, 164–165.

35. See *ibid.*, pp. 97–165.

36. Gamal Abdel Nasser, "The Egyptian Revolution," *Foreign Affairs*, 33 (January, 1955), 208.

37. "Nasser Replies to Questions of U.S. Editors," *Egypt News*, 5 (Washington, D.C.: Embassy of United Arab Republic, February 12, 1958), 1.

38. *Documents on International Affairs: 1958* (London: Oxford University Press, 1962), p. 245.

39. "The Foreign Policy of the Iraqi Republic," *New Iraq* (New Delhi: Embassy of Iraq, no date), 5.

40. *The New York Times,* March 21, 1958.

41. "Abdel-Nasser Says 'Russia Took Our Hand.'" *Mideast Mirror,* 12 (July, 1960), 2.

42. Dwight D. Eisenhower, *Mandate for Change: 1953–1956* (Garden City, N.Y.: Doubleday, 1963), p. 154.

43. *Egyptian Mail,* November 18, 1961.

44. Quoted in "Syria and the United States," *The Arab World,* 3 (New York: Arab Information Center, November, 1957), 4.

45. *The Hindustan Times* (overseas edition), January 17, 1957.

46. *Documents on International Affairs: 1957* (London: Oxford University Press, 1960), p. 216.

47. Department of State, *United States Policy in the Middle East, op. cit.,* pp. 152–153.

48. Senate Foreign Relations Committee, *International Development and Security,* Hearings, 87th Congress, 1st Session (Washington, D.C.: 1961), p. 761.

49. House Foreign Affairs Committee, *Foreign Assistance Act of 1962,* Hearings, 87th Congress, 1st Session (Washington, D.C.: 1962), pp. 564, 566.

50. House Foreign Affairs Committee, *Foreign Assistance Act of 1963,* Hearings, 88th Congress, 2nd Session (Washington, D.C.: 1963), p. 2.

51. House Foreign Affairs Committee, *Foreign Assistance Act of 1962, op cit.,* Part 2, p. 213.

52. *Documents on International Affairs: 1957, op. cit.,* p. 322.

53. Quoted in *Egyptian Gazette,* August 6, 1961.

54. "Iraqi Coup Explained," *News of the United Arab Republic,* 5 (Washington, D.C.: Embassy of the United Arab Republic, July 23, 1958), 1.

55. *The Asian Recorder,* 3 (April 6–12, 1957), 1386.

56. Senate Foreign Relations Committee, *Review of Foreign Policy, 1958,* Hearings, 85th Congress, 2nd Session (Washington, D.C.: 1958), p. 565.

57. Khalid I. Babaa, *Arab Positive Neutralism* (New York: Arab Information Center, no date), p. 9.

58. *The Asian Recorder,* 8 (October 22–28, 1962), p. 4855.

59. See *Iraq Times* (Baghdad), January 1, 10, and 29, 1961.

60. See the testimony of USIA officials in in House Foreign Affairs Committee, *U.S. Information Service Activities in Africa,* Hearings, 88th Congress, 1st Session (Washington, D.C.: 1963), p. 32.

61. *Egyptian Mail,* December 16, 1961.

62. "Communism and Us," *The Scribe* (Cairo), 2 (May–June, 1961).

63. Charles O. Cremeans, *The Arabs and the World* (New York: Praeger, 1963), pp. 288–289. Cremeans's study is an outstanding analysis of Arab attitudes on a variety of regional and global issues.

64. Quoted in *ibid.,* p. 291.

65. Leon M. Herman, "The Soviet Oil Offensive," *The Reporter,* 26 (June 21, 1962), 26–28.

66. Andrew H. Berdung, "The Crucial Decade," *Department of State Bulletin,* 43 (October 31, 1960), 6756; and House Foreign Affairs Committee, *Foreign Assistance Act of 1962, op. cit.,* p. 564.

67. *Documents on American Foreign Relations: 1960* (New York: Harper & Row, 1961), p. 97.

68. "New U.S. Approach to Positive Neutralism?" *Arab Observer,* 4 (February 26, 1962), 12.

69. *The New York Times,* September 11, 1963.

70. *The New York Times,* January 26, 1964.

71. Walter Goldschmidt, ed., *The United States and Africa* (New York: Praeger, 1963), p. 4. This is an illuminating symposium, containing papers prepared for the 13th American Assembly discussion of African problems.

72. Chester Bowles, *Africa's Challenge to America* (Berkeley, Calif.: University of California Press, 1956), pp. 51–52; Calvin W. Stillman, *Africa in the Modern World* (Chicago: University of Chicago Press, 1955), p. 10.

73. Bowles, *op. cit.,* p. 2.

74. Goldschmidt, *op. cit.,* p. 162.

75. W. S. Woytinsky and E. S. Woytinsky, *World Population and Production: Trends and Outlook* (New York: Twentieth Century Fund, 1953), p. 695.

76. Stillman, *op. cit.,* pp. 34–37.

77. Robert L. Heilbroner, *The Great Ascent* (New York: Harper & Row, 1963), pp. 39, 41. This study provides a succinct treatment of problems facing Africa and other underdeveloped areas.

78. George T. Kimble, *Tropical Africa,* I (New York: Twentieth Century Fund, 1960), 165.

79. Elliot J. Berg, "The Character and Prospects of African Economies," in Goldschmidt, *op. cit.,* p. 129. This essay is an

illuminating treatment of African economic problems.

80. Kimble, *op. cit.*, I, 121–129.
81. Rupert Emerson, "The Character of American Interests in Africa," in Goldschmidt, *op. cit.*, p. 3. Provides background on American contacts with Africa.
82. For the evolution of official American concern with Africa, see Vernon McKay, "The African Operations of United States Government Agencies," in Goldschmidt, *op. cit.*, pp. 273–296.
83. Cited in Goldschmidt, *op. cit.*, pp. 31, 285–286, 288.
84. *The New York Times*, January 20, 1964; Goldschmidt, *op. cit.*, p. 282.
85. *The New York Times*, January 20, 1964; Goldschmidt, *op. cit.*, pp. 24–25.
86. House Foreign Affairs Committee, *Foreign Assistance Act of 1962*, *op. cit.*, p. 395.
87. Cited in Goldschmidt, *op. cit.*, pp. 29, 161, 171.
88. The rationale of aid to these and other African states is set forth in a document submitted by foreign aid officials, in House Foreign Affairs Committee, *Mutual Security Act of 1958*, Hearings, 85th Congress, 2nd Session (Washington, D.C.: 1958), pp. 1709–1770.
89. House Foreign Affairs Committee, *Foreign Assistance Act of 1963*, *op. cit.*, p. 333.
90. See the views of executive officials, in Senate Appropriations Committee, *Mutual Security Appropriation for 1960*, Hearings, 86th Congress, 1st Session (Washington, D.C.: 1960), p. 301.
91. David Hapgood, "Guinea's First Five Years," *Current History*, 45 (December, 1963), 359. This entire issue is devoted to recent developments in West Africa.
92. *The New York Times*, July 30, 1963, and February 4, 1964.
93. Quoted in Collin Legum, *Pan-Africanism* (New York: Praeger, 1962), p. 128. This is an extremely helpful semidocumentary treatment of an important African concept.
94. Berg, in Goldschmidt, *op. cit.*, p. 140.
95. Quoted in Legum, *op. cit.*, p. 121.
96. Herbert J. Spiro, *Politics in Africa* (Englewood Cliffs, N.J.: Prentice-Hall, 1962), p. 10. A succinct appraisal of Africa's political evolution.
97. Keith Kyle, "This Strange Thing Called African Socialism," *The Reporter*, 28 (June 6, 1963), 28. An illuminating evaluation of this leading African concept.
98. Ronald Segal, *African Profiles* (Baltimore: Penguin Books, 1962), p. 270. An interesting and illuminating treatment, focusing upon African political elites.

99. J. Nyerere, "Will Democracy Work in Africa?" in Peter R. Gould, *Africa: Continent of Change* (Belmont, Calif.: Wadsworth, 1961), pp. 53–54. This is a helpful collection of essays on African problems.
100. For African practice in applying its version of socialism see Goldschmidt, *op. cit.*, pp. 115–155.
101. "Sékou Touré in America," *Africa Special Report*, 4 (November, 1959), 9.
102. *Egyptian Gazette*, September 8, 1961.
103. Emmet V. Mittlebeeler, "Africa and the Defense of America," *World Affairs*, 121 (Fall, 1958), 82. Italics in original.
104. Mahmoud Bey Muntasser of Libya at the Bandung Conference, as cited in *Report on Indonesia*, 6 (June, 1955), 22–23.
105. Kwame Nkrumah, *I Speak of Freedom* (New York: Praeger, 1961), p. 128. An invaluable primary source on African attitudes.
106. *Ibid.*, pp. 201, 217–218.
107. *The New York Times*, February 20, 1964.
108. *The New York Times*, October 7, 1963.
109. See the statement of George V. Allen, Director of USIA, in Senate Foreign Relations Committee, *Review of Foreign Policy*, Hearings, 85th Congress, 2nd Session (Washington, D.C.: 1958), p. 218.
110. *Daily Times* (Lagos, Nigeria), July 12, 1961.
111. Nkrumah, *op. cit.*, p. 271.
112. Senate Foreign Relations Committee, *Review of Foreign Policy*, *op. cit.*, p. 736.
113. See the appraisal of African views of American behavior at the UN presented by George M. Houser, "Cause for Concern," *Africa Today*, 8 (January, 1961), 5–6, 10. Thus, one African friendly to the United States said, America "suffered a disastrous political and ideological defeat" at the 15th General Assembly, largely because of its record on colonialism.
114. *The New York Times*, October 25, 1959.
115. Quoted in *Iraq Times*, September 25, 1961.
116. *The African Recorder*, 1 (January 1–14, 1962), 56.
117. The views of Balewa and other African leaders are cited in Legum, *op. cit.*, p. 112; see also Sanjiva Nayak, "Foundations of the Foreign Policy of Nigeria," *Africa Quarterly*, 2, No. 2, 118–124.
118. For these and comparable African views, see Legum, *op. cit.*, pp. 112–113; Sir Abubakar T. Balewa, "Nigeria Looks Ahead," *Foreign Affairs*, 41 (October, 1962), 139.

119. Balewa, *op. cit.*, p. 139.
120. *The New York Times*, August 12, 1963.
121. James K. Penfield, "Africa: A New Situation Requiring New Responses," *Department of State Bulletin*, 43 (June 6, 1960), 923.
122. House Foreign Affairs Committee, *Mutual Security Act of 1958, op. cit.*, p. 582.
123. Speech by Assistant Secretary of State G. Mennen Williams, cited in *Morning News* (Khartoum, Sudan), June 2, 1961.
124. House Foreign Affairs Committee, *Foreign Assistance Act of 1962, op. cit.*, p. 83.
125. Quoted in Goldschmidt, *op. cit.*, p. 74.
126. *The New York Times*, February 23, 1958.
127. Tai Solarin, "A Personal View of Nigerian Independence," in Peter Judd, *African Independence* (New York: Dell, 1962), p. 245. This symposium offers comprehensive appraisals of Africa's political evolution. See also *Daily Times* (Lagos, Nigeria), July 11, 1961.
128. Quoted in Legum, *op. cit.*, p. 117.
129. Quoted in House Foreign Affairs Committee, *Foreign Assistance Act of 1962, op. cit.*, p. 614.

12 → THE WESTERN HEMISPHERE → vicissitudes of the good neighbor policy

Preoccupied in recent years with the all-pervading cold war, the people of the United States and their leaders have been prone to neglect one of the most crucial areas in world politics: the Western Hemisphere. Though fairly well insulated from the eddies of great-power antagonisms witnessed in Europe, the Middle East, and Asia, the Western Hemisphere is nevertheless of fundamental importance to policy-makers in Washington.

It would be difficult to justify the neglect of this hemisphere on rational grounds. By the early 1960s, almost half the imports into the United States came from nations in the Western Hemisphere, and approximately one-third of its exports were sent to these nations.[1] About half of American private investment funds each year went into Latin America or Canada.[2] Out of some $35.5 billion in total private investment overseas, $21.7 billion in funds from the United States were invested in Canada and the Latin American republics.[3] Measured solely by such statistics, Canada and Latin America are about as important to the United States as Western Europe and considerably more important than Asia or Africa.

Furthermore, Latin America is an area of outstanding potential, and a great deal of actual, economic growth. Spectacular economic expansion has occurred in the past quarter-century. Per capita income has grown 2.25 percent a year. From 1946 to 1952 it grew 2.5 percent annually. These gains become all the more impressive in light of the fact that population increases in that region are nearly the highest in the world; the population doubled from World War II to the late 1950s, and is expected to double again in the next quarter-century. If Latin American countries succeed in carrying forward programs of economic advancement, in which they will have to maintain the 2.5 percent annual economic growth rate, then the Gross National Product throughout these countries will have to triple in the next 25 years.[4] Convinced that they have been "neglected" by Uncle Sam in recent years, citizens and leaders in Latin America believe that their future welfare will hinge upon generous assistance extended by the United States government and by the investment activities of private business concerns.

The over-all strategic importance of Latin America to the United States has already been discussed at length in Chapter 1 and reviewed in Chapters 8 and 9. We shall not cover that ground again, except to stress once more that the security of the United States is dependent to a high degree upon keeping the military approaches to the Western Hemisphere in friendly hands and protecting the vital hemispheric lines of communications and trade from threats by the nation's avowed diplomatic enemies. For instance, of the imports needed by the United States in recent years for defense purposes, a goodly share comes from Latin America: 100 percent of vanadium and quebracho (used for tanning), 90 percent of quartz crystals, 80 percent of castor bean oil (used as aircraft lubricant), crude petroleum and fuel oil, and 40 percent of the tungsten and zinc.[5]

The development of nuclear weapons and guided missiles has vastly enhanced the importance of Canada and the Arctic region for Washington's defense policy. The United States and Canada developed close defense ties during World War II. These have been greatly strengthened under the necessity to build effective defenses in the nuclear-missile age. "The Arctic," writes one geographer, "may become to the future what the Mediterranean was to the past—the axis of world power. . . . This is the new strategic center of the world. It is the new Pivot Area, which has made the old Heartland eccentric."[6] A former chief of the United States Air Force, General Spaatz, has asserted that: "Whoever controls the Arctic air lanes controls the world today."[7] The new strategic significance of North America has been reflected in postwar agreements between the United States and Canada providing for joint construction and maintenance of a three-stage radar defense network extending into the Arctic and for general United States-Canadian cooperation in the field of defense planning. The St. Lawrence Seaway project also demands closer ties than ever before between the United States and Canada, especially in the sphere of expanding commercial cooperation. New vistas are thus opening up in the relations between the United States and its northern neighbor. Some authorities even foresee a gradual weakening of Canada's historic ties with the British Commonwealth and its ever closer association with the United States.[8*]

This chapter will focus on the response of the United States to three problems: hemispheric security and solidarity, problems of

foreign trade and aid, and the communist movement in the Americas.[**]

HEMISPHERIC SECURITY AND SOLIDARITY

The Monroe Doctrine

For over a century the Monroe Doctrine defined the diplomatic behavior of the United States toward the Western Hemisphere. Two developments in the third decade of the nineteenth century induced President Monroe to enunciate what came to be the most famous principle of our foreign policy. There were, first of all, Russian colonial activities in the West. Especially significant was the tsarist Imperial Ukase of 1821. It virtually declared the Pacific waters around these Russian colonial outposts a closed sea, a pronouncement that seemed to the United States to presage renewed Russian colonizing efforts in North America. A second danger arose from the threatened intervention of the Holy Alliance in the affairs of the former Spanish colonies in Latin America. The United States feared that the Holy Alliance would invoke the principle of "legitimacy" in an attempt to reimpose Spanish hegemony over newly independent American possessions; or failing this, that another European country might supplant Spain as a colonial power in the Western Hemisphere.

---

* Canada receives peripheral attention in this chapter. Extended treatments of relations between the United States and Canada historically and in recent years are: Hugh L. Keenlyside, *Canada and the United States* (New York: Knopf, 1952); Tom Kent, "The Changing Place of Canada," *Foreign Affairs*, 35 (July, 1957), 581–592; Walter O'Hearn, "How We Stand with the Canadians," *The Reporter*, 18 (March 6, 1958), 22–25; William W. Willoughby, "Canadian-American Defense Co-operation," *Journal of Politics*, 13 (November, 1951), 675–696; John W. Holmes, "Canada in Search of Its Role," *Foreign Affairs*, 41 (July, 1963), 659–672; R. J. Sutherland, "Canada's Long Term Strategic Situation," *International Journal*, 17 (Summer, 1962), 199–224.

** In discussing relations between the United States and Latin America it is sometimes difficult to follow a satisfactory scheme of nomenclature without resorting to cumbersome phraseology. Our Latin American friends resent the fact that usage in the United States applies the term "American" to the United States alone. The people of Central and South America are fully as entitled to use this term as are the people of the United States.

Because it accords with popular usage, in other chapters of this book I have used the term "American foreign policy," to refer solely to the policy of the United States. To avoid confusion in this chapter, however, I have avoided such terms as "American foreign policy," which could conceivably mean the foreign policy of other countries in the Western Hemisphere. Instead I have spoken of the foreign policy of the United States or the diplomacy of the State Department. Elsewhere in the book, the adjective "American" refers to the United States, on the theory that in those chapters there is minimum risk of confusion. The reader may wish to pursue the question of accurate nomenclature further in Samuel F. Bemis, *The United States as a World Power* (New York: Holt, Rinehart & Winston, 1955), p. 32 n, and E. C. Burnett, "The Name 'United States of America,' " *American Historical Review*, 31 (October, 1925), 79–81.

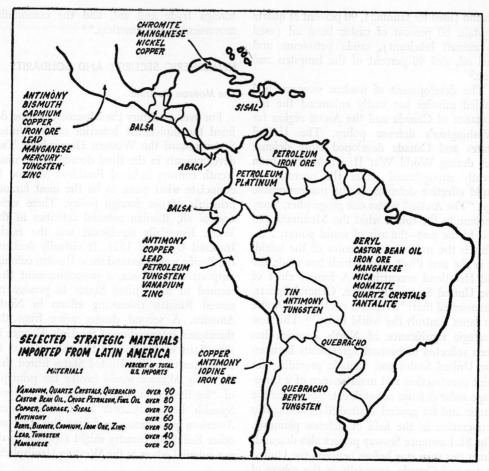

SELECTED STRATEGIC MATERIALS
IMPORTED FROM LATIN AMERICA

MATERIALS	PERCENT OF TOTAL U.S. IMPORTS
VANADIUM, QUARTZ CRYSTALS, QUEBRACHO	OVER 90
CASTOR BEAN OIL, CRUDE PETROLEUM, FUEL OIL	OVER 80
COPPER, CORDAGE, SISAL	OVER 70
ANTIMONY	OVER 60
BERYL, BISMUTH, CADMIUM, IRON ORE, ZINC	OVER 50
LEAD, TUNGSTEN	OVER 40
MANGANESE	OVER 20

Industrial Raw Materials Available in Latin America. (Source: House Foreign Affairs Committee, Hearings on the Mutual Security Act of 1958, Part 12, p. 1501.)

The key portion of Monroe's message of December 2, 1823, was that:

The political system of the allied powers is essentially different . . . from that of America. . . . We owe it, therefore, to candor, and to the amicable relations existing between the United States and those powers, to declare that we should consider any attempt on their part to extend their system to any portion of this hemisphere as dangerous to our peace and safety. With the existing colonies or dependencies of any European power we have not interfered and shall not interfere. But with the governments who have declared their independence and maintained it . . . we could not view any interposition for the purpose of oppressing them, or controlling in any other manner their destiny, by any European power, in any other light than as the manifestation of an unfriendly disposition toward the United States.[9]

Several points about Monroe's pronouncement require emphasis.* The first is that this was a *unilateral* declaration by the United States. The noncolonization principle, to be sure, was also supported by the British Foreign Office and, what was much more crucial for the continued independence of the Latin American states, enforced on several significant occasions

* Here our concern is with the Western Hemispheric aspects of the Monroe Doctrine. The European aspects, by which the United States pledged itself not to interfere in wars on the continent of Europe, are discussed in Chapter 10.

The historic meaning and evolution of the Monroe Doctrine are ably treated in the studies by Dexter Perkins: *The Monroe Doctrine, 1823–26* (Cambridge, Mass.: Harvard University Press, 1927); *The Monroe Doctrine, 1826–67* (Baltimore: Johns Hopkins University Press, 1937). James W. Gantenbein, *The Evolution of Our Latin-American Policy* (New York: Columbia University Press, 1950), pp. 301–425, provides documentary materials on the Monroe Doctrine.

by the Royal Navy. Yet other powerful nations were not inclined to regard the doctrine as a fixed canon of international law, much less as a precept to which they had freely given consent. As the history of the Monroe Doctrine made clear, its effectiveness depended predominantly upon one factor: the willingness and ability of the United States, backed in some instances by Great Britain, to enforce compliance with it. Second, as originally expressed, the noncolonization principle of the Monroe Doctrine prohibited *future* colonization by European countries. It did nothing to interfere with *existing* colonies; nor did it proscribe European diplomatic or economic influence throughout the New World. Later amplifications and corollaries of the Monroe Doctrine, which we shall treat below, broadened the scope of the noncolonization principle and introduced new prohibitions against European diplomatic activity in the Americas. But no such sweeping prohibitions were included in the original message.

Third, in the years following Monroe's proclamation the United States was unprepared on a number of occasions to back up the Monroe Doctrine with military and diplomatic force. This became evident almost immediately after 1823, when Latin American diplomats asked Washington for treaties of alliance that would commit the United States to support their continued freedom from Spanish colonial rule. These requests met with an unenthusiastic reception on the part of the State Department. Moreover, when the nations of Latin America sought to cement closer hemispheric relations at the Panama Congress of 1826, the United States held aloof from the meeting. The viewpoint of the new President John Quincy Adams —"There is no community of interest or of principle between North and South America"— was in strange contrast with the community of interest which had seemingly been postulated by Monroe's message of 1823.[10]

From the time of its inception, and even after its scope had been broadened in the light of experience, the Monroe Doctrine remained essentially a unilateral response by the United States to conditions believed to threaten its security. In substance, wrote Robert Lansing in 1914, it reflected the view that "the United States considers an extension of political control by a European power over any territory in this hemisphere, not already occupied by it, to be a menace to the national safety of the United States." Compliance with the doctrine

in the last analysis rested upon the "superior power of the United States to compel submission to its will. . . ."[11] That the Monroe Doctrine had been proclaimed unilaterally by the United States meant, in the words of Secretary of State Charles Evans Hughes in 1923, that

the government of the United States reserves to itself its definition, interpretation, and application. . . . Great powers have signified their acquiescence in it. But the United States has not been disposed to enter into engagements which would have the effect of submitting to any other power or to any concert of powers the determination either of the occasions upon which the principles of the Monroe Doctrine shall be invoked or of the measures that shall be taken in giving it effect.[12]

Schooled as they are in the idea that Monroe's classic foreign policy principle was ideally suited to their country's historic desires and needs, North Americans find it difficult to understand that the doctrine could arouse apprehension in their neighbors south of the border. Over the course of time, however, Latin American nations often viewed "Yankee imperialism" as a more imminent threat than reimposition of European colonial domination. Occasionally, Latin American countries were inclined to regard the doctrine as nothing more than a thinly veiled scheme whereby the United States invoked hemispheric security as a pretext to exercise a *de facto* protectorate over weaker American states and, under the guise of protecting them from European intervention, practiced intervention itself in the affairs of nations to the south. In recent years, therefore, one recurring task of United States foreign policy-makers has been to try to convince the countries of Latin America that the Monroe Doctrine has not been directed against them but against powerful nations in Europe. Later portions of the chapter will illustrate how the United States has sought to translate the unilateral guarantees contained in the Monroe Doctrine into guarantees supported and enforced by all the countries belonging to the Inter-American System.

Corollaries of the Monroe Doctrine

Today, when the student of American foreign policy studies the Monroe Doctrine, in reality he is studying an aggregate of diplomatic pronouncements and actions based upon President Monroe's message to Congress in 1823. Collectively, these have vastly expanded and modified the original meaning of the Monroe Doctrine in order to cover specific diplomatic situations that have arisen in the Western Hemisphere. Let us look briefly at some of the more important highlights in the evolution of this cardinal principle of American foreign policy.

The first important amplification of the Monroe Doctrine was the *Polk Corollary* in the period 1845–1848. President Polk declared that the noncolonization principle of the Monroe Doctrine "will apply with greatly increased force, should any European power attempt to establish *any new colony* in North America. . . . "[13] A half-century later, in the midst of the Venezuelan boundary dispute with Great Britain, Secretary of State Richard Olney informed the British that the non-colonization principle of the Monroe Doctrine had been "universally conceded" and that it had been the "controlling factor" in the "emancipation of South America" from Spanish rule. Olney, more gifted in the role of prosecuting attorney than historian or diplomat, went on to inform the British Foreign Office categorically that:

Today the United States is practically sovereign on this continent, and its fiat is law upon the subjects to which it confines its interposition. Why? . . . It is because . . . its infinite resources combined with its isolated position render it master of the situation and practically invulnerable as against any or all other powers.[14]

The Olney letter translated the Monroe Doctrine into a pronouncement that in effect designated the Western Hemisphere as a Yankee sphere of influence, a claim which the nations of Europe and of Latin America were reluctant to accept.

Coincident with the age of "dollar diplomacy" toward Latin American and Asian affairs in the early 1900s was the *Roosevelt Corollary* to the Monroe Doctrine. Certain Latin American nations, chiefly in the Caribbean region, were notoriously lax in the management of their governmental and fiscal affairs. Outside intervention in their affairs for the purpose of collecting legitimate debts was consequently a perennial risk. President Theodore Roosevelt concluded that the United States could not prohibit foreign intervention to enforce payment of debts unless it were willing to assume responsibilities itself for preventing gross fiscal mismanagement by its southern neighbors. In 1901, Roosevelt stated that the Monroe Doctrine did not protect any Latin American coun-

try "against punishment if it misconducts itself. . . ." A year later he warned that it behooved each country in Latin America to "maintain order within its borders and to discharge its just obligations to foreigners." This line of reasoning ultimately led him to the conclusion in 1904 that any nation that "knows how to act with reasonable efficiency and decency" need not fear intervention. But:

Chronic wrongdoing, or an impotence which results in a general loosening of the ties of civilized society, may in America, as elsewhere, ultimately require intervention by some civilized nation, and in the Western Hemisphere the adherence of the United States to the Monroe Doctrine may force the United States, however reluctantly . . . to the exercise of an international police power.[15]

This then was the first Roosevelt's characteristically forthright response to the threat of intervention in Latin American affairs by European countries. Either the southern neighbors of the United States would keep their own affairs in order, thereby minimizing the risk of such intervention, or else the United States would be compelled under the Monroe Doctrine to undertake necessary housecleaning duties in such countries. This was no idle boast. On repeated occasions after 1904, the United States invoked the Roosevelt Corollary to justify intervention in Latin American affairs. This fact inevitably conveyed the impression to the other American republics that the Monroe Doctrine might protect them from the diplomatic ambitions of countries outside the Western Hemisphere, but that it could also be invoked to rationalize control over them by the United States, and to their minds this was often a distinction without a difference. Not until the administration of the second Roosevelt were all the military contingents of the United States finally withdrawn from Latin America.

The scope of the noncolonization principle contained in the Monroe Doctrine was also broadened by the *Lodge Corollary*, expressed in a Senate resolution of August 2, 1912. Prompted by threatened Japanese acquisition of parts of Lower California, this corollary held that the United States could not permit occupation of harbors within the Western Hemisphere "for naval or military purposes" by a foreign power, if such occupation would "threaten the communications or safety of the United States. . . ."[16]

The Good Neighbor Policy

The impact of Wilsonian idealism, along with the evident deterioration in relations between the United States and its hemispheric neighbors as a result of the Roosevelt Corollary from 1904 onward, demanded corrective measures on the part of the State Department. Recurrent outcries from the south against "Yankee imperialism" could no longer be ignored in Washington. A significant change in the foreign policy of the United States was therefore presaged by the "Clark Memorandum" of 1928, the gist of which was that the Roosevelt Corollary had been a perversion of the original intention of the Monroe Doctrine. Then with the election of Franklin D. Roosevelt came the "Good Neighbor" policy, enunciated in FDR's First Inaugural Address and reiterated in a series of messages thereafter by Roosevelt and Secretary of State Cordell Hull. The first step in establishing good neighborly relations was to reassure the Latin American countries that the Monroe Doctrine was not a pretext to conceal Yankee imperialistic ambitions toward them. Secretary Hull stated in 1933 that the people of the United States believed that the so-called right of conquest "must be banished from this hemisphere and, most of all, they shun and reject that so-called right for themselves." In the same year, FDR repeated Wilson's earlier pledge that the United States would never again seek additional territory by conquest. Paving the way for an effective inter-American system of defense and solidarity, Roosevelt observed that political turbulence and threats to hemispheric security were no longer of special concern to the United States alone, but that they were "the joint concern of a whole continent in which we are all neighbors."[17] As it related to the Monroe Doctrine, the new good neighbor policy came down to this: the traditional interest of the United States in Western hemispheric security must be translated into a policy shared by all the American countries. All must support it and all must act in concert to deal with conditions threatening the peace and stability of the hemisphere. This was in substance the purpose of the Inter-American System.

The Pan-American Movement

No sooner had the countries of Latin America won their independence in the early 1800s than their leaders began to think in terms of a Pan-American movement to preserve their freedom, not alone from Europe but from their northern neighbor, the United States, as well. The great South American leader Simon Bolivar early took the lead in laying the basis for the Pan-American movement. The United States, largely for reasons of domestic politics and the desire to preserve an attitude of non-entanglement with other countries, did not participate in the first Panama Congress of 1826. As was often characteristic of such conferences in the years that followed, the delegates were quick to pass resolutions proclaiming their mutual attachment to idealistic goals, such as political nonintervention and economic cooperation. But in this and later instances, such resolutions frequently received little or no tangible support afterwards from the governments concerned. The first attempt to establish a Pan-American System therefore was a failure. For a half-century thereafter, the dream of Pan-Americanism languished, despite the fact that considerable support for it existed in Latin America and within the United States.

Fifty years later the movement received new impetus under Secretary of State James G. Blaine, who proposed a meeting of all the American republics in Washington in 1881 for the purpose of preventing war in the Western Hemisphere and of promoting closer economic collaboration among the nations of the region. A change in political administrations within the United States delayed these plans for eight years. But finally, in 1889, the conference was held. This conference was also devoid of tangible results, except for one: establishment of the Bureau of American Republics, later renamed the Pan-American Union, which in time evolved into one of the principal organs of the Inter-American System.[18]

The pace by which the Pan-American movement grew from little more than expressions of affinity among the American republics, accompanied by occasional conferences at which actual gains were usually negligible, was leisurely between the late 1800s and the New Deal. Interventions carried out by the United States under the Roosevelt Corollary understandably made the other American republics highly suspicious of Uncle Sam's intentions. Uppermost in the minds of Latin American statesmen was the ubiquitous specter of Yankee domination; they consequently looked askance at frequent endorsements of the ideal of Pan-Americanism by the United States because they feared domination of Latin American affairs by an international body controlled from Washington.

Repudiation of the Roosevelt Corollary and the inauguration of the Good Neighbor policy were therefore necessary before significant progress could be expected toward establishing more intimate relations among countries in the Western Hemisphere.

Once the diplomatic atmosphere had cleared after 1932, Pan-American cooperation gradually became a reality. The threat of Axis aggression provided another stimulus, by binding the nations of the Western Hemisphere together against a common enemy and by emphasizing their economic interdependence. Beginning with the conference at Montevideo in 1933, the Inter-American System began to take shape. Here the United States accepted a resolution directed principally at itself, pledging all American republics to a policy of nonintervention in the affairs of their neighbors. In return, the United States received widespread support by the Latin American governments for the New Deal principle of reciprocal trade, whereby national tariffs were lowered on the basis of mutual concessions. Three years later, at the Inter-American Conference in Buenos Aires, the American republics accepted the principle of joint consultation among all the American countries in the event of a threat to the security of the hemisphere. Additional conferences were held in 1938, 1939, 1940, and 1942. An important milestone was the conference at Mexico City in 1945, at which the Act of Chapultepec was adopted, formally declaring the determination of the American republics to pursue a common policy in meeting any threat to their security from abroad.[19]

Building on these foundations, the Rio Conference of 1947 resulted in the Treaty of Reciprocal Assistance, signed on September 2. This regional defense agreement, like NATO and similar agreements, was drawn up under Article 51 of the United Nations Charter, providing for the right of individual and regional self-defense. Pending action by the Security Council of the UN, threats to the peace within the Americas were to be dealt with by the Inter-American System.[20] Then at the Ninth Inter-American Conference at Bogotá in the spring of 1948, the formal machinery necessary to make these goals a reality—the Organization of American States (OAS)—was established. Finally, the Pan-American movement had come to fruition. After nearly a century and a quarter, the American republics had moved from highly generalized and usually ineffectual declarations of mutual affinity to the creation of a regional defense system, containing permanent machinery for dealing with threats to the security and stability of the Western Hemisphere that might arise from such diverse sources as the activities of international communism, conflicts among individual American states, or widespread hemispheric economic dislocations.

OAS—Procedures and Principles

The Inter-American System rests upon three basic "charter documents" defining its scope and procedures. First, there is the Rio Treaty of mutual assistance, safeguarding the defense of the Americas from an attack originating outside or inside the hemisphere; second, there is a document specifying the scope, organs, and duties of OAS; and third, there is a document setting forth procedures to be followed for bringing about the pacific settlement of disputes among members of the system. Similarly, the Inter-American System has three principal organs: international conferences, the Pan-American Union, and specialized agencies. The high-level policy-making body is the international conference. General conferences are supposed to be held at five-year intervals. Within shorter periods, lower-level conferences dealing with limited, sometimes highly technical, subjects are held. In the event of a threat to the security of the Americas, Meetings of Consultation are summoned immediately to deal with the threat. The foreign ministers of the member states attend these meetings. The purpose of such meetings, in the words of a State Department document, is "to bring together on short notice the top spokesmen on foreign affairs of the executive branches of the 21 governments for rapid discussion and resolution of emergency issues." We shall see how the Meeting of Consultation dealt with a specific complaint brought before the OAS in 1955.

The Pan-American Union is the permanent organ of the Inter-American System. PAU maintains its headquarters in Washington. Its governing board consists of representatives chosen by each member state. Frequently, the state's highest diplomatic representative in the United States is selected. To assure that PAU would not become the diplomatic organ of one country alone, or would be too strongly influenced by one country, such as the United States, the chairman of PAU's governing board is not eligible for re-election. The Director General and his assistant, the highest administrative officials, serve for ten years, and they, too, are ineligible for re-election, nor can their successors be of the same nationality as the incumbents.

Established in 1910 primarily as an information-gathering and information-disseminating body, PAU's functions were largely confined to this task until after World War II. Much of its activity today is still devoted to the collection and spread of information of common interest to the American states in economic, social, technical, scientific, cultural, and legal fields. In addition, it has become the secretariat of OAS. It arranges for inter-American conferences, provides the required staff, and does the paper work that invariably accompanies such meetings. Moreover, many of the scientific and technical bodies associated with OAS operate under the supervision of the Pan-American Union. After the Rio Treaty of 1947, for the first time PAU acquired important *political* duties. Now it is empowered to act in response to a threat to the Inter-American System, until a Meeting of Consultation can be convened.[21]

The guarantees of hemispheric security contained in the Monroe Doctrine and its corollaries have been assumed by the Inter-American System. Certain precepts have emerged to guide OAS in dealing with threats to the peace. As far back as the end of the nineteenth century, the states in the Western Hemisphere agreed to abstain from using force unilaterally in settling disputes among themselves. This principle was translated into a series of treaties during the 1920s and 1930s, providing that each state would rely upon the "good offices" of other countries, mediation, conciliation, and the like, in settling conflicts within the Inter-American System. Then, during World War II the principle of "all for one, one for all" was incorporated into the Inter-American System. Any attack or threat against any part of the hemisphere would be regarded as an attack against all the American republics. Under the Rio Treaty of 1947, therefore, OAS is empowered to deal with any threat to the hemisphere, irrespective of whether the threat arises from within or outside the American System. Decisions taken by the Meetings of Consultation are binding on all members, regardless of whether they voted for the decision or not, provided the decision was taken by a two-thirds vote and with the further qualification that no state can be required to use armed forces without its own consent.

The five most salient features of the Inter-American System as it has evolved throughout a long, and sometimes discouragingly slow,

historical process are: each member of the system is obligated to cooperate in resisting an actual or threatened attack against any American country; a two-thirds vote of a Meeting of Consultation is binding on all members; no distinction is made between a threat to the peace arising from outside or inside the hemisphere. The Pan-American Union now exercises political responsibilities, along with those in the cultural, social, economic and related fields; and finally, the Inter-American System is firmly integrated with the United Nations.[22]

OAS in Action—A Case Study

The machinery established under OAS to facilitate the peaceful settlement of disputes has been utilized on a number of occasions in recent years, with an impressively high level of success. Several specific disputes might be cited. We shall confine our attention to a single example. Let us look at the dispute between the United States and Panama over the Canal Zone.

Early in 1964, riots and demonstrations against the United States, triggered by a minor incident among school children involving the right to display the American flag in the Canal Zone, erupted in Panama. In the ensuing melee, several people were killed, several hundred wounded, and considerable property destroyed. Panama's President Roberto Chiari broke relations with the United States. This was but the latest in a series of episodes within recent years indicating mounting Panamanian displeasure with the terms of the Treaty of 1903, whereby the United States acquired in perpetuity the right to act "as if it were sovereign" within the Canal Zone. By 1955, the rental paid by the United States for this concession had been raised to $1.9 million annually; Washington had made other concessions to Panamanian nationalism, such as granting equal pay to Panamanians and citizens of the United States for equal work within the Zone, and the right to display Panama's flag side by side with the Stars and Stripes, to symbolize Panama's "titular" sovereignty over the territory. Yet these concessions obviously did not satisfy the demands of Panamanian nationalists or prevent a mounting crescendo of resentment, within this small country of just over one million people, against "Yankee imperialism."

After breaking relations with the United States, the government of Panama initially brought charges of "aggression" against it in the United Nations; simultaneously, it requested a five-nation Peace Committee of the Organization of American States to seek a basis for conciliation. By common consent, the UN left the OAS to work out a modus vivendi. Within a few days, the OAS had established a new commission called the Joint Cooperation Commission, to "adopt measures to prevent and resolve any new disorders as well as to determine what places [in Panama] require special vigilance."

Meanwhile, the Peace Committee sought to bring the United States and Panama to the conference table to effect a lasting settlement of the differences between them. Throughout the weeks required for the representatives of OAS to achieve a compromise between Washington and Panama City, a remarkable aspect of the quarrel was the extent to which responsible opinion in both the United States and Latin America counseled moderation and urged the necessity for a calm and constructive approach to the conflict. Despite efforts by Communist and other extremist elements to inflame Latin American passions against the United States, the keynote of the deliberations was sounded by a Panamanian publication, which said: "In order to create an atmosphere which would give the Inter-American Peace Commission an opportunity to function there should be no more mass meetings or popular manifestations. . . . Agitators and other undesirable elements easily infiltrate such events and hurt Panama's position. Inflamed oratory damages our cause." A Chilean source likewise called upon the OAS and the parties to the dispute to "employ a peaceful formula to bring about understanding, thereby returning early normalcy."[23] At the same time, almost instinctively, Latin American opinion tended to side with Panama in its grievances. Even friends of Washington, like President Betancourt of Venezuela, stated openly that "the only possible solution" was a revision of the Panama Canal Treaty of 1903. The former President of Colombia Alberto Camargo agreed that the "origins of the conflict are founded" in the treaty agreements between the United States and Panama, and that these agreements had to be "discussed and solved."[24]

In the ensuing weeks, the diplomatic seesaw went up and down, as OAS attempts to secure agreement appeared successful, only to have either Panama or the United States reject the wording of the compromise proposal. A fine semantical distinction, involving whether the two countries would "discuss" or "negotiate" with respect to the Canal Zone Treaty, concealed divergent national attitudes and goals. Both countries were in the early stages of a national election; officials in both were, therefore, acutely sensitive to charges of "appeasement" or "surrender" in the controversy. Beyond that, extremist groups in Panama at least, if not President Chiari's regime, demanded outright "nationalization" of the Panama Canal, a move which no American administration would contemplate, especially not in an election year. Consequently, the State Department refused to commit itself in advance to "negotiate" with Panama about the Canal Treaty, since such wording at least implied a willingness to discuss nationalization or some new scheme for the canal, that was unacceptable to official and public opinion in the United States. Panamanian nationalists demanded, on the other hand, that the possibility of writing a new treaty at least be kept open and insisted that Washington could not unilaterally prescribe the terms of negotiation carried out under OAS auspices.

As OAS mediatory efforts bogged down over semantics, sentiment in Panama rose for charging the United States with "aggression" before the OAS and for invoking the machinery established under the Rio Treaty of 1947; if the OAS did not give prompt attention to Panama's complaint, then the same charge would be taken to the United Nations. Confronted with such militancy, on February 4 the Council of the OAS constituted itself an "organ of consultation" and voted 16–1 (Chile alone dissenting) to consider Panama's complaint. The United States expressed itself as being "perfectly agreeable" to full OAS consideration of Panama's complaint. For the majority of OAS members, spokesmen for Argentina, Brazil, Colombia, and Venezuela emphasized that this step in no way prejudged the quarrel between Panama and the United States. It was taken merely out of the deep conviction prevailing throughout Latin America that *any* member of OAS had the right to avail itself of the organization's facilities for peaceful settlement. In reality, there was no question that widespread sentiment existed throughout Latin America that OAS must deal with complaints brought *against* the United States just as fully and as impartially as it traditionally dealt with complaints brought *by* (or supported by) the United States against countries like Castro's Cuba.

By February 6, the OAS had agreed to establish a 17-nation committee to investigate and mediate the controversy between the United States and Panama. This new committee was charged with responsibility for: (1) investigating Panama's accusations against the United States; (2) appraising the efforts of both countries to reach a satisfactory agreement; and (3) assisting in enabling both countries to arrive at a final solution to their long-standing differences. Intensive diplomatic activity and consultations by OAS representatives with Washington and Panama City ensued. Yet the earlier deadlock remained: Washington consented merely to "discuss" outstanding differences with Panama, while the latter demanded that the two countries "negotiate" the issues between them, chiefly the Treaty of 1903. President Johnson and his advisers repeatedly underscored the fact that the United States would not commit itself in advance to negotiate a new treaty for the Canal Zone; Panamanian officials would settle for nothing less.[25]

Policies Toward Dictatorial Governments

At the fifth Inter-American Meeting of Consultation of the Organization of American States, held at Santiago, Chile, in August, 1959, the urgent problem on the agenda was one that has perennially troubled the waters of hemispheric relations in the modern period: What policies ought to be followed in dealing with dictatorial regimes throughout Latin America? By the mid-1960s, the problem appeared to be no closer to satisfactory resolution than before.

In dealing with this problem, the United States, now as in the past, was in a quandary. Firmly committed to the principle of "non-intervention" in the internal affairs of other countries, Washington was reluctant to take any step that might seem to violate this principle. Yet policy-makers in the United States were deeply troubled by conflicts between states like Cuba and the Dominican Republic and the activities of "rebel" groups against established political orders, when these groups were plainly supported and equipped by other countries. As expected, the Meeting of Consultation of the OAS found no clear-cut answer to this problem. Its response—setting up an "American Peace Commission" to observe, and perhaps mediate, recurrent tensions—testified to the durability and complexity of the issue in hemispheric relations.[26]

By the end of the 1950s, policy-makers in

Washington conceded freely that the nation's position on the issue of dictatorships in the Americas remained ambiguous. In a report to the President on December 27, 1958, Milton S. Eisenhower stated that in his recent tour of Central American countries, "I pointed out with candor that from the beginning of our history until 1933, we had not been very consistent in our policies toward Latin America and that some of our actions in that period had clearly strengthened the hands of dictators. But I also pointed out that at Montevideo in 1933, we agreed to a vital change in policy. We agreed thereafter not to intervene in the internal affairs of our sister republics."[27] The "vital change" occurring after 1933 was perhaps more apparent to Washington than to other capitals in the hemisphere. At intervals thereafter, Washington was accused of too intimate relationships with dictatorial regimes, if in no other respect than that it did little or nothing to oppose them and that its usually "correct" policies toward them suggested indifference toward the kind of internal political orders prevailing in countries to the south. An illustration of the difficult policy choices involved is seen in the case of Fulgencio Batista, whose regime in Cuba was overthrown by the revolution led by Fidel Castro in 1959. Castro later generated considerable support for his anti-United States propaganda by referring continually to the "cordial" relations that had prevailed between the State Department and Batista. Batista had been the recipient of economic and military aid from the United States; the State Department did little (conspicuously less than it did when Castro came to power) to protest against Batista's political excesses, his ruthless suppression of political opposition groups, and his use of violence and intimidation to consolidate his hold upon the Cuban society. In Castro's view—and in this respect, his judgment was widely shared by non-Communist critics of the United States throughout Latin America—the State Department appeared to object only to *Marxist* dictatorships in the hemisphere.*

* That official American attitudes toward Batista were part of a general phenomenon in State Department policies toward Latin America has been emphasized by many informed commentators. Thus, in 1954, the United States named the Venezuelan dictator Peres Jiménez an "Honorary Submariner"; his ruthless police chief, Pedro Estrada, was similarly honored. For these and other examples, see Herbert L. Matthews, ed., *The United States and Latin America* (Englewood Cliffs, N.J.: Prentice-Hall, 1963), p. 163.

Intelligent insight into the complexities of the issue for the United States can only be gained when the problem of dictatorships throughout Latin America is viewed against the background of the area's recent history and of the principles governing the United States in its response to historical developments in this region.

Revolution is more often than not the means by which political changes are made within Latin American countries. Most of these countries exhibit and venerate the outward trappings of political democracy. As an illustration, the constitution of Argentina under the late dictator Juan Perón resounded with guarantees of civil liberties, restraints on autocratic governmental power, and other professed safeguards of freedom. In reality, elections and other practices which citizens of the United States regard as indispensable to democratic government have customarily been resorted to in Latin America to ratify and maintain the authority of the latest revolutionary regime. Frank Tannenbaum noted that from 1930 to 1956 there were "over fifty violent, mainly military, upsets of government in Latin America, and many more abortive attempts that ended in failure."[28] This pattern of course does not fit all Latin American states equally. Some, like Uruguay, are comparatively quiescent and democratically inclined; others, like Paraguay and Bolivia, appear to be addicted to perpetual revolutionary turmoil.

Throughout the region as a whole, there is no very reassuring evidence that societies have abandoned revolutionary ferment and *coups d'état* as their principal methods for effecting political change. Thus in an 18-month period during 1962–1963, five Latin American countries—Argentina, Peru, Guatemala, Ecuador, and the Dominican Republic—witnessed the overthrow of elected governments; in every case, military elements either led the revolution or provided the principal support for the elements that seized power.[29]

The problem of chronic revolutionary ferment in the Latin American states has confronted the United States ever since these countries began to throw off the colonial yoke in the early decades of the 1800s. The diplomatic response of the United States to the pattern of shifting political tides in these countries has been productive of endless controversy and misunderstanding within the Western Hemisphere.

Many of the complexities and hard choices involved in the problem of relationships between the United States and dictatorial political systems in Latin America also came into sharp focus early in 1958 in regard to Venezuela. On January 23, a popular uprising ousted the dictatorship of General Marcos Pérez Jiménez. Until the time of Jiménez's overthrow, the United States had been careful to maintain "correct" relations with his government. At least publicly, the State Department refrained from any action that might seem to support the dictator's political opponents; and in some cases, as in Washington's awarding him a "Legion of Merit" and extending hospitality to his ruthless chief of police upon the latter's visit to the United States, it was apparent that Washington was "cultivating" harmonious relations with Venezuela.

After Jiménez's overthrow, resentment toward the United States mounted steadily—until it exploded into a bitter demonstration against Vice-President Nixon, who visited the country in May. The United States was accused of having consorted with dictators and, by failure to act *against* Jiménez, of having helped maintain him in power. Letters were circulated purporting to show how diplomatic officials from the United States had sided with the dictator against his opponents. Meantime, actions taken in Washington seemed to lend credence to this view. As part of its attempt to curtail imports competing with domestic oil production, the United States began to impose "quotas" against the importation of Venezuelan oil—a move it had never taken when Jiménez was in power! On top of this, the United States, following precedents adhered to in many other such cases, granted political asylum to Jiménez and his notorious chief of police, a move that further inflamed popular antagonisms in Venezuela. As interpreted by many groups in Latin America, the actions of the United States had been dictated simply by a desire to safeguard access to Venezuelan oil.

A more recent case in point involved the response of the United States to a military-led coup that overthrew the elected government of the Dominican Republic on September 25, 1963. As a token of its displeasure, the State Department broke diplomatic relations with the Dominican Republic and cut off military and economic aid to the new regime. At his press conference, President Kennedy stated unequivocally that the United States was "opposed to an interruption of the constitutional system by a military coup" anywhere in Latin America; military juntas, he emphasized, provided "seedbeds from which . . . communism ultimately springs up." Consequently, the United States was using its influence overtly in countries such as the Dominican Republic and Peru (which had experienced a similar military takeover) "to provide for an orderly restoration of constitutional processes."[30]

Yet within a few months, the Johnson Administration had reconsidered the policy of indiscriminate and implacable opposition to military-sponsored regimes in Latin America. News reports noted that the State Department was "moving quietly" to restore economic and military assistance to the Dominican Republic and that the Johnson Administration was adopting a "flexible policy" toward Latin American dictatorships. Then a few weeks later, a high State Department official announced that henceforth the United States would continue to oppose outright only *communist* dictatorships in the Western Hemisphere; it would endeavor to avoid involvement in the internal political affairs of other Latin American states. Except for Marxist regimes, the United States would no longer distinguish officially between dictatorships and democratic systems among its American neighbors. This official suggested that in the future the United States might be guided by the Estrada principle, which we shall discuss presently, whereby the *stability* of the government was made the chief criterion for recognition by the United States.[31]

The policy problem confronting State Department officials in their attempt to evolve a satisfactory approach to Latin American dictatorships bristled with complexities and difficulties. Several antagonistic, almost mutually exclusive, principles of foreign policy and diplomatic interests must be reconciled. In some instances, the problem virtually defies satisfactory solution. Throughout the course of its diplomatic experience, the United States has sympathized with movements in other countries directed at expanding political freedom and widening popular participation in governmental affairs. At the same time, the principle of nonintervention in the internal affairs of other countries has demanded that the United States remain aloof from internal political struggles of other nations. It would not be amiss to say that the concept of nonintervention is the cornerstone of the edifice of hemispheric cooperation which the United States has tried to erect since it began advocating the policy of the Good Neighbor early in the 1930s.

Certain other strands in American foreign policy towards Latin America have tended to weaken the principle of nonintervention. And against this principle, for example, has been the recognition policy of the United States, which has been used to strengthen or weaken political movements in the hemisphere. Over the years, the United States began to evolve a set of principles to guide it in extending or withholding recognition. Before it would accord recognition to the newly independent countries in Latin America in the early 1800s, the United States demanded: (1) that the government in power actually exercise effective control over the country in question; (2) that it have a reasonably good prospect for continued stability; and (3) that it be willing and able to carry out its commitments and obligations toward other nations.[32]

In the Wilsonian era, a fourth criterion was added, when the United States was once again confronted with a revolutionary situation in Latin America, this time in Mexico. Wilson refused to recognize the Huerta regime because, in the President's words, it was a "government of butchers," which had come into power through violence and was, to Wilson's mind, antagonistic to the principles of democracy. Ultimately, Wilson intervened directly in Mexican internal affairs with the avowed purpose of overthrowing the Huerta government, on the dubious ground that in this way he would be advancing the welfare of the Mexican people.[33] Wilson's viewpoint—that the United States should recognize only those governments whose character it approved—was incorporated into United States recognition policy, and on a number of occasions thereafter it became the dominant element in that policy.

Despite the idealism periodically expressed by the United States toward Latin America since 1932, Washington's unwillingness to recognize new governments in the American republics unless they enjoy the State Department's approval has been productive of recurrent disagreements in inter-American relations. Pan-American conferences held during the 1930s, for instance, as a rule devoted considerable attention to the question of recognition. Other American countries sought to secure agreement on common principles of recognition policy that would prevail throughout the Inter-American System. Considerable support existed in Latin America for the Estrada Doctrine, named for a Mexican statesman, the gist of which was that recognition of new governments necessarily implied neither approval nor disapproval. The United States, however, consistently refused to endorse this doctrine. Each country within the Inter-American System continues to follow its own diplomatic precedents and inclinations in respect to recognition. And, although it amounts to intervention in the affairs of Latin American states, the United States continues on occasion to invoke Wilson's idea that a new government must be committed to democratic precepts and practices before cordial relations will be established and maintained with it.[34]

The nonintervention principle also faces a severe test when governments which have already been recognized embark upon policies held to be injurious to the diplomatic interests of the United States—perhaps by nationalizing foreign-owned corporations or becoming too closely identified with international communism or engaging in virulent propaganda against the United States.* An illustration is afforded by the history of relations between the United States and Argentina during and after World War II. Throughout most of the war, Argentina was openly pro-Axis. Belatedly, and with visible reluctance, Argentina finally declared war on the side of the Allies; its contribution to the Allied victory, however, was minimal. Then after the war, the internal and external policies of the dictator Juan Perón alienated official and public opinion within the United States. Perón was skilled in exploiting Yankee-phobia for his own political advantage. In time it became apparent that Perón was using Uncle Sam as a scapegoat for Argentina's increasingly critical economic situation. Perón's fulminations against United States intervention did possess some validity, since State Department officials had intervened repeatedly in an effort to change the policies of the Argentine government. Despite United States intervention to discredit Perón and make him lose in the national elections of 1946, Perón won decisively, in part because he was adept at exploiting residual resentment against the United States to full advantage.[35] Not until Perón's overthrow in 1955 did relations between the United States and Argentina improve materially.

An Assessment of Policy Alternatives

Under optimum circumstances, the question of relations between the United States and outright or camouflaged dictatorships throughout Latin America remains one of the most delicate

* In recent years, the best illustration of the problem described here is of course relations between the United States and Castro's Cuba. We have reserved consideration of the issue of communism in Cuba for a later stage in the chapter.

and difficult issues that continues to confront State Department officials. Even more than in most foreign policy decisions, the problem admits of no easy and clear-cut answers, guaranteed to achieve the national interest. Indeed, perhaps the bedrock question in the problem is: What *is* the national interest of the United States with respect to this recurrent political crisis in the Western Hemisphere?

Two oversimplified approaches must be clearly rejected as incapable of achieving the diplomatic goals of the United States in its relations with Latin American governments. One is the path of indifference or isolationism. Only the politically naïve would contend that Washington can be indifferent or insensitive to political currents on the Latin American scene or that it ought to treat all Latin American regimes equally, regardless of their political complexion or national policies. The United States cannot be apathetic about the future of democracy in Latin America any more than it can be insensitive to it in the Middle East or Asia. A second approach would have American policy-makers go to the opposite extreme by seeking to intervene *directly and openly* in the political affairs of Latin American states. According to this view, the State Department ought to operate upon the explicit Wilsonian principle of cooperating only with "democratic" political orders; implicitly at least, it would oppose all others in Latin America. A not inconsequential drawback of this approach is that its implementation would mean in practice that the United States opposed *most* governments in Latin America! But its most serious deficiency lies in its underlying rationale. The days of the Roosevelt Corollary and the "big stick" are over. Any effort by the State Department to return to them would signal the end of the OAS; at best, it would probably convert that organization into an instrument used collectively by the Latin American governments for protection against the United States. Moreover, this approach would blur the distinction between the principles actuating the United States and the Soviet Union or Red China in world affairs and would go far toward undermining the State Department's indictment of Castro's "interventionism" in the affairs of neighboring American republics. In short, this path risks the total alienation of Latin America, perhaps followed by assiduous Soviet or Chinese efforts to identify with countries threatened anew by "American imperialism."

Whatever the correct course may be, this much is clear: there is no simple or self-evident principle that offers a prospect of automatic success. The policy pursued will most likely have to be worked out on the basis of trial and error. To be successful, it will have to reflect recognition of three dominant realities. First, it must always be remembered that *whether* the United States attempts to influence the course of events in the other American republics is perhaps not so important as *how that influence is exercised*. Given the deeply ingrained and lingering sensitivity of the Latin American states to being dictated to by the United States, extreme tact, endless patience, and reliance upon persuasion and conciliation will likely accomplish far more than bluster and crude diplomatic pressure exerted upon the Latin American countries. John M. Cabot, former Assistant Secretary of State for Inter-American Affairs, has cautioned that:

> We cannot take the attitude that what is good for us is necessarily good for other nations under vastly different circumstances; that Uncle Sam knows best what is good for others, and will assume the responsibility for seeing that they get it; that it is wrong for Soviet Russia to impose Communism on foreign nations but permissible for us to impose democracy on them; that in the present state of international affairs we can afford to feud with every government whose internal policies don't altogether meet our approval.[36]

Admittedly, it is a source of embarrassment for the United States to seem to be closely identified with Latin American dictators whose actions sometimes are little different from those of Hitler or Stalin. Some might raise the question: how can the United States simultaneously condemn Soviet oppression behind the iron curtain and in recent years condone or, at any rate, do very little to interfere with dictatorships in Cuba or Bolivia or Venezuela? The answer is as simple as it is fundamental. The United States government does not today, nor has it historically, opposed dictatorships in Russia or Germany or Japan or elsewhere merely because of the form of the existing government but because ultimately dictators in these countries endangered the security of the United States and of the international community as a whole. As a rule, no such threat has arisen from totalitarian orders in the Western Hemisphere.

This is an essential distinction to keep in mind about the response of the United States to Castro's Cuba. It is one thing to say that the United States dislikes dictatorships, and that it is especially antipathetic to communist dictatorships, in Latin America. It is quite another thing to advocate that the United States intervene openly against a regime, such as Castro's in Cuba, because of its internal character or ideology. Whatever direct force the United States has brought to bear against Cuba can be justified primarily by two other factors: the Soviet Union sought to turn Cuba into a missile base to impair the security of the United States and the Inter-American System generally; and Castro has sponsored subversive activities against governments in neighboring Latin American states. In other words, direct State Department intervention against Castro was resorted to because Havana was pursuing policies that threatened the security of the hemisphere. In whatever degree citizens of the United States dislike Castro's communist program, this alone would not justify efforts to overthrow him, nor would such animosity alone prove sufficient to rally most other American republics behind the policies of the State Department.

The United States would obviously prefer to see democratic governments flourish in the Americas, as in other regions. What specific policies are calculated to serve this end? Vice-President Nixon and Milton S. Eisenhower, brother of President Eisenhower, recommended to the President in the late 1950s that the United States enthusiastically greet democratic systems in the Americas but that it have merely "a formal handshake for dictators." This means more concretely, in Milton S. Eisenhower's words, that

> . . . we refrain from granting special recognition to a Latin American dictator, regardless of the temporary advantage that might seem to be promised by such an act. I most emphatically do *not* believe that we should withdraw our programs from Latin America countries which are ruled by dictators. Nonrecognition and noncooperation would not help another nation achieve democracy. . . . By cooperating with them, even through dictators—by keeping open the lines of communication—one may hope that a growing understanding of the strength, glory, and basic morality of democracy will enable the people of a harshly ruled country to achieve and maintain democratic institutions of their own design.[37]

A second reality governing the policies of the United States toward dictatorships concerns the pivotal role of military elements in contemporary Latin American political behavior. During the 1940s and 1950s it was fashionable, even among well-informed students of Latin American affairs, to believe that "the hour of democracy had finally arrived in Latin America." Latin America, many observers widely supposed, had at last awakened from its political torpor; the era of the old-style military *caudillos* who had long dominated the political scene was at an end.[38] If subsequent events indicated that this view was premature and overly sanguine, it was not totally incorrect. For few outright military dictators, possessing virtually unlimited political power, remained. The military-inspired coups that overthrew popular governments during the early 1960s were, in many respects, fundamentally different in their methods and their goals. The military was still—and for many decades was likely to remain—a dominant force in Latin American politics; yet the "winds of change" were also sweeping this region and destroying old political patterns and ideologies. Gradually, Latin America has begun to feel the impact of twentieth-century life. Industrialization, greatly accelerated by World War II; urbanization, witnessing a flood of rural migration into overcrowded cities; education, in which opportunities are finally being extended to the masses; the impact of Arab, African, and Asian nationalism upon the Latin American mind—these and many other forces have coalesced to bring about a new context of political development in which the old-type military dictator, who used his power largely for personal or family aggrandizement, is being replaced by military juntas with quite different goals. If few political regimes in Latin America can survive *without* military support or in the face of outright military opposition, this fact should not mislead us into believing that nothing has really changed since the nineteenth or early twentieth century in the Latin American political context.

Paradoxically, it is from the ranks of the military (particularly from middle-grade officers, such as captains, majors, and colonels) that a new concern for the welfare, progress, and independence of Latin America has largely come. And it is from this class that democracy —if it is capable of emerging at all in what is, at best, an extremely hostile environment—may well evolve. Latin Americans are determined to break the long-dominant power of the Church, the landed aristocracy, the economic upper classes, and other entrenched elites who have traditionally dictated the course of political events. Traditionally lacking the support of a middle class, and only now beginning to develop one, nationalist groups in Latin America tend to look to, and make common cause with, ambitious, well-educated, intensely patriotic army officers, as one of the only forces capable of leading the nation forward.* Significantly,

* Specific examples of the new role of the military in Latin American politics are afforded by the movement that overthrew the dictatorship of Juan Perón in Argentina in September, 1955. A coalition of students, intellectuals, military leaders, and (perhaps most revolutionary of all for Latin American politics) the Roman Catholic Church joined to oust Perón, who had based his regime upon an ostensible platform of social justice, but who had in reality converted Argentina into his personal fief, for his own aggrandizement and self-indulgence. Powerful military units joined with students in raising the flag of rebellion; after victory, the military initially installed General Lonardi as Provisional President, only to oust him later in favor of the more moderate General Aramburu. This official governed for the next three years at the head of a civilian regime, whose declared aim was to restore democracy to Argentina. In the elections of 1958, Arturo Frondizi, a left-wing intellectual, was elected overwhelmingly; although military elements preferred another candidate, they accepted Frondizi, who governed reasonably well until 1962.

These events had a powerful impact in other Latin American countries. In Colombia, for example, military officials similarly bowed to popular demand and opposed the regime of General Rojas, which had governed since 1953. It was largely at the instigation of the military that an agreement was reached lifting the ban on political parties and allowing the powerful Liberals and Conservatives to alternate in office under a "National Front" policy.

In Venezuela, a military-inspired coup against the corrupt dictatorship of General Marcos Pérez Jiménez early in 1958 failed. One writer has commented: "The rebel pilots, safe in Colombia . . . wondered aloud why the United States was not supporting the revolution. They told of their training in the United States, where they were taught democracy along with flying, and that their action against . . . Jiménez had been inspired by these Stateside teachings about liberty." For these and other examples, see Tad Szulc, *The Winds of Revolution: Latin America Today—and Tomorrow* (New York: Praeger, 1963), pp. 86–100. Other examples are set forth in detail in Edwin Lieuwen, *Arms and Politics in Latin America* (New York: Praeger, 1963), pp. 59–101. A succinct and well-documented study of the trends we are discussing here is provided in Senate Foreign Relations Committee, *United States-Latin American Relations: Post-World War II Political Developments in Latin America*, 86th Congress, 1st Session (Washington, D.C.: 1959). This study, prepared by the School of Inter-American Affairs in the University of New Mexico, is one of a series of background reports on Latin America published for the committee.

the military elite in many Latin American countries was often willing to give civilian policy-makers a chance to resolve the nation's problems and lead the way to a better life. Thus, a succession of new civilian regimes came out of the wartime and early postwar era in countries including Bolivia, Ecuador, Guatemala, Cuba, Venezuela, Brazil, Peru, Panama, and Colombia.

Nowhere did the fundamental realignment of political forces within Latin American countries take place smoothly; nor was progress recorded in a straight line. Some civilian regimes attempted to do too much too quickly and inevitably failed. Adverse economic conditions at home and abroad sometimes undermined their popular support. Communist and other leftist elements almost everywhere agitated against them. In still other cases, military elements themselves overthrew the very regime they had earlier installed or supported, often because there seemed no other alternative to direct military rule. The political turmoil, and bewildering array of governments that came and went in postwar Latin America, symbolized "a painful process of social, economic, and political transformation." If the armed forces still exercised control, sometimes dominant control, over Latin American political developments, it was no less true: (1) that the goals and ideologies embraced by these forces were themselves undergoing far-reaching change; (2) that, on balance, their *relative* influence in increasingly pluralistic Latin American societies was slowly declining; (3) that the military elements themselves were usually the objects of highly disparate contending political forces, represented by right-wing traditionalists or Communists and other left-wing groups, that tried to gain their support in behalf of diverse national policies.[39]

Mindful of these tendencies, policy-makers in the United States thus concluded by the early 1960s that a government in which the influence of military elites figured prominently was not *per se* objectionable in Latin America. Indeed, as we shall see, the principal American diplomatic strategy became that of working with indigenous regimes, through programs like the Alliance for Progress, to lay the foundations for the gradual emergence of more democratic political and economic systems throughout Latin America.

The third reality of which American policy was obliged to take account was the fact that, in the final analysis, only the Latin American peoples themselves could decide the kind of political systems under which they desired to live. Neither in Latin America nor elsewhere did the United States possess the power to make such decisions for other societies. Ideologically, no other principle accorded with the professed ideals of the United States in global affairs. Even on the level of diplomatic expediency, as Dexter Perkins has observed, "it is extremely doubtful whether the United States strengthens democracy in fact by active participation in the affairs of other states. Appeals from the outside by a government over the head of constituted authority in another country seem in general to have been unsuccessful in the past, and are likely to be unsuccessful in the future."[40] This observation applies with special pertinence to an area that remains keenly sensitive to the real or imagined ambitions of the "North American Colossus"; to countries in which there are always groups willing and ready to fan the flames of xenophobia and to revive memories of State Department "big stick" diplomacy of an earlier era; and where, in at least some contexts, the alternative to authoritarian regimes might well be chaos.

Patiently, sympathetically, and with a minimum of fanfare, the United States can and must endeavor to assist in raising the level of political morality and enlightenment throughout Latin America, realizing all the while that political freedom and stability are not likely to endure unless there are firm socioeconomic foundations and that, in most crucial respects, the future of Latin American countries will be determined by the populations of these countries. In many if not most instances, the influence of the United States is likely to be marginal. Any new flare-ups of xenophobia, triggered by genuine or fancied threats of intervention by the United States, will assuredly solidify latent anti-democratic tendencies and will postpone the emergence of orderly and effective governments, based upon respect for human freedoms.

PROBLEMS OF HEMISPHERIC TRADE AND AID

U.S. Assistance to Latin America

When Milton S. Eisenhower returned from a good-will tour of Latin America in 1953, he reported widespread misunderstanding of the United States in southern countries, "misunderstanding especially of our economic capacity and an underestimation of the degree of the sacrifices the people of the United States have made since 1941."[41] Succeeding years witnessed no appreciable improvement in this aspect of American Hemispheric relations. A reporter found the attitude prevailing at an Inter-American Economic Conference, held in Washington late in 1958, to be "a sullen and growing revolt against economic conditions for which the United States, whether justly or unjustly, was somehow held partly responsible." Expressing a complaint voiced widely throughout Latin America, one delegate stated: "The economic measures taken toward Latin America by the United States have always been very small ones, without the importance or magnitude required by the problems to be solved in Latin American countries."[42]

Living in an area comparatively insulated from the cold-war tensions that have heavily shaped the foreign policy of the United States toward other major regions, and yet sharing in the expectations commonly held by other underdeveloped areas, officials and citizens in Latin America have been unable to comprehend why foreign assistance to their countries has been a small part of the foreign aid total extended by Washington since World War II and why Uncle Sam has often appeared far more generous toward its former enemies, such as Germany, Italy, and Japan, than toward its professed southern friends. In Latin American eyes the limited amount of foreign aid provided them since 1947 has seemed to imply that the United States has only a subordinate interest in helping these economically backward nations elevate their standards of living and levels of productivity.[43]

Down to the early 1960s, statistical data tended to support Latin America's claim that the lion's share of foreign assistance by the United States has gone to Western Europe, the Middle East, and Asia. In postwar foreign aid provided by the United States through 1957, less than $2 billion, or a little over 3 percent of a total of $62 billion, went to Latin America. Out of the total flow of foreign capital into Latin American countries in the period 1950–1958, grants by the United States government totaled $2.3 billion, or 22.5 percent of the total flow of $10.2 billion received by countries in this region. Latin American nations were keenly sensitive to the fact that this total from *all* sources was less than the United States government alone furnished Western Europe under the Marshall Plan, and that grants from Washington to Latin American governments over this eight-year period were equal to about one-sixth of the total extended to promote European recovery.[44] As for military aid, Latin American countries contended that they had been virtually omitted altogether from Washington's largess, as indicated by the fact that these nations normally received 2 or 3 percent of the total military assistance budget of the United States.

Latin America's role in the foreign assistance program under the Truman and Eisenhower Administrations may be highlighted by looking at the Mutual Security Act for fiscal year 1960. The act entailed a total of $3.6 billion in foreign aid. Direct military support ($1.4 billion) and support for defense activities of other free nations ($0.751 billion) made a combined military aid program of $2.151 billion. Of this total, Latin America was granted $0.67 billion, or 3.1 percent of the funds earmarked for military assistance throughout the world. Although this percentage had remained fairly constant in recent years, considerable opposition had developed in Congress to providing military aid to Latin American countries, and the amount finally authorized was less than the Eisenhower Administration had recommended. Thus Congress cut out a proposal, endorsed by the Senate Foreign Relations Committee, that $31.5 million be given to the Organization of American States to encourage the creation of an international police force under OAS auspices. Furthermore, Congress believed that more stringent criteria ought to govern provision of military assistance to Latin America; it inserted a provision in the act specifying that "internal security requirements" within Latin American countries "shall not, unless the President determines otherwise, be the basis for military assistance to American Republics." The act stipulated further that "military equipment and materials may be furnished to the other American Republics only in furtherance of missions *directly relating to the common defense of the Western Hemisphere* which are found by the President to be important to the security of the United States."* Such pro-

* The text of the Mutual Security Act of 1959, amending the same act for 1954, may be found in House Report No. 695, 86th Congress, 1st Session, 1959.
    In addition to the provision of technical-economic assistance discussed above, Latin America shared in various multinational projects to which the United States contributed, such as technical assistance programs carried on by the UN and the Atoms for Peace program.

visions would almost certainly generate dissatisfactions south of the border.

Intensely proud and desirous of building up their prestige in the community of nations, Latin American countries could not be expected to react sympathetically to any move in Washington that detracted from the strength of their already weak military forces. Tempers in these countries were not likely to be improved either by the fact that Latin America was omitted entirely from the list of countries scheduled to receive $751 million in defense support funds.

The Mutual Security Act of 1959 provided $179.5 million for bilateral technical cooperation or economic assistance to foreign countries, out of which Latin America was slated to receive $43.7 million, 24.3 percent of the total. In addition, the United States contributed $1.5 million to the technical assistance program carried on by the Organization of American States. Limited by law to a ceiling of no more than 70 percent of the total budget of OAS-sponsored projects, the United States had contributed approximately that percentage in preceding years. Such projects involved activities like public health teaching programs, statistical training, construction of new housing, establishment of normal schools in rural areas, and encouragement of scientific practices in agriculture.*

Nations in the Caribbean, Central and South America have also received financial assistance from other sources that are heavily supported by the United States government. Both the International Bank for Reconstruction and Development and the Export-Import Bank, the latter being an agency of the United States government, had advanced sizable loans to countries in this area. The newer Development Loan Fund, established specifically to make capital available to underdeveloped nations, by 1959 had provided over $63 million in loans to 14 Latin American nations. Yet, according to the Senate Foreign Relations Committee,

* Special Committee to Study the Foreign Aid Program, *Foreign Aid Activities of Other Free Nations*, 85th Congress, 1st Session (Washington, D.C.: 1957), pp. 31–32. For several years, the United States had also endeavored to make "emergency assistance" available to Latin American governments to deal with extraordinary situations prevailing in that region. For 1960, such special assistance sought to alleviate hardship situations in Bolivia and Haiti; the former was hard-pressed to maintain economic viability because of its undue reliance upon the tin industry, while the latter had been severely hit by hurricane damage.

DLF's resources were inadequate to the existing need, with requests for loans "increasing far beyond its capacity to provide assistance."[45]

The Alliance for Progress

Valuable as they were in assisting with Latin American economic progress, foreign aid programs by the United States down to the late 1950s remained limited and incommensurate with the region's pressing needs. After a tour of the area during 1960, an experienced public servant in the United States observed:

> During the next decade and thereafter the fight against communism in and by Latin America may turn out to be as important to the U.S. and to the free world as that in any other part of the globe.[46]

In the same period, Milton Eisenhower described Latin America as "a continental area in ferment." Senator George D. Aiken (Republican of Vermont) noted that ". . . Latin America is in a race between evolution and revolution. The crucial question is whether Latin American democratic political institutions are sturdy enough to bring about the needed economic and social reforms quickly enough. U.S. policy should be directed to helping this process through any appropriate means available."[47] Citing conditions within individual Latin American countries, this legislator noted that: "Nowhere is the race between economic growth and economic chaos more evident and dramatic than in Brazil." In Peru, the overriding issue was "whether or not the Indian half of the population will enter modern society on the democratic side of the fence." Bolivia had "produced a political miracle and is now waiting for an economic one." In Panama, a country having few resources, this observer found "widespread unrest" and concluded that "the surprising thing is that there has not been more."[48] In brief, the "revolution of rising expectations" throughout Latin America was fomenting rising social and political tensions. Ample evidence could be found for supporting the judgment of the former President of Colombia Eduardo Santos: "As things are going now, the greatest outburst in history is brewing in Latin America. In 5, 10 or 15 years, unless the United States acts, you'll see country after country explode. The Cuban upheaval will seem mild in comparison."[49]

Statistical indicators of economic levels throughout Latin America confirmed the fact that a far greater effort was required than had been made thus far to deal successfully with the region's massive problems. Nowhere in the world perhaps, at least not on a comparable scale, was the "population explosion" generating such a vicious spiral of economic, social, and political dislocations. In the decade 1953–1963, Latin America's population increased about 30 percent. By the latter date, the region had approximately 200 million people—destined, at present population growth rates, to reach 400 million by the 1980s! With one of the most rapid population growth rates in the world, Latin America found its per capita income level declining in some countries; in others, incumbent governments were hard-pressed to show any significant improvement in income levels. Illiteracy rates were extremely high in countries such as Bolivia (60 percent), the Dominican Republic (58 percent), Guatemala (70 percent), and Haiti (85 percent); even in the more advanced Latin American states such as Brazil, Colombia, and Venezuela, they were 50 percent, 48 percent, and 18 percent respectively.

Per capita income ranged from under $200 annually in such countries as Honduras, Peru, and Paraguay, to $200–399 annually in Mexico, Colombia, and Brazil, to over $400 in Venezuela, Argentina, and Uruguay. The region's average annual per capita income was $280; in some of the larger cities, it was below $70 annually! President Kennedy described the situation prevailing widely throughout Latin America in the early 1960s by saying that, for millions of people in this area,

> life expectancy . . . is less than 50 years . . . half the children have no schools to attend . . . almost half the adults cannot read or write . . . tens of millions of city dwellers live in unbearable slums . . . millions more in rural areas suffer from easily curable diseases without hope of treatment. . . .

He cautioned that such problems "will not be solved simply by complaints about Castro, by blaming all problems on communism, or generals, or nationalism."

Compounding their problems were the adverse tendencies to which Latin American states were subjected in world trade and investment. For years, the prices of goods these countries bought in the world market were rising, while the price of the commodities they sold was declining. In addition, from a peak of $1.5 billion annually, private investment in Latin America by sources in the

United States also declined, totaling only $0.2 billion in 1962.[50]

With these realities in mind, the Kennedy Administration concluded that the time was overdue for a fundamental reorientation in concern with the problem of Latin America by the United States. North Americans, the President confessed, had "not always grasped the significance" of the needs of their southern neighbors, just as the latter had "not always understood the urgency of the need to lift people from poverty and ignorance and despair." Accordingly, on March 13, 1961, Kennedy proposed what he labeled "a vast new 10-year plan for the Americas, to transform the 1960s into a historic decade of democratic progress." If successful, at the end of the decade the plan would witness "the beginning of a new era in the American experience . . . every American republic will be the master of its own revolution and its own hope and progress." Kennedy's proposal was soon known as the Alliance for Progress. Like the Marshall Plan that had revitalized Western Europe in the early postwar period, the Alliance for Progress emphasized *mutual collaboration* among the participants and accorded a key role to maximum self-help by the recipients of American economic aid. The President was convinced that "only the most determined efforts of the American nations themselves can bring success to this effort." Without such an effort, "no amount of help will advance the welfare of the people." Among the 10 points cited by the President as fundamental to the plan, key ones were: regional planning by the Inter-American Economic and Social Council; an initial allocation by the United States of $500 million to launch the Alliance for Progress; increased economic integration and cooperation among nations in the Western Hemisphere; and an attempt to stabilize the commodity market for Latin American exports.

The most far-reaching change contemplated by the Alliance for Progress, however, was its implicit demand for nothing less than a social and economic revolution throughout Latin America. It demanded "vital social change" in this region; its funds would be used to "improve productivity and use of . . . land," to "attack archaic tax and land-tenure structures," and to assure "abundance to all" throughout the region. In short, successful fulfillment of the projected goals demanded a radical reconstruction of traditional Latin American society, in which oligarchies based upon vast land holdings and ancient privilege would be eliminated, personal fortunes that had traditionally been used for luxuries or had been invested overseas would be directed into national development, and sweeping transformations in all levels of society would usher in an age of equal opportunities for all. To Congress, Kennedy reiterated that the Alliance's "effectiveness depends on the willingness of each recipient nation to improve its own institutions, make necessary modifications in its own social patterns, and mobilize its own domestic resources for a program of development."[51]

To carry out this ambitious scheme, President Kennedy pledged the United States to supply $10 billion in governmental funds, to be supplemented by an additional $10 billion from other public and private sources for Latin American economic development. Thus from the beginning, the role of *private investment capital* was recognized as indispensable in promoting economic progress in the southern zone of the hemisphere. The charter formally establishing the Alliance for Progress was signed by all the American republics (except Cuba) at Punta del Este on August 17, 1961. Under this agreement a "Panel of Nine" was established to advise governments on plans submitted for Alliance support and to promote hemispheric economic cooperation and commodity price stabilization. Under the plan ultimately adopted to implement the Alliance, Latin American countries themselves were expected to furnish some 80 percent of the resources needed to achieve its goals.[52]

Launched with considerable public fanfare and in an atmosphere of high idealism, the Alliance for Progress from a very early date faced sharp criticism both within the United States and south of the border. At home, it encountered vocal opposition from a growing circle of opponents to *all* foreign aid. Both Presidents Kennedy and Johnson conceded publicly that foreign aid programs *per se* faced tough legislative scrutiny. We have analyzed the forces in the anti-foreign aid movement elsewhere, so that we shall not examine them here.* It is enough to emphasize that, before his death, President Kennedy became deeply concerned about the future of the Alliance for Progress, so much so that he bluntly warned critics:

* The mounting opposition to foreign aid within the United States is discussed in Chapter 15.

Had the needs of the people of Cuba been met in the pre-Castro period—their need for food, for housing, for education, for jobs, above all, for a democratic responsibility in the fulfillment of their own hopes— there would have been no Castro, no missiles in Cuba, and no need for Cuba's neighbors to incur the immense risks of resistance to threatened aggression from the island.[53]

For essentially different reasons, the Alliance for Progress also encountered difficult obstacles in Latin America. Let us briefly examine some of the difficulties it faced in the mid-1960s, in an effort to assess its future.

The Future of the Alliance for Progress

Reporting to Congress two years after he presented his Alliance for Progress idea, on April 2, 1963, President Kennedy called attention to "striking accomplishments" that had been achieved in that period. Among the more outstanding accomplishments were intensive housing programs—producing 140,000 new homes for Latin Americans; over 8000 new classrooms; the distributions of some 4 million textbooks; the construction of 700 community water systems throughout Latin America; the extension of 160,000 loans to improve agricultural production throughout the region; and the erection of some 900 new hospitals and health centers; the improvement of the diets of over 8 million families, with this figure slated to rise to 16 million families by 1964. Impressive progress had also been made in projects tailored to the needs of individual Latin American countries, such as a program to train some 3000 new teachers in northeastern Brazil and a $30 million scheme for slum clearance in Bogatá. In other countries, like Argentina, Bolivia, and El Salvador, steps had been taken toward a revision and improvement of antiquated tax structures. Land reform and agricultural productivity programs had been launched in such countries as Venezuela, Chile, and Uruguay. Above all, executive officials detected "a change in the hearts and minds of the people—a growing will to develop their countries."[54] A study submitted to the Senate Foreign Relations Committee in this same period found that the *Alianza para Progreso* had "taken a giant leap forward."[55] That progress continued to be achieved throughout the months that followed was indicated by President Johnson's address on the third anniversary of the program, when he told a gathering of Latin American diplomats that: "In the last

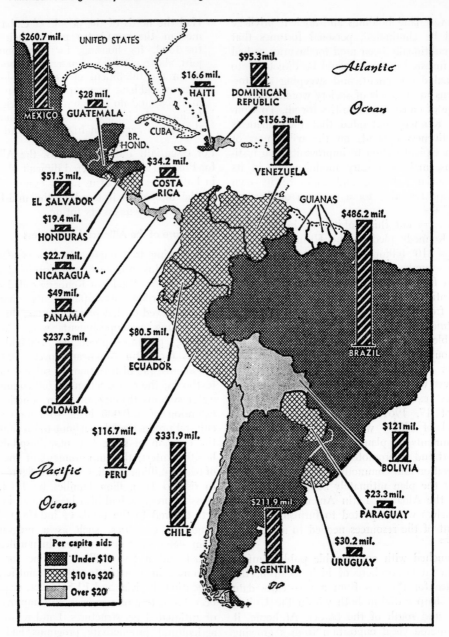

Alliance for Progress—United States Aid to Latin America, from July, 1961–January, 1964. (Source: *The New York Times*, March 15, 1964. © 1964 by The New York Times Company. Reprinted by permission.)

three years we have built a structure of common effort designed to endure for many years." Citing continued gains in school construction, industrial and agricultural expansion, housing, hospital and health programs, land and tax reform, President Johnson observed that all Americans could be "proud of these achievements."[56]

Yet by the mid-1960s, there was no denying the fact that the Alliance for Progress had lost much of its momentum and that officials in the United States were apprehensive about its future. The legislative report cited earlier thus characterized the early gains in the program as "only a short faltering step," in the light of the projected goals.[57] Before his death, President Kennedy called for all participants in the program to attack problems endemic in Latin America with "continuing urgency." President Johnson urged governments in all the American republics to concentrate on the "unfinished business" remaining, in order that "we can make our Alliance succeed in the years ahead." Still ahead lay the "complex and sometimes painful and difficult task of basic social reform and economic advance."[58]

The White House thus referred publicly, if indirectly, to a fact that had become abundantly apparent to informed observers of Latin American affairs in the mid-1960s: the Alliance

We're Taking a New Look at It. (Source: Herblock in *The Washington Post*, reproduced in *The New York Times*, February 23, 1964.)

for Progress was lagging, and it was at best problematical whether many of its principal goals could be achieved at all, before severe economic dislocations and political eruptions in Latin America rendered their achievement all but impossible. From the beginning, the program had rested upon the precept, as one State Department official phrased it, that "a people cannot be saved—people save themselves." And it was chiefly in this area—the unwillingness or inability of regimes throughout Latin America to make the sweeping reforms indispensable for the success of the

program—that was the greatest obstacle to the "decade of progress" in the Western Hemisphere.

Full allowance of course had to be made for the fact that even successful reforms were not *immediately* translated into greater economic production within the countries concerned. Moreover, the United States had to restrain a tendency to become impatient, to expect *all* or even most of the measures required for the success of the Alliance for Progress to be taken in the first third or half of the decade allocated for its fulfillment. Nor could it be forgotten that, in light of the magnitude and scope of Latin America's problem, progress under optimum circumstances was likely to be slow, if indeed for many years it might not be extraordinarily difficult even to achieve any significant gains in the face of the population explosion occurring throughout the region. It also had to be recognized that many of the very conditions in Latin America that made the Alliance for Progress necessary—antiquated and bureaucratic administrative systems, chronic inflation, the "flight" of native capital outside the countries, prevalent political turbulence—also militated strongly against the ability of these countries to draw up and carry out realistic development plans acceptable to Washington. There was also the inevitable tendency for observers in the United States to dwell upon continuing and graphic evidences of economic and political instability (like mounting inflation in Brazil, the near-stagnation of Bolivia's economy, or a military *coup d'état* in Peru) and to gloss over less spectacular, but perhaps more fundamental, developments that illustrated Latin America's progress in achieving the Alliance's underlying goals.

After allowing for these admonitions, it remains true that progress in implementing the Alliance's goals remained distressingly slow in many Latin American countries. In most Latin American countries, the Alliance had profound political implications, as reformers vied with entrenched conservative elements over whether to carry out or to block the measures required by the program. The "national planning" demanded to fulfill the program's objectives often added new fuel to what was already an inflammatory political situation. Since the Alliance called for nothing less than a "democratic revolution" throughout Latin America, in the short run at least it was bound to prove a highly controversial and unsettling political force. For many countries of Latin America, there was the inescapable reality that powerful, deeply entrenched political elements *preferred* the *status quo*, even if it meant losing substantial outside assistance to promote national development. Thus, as one observer put it, in many of the American republics the Alliance was encountering

> . . . stubborn resistance to change by a small but obdurate oligarchy that would prefer a return to dictatorship rather than accept reforms. . . .

Even by the mid-1960s, for the masses in Latin America, the "irrational throbbing of nationalism" often directed against the United States sometimes still had far more appeal than did the "unromantic appeal for responsible fiscal policies as a prerequisite for sound development." Although individual instances of progress could be cited, it remained true that, after three years of the Alliance, "The material conditions of the masses in most of the hemisphere have continued to deteriorate as populations soar and the income of the raw-materials producing countries declines further." Prevailing public "disenchantment" with Alliance achievements meant that: "Political demagogues are beginning to shop around for politically more attractive short cuts, even though they may lead nowhere."[59]

Certain economic indicators also suggested that many of the gains achieved by the Alliance for Progress were thus far superficial and extremely limited. After three years, the economic growth rate for the Latin American countries as a whole showed little improvement, in spite of the fact that 10 of the 19 participating countries exceeded the projected goal of a 2.5 percent annual per capita increase in income. Acute and persistent dislocations in Brazil and Argentina (with half of Latin America's population) pulled regional averages down. During 1963, in Chile, Bolivia, Mexico, the Central American republics, Venezuela, Colombia, and Peru, the rate of economic growth either was less than, or did not exceed, the rate attained the preceding year. Moreover, economists detected a considerable disparity between the economic progress achieved in the urban areas of Latin America, as opposed to the results witnessed in rural areas. A State Department official thus pointed to "a marked lag in the development of the rural areas." Events in Brazil (sometimes looked upon as the key to the future political direction of Latin America) highlighted existing problems.

Writing in 1964, one experienced observer of Latin American affairs described "the steadily deteriorating political and economic situation of Brazil"; in that country "rising agitation and unabating inflation have combined to create Latin America's potentially most dangerous and explosive crisis." With runaway inflation doubling the cost of living in a single year, Brazil had done little or nothing to effect reforms required by membership in the Alliance; it had in effect "read itself out of the program."[60]

Wave of Revolution Versus Flower of Reform. (Source: Mauldin in *The St. Louis Post-Dispatch*, March 25, 1962.)

Equally distressing to observers in the United States was the rate at which *private* investment in Latin America, regarded as playing a vital role in the Alliance for Progress, had sharply *declined* by the mid-1960s. After achieving a peak in 1957, private investment from the United States fell off sharply; by 1962, it was entering Latin America at a slower rate than in the early 1950s. For many years, State Department officials had stressed the contribution to be made by private capital in the economic development of the Western Hemisphere. By the end of the 1950s, approximately 80 percent of all capital investment from the United States in Latin

American countries came from private sources. In 1958, Dr. Milton Eisenhower warned the Latin Americans bluntly that: "Private capital cannot be driven. It must be attracted." In view of the tendency of private investors to seek "safer" political environments within the United States itself or Western Europe, he was convinced that "attracting private capital to Latin America . . . is not an easy matter."[61]

Throughout the years that followed, the environment needed to induce an expansion of private investment in Latin America became, if anything, even more unattractive than before. Endless political ferment, the tendency of political groups to denounce "Yankee imperialism" and to call for the nationalization or expulsion of foreign corporations, expropriations of foreign properties, rampant inflation, lingering governmental corruption, oppressive tax burdens, limitations upon the repatriation of profits—these did not coalesce into an atmosphere conducive to the attracting of foreign development funds. Repeatedly, State Department officials were required to underscore the central importance of private capital in promoting Latin America's economic development, as when Under Secretary of State Harriman told an audience in Brazil that governmental and private development activities were complementary approaches and that: "The choice between public and private means is not a matter of theology. It is the pragmatic question of how resources can best be used to hasten national growth." Harriman emphasized that "freedom and efficiency are most likely to flourish when economic decision, ownership and power are widely distributed" between the public and private sectors.[62] A few months later, President Johnson once more emphasized that "public funds are not enough. We must work together to insure the maximum use of private capital. . . . Without it growth will certainly fall far behind." Again he underlined the fact that: "Such capital will respond to a stable prospect of fair earnings and a chance to create badly needed industry and business on a responsible, safe, and sound basis." He warned against those groups in Latin America "who destroy the confidence of risk capital," since they "endanger the hopes of their people for a more abundant life" throughout the region.[63]

By the mid-1960s, only one thing seemed certain about the Alliance for Progress. Results would continue to be slow, characterized by numerous setbacks in individual Latin American countries, and in some instances perhaps even insufficient to stem the tide of economic stagnation and of accompanying political turbulence. Launched as a kind of Marshall Plan for the Western Hemisphere, the Alliance for Progress faced two hurdles that differed, at least in marked degree, from the earlier program designed to reconstruct Western Europe. Latin America's problems were far more critical and obdurate, and its resources for solving its problems much more limited, than had been true of Europe; and, perhaps even more crucially, successful implementation of the *Alianza para Progreso* demanded a thoroughgoing social and economic revolution, which in itself was not likely to promote (at least in the short run) political *stability* in a region where democratic political processes had traditionally been used to disguise authoritarian political power. Perhaps even more than in a region like Southeast Asia, friends of democracy and political stability in Latin America were in a race against time. They had entered the race with an extremely ambitious program, at a very late stage; the forces they opposed had many advantages. Whether they could win the race and usher in the "decade of progress" remained at best an open question. When President Johnson declared, late in 1963, that "no work is more important for our generations of Americans than our work in this hemisphere," he acknowledged that the outcome was likely to prove crucial for inter-American relations, and for international politics generally, for generations to come.[64]

COMMUNISM IN LATIN AMERICA

The importance of Latin America as an arena of cold-war hostilities may be gauged by recalling briefly the Nazi menace to the Western Hemisphere during World War II. Nazi agents were active in a number of Latin American states, particularly Argentina. There was perhaps never a time when the Axis powers were in danger of gaining control over Latin America—nor could the threat to the security of the United States existing in that quarter compare with the danger from Europe or Asia—but the United States was nonetheless compelled to divert over 100,000 troops for protection of that vital region.[65] Today, according to a high Defense Department spokesman, "In enemy hands the Latin American countries could provide bases for attack which would be dangerously close to the United

States"—a fact that was borne home with the utmost gravity to citizens of the United States, when aerial photographs showed Soviet guided missiles being installed by Castro's regime in Cuba. These weapons were capable of bringing the great industrial northeastern heartland of the United States within their field of fire. Similarly, a potential aggressor would find that the "bulge" of Brazil affords a tempting foothold for any enemy seeking to penetrate the Western Hemisphere across the South Atlantic, especially if the Middle East and northern and western portions of Africa were in hostile hands. Conversely, Brazil and its neighbors offer needed bases for air power and for radar defense units to safeguard the Americas and the South Atlantic sea lanes. Latin America also supplies the United States a number of strategic imports. One of the most important now is thorium from Brazil, used for thermonuclear technology. The states along the northern periphery of the South American continent and in Central America are in close proximity to the Panama Canal, while those along the continent's western fringe can protect vital sea and air approaches to the hemisphere. Moreover, with its own domestic petroleum reserves being rapidly depleted, the United States is becoming more than ever dependent upon oil from Venezuela; these reserves would also be vital in maintaining the security of the Western allies, if an enemy blocked access to the oil supplies of the Middle East.

Because of Latin America's strategic-military importance to the United States, Washington has regarded the successful establishment of a communist bridgehead in the American republics with the utmost gravity. Just how strong is the communist movement in Latin America? Measured solely by the size of national Communist parties, there is no cause for alarm within the United States. Membership varies from around 50,000 in Argentina and Brazil, to 30,000–40,000 in Chile and Cuba, to 500–1000 in El Salvador, Guatemala, and Honduras, to negligible membership in Haiti and the Dominican Republic.[66] Yet a quantitative standard alone would be misleading as an indication of the threat posed by the intrigues of the communist movement in South America and the Caribbean. It is profitable to recall that communist groups in most countries, including Soviet Russia, are small minorities and that Marxist-Leninist-Stalinist theory supports this phenomenon. Communist infiltration of *other* political parties, utilization of

popular social and economic reform movements to advance the Kremlin's diplomatic ambitions, gradual infiltration of governments through "united fronts," skillful propaganda moves calculated to undermine the prestige and influence of the United States and to increase that of the Soviet Union, sabotage and espionage activities directed from Moscow—these are the dangers inherent in the presence of comparatively small, but dedicated and tightly disciplined, Communist party and Communist front organizations in the American republics.

Politico-economic conditions in Latin America often provide a fertile seedbed for the germination of communism. Poor, sometimes to the point of being poverty-stricken, dependent upon one-crop economies, saddled with antiquated social structures that favor privileged classes while depressing those at the bottom of the scale, handicapped by formidable geographical obstacles to economic betterment, and yet all the while believing in the desirability and possibility of material advancement, citizens in these countries can be expected to listen sympathetically to the siren song of the Kremlin that Marxism will fulfill their long-cherished dreams. As an example, a report by the International Cooperation Administration in 1957 characterized the favorable environment for the existence of communism in Boliva as one in which:

> Widespread poverty, the political inexperience of the population, the existence of a large poorly paid working class, a civilian militia not wholly under Government control, and the low morale of the small national army and air force were factors which favored extremists. If the moderate forces had not been able to prevent economic deterioration, they would probably have lasted about as long as the Kerensky regime in Russia in 1917.[67]

Two crises in recent years have called attention dramatically to the problem of communist infiltration of Latin America and provide case studies for evaluating the response of the United States to this threat. They are the crisis in Guatemala under the Eisenhower Administration and the Soviet-American confrontation in Cuba under the Kennedy Administration.

Crisis in Guatemala

The emergence of the communist movement in Guatemala cannot be divorced from the context of political events there within recent history. Revolutionary ferment had long marked the political scene in Guatemala, as elsewhere in Latin America, in large part because non-communist groups had been unable to effectuate lasting socioeconomic reforms. Like its counterparts in Asia, the Middle East, and other Latin American nations, the Guatemalan Communist party was able to pose as the champion of nationalist aspirations while promising progress in solving bedrock economic problems. In the words of a British observer, "It is impossible to draw an exact boundary-line between nationalism and communism in Latin America today."[68]

The year 1944 witnessed the beginning of a new revolutionary regime under Juan José Arévalo, who overthrew the government of the military dictator Jorge Ubico. The new government received substantial support from the lower middle classes and from the intellectuals, with many of the latter believing that a Marxist approach offered the best hope of progress for Guatemala. As is customary following revolutions in Latin America, a number of prominent and less prominent political exiles returned to Guatemala. Among these were influential individuals who espoused communism; some of these had received revolutionary training in Moscow. Until the early 1950s, however, Guatemalan Communists tended to operate clandestinely and to work through popular movements to advance their goals.

As time passed, Communists infiltrated the Guatemalan labor movement and other organizations commanding wide popular support. Through such groups Communists carried on intensive propaganda campaigns closely paralleling the diplomatic line of the Kremlin. The equivocal policies of President Arévalo, who encouraged "participation of Communists as individuals" in the government and labor movement while "discouraging the formation of an open organized Stalinist party," enabled communist groups to gain more and more control over Guatemalan affairs.[69] As the time for the national elections of 1951 drew near, the tempo of communist agitation and propaganda greatly increased. Election of the Communist-sponsored candidate, Colonel Jacobo Arbenz, as President was soon followed by the open establishment of the Guatemalan Communist party (Partido Communista de Guatemala, PCG). At home Arbenz, supported by the PCG, embarked upon a long overdue program of land reform. As the largest landholder

in the country, the United Fruit Company—with headquarters in Boston—became the principal target of Arbenz's reform measures. Guatemalan nationalism was also directed against the alleged power of the *Empresa Eléctrica*, owned by investors within the United States, that generated four-fifths of the country's electric power.[70]

In external affairs, the Arbenz government was making little effort to conceal its growing hostility toward the United States. On a number of occasions Guatemala gave the appearance of deliberately seeking to provoke the United States into some kind of ill-advised intervention in Central America. As an illustration, Guatemala dramatically withdrew from the Organization of Central American States —a regional grouping that had long been actively encouraged by officials in Washington —charging that OCAS had become merely a tool of State Department propaganda and an instrument whereby Uncle Sam dominated the affairs of weaker Central American countries. As the months passed, policy-makers in the United States were convinced they detected the hand of Guatemalan Communists in fomenting political unrest in such countries as British Guiana and British Honduras. Guatemala provided a base for Communist-inspired intrigue throughout all the neighboring Central American states. In international affairs Guatemala's position coincided with the Kremlin's with remarkable frequency, notably in respect to virulent propaganda attacks against alleged "Wall Street imperialism" and in denunciations of free-world defense efforts generally.[71]

Quite naturally then, developments in Guatemala were viewed with grave misgivings in Washington. On June 30, 1954, Secretary of State Dulles publicly called attention to the "evil purpose of the Kremlin to destroy the inter-American system. . . ." He noted that "For several years international communism has been probing . . . for nesting places in the Americas. It finally chose Guatemala. . . ."[72] Side by side with the consolidation of Communist power in Guatemala therefore went increasing diplomatic activity to deal with what the United States regarded as a menace to hemispheric solidarity and security. In an earlier period the United States would most probably have invoked the Monroe Doctrine unilaterally. Now it sought to work through the Inter-American System. As early as April 7, 1951, the foreign ministers of the American republics, largely at the instigation of the

United States, had issued the "Declaration of Washington," calling for "prompt action . . . against the aggressive activities of international communism. . . ."[73] But as it watched the steady accretion in the influence of Guatemalan communism, the Eisenhower Aministration was persuaded that stronger measures were demanded. Hence Secretary of State Dulles personally attended an OAS meeting in Venezuela on March 28, 1954, where he was successful in getting the "Caracas Declaration" approved by an overwhelming vote. This sharply worded resolution declared that

> the domination or control of the political institutions of any American States by the international communist movement . . . would constitute a threat to the sovereignty and political independence of the American States, endangering the peace of America, and would call for a Meeting of Consultation to consider the adoption of appropriate action in accordance with existing treaties.[74]

The Caracas Declaration was widely hailed in the West, most especially in militantly anti-communist circles, as an outstanding diplomatic victory for the United States on the cold-war front. Now the weight of the entire Inter-American System could be thrown against the "communist beachhead" in the Western Hemisphere. Discriminating observers, however, pointed to a number of signs indicating significant differences of opinion among the American republics about the proper attitude toward Guatemalan communism. It was clear that Latin America was much less concerned about the threat of communism in Guatemala, and much more alarmed about State Department interference in hemispheric affairs, than the United States.*

* At this meeting of the OAS, Latin American delegates voiced a theme that was recurrent in their attitudes about the communist problem in the Americas. Although the Caracas Declaration had been approved by a vote of 17 to 1 (with Guatemala predictably voting no, and Mexico and Argentina abstaining), many Latin American spokesmen expressed strong reservations about Washington's preoccupation with the issue of communism. Justifiably or not, then and throughout the years that followed, Latin American states believed that the interest of the United States in their problems tended to vary directly according to the intensity of the communist threat to the hemisphere. Put differently, they often gained the impression that Latin America was "useful" to the United States only in the degree to which it played a role in "containing" communism. Thus a Bolivian delegate to the conference demanded "something more than a new way of fighting communism . . . something

Events moved toward a climax in the spring and summer of 1954, when Guatemalan Communists supported a strike in Honduras and when a shipload of arms from behind the iron curtain arrived in Guatemala. Denouncing Guatemala as already the "heaviest armed state" in Central America, the State Department moved immediately to increase the flow of armaments to other countries in that area.[75] In the ensuing diplomatic tug of war, Guatemala, supported by the Communist bloc, sought to have the United Nations consider alleged United States intervention in Guatemala's affairs; Washington, on the other hand, was insistent that the United Nations did not have initial jurisdiction in the matter and demanded that it first be considered by the Organization of American States. Meanwhile, tension was growing in Central America. On June 18 an anti-communist force under Colonel Castillo Armas crossed into Guatemala from Honduras. Within a short time the pro-communist Arbenz government collapsed. "Each one of the American States has cause for profound gratitude," said Secretary of State Dulles. The "impressive solidarity" of the Inter-American System, he continued, "undoubtedly shook the Guatemalan Government." All Americans could rejoice that the citizens of that country "had the courage and

appropriate to improve welfare and progress" in the Americas. A delegate from Uruguay confessed that he supported the Caracas Declaration "without enthusiasm, without optimism, without joy and without feeling that we were contributing to the adoption of a constructive measure." That this sentiment did not disappear throughout the months that followed was indicated by the view of José Figueres, a former President of Costa Rica, who told two visitors from the United States several years later: "Unless there is a change in United States policies in relation to the hemisphere, there is the absurd possibility that Latin America may turn toward the Soviet Union." William Benton, The Voice of Latin America (New York: Harper & Row, 1961), p. 73.

Long-standing resentment and fear that Latin America was being "used" as a cold-war instrument by the United States undoubtedly was one reason why General de Gaulle struck a responsive chord during his tour of Mexico early in 1964. His plea for greater Latin American diplomatic "independence" expressed a yearning that was deep-seated throughout the region. One commentator has observed: "General de Gaulle's trips to Latin America, with a message to the region to 'follow me,' are only minor symptoms of the independence of Washington that he preaches and, increasingly, practices." The New York Times, March 16, 1964, dispatch by Max Frankel.

the will to eliminate the traitorous tools of of foreign despots."[76]

From one perspective—that of a dramatic victory of the free world against communism —the United States had scored an impressive diplomatic coup in the Guatemalan affair. Whatever else Armas was, and we shall examine this question more fully below, he was certainly anti-communist. Temporarily at least, the "communist beachhead" in Guatemala had been eliminated.

But many Latin American countries, joined by some of the United States's Western allies, were less given to unqualified rejoicing than were supporters of Secretary Dulles. If joy among the allies was noticeably restrained, there were several reasons why it should be. Skepticism, in the first place, was directed against State Department complicity in the counterrevolution that had ousted the Arbenz government. The exact nature and scope of United States involvement in the movement that overthrew the Arbenz regime may never be known, although there seems little question that the Central Intelligence Agency was highly active in the affair and that it perhaps supplied the increment of power needed by the anti-communist forces under Colonel Castillo Armas to achieve victory.*

In the second place, there was the un-

* In his memoirs, former President Eisenhower does not conceal the fact that CIA Director Allen Dulles played a key role in the White House deliberations on this issue. Upon his recommendation, Eisenhower agreed to supply the anti-communist forces with aircraft, to replace those that had previously been lost. Eisenhower was convinced that: "The major factor in the successful outcome" of the struggle in Guatemala was "the disaffection of the Guatemalan armed forces and the population as a whole with the tyrannical regime of Arbenz." His judgment upon the new President Armas was that he proved "a farseeing and able statesman, who enjoyed the devotion of his people." Dwight D. Eisenhower, *Mandate for Change* (Garden City, N.Y.: Doubleday, 1963), pp. 424–426. The judgment of more disinterested observers is rather different. One authority, for example, noted that it was easy for Armas "to crush the Communists and the radical left" in Guatemala; it was a different matter for him to implement the principles of the country's revolution of 1944, in the face of the entrenched oligarchy's opposition. Indeed, Armas's seizure of power "was a genuine counterrevolution." Lieuwen, *op. cit.*, p. 94. Significantly, Castillo Armas was assassinated in 1957; there followed a period of political turbulence, in which General Ydígoras was installed by the armed forces. As with many other Latin American countries, the armed forces still dictate the nation's political course. *Ibid.*, pp. 164–165.

mistakable determination of the United States to prevent the United Nations from considering the Guatemalan issue. The State Department's view was that the UN could not properly take jurisdiction in the affair until the OAS had disposed of it—which was, to say the least, a novel interpretation of the power of the international organ charged with preserving global peace and security.[77]

Finally, there was the strong belief, shared by critics of Washington's policy inside and outside the hemisphere, that the victory against communism in Guatemala might prove short-lived and self-deceiving. As one commentator wrote of the Guatemalan conflict: "The real issues antedate the anti-communist crusade; indeed, they antedate communism."[78] In Guatemala, as elsewhere in Latin America, the only lasting anti-communist measures would be those that were directed against the conditions within which communism and other extremist movements thrive. Conversely, by arousing lingering apprehensions about "North American interventionism," America's response to events in Guatemala might well have complicated the task of generating concern about communist inroads in the Western Hemisphere.

The Cuban Missile Crisis

From 1933 to 1944, the island of Cuba was the personal enclave of a *caudillo*, former army sergeant Fulgencio Batista. Like most Latin American dictators of his ilk, Batista depended heavily upon military support; under his administration, the Cuban army was pampered with pay increases, lucrative appointments, and access to graft. Surprisingly, in 1944, Batista accepted the defeat at the polls of his own hand-picked candidate for President; shortly thereafter, the *caudillo* announced his "retirement" from the army and subsequently moved to Florida, leaving Cuba for the next eight years to be governed by civilian leaders. Batista's successors, however, either could not or would not drastically alter the pattern of military dominance over Cuban life, eliminate the wholesale corruption that infused the island's government, or concern themselves with needed reforms. By a coup carried out in 1952, Batista took back the reins of power. Thereafter, opposition to his regime—now widely hailed by conservative circles in the United States because of its "stability" and its anti-communist complexion—steadily mounted. Student disturbances broke out in 1955, followed by signs of discontent among the military, attempted assassinations, and invasions by rebel groups led by a man who was soon to dominate the center of the Cuban stage—Fidel Castro.

As the pressure in the Cuban political boiler rose, Batista reacted in traditional *caudillo* fashion by instituting sweeping purges of the army, revoking one Cuban liberty after another, and clamping a ruthless despotism upon the Cuban people. But the end was not far away. Relying chiefly upon rural support, Castro's rebellion in the eastern section of the island slowly gained momentum. As one element of Cuban society after another defected from Batista's camp, Castro advanced upon Havana. On January 1, 1959, the dictator left Havana and went into exile. On January 7, the United States recognized Castro's regime, under President Manuel Urrutia, as the government of Cuba.* Although the Eisenhower Administration had not suspended arms shipments from the United States to Batista until March 14, 1958, it extended cordial greetings to Cuba's new revolutionary government and gave every indication of seeking to cooperate with Castro's regime to achieve many of its stated goals.

Within a few weeks, however, relations between the United States and Cuba began to sour. By the end of 1959, Castro's government had executed over 600 Cubans for counterrevolutionary and pro-Batista activities. Very soon after taking office, Castro began a program of expropriation and nationalization of foreign properties on the island. By mid-1960, the State Department estimated that some $1 billion in U.S.-owned properties had been seized; in addition, Cuban authorities denied U.S. exporters some $100 million in debts owed them. Throughout this period, State Department officials repeatedly emphasized that the United States supported many of the goals of Castro's regime, such as land reform;

* For the background to Castro's successful revolution in Cuba, see Lieuwen, *op. cit.*, pp. 97–100.

Our discussion of the Cuban crisis relies heavily upon studies prepared for the Senate Foreign Relations Committee, particularly: *Events in United States-Cuban relations: A Chronology*, 88th Congress, 1st Session (Washington: 1963). An excellent documentary source is David L. Larson, *The "Cuban Crisis" of 1962* (Boston: Houghton Mifflin, 1963). This source contains relevant documentary materials, beginning with September 4, 1962, and extending through the denouement achieved in U.S.-Soviet relations by UN Secretary General U Thant early in January, 1963.

nor did it contest Castro's right to expropriate private property in Cuba, provided just compensation were paid for properties seized, as international law required.

In whatever degree such quarrels alienated the United States and Cuba, the most serious issue became Castro's perceptible gravitation toward the Communist bloc. A few days after his regime seized power, Ernesto Guevara, one of Castro's most trusted lieutenants, said that the Communist party had a right to operate legally in Cuba, along with all other parties— an allegation that was sharply challenged in July by President Urrutia, who condemned the Communist party as a threat to the welfare of the Cuban people and to the revolution. Four days later, President Urrutia resigned and shortly thereafter was superseded in office by Fidel Castro himself.

The ensuing months witnessed mounting tensions between Havana and Washington, as Castro accused the United States of supporting counterrevolutionary activities against him and as the Eisenhower Administration watched with deep concern Castro's evident determination to alienate the United States completely. A trade agreement between Red China and Cuba at the end of 1959 did not improve the atmosphere of Cuban-American relations. Nor did Castro's charge early in 1960 that the United States had "exploited" Cuba for 50 years and that the State Department was implacably opposed to his revolutionary program. Within a few weeks, Castro had received a visit from Soviet First Deputy Premier Anastas Mikoyan; on February 13, the first of a series of Soviet-Cuban trade agreements was announced. Early in March, the French ship *La Coubre* exploded in Havana harbor, an event for which Cuba held the United States completely responsible. On March 20, "Ché" Guevara stated openly that: "Our war . . . is against the great power of the North." This announcement was followed by the statement of another Cuban official in June that Cuba was "the Soviet Union's greatest and most loyal friend." Next came an assertion by Cuban Minister of State Roa that a major goal of Cuban policy was "to break the structure of its commercial relations with the United States." Congress responded to these provocations by giving the President the authority to reduce Cuba's sugar quota in the United States, a power first invoked by President Eisenhower on July 6. The Kremlin's answer to this gambit was to inform the world that the USSR was "raising its voice and extending a helpful hand to the people of Cuba." Ominously, Khrushchev added that "Soviet artillerymen can support the Cuban people with rocket fire." This brought the assertion by officials in Havana that the USSR was "the greatest military power in history."

By August 1, the United States had become sufficiently disturbed by these evidences of Cuban-Soviet collaboration to submit a lengthy document concerning communist infiltration of the Western Hemisphere to the Inter-American Peace Committee of the OAS. By the end of the month at a meeting in San José, Costa Rica, the foreign ministers of the American republics condemned extrahemispheric intervention in American affairs. Castro's reply was to castigate the United States anew for its "intervention" in Cuban affairs and to reaffirm Havana's close ties with the Communist world. These charges were dramatically repeated by the Cuban delegate before the UN General Assembly late in September.

The early months of 1961 might well be taken as marking the turning point that led to a complete rupture between the United States and Cuba. Two developments, occurring more or less simultaneously, led to the final break. One was the disastrous "Bay of Pigs" episode, in which a small group of anti-Castro forces, morally and materially assisted by agencies of the United States government, endeavored to invade Cuba and topple Castro's regime. After months of preparation (in which nearly all their plans became known to the public, and to Havana as well), early in the morning of April 17 this group landed in Cuba at the Bay of Pigs. From the beginning, the invasion force had no chance. Counting on air cover by the United States, which was never supplied, within a few days this pathetic force was expeditiously liquidated by Castro's army. In the process, the United States was administered a humiliating diplomatic defeat. That the Kennedy Administration would even permit and sanction such an invasion from Florida, much less give it nominal but totally inadequate support, indicated both the implacable opposition of the United States to Castro's regime and its apparent unwillingness to take firm measures to oppose it.[79]

In the same period, unmistakable evidence appeared of Castro's gravitation toward the Communist bloc. The first in a series of Soviet arms shipments arrived in Cuba on November 18, 1960. Throughout the weeks that followed,

Cuban officials openly proclaimed their allegiance to the communist cause. On January 3, 1961, the United States broke relations altogether with Castro's regime. Then by spring, Cuban officials publicly admitted a fact that State Department officials had long since accepted. On April 16, Castro described his regime as "socialist." A few days later, his lieutenant Guevara disclosed that Castroism constituted "the first socialist revolution in Latin America." Finally, on December 2, Castro openly admitted that: "I believe absolutely in Marxism. . . . I am a Marxist-Leninist and will be a Marxist-Leninist until the last day of my life." He confessed that this had been his "true" political ideology ever since he embarked upon his revolutionary course. Early in 1962, the Inter-American Peace Committee found Castro's ties with the Communist bloc incompatible with its obligations under the Inter-American System; this judgment was formally confirmed when the foreign ministers of the American republics, meeting at Punta del Este, on January 31 formally expelled Cuba from the Inter-American System.* On February 3, the United States proclaimed a total embargo on trade with Cuba.

Throughout the weeks that followed, Havana received new shipments of arms from the Communist world, together with "technical advisers" from behind the iron curtain. On September 4, President Kennedy finally warned Castro's government that the United States was determined to take whatever steps were necessary to prevent the installation of offensive

---

* From the San José meeting onward, however, many Latin American Republics took a view of communism in Cuba which differed from that of the United States. On the crucial vote in the OAS, requiring a two-thirds majority, to expel Cuba from the Inter-American System, six countries (Argentina, Bolivia, Brazil, Chile, Ecuador, and Mexico) abstained; these countries have two-thirds of the population of Latin America. Since they had earlier voted that communism was incompatible with membership in the OAS, their abstention was not motivated by lack of support for this doctrine. Rather it stemmed from doubt that, at this time, Castro's Cuba represented a threat to hemispheric solidarity and security, doubt that it was legal to expel a country from the OAS, and belief that the Cuban people had a right to adopt a communist system. Most basically, as one observer has put it, these six countries believed that "nonintervention still weighed more heavily than any fear of aggression by Communist powers or by Fidelismo." John C. Dreier, The Organization of American States (New York: Harper & Row, 1962), p. 112. This study provides a recent, succinct appraisal of the OAS in the postwar period.

weapons on Cuban soil; this was followed on September 13 by another warning that the United States would do whatever was necessary to protect its own security and the security of other American republics from a Cuban-instigated threat. In the same period, the OAS called upon its members to take intensified measures to safeguard their security against communist inroads in the Americas.

Then, on October 22, came the long-deferred showdown: in a dramatic coast-to-coast television appearance, President Kennedy announced that communist missiles had been installed in Cuba, that these were capable of launching nuclear weapons at the United States and other American states. Kennedy outlined seven steps the United States was taking to deal with this threat to hemispheric peace and security. These included a naval blockade against the shipment of offensive weapons to the island; re-enforcement of American strength at the Guantánamo Bay naval base; a request for an immediate meeting of the OAS; and a similar request for an emergency session of the UN Security Council. To Soviet Premier Khrushchev, President Kennedy issued a warning that the United States would retaliate against the USSR itself if any Soviet missiles were launched from Cuba; and he urged the Kremlin to eliminate this dangerous threat to global peace. Concurrently, Congress prohibited the extension of American foreign aid to any country that carried on trade in arms, strategic goods, or articles of economic value with Cuba, unless the President specifically found such trade in the interests of the United States.

The controversy between Washington and Havana had now become openly transformed into a major cold-war confrontation between the United States and the Soviet Union. This "secret, swift, and extraordinary build-up of Communist missiles" in Cuba, President Kennedy told the American people, "in an area well known to have a special and historical relationship to the United States . . . is a deliberately provocative and unjustified change in the *status quo* which cannot be accepted by this country. . . ." The United States "will not prematurely or unnecessarily risk the costs of worldwide nuclear war . . . but neither will we shrink from that risk at any time it must be faced."[80]

Some 48,000 telegrams from citizens in the United States, supporting the President's stand 10 to 1, poured into the White House.[81] At

no time in the postwar period had the United States gone so perilously to "the brink of war." As tense White House and State Department officials awaited the next moves by Havana and Moscow, they feared that an outright military invasion of Cuba might soon be required.[82] Meanwhile, the UN Security Council was summoned into extraordinary session, where the United States presented incontestable proof of Soviet missile sites inside Cuba. Contemporaneous with these developments, the OAS demanded the immediate and total dismantling of communist missiles in Cuba and called upon its members to resist, by force if necessary, any further Cuban importation of communist arms. At the same time, Soviet ships bearing new arms shipments from behind the iron curtain held their course for Havana; heavily armed naval forces of the United States waited to intercept them.

The first break in the crisis came when these Havana-bound ships finally altered course and turned back with their lethal cargoes. Then, in a succession of swiftly-moving events, the crisis receded: the State Department received an unusually conciliatory message from the Kremlin, indicating its desire to avoid provocations against the United States; both the United States and the USSR (if not Cuba) indicated their readiness to have UN Secretary General U Thant mediate the crisis; non-aligned countries in the UN called on the parties to the conflict to avoid provocative actions and used their influence heavily in behalf of peaceful settlement; Khrushchev pledged that no further arms from behind the iron curtain would be sent to Cuba, and this assurance was followed on October 27 by a new pledge that all offensive weapons would be removed from the island; with this assurance, and upon the understanding that the removal of such weapons would be clearly verified, the United States agreed to lift its naval blockade. By November 20, President Kennedy announced that all communist missiles had been dismantled and that Premier Khrushchev had pledged to have remaining IL-28 bombers removed speedily. With that announcement, the White House also declared that it had ordered the termination of Cuba's naval quarantine. On December 12, the White House stated that the evidence indicated all offensive missiles and aircraft had been dismantled in Cuba; thereafter, as in the preceding weeks, American high-level reconnaissance aircraft kept up a constant inspection of the island to assure that there was no clandestine violation of the *détente* that had led to a resolution of the crisis.

The Kennedy Administration's handling of the Cuban missile crisis must surely be ranked as one of the most spectacular cold-war diplomatic victories the United States has scored in recent years. It revealed a remarkable degree of astuteness and adroitness in policy formulation and execution. Nearly every American goal was achieved, as Soviet machinations were dealt one of their most severe setbacks since World War II. For once, a major diplomatic undertaking by the United States won approval by the overwhelming majority of countries in the OAS and in the United Nations; even many of the neutralist countries of Africa and Asia, formerly sympathetic to Castro in his David-and-Goliath drama with the United States, were remarkably uncritical of the United States and notably passive in championing Cuba's cause before the bar of world opinion. Among other results, the Soviet-American confrontation over Cuba exploded many myths, such as the bogy of Soviet missile invincibility, the hollowness of Khrushchev's pledges to defend Castro's regime with rockets, and the stereotype of the United States as a wavering democracy unable to take a firm stand when its vital interests are at stake.

Yet there was the danger that the very success of the United States in frustrating the Soviet Union's plans in Cuba might pose a significant obstacle for the nation's future relations with the other American republics. Official and public opinion in the United States might attribute too much to this victory; they might forget precisely what had been achieved in Cuba. For a society prone to oscillate between apathy and passionate intervention in dealing with the outside world, to move hurriedly from neglect to crisis-oriented alarm, clarity on this question was a vital requirement. The United States had successfully prevented the conversion of Cuba into a Soviet air and missile base. This was no inconsiderable accomplishment.

At the same time, it was necessary to realize constantly what the United States had *not* accomplished. It had not "saved" the whole of Latin America, or even Cuba, from communism. It had not discredited Marxism—or its Cuban variant, *Fidelismo*—throughout the Western Hemisphere. It had not guaranteed political stability or the absence of authoritarian regimes from Mexico to Argentina. It was equally imperative for citizens of the United States to be clear *why* the vast majority

of countries in the OAS had supported the Kennedy Administration's policies in the Cuban crisis. One observer has aptly commented: "The unanimous hemispheric support of the United States in the Cuban missile crisis concerned military self-defense; it was not a condemnation of Cuban communism as such."[83] That is to say, Castro had alienated Latin American opinion not primarily because he was a revolutionary leader, or because he declared himself a "Socialist" and later an avowed "Marxist," or because he seized foreign corporations and landholdings in Cuba—but because he had in effect largely forfeited his claim as a "nationalist" leader by giving over the direction of Cuba's foreign and defense policies to the Kremlin. In brief, he had allowed Cuba to become a pawn in a great-power contest.*

It followed, as several well-informed students of Latin American affairs have suggested, that the United States could not afford to be indifferent to the long-range implications of Castroism or the Cuban revolution for the Western Hemisphere. Castro had made a near-fatal mistake in relying upon the Soviet Union for security—thereby giving the United States irrefutable evidence to support its claim that communism threatened the peace and security of the hemisphere. Nevertheless, it might be a no less costly mistake for North Americans to imagine that the resolution of the crisis witnessed the disappearance of the underlying forces that had brought *Fidelismo* to the center of the Latin American stage. For several years, it had been a theme of official American opinion that the basic principles of Castro's revolution were sound and praiseworthy, but that Fidel had "betrayed the revolution" that swept him into power. However much they might deplore his military association with the USSR, probably a majority of Latin Americans did *not* basically oppose Castro's seizure of foreign enterprises, his sweeping internal reforms measures, his stern handling of Batista's supporters, or his determination to terminate Cuba's long diplomatic and economic dependence upon the United States. In pursuing these goals,

---

* This was a point made repeatedly to the author by representatives at the United Nations from countries throughout the Afro-Asian world, in interviews during 1963. The prevailing belief that Castro had betrayed his own "nationalist" claims by becoming the junior member of an alliance with the Kremlin was a major reason why Cuba's cause received relatively little overt support from formerly sympathetic countries in the UN.

Fidelismo often received the widespread approval of the Latin American masses, who did not interpret the State Department's "victory" in the missile crisis as necessarily reflecting upon their inherent validity. However spokesmen in Washington might view him, Herbert L. Matthews has written: "Fidel Castro has become a figure of worldwide fame"; his "model" for effecting basic social, economic, and political reforms is undeniably appealing for groups in Latin America and for newly independent countries, such as Ben Bella's Algeria. Ultimately, the only plan for destroying the attractiveness of Castroism on this level is "by satisfying, or offering the hope of satisfying, Latin American demands for social justice, industrialization and higher standards of living."[84] Inadvertently, Castro may have supplied the one element that was often lacking in the approach of the United States toward Latin America in the contemporary era: a visible, easily comprehended symbol of what might happen throughout the entire hemisphere if programs like the Alliance for Progress *fail* to fill the vacuum that *Fidelismo* filled in Cuba.

NOTES

1. *The World Almanac: 1964* (New York: The New York World-Telegram and the Sun, 1964), p. 691.
2. Fred Cutler and Samuel Pizer, "Foreign Operations of U.S. Industry," *Survey of Current Bussiness*, 43 (October, 1963), 16.
3. "The Global Stake of U.S. Business," *Fortune*, 67 (December, 1963), 130–131.
4. *The New York Times*, November 28, 1958, dispatch by E. W. Kenworthy.
5. Department of State, *Military Assistance to Latin America* (Washington, D.C.: Publication No. 4917, "Inter-American Series" 44, 1953), p. 7.
6. Hans W. Weigert *et al.*, eds., *New Compass of the World* (New York: Macmillan, 1953), p. 40.
7. *Ibid.*, p. 55.
8. *Ibid.*, p. 58.
9. James W. Gantenbein, *The Evolution of Our Latin-American Policy* (New York: Columbia University Press, 1950), p. 324. A helpful compendium of official sources on historic U.S. policy in Latin America.
10. Julius W. Pratt, *A History of United States Foreign Policy* (Englewood Cliffs, N.J.: Prentice-Hall, 1955), pp. 180–181.

11. Gantenbein, *op. cit.*, pp. 371–372.
12. *Ibid.*, pp. 387–388.
13. *Ibid.*, p. 330 (italics added).
14. *Ibid.*, pp. 344–348.
15. *Ibid.*, pp. 360–364.
16. *Ibid.*, p. 208.
17. *Ibid.*, pp. 401–407, 165–166.
18. Pratt, *op. cit.*, pp. 181–183, 346.
19. *Ibid.*, pp. 610–611, 765; Gantenbein, *op. cit.*, p. 285.
20. Pratt, *op. cit.*, pp. 767–768.
21. Department of State, *Sovereignty and Interdependence in the New World* (Washington, D.C.: Publication No. 3054, "Inter-American Series," 35, 1948), pp. 157–163. This document traces out the evolution and operation of the Inter-American System.
22. *Ibid.*, pp. 165–168.
23. These and other Latin American press reactions are cited in *The New York Times*, January 19, 1964.
24. Quoted in *The New York Times*, January 19, 1964.
25. Our discussion of the Panamanian crisis is based upon *The New York Times*, January 12, 14, 19, 26, 28, February 3, 7, 9, 27, March 14, 15 and 16, 1964.
26. *The New York Times*, August 9 and 16, 1959, dispatches by Tad Szulc.
27. *The New York Times*, January 4, 1959.
28. *Yearbook of World Affairs: 1956* (London: Stevens and Sons, 1957), p. 45.
29. *The New York Times*, October 26, 1963.
30. Text of President Kennedy's press conference, in *The New York Times*, October 10, 1963.
31. See *The New York Times*, January 5, March 19, 20, 1964.
32. Pratt, *op. cit.*, p. 174.
33. *Ibid.*, pp. 426–431.
34. Department of State, *Sovereignty and Interdependence in the New World*, *op. cit.*, p. 173.
35. R. Patee, "The Argentine Question: The War Stage," *Review of Politics*, 8 (October, 1946), 475–500. Analyzes U.S.-Argentine relations during the war years.
36. John M. Cabot, *Toward Our Common American Destiny* (Medford, Mass.: The Metcalf Press, 1955), p. 90. A series of speeches and addresses by a former Assistant Secretary of State.
37. *The New York Times*, January 4, 1959.
38. Tad Szulc, *The Winds of Revolution: Latin America Today—and Tomorrow* (New York: Praeger, 1963), p. 79.
39. Edwin Lieuwen, *Arms and Politics in Latin America* (New York: Praeger, 1963), pp. 123–125; Senate Foreign Re-

lations Committee, *United States-Latin American Relations: Post-World War II Political Developments in Latin America,* 86th Congress, 1st Session (Washington, D.C.: 1959), pp. 24–26.

40. Dexter Perkins, *The United States and the Caribbean* (Cambridge, Mass.: Harvard University Press, 1947), p. 165.

41. Department of State, *United States-Latin American Relations* (Washington, D.C.: Publication No. 5290, "Inter-American Series" 47, 1953), p. 7.

42. *The New York Times,* November 23, 1958, dispatch by E. W. Kenworthy.

43. Department of State, *United States-Latin American Relations, op. cit.,* p. 7.

44. *The New York Times,* May 17, 1959, dispatch by Tad Szulc.

45. Senate Foreign Relations Committee, *Mutual Security Act of 1959,* Hearings, 86th Congress, 1st Session (Washington, D.C.: 1959), Part 1, p. 540.

46. William Benton, *The Voice of Latin America* (New York: Harper & Row, 1961), p. xiii.

47. Senate Foreign Relations Committee, *Latin America: Venezuela, Brazil, Peru, Bolivia, and Panama,* 86th Congress, 2nd Session (Washington, D.C.: 1960), p. 1.

48. *Ibid.,* pp. 7, 9, 11, 14.

49. Quoted in Benton, *op. cit.,* p. 147.

50. See the text of President Kennedy's speech on November 18, in *The New York Times,* November 19, 1963; see also *The New York Times,* August 18 and November 17, 1963.

51. See text of President Kennedy's message outlining the Alliance Progress in *Documents on American Foreign Relations: 1961* (New York: Harper & Row, 1962), pp. 395–408.

52. Department of State, *Report to the Congress on the Foreign Assistance Program for Fiscal Year 1962* (Washington, D.C.: 1963), pp. 7–8.

53. *The New York Times,* April 3, 1963.

54. See text of President Kennedy's message to Congress on foreign aid, in *The New York Times,* April 3, 1963, and *The New York Times,* August 18, 1963, dispatch by Tad Szulc.

55. Senate Foreign Relations Committee, *A Report on the Alliance for Progress, 1963,* 88th Congress, 1st Session, Document No. 13 (Washington, D.C.: 1963), p. 1.

56. See text of President Johnson's address to the Pan American Union, in *The New York Times,* March 17, 1964.

57. Senate Foreign Relations Committee, *A Report on the Alliance for Progress, op. cit.,* p. 1.

58. *The New York Times,* April 3, 1963 and March 17, 1964.

59. *The New York Times,* November 17, 1963, dispatch by Henry Raymont.

60. *The New York Times,* January 17 and March 15, 1964.

61. *The New York Times,* January 4, 1959.

62. See text of Harriman's speech in *The New York Times,* November 14, 1963.

63. *The New York Times,* March 17, 1964.

64. *The New York Times,* December 16, 1963.

65. House Foreign Affairs Committee, *Mutual Security Act of 1957,* Hearings, 85th Congress, 1st Session (Washington, D.C.: 1957), Part 5, p. 925.

66. *Ibid.,* p. 941.

67. House Foreign Affairs Committee, *Building A World of Free People,* 85th Congress, 1st Session (Washington, D.C.: 1957), pp. 87–88.

68. *Survey of International Affairs: 1954* (New York: Oxford University Press, 1956), p. 368.

69. Department of State, *Intervention of International Communism in Guatemala* (Washington, D.C.: Publication No. 5556, "Inter-American Series" 48, 1954), p. 49. This document presents the State Department's "case" against the Arbenz regime in Guatemala.

70. *Survey of International Affairs: 1954, op. cit.,* pp. 376–378.

71. *United States in World Affairs: 1954* (New York: Harper & Row, 1955), p. 372.

72. Dept. of State, *Intervention of International Communism in Guatemala, op. cit.,* p. 30.

73. Department of State, *American Foreign Policy: 1950–55,* I (Washington, D.C.: Publication No. 6446, "General Foreign Policy Series" 117, 1957), 1292.

74. *Ibid.,* p. 1301.

75. *Ibid.,* p. 1308.

76. *Ibid.,* p. 1315.

77. Frederick B. Pike, "Guatemala, the United States, and Communism in the Americas," *Review of Politics,* 17 (April, 1955), 258–259. An illuminating analysis of many aspects of the Guatemalan crisis.

78. Bernard Rosen, "Counter-Revolution: Guatemala's Tragedy," *The Nation,* 179 (July 31, 1954), 87–89.

79. The Bay of Pigs episode is described more fully in Hugh Sidey, *John F. Kennedy: President* (New York: Atheneum, 1963), pp. 124–144.

80. See the text of President Kennedy's broadcast to the American people on October 22, 1962, in David L. Larson, ed., *The "Cuban Crisis" of 1962* (Boston: Houghton Mifflin, 1963), pp. 41–46.

81. Sidey, *op. cit.*, p. 344. Sidey's discussion of the Cuban crisis provides many insights into policy formulation under Kennedy. See pp. 323–349.

82. Sidey, *op. cit.*, p. 346.

83. Herbert L. Matthews, ed., *The United States and Latin America* (Englewood Cliffs, N.J.: Prentice-Hall, 1963), p. 144.

84. *Ibid.*, p. 159.

13 ⟶ ASIA ⟶ new nations and
ancient problems

In the turbulent postwar period no region has presented the United States with so many diplomatic challenges as has that far-flung arc of territories extending from Afghanistan to Japan and southward to Indonesia and the Philippines. As in the Middle East, the United States has been compelled to formulate viable policies toward countries and problems in this area when the swift unfolding of events often left very little time for working out intelligent decisions.

Guidelines from earlier diplomatic experience toward Asia unfortunately offered minimum help to American policy-makers in today's world. Some authorities doubt whether, prior to World War II, the United States ever possessed what can meaningfully be called a "foreign policy" toward Asia in the sense of a realistic conception of its diplomatic interests there, together with reasonably effective methods for advancing them. Broad segments of American public opinion and even influential political and government leaders tend to seek guidance for contemporary policy in America's historic relations with Asia. Their attachment to images and conceptions derived from this experience goes far toward explaining many of the nation's policy inadequacies in that vital region during recent years. Let us look briefly at the highlights of America's relations with Asia in the past.

Three episodes were of singular importance: Commodore Perry's opening of Japan to Western influence; proclamation of the Open Door policy toward China; and America's acquisition of the Philippines and other strategic bases in the Pacific. The visit of an American naval ex-

pedition under Commodore Perry to Japan in the mid-1850s climaxed a period of westward continental expansion at home. By 1848 the United States had acquired a 1200-mile Pacific coastline, thereby whetting its interest in the affairs of Asia. Perry's visits in 1853–1854 at last forced the hermitlike kingdom of Japan to open its doors to Western influence and, more specifically, to trade with the outside world.[1] In the years following Perry's visit, Japan became America's protégé in the Orient. Long after contrary evidence had accumulated, the American people and their leaders continued to believe that the interests of the United States and Imperial Japan in the Orient were compatible. Only after Tokyo had dropped even the pretext of a pro-American, generally pro-Western, policy and embarked upon a course of outright military conquest in Manchuria early in the 1930s did Americans forsake their image of Japan as a benign, pacifically inclined, crypto-Western country. Much the same image of Japan, however, reappeared during the period of the American occupation following World War II. Tokyo's apparent willingness to accept sweeeping occupation-imposed changes in social, economic, and political affairs convinced many Americans that Japan's aggressive moves during the 1930s and 1940s had not really accorded with the wishes of the Japanese people.

The second historic landmark in American policy toward Asia was proclamation of the Open Door policy toward China at the end of the nineteenth century. Preservation of the Open Door remained a professed goal of American foreign policy until World War II. Even after the victory of communism in China in the period 1949–1950, part of America's resentment toward the communist government derived from the fact that Soviet Russia enjoyed a preferential position in Chinese affairs. Peiping had abandoned the Open Door policy. Just what was this policy? What were its implications for later American-Asian relations?

Strict accuracy should make us hesitate to call the Open Door a policy at all. In a brilliant diplomatic coup, on March 20, 1900, Secretary of State John Hay announced that he had been able to secure British, German, Japanese, and American concurrence to a pledge which, in the words of a British diplomat, assured that these countries would "maintain free and equal commercial relations for all time in the Orient."[2] More concretely, Hay professed he had secured agreement to the general principle that future economic concessions granted to one of these governments by China must be granted on the same basis to the other governments. The gist of the threefold pledge was that: each party agreed not to interfere with commercial spheres of influence currently maintained by other powers in China; Chinese tariffs would apply equally to the goods imported from these countries; and harbor dues, railroad charges, and the like, within any power's sphere of influence would be the same for other powers using these facilities.[3]

Actually, Hay had not secured the agreement of the powers to these terms, but after his public announcement the countries involved hesitated to deny their acceptance of what appeared to be a fair, almost idealistic, agreement respecting diplomatic rivalry in China.

Historical scholarship has shown convincingly that the Open Door policy grew out of competing diplomatic ambitions in China, not the least of which were ambitions entertained by the United States. The policy was aimed specifically at tsarist Russia, whose advances in the Orient caused widespread alarm among other imperialistic countries, not so much out of abstract concern for the territorial integrity of China as out of fear that Russia's seemingly insatiable diplomatic appetite might eventually close China, Manchuria, and Korea to Western influence.[4] The United States was insisting upon equality of treatment chiefly because recent concessions wrested from China by other countries threatened to imperil America's position in the current economic rivalry and, most especially, to jeopardize American access to the lucrative Chinese trade. The Open Door was Washington's way of trying to safeguard its own political and economic interests in China at a time when an all-out diplomatic struggle for control of that country—in which America had neither the inclination nor the means to compete vigorously—would almost certainly result in the disappearance of American influence. Says Werner Levi of the Open Door: ". . . every nation sought its own advantage in the policy, not the least its official originator. . . ."[5]

In the light of these facts, it may seem strange that over the course of time the Open Door policy came to be widely regarded by the American people as the quintessence of a moral, unselfish foreign policy whose dominant purpose was preservation of Chinese territorial integrity against powerful imperialist forces. Several reasons explain what amounted to a kind of sanctification of the Open Door policy by the American people. Americans were unwilling to comprehend or admit that insistence upon the Open Door accorded with their own nation's diplomatic ambitions in China, the chief one of which was maintenance of unimpaired trade relations. This mentality was part of the larger and persistent belief that only other countries were capable of "imperialistic" motivations. Then, too, the Open Door policy seemed to foreshadow certain idealistic Wilsonian principles such as self-determination. In time the American people tended to ascribe to the Open Door policy a much wider and more humanitarian compass than its instigators had intended, converting it ultimately into a blanket guarantee of Chinese economic and political integrity.

Yet the Open Door policy did nothing whatever to interfere with *existing* foreign concessions in China; nor did it prevent future ones, so long as the countries enumerated above were treated *equally* by China. A four-way monopoly of Chinese trade was by no means prohibited under the Open Door policy—if indeed this was not what its framers ultimately anticipated. The Open Door policy said nothing about the *political* inviolability of China. The principle of equal concessions applied to commercial matters only, and it did not apply to all of them. For instance, future industrial or railroad concessions were excluded. Whatever influence the Open Door may have had in protecting Chinese sovereignty was therefore largely incidental. The objective was to assure equality of treatment for the United States in the midst of an impending imperialist struggle on the Chinese mainland.[6] That China itself greeted the Open Door with something less than unrestrained enthusiasm was indicated by the fact that it did not formally adhere to the principle until it signed the Nine-Power Treaty in 1921.[7]

More basic still in evaluating the implications of the Open Door policy in shaping the future American outlook toward Asia is the fact that neither at the time nor later was the United States prepared to take steps to enforce compliance with its provisions. Chester Bowles equates the Open Door policy with "so many of the statements of moral principle which we too frequently like to identify with foreign policy. It amounted to no more than a pious wish that the great powers should refrain from carving up China." As the years passed after 1900, American foreign policy in the Far East sometimes appeared deliberately designed to undermine the Open Door, perhaps not so much by commission as by omission. The United States was either unwilling or unable to halt progressive Japanese encroachments against the Open Door principle; and willfully or through ignorance, American policies sometimes actually facilitated Japanese expansionism at the expense of the Open Door.[8]

Nevertheless, the Open Door policy was one of the most profound influences which shaped popular attitudes toward China and, more broadly, toward Asia as a whole. Its most lasting consequence was to inculcate the view that in China's relations with the outside world, the United States occupied a preferential position. This idea had a number of important corollaries: that China was a kind of "ward" of the United States and that it looked to Washington for guidance in its internal and external affairs; that China's leaders were highly amenable to American suggestions and leadership in all fields; that China was unshakably pro-American in its attitudes and could be counted on to remain America's firm ally in Asia; that China was moving slowly but perceptibly down the path of political democracy and economic stability; that China owed a great "debt of gratitude" to the United States for moral and material help extended to it after 1900, and that this debt would weigh heavily in shaping China's attitudes toward domestic and foreign issues.

Since World War II, Americans have been psychologically unable to accept the fact—and this has been a key element in explaining the ineffectuality of their policies—that events in-side and outside China have long since overtaken the Open Door policy. That policy was postulated upon the existence of a weak, internally divided China which was an easy prey to foreign influence. In general these conditions persisted until the end of World War II. Even during the war and in the immediate postwar period, however, Chiang Kai-shek had demonstrated time and again that *China's interests* were uppermost in his mind and that in critical areas of policy the United States and other foreign countries could be expected to exert minimal influence over Chinese affairs. This fact was made even plainer after communism's victory under Mao Tse-tung. The American people have been unable to adjust their thinking and their policies to the existence of a politically unified, ambitious, self-confident China. Deriving their images of China from the bygone (and what history is likely to show as a most untypical) era of the Open Door policy, Americans have been left with a policy vacuum. They have demonstrated very little ability to fill that vacuum with constructive policies in recent years. Current American policies toward China are still groping for a new approach to replace the Open Door.

The third landmark in American Far Eastern policy before World War II was acquisition of the Philippines in 1899. This climaxed the acquisition of other Pacific islands such as Midway and Hawaii, obtained in 1867 and 1898, respectively. Its new strategic island bases for the first time made the United States a "Pacific power" in the military sense.[9] This fact drew America deeper and deeper into the vortex of great-power rivalry there, ordaining that sooner or later conflict would arise between the United States and the rising Imperial Japanese Empire, whose diplomatic ambitions led it eventually to challenge the United States and Great Britain for mastery over the western Pacific area.

With other territories in Asia—India, Burma, Southeast Asia, Indonesia—the United States had no significant and direct relations at all before World War II. Washington recognized British primacy in India and Burma, French in Indochina, and Dutch in Indonesia. At intervals the United States did not hesitate to offer gratuitous advice to European countries about the management of their colonial affairs. But it was not until former dependencies emerged as independent nations after World War II that the United States established formal and direct diplomatic relations with them.

The principal elements of American foreign policy toward the Far East in the prewar period afforded very poor preparation for the new role of responsible American leadership of the West's policies toward Asian affairs throughout the postwar period. Novel and complex problems, often totally alien to American experience and arising under conditions of unprecedented urgency, required a fundamental reorientation in American policies. We may conveniently discuss postwar American relations with Asia by examining three categories of issues confronting policy-makers in the United States: Sino-American relations since the Communist victory on the Chinese mainland; Asian neutralism, as symbolized by the problem of American-Indian relations; and rival cold-war strategies in Asia, as illustrated by the crisis in Laos and the conflict in South Vietnam.

THE UNITED STATES AND COMMUNIST CHINA

In the light of the historic background of Sino-American relations that we described earlier, it is not surprising that with the Communist victory in China at the end of 1949, the United States suffered one of the most far-reaching diplomatic reverses in its history. Morally, economically, and militarily, the United States had supported the regime of Chiang Kai-shek in its struggle against Mao Tse-tung's Communist forces. With Chiang's defeat, and his subsequent retreat into exile on Formosa (Taiwan), a breach appeared in Sino-American relations that has proved unbridgeable down to the present day.

Space is not available to discuss the course of the Chinese civil war, or even to analyze in detail why Communist forces ultimately won this contest. Basically, Mao Tse-tung's movement emerged victorious because, in spite of massive quantities of American aid to Chiang's regime, the Nationalist Government was unable to hold the allegiance of the Chinese masses, unwilling to eliminate corruption from its own ranks, and incapable of offering a constructive program to the people of China as an alternative to Mao's forward-looking, if ruthlessly autocratic, platform.*

The Deadlock in Sino-American Relations

Following the Communist victory in China, relations between Peiping and Washington en-

* Political developments in China during and after World War II, and America's relations

tered a stage of intense animosity, suspicion, and recrimination that has endured into the 1960s. The thaw that became conspicuous in Soviet-American relations during the era of "peaceful coexistence" after 1955 had little effect upon the Sino-American deadlock. Mao Tse-tung's regime regarded the United States as the embodiment of a "capitalist warmonger"; Washington, in Peiping's view, manifested a degree of enmity toward Red China that it did not exhibit even toward Soviet Russia. Nearly every week after 1949 witnessed vitriolic outbursts of intemperate Chinese propaganda against the United States. A Chinese celebration marking the tenth anniversary of the Korean War, for example, witnessed headlines in official Chinese news journals calling upon the masses to "Drive U.S. Imperialism out of Asia." The official *People's Daily* announced that a communist "victory" over American imperialism could only be attained by "countering an unjust war launched by U.S. imperialism [i.e., the Korean War] with a just war." It continued: "Only by beating U.S. imperialism black and blue can its plan of aggression and war be frustrated." Repeating a recurrent theme of Chinese propaganda, this source observed that American "imperialism" was "merely outwardly strong but internally a brittle paper tiger. . . ." Since the Korean War had forever destroyed the "myth of the so-called invincibility of the U.S.," Washington was cautioned that it faced "utter defeat" if it launched another war against Red China.[10]

Such appraisals have been paralleled in American statements describing the government and policies of Communist China. Thus a major

with China during this period, are discussed in the following sources: Department of State, *United States Relations with China* (Washington, D.C.: Publication No. 3573, "Far Eastern Series" No. 30, 1949). This is the Truman Administration's "white paper" on China, tracing the course of Sino-American relations since the era of the Open Door. Werner Levi's *Modern China's Foreign Policy* (Minneapolis: University of Minnesota Press, 1953) appraises China's foreign relations from around 1900 to the early postwar period. Herbert Feis, *The China Tangle* (Princeton: Princeton University Press, 1953). An authoritative and dispassionate discussion of the Chinese civil war and America's role in it. John K. Fairbank, *The United States and China* (New York: Viking, 1962, revised ed.). A succinct and illuminating treatment, by one of America's foremost authorities on China. Foster Rhea Dulles, *China and America* (Princeton: Princeton University Press, 1946). A historical account, focusing on the prewar period.

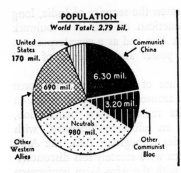
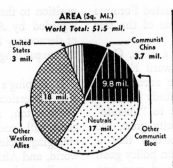
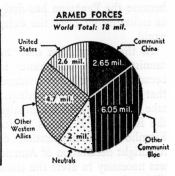

Communist China: Power Giant of Asia. (Source: *The New York Times*, September 7, 1958. © 1958 by The New York Times Company. Reprinted by permission.)

State Department policy statement in 1958 took the view that Communist China was engaged in a long-range struggle to "destroy the way of life of the free countries of the world and bring about the global dominion of communism." China's rulers did not disguise their "hostility to the United States and the free world as a whole nor their avowed intention to effect their downfall." The "primary purpose" of Mao's regime in foreign affairs was to "extend the Communist revolution . . . to the rest of Asia and thence to the rest of the world." Consequently, a prime objective of American policy in Asia was to "neutralize" Red China's influence and "to deter Communist aggression." In pursuit of this goal, the United States proposed to withhold diplomatic recognition of Red China, to contest its admission to the United Nations, to maintain relations with the government of Chiang Kai-shek on Formosa, and to encourage "the hopes of those Chinese who are determined eventually to free their country of Communist rule." A basic premise of American policy was that "there is . . . no reason to accept its [communism's] present rule on mainland China as permanent." Indeed, the State Department was convinced that "communism's rule in China is not permanent and that it one day will pass." The United States sought "to hasten that passing."[11]

The extremely tense atmosphere surrounding Sino-American relations since 1949 has been aggravated by several developments. Red China's entry into the Korean War late in 1950 turned what looked like a certain United Nations victory over the entire peninsula into a stalemate truce settlement along the 38th parallel. American diplomatic initiative was in turn responsible for a United Nations resolution which branded Red China an "aggressor"

in Korea. More than ever, Americans became convinced that China could not be permitted to "shoot its way into the United Nations," a feeling which was re-enforced by repeated Chinese violations of the armistice negotiated in 1953. As a result of Red China's intervention in Korea, the United States took the lead in endeavoring (with only partial success) to impose a free-world trade embargo against Mao's regime. While Washington was eventually compelled to accept expanding trade in "nonstrategic goods" between most of its free-world allies and friends and Communist China, it continued to maintain a total embargo upon American trade with the Chinese mainland.* Moreover, successive administrations in Washington prohibited travel by newsmen and other citizens to the Chinese mainland. The result was that Americans were required to depend upon second- and third-hand accounts for their information about developments and attitudes on the Chinese mainland.

A persistent source of Sino-American friction since 1949 has also been the future of Formosa, to which Chiang Kai-shek's government fled when it was defeated on the Chinese mainland. Periodically, Peiping has declared its determination to "liberate" Formosa. Early in 1964, for example, it reiterated its pledge to "liberate Taiwan [Formosa] without fail" from the grip of the American imperialists.[12] Since the end of the Chinese civil war, the United States has been determined to protect the security of Formosa in the face of Mao's threat to engulf it, both because Communist hegemony over the island would inflict a severe psychological defeat upon the United States and

* The problem of East-West trade is discussed in greater detail in Chapter 15, dealing with American foreign economic policy.

because the Pentagon has designated Formosa as militarily vital for the defense of the free world.

As the Korean War drew to a close, Communist Chinese belligerancy toward Formosa became more intense; evidence accumulated that Mao Tse-tung was perhaps ready to undertake his long-awaited campaign to "liberate" the island. As Peiping's bellicosity grew, the Eisenhower Administration decided that a forthright declaration of American policy goals was necessary to avert the threat of open hostilities. In a message to Congress on January 24, 1955, President Eisenhower declared that Red Chinese military activities in the Formosa Straits posed a "serious danger to the security of our country and of the entire Pacific area and indeed to the peace of the world." He requested Congress to pass a resolution which would "reduce the possibility that the Chinese Communists, misjudging our firm purpose and national unity," might attempt to challenge the strength of the free world.[13] Congress responded four days later by approving the "Formosa Resolution" authorizing the President to "employ the Armed Forces of the United States as he deems necessary for the specific purpose of security and protecting Formosa and the Pescadores against armed attack. . . ." In the same period, Washington issued blunt warnings to Peiping that new outbreaks of Chinese aggression anywhere in Asia—the most likely point was Indochina—would encounter firm American resistance which would not necessarily be confined to the immediate territory in which aggression took place nor be limited solely to the use of conventional, non-nuclear, weapons.[14]

By the late 1950s and early 1960s, other issues aggravated Sino-American relations. With the liquidation of French colonial control in Indochina in 1954, the Communist Chinese, working with Ho Chi Minh's regime in North Vietnam, supported a campaign of subversion against the government of South Vietnam. Similarly, in Laos—supposedly "neutralized" by the great powers in 1954—Red China supported communist elements seeking to defeat both the "neutralist" and right-wing forces in the country and to establish a communist regime oriented toward Peiping. Then, in 1962, came the most daring and dangerous Communist Chinese attempt to expand into the free world: Peiping's move against India's Himalayan provinces. After a de facto ceasefire, this venture left Chinese troops in a position to threaten the security of India, long regarded by American officials as a bulwark of democracy in Asia and as a counterpoise to the expanding power and influence of Red China.

If Peiping's use of outright military force and subversion aroused deep apprehension in Washington, its reliance upon conciliation, good will, and an effort to "identify" with emerging societies throughout Asia, the Arab world, and Africa were scarcely less disconcerting. Beginning with the Afro-Asian conference at Bandung in 1955, Mao's regime sought to generate good will among neighboring Asian countries, to convince them that Communist China was "sympathetic" to their problems, and (even while it suffered acute economic problems at home) to extend limited economic assistance to developing countries requiring massive injections of foreign capital. As part of its "soft" approach to the underdeveloped world, Red China concluded border agreements with countries such as Burma and Pakistan. It endeavored to arrive at a détente with Jakarta concerning the citizenship of the three million Chinese living in Indonesia. By the mid-1960s, Chinese leaders had extended their orbit to Arab and African states. Thus, in a visit to the Arab world and North Africa late in 1963, Chinese Foreign Minister Chou En-lai sought to get Red China accepted as a "good, reliable friend" of Arab societies. On his tour, Chou sought to cultivate the impression among Africans that China was ready to supply their needs in foreign aid and favorable trade agreements. Throughout his tour, Chou stressed the theme of "Afro-Asian solidarity" and sought (with no notable degree of success) Arab and African support for the calling of another Bandung Conference.[15]

The Sino-Soviet Axis

China's own diplomatic ambitions in Asia would have been sufficient to create great tension between Washington and Peiping after 1949. American apprehensions about China's intentions, however, were re-enforced by the Sino-Soviet alliance. China's accession to the Communist camp raised the number of people within the Communist orbit to around one billion; territorially, the Communist empire now extended from the Pacific and the China Sea to the Adriatic, the gates of Berlin, and the Baltic Sea. Not since the time of Genghis Khan has such an empire appeared in history.

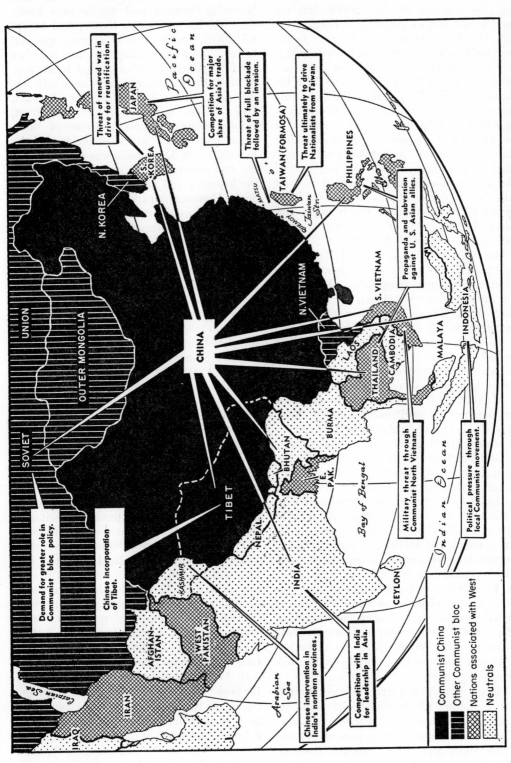

Communist China Presses Outward. (Source: *The New York Times*, September 7, 1958. © 1958 by The New York Times Company. Reprinted by permission.)

Labels within the map:

Threat of renewed war in drive for reunification.

Competition for major share of Asia's trade.

Threat of full blockade followed by an invasion.

Threat ultimately to drive Nationalists from Taiwan.

Propaganda and subversion against U. S. Asian allies.

Demand for greater role in Communist bloc policy.

Chinese incorporation of Tibet.

Chinese intervention in India's northern provinces.

Competition with India for leadership in Asia.

Military threat through Communist North Vietnam.

Political pressure through local Communist movement.

Legend:

Communist China
Other Communist bloc
Nations associated with West
Neutrals

Down to the late 1950's, the official American view was that the Sino-Soviet Axis was durable and that its policies were highly unified. The American tendency to refer to the machinations of "international communism" in Europe or the Middle East or Asia indicated a belief in the United States that the Communist conspiracy against the free world was monolithic. A State Department memorandum of 1958 held that "the two partners in the Sino-Soviet alliance clearly realize their mutual dependence and attach great importance to bloc unity vis-à-vis the free world." The memorandum detected "no evidence" for believing "it would be possible to exert leverage on the Peiping regime which might ultimately be successful in weakening or even breaking the bond with Moscow."[16]

The Kremlin's policies toward its increasingly powerful Asian ally were designed to take account of Chinese viewpoints and to maintain intimate relations between the two power giants of the Communist movement. In ideological affairs, the doctrine of "different paths to socialism" was designed to accommodate the fact that Chinese communism—based upon the peasantry, instead of the urban proletariat— was a legitimate, if different, manifestation of Marxism. This meant, in the words of an announcement from Peiping in 1951, that: "The classic type of revolution in the imperialist countries is the October revolution" in Russia. But the "classic type of revolution in the colonial and semi-colonial countries is the Chinese revolution, the experience of which is invaluable for the peoples of these countries."[17]

Similarly, in economic affairs, during the early and mid-1950s the USSR provided massive economic aid to Peiping and negotiated generous trade agreements, in assisting Peiping with its "great leap forward." Diplomatically, the Kremlin was at the forefront of countries calling for the admission of Red China to the United Nations and denouncing American "imperialistic" intervention in Chinese affairs, as exemplified by Washington's determination to prevent Formosa from passing under Red China's hegemony.

These moves did not serve, however, to prevent a growing rift in Sino-Soviet relations, which many well-informed observers of Communist affairs contended was present as early as the 1920s and 1930s, however much it might be concealed by outward signs of Sino-Soviet solidarity. Following the death of Stalin in 1953, evidence accumulated that relations between Khrushchev and Mao Tse-tung were becoming distinctly cool. By the early 1960s, they had become openly hostile. And by the mid-1960s, the Sino-Soviet alliance appeared to have disintegrated altogether, as a tendency toward "polycentricity" appeared to be fragmenting the Communist movement into several more or less influential poles of power. Using epithets usually reserved for the West, Peiping accused the Soviet Union of "anti-China propaganda" which—in the face of the Kremlin's call for a rapprochement between the two countries—"has completely laid bare the hypocrisy and ulterior motives behind the Soviet Communist party leaders' so-called call for a halt to open polemics." Early in 1964, Peiping accused Moscow of having "completely reversed enemies and comrades." Under Khrushchev, the USSR had "directed the edge of struggle which should be against United States imperialism and its lackeys, against the Marxist-Leninist fraternal parties and countries," meaning principally Red China and its chief European supporter, Albania. The Kremlin was openly indicted for having joined with "United States imperialism, the reactionaries of various countries, the renegade Tito clique and the right-wing Social Democrats . . . against the Socialist fraternal countries . . . the Marxist-Leninists and the revolutionary people of all countries." In the same period, Peiping asserted that Red China proposed to lead a new Communist bloc, against what it labeled Soviet heresy and "opportunist revisionism." Khrushchev and his followers, the leaders of Red China declared, were put on notice that "we do not recognize their majority" in the global Communist movement.*

The Kremlin naturally did not let such challenges pass uncontested. By 1963, Mao Tse-tung and his followers in China were labeled the "heirs" of Trotsky in the international Communist movement; they were members of the "anti-party group" that sought to disrupt the unity of the Marxist movement. Several weeks later, the Kremlin denounced Mao Tse-tung's Communist program as "incompatible with Marxist-Leninism"—signifying a shift in the Soviet line from a condemnation of *specific* features of Red China's version of communism to a blanket indictment of it as heretical. Peiping was accused of carrying on "subversive

* For Chinese viewpoints in the dispute with the Soviet Union, see the texts of official Chinese statements in The New York Times, July 5, 1963, February 4 and 7, 1964.

activities against the international Communist movement." As the weeks passed, Soviet invective became sharper. By 1964, the Kremlin lamented that the "Chinese directors" were seeking the "conversion of Mao Tse-tung" into a god and were leading a movement that sought "to replace Leninism with Mao Tse-tungism." Moscow cautioned its supporters that: "We are witnesses to a crusade against Marxism-Leninism such as has not been seen since the time of Trotsky."[18]

The Sources of the Sino-Soviet Dispute

What factors had produced this schism in the Marxist family? A number of long-range

Who's Burying Whom? (Source: *The San Francisco Chronicle*, reproduced in *The New York Times*, August 4, 1963.)

and short-range influences could be identified. In the first place, Western observers had perhaps always been prone to attribute greater cohesiveness to the Sino-Soviet alliance than the facts warranted. As far back as the 1920s, and continuing through the 1930s and the period of World War II, fundamental differences existed between the Soviet and Chinese Communist parties. On numerous occasions, Moscow sacrificed the interests of the Chinese Communists to achieve goals deemed important by the Kremlin. Not only did Mao Tse-tung finally win in China with minimum assistance from Stalin; he did so in the face of attempts by the Kremlin to impede Mao's campaign and to encourage his principal enemy, the Kuomintang movement headed by Chiang

Kai-shek.* Having successfully established itself as the dominant political force on the Chinese mainland, Mao Tse-tung showed no inclination after his victory to become subservient to the Kremlin. Moreover, after Stalin's death, Mao became the "senior member" of the Communist partnership. In whatever degree he might have been inclined to acknowledge Stalin's pre-eminent position in the international Communist movement, there was no reason whatever why he should accept Khrushchev's claim to that position, especially in view of the latter's inconspicuous role in leading the communist revolution within the USSR. One issue in the current debate between Moscow and Peiping—the Kremlin's efforts to villify Stalin versus Peiping's obvious resistance to accepting "de-Stalinization"—provided a key to Mao's appraisal of these two Soviet leaders.

Ideological issues also furnished ammunition for continuing philosophical discord between the USSR and Red China. Although the Kremlin accepted the theory of "different paths to socialism," it was obviously unwilling to accept a Chinese corollary to this idea, assiduously advanced by Mao's regime. This was the idea that Red China had succeeded—where the Soviet Union had earlier failed—in finding the path that permitted a prompt and direct transition to the communist utopia. This was the "commune" system for agriculture, progressively abandoned by the Kremlin. Mao Tse-tung offered the commune system as the long-missing key that would open the door to the communist utopia of material plenty and the "classless society." In effect, as Harry Schwartz has observed, this amounted to claiming "ideological leadership of world communism, since it implied that Peiping had found a magic formula for doing in a few years what Moscow has not been able to do in more than four decades."[19] Khrushchev joined Western observers in predicting openly that Mao's commune system would ultimately fail.

Another source of doctrinal discord, more

* The origins of the Sino-Soviet split in the recent period are related to political and diplomatic developments in China before World War II, in George F. Kennan's perceptive treatment, *Russia and the West Under Lenin and Stalin* (Boston: Little, Brown & Co., 1961), pp. 241–278. See also: Louis Fisher, *Russia, America, and the World* (New York: Harper & Row, 1961), pp. 52–79; G. F. Hudson, "Russia and China: The Dilemmas of Powers," in Philip E. Mosely, *The Soviet Union: 1922–1962* (New York: Praeger, 1963), pp. 417–428.

directly relevant for East-West relations, lay in differing Soviet and Chinese assessments of the prospect and implications of nuclear war between the non-Communist and Communist worlds. In 1963, the Kremlin released a statement attributed to Mao Tse-tung at an earlier conference in Moscow, in which the Chinese leader deprecated the dangers of a nuclear holocaust, particularly for the future of global communism. The leader of China purportedly acknowledged that in a full-fledged nuclear contest between East and West, "a half of humanity, and perhaps even more than a half, will perish." Yet he contended that "if a half of humanity were destroyed, the other half would still remain, but imperialism would be destroyed entirely and there would be only Socialism in all the world and within a half of a century or a whole century the population would again increase even by more than a half."[20] Moscow heatedly denounced China's "erroneous and adventuristic platform on questions of war and peace, which was emphatically rejected by the peace-loving peoples." Severely criticizing Peiping's manifest desire to "acquire their own atomic bomb at any cost," the Kremlin reiterated its conception that "in modern conditions the forces of peace, of which the mighty community of Socialist states is the main bulwark, can, by their joint efforts, avert a new world war." Since fusion and fission weapons "possess an unheard of devastating force," Moscow believed it was incumbent upon Communist groups "to organize and head the struggle of the peoples for averting a thermonuclear war." Peiping's tendency to believe that "the atomic bomb is a paper tiger" was held to be "in crying contradiction with the ideas of Marxism-Leninism."[21] As in the conflict over agricultural communes, Moscow's insistence upon "peaceful coexistence" versus Peiping's insistence upon continuing the "revolutionary struggle," even at the risk of nuclear war, amounted to a contest over whether the Soviet or the Chinese version of Marxism-Leninism would become the authoritative interpretation of communist principles for the conduct of international relations in the nuclear age.

Behind such ideological disputations there was increasingly emerging what one commentator called "the respective dynamism of the two great Communist states."[22] By the 1960s, an ancient theme had come prominently to the fore in Asia: the rivalry between the Russian and Chinese empires, each of which sought to expand its influence, sometimes at the expense of the other. It was largely to prevent *Russian* hegemony over China, for example, that the United States proclaimed, and the powers of Europe supported, the Open Door policy at the turn of the century. Throughout history, Russian and Chinese interests have conflicted over important territories such as Manchuria, Outer and Inner Mongolia, Sinkiang, and Tibet. Nathaniel Peffer has pointed to the congruence of ideological and national goals in Soviet policy in Asia by saying: ". . . the strategy for world revolution coincided point for point with the historic strategy of old Russia. It worked to the interest of world revolution to strike at Great Britain in Asia; but it had also worked to the interest of tsarist expansion to strike at Great Britain in Asia." Thus, imperialist-minded Russian tsars "might gleefully have burned Lenin at the stake, but they would also have applauded his foreign policy." Referring to certain concessions exacted at China's expense, as Moscow's price for entering World War II against the Japanese, Peffer notes that Russia "got back all of its classical imperialist tokens. In this respect in the Far East Russia has never acted out of its traditional character since the Bolshevik revolution."[23]

As for China's goals in Asia, one authoritative study has concluded that its dominant ambition is:

> the establishment of China as a recognized world power with a position of primacy in East Asia. This is not a uniquely Communist aim; it is one which has deep roots in traditional Chinese thinking. . . . Traditional Chinese attitudes have led many Chinese to believe that their country naturally deserves leadership in Asia and hegemony over surrounding areas. Chinese do not forget that if one views the last two millennia rather than the past century, China had been the strongest country in Asia over long periods, and many Asian countries have at some time been tributary to China.[24]

Werner Levi points out that since 1949, Red China has presented itself as "the savior of all Asia, leading its peoples to a glorious future." Especially significant to an understanding of present-day Chinese policy is the fact that "the area of major interest, Southeast Asia, is also the area in which imperial China had or claimed a paramount position. . . ."[25] Traditionally conceiving of itself as the "Middle Kingdom," throughout history Imperial China sought to create and to maintain a system of political dependencies—known in earlier diplomatic parlance as "client states"—around the periphery of the Chinese heartland. At various stages in history, Chinese dominion has extended over what are now the states of North and South Korea, North and South Vietnam, Laos, Cambodia, Thailand, Burma, Tibet, Nepal, and parts of Malaya and Indonesia. Relating this fact to contemporary Chinese diplomatic behavior, an authoritative British study group summarized Chinese ambitions in Asia by concluding that "the Central People's Government will aim at the formation around China of a ring of satellites under Chinese influence, following in many respects the Chinese

Magnetism. (Source: Peb in *The Philadelphia Inquirer*, reproduced in *The New York Times*, May 10, 1964.)

political way of life, insulating China's borders from undesirable contacts."[26]

Events following Mao Tse-tung's victory in China have tended to corroborate this prediction. North Korea has become a *de facto* Communist Chinese satellite; North Vietnam is not perhaps, strictly speaking, a "satellite," but Ho Chi Minh's regime has maintained intimate ties with Peiping and has in most instances accepted its interpretations of the Marxist creed over competing Soviet interpretations. On most counts, the Communist party of Indonesia (PKI)—the largest Communist organization outside Russia or China—has also sided with Mao Tse-tung in his contest with the Kremlin. As we shall see, Western observers were persuaded that it was Mao's China, rather than Khrushchev's Russia, that sought

to undermine a great-power agreement calling for "neutralization" of Laos. Chinese power also actively supported a campaign of subversion against the government of South Vietnam. In the face of evident Soviet embarrassment, late in 1962 Peiping launched an attack against India's Himalayan frontier, thereby risking a cold-war confrontation in the Himalayas, at the very time the United States and the USSR were embroiled in the Cuban missile crisis.

By the mid-1960s, conflicting territorial claims along the 4000-mile border between Russia and China created extremely tense relations on the frontier of Sinkiang and in the disputed Amur river district of Manchuria. Now it was the Kremlin's turn to be subjected to Chinese "map diplomacy." Peiping vocally complained about old and "unequal" treaties, supposedly alienating Chinese territories at a time when China was too weak and too internally divided to protect its territorial integrity. Thus, an Indian source took note of a report that the Chinese were studying history in order to revive claims to territory in Eastern Siberia, notably areas originally colonized by Chinese during the seventeenth century! Concurrently, the Soviet press was filled with reports about Chinese "saboteurs" who were violating the Soviet frontier in Asia. This Indian observer detected ample realization among Chinese officials that their "biggest territorial loss in the latter half of the last century was in the north at the hands of tsarist Russia." An initial surrender of 93,000 square miles of Chinese territory to Moscow was followed by other cessions that proved highly deleterious to China's interests.[27]

China's growing inclination to "discover" some ancient and allegedly authoritative map, substantiating its "border claims" to Russian or Indian or Burmese territory, was but one response that Mao's regime was making to a problem that could be expected more and more to color China's relations with the outside world. This was the fact that by the mid-1960s, China had a population of around 700 million —close to one-fourth of the human race! Moreover, the population of China was expanding at a rate well above the world average. United Nations studies indicated that by 1975, Red China would likely have a population of 900 million people; by the end of the century it might well reach 1.5 billion people. As China's mushrooming population pressed against the country's limited food supplies—and as Mao's regime encountered severe difficulties in its efforts to expand productivity significantly by its "great leap forward"—internal population pressures would well-nigh dictate expansionist policies abroad. With India and most of Southeast Asia already severely overcrowded, Russian provinces in East Asia offered the most inviting sites for untold millions of Chinese settlers.

American Appraisals of Sino-Soviet Relations

Down to the early 1960s, policy-makers in Washington were inclined to discount the prospect of acute tension between Moscow and Peiping and to detect few major implications for American policies in Asia in the schism between the two centers of world communism. A recurrent theme in official and public American reactions to the Sino-Soviet conflict was expressed by John J. McCloy, a former diplomatic official: "I do not take much comfort from that schism . . . when the chief issue between them seems only to be the speed and manner with which the rest of us should be overcome."[28] Gradually, among informed students of Asian affairs and many governmental leaders, this view came to be rejected as highly oversimplified and as glossing over several important implications for the United States of the tendency toward "polycentricity" within the Communist bloc. Thus, in mid-1963, President Kennedy differentiated sharply between the policies of the USSR and Red China, labeling those of the latter capable of producing a situation "potentially more dangerous . . . than any we faced since the end of the second war." Noting that in recent years the Kremlin had tended to pursue its goals "with some caution," the President contrasted the conduct of Peiping, which continued to pursue policies in Asia that created a "menacing situation" for the West. President Kennedy speculated that mutual concern about Peiping's ambitions might conceivably have had some role in inducing the United States and the Soviet Union to conclude a nuclear test-ban agreement. Soviet Russia, the President surmised, may have been seeking to undermine Red China's influence among the diplomatically uncommitted states (where sentiment in favor of a nuclear test-ban accord was high) and to prevent the Chinese acquisition of nuclear weapons.

Several months later, American officials also referred openly to the relationship between the Sino-Soviet dispute and the position of the Communist satellite states in Eastern Europe. Recent years had witnessed considerable "lib-eralization" of regimes in such countries as Bulgaria, Czechoslovakia, and Hungary. American officials were concerned that a total rupture between Moscow and Peiping might reverse this trend in Eastern Europe and—in reaction against the failure of its attempts to conciliate Mao Tse-tung—lead the Kremlin to insist upon more "orthodox" adherence to the Kremlin's line among its remaining satellites than it had insisted upon in recent years. Still later, Secretary of State Dean Rusk acknowledged that the "Communist world is no longer a single

We Can Always Expand into Russia. (Source: New York Herald Tribune, 1958.)

flock of sheep following blindly behind one leader." In opposition to Red China's militant brand of "revolutionary" Marxism, Rusk declared, the Soviet Communist elite has "begun to realize that there is an irresolvable contradiction between the demands to promote world communism by force and the needs and interests of the Soviet state and people." Conceding that the American "capacity to influence events and trends within the Communist world is very limited," Rusk stated that the policy of the United States was "to do what we can to encourage evolution in the Communist world toward national independence and open societies."

In the same period, another State Department official called attention to differing

American appraisals of Soviet and Chinese diplomatic goals and methods by saying that both countries unquestionably shared "the goal of communizing the world." Nevertheless, the United States detected "important difference in the thinking and tactics of the two. . . . The Soviet leadership seems to have absorbed certain lessons . . . as to the values and priorities which one may safely pursue on a small planet, and as to the price of miscalculating the nature of the outside world." In the light of such divergencies, American policies ought to "be adopted to the differences in behavior between the two, as they relate to our national objectives."[29] Two events in earlier months—the Soviet-American confrontation in Cuba and the Sino-Indian conflict in the Himalayas—had witnessed attempts by the United States and the USSR to mitigate cold-war tensions, in a period when ideologically and practically Peiping seemed indifferent to them. So divergent were Soviet-American and Chinese interests in these crises that, by early 1964, official Chinese journals openly accused Soviet Premier Khrushchev of "plotting with Washington" and of yielding supinely to "United States imperialist policies of nuclear blackmail and 'peaceful evolution.'" Moscow, in the Chinese view, had substituted "class collaboration or class capitulation for class struggle and social reformism" by making common cause with the United States in approaching a number of international issues.[30]

One result of the Sino-Soviet quarrel was thus to make American policy-makers mindful of a fact that had frequently become obscured during the late 1940s and the 1950s. This was that throughout history ideological affinities among powerful nations were often incapable of preventing the emergence of clashing *national* goals and interests; in a contest between the two, the latter more often than not eclipsed the former. The rupture between Moscow and Peiping had thus opened up a possibility that many Americans would have thought inconceivable a decade earlier: the prospect of growing Soviet-American cooperation in the face of intense Chinese animosity toward both countries. For the same reasons that the Western allies and the USSR collaborated against Hitler during World War II, now Soviet and Western policy-makers discovered new common ground, within a context of rising Chinese assertiveness and determination to pursue a policy that was "independent" of both Russia and the West.

If official American acknowledgement of deep-seated Sino-Soviet differences showed greater policy realism than had prevailed earlier, policy-makers and competent students of Asian affairs alike remained conscious of several other major implications of the dispute between Moscow and Peiping. The ability of the United States to influence the direction of Sino-Soviet relations, as State Department officials repeatedly emphasized, was minimal. Any overt American attempt to "exploit" the rift between the USSR and Red China would almost certainly prove unsuccessful. In addition, such a move might supply the only force capable of bringing a new *rapprochement* between the two countries—a visible attempt by "American imperialists" to take advantage of the conflict and to convert it into a dramatic cold-war "victory" for the West. As much as any other development, such a strategy would most likely once more bring the ideological affinities between Russia and China to the fore and forge a new bond between them, effectively subordinating their many differences. American policy-makers thus sought to prevent two extremes in Sino-Soviet relations: (1) a new tightly knit and dangerous Sino-Soviet alliance that had confronted the West in the early 1950s; and (2) a totally divisive, hostile relationship between Moscow and Peiping, in which the Kremlin all but lost its ability to influence Chinese diplomatic conduct. If the United States had an obvious interest in preventing the creation of a new Sino-Soviet entente, it had no less an interest in preventing the rift between Russia and China from reaching a stage in which unilateral Chinese policies, pursued in total disregard for the Kremlin's wishes, threatened new cold-war crises, in which Moscow might be compelled for reasons of international prestige to support its reckless Asian ally. We shall examine some of the consequences implicit in this latter possibility in our discussion of the Sino-Indian Himalayan encounter.

American Policies Toward China in the Balance

In its fundamental elements, by the mid-1960s American foreign policy toward Red China remained essentially what it had been since 1949. Washington continued to withhold diplomatic recognition from Mao Tse-tung's regime and to lead the movement against Red China's admission to the United Nations. A total embargo remained in force against American trade with the Chinese mainland. American citizens and newsmen were prohibited from traveling to Red China. And the Pacific fleet continued to safeguard the security of Formosa and adjacent islands from communist domination. How successful had these policies been in achieving American objectives in Asia? Were American policies being perpetuated by sheer inertia and diplomatic vested interest, or were there still sound reasons for their continuation, some 15 years after Mao's Communist government gained control of the Chinese nation?

Such questions came prominently to the fore in 1964, when—as part of its declared policy of *l'independance* in foreign affairs—General de Gaulle's government in France announced its recognition of Communist China. This French move was widely interpreted as a severe setback for American foreign policy in Asia and as another instance in which de Gaulle threatened to seize the initiative in the Western alliance away from the United States. Recent developments within the United Nations also tended to call the adequacy of American policy into question. Every year since 1949 the United States had been successful in preventing Red China's admission into the UN. Yet the trend of voting behavior in the General Assembly on the issue since 1951 was clearly against the American position. In 1953, for example, approximately 70 percent of the Assembly members voted with the United States; by 1963, that majority had fallen to slightly over 50 percent. Relying upon a coalition of 35 Western votes, 12 votes in the former French possessions of Africa, and 10 additional votes, the United States had successfully blocked Red China's admission. A change of only a few votes—and with France's recognition of Red China, this change might well soon occur among the former French colonies of Africa—would create an Assembly majority in favor of Communist Chinese admission to the UN.[31] Informed observers therefore believed that, within a relatively brief period of time, the United States would likely find itself outvoted in the UN, on an issue concerning which Americans have tended to react with deep emotion. Time and changing circumstances in the global community were about to overtake American foreign policy on this question.

Proponents of long-standing American foreign policy toward Communist China cite several fundamental reasons for its continu-

ation throughout the years ahead. Red China was labeled an "aggressor" because of its intervention against the UN in the Korean War. Peiping's continuing involvement in Laos and South Vietnam, along with its military intrusions into Tibet and northern India, testify to its continued addiction to aggressive policies. Since the United Nations supposedly consists of "peace-loving states," it would contravene the spirit of the Charter to admit Red China. Moreover, in this view, the United States must not contemplate the "abandonment" of Chiang Kai-shek's regime on Formosa. Such a step would inflict a severe psychological defeat upon the free world, call into question the reliability of Western alliances, and greatly aggravate the problem of preserving free-world military security. The problem created by the "overseas Chinese" also persuades many Americans that current policy toward China must be maintained. Politically and economically, this group is highly influential throughout Southeast Asia. If the United States recognized Mao's regime on the mainland, and permitted Formosa to pass behind the Bamboo Curtain, this influential Chinese minority might well become a fifth column in vulnerable Asian countries. In addition, millions of Americans remained convinced that Red China's aggressive conduct could not be "rewarded" by granting Peiping concessions that amounted to "appeasement" of what might some day prove the most dangerous country within the Communist orbit.

Critics of contemporary American policy toward China were not unaware of the cogency of many of these arguments; nor did they minimize the difficulties in the path of any fundamental change in American relations with Mao's regime. Admittedly, in the United States very little support could be found for the idea, for example, that Chiang Kai-shek's government on Formosa ought to be deserted by the United States or that American recognition of Red China, coupled with willingness to grant it a seat in the UN, ought to be extended unconditionally or at once. It was no less clear that, for its part, Mao Tse-tung's government evinced no discernible interest in improving relations with the United States, as judged by its behavior in Asia and on the global scene. Just as the existence of Israel sometimes served convenient purposes in the Arab world, the omnipresent specter of "American imperialism" afforded officials in Peiping ready-made and effective propaganda raw materials with which to generate mass loyalties behind their internal programs. If "aggressive" American intentions toward China did not exist, in all probability it would be necessary for Mao Tse-tung to invent them in order to elicit maximum popular support for his policies.

Even so, critics of current American policy toward China contended that the guiding principle upon which any foreign policy must be assessed is the extent to which it achieved the nation's *own interests*, irrespective of the way it might serve the purposes of other countries, including the nation's enemies. By this criterion, American policy appeared stagnant, unimaginative, and increasingly ineffectual, no matter how much it served as a visible symbol of the profoundly anti-Communist impulses of the American society. Indeed, it stood as a classic example of a foreign policy supported almost exclusively by popular emotions and domestic political considerations. As the years passed, American policy-makers found themselves in a diplomatic strait jacket that greatly inhibited their flexibility and impeded their ability to achieve national policy objectives under new conditions. Paradoxically, a policy that was initiated in the late 1940s to "isolate" China in the global community threatened, by the mid-1960s, to "isolate" the United States from its principal allies and friends and to freeze it in a position in which diplomatic reverses were becoming well-nigh inevitable.

The most fundamental defect in American policy, as Fairbank emphasized, was that: "Our thinking, in conservative America, has not kept pace with China's revolution." All of the images, stereotypes, and mythology surrounding American policy toward China in recent years —such as the idea that China was "lost" to communism, or that Chiang Kai-shek's government was "sold out" by subversive influences in America or elsewhere—betrayed what Fairbank has labeled "an attempted rejection of reality" by the American mind and a retreat into a shell of national anger, revulsion, and frustration about events on the Chinese mainland that Americans did not fully understand. Under Mao Tse-tung, China is not conducting itself as Americans had long convinced themselves China *ought* to conduct itself, on the basis of their experience with a weak, internally divided, seemingly pro-American country during the period from 1900 to World War II. Even into the 1960s, what might be called the "Open Door mentality" about China prevented Americans from bridging the gap between their own conceptions of expected Chinese national policies and aspirations, and the actual behavior of Mao Tse-tung's government. The result was that America's China policy came to possess a high inertia of its own, preventing foreign policy officials from even discussing its advantages and disadvantages publicly or suggesting that, in many crucial respects, it might no longer achieve American diplomatic objectives.

One fundamental difference between the way Americans looked at events in China and the way most other societies in the free world looked at these same events may be cited to illustrate the point. To Americans, Mao Tse-tung's victory in China was explained by reference to the machinations of "international communism." This oversimplified approach glossed over, if it did not totally submerge, the fact that if Mao was admittedly a Communist, he was no less a revolutionist and Chinese nationalist, who used Marxist ideology (greatly modified to fit conditions in China) to achieve his goals. It became plain in the 1950s and 1960s, if it was not always clear earlier, that from the *beginning* of his revolutionary movement in the late 1920s, Mao had no intention of becoming subservient to Moscow and that he had achieved his victory almost entirely by his own efforts. Most of America's cold-war allies, along with the great majority of nations throughout the Afro-Asian world, thus took the view that the emergence of a communist regime in China must be seen as the culmination of a great nationalist ferment in China, leading to a civil war that began in the late 1920s and was not completed until the late 1940s. America's implacable opposition to Mao's regime was thus widely regarded as *de facto* intervention in China's internal affairs.

Whatever the outside world may think of Mao's movement, there was no real doubt that it was chosen by the Chinese in preference to Chiang Kai-shek's Kuomintang organization; nor was there any real question that today Peiping's rule is effective throughout the country. While Americans have tended to think that intervention in Chinese affairs is justified as part of its global response to "international communism," other nations throughout the free world regard it as interference in Chinese internal politics—a course which, by the 1960s, was perhaps condemned as much for its demonstrated futility as for its departure from America's own ideological principles. Persistence in the policy, other governments have tended to think (in part on the basis of a comparable policy pursued toward the Soviet Union for many years after 1917), not only tended to lose touch with reality, but tied the hands of American policy-makers by preventing them from adopting *other* approaches that might much better achieve Western objectives in Asia. If Americans have accepted the fact that a policy of widening contacts and *détentes* with the communist regime of the USSR benefits both East and West, why would not such a policy eventually pay dividends with respect to China?

The long overdue necessity for a reformulation of American foreign policy toward Red China did not necessarily indicate, much less require, wholesale American "concessions" to Peiping, such as immediate recognition of Mao's government, outright "abandonment" of Chiang Kai-shek's regime on Formosa, or any other particular steps that might conceivably improve the atmosphere of prevailing Sino-American relations. It was no more realistic to expect the United States to make concessions of this kind unilaterally than it was to anticipate that Peiping would terminate its "Hate America" campaign or cease supporting subversive movements in Southeast Asia. These and other concrete issues dividing America and China were properly the subject for careful study and negotiation. And as in all diplomatic bargaining, in any attempt to bring about a "thaw" in Sino-American relations, the United States would expect to receive equivalent concessions for any it was prepared to grant the other side. Lasting diplomatic accords, like trade agreements, usually are negotiated because each side gains something it did not have before and, in the process, relinquishes something that is less important to it than what it gains. The precise elements in any future *détente* between Red China and America would largely depend upon: (1) the circumstances prevailing at the time of its negotiation, and (2) the bargaining positions of both sides at the conference table.

These considerations, particularly the latter, dictate renewed concern about American foreign policy toward Red China. By the 1960s, events were rapidly eroding America's bargaining position. In one instance after another, Washington was finding itself increasingly compelled to "accept" major international decisions respecting Red China and Asia generally, made by countries which were no longer prepared to support hallowed and rigid American policies. Trade and cultural contacts between countries throughout the free world and Communist China was constantly expanding. France was but the latest American ally to extend recognition to Peiping and, indirectly at least, to focus global attention upon the anomaly of two governments purporting to represent mainland China. As we have seen, it was problematical how long the United States could successfully stem the rising tide of opinion in the United Nations in favor of seating Red China in that organization. By 1964, General de Gaulle threatened to wrest the diplomatic initiative altogether from the United States by endeavoring to achieve an Asian settlement that would bring stability to this turbulent area. In brief, the United States—wedded to a policy whose foundations were images and expectations about Chinese behavior applicable to a bygone era—was in danger of being relegated to the diplomatic sidelines and of having decisions in Asia affecting its interests made by countries whose approach was geared to the realities of contemporary international life.*

THE CHALLENGE OF ASIAN NATIONALISM AND NEUTRALISM

Over one billion people in Asia have been involved in nationalist movements since World War II. Out of the fires of Asian nationalism, 13 newly independent nations have been forged: Pakistan, India, Burma, Ceylon, Laos, Cambodia, North and South Vietnam, Malaysia, Indonesia, the Philippines, and North and South Korea. In addition, profound social, economic, and political transformations have taken place as a result of the Communist victory in China and changes carried out in Japan by the American occupation authorities and by successive Japanese governments. No nation in the Orient has escaped nationalist

* A penetrating and comprehensive analysis of the pros and cons of American foreign policy toward Red China since 1949 is provided in Robert P. Newman, *Recognition of Communist China?* (New York: Macmillan, 1961). For briefer treatments, see A. Doak Barnett, *Communist China and Asia: A Challenge to American Policy* (New York: Random House, 1961), pp. 430–476; Fairbank, *op. cit.*, pp. 307–322; Edward Crankshaw, *The New Cold War: Moscow v. Peking* (Baltimore: Penguin Books, 1963), pp. 136–164.

ferment. A leading student of Asian affairs has thus said that nationalism may still prove "the nuclear weapon of the situation in Asia."[32]

As far as the domestic programs and policies espoused by nationalist regimes in Asia are concerned, the dominant interest of the United States might be said to consist of two closely related goals: to encourage, and assist with, the maintenance of *stable* political regimes throughout Asia, capable of enforcing central governmental authority over what is, in nearly every case, a sharply divided and fragmented society; and to create the conditions under which Asian governments may progress in the achievement of a "democratic" political order, accompanied by rising standards of living, a goal to which every Asian nation from Pakistan to the Philippines is committed. A major technique of American foreign policy in pursuing these goals, to which we shall refer in more detail presently, has been the extension of economic and technical assistance to Asian governments to enable them to overcome formidable social and economic problems impeding their quest for modernization.

As in the Arab, or African, or Latin American contexts, great diversity has characterized the political orders appearing on the Asian scene. Military dictatorships, exercising greater or lesser authoritarian powers, govern such countries as Pakistan, Burma, Thailand, South Vietnam, and South Korea. The government of Cambodia is a constitutional monarchy. In Indonesia, President Sukarno's "guided democracy" possesses many of the earmarks of strong presidential governments in Egypt and Ghana. Only in India, Malaysia, the Philippines, and Japan did regimes adhere to constitutional and political precepts long viewed by the West as integral features of democratic systems. Even so, widespread agreement existed among newly independent states of Asia upon two propositions. One was that "democracy" had to be defined fully as much in social and economic terms as it was in political terms. Asian nationalists tended to believe that democratization of the social and economic systems prevailing in their countries was perhaps an indispensable *prerequisite* for the achivement of political democracy. This led to the second dominant idea: *ultimately* Asian states hoped to achieve a substantial measure of political democracy. Progress toward that goal remained a fixed objective of all governments on the Asian scene.

Our concern with Asian nationalism, however, is more with its diplomatic than its internal aspects. In this respect, a dominant fact about contemporary Asia was widespread attachment to a neutralist or nonaligned position in world affairs. Pakistan, Thailand, South Vietnam, South Korea, Japan, and the Philippines had defense ties with the United States. North Vietnam and North Korea were members of the Communist bloc; they were oriented chiefly toward Peiping, rather than Moscow. The largest and most influential non-Communist countries of Asia—India and Indonesia—along with Burma, Ceylon, Laos, Cambodia, and Malaysia, adhered to the principle of nonalignment with rival cold-war power blocs. Moreover, by the mid-1960s, in other countries that were formally "aligned" with the West (like Pakistan, Thailand, and South Vietnam) neutralist currents were strong. After the Sino–Indian Himalayan crisis of 1962–1963, the government of Pakistan assumed a *de facto* position of diplomatic nonalignment by signing a border agreement with Red China and by reaching other accords with Peiping, in the face of evident American opposition. The evidence therefore indicated that, as in regions like Africa and Latin America, nonalignment was gaining converts in Asia and that the United States would most likely be confronted with new manifestations of this diplomatic ideology in the Asian context.

What were the leading ingredients in the concept of neutralism or nonalignment in Asia? What were some of its more important regional variations? How did it compare with Arab or African manifestations of the idea? What were the principal implications of the trend toward nonalignment for the United States? These questions may be most meaningfully evaluated as we focus upon the one Asian country that, throughout the postwar period, epitomized the concept of nonalignment and provided guidance in its expression and application to many other newly independent countries—the Republic of India.

The Indian Conception of Nonalignment

An editorial appearing in the Ceylon *Daily News*, commemorating Indian Prime Minister Nehru's 74th birthday on November 14, 1963, referred to Nehru as "one of the dominating figures of the age." Among his achievements was listed "the influence he has exerted in international affairs as initiator of [the] neutralist policy so favored by newly independent countries." This tribute (written after the Chinese attack late in 1962) commended Nehru because he "constantly adhered to the policy of neutralism."[33] Several years earlier, Woodrow Wyatt, a Member of the British Parliament, observed that India

> has set the pattern by which states that are numerically strong but weak as yet in physical resources can "live with all" and find the means of developing themselves economically while retaining independence of judgment and maintaining democracy.[34]

And an American Ambassador to India, Chester Bowles, has said that Nehru of India expressed "not only his own convictions but also the yearnings and the attitudes of the vast majority in free Asia and in Africa. . . . I am convinced that what Nehru says, most free Asians think."[35] In no sphere are such comments more relevant than in the area of foreign relations. Nehru of India emerged as the architect of the policy of nonalignment, that has gained a growing circle of converts throughout the Afro-Asian world. Many of the misgivings American officials and citizens have felt about the concept of neutralism or non-alignment often centered upon Nehru of India, who symbolized a diplomatic credo many Americans neither understood nor accepted.

The great variety of viewpoints and practices associated with neutralist or nonaligned foreign policies in Asia, and in other regions in the contemporary world, lends considerable credence to the judgment expressed by an Indian observer in 1961: "There is no measuring tape for determining nonalignment."[36] Asian versions of the concept—ranging from the "nonalignment" professed by India, to the "neutralization" imposed upon Laos, to the "positive neutralism" espoused by Indonesia—reveal numerous differences, both in principle and in practice. At the same time, there is a substantial consensus among states in Asia and elsewhere devoted to nonalignment about its central ingredients. As in the Arab world and Africa, the core of the doctrine is the idea that genuine national independence both makes possible and demands nonalignment in foreign affairs. One student of Asian affairs has thus linked the emergence of the neutralist credo with the nationalist ferment that swept Asia during and after World War II:

> The policy of nonalignment with power blocs was an offshoot of the strong sentiments of nationalism in these countries. The pursuit of an "independent" foreign

policy provided a tremendous satisfaction to their national pride and sense of independence. . . . such a policy makes a tremendous mass appeal in all these countries. . . . Nonalignment . . . was seen to be the best possible guarantee by these states to preserve . . . their national integrity and independence.[37]

In the same vein, the editor of the *Times of India* declared in 1961 that for India a policy of nonalignment "in world politics . . . is an insurance against being treated lightly or with calculated disrespect."[38] Echoing this view, the Foreign Minister of Nepal has said that: "We have passed the age when smaller nations existed only as satellites of a Great Power. . . . We regard the concept of the buffer state as outmoded." The Prime Minister of Malaya has explained his country's adherence to nonalignment by saying: "We faced up to the fact that with independence, we should develop our Malayan political point of view in foreign affairs." Defending this approach to foreign relations, he observed that "Britain and the United States have been doing our thinking for us for a long time. Sooner or later we have got to stand on our own two feet and work out our own salvation."[39]

The crux of the doctrine of nonalignment was thus identified by Nehru in 1957, when he declared that such a policy "seems to me as the natural consequence of an independent nation functioning according to its own lights. After all, alignment means being regimented to do something you do not like and thereby giving up a certain measure of your own independent judgment and thinking."[40] On another occasion Nehru asked:

> Are we copies of Europeans, Americans or Russians? We are Asians or Africans and none else. For anyone to tell us that we have to be camp-followers of Russia or America or any country in Europe is not very creditable to our new dignity, our new independence, our new freedom, our new spirit.

To Nehru's mind—and in this, he was unquestionably voicing the dominant sentiment prevailing in Asia—*permanent* diplomatic or military identification with either cold-war power bloc would be "most degrading and humiliating to any self-respecting people or nation. It is an intolerable thought to me that the great countries of Asia and Africa should come out of bondage only to degrade themselves in this way."[41] As early as 1946, therefore, Nehru declared that in foreign affairs India proposed to "keep away from power politics of groups aligned against one another" in the world community. Within a few months, the government of nearby Burma also announced its intention to avoid "alignment with a particular power bloc antagonistic to other opposing blocs."[42] Several years later, Nehru reiterated that military or diplomatic "alignment" with a great power would reduce India to the status of a "camp-follower"; Indian policies would then become shaped by its more powerful allies. Although India by no means ruled out the possibility that "we will not align with other countries for friendly purposes," he insisted that "we will not have alignment for military purposes." Fervently, Nehru told the Indian Parliament, "I would rather India sank and died than she should be a camp-follower of other nations."[43]

Implicit in this conception of foreign affairs is the idea of diplomatic *freedom of choice* as the hallmark of a nonaligned foreign policy. *Permanent* identification with the East or West (or, as each bloc has tended to lose its monolithic character, with powerful countries within them) is prohibited by a policy of nonalignment. *Temporary* cooperation or association with great powers in military, economic, diplomatic, or other affairs is permissible without departing from a "nonaligned" diplomatic status. Thus, for India and other states espousing this principle, four alternatives are available: (1) to formulate policies of their own toward major global issues; (2) to agree on some issues with the West; (3) to agree with the Communist bloc on other issues; and (4) to agree in part with the West and in part with the East on some issues, such as disarmament.

Indian officials, along with those in almost all other nonaligned states, have repeatedly rejected what they deem to be a deep-seated Western misconception about the concept of nonalignment. This is the expectation (to use a phrase conspicuous in Yugoslav formulations of the doctrine) that nonaligned countries must asume a position of "equidistance" between the diplomatic positions of the great powers. Adherence to nonalignment neither demands a "middle-of-the-road" diplomatic course between cold-war contestants, nor do states professing this doctrine actually follow such a course, since each nonaligned country "takes a different attitude on a number of questions, in keeping with its geographical posi-

tion, its special interests, concepts, traditional ties" and other factors.[44]

Indian voices have been conspicuous in making another distinction deemed essential by nonaligned states broadly throughout the Afro-Asian world. This is the difference between "neutralism" (or nonalignment) and "neutrality." For two reasons, advocates of nonalignment reject the label "neutral" to describe their position. First, under international law "neutrality" has a fairly precise meaning; it describes the position of a country toward *belligerents in a war*. Hence it is inapplicable to East-West relations in the contemporary era. Second, neutrality implies a kind of ethical-moral indifference or relativism, a lack of concern about major global issues, that nonaligned states believe is in fact directly contrary to the objectives they actually pursue. For this reason, New Delhi and many other capitals throughout the Afro-Asian world prefer "nonalignment" to describe their foreign policy orientation. The Indian Ambassador to the United States declared in 1959:

> It is a grave error to accuse India of neutralism. Neutralism means knowing the difference between right and wrong and refusing to side with either. It is an obnoxious expression which can only be true of cowardly people without a backbone.

Nehru once said categorically: "One cannot be neutral to right or wrong." And he emphasized that "neutralism . . . means a person who sits on the fence and who cannot decide between right and wrong. India is certainly not neutral, and her policy of nonalignment is anything but a neutral policy."[45]

A corollary of this idea is that nonalignment does not entail isolationism, noninvolvement in global affairs, or passivity toward major international developments. Suggestions (prevalent in the West) that nonalignment implies an isolationist or passive stance, President Sukarno of Indonesia has said, "is wrong and altogether beside the point." Asian countries dedicated to nonalignment "are not neutral; we are not passive spectators of the events happening in the world; we are not without principles, we are not without a standpoint. We do not conduct the independent policy just for the sake of 'washing our hands clean' " in the face of thorny international issues.[46] Instead, a major goal of nonaligned states, an Indian spokesman has said, is to restrict the area of the cold war and to work in behalf of international peace and stability "by persuading other countries also to remain unaligned." India was "actively and vividly interested in improving the climate of the world by bringing about more tolerance and understanding" among powerful nations professing different ideologies.[47] A desire to call attention to such goals has induced some nonaligned countries to designate their foreign policy as "positive neutralism," to distinguish it from "neutrality" or mere passivity in global affairs.

If these were the leading elements in non-alignment, as defined by one of its outstanding exponents, the Republic of India, brief mention must be made of some of the more distinctly *Asian* characteristics of the doctrine. In the spectrum of viewpoints and policies embraced under the concept of nonalignment, by the 1960s India and Asian states generally (with the exception of Indonesia) had gained the reputation for being among the "moderate" neutralist countries. On the one hand, as time passed, officials in India were much less inclined than "radical" neutralist countries (like the "Casablanca group" on the African scene, led by Ghana, Guinea, and Egypt), to engage in intemperate denunciations of Western "colonialism," while giving minimum attention to Communist oppression behind the Iron Curtain. While Nehru insisted that, literally speaking, it was incorrect to call communist domination of European countries "colonialism," he nonetheless endorsed the principle of self-determination for Communist satellites and stated that communist rule was "even worse from the human point of view" than Western-style colonialism. Nehru denounced Moscow's suppression of Hungarian freedom as a "terrible thing" and condemned the USSR for behaving "in a brutal manner in Hungary." Moreover, Nehru often repeatedly criticized the agitational tendencies of some of India's neutralist partners, leading to fiery "resolutions" on subjects like colonialism that did little more than alienate the countries they were endeavoring to influence. To his neutralist compatriots, Nehru had cautioned:

It is rather difficult to deal with these matters in this way. There are what might be called a diplomatic approach to these problems, and an agitational approach and various other approaches. Now as a nation grows in maturity, it adopts a mature approach to these problems. It may be occasionally satisfying to a country to utter condemnations of other countries, but if it wants to achieve results that is hardly the shortest way. Sometimes silence is a little bit louder than noise.[48]

Nehru's reluctance to engage in, or support, a flamboyant approach to issues such as colonialism or disarmament had unquestionably tarnished India's image among newer, more overtly anti-Western states in Africa. One Indian source in the early 1960s, for example, reported that on the basis of an Afro-Asian conference on colonialism, many African countries "did not conceal their feeling that India's passion against colonialism had undergone a substantial watering down in the years of freedom. . . ." New Delhi's "moderate" position on colonialism, said another observer, found "little positive support for the Indian stand on various issues among the African invitees."[49] Nehru's version of nonalignment—widely praised throughout the West as a moderating and conservative influence at gatherings like the neutralist Belgrade Conference in 1961— had increasingly come to be widely criticized by such countries as Indonesia, Ghana, and Egypt for its lack of dynamism and "commitment" to causes high on the list of neutralist priorities.

At the same time, the nonalignment avowed and practiced by Nehru's government also differed fundamentally from the "pro-Western neutralism" of such countries as the former French states of West Africa, Tunisia, or Malaysia. New Delhi's resort to military force to liquidate the Portuguese enclave in Goa illustrated, even to the satisfaction of Indonesians, that Nehru believed: "There can be no compromise with colonialism" and that "when it becomes evident that the colonial Power in question does not intend to give way, all means must be used to resolve the situation." To the Indian mind, once Portugal joined NATO, then the existence of Goa as a colonial enclave on Indian soil not only signified the perpetuation of Portuguese colonial rule; it also meant that the dispute over Goa might sooner or later involve the intervention of NATO powers in the controversy.[50]

Nehru's middle-of-the-road conception of nonalignment, and his reluctance to engage in histrionic and, in his view, usually futile neutralist demonstrations against either East or West, thus enabled India to serve a valuable role in mediating and ameliorating cold-war tensions. Being neither overtly pro-Western nor pro-Communist in its practice of nonalignment, New Delhi was acceptable to all belligerents in the Korean War. Nehru's government made a valuable contribution in bringing about negotiations that finally broke the deadlock in the truce negotiations. Similarly, Western and communist countries alike have been willing to accept Indian membership on the Control Commission supervising the settlement arrived at for Southeast Asia in 1954.

The Sources of Indian Neutralism

We have already identified what is undoubtedly the strongest impulse toward a neutralist or nonaligned diplomatic position throughout the Afro-Asiam world: belief that genuine political independence both permits and requires a position of diplomatic independence, or nonalignment. We may briefly note other sources that engender support for the doctrine in India and elsewhere in Asia.

One of these is geographic location. According to an Indian spokesman, India is "the center of gravity of the ideologies of the world."[51] Geographically, it is exposed to communist influences from the Asian hinterland and to Western influences. In common with many countries professing nonalignment, until the Chinese attack in 1962, Indians were inclined to believe that their country was remote from cold-war military tensions or subversive activities.

An outgrowth of India's geography has been its tradition of *cultural and philosophical diversity,* fostering a broad tolerance for heterogeneous ideas and value systems. Indian officials and writers have called attention to the key role of Hinduism in conditioning the Indian mind for the assumption of a nonaligned diplomatic role. Hinduism is an eclectic, highly individualistic, nondogmatic faith permitting— if not encouraging—its adherents to tolerate different beliefs, to avoid dogmatism, to find truth in other points of view, and to eschew efforts to "convert" individuals holding contrary beliefs. India prides itself upon a tradition of religious and philosophical "toleration" and upon its ability to "absorb" and "harmonize" divergent belief systems. Hence, Hindus are inclined to deprecate efforts to wage ideological crusades or to insist that there is only one "correct" path to ideological, economic, political, or diplomatic truth.[52] For quite different reasons, Buddhism in countries like Burma provides a similar impetus to diplomatic nonalignment. Buddhism, in the words of an

adherent, emphasizes the "fundamental sameness in all beings," regardless of their nationalities; it regards national or ideological differences as "superficial and not fundamental," as "temporal and not everlasting"; and it encourages a philosophy of "live and let live" among its disciples. A Buddhist thus reveals a "genius for the assimilation and acclimatization of foreign influences"; his attitude toward foreign ideologies is one of "tolerant assimilation."[53]

It must also be emphasized that for India, as for many other countries dedicated to nonalignment, the energies of its officials have been concentrated heavily upon *domestic* policies. Nehru once declared that: "Ultimately foreign policy is the outcome of economic policy"—a judgment which leaves much to be desired as a general principle, but which is clearly indicative of the Indian conception that deep-seated domestic problems have first claim upon the attention of the nation's leaders and masses. Part of India's "awakening" after the Chinese aggression in 1962 entailed redressing the balance between foreign and domestic programs. Nevertheless, even *after* the Chinese attack, Indian spokesmen continued to believe that India's destiny would depend fully as much upon its success in solving internal problems as in providing for external security. Put differently, in the Indian view—and in the view of perhaps a majority of other countries that looked to New Delhi for diplomatic guidance—whether the nation succeeds in preserving its free political institutions or whether it succumbs to communism or another form of totalitarian system will depend chiefly upon its success in modernizing its primitive economy and in convincing the masses that "independence" is being successfully translated into a new era of expanding human welfare.

Still another influence impelling India along the path of diplomatic nonalignment has seldom been sufficiently understood in the United States. This is the *domestic political environment* prevailing in nonaligned countries. Whether it is India or Morocco or Iraq or Indonesia, three groups of political forces have tended to contest for control of the government since the country received its independence. One is the Western-educated and Western-oriented political elite that usually led the struggle for freedom and, in the post-independence era, assumed direction of the government. If this group is much more pro-Western than many other groups within the society, it is: (1) at the same time determined to preserve the country's independence from Western domination and control, and (2) inherently *suspect* by other groups within the society because of its identification with the West. For political survival, this group must constantly *demonstrate* its freedom from direct or indirect Western domination. Thus, an American official pointed out in 1956 that in evaluating anti-Western sentiments and demonstrations abroad it had to be remembered that:

> there is political vote-getting appeal . . . in a number of countries in defying the United States. Politicians know they can get a lot of cheers as stout fellows who are defending the new independence of their country by shaking their fist at the United States. They get votes, not so much because they condemn the United States . . . but because they show themselves as great leaders of an independent country, not bound to anybody and not even afraid of the country which gives them aid.[54]

It may be added that it was more than ordinarily essential for leaders such as the late Nehru of India, who have not disguised their affinity for Western political ideologies, to prove their lack of dependence upon, or subservience to, the Western powers.

Second, there are tradition-oriented groups in neutralist countries that often condemn *all* ties with foreign countries and are frequently xenophobic in their attitudes. Right-wing extremist Hindu elements in India, or the Moslem Brotherhood in Egypt, deplore any cooperation with, or reliance upon, foreign countries. Third, there are various left-wing forces, like Communist and crypto-Communist groups in India and other nonaligned countries, that favor intimate relations with the Communist bloc. Obviously, such a group is militantly anti-Western and always ready to criticize the government for any overt inclination to become identified diplomatically or militarily with the West.

This confluence of political forces provides a powerful impetus for a foreign policy of nonalignment as *the only policy all three important elements can agree upon*. It satisfies the minimum demands of all three, without infringing upon their deeply held prejudices and convictions. In India's case, and in the case of such countries as Burma, Ceylon, Malaysia, Indonesia, and other nations in the Arab world

and Africa, the necessity for national leaders to keep centrifugal and fissiparous political tendencies in check has, as much as any other factor, demanded adherence to a foreign policy of nonalignment.

Finally, we may make more explicit a point suggested earlier. In pursuing a foreign policy of nonalignment, India is at the forefront of countries that believe the policy must be viewed *positively* and not negatively. If they are opposed to permanent diplomatic identification with contending cold-war belligerents, they are *for* amelioration of regional and international conflicts and are convinced that their "nonaligned" status permits them to make a unique contribution in achieving this goal. As long as their *bona fides* is accepted by East and West alike, nonaligned countries can sometimes do what diplomatically "committed" nations cannot do. The contributions of UN Secretary General U Thant, the role of neutralist states in the Congo Crisis, and neutralist pressure upon America and Russia to negotiate their differences over Cuba in 1962 afford illustrations of this contribution.

Himalayan Encounter: The Testing of Indian Principles

Indians had been living, Prime Minister Nehru said late in 1962, in an "artificial world of our own creation," and "we have been shocked out of it." New Delhi, the President of the Republic of India agreed, had been shaken out of a "false sense of security" into which the country had lapsed since independence.[55] There comes a time, the *Hindustan Times* lamented grimly, when a nation's "independence is tested in the fire of unexpected peril." India, said the *Statesman*, was now confronted by "a powerful and unscrupulous opponent." The danger, said the *Tribune*, was "not only to this country but also to all those in the East and West who believe in peace and freedom, to the Soviet Union as much as to the USA."[56]

Such indications of diplomatic trauma followed the massive Red Chinese attack upon India on October 20, 1962. Within a few weeks, Peiping's Himalayan battalions had penetrated India's northern provinces and threatened to break through into the plain of Assam, leaving the whole of the Indian subcontinent exposed to further Chinese aggression. To Americans, this military debacle not only jeopardized the security of the free world; it symbolized what Americans widely interpreted as a much more fundamental wreckage of the foreign policy with which New Delhi was so conspicuously identified. Quite a few American observers referred to the "collapse" of India's nonalignment policy. New Delhi's "great awakening," American commentators were prone to believe, signified the end of Indian espousal of "peaceful co-existence," "neutralism," and of other foreign policy precepts which, in the American view, had been responsible for the catastrophic events in the Himalayas. Finally, Nehru and all other proponents of nonalignment had been brought face to face with the "reality" of communist expansionism; that encounter, Americans supposed, unmistakably and painfully highlighted the inadequacies of the neutralist credo.

A detailed recapitulation of the events following Red China's Himalayan aggression is not necessary for our purposes. It must suffice to note briefly that within a few days after Peiping's attack, the United States and Britain offered large quantities of military supplies and other assistance to Nehru's government. In time, Western and Indian defense cooperation was extended to joint air training programs and expansion of India's radar facilities. By mid-1963, America, Britain, and other Commonwealth countries had agreed to extend military aid valued at $500 million during the next five years. As India's defenses stiffened, just as unexpectedly as Peiping had invaded Indian territory, on November 22 it announced a unilateral cease-fire on the Himalayan front. Thereafter, Sino-Indian relations were characterized by intermittent and isolated military engagements, alarms about impending Chinese incursions, and propaganda exchanges between Peiping and New Delhi. Concurrently, a representative group of neutralist countries met at Bandung and sought to produce a formula that would effect a peace in the Himalayan episode.[57]

Our interest in the Himalayan controversy centers upon a question that is crucial for intelligent understanding of the foreign policy precept with which New Delhi has been so conspicuously identified and which was tried in the fires of the Himalayan contest with China. Why, after India's encounter with Chinese aggressiveness, did New Delhi not only fail to "abandon" nonalignment as the keystone of its foreign policy, but instead reiterated it and discovered new reasons why this philosophy served India's national interest? Why, in other words, did the Himalayan crisis reveal a sharp divergence between the Indian (and, more broadly, neutralist) appraisal of nonalignment and the American appraisal of that doctrine? And why, with the passage of time, did other neutralist countries follow India's lead, both in proclaiming the continued validity of this diplomatic principle and in reasserting their own devotion to it? Attention to such questions affords an unparalleled opportunity to evaluate the postulates underlying the neutralist ideology and of discovering the relationship of these postulates to American foreign policy objectives.

A major implication of India's response to the Himalayan crisis related to a point about the concept of nonalignment that had seldom been appreciated in the United States. This was that, in arriving at a philosophy of foreign affairs that safeguarded their vital interests, India and other countries adhering to the doctrine had never been as "indifferent" or as "insensitive" to their security requirements as Americans had been inclined to suppose. Americans widely attributed attachment to nonalignmet to a pervasive lack of diplomatic "realism" throughout the Afro-Asian world, to a neglect of those elementary principles of statecraft that took full account of the security needs of the nation and endeavored to evolve guidelines for foreign policy that protected those needs. In brief, Americans had tended to equate the concept of nonalignment with the absence of a foreign policy, to regard the prevalence of the doctrine as signifying a kind of foreign policy vacuum, which would now be filled with "sound" and "realistic" doctrines as a result of China's aggression at India's expense. As we shall see, the Himalayan crisis made much clearer than before (perhaps even to Indians) that attachment to nonalignment did not spring from a total disregard for the problem of military security; rather, it emerged after a careful weighing of alternative policies, leading to the decision that nonalignment could be defended as much on the grounds of its contribution to national security as on other grounds. The Himalayan episode called attention to the fact that it was precisely in the midst of diplomatic crises that the virtues of nonalignment—both for its adherents and for the United States— often stood most sharply revealed.

The crisis also underscored another fact about nonalignment. This was that the longstanding distinction between "aligned" or "committed" and "nonaligned" or "uncommitted" nations in the contemporary world had become severely eroded, to the point perhaps of becoming almost meaningless. Paradoxically, India emerged from the crisis both "aligned" and "nonaligned." Conversely, one of America's principal allies in Asia, Pakistan, remained a member of the SEATO defense system, but it utilized the Sino-Indian crisis to "normalize" its relations with Red China, by negotiating a border agreement that prejudiced the goal of free-world defense on the Indian subcontinent.

Another generalization that could be made about the implications of diplomatic nonalignment before and after the Himalayan crisis was that there were in reality several *levels* or *categories* of "nonalignment." Countries might, in varying degrees, be aligned or nonaligned with cold-war power blocs in ideological, political, diplomatic, economic, and military affairs. Like India, they might be aligned in some of these respects and not in others. For the United States and the West as a whole, the Himalayan contest raised the question of the relative importance of these levels and the criteria by which such judgments were made.

The relevance of such general implications of the Himalayan dispute becomes clearer as we analyze several influences that were crucial in the re-examination of Indian foreign policy following Red China's expansionism. In reassessing the value of the nonalignment policy during the crisis with Peiping, Nehru's government was guided by a number of fundamental considerations. A dominant one was the belief —widely held in India and throughout the Afro-Asian world as a whole—that in attacking India, Peiping intended to *attack the concept of nonalignment itself*. In discussing Peiping's goals, Nehru placed considerable emphasis upon the often-repeated Chinese doubt "that a country can pursue an uncommitted policy." Prime Minister Nehru himself explained that China had sought to demonstrate that "our policy of nonalignment is hypocrisy, that we are already aligned to the Western bloc, and this war . . . is induced by the Western bloc. . . ."[58] Whatever Peiping's precise objectives (and even today, they are not altogether clear), Red China sought in part to humiliate India and to discredit Nehru's government. Peiping, said the Indian commentator Asoka Mehta, desired "a weakening of the will of India," and a "confusing of its sense of identity." The *Weekly Tribune* of Ceylon believed Red China was trying to

"bring a nonaligned country to its knees."[59] The Chinese assault on India was more than a physical invasion of territory; it was an overt attack, said the Vice-President of India, "on nonalignment itself."[60] India's humiliation was intended as a dramatic "lesson" to other countries espousing this doctrone. Since India was widely regarded as "the voice of resurgent Asia, and even Africa," China was expressing "transparent contempt for Asia and Africa" by attacking the country that provided this zone with its dominant diplomatic philosophy.[61]

For many months prior to the Himalayan crisis, Chinese propaganda organs had kept up a drumfire of denunciation against Nehru's government. A favorite Chinese propaganda theme was that New Delhi's advertised policy of nonalignment was a sham and a fraud; that Nehru was a "running dog of American imperialism" and a "follower of the capitalist warmongers." India, said Chinese sources, was in reality "aligned" with the Western camp. However tempting it might be for Westerners to dismiss such allegations merely as efforts to rationalize China's own expansionism, this explanation was much too simple. The Chinese, for example, could not be unmindful that American foreign policy officials repeatedly referred to India as the "bastion of democracy" in Asia and had justified massive American aid to New Delhi by reference to the "contest for leadership in Asia" going on between India and China. Moreover, India *was* heavily dependent upon Western countries financially— and this dependence was growing, not decreasing. Nor could Chinese policy-makers be unaware of the evolution in official (if not always popular) thinking in the United States about the concept of neutralism or nonalignment. From Secretary of State Dulles's widely circulated statement in 1956 that neutralism was "immoral," executive policy-makers had increasingly come to terms with the neutralist movement. Thus, W. Averell Harriman told a congressional committee in 1959, after a visit to India, that New Delhi will be allied

to us in the fundamentals of our objectives —namely, independence of countries from outside interference and individual dignity and personal freedoms. However, India will not join in military alliances and is not impressed by those statements that have been made that "they are either for us or against us."

In 1962, Secretary of State Rusk spoke of the "enormous stakes" of the United States in the welfare of India—a "country of over 400 million people situated in a most strategic part of the world, committed to constitutional and democratic government, and traditionally associated with the free world. . . ."[62] Mao Tse-tung's government, in other words, could not fail to be aware that the United States increasingly regarded India and other nonaligned countries as members of the free-world community and that American policies, by the 1960s, were much more geared to that fact than had been the case in the 1950s.

Moreover, Peiping's assault upon the foreign policy principle so prominently identified with India had to be understood against a background of accelerating tensions between the USSR and Red China, as we described them earlier in the chapter. Ever since 1955, the Soviet and Chinese evaluations of neutralism had diverged; by the early 1960s, they were virtually antithetical. In the Himalayan crisis, said the Prime Minister of Malaysia, India had become "the guinea pig in the search for truth between Russia and China." In Khrushchev's reformulation of the Communist program in the USSR, there was room for "the pursuit of an independent [or nonaligned] foreign policy" by "young sovereign states" that had recently completed nationalist revolutions. The Kremlin believed a "fraternal alliance" existed between such countries and the Communist bloc. This led to a Soviet strategy of "coexistence" with such countries, whereby liberal foreign aid and trade programs, cultural exchange, and other gestures of friendship were designed to win and hold the good will of the neutralist zone.[63] Concurrently, the USSR was *reducing* its foreign assistance to Red China, at the very time Peiping was encountering serious problems in its "great leap forward" and in its attempt to communize agriculture. By humiliating India, China therefore hoped to prove the "correctness" of its hard, uncompromising diplomatic line and to force a reorientation in the Soviet Union's policies toward the neutralist world. It followed that an Indian repudiation of nonalignment would, therefore, go far toward substantiating Chinese claims, by providing proof that India was in reality merely a "running dog of imperialism" and a "stooge of the West." The unmistakable implication would be that massive Soviet aid to countries such as India was detrimental to Communist diplomatic interests and that such aid might much more usefully be directed to countries belonging unequivocally to the Communist cause.

Indian policy-makers also appraised the adequacy of nonalignment in the light of strategic and military alternatives available for best promoting national security. Americans had seldom been aware of the strategic-military arguments supporting nonalignment throughout the Afro-Asian world; the cogency of these arguments become much more evident after India's Himalayan encounter with Red China. Ultimately, India, along with a majority of states throughout the Afro-Asian world, concluded that the underlying military-defense postulates supporting the concept of nonalignment remained sound, even after Red China's Himalayan attack.

What considerations led New Delhi to this conclusion? First, there was the transcendent danger recognized in neutralist, Western, and Communist capitals alike: the risk that the Himalayan conflict might "escalate" into a regional or global holocaust. Thus, Nehru repeatedly stated that India wanted nothing to do with nuclear weapons or foreign troops on Indian soil. An Indian diplomat in Washington stated that:

India wishes above all to keep the Communist Chinese attack from escalating into a major war. Hence, India is refusing Britain's proffers of specialized troops and is avoiding anything like bombing raids into China. . . . [Indians] also strongly reject any talk of resort to nuclear warfare, including the use of tactical atomic weapons . . . assuming these should be offered by the United States.[64]

This concern was also shared by officials of the Kennedy Administration, which during this period was deeply involved in the Cuban Crisis with the Soviet Union. On the basis of official reaction in Washington, a dispatch to a leading Indian journal concluded:

When we tell them that we do not seek tactical nuclear weapons, the Pentagon heaves a sigh of relief. When we proclaim that we have adequate manpower and we need only weapons, Americans say, "Thank God."[65]

Not only was New Delhi determined not to expand the war in the Himalayas. Its reaffirmation of nonalignment could also be accounted for by its conception of the military effort required to contain, and ultimately to liquidate, the Chinese intrusion onto Indian soil. A pivotal consideration in this respect was the nature and extent of expected Western military involvement in India. Suppose New Delhi, at long last, *did* announce its intention to become militarily "aligned" with the West, perhaps by requesting membership in SEATO. What kind of military assistance could it expect from the West, and how decisive would that assistance be in the outcome of the contest with Red China? Two major possibilities existed. Either the West (meaning principally the United States) would intervene *decisively* in the Himalayan conflict with overwhelming *nuclear* force. Or, it would intervene *indecisively* with limited *conventional* forces and supplies to augment India's own defense effort. Given the fact that the United States was currently involved in the Cuban Crisis, and was also committed militarily in South Vietnam, Indian officials were convinced that limited Western involvement—entailing principally the supplying of military equipment to Nehru's government—in the Himalayan contest was the most likely expectation. This assistance could be obtained *without* abandoning a policy of diplomatic nonalignment, just as Tito of Yugoslavia accepted Western arms to bolster his nation's security and as Nasser of Egypt had relied upon the threat of "Soviet volunteers" during the Suez Crisis of 1956 to liquidate the Anglo-French-Israeli invasion of his country.

These military considerations led to a corollary conclusion, re-enforcing the Indian decision to remain nonaligned. This was that the primary effort in dealing with the Chinese threat *had to be borne by the Indian people themselves*. In the last analysis, Nehru declared, "it is our determination to defend the freedom and security of our country and our self-reliance that is going to be the deciding factor" in the contest with Red China. "No nation," said another Indian official, "can maintain its freedom with blood . . . borrowed from other countries."[66] In maintaining the "new spirit" that was required if the Indian society were to defeat the Chinese aggressor, continuance of the nation's policy of nonalignment—long a hallmark of national "independence"—was viewed by New Delhi as crucial.

The Indian decision coincided exactly both with the scope of the commitment the United States was prepared to make for bolstering Indian security and with the ideal American policy-makers held up for other countries threatened by Chinese aggression. The *Times* *of India* observed: "The consolidation of Indian strength by internal mobilization and as large a measure of self-help as possible would be a far more helpful policy than one of starry-eyed dependence on so-called massive Western aid." This idea accorded with American Secretary of Defense McNamara's judgment that Peiping's bid to expand into India would ultimately fail because of "India's determination to defend its freedom and Western determination to help it do so."[67] Ironically, nonaligned India had supplied the one vital ingredient—a national resolve to assume most of the burden against expansive communism—that Americans found lacking in "aligned" South Vietnam, in Laos, and sometimes in other settings.

India's decision to rely principally upon its own efforts to deal with the Chinese foray into its northern provinces stemmed from another military-defense reality. Relations with Red China, in the Indian view, would remain hostile for an indefinite period in the future; the Indian military buildup would therefore have to continue for many years. As New Delhi doubled its defense budget to a total of $1.8 billion annually, it was a basic premise of Indian military planning that the necessary new defense effort must not be made at the expense of India's ambitious development schemes, deemed no less vital for survival than a program of defense expansion. Moreover, a new financial crisis threatened to impair India's balance of payments. More than ever, India depended upon outside assistance. Indian officials freely acknowledged that Western countries had been unstinting in providing *military* equipment to India in its hour of need. As the weeks passed, however, there was no indication that Western *economic* assistance would be significantly expanded to meet India's new requirements. Indeed, in this period the United States was seeking to *curtail* its overseas assistance programs. Under these conditions, continued Soviet assistance to India became indispensable. In their efforts to secure commitments for greater assistance from the iron curtain countries, Indian officials emphasized that:

. . . nonalignment and peaceful co-existence would continue to be the basic features of India's foreign policy. If India was obtaining military assistance from the West . . . it did not in any way conflict with its policy of nonalignment. . . . For nonalignment did not mean surrender to aggression.[68]

Indian officials not only had to persuade Soviet officials that acceptance of Western arms marked no departure from their position of diplomatic nonalignment. They could not, even by inadvertence, embarrass the Soviet Union in its own ideological dispute with Red China, by lending credence to the militant Chinese view that nonalignment was tantamount to membership in the "imperialist" camp. In the Indian view, seconded by observers throughout the Afro-Asian world, such a course could have no other result than to encourage Chinese "adventurism" and to reduce even further any remaining Soviet influence over its reckless Asian ally. Such developments would neither help India nor promote the over-all policy of global peace and good will to which neutralist states generally were committed. Noting that outside aid "can at best be a supplement, a marginal supplement, to our own efforts," G. L. Mehta, former Indian Ambassador to the United States, nevertheless observed:

> . . . we have necessarily to rely on friendly countries both during a period of emergency and as a long-term policy. There is nothing humiliating or derogatory in such cooperation. Britain with all its imperial possessions had to depend on the resources of the United States during the two world wars and even Soviet Russia borrowed arms and ships from the United States to fight Hitler.

Other Indian observers noted that "Yugoslavia also, has received offensive arms only from the West; while for many years now the UAR, Iraq, and Syria have done so exclusively from the East. Yet all are equally nonaligned. . . ."[69]

Still another aspect of the security problem facing India led New Delhi to reaffirm its commitment to nonalignment after Red China's attack. Whatever China's precise objectives in attacking India, they unquestionably included the goal of seeking to undermine India's position in Southeast Asia. It was, therefore, incumbent upon India to strengthen its relations with Asian governments. Any stabilization of India's or the free world's position in Asia also demanded what one Indian observer described as "a tacit understanding between the USA and the USSR" if Chinese expansionism were to be checked.[70] In this commentator's view, India had to encourage a policy of Soviet-American "disengagement" in Asia and, concurrently, foster the emergence of four major foci of Asian power: the Arab states in West Asia, Japan in East Asia, the emergent

nation of Malaysia in Southeast Asia, and India itself. Soviet-American disengagement would in turn be facilitated by India's continued reliance upon nonalignment, thereby avoiding the implication that New Delhi was motivated primarily by cold-war considerations in reconsidering its Asian policies.[71]

Ample awareness of the consequences likely to attend abandonment of a nonaligned position in world affairs accounted for the fact that the vast majority of countries throughout the Afro-Asian zone fully supported New Delhi's decision. One of China's objectives, said a Nepalese source, had been "to inflict a severe blow to the neutral side and weaken it . . . whatever India was doing for her defense by sticking to her neutrality strengthened to a great extent the cause of neutral nations. . . ." Agreeing that China's attack was a "blow to the concept of nonalignment," an Egyptian source observed: "Even while receiving aid from the West, Nehru made clear his policy of nonalignment would remain unchanged. . . ." A journal reflecting the views of Tito's regime in Yugoslavia commended Nehru's statement that India had " 'so far . . . pursued a policy of non-alignment and I still believe in it.' " A Lebanese journal concluded that "the best way to retain self-dignity is to be nonaligned." An Iraqi source praised Nehru for reiterating his belief in nonalignment and added: "His declaration should be taken not only as a declaration by India alone but as an affirmation of faith in nonalignment by the entire nonaligned world."[72]

In some respects, the "rude awakening" Red China's attack induced throughout India had its counterpart in the United States concerning the concept of nonalignment and the extent to which continued adherence to the precept served *American* as well as Indian interests in global affairs. On November 6, 1962, American Ambassador Galbraith declared in New Delhi:

> The military assistance which the United States is giving India is not intended to involve India in a military alliance or otherwise influence her policy of nonalignment. We have often said that we accept India's policy in this regard. . . . Our aid is designed to help defend India's independence and not to compromise it.[73]

Speaking on August 23, 1963, Nehru commented that an agreement for joint defense planning between India and Western nations rested upon the premise that "the defense of India, including its air defense, is wholly and solely the responsibility of the Indian Government."[74] In a statement widely circulated in India, early in 1963, President Kennedy declared: "We have gone to the aid of imperilled nations, neutrals and allies alike. What we do ask—and all that we ask—is that our help be used to best advantage and that our own efforts not be diverted by needless quarrels with other independent nations."[75]

Kennedy's reference to "needless quarrels" was obviously to India's long-standing dispute with Pakistan over Kashmir. American officials repeatedly emphasized the urgent necessity for an Indo-Pakistani agreement on this issue—if for no other reason than that it was vital for the security of the Indian subcontinent. Yet Indian sources conceded that the United States made no effort to condition its military or economic aid to India upon such a settlement; they also admitted that official American viewpoints toward India's case in the Kashmir dispute had become more sympathetic, especially since Pakistan used the Sino-Indian dispute to arrive at a *détente* with Peiping, in the face of evident American displeasure.* India's un-

swerving determination to bear the main responsibility for protecting its freedom—coupled with America's and Britain's willingness to assist it in doing so—the *Indian Express* concluded, revealed "the pointlessness of military pacts and alliances. . . . Mr. Kennedy has rightly pointed out that not one of the 50 new nations since World War II had succumbed to Communist control."[76] Supporting India's continued attachment to nonalignment, an editorial in the *Times of India* urged that the concept from now on be looked at not so much as a "moral virtue," but as a policy that "yields the greatest advantage to this country"; essentially, it had meant, and continued to mean, an Indian rejection of "military alliances and an . . . assertion of the right to judge every issue on merit in the light of the nation's interests." The same journal also underscored the fact that "Washington's reluctance to accept far-reaching commitments of any kind [in India] is certainly not incompatible with New Delhi's interests."[77]

Earlier, we observed that the Himalayan crisis highlighted the existence of several *levels* of nonalignment. Surely, one lasting consequence of the crisis was to underscore the fact that in America's relations with such countries as India—in marked contrast to the situations confronting the United States in Laos or South Vietnam—the most durable bonds between countries throughout the free world grew out of their common dedication to freedom and independence and their determination to maintain it, irrespective of their willingness or unwillingness to enter military alliances. Thus, the Himalayan crisis called attention to a reality that had existed ever since 1947 but which—because of American irritation with India or vice versa over specific policy questions since then—had become obscured down to 1962. Nehru's India had *always* been "aligned" with the free world in the sphere that counted most: its dedication to the principles of free government and its determination to defend those principles. The Himalayan crisis thus provided graphic proof of Vice-President Richard M. Nixon's observation in India in 1953:

> . . . there might have been a tendency in recent months to emphasize the differences that exist between the USA and India, as far as our international policy is concerned. I think it is important for us to bear in mind that the objective of the USA and the objective of the Government of India are the same. We both desire that we can live

* The course of relations between "aligned" Pakistan and Red China during the Himalayan imbroglio provided further evidence of how tenuous the distinction between "neutralist" and "committed" countries had become by the early 1960s. From the beginning of the Sino-Indian crisis, Pakistani sources strongly denounced American arms aid to India as encouraging "Hindu imperialism" —deemed to be a more serious threat to Pakistan's security than communism. On December 27, 1962, Ayub Khan's government in Pakistan arrived at a border agreement with Red China. At the meetings of the Central Treaty Organization the following spring, Pakistan continued to denounce American arms aid to India and to express its evident dissatisfaction with CENTO. Ayub Khan was under extreme pressure within Pakistan to withdraw altogether from Western-sponsored security pacts. Then, early in 1964, Chinese Foreign Minister Chou En-lai visited Pakistan, where Pakistani sources once more publicly condemned American arms aid to India and called for negotiations between India and China. Within a few days, Red China publicly supported Pakistani claims to Kashmir, abandoning its formerly "neutral" position on this controversy. The Soviet Union, meanwhile, continued to support Indian claims to this strategic area. In brief, the "normalization" in Pakistan's relations with Red China raised real questions about its "alignment" with the West and tended to cast greater doubt than ever upon the value of regional security pacts like CENTO and SEATO. See *The New York Times*, November 25, 1962; May 4 and July 19, 1963; February 10 and 24, 1964. Such developments went far toward explaining why the United States did not "tie" American aid to India to a settlement of the Kashmir question. *India News*, 2 (May 10, 1963), 6.

in a world of peace with our neighbors and we both recognize that only when nations are aggressive is the peace threatened. . . . I am confident that in the end, we shall find general agreement among the free nations on both the objective and the means to reach that objective. That is, of course, what our Governments are working towards.[78]

DEFENSE AND SECURITY IN THE PACIFIC

The strategic importance of Asia arises from a number of factors. India and Southeast Asia, along with Indonesia, lie athwart the main sea and air routes connecting Europe and the Middle East with the Far East. Japan, Formosa, Okinawa, the Philippines, and many lesser Pacific islands, form links in the defense chain safeguarding the military approaches to the Western Hemisphere and to two stalwart Western allies, Australia and New Zealand. Southeast Asia offers sources of food and raw materials needed both within and outside Asia. This region, for instance, supplies 90 percent of the world's natural rubber and 55 percent of its tin. Added to these considerations is the fact that the outcome of the ideological conflict that has divided the world since World War II could well be decided by the ultimate direction taken by several key nations in Asia.

As our discussion thus far has indicated, threats to the peace and stability of Asian countries can arise from a variety of causes: economic dislocations; deep ethnic and other social divisions; the prospect of communist military aggression; subversive and infiltration campaigns waged by Communist groups and their supporters; ideological contests between the West and the Communist world for the allegiance of the Asian masses. In the remainder of the chapter, our interest will center upon the cold-war confrontation in Asia, particularly the efforts of the West to create a viable regional defense system for dealing with direct and indirect communist efforts to penetrate Southeast Asia.

The Appeal of Communism in Asia

Closely allied to the danger of outright aggression by communist powers in Asia is the imminent threat of widespread communist infiltration and subversion of free governments in the Orient. In many of these countries the harvest is ripe and the communist laborers are many, dedicated, and exceedingly capable.

A number of intertwined and mutually de-pendent factors coalesce to make Asia peculiarly vulnerable to communist penetration. Uppermost, because it is probably the most basic condition favoring communism, is the continuing nationalist ferment in Asia, especially in its more extreme manifestations. Communists have had significant success in identifying their cause with the aspirations of hundreds of millions of Orientals. Countries like India, Indonesia, Burma, and Laos do not disguise their open admiration for at least certain features and achievements of the Soviet state since 1917. Political leaders in these countries find many parallels between problems confronting their own people and those faced throughout recent history by the Soviet society. Particularly impressive to their minds has been the USSR's ability to deal with age-old agrarian problems, to make spectacular progress toward industrialization, and to abolish racial and ethnic discriminations, at least officially. To a greater or lesser degree, these goals are common to every country in Asia. Even more than Russia's, however, Red China's record has been closely watched throughout Asia. China's problems—landlords versus peasantry, poor agricultural yields, the pressure of population on food supplies, the termination of foreign concessions within the country—are more common to Asia than are many of Russia's problems.

Referring to communism's appeals to Asians, Van Der Kroef observes that:

no other ideology, religious or political, has offered as understandable an explanation of their present predicament, or has stressed so heavily the need for loyalty and sacrifice to a program of action designed to solve their problems.[79]

Communist groups in Asia have experienced considerable success in "running against" the bogy of Western colonialism, long after many Western colonial empires in Asia and elsewhere had been liquidated or were in the process of liquidation. The anticolonialist issue has persisted, because it is emotionally satisfying to certain groups and peoples in Asia and because it has its roots in widespread Asian disillusionment over the continued existence of deeply imbedded social cleavages, formidable economic difficulties, and conditions of political disequilibrium. Asian nationalist groups held high hopes for their countries after colonial domination had been terminated. Many of these hopes were undoubtedly utopian and have not been realized. According to Van Der Kroef, "The bright greeting of the Millennium did not await Southeast Asians on the day of liberation, as so many of them had confidently expected." The morning after, so to speak, has brought realization that bedrock problems remain to be solved and that most Asian societies will be sorely challenged to solve them for an indefinite period in the future.

This condition is ready-made for successful and prolonged communist agitation throughout Asia. Communist spokesmen can assert that nationalist revolutions must be continued under their direction, that they must be "completed" by those uniquely fitted for such tasks. Pending creation of stable conditions in Asia, Communists exploit the omnipresent specter of Western imperialism, a force supposedly ever-vigilant for new opportunities to reimpose colonial bondage on Asia. Communists contend that they alone possess the leadership qualities and insights necessary to achieve nationalist demands and, in the process, to preserve national security in the face of the ubiquitous imperialist threat.[80]

Yet, whatever its current appeal for Asians, Americans ought to be wary of overemphasizing international communism's role in *creating* disequilibria throughout the Far East. For it was Western countries that initially ignited the fuse of Asian nationalism and held out a new vision of material progress; and in this process the United States played a central role. In providing an impetus for nationalism in Asia, no force was more revolutionary than Wilsonian idealism. Referring to the reception accorded Wilson's Fourteen Points in politically backward areas, Nathaniel Peffer has written that: "It may not be an exaggeration to say that in modern times only the Communist Manifesto of Karl Marx was more subversive. Indeed, in the relations of empires and colonies Marx was probably less subversive than Wilson." Peffer was convinced that idealists like Wilson did more to bring about political ferment in Asia "than Nikolai Lenin and Josef Stalin. Certainly he prepared the ground for Lenin and Stalin."[81]

Nationalist demands in Asia then originated from Western sources. The Kremlin did not create widespread unrest in political, social, and economic affairs in Asia. Nor would conditions in many Asian countries necessarily be more favorable for the West if the Communist Revolution in 1917 had never occurred. Asia's problems have their roots in many of the same conditions that prepared the way for communism in Russia and later in China. Surely this

is one key to Communist success on the Asian scene. One of these conditions is the wide gulf in most Asian countries separating a handful of well-educated, capable leaders from illiterate, poverty-ridden multitudes. This situation naturally facilitates the imposition and maintenance of a political oligarchy on Asian masses. Lenin's conception of the Communist party as the "vanguard of the proletariat" has its counterpart in widespread Asian acceptance of a political elite and the necessity for prolonged "tutelage" before mass participation in politics and government can be achieved. Edwin O. Reischauer thinks that communism

> forms in some respects an almost perfect continuity of tradition with the supposedly benign autocracies of Asia's past. . . . There is no part of Asia in which democratic methods of organization and control do not represent a far greater and more difficult break with past political practices than does Communist dictatorship.[82]

Origins of a Pacific Defense System

Military aid was but part of the larger pattern of the total American response to defense problems in the Pacific area. Following the outbreak of the Korean War in 1950, the step-up in communist activities in Indochina, and the growth of neutralist sentiment in other parts of Asia, the United States began to lay the basis for a Pacific security system. Creating a more durable basis for free-world defense efforts required negotiation of a treaty to end the war with Japan, followed by the termination of the American occupation. Studies toward that end were carried on during 1950–1951. Sovereignty was finally restored to Japan by the San Francisco Conference during the fall of 1951. Concurrently, a new treaty of defense between the United States and Japan was drawn up giving the United States the right to "dispose . . . land, air and sea forces in and about Japan."*

The end of the occupation in Japan raised the issue of safeguarding Far Eastern countries from a renewal of Japanese aggression, a matter causing apprehensions particularly in Aus-

* Quotations from the texts of treaties between the United States and Asian countries here and in the remainder of the chapter are taken from House Foreign Affairs Committee, *Treaty Provisions Relating to the Use of United States Forces for Mutual Defense*, 84th Congress, 2nd Session (Washington, D.C.: 1956). This document provides a valuable comparative study of all defense treaties to which the United States is a party, pointing out significant differences in the obligations assumed under them.

tralia and New Zealand. Accordingly, a security treaty among Australia, New Zealand, and the United States—popularly called ANZUS—entered into force on April 29, 1952. Under Article 5, each party recognized that "an armed attack in the Pacific Area on any of the Parties would be dangerous to its own peace and safety and declares that it would act to meet the common danger in accordance with its constitutional processes." Then on August 27, 1952, a United States-Philippine treaty of defense became operative. Article 4 of this treaty duplicates Article 5 of the ANZUS treaty. On November 17, 1954, following the armistice in the Korean War, a mutual defense treaty between the United States and the Republic of South Korea entered into force. Article 3 of this treaty contained the same key stipulation as found in the ANZUS and Philippine treaties. Then on March 3, 1955, a new defense treaty was signed between the United States and the Republic of China on Formosa. Article 5 of this treaty was similar to the articles contained in the treaties cited above.

SEATO—Organization and Principles

During this period, sentiment was growing both within the United States and within allied countries in the Pacific in favor of a regional security system modeled after the earlier NATO pattern. Far Eastern security problems assumed new urgency after the French military collapse in Indochina in the summer of 1954, which raised the possibility that renewed communist agitation might erupt somewhere else in Asia. Consequently, after extended consultations, the South East Asia Collective Defense Treaty was signed at Manila on September 8, 1954, by the governments of the United States, United Kingdom, France, Australia, New Zealand, the Philippines, Pakistan, and Thailand. The South East Asia Treaty Organization (SEATO) began operating on February 19, 1955. To allay apprehensions among neutralist countries that SEATO threatened their freedom, there was attached a "Pacific Charter," which put the signatories on record as favoring the principle of self-determination and pledging to assist Asian states in maintaining it.

While SEATO bears a superficial resemblance to NATO, there are several fundamental points of contrast. The heart of SEATO is Article 4, providing that in case aggression occurs each party will "act to meet the common danger in accordance with its constitutional

processes." The same article declares that threats of internal subversion or other threats to the peace, shall oblige the signatories to "consult immediately in order to agree on the measures which should be taken for the common defense." The treaty area is defined as the general area of Southeast Asia up to 21 degrees 30 minutes north latitude. A separate protocol to the treaty, however, designates the states of Cambodia, Laos, and South Vietnam as lying within the treaty area. In still another protocol the United States expressed its understanding that references in the treaty to aggression and armed attack apply only to *Communist-instigated* attacks. If aggression arises from any other quarters, the United States will consult with the SEATO powers concerning appropriate steps to be taken.

Several points require elaboration. First of all, the obligation assumed by the United States actually commits it to nothing more than to "act to meet the common danger in accordance with its constitutional processes" —action which the United States could, and undoubtedly would, take in the absence of SEATO. As a practical matter, American intervention in the Korean War, along with repeated unilateral warnings against a resumption of communist aggression elsewhere in Asia, have left no doubt what the United States would do if there were a renewal of outright, undisguised communist aggression. Repeatedly, since the end of hostilities in Korea and Indochina, the State Department has warned both Russia and China that a new wave of communist aggression would encounter the resistance of the free world which would not necessarily be confined: (1) to the immediate area of aggression or (2) to use of so-called "conventional" weapons. The Communist bloc, in other words, has been warned that new threats to the peace might encounter retaliation at points, and by methods, of the West's own choosing.[83]

As regards the threat of subversive activities carried out against non-Communist governments, the SEATO agreement, in the words of one study, "bristles with difficulties." The treaty binds the parties to "consult immediately" to counter such threats. Moreover, at the meetings of the SEATO Council, and at more frequent lower-level meetings, representatives of the SEATO powers have carried on continuing studies of defense and security problems in Asia. How effective have these measures been in countering communist penetration of Asian countries? We may most meaningfully answer that question by looking at what had become, by the mid-1960s, the most serious challenge to SEATO's effectiveness: the communist campaign to subvert the government of South Vietnam.

The Crisis in South Vietnam

"The history of United States involvement in the fortunes of Vietnam," wrote one observer in 1964, "has largely been one of misfortune."[84] From World War II to the mid-1960s, the United States was directly or indirectly involved in a series of internal crises in this pivotal Asian country. During World War II, President Roosevelt endeavored to persuade the French to make concessions to Indochinese nationalist demands, most militantly expressed by the Viet Minh led by Moscow-trained Ho Chi Minh. Despite mild American opposition, in 1946 Paris asserted its authority over the country once more, although France admitted Indochina into the newly formed "French Union." Such concessions (leaving the exact status of Indochina highly ambiguous) did not satisfy nationalist demands; at the end of 1946, the Viet Minh spearheaded a revolt against French rule that lasted until 1954, when the French were finally defeated in a decisive military contest at Dienbienphu. At the ensuing Geneva Conference of 1954, Indochina was partitioned at the 17th Parallel, into the State of Vietnam (South Vietnam) and the Democratic Republic of Vietnam (North Vietnam). Other articles in the Geneva accord called for the independence and "neutralization" of neighboring Laos and Cambodia.

As the first independent leader of South Vietnam, President Ngo Dinh Diem, a Western-trained and Western-educated figure, endeavored to unify the country, to eliminate pervasive corruption, and to impose a modern system of administration. Meanwhile, approximately a million refugees from Communist North Vietnam poured across the border into South Vietnam. This group both imposed enormous economic and social strains upon Diem's new regime and introduced Communist infiltration into the country, who later served as a nucleus for Communist-led Vietcong forces. Under Diem, Vietnam undoubtedly made some progress in economic modernization and in laying the basis for a stable political order. Such gains were imperiled, however, by the growing es-

trangement between Diem's regime and the masses. From the beginning, Diem was suspect because of his ties with, and active encouragement by, the West. Moreover, nepotism became rife under his administration, as the government of South Vietnam became a personal enclave of Diem and his relatives. Nor was Diem receptive to suggestions involving the liberalization and reform of his government made by officials in Washington. In whatever degree Diem was prepared to accept vast quantities of American aid, he was never prepared to introduce measures that would curtail his own extensive authority or in any way satisfy the growing dissatisfactions of diverse groups within the country.

By 1959, Communist-led Vietcong forces—materially and morally aided by North Vietnam and by Red China—opened a drive to subvert Diem's government. As the months passed, in spite of growing assistance—reaching $1.5 million daily by the early 1960s and including an American military "advisory group" that numbered about 16,500—the Vietcong steadily consolidated its position. The government in Saigon was losing the loyalty of the masses. As the Vietcong's activities mounted, the United States in turn became openly insistent that radical changes be made by Diem's administration while there was still time to defeat the insurgents.* Finally, at the end of 1963, a military-led *coup d'état* overthrew the Diem government; within a few weeks, another coup, also carried out by military officers, again shifted control of the country's political affairs. Meanwhile, officials of the Kennedy and Johnson Administrations began to concede publicly that the conflict in Vietnam was becoming acute and that prospects for a Western victory were progressively unfavorable. Early in 1964, Defense Secretary McNamara described the situation in Vietnam as "very grave."[85] French President Charles de Gaulle, who in the same period recognized Red China, offered a plan for the "neutralization" of

---

* *The New York Times*, August 28, 1963; January 31, March 1, and March 6, 1964. For a detailed appraisal of American experience in extending various kinds of foreign aid to the government of Vietnam, see John D. Montgomery, *The Politics of Foreign Aid* (New York: Praeger, 1962), pp. 43–83, 224–243. A succinct discussion of postwar developments in Southeast Asia is given in Claude A. Buss, *Southeast Asia and the World Today* (Princeton, N.J.: Van Nostrand, 1958), pp. 70–80. The text of the Geneva agreement on Southeast Asia, along with other relevant documentary materials, is included in *ibid.*, 157–168.

Southeast Asia. De Gaulle's proposal stemmed from the conviction that the West could not defeat the Vietcong in the kind of guerrilla contest in which they, and their North Vietnamese and Chinese supporters, had become expert.[86] On the basis of the reverses suffered by one of America's principal SEATO allies, Peiping called upon Communist groups throughout Asia to emulate the Vietcong and declared that in the contest in Southeast Asia the "U.S. paper tiger had been punctured and exposed." The Soviet Union, meanwhile, joined French officials in calling for an East-West *détente* that would "neutralize" South Vietnam and adjacent countries.[87]

How Deep You Figure We'll Get Involved, Sir? (Source: Canfield in *The Newark Evening News*, reproduced in *The New York Times*, July 22, 1962.)

For American policy-makers, the struggle in Vietnam had proved a frustrating and baffling experience. After expending well over $3 billion to keep Vietnam out of the Communist orbit, by 1964 Washington found prospects for victory dimmer than they had been at any time since 1954. The crisis in Vietnam confronted the United States with two paramount realities sharply limiting its ability to achieve results in the realm of external affairs that coincided with its own diplomatic interests. Public officials might be fully aware of these inhibiting factors; it was extremely difficult to secure widespread public awareness of them.

One reality was that, vast as it is, American power is *finite*, not infinite. The "illusion of American omnipotence," as we observed in Chapter 2, has conditioned the American mind to expect that once the resources and energies of the United States were directed toward the solution of an international problem, the problem would sooner or later be "solved" in a manner acceptable to Americans. The second reality was that the situation in South Vietnam differed in a most fundamental respect from the Sino-Indian crisis that we examined earlier. Speaking of the problem in Southeast Asia, Secretary of Defense Robert McNamara declared early in 1964: "I think the problem . . . is very clearly a political-economic-military problem. It is a problem that requires the support of the people if it is to be solved."[88] This was indeed the key to the unhappy course of events in Vietnam. The Western-supported "containment" effort in that country had never had the "support of the people," in contrast to the defense effort mounted by Nehru's government to cope with, and ultimately to liquidate, the Chinese invasion of its northern territories. By the time President Diem's regime was overturned, it was perhaps too late for a new political elite to win popular support, particularly in the rural areas, where the Vietcong was making its heaviest inroads. The result was that even heavily armed, American-trained Vietnamese military units made little headway against poorly armed, outnumbered, but skillful Vietcong guerrillas, who had gained widespread support among the villagers.

Under these conditions, the limitations inherent in the SEATO pact were starkly revealed. Aside from the fact that the usefulness of SEATO had always been curtailed because some of the most influential countries in Asia did not belong to it and questioned its value, the Vietnam crisis highlighted what was perhaps an even more serious deficiency. This was that SEATO was directed against the *least likely* danger to Asian security—an overt communist military attack—and was ill-equipped to deal with what was the most likely threat to regional security—Communist-instigated subversion and guerrilla campaigns against free Asian governments. The severely limited usefulness of SEATO became even more evident as American policy-makers considered alternative responses to the deteriorating situation in South Vietnam. In evaluating the steps that might be taken to reverse the Communist tide, Washington had to formulate its policies in the light of several indisputable, if painful, facts.

An expanded American military campaign against the Vietcong and their supporters in North Vietnam would have to take place without the support of the NATO allies. France, as we have noted, regarded the war as already lost and advocated neutralization of the area. Among the other NATO allies, only Britain and Italy were known to favor an expanded military effort in Southeast Asia; Britain was ready to back the United States in this step only if Washington also committed itself irrevocably to supporting the new Federation of Malaysia, against Indonesian threats to destroy it.[89] Another inescapable fact was that SEATO remained as unpopular as ever among the neutralist states of Asia. There was still no inclination on the part of India, Indonesia, Cambodia, Burma, or Ceylon to ask for membership in SEATO, or otherwise to cooperate with it, even after Red China's Himalayan thrust into India. Still another fact was that, despite growing American disillusionment with the trend of events in Vietnam, there was overt opposition on Capitol Hill against wholesale American military involvement in Southeast Asia. Influential legislators like Senator Mike Mansfield (Democrat of Colorado) vocally opposed "the issuance of a new blank check on our aid funds and on the lives of American servicemen" to the government in Saigon.[90] Moreover, growing sentiment existed throughout Asia for the scheme of "neutralization" proposed by General de Gaulle. Prince Sihanouk of Cambodia, for example, agreed fully with Paris that "peace and stability could be restored to South Vietnam only by neutralization of that country."[91]

Within this over-all context, three alternatives—all of them painful and all of them involving a calculated policy risk—confronted American officials. First, they could continue the *status quo* in the contest against communism in South Vietnam, by supporting the government in Saigon with funds, military equipment, and military "advisers" for the Vietnamese army. In brief, they could continue the policy the United States had followed since 1959. Events by 1964 strongly suggested that this policy offered scant hope of ultimate victory, as each passing week witnessed some new victory by the Vietcong. Its most crucial defect was that this policy would do little (or, at least, little that was immediate and graphic) to generate mass support for the Saigon government or to deny the insurgents virtually unhampered freedom in the rural areas. A basic premise of this policy was that sufficient time remained to defeat the Vietcong by relying upon the same policies that had been followed since 1959. This was at best a highly questionable assumption.

Second, American policy-makers could "expand" the war against communism in South Vietnam into North Vietnam, perhaps even into Red China itself. This course would at least satisfy a growing public demand that Washington "do something" about impressive communist inroads in Southeast Asia. Beyond that, the proposal to broaden the war suffered from serious shortcomings and abounded with policy dilemmas. Innumerable questions had to be asked, and answered, before this course offered a way out of the difficulty. Against what forces specifically would the war be "expanded"? Would an intensified military campaign be directed only against the Vietcong in the south? Would a Western-instigated invasion of North Vietnam be attempted? Would an effort be made to interdict Chinese support of Communist elements in Southeast Asia, even if this required an attack upon Communist China itself? From a military point of view, what kind of "intervention" would achieve American objectives in Southeast Asia?

Broadly speaking, there were two possibilities: (1) the United States might use its strongest and presumably decisive weapon—its nuclear arsenal—against North Vietnam or possibly Red China; or (2) the United States might confine its "intervention" to a limited war campaign against the Vietcong, coupling this with a strategy of harassment and "pinpricks" against North Vietnam, by blockade of the coastline, isolated air strikes, border incursions and guerrilla raids, and other measures designed to "persuade" Communist countries that their subversive efforts in Southeast Asia could not succeed. No responsible officials in the United States or competent students of Asian affairs proposed that America initiate nuclear war against the Communist heartland of Asia. Washington had deliberately refrained from that course in the Korean War; the prospect was no more attractive in the mid-1960s. For if the United States did so, it would assuredly fight alone. And if it did so, it would be required—in order to eliminate the danger indefinitely—to *occupy* North Vietnam and perhaps Red China as well! Moreover, this proposed strategy confronted American policy-makers with a dilemma that always arose whenever reliance upon "massive retaliation" was suggested for dealing with localized communist incursions into the free world. This was the prospect that South Vietnam itself risked nuclear devastation in the course of "liberating" it from the communist enemy entrenched in its borders.

For essentially different reasons, a policy of *limited* military harassment had no great appeal among American defense officials—chiefly because it offered no clear prospect of achieving American objectives. Strong American air and naval units in the Pacific were perfectly capable of launching air strikes against North Vietnam, of blockading the coastline, and of supporting guerrilla raids into communist territory. The dominant question that remained, however, was: How would such a strategy undermine the position of the Vietcong *in South Vietnam?* Ever since World War II, insurgency movements in Southeast Asia had been an amalgam of nationalistic demands for freedom from French (and now American) control, of popular demands for governmental reform, economic progress, and religious freedom; of long-standing tribal and ethnic conflicts; and of Communist-inspired subversive activities. By the 1960s, it was perhaps impossible to disentangle these separate elements. Communist groups in South Vietnam both led, and were in turn led by, nationalist and reformist groups.* In any case, there was no assurance that, even if it were denied its usual supply and communications routes to North Vietnam and Red China, the Vietcong could be defeated in the south or that the loyalties of the villagers could finally be won over by the government. Even if there were a chance these things could be done, there remained the strong probability that Red China would not, and for prestige reasons could not, permit the

defeat of the Vietcong movement or allow Western intimidation of North Vietnam. In brief, there was no assurance: (1) that a policy of "limited" war would work or (2) that such a war would *stay* limited. After evaluating various proposals designed to win the contest by expanding the war in South Vietnam, the military analyst Hanson W. Baldwin concluded: "All the offensive measures . . . that have been seriously discussed pose problems. None could end the war quickly. All, to varying degree, entail greater political risks and some might be militarily ineffective."[92]

Third, there remains General de Gaulle's proposal for the "neutralization" of South Vietnam and of Southeast Asia as a whole. On three grounds, this did not appeal to American policy-makers; the response from the State Department to General de Gaulle's proposal was overwhelmingly negative.** One objection was that the Communist bloc had been seeking such a solution to the conflict in South Vietnam for many months. This inherently made the proposal suspect in Western eyes. Another objection was that, even in the 1960s, Americans remained skeptical about concepts such as "neutralism" and "neutralization." When such postures were not believed to be equivalent to *de facto* membership in the Communist bloc, they were viewed as "the next thing to communism" or as perhaps "the first step toward communism."

Yet, the most persuasive influence predisposing American official and public opinion against neutralization for Southeast Asia was recent experience in the tiny kingdom of Laos. This new Asian state had supposedly been "neutralized" by the great-power agreement in 1954 that ended the war in Indochina. This understanding called for the withdrawal of all foreign forces from Laos, and the administration of the country by a coalition of political forces, led by neutralist Premier Souvanna Phouma. Subsequent developments in Laos did not convince Americans that this scheme held promise of protecting the territorial integrity and stability of Laos or of Southeast Asia as a whole. The precarious balance of political forces in Laos was jeopardized by a twofold threat to the regime of Souvanna Phouma. On

---

* Speaking of the deterioration of the French position in Indochina, former President Eisenhower has said that a French unwillingness to grant independence to this dependency only served "to bolster the Communist claim that this was in reality a war to preserve colonialism." It was thus "almost impossible to make the average Vietnamese peasant realize that the French . . . were really fighting in the cause of freedom. . . . It was generally conceded that had an election been held, Ho Chi Minh would have been elected Premier." Dwight D. Eisenhower, *Mandate for Change: 1953–1956* (Garden City, N.Y.: Doubleday, 1963), pp. 337–338. Little perceptible change could be noted in this situation after South Vietnam received its independence in 1954.

** *The New York Times*, March 6, 1964, dispatch by David Halberstam. This reporter detected "wide agreement among experienced observers that neutralization of the south would mean an almost certain Communist take-over of the country and a withdrawal of the vast American mission" in South Vietnam.

the one hand, in the period 1955–1961, the United States rendered the experiment in neutralization of Laos all but impossible by massively supporting right-wing and pro-Western elements in the country, led by Boun Oum. In this period, the United States supplied a subsidy totaling some $300 million to Boun Oum's movement, in an unsuccessful attempt to install a conservative, Western-oriented regime.* On the other hand, left-wing elements —led by the Pathet Lao (Land of Laos) movement—also sought to control the country. The Pathet Lao was Communist-infiltrated and had close links with North Vietnam and Red China. At the same time, it was intensely nationalistic, favored sweeping reforms, called for the elimination of governmental corruption, and advocated a foreign policy of intimate friendship with (if not necessarily subservience to) the Communist bloc.

After 1961, in the face of substantial gains by the Pathet Lao in the northern and central regions of Laos, the United States despaired of a rightist victory and belatedly shifted its support to neutralist Souvanna Phouma, regarded as the only Laotian leader capable of unifying the country and of assuring its genuine "neutralization." American officials had come to see that there were basically two alternatives in Laos: either they could cooperate with Souvanna Phouma's attempt to keep Laos out of both cold-war camps, or they would be compelled to accept what seemed an inevitable victory by the Pathet Lao, entailing the country's gravitation toward the Communist bloc. Ironically, even the ability of the United States to achieve the former alternative had, by the mid-1960s, been severely impaired by Washington's *tardiness* in recognizing the realistic courses available, thereby giving the Pathet Lao a period of several years within which to consolidate its

position and perhaps to render the position of Phouma's neutralist regime untenable.**

However events turned out in Laos, they did not elicit American enthusiasm for a comparable experiment in neutralization for South Vietnam. For events in that country had highlighted another prospect that made de Gaulle's suggestion unappealing to the State Department. By early 1964, Soviet policymakers joined de Gaulle's government in calling for a great-power agreement to "neutralize" South Vietnam. In the view of many Western observers, the Kremlin had also tried to achieve the neutralization of Laos since 1961. The accelerating crisis in that country, and analogously in a "neutralized" South Vietnam, stemmed therefore largely from Red China's militant opposition to neutralization and its determination to reduce peripheral states in Asia to a position of political and diplomatic dependency. In view of the widening rift between Red China and the USSR, there was no guarantee that any East-West agreement to neutralize South Vietnam would be respected by Peiping, especially (as the United States was likely to insist) when Chinese representatives had no part in reaching the agreement.†

** Events in Laos, focusing upon American policy in that country, are discussed in: Philip Wright, "Laos: Wrong Place for a War," *The Reporter*, 24 (February 16, 1961), 20–30; Denis Warner, "The Loss of Laos," *The Reporter*, 25 (July 6, 1961), 21–24; Frank N. Trager, "The Importance of Laos in Southeast Asia," *Current History*, 46 (February, 1964), 107–112.

† Asian sources tended to differentiate sharply between Soviet and Chinese policies in Southeast Asia. Speaking of Moscow's views of the situation in Laos, the *Indian Express* on April 29, 1963, concluded that in his diplomacy, Khrushchev "never gets to a point where there might be a showdown with the West." Thus, in Laos, "The interest of Mr. Khrushchev and of Mr. Kennedy are identical . . . for neither would like to see Peking get the upper hand in this strategic region"; it felt that: "A stable and neutral Laos is in the interests of both." Quoted in *India News*, 2 (May 10, 1963), 2. Another Indian source observed that: "Communist China was never happy over the agreement for establishment in Laos of a coalition government pursuing a neutralist policy, because such an agreement went against the Chinese belief that no agreement was possible between socialist and capitalist countries. This ran contrary to the veiws held by the Soviet Union." Indian observers discerned a correlation between renewed conflict in Laos and progress between the United States and the USSR in resolving their outstanding differences. *India News*, 1 (April 19, 1963), 8. In the same period, Indian officials communicated to Washington their view that the

* Technically, the American support of Boun Oum's right-wing regime in Laos could not perhaps be called a violation of the Geneva accord of 1954, since the United States was not formally a party to the agreement. Yet, in a later policy declaration, the United States did "take note" of the agreement and pledged itself not to "disturb" it by force. Article 12 of the Geneva accord bound the signatories to "respect the sovereignty, the independence, the unity, and territorial integrity" of Laos, Cambodia, and Vietnam, and "to refrain from any interference in their internal affairs." Buss, *op. cit.*, pp. 159, 163. The American view was that alien Communist forces had never terminated their "intervention" in Laos; this justified continued American intervention.

The three basic policy alternatives available—to continue the *status quo* in South Vietnam, to adapt a policy of expanded American intervention in the contest, or to support the country's neutralization—thus presented American officials with hard, unpalatable choices. No course guaranteed success; each entailed many risks. After a visit to South Vietnam by Secretary of Defense McNamara, by mid-1964 American officials had decided to pursue a strategy of continuing to support Saigon's efforts to defeat the Vietcong; the possibility of limited incursions against North Vietnam was not altogether ruled out. At the same time, the Johnson Administration continued to avoid direct American military involvement against Communist forces in the Southeast Asian peninsula.[93] This policy involved in effect a race with time. By the mid-1960s, many qualified students of Asian affairs were skeptical that the West had sufficient time left in which to make it work.

NOTES

1. Julius W. Pratt, A History of United States Foreign Policy (Englewood Cliffs, N.J.: Prentice-Hall, 1955), pp. 270–278.
2. Foster R. Dulles, China and America (Princeton, N.J.: Princeton University Press, 1946), p. 107.
3. Ibid., pp. 109–110.
4. Ibid., p. 107.
5. Werner Levi, Modern China's Foreign Policy (Minneapolis: University of Minnesota Press, 1953), p. 52. A leading authority appraises China's foreign relations.
6. Dulles, op. cit., pp. 110–111.
7. Levi, op. cit., p. 55.
8. Ibid., pp. 287–297.
9. Pratt, op. cit., pp. 387–392.
10. The New York Times, June 26, 1960.
11. The New York Times, August 10, 1958.
12. The New York Times, February 20, 1964.
13. Department of State, American Foreign Policy, 1950–1955, II (Washington, D.C.: Publication No. 6446, "General Foreign Policy Series" No. 117, 1957), 2485. Contains numerous documentary materials on Asia.

14. Ibid., II, 2487, 2370–2371, 2373–2376.
15. The New York Times, December 22 and 29, 1963.
16. The New York Times, August 10, 1958.
17. Howard L. Boorman et al., Moscow-Peking Axis (New York: Harper & Row, 1957), pp. 42–43.
18. See the texts of official Soviet statements, along with commentaries, in The New York Times, July 31, 1963, October 4, 1963, and February 9, 1964.
19. The New York Times, February 19, 1959.
20. See the text of the Kremlin's record of this statement in The New York Times, September 23, 1963.
21. The New York Times, July 15, 1963.
22. Christian Science Monitor, February 5, 1959, dispatch by Paul Wohl.
23. Nathaniel Peffer, The Far East (Ann Arbor, Mich.: University of Michigan Press, 1958), p. 421. A succinct and readable historical account of the political evolution of Asia.
24. American Assembly, The United States and the Far East (New York: Columbia University Press, 1956), p. 147. Papers presented to an Arden House conference on Asia.
25. Levi, op. cit., p. 329.
26. Royal Institute of International Affairs, Collective Defense in South East Asia (London: Oxford University Press, 1956), pp. 58–59.
27. See the dispatch entitled "Sino-Soviet Border Tensions," in Hindustan Times, May 6, 1963; "Where Troops of Red China and Soviet Stand Toe to Toe," U.S. News and World Report (January 6, 1964), pp. 53–54; The New York Times, February 9, 1964; R. Vaidyanath, "Exodus from Sinkiang," Indian and Foreign Review, 1 (January 1, 1964), 18–20.
28. The New York Times, December 22, 1963.
29. For recent official American statements on the Sino-Soviet dispute, see The New York Times, August 2, and December 2, and 14, 1963; February 26, 1964.
30. The New York Times, February 5, 1964.
31. The New York Times, February 2, 1964.
32. Edwin O. Reischauer, Wanted: An Asian Policy (New York: Knopf, 1955), p. 269. An illuminating background study of Asian affairs.
33. Text in Indian News, 2 (Embassy of India, Washington, D.C.), (November 22, 1963), 2.
34. Cited in Times of Indonesia, March 10, 1960.
35. Chester Bowles, Ambassador's Report (New York: Harper & Row, 1954), p. 111. A valuable first-hand appraisal of India's

Pathet Lao forces had been taken over by "hardcore Peking Communists." *The New York Times,* May 12, 1963. General de Gaulle's move early in 1964 to "normalize" French relations with Red China grew out of a belief that France would then be in a position to arrive at an "understanding" with Red China to respect the neutralization of Laos. *The New York Times,* February 10, 1964.

problems and outlook by a former American ambassador.

36. *Hindustan Times* (overseas edition), June 22, 1961. The concept of neutralism or nonalignment in the Arab world and in Africa is discussed in Chapter 11.

37. N. P. Nayar, "Non-Alignment in World Affairs," *India Quarterly*, 18 (January–March, 1962), 30, 32. An excellent appraisal of the evolution of the neutralist mentality.

38. *Times of India*, November 7, 1961, dispatch by Prem Bhatia.

39. See *Asian Recorder*, 8 (August 6–12, 1962), 4726; the *Straits Times* (Singapore), October 7, 1961; and *Times of Indonesia*, August 1, 1960.

40. *Asian Recorder*, 3 (July 6–12, 1957), 1531.

41. See Nehru's remarks to the Bandung Conference in 1955, as reported in *Hindustan Times* (overseas edition), April 28, 1955.

42. Quoted in Nayar, *op. cit.*, p. 33.

43. See Nehru's speech to the Lok Sabba on May 14, 1962, as reported in *India News*, 1 (May 28, 1962), 1.

44. Dr. Ales Bebler, "Role of the Non-Bloc Countries," *Review of International Affairs*, 9 (Belgrade, Yugoslavia: January 1, 1958), 1–2.

45. See *India News*, 4 (March 1, 1959), 1, and 6 (January 1, 1961), 1; *Egyptian Gazette*, November 17, 1961.

46. *Times of Indonesia*, August 19, 1960.

47. *India News*, 4 (January 26, 1959), 1; and *India News*, 5 (February 15, 1960), 2.

48. *Hindustan Times* (overseas edition), August 16, 1956.

49. "Portuguese Colonies: The Boomerang," *Eastern Economist*, 37 (October 27, 1961), 779; *Times of India*, June 20, 1961, dispatch by Prem Bhatia.

50. See the reaction of an Indonesian official in the *Asian Recorder*, 8 (January 15–21, 1962); *Asian Recorder*, 8 (February 5–11, 1962), 4404–4405.

51. B. S. N. Murti, *Nehru's Foreign Policy* (New Delhi: Beacon Information and Publication Co., 1953), p. 42. A semi-documentary account, written from a pro-Nehru point of view.

52. For fuller treatment of this point, see Taya Zinkin, "Hinduism and Communism: Are They Compatible?" *Eastern World*, 9 (January, 1955), 16–17; *India News*, 3 (March 15, 1958), 2.

53. See U Khim Zaw, "Aspects of Burmese Culture," *Forward*, 1 (Rangoon: Government of Burma, December 7, 1962) 18–20; and "The Buddhist Doctrine of Peace," *New Times of Burma* (Rangoon), May 9, 1960.

54. See the view of George V. Allen in House Foreign Affairs Committee, *Mutual Security Act of 1956*. Hearings, 84th Congress, 2nd Session (Washington, D.C.: 1956), pp. 586–587.

55. *The New York Times*, November 4, 1962; *India News*, 1 (Dec. 28, 1962), 7.

56. Quoted in *India News*, 1 (November 5, 1962), 2.

57. Our discussion of the Himalayan crisis, particularly as it relates to American foreign policy, draws heavily upon the author's more extended discussions of this episode in "The Testing of Non-Alignment," *Western Political Quarterly*, 17 (September, 1964), 517–542; "An 'Agonizing Reappraisal' for Nonalignment?" *Christianity and Crisis*, 23 (July 8, 1963), 118–132; and "The Two Faces of Non-Alignment," *The Progressive*, 17 (April, 1963), 24–28.

58. *India News*, 1 (February 8, 1963), 8; and *India News*, 1 (February 15, 1963), 1, 6.

59. *Hindustan Times*, January 21, 1963; *India News*, 1 (December 28, 1962), 2.

60. *Times of India*, March 9, 1963.

61. B. Krishna, "Mr. Nehru: An Appraisal," *Eastern World*, 14 (August, 1960), 15; Prem Bhatia, "China's Aggression—Its Impact on Non-Aligned Nations," *India News*, 1 (December 21, 1962), 7.

62. House Foreign Affairs Committee, *Mutual Security Act of 1959*, Hearings, 86th Congress, 1st Session (Washington, D.C.: 1959), p. 775; and *India News*, 1 (September 24, 1962), 1.

63. The Soviet Communist party's views on neutralism are presented in the program adopted at the 22nd Party Congress in 1961. The text of the program is reproduced in Harrison E. Salisbury, *Khrushchev's "Main Kampf"* (New York: Belmont Books, 1961). See especially pp. 31–36; 45–52; 73–81; 87–94; 170–174.

64. *Christian Science Monitor*, November 3, 1962.

65. *Indian Express*, November 16, 1962.

66. *Foreign Affairs Record*, 8 (New Delhi: Ministry of Foreign Affairs, August, 1962), 169–170; *Times of India*, February 5, 1963.

67. *Times of India*, February 4 and 5, 1963.

68. *Times of India*, March 7, 1963; *Hindu*, January 13, 1963.

69. G. L. Mehta, "Defense and Development," *India News*, 1 (June 7, 1963), 4; *Statesman*, May 2, 1963, dispatch by G. H. Jansen. After a period of considerable uncertainty—growing out of Moscow's obvious embarrassment over Peiping's expansionism into India—the Kremlin announced its intention to supply New Delhi

a limited quantity of MIG aircraft and a factory for producing such aircraft. By the summer of 1963, the Kremlin offered India guided missiles and other military equipment that New Delhi had requested for use against a renewed Chinese attack. In the same period, Russia authorized loans to India of $100 million annually, to support its Third Plan for national development. I. M. D. Little, "Why Not Help India More?" *India News*, 1 (May 31, 1963), 5; *The New York Times*, August 2, and August 16, 1963.

70. *Hindustan Times*, May 28, 1963, dispatch by Asoka Mehta.
71. *Hindustan Times*, May 28 and 29, 1963, dispatch by Asoka Mehta; *Indian Express*, April 3, 1963, dispatch by D. R. Mankekar.
72. These and other global reactions to the Indian government's reaffirmation of non-alignment are cited in: "Non-Alignment Since Chinese Aggression" (New Delhi: Indian Ministry of External Affairs, mimeographed document, 1963).
73. Quoted in *ibid.*, p. 13.
74. *India News*, 2 (August 23, 1963), 1.
75. *Hindustan Times*, January 16, 1963.
76. *Indian Express*, January 16, 1963.
77. *Times of India*, January 30 and February 5, 1963.
78. Quoted in *Hindustan Times* (overseas edition), December 3, 1953.
79. J. M. Van Der Kroef, "The Appeals of Communism in Southeast Asia," *United Asia*, 7 (December, 1955), 297.
80. *Ibid.*, pp. 291–297; John Kerry King, *Southeast Asia in Perspective* (New York: Macmillan, 1956), pp. 74–105.
81. Peffer, *op. cit.*, pp. 272–273.
82. Reischauer, *op. cit.*, p. 165.
83. Department of State, *American Foreign Policy: 1950–1955*, II, *op. cit.*, 2326–2328; 2370–2371; 2373–2376; 2388–2390.
84. *The New York Times*, January 31, 1964, dispatch by Paul Grimes.
85. *The New York Times*, March 6, 1964.
86. *Idem.*
87. Quoted in *The New York Times*, March 4 and 5, 1964.
88. *The New York Times*, March 6, 1964.
89. *The New York Times*, March 2, 1964.
90. *The New York Times*, February 20, 1964.
91. *The New York Times*, February 29, 1964.
92. *The New York Times*, March 6, 1964.
93. *The New York Times*, March 14, 1964.

14 → PSYCHOLOGICAL
WARFARE → logomachy
at midcentury

Late in 1960, a committee appointed by President Eisenhower to investigate the operation of American overseas information programs reported that: "The eventual outcome of the struggle, assuming that general war can be avoided, and that Communist subversion can be countered, will depend in considerable degree on the extent we are able to influence the attitudes of people."[1] Three years later, the authors of a study of American cultural and informational programs abroad concluded that these activities consituted "the most critical component in U.S. relations" with countries throughout the underdeveloped world.[2]

These two judgments focus upon a noteworthy feature of international affairs since World War II: the growing extent to which cultural, informational, and broad psychological aspects of foreign policy are being utilized by nations on both sides of the iron curtain to achieve their diplomatic goals. Policy-makers in Washington and Moscow alike have increasingly operated upon the premise that influencing "the attitudes of people" could prove the decisive element in the outcome of the cold war. Even for governments of countries within the Western alliance—as Washington has discovered in dealing with such diverse phenomena as the growing independence of de Gaulle's Fifth Republic or the attitude of the European allies toward colonial and racial issues—attitudes, sentiments, and images existing in the minds of citizens decisively influence policies, at times in a manner highly deleterious to American diplomatic interests.

Military commanders have long known that the morale of soldiers, and of civilians behind the lines, can be the decisive element in the outcome of battles. So it is with the paramilitary conflict which today is designated the cold war. The morale on both sides over extended periods, the predispositions of hundreds of millions of peoples in the uncommitted nations, the ability of both sides to keep their citizens psychologically prepared for the sacrifices required while at the same time attempting to promote defections within the enemy's camp—these may turn out to be the crucial determinants of the cold-war conflict.

Our analysis of the informational-psychological aspects of American foreign relations will be conducted within a threefold frame of reference: first, we shall discuss the nature and uses of psychological warfare, with emphasis upon propaganda as an instrument of foreign policy; next, we shall describe and appraise the Communist psychological offensive against the West; and finally, we shall evaluate America's own psychological and propaganda activities, chiefly as conducted by the United States Information Agency.

PSYCHOLOGICAL WARFARE: ITS NATURE AND USES

Psychological warfare is as old as history. When the Greeks failed to capture Troy by force of arms, they resorted to skillful deception—the Trojan Horse—to bring them victory. In early American history, one purpose of the Declaration of Independence was to gain widespread support in England and Europe for the colonial cause by identifying it with the political aspirations of Western society as a whole. One of the most famous books in American literature, *Uncle Tom's Cabin*, probably did more to arouse public support for the antislavery cause than the thousands of impassioned speeches made by all the Abolitionists combined. During World War I, tons of propaganda in the form of press releases, leaflets, posters, booklets, pictures, and the like, emanated from the Allied side. These were acknowledged by German military leaders as having been singularly effective in undermining the military and civilian morale of the Central Powers and in turning neutral opinion against their cause. One of the most brilliant Allied propaganda victories in the period was won through the proclamation of President Wilson's "Fourteen Points," which were of inestimable value in shortening the war by weakening the will to resist among populations in the enemy camp.[3]

Some Basic Concepts

No universally accepted definition of psychological warfare exists; and, indeed, it is difficult to formulate an altogether satisfactory definition of the concept. Its goal can be stated quite simply: to persuade other countries—especially the nation's diplomatic enemies—to accept one's own point of view as a basis for action. Nations utilize psychological warfare during periods of military hostilities to undermine the enemy's will to fight, thereby hastening his capitulation. In periods of peace or cold war, psychological warfare techniques are valuable diplomatic tools used: (1) as a substitute for military hostilities altogether; (2) to assure victory for one's own country if war comes; and (3) to assure that diplomatic victories won with or without resort to arms will be achieved as inexpensively as possible.

Today, the traditional line between war and peace is exceedingly difficult to draw precisely. Most ordinary diplomatic contacts among powerful countries contain at least rudimentary elements of psychological warfare; and in some periods, relations among these countries can have many of the earmarks of relations customarily prevailing during time of war. So variegated are these relationships that it is even possible to have war on the ideological plane at the very time leaders are attempting to cultivate "better understanding" through devices like cultural exchange.

In this chapter we shall concentrate upon propaganda as a major technique of psychological warfare, defining it as the effort of one group or nation to influence the actions of another group or nation *by primary reliance upon methods of systematic persuasion, including methods of verbal coercion and inducement.** Propaganda is to be distinguished from other forms of psychological warfare by its utilization of the written and spoken word. Successful utilization of methods of persuasion depends in no small degree upon the effectiveness of other weapons in the arsenal of national power, such as economic strength and military force. Threats, unsupported by the requisite military power, are usually ineffectual; promises and inducements, without the willingness and capacity to make good on them, are equally worthless as diplomatic tools.

The successful propagandist is required to have a well-stocked and versatile arsenal and to be skilled in the use of these weapons. Among the variety of weapons available are radio broadcasts, television programs, speeches, films, public rallies and demonstrations, various symbols like armbands, flags, slogans, or buttons, posters, cartoons, comic books, newspapers, timely "leaks" of official infor

* In common with many other general concepts, definitions of such terms as psychological warfare and propaganda often vary widely; frequently they reflect the emphases that the user thinks most basic and important. Numerous definitions are thus available, including broad definitions of psychological warfare like "the use of propaganda against an enemy, together with such other operational measures of a military, economic or political nature as may be required to supplement propaganda." Similarly, propaganda may be conceived of as "the planned use of any form of public or mass-produced communication designed to affect the minds and emotions of a given group for a specific public purpose, whether military, economic or political." These and other definitions are cited in Urban G. Whitaker, Jr., *Propaganda and International Relations* (San Francisco: Chandler, 1962), pp. 4–5. Qualter expresses the essential point succinctly when he observes that: "The purpose of propaganda is to control actions by influencing attitudes." He emphasizes that it is the "deliberate attempt" to control the actions of others, rather than the unintentional or accidental result of controlling action, that is the hallmark of propaganda. Terence H. Qualter, *Propaganda and Psychological Warfare* (New York: Random House, 1962), pp. 15, 27.

mation, libraries, lectures, seminars, clandestine radios, articles in magazines, news conferences, and a host of other techniques.[4] In successfully employing any or all of these techniques, the propagandist is continually conscious of a fact that is at the center of his operations. This is that propaganda is merely a *single instrument* of foreign policy; as such, it is intimately related to, and its success ultimately depends upon, the effective use and skillful coordination of other instruments to achieve diplomatic goals, such as foreign aid, reliance upon (or the threat to rely upon) military force, negotiating skill, and perhaps above all, a clear sense of what the nation is seeking to achieve in its relations with other countries.

Several further points about propaganda require emphasis. A popular misconception is that propaganda is inherently false. This misconception explains in some measure why Americans have often been loath to support the propaganda activities of their government. Knowing that certain information is "propaganda" tells us nothing about the veracity or falsity of that information. The etymology of the word propaganda enables us to keep this point clearly in mind. Its root is the Latin verb *propagare*, meaning to propagate, to spread, to disseminate, to extend, to transmit. The term first came into historical currency after the establishment of the College of Propaganda by Pope Urban VIII (1623–1644), to promote the missionary activities of the Roman Catholic Church. Throughout the greater part of history, propaganda possessed none of the insidious connotations later associated with it in the Nazi or Communist periods. It meant merely the process of trying to gain converts to a particular cause, initially the Christian gospel as expounded by the Vatican. The process of propaganda then is the act of disseminating a belief; or propaganda may describe the belief so disseminated.[5]

Confusion can enter into any discussion of propaganda, however, when we inquire: what is good and bad propaganda? In a *tactical* sense, good propaganda is that which attains its intended result—gaining converts for the belief in question—and bad propaganda is that which fails to attain this result. In an *ethical* sense, according to the Judaeo-Christian tradition prevalent in the West, good propaganda is that which accords as nearly as possible with objective truth, and bad propaganda is that which relies heavily upon various forms of deception, falsehood, and chicanery. Whatever the ethical standards by which propaganda is judged, however, *any* propaganda, including of course American, is to be distinguished from an objective search for truth. Irrespective of whether it is the lobbyist trying to influence the legislator, the advertising agency trying to influence the consumer, or the Voice of America trying to influence public opinion in Indonesia, the object of all propaganda is to utilize *carefully selected* data to induce the hearer to accept a predetermined point of view. The propagandist may *use* the truth—in fact, successful propaganda nearly always necessitates its use—but he is not *seeking* it objectively, nor is he prepared to follow where a dispassionate search for truth may lead. This is the cardinal distinction between propaganda and education.[6]

Propaganda, as we have suggested, often arouses a feeling of revulsion among individuals steeped in the Western liberal or Judaeo-Christian traditions, particularly if it is equated with outright falsehood. These feelings are re-enforced by widespread antipathy to the methods of Nazi or Communist propagandists in recent history, whose conduct frequently has violated standards of behavior deemed acceptable among civilized societies. Yet, from another perspective, propaganda can properly be regarded as an alternative to military force in the conduct of international affairs. Organizations like the United Nations and the World Court exist to confine disputes among nations to the arena of persuasion and argumentation—which is the arena of propaganda. Conversely, wars occur when argumentation and negotiation *fail* to safeguard the vital interests of nations, leaving them no alternative but recourse to armaments. The ultimate objective of the United States therefore is not the elimination of propaganda *per se* as a permissible technique of international relations; rather, it is the substitution of words for bullets, so that propaganda and other forms of nonviolent techniques may accomplish in the future what machine guns, howitzers, and, in the contemporary era, nuclear weapons accomplish in safeguarding the nation's interests and promoting its diplomatic objectives.

This is not to imply that the *methods* utilized by propagandists in the global arena are always ethically defensible; nor is it to suggest that the techniques employed by the propagandists of one nation are ethically equivalent to those employed by other nations.

Western political leaders and informed citizens particularly have been disturbed for many years by the kind of psychological "total war" waged by Moscow and Peking, the hallmarks of which have been duplicity, blatant distortions of the truth, repeated imputations of bad faith, and other techniques poisoning the atmosphere of international relations and sometimes rendering any settlement of outstanding global issues all but impossible. Responsible leaders and observers have long recognized the need for agreement upon the kind of propaganda that is permissible in international affairs. Nevertheless, it remains true that words, however false and malicious, are always preferable to bombs, and that the more conflicts among nations can be confined to propaganda exchanges, the less likely that the future of civilization itself will be imperiled by global and regional animosities.

Americans particularly are prone to derogate "mere talk," to believe that "talk is cheap" and to call for "action instead of words." Historically, Americans have been doers, not philosophers; they have admired the man who "gets things done" more than the man who looks for the meaning in action or who seeks to change the thought patterns upon which past or future action takes place.* Americans are, therefore, suspicious of diplomats who "do nothing but talk," often about highly technical, dull subjects, frequently beyond the comprehension of a majority of citizens. This attitude inevitably places barriers in the way of those who urge greater national efforts in psychological warfare.[7]

The Interdependence of Diplomatic Weapons

In common with all aspects of national power, the effectiveness of propaganda as an instrument of foreign relations is heavily con-

* Paradoxically, no nation known to history has geared its economic life so closely to the efforts of the advertising industry, which deals in only one product: persuasion. Somehow, Americans see very little connection between the role of advertising in the economic field and what is essentially the same task in the diplomatic field.

The story is told that one day the great British Prime Minister Benjamin Disraeli was accosted in the halls of the House of Commons by an individual who had listened to hour after hour of dull debate on the floor. This individual was condemning the futility of "mere talk" and was highly resentful of the fact that his time had been taken up in lengthy discussions that involved "only matters of opinion." Disraeli finally bested his tormentor by saying: young man, opinion rules the world!

ditioned by the *totality* of the nation's response to the outside world. Nearly every action undertaken by a state in world affairs has propaganda connotations in terms of creating a favorable or unfavorable image of that country in the minds of foreigners. That image is an amalgam of a large number of diverse influences, most of which bear no relation to deliberate efforts by the country in question to create an attractive image of itself abroad. To illustrate, if the United States promises economic assistance to such countries as Bolivia, Turkey, or South Vietnam, its ability to make propaganda capital out of this fact will be determined by the following major considerations: whether the United States has the resources to make good on its promise; whether public opinion and Congress will support the pledges given by executive officials; whether such aid is administered so as to advance the program's objectives; whether American aid is compatible with or, at a minimum, does not conflict with the national aspirations of the peoples concerned; and whether American aid is visualized by the recipients as meeting their needs more constructively than perhaps Soviet or Chinese aid.

Propagandists are much like individuals engaged in retouching photographs. In their effort to create as pleasing a likeness as possible, they are limited by the quality of the original picture. No amount of retouching can compensate completely for an unflattering image conveyed by words and deeds which paint a totally adverse portrait of the nation abroad. Similarly, as the United States has discovered repeatedly in recent years, a favorable image of the country may survive, even after propaganda efforts have been feeble and uninspired. A strategically timed announcement, such as President Eisenhower's "Open Skies" disarmament proposal at the Geneva Conference in 1955, can be worth more than a hundred routine Voice of America broadcasts, in turning the propaganda tide in favor of one's own country.

These considerations suggest that propaganda *is not a policy itself but merely a reflection of a policy*. Nations do not engage in propaganda for its own sake. They do so to advance some pre-existing goal of statecraft. Thus success in the psychological warfare field will be determined to an important degree by prior success in clarifying the basic goals of policy toward major issues and areas. If American policy toward colonial peoples is vague and contradictory, American propaganda efforts will inevitably reflect this weakness and, for that reason, will be only moderately successful. Technicians in psychological warfare can perhaps tell the State Department how to put across a certain viewpoint most effectively in Saudi Arabia or Thailand; they cannot tell the State Department what viewpoints ought ultimately to be propagated as reflections of basic national policies.

THE COMMUNIST IDEOLOGICAL OFFENSIVE

Few Americans in the contemporary age need to be reminded of the central place ideological hostility among nations occupies on the current international scene. Hardly a day passes without efforts by one or more of the 91 Communist parties, embracing over 40 million people throughout the world, to undertake some new psychological or propaganda offensive against non-Communist nations.[8] In spreading the Marxist gospel, these parties, led by Moscow and Peiping, have raised psychological warfare to a pinnacle it perhaps did not even attain under Hitler's Nazi regime.

Communist Ideology and the Outside World

Chapter 9 discussed the nature of communist ideology and assessed its implications for Soviet foreign policy. Here our interest centers upon examining efforts made by Moscow and its supporters since World War II to wage an intensive psychological warfare offensive against the non-Communist world.

Central to the Marxist-Leninist-Stalinist conception of world affairs is the idea, expressed by Stalin in 1950, that: "History never does anything of moment without some particular necessity."[9] Events in history are governed by the "laws of dialectical materialism," as expounded by Marx and his latter-day disciples. History is supposedly moving toward a mighty denouement which will witness the collapse of capitalism and the ultimate victory of communism. As long as capitalism and communism continue to exist, said Lenin in 1920, "We cannot live in peace; in the end, one or the other will triumph—a funeral dirge will be sung either over the Soviet Republic or over world capitalism."[10]

Communist thought of course admits of no doubt concerning the system which will ultimately triumph. But meanwhile the "revolu-

tionary struggle" must go on. Devoted Communists must simultaneously consolidate their own position while trying to weaken the position of the enemy. How long will this state of conflict last? There is no predetermined timetable. Stalin declared in 1925:

> The epoch of world revolution . . . may occupy years or even decades. In the course of this period there will occur, nay, must occur ebbs and flows in the revolutionary tide . . . The revolution does not develop along a straight, continuous and upwardly aspiring line, but along a zigzag path . . . an ebb and flow in the tide. . . .[11]

The absence of a precise timetable—coupled with an unshakable belief in the historic "inevitability" of Communist victory—means that the communist movement relies upon a continuous, highly diversified, and often ingenious psychological campaign against its ideological enemies. The Khrushchev era of "peaceful coexistence" witnessed far greater emphasis than in the Stalin period upon psychological techniques to advance Communist goals. For it was a cardinal axiom of Khrushchev's regime that in the battle with capitalism for the minds of men, communism will successfully demonstrate its "superiority" as a social, economic, and political system; this will induce societies throughout the world to "bury" capitalism as an antiquated, deleterious system of social and economic organization.

The Soviet Propaganda Apparatus

A detailed discussion of the Soviet propaganda apparatus, and its manifold relationships to other organs of the Soviet state, would carry us beyond the compass of our study.* At the center of the Soviet propaganda effort stands the Communist Party of the Soviet Union (CPSU), the "vanguard of the proletariat." Lenin likened the party to an army which, "inspired by a single will," leads "millions of people" to change their minds and actions "in accordance with the changing circumstances

---

* The organizational machinery for conducting Soviet propaganda, and for coordinating the worldwide network of Communist propaganda efforts, is described in Evron Kirkpatrick, *Target the World* (New York: Macmillan, 1956), and *Year of Crisis* (New York: Macmillan, 1959), pp. 1–35 and 28–43, respectively. For a case study involving propaganda activities concerning a meeting of Communist leaders in Moscow late in 1960, see Marvin L. Kalb, "Agitprop Goes to Work," *The Reporter*, 24 (January 5, 1961), 32–33.

and demands" of the class struggle.[12] The Communist party is the repository of Marxist truth. Its monolithic nature assures that this truth will filter down to, and be binding upon, all inferior organs of the Communist state. The National Party Congress theoretically chooses—in reality, its actions are governed by—the ruling bodies of the party, such as the Central Committee, whose Presidium is the policy-determining body of the party, and hence of the entire Soviet state. Lower-echelon party organs like the Cadre Department train Communist leaders and oversee the execution of party directives throughout the Soviet government.[13]

Specifically charged with propagating the communist faith around the world is the organ known as Agitprop, which is responsible directly to the Central Committee of the CPSU. After the "party line" toward any domestic or foreign issue has been determined, it is incumbent upon Agitprop to act as planner, director, and watchdog of all Communist media engaging in propaganda dissemination. Agitprop directs the flow of information to important Communist news media like *Pravda* and *Izvestia*; supervises the preparation of films; supplies information on the correct party line to foreign Communist operatives by means of radio broadcasts, Communist theoretical journals and publications, conferences among leading Communists, sponsorship of exhibits and cultural exchanges, and in many other ways. One highly important agency operating under Agitprop's direction is VOKS (the All-Union Society for Cultural Relations with Foreign Countries) which, though it feigns an autonomous status, is in reality a subordinate body within the total Communist propaganda structure.[14]

Supplementing the propaganda activities within the Soviet state are the attempts by Communist groups to infiltrate non-Communist bodies within the free world. Such infiltration has a number of objectives: to promote person-to-person contact with non-Communists, to provide popular support for Communist causes, to conceal Communist operations behind a façade which makes them acceptable to ignorant peoples, and to recruit and train future party members. Among these Communist-infiltrated groups are such organizations as the World Peace Council, the World Federation of Trade Unions, the International Union of Students, and the World Federation of Teachers' Unions.[15]

Some Characteristics of Soviet Propaganda

Steeped in the view that Marxist-Leninist-Stalinist canons can unlock all mysteries of human experience, Communists naturally place a high premium upon mastering the "techniques" of revolutionary agitation, in which propaganda has a high place. Technique of course includes a variety of skills in knowing when to attack and when to retreat, how to adapt revolutionary activity so as to make the most effective use possible of prevailing environmental factors, how to undermine morale in the enemy's camp, how to recognize vulnerabilities in both one's own position and the enemy's position, and how to utilize this knowledge successfully. Another conspicuous, and often highly successful, feature of Soviet propaganda is its ability to "adjust" to different audiences and conditions. It may present an entirely different—and often contradictory—message to a French intellectual, a Greek peasant, an Arab student, an African labor leader, or an Asian nationalist.[16]

Communist propaganda efforts are governed by the same principles that we have emphasized earlier in discussing American foreign policy: the deeds and conduct of the Communist world, particularly the Soviet Union, constitute much more eloquent testimony about its beliefs and values than does its official propaganda to the outside world. In that connection, it must be realized that the Soviet Union possesses certain advantages skillfully exploited by its propaganda mechanism. Widespread admiration unquestionably exists throughout Africa, the Arab world, and Asia, for example, for the impressive economic progress attained in the USSR since 1917, although (especially in countries like India) there is also widespread recognition that the methods employed by the Soviet state to attain it were harsh and sometimes barbarous. Since the 1950s, Moscow has also made spectacular propaganda capital out of its scientific and technological prowess, notably because of the Sputniks and other space programs.[17] In certain aspects of space exploration (like the total thrust of Soviet rockets), the alleged "superiority" of the Communist system was incontestably demonstrated to societies in the ideologically uncommitted world. Moreover, propagandists behind the iron curtain can assume a much closer affinity between the Communist world's experiences and problems and those of countries such as Ghana, Iraq, or

Burma than is the case with Western, particularly American, propagandists. However much Americans are convinced that their way of life is superior, the fact is that there is virtually no prospect that it can be duplicated throughout the underdeveloped world. The broad pattern of Soviet or Chinese (and increasingly, Yugoslav) experience, however, is often highly relevant for such societies.

Tactically, Communist propagandists also possess potent weapons growing out of the Marxist theory of "Communist morality." Lenin declared unambiguously in 1921 that:

> our morality is entirely subordinated to the interests of the class struggle. . . . We say: morality is that which serves to destroy the old exploiting society and to unite all the toilers around the proletariat. . . . Communist morality is the morality which serves this struggle. . . .[18]

Thus, the free world faces an unscrupulous diplomatic opponent who is prepared to ignore the ordinary amenities of international conduct and morality; who, except as a matter of tactical importance, cares nothing for "a decent respect for the opinions of mankind," and who is ready to invoke every Machiavellian device which seems suitable for realizing his aggressive foreign policy ambitions.

One of Lenin's publications was entitled *Two Steps Forward, One Step Backward*, calling attention to the ebb tides and flood tides in the revolutionary struggle. Communist policy-makers are expert in adapting their methodology to the exigencies of the hour; and indeed, in this process, they have had few equals throughout history. A striking characteristic of Bolshevik propaganda since 1917 has been the Kremlin's ability to shift from a "hard" to a "soft" propaganda line, in much the same way as an individual might alternately open and close the hot and cold taps of a faucet.

When external conditions favor launching a militant psychological offensive—usually when the Communist world is strong and its enemies weak—the men in the Kremlin open the spigot marked "hot." There pours forth a stream of propaganda abuse and belligerent ideological declarations aimed at non-Communist countries. High on the list of propaganda themes during such periods are the "inevitable conflict" between Communist and non-Communist societies; the ultimate consummation of the "world revolution"; the inevitability of "frightful clashes" before communism emerges victorious; the perfidy and unalterable hostility displayed by capitalist countries toward the USSR and its followers; and the necessity for stepped-up revolutionary agitation throughout the world. Interspersed among these themes is emphasis upon the "durability" of the communist system and its ability to survive even military conflict with its enemies.

Different conditions in the external environment—for example, when the Communist world and its enemies are nearly equal in strength or possibly when the former may be weaker than the latter—can prompt the Communist hierarchy to turn on the "cold" propaganda spigot. Then there emanates from Communist propaganda organs a soothing "soft" line, calculated to advance Moscow or Peiping's interests by reliance upon methods of persuasion, conciliation, compromise, and reasonableness. "Nods and becks and wreathéd smiles" become the order of the day for Communist diplomats.

Outstanding themes of Communist propaganda during such periods, as Westerners have become amply aware since the mid-1950s, are the necessity for "peaceful coexistence" and for "competition" between differing ideological and socioeconomic systems; the necessity for a "relaxation of tensions" in the global community, coupled with diverse Communist maneuvers such as calls for summit meetings, disarmament agreements, and cultural exchange programs, to achieve this goal; the acceptance of the principle within the communist system of "differing paths to socialism," dictating attempts by Moscow to maintain amicable relations with such former Marxist "heretics" as Tito of Yugoslavia and to propose schemes for a Sino-Soviet ideological reconciliation; the encouragement of diverse measures, including stepped-up foreign aid programs, cultural missions, regional tours by high-ranking Communist leaders, and championship of causes such as anticolonialism in the United Nations, to convince societies throughout the free world that communism represents the "wave of the future" and that the "progressive" forces of human society are led by the Communist camp.

The Communist Ideological Crusade in the Balance

Policy-makers within the Communist world, as we have noted, possess certain very tangible advantages in waging psychological warfare against the West, chiefly the United States. One of these is the great backlog of experience

Bolshevism accumulated in its efforts to overthrow tsarism within Russia and, after that, in successfully undermining the moderate Kerensky regime that came into power after the tsarist government was overthrown. Thereafter, both in dealing with their own citizens and with the outside world, Communist policymakers have carried on intensive propaganda activities now for almost a half-century.

Moreover, advocates of the communist cause espouse a faith they propagate with all of the fervor and dedication usually associated with religious fanatics. Their indoctrination in the "science" of Marxism-Leninism has convinced them that their cause is both intellectually defensible and that its victory is assured by the inexorable unfolding of history. Communists are prepared to sustain setbacks of varying duration, in full confidence that Marxist goals will ultimately be achieved. In propagating their faith, they have evolved, and skillfully utilize, a technique that is often crucial in any successful propaganda campaign: setting up personalized "devils" like "capitalist warmongers," "enemies of the people," "Wall Street imperialists," "paper tigers" and "fascist beasts." In uneducated or credulous individuals, Communists are able to inculcate the idea that problems like poverty or racial discrimination or chronic political instability stem from the machinations of Western "monopolists" or some other group that is the target of Marxist animus. The inference is that elimination of this group—rather than prolonged attention to underlying national problems, coupled with massive efforts to overcome them—will automatically bring social and economic progress.

Communist propaganda experts also hold advantages over their counterparts in the free world, as we have suggested, by the freedom with which they can employ any suitable technique—not excluding outright falsehood, slander, various degrees of distortion, obstructionism in bodies like the UN, threats, promises, alternating programs of ideological hostility and of reconciliation, as well as truth itself—to undermine and weaken societies outside the Communist bloc. In turn, this involves still another factor favoring Communist propagandists: the enormous advantage accruing to Moscow or Peiping from a monolithic political system enabling policy-makers to make required adjustments in their diplomatic offensive and to coordinate a great variety of propaganda, political, diplomatic, or economic moves in behalf of a unified policy, with a minimum of delay, disunity, or fear of repudiation by public opinion.

Yet, it must not be supposed that Communist propaganda programs have met with unqualified success in the recent period or that the real advantages favoring Moscow and Peiping in propaganda warfare give the Communist bloc a decisive lead in the battle for the minds of men. In company with their Western counterparts, Communist propagandist efforts have experienced several greater or lesser failures.*

Far more crucial than momentary lapses in Communist propaganda efforts in determining the success or failure of the Soviet psychological attack, however, is another consideration. Since propaganda is an integral part of the total pattern of a nation's responses to the outside world, what the Soviet Union and its satellites *do* in world affairs, testifies much more eloquently about the nature of the communist system *than what they say they do or are going to do.*

Prodigious propaganda efforts are required to erase vivid impressions of the ruthless Soviet suppression of the Hungarian Revolt in 1956, of widespread realization that the USSR holds millions of Eastern Europeans in economic vassalage, and of Russian and Chinese aggression in Korea. Communist propaganda experts may repeatedly emphasize the

* Among the more spectacular setbacks for Communist (particularly Soviet) propaganda efforts in recent years might be listed the following: the USSR's brusque rejection of serious American disarmament proposals in 1951; the revelations under Khrushchev of the "crimes" committed by Stalin and his henchmen; the Kremlin's ostracism of, and vituperation against, Tito of Yugoslavia; the revolts and political unrest in Poland, Hungary, and other European satellites; the erection of the Berlin wall; the Soviet Union's resumption of nuclear testing in 1961, after demanding the cessation of testing; the vetoes cast by the USSR and other Communist countries in the UN, which have all but deadlocked the Security Council; the continual flow of refugees to the West from the Soviet Union, Red China, and other Communist nations; the censorship and thought control exercised, often against foreigners, behind the iron curtain; the Kremlin's disreputable treatment of Boris Pasternak and other writers who have achieved world recognition; and the apparently mounting discrimination that African students have met with when they attended universities in the Soviet Union and Eastern European nations. These and other instances are discussed more fully in: Edward W. Barrett, *Truth Is Our Weapon* (New York: Funk & Wagnalls, 1953), pp. 135–137; Whitaker, *op. cit.*, pp. 136–137; *The New York Times*, December 19, 1963.

theme of "different paths to socialism"; yet the Kremlin's ostracism of Tito's regime in Yugoslavia in certain periods afforded graphic refutation of Moscow's preachments about freedom and self-determination. Similarly, much of the propaganda capital that may accumulate to the Kremlin from time to time because of its stress upon the theme of peace and "coexistence" was dissipated by Moscow's efforts to implant missile bases in Cuba and to carry on a dangerous campaign of harassment against the Western position in Berlin. For many nonaligned nations, Communist deeds have often succeeded, where Western warnings have failed, to instill a heightened appreciation of Moscow's or Peiping's ambitions in Africa, the Arab zone, and Asia. Even a regime ideologically predisposed toward Marxism, like the new African state of Guinea under President Sékou Touré, would not tolerate massive efforts by the Communist bloc to infiltrate the society and openly to intrigue against the established government. Arab states, like Egypt and Iraq, have likewise been unwilling to countenance repeated Communist interventions in Middle Eastern affairs—especially in countries that had experienced nationalist revolutions—on the basis of an alleged affinity between communism and nationalist movements in the recent period. Similarly, the Kremlin's efforts to hamstring the United Nations by insisting upon replacement of the Secretary General with a "troika" scheme have alienated many countries, particularly small, nonaligned states that often seek to *increase* the UN's global effectiveness.

Much as the disciples of Marx scoff at the "bourgeois" idea of objective truth, their own rejection of this idea does not prevent other countries from evaluating Moscow's or Peiping's diplomatic record and from basing their assessment of communism upon this evaluation, rather than upon ideological pronouncements emanating from Communist sources. The injunction that "faith without works is dead" is a central precept for succesful propaganda. More than at any time in history, instantaneous and worldwide methods of communication render it all but impossible for nations to conceal discrepancies between word and deed from the scrutiny of other societies. As never before, outright falsehood and duplicity are poor ingredients for propaganda, if for no other reason than that the liar will almost certainly be exposed. Thereafter, he will face a difficult challenge in maintaining

credibility in his propaganda campaign. When hypocrisy is revealed, the net result is likely to be a psychological defeat for the country whose deeds and behavior do not accord substantially with its ideological professions.

THE AMERICAN "CAMPAIGN OF TRUTH"

. . . we seek to encourage constructive public support for what the President has described as "a peaceful world community of free and independent states, free to choose their own future and their own system so long as it does not threaten the freedom of others." We present the United States as a strong, democratic, dynamic nation qualified to lead world efforts toward this goal. We emphasize the ways in which U.S. policies harmonize with those of other peoples and governments, and underline those aspects of American life and culture which facilitate sympathetic understanding of our policies. We endeavor to unmask and counter hostile attempts on the part of Communists and others to distort or frustrate American objectives and policies.
. . . in this age of swift communication and swift reaction, our Government tries to present its policies and programs in as understandable and palatable form as possible—understandable and palatable to those millions abroad, friend, foe and neutral, whose lives and fortunes are affected by what we do.[19]

This statement by former United States Information Agency Director Edward R. Murrow defined the goals of America's chief propaganda agency during the 1960s. Implicit in his formulation of the challenge was recognition that the United States was engaged in a crucial propaganda contest, against resourceful and skilled diplomatic enemies, that extended to every major region and country of the world. It was a conflict that would likely continue indefinitely and would determine the over-all direction of great-power relations for decades to come.

Forerunners of Postwar Propaganda Efforts

The United States was a comparative latecomer in recognizing the centrality of psychological warfare as an instrument of foreign policy. During World War I, the Creel Committee carried on an intensive campaign of propaganda which made a significant contribution to the Allied war effort. But from 1919 until the late 1930s, the United States carried on no noteworthy psychological warfare activities as a part of its foreign relations. Then in the late 1930s, several agencies within the government, particularly the Division of Cultural Relations in the State Department, began to undertake propaganda operations directed toward Latin America, where the threat of Axis penetration had become imminent.[20]

A host of civilian and military agencies with responsibilities in the propaganda field emerged during World War II. Among the more important of these were the Office of Strategic Services, the Office of War Information, branches of army and navy intelligence, and the Coordinator of Inter-American Affairs who took the place of the Division of Cultural Relations mentioned above. All of these carried on psychological warfare activities designed to shorten the war and to assure ultimate victory by the Allies. In the process, many valuable insights into the nature of such warfare were obtained, and for the first time the United States began to acquire a backlog of experience and of personnel trained in the propaganda field. These were to pay enormous dividends when cold-war compulsions finally forced the United States to initiate its first peacetime campaign of systematic propaganda operations.

After the war, many of the functions of these agencies were either eliminated altogether or transferred helter-skelter to the Department of State. Yet neither in the government nor in public opinion during this period was there any noteworthy support for continuance of psychological warfare activities. During the late 1940s and early 1950s, White House efforts to expand propaganda operations encountered extreme budgetary difficulties on Capitol Hill, as well as undisguised legislative hostility toward certain officials engaged in such activities. Events during the period of the Greek-Turkish Aid Program and the Marshall Plan nevertheless made it painfully clear that a greatly augmented informational and propaganda program was a diplomatic necessity, if the free world was to counter the expansive tendencies of the Communist bloc.

Propaganda aspects of foreign policy, however, remained secondary until the era of the Korean War, when President Truman committed the nation to a "Campaign of Truth" abroad. Disturbed by enhanced Soviet prestige in exploding a nuclear bomb, and by initial Communist victories in Korea, Truman launched a propaganda campaign whose stated goals were:

. . . to present the truth to the millions of people who are uninformed or misinformed or unconvinced . . . to reach them in their daily lives, as they work and learn . . . to show them that freedom is the way to economic and social advancement, the way to political independence, the way to strength, happiness, and peace . . . [to] make ourselves known as we really are—not as Communist propaganda pictures us.[21]

The United States Information Agency

Yet these efforts by the Truman Administration to strengthen American propaganda efforts proved only partially successful. After President Eisenhower took office in 1952, evidence mounted that the United States was lagging behind its ideological opponents in presenting its point of view to the outside world. Administratively, as one study has concluded, the American propaganda campaign in this period consisted chiefly of a "patchwork of pieces." Organizational responsibility for conducting programs remained scattered, and the programs themselves were inadequate to meet the challenge.[22] Consequently, upon the recommendation of President Eisenhower, the United States Information Agency (USIA), headed by a director appointed by the President, was established on August 1, 1953. The State Department was divested of operating responsibility for propaganda and informational programs, although USIA remained under the supervision of the State Department for over-all policy guidance.

A USIA publication early in the 1960 asserted that, once American policies have been decided upon, it was this agency's responsibility "to influence foreign public opinions and attitudes in order to advance these policies." To achieve this goal, USIA "is charged with depicting America and American policies and goals to the peoples of other lands in terms that will generate understanding, respect, and, to the fullest extent possible, identification with their own legitimate aspirations." In addition, USIA seeks to "demonstrate and document before the world the designs of those who would threaten our security and seek to destroy freedom."[23]

To carry out its assigned duties, by the mid-1960s USIA maintained nearly 250 posts in over 100 foreign countries, ranging from Finland to Argentina and from the Philippines to Great Britain. The operating budget of USIA rose from almost $85 million in 1954 to nearly $125 million in 1964. Almost half of its annual budget was expended to operate its overseas missions; a fourth of the budget paid for operation of the Voice of America, USIA's widely-known global broadcasting service; the remainder went for other services and for the administration of propaganda programs.[24] As its responsibilities grew, USIA established its own Foreign Service, closely resembling the diplomatic Foreign Service; by the 1960s, candidates for both services took identical qualifying examinations.*

Serving in more than 100 countries, USIA officials manned nearly 200 libraries and close to 150 binational centers around the world. In most instances, these centers conducted or supervised a broad range of activities, utilized by more than 30 million visitors annually. USIA's English language courses have attracted well over a million students since 1953. In addition, numerous lectures, exhibitions, and concert programs have been sponsored by USIA.

The Voice of America is USIA's broadcasting arm. Every day, 24 hours a day, VOA's powerful transmitters are beamed behind the iron curtain and to other regions of the world in which it is vital to present American viewpoints overseas. By the mid-1960s, VOA maintained the following schedule.

TABLE 5.   VOA Schedule of Broadcasting

VOA Target Area	Hours Broadcast Weekly
Worldwide	
English language programs	184
Music	73
Eastern Europe—Far Eastern USSR[a]	214
Arab World	49
South Asia	21
Africa	28
Far East	133
Latin America	88
Total hours of VOA broadcasting[b]	790

[a] For this area and all others, figures cited refer to vernacular languages only; they do not include English *language* programs audible in the area.
[b] Includes English and all other languages utilized.
SOURCE: USIA, *20th Review of Operations,* p. 49.

* Details concerning the scope and range of USIA's programs are set forth at length in a pamphlet, *United States Information Agency,* published by the agency in 1962, and in USIA's semi-annual report, *Review of Operations.* These reports also give detailed breakdowns on USIA's budget and the schedule of the Voice of America's broadcasting program to major regions of the world.

VOA's radio transmission facilities have been steadily improved. By the mid-1960s, after a decade of construction, their total output was 4.8 million watts—equivalent to the strength of America's 96 strongest radio stations! From an Indonesian student in Moscow University came the remark: "I hear the Voice of America every day in my room." From Leopoldville in the Congo, another listener wrote VOA that its broadcasts were "often the top station on the band." With its powerful transmission facilities, VOA was literally able to overwhelm Castro's attempt to "jam" its programs in Spanish to the Cuban people. In time, Havana abandoned its jamming activities altogether.[25] Other newly developed or scheduled improvements in VOA's transmission network will make possible vastly enhanced reception of programs in East Germany, Africa, the Balkans, and the South Pacific.

The intensive coverage USIA is able to give an event of worldwide interest and of great consequence for American foreign policy is illustrated by the agency's own account of its efforts to publicize President Kennedy's message of civil rights on June 11, 1963:

The President's June 11 speech to the Nation on civil rights was reported worldwide by all media. Far East and Latin America broadcasts of the Voice, on the air at the time, carried the message live. Broadcasts to other areas repeated extensive excerpts as they came on the air. The full text was transmitted by radio-teletype to 111 posts the same evening for distribution to all the news media, important government officials and others. The 3 USIA regional printing plants at Manila, Beirut, and Mexico City reproduced it as a leaflet in various languages. A color film was made and excerpts were dispatched by air for newsreel and TV showings throughout the free world.

The Agency has a continuing responsibility of supporting the Government's foreign policy objectives. Handling of the President's June 11 speech is a good example of the way in which it carries out this mission.[26]

What is the size and nature of the audience that VOA's programs command? How influential is its message in other societies? To what extent is VOA contributing positively to the achievement of American foreign policy goals? Such questions are inordinately difficult. Often they cannot be answered definitively or to

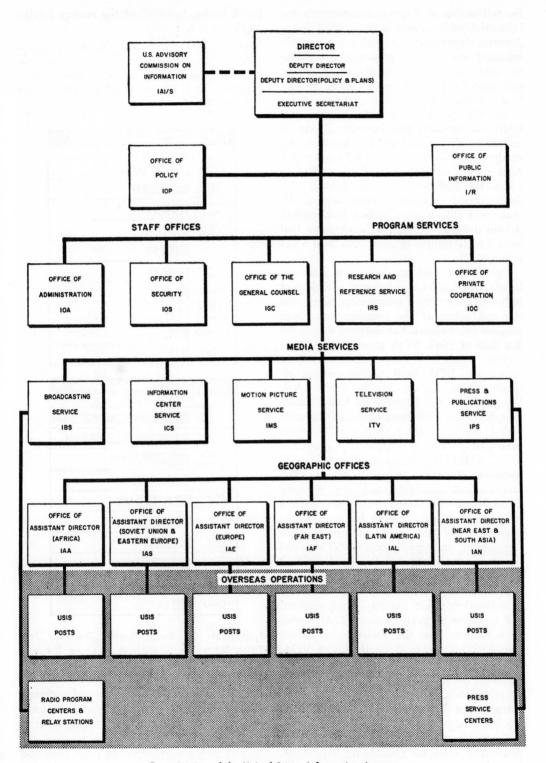

Organization of the United States Information Agency.

the satisfaction of skeptical congressmen and influential public groups in the United States. Accurate measurement of results, as most well-informed students of propaganda activities are aware, remains one of the most baffling and complex tasks connected with psychological warfare. We shall have more to say about the problem presently. Meanwhile, USIA has estimated that between 17 and 26 million people listen to VOA broadcasts daily; nearly twice this number listen to some program during an average week. According to USIA, the audience "increases dramatically" during periods of crisis or when some significant event (like a space probe) is scheduled. Behind the Iron Curtain, it is calculated that from 5 to 10 million listeners daily hear VOA broadcasts.[27]

Upon what evidence are such estimates based? USIA officials rely upon a variety of techniques to supply information about the size and nature of the audience and about program effectiveness. For instance, during the first half of 1963, VOA received more than 50,000 unsolicited letters from listeners. Sometimes, VOA itself solicits listener responses. One request in the early 1960s brought in 35,000 letters from Latin Americans, including 1500 from Cuba. In the same period, another request elicited 5000 letters from widely scattered listeners throughout the Arab world. Refugees and immigrants provide testimony about the extent to which VOA programs are available and are regularly listened to within their former homelands. A rough measurement of VOA influence is also afforded by the *reaction* to its broadcasts from Communist propaganda organs. VOA news reports on the Hungarian Revolt of 1956, it is believed, ultimately compelled Radio Moscow and other Communist propaganda media to acknowledge that the revolt had occurred and to release information about it. Moreover, from time to time the Soviet press devotes considerable space to the activities of VOA, describing the agency as "an instrument for poisoning the minds of the people with deceitful propaganda," as promoting "the ideological corruption of the population," and as inducing "sleepless nights in Socialist countries"—all indirect tributes to VOA's effectiveness in penetrating extensive Communist "jamming" operations and of achieving at least some success in disseminating the Western point of view behind the Iron Curtain.[28]

Out of its experience, USIA has constructed

the following "profile" of the average foreign VOA listener.

He tends to be in the 18–30 age group; he is a student, either at a formal educational institution or in a home study course; he listens to many foreign political broadcasts.[29]

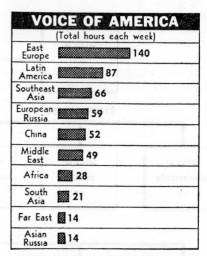

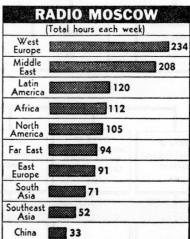

Propaganda Broadcasts. (Source: *The New York Times,* September 8, 1963. © 1963 by The New York Times Company. Reprinted by permission.)

Other major USIA activities and programs overseas may be mentioned briefly. In some countries, films have proved a highly effective medium for presenting information about the United States, particularly in rural areas and among largely illiterate masses. Former Ambassador to India, Chester Bowles, has singled out this approach as unusually effective on the Indian subcontinent.[30] Booklets, pamphlets, comic books, posters, and other publications are also widely distributed by USIA. For example, during the first half of 1963, some 7 million copies of a simple and graphic booklet on how Fidel Castro betrayed the Cuban revolutionary movement were distributed to readers throughout Latin America—making a total of 20 million copies distributed during a two-year period.[31] A USIA magazine, *Sports*, presents news of the American athletic scene and capitalizes upon the intense interest (particularly in newly emerging countries) about athletic events. Another regular publication, *It's a Fact*, presents up-to-date information about American scientific progress and programs. On a worldwide basis, USIA publishes a total of 66 magazines and other periodicals, collectively totaling 30 million copies annually, in 28 different languages.[32]

Another significant dimension of the American psychological campaign involves cultural and educational exchange programs. By the 1960s (in part because of growing Communist emphasis upon such programs), cultural and educational exchange had emerged as an increasingly important aspect of American foreign policy. The Fulbright Act of 1946, broadened by the Smith-Mundt Act of 1948, inaugurated educational exchange programs. The former provided funds for the exchange of students and professors between the United States and other countries; the latter encouraged broad cultural exchange programs designed to foster better understanding among nations. Still other cultural programs have been supported overseas by the sale of surplus American agricultural commodities abroad.[33]

The Peace Corps

The most recent, and in its brief existence already one of the most effective, innovations in the American psychological campaign was establishment of the Peace Corps by President Kennedy in 1961. Envisioned officially as "a pool of trained American men and women sent overseas by the U.S. Government or through private institutions and organizations to help foreign countries meet their urgent needs for skilled manpower," the Peace Corps quickly established itself as an organization that generated good will for the United States from Latin America to East Asia. Relying upon nonsalaried volunteers, who lived and worked under normal conditions prevailing within the country to which they were sent,

the Peace Corps found the demand for its services continually growing more rapidly than its ability to meet it. Under both Presidents Kennedy and Johnson, the agency was repeatedly obliged to send out new calls for volunteers; even then, it could not supply personnel as rapidly as other countries asked for American teachers, doctors, farmers, mechanics, engineers, and literally hundreds of other specialists. The Peace Corps appeared to be one governmental program that commanded enthusiastic support among executive and legislative officials, and among public opinion in the United States as well as among foreign societies to which its volunteers were sent.[34]

Private Propaganda Activities

American propaganda, cultural, and informational activities are not confined to those carried on by governmental agencies. Private organizations have always been active in this field. Sometimes, their activities afford valuable supplements to official programs, while at other times private groups have greatly complicated the job of official policy-makers. Two privately sponsored radio networks—Radio Free Europe and Radio Liberation—have broadcast intensively across the iron curtain. Their approach has been militantly anti-Communist; they have sought to encourage defection behind the Iron Curtain; and at some periods, as in the weeks leading up to the Hungarian Revolt of 1956, they have made explicit or tacit promises concerning America's willingness to "liberate" Eastern Europe from Communist domination and to "roll back" the Iron Curtain, that were at variance with the policies of the United States.

For many years, philanthropic organizations like the Ford Foundation and the Rockefeller Foundation have sponsored programs designed to assist economically backward societies raise educational, health and sanitation, and economic standards.[35] Such programs have sometimes been outstandingly successful and have paid rich dividends in promoting good will for the United States. Similarly, organizations like the People-to-People movement endeavor to promote mutual international understanding by supporting visits by foreigners to the United States.[36] Many American communities also have "Community Ambassador" programs involving individuals selected to live with a foreign family for a brief period of time. While abroad, he interprets the United States to other societies; when he returns, he interprets the foreign society to his American associates.

A recent innovation in American propaganda activities has consisted of much greater emphasis than in the early postwar era upon cultural exchange programs, in which outstanding artists in diverse fields are sent abroad, under State Department auspices and encouragement, to demonstrate American cultural achievements (in part to counteract the widely prevalent idea that American cultural attainments are inferior). Thus, beginning with the late 1950s, symphony orchestras and smaller groups of musicians, dancers, actors and actresses, writers and poets, lecturers, painters and sculptors, and other outstanding artists have increasingly been called upon to generate good will for the United States in foreign countries.[37]

Past Patterns and Future Problems

After evaluating Western, chiefly American, propaganda activities toward the Communist bloc, a correspondent for the French newspaper *Le Monde* wrote early in the 1960s: "In the huge task of mobilizing all the resources of the United States and those of its allies to meet the Berlin crisis, the psychological field is one of the thorniest but perhaps the most decisive. It is also the field in which this country is the least prepared."[38]

Our treatment thus far has called attention to a number of problems that have confronted, and will continue to confront, the United States in its efforts to wage successful psychological warfare in the global arena. Even by the mid-1960s, the American still held an inadequate view of the *necessity* for interpreting American goals and aspirations to other countries. With a majority of citizens relatively apathetic about world affairs generally, there prevailed a tendency to believe that the American attachment to democracy, the nation's historic antipathy to foreign entanglements, its humanitarian impulses, and its championship of principles such as self-determination would "speak for themselves" in convincing foreigners about America's dedication to freedom and its underlying identification with the goals of human progress and welfare. Consequently, the American people and their representatives in Congress evinced a minimum awareness of an obligation to "sell" their ideological cause to the outside world. For many citizens, it was sufficient merely to *deny* Communist propaganda mili-

tantly and to point out the often absurd claims and philosophical contradictions infusing it.

Postwar events, however, have repeatedly exposed the inadequacy of this approach in achieving American global objectives. Justifiably or not, other societies often have highly unflattering ideas and conceptions about the United States, that sometimes interfere seriously with the successful pursuit of external goals. Public opinion surveys and other studies have called attention to the presence of deeply embedded stereotypes and distortions in the minds of foreigners about the American society, that will require intense efforts, spread over many years, to correct. Whether these images and impressions are true or false is not, for our purposes, the essential point. The point instead is that they unquestionably exist and that they can sometimes influence decisively the ability of the United States to accomplish its diplomatic purposes.*

Widespread public skepticism in the United States about the necessity or desirability for waging an ongoing propaganda campaign overseas has often interfered seriously with the effectiveness of USIA's operations. Throughout the 1950s and into the 1960s, USIA enjoyed the dubious distinction of being one of the

---

* A brief indication of the nature of the problem is afforded by the following examples. A UN-sponsored study showed that people in other societies often applied words like "practical" and "progressive" to the American society. Words *not* applied to America, often used to describe other societies, were "brave," "self-controlled," and perhaps most crucial from a propaganda point of view, "peace-loving." French attitudes have conspicuously emphasized the extent to which Frenchmen fear becoming "Americanized"; one study summarized French viewpoints by saying that Americans were looked upon as "politically maladroit and lacking in experience." Studies of British attitudes have found a feeling that Americans are "a lot of simple plebeians" who often act like "an overgrown child"; America is "an impulsive nation, composed of decidedly immature people." Germans have characterized American society as "superficial, fickle, unprincipled, extremely naive at best. . . ." Japanese students in America have found the American people "subject to changing whims," as well as "overly materialistic, uncultured, impulsive, disorderly, shallow, superficial, too individualistic." For the Japanese as for many other societies, antiracial and anti-intellectual currents run deep in American life. See William Buchanan, "How Others See Us," *Annals of the American Academy of Political and Social Science*, **295** (September, 1954), 1–11; Jacques Freymond, "America in European Eyes," *ibid.*, pp. 33–41; Nobert Muhlett, "America and American Occupation in German Eyes," *ibid.*, pp. 52–61; Herbert Passin and John W. Bernett, "The American-Educated Japanese," **I**, *ibid.*, pp. 83–96.

most unpopular agencies in Washington. Newspaper headlines like "U.S. Propaganda Post Called Thankless Job" highlighted its lack of rapport with Congress and the public, and underscored the difficulty it faced in finding well-qualified personnel to staff its operations. During the early 1950s, USIA, along with the State Department and other governmental agencies, came under heavy attack for allegedly harboring pro-Communist subversive elements. An almost endless series of "investigations," conducted with great fanfare, threatened to undermine the morale of its staff and to impair its administrative efficiency. Even after the era of "McCarthyism" came to an end, USIA continued to find the public largely indifferent to its responsibilities. Congress tended to remain parsimonious in providing funds and critical in evaluating the agency's needs. Like the State Department, USIA is an agency that has no "constituents" in the United States to champion its cause, among the competing demands made upon Congress for money. The problem confronting USIA in this respect has been aptly formulated by a former State Department official, Edward Barrett, who has said that in presenting the case for expanded propaganda activities:

> No one could prove last year's funds had been well spent by producing a cage filled with 7000 Russians who had deserted Communism. The committee could see and touch new post offices; it could not see 10 million Indians or Britons who had been made a little less suspicious of America than they were a year earlier.[39]

Or, as former USIA Director Edward R. Murrow, said in 1963: "No computer clicks, no cash register rings when a man changes his mind or opts for freedom."[40]

The result has been an over-all propaganda effort throughout the postwar era that has admittedly been strengthened, but which still lags behind the kind of program increasingly demanded in an era of "peaceful coexistence" or "competitive competition" with the Communist bloc. USIA's entire budget of approximately $125 million for 1963 was considerably less than the cost of several modern bombers, a single space program, and infinitely smaller than the cost of waging the Korean War for a few days. Even more significantly perhaps, this total was equal to the amount the Soviet Union spent merely to "jam" Voice of America broadcasts. Altogether, the USSR expended four times as much on its propaganda campaign as did the United States.[41] In the light of these facts, several studies by individuals and committees have recommended a significant expansion in American psychological warfare activities.[42] Yet even by the mid-1960s, national propaganda and psychological efforts remained inadequate, particularly in the face of intensified use of such weapons by the Communist bloc to turn the tide of ideological battle.

Another continuing problem sometimes impeding successful American efforts in the propaganda field is inherent in the very concept of the "open society" existing in the United States. If fundamental liberties, like freedom of speech and of the press, are the essence of the democratic process, the exercise of such freedoms presents a greater challenge than ever for USIA and other agencies endeavoring to create good will for the United States abroad. Socioeconomic problems in America—from racial incidents, to the presence of slums, to occasional high levels of unemployment—cannot be concealed from the eyes of the world, any more than they can be hidden from the American people themselves. The failure of a space probe, or discrimination against a diplomat from an African country, or acrimonious controversies and lack of cooperation between the White House and Capitol Hill over a major piece of legislation, or public revelations of political corruption—these become quickly known and are publicized, often with great fanfare, throughout the world. *Pravda's* correspondent in Washington has almost the same access to news about the United States as does a correspondent for *The New York Times*. By contrast, American and other foreign commentators in the USSR, and even in such countries as Ghana, Egypt, and Indonesia, find their activities sharply circumscribed; their dispatches, particularly when they deal with unflattering aspects of the society, are often subjected to heavy censorship.

The single most difficult problem for USIA and the State Department in this respect is, of course, the issue of racial conflict in the United States. Almost every day, some high American official is quoted as characterizing it as the "chief propaganda problem abroad, especially in Africa."[43] Its serious implications for the United States on the propaganda front cannot be minimized. Yet, by the mid-1960s it also had to be recognized that leaders and informed citizens in other countries had acquired a much more balanced and sophisticated viewpoint toward racial conflict in America than was the case in the 1950s. Indicative of this trend was the viewpoint expressed by President Sékou Touré of Guinea: "We cannot say that the American people are racists—racism exists everywhere, even in Guinea." Increasingly, observers in countries keenly sensitive to racial discrimination were recognizing the difference between isolated instances of racial discrimination and *governmentally sponsored* policies and programs that fostered discrimination. Moreover, USIA officials found growing understanding, and acceptance, for the fact that the influence of the United States government was being used to eradicate racial discrimination—a fact that often itself fostered newsworthy incidents.* In other words, foreign societies were more and more grasping the distinction between an "open" society that admitted its defects publicly and endeavored to correct them, and various kinds of "closed" societies that neither admitted the existence of social problems (especially not to foreigners) nor publicized their efforts to solve them.

Yet it remains true that in reality there are many "voices of America" that compete with, and sometimes drown out, official propaganda statements. There is, as we have described at length, the official voice of the United States, as embodied in the President and as expressed by officials under his jurisdiction. Even within the executive branch there has appeared an ever-widening circle of voices that can occasionally produce a confusing and displeasing cacaphony for foreign listeners. In addition, there are 535 voices in Congress, expressed individually or in legislative committees or collectively in each house. Legisla-

* Thus the following foreign reactions to events in Oxford, Mississippi, during 1962 illustrate the point. The *Ethiopian Herald* said that "President Kennedy's latest action in ending segregation in Mississippi's state university should be viewed as paving a way broad and smooth enough for others to follow." The racial conflict that followed the attempt to integrate the university was described by the *Daily Nation* of Kenya as "a vindication of American democracy"; the publication *Yuwadi* of Burma said: "The U.S. Government is trying to suppress racial discrimination and it is only a handful of American reactionaries who . . . are defying the law." These and other reactions are quoted in USIA, *19th Review of Operations: July 1–December 31, 1962* (Washington, D.C.: Government Printing Office, 1963), p. 17. See also *The New York Times*, May 29, 1963.

tive voices testify about the United States in many ways: by legislative investigations, by the activities of legislators traveling abroad, by laws and resolutions passed in each chamber, by the opinions expressed by individual members of Congress. Sometimes, as when an influential legislator publicly makes disparaging remarks about the ability of African nations to govern themselves successfully, or conversely, when the political leadership of Congress gives its united support to the President in the midst of a crisis, these voices can be infinitely more influential than the Voice of America.

Added to this chorus are the voices of thousands of groups and millions of individual citizens in the United States. There are the voice of competing interest groups calling for the raising or lowering of tariff barriers; groups demanding militant policies toward, or a reconciliation with, Red China; groups calling for stepped-up anti-Communist campaigns in Southeast Asia or for a curtailment of American military involvement there; groups advocating withdrawal from the United Nations or strengthening the UN; groups calling for greater progress toward world government, while other groups demand that the United States zealously defend its "national sovereignty." In the midst of this babble of voices, there are the millions of citizens who ordinarily play little role directly in foreign relations, but who occasionally bring their influence to bear decisively in demanding that the United States "do something" about Soviet military intrusion in Cuba, or about repeated Communist harassment of Allied access routes to Berlin, or about what is regarded as exorbitance and waste in the field of foreign aid.

Finally, there is another voice of America that frequently transcends this cacaphony, to produce the clearest and most expressive voice audible overseas: *the deeds and conduct of the United States in the international community*. Almost all propaganda experts agree with a State Department conclusion that: "Propaganda is 90 percent deeds and only 10 percent words." As with the Soviet Union or any other country, what the United States *does* in world affairs testifies much more eloquently about its claimed attachment to freedom, or its concern for the problems of the underdeveloped world, or its respect for the principle of self-determination than what its officials *say* about such principles. Thus, many hours of broadcasting by the Voice of America concerning Western dedication to political liberty, versus Communist attachment to totalitarian methods, can be more than counteracted by oppressive political policies carried out by an ally of the United States, and a member of the "free world," in Southeast Asia. Similarly, USIA may endeavor by various means to establish a rapport between the United States and economically underdeveloped countries; it may try to convince the people of such countries that the United States is more deeply concerned about age-old human problems than is the Soviet Union or Red China. This message can largely be nullified when Congress slashes the foreign aid budget, or when it seeks to "discipline" some foreign government that has nationalized American business holdings by denying it economic assistance, or when a legislative committee recommends cutting American aid to regimes that have adopted a "socialist" program. Conversely, one of the most convincing testimonies the United States can offer about its attachment to freedom is for its delegates at the United Nations to vote against the apartheid policies of South Africa or vote to support a UN investigation of Portugal's African policies. By the same token, steadfast Western resistance to Communist encroachments in Berlin furnishes continuing evidence of America's determination to preserve the security of the free world, even at the cost of possible war.

Our discussion has suggested that in their propaganda activities, both the American-led free world coalition and the Soviet-led Communist bloc possess certain strengths and weaknesses. In waging psychological warfare, the Communist world has all of the advantages traditionally possessed by the patent medicine man. It is seeking to dispense globally a political nostrum designed to cure all the assorted ills of human society—from problems of poverty, to labor-management relations, to the desire for political "democracy." In certain regions, the Soviet Union and Red China have substantial advantages by virtue of the fact that they are not identified as a "colonial power." Throughout Africa, the Arab world, Asia, and Latin America, colonialism has traditionally meant *Western* colonialism. Nor has the Communist world had the record of overt and well-publicized racial discrimination often identified with America and other Western societies. The Soviet Union's record of discrimination against Jews and other ethnic and national minorities has often either remained

virtually unknown or has been disregarded throughout many areas of the diplomatically noncommitted world.*

Communist propagandists also hold another advantage that has proved extremely useful in their efforts to maintain diplomatic rapport with the underdeveloped world: in general, the experiences and problems faced by societies behind the Iron Curtain are more applicable to conditions in Guinea or Nigeria or the Sudan or Burma than is the case with American or European experience. In many cases, emerging countries are seeking to reproduce the record of industrialization and modernization that Soviet Russia has made since 1917 and that Red China is endeavoring to make in the contemporary era.

In recognizing these facts, it remains true that certain other factors frequently tip the propaganda scales in favor of the United States. High on the list is America's well-known anticolonial heritage and its favorable record as a colonial power. While many nations have deplored the tendency of the United States to support (or not oppose) its European allies on colonial issues since World War II, they remain aware that the United States nevertheless opposes colonialism and that it has not been known historically as a colonial power. Political leaders outside the United States are usually aware that the United States exerted pressure upon its allies to liquidate their empires and to come to terms with nationalist movements. More often

---

* By the 1960s, however, events indicated that this situation was undergoing significant change. As part of its strategy of "peaceful coexistence," the USSR was endeavoring to demonstrate its "sensitivity" to public opinion in the outside world about alleged incidents involving discrimination toward Jewish groups and other minorities behind the iron curtain. Press dispatches from Moscow declared that "Soviet leaders and the press have been stung by criticism abroad into denying that anti-Semitism exists in the Soviet Union. Previously the subject was taboo here." The Kremlin had evidently been acutely embarrassed by accusations that 60 percent of all persons executed for crime were Jewish. Soviet publications like *Pravda* and *Izvestia* were frequently prompted to refute charges of religious or racial discrimination; in response to unfavorable world publicity, the Communist regime apparently was endeavoring to modify certain policies toward minorities, intellectuals, and other groups, to avoid even the *appearance* of discrimination. *The New York Times*, June 5, 1963. Racial incidents involving Africans behind the Iron Curtain are described in David Hapgood, "The Competition for Africa's Students," *The Reporter*, **29** (September 12, 1963), 41–42.

than not, diplomatically uncommitted countries are familiar with America's "revolutionary" heritage. Nationalist leaders in the recent period look upon the Declaration of Independence and the American Constitution as beacons to light their own country's path toward genuine independence; frequently, they base their own constitutional and governmental system upon principles taken from American or Western parliamentary models. The conception of "democracy" prevailing in countries that have experienced nationalist movements draws heavily upon American and other Western sources. President Wilson's Fourteen Points or the Atlantic Charter are cited from Morocco to Indonesia as embodying the highest ideological and political ideals. Frequently, private and official spokesmen in these countries criticize the United States and its allies for failure to *adhere* to their own announced ideological principles!

Despite propaganda setbacks from time to time, American officials have become convinced that political leaders throughout the zone of nonaligned countries are manifesting increasing sophistication and discrimination in evaluating Western and Communist propaganda claims. This does not mean that in every respect such leaders always accept Western assertions *in toto*; much less does it imply that Ghana or Egypt or Iraq or Burma or Indonesia is on the verge of embracing the Western conception of political "democracy," of severing all their relations with the Communist bloc, or of entering a Western military alliance. Certainly it should not be construed as suggesting that the West has already won a decisive victory on the ideological front of the cold war. It does mean that, with the passage of time, leaders and political elites within these societies have become much more critical than formerly of the divergence between Communist propaganda claims and Communist behavior in internal and external affairs; that they are much more realistically aware than in the 1940s or early 1950s of underlying Communist objectives in dealing with their country; that they are as determined to resist Communist-instigated encroachments upon newly gained freedom as to preserve their independence from Western colonialism; that they have frequently become disillusioned with Communist maneuvers that seek to identify with, and use, nationalist movements merely as *tools* to achieve goals defined in Moscow or Peiping. It does mean that a basic

identity of interests has increasingly become apparent between the nonaligned countries and the West. It lies essentially in the extent to which both desire that the nonaligned nations *maintain* their freedom in the face of Communist efforts to subvert it. It is perhaps this conviction as much as any other—the idea that the tide of battle will ultimately shift decisively in favor of the free world, to the degree that the independence of nations within the non-Communist zone is successfully preserved—that may tilt the scales overwhelmingly against the Communist bloc.

NOTES

1. See the text of the Sprague Committee's report in Urban G. Whitaker, Jr., *Propaganda and International Relations* (San Francisco: Chandler, 1962), pp. 38–61.
2. Charles A. Thomson and Walter H. C. Laves, *Cultural Relations and U.S. Foreign Policy* (Bloomington, Ind.: Indiana University Press, 1963), p. 173.
3. Daniel Lerner, ed., *Propaganda in War and Crisis* (New York: Stewart, 1951), pp. 72–73, 84–85, 276.
4. For a more complete listing of the weapons of psychological warfare, see Terence H. Qualter, *Propaganda and Psychological Warfare* (New York: Random House, 1962), p. 74.
5. *Ibid.*, p. 3.
6. *Ibid.*, pp. 8–14.
7. Lerner, *op. cit.*, pp. 345–346.
8. *The New York Times*, April 7, 1963.
9. Nathan Leites, *A Study of Bolshevism* (New York: Free Press of Glencoe, 1953), p. 67.
10. Quoted in *ibid.*, p. 415.
11. Quoted in *ibid.*, p. 478.
12. Evron Kirkpatrick, *Year of Crisis* (New York: Macmillan, 1959), p. 34.
13. Evron Kirkpatrick, *Target the World* (New York: Macmillan, 1956), pp. 34–37.
14. Kirkpatrick, *Year of Crisis*, *op. cit.*, pp. 38–40.
15. Kirkpatrick, *Target the World*, *op. cit.*, p. 43.
16. Whitaker, *op. cit.*, pp. 223–224.
17. *Ibid.*, pp. 133–134.
18. Quoted in Leites, *op. cit.*, p. 103.
19. United States Information Agency, *Foreign Service: USIA* (Washington, D.C.: no date), p. 1.
20. The history of American propaganda activities before World War II is described in Thomson and Laves, *op. cit.*, pp. 27–56 and Whitaker, *op. cit.*, pp. 28–38.

21. Department of State, *American Foreign Policy, 1950–1955*, Publication No. 6446, "General Foreign Policy Series" 117, **II** (Washington, D.C.: 1957), 3165.
22. Thomson and Laves, pp. 97, 119.
23. USIA, *op. cit.*, p. 3.
24. United States Information Agency, *20th Review of Operations: January 1–June 30, 1963* (Washington, D.C.: 1963), p. 51.
25. *Ibid.*, pp. 6–7.
26. *Ibid.*, p. 5.
27. *Ibid.*, p. 11.
28. *Ibid.*, pp. 6–12.
29. *Ibid.*, p. 10.
30. Chester Bowles, *Ambassador's Report* (New York: Harper & Row, 1954), pp. 305–311.
31. USIA, *20th Review of Operations, op. cit.*, p. 22.
32. *Ibid.*, pp. 23–24.
33. Department of State, **II**, *op. cit.*, 3198–3199; Thomson and Laves, *op. cit.*, pp. 59–69.
34. Whitaker, *op. cit.*, pp. 227–242; *The New York Times*, January 14, 1962.
35. Qualter, *op. cit.*, pp. 130–131; John Scott, *Political Warfare* (New York: Day, 1955), pp. 33–36, 219–220.
36. Thomson and Laves, *op. cit.*, pp. 131–133.
37. *Ibid.*, pp. 122–126.
38. Edmond Taylor, "Political Warfare: A Sword We Must Unsheath," *The Reporter*, **25** (September 14, 1961), 27.
39. Edward W. Barrett, *Truth is Our Weapon* (New York: Funk & Wagnalls, 1953), p. 85.
40. *The Washington Post*, March 29, 1963.
41. *Idem; New York Herald Tribune*, November 27, 1961.
42. Sherman Adams, *First-Hand Report: The Story of the Eisenhower Administration* (New York: Harper & Row, 1961), p. 115; Thomson and Laves, *op. cit.*, pp. 186–195.
43. *The New York Times*, November 27, 1961, and May 29, 1963.

15 ➞ FOREIGN ECONOMIC

POLICY ➞ the world's creditor

on trial

As one of the supporting pillars of a nation's diplomacy, foreign economic policy is of utmost concern to students of international affairs. An example from recent American diplomatic experience will illustrate the centrality of the subject.

Dollars and Diplomacy

In the spring of 1958, Vice-President Richard Nixon undertook a "good will tour" of Latin America. Throughout his tour Mr. Nixon encountered anything but good will toward the United States. Extreme anti-American sentiment time and again was manifested by masses in Latin America. Mobs in countries such as Peru and Venezuela heaped indignities upon him and the country he represented, and threatened his very life. Behind these incidents lay many contributing causes: resentment because the United States often appeared to sanction dictatorial regimes in countries to the south; prolonged efforts by Communist-led groups to discredit the United States; festering grievances which have led to sporadic outbursts of Yankeephobia in the past.

The cause relevant to our discussion here, however, was a deeply imbedded disillusionment with certain aspects of the foreign economic policy adopted by the United States. Latin Americans had long been chafing under the conviction that the United States was "taking them for granted," that their region had consistently played second fiddle to Europe and Asia in most phases of American

foreign economic relations, and that Uncle Sam had been penurious and self-centered in his policies relating to foreign aid and trade questions. Most Latin American countries rely heavily upon single commodity exports. They have experienced foreign exchange dificits, as the value of their exports to the United States has declined. And because foreign trade was vital to their continued economic well-being, economic crises aggravated existing political turbulence.[1]

All these grievances and apprehensions coalesced in the hostile reception manifested toward Vice-President Nixon. Nixon's tour resulted in intensive soul-searching in high diplomatic circles in Washington over United States-Latin American relations, particularly economic aspects of those relations. Yet Washington realized that more than Latin America's problems and needs had been highlighted by the Nixon tour. Problems there mirrored those of underdeveloped areas as a whole. As was emphasized by our discussion of Africa and Asia, the formulation of effective policies toward underdeveloped regions will present a continuing challenge to American officials for the indefinite future. In dealing with these areas, economic issues are likely to be of paramount importance.

In this chapter our approach will focus upon three broad categories of problems: American tariff and trade policies, foreign assistance programs and their consequences, and miscellaneous other problems in American foreign economic relations. Analysis of these subjects will be more meaningful, however, if we first discuss them in an historical context.

Basic Economic Trends

Basic to an understanding of contemporary economic issues is America's transition from a debtor to a creditor—in the modern period, the richest creditor—in the international community. From World War I onward, there was an outflow of American capital to other countries. Economic dislocations caused by two world wars and by the Great Depression destroyed Great Britain's historic position as the world's creditor. As was the case in other aspects of international affairs, Britain's former role was assumed by the United States. With the precipitous decline in world trade during the 1930s, much of the world's gold supply flowed into the United States. Consequently, by the late 1950s the United States held nearly $23 billion worth of gold, out of a total world supply of nearly $39 billion.[2] Having depleted their gold reserves—and World War II took most of the reserves which had been maintained through the Great Depression—and having cashed in their foreign investments to finance the war, the nations of Western Europe emerged in the postwar period near the brink of bankruptcy. Yet they were faced with the prodigious challenge of reconstructing their economies and of attempting to restore normal patterns of economic intercourse upon which their future prosperity depended. Had it not been for vast quantities of American assistance to such countries, and to more backward countries in Latin America, the Arab world, and Asia, many of these nations might not have survived. The worldwide demand for capital goods and raw materials in war-devastated countries, joined with the inability of these countries to pay for required imports, led to the so-called "dollar gap" which was a more or less consistent feature of the patterns of international economics down to the 1950s.[3]

A second trend of fundamental significance in shaping America's response on questions of international economics has been the increasing dependence of the United States upon imports of raw materials and commodities needed both for civilian consumption and for national defense. A cessation of imports of such consumer goods as coffee, pineapples, tea, spices, cocoa, olives, tuna fish, sugar, and many more, would cause the American housewife discomfiture and would also have adverse repercussions for certain segments of the American economy. Far more crucial, however, is America's reliance upon foreign trade to maintain a strong defense posture. America's growing dependence upon imports, and the implications of this fact for national security, were discussed at length in Chapter 1. We shall not reproduce that data in our discussion here. Suffice it to emphasize that, as weapons become more complex and as the standard of living in the United States continues to rise, national security depends as never before upon unimpeded access to strategic raw materials such as ferroalloys, aluminum, asbestos, and a variety of other commodities which are either lacking altogether in the United States or for which supplies are dwindling. A State Department publication has highlighted the extent of this dependence by pointing out that a particular type of jet aircraft required the following imported metals:[4]

Material	Pounds Utilized	Percent Imported
Chromium	3,659	92
Nickel	2,117	97
Aluminum (bauxite)	46,831	76
Copper	436	88
Cobalt	2,309	35

These are, or ought to be, sobering figures. They indicate the degree to which the United States is at present dependent upon the outside world for some of its most basic security needs. They constitute perhaps the most convincing refutation possible of an "isolationist" approach to foreign affairs. Projections for the future anticipate ever-increasing reliance upon imports in such categories as iron ore, crude oil, aluminum (bauxite ore), copper, lead, zinc, and virtually all the other ferroalloys.[5]

Third, economic aspects of foreign policy have assumed unprecedented importance because of the Communist bloc's emphasis upon economic weapons to achieve victory in the cold war. This trend emerged strikingly after the Geneva Conference of 1955, when Soviet Premier Khrushchev began to rely upon nonmilitary techniques to advance the Communist cause throughout Africa, the Arab world, Asia, and in more recent years, Latin America. During the new era of "peaceful coexistence," trade and foreign assistance emerged as primary Communist instruments of foreign policy. Khrushchev candidly admitted to a group of visiting American legislators that:

"We value trade least for economic reasons and most for political reasons."[6] That this was no idle comment became clear by the rapidity with which the Kremlin moved during the late 1950s and early 1960s to conclude trade agreements with nations throughout the underdeveloped world. Swarms of Communist "technicians" followed in the wake of such agreements; eye-catching displays—like newly paved streets in Kabul, Afghanistan, or the Aswan High Dam in Egypt—served as constant reminders of the Communist world's interests in the problems of economically backward societies; countries behind the iron curtain stepped up their participation in world trade fairs and industrial exhibitions, to demonstrate the "superiority" of communism over capitalism. In the period 1954–1960, the Communist bloc increased the number of its trade agreements with the underdeveloped world from 87 to 206 and raised the total volume of its trade with these countries from $860 million to $2.7 billion annually.[7] Concurrently, Communist propaganda organs and groups espousing the Communist cause mounted vigorous attacks upon Western trade and aid programs, labeling them "neocolonialist" schemes designed to reimpose a new form of economic bondage upon newly independent societies. The net result of these moves was to put the Western alliance on the defensive in its relations with neutralist countries and other nations in the free world.

Domestic Policy and Foreign Policy

Finally, mention must be made of the extent to which economic developments within the United States affect, and are in turn affected by, international trade and finance. The aphorism that "When the United States catches a cold, Europe sneezes," has no greater validity than in the economic realm. In the postwar period, fundamental economic trends within the United States have had a far broader impact than upon Europe alone; their ramifications have extended throughout the civilized world. The total level of spending by the United States government, the proportion of the federal budget devoted to national defense, the national income generated in any given year, the number and composition of the civilian labor force, the level of domestic prices, the depletion of natural resources, the present and future well-being of domestic agriculture—all of these enter into calculations of national power capabilities and intentions.

Capitals like Moscow, London, Paris, New Delhi, and Tokyo are keenly interested in the entire gamut of so-called "domestic" issues within the United States. Thus, effective American consumer demand for textiles will in turn affect the level of Japanese industrial production, which will go far toward shaping the total pattern of Japanese foreign trade, which will be a significant element in determining Japan's relations with Southeast Asia and Red China, and so on. While the long-run consequences of economic phenomena within the United States may pass through a number of intermediate stages before they trigger major developments on the world scene, their ultimate effect upon the course of international affairs cannot be doubted. The lack of meaningful distinction between what were formerly "internal" and "external" policy matters is surely one of the most fundamental trends in contemporary global affairs.

Furthermore, if it is of the utmost importance that the United States maintain a position of strength from which to lead the free-world coalition, problems of international trade and finance become high priority issues. Few Americans realize how much their own security and the security of their diplomatic friends are tied up with the maintenance of a high level of American exports. Looked at purely from the point of view of domestic economic welfare, exports have played a progressively more important role in creating a position of economic strength and in supporting a high standard of living. Even "isolationists" would agree to the principle that full production and employment cannot be maintained within the United States without access to the world market though, as we shall see, they often do not see the companion necessity for a high level of imports.

With these broad considerations in mind, we turn now to an examination of specific issues in American foreign economic policy that have been important since World War II and that constitute significant continuing issues in American relations with the outside world.

AMERICAN TARIFF AND TRADE POLICIES

Few issues have engendered such political controversy throughout American history as the tariff. Significantly, the second law passed by Congress under the Constitution was the Tariff of 1789, upon which the government was heavily dependent for revenue. Major stages in the development of United States tariff policy thereafter occurred in 1816, when the first tariff for the protection of American domestic industry from foreign competition was passed; in 1890, when President McKinley was given limited authority to adjust tariff rates after tariff concessions had been obtained from other countries; in 1916, when the United States Tariff Commission was created to study trade questions and make recommendations to the President concerning rate adjustments; in 1930, when American tariff rates under the Smoot-Hawley Tariff reached their highest level in history—52.8 percent of the value of dutiable imports. Thereafter, in large measure as a result of the Great Depression, of the barriers erected by the Smoot-Hawley Tariff, and of retaliatory steps taken by other countries against American imports, the foreign trade of the United States declined spectacularly, dropping from over $10 billion in 1930 to less than $3.5 billion in 1933. The early 1930s also witnessed a proliferation of trade restrictions throughout the international community. This was the period, for example, of the emergence of the "British Imperial preference system," whereby more favorable tariff rates were applied to nations within the British Empire and Commonwealth than to nations outside it.[8]

The Reciprocal Trade Program

It was against this background of virtual stagnation of international trade, accompanied by the multiplication of barriers to its revival, that President Roosevelt and Secretary of State Cordell Hull proposed a reciprocal trade program. After vigorous leadership by the White House, Congress inaugurated the program in 1934 as an amendment to the Smoot-Hawley Tariff. The President was authorized for a three-year period to enter into trade agreements with other countries. He was permitted to reduce American tariff rates to a limit of 50 percent of prevailing rates, provided that other countries made equivalent concessions in their tariff rates on American goods.

The reciprocal trade program, technically known as the Trade Agreements Act of 1934, was renewed at intervals, and with some modifications, over the course of the years which followed. The apex in a philosophy of free trade was reached in the TAA renewal of 1945,

when the President was given authority to cut tariff rates on a reciprocal basis up to 75 percent of prevailing 1934 rates.

Significant developments in global economic relations in the early postwar period also included the negotiation between the United States and 22 other countries in 1947 of the General Agreement on Tariffs and Trade (GATT); its purposes and provisions will be described below.

Meanwhile, within the United States, Congress periodically renewed the reciprocal trade program, for one, two, or three years. The Trade Agreements Act was renewed eleven times from 1934 to 1958. Depending upon the political composition of the national legislature when the Trade Agreements Act came up for renewal, Congress's approach was alternatively "protectionist" or "liberal" in giving the President authority to negotiate tariff reductions on a reciprocal basis with other countries. In 1948, and again in 1951, for example, Congress inserted certain protectionist features into the trade program.* In 1958, on the other hand, Congress substantially acceded to President Eisenhower's request for a long-term renewal of TAA, by which the chief executive would be given broad latitude to lower American tariff rates, provided other

---

* In 1948, Congress added the "peril point" provision to the TAA. Under this provision, *new* trade agreements with other countries could not lower American tariff rates below a level that would seriously damage American domestic industry. The Tariff Commission was required to determine the "peril point"—the tariff rate below which injury would be sustained by American manufacturers. The commission was required to make its findings public and to inform the President of them; in turn, executive officials were supposed to take them into account when they negotiated new tariff agreements. In 1951, Congress also inserted the "escape clause" provision into tariff legislation. Closely akin to the "peril point" idea, this provision applied both to new trade agreements and to those already in force, as soon as executive officials could get them incorporated into existing agreements. The basic idea was that if imports were found to be injuring American producers, tariff rates would be raised to give relief to domestic producers. The Tariff Commission was required to carry on continuing studies of the impact of imports upon the American economy and to report its findings to the White House and to the public. Under this clause, industries in the United States could request "relief" from the White House; if their request was granted, tariffs would be raised against those imports causing economic injury at home. In the vast majority of cases since 1951, the White House has denied such requests for relief. For examples, see the volumes in the *Annual Reports* of the United States Tariff Commission.

countries did likewise. Even then, the Eisenhower Administration was required to make concessions to "protectionist" attitudes by accepting various provisions in the law, designed to cushion the impact of expanded imports upon American domestic producers, particularly those hard-hit by foreign competition.[9] By the end of the 1950s, the United States had trade agreements with more than 40 countries.

The General Agreement on Tariffs and Trade

In 1947 the United States and 22 other countries signed an agreement to promote world trade, known as the General Agreement on Tariffs and Trade (GATT). Created to foster expanded trade among its members (expanded by 1964 to 58 countries) GATT was concerned specifically with such concrete issues as negotiating tariff adjustments between the United States and the members of the European Common Market; promoting agreements among its members to accept voluntary restrictions upon exports (such as textile imports into the United States) that might damage domestic producers and, in turn, might engender demands for higher tariffs; encouraging the economic diversification of underdeveloped countries and the exportation by such countries of a broad range of goods and services; and trying to secure agreement on one of the most controversial problems confronting GATT's members: tariff reductions on highly "protected" agricultural commodities. As a leading member of GATT, the United States joined other nations in meetings and negotiations, such as the Geneva meeting in 1963, calling for further reductions in world trade barriers, negotiated on a reciprocal basis. By 1964, the Common Market members of GATT sought an over-all 50 percent reduction in tariff rates, coupled with other steps designed to eliminate trade restrictions.[10]

The Trade Challenge of the 1960s

By the early 1960s, many of the long-range factors influencing America's international economic relations were of sufficient urgency to convince the Kennedy Administration that a new approach to tariff and trade questions was demanded. Instead of asking Congress for another renewal of the Trade Agreements Act, executive policy-makers formulated another program that embodied some features of TAA and certain innovations as well. What were the conditions engendering the conviction that

traditional policies were out-of-date and inadequate for the 1960s? Several considerations coalesced to support this conclusion.

First, and possibly foremost, was increasing official awareness of the implications for the United States inherent in the emergence and successful operation of the European Economic Community or Common Market.* Established in 1958, by the early 1960s the Common Market was on the verge of becoming the "world's largest single international trading unit" and potentially the most influential trading nexus on the globe.[11] Without reproducing material presented earlier, we may observe here that from its inception, EEC was remarkably successful in lowering trade barriers among its members, in stimulating European economic production, in raising living standards, and in coordinating the trade activities of its members toward the outside world. By the mid-1960s, the economic and financial position of EEC rivaled, and in some respects surpassed, that of the United States. For instance, the Common Market had monetary reserves of about the same magnitude as the United States; it had a strong balance-of-payments position, whereas the United States had a weak position; it was accumulating gold surpluses, while the United States was experiencing a gold outflow; capital investment funds were flowing out of the United States into Common Market countries, while the counterflow of funds from EEC to the United States was relatively insignificant; the members of EEC had economic growth rates of from 4 to 6 percent annually, while the rate for the United States was about half this level; total imports and exports for EEC members in the early 1960s were running about $40 billion annually, while they were about $33 billion for the United States.[12] These developments called forceful attention, at least so far as Western Europe was concerned, to the end of the era of the "dollar shortage," during which Europe was economically prostrate, dependent upon the United States, and unable to purchase American goods without massive outside assistance.

Emergence of an increasingly prosperous,

* The evolution, structure, and goals of the European Economic Community are described at length in Chapter 10. For the year 1963, EEC had total imports of some $37.5 billion, of which $5.2 billion was from the United States; its total exports were $36.9 billion, of which $2.3 billion was to the United States. *The New York Times*, January 10, 1964.

internally cohesive European Common Market, in fact, signaled the end of a long era in American international economic relations. As a high State Department official observed in 1963, from 1940 (if not earlier) until 1954, American business concerns enjoyed "what amounted to almost total and absolute protection" in the world market, owing to the virtual elimination of their two principal economic rivals—Western Europe and Japan—as a result of World War II. During that period, which many Americans had perhaps unconsciously come to accept as normal, the United States had no effective competition for about two-thirds of the goods and services it produced for the foreign market.[13] A global shortage of dollars had meant that America's trade problem was precisely the opposite from what it became by the late 1950s and early 1960s. Then other countries were unable to *purchase* American goods and services, because of the scarcity of dollars due to their inability to sell their own goods on a competitive basis with the United States. By the end of the 1950s, however, many Americans had become conscious of the profound transformation that had occurred within the environment of global trade. American business concerns were facing keen competition from nations such as the members of the EEC and Japan; instead of a "dollar shortage," many industrialized countries were accumulating dollar balances, sufficiently to bring the soundness of the dollar vis-à-vis other currencies into question. A State Department official summarized the new conditions by saying: "In our tariff negotiations with this strong new Europe we will have to make concessions to gain concessions."[14] Europe was no longer a supplicant for American favors. At America's own instigation, it had successfully overcome national interests and animosities and in economic affairs, had achieved a viable form of European "unity" undreamed of in the immediate postwar period. If statesmen in Europe were acting more and more "independently," it was in part because Europe *was* very largely independent economically.

These facts posed two basic choices for American policy-makers. Either they could follow the course of "protectionism" and narrow nationalism, endeavoring to insulate the American economic system from the impact of growing competition abroad. Or they could chart a new course in the direction of liberalized and expanded trade opportunities by endeavoring

to promote the maximum exchange of goods and services throughout the free world. Under Presidents Eisenhower, Kennedy, and Johnson, a number of advisers and influential public groups vigorously advocated the former course. According to this point of view, America's economic welfare would be promoted to the extent that communities experiencing unemployment, and segments of American industry damaged by imports, were shielded by high tariffs or various other devices designed to protect the American economic system from "unfair" foreign competition.*

As with the Eisenhower Administration before it, the Kennedy Administration decided against this policy. In its view, the national interest would be far better served by vigorous and imaginative policies seeking to *expand* global trade—even if this meant, as it inevitably did mean, significant reductions in American trade barriers. A policy of active (or threatened) trade "retaliation" against other countries was rejected as not only incompatible with the philosophy of reciprocal trade, with which the United States had long been identified, but also as contradictory to the ideals the United States advocated vis-à-vis the Communist bloc, and as antithetical to the spirit of regional economic "cooperation" the United States had urged upon Western European nations throughout the postwar era. If for no other reason, a policy of economic provincialism was inadvisable because it simply would not work. For the first time in many years, EEC nations were in a position to retaliate effectively against American goods and services. If they did so—if the Common Market, so to speak, "turned inward" and pursued discriminatory trade policies toward nonmembers, including the United States—this course could jeopardize American economic well-being perhaps even more crucially than a rising level of imports into the United States. Thus one economist estimated that, without tariff accommodations with the Common Market, the United States stood to lose about $2 billion in trade with Europe—at the very time increased exports were needed to cut down the outflow of American gold reserves.

Similarly, about one-fourth of all American agricultural exports (valued at some $1 billion

* For a discussion of the Eisenhower Administration's relatively successful battle against "protectionist" forces at the end of the 1950s, see Sherman Adams, *First-Hand Report: The Story of the Eisenhower Administration* (New York: Harper & Row, 1961), pp. 381–395.

annually) went to countries belonging to EEC. Restrictive policies against American agricultural commodities by members of EEC could thus seriously menace the prosperity of American farmers.[15] The over-all conclusion emerging from these data, in the words of a writer for the *Wall Street Journal*, was that "it would be folly to suppose that other nations will lower their tariff barriers against American goods while the U.S. is putting fresh obstacles in the way of imports."[16]

Many of these same considerations applied to economic relations between the United States and other trading nations such as Japan, Canada, and Latin American states. While these countries did not perhaps possess the actual or potential economic power represented by EEC, America's own internal and external interests dictated basically the same course: expanded opportunities for the exchange of goods and services. Executive officials in the United States were fully mindful that the military and diplomatic positions of the free world demanded a continuation of unimpeded economic growth, particularly with countries like Japan that depended heavily upon trade to maintain domestic prosperity and employment.

The approach of the United States to tariff and trade questions in the 1960s was also compelled to take account of the demands, expressed with growing regularity and intensity, of the economically underdeveloped countries, many of which occupied diplomatically non-aligned positions. Industrialized Western countries found themselves sometimes severely criticized for following restrictive trade policies that were injurious to the often fragile economies prevailing in developing societies. In their quest for modernization, nations throughout the Southern Hemisphere required new trade vistas, stable prices for commodity exports (particularly for primary raw materials and agricultural goods), and Western policies that encouraged, rather than inhibited, the maximum exchange of goods and services. Communist propaganda organs exploited existing apprehensions about restrictive Western trade policies.[17] Aside from posing difficult obstacles to the economic development of such countries, narrowly nationalistic trade policies by Western nations would almost certainly drive many of these countries to closer economic dependence upon the Communist bloc.

America's own balance-of-payments problem also dictated a new course in trade policy. Since 1950 the United States had incurred a drain upon its gold reserves, stemming from an excess of liabilities over credits in its international financial transactions. By the early 1960s, as we shall see, the gold loss had been slowed down. Yet it also seemed clear that radically different approaches were required to solve the balance-of-payments problem throughout the years ahead. For reasons that we shall examine later, the Kennedy and Johnson Administrations decided to depend chiefly upon expanded exports to check the gold loss. Implementation of this policy in turn necessitated new departures in tariff and trade relations with other countries.

Still another factor inducing policy-makers in the early 1960s to formulate a new set of guiding principles for American trade relations was highlighted by two events occurring within a few months of each other at the end of 1963. The Soviet Union announced the extension of a credit totaling almost $100 million to the Republic of Algeria to promote its economic advancement. In the same period, Premier Chou En-lai of Red China toured the Arab world. In Morocco he emphasized his desire to expand Moroccan-Chinese trade relations.[18] Loans offered by Communist countries —featuring low interest rates, long repayment periods, and low collateral requirements —proved extremely attractive to countries that were often unable to raise their capital requirements in the West or from multinational and international institutions. Another hallmark of the Communist approach was willingness to purchase, or accept as payment, commodities produced by underdeveloped nations—like Egyptian cotton, Burmese rice, or Ceylonese rubber—which the United States and its allies either did not want at all or were willing to purchase on terms that were unfavorable to the sellers. Growing reliance upon economic instruments of diplomacy by Communist regimes raised the question of whether the United States and its Western partners were willing to "compete" with Moscow and Peiping in responding to the needs of developing societies.[19]

The Trade Expansion Act of 1962

These were the principal factors inducing the Kennedy Administration to sponsor a new tariff measure, called the Trade Expansion Act of 1962. TEA preserved the earlier idea of reciprocal tariff reductions, but it also added new features not found in former trade legislation. Significant features of this new bill were: (1) authority granted to the President to reduce tariff rates on a reciprocal basis by 10 percent annually, or a total of 50 percent over the five-year life of the bill; (2) authority to the President to eliminate tariffs altogether over a five-year period on products in which the United States and Common Market countries collectively account for more than 80 percent of global trade;* (3) authority for American negotiators to secure reciprocal tariff agreements on broad *categories* of products (like motor vehicles or rubber products) instead of having to secure agreements on hundreds or thousands of individual items that might be traded between the United States and other countries; (4) a "trade adjustment" plan involving an expanded variety of governmental programs to assist American industries hard-hit by foreign competition; (5) retention (in modified form) of protectionist features like the "peril point" and "escape clause" provisions that would afford tariff relief to industries seriously injured by foreign competition.[20]

Certain other steps were crucial in gaining legislative support for the new trade bill. These included American efforts to negotiate agreement among cotton-exporting nations to limit their exports to the United States *voluntarily*, to forestall domestic demands that tariff rates be raised to protect American cotton growers. Textile manufacturers in the United States were reassured by two steps designed to cushion the impact of imports on this long-depressed industry. As with cotton imports, agreements were secured with textile-exporting nations (notably, Japan) to limit their shipments to the United States; and liberal tax credits were granted firms in this industry for plant modernization, thereby enhancing the competitive position of American producers in the world market. Another category of industries deemed vital to American security—such as producers of oil, lead, zinc, and other minerals—was accorded protection by a stipulation in TEA that barred tariff cuts on imports, when a danger existed that defense industries in the United States might be damaged by tariff reductions. Besides raw materials industries, this prohibition also afforded some protection to a wide variety of domestic producers, from dried figs to fur-felt hats, and from sheet glass to umbrella frames. Moreover, one of the most politically influential groups in the United

States, the farm lobby, was conciliated by provisions of TEA prohibiting tariff cuts for the products of any country that discriminated against the importation of American agricultural products. In spite of these and other concessions to "protectionist" demands, the Trade Expansion Act of 1962 substantially fulfilled President Kennedy's conception of a "bold new instrument" for achieving American goals in international economic affairs.[21]

Armed with unprecedented negotiating powers to arrive at trade agreements with other countries, American policy-makers in the mid-1960s sought to open new trade vistas, while at the same time inflicting minimum damage upon domestic producers. The radically changed environment within which they were required to negotiate was illustrated graphically by the "chicken war" between the United States and the members of the European Common Market late in 1963, involving a mere $50 million in American poultry exports to Europe, out of a total of $1.25 billion in agricultural exports to that region. Unable to secure EEC acceptance of low tariff rates on American poultry products, the United States for a time threatened to retaliate against a wide assortment of European exports to the United States. Yet the "chicken war" was symptomatic of a larger problem that would confront American policy-makers throughout the months and years ahead: gaining acceptance among nations in the free world of agreements covering the exchange of agricultural commodities generally. Almost without exception, every nation "protected" agriculture by various devices that shielded farmers from the vicissitudes of a free market in agricultural products. Moreover, throughout the free world, agricultural production was expanding. As the *Times* of London said about farm production in the EEC area: "What agricultural efficiency has achieved in North America in the past decade —far too much grain and other agricultural products—a similar European efficiency is bound to produce in the next decade."[22] This meant that hard bargaining, inevitably requiring as many concessions from America as America expected from Europe, would be required in the years ahead to arrive at trade agreements permitting a maximum exchange of goods and services throughout the free world.

The Trade Expansion Act of 1962 stands as a fascinating and instructive case study in the formulation of national policy, illustrating

* The effect of this provision was largely nullified by French President de Gaulle's veto of British membership in the Common Market.

many recent and powerful techniques of presidential leadership. Particularly noteworthy was the Kennedy Administration's success in undertaking an "educational campaign" designed to acquaint the American people and their representatives in Congress about the extent of American involvement in world trade, the importance of expanding trade for continued American prosperity, and the key role played in this process by *exports*. An outstanding feature of this successful campaign was the alliance forged between executive officials and certain influential pressure groups (such as the Committee for a National Trade Policy and the AFL-CIO) to generate public and legislative support for the new trade bill. Individual legislators, for example, were furnished evidence of the extent to which the prosperity of their districts was linked to sales in foreign markets and the degree to which their districts would suffer economically if American exports were contracted. Legislators representing constituencies peculiarly vulnerable to imports, on the other hand, were promised a variety of measures for cushioning the impact of foreign competition; as we have seen, many of these measures were ultimately embodied in the Trade Expansion Act. All in all, the Kennedy Administration's victory on TEA—in the face of widespread predictions of failure, based upon still-intense "protectionist" sentiment throughout many sections of the United States—represented skillful utilization of a great variety of techniques available to executive policy-makers for marshaling public and legislative support for needed programs in foreign affairs.*

* The Kennedy Administration's campaign to secure legislative adoption of TEA is described at length in: *Congressional Quarterly Almanac: 1962*, **18**, 249–295; *The New York Times*, January 28, February 4, and September 23, 1962.
    One key to the administration's success, in spite of early predictions of failure, in overcoming protectionist opposition to trade liberalization lies in the changing character of American industry itself. By the early 1960s, approximately 70 percent of the largest 1000 American corporations had established foreign branches, giving them a stake in the maintenance of unimpeded trade they did not possess before. Moreover, many American corporations had increasingly come to see that rising imports *per se* were not necessarily detrimental to American prosperity. Thus the Detroit Chamber of Commerce continued to endorse liberalized trade, even in the face of steadily rising foreign automobile imports; American automobile producers were themselves selling more products than ever before. Louis Banks, "What Kennedy's Free-Trade Program Means to Business," *Fortune*, **66** (March, 1962), p. 214.

"Protectionism" Versus Free Trade— The Continuing Debate

Although the Trade Expansion Act of 1962 determined the scope of presidential negotiating power in tariff issues until 1967, the conflict between "protectionists" and advocates of free trade has endured throughout American history. There is no reason to suppose that the controversy will not recur throughout the years ahead. Before a new trade bill is debated in 1967, it is safe to predict, each side will make an intensive effort to rally support for its point of view and to have it incorporated into law. A knowledge of the essential issues in the debate therefore remains indispensable for any intelligent understanding of international economic policy.

In the contemporary period, as in years past, advocates of protectionism are convinced that presidential freedom to negotiate sweeping tariff reductions endangers economic prosperity at home. Pointing to high levels of domestic unemployment in the textile, watch, toy, ceramics, or other industries damaged by imports, the protectionist contends that American industry—required to pay the highest wage levels in the world—cannot successfully compete with "unfair" foreign competition, when workers in other countries are paid a fraction of what the American worker earns. Frequently, local labor unions, whose officers and members are deeply disturbed about rising unemployment, join with spokesmen for industry in demanding higher tariff rates. Even on diplomatic grounds, the protectionist argument contends that the United States cannot provide the mainstay of free world defense against Communist encroachments unless it successfully maintains its own economic and political stability. In brief, protectionism rests upon the premise that the first consideration in formulating national tariff and trade policy must be the economic well-being of the American society. Practically, this belief is translated into intense pressure upon Congress and executive officials to raise (or, at a minimum, to maintain) tariff rates against a rising volume of imports.

Proponents of free (or freer) trade, on the other hand, base their case ultimately upon the basic economic principle that unencumbered trade—promoting the maximum exchange of goods and services among nations—is ultimately the most beneficial course available to the

United States and to all other nations. This conclusion is derived from the concept of "comparative advantage," according to which each society specializes in the production of those goods and services it can make most cheaply, and exchanges these for needed goods and services other societies can produce more cheaply. Exchange on this basis is most profitable for all countries concerned. Even if it were possible (and of course it is not) for a country to produce *every* commodity more cheaply than other countries, trade would still be profitable; for this country would then concentrate upon the production of goods and services in which its productive advantages were greatest, and it would trade for goods and services in which its comparative advantages were relatively less.

Moreover, the advocate of liberalized trade is aware of a reality frequently omitted from the arguments of protectionists: no nation can *export* in the world market (which even protectionists continue to advocate) without being willing to *import* from other countries. A conception of trade that visualizes unimpaired, not to mention expanded, exports without correspondingly expanded imports is the economic equivalent of trying to square the circle. It follows also that any significant *contraction* in imports sooner or later brings a corresponding contraction in exports, as foreign countries are denied the ability to acquire dollars for the purchase of American goods and services. Consequently, the advocate of free trade believes, in lieu of higher American tariff barriers, continued American prosperity demands an expansion in both imports and exports. When tariff rates are raised to "protect" some segment of domestic industry, in effect such protection is afforded at the expense of another segment of industry engaged in selling abroad. The relevant inquiry thus becomes: *Which* segment of American industry ought to be "protected" and encouraged by governmental policy—that segment that cannot compete abroad, or that segment which is successfully maintaining its position in the world market, as measured by an expanding level of foreign sales?

In spite of the fact that the arguments in favor of unhampered global trade seem, on balance, compelling, tariff reductions (particularly *sudden* tariff reductions) unquestionably create or compound problems faced by American producers having foreign competition. For thousands of American workers, managers,

and investors involved in industries producing textiles, toys, electronic components, pottery, and a variety of other goods, rising unemployment and shrinking domestic markets pose real hardships, which no amount of argument about the over-all benefit accruing to the nation from expanded trade can mitigate. Moreover, it is incontestably true that the defense requirements of the United States demand that manufacturers of steel, watches, optical equipment and other strategic materials maintain their ability to produce such commodities on short notice. In the event of general war, for example, it would be prudent to assume that the formidable Soviet submarine fleet would deny the United States access to many of its customary sources of supply overseas. Moreover, it would be equally realistic to suppose that much of Europe's industrial complex would be rendered inoperative, or otherwise unavailable, for the defense of the non-Communist world.

Such considerations, however, do not necessarily argue in favor of high tariffs to afford the protection needed for selected segments of American industry. As the Trade Expansion Act of 1962 recognizes, numerous other—and in many cases, much more effective—measures are available for this purpose, including: a continuing program of government "stockpiling" to assure that an adequate supply of defense commodities and goods are available; governmentally assisted programs of industrial modernization to enable domestic manufacturers to improve their competitive positions; local, state, and federal activities, coupled with massive private efforts, to promote economic diversification, market analysis, research and development and other steps for industries vulnerable to competition from abroad; retraining and industrial relocation programs for industries injured by imports; tax credits and other devices to permit American producers to improve their competitive position; governmental and private activities designed to increase exports, thereby giving employment to workers displaced in industries injured by foreign competition; perhaps, in selected cases, outright governmental subsidy to certain industries that cannot compete with foreign producers under any circumstances. These steps, singly or in combination, would go much further than higher tariff rates to get at the root of the difficulty faced by American producers in an increasingly interdependent global order.

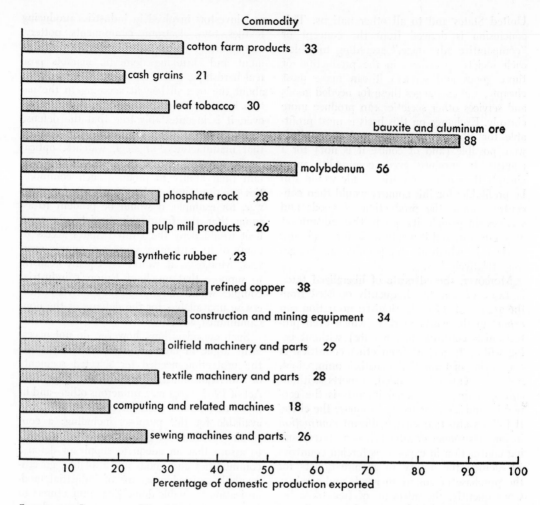

Exports as a Percentage of Total Domestic Production, 1961. (Source: *Statistical Abstract of the United States, 1963, p. 873.*)

The Problem of East-West Trade

In his 1964 New Year's message to the American people, Soviet Premier Khrushchev renewed a plea he had made many times earlier. Lamenting the fact that "there has been practically no trade between our countries for a great many years," Khrushchev believed "the cause of peace and relationships between our two countries do suffer because the absence of trade creates an abnormal situation. . . ."[23] The Soviet leader's plea fell on receptive ears in Washington and in certain American business circles. A few months earlier, a White House conference of businessmen urged executive policy-makers to re-examine national policy on trade with the Communist bloc. Citing "changed world conditions," business spokesmen lamented the fact that the United States share of some $5 billion in Western sales behind the Iron Curtain amounted to a mere $200 million annually.[24] A degree of thawing on the trade front of the cold war was symbolized by the negotiation late in 1963 and early 1964 of a Soviet-American wheat sale, initially involving some four million tons of American wheat valued at $250 million, exclusive of shipping charges.[25]

These events signified a fundamental modification in long-standing American policy toward East-West trade. Throughout most of the postwar period the United States had virtually imposed a trade embargo on its own economic relations with the communist bloc and had encouraged its allies and other nations in the free world to do the same. Following the Greek crisis of 1947, the United States instituted a series of measures designed to prohibit outright, or severely restrict, East-West trade.

The "Battle Act" (officially called the Mutual Defense Assistance Control Act of 1951, enacted after the Korean War erupted), required the imposition of an embargo on American trade in strategic or semistrategic goods with Communist countries, although limited trade was permitted in nonstrategic goods. The act required the termination of American foreign assistance to any countries maintaining trade that contravened Battle Act provisions, unless the President felt that an "exception" to the prohibition promoted America's own interests.* American efforts to inhibit East-West trade were especially stringent with respect to Red China. After Chinese entry into the

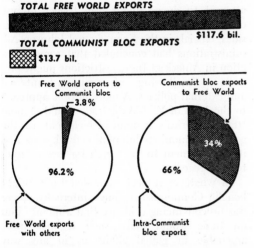

East and West Trade Compared. (Source: The New York Times, March 1, 1964. © 1964 by The New York Times Company. Reprinted by permission.)

* In the administration of the Battle Act, despite considerable pressure from Congress to the contrary, "exceptions" have been the rule. Executive officials have been amply aware, if legislators have not, that a cessation of American assistance to such countries as Yugoslavia, Ghana, Egypt, Iraq, or Indonesia would most likely serve Communist interests more than American interests. National leaders in such countries are determined to trade somewhere. If avenues for trade in the West are blocked, they will turn to the East to meet their economic needs, even though many such countries would prefer cordial relations with the West or would, at a minimum, like to "balance" their economic relations between East and West. What possible advantage would thus accrue to the United States from compelling developing countries to rely exclusively upon the Communist bloc? Executive officials have also been mindful that some countries, like Guinea, have developed close ties with the West, after an initial period of heavy economic reliance on the Communist bloc.

Korean War, Washington embargoed all American trade with China; American leadership was instrumental in successfully sponsoring a UN General Assembly resolution in 1951 calling for a general embargo on trade bound for Red China and North Korea.[26]

Periodically, the issue of East-West trade has fomented sharp controversies within the Western alliance. From the beginning, America's principal allies have not shared Washington's enthusiasm for a trade embargo as an instrument of cold-war diplomacy, nor have they accepted the underlying rationale supporting the State Department's policies. Increasingly, the United States has found itself compelled to make concessions to the viewpoints of its allies and friends in the international community, if in no other respect than acquiescing in a growing volume of trade between the Communist world and other free-world countries. By the mid-1960s differences on this issue came into sharp focus over the question of granting long-term credits to Moscow and Peiping for the purchase of agricultural commodities and other imports from the West. The United States was willing neither to grant such credits itself, nor did it favor generous credits by its cold-war allies. Yet by 1964, France was but the most recent country to offer Moscow liberal trade terms to enable the Kremlin to expand its purchases in the West. A majority of Western countries was prepared, in the face of evident American displeasure, to grant the USSR up to five years in which to make payment and to impose no limit on the total amount of credit which the Kremlin might obtain from Western sources.[27]

This was merely one development highlighting the fact that, by the mid-1960s, the United States was virtually the *only* nation in the free world advocating stringent limitations upon East-West trade. For the allies, the issue was relatively simple and clear-cut. Their own national interests demanded extensive and expanding trade across the Iron Curtain; without it, their economic progress would be hampered and their ability to contribute to free world security severely jeopardized. A widespread conviction prevailed among official and unofficial circles in the United States that East-West trade inherently benefited the Communist world more than it benefited the West. The rationale behind the American embargo policy was that trade in a wide variety of strategic goods enhanced Communist military potential and enabled Soviet Russia and Red China to secure Western assistance in solving many internal problems (like the chronic agricultural shortages in Russia and China) that otherwise would serve to check Communist-instigated foreign adventures.

The Allies, on the other hand, tended to cite an elementary economic principle: when trade is *voluntarily* conducted, it occurs only when each party believes it to be advantageous. It follows that East-West trade is equally beneficial to Western or free-world countries, in enabling them to maintain a high standard of living, full production and employment, and a strong defense position. The Allies concede that, by securing needed goods and commodities in the West, Communist nations were to some degree enhancing their economic and military positions. Almost every article of trade in the mid-twentieth century had some military or defense application. By the same token, the *absence* of expanding trade opportunities had no less vital defense implications for the free world. For an economic contraction in a country such as Britain, France, Ghana, or India could both trigger dislocations that created a conducive atmosphere for communist intrigue and expansionism, and ultimately bring about a weakening in the military strength of non-Communist countries.

These considerations were exemplified in the dilemma that increasingly confronted Japan, perhaps America's strongest and most reliable ally in Asia. For many years, with strong American encouragement, Japanese officials had successfully resisted growing pressures to expand trade with the country's traditional customer, mainland China. By the 1960s, Japan found itself in a frustrating economic "squeeze." On the one hand, to maintain domestic prosperity, it required a steadily mounting volume of trade. On the other hand, it experienced mounting resistance to Japanese imports on the part of its best customer, the United States, and encountered new barriers to Japanese trade among the members of the European Common Market.* Equally diffi-

cult obstacles often beset Japan's effort to build up trade with developing nations.[28]

Japan's dilemma posed hard choices for American policy-makers. For Japan, as for most of the other Allies in greater or lesser degree, trade was a vital necessity. American policy-makers confronted the question: Was the United States willing to expand imports appreciably—in the midst of its own balance-of-payments crisis—in order to provide its allies with an alternative to trade with the East? Obviously, the answer in most cases was no. In dealing with Japan's difficulty, and the cases of other countries comparably situated, the United States was not inclined, nor did it have the power if it were, to impose a tight trade embargo on East-West trade. Even an attempt to do so might well trigger intense controversies within the Western alliance. Besides, officials in the Kennedy and Johnson Administrations had concluded that some relaxation in American trade restrictions might promote a "mellowing" of communist internal and external policies. A more flexible approach to the issue of East-West trade would demonstrate America's genuine attachment to the goal of harmonious international relations and its commitment to the search for new avenues toward peace.

In whatever respect expanded trade might benefit Communist regimes internally, there was no convincing evidence that a moratorium on trade would make such regimes more amenable in global affairs or in any way mitigate the harsh features of communist totalitarianism. Still another hope was that liberalized trade with the Communist satellites in Eastern Europe, such as Poland and possibly Hungary, might well encourage growing polycentricity within the Communist bloc and induce greater "independence" in policy formulation within societies that had demonstrated a desire to loosen Moscow's grip upon their affairs. For these reasons, in the Foreign Aid Act of 1964, Congress, after lengthy and often acrimonious debate, granted the White House new authority to negotiate trade agreements with Communist nations whenever the President believed such agreements promoted American diplomatic objectives.[29]

---

* For a number of years, Japanese exporters have accepted "voluntary" quotas on shipments to the United States. About 30 percent of all Japanese exports were sold in American markets. By 1964, press reports indicated rising Japanese resentment against the prospect "of an American tariff raise." Japanese business groups were distressed that a new three-year trade agreement with the United States, negotiated in 1963, permitted only a slight expansion in Japanese exports to America. With only 4 percent of its total trade carried on with the

Communist bloc, Japanese groups were exerting intense pressure upon the government to pursue a more "independent" trade policy, particularly in relations with Communist countries. *The New York Times,* January 13, 1964.

Promoting "Liquidity" in World Trade

In a manner roughly comparable to private business firms, nations must maintain a fund of "reserves" or operating capital to finance current international trade transactions. The sale of exports adds to the fund; the purchase of imports depletes it. When adverse economic or political conditions in the outside world compel reductions in a country's exports, while imports remain stable or perhaps even increase, then that country will be required to draw upon its reserves to pay for purchases abroad. The extent to which its reserves are adequate to pay for necessary imports determines a country's "liquidity" in international trade and commerce. If its imports and reserves both equaled X amount of currency units, then the country would be 100 percent "liquid"; if its imports were valued at X currency units and its reserves at one-half X, then it would be only 50 percent liquid.

The problem of maintaining adequate liquidity in the face of a rising volume of world trade, in an environment of rising prices and depleted reserves, had become a critical issue in international economic relations by the end of the 1950s. By that period, the gap between global imports and global reserves was widening. Collectively, the trading nations of the world were only 50 percent liquid in their international transaction.[30]

This problem assumed more important dimensions than ever for the United States. Two facts dictated this result: the continuing deficit in the American trade balance and the long-accepted position of the dollar (along with the British pound sterling) as one of the two "reserve currencies" in world trade, meaning that dollar reserves could be converted into gold by countries holding them. America's own trade deficit added to the pressure on available reserves, thereby decreasing global liquidity; growing dollar reserves by other countries, coupled with the decline in American gold stocks, at least raised the question of how long the dollar could serve as a "reserve currency." If no genuine apprehension existed about the future soundness of the dollar, or about the risk that a sudden "run" on available reserves by countries holding dollars would precipitate a global depression, these possibilities at least had to be considered by the leading trading nations of the world. Obviously, the problem of assuring the necessary degree of liquidity in world trade was intimately related to the problem of trying to close the gap in America's balance of international payments. In addition, the United States and other industrialized countries were seeking to strengthen the International Monetary Fund, an institution set up after World War II to facilitate international commercial transactions. By the mid-1960s, negotiations were proceeding to give IMF larger resources and to attack the liquidity problem in other ways.[31]

THE FUTURE OF FOREIGN AID

By fiscal year 1964, the United States had extended over $100 billion in foreign assistance to foreign countries since the end of World War II.[32] Earlier chapters dealing with Western Europe, the Middle East and Africa, Latin America, and Asia have focused upon American postwar foreign assistance programs as they related specifically to these areas. In this chapter our interest centers upon *over-all* aspects and implications of foreign aid. What have been the extent, nature, and changing emphases in the program? How does foreign aid affect the American domestic economy? What have been significant strengths and weaknesses in the foreign aid program? What is the future of foreign aid, as an instrument of American foreign policy? These are some of the dominant questions which must be discussed if our treatment of the foreign aid problem is to be complete.

Scope and Nature of U.S. Aid

Extensive foreign assistance is no new phenomenon in American history. In the post-World War I period the United States advanced nearly $10 billion in loans to some 20 countries. Most of these loans were never repaid. Negotiated agreements between America and its debtors, coupled with the Hoover debt moratorium during the Great Depression, turned most of these loans into outright grants.

Huge sums were advanced by the United States to its allies during World War II and to deal with severe crises in the immediate postwar period. The Greek-Turkish Aid Program and the Marshall Plan inaugurated continuing programs of economic and military assistance. These programs differed somewhat from later foreign aid ventures, however, in that they were designed to deal with a specific, relatively short-lived crisis. Continuing *military* assistance to other governments began with the Mutual Defense Assistance Program to bolster the defense of Western Europe, following ratification of the North Atlantic Treaty in 1949. Global *economic and technical* assistance programs evolved out of President Truman's "Point Four" program of aid to underdeveloped countries in 1949.

From the mid-1950s to the mid-1960s, the largest beneficiary of American military and economic assistance combined has been the Far East, which received almost $17 billion in aid; next came Western Europe and the Near East-South Asia, each of which received approximately $16 billion; Latin America received over $8 billion; Africa got some $2.3 billion; and other countries, over $2 billion.[33]

Several significant trends in the formulation and administration of American assistance programs have proved noteworthy. A fundamental one has been the evolution from primary reliance upon *economic* assistance (from 1948 to 1952), to primary reliance upon *military* assistance (from 1952 to 1959), to establishment of a rough equilibrium between these two categories or aid (in the early 1960s). From 1948 to 1952, the Marshall Plan for the reconstruction of war-devastated Europe was the principal channel of American foreign assistance. With the outbreak of the Korean War in 1951, the emphasis changed radically to the extension of military aid to countries threatened by communist expansionism—a tendency that reached its peak in 1953, when military aid was more than double economic aid. Thereafter, as a truce was achieved in Korea, and as the Khrushchev era of "peaceful coexistence" witnessed a relaxation of international tensions, American military assistance declined, to reach about $1.5 billion annually in the early 1960s. After reaching its lowest point in the postwar era in 1954 ($1.4 billion), economic and technical assistance assumed a growing percentage of the foreign aid budget, averaging between $1.5 and $1.8 billion by the early 1960s.[34]

Second, the shift in the geographic direction of American aid has been pronounced. Down to the mid-1950s, the preponderance of American military and economic assistance went to Western Europe, as the twofold realization prevailed that American diplomatic interests demanded the economic reconstruction of this vital region, along with measures to enhance its defenses against a possible communist military thrust across the Iron Curtain. After 1955 (when aid to Europe totaled just over half of the annual foreign aid budget of nearly $5 billion), over-all assistance to Europe

declined, totaling less than $500 million annually by 1963. By this date, economic assistance to Western European countries had all but ceased.

From the middle of the 1950s to the opening of the 1960s, a proportionately larger share of American foreign assistance was directed to the Far East, South Asia, the Middle East, Africa, and Latin America. Most countries in these regions of course were classified as "underdeveloped" economically; some—like Turkey, Iran, Pakistan, Thailand, and Taiwan (the Republic of China on Formosa)—were actual or potential cold-war trouble spots, necessitating large military outlays for free world defense. After 1956, the relative share these countries received from American foreign assistance programs grew steadily; by 1961, nearly all American economic and military assistance combined went to countries in these regions.

The place of Africa in American assistance programs deserves special mention. In contrast to other economically backward regions, Africa has always received, and continues to receive, a relatively insignificant share of American foreign aid. From 1945 to 1962, Africa received a total of $1.8 billion in American foreign aid. During 1962, for example, the United States granted the whole of Africa a total of $350 million in foreign aid, divided into $315 million for economic aid and $35 million for military aid. Thus, American assistance to the African continent was less than that provided for Pakistan alone and approximately equal to the aid granted to Turkey or to the Republic of South Korea. This apparent "neglect" of Africa, as American officials have repeatedly emphasized, implies no lack of concern about developments on this continent or indifference toward the monumental problems confronting newly independent nations in this area as they push forward in their quest for economic modernization. The basic explanation is that the United States has left the provision of massive quantities of aid to African nations to former colonial countries, its increasingly prosperous NATO allies. As we shall see, despite a widespread lack of understanding in the United States, countries like Britain, France, and West Germany have responded massively to African needs.

Another significant trend in American foreign aid programs has been the shift from outright "grants" to "loans" as the basic element in assistance provided to other coun-

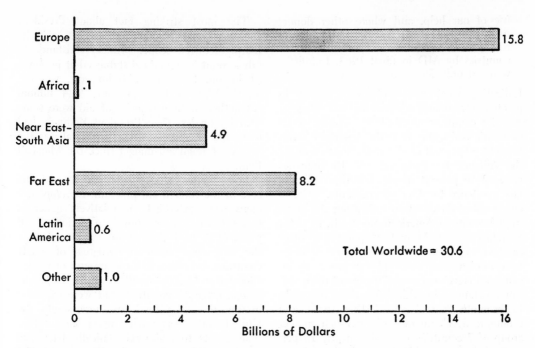

Europe — 15.8

Africa — .1

Near East–South Asia — 4.9

Far East — 8.2

Latin America — 0.6

Other — 1.0

Total Worldwide = 30.6

0   2   4   6   8   10   12   14   16
Billions of Dollars

United States Military Programs, 1950–1963. (Source: Adapted from the U.S. Department of State, *Mutual Security Program, 1959;* 1963 figures from *Statistical Abstract of the United States, 1963,* p. 259.)

tries. During the era of the Marshall Plan (1948–1952), some 90 percent of all American aid consisted of grants to other governments; by 1964, 60 percent of all aid consisted of loans, often made on a long-term basis, at low interest rates.[35]

A more recent tendency has been the trend toward greater selectivity in the provision of American foreign assistance. In the face of mounting legislative criticism of the foreign aid program—engendered in part by critical novels such as *The Ugly American* and studies like the Clay Report in 1963, that urged greater discrimination in the administration of aid funds—executive officials have carried out repeated organizational reforms and reformulations of the principles that ought to guide the extension of assistance to other governments.* By 1963, five major working concepts guided the Agency for International Development in its provision and supervision of economic and technical assistance:

* The organizational structure for the administration of foreign aid programs was discussed in Chapter 3. The latest organizational change was the establishment of the Agency for International Development in 1961. This agency was given responsibility for administering economic assistance and for coordinating the administration of military assistance by the Pentagon.

1. Long-range development assistance, on the basis of soundly conceived plans, was extended to underdeveloped countries to encourage their progress toward self-sustaining economic growth.

2. American assistance was deemed to be successful "in relation to the ability and willingness of developing countries to help themselves."

3. Aid programs were tailored to the needs of, and conditions prevailing within, particular countries.

4. Loans on reasonable terms were favored over grants, and repayment in dollars rather than local currencies was postulated as a goal.

5. Since promotion of economic progress in the underdeveloped world was viewed as a "collective responsibility" of nations within the free world, the United States sought expanded participation in foreign aid programs by the cold-war allies.[36]

The keynote of the American philosophy of foreign aid by the early 1960s was expressed by David E. Bell, Administrator of AID, who said that his agency was following a policy of "careful selectivity" in making aid allocations.

We are stressing aid to those countries where the U.S. interest is most urgent, which are in a position to make the best use of our help, and where other donors cannot supply all the aid needed. As a result, of the $2.2 billion committed to 82 countries by AID in fiscal 1963, four-fifths went to only 20 countries.[37]

Indicating what this philosophy meant in practice were figures released in 1963, showing that 20 countries received 80 percent of all economic assistance; 6 Latin American states received 80 percent of all funds allocated under the Alliance for Progress; and 10 countries received 80 percent of all allocations of military assistance to other governments.[38] Or, to cite another classification indicating the growing selectivity of American aid funds, in 1963, Secretary of State Dean Rusk pointed to three categories of countries benefitting from American foreign assistance: (1) a group of 30 countries (receiving some 70 percent of American assistance) in which American aid seeks to promote "sound and lasting social and economic development"; (2) a much smaller group of 7 countries (receiving nearly 19 percent of American aid) in which the primary goal is promotion of internal and external security; and (3) a final category of 40 nations (receiving approximately 11 percent of American aid funds) in which assistance by the United States is very limited.

Many of these trends and guiding principles were highlighted by the foreign aid budget submitted to Congress by President Johnson for fiscal year 1965. The following chart presents basic data about foreign aid for that year and for the two preceding years.

TABLE 6.   American Expenditures for Foreign Aid
millions of dollars

	1963 (actual)	1964 (est.)	1965 (est.)
Military assistance	$1,500	$1,100	$1,100
Economic and Financial programs			
Development loans	760	790	850
Development grants	245	230	225
Alliance for Progress	260	325	405
Supporting assistance	494	415	335
Contingencies and other	284	340	335
Subtotal	3,543	3,200	3,250
International financial institutions	122	112	62
Peace Corps	42	73	90
Food for Peace program	216	246	244

SOURCE: Adapted from the text of President Johnson's Message to Congress, as reprinted in *The New York Times*, January 22, 1964.

The most striking fact about President Johnson's first foreign aid budget was its sharply reduced scope. Military assistance to other countries remained stabilized at just over $1 billion. Economic aid, however, was cut drastically to a total of some $2.4 billion. Altogether, both categories of aid were some $1.5 billion less than President Kennedy had requested the previous year; the total was the smallest foreign aid budget since the Marshall Plan.

Four major categories of aid formed the core of the foreign aid program. *Development loans* were extended on relatively generous terms (with a maximum loan period of 40 years, at ¾ of 1 percent interest) to finance the long-range economic progress of needy countries. Less than half the amount of money allocated in loans was available in *development grants*, given to countries that were expected in time to qualify for loans. Increasingly, the United States was relying upon loans rather than grants to assist economically backward countries. The *Alliance for Progress* for the American republics constituted a third major category of foreign assistance.* Finally, *supporting assistance* was provided to enable especially vulnerable countries along the rim of the free-world defense perimeter to maintain the burden of a disproportionate defense effort. Again, recipients of supporting assistance were being encouraged to turn from American grants to loans to meet their needs.[39]

Beginning with fiscal year 1965, military aid was allocated to the Defense Department budget. A total of $1.1 billion was utilized to bolster the defense of over 60 cold-war allies and other countries within the free world. Military aid to the Western European allies had all but ceased. By 1965, nine countries—Greece, Turkey, Iran, India, Pakistan, Thailand, Vietnam, the Republic of China (Taiwan), and the Republic of South Korea—received 70 per cent of all military assistance from the United States.[40]

The Food for Peace Program

In spite of acreage limitations, a declining farm population, a lowering of man-hours devoted to farming, and other inhibiting influences, almost every year American agricultural productivity has surged to a record high. For the year 1963, for example, agricultural production was 12 percent above the

* The origins and guiding principles of the Alliance for Progress are dealt with in Chapter 12.

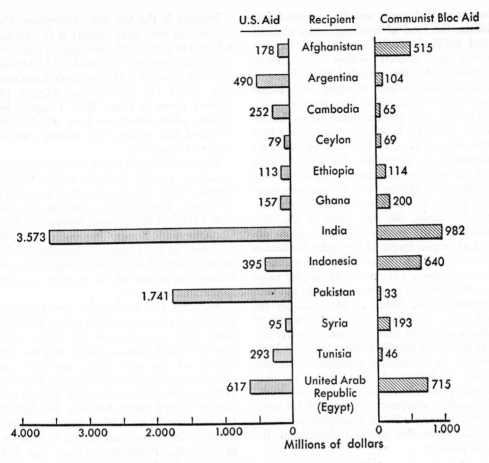

U.S. Aid	Recipient	Communist Bloc Aid
178	Afghanistan	515
490	Argentina	104
252	Cambodia	65
79	Ceylon	69
113	Ethiopia	114
157	Ghana	200
3.573	India	982
395	Indonesia	640
1.741	Pakistan	33
95	Syria	193
293	Tunisia	46
617	United Arab Republic (Egypt)	715

4.000   3.000   2.000   1.000   0   0   1.000
Millions of dollars

American and Soviet Aid to Selected Countries, 1954–1963.

1957–1959 average. This has meant that ever since World War II, the United States has experienced steadily mounting agricultural surpluses. The ability of the United States to produce food and other agricultural commodities is, of course, one of the sinews of national power; in time of war, as both World War II and the Korean conflict demonstrated, this productive capacity proved a vital element in free-world defense. In more normal times, however, the Commodity Credit Corporation (the agency charged with storing agricultural surpluses) has found its facilities overflowing and the costs of storing rising agricultural stockpiles moving steadily upward. At the same time, a conviction has come to prevail among executive and legislative officials, joined by many public groups, that America's vast agricultural wealth must be utilized more effectively to meet global needs and to achieve diplomatic purposes.

Yet the ideal has been easier to state than to translate into a successful program. A high official of the Eisenhower Administration stated the dilemma by saying, "We could find no domestic use for the billions of dollars' worth of farm commodities in government warehouse and storage bins, but to dump them on foreign markets would have raised havoc with some of the best friends we had in the world."[41] Apprehensions about proposed American "dumping" prevailed in Canada, Egypt, and other nations depending heavily upon agricultural exports to maintain economic prosperity. Unless carefully formulated, an American program of agricultural disposal might well cancel out the gains made by friendly countries through American foreign assistance programs and other measures designed to engender their economic stability and advancement. With these limitations in mind, the Eisenhower Administration sponsored, and in 1954 Congress enacted, Public Law 480, authorizing the disposal of surplus American agricultural products abroad. Initially, such products could be sold for local currencies that could not be converted into dollars; the fund of local currencies accumulated could, however, be reloaned for economic aid projects within the country concerned. In the period 1954–1958, agricultural goods valued at some $1.5 billion were sent overseas under this program.

In time, this scheme came to be known as the "Food for Peace" program. Under later extensions of PL 480, executive officials were empowered to draw upon the stock of agricultural surpluses to achieve a variety of diplomatic goals. During 1964, for example, some $2.4 billion worth of such commodities were available under the four titles of PL 480, authorizing the executive department to dispose of surplus crops: (1) by sales for foreign currencies, (2) to make emergency grants in other countries, (3) to donate surplus crops to private welfare groups, and (4) to sell such commodities on liberal credit terms. By the mid-1960s, more than $20 billion worth of surplus crops had been disposed of under this law, benefiting over 90 million people.[42] India afforded an outstanding example of the program's usefulness. Surplus American agricultural commodities provided over 60 percent of American assistance to this key Asian country.[43] Executive officials anticipate increasing reliance upon this program throughout the years ahead.[44]

Private Aid Activities

For many years, executive and legislative officials alike have emphasized the role of private capital in contributing to the economic advancement of nations in Latin America, Africa, the Middle East, and Asia. By 1964, Americans held a total of well over $52 billion in overseas investments—an increase of some $20 billion since 1950. This $52 billion total was in turn divided between $37 billion in *direct* investments (outright ownership of business enterprises abroad) and $15 billion in *indirect* investment (portfolios of foreign stocks and bonds).

A breakdown of the geographical distribution of American private investment funds affords interesting insight into the scope of private business activities overseas and lays the groundwork for an understanding of the problems besetting greater dependence upon private sources to supply development capital. This breakdown applies to *direct* investment only. More than half of all private American business holdings overseas (nearly $22 billion)

is invested in the Western Hemisphere. Over half of this total ($12 billion) is in American holdings in Canada; the next largest concentration of holdings is in Venezuela ($2.8 billion). Holdings in other Latin American states range from Brazil ($1 billion) and Mexico ($.9 billion) down to Costa Rica, Uruguay, and Bolivia, where Americans have direct investments of $63 million, $53 million, and $32 million, respectively.

The second-largest regional concentration of American private investments is Western Europe, where American holdings are close to $9 billion. Great Britain accounts for more than a third of this amount, followed by West Germany and France. Especially since the formation of the European Common Market, American firms have sought to expand in what is emerging as one of the greatest consumer markets on the globe.

American private business investments in the southern zone from Morocco to the Philippines total approximately $5 billion, about equally divided between Africa and the Arab region, on the one hand, and Asia and Oceania, on the other. Holdings by Americans in the entire Arab world ($1.2 billion) only slightly exceed their holdings in Australia ($1.1 billion). In Africa, the Republic of South Africa, Libya, and Liberia lead the list; in Asia, the Philippines, Japan, and India have been the largest beneficiaries from American business expansion overseas.[45]

These data suggest some of the hard realities confronting proposals that the United States rely primarily on private sources to assist underdeveloped countries. One of the most striking facts is that the largest *growth* in American foreign investment has come in regions such as Canada (with American investment almost doubling from 1957 to 1963) and Western Europe (with American investments expanding at roughly the same rate in this region). By contrast, in this period American holdings in the Middle East remained relatively stable, while investments in other economically backward regions showed only moderate increases. In other words, American businesses have committed investment capital abroad in those contexts, as one source has put it, "where the chances of gain are maximal and the risks minimal."[46]

Understandably, if regrettably for countries that need such capital, American businessmen have shunned environments where governments are hostile (or thought to be hostile) to private enterprise; where there is a deeply rooted anti-Western, or generally xenophobic, tradition; where there is a threat of expropriation of foreign business concerns or where it may be difficult to repatriate profits; and where American firms face harsh and discriminatory taxation. In brief, American capital has avoided those countries in which the investment climate is unattractive. Yet these tend to be the very countries that *need* massive amounts of outside development and are often unable to raise even a portion of the funds required from other governments or from international sources. Even when American private capital is invested in such countries, the tendency is for it to be centered in extractive and raw materials industries—such as oil in Venezuela and Saudi Arabia, iron and rubber in Liberia, and bauxite in Ghana and Guinea. This fact often encourages political groups within such countries, aided by Communist or other extremist groups outside it, to accuse the United States of "neocolonialist" exploitation of weak countries.

It must not be thought that nongovernmental activities contributing to the economic progress of backward countries are confined merely to business groups. Increasingly, a host of private and nonfederal agencies and groups have become active in this field—like cooperative societies, savings and loan associations, landgrant colleges and universities, labor unions, philanthropic organizations, professional societies, and private citizens. To a greater extent than ever, such groups are establishing contacts overseas and are making available capital and technical know-how to societies that require them.[47]

The Investment Guaranty and Survey Programs

As one means of overcoming many of the impediments to the expansion of American business enterprise abroad, beginning in 1948 successive administrations in Washington have made available a "guaranty program" to protect businessmen from risks in other countries. Upon payment of a premium, businessmen are afforded full or partial compensation for losses growing out of currency inconvertibility, expropriation or confiscation, wars, revolutions, and insurrections in other countries. By the 1960s, the program offered all-inclusive, "extended" protection against *any* loss, other than normally insurable risks, up to 75 percent of the value of the investment. Under this option, no single business investment could be

protected for more than $10 million. This approach was being utilized particularly to encourage the investment of American funds in housing projects in Latin America. That investment guaranty fulfilled a basic need in enabling many countries to attract outside capital was indicated by the extent to which applications to AID (the administering agency) had grown throughout the late 1950s and the 1960s.

For several years after its inception, many foreign countries were apprehensive about certain features of the investment guaranty program. In the event of confiscation of American assets covered by an investment guaranty, title to the assets passes to the United States government, after which Washington negotiates directly with the foreign government concerned to reclaim its assets or to recover damages.[48] Countries throughout the underdeveloped world have often been cautious about the United States acquiring title to business holdings within their borders, fearing a return of Western "colonialism" or of American "dollar diplomacy." One study group found this fear a real barrier to widespread use of the investment guaranty approach.[49] Although such apprehensions undoubtedly continue to exist in many needy societies, by the early 1960s some 44 countries had entered into agreements with the United States to permit the guaranty program to operate within their borders in respect to currency inconvertibility; a smaller number had accepted the program in respect to expropriation and damage to foreign business because of war. Officials in AID believed that the number of countries participating in the guaranty program would most likely expand in the years ahead.[50]

A recent innovation in governmental efforts to encourage overseas business expansion was the "investment survey" program, inaugurated in 1961. Under this program—growing out of the realization that frequently American business concerns are ignorant of business conditions, opportunities, and risks in other countries—the Agency for International Development pays up to 50 percent of the cost of such surveys. Several hundred applications to AID for this service by the early 1960s indicated that this approach was a valuable contribution for American business firms.[51]

Foreign Assistance in the American Context

The effects of American foreign assistance upon the recipient nations has been in the main highly beneficial. But what has been its impact upon the United States itself? This question receives very little attention on the part of commentators and writers interested in American foreign policy, yet its implications for future American foreign policy may be far-reaching.

Individuals and groups who attack foreign aid programs as "give-aways," who think that "charity begins at home" and that money expended for foreign aid ought to be used instead for tax cuts or possibly subsidies for depressed segments of American industry, overlook one fact about the foreign aid program which is of cardinal importance in evaluating its worth. This is that from the beginning the United States has provided assistance to other countries *predominantly to advance its own national interest and secondarily to benefit the countries receiving such aid.* Whether this impulse *ought* to be the basic philosophy of the foreign aid program is of course debatable. But that it has been the guiding philosophy, especially since the Greek-Turkish aid program of 1947, is not open to serious challenge. Prevention of communist penetration through the Balkans to the Mediterranean, reconstruction of Western Europe, elimination of malaria in countries such as Iran, steady improvement in India's productive capacity under New Delhi's development plans, attempts to stabilize the tin industry in Bolivia—the United States has contributed funds for these purposes chiefly to promote its own security and diplomatic interests. To the extent that these goals have been achieved, the United States has thus been the main beneficiary of foreign aid programs.

These considerations have been consistently overlooked by opponents of foreign aid. Nor have the domestic economic implications of foreign aid been sufficiently appreciated by critics of the program. The fact is that foreign aid has been highly instrumental in maintaining the prosperity of several key segments of the American economy. By 1962, AID procured 50 percent of the commodities furnished under the foreign aid program from American suppliers; the agency planned to increase this percentage to 70 percent by 1964. After that, it was planned to procure 80 to 85 percent of all commodities shipped by AID from the United States.[52] By the early 1960s, 12 percent of all American exports were financed by foreign aid. More specifically, this meant that of $2.4 billion committed by AID for procure-

ment in fiscal year 1963, $1.9 billion was spent in the United States. Certain products especially depended heavily upon the foreign assistance program to maintain a high level of sales. Thus, 87 percent of iron and steel products needed by AID, 92 percent of the nonferrous metals, and 97 percent of the fertilizers were purchased from American firms.[53]

A closely related consideration is the extent to which foreign aid, as its critics have widely charged, has fostered increasingly intense competition for American manufacturers and producers in foreign markets. Has the recent prosperity, achieved in part by American foreign aid funds, of countries such as Britain, France, West Germany, and Japan injured the prosperity of the American economy? To this question, several answers must be given. In the first place, there is no assurance that such competition would not have appeared sooner or later, in the absence of American assistance. Given the fact that many of these countries were obliged to replace war-devastated industries with new and modern equipment, there is every reason to believe that the competition the United States faces abroad has little or nothing to do with the provision of foreign aid, however much the *rate* of industrial modernization in these countries was accelerated by American assistance. In the second place, the relatively low over-all percentage of American aid—in terms of the *total* funds committed to modernization in France, Germany, or Japan—has meant that American assistance was always a small part of the comprehensive national effort required to make these countries once more competitive in the world market. In the third place, there is a definite correlation between the provision of American assistance to other countries and the expansion of American *exports* to those countries. In answer to the accusation that foreign aid has been used to undermine the competitive position of American business firms, President Kennedy pointed out that, in spite of massive assistance to Western Europe since World War II, American exports to Europe from 1953 to 1963 doubled, while those to Japan increased fourfold.[54] These data suggest that —far from injuring the American economy— foreign aid has contributed significantly to creating the only conditions under which American prosperity can be indefinitely maintained: creation of prosperous economic conditions in the outside world, enabling other societies to acquire the purchasing power to *buy* from the United States and other highly industrialized nations.

These data indicate that one of the steps advocated by many Americans for reducing America's gold outflow—drastic cuts in the foreign aid program—would in fact have very little constructive effect upon the balance-of-payments deficit. With upwards of 90 percent of all American foreign aid funds expended within the United States, a reduction of $1 billion in foreign aid would reduce the deficit in America's international accounts by something like $100 million, while it would cut $900 million from expenditures for exports. As David E. Bell, Administrator of Aid under the Kennedy and Johnson Administrations, has observed: "An appropriation cut intended to reduce the balance-of-payments deficit would in fact mainly reduce U.S. exports."[55] Unless an equivalent quantity of exports replaced those eliminated, the immediate effect of a substantial reduction in foreign aid would be to *widen* the gap between income and outgo in America's international accounts!

The Future of Foreign Aid

By the mid-1960s, the future of the foreign aid program was highly uncertain. With some segments of the American society and with some legislative groups, the foreign aid program had been unpopular ever since the inauguration of the Marshall Plan in 1948. The program had survived innumerable attempts to reduce its scope, if not to eliminate it altogether. Moreover, opposition to the program had gathered momentum throughout the late 1950s and early 1960s. By 1964, its future was perhaps more in jeopardy than at any time since its inauguration. Headlines like "Bitter Foreign Aid Battle Reflects an Intense Hostility" or "House Pressing Large Foreign Aid Cut" testified to the durability and growing influence of the movement to curtail foreign aid sharply. For 1964, for example, President Kennedy had asked Congress for almost $5 billion to support foreign aid; after his death, President Johnson was required to settle for a final appropriation of $3 billion. Even then, the White House was widely believed to have won a victory in the tug of war over foreign aid with an increasingly critical Congress.

What factors account for the growing intensity of opposition to the foreign aid program? How does this opposition in the mid-1960s differ from that existing toward the Marshall Plan or Point Four program earlier? In general

terms, a variety of influences—deriving from deficiencies in the conception and administration of previous aid programs, to widespread public and legislative misconceptions about its scope and purpose—account for the phenomenon.[*]

A number of more specific criticisms may be mentioned briefly. First, there is a category of arguments against foreign aid directed at, or derived from, the underlying goals associated with the program. Much of the private and official disillusionment about foreign aid springs from skepticism about the "results" achieved by the extension of some $100 billion in assistance to other countries since World War II. Critics contend that this massive assistance has done little to reduce the danger to American security posed by expansive communism; that it has won few steadfast "friends" for the United States throughout Africa, the Arab world, Asia, and Latin America; that it has had no appreciable effect in reversing the tide of diplomatic "neutralism" sweeping these regions; and that thus far, it has made a minimum contribution in enabling newly emergent countries to solve their own economic and social problems without continuing reliance upon outside assistance. On the contrary, opponents of foreign aid have contended, the provision of several billion dollars annually to other governments has fostered the expectation abroad that foreign countries are *entitled* to American help; that they will receive it, irrespective of the extent to which their internal and external policies are compatible with American interests; that they are obliged to render no "accounting" or permit no outside supervision over the use of American funds; and that they are expected to exert a minimum of "self-help" in overcoming their internal economic and social problems.

Still another category of arguments against foreign aid derive from apprehension over America's continuing balance-of-payments deficit producing a steady drain on the nation's gold reserves. The conviction exists that the most promising method of reversing the gold drain is to reduce, if not to eliminate altogether, the one item—foreign aid—constituting the largest liability in America's international accounts.

---

[*] Many legislative objections to foreign aid are summarized in the report by the Senate Foreign Relations Committee, *Foreign Assistance Act of 1963,* 88th Congress, 1st Session (Washington, D.C.: 1963), pp. 1–7.

Another category of objections to continuing foreign aid stems from the belief, shared by study groups such as the Clay Committee in 1963, that serious mistakes have been made in the past administration of aid programs and in the underlying conceptions of the programs held by the Truman, Eisenhower, and Kennedy Administrations. Thus, the accusation is made—and executive officials have sometimes admitted its validity—that the foreign aid program has been laxly administered in some countries, that its goals have often been ill-defined or unrealistic, that it endeavored to do "too much" in too many different societies, that the organizational pattern for the administration of aid was chaotic and needed drastic overhauling, that higher "standards" ought to be imposed upon recipient countries as regards obligations they assumed for utilizing aid funds constructively and for instituting necessary domestic reforms, that aid for certain countries ought to be terminated altogether and for all countries ought to be scheduled with a definite termination date in mind. In brief, the conviction has prevailed that the guiding philosophy and administration of the foreign aid program required redefinition and reform.

Opposition to foreign aid has also unquestionably sprung from a political reality that, to a greater or lesser degree, affects all aspects of foreign policy: foreign aid has no "constituency" in the United States to bring pressure to bear upon Capitol Hill for its adoption. Support for foreign aid (or so legislators are inclined to believe) does little or nothing to help the re-election of congressmen, and it may do a good deal to prevent their re-election. Executive officials have been aware for years that this conviction, whether justified or not, is one of the most durable obstacles to legislative support for foreign assistance programs. As we shall see, the extent of public opposition in the United States to foreign aid may well be exaggerated by critics of the program on Capitol Hill. Nevertheless, if many legislators believe that support for foreign spending is a political millstone, if they correctly or incorrectly think that a majority of their constituents opposes foreign assistance, they are likely to be guided by their beliefs, despite what more objective data might indicate about public attitudes. In the light of this conviction, legislators are often prone to focus upon foreign aid as an expendable budgetary item, in the perennial quest for "economy" in federal spending. Lacking constituents in

America, recipients of foreign aid can make little effective protest when Congress cuts out a steel mill for India, eliminates technical assistance to Indonesia, or refuses to construct a dam in Ghana.

Opposition to foreign assistance has also derived from another phenomenon that has received central attention in this chapter: the growing conviction that, with productive levels and standards of living in areas such as Western Europe and Japan at an all-time high, America's cold-war allies ought to assume a far heavier burden of providing the capital and other help required by developing countries than has been the case over the past several years. Many legislators believe that, in the absence of reductions in American aid, the allies will be content indefinitely to permit an apparently willing United States to carry a burden that ought to be shared more widely among nations which themselves were once primary beneficiaries of American assistance.

We may fairly summarize the mounting opposition to foreign aid by saying that after more than a decade and a half, its failures are widely believed to be more spectacular and far-reaching than its successes.*

Finally, note must be taken of a comparatively recent phenomenon associated with legislative debate on foreign aid: the growing opposition to the program to be found among many "liberal" and "internationalist" senators and representatives who have formed the nucleus of support for foreign aid in earlier years. By the 1960s, even members of the Senate Foreign Relations Committee—perhaps the most internationalist-minded group on Capitol Hill, including such leading Democrats as Senators J. William Fulbright of Arkansas and Wayne Morse of Oregon—have opposed some aspects of the foreign aid program outright and have demanded drastic reforms and modifications in the program as a whole. Their criticism has been directed at two points in particular. They have demanded that the scope of the program be reduced and that its over-all purposes be clarified; and they have insisted that economically backward countries

* The following sources deal with the arguments against foreign aid advanced in the early 1960s: *The New York Times*, September 19, 23, and 30, 1962; July 31, August 11, October 23, and 25, and December 22, 1963. For summaries of legislative debate, illustrating many prevalent criticisms on Capitol Hill, see the discussions of the President's foreign aid budget in annual installments of the *Congressional Quarterly Almanac*.

rely more heavily upon multinational institutions such as the United Nations, the World Bank, and upon the prosperous nations of Western Europe to raise their capital requirements.

Executive policy-makers have not been insensitive to the criticisms voiced about the foreign aid program on Capitol Hill and by public groups. As we have seen in this chapter and in Chapter 4, a number of organizational reforms and of redefinitions in the philosophy of the foreign aid program have occurred in recent years to reflect such criticism. Yet in making these concessions, the Eisenhower, Kennedy, and Johnson Administrations have operated upon the firm conviction that, however valid certain criticisms of the aid program have been, there remains no question that the extension of economic and military assistance to other governments continues to achieve American diplomatic goals. As far as economic aid is concerned, executive officials are mindful of the dictum expressed by the British diplomat Sir Oliver Franks, who observed that for many decades, the course of global affairs would likely turn "on a right relationship of the industrial north of the globe to the developing south."[56] Nor, by the 1960s, could executive officials discern any significant diminution in the *need* for economic and technical assistance by African, Arab, Asian, and Latin American states. President Kennedy, for example, identified the gap between rich and poor nations as one of the two dominant problems of international affairs (the other being the cold war). As evidence, the President and his subordinates cited the fact that one-third of the world's richest nations have five-sixths of its total output of goods and services; one-third of mankind has a life expectancy of 67 years, whereas two-thirds has a life expectancy of 38 years; and one-third of human society has an illiteracy rate of around 70 percent.[57] Legitimate and illegitimate criticisms of the aid program aside, executive policy-makers were convinced that the necessity for constructive aid programs for other countries was as great as ever.

These considerations induced President Kennedy to devote a substantial portion of one of his last press conferences to the issue of foreign aid. Conceding that his foreign assistance budget was encountering "the worst attack on foreign aid that we've seen since the beginning of the Marshall Plan," the President pointed out that foreign aid has been regarded by Presidents Truman and Eisenhower, by all presidential candidates during this period, and by himself as a vital instrument to safeguard American diplomatic interests from Western Europe to South Vietnam. In answer to the often-reiterated charge that Americans were "tired" of supporting the foreign assistance program, the President emphasized a fact that seemed only dimly understood on Capitol Hill and throughout the nation. This was that since the late 1940s, the annual foreign aid budget had not only declined *actually*; it had also declined *relatively*, in terms of the nation's ability to carry the burden of $3–4 billion annually the foreign aid budget normally entailed. By 1963, as a percentage of the federal budget, expenditures for foreign aid were proportionately about one-fourth what they had been in the beginning of the early postwar era. In 1951, foreign aid comprised 20 percent of the federal budget; in 1963, it comprised 4 percent. In 1963, executive officials asked the American people to devote 7/10 of 1 percent of the Gross National Product to foreign aid; in 1951, this percentage was four times higher. With respect to $600 million that Congress had recently eliminated from his latest foreign aid budget, President Kennedy noted that this amount was "less than this country's annual outlay for lipstick, face cream, and chewing gum." Challenging the American society of the 1960s to do "half as well as the Americans of the 1950s," President Kennedy asserted that "the need is greater" for foreign aid than ever before, owing to the number of newly independent governments that have appeared within recent years and that "I don't regard the struggle [to promote the economic progress of these countries] as over, and I don't think it's probably going to be over for this century."[58]

In evaluating the criticisms made of the foreign aid program, executive policy-makers were prone to emphasize several points. One was that the extent of public opposition to foreign aid, a favorite theme with legislative critics, was often highly exaggerated. Gallup polls during 1963, for example, showed that from 58 to 70 percent of the American people *supported* the extension of foreign assistance to other countries.[59] Furthermore, executive officials believed that much of the opposition to foreign aid had its origins in highly unrealistic, not to say Utopian, expectations about what American assistance is capable of accomplishing in other societies. Thus, a high-ranking official in the Kennedy and Johnson Administrations cautioned against a widespread tendency to expect that foreign aid could control events in other countries in a manner always consonant with American diplomatic objectives; or to expect that foreign aid can "buy allies and votes in the UN"; or to believe that it would assure the United States "first place in a global popularity contest." The most that successfully administered foreign aid could achieve—and this was a great deal—was to help create conditions by which other countries "that are increasingly prepared to defend their independence against totalitarian enemies—external or internal, overt or covert" and are "prepared to work with us as partners" could move closer to their goal.[60]

This conception of the basic objective, in turn, implied several corollaries. It meant that results achieved with foreign aid would be partially (and sometimes heavily) dependent upon steps taken by other countries. It meant that recipients of aid were "partners" of the United States and not satellites whose policies coincided at every point with Washington's. It meant that the ultimate goal was promotion of genuine *independence* for such countries as Ghana, Morocco, Iraq, and Indonesia—with all that implied about the exercise of "independence" in the management of their own political and diplomatic affairs. In brief, it meant something that had been grasped only dimly by many Americans: the goal was creation of a truly pluralistic free-world society of nations, capable of formulating their own policies at home and abroad, without interference by Washington, Moscow, or Peiping. To the extent that this goal was achieved, the foreign aid program could be called a success; and, within the more limited context of the cold war, to the extent that it was achieved, communist expansionism would be thwarted.

Confronted with widespread allegations of "waste, mismanagement, and failure," in the foreign aid program, executive policy-makers also underscored another fact that has been seldom publicized sufficiently about American foreign assistance programs throughout the postwar era. This is the number and magnitude of the *successes* achieved by the expenditure of American funds in other societies. At the outset, officials in the executive branch have been conscious of a psychological difficulty that has always faced proponents of foreign aid. Failures inherently make better headlines than successes. A scandal in the administration of aid

funds in a Southeast Asian country always receives greater publicity than does the success achieved in raising agricultural productivity in an Arab country. Or, as Secretary of State Dean Rusk expressed the point in testimony before the Senate Appropriations Committee in 1963: ". . . the closest we come to showing you a great foreign aid victory is to point to the absence of a defeat." A supporter of foreign aid on the committee replied: "In other words, what you are saying is that we have been buying fire insurance for many years and just because the house has not burned down we [i.e., critics of the program] want to abandon the policy?"[61] The fact that Syria or Nigeria or India has *not* succumbed to communism or some other form of expansive totalitarianism—and that these and other recipients of foreign aid are in the main demonstrating an ability to safeguard their own security against internal and external threats—was neither widely understood nor publicized throughout the United States.

Even so, the record of "achievements" with foreign aid since the early 1940s has been impressive. Space does not permit us to do more than present a random sample of cases from this record. Sufficient progress had been made in promoting the economic and military stability of Greece, Israel, Taiwan (Republic of China on Formosa), Venezuela, Mexico, and the Philippines to enable the executive branch to schedule the termination of American assistance to these countries by 1965 (a goal that may have been impaired by substantial legislative reductions in the foreign aid budget in the years preceding that date).[62] Some $13 billion in American assistance to Western Europe had contributed to building a thriving economy in that region, so much so that European countries were able to supply assistance to other countries throughout the underdeveloped world. Except for an insignificant amount of military aid, economic assistance to Europe had been altogether terminated. In the poorer countries of Africa, the Arab world, Asia, and Latin America, spectacular progress had been made in campaigns such as the one launched against malaria. India, for instance, had one million deaths from malaria in 1953; in 1962, India reported fewer than 2000 *cases* of malaria altogether! Similarly, on Taiwan, in 1950, there were 1.2 million cases, resulting in 12,000 deaths, from malaria; in 1961, there were only 61 cases and no deaths from this disease.

In Nigeria, programs operated by AID have trained 150 school instructors, who in turn have trained 5000 native teachers. Throughout Latin America, AID funds have constructed 18,000 classrooms and distributed 4 million textbooks to raise educational levels. In Chile, several thousand small, private homes have been constructed by citizens, using materials supplied by AID. In Peru, 1500 families have been resettled in what was once an arid wasteland north of Lima. In Brazil, a program calling for the construction of 120 community water-supply systems, as well as a project to construct over 1200 new classrooms for nearly 250,000 elementary school children, was proceeding apace. In Thailand, progress was being made in supplying one of the country's most vital needs—an adequate internal transportation system; by 1963, more than 135 bridges had been built or replaced in the country. In Indonesia, assistance from AID continued to make possible the improvement of higher education in areas where the Indonesian state's facilities remained inadequate.

In Africa, AID funds enabled Nigeria to refinance its own economic development plan and to move closer toward economic self-sufficiency; for Chad, Nigeria, Cameroon, and Niger, AID programs financed a three-year campaign against a traditional African scourge —rinderpest, a disease that sometimes wipes out livestock holdings—by distribution of vaccines; the goal of the program is to wipe out rinderpest altogether. In poverty-stricken Iran, American foreign aid teams worked with more than 1.3 million farmers, housewives, and children, to improve basic standards of agricultural production, home economics, and sanitation. In Jordan, American assistance succeeded in providing the country a pure and adequate water supply. In India, American assistance (in conjunction with massive Indian efforts) contributed to a threefold expansion of the number of children in school since 1947, to a doubling of agricultural and industrial production, and to a threefold increase in electric power generation.

Countless other individual cases illustrating the accomplishments of foreign aid could be cited. As general indications of the gains achieved with foreign economic aid, executive officials cite two facts. The first is that among 41 countries that have received "substantial" economic aid from the United States ($300 million or more per country), 33 achieved an economic growth rate of at least 1.5 percent

annually for five years. This is an admittedly low figure; yet it is approximately half the recent annual economic growth rate for the United States itself. For such countries as Egypt or India or Indonesia, it is perhaps a remarkable achievement since, left to their own devices and forced to cope with a burgeoning population, they would likely have experienced a *declining* economic growth rate. Second, economic aid from the United States has been terminated altogether for 14 Western European nations, Japan, and Lebanon. It is scheduled to be terminated wholly or substantially for Greece, Israel, Free China (Taiwan), Mexico, and the Philippines.*

Proponents of foreign aid concede the merit of one argument advanced by the program's critics. Indeed, this point has been emphasized repeatedly by Presidents Eisenhower, Kennedy, and Johnson. This is that the increasingly prosperous NATO allies ought to carry a proportionately greater burden of providing economic and technical assistance to nations throughout the free world. At the same time, it has been insufficiently recognized within the United States that the allies *are* providing large quantities of aid to other governments and that in some instances their efforts, expressed as a percentage of their Gross National Product, exceed our own. The following chart highlights this fact.

TABLE 7.   Economic Assistance as a Percentage of the Gross National Product

France	1.6 %
Belgium	.85%
United Kingdom	.64%
United States	.59%
West Germany	.56%
Netherlands	.47%
Japan	.44%

SOURCE: Agency for International Development, 1963.

From 1956 to 1962, nations in Western Europe and Japan doubled their foreign assist-

* Data on the accomplishments of foreign aid have been drawn from a wide variety of sources. See particularly: Agency for International Development, *The Foreign Aid Program Today: Answers to Four Basic Questions* (Washington, D.C.: 1963), pp. 2–7; *The Story of A.I.D.* (Washington, D.C.: no date) and *Report to the Congress on the Foreign Assistance Program for Fiscal Year 1962* (Washington, D.C.: 1962), pp. 7–32; Chester Bowles, "Foreign Aid: The Essential Factors for Success," *Department of State Bulletin*, 48 (June 17, 1963), 940; U. Alexis Johnson, "Aid—Investment in the Future," *Department of State Bulletin*, 48 (May 27, 1963), 830–833.

ance to other countries. By the early 1960s, the United States provided about 60 percent of all governmental assistance from industrialized countries; other countries provided about 40 percent. This was about the same as the ratio of the Gross National Product of the United States to the combined national products of all other industrialized states in the free world.[63] In one region particularly—the continent of Africa—other advanced nations in the free world carried the burden of foreign assistance. Aid programs operated by France, Britain, West Germany, and Israel eclipsed those operated by the United States. American programs in Africa have been, and because of efforts made by the cold-war allies are scheduled to remain, limited in quantity and scope. In spite of past efforts by the allies, it was reasonable to suppose that the United States would continue to exert pressure upon London, Paris, and Bonn to expand the scope of their assistance programs to needy countries.

In concluding our analysis of the pros and cons of foreign aid, one development may be considered well-nigh inevitable, on the basis of past experience. Modifications will continue to be made in the principles, scope, and organizational machinery of the foreign aid program. Indeed, one of the first official acts of the Johnson Administration was to appoint a top-level executive committee to study the program anew and to bring in recommendations for its improvement; this move was unquestionably induced by the opposition to foreign assistance existing on Capitol Hill. In establishing the committee, President Johnson emphasized that one goal was to gain greater legislative support for the program. At the same time, executive officials were fully aware that critics of foreign aid themselves were sharply divided over the kind of program they desired and over the precise organizational pattern they favored. The results of further study were almost certain to be, first, that this new committee would encounter limited success in winning converts among opponents of foreign aid and, second, that other studies would continue to be made to formulate a program that could command wider executive, legislative, and public support.[64]

Multinational and International Assistance Programs

A noteworthy trend has been the extent to which multinational and international organi-

zations have evolved foreign assistance programs of their own, often providing aid to meet specialized problems. Frequently, American assistance programs are coordinated with the efforts of these groups.

The Development Assistance Committee of the Organization for Economic Cooperation and Development (OECD)—composed of all European countries extending foreign assistance, the United States, Canada, and Japan—was established in 1960.* OECD has sought to increase the total amount of aid made available by its members, to coordinate their aid activities, to liberalize the terms of loans to needy countries, and to set up consortia to facilitate multinational aid activities and to integrate multinational activities with international institutions such as the World Bank. By 1963, at the suggestion of President Kennedy, OECD had set up a "development center" to study the needs of economically backward countries and to propose coordinated steps for meeting them.

The World Bank has become increasingly active in supporting long-range development programs in needy countries, in part by encouraging the formation of consortia among aid-supplying nations to plan coordinated assistance projects. A conspicuous example has been the "Aid India Club," consisting of nations providing assistance to enable India to achieve its ambitious economic development goals. For many years, the United States has been the leading member of this consortium. On the regional level, the Inter-American Development Bank, supported by all the American republics, promotes long-term economic progress within the Western Hemisphere. The International Finance Corporation seeks to expand the role of *private* business activity in developing societies. The Export-Import Bank, an instrumentality of the American govern-

* OECD was the successor to the Organization for European Economic Cooperation (OEEC), set up initially to formulate long-range plans for European economic recovery during the era of the Marshall Plan from 1948 to 1952. By 1964, OECD had 20 members, including the United States, Canada, and 18 Western European countries. It was set up in 1961 to coordinate the economic policies of its members, particularly their foreign aid activities. It was expected that Japan (which had participated in many of OECD's activities) would be admitted eventually to formal membership in the organization; this step would help Japan terminate or prevent "discrimination" against its goods by members of the European Common Market. *The New York Times*, January 10, 1964.

ment, provides financing for foreigners to purchase American goods.

Finally, the United Nations conducts numerous activities that furnish direct and indirect assistance to other governments. In promoting the "Decade of Development" launched for the 1960s, the UN's Special Fund and its Expanded Program for Technical Assistance (EPTA) were supported by the United States.* By the mid-1960s, the UN was inaugurating a new world food program, to which the United States also contributed.[65] In addition, the United States normally supplied 30 to 40 percent of the budget for many of the UN's specialized agencies. For example, it was announced early in 1964 that the United States had contributed a total of $17.5 million to the World Health Organization's campaign to eradicate malaria. A portion of those funds had been raised by private donations from Americans.[66]

THE BALANCE-OF-PAYMENTS DEFICIT AND OTHER FOREIGN ECONOMIC PROBLEMS

The Balance of Payments in Perspective

Every citizen who has the most cursory understanding of contemporary foreign policy is aware that within recent years the United States has experienced a chronic deficit in its balance of international payments, resulting in a continuing drain upon its national gold reserves. From 1950 through 1963, the trade deficit ran from less than $1 billion to as much as $4 billion annually (with the exception of 1957, when there was a slight surplus in America's international accounts).[67] American gold stocks have consequently fallen from around $22 billion in 1953 to less than $16 billion in 1963, with Western European countries—chiefly France, Italy, Switzerland, the United Kingdom, and West Germany—greatly expanding their gold holdings.[68]

What factors accounted for this phenomenon? What implications did the gold loss

* These programs—along with another proposal which the United States has not supported, the Special United Nations Fund for Economic Development (SUNFED)—are discussed in detail in Chapter 16. Although the United States has cooperated closely in joining in certain UN programs, it has been at best lukewarm about diverting massive amounts of American assistance to ambitious UN programs such as SUNFED, at least until significant progress is made in reducing the scale of national defense budgets through a viable disarmament agreement.

have for the American domestic economy and for related issues such as the American position on tariff and trade questions? What steps could be taken to narrow the trade gap? These were questions which, by the mid-1960s, engaged the attention of American officials and of serious students of foreign policy.

At the outset, it is necessary to deal briefly with certain basic economic concepts. The "balance of payments" in effect is a system of double-entry bookkeeping, affording a record of a nation's total international transactions during a specified period, normally one year.** Every transaction that entails an outflow of dollars from the United States—including the purchases of imported goods and services, the investment of American capital abroad, military and economic assistance, money spent by American tourists overseas, the temporary flow of short-term capital to foreign money markets—constitutes a *deficit* in the balance of payments. Every transaction that entails an inflow of dollars to the United States—including purchases by foreigners of American goods and services, the income from American overseas investments, expenditures by foreign tourists in the United States, repayments of loans by foreign governments, foreign investments in the United States—constitutes a *credit* in the balance of payments. Now let us assume that, in any given year, Americans incurred total liabilities of $20 billion in their foreign

** Students are cautioned about the necessity for precision in the use of phrases often used interchangeably and, when this is the case, inaccurately. As indicated, the "balance of payments" refers to the *sum total* of a nation's international transaction. In this sense, "credits" (what it received from other countries) must by definition equal "debits" (what it bought from or lent other countries). In its simplest terms, for everything of value the United States gives other countries, it receives something of value in return. Consequently, its total transactions must in the nature of the case always "balance." The term "balance of trade," however, is a much narrower concept, usually referring to the difference in value between *exports* of goods and services, on the one hand, and of *imports* of goods and services, on the other. When it is said that a nation has an "unfavorable balance of trade," this means that its imports ("debits" in the balance of payments) exceed its exports ("credits" in the balance of payments). A "favorable" balance of trade refers to the reverse of this situation. Since other items besides imports and exports are included in the balance of payments, the idea of a "favorable balance of trade" (or an "unfavorable" one) often means little in determining whether there is an over-all trade deficit that must be paid for with gold.

accounts and that they had total credits of $16 billion. An outflow of $4 billion in gold from American reserves would be required to satisfy foreign claims, thereby "balancing" credits and debits in the nation's international accounts.

By all odds, the two most significant categories of items affecting the American balance of payments are trade (or imports and exports), and foreign military and economic aid. For the period 1959–1962, for example, the sale of American goods and services abroad yielded an annual credit to the United States ranging between $16 billion and over $20 billion. By contrast, American purchases from foreigners were almost always less, ranging from $15 to $16 billion annually. In other words, in every year during this period, Americans sold more to foreigners than they bought from them; if trade alone is considered, America would therefore accumulate a surplus in its international accounts, equaling from $2 billion to more than $6 billion annually, with other countries required to ship gold to America to meet their indebtedness.

This is an extremely significant fact, poorly understood by many Americans. For it indicates that America's gold loss has its origins in something other than trade transactions. This leads to the second category of items in the balance of payments which, in the main, accounts for America's gold loss: foreign military and economic aid. For the year 1962, for example, the total amount of American foreign aid—constituting the largest liability in its foreign accounts—was close to $6 billion. This meant that Americans had to generate an equivalent amount of credits abroad, if the nation were not to lose gold. As it was, the United States lost $2.3 billion in gold that year; less than half the total funds extended in foreign aid was offset by the excess of American exports over imports or by other transactions generating credits in the balance of payments. Put differently, the total value of foreign aid extended by the United States to other governments in that year was more than double the value of the gold loss. A logical corollary to be drawn from these facts, as many Americans have concluded, is that the gold outflow could be halted readily by eliminating foreign aid. The implications of this proposal will be considered below.

Other items affecting the American balance of payments require brief mention. For 1962, the United States received credits of over $3.5 billion derived from the income on its overseas investments. By contrast, a liability of almost $3 billion was incurred because of the outflow of American capital in investments overseas. Nearly $1.5 billion in short-term capital also left the country, to be invested temporarily in areas such as Western Europe, where interest rates were more attractive. American tourist spending overseas also resulted in a loss of approximately $1.5 billion. Using the year 1962 as an example, the American balance of payments showed a total of $7.6 billion paid *to* the United States, $9.9 billion paid *by* the United States, leaving a deficit of $2.3 billion that had to be met by transfers from American gold reserves to foreigners.*

Alternative Approaches to the Trade Deficit

By the mid-1960s, American officials and economists were encouraged about the overall trend of the nation's international accounts, leading some observers to believe that 1964 would mark a "turning point" in reversing the deficit in the balance of payments. If improvement witnessed in the early 1960s could be maintained, the gold loss would be reduced to relatively insignificant proportions. On the surface, the statistics perhaps do not reflect this change. From 1957 to 1962, the United States lost between $3 billion and $4 billion annually from its gold reserves; the gold deficit for the year 1963 was estimated at approximately $3 billion. The early months of 1963 witnessed an accelerated drain on American gold reserves. Yet, by the end of the year, nothing less than spectacular improvement occurred, engendering the belief that in the years that followed the gold loss would be substantially halted.

As we have indicated, the payments deficit had already been reduced to $2.3 billion for 1962. This meant that relatively small changes in the individual items in the balance of payments could virtually eliminate the deficit. Such changes occurred in three categories of transactions: owing to a proposed new tax designed to check the purchase of foreign securities, the amount of dollars spent on foreign securities during 1963 declined sharply; interest rates within the United States became

* See the chart in *The New York Times*, July 21, 1963. These totals are "net" totals, meaning that the sums cited represent the differences between offsetting items such as merchandise exports and imports, or the amount of American capital sent overseas, versus the amount of foreign capital invested in America.

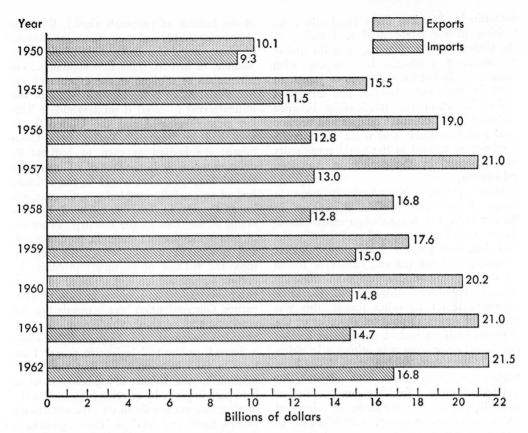

Merchandise Imports and Exports of the United States, 1950–1962. (Source: *Statistical Abstract of the United States, 1963*, p. 850.)

competitive with those in Europe, thereby reducing the outflow of short-term investment funds; and the volume of bank loans to foreigners also declined.[69]

Beyond these developments, there exists the continuing question: What steps can be, and ought to be, taken to avert further American gold losses? Before examining possible alternative approaches, let us note that the magnitude of the problem is not at all as great as is sometimes imagined. By 1963, the Treasury Department still had some $15.5 billion in its gold reserve—about 37 percent of the free world's gold supply. Some observers were inclined to believe that economically this was a much more "healthy" situation than when the United States held a much larger percentage of the world's reserves of gold. Moreover, while the continuing depletion of American gold reserves occupied the attention of policymakers, there was no indication that the gold loss jeopardized the stability of the dollar, necessitating its devaluation. Theoretically, if a significant annual gold drain occurred in-

definitely, devaluation of the dollar might become inevitable. In actuality, there was no evidence that this stage had been reached or was likely to be reached in the future.

America's trade deficit was no less a matter of continuing concern because of the continuing gold outflow than for another reason that foreign policy officials emphasized repeatedly to Congress and to the public. The loss of gold was fully as much a *symptom* as a cause of problems besetting America's international economic relationships. For the gold drain signified the end of the long era of American economic dominance in global affairs, when the United States almost alone had large gold holdings and when it could compete with remarkable success in the world market, often on its own terms. This era had been characterized by large credits in America's international accounts and by a position of economic dependency on the part of other countries. By the 1950s, a new, more normal pattern of global economic relations was emerging. The dollar shortage had ended.

Increasingly, American firms faced stiff competition in the world market. Inflation in the United States further impaired the ability of American producers to compete with modernized industries in Europe or Japan. In brief, by the 1950s, America had entered a period in which the relationship between "internal" and "external" policies had become clear and inescapable and when the interdependence of nations in the world community was illustrated by the decline in American gold stocks.

What do these generalizations mean in terms of the most feasible alternatives in dealing with the balance-of-payments issue? At the outset, a widespread realization exists that America's problem is in many respects unique, that it will not and cannot be solved by resort to many "classic" steps normally taken by countries confronted with the same difficulty. If for no other reason, this was because of America's position as leader of the Western coalition and of the role of foreign aid in achieving American diplomatic objectives. Nevertheless, several steps have been proposed, and some have been adopted, for dealing with the crisis, like implementation of a "tight money" policy at home, reform of the international currency, establishment of higher interest rates in the United States, curtailment of overseas spending, reduction in defense expenditures abroad, and efforts to get the cold-war allies to assume a larger proportionate share of foreign aid spending. Two proposals in particular—drastic reductions in foreign aid and increased tariff barriers to curtail imports—have commanded widespread public and legislative support.

Conceivably, a substantial reduction in foreign aid would reduce American international liabilities by as much as $4 to $6 billion annually. At the same time, as we have noted earlier, it would also reduce American *exports*, since a large percentage of many categories of exports is paid for out of foreign aid funds spent in the United States. This is notably the case with agricultural commodities. Executive officials, for example, calculated that out of $2.4 billion spent for foreign aid in 1963, almost $2 billion was expended in the United States, leaving $400 million to be credited against the payments deficit if foreign aid were completely eliminated.[70] Moreover, if economic and military aid were cut out, or drastically reduced, on economic grounds alone (and even, more narrowly, from the viewpoint

of the balance of payments alone), this step might conceivably cost many times the amount of money saved if a curtailment of aid made possible, or invited, some new communist expansionism or intrigue at the expense of the free world. As an example, what would be the ultimate cost involved if military aid to Turkey were eliminated and the United States then had to "liberate" Turkey from Communist domination or even to buttress its defenses massively in the face of a Communist threat? Similarly, what would be the ultimate cost of successfully countering a Communist-inspired coup in Iraq, engendered by economic dislocations in the country? There are of course many other strategic, psychological, and diplomatic reasons why attempting to solve the balance of payments problems by cutting foreign aid has not appealed to executive policy-makers and leaders in both political parties. Our contention here is merely that for economic reasons alone, this course does not, as widely imagined, offer a promising solution.

Second, public and legislative groups from time to time have proposed that the logical solution to the balance-of-payments problem is to pare imports, by erecting high tariff walls or otherwise cutting down on expenditures for foreign goods and services. This approach, it is widely supposed, would eliminate from $16 to $20 billion annually in international liabilities, leaving the United States a sizable surplus in its foreign accounts. Again, officials in the Eisenhower, Kennedy, and Johnson Administrations have rejected this approach.

However plausible it sounds, this approach suffers acutely from several fundamental drawbacks. Ideologically, it would be totally antithetical to the historic American position of reciprocal trade; it would violate the ideals of economic "cooperation" that the United States has urged upon countries in Western Europe since World War II; it would alienate the underdeveloped nations, by seeming to confirm Communist allegations about capitalist "neocolonialism" and insensitivity to their needs; and, generally, it would imply American indifference to the necessity for national and international cooperation to resolve mutual problems. Such action would be interpreted as a resurgence of isolationism in the United States, engendering the belief that Washington was, in effect, forfeiting its responsibilities in leading the free world.

On economic grounds alone, an attempt to curtail imports seems a dubious approach to the balance-of-payments problem. Two major considerations dictate this verdict. First, other countries, particularly the ones in the European Common Market, could and doubtless would retaliate in kind against American imports—thereby ushering in a new age of economic nationalism and open trade warfare. In any case, there are no grounds whatever for believing that America could impose trade restrictions upon foreign goods with impunity, while its own goods continued to find wide markets abroad. Even more basically, in the second place, this approach violates an axiom of international trade that we emphasized earlier in the chapter. A shrinkage in imports inevitably and inescapably produces a corresponding contraction in exports. If imports decline, exports must correspondingly decline, because other countries do not have dollars with which to purchase American goods. The only way they acquire dollars is by selling goods and services to the United States (or to third countries that have accumulated dollars). Thus, it is totally unrealistic to imagine that some quantity of imports (say, up to $16 billion annually) could be eliminated from the balance of payments without at the same time eliminating an equivalent amount of exports, assuming that the United States did not give or lend other countries the dollars they lost through curtailed foreign trade. Ironically, if trade restrictions were imposed to cure the balance-of-payments difficulty, the United States might, in fact, lose *more* gold than it has been losing, since it customarily sells more in the world market than it buys!

These considerations thus suggest the most promising course for correcting the nation's trade deficit, an alternative that the Kennedy and Johnson Administrations emphasized repeatedly in discussions with American business and labor groups and with the general public. This is a significant expansion *in American exports*. Thus President Kennedy told a White House trade conference late in 1963 that if business firms could raise the level of their exports by 10 percent, this would cover the gold loss arising from the trade deficit. The President pointed out that American exports were currently about 4 percent of the Gross National Product—about half the ratio to the GNP recorded a century ago! He also noted that if American exports had held at the level attained in 1957, the United States would have no balance-of-payments problem.[71] Throughout the late 1950s and early 1960s,

in other words, the United States had not only failed to maintain its earlier export growth; exports had actually declined, as a percentage of the GNP.

What are the prospects that such a modest expansion in exports can be achieved? Does a recently declining export rate mean that the United States is losing its ability to compete with foreign producers, whose wage levels are significantly lower than those paid in the United States? This conclusion is often drawn by groups advocating higher tariffs or other measures to restrict imports. Yet there is perhaps no more deeply ingrained and widely cultivated myth in the American mind than the idea that high wage levels and the standard of living prevailing in the United States prevent American producers from competing successfully against foreigners in the world market. Even when this idea is sincerely believed (and often it is disseminated by propagandists), it derives from a lack of understanding of the forces affecting a nation's competitive position in world trade. It overlooks the fact that one element alone affecting productive costs—in this case, wage rates—signifies little or nothing about a nation's ability to compete successfully. What counts is the *over-all cost of production*. Labor and business leaders alike are agreed that in the production of many commodities, the United States has the strongest competitive position of any leading industrial nation. As George Meany, head of the AFL-CIO, said in 1962:

> We can compete with anyone because we have the skill and the know-how to do it. I have no apology to make for high wages in the United States. These high wages are based on performance, and every progressive employer knows it.[72]

In the same period, a leading business spokesman, Eric Johnston, lamented the prevalence of the "myth" that American firms cannot compete in the world market. He observed that for a nine-month period in 1961, "our total exports to Western Europe were 59 percent greater than our total imports from that region, and our exports to Japan were 73 percent greater than our total imports from there." Mr. Johnston went on to identify the only significant criterion for comparing the competitive positions of nations: their *productivity* or output per man-hour. He cited the case of Japan, often viewed as one of America's foremost competitors in foreign markets. Overlooking the fact for the moment that Japan normally buys a much larger quantity of goods than it sells in American markets, it is a total misconception to think that American wage rates give Japan an unfair advantage in trade competition. As Mr. Johnston explained:

> A study some time ago showed that when the average Japanese worker was earning 22 cents an hour, his American counterpart was receiving $1.95 an hour. But the Japanese worker produced 30 cents' worth of merchandise an hour, while the American produced $3.19 worth an hour.

Another study showed that "a coal miner in the United States is paid eight times as much an hour as a Japanese coal miner, but produces fourteen times as much coal per hour."[73] Yet another study has shown more generally that in many broad industrial segments—processed food, paper and paper products, chemicals, rubber products, electrical and other kinds of machinery—the United States either has an advantageous competitive position in the world market or its position is roughly comparable to those of other industrialized nations.[74] In agricultural commodities, there is no question of the American farmer's ability to produce a wide variety of crops more cheaply than can farmers of other countries. In fact, a deep concern expressed by countries exporting agricultural goods is that the United States may impair their economic stability by offering its large agricultural surpluses for sale on the world market.

If it is clear that in many economic sectors, American producers are capable of competing successfully with foreigners, it is also plain: (1) that their position cannot be maintained without constant efforts to raise productive levels in the United States, and (2) that the differential between American productivity, giving firms in the United States a competitive advantage, and that of other industrialized countries is diminishing. This is suggested by the fact that by the mid-1960s, American sales abroad were expanding only slightly; the improvement in the balance-of-payments position by 1964 was produced by factors other than expanding exports. All of this means that, perhaps more than in any other period of American history, all segments of American society were required to be continually aware of the connection between "internal" and "external" affairs. If the actions and policies of government, and of influential groups within the American society, could ever be meaningfully separated into domestic and foreign developments, the balance-of-payment issue meant that this era had passed. The Kennedy and Johnson Administrations were amply aware that a variety of steps had to be taken to enhance the competitive position of American producers. These included negotiation of favorable trade agreements, expansion of foreign markets, modernization of plant and equipment, reduction of obstacles to increased trade, creation of new credit facilities for business firms wishing to expand foreign sales, and research and development to create new products. Above all, any significant expansion in exports would require a new concern for *wage and price stability* at home, particularly when wage and price increases tend to outstrip gains in productivity. This was the challenge that confronted the American nation in its international economic affairs in the 1960s. The extent to which Americans successfully responded to it would determine in no small measure the ability of the United States to lead the free world politically and diplomatically.

NOTES

1. *The New York Times*, May 18 and May 25, 1958.
2. Michael A. Heilperin, "U.S. Foreign Economic Policy," *Fortune*, **57** (June, 1958), 134.
3. J. Frederick Dewhurst and associates, *America's Needs and Resources* (New York: Twentieth Century Fund, 1955), pp. 668–676.
4. Department of State, *Together We Are Strong*, Publication No. 6571, "Commercial Policy Series" (Washington, D.C.: 1958), p. 11. Highlights America's growing dependence on foreign trade.
5. Dewhurst, *op. cit.*, p. 716.
6. Christian A. Herter, "International Trade and Our National Security," *Department of State Bulletin*, **38** (May 5, 1958), 732.
7. *The New York Times*, February 4, 1962.
8. Thomas C. Mann, "American Trade Policy and the Lessons of the 1930's," *Department of State Bulletin*, **38** (June 2, 1958), 895–898.
9. "Congress and the Reciprocal Trade Act," *Congressional Digest*, **37** (April, 1958), 97–99; *The New York Times*, August 10, 1958.
10. "White House Holds Conference on Export Expansion," *Department of State Bulletin*, **49** (October 14, 1963), 602–

604; *The New York Times*, January 10, 1964.

11. Philip H. Trezise, "The Trade Expansion Program," *Department of State Bulletin*, 48 (April 1, 1963), 497.

12. Philip H. Trezise, "The United States and the European Economic Community," *Department of State Bulletin*, 48 (June 24, 1963), 973.

13. Douglas MacArthur, II, "United States Trade Relations with the New Europe: The Challenge and the Opportunities," *Department of State Bulletin*, 48 (February 4, 1963), 178.

14. *Ibid.*, p. 176.

15. Trezise, "The United States and the European Economic Community," *op. cit.*, p. 974, and Louis Banks, "What Kennedy's Free-Trade Program Means to Business," *Fortune*, 66 (March, 1962), p. 104.

16. *Wall Street Journal*, August 28, 1961, dispatch by Lindley H. Clark, Jr.

17. *The New York Times*, November 20, 1963.

18. *The New York Times*, December 30, 1963.

19. The ideological rationale behind this expanded Communist economic offensive, involving careful attention to the needs of the underdeveloped countries, is set forth in the following source, which provides the text of the Communist party program adopted in 1961: Harrison E. Salisbury, *Khrushchev's "Mein Kampf"* (New York: Belmont, 1961).

20. These and other provisions of the TEA are discussed in *Congressional Quarterly Almanac: 1962*, 18, 249–295.

21. *The New York Times*, September 23, 1962.

22. Peter Hendry, "The Chicken-War Stew," *The Reporter*, 29 (November 7, 1963), 31. See also Michael A. Heilperin and Robert Lubar, "It's an International 'Farm Mess' Now," *Fortune*, 67 (May, 1963), 135–137, 210–216.

23. *The New York Times*, December 31, 1963.

24. *The New York Times*, September 19, 1963.

25. "U.S. Grain Dealers to be Allowed to Sell Wheat to Soviet Union and Eastern Europe," *Department of State Bulletin*, 49 (October 28, 1963), 660.

26. International Cooperation Administration, *The Strategic Trade Control System, 1948–1956* (Washington, D.C.: 1957), pp. 1–13, 33–34.

27. *The Nashville Tennessean*, January 9, 1964.

28. *The New York Times*, January 13, 1964.

29. *The New York Times*, December 23 and 29, 1963; January 5, 1964.

30. *The New York Times*, June 15, 1958.

31. *The New York Times*, October 6, 1963.

32. *Congressional Quarterly Weekly Report*, May 24, 1963, p. 801.

33. See the chart in *The New York Times*, November 3, 1963.

34. Agency for International Development, *The Story of A.I.D.* (Washington, D.C.: no date).

35. Agency for International Development, *The Foreign Aid Program Today: Answers To Four Basic Questions* (Washington, D.C.: 1963), p. 9.

36. Agency for International Development, *Report to the Congress on the Foreign Assistance Program for Fiscal Year 1962* (Washington, D.C.: 1963), p. 4.

37. AID, *The Foreign Aid Program Today*, *op. cit.*, p. 10.

38. *The New York Times*, December 22, 1963.

39. AID, *The Story of A.I.D.*, *op. cit.*, and see the text of President Johnson's budget for 1965 in *The New York Times*, January 22, 1964.

40. AID, *Report to the Congress*, *op. cit.*, pp. 32–33; *The New York Times*, January 22, 1964.

41. Sherman Adams, *First-Hand Report: The Story of the Eisenhower Administration* (New York: Harper & Row, 1961), pp. 389–390.

42. *United States in World Affairs: 1962* (New York: Harper & Row, 1963), p. 369; AID, *The Foreign Aid Program*, *op. cit.*, p. 3.

43. *United States in World Affairs: 1962*, *op. cit.*, p. 369.

44. AID, *Report to the Congress*, *op. cit.*, pp. 52–53.

45. "The Global Stake of U.S. Business," *Fortune*, 67 (December, 1963), 129, and accompanying charts.

46. *Idem.*

47. President John F. Kennedy, "Free-World Defense and Assistance Programs," *Department of State Bulletin*, 48 (April 22, 1963), 595.

48. Special Committee To Study the Foreign Aid Program, *American Private Enterprise, Foreign Economic Development, and the Aid Programs*, 85th Congress, 1st Session (Washington, D.C.: 1957), p. 56.

49. *Ibid.*, pp. 57–58.

50. AID, *Report to the Congress*, *op. cit.*, pp. 43–45.

51. *Ibid.*, pp. 45–46.

52. *Ibid.*, p. 58.

53. AID, *The Story of A.I.D.*, *op. cit.*; and David E. Bell, "The Impact of Foreign Aid on the American Economy," *Department of State Bulletin*, 49 (November 25, 1963), 830.

54. President Kennedy, "Free-World Defense and Assistance Programs," *op. cit.*, p. 594.

55. AID, *Foreign Aid Program Today, op. cit.,* p. 7.
56. *The New York Times,* March 26, 1961.
57. Quoted in Robert J. Manning, "U.S. Foreign Policy: Problems and Challenges for 1963," *Department of State Bulletin,* 48 (January 28, 1963), 140.
58. *The New York Times,* November 9 and 15, 1963.
59. *The New York Times,* December 22, 1963; Chester Bowles, "Foreign Aid: The Essential Factors for Success," *Department of State Bulletin,* 48 (June 17, 1963), 939.
60. Bowles, *op. cit.,* p. 940.
61. *The New York Times,* December 22, 1963.
62. *Idem.*
63. AID, *The Foreign Aid Program Today, op. cit.,* pp. 8–9.
64. *The New York Times,* December 27, 1963, and January 12, 1964.
65. AID, *Report to the Congress, op. cit.,* pp. 40–43.
66. *The New York Times,* January 4, 1964.
67. *The New York Times,* January 6, 1964.
68. *The New York Times,* September 30, 1963.
69. *The New York Times,* January 6, 1964.
70. Bell, *op. cit.,* p. 830.
71. "White House Holds Conference on Export Expansion," *Department of State, op. cit.,* p. 595.
72. *The New York Times,* March 25, 1962.
73. Eric Johnston, "America Can't Compete? 'A Myth,' " *New York Times Magazine,* March 11, 1962, p. 17.
74. Banks, *op. cit.,* p. 104.

16 ➡ THE QUEST FOR WORLD
PEACE AND SECURITY ➡

Over two millennia separate the mutual defense leagues established by the ancient Greeks
from the United Nations organization set up
at the end of World War II. Yet statesmen
dedicated to the goal of world peace and
security in the modern period follow a path
through the jungle of international anarchy
which has been blazed by countless predecessors. Oftentimes the trail has grown dim; frequently it has veered off into the tangled
thickets of wars and the quagmires of competing national interests. The ultimate destination
has sometimes been obscured by clouds of
suspicion, hate, ignorance.

But the vision has persisted and, in spite of
obstacles and digressions in the unfolding of
historical events, the quest has gone on. Gradually, mankind has acquired renewed faith in
its ability to reach the final goal, greater skill
in the use of techniques and institutional
devices to cultivate harmonious intercourse
among nations, and heightened awareness that
the abolition of war as an instrument of national policies may well be a prerequisite for
survival of civilization on the planet. Every
age has added its legacy to the reservoir of
insights and tools available to contemporary
statesmen. We must confine our attention to
those most directly relevant to American foreign relations.*

* Limitations of space prevent us from dealing
extensively with pre-United Nations efforts to
achieve workable international organization and
respect for world law. Students are strongly urged,
however, to familiarize themselves with these earlier
movements by reading some of the worthwhile
studies available, such as: American Association for
the United Nations, An Eleven Year Review of the

INTERNATIONAL ORGANIZATION BEFORE WORLD WAR II

Nineteenth-Century Antecedents

Conditions in the nineteenth century were
peculiarly conducive to impressive strides
toward reaching the goal of effective international organization and toward inculcating
acceptance of world law. After 1815, techniques for "consultation" among powerful
European countries emerged within the Concert of Europe. The Holy Alliance sought,
admittedly with limited success, to inject
Christian principles into the conduct of international affairs. Significant progress came
about in socioeconomic-administrative aspects
of interstate relations by agreements establishing such bodies as the Rhine River Commission (1868), the International Telegraphic
Convention (1865), the Universal Postal
Union (1874), and many others.[1]

Meantime, international law was being
strengthened. Noteworthy developments in-

League of Nations (New York: League of Nations
Association, 1931); Edgar E. Davis, Pioneers of
World Order (New York: Columbia University
Press, 1944); D. F. Fleming, The United States
and the League of Nations, 1918–1920 (New York:
Putnam, 1932); the same author's The United
States and World Organization (Garden City,
N.Y.: Doubleday, 1945); Institute on World Or-
ganization, World Organization: A Balance Sheet
of the First Great Experiment (Washington, D.C.:
American Council on Public Affairs, 1942); Ger-
ald J. Mangone, A Short History of International
Organization (New York: McGraw-Hill, 1954);
Gilbert Murray, From the League to the U.N.
(New York: Harper & Row, 1951).

cluded international agreements on the abolition of the slave trade; various conventions dealing with fisheries and marginal territorial waters; agreements aimed at mitigating the barbarities of naval and land warfare; and the Hague Conferences late in the nineteenth century, which established machinery for arbitrating disputes among nations and for reducing armaments.[2]

By 1900, the United States had assumed an active role in these activities. It supported the Permanent Court of Arbitration at the Hague by submitting cases to it. An attempt was made by President Taft to broaden the area of disputes which the United States would submit to arbitration; but it encountered formidable resistance in the Senate, where so many exceptions were demanded that Taft finally abandoned the effort. President Wilson's idealistic and pacifistically inclined Secretary of State, William Jennings Bryan, resumed the crusade. Eventually, 30 "cooling-off treaties" were negotiated between the United States and other countries, of which 21 were ratified by the Senate and proclaimed. These provided for arbitration of disputes by impartial bodies. The signatories were not required to accept recommendations made, but they pledged not to begin hostilities until after the arbitration commission had submitted its report.[3]

The League of Nations

The League of Nations was the culmination of an evolutionary movement often proceeding on many fronts at once, directed at gaining adherence to principles of international law and at securing formal and informal agreements for the peaceful settlement of disputes among nations. What looked like the total collapse of efforts to avert war in the period 1914–1918 was in reality but a temporary though crucial deviation from the charted course in the history of international organization. World War I witnessed physical destruction, bloodletting, and social disorganization on a scale seldom equaled in human society to that time. It furnished a powerful stimulus to an often complacent Victorian world for eliminating war and creating machinery for nonviolent adjustment of disagreements in the world community. Out of the "war to end wars" and to "make the world safe for democracy" came intensive and widespread study of methods for setting up a viable international organization. From numerous sources, both of-

ficial and private, suggestions and proposals were made which finally coalesced into the Covenant of the League of Nations, the first international organization in history providing a continuously functioning body to study and deal with issues affecting peace and security for all nations.

In many respects, the structure and operating principles of the League of Nations foreshadowed that of its successor, the United Nations. Three major organs were created. The *Council*, a revised version of the Concert of Europe, consisted of Britain, France, Italy and Japan, plus four smaller nations elected by the Assembly. The *Assembly* embraced the total membership of the League, initially 42 countries; it was roughly analogous to national legislatures. The *Secretariat* was the permanent administrative body, whose head, the Secretary-General, was nominated by the Council and approved by the Assembly. The World Court was the League's legal tribunal. In addition, there grew up a host of lesser agencies in the economic-social field.

An imprecise boundary separated the functions of the two major policy-making agencies, the Council and the Assembly. The Covenant gave both certain independent functions; yet both were also empowered to deal with any question affecting world peace and security. Theoretically, the Council was expected to address itself to issues *directly* affecting peace and security, such as disarmament and the threat of war, while the Assembly was to consider more indirect contributory causes of international instability. The founders of the League, like the founders of the UN, envisioned that the smaller Council, where the great powers had a preponderant voice, would provide leadership and guidance to the larger Assembly in arriving at decisions on major causes of international tension.[4] And in time the Council indeed came to speak for the League, as corroborated by the fact that it held 106 meetings throughout the League's existence, whereas the Assembly met only once a year from 1920 to 1940.[5]

Uppermost among the League's objectives was the maintenance of peace. The Covenant required members to submit disputes to judicial organs or to the League Council and to observe a 90-day "cooling-off" period before resorting to hostilities over a dispute. The League's fatal weakness showed up when it had to grapple with aggressions by ambitious dictators after Japan's invasion of Manchuria in 1931. The League possessed no independent power to *compel* acceptance of its decisions by recalcitrant members and nonmembers. Recommendations by the Council, reports by fact-finding commissions, impassioned appeals to protect the "sovereign rights" of weaker countries, aroused public opinion, moral suasion, conferences among the great powers—all of these were used to no avail by the League to dissuade aggressive countries. Dictators in Germany, Italy, and Japan continued to defy the League with impunity, because the great powers hesitated to use collective force to stop them. With each successful aggression the League was rendered more and more impotent.

In some fields, however, the League of Nations accomplished lasting good. Its subsidiary organs vigorously and often successfully attacked problems like widespread disease, narcotics traffic, government barriers to communications, substandard conditions of labor, and the slave trade. Many of the League's less publicized activities made an undeniably valuable contribution in eliminating underlying causes of war and human misery. Moreover, the League's contribution was of inestimable importance in another respect: experience gained in establishing and successfully operating the first permanent international organization in history provided a rich backlog of precedents and insights which was drawn upon in innumerable instances by the founders of the United Nations.

The United States did not join the League of Nations, in spite of the fact that one of its greatest Presidents had secured Allied acceptance of it at the Paris Peace Conference. The overwhelming election of Republican President Warren Harding in 1920 was widely—and probably incorrectly—interpreted as a resounding public rejection of the League. The Senate refused to ratify the Treaty of Versailles as submitted by President Wilson, and Wilson refused to accept modifications which would make it palatable to the Senate. The impasse was never resolved, dooming the United States to remain outside the League.

Nevertheless, as time went on, the United States sent "unofficial observers" to Geneva. Working without fanfare, the observers cooperated with certain League activities, particularly in fields such as suppression of narcotics rings and white-slave traffic. They were able to communicate the American government's position on prevailing international issues to statesmen at Geneva. In 1934, the United States finally joined the International Labor Organization, which was loosely affiliated with the League, and in the same year it agreed to register its treaties at League headquarters.[6] That isolationism still was the dominating impulse in American foreign affairs, however, was indicated in 1935, when not even the politically adroit President Roosevelt could prevail upon two-thirds of the Senate to approve American membership in the World Court.

The United States held officially aloof from the proceedings of the League of Nations dealing with global political developments after 1920. American initiative in sponsoring the Washington Naval Armaments Conference (1921) and the Kellogg-Briand Pact (1928) denouncing war as an instrument of national policy, however, was indicative of America's willingness to work for peace. In the critical decade of the 1930s, the United States as a rule applauded efforts by the League to deal with aggression in Europe and Asia; and occasionally, Roosevelt and Secretary of State Hull took the initiative in trying to prod the League to even greater efforts. From time to time, vigorous condemnations of German expansionism and of Japanese perfidy emanated from Washington. But American officials were always restricted by two prohibitions: they dared not commit the country to a policy which demanded action, and particularly military action, to halt aggression, nor could they risk the accusation that American policy was being "dictated" by the rejected and still unpopular League of Nations.[7] These limitations, coupled with prolonged indecision in Washington regarding the long-run implications of Japan's expansionism in the Orient, meant that the United States was unprepared to render any tangible assistance to the League of Nations in a showdown and that its own unilateral response to repeated international crises was seldom an improvement over the growing paralysis displayed by the League of Nations. Considering the profound isolationist propensities of the American people, it was perhaps of no crucial significance that the United States failed to join the League of Nations. There is no evidence that, had the United States been a member, it was prepared to go beyond the feeble efforts exerted by England, France, and Russia in meeting the challenge of aggression head-on, with military force if necessary. Anything less could scarcely have averted the League's eventual demise.

The United Nations

Hitler's attack against Poland in the fall of 1939 ignited World War II. Soon every major power of the world was drawn into the vortex of that struggle. After the United States entered the war, following the Japanese attack against Pearl Harbor on December 7, 1941, American officials moved rapidly to integrate Allied war efforts and, more importantly for our subject, to lay the basis for a durable peace in the postwar era. By 1942, the State Department had initiated intensive preliminary studies of problems that would be encountered in assuring international stability after the Axis defeat. Executive and legislative officials collaborated intimately to generate support within the government and throughout the country at large for an international organization to facilitate maintenance of world peace. Careful attention was paid to the experience of the League of Nations.

In a series of conferences dating from early 1942, step by step the contours of the nascent United Nations emerged, as agreements were secured among the Allies concerning its purposes and guiding principles. At Moscow in the autumn of 1943, at Tehran in December, and finally at Dumbarton Oaks in the autumn of 1944 the "Big Five" (Great Britain, France, China, Soviet Russia, and the United States) negotiated agreements laying the foundations for the United Nations. The Dumbarton Oaks agreements indicated that the UN was to be much like its predecessor. The two major policy-making bodies were to be the Security Council and the General Assembly. The former, possessing primary responsibility for dealing with questions of international peace and security, was to reflect the preponderant influence of the Big Five in world affairs. These states were to be the "permanent" members, and seven smaller countries were to be rotating "nonpermanent" members elected for two years by the General Assembly. The Assembly's function theoretically was confined to discussing all other matters within the jurisdiction of the UN and, more broadly, to promoting human welfare. The League's Permanent Court of International Justice, renamed the International Court of Justice, was retained as the judicial organ of the new international organization.

Finally, the Dumbarton Oaks proposals included a Secretariat, to be headed by a Secretary-General who, according to Article 97 of the UN Charter, is designated "chief administrative officer of the Organization." The Secretariat was to be the UN's continuing executive office, charged with facilitating the carrying out of policies and taking an active part in their formulation. As we shall see, one of the most profound changes in the UN after 1945 was the emergence of the Secretary-General as an active force in negotiations seeking to eliminate causes of international tension.

After Dumbarton Oaks there remained the crucial question of voting within the Security Council—a question involving the guiding philosophy upon which the United Nations was to be constructed and operated thereafter. The great powers had been primarily responsible for the impending Axis defeat. Moreover, they had taken the initiative in planning for the UN, virtually presenting the smaller powers with a *fait accompli*. Two extreme alternatives were possible: either the emergent UN, following in the footsteps of the Concert of Europe after the Congress of Vienna, might become merely a mechanism whereby the great powers imposed their will upon the international community. Or else the UN would accept the principle of "one state, one vote," carrying the concept of the equality of nations to the point of giving all states, regardless of size and power, an equal opportunity to shape decisions. The first course led back to the wastelands of a world dominated by the great powers, in which global decisions were made by a handful of governments representing a small minority of the earth's population. The second path led to the swamp of futility, with the new international organization rapidly becoming impotent because decisions were made by a preponderance of weak states which possessed neither the power nor inclination to carry them out in the face of great-power opposition. In short, a formula had to be found which in some way would blend the realities of the existing international power structure with the broad principles of equality, responsibility, and respect for the rights of weaker countries.

Such a formula was agreed upon at the Yalta Conference in February, 1945. Here it was decided that Security Council decisions involving *procedural* (i.e., presumably minor) questions could be made by a majority of any seven members of the Council. But on *substantive* matters (i.e., highly important questions affecting peace and security) decisions could only be reached by the *unanimous* vote of the great powers, plus the affirmative votes of at least two of the nonpermanent members. Parties to a dispute before the Council, however, were prohibited from voting. Each permanent member in effect possessed a "veto" —a term not mentioned in the Charter. If the Security Council could not act in matters affecting peace and security with the concurrence of *all* the great powers, then it could not act at all.

The UN Charter was drawn up and signed at the 50-nation San Francisco Conference held April 25–June 26, 1945. The smaller states objected vigorously to the preponderant voice given to the Big Five in the Security Council. While the great powers remained adamant on retention of the veto, other concessions were made to accommodate the viewpoints of smaller countries. As an example, the draft Charter was amended to make more forceful the UN's concern for "fundamental human rights," "social progress" and "better standards of life"—matters of the highest concern to newly independent and dependent countries throughout Asia and Africa. A vastly strengthened Economic and Social Council, was elevated into a major organ of the UN.*

* The Charter provision permitting the Economic and Social Council to negotiate working relationships with specialized agencies active in the economic-social field proved especially important. In some cases, these agencies already existed; after 1945, their efforts were coordinated as closely as possible with the UN. In other cases, the UN created certain specialized agencies. Agencies already in the field, and later brought under the jurisdiction of the UN, include the Universal Postal Union (UPU), the International Labor Organization (ILO), the Food and Agriculture Organization (FAO), the International Monetary Fund (IMF), and the International Bank for Reconstruction and Development (IBRD). Agencies which were in the formative stage or were created after 1945 include the International Civil Aviation Organization (ICAO), the UN Educational, Scientific and Cultural Organization (UNESCO), the World Health Organization (WHO), the International Refugee Organization (IRO), and the International Trade Organization (ITO). A total of 11 "specialized agencies" of the UN exist. While they possess a certain degree of autonomy, they are also loosely under the jurisdiction of the General Assembly and the Economic and Social Council. For a fuller treatment of their precise relationship to the UN, see Leland M. Goodrich and Edward Hambro, *Charter of the United Nations* (Boston: World Peace Foundation, 1949), pp. 73–78. An informative treatment of the activities of these agencies is contained in Graham Beckel, *Workshops for the World: The Specialized Agencies of the UN* (New York: Abelard-Schuman, 1954).

A completely new body, the Trusteeship Council, was also added and given responsibilities for supervising governments of dependent people and of advancing their welfare.

The UN—Basic Assumptions and Underlying Concepts

For a proper understanding of the United Nations and of America's relationship to it, it is essential to grasp certain assumptions and underlying concepts upon which the UN was founded. Failure to understand these and their implications has often led to widespread confusion in American public attitudes toward the UN and has sometimes placed unnecessary obstacles in the path of the successful utilization of the UN as an instrument for world peace and security.

First, the United Nations was designed to be, and it remains, *a league of sovereign states, not a world government.* This distinction has sometimes been blurred by both advocates and critics of international organization. The UN was established to facilitate harmonious relationships among *sovereign* countries to achieve ends specified in the UN Charter. While the Preamble to the Charter speaks of "the *peoples* of the United Nations," it goes on to observe that "our respective *Governments* . . . have agreed to the present Charter . . . " (italics added).

The UN possesses virtually none of the attributes associated with sovereign political entities: the power to tax, to pass laws, to impose its will directly upon citizens, and to punish *individuals* who violate its laws. Exceptions exist in one sphere only: enforcement of Charter provisions against violators of international peace and security. Article 2 of the Charter expressly prohibits the UN from intervening "in matters which are essentially within the domestic jurisdiction of any state," leaving it to the states concerned to decide what these matters are. A committee of the San Francisco Conference held that any nation would be free to withdrew from the UN "if its rights and obligations . . . were changed by Charter amendment in which it has not concurred and which it finds itself unable to accept."[8] In countless ways, the preliminary wartime studies of the UN, the debates at San Francisco, and the Charter itself leave no doubt that the founders were establishing an institution which accepted national sovereignty as supreme except in the case of threats to the peace. They sought to create an international environment in which sovereignty could be exercised more beneficially for the welfare of mankind.[9]

In the second place, the United Nations was envisioned by its originators as predominantly an instrumentality *to preserve and maintain peace and security.* The implications of this fact for the later development of the UN, and for its subsequent influence upon world affairs, can hardly be exaggerated. For in many crucial respects, the United Nations presupposed the existence or the early establishment of the peace it was expected to preserve; it was not designed to bring that peace into existence.

In at least three important respects, however, the peace which the UN was expected to preserve was not achieved after 1945 and has not been altogether achieved today. The most obvious instance was in relations among the great powers themselves. "Great-power unanimity," the keystone of the arch of collective security, began to disintegrate after 1945 in the face of cold-war antagonisms between two rival diplomatic blocs. Having postulated its existence and future effectiveness upon a continuation of wartime unity among the great powers, the UN possessed very few methods for creating an essential condition which its founders had taken for granted. The United Nations was set up to deal with *future* threats to the peace which met a twofold definition: (1) situations which the great powers *unanimously* recognized as endangering international tranquility; and (2) those with which the great powers were prepared to deal on a basis of *collective action.* Quite obviously, disputes among the great powers themselves do not meet this test—a fact which as much as any other explains why the UN's influence in settling cold-war disputes since 1945 has often been peripheral.

By contrast, it was significant that the *rapprochement* in Soviet-American relations that began to appear by the late 1950s largely evolved *outside* the United Nations. Whether in East-West negotiations over the Berlin Crisis, or in efforts to stabilize a turbulent situation in Southeast Asia, the UN tended to play an incidental role. When it was in some measure effective, as in the Cuban controversy, it was utilized as a mechanism for giving expression to and carrying out great-power agreements largely arrived at by direct diplomatic negotiations.

Another sphere in which the UN presupposed an established peace was in restoring defeated Axis countries to the family of nations. The founders deliberately divorced the UN Charter from the peace treaties for all defeated Axis powers, in order to escape the stigma attached to the League of Nations because of its intimate identification with what proved in some countries a highly unpopular peace settlement. The UN has taken no role in negotiating Axis peace treaties since World War II. One of the issues which lies at the heart of continued cold-war tensions—the territorial division of Germany—remains an issue toward which the UN has made, and can make, little positive contribution, so long as the great powers remain divided.

Still another sphere in which the peace the UN was supposed to safeguard did not materialize was in relations between colonial countries and their possessions. Here again, the founders of the UN either did not anticipate postwar tensions over colonial questions, or else they counted on "great-power unanimity" to resolve problems which might arise. In any event, the UN was given no formal jurisdiction over the vast majority of pre-existing colonial relationships. Charter provisions pertaining to dependent areas, in the words of one commentary, applied only to a limited number of "territories administered under League mandates or for which at a later time trusteeship agreements might be negotiated."[10] While certain obligations were assumed by all members of the UN in administering their colonial affairs, no mechanism or procedures were set up whereby international control could be exerted to assure compliance with Charter obligations.

Immediately after the war, the UN did experience some success in dealing with colonial disputes, as in Indonesia, Syria, and Lebanon. But in many other critical instances, involving French colonialism in Indochina and North Africa, British colonialism in Kenya and Cyprus, and what can be correctly designated as Russian colonialism in Eastern Europe, the UN has been conspicuously unsuccessful in preserving the peace. Largely because peace did not exist in many of these areas at the time of the UN's establishment and, throughout the years that followed, the UN possessed very few facilities for resolving these tensions. When colonial conflicts became intertwined with cold-war issues, progressively involving the diplomatic ambitions and interests of the great powers, the difficulties facing the UN became well-nigh insurmountable.

Admittedly, the UN's record in dealing with colonial disputes, or with the consequences of colonial discords, has by no means been totally negative. By the late 1950s, two tendencies combined to inject the UN more than ever into colonial controversies: the increasing influence of the Afro-Asian world in the General Assembly, and the emergence of that organ as, in most important respects, the dominant agency of the United Nations. Newly independent states of Africa, the Middle East, and Asia have tended to take a "dynamic" view of the United Nations, leading them to favor greater reliance upon the UN, and to encourage a more liberal interpretation of the scope of its powers under the Charter, than the great powers often are willing to accept.* Hence, such states have often converted the UN into a forum for denouncing Portuguese or French colonialism, for demanding a speedup in the "timetable" of independence for dependent societies, and for calling for outright UN intervention in disputes such as the Congo Crisis of the early 1960s. It is noteworthy, however, that even in the Congo discord, direct UN involvement came only *after* the Congo received its independence and after it was clear that a "threat to the peace" existed in the center of Africa.

THE UN AND THE POSTWAR WORLD

Since our task is confined to describing and assessing problems of international organization as they bear upon the foreign policy of the United States, we cannot undertake a comprehensive treatment of the evolution and

major activities of the United Nations after 1945.** Nevertheless, some familiarity with the UN's development and its efforts to cope with leading international issues is indispensable for our purpose.

Decline of the Security Council

Critics of the UN often overlook the solid record of accomplishment which it has amassed throughout the postwar period. Notable achievements have been the withdrawal of Soviet troops from Iran's northern provinces in 1946; termination of colonial rule over Syria and Lebanon in the same year; resolution of the conflict between Indonesia and the Netherlands in the period 1947–1949; successful adjudication of a dispute between Great Britain and Albania in 1947; assistance in preserving the sovereignty of Greece in 1946–1948; prevention of war between India and Pakistan over Kashmir after 1948; partial responsibility for ending the Berlin blockade in 1949; resistance to armed Communist attack against South Korea from 1950 to 1953, and supervision of the Korean truce; conclusion and subsequent supervision of an armistice between Israel and the Arab states in 1950; termination of hostilities growing out of the Anglo-French and Israeli invasion of Egypt in 1956 and continuing enforcement of the armistice agreement by a United Nations Emergency Force stationed on the Israeli-Egyptian border; intensive efforts late in 1958 to deal with crises in the Middle East involving Iraq, Lebanon, and Jordan; the prevention of anar-

* Dramatic testimony concerning the viewpoints of the neutralist world toward the United Nations was furnished by the Declaration adopted by the Conference of Non-Aligned Countries in Belgrade on September 6, 1961. Nearly every article in this document directly urged or implied a greater reliance upon the UN to resolve pressing international and regional problems, as in the demand of the conference for the "immediate termination of all colonial occupation"; intensified UN pacification efforts in the Congo; condemnation of South Africa's racial policies; stepped-up disarmament activities, under UN auspices and with participation by neutralist countries; establishment of a UN Capital Development Fund to render greater assistance to the underdeveloped world than was currently being furnished by other programs; expansion in the membership of subsidiary organs of the UN; and a reorganization of the UN Secretariat, in which Afro-Asian membership would be increased. See the text of this declaration in *Documents on American Foreign Relations: 1961* (New York: Harper & Row, 1962), pp. 464–473.

** Bibliography on the United Nations is copious. Aside from the *Official Records* of the UN's principal organs, described in the *United Nations Documents Index* issued monthly, a number of valuable summaries and commentaries exist. Official publications include the *Yearbook of the United Nations*, summarizing annual activities; the *United Nations Bulletin*, issued bi-weekly; and the *Annual Report of the Secretary-General on the Work of the Organization*. These also cite relevant documentary materials for further reading in selected cases. Also valuable is the State Department's publication entitled *U.S. Participation in the United Nations*, issued annually, summarzing the UN's activities with emphasis upon America's role.

Helpful secondary studies include the summaries and articles appearing in the journal *International Organization*, which contains resumés of UN activities in its quarterly issues; publications in the Carnegie Foundation's series *International Conciliation*, which contains a number of illuminating studies on selected cases involving the UN; studies in the State Department's "International Organization and Conference Series"; and the summaries and essays in New York University's series *Annual Review of United Nations Affairs*.

chy in the Congo in 1960 and thereafter; and attempts to prevent Greeks and Turks from carrying on a war of mutual extermination on Cyprus during 1964.

While these achievements are an eloquent tribute to the contribution of the United Nations in its comparatively brief existence, it cannot be denied that in one vital area—mitigating tensions between the Soviet-led Communist world and the American-led free-world coalition—the UN's role has often been minimal. With rare exceptions, such as ending the Berlin blockade, the Security Council has been able to accomplish very little in adjusting disagreements between these two antagonistic power blocs. Time and again, Soviet vetoes have prevented the Security Council from taking action in critical international disputes. In the face of a relentless bombardment of Russian *nyet's*, the Council's ability to discharge its duties under the Charter has inevitably declined and the over-all prestige of the United Nations has been seriously impaired. Yet, as we shall see, the United States cannot wholly escape responsibility for the growing paralysis of the Security Council. The United States has never vetoed an important measure dealing with peace and security. More perhaps by omission than by commission, by subtle means rather than by deliberately obstructionist tactics, the United States has also played a part in weakening the Security Council's influence. The Council's decline is reflected in the decrease in the number of its meetings. In 1946, the Security Council held 88 meetings; in 1948, 168 meetings; in 1950, 73 meetings; in 1952, 42 meetings; and in 1954, 32 meetings.[11] Repeated deadlocks in the Council over inflammatory cold-war issues at length resulted in a kind of constitutional revolution whereby the Council's functions have more and more been assumed by the General Assembly.

What factors explain this profound change in the character of the United Nations? The obvious answer is to point to instance after instance in which the Security Council was immobilized by the Soviet veto. Yet this is a superficial explanation which mistakes symptoms for causes. Excessive Soviet use of the veto is not in itself the *cause* of the Council's inability to deal with threats to the peace involving the great powers. Impotence stems from the fact that the world remains divided into powerful sovereign nations which are prepared to fight, if necessary, rather than to see their "vital interests" infringed, whether by nations acting jointly under UN auspices, or acting in coalition, or acting unilaterally. Under these conditions, the veto furnishes the only possible way out for an international organization which must depend upon the voluntary consent and strength of its members for its enforcement powers. When UN action is contemplated against one of the strongest members as, for example, was widely advocated in the case of Soviet intervention in Hungary in 1956, then one of two possible alternatives exists: either the UN attempts to compel acceptance of its decrees by international malefactors at the risk of starting the third world war, or else it agrees that enforcement action under the circumstances is impracticable.

Abuse of the veto then can only be interpreted as symptomatic of the fact that peace does not exist among the great powers and that the UN was not designed to achieve it. Outright abolition of the veto in the Security Council would in no way alter the underlying international power structure which has contributed to the Council's ineffectualness in the face of recurrent cold-war tensions. If the Council were permitted, by a simple majority vote, to take a decision, let us say, on Soviet intervention in the affairs of the Baltic states, the Council would sooner or later have to make the choice of fighting Russia to enforce the decision or of giving up the proposed action as unattainable. Little is to be gained, therefore, in blaming the veto for the Security Council's impotence. Assuming the continuance of the cold war, there is virtually no prospect that elimination of the veto would restore the Council to the position originally assigned to it by the founders.

Emergence of a Strengthened General Assembly

Contemporaneous with the eclipse of the Security Council has been transformation of the General Assembly into the UN's most influential organ. Our discussion has called attention to attempts in the Charter to distinguish rather sharply between the functions of the Council and the Assembly, assigning primary responsibility to the former for dealing with issues affecting peace and security. The Assembly, on the other hand, in the words of Article 10 of the Charter,

> may discuss any questions or any matters within the scope of the present Charter or

relating to the powers and functions of any organs provided for in the present Charter, and, except as provided in Article 12 [prohibiting the Assembly from making recommendations on issues pending before the Security Council], may make recommendations to the Members of the United Nations or to the Security Council or to both on any such questions or matters.

Save for questions directly pertaining to peace and security, therefore, the founders intended that the General Assembly should possess very broad powers and that it should deal with sundry "indirect" and long-range causes of international instability. However, the Assembly is limited to "making recommendations" on matters within its jurisdiction.

Founded upon the principle of the equality of all members, the General Assembly was to be a great international forum in which countries great and small would have an opportunity to discuss any subject within the purview of the Charter. Military behemoths and pygmies alike were given an equal voice and an equal vote. At San Francisco, the United States had joined with the small states in demanding broad powers and equality of voting in the Assembly. One of the crises at the Conference had come when Soviet Russia refused to accept such a conception, only to give way in time to avert a total impasse.[12] A significant advance was made over the Assembly of the League of Nations, where unanimity was required for decisions, by the Charter provision that the Assembly could make decisions on an "important matter" by a two-thirds majority and on less important questions by a simple majority (Article 18). Apprehensive lest some of the smaller states lead the Assembly to discuss questions not properly within the competence of the United Nations, the American delegation at San Francisco took the initiative in inserting the Charter provision already cited (Article 2, Section 7) prohibiting *all* organs of the UN from intervening in matters which were "essentially within the domestic jurisdiction of any state."[13]

As cold-war antagonisms increasingly paralyzed the Security Council, the General Assembly began to emerge as the authoritative voice of the United Nations. A critical period was 1947–1948, when the General Assembly voted to partition the strife-torn land of Palestine into separate Jewish and Arab states and was called upon to deal with the violence which this act precipitated. After the Communist attempt to gain control over Greece in 1946–1948, the United States took the initiative in converting the Assembly into the UN's primary organ for dealing with political tensions and possible causes of war.

An important evolutionary step was the American-sponsored "interim assembly" plan introduced in 1947, whereby an interim committee could deal with inflammable international issues between sessions of the Assembly.[14] This was merely the forerunner of a much more sweeping transformation of the Assembly's powers. That step was the American-initiated "Uniting for Peace" resolution, presented in the fall of 1950 and passed by the General Assembly on November 3. Carefully taking note of the Security Council's inability to discharge its primary obligations under the Charter, the resolution observed that this did not "relieve Member States of their obligations or the United Nations of its responsibility under the Charter to maintain international peace and security." The resolution therefore provided that when the Security Council was deadlocked or failed to act "where there appears to be a threat to the peace," then the General Assembly

shall consider the matter immediately with a view to making appropriate recommendations to Members for collective measures, including in the case of a breach of the peace or act of aggression the use of armed force when necessary, to maintain or restore international peace and security.

If the Assembly were not in session when a threat to the peace occurred, it could meet in emergency special session within 24 hours; the request for an emergency meeting could be made by any seven members of the Security Council or by a majority of the members of the United Nations. Other important provisions of the resolution were establishment of a Peace Observation Commission under the auspices of the Assembly; recommendations that all governments cooperate with the commission; requests to each member to survey the resources it could make available to support efforts of the Council or the Assembly for enforcing peace; and establishment of a Collective Measures Committee to study and report on methods for strengthening international peace and security.[15]

The impact of these changes, in the words of Clark M. Eichelberger, was that the General Assembly became the "paramount organ" within the United Nations for adjusting international disputes. Eichelberger believes that the old balance between the Security Council and the Assembly "is not likely to be restored." Increasingly, it has fallen to the Assembly's lot to take over responsibility from the Security Council, as when the Assembly stationed a commission along the Greek border in 1947 to observe conditions there after the Council refused to act; when it gradually assumed the burden of successfully prosecuting the Korean War; and when it sought to enforce compliance with the Korean armistice agreement after 1953.[16]

When the Assembly had to deal with successive crises in Egypt and Hungary in 1956, the "Uniting For Peace" resolution was put into effect for the first time. It was of no avail in attempting to terminate Soviet oppression of the Hungarian revolutionary movement. This proved once again that the Assembly, where there is no veto, was no more successful than the Security Council, in dealing with issues on which one of the world's two power giants refused to accept UN directives.[17] The Assembly debates on the Suez dispute left no doubt that public opinion the world over was opposed to the Anglo-French and Israeli invasions of Egypt. As a result of negotiations which took place both inside and outside the UN, these countries agreed to withdraw their troops. For the first time in history, a "United Nations Emergency Force," consisting of military contingents from ten member-states, was created. Its task was to patrol the always tense Israeli-Egyptian frontier and to prevent further hostilities from erupting between these countries.[18] Whatever other results the Suez crisis of 1956 may have had, one of them was to enhance the prestige of the United Nations and to revivify its sometimes waning fortunes. In turning to the General Assembly in this crisis, it was the United States as much as any other country which took the lead in giving the UN responsibility for restoring stability to the Middle East.[19]

Yet, perhaps somewhat to the surprise of many students of international organization, the Congo Crisis that erupted in 1960 and continued for many months thereafter, demonstrated that the UN Security Council was not totally moribund. For it was under Security Council auspices that the UN Operations in the Congo (ONUC) were carried out. After the crisis had continued for several months, the General Assembly also took cognizance of the question and passed resolutions seeking to clarify the UN's role in the country. Debate on the floor of the Assembly over the activities of ONUC became heated and intense. Still, technically, it was the Security Council that supervised UN activities in this controversy.*

With the admission of Zanzibar and Kenya at the end of 1963, the United Nations contained 113 member states. The United States, which had taken the initiative in enhancing the General Assembly's role in the UN, found itself confronted with a vastly altered international organization. For among the 113 members of the UN, the Afro-Asian group (as we shall see, it would be incorrect to designate it as a "bloc") now commanded more than half of the Assembly's votes; approximately one-third of the nations represented in the Assembly (35 countries) were on the African continent. This signified a drastic quantitative change in the UN's membership from its foundation in 1945, when there were 13 Afro-Asian members, out of a total of 51 countries. Much more fundamentally, however, this phenomenon had transformed the character of the United Nations, by converting it from an instrument in which the great powers either had their way or could prevent action deleterious to their interests, into a world forum in which small, militarily weak nations possessed an unprecedented power to bring their influence to bear upon global affairs, and, more specifically, to utilize the General Assembly as a mechanism for expressing the neutralist viewpoints about dominant international issues.**

Evidence of the profound changes that had taken place within the UN was provided in the 18th Session of the General Assembly in 1963. Here, the Afro-Asian states insisted

---

* For a detailed treatment of UN handling of the Congo crisis, see Stanley Hoffman, "In Search of a Thread: The U.N. in the Congo Labyrinth," in Norman J. Padelford and Rupert Emerson, eds., *Africa and World Order* (New York: Praeger, 1963), pp. 63–94; and Colin Legum, *Congo Disaster* (Baltimore: Penguin, 1961).

** Secretary of State Dean Rusk pointed out early in 1964 that: "Theoretically, a two-thirds majority of the General Assembly would now be formed by nations with only 10 percent of the world's population, or who contribute, altogether, 5 percent of the assessed budget" of the United Nations. Rusk, however, in company with many other officials and observers of UN affairs, went on to add: "In practice, of course, this does not happen; and I do not share the dread expressed by some that the General Assembly will be taken over by its 'swirling majorities.' " In some measure, Rusk was answering sharp criticism that had been expressed about the UN by General de Gaulle's government within preceding months. *The New York Times*, January 11, 1964.

upon certain procedural and organizational reforms that they had sought for many years, particularly a reorganization of the great-power-dominated Security Council. Under Afro-Asian (joined by Latin American) impetus, the Assembly for the first time passed an amendment to the Charter that would increase the 11-nation Security Council to 15 members and that would similarly expand the 18-member Economic and Social Council to 27 members. In the reconstituted Security Council, Afro-Asian countries would get 5 of 10 elective seats, thereby changing an understanding that had prevailed since 1946, whereby the 6 elective seats on the Council had gone to Latin America (2 seats), Western Europe, Eastern Europe, the Middle East, and the British Commonwealth. Under the new arrangement, the veto would in effect be abolished; the Council could act if a measure received an affirmative vote from any 9 out of the 15 members. Writing at the end of 1963, one observer stated that "it appears to be foreordained that the African and Asian members will achieve their demands by one means or another, and that they will have a third of the votes in the Security Council within another year."[20]

Not only has the weight of increased Afro-Asian influence in the UN been cast behind far-reaching procedural and organizational changes. The emergence of an Afro-Asian majority in the General Assembly has also injected the United Nations as never before into the midst of global issues that often tended to be eclipsed by cold-war antagonisms before the 1960s. The small nations have taken advantage of their new majority in the Assembly to air their own grievances and demands. Increasingly, the UN has become their instrument for waging their own cold war against colonialism and economic backwardness, against the threat of nuclear annihilation, against racial discrimination, and disregard for human rights. The United Nations has thus evolved as an agency in which the full panoply of international issues is debated and acted upon, and in which the "have-not" nations of the world, a majority of whom espouses a neutralist position vis-à-vis cold-war power blocs, can make their voices heard. The United States, in other words, has discovered that a strengthened General Assembly is a double-edged sword. If it could cut the shackles that bound the UN as long as the Security Council was veto-ridden, today it can also slash away at the bonds of colonialism and racism, and it can occasionally be utilized to prod the great powers themselves into taking more vigorous action on matters of deep concern to a majority of UN members.

This is not to say or imply that under these circumstances the UN is *per se* detrimental to American diplomatic interests. Theoretically, with only one vote among 113, the United States is on a par in the General Assembly with such countries as Costa Rica, Dahomey, Kenya, and Cambodia. Allowing for occasional demagoguery and flamboyant speechmaking, most members of the UN are thoroughly aware of the realities of global politics. Their delegates are cognizant that effective UN action—at least, with respect to action affecting the interests of a great power—depends upon the concurrence of the United States, Western Europe, and the USSR. At a minimum, such activities are not likely to be effective in the face of outright opposition by one of the great industrial nations. Believing firmly in a *strengthened* United Nations, the smaller countries are usually mindful that totally irresponsible use of their majority in the Assembly could, in the end, destroy the very organization whose powers they wish to enhance. However psychologically unpalatable the fact may be, such countries are aware that the richer nations of the West and the Communist bloc cannot be coerced or intimidated; they must be persuaded and made to see that their own diplomatic interests are served by conciliation of the neutralist world on issues such as colonialism, economic development, or disarmament. To Americans who have become apprehensive about the implications of growing Afro-Asian influence in the UN, Ambassador Adlai Stevenson declared late in 1961:

There is an illusion in some quarters that the so-called "Afro-Asian bloc" always votes with the Soviet Union against the so-called "Western bloc." This is three mistakes in one, since, in the first place, neither the Afro-Asians nor, in the second place, the Western nations vote mechanically as blocs in the United Nations—and as long as each member is free to think for itself they never will.

Furthermore, the record abundantly proves that the members from Africa and Asia have not been afraid to find themselves voting on the same side as the United States; indeed, on great issues they have been doing so very often.

The Soviets do the best they can to put Africa and Asia against the West, and to side with the Africans and Asians. And one of the great untold stories of the United Nations—a story which I hope will one day be told in full—is the failure of this divisive strategy.[21]

In whatever degree it was incorrect to speak of the Afro-Asian "bloc" in the UN, it was nonetheless true that the emergence of an Afro-Asian group in the UN presented many new challenges to American policy-makers. If the United Nations had not become, and showed no sign of becoming, an instrument that regularly collided with American diplomatic interests, neither was it an instrument whose primary purpose was to *achieve* American foreign policy goals, particularly those directed against the Communist bloc. To an unprecedented degree, the UN would likely serve as a mediator between cold-war antagonists. More than ever, the diplomatically uncommitted states—whose new role was symbolized by Secretary General U Thant—would bring their influence to bear upon *both* cold-war power constellations. U Thant's mediatory role in achieving a peaceful resolution of the Cuban missile crisis in 1962 typified the function that the UN was likely to serve in response to the demands of its Afro-Asian members. As in that crisis, the UN may have permanently "solved" few problems that engendered cold-war animosities. Neither U Thant, nor the Afro-Asian majority in the General Assembly, nor any other UN agency was capable of eliminating the ideological conflict between the West and the Communist bloc. They could, however, alleviate great-power conflicts, confine them to nonviolent channels, insist upon continuing efforts to arrive at a modus vivendi, and make them generally more tolerable for the international community.

Economic and Social Activities

Sometimes overshadowed by the activities of the United Nations in peace and security matters are the myriad activities carried on by the UN in economic and social affairs touching hundreds of millions of people. An earlier portion of the chapter called attention to the fact that, to conciliate the small states, provisions for a strengthened Economic and Social Council were added to the Charter at San Francisco. The Economic and Social Council consists of 18 members elected by the General Assembly, each member serving for three years. As defined in Article 62, its province is sweeping, permit-

ting it to "make or initiate studies and reports" relating to "international economic, social, cultural, educational, health, and related matters"; to "make recommendations . . . to the General Assembly, to the Members of the United Nations, and to the specialized agencies"; and to "make recommendations for the purpose of promoting respect for, and observance of, human rights and fundamental freedoms for all."

Under the Economic and Social Council are eight functional commissions and three regional bureaus. In addition, it has several "operating bodies" like the UN International Children's Emergency Fund (UNICEF), the UN Relief and Works Agency for Palestine Refugees, and the UN Korean Reconstruction Agency. There are also 11 semiautonomous "specialized agencies," which were enumerated earlier in this chapter. Measured by the volume and quality of studies and publications turned out, the subsidiary organs of the Economic and Social Council have done a staggering and immensely valuable job. Frequent publications include a *World Economic Report, Review of International Commodity Problems, Statistical Yearbook, Demographic Yearbook, and Yearbook of International Trade*, to list merely a few titles from among the hundreds of comprehensive and specialized studies released so far.

Two broad concepts have thus guided United Nations activities in social and economic fields. One involves those activities carried on directly by the United Nations itself, through a centralized system of administration. Such operations include the Children's Fund (established in 1946), the Relief and Works Agency for Palestine Refugees (established in 1949), and the High Commissioner for Refugees (established in 1950). Another ambitious program was undertaken in 1950, when the Expanded Program of Technical Assistance (EPTA) was established. Down to 1962, the members of the UN voluntarily contributed $235 million for its operations.[22]

The second administrative concept is followed by the UN "specialized agencies," which largely function autonomously, with their own headquarters, secretariats, budgets, and programs. Some of these agencies, like the International Telecommunications Union, antedate the UN; in 1945, they were brought under UN jurisdiction. Others include the Food and Agriculture Organization, the International Monetary Fund, the World Health Organization, and the International Atomic Energy Agency. The principal reason for giving such agencies administrative independence was to free them from the diplomatic and political pressures that are felt within the UN itself and to enable them to carry on "professional" programs that are not affected by diplomatic differences dividing the world.[23]

That the work of the UN directly, and of its specialized agencies, in attacking social and economic problems in the underdeveloped world has been extremely valuable can hardly be doubted. The list of achievements is long and impressive—ranging from the assistance provided in reconstructing war-devastated South Korea, to a phenomenally successful antimalaria campaign in India, to continuing work against chronic diseases in the Nile valley, to efforts to eradicate rinderpest and other scourges to livestock in Africa. These and other programs, like the UN Children's Fund, have received the generous support of the American government and of millions of American citizens. This is not to say that such programs have not sometimes encountered organizational bottlenecks that impaired their effectiveness. One experienced American official at the UN, for example, has pointed to the "confusion implicit in working simultaneously on two divergent principles of organization" and to the "unavoidable jurisdictional friction" that sometimes characterizes UN programs. Nor have such programs always succeeded in escaping cold-war conflicts, as in the contest between the United States and the Soviet Union over the Director-General of the International Atomic Energy Agency, or Soviet failure to participate in the International Bank for Reconstruction and Development.[24] Nevertheless, these have proved essentially minor problems that have not, in the main, detracted from continuing UN programs in the social and economic field or produced serious American apprehensions about their value.

The UN and Global Economic Development

The United Nations, said a Bolivian delegate in 1957, "must assume the responsibility for seeing to it that living standards in the poorer countries gradually reach those of more prosperous states." Referring to the same problem a year earlier, Secretary of State Dulles declared that: "I would be in favor of seeing the United Nations take a more active interest in this business." And in 1959, a study by the Rockefeller Brothers Fund urged the United States to "make additional use of the United Nations in its aproach to economic aid."[25]

Few areas of United Nations concern have felt the impact of expanded Afro-Asian, supported by Latin American, membership as much as its operations in the field of economic development. In 1959, the underdeveloped world—with nearly half the earth's land area and almost half of its population—had an average per capita income of $120 annually, as contrasted with $1400 in the developed nations.[26] Since that time, the disparity between these two groups of countries in the global community has widened, as the industrialized countries of the world increased their economic growth rates more rapidly than did the poorer countries.

By the late 1950s, these considerations led the Afro-Asian members of the UN to launch a campaign for a vastly stepped-up program to promote the economic advancement of poorer countries. In time, these nations proposed the creation of a Special UN Fund for Economic Development (SUNFED), whose budget would be subscribed chiefly by the industrialized nations of the world. As alternatives, the United States proposed expanded activities by the UN Expanded Program of Technical Assistance (EPTA), created in 1949; EPTA received its impetus in part from the Truman Administration's Point Four program in the same period. Washington also urged the creation of a new technical fund (called the Special Fund) that would endeavor to raise development capital from sources not available through the United Nations.[27] American officials opposed SUNFED, ostensibly on the grounds that the United States could not make the kind of contribution visualized by its sponsors unless a global disarmament agreement permitted the diversion of funds now required for defense to expanded development programs. In reality, American opposition to SUNFED perhaps stemmed more directly from a variety of other factors: disillusionment about the UN in the United States, particularly as regards the failure of many of its members to support UN military efforts in the Korean War; American apprehension about Communist influence in the allocation of aid funds; growing opposition within the United States to foreign aid programs generally; legislative unwillingness to expand the contribution of the United States to UN operations (often growing out of a belief that its share was already too large); and widespread official and public opposition to relinquishing American control over aid funds provided other countries.

Official American coolness toward SUNFED and other suggestions contemplating a vastly expanded UN effort in development assistance programs, however, did not dampen the ardor of Afro-Asian advocates of such proposals. Faced with a widening disparity between the prices of goods they sold and goods they were required to buy in the world market, saddled with rising national indebtedness, and confronted with other evidences of acute economic need, by the mid-1960s such countries had become more inclined than ever to look to the United Nations for help in solving their economic problems. The crescendo of demands from the underdeveloped nations was highlighted by a UN Conference on Trade and Development, scheduled to meet in Geneva in the spring of 1964. Perhaps extravagantly described as "the biggest conference ever held anywhere on anything," this gathering, one commentator observed, was "a mass demonstration by the world's underdeveloped countries. They want more help." Their objectives included greatly augmented UN assistance programs, guaranteed price stability for their primary exports, and other steps calculated to enhance their economic conditions. The industrial nations of the world, on the other hand, had not concealed their opposition to such a conference; they had sought to defeat the idea for nearly three years.[28]

Increasingly vocal demands by the underdeveloped world for UN-sponsored development assistance and other economic measures placed the United States in an extremely awkward policy dilemma, by focusing attention upon ambivalences that had been present in the American position on this issue for many years. In an appearance before the UN General Assembly on September 25, 1961, for instance, President Kennedy had dramatically designated the 1960s as the "United Nations Decade of Development." He urged that the UN's role in this field be expanded and more closely coordinated with existing national, regional, and private efforts.[29] Yet, American officials made no secret of their lack of enthusiasm for meetings such as the conference in Geneva, since they did not "relish being in the position of saying 'no' to practically everything that will be proposed by the poorer countries. . . ."[30] Policy-makers in the United States did not contest the legitimacy of many of the grievances held by spokesmen for the Afro-Asian and Latin American nations. They freely admitted that the terms of trade offered

to these regions had deteriorated during the past decade; that national development programs in such countries sometimes faced what seemed almost insuperable hurdles; and that policies followed by regional organizations such as the European Common Market often placed underdeveloped countries at a severe economic disadvantage.

The State Department nevertheless held to its basic conviction that America could not support or contribute to ambitious UN development schemes, in which the United States and other advanced societies would pay a disproportionate share (if not almost all) of the bill. Nor was Washington prepared to forsake longstanding principles of free trade, like those embodied in the General Agreement on Tariffs and Trade (GATT),* even though such agreements might prove disadvantageous to developing countries, which depend heavily upon exports of primary products. Similarly, Washington was not enthusiastic about "rigged" or artificially supported price levels for commodities sold by nations throughout Latin America, Africa, and Asia. Instead, State Department officials emphasized: (1) that a nondiscriminatory system of global trade would ultimately work to the best advantage of developing nations; (2) that the primary responsibility for raising economic levels in the underdeveloped world had to be borne by the countries themselves, rather than by the industrialized West; and (3) that the American record—of providing more than $100 billion in various kinds of foreign assistance to other countries since World War II—afforded incontrovertible evidence of America's continuing interest in the needs of economically backward societies.[31] Neither in this period nor earlier, however, was this approach by the United States likely to elicit enthusiastic endorsement from the countries comprising the Afro-Asian majority in the United Nations; nor could it be expected to end their agitation for greatly augmented UN activities in the field of economic development.

Human Rights and Self-Determination

Also less well publicized than the UN's efforts to deal with situations endangering world peace are activities carried out in the Nations has had before it for consideration two realm of human rights. Since 1953, the United

---

* The General Agreements on Tariffs and Trade is discussed in Chapter 15.

documents, a draft covenant on civil and political rights and another on economic, social and cultural rights. Discussion of these documents within the UN has sometimes been stormy, paralleling in many respects public consideration of them within the United States. To the United States, a particularly controversial provision of the draft on economic rights has been Article 1, Section 3, providing that: "The right of peoples to self-determination shall also include permanent sovereignty over their natural wealth and resources. In no case may a people be deprived of its own means of subsistence on the grounds of any rights that may be claimed by other States."[32] Support for this idea, and for even stronger expressions of it after 1953, has naturally come chiefly from the underdeveloped countries, which have sought to apply the principle of "self-determination" broadly. By contrast, the United States and its European allies have feared that such a conception of self-determination might encourage nationalization or otherwise lead to expropriation of foreign corporate holdings in other countries. Among the deleterious consequences of such action, one would be to impair the investment climate in many of these countries and to reduce the prospect of attracting increased private overseas investment.[33]

Despite strong official support from time to time for the human rights activities of the UN,[34] the United States has taken a conservative position both on what the UN can and ought to try to accomplish in this field. Few activities of the United Nations have engendered so much apprehension within American public opinion concerning possible infringements upon national sovereignty and loss of constitutional guarantees than those carried on in the field of human rights. Deep public concern about this issue underlay much of the agitation in favor of the "Bricker Amendment" and other efforts to limit the treaty-making powers of the national government late in the Truman Administration and early in the Eisenhower Administration. Because of widespread citizen misgivings, and because American officials challenged the UN's authority to deal with essentially "domestic" questions, the United States has not ratified the two covenants on human rights alluded to above, the Convention on Genocide adopted by the Assembly in 1948, or the Convention on the Political Rights of Women adopted by the Assembly in 1952.

The largely negative attitude displayed by American officials, and most probably by a majority of American citizens, toward UN activities in the field of human rights has undeniably tarnished the national image in the outside world, particularly among the newly independent countries in the global community. One highly competent observer has labeled American attitudes on the issue of UN human rights activities "disdainful" and has urged the United States to re-examine its policies toward this "largely symbolic but nonetheless psychologically crucial" issue.[35] Another experienced American official has noted: "Condemnation by the United States of genocide in Tibet or Hungary would have a more convincing ring if the United States were to ratify the Genocide Convention outlawing such practices."[36] Yet favorable American action on such proposals appears no more likely today than ever. Public and official distrust of the UN, particularly the fear that its jurisdiction might be extended to "domestic" problems in the United States, such as racial disorders; long-standing disillusionment with idealistic pronouncements (such as the 1928 Kellogg-Briand Pact to "outlaw" war) that did nothing in practice to alleviate growing international tensions; fear that many UN activities in the sphere of human rights might be Communist-inspired; legitimate doubts about the lasting value of such documents as the Universal Declaration of Human Rights; unwillingness to transfer American sovereignty to an international organization—these and other considerations now, as in the past, dictate a predominately negative (or, at best, indifferent) American attitude toward UN human rights activities.

The United States and Colonialism

Caution by American officials, and divergent attitudes between industrialized and underdeveloped countries, have also characterized UN consideration of political self-determination for still-dependent peoples. When they ratified the Charter, all members of the United Nations pledged themselves to support Article 73, setting forth principles to govern colonial relationships. According to these principles the interests of the inhabitants living in dependencies "are paramount," colonial responsibilities are a "sacred trust," the ultimate goal is to "develop self-government." Articles 75 through 91 set forth provisions regulating the international trusteeship system established under the UN for territories placed directly under international control. These territories are supervised by the Trusteeship Council.

As would be expected, the Afro-Asian preoccupation with colonialist issues has found reflection both within Trusteeship Council discussions and in General Assembly discussions dealing with colonial issues not under the Council's jurisdiction. "The United Nations," said an Indonesian delegate, "is the best agency through which a burial of colonialism could be sought,"[37] a viewpoint widely accepted throughout the Afro-Asian countries. Within the Trusteeship Council, discussion has often centered on the pace with which independence ought to be granted to trust territories.[38]

Perhaps in no sphere has American policy in the United Nations come under sharper attack in recent years than in the matter of colonialism. Expressing a viewpoint widely in evidence throughout the Afro-Asian world, one observer commented in 1962: "The most characteristic and the most important element in the evolution of the United Nations during the last few years has undoubtedly been its growing importance as a factor of anticolonial policy." On September 23, 1960, President Nkrumah of Ghana called upon the members of the North Atlantic Treaty Organization to honor the preamble of their treaty, which pledged the signatories to "safeguard the freedom, common heritage and civilizations of their peoples. . . ." Before the UN General Assembly, Nkrumah asked the members of NATO to point to "any single instance where Portugal has observed the NATO principles in regard to her colonies in Africa. . . ." He urged other NATO members to "bring pressure to bear on Portugal to accord the same independence to her colonies in Africa as other North Atlantic Treaty powers have granted to their former colonial possessions."[39]

To whatever extent American officials have tended to regard such viewpoints as immoderate, oversimplified, doctrinaire, or otherwise impractical, there is less doubt about the fact that they are typical of opinion prevailing from Morocco to the Philippines. Nor is there any real doubt that the American record on colonialism has severely detracted from the ability of the United States to win acceptance for the idea that Western and Communist diplomatic behavior was actuated by different principles, or that the world could be divided between those nations favoring "democracy" and freedom and those favoring despotism and human bondage. Informed citizens in Asia,

the Arab world, Africa, and Latin America are, of course, aware of America's own historic record of anticolonialism, of its grant of independence to the Philippines, and of its efforts during and after World War II to promote rapid independence for societies in the British, French, or Dutch empires. Moreover, spokesmen for societies that have recently acquired, or are still in the process of acquiring, their political independence are mindful that the issue of colonialism often presents American policy-makers with unpalatable choices. They know that the United States is the leading member of a network of military alliances that Washington deems vital in protecting the security of the non-Communist world; the successful functioning of these alliances presupposes at least a semblance of diplomatic consensus among the major Western allies.

Yet after allowances are made for these realities, it remains true that as much as any other single issue, the issue of colonialism has created a wide gulf between American officials and those from the Afro-Asian and Latin American worlds. On this question, the United States has often let the Soviet Union gain propaganda victories at the UN almost by default. As one African delegate to the UN said in 1961: "Those of us who have been friends of the United States are almost ashamed of that fact now. . . . It is detrimental to our position at the UN for our representatives to be seen too frequently talking to members of the United States delegation." He continued that: "We used to have reservations when the Soviet Union said the U.S. was colonialist. Now we are ready to believe it." On the basis of such verdicts, one commentator concluded that "the United States suffered a disastrous political and ideological defeat" at the 15th General Assembly of the UN in 1960.*

---

* George M. Houser, "Cause for Concern," *Africa Today*, 8 (January, 1961), 5. More specifically, Houser cites the following actions (or inactions) taken by the United States at this session which gave "the lie to American pronouncements and severely tarnished its already cloudy image." The United States abstained on the General Assembly resolution denouncing colonialism and calling for its "speedy and unconditional end . . . in all its forms and manifestations." American delegates explained that they did not disagree with the principle of the resolution, but only with its wording. Again, the United States abstained on a crucial vote calling for self-determination for Algeria, and proposing a UN-sponsored plebiscite for the country. Once again, the United States abstained from voting on a resolution calling on Portugal to transmit information to the UN about its colonies

A turning point in American policy toward colonialism came in 1961, under the Kennedy Administration. Long aware that America's position on colonial questions had won few friends throughout the Afro-Asian world, the Kennedy Administration decided to reverse the position held for many years in the Eisenhower-Dulles era. The new direction in American policy became evident in June, 1961, when the United States voted in the Security Council to condemn Portugal's "repressive measures" in Angola.[40] Such indications of American concern for societies still in a position of colonial dependency helped to alter the image of the United States as a country that either supported outright, or was closely identified with, Western colonial systems. Yet it was doubtful that the change in American policy had come soon enough to counteract the good will that often accrued to the Communist bloc because of its vocal support for anticolonial causes. It would likely be many years before the United States was completely successful in disassociating itself from the colonial records of its major European allies.

THE U.S. AND THE UN: SOME PERSISTENT ISSUES

In tracing out the movement toward world international organization and world law before World War II, and in treating the establishment and evolution of the United Nations, we have attempted to lay the groundwork for more intelligent understanding of America's relationship with the United Nations in the postwar period. We have already suggested some of the key elements in that relationship. In the remainder of the chapter, we shall explore that subject in greater detail. Important questions guiding our inquiry will be: To what extent has America's membership in the UN posed problems for the foreign relations of the United States? What is the nature of these problems and what are their implications for the present and future? What are likely to be some of the more significant factors shaping public and official attitudes within the United States toward the United Nations throughout

the years ahead? Our discussion will focus particularly upon those aspects of America's relationships with the UN which have tended to detract from the UN's usefulness and from enlightened American leadership in the realm of international organization.

American Policy Formulation and the UN

The United States is represented at the United Nations by the U.S. Mission to the UN, which has two separate but intimately related functions: to provide representation at annual and special meetings of the General Assembly and to provide continuous representation to all other UN agencies.[41] Heading the Mission is the United States Representative to the United Nations, appointed by the President and confirmed by the Senate.

Officials representing the United States at UN Headquarters in New York are "instructed" officials, which is to say that their function is to carry out American foreign policy as formulated in Washington under the ultimate supervision of the President. During the preliminary planning leading to the San Francisco Conference in 1945, machinery had already been created within the State Department to provide guidance and continuity for American foreign policy in the field of international organization. After several organizational changes, some of which were prompted by the Hoover Commission's recommendations in 1949, a bureau now called the Office of International Organization Affairs, headed by an Assistant Secretary of State, was established. This office became the focal point for coordinating policy in Washington with policy in the United Nations.[42] Theoretically, policy decisions affecting the UN flow from the Office of International Organization Affairs in the State Department to the U.S. Mission in New York. Sometimes, broad principles of policy are passed on to the mission, with the latter applying these to specific issues which arise within the United Nations. In other cases policy-makers in Washington may issue detailed instructions to the UN Mission.[43]

In practice, however, there is an interchange of ideas and recommendations between officials in Washington and New York in arriving at positions on important questions.

The existence of recognized machinery and procedures for coordinating diplomatic efforts in Washington and New York, however, has not always guaranteed effective liaison or fully concerted policies. Some informed commen-

---

in Africa, principally Angola. Nor did the United States support a proposed effort to have a UN inspection team visit South West Africa, since presumably the Union of South Africa would not accept this mission. On the other hand, in this session, the Soviet Union voted with African countries on colonial questions a total of 13 times. *Ibid.*, pp. 5–10.

tators have called attention to the anomalous position occupied by the Office of International Organization Affairs within the State Department. This bureau is theoretically on a par with the geographical bureaus in formulating American foreign policy. Two factors, however, have detracted from its position. First, the Assistant Secretary of State for International Organization Affairs has sometimes been outranked by the U.S. Representative to the United Nations. Under the Eisenhower Administration, for example, Henry Cabot Lodge held the rank of Ambassador to the UN; he was a close political confidant of the President and a member of Eisenhower's Cabinet. Ambassador Lodge therefore had access to the President almost equal to that of the Secretary of State, and far greater access than almost all subordinate executive officials within the government. Thus the channels of communication between the State Department in Washington and the UN Mission in New York appear to be as much an outgrowth of the impact of key personalities on the foreign policy process as the result of precise legislative or executive determination.*

A second factor tending to interfere with smooth coordination of policy between Washington and New York since 1945 has to do with relationships between the Office of International Organization Affairs and other execu-

* One commentator has written that shortly after his appointment, Ambassador Lodge let it be known that he did not intend to function on the basis of detailed "instructions" from IOA in the State Department. *Time* magazine's account holds that Lodge frequently got his instructions changed and "usually wins his point" in differences with the State Department. It continues that: "Sometimes the 'instructions' he gets from Washington are verbatim playbacks of what he wrote himself," in part because developments "happen too fast to rely upon specific instructions."

Insight into the part played by Mr. Lodge in his interesting role as a member of the Cabinet is afforded by Robert J. Donovan's account of Eisenhower's first term. In the vast majority of cases, Mr. Lodge's remarks in Cabinet meetings pertained to subjects such as social security, highway construction, or taxes. Not once did he present a critique of problems within the UN, which may be perhaps explained entirely by the fact that the National Security Council is the highest governmental agency concerned with foreign policy and defense issues. See: Lincoln P. Bloomfield, "American Policy Toward the UN—Some Bureaucratic Reflections," *International Organization*, 12 (Winter, 1958), 10; *Time*, 72 (August 11, 1958), 11–14; Robert J. Donovan, *Eisenhower: The Inside Story* (New York: Harper & Row, 1956), pp. 14, 16, 27, 32, 61, 64–65, 86, 141, 157, 387, 394.

tive agencies. The prestige of IOA, and of the UN itself, was heavily damaged by disclosures and allegations made at the time of the "Hiss case" in the period of intense anti-Communist agitation which gripped the country in the late 1940s and early 1950s. One result was that IOA experienced difficulty in becoming fully assimilated and "accepted" within the State Department because of the taint derived from its close connection with an organization many people believed to be heavily Communist-infiltrated. The change in its earlier title, Office of United Nations Affairs, to IOA in part symbolized the department's awareness that many activities of the UN had become controversial public issues and that within Congress "the United Nations" was not always a psychologically acceptable term.

The influence of IOA upon American policy in the UN was further weakened by the gradual replacement of "specialists" on the United Nations—who had entered the State Department by means of civil service appointments during and after the war—by field officers from the Foreign Service. A similar process has taken place within the U.S. Mission. Both IOA and the mission have lost many of their highly trained experts on the United Nations. Their successors from the Foreign Service sometimes appear to have neither the knowledge nor the inclination requisite for forthright and dynamic American leadership on the plane of international organization.[44]

Despite continuing efforts to assure the smooth coordination of policy between Washington and the UN Mission in New York, breakdowns in communications—sometimes creating the appearance of an internally divided government—continue to hamper the effectiveness of American diplomatic activities in the United Nations. A particularly glaring example of such an organizational breakdown occurred early in 1961. For weeks, the Kennedy Administration had denied any complicity in attempts by Cuban refugees to invade Cuba and "liberate" the island from Fidel Castro's control. On April 15, Ambassador Stevenson at the UN made an impassioned speech denying any intention by the United States to intervene in Cuban affairs and categorically rejected Cuban accusations concerning such interventionism. Forty-eight hours later came the disastrous "Bay of Pigs" invasion of Cuba, in which State Department involvement was too obvious to be denied. Moreover, it was plain that agencies such as the Central Intelligence Agency had been planning for months to carry out an invasion of Cuba. The result was that Stevenson's denials of American complicity in plots against Castro's regime were not only belied. The American position in the UN was seriously damaged by what could only be explained on the basis of: (1) a flagrant and cynical American resort to falsehood to cover up its anti-Castro activities, or (2) a serious impairment in the process of policy consultation and communication between Washington and New York, so that Ambassador Stevenson was himself not actually aware of the degree of official involvement in the Bay of Pigs fiasco. Either way, the United States suffered a dramatic propaganda defeat because of the episode.[45]

Finally, maximum United States participation and leadership within the United Nations has inevitably been hampered by the growing complexity of foreign affairs, as reflected in the increasingly intimate connection between foreign and domestic policies. One result has been the continuing necessity to integrate the efforts of an ever-widening circle of executive and legislative agencies involved in major foreign policy decisions. Harmonizing and dovetailing the interests and demands of a large number of such agencies—and to do this sometimes under conditions of global crises—have clearly emerged as most difficult, and yet most urgent, continuing tasks facing officials dealing with foreign relations. New proposals, suggested modifications in existing policy, countermoves to answer communist strategy or the latest moves of neutralist countries—all of these must be referred to the State Department and possibly to the National Security Council for study and consultation by an expanding number of departments, bureaus, and commissions within the national government. After a decision is eventually reached and passed on to the U.S. Mission in New York, which in turn presents it before the appropriate UN organ, the process may have to be repeated before major modifications can be made to accommodate the wishes of countries with which the United States desires to preserve friendly relations.

The necessity for almost endless coordination of policy within the government means that proposals sometimes become blunted and watered down, lose their dynamism and originality in their passage through the bureaucratic labyrinth. As often as not, bargains are arrived at and compromises are reached, producing a kind of lowest-common-denominator policy, acceptable to agencies because it proposes nothing startlingly new nor requires too many adjustments in prevailing policies. There comes about what Bloomfield has aptly described as a "cross-sterilization of ideas."[46] The final resolution of conflicting viewpoints within the government on any important issue pending before the United Nations, such as cessation of nuclear weapons testing or expanded UN technical assistance efforts, not infrequently leaves the United States resting on dead center. By first trying to evolve a widely acceptable position *within* the government, and then in the next stage trying to reach a mutually agreeable solution with *other* governments, the result is sometimes a policy which does not *offend*—but yet at the same time does not *please*—groups at home and abroad concerned with the issue. The end product is often a middle-of-the-road policy, which is perpetually in danger of colliding with traffic going in both directions.

The knowledge that greater reliance upon the United Nations will add still another dimension to the already extremely complicated process of coordinating foreign policy may thus encourage a "standpat" philosophy among American officials both in Washington and New York. Within the United Nations, the strategy of the United States has sometimes been to "let sleeping dogs lie" on a number of vexatious issues. This propensity can be attributed at least partially to bureaucratic inertia, to an understandable reluctance on the part of responsible officials to raise questions which will precipitate interminable consultations among governmental agencies, when the final result of countless meetings and mountains of paperwork may be the quiet interment of new proposals and the reiteration of declared policy.[47]

Changes in the UN and American Policy

A number of implications for American policy inherent in the rise of a vastly strengthened General Assembly have already been suggested. Let us review these very briefly and add others that are basic to an intelligent appraisal of the transformations witnessed within the UN since 1945.

The Assembly's enhanced position means that nations associated with neither the free-world coalition nor the Communist bloc now possess greater influence in the deliberations and actions of the United Nations. A diplomatic third force has arisen in recent years, a force whose urgent problems and demands in the world community are often quite different from those of Washington, Moscow, London, or Paris. The newly found strength of the neutralist position has also come to the fore in some aspects of the increased influence of the Secretary-General in international negotiations aimed at eliminating and mitigating sources of global tensions.* In 1958, Secretary-General Dag Hammarskjöld noted that: "Over the years, the weight of the work of the Secretary-General has increasingly moved from what are conventionally regarded as political and administrative tasks to the diplomatic ones." More and more, Mr. Hammarskjöld found himself devoting his time to mediating between the two great-power blocs and to extending his "good offices" in resolving international controversies.[48]

What Mr. Hammarskjöld's predecessor called the "United Nations view" has progressively been brought to bear upon international conflicts, especially those involving the Communist world and the free world. Mr. Hammarskjöld experienced limited success in resolving such issues as continued Red Chinese imprisonment of American soldiers, in bringing about British-French-Israeli withdrawal from the Suez area in 1956, and in persuading the Soviet Union to participate more wholeheartedly in disarmament discussions. In a new outbreak of Middle Eastern crises in mid-1958, it was again the Secretary-General who took the initiative in finding solutions acceptable to the countries concerned.

Yet it really was not until the appointment

* An illuminating account of the rise of the Secretary-General as a force in global political affairs can be found in the memoirs of former Secretary-General Trygve Lie. Mr. Lie makes clear that all along he favored a *maximalist* conception of the Secretary-General's powers, i.e., that he ought to "influence the course of debates" and "emerge as a bold leader of international thought and action, as a genuinely international figure stimulating the Member States to rise above their nationalistic dispositions." This role found graphic expression in the "peace mission" undertaken by Mr. Lie in the spring of 1950, when he made the rounds of the world's capitals in an attempt to find bases for lessening world tensions. In Washington, he told President Truman that "the trend of discussions" in the UN "seems to relate to means for *winning* the 'cold war' instead of *ending* it." In Moscow, he strongly urged Soviet leaders to take a more conciliatory attitude in dealing with still unsolved global problems. See Trygve Lie, *In the Cause of Peace* (New York: Macmillan, 1954), pp. 41, 283–293, 307.

of U Thant as Secretary-General in 1961 that the "United Nations view" emerged forcefully or that the Secretary-General became an international figure whose function, as much as anything else, was to mediate between the two contending cold-war power blocs. Trygve Lie became *persona non grata* to the Communist bloc; his successor, Mr. Hammarskjöld, was not always supported by the Communists or by the growing neutralist group within the UN. U Thant's appointment, however, symbolized the new power of the neutralist nations and their determination to make the UN an instrument for ameliorating cold-war tensions, as well as one within which cold-war diplomatic jockeying could occur. As an Asian and citizen of a leading neutralist country (Burma), Mr. Thant was acceptable to both cold-war power groupings, as well as to the nonaligned countries. Consequently, he was in a position to bring UN influence to bear upon causes of global tension in a manner that could not be equaled by his predecessors. His role in effecting a *détente* in the Cuban missile crisis of 1962 attested to his acceptability to both sides in the controversy. Significantly, in this case the neutralist countries were prepared to await the outcome of the kind of "quiet diplomacy" for which Mr. Thant quickly became known, instead of intruding themselves forcefully into an extremely delicate dispute, in which ill-timed and flamboyant activities might render an East-West settlement infinitely more difficult.

Other ramifications of the Assembly's new role in the UN relate to the broad field of diplomatic method and procedure. Here we can only suggest some of the most direct connotations for American foreign policy. America's role in expanding the powers of the General Assembly is but one manifestation of a movement visible in American diplomatic history over the past half-century, aimed at "democratizing" the conduct of international affairs. This movement found its most outspoken champion in Woodrow Wilson, whose insistence upon "open covenants, openly arrived at" was a key provision of his famous Fourteen Points. Owing at least partially to popular disillusionment following World War I and to Wilson's crusade against "secret diplomacy," Americans have become highly suspicious of professional diplomats, whose natural propensity, in the existing folklore, is to make nefarious deals giving away sovereign rights or perhaps selling out weaker countries.

Lingering citizen misgivings about the Yalta and Potsdam Conferences of World War II have intensified public apprehensions about secret diplomacy in the modern period.

In recent years, informed students of international affairs have challenged the efficacy of "open diplomacy," as epitomized by discussions in the UN General Assembly. Particularly when deliberations are televised to millions of viewers and the galleries are open to the public, proceedings are apt to degenerate into propaganda contests, in which each side tries to outscore the other in verbal sparring. Officials from democratic countries are peculiarly tempted to pursue such tactics because of the ubiquitous influence of public opinion. Above all, officials think they must avoid the slightest intimation that they are "appeasing" the enemy or failing to "protect" the national honor. Some insight into what passes for diplomacy under these circumstances can be gauged from a *Time* magazine article in 1958. It attributed mounting public confidence in the United Nations to the fact that America's chief spokesman "answers every Russian thrust with a hard-hitting counter-thrust." The public could be assured that "the U.S. is not being pushed around in the UN and is not likely to be." Frequently, after lively propaganda exchanges, Ambassador Lodge would be greeted by citizens who said, "Good work, Mr. Lodge" or, "Keep giving it back to them, Ambassador."[49]

Propaganda duels in the UN may provide a scintillating hour of television, but can they properly be called diplomacy? Do they really fulfill the purposes for which the UN Charter was drawn up and signed? The answer is obvious when we recall that the chief purpose of diplomacy is to *settle* outstanding disagreement among nations, to find a basis upon which negotiations can be successfully carried through to a mutually satisfactory result. The essence of the diplomatic method is a willingness to make concessions in the expectation that the other side will also make concessions. This process becomes virtually hopeless in televised and public meetings. An experienced American diplomatic official has stated that "it is extremely difficult—often impossible—to retreat from a position taken in public."[50] Positions taken in public quickly become encrusted with considerations of the nation's "honor and prestige"; for that reason they tend to become rigid and frozen. The customary process of reaching diplomatic agreements, in which almost invariably both sides state certain maximum demands and then retreat to their minimum demands, is replaced by dogged attachment to, and tiresome reiteration of, positions announced before the entire world. An eminent British scholar, Sir Harold Nicholson, has stated that genuine progress in resolving international disputes cannot be made before public assemblies in the United Nations, but that it must be made "elsewhere, in accordance with those principles of courtesy, confidence, and discretion which must forever remain the only principles conducive to the peaceful settlement of disputes."[51] Attempts to follow the concept of "open covenants, openly arrived at," more often than not end in open disagreements, openly arrived at; in most cases the best interests of the international community are served by following the principle of *open agreements, secretly arrived at,* whereby results are made public, but deliberations leading to results are conducted in private, away from the corrosive influence of television cameras and a powerful, if often impatient and poorly informed, public opinion. By the mid-1960s, there was evidence for believing that American officials accepted the case for "quiet diplomacy" much more than had been the case in the 1940s and 1950s.

The UN in the Cold-War Context

Soviet Russia, far more directly and dramatically than any other country, has frustrated the operation of the UN and thwarted collective action against machinations of the Communist bloc. The latest Soviet veto in the Security Council or the most recent "walkout" by tight-lipped Soviet officials or the Kremlin's unwillingness to pay its bills are featured in headlines around the world. Our concern here, however, is not with Soviet culpability on this point, nor with trying to draw up a balance sheet between Soviet and American derelictions in the United Nations. While acknowledging wholesale Soviet iniquities, we must move on to deal with inadequacies in America's own role in the United Nations. For in less spectacular, but perhaps no less fundamental ways, the United States has also weakened the United Nations. On a number of occasions it has failed to exhibit the statesmanship which both its own citizens and its friends in the international community might reasonably have expected from what is in most respects the most pacifically inclined and overtly idealistic great power known to history.

It is primarily in utilizing the United Nations as an adjunct of the State Department, to carry out America's cold-war strategy against the Communist bloc, that American policy toward the UN is most vulnerable.

This tendency has been manifested in several ways. First, mention can be made of the extent to which the United States has consistently bypassed the United Nations in the postwar period. Beginning with the Greek-Turkish Aid Program of 1947, marking the official inauguration of the American policy of containment, and going through the China Aid Program of 1948 and the European Recovery Program of the same year, the Mutual Defense Assistance Program and the Point Four Program in 1949, the United States embarked upon programs and policies which were of lasting importance in shaping the course of international economic and political developments. All of these programs were undertaken outside the United Nations; and some were inaugurated in the face of visible opposition on the part of important countries within the United Nations. Admittedly, there was considerable evidence to support the viewpoint of American officials that the UN was too weak and inexperienced—and, when programs related intimately to the cold war, too hindered by the veto—to carry out some of these undertakings successfully. Yet there was an evident predisposition on the part of the United States to conclude that the UN was incapable of administering many of these programs, without seriously testing the UN's ability or willingness to handle them. American policy-makers seemed largely unaware of what bypassing the UN would do to that body's prestige or that, in some cases, UN action might actually be more effective for some problems than unilateral administration.

A case whose consequences ultimately proved far-reaching involved simultaneous American neglect of the United Nations and impressive American statesmanship in elevating that body to the highest pinnacle ever reached by an international organization in meeting threats to the peace through the collective action of its members. This occurred during the course of the Korean War. The dualism characteristic of America's approach to the UN during that conflict is not untypical of America's approach toward a number of other issues relating to international organization in the postwar period. When the communist state of North Korea attacked South Korea, the United States

moved rapidly to meet this aggression head-on, without waiting for the sanction of the United Nations. Then, in what may well have been a turning point in the history of international organization, on June 25, 1950, the day when U.S. troops had moved into Korea, President Truman requested the Security Council to find that the communist invasion of South Korea constituted a "threat to the peace" and to invoke Charter provisions for dealing with such threats. Thanks to an earlier Soviet "walk-out," the Security Council was able to respond promptly and effectively. It called upon members to render all possible assistance to the United States. By the end of the war, contributions had come from almost 40 countries, with the United States of course carrying the principal burden of the military commitment demanded in Korea. For the first time in history, an international organization met gangsterism in the world community with adequate force, made possible by the collaborative efforts of its members. In retrospect, the Korean War may well have been a test case in the precarious existence of the United Nations, and it was largely owing to American leadership that it met that test forthrightly.

Then, having converted what began as unilateral American resistance to communist expansionism into a collective UN effort, officials in Washington throughout the ensuing months appeared to relegate the UN more and more to the sidelines, while American military commanders in the field carried out vital decisions affecting politico-diplomatic questions. None had more profound consequences for the international community as a whole than General Douglas MacArthur's crossing of the 38th Parallel into North Korea, after which he pursued retreating Communist armies up to the Yalu river border of Red China. Not only was there no clear UN mandate for such action, but in all probability a majority of the members opposed it. Red China's subsequent entry into the war converted what had been a spectacularly successful UN operation to "repel aggression" into a protracted, bloody, and probably avoidable military conflict which eventually ended in stalemate and, in the process, intensified hostilities between the United States and Red China, inflaming global tensions for an indefinite period thereafter. Official American reluctance to consult with the United Nations, partly stemming from the public aversion to "interference" on the part of the UN's members, was also apparent in arranging for truce negotiations in the Korean conflict and in determining the composition of the UN truce negotiating team.

The United States, in other words, sought the moral sanction and broad support of the United Nations in meeting aggression head-on in Korea; at the same time, it did not want to relinquish any significant control to the UN in shaping military strategy, which often involved global and regional *political* issues of vital concern to other countries, or to permit extensive United Nations' participation in the resultant truce negotiations. In some cases, it appeared that the South Korean government of Syngman Rhee had considerably more voice in shaping American policy than did the United Nations.[52]

It must be conceded that numerous obstacles have existed for relying upon the United Nations in every major instance involving global conflicts since 1945. Admittedly, as one American diplomatic official has phrased it, the United States sometimes had no choice but to "work outside the United Nations in our continuing efforts to assure a just peace. . . ." In many other cases, however, Swift's judgment is substantially correct when he asserts that "unfortunately, we never really gave the United Nations a chance to do some jobs we have undertaken ourselves. . . ."[53]

America's neglect of the United Nations in matters affecting its cold-war strategy is also apparent in other ways. By the late 1950s, when American officials considered holding high-level or lower-ranking diplomatic conferences with the Communist bloc, the United Nations was seldom mentioned as a possible meeting place; and no evidence existed from official American statements on this subject that the UN was even being seriously considered as a place in which global tensions might be reduced. Then in the summer of 1958, President Eisenhower surprised the world, and in the process scored a dramatic propaganda coup for his country, by inviting Communist party boss Khrushchev to a heads-of-state meeting at UN headquarters in New York. Khrushchev's final reaction was to decline the invitation. For once, this put the onus squarely on Russia for bypassing the UN and for "blocking the road to peace." In many earlier instances, it had been the United States which had too often taken the lead in arranging major diplomatic conferences, affecting political developments throughout the world, outside the United Nations.

Two international crises in the early 1960s —the Congo Crisis and the Soviet-American confrontation in Cuba—witnessed intensified efforts by the United States to rely upon the UN to avert a tendency toward political chaos and perhaps regional or global war. In both instances, Washington found that its own interests coincided with those of the neutralist countries in turning to the UN to ameliorate regional and global tensions. Admittedly, in the Congo Crisis at least, a condition was present that had been lacking in earlier efforts by the UN to cope with threats to international peace and security. A vital new element was the willingness of the nonaligned states to assume the military burden required for pacification in the Congo, coupled with their evident opposition to intervention in that crisis by either the Western or the Communist blocs.

American foreign policy has also tended to convert the United Nations into a propaganda forum in which to indict Soviet Russia, while justifying America's own policies before the world. Sonorous pronouncements, typified by Secretary of State George C. Marshall's view that the UN "is the symbol of the aspirations of mankind," President Truman's view that the Charter is "an expression of the moral nature of man's aspirations,"[54] and Secretary Dulles's view that the Charter "represents man's most determined and promising efforts to save humanity. . . ."[55] have emanated from American officials at periodic intervals. Official assurances that the UN is the "cornerstone of American foreign policy" have, over the years, become part of the liturgy of American foreign relations.

Yet on occasion, American officials have also been candid enough to admit some of the less exalted objectives which the United States pursues within the United Nations and which were not envisioned by the Charter. Thus, Secretary of State Marshall in 1948 conceived it to be a "fundamental task" of the UN to "dispel the misconceptions of the Soviet leaders and to bring about a more realistic view of what is impossible in the relationships between the Soviet Union and the world at large."[56] President Eisenhower in 1954 called the United Nations "the only real world forum where we have the opportunity for international presentation and rebuttal. . . . It is a place where the guilt can be squarely assigned to those who fail to take all necessary steps to keep the peace. . . ."[57] A report to Congress on the Tenth Session of the General Assembly in 1955 asserted that "the fundamental, although not the sole, value of the United Nations to the United States is that it provides us with a forum where we can meet the Soviet threat to the free world and expose that threat for what it is before the whole world."[58]

While it must be admitted that American officials can hardly do otherwise than "answer" Soviet propaganda outbursts against the United States, and that the United States is by no means unilaterally responsible for the extent to which propaganda exchanges often substitute for serious negotiations, it is also true that the United States has, at times, stooped too far to the level of its enemies. Policies and conduct based upon propaganda objectives are not calculated to *reduce* tensions and to advance the evolutionary process by which the UN becomes a more active influence in global affairs, in time perhaps acquiring some capacity to deal with disputes among the great powers. In pursuing its national objectives, the United States has sometimes resorted to tactics to which it and its allies have objected vigorously when applied to themselves and that are of doubtful constitutionality under the Charter. This has been notably true of issues that lie exclusively or predominantly within the domestic jurisdiction of states. The United States has pushed studies of "genocide" which were clearly aimed at exposing oppressive Soviet policies toward cultural and economic minorities within the USSR, many of whom have been virtually liquidated by the communist regime since 1917. To say the least, international law relating to genocide is cloudy. Many activities of the Soviet government, morally reprehensible as they may be, cannot legally be called genocide and condemned as such. An even clearer case has been American advocacy of UN-sponsored studies of Soviet "slave labor" and other iniquitous features of the communist system. In such activities, Western officials have drawn hasty and inexact analogies with international law prohibitions against "slavery." The same officials have not protested far more flagrant cases of slavery in the Arab world. However much the free world is repulsed by barbarous treatment of citizens of other countries, it must be remembered that these matters are in the vast majority of cases excluded from the jurisdiction of the United Nations under Article 2, Section 7, of the Charter—a prohibition which the United States took the lead in inserting into the Charter.

One final aspect of America's often dominant concern for cold-war considerations in its approach to the United Nations remains to be examined. The United States on many occasions has looked upon the UN as a place in which to register resounding "majorities" against the Communist bloc in behalf of policies and programs sponsored by Washington. Perhaps out of a desire to convince critics at home that American participation in the UN does not jeopardize national sovereignty or give communist nations control over American foreign policy, official publications have made statements like the following: "The United States has never been defeated on any important political question in the United Nations. On the other hand the Soviet Union can usually count on only 5 out of 60 votes [before 1955] in the General Assembly."[59] A report submitted to Congress on the Twelfth Session of the Assembly in 1957 makes the statement that: "On nearly all issues . . . where the Soviet Union vigorously attacked our position, the majority of the United Nations members supported the United States."[60]

Such statements, while perhaps comforting to groups within the country which are apprehensive about the UN, inescapably raise the question: What would be the attitude of the United States toward the UN if the American position on most issues did *not* command overwhelming majorities? Does the thinking behind such statements imply that the United States ought to support the UN because, after all, the United States usually gets its way there? These questions are far from academic. With the growth in power of the 113-nation General Assembly, able as never before to subject the foreign policies of free world and communist countries alike to searching examination, such questions will become more and more pertinent to American policy-makers and may well require a new appraisal of certain objectives present in the American approach to the United Nations.

As control of the General Assembly has shifted to the neutralist zone, the likelihood of the United States receiving an "automatic majority" in support of its policies inevitably declined. Now, said an American official in 1962, "we have to fight for everything we get" in the UN.[61] At the same time, as we have emphasized earlier, this in no sense meant that the United States had entirely "lost control" of the UN or that it was in any serious danger of regularly confronting anti-American majorities on vital diplomatic issues. If the United States still found itself voting with the majority in the great preponderance of cases, it was only because on a number of outstanding international questions, such as colonialism or racial discrimination, it had re-examined its own past policies and had taken pains to align itself with the Afro-Asian states, whose influence (often supplemented by the votes of Latin American countries) was great enough to secure favorable Assembly action.

The UN Financial Crisis

It was perhaps ironic that in the very period when the United Nations was evolving into an international organization capable of making its influence felt in the Middle East and in the Congo, it was also gripped by a "crisis of confidence" that raised questions about its own future. To a significant degree, this crisis was an outgrowth of progressively acute fiscal problems the UN encountered, as a result of its expanded peacekeeping role in global troublespots, particularly in Africa. The financial tribulations of the UN were not only serious in their own right; they afforded an occasion for a sweeping re-examination in the United States of the UN's value and its compatibility with national foreign policy goals.

By early 1964, the UN's books showed some $138.6 million in unpaid "assessments" to finance its extremely costly operations along the Arab-Israeli frontier and in the Congo. This deficit arose chiefly out of the unwillingness of the Soviet Union, Britain, France, Belgium, and other countries to pay their prescribed costs; by 1964, the USSR had acquired a deficit at the UN of over $52 million.[62] Aside from the strain imposed upon the UN by its financial straits, the growing deficit also had important diplomatic implications. The Charter provided that delinquent nations might be denied their vote in the General Assembly, when their indebtedness equaled or surpassed "the amount of the contributions due from it for the preceding two full years." A ruling by the International Court of Justice in 1962 held that special assessments upon members for extraordinary peacekeeping operations were covered by this provision in Article 19, thereby negating the legal pretext invoked by the USSR, France, and other countries to

justify their failure to pay their assessments.

The financial troubles besetting the UN's operations had become sufficiently grave by 1962 to require new measures for raising funds, if the organization's activities were not to founder on the rocks of bankruptcy. Accordingly, the United States proposed the floating of a $200 million bond issue (American officials proposed that the United States itself purchase half the bonds), together with a series of other steps designed to retrieve the UN from its financial distress. When this request was presented to Congress, it precipitated a lengthy and sometimes heated exchange of opinion on Capitol Hill, and between legislative and executive officials, concerning the American role in an organization that, as we have seen, tended to be controlled by non-Western nations. Legislative deliberations over the UN bond issue brought to the surface latent, oftentimes highly emotional, criticisms of the UN in Congress. As usual, it seemed clear that similar misgivings prevailed throughout the nation as a whole. A vocal body of American opinion, it became apparent, was disturbed about the evolution of the UN and about what was thought to be a growing tendency by the United States to rely upon it for the achievement of national diplomatic objectives.

Thus, ex-President Herbert Hoover deplored the fact that the UN "has failed to give us even a remote hope of lasting peace. . . . Instead, it adds to the dangers of wars which now surround us. . . ." A group of Republican legislators concluded that: "This country's responsibility of free world leadership must not be abdicated to the United Nations. . . ." Leading Democrats, like Senator Henry M. Jackson of Washington, asserted that "the best hope for peace with justice does not lie in the United Nations." He called upon executive policy-makers to realize that: "The best hope for the United Nations lies in the maintenance of peace [and] peace depends on the power and unity of the Atlantic community and on the skill of our direct diplomacy." He deplored any tendency to regard the American Ambassador to the UN as "a second Secretary of State." Senator George D. Aiken (Republican of Vermont) called upon members of the UN to "take heed of what we are doing and saying here in Congress"; he urged the UN to "adopt sound methods in conducting its business," and called upon it to "stand undeviating for the purpose for which it was organized."*

In the end, Congress reluctantly accepted a modified version of the Kennedy Administration's request for massive American support in solving the UN's financial crisis. Congress authorized the Treasury Department to purchase up to one-half of all UN bonds sold, up to a total of $100 million; the Treasury was prohibited, however, from making total purchases in excess of the total purchases by all other countries. As we have seen, this step in no sense "solved" the UN's long-term problem, although it did relieve the immediacy of its financial need.

Meanwhile, executive officials were not idle in meeting legislative and public criticisms expressed about the UN and about America's relationship to it. Executive officials emphasized several facts that were often ignored or glossed over by critics. One of these was that the United States had never "depended" upon the United Nations for its security; to pretend that it did was to perpetrate an illusion. The UN, said Ambassador Stevenson, is "not an alternative to NATO." The foreign policy of the United States was in reality conducted at "several levels"; one level was the plane of international organization. Senator Hubert Humphrey (Democrat of Minnesota) deplored the tendency to believe that "there is a conflict between our allegiance to NATO and to the United Nations." Another myth was the idea that UN activities were always or inherently inimical to American interests in world affairs. Senator Mike Mansfield (Democrat of Montana) observed that ". . . in the countless votes in the General Assembly since Korea there have been few, very few decisions which were not identical with or reasonably reconcilable with our national policies." In urging favorable legislative action upon his request, President Kennedy summarized many of the accomplishments of the UN in safeguarding peace and alleviating global tensions. He observed that: "Whatever its imperfections, the effectiveness and existence of the UN are an essential part of the machinery to bring peace out of this world of danger and discord." And he injected a note almost certain to override legislative objections to the bond issue by underscoring the fact that: "Failure

to act would serve the interests of the Soviet Union, which has been particularly opposed to the operation in the Congo and which voted against this plan as part of the consistent Communist effort to undermine the United Nations. . . ." In New York, Ambassador Stevenson said that: "If the United Nations has not succeeded in bringing the great powers together, it has often succeeded in keeping them apart—in places where face-to-face confrontation might have changed difficult situations into impossible situations." He freely admitted that the UN "has not succeeded in settling all international disputes"; yet "it has prepared the way for the peaceful evolution of an international order." At the close of the 17th General Assembly Session late in 1962, he reiterated one of his earlier statements that American officials were "more than ever convinced that the success or failure of this organization could well mean the difference between world order and world anarchy."**

The contention of executive officials, in brief, was that however valuable they believed the UN to be, they did not expect miracles from it; they did not rely upon it excessively, certainly not to the detriment of the nation's alliances and other measures designed to safeguard the security of the free world; in spite of obvious changes in the character of the UN, the organization was in no sense endemically anti-American, nor was the United States in danger of being outvoted consistently on major international issues; and, deplorable as the unwillingness of the USSR and other countries to pay their debts might be, American failure to help the UN extricate itself from a financial morass could only help the Communist bloc achieve its objectives in the Congo and elsewhere.

Perhaps the most remarkable aspect of the UN's "crisis of confidence" in American opinion was not that strong anti-United Nations sentiments were expressed during the debate that had occurred periodically since 1945. It was that, in spite of such misgivings, Congress ultimately supported the Kennedy Administration's request—indicating that, now, as in the past, opposition to the United Nations within America has often been vocal, highly organized, and skillful, but has always

---

* These and other legislative criticisms of the UN are cited in *The New York Times*, April 8, 1962, and in *United States in World Affairs: 1962* (New York: Harper & Row, 1963), pp. 315–316.

** See the texts of speeches by President Kennedy and Ambassador Stevenson in *Documents on American Foreign Relations: 1962* (New York: Harper & Row, 1963), pp. 413–416, 416–439; and remarks by other executive officials in *The New York Times*, April 8, 1962.

remained an expression of a small minority of the population. In this period, for example, President Kennedy revealed that polls had showed that "80 to 85 percent of the American people realize the importance of the United Nations."[63] By providing an opportunity for prevalent official and public doubts and frustrations about the UN to be aired, and to be analyzed publicly by executive policy-makers, the debate over the UN deficit was in the long run an extremely healthy phenomenon. For it proved overwhelmingly that official American support for the UN had a broad base of public support. And it called attention to the fact that extremist opposition to the United Nations within the United States remained in the 1960s what it had always been—a minority opinion, which executive officials were always required to listen to but never required to accept as typical of national sentiment.

One final aspect of the UN's financial crisis requires brief mention. As we observed earlier, according to a ruling by the International Court of Justice in 1962, UN members whose accounts were over two years in arrears risked the forfeiture of their vote in the General Assembly. The Court's decision did nothing to make the USSR, France, and other delinquent members pay their assessments. Consequently, in preparation for the forthcoming meeting of the Assembly late in 1964, the United States suggested that delinquent countries ought to be deprived of their Assembly vote, as the Charter provided.

That this proposal was seriously advanced by executive policy-makers in an effort to "force" the Soviet Union out of the UN may be seriously doubted. The State Department knew full well, Secretary of State Dean Rusk declared early in 1964, ". . . that the United Nations simply cannot take significant action without the support of the members who supply it with resources and have the capacity to act."[64] On this issue, as on many others since 1945, the State Department had long ago decided that it was preferable to have a recalcitrant, uncooperative USSR inside the UN than outside. In whatever degree his shoe-pounding and generally obstructionist tactics irritated Americans, Premier Khrushchev had demonstrated on several occasions that the USSR was not totally insensitive to the force of global opinion, as expressed in the United Nations. The Soviet Union, no less than the United States, had been compelled to come to terms with neutralist opinion in the UN and to adjust its policies to the reality that the UN was likely to be controlled by neither the Communist nor the Western bloc. American policy-makers were fully conscious of the fact that perhaps the most certain road to oblivion and futility for the UN was to convert it (or even to try to convert it) merely into an instrument of anti-communism.

It could reasonably be anticipated therefore that some kind of compromise would be reached upon the issue of the deliquency of Russia and other countries in paying their bills at the UN, that would permit their unhampered participation in UN deliberations. This result seemed certain, if for no other reason than that in endeavoring to disfranchise the USSR in the Assembly, the United States would inescapably be required to ask for the similar disfranchisement of allies such as Britain, France, and Belgium, as well. Without a compromise on the issue, the financial "crisis of confidence" would pale into insignificance, as the UN became relegated more and more to the sidelines of history.

NOTES

1. Gerald J. Mangone, A *Short History of International Organization* (New York: McGraw-Hill, 1954), pp. 67–90.
2. *Ibid.*, pp. 105–120; Inis L. Claude, *Swords into Plowshares* (New York: Random House, 1956), pp. 19–42. An incisive analysis of the theory and practice of international organization.
3. Julius W. Pratt, A *History of United States Foreign Policy* (Englewood Cliffs, N.J.: Prentice-Hall, 1955), pp. 454–460.
4. James T. Watkins and J. William Robinson, *General International Organization* (Princeton, N.J.: Nostrand, 1956), pp. 81–84. Provides historical background on the UN and its functions.
5. Mangone, *op. cit.*, pp. 132–133.
6. Pratt, *op. cit.*, pp. 527–558.
7. *Ibid.*, pp. 580–581.
8. Leland M. Goodrich and Edward Hambro, *Charter of the United Nations* (Boston: World Peace Foundation, 1949), p. 21.
9. *Ibid.*, pp. 20–21; Claude, *op. cit.*, pp. 76–77.
10. Goodrich and Hambro, *op. cit.*, p. 408.
11. Clark M. Eichelberger, UN: *The First Ten Years* (New York: Harper & Row, 1955), p. 14. An illuminating interpretive study.
12. H. Field Haviland, Jr., *The Political Role of the General Assembly* (New York:

Carnegie Endowment for International Peace, 1951), pp. 11–18.

13. *Ibid.*, pp. 18–20.

14. *Ibid.*, p. 37.

15. Department of State, *American Foreign Policy, 1950–1955*, Publication No. 6446, "General Foreign Policy Series" 117, **I** (Washington, D.C.: 1957), 187–192.

16. Eichelberger, *op. cit.*, p. 16.

17. "The Situation in Hungary," *United Nations Review*, **3** (December, 1956), 46–71, *passim.*

18. William R. Frye, A *United Nations Peace Force* (New York: Oceana, 1957).

19. *United States in World Affairs: 1956* (New York: Harper & Row, 1957), pp. 358–360.

20. *The New York Times*, December 9 and 15, 1963, dispatches by Thomas J. Hamilton.

21. *Documents on American Foreign Relations: 1961* (New York: Harper & Row, 1962), p. 491.

22. Ernest A. Gross, *The United Nations: Struggle for Peace* (New York: Harper & Row, 1962), pp. 86–87. A distinguished American public servant reviews the record of the UN.

23. *Ibid.*, pp. 89–90.

24. *Ibid.*, pp. 90–91.

25. Cited in Lincoln P. Bloomfield, *The United Nations and U.S. Foreign Policy* (Boston: Little, Brown, 1960), pp. 174–176. A valuable study by a former member of the U.S. Mission to the UN.

26. *Ibid.*, p. 172.

27. *Ibid.*, p. 175; House Foreign Affairs Committee, *Report on the Twelfth Session of the General Assembly of the United Nations*, 85th Congress, 2nd Session (Washington, D.C.: 1958), pp. 24–68. Reports in this series provide valuable material on legislative viewpoints toward the UN.

28. *The New York Times*, March 22, 1964.

29. *Documents on American Foreign Relations: 1961*, *op. cit.*, p. 480.

30. *The New York Times*, March 22, 1964, dispatch by Edwin L. Dale, Jr.

31. *Idem.*

32. Senate Foreign Relations Committee, *Review of the United Nations Charter, A Collection of Documents*, 83rd Congress, 2nd Session (Washington, D.C.: 1954), p. 267. A valuable documentary collection.

33. Department of State, *U.S. Participation in the UN, 1955*, Publication No. 6318, "International Organization and Conference Series, III," 115 (Washington, D.C.:

1956), pp. 166–168. This series provides a valuable summary of U.S. participation in the UN.

34. Department of State, *American Foreign Policy, 1950–1955*, **I**, *op. cit.*, 228–231.

35. Bloomfield, *op. cit.*, p. 205.

36. Gross, *op. cit.*, p. 105.

37. Quoted in Coral Bell, "The United Nations and the West," *International Affairs*, **29** (October, 1953), 467.

38. Ernst B. Haas, "The Attempt to Terminate Colonialism," *International Organization*, **7** (February, 1953), 9–21.

39. See, respectively: L. Erven, "The United Nations and Anti-Colonialism," *Review of International Affairs* (Belgrade), **13** (February 20, 1962), 1; and Kwame Nkrumah, *I Speak of Freedom* (New York: Praeger, 1961), p. 271.

40. *The New York Times*, June 11, 1961.

41. Channing B. Richardson, "The United States Mission to the United Nations," *International Organization*, **7** (February, 1953), 22–23.

42. Lincoln P. Bloomfield, "American Policy Toward the UN—Some Bureaucratic Reflections," *International Organization*, **12** (Winter, 1958), 7–9.

43. James N. Hyde, "United States Participation in the United Nations," *International Organization*, **10** (February, 1956), 22–28.

44. Bloomfield, "American Policy Toward the UN—Some Bureaucratic Reflections," *op. cit.*, pp. 12–13.

45. *United States in World Affairs: 1961* (New York: Harper & Row, 1962), pp. 314–315.

46. Bloomfield, "American Policy Toward the UN—Some Bureaucratic Reflections," *op. cit.*, p. 15.

47. *Ibid.*, pp. 3–4, 15.

48. Dag Hammarskjöld, "Why the United Nations?" *United Nations Review*, **5** (July, 1958), 15.

49. *Time*, **72** (August 11, 1958), 11.

50. Ernest A. Gross, "Five Rules for Diplomatic Diplomats," *New York Times Magazine*, October 25, 1953, p. 12.

51. Harold Nicholson, "An Open Look at Secret Diplomacy," *New York Times Magazine*, September 13, 1953, p. 58.

52. Eichelberger, *op. cit.*, pp. 22–23; Richard N. Swift, "United States Leadership in the United Nations," *Western Political Quarterly*, **11** (June, 1958), 186–188.

53. Swift, *op. cit.*, pp. 184, 193.

54. Department of State, *Principal Statements Regarding the United Nations* (Washington, D.C.: Office of Public Affairs, 1950), pp. 14, 18.

55. Department of State, *American Foreign Policy, 1950–1955*, I, *op. cit.*, 323.
56. Department of State, *Principal Statements Regarding the United Nations, op. cit.*, p. 12.
57. *United States in World Affairs: 1954* (New York: Harper & Row, 1955), pp. 431–432.
58. House Foreign Affairs Committee, *Report on the Tenth Session of the General Assembly of the United Nations*, 84th Congress, 2nd Session (Washington, D.C.: 1956), p. 11.
59. Department of State, *You and the United Nations*, Publication No. 5887, "Interna-tional Organization and Conference Series, III," 105 (Washnigton, D.C.: 1955).
60. House Foreign Affairs Committee, *Report on the Twelfth Session of the General Assembly op. cit.*, p. 43.
61. See the remarks of Assistant Secretary of State Harlan S. Cleveland, as quoted in *United States in World Affairs: 1962* (New York: Harper & Row, 1963), p. 317.
62. *The New York Times*, March 22, 1964.
63. *United States in World Affairs: 1962, op. cit.*, p. 315.
64. *The New York Times*, January 11, 1964.

17 ➞ DISARMAMENT ➞ turning

swords into plowshares

When the League of Nations was founded, no one anywhere doubted that the race in armaments had been largely responsible for the first World War. Therefore, "disarmament" was the largest single item in the peace movement of that time, and there was universal agreement that the first and greatest test of the Legaue of Nations would be its ability to carry out a "reduction and limitation of armaments," which was the more cautious expression for the popular term, disarmament.[1]

That the disarmament question had lost none of its urgency in the intervening years was indicated by President John F. Kennedy's speech to the United Nations on September 25, 1961, when he declared:

Today, every inhabitant of the planet must contemplate the day when this planet may not longer be habitable. Every man, woman and child lives under a nuclear sword of Damocles, hanging by the slenderest of threads, capable of being cut at any moment by accident, or miscalculation or by madness. The weapons of war must be abolished before they abolish us.[2]

With the constantly increasing destructive power of modern weapons and the growing stockpiles of arms in the hands of rival nations, disarmament had clearly emerged as one of the paramount issues in world politics. "The Powers' inability to agree on the regulation of armaments, and particularly on the control of atomic energy," has been called "the greatest single obstacle to the full implementation of that system of security . . . so carefully and hopefully planned in 1945," when the United Nations was established.[3] If collective

endeavors to assure peace through international organization is one side of the coin of the quest for world peace, disarmament is surely the opposite side of the same coin. No problem possesses more of a life-or-death quality, bristles with more formidable difficulties, and has proved so unyielding before the earnest efforts of statesmen throughout history.

DISARMAMENT IN HISTORICAL PERSPECTIVE

Some Basic Concepts

Several factors explain the unyielding nature of the disarmament problem. First, the very term disarmament is, literally speaking, a misnomer. No nation has ever advocated *total* abolition of military force from the world scene. The ultimate goal was clearly expressed by the League of Nations Covenant, which called for "the reduction of national armaments to the lowest point consistent with national safety and the enforcement by common action of international obligations." The juxtaposition of this provision—just preceding Article 10, providing for collective action against aggression—is a key to the intimate relationship described here.[4] The many-faceted nature of the disarmament problem was illustrated even more sharply by a League of Nations Assembly resolution in 1922, which specified a four-step process by which the levels of armaments might be lowered: agreements by all countries to cut military force levels; a satisfactory guarantee of the security of each country; a plan for collective action against aggression; and adherence by all countries to a mutual defense treaty.[5]

The League Covenant identified three cardinal ingredients in any successful approach to disarmament: agreement that arms limitation would entail significant benefits for mankind; belief that effective alternatives to armaments must be found and made operable in the international community; and conviction that the vital interests of nations, most fundamentally their right of self-preservation, must be safeguarded. Disarmament thus is really not a *single* problem, but a *cluster* of intimately related problems. Progress in resolving any one will likely determine the extent to which progress can be made in resolving closely associated ones. The attack against the causes of war and global insecurity must therefore proceed on many fronts at once.

The often bewildering intricacy of disarmament negotiations springs from the fact that few issues in global affairs have such widespread and important ramifications for the entire spectrum of problems and relationships existing among nations as does the question of arms limitation. This is why it has proved so difficult for statesmen to make the transition from almost universal support for the *principle* of disarmament to detailed plans carrying out that principle in different historical periods and under highly varied circumstances.

Do high levels of armaments actually *engender* conflicts in the international community? Or are they merely reflections of the fact that hostilities *already exist* among nations, expressed in an increasing reliance upon military force among powerful countries? Impressive evidence can be cited to support both viewpoints. Statesmen and competent observers of international affairs have generally accepted the view that high levels of armaments are at once both a *cause* and a *symptom* of global tensions. In the present stage of knowledge, there appears to be a well-nigh indissoluble cause-and-effect relationship between world tensions and growing stockpiles of armaments. Perhaps in time the advancing frontiers of knowledge will impart greater precision in diagnosing the exact role of armaments as a cause and as an effect. Meantime, statesmen must continue to deal with the armaments problem in all its complex ramifications.

Would the total abolition of armaments *per se* restore stability, and greatly enhance the chance for peace, in a strife-torn world? Several answers are suggested on the basis of experience. Armaments usually are not an end in themselves. Normally, nations seek power—a central ingredient of which is armaments—to achieve certain goals in international affairs, such as security, a more favorable strategic position, colonies, greater territory, an enhanced economic position, revenge for past hurts and slights against national honor, and a variety of other objectives. Implicitly or explicitly, every nation establishes some kind of scale by which an order of priority among its goals is determined. Its attachment to military force, as with all other kinds of power, will be determined in large measure by: (1) the extent to which it is determined to realize its diplomatic goals in the face of possible opposition by other countries and (2) the precise nature of these goals and their amenability to being achieved by military, violent means.

The mere possession of impressive military force does not *per se* guarantee that a nation will be successful in achieving its goals of statecraft. The United States has become very conscious of the inherent limitations of military force, for example, in dealing with widespread anti-Western sentiment throughout the Afro-Asian bloc in recent years. America's great stockpile of nuclear weapons does not make Cambodia or Iraq more favorably disposed toward the free-world coalition, nor does it help solve problems of poverty in Africa. Consequently, it is reasonable to think that the reduction or even the total abolition of armaments would have no significant impact upon a number of enduring sources of tension and instability in global affairs.

Total or partial disarmament might usher in a breathing spell in which these issues could be attacked; and unquestionably, it might impart a different tone to international negotiations, perhaps cooling tempers among hostile countries and greatly reducing the chance that an "incident" could set off a world conflagration. A prolonged period of disarmament conceivably could permit human and national behavior to change sufficiently so that a new era might dawn in the conduct of relationships among nations. Invaluable byproducts of disarmament might also be strengthening international organization and gaining useful experience in the use of such techniques as global "inspection" to facilitate maintenance of peace. But sooner or later, the frustrating spiral is encountered: significant progress toward disarmament would foster progress in solving major political problems; but the solution of many of these problems is usually a prerequisite for commencing significant disarmament. Disarmament alone affords no guarantee that war would be abolished or that feelings of insecurity might not trigger a new arms race. If history affords a reliable guide, disarmament instead could, under some circumstances, furnish new impetus to reliance upon military force, if nations believed their vital interests were in jeopardy. This was the case with the United States in the immediate postwar era, when its military weakness compared with the USSR forced a new buildup in American armed strength, which most probably set off renewed activity in military technology in the Communist world. As an astute observer of international organization has commented: "The experience of the interwar years had weakened enthusiasm for disarmament *per se*; the events of the thirties seemed to suggest that it was not armaments as such, but armaments in the wrong hands which endangered peace. . . ."[6]

In addition to the belief that a reduction in the level of global armaments will contribute to strengthening the prospects for peace, and that it accords with broad ethical-humanitarian aspirations, disarmament movements throughout history have often been motivated by still other goals. One motivation has been the desire to divert huge expenditures for armaments to projects designed to promote human welfare. Today this has become one of the most persuasive arguments advanced in behalf of disarmament. The United States, for example, has repeatedly stated that it cannot support the proposed Special United Nations Fund for Economic Development (SUNFED), vigorously espoused by nations in the Afro-Asian bloc, until the economic burden necessitated by high levels of armaments has been reduced.[7]

Propaganda motivations are almost always present in proposals advocating disarmament. Indeed, throughout the postwar period, it has sometimes seemed that propaganda considerations were uppermost in positions assumed by the two power giants, Soviet Russia and the United States. President Eisenhower's "Open Skies" plan and his later offer to establish an "Arctic Inspection Zone" were in large measure designed to enhance the position of the United States on the propaganda front, where Soviet Russia had scored impressive victories in preceding months. The value of both proposals to the United States lay more in the realm of psychological warfare than as measures calculated to break the stalemate reached in disarmament negotiations. The Soviet approach, too, has been heavily colored by propaganda overtones. The Kremlin's insistence upon such steps as outright prohibition of nuclear weapons and destruction of existing stockpiles, its call for cessation of nuclear weapons testing, its unilateral reductions in Soviet armed force levels, and its assaults against the West for alleged "germ warfare" in Korea have all been undertaken at least partially to cultivate a favorable reaction among neutralist countries, to undermine the military strength of the free world, and as part of the familiar postwar Soviet-instigated "peace offensive."

Propaganda overtones abounded in Premier Khrushchev's dramatic appearance before the UN General Assembly in September, 1959. Khrushchev's grandiose scheme for immediate and total disarmament; his skillful and lengthy association of this plan with the "needs" of the underdeveloped countries and the crushing "armaments burden"; his choice of the General Assembly for a platform, instead of the disarmament sessions that had been in progress for some time in Geneva; subsequent insistence by Soviet diplomats that the proposal be fully discussed in ensuing Assembly meetings—these moves were calculated to have the maximum propaganda effect in cultivating the image that Russia was in the forefront of nations seeking the goal of peace. This of course does not necessarily suggest that the Soviet proposal was "nothing but propaganda," that there were not some worthwhile suggestions in it. It is merely to underscore the fact that because of its pre-eminence as an issue confronting mankind and its sweeping ramifications for other thorny global issues like national economic progress, the disarmament question lends itself admirably to the reaping of maximum propaganda capital.

Finally, in evaluating disarmament efforts undertaken in recent years, account must continually be taken of another motivation almost invariably present in such efforts. Practically without exception, nations formulate their positions on arms limitation in terms of how progress toward that goal affects their power position generally and, more specifically, how agreements reached leave them vis-à-vis potential enemies. Thus, President Coolidge lamented, concerning an Anglo-French disarmament understanding in 1928, that "foreign governments made agreements limiting that class of combat vessels in which we were superior, but refused limitation in the class in which they were superior."[8] Countries routinely demand sweeping reductions in weapons in which their enemies are strong, while finding convincing reasons why there is no urgency about reducing weapons in their own arsenals, perhaps on the ground that such weapons are "defensive" or because the "right of self-defense" demands that they be retained.

Let us now focus more sharply on three aspects of the arms limitation problem: basic trends in disarmament negotiations throughout modern history; enduring issues encountered throughout the postwar period; and implications of the peaceful utilization of nuclear energy.

Canada, the United States, and the "Unguarded Frontier"

It is a curious fact that one of the most effective disarmament plans ever carried out in international affairs is also the oldest agreement in existence. This is the demilitarization of the Canadian-American border, provided by the Rush-Bagot agreement of 1817 and agreements growing out of that accord. The ideal of demilitarization stemmed from settlement of the War of 1812 and from suggestions made by John Jay and John Adams much earlier. Within England the realization was growing that if a race ensued for naval supremacy on the Great Lakes, the United States would most likely win eventually. For its part, the United States was glad to arrive at an understanding which prevented an arms race along its northern frontier. The Rush-Bagot agreement therefore provided that warships on the lakes would be limited solely to those required for patrol duty and customs inspection, an agreement which has remained in effect ever since.

Starting with an initial accord governing only *naval* armaments, agreements were later formulated which, at least by tacit consent, covered land armaments and fortifications along the border as well. Significantly, broadening of the Rush-Bagot agreement was accompanied by the evolution of arbitration and other nonviolent methods for settling disputes between the two nations.[9]

The "unguarded frontier" between the United States and its northern neighbor has not always enjoyed as peaceful a history as is sometimes supposed. Periodically, strife between the two countries has threatened to abrogate the demilitarization accord. The United States, for example, was on the verge of terminating the agreement during the Civil War.

How much relevance has the history of the Canadian-American "unguarded frontier" for the broader problem of arms limitation within the international community at large? A number of special features in Canadian-United States relations caution against uncritical attempts to hold this out as a "model" to be applied generally throughout the world. With rare exceptions, neither the United States nor Canada has regarded the other as a threat to its existence, has nurtured ancient grievances toward the other or coveted the other's territory. To the contrary, over the course of time, each has come to feel a community of interest with the other and to appreciate the extent to which the security of both countries was indissolubly linked. By the late 1950s, there had come about a virtual merger in the two nations' strategic defense system established to protect the Northern Hemisphere from surprise attack.

The Hague Conference

If we view the Rush-Bagot agreement as a special case, then we must date systematic disarmament proposals among the great powers from the emergence of the Hague Tribunal in the late nineteenth century. In 1898, the government of Tsar Nicholas II, alarmed by the rapid expansion in German military technology, especially by the spectacular buildup in artillery firepower, proposed an international conference to deal with the rising spiral of armaments. All of the arguments heard today—that ever more destructive armaments were increasing the likelihood and barbarity of war, that funds and energies could better be devoted to more beneficial purposes, that mankind yearned for a better way to settle world conflict—were voiced by advocates of disarmament in this period. A British scholar has written: "To these arguments, which were as cogent at the time as they are today, the Powers reacted in a manner that set the pattern for the next 50 years. They did accept the principle; they did not allow the preparations for the conference to interfere with the execution of their existing [armaments] programmes." The Hague Conference sought a modest beginning: merely a moratorium on the *future* production of weapons, without proposing the abolition of existing military forces.

Concurrently with this limited beginning, it was hoped that an alternative for force could be found in greater reliance upon arbitration procedures for settling differences among countries.[10]

Yet, in microcosm, the Hague Conferences of 1899 and 1907 mirrored tendencies typical of disarmament negotiations throughout the years that followed. Not even the limited hope of freezing existing levels of armaments and of gradually substituting organized procedures for the peaceful settlement of disputes proved attainable. The most that could be accomplished was acceptance of rules designed to "humanize war," such as pledges not to use expanding ("dum-dum") bullets and asphyxiating gases.[11] That such rules were valuable in later years is conceded. But in the judgment of Martin, the Hague Conferences nevertheless diverted attention from the primary problem of *avoiding* war to the distinctly secondary problem of "humanizing war," and "by so doing they . . . helped to delay political and social pressures for the setting up of a strong and comprehensive international organization for peace."[12]

Disarmament Movements in the 1920s and 1930s

Sporadic and unsuccessful attempts were made to gain support for disarmament proposals from 1907 down to World War I.[13] The next stage of importance dates from President Wilson's proposals relating to the League of Nations and disarmament. Four ideas were emphasized: compulsory adjudication of international disputes; a scheme whereby the security of large and small states was to be guaranteed; a new institutional framework, the League of Nations, whereby these goals could be carried out; and, finally, immediate adoption of a disarmament plan upon termination of hostilities, to be applied first to Germany, Austria, and the other defeated countries. It would be an oversimplification to say that disarmament failed in this period because the League of Nations ultimately failed; to some degree it might have been the other way around. In any case, the whole "package deal" envisioned in Wilson's proposals eventually broke down for a number of reasons, most fundamentally perhaps because nations were unwilling to make a wholehearted commitment to its requirements. Even granting a sincere desire on the part of certain League members to achieve disarmament within a context of

functioning collective security, the chances for success were dim on a number of thorny "technical" questions inherent in disarmament schemes. These had to do with such issues as establishing a system of inspection to determine violations, a method for carrying out sanctions and punishments against lawbreakers, an equitable formula for determining the military force levels necessary for maintenance of internal order and defense, and criteria for determining comparability of various categories of weapons.[14] However, League of Nations disarmament efforts served to dispel the notion that the only major barriers to arms limitation were technical ones. It became clear that the thorniest issues associated with disarmament were "political" questions. Ancient national rivalries like that between France and Germany had to be set at rest before disarmament could be successful, and there had to be workable machinery to facilitate application of nonviolent methods of international intercourse.[15]

As a nonmember of the League of Nations, the United States was not a party to disarmament deliberations undertaken within that body. Yet it was highly desirous of reducing the level of world armaments. Consequently, the United States sponsored and participated in a number of developments during the interwar period which sought to eliminate the scourge of war. As an outgrowth of the Hague Conferences, the United States had taken a leading role in sponsoring arbitration treaties. Although the United States had refused to enter the League of Nations, these treaties indicated that it shared many of the goals expressed in the League Covenant. Furthermore, its initiative in sponsoring disarmament negotiations testified to its acceptance of many of the League's professed purposes.

Perhaps the most impressive beacon of disarmament in the troubled seas of arms competition was the Naval Armaments Conference of 1921. Significant results included the establishment of a ratio of 10:10:7 for Great Britain, the United States, and Japan, respectively, for capital ships; an agreement to scrap certain types of older ships and to declare a ten-year moratorium on the construction of new capital ships; limitations on the total tonnage and the armaments of certain kinds of existing capital ships; and a pledge by the United States, Great Britain, and Japan not to strengthen fortifications on their possessions in the Pacific. The agreement was to remain in force until the end of 1936, whereupon it could be terminated by two years' notice from any of the signatories. Following its aggressive moves in Manchuria in the early 1930s, Japan gave notice in 1934 that it would no longer honor the treaty obligations after 1936.

A Decade of Failure

Two other attempts to reach disarmament agreements before World War II deserve brief mention. Owing to expanded construction of certain types of cruisers, destroyers, and submarines exempted from the Washington agreements, the United States had come to believe that the prohibitions laid down in 1921 ought to be broadened. This led to the calling of the Geneva Conference in 1927. As events turned out, the atmosphere could hardly have been more prejudicial to success. France and Italy refused to attend; jealousy and suspicion colored the approaches of the erstwhile Atlantic allies, Britain and America. Each country pursued the customary policy of trying to "regulate" armaments which were conspicuous in the other country's arsenal, while showing no particular propensity to reduce its own. The conference ended in total failure.

One development in this same period prevented failure of the Geneva Conference from triggering a renewed race for military supremacy.[16] That was the signing of the Kellogg-Briand Pact (or Pact of Paris) on August 27, 1928. This agreement, ultimately signed by nearly all civilized countries in the world, solemnly condemned "recourse to war for the solution of international controversies" and pledged the signatories to "renounce it as an instrument of national policy in their relations with one another." Numerous powerful signatories accepted the pact only after attaching various "qualifications" and "understandings." The United States, for instance, declared that the pact did not impair the "right of self-defense," did not exclude the use of force to uphold the Monroe Doctrine, or entail any obligation to participate in sanctions against countries violating the pact. Furthermore, American officials rated the pact of marginal importance in attacking the root-causes of war and violence in world affairs. According to the diplomatic historian Julius Pratt, it was perhaps indicative of prevailing attitudes in the Senate that, immediately after ratification of the pact, the Senate voted appropriations to construct 15 new 10,000-ton cruisers to add to the nation's naval strength.[17]

The last significant act in the drama of disarmament negotiations before World War II was the London Conference of 1930, at which the United States and Britain manifested as much of a spirit of conciliation as they had shown suspicion and hostility earlier. The old 10:10:7 ratio set by the Washington Conference for the United States, Britain, and Japan, respectively, was preserved and applied now to cruisers. Japan, however, gained a position of parity in submarines, a fact which strengthened its naval position in the Orient even more than formerly. Agreement was also reached that submarines should not be used against passenger shipping and should be used in accordance with rules already recognized in international law. An "escalator clause" permitted the great naval powers to exceed adopted quotas if countries not party to the accord embarked upon a naval arms race.[18]

The London Conference marked the finale in progress toward disarmament in the interwar period. Following Japanese invasion of Manchuria in 1931–1932, the world drifted inexorably toward the abyss of war. Japan gave notice of withdrawal from treaty prohibitions upon naval construction, effective at the end of 1936. Thereafter, the level of armaments began to climb toward the peak reached in World War II. Not until the postwar period were sustained efforts made to initiate new disarmament negotiations.

Disarmament Efforts in the Early Postwar Period

In evaluating progress made throughout recent history in the vexatious disarmament issue, Inis Claude cautioned in 1956 that:

It is important to avoid confusing long hours of international debate, vast piles of printed documents, and elaborate charts of institutional structure with meaningful accomplishment. Aside from certain limited and ephemeral successes which were achieved outside the League structure in the interwar period, the movement for arms reduction and limitation has been as unproductive of results as it has been productive of words. The tremendous display of military fireworks from 1939 to 1945 was only the final and most tragic bit of evidence that the League's efforts had been an abject failure, and the equally complete sterility of the work thus far undertaken by the United Nations in this field is one of the most glaring facts of international life.[19]

As the destructive power of modern weapons has risen by almost geometric proportions since

World War II, the postwar period has been characterized by interminable and highly technical meetings of negotiators from powerful countries; by carefully drafted and exceedingly complex disarmament proposals and counterproposals; by mounting pressure from public opinion around the world for renewing the search for a way out of the disarmament impasse; and, down to the 1960s, by minimum progress in resolving the issues which have blocked great-power acceptance of an operable disarmament plan.

The postwar period began auspiciously enough with the total demilitarization of such once-powerful Axis countries as Germany and Japan, followed by significant reductions in the military forces of the Allied governments. In hindsight, it is clear that the United States government, bowing to insistent public demands, reduced its armed strength to levels dangerously below those consistent with the nation's security and its expanding diplomatic commitments around the world. Alone among the great powers, only Soviet Russia continued to maintain a large military establishment, although there was some reduction from the peak reached during World War II.

But a new element had entered the picture. Toward the end of the war, the United States had perfected the atomic bomb, using it to administer the military *coup de grâce* to the Japanese Empire. The awesome power of what came to be called the "absolute weapon" for a time focused world opinion on the compelling urgency of controlling nuclear weapons. In the new era—the nuclear age—the problem of nonnuclear (or "conventional") weapons for many years seemed insignificant compared with the necessity of assuring that nuclear energy was utilized for human welfare.

As the only country which had actually produced atomic bombs, and the one which possessed a clear headstart in nuclear technology, the United States took the initiative in presenting a plan for international control of atomic energy. The American position was based upon an Anglo-Canadian-American declaration of November 15, 1945. This statement described the atomic bomb as a "means of destruction hitherto unknown, against which there can be no adequate military defense. . . ." It held that only the "prevention of war" offered genuine protection to civilization. It declared further that dissemination of information about its manufacture "before it is possible to devise effective, reciprocal, and enforceable

safeguards" might intensify feelings of insecurity throughout the world. The statement therefore proposed immediate establishment of a UN commission to prepare recommendations aimed at utilizing nuclear energy solely for peaceful purposes. Enunciating a principle which has been consistently advocated by the United States throughout the greater part of the postwar period, the statement held that: "The work of the Commission should proceed by separate stages, the successful completion of each one of which will develop the necessary confidence of the world before the next stage is undertaken." As we shall see, the matter of "staging" has proved one of the most controversial issues associated with disarmament within recent years.[20]

Following this tripartite declaration, on June 14, 1946, elder statesman Bernard Baruch presented a proposal—later known as the "Baruch Plan"—to the newly created Atomic Energy Commission of the UN. The plan provided for establishment of an International Atomic Development Authority with broad powers to own and control all nuclear energy facilities "potentially dangerous to world security." The agency would control, inspect, and license all nuclear activities, would foster beneficial uses of nuclear technology, and sponsor research and development basic to scientific progress. After these steps had been taken, there would be cessation of production of all nuclear weapons, disposal of all existing stockpiles of such weapons, and transmission to the Authority of complete information concerning nuclear technology. The proposal envisioned rigid enforcement of the provisions of any disarmament proposal adopted, with "immediate, swift, and sure punishments," on the order of the Nuremberg war crimes trials, to be meted out to violators. The Security Council would have no veto of the Authority's findings and operations.[21]

On June 19, Soviet Russia offered a counterproposal to the Baruch Plan. Cardinal features were: an immediate international agreement pledging nations "not to use atomic weapons in any circumstances whatsoever," and requiring them to terminate current production of nuclear weapons and to dispose of existing stockpiles of nuclear weapons within three months after the agreement was reached; a pledge that signatories would regard violation of the agreement as a crime against humanity; and a further pledge that within six months the signatories would "pass legislation providing severe penalties" for violations of the provisions of the agreement.[22]

These two proposals were of lasting significance in shaping the course of disarmament negotiations over the next several years. The proposals defined the positions of the two rival power blocs whose relations colored most global political issues. Each plan reflected certain underlying assumptions indicative of each side's approach to disarmament and closely related questions in international affairs. Although there were some modifications on the part of each side in the years ahead, the deadlock on disarmament which ensued over these two conflicting proposals remained essentially unchanged thereafter.

The cardinal ingredients in the American plan were establishment of foolproof international inspection and control over all phases of nuclear technology, cessation of nuclear weapons production, disposal of accumulated atomic weapons stockpiles, and surrender of full information concerning nuclear technology to the Authority—in that order. The fundamental elements in the Soviet plan were immediate and unconditional prohibition of the use and manufacture of atomic weapons, destruction of existing stockpiles, and establishment of a nationally operated inspection and control system—in that order.

Behind each of these proposals were certain hard realities. The United States possessed the atomic bomb; the USSR did not. Therefore, America was unwilling to relinquish its advantage until international control over nuclear processes had been guaranteed. Lacking the atomic bomb, but possessing formidable ground- and air-forces, the USSR was following the ancient stratagem of seeking to deprive its opponent of its strongest weapon, thereby leaving the Communist bloc an overwhelmingly advantageous position in nonnuclear weapons. Meantime, pending negotiation of an acceptable disarmament scheme, Russia would press on rapidly to expand its own scientific-technological knowledge in the field of nuclear energy.

The American-sponsored Baruch Plan was widely hailed as a generous and statesmanlike gesture designed to assure that nuclear energy would forever be used for the benefit of mankind. Few other great powers would have been prepared to relinquish control over the greatest destructive force ever developed, especially when they were beginning to have serious doubts about the intentions of their most powerful diplomatic rival. Generous as it may have been from an American point of view, however, the Baruch Plan was probably foredoomed to failure as a measure acceptable to the Soviet Union. Two features of the plan virtually guaranteed this result. One was insistence upon "ironclad" inspection and control by the Authority as a prerequisite to any functioning disarmament agreement. The other was that the efficacy of the inspection-control system had to be clearly demonstrated *before* the United States was prepared to relinquish its atomic monopoly. Given the extreme sensitivity Russia has displayed throughout history about the security of its borders and the hostility it has demonstrated toward foreigners, coupled with more recent re-enforcement of these anxieties and propensities by communist ideological preachments, it is extremely doubtful whether Russia would have accepted any plan calling for hordes of foreign "inspectors" in Russia, who possessed sweeping powers to inquire into virtually every aspect of Soviet society and industry. Under the Baruch Plan, the powers envisioned for the nuclear Authority were vast and without any very clearly specified limits.[23]

But it was perhaps the second requirement which posed the most enduring obstacle to agreement in 1946 and in the years thereafter. America's insistence that successive stages in the disarmament agreement be completed before its own monopoly of nuclear weapons would be relinquished amounted to saying to the USSR: If you are willing to demonstrate your "good faith" by satisfactory compliance with the Baruch Plan; if we are completely convinced that you are genuinely endeavoring to meet its requirements; if, in short, the USSR's conduct over the course of months or possibly years is acceptable to the United States—then, and *only then*, will the American government place itself on a plane of nuclear parity with other great powers. If, however, at any stage, Soviet behavior does not meet with American approval, then "the deal is off," and the United States is left free to exploit the advantage which its prior stockpiling of nuclear weapons and its headstart in nuclear technology have given it. The Soviet Union, that is to say, was to be put on probation for an unspecified period, with the United States acting as probation officer to decide whether Soviet behavior met required standards. If it did not, if for any reason the step-by-step disarmament plan did not prove feasible, then the United States would be left in a clearly superior position in any ensuing arms race.

From the point of view of Soviet national interest, there was little incentive for the Kremlin to accept the Baruch Plan. The United States was asking its most powerful antagonist to do something which it would never itself have contemplated doing if the roles had been reversed: to trust America not to exploit the great advantage its atomic monopoly gave it in world affairs, pending ultimate conclusion of an international disarmament agreement. In later years it became a cardinal principle of American foreign policy that no disarmament agreement could rest upon "mere promises"; yet this was in effect what Washington was prepared to offer Moscow for an indefinite period in the future. When the stakes were nothing less than the global balance of military power, this was asking a good deal of *any* state and entirely too much of a state whose outlook on world affairs had been conditioned by centuries of suspicion and hostility toward the outside world and whose ideology permitted no room for doubt about the hostility of other countries toward the Communist bloc.

As for the Soviet counterplan, its weaknesses were even more glaring and just as fundamental as those of the Baruch Plan. The Kremlin wanted the United States to relinquish its monopoly in atomic weapons—virtually the *only* weapons available to the West as a counterpoise against the crushing might of the Red Army—in exchange for vague Soviet promises of future compliance with an international disarmament agreement and bland assurances that in good time an effective system of global inspection and control would be set up and function satisfactorily under purely *national* auspices. The Soviet proposal required an even greater act of faith than the American, especially in view of recent Soviet machinations in Eastern Europe, indicating to the West the Kremlin's patent unwillingness to be bound by solemn promises made earlier in the Yalta and Potsdam agreements. Whatever weaknesses might be singled out in the Baruch Plan, no impartial student of American diplomatic history would seriously contend that the United States was contemplating a surprise attack against Russia in some future period, or that it was plotting to impose its rule over debilitated countries in Europe and Asia. The same could not be said for the Kremlin's intentions toward weaker nations. Already, these were be-

ginning to be widely suspected in the Western world; and having demobilized their armies, Western officials could never give up their only protection against the overwhelming superiority of the Red Army in exchange for paper promises of Soviet good behavior in the future.

PERSISTENT ISSUES IN DISARMAMENT NEGOTIATIONS

The positions taken by the two superpowers, and their allies and satellites, in the period of UN debate on the Baruch Plan were, in most particulars, identical with positions held throughout the disarmament negotiations in the years thereafter. Proposals, counterproposals, and attempts to create syntheses between them, resulted in negotiations that were as prolonged and intricate as they were usually fruitless in halting the steady accretions in national armaments and the destructive power of modern weapons. In the absence of a workable disarmament agreement, both sides pressed forward rapidly in the field of nuclear technology. Soviet Russia broke America's monopoly of the uranium bomb in 1949. The United States, meanwhile, was developing the thermonuclear (hydrogen) bomb, which it perfected in 1952. Less than a year later, the USSR had succeeded in making a "hydrogen device," thereby re-establishing approximate nuclear weapons parity with the United States. The Korean War prompted a considerable increase in the level of "conventional" weapons* throughout the non-Communist world. Furthermore, East and West alike

---

* The term "conventional" weapons does not have a universally accepted definition. In Martin's words, it means "all armaments and armed forces except atomic, radioactive, lethal-chemical and biological weapons, and all future weapons having comparable destructive characteristics." Andrew Martin, *Collective Security* (Paris: UNESCO, 1952), p. 81. The principal point of ambiguity arises, however, about tactical nuclear weapons intended chiefly for use against troop concentrations on the battlefield. If these are looked upon as simply highly destructive "conventional" weapons, ironically the destructive force of *several* of these could easily exceed that of a single nuclear bomb used against enemy cities!

For that matter, the definition of "armaments" themselves is extremely difficult to draw precisely and meaningfully. Is the steel-making potential of a nation part of its "armaments"? Normally, it would not be so regarded. Yet in any future military conflict, the side that possesses the greatest economic potential—the greatest ability, that is to say, to "bounce back" from a nuclear attack—could be expected to win the conflict in the end.

pressed forward with the development of a category of weapons fitting neatly into neither classification: "tactical" nuclear weapons, designed for use on the battlefield or against enemy submarines or (potentially, if not by the mid-1960s, actually) as "antimissile" missiles for defense. The result was that the destructive power of *all* categories of weapons was at a new high. One thermonuclear bomb dropped on New York or Moscow, for example, would exceed the total destructive power of all bombs used in World War II.[24]

The ebb and flow of tensions between rival, heavily armed power blocs both caused, and were in some measure caused by, the stalemate over disarmament questions within the United Nations. Now, as in earlier eras, nations always had to consider the diplomatic context within which decisions respecting disarmament were to be made. How would acceptance of a particular disarmament scheme alter the nation's power relative to the power of its diplomatic opponents? How would reductions in specified categories of weapons affect the capacity of the nation to carry out its diplomatic commitments? These and many other questions weighed heavily in the approaches of all countries involved in the disarmament discussions. As rapid progress was made in nuclear technology, and as powerful nations perfected new methods, particularly missiles, for delivering nuclear weapons, the urgency of discovering fruitful approaches to the problem of arms limitation mounted.

Throughout months and years of prolonged and often sterile negotiations, certain key issues persisted. Insight into the intricacies of the disarmament question since World War II can more profitably be gained by focusing our attention on these questions instead of tracing out chronologically the pattern of disarmament negotiations since 1946.*

The Scope of Disarmament Proposals

An issue at the center of all disarmament negotiations is the question: Shall statesmen

* A variety of sources is available to students who wish to follow disarmament negotiations on a year-by-year basis. Annual developments are summarized in the official *United Nations Yearbook*; good secondary accounts are the annual volumes in the series, *Annual Review of United Nations Affairs*, published by New York University. Informative sources for American policy toward disarmament are the annual installments in the State Department's series, *U.S. Participation in the UN*, and a number of titles in its "International Organization and Conference Series."

strive for *total and comprehensive* agreements, covering all major aspects of the armaments problem, or shall they seek separate agreements covering only *limited* aspects of the problem?

The former procedure was epitomized by the remark of Soviet Foreign Minister Maxim Litvinov during the 1930s that "the way to disarm is to disarm." This same mentality was reflected more than two decades later in Soviet Premier Khrushchev's dramatic plea before the UN General Assembly late in 1959, when he presented a new Russian proposal calling for total disarmament within four years. Schemes advocating total disarmament have the merit of simplicity: they urge powerful countries, by a supreme act of self-abnegation, to scrap their military forces at one blow, thereby relieving mankind of the evils growing out of the existence of large armaments stockpiles and military forces.

In view of the evident reluctance of powerful, often hostile countries to take so radical a step in the absence of settlements of vital political issues, the greatest weakness of total disarmament schemes is the fact that their comprehensiveness is their undoing. Whatever merits such plans possess because of their simplicity, experience in recent history affords very little evidence for believing that heavily armed nations are prepared to accept such schemes. As with many "all or nothing" proposals, insistence upon *complete* reform as often as not results in *no* reform. A limited disarmament scheme, on the other hand, recognizes that some *actual* progress is better than mere theoretical agreement on the desirability of sweeping disarmament measures. Modest beginnings which are successful may pave the way for more far-reaching steps in the future. Said Secretary of State Dulles in 1955: " . . . it is the beginning, the initial breakthrough, that is often decisive."[25] The same attitude was expressed by President Kennedy in his report to the American people after the signing of the nuclear test-ban agreement in Moscow, on July 25, 1963. This accord prohibiting ground and atmospheric testing, said the President, was "a shaft of light out into the darkness"; it could be "a step toward reduced world tensions and broader areas of agreement."[26] Throughout the postwar period, American officials remained convinced that, as a practical matter, limited and "first-step" proposals offered the only promise of making genuine progress in achieving significant arms reduction.[27]

Just Agree in Principle, Step In and We'll Find the Way to Controls and Inspection. (Source: Valtman in *The Hartford Times*, reproduced in *The New York Times*, October 18, 1959.)

At the same time, the United States remained amply aware that in its repeated and dramatic calls for "general and complete disarmament," the Communist bloc had scored propaganda victories over the West. "GCD," as it came to be abbreviated, unquestionably had worldwide appeal, especially among the neutralist countries. That Communist negotiators always remained evasive and vague on the steps by which it was to be achieved did not dampen the ardor of some countries for the principle, nor did it prevent a skeptical American government sometimes from *appearing* to oppose the principle itself when it called for clarifying details from Moscow. Moreover, despite the admittedly remote prospect of achieving it, the United States, no less than the USSR, supported GCD as an ultimate goal. By the early 1960s, the United States reiterated its dedication to the ideal of general and complete disarmament. President Kennedy, late in 1961, challenged the USSR "not to an arms race but a peace race"; he proposed that both countries "advance together step-by-step, stage-by-stage, until general and complete disarmament has been achieved."[28] If the President's speech did nothing else, it at least went far toward satisfying other countries about America's commitment to the principle of GCD, although the thorny issues of how to reach the goal remained as difficult as ever.

Political Issues and Agreement on Disarmament

The necessity for a "relaxation of tensions" throughout the international community has been a motif in Comunist propaganda within recent years. For example, a Soviet statement on disarmament made before the United Nations on May 10, 1955, expressed the view that:

Until an atmosphere of trust has been created in relations between states, any agreement on the institution of international control [of national armaments] can only serve to lull the vigilance of the peoples. It will create a false sense of security, while in reality there will be a danger of the production of atomic and hydrogen weapons and hence the threat of surprise attack and the unleashing of an atomic war with all its appalling consequences. . . .[29]

This theme has likewise been prominent in Western, and especially American, foreign policy. An atmosphere of trust has been viewed as indispensable to any kind of permanent resolution of cold-war issues. Yet agreement upon sonorous principles, such as those enunciated in the Soviet statement just cited, can be, and often has been, followed by violent disagreement over the precise steps needed to create the atmosphere conducive to harmonious international relations.

The American approach to disarmament is part of a pattern of the nation's diplomatic response to the communist challenge in the postwar era. A consistent element in this response has been insistence upon "deeds and not words" on the part of the Communist world. Said Secretary of State Acheson in 1950, in dealing with tensions between the United States and the USSR:

No one who has lived through these postwar years can be sanguine about reaching agreements in which reliance can be placed and which will be observed by the Soviet leaders in good faith. We must not, in our yearning for peace, allow ourselves to be betrayed by vague generalities or beguiling proffers of peace which are unsubstantiated by good faith solidly demonstrated in daily behavior. . . . What is required is genuine evidence in conduct, not just in words, of an intention to solve the immediate problems and remove the tensions which divide us.[30]

Repeatedly, American officials have underscored the fact that disarmament agreements with the Communist bloc, especially *limited* accords like a test-ban treaty, settled no fundamental political differences between East and West. Peace, said President Kennedy, in 1961, "is not solely a matter of military or technical problems, it is primarily a problem of politics and people." Unless progress could be made in social and political spheres, he told the United Nations, "our great strength, like that of the dinosaur, will become incapable of proper control and, like the dinosaur, vanish from the earth."[31] Again in 1963, President Kennedy observed that the recently concluded nuclear test-ban agreement did not usher in "the millennium. It will not resolve all conflicts, or cause the Communists to forego their ambitions, or eliminate the dangers of war. It will not reduce our need for arms or allies or programs of assistance to others."[32]

Implicit in the American approach to disarmament throughout the postwar period has thus been an underlying conviction that an indissoluble relationship exists between the level of national armaments and fundamental differences between powerful, ideologically hostile states over a host of outstanding diplomatic questions. In this complex relationship, which is essentially cause and which effect? However the question might be answered by informed students of disarmament negotiations throughout history, American policy-makers have been conscious of one paramount reality since World War II: massive Western rearmament was precipitated by increasingly ominous Soviet and Red Chinese threats against the security of the free world. Unquestionably, after East and West had acquired high levels of armaments, the arms race took on a certain momentum of its own, with each side increasingly apprehensive about the adequacy of its defenses. This led to the paradox described by Secretary of Defense Robert McNamara in 1963: ". . . I cannot allege that the vast increase in our nuclear forces, accompanied as it was by large increases in Soviet nuclear stockpiles, has produced a comparable enhancement in our security." He continued that "the sheer multiplication of a nation's destructive nuclear capability does not necessarily produce a net increase in its security."[33]

Yet a central ingredient in American disarmament proposals since World War II has been that the problem of rising levels of armaments and of national conflicts over global political issues cannot be rigidly separated. Limited progress, as examplified by the test-ban agreement in 1963, can perhaps be made in one sphere without corresponding progress in the other. Moreover, President Kennedy declared in 1961 that: "Men no longer maintain that disarmament must await the settlement of all disputes, for disarmament must be a part of any permanent settlement."[34] Even so, the American approach has been geared to the assumption that more or less parallel progress in resolving global political disputes was indispensable to any significant reduction in armaments. Western officials want no more vaguely worded, elastic pledges like those contained in the Yalta and Potsdam agreements of 1945, which supposedly bound the Soviet Union to certain mutually acceptable steps in areas like Eastern Europe, but which in reality bound it to nothing at all that could be enforced. Later experience in the truce negotiations following the Korean War demonstrated that agreements "in principle" between East and West provide no assurance that the all-important *details* of an acceptable accord will be forthcoming. Nor, on the basis of such earlier experiences, are Western statesmen inclined to put stock in pledges that rely upon nothing more than the good faith of the Communist world for compliance. In brief, Western governments have demanded, and by the mid-1960s continued to demand, tangible evidence of a genuine Communist desire to reach lasting international agreements before they commit themselves to steps that might imperil their military security.

"Staging" as an Issue in Disarmament

A staff study written for the Senate Foreign Relations Committee holds that: "At the present time, some of the issues of disarmament revolve less around what is to be done than when it is to be done."[35] The matter of "staging" (sometimes called "phasing") has caused endless controversy among the great powers. The American position, as stated by Secretary of Defense Charles E. Wilson in 1956, is that:

> Any agreement for reductions under the terms of a comprehensive disarmament program must be carried out by stages. These stages must be clearly defined and should be progressive, beginning with areas of least sensitivity. Each of the succeeding stages should only be initiated after the preceding stage has been satisfactorily completed.[36]

By 1961, in a series of new proposals designed to break the disarmament deadlock and to convince neutralist countries that the United States was genuinely endeavoring to produce a "fresh" approach to the problem, President Kennedy modified the American viewpoint on staging to meet many communist and neutralist demands. His new suggestions contemplated a five-stage disarmament accord: (1) a nuclear test-ban agreement; (2) a cessation of production of nuclear materials for war; (3) a prohibition upon the transfer of nuclear weapons to countries not presently possessing them; (4) an East-West agreement to ban nuclear weapons in outer space; and (5) the destruction of existing stockpiles of nuclear weapons and conversion of fissionable materials for peaceful uses.[37] While this represented a significant modification in earlier American demands, the American position, as we shall see more fully below, continued to regard an international inspection and control system as a vital component of any disarmament accord; it was unwilling to go beyond the first of the above phases (which was largely self-enforcing) with-

out Communist acceptance of such a system.[*]

Throughout the postwar era, Soviet proposals on staging have never been as explicit as Western proposals; a major drawback to them, in the Western view, is that they have always been vague on the "timing" of transition from stage to stage and on the circumstances under which such transitions would be made. By the mid-1950s, the contours of a three-stage scheme could be detected in Communist proposals. Implicitly at least, the Communist world seemed to anticipate the following sequence of stages: (1) total prohibitions against the manufacture of nuclear weapons and the use of existing ones; (2) reductions in the stockpiles of both conventional and nuclear weapons, together with cuts in military manpower; and finally (3) establishment and operation of a system of international inspection and control.[38] Down to the mid-1960s, Communist officials gave much more emphasis to the first two than to the last of these stages. As part of his stress upon "peaceful coexistence," and as an outgrowth of the *détente* with the United States over Cuba in 1962, Khrushchev admitted his willingness to accept the *principle* of limited inspection as an element in first- or second-stage proposals. Since we shall discuss this issue in detail below, we shall note here only that the Soviet position on disarmament appeared to be more flexible, and more inclined to conciliate the West on the inspection issue, than at any time in the postwar era. To date, however, no specific and satisfactory agreement on the matter of inspection and control of disarmament has been reached.

Great controversy has not only surrounded the exact *order* of stages to be followed, but it has also prevailed over the circumstances under which transitions will be made from one stage to the next. Three attitudes on this question may be discerned. The USSR has favored *automatic* transition from one stage to the next. Britain and France have tended to favor *semi-automatic* transition. The United States, on

---

[*] As with all aspects of the disarmament issue, the American position on staging was directly linked to the problem of maintaining national security unimpaired, as step-by-step arms reduction was carried out. The aim of the American approach, said a State Department publication, was "to keep the relative military positions of the parties as closely as possible to what they were at the beginning" of any disarmament accord. A key consideration, in the Western view, was that throughout early stages, NATO's military power—particularly its nuclear deterrent—must not be jeopardized, thereby

risking an attack by overwhelming Communist "conventional" forces against the free world. Thus, the West and its NATO allies repeatedly rejected Soviet first- or second-stage proposals intended to eliminate nuclear weapons or the means for delivering them, before an effective international inspection-control system was established or had become operational. See *Documents on American Foreign Relations: 1962* (New York: Harper & Row, 1963), pp. 81–82, and *The New York Times*, July 22, 1962, dispatch by Sidney Gruson.

the other hand, has insisted upon the idea (as expressed in its proposed draft of its treaty for general disarmament in 1962) that:

> Transition from one stage of disarmament to the next would take place upon decision that all measures in the preceding stage had been implemented and verified and that any additional arrangements required for measures in the next stage were ready to operate.[39]

In conformity with its over-all demand for convincing evidence of Communist good faith, Washington called for demonstrated national *compliance* with the requirements of one stage before the transition was to be made to the next. Moreover, the United States had been unwilling to accept the unsubstantiated word of Communist officials regarding the extent of such compliance; it demands that, in accordance with its proposals on inspection and control, this evidence be verified by impartial inspectors, unimpeded by a possible Soviet veto on the control commission.

If, as we have noted, the American position on staging is an outgrowth of the free world's insistence upon evidence of good faith on the part of the Communist bloc, and of unwillingness to risk impairment of its nuclear deterrent, different motivations have been present in the Communist conception of staging. Repeatedly, the USSR has invoked the principle of noninterference in the internal affairs of countries to oppose any inspection by other nations or an international agency to evaluate Soviet compliance with various stages of an arms limitation agreement. It has been unwilling especially to leave that judgment to its archrival, the United States, since Washington might conceivably decide that Soviet behavior at any stage was unacceptable, leaving America with its postwar superiority in nuclear stockpiling and technology. Two interpretations of the Soviet Union's attitude on staging are possible. Many leading authorities on the USSR, joined by many governmental officials and laymen, have doubted that the Kremlin is sincerely interested in *any* binding disarmament scheme involving international inspection and control.[40] If so, the Kremlin's reluctance to accept a requirement of full compliance with first-stage provisions is fully explicable. Or, if Soviet good faith in approaching disarmament negotiations is conceded, the USSR may be taking out a kind of insurance to guarantee that breakdown of an arms limitation agreement at some later point would not leave Russia in an inferior military position. It is conceivable, of course, that both of these motivations are present in some degree.

Conventional Weapons and Disarmament

So preoccupied were the great powers with the new magnitude of destructive force attained in nuclear and thermonuclear weapons in the years following World War II that for many years they gave only incidental attention to the problem of conventional armaments. In 1947 a Commission for Conventional Armaments had been established under the United Nations; meantime, its companion body, the UN Atomic Energy Commission, was considering the problem of nuclear weapons. Negotiations in each body were carried on without any significant liaison and coordination with the other agency. Deliberations in the Commission for Conventional Armaments lagged throughout successive months, indicating that the great powers were almost exclusively concerned with the threat of nuclear devastation.[41]

As always, positions on disarmament, however, were responsive to important developments in the international environment. Three such developments were of particular significance: by acquiring the uranium bomb (1949) and the hydrogen bomb (1953), the Soviet Union finally achieved at least approximate parity with the West in nuclear weapons; over this same period, the Western countries themselves raised their levels of conventional weapons and military manpower, thereby narrowing the gulf between themselves and the Communist bloc in ground forces; and despite a widely prevalent conception in the West that the atomic bomb was the "absolute weapon," the Korean War, along with later conflicts in South Vietnam and Laos, demonstrated graphically that control over conventional armaments was indispensable to further progress toward world peace and security.

In 1950, President Eisenhower proposed that the two questions of controlling nuclear and conventional armaments be considered jointly. This change in the American position led in 1952 to amalgamation of the two separate disarmament bodies into a new agency, the UN Disarmament Commission, charged with considering the entire spectrum of problems associated with disarmament.

Before this move, the United States and the Soviet Union had taken widely divergent positions on the relationship between conventional and nuclear weapons. From the beginning of postwar disarmament talks, the USSR has linked the two categories of weapons closely together and demanded simultaneous cuts in both categories—a demand which led to the specific proposal in 1948 and subsequently that the great powers cut their ground, sea, and air forces by one-third and, at the same time, unconditionally ban nuclear weapons. The American position, on the other hand, tended to be that controlling conventional armaments was secondary to controlling nuclear weapons; once the latter had been achieved, then the former problem could be dealt with constructively.[42]

A joint Anglo-French-American proposal to the Disarmament Commission in 1951 marked a fundamental modification in the Western view. At least some of the elements in earlier Soviet proposals were accepted by calling for a census of *all* military forces and armaments and for imposition of a "ceiling" on armed force levels and future weapons production.

Yet, until 1955, the Kremlin merely reiterated its familiar demand for an *immediate* one-third reduction in the force levels of all great powers. This demand came to have a greater than ordinary appeal for neutralist countries when, in the months that followed, the USSR announced that Russia and its Eastern European satellites were making unilateral cuts in their military manpower. The West, however, continued to reject across-the-board percentage cuts in armaments, because this move would merely perpetuate the Communist bloc's preponderance in ground forces; nor would the West accept any approach based upon unilateral disarmament, when such a move was unaccompanied by international inspection and control.[43]

Finally, in 1955, the Soviet Union expressed its willingness to accept the principle of armed force "ceilings" as suggested by Anglo-French-American proposals. Premier Khrushchev before the UN in 1959 proposed limits of 1.7 million men each for Russia, the United States, and Communist China, leaving Britain and France 650,000 men each. Although the difference between Communist and free-world positions was considerably narrowed by this suggestion, the disarmament deadlock continued because of disagreement over the pivotal question of inspection and control. The West insisted upon two preconditions: a military census to determine existing national force levels and, in the light of information obtained, as-

surance that the Soviet Union would not be left in a position of preponderance in ground forces.[44]

Establishing an Inspection-Control System

Along with the question of staging, the issue of an effective inspection-control system has proved to be a rock against which disarmament negotiations have broken within recent years. Not only have the free-world coalition and the Communist bloc differed over the stage at which a system of inspection-control ought to be inaugurated; they have also differed widely over many other fundamental issues associated with such a system. Basically, their positions today have changed little from positions assumed at the time of the Baruch Plan and the Soviet counterproposal in 1946.

The powers to be exercised by an international control agency are a source of great controversy. Should it have sweeping powers, to investigate *all* national activities that might conceivably entail a violation of a disarmament scheme? Or should its powers be confined to clearly designated sites and to specified activities within national territories? The United States has favored sweeping powers for the control agency. Said Secretary of Defense Charles E. Wilson in 1956, "it would be illusory to condition the execution of an arms-limitation agreement solely upon the good faith of the contracting parties. This emphasizes the requirement that any arms-limitation agreement be safeguarded by an effective inspection and control system which does not depend upon good faith alone for effective operation."[45] The Soviet Union has assigned no such priority to the question of inspection and control, believing that: (1) establishment of such a system should *follow* a ban upon the use and manufacture of nuclear and conventional weapons and (2) that the powers given to such a system ought to be carefully specified so as to prevent any infringement upon national sovereignty.

It would be no exaggeration to say that disagreement between the free world and the Communist bloc over the issue of inspection and control has been the ultimate source of the deadlock in disarmament deliberations since World War II. The impasse involves disagreement over two basic questions: the *scope* of the powers to be possessed by an international control agency in verifying compliance with a disarmament accord, and the ability of this agency *to deal with violations which are uncovered.* American officials demand sweeping powers of inspection, together with sufficient power to deal effectively with violations—which means that the agency's operations must not be subject to veto in the Security Council of the UN. The USSR favors limited and selected inspection; its few statements on the matter of control indicate that it would leave violations largely to be dealt with by the countries themselves.

While these have been the basic positions of East and West throughout the postwar era, by the late 1950s and 1960s, negotiators from each side sought intermediate positions that would at least partially satisfy the demands of the other side. Several possibilities existed for narrowing prevailing differences. One approach was embodied in President Eisenhower's "Open Skies" proposal in 1955, calling for reciprocal and unimpeded aerial inspection by Russia and America of each other's security zone. As a countermove, the Soviet Union advanced a plan for "ground inspection," in which each side would provide opportunities to the other to inspect designated land areas under its military control. These proposals stemmed from a realization that was more and more at the forefront of disarmament negotiations: protection against *surprise attack* had become, in the nuclear missile age, a key ingredient of any disarmament scheme capable of safeguarding the military security of its adherents. This realization in turn rested upon the tacit assumption that there was no known or foolproof way of preventing countries from secreting stores of arms, however effectively the future production of armaments might be controlled. The United States thus believed that reciprocal aerial inspection, accompanied perhaps by an exchange of military blueprints, would go far toward alleviating the danger that either side could successfully mount a military offensive against the other. The Kremlin, however, greeted this proposal by reiterating its all too familiar accusation that "Open Skies" was merely one more American-instigated plot to carry out espionage activities within the Communist security zone.[46]

Many of the same considerations underlay another proposal that gained wide attention during the early 1960s—the so-called "black box" system of inspection. Essentially, this entailed installation of sealed scientific devices within the borders of the nuclear powers, that would enable observers to determine whether nuclear testing was being carried on, in defiance of an agreement prohibiting it. As usual, this proposal also abounded with difficult technical questions engendering controversy between East and West. What kind of, and how many, "black box" devices would be installed in America and the Soviet Union? Who would decide *where* they should be installed? How often could they be inspected? What routes, and what methods of transportation, would inspecting teams utilize in carrying out their duties? What happened if evidence of violation were uncovered? These and a multitude of other technical issues, as with almost all other aspects of the larger disarmament question, engendered controversy between negotiators from Western and Communist nations, sufficient to forestall any significant agreement upon the principle of "black box" inspection.[47]

After nearly 20 years of discussion on the question of arms control since World War II, both East and West had evinced some willingness to modify long-held demands on inspection and control. Under Khrushchev, the Soviet Union expressed its readiness to consider establishment of a limited inspection system during an early stage of disarmament. Moreover, by the 1960s, the Kremlin had retreated from its dogged attachment to unsupervised national compliance, instead of inspection and control by outside observers. For its part, the United States was willing to consider more or less simultaneous disarmament and establishment of a limited inspection-control system, instead of adhering to its long-held demand that the latter precede the former.[48] By signing the nuclear test-ban agreement of 1963, it also signified its readiness to take a limited step toward disarmament that depended chiefly upon self-regulation exercised by the parties to the accord, rather than upon coercive measures exercised by an impartial international control agency.

Despite such progress, the basic deadlock over inspection and control largely remained. The Communist world adhered fundamentally to the position expressed by Khrushchev in 1959:

> We are in favor of strict control over the implementation of a disarmament agreement when it is reached. . . . We are in favor of general disarmament under control, but we are against control without disarmament.[49]

And by the mid-1960s, there were indications that the Soviet approach had moved closer to the American position in acknowledging that inspection and control was a *sine qua non* of general disarmament, as when high-level Soviet sources declared: "It is our belief that under general and complete disarmament there can and must be complete control in order to guarantee that the world remains disarmed."[50] Yet it was difficult to determine whether these concessions represented merely propaganda gestures or whether a significant change had actually occurred in the Communist bloc's position on inspection and control. Irrespective of such statements, the Communist bloc's negotiating position continued to be that: (1) any inspection-control system contemplated must be of limited scope and authority, so limited that it fell far short of American demands; and (2) that a substantial degree of *actual disarmament* must occur prior to establishment of a system for inspection and control. By the same token, American proposals continued to insist upon an inspection-control system that was given ample scope and authority to carry out its duties; they also demanded that such a system be established and demonstrate its viability *before* the great powers reduced their armaments level appreciably. Thus, President Kennedy declared in 1963 that the United States fully endorsed "general and complete disarmament," but that the Soviet Union "is still unwilling to accept the inspection such goals require."[51] In the light of this impasse, it could safely be predicted that fundamental disagreement between East and West over inspection and control would pose the most formidable obstacle to progress in reducing the level of global armaments.

Proposals for an Experimental "Test Zone"

The last half of the 1950s witnessed intense preoccupation among disarmament negotiators with still another approach that for a time presaged a breakthrough in achieving genuine arms limitation. This was some kind of "pilot project," as exemplified by President Eisenhower's proposal in 1958 that an "Arctic Inspection Zone" be created, to include territories adjacent to the Arctic Circle within the Western and Soviet security zones. The basic idea was that within a specified area, the great powers would report the location of their military bases and the disposition of their armed forces; international inspection teams would supervise whatever degree of disarmament was actually carried out within the zone. In spite of world-wide interest in the possibilities of this

approach, Soviet Russia's eighty-third veto in the Security Council of the UN prevented its adoption.[52]

Yet the basic idea embodied in an experimental "test zone" was not totally abandoned. In the months that followed, discussion centered upon the possibility of extending the idea to continental Europe, where a belt of territories in the center of Europe—embracing areas within the NATO alliance and the Communist bloc—might be used to test limited disarmament agreements and the viability of an inspection-control system.[53] Despite favorable indications, by the early 1960s this plan too had obviously failed to break the deadlock between East and West—indicating, as postwar experience had made abundantly clear, that it was not for lack of detailed and imaginative plans, but for lack of a real commitment to the basic goal, that disarmament schemes covering many different approaches and possibilities had failed to receive great power support.

Nuclear Test-Ban Accord and Agreement on Outer Space

Bleak as it was, the record of postwar disarmament negotiations was not totally unproductive. Enough progress had been achieved at least to convince governmental leaders on both sides of the iron curtain that the search for agreement must continue. Aside from widespread awareness of the catastrophic consequences of nuclear war, two specific agreements fostered the hope that eventually a major disarmament accord might still be negotiated. One of these was the nuclear test-ban treaty, signed in Moscow on July 25, 1963, among the United States, the Soviet Union, and Great Britain. The treaty banned atmospheric and ground tests of nuclear weapons by the signatories. It did not prohibit underground tests of such weapons. In one sense, it did not qualify as a "disarmament" agreement at all, since it did nothing to reduce stockpiles of existing nuclear weapons, nor did it prohibit the production of these weapons.*

---

* This point was underscored by high-ranking American officials, who emphasized to skeptical legislators that the agreement would in no way impair the American nuclear deterrent, tilt the military balance in favor of the Communist bloc, or hinder what some officials in the executive and legislative branches regarded as a military necessity—development of a nuclear "antimissile missile" to safeguard the free world from a possible surprise attack by Communist nations. Secretary of Defense Robert

American officials were nonetheless convinced that the agreement was in the national interest for several reasons. First, it marked at least a limited "breakthrough" in the disarmament stalemate and offered renewed hope that a more comprehensive agreement might be reached. Second, it went far toward eliminating a danger that had increasingly aroused apprehension throughout the world, particularly among societies in Asia that were uniquely vulnerable: the hazards posed by cumulative radioactive fallout from the atmosphere that threatened not only to imperil the health of millions of people on the planet but perhaps also to jeopardize the physical and mental wellbeing of future generations. Although it had been inclined for many years to minimize these dangers, by the 1960s the United States was compelled to accept the fact that, scientifically justified or not, fears about fallout were prevalent among countries in the neutralist zone. The United States was obliged for propaganda reasons, if for no other, to take account of them.* Third, the nuclear test-ban agreement

ought to contribute toward another long-standing American goal: prevention of the "proliferation" of nuclear weapons among countries not already possessing them.[54] No less important than these reasons, another consideration influenced American foreign policy officials. From a propaganda and psychological standpoint, the United States could not lose, irrespective of whether the Communist world complied with the terms of the agreement or did not comply. If the agreement were honored, as we have seen, the United States would continue to maintain the "credibility" of its deterrent and would have at least shared with the Soviet Union in the propaganda credit for reaching an accord long demanded by the diplomatically uncommitted nations. If, on the other hand, the Communist bloc did *not* adhere to the agreement, American military security would not be appreciably impaired; even more significantly, the onus would then fall squarely upon the Soviet Union and its satellites for abrogating an agreement seeking to resolve cold-war tensions. In brief, if the Communist world violated the accord, it risked exposing the falsity of its devotion to "peaceful coexistence" and the spuriousness of its claim to being at the forefront of the "peace-loving" nations of the world.

A second area in which common ground existed between East and West was in acceptance of the idea that nuclear weapons must be excluded from outer space. The United States and the Soviet Union acceded to the overwhelming sentiment of nations in the UN General Assembly that neither East nor West should utilize outer space for its own military advantage.[55] By the mid-1960s, the evidence indicated that this agreement was being adhered to as each side pressed forward with its space exploration programs.**

Representation in Disarmament Negotiations

By the end of the 1950s, disarmament negotiations had proved responsive to a funda-

---

McNamara thus testified concerning the way this agreement would affect America's defense effort: "I can say that most of the factors [in America's armed strength] will not be affected at all—not accuracy of missiles, not variety of systems, not their dispersal or mobility, and not numbers." Assuming that the USSR or another Communist country secretly violated the agreement, McNamara was convinced, violations "could not produce significant advantages" for the country concerned. For the text of McNamara's statement, see *The New York Times*, August 14, 1963.

* Throughout the 1950s and early 1960s, American officials, particularly in the Atomic Energy Commission, denied that nuclear testing constituted a significant danger to health, either for people living or those unborn. This verdict enjoyed very little support among nations through the Afro-Asian-Arab world. Most especially in Asia (where two atomic bombs had already been exploded, and where dietary habits and climate made populations unusually susceptible to fallout contamination), governmental and popular sentiment was strongly against continued testing by the United States or other governments. Global apprehensions were confirmed by a UN-sponsored scientific study, released in 1958, sharply challenging the American view that testing posed no real health hazards. It predicted, for example, that from 2500 to 100,000 babies would be born with genetic defects because of testing thus far; it also predicted that from 400 to 2000 cases of leukemia would be caused directly by such testing. It underscored another fact that received minimum attention from American officials: that the damage from testing *varied widely* around the world, depending upon factors such as prevailing winds and dietary patterns. Asians, for example, depended heavily upon rice as a staple—a fact that meant that highly dangerous strontium-90 from

fallout was assimilated much more easily into the human body among them than in other societies. *The New York Herald-Tribune*, August 11, 1958, and *The New York Times*, August 17, 1958.

** The agreement on outer space was paralleled by a comparable understanding, accepted by tacit consent on all sides, that military bases and weapons ought to be excluded from Antarctica and that this region should be reserved for scientific research by all nations. By the mid-1960s, considerable cooperation in scientific ventures in this region prevailed between Communist and non-Communist countries.

mental tendency in the international community: the emergence and growing influence of a body of diplomatically nonaligned states that demanded the right to have their viewpoints considered seriously by the great powers. Genuine progress on arms control was an item high on the agenda of demands made upon the nuclear giants by such countries as Yugoslavia, Egypt, Ghana, India, and Indonesia. The neutralist nations insisted also that they be given a formal role in disarmament talks, in the obvious expectation that they could successfully break the deadlock that had long characterized deliberations among the great powers.

Coming at a time when UN-sponsored disarmament negotiations had bogged down into a reiteration of long-familiar proposals and counterproposals, the neutralist demands at length were substantially accepted by Washington and Moscow, partially out of the conviction that nothing would be lost by acceding to them. For many months the UN Disarmament Commission had proved incapable of producing agreement, particularly after 1957 when it was "boycotted" by the Soviet Union. Accordingly, disarmament negotiations were shifted to Geneva. By the early 1960s, the Geneva disarmament negotiations had been broadened to include 18 countries, with eight Asian, African, and Latin American countries represented (although France, engaged in producing its own nuclear *force de frappe*, boycotted the Geneva discussions). It could not be said that this reliance upon "multilateralism" to break the disarmament stalemate achieved results any more notably successful than had been achieved earlier under the United Nations. Significantly, the nuclear test-ban accord of 1963 was negotiated bilaterally by the United States and the Soviet Union, with minimum reference to the Geneva disarmament proceedings—a fact that brought vocal complaints from neutralist governments about the extent to which their viewpoints were being "ignored" by the great powers.[56]

Even so, it could not be maintained that the trend toward multilateralism was totally without important consequences for disarmament negotiations. As with its over-all assessment of "neutralism" down to the early 1960s, the United States viewed the intrusion of the neutralist world into disarmament talks with misgivings, however much it conceded that propaganda considerations required some concessions to neutralist demands. Neutralist reaction to the Soviet resumption of nuclear testing in September, 1961—producing few vocal remonstrances from the Belgrade Conference of Nonaligned States during this period—re-enforced prevailing American apprehensions that on the thorny issues surrounding arms control the neutralist world agreed substantially with the position of the Communist bloc.[57] On such problems as inspection and control, for example, spokesmen for the neutralist cause seemed much more inclined than American officials to rely upon Soviet professions of good intentions and promises of compliance with any agreement reached.

Nevertheless, events revealed that diplomatically nonaligned states were not as naïve about Communist intentions, or as inherently skeptical of Western good faith, as Americans often imagined. The Geneva forum admittedly provided the Communist bloc with a propaganda platform for advertising its attachment to the cause of peace that it exploited skillfully. At the same time, according to a State Department evaluation, the Soviet approach was also revealed as "superficial and propagandistic" before the eyes of the world.[58] American officials were thus inclined to view the shift to Geneva as beneficial in that it offered "useful opportunities to advance United States interests by communicating our point of view to other nations, by demonstrating that disarmament is a complicated task which cannot be achieved by sweeping and propagandistic proposals, by establishing the common interests of all nations in turning down the arms race, and by defining the issues properly so that practical steps can be taken toward their resolution." By the early 1960s, the State Department regarded the Geneva meetings as "one of the best available methods of prevailing upon the Soviet Union to accept its responsibility to heed the conscience and aspirations of the world community. . . ."[59] In brief, by being given a participating role, neutralist countries had received a thorough indoctrination into the complexities of the many-faceted problem of arms reduction. Increasingly, this engendered greater responsibility on the part of these countries and promoted growing receptivity for the realization that prolonged, serious, and detailed negotiations over concrete *plans* were required to achieve the goal, rather than general and dramatic statements calling for "complete and general disarmament."[60] If, as the Anglo-American-Soviet test-ban agreement illustrated, serious disarmament negotiations were likely to remain chiefly in the hands of the great powers, the neutralist countries nevertheless succeeded in airing their demands and in compelling Washington, Moscow, and other capitals to take their opinions more and more into account.

Disarmament and American Policy Machinery

The difficulty of finding a satisfactory organizational pattern for carrying on international disarmament negotiations had been paralleled within the United States, where numerous efforts have been made to discover the most effective machinery for formulating and carrying out American policy on arms limitation. By the mid-1960s, direct responsibility for disarmament policy was lodged in the Arms Control and Disarmament Agency (ACDA), established in 1961 by President Kennedy as a semiautonomous organization, functioning under the broad policy guidance of the State Department. ACDA, in turn, grew out of President Eisenhower's appointment of Harold Stassen to be his Special Assistant for Disarmament, from 1955 to 1958.[61] The conviction that a separate agency ought to be established, according to one authority, stemmed from the belief that "only an independent agency with representation at the highest level [of government] could ensure that the disarmament point of view was not suppressed within any agency with vested interests of its own."[62]

Throughout the postwar period, American policy on disarmament has been plagued by a greater or lesser degree of interagency disagreement over the nature of the disarmament proposals the United States ought to support— and, indeed, over whether its security interests were served by offering any at all. Officials on the Atomic Energy Commission, for example, have been conspicuously cool about a cessation of nuclear weapons testing; their viewpoints were often seconded by spokesmen for the military establishment. In the Pentagon, a belief prevailed that in their zeal for progress in arms control, ACDA was insensitive to the security needs of the nation. One observer reported a deep apprehension among Defense Department officials that "in their ignorance," advocates of disarmament "could turn the balance against us overnight."[63] For its part, during its relatively brief existence, ACDA suffered from chaotic organizational structure, low morale, and an over-all feeling that its viewpoints were being neglected by more influential executive agencies and by Congress,

where the agency's proposals often received little serious attention. To a significant degree, organizational malfunctioning and interagency friction in Washington reflected a much deeper problem: the frustration occasioned by policy-makers because of their sincere *desire* to achieve general and complete disarmament and their ample awareness, in view of the manifold difficulties involved, there was virtually no chance of attaining it. ACDA thus found itself in a dilemma that weakened its morale and involved it in controversies with other agencies. This was whether to endorse broad, humanitarian goals that were not likely to be achieved, and that ACDA officials *knew* full well would not be achieved, or whether to settle for very limited, unspectacular gains in the sphere of arms reduction that, for many years at least, would likely do little or nothing to reverse the tide of mounting, and ever more destructive, levels of armaments. At some risk to the nation's propaganda and psychological campaign, by the mid-1960s ACDA apparently had decided to concentrate its efforts in seeking the latter alternative.

By the beginning of 1964, one other development required brief mention. In view of the fact that over half of federal expenditures (around $50 billion annually, or about $1 billion per week) were devoted to national defense, President Johnson believed that the domestic *economic* implications of arms reduction required intensive continuing study. Accordingly, at the end of 1963, he appointed a high-level governmental committee to investigate these implications of disarmament and to make recommendations designed to mitigate adverse economic effects accompanying significant arms reduction, especially for those communities that were heavily dependent upon defense spending to maintain prosperity.[64]

Disarmament—Retrospect and Prospect

What have innumerable and frequently highly technical disarmament negotiations carried on since World War II actually accomplished? In view of the inordinate complexity of the disarmament problem, and the great variety of relationships which exist among constituent parts of that problem, it may be well to recapitulate very briefly progress made to date.

We have already identified three specific formal or tacit agreements reached between East and West on arms control: the nuclear test-ban treaty of 1963, the agreement to bar nuclear weapons from outer space, and the agreement to refrain from turning the Antarctic into military bases. Besides these specific understandings, considerable progress had been made in narrowing differences between Western and Communist proposals, in contrast to the rigid and apparently antithetical positions prevailing during the 1940s and early 1950s. Thus far, for example, in spite of Soviet Russia's return to the concept of total disarmament in 1959, the great powers have concentrated upon partial disarmament in preference to comprehensive disarmament. Partial disarmament has been chosen out of widespread realization that more sweeping proposals have little or no chance of being universally accepted. Moreover, it seems widely conceded that experience gained in putting partial disarmament schemes into operation will provide statesmen with valuable lessons and will perhaps increase confidence that greater progress can be made.

No clear-cut agreement has emerged on the always controversial question of the relation of armaments to collateral political issues. Each side has tended to abandon an either-or position: Russia has expressed its willingness to relate such issues intimately to disarmament and perhaps to let negotiations over them proceed *concurrently* with reductions in weapons and manpower; America has expressed its willingness to take at least *limited* steps toward disarmament before or while political issues are being negotiated. A fundamental divergence is still discernible, however, in the weight accorded solution of political issues by each side. The free world continues to demand significant progress before embarking upon extensive arms limitation programs; the Communist world is willing to make some concessions, but demands that substantial arms reduction come first.

Compromises have been made on staging also, with the position of neither the United States nor the Soviet Union as inflexible as it was during the 1940s. America has agreed to the principle that limited disarmament can take place before an effective inspection system is established, or perhaps while such a system is in the process of establishment. Nevertheless, the United States has made it clear that it wants to see early evidence of Soviet good faith before it proceeds very far with arms reduction. The Soviet Union has modified its earlier insistent demand that the West agree

to elimination of nuclear stockpiles and conventional weapons, and that it liquidate foreign bases, before an inspection-control system comes into being. It has accepted the idea in principle that inspection can be carried on within a specified geographical area *concurrently* with an actual reduction in armaments and that the powers of an inspection-control agency can grow apace with the lowering of arms levels. Recent Soviet statements on the question of inspection are, on the whole, less belligerently negative than they were during the 1940s and early 1950s. Yet, formidable differences on the question of staging remain to be overcome. American insistence that transition from stage to stage be certified by an international agency unhampered by veto, and Soviet insistence that certification be by each country or by an agency under the Security Council's auspices, seem almost as irreconcilable as ever. The same can be said about the matter of control. No consensus has emerged concerning what measures ought to be taken, and by whom, against violators of an international arms limitation agreement.

Inspection and control, as we have already suggested, is perhaps the most firmly embedded obstacle to agreement on disarmament. Some progress has been made. Each side has moved closer to the position of the other side —but it is still a long way from American insistence upon genuinely effective inspection-control and Soviet insistence upon preserving the "sovereignty" of nations by curtailing the activities of an international inspectorate, perhaps to the point that its powers could become nil. The most heartening development on this issue is the continuing interest expressed by both sides in launching some kind of experimental plan whereby an inspectorate would gain experience in supervising an "arms-free zone" in an area such as the Arctic or Europe. Implementation of such a plan could go far toward clarifying the actual problems an inspectorate would encounter with disarmament schemes on a larger scale.

Despite such progress, it also had to be recognized that by the mid-1960s two similar phenomena tended to cast an ominous shadow over East-West disarmament negotiations and to compound many of the problems we have discussed in this chapter. Within each great-power bloc, internal stresses and strains increasingly called into question the ability of the United States and the Soviet Union to control the policies of its military allies. The

United States was disconcerted by French President de Gaulle's determination to forge ahead in developing a nuclear *force de frappe* and in pursuing a military strategy that envisioned considerable national independence in employing France's nuclear arsenal. De Gaulle refused outright to participate in the Anglo-American-Soviet nuclear test-ban agreement; more generally, he was known to be exceedingly skeptical about the desirability of continuing disarmament negotiations with the Communist bloc. There was no guarantee, therefore, that an East-West disarmament accord could be made binding upon the French Fifth Republic. Moscow was confronted with much the same problem in its relations with Red China, whose nuclear technology by the mid-1960s lagged far behind that of the USSR and Western countries, but whose determination to create its own nuclear force remained undiminished. Eventual Red Chinese membership in the "nuclear club" was only a matter of time. Given Mao Tse-tung's well-known callousness toward the prospect of nuclear war, the problem of arriving at an arms limitation accord that embraced Red China might well prove insoluble, at least until there was some mitigation in the tensions that had prevailed for many years between Washington and Peiping.

"ATOMS FOR PEACE"

By 1953, after witnessing close to a decade of deadlock in disarmament discussions, President Eisenhower was persuaded that "the world . . . was courting disaster in the armaments race, that something must be done to put a brake on this momentum." For many months, the President had been searching "for any kind of an idea that could bring the world to look at the atomic problem in a broad and intelligent way and still escape the impasse to action created by Russian intransigence. . . ."[65] The President's concern reflected realization that America's early postwar policies of "atomic secrecy" were more and more alienating its friends in the international community. As a country professing lofty ideals for international conduct, and as the nation at the forefront of nuclear technology, the United States was expected to find some way of making the benefits of the nuclear age available for the improvement of human society, even in the absence of a disarmament accord. Nuclear energy was widely regarded, however mistakenly, as the answer to the economic needs of underdeveloped nations.

The "Atoms-for-Peace" Proposal

Briefly, this was the background against which President Eisenhower on December 8, 1953, made what was widely interpreted as one of the most statesmanlike proposals advanced by the United States in the postwar period. This was the "Atoms-for-Peace" plan, outlining steps which might be taken under the United Nations to extend the benefits of nuclear technology to all countries.[66] Apart from the belief that the President's proposal would have wide appeal and utility for the underdeveloped regions, Eisenhower's speech scored at least a temporary victory for the United States on the propaganda front by undercutting what was up to that time a highly successful Communist propaganda offensive depicting Uncle Sam as animated by "atomic imperialism" and determined to deprive other countries of the benefits of nuclear technology by clinging doggedly to a policy of "atomic secrecy." Within the UN, the initial response to the President's plan was instantaneous and, almost without exception, favorable.[67]

Unfortunately from a propaganda viewpoint, several months elapsed between President Eisenhower's dramatic suggestion and the presentation of a concrete plan designed to carry out his proposal. In explanation, American officials stated that the President had anticipated that *all* nuclear powers would make contributions to the atoms-for-peace plan and that the Kremlin had given no indication of its willingness to participate. Finally, late in 1954, the United States scored another propaganda coup when it announced its willingness to contribute to the atoms-for-peace program even if the Kremlin did not; within a few days, the USSR declared its willingness also to participate.[68]

The International Atomic Energy Agency

Ever since the President's speech in 1953, negotiations had been carried on to create an international agency to operate and supervise the atoms-for-peace proposal. Negotiations were prolonged and exceedingly technical, but finally a draft agreement was drawn up and signed at a conference held at UN Headquarters from September 20 to October 26, 1956. Signatories were the USSR, Great Britain, France, the United States, and eight lesser powers.[69] On June 18, 1957, after lengthy committee consideration and floor debate, the Senate by a vote of 67–19 ratified the treaty establishing the International Atomic Energy Agency. In response to prevalent fears that national security might someday be imperiled by American membership in IAEA, the Senate appended a reservation to the effect that if the treaty were ever amended in a manner unacceptable to the Senate, then the United States would be required to withdraw from the agency.

The highest governing body of the IAEA is the General Conference, consisting of one representative from each member state. The Conference meets annually or more often if necessary. The Board of Governors carries on the day-by-day activities of the agency; its members are chosen by a complicated formula to assure majority control by countries in the forefront of nuclear development.[70]

The treaty establishing IAEA specifies that the transmission of nuclear information to it by member states is purely *voluntary*; information acquired by the agency, as a result of assistance to members, however, must be shared with all member states. Members agree to notify the agency concerning the quantity and quality of fissionable materials they are prepared—in conformity with regulations laid down in their own domestic law—to make available under the atoms-for-peace agreement. After studying the treaty's provisions, the Senate Foreign Relations Committee concluded that: "Contributions are on a completely voluntary basis. Members are free to supply or to withhold materials, or to make available such quantities as they deem advisable, and on such terms as are agreed with the Agency. . . ."[71]

The Committee's report continues that the heart of the treaty is Article XII, "which contemplates a system of safeguards and security to prevent materials and facilities furnished for a particular project by the Agency from being diverted to a military use, and to require observance of any health and safety standards prescribed by the Agency." Under the treaty, IAEA possesses the right to examine and approve equipment and reactors used under its auspices by member states, to require strict accounting for all fissionable materials granted to members, to demand project reports, and to demand return to the agency of any excess fissionable materials produced or reserved by member states. The agency may

employ inspectors to verify compliance with its regulations and to report any suspected diversion of fissionable materials for military use. Reports of suspected noncompliance are made to the Board of Governors and to the General Conference; ultimately, the UN Security Council and General Assembly are notified. If a state fails to take corrective measures after a finding of noncompliance has been made, it is denied further participation in the atoms-for-peace plan and, in case of flagrant wrongdoing, it may be suspended from membership.[72]

As is apparent, the atoms-for-peace program thus has lasting implications for the corollary field of disarmament. The agency's inspection-control powers are far from ironclad; they probably are not sufficient to prevent a country from violating the agreement at least the *first* time. Thereafter, of course, that country would be denied any further participation in the benefits of the atoms-for-peace proposal. According to Secretary of State Dulles, conformity derived essentially from two forces: the reluctance of countries to cut themselves off from any further benefits of the plan for the sake of a temporary and probably indecisive advantage in nuclear weapons; and the moral suasion which would be exercised against such a country by the rest of the world. While there is always the risk that a country can violate the agreement, there is, in the words of one American official, "no possible way to prevent peaceful atoms from being perverted to warlike purposes if someone wants war badly enough. . . . But if we are going to live in the atomic age, we have to take the risks that are normal to that age."[73] The most significant thing about the inspection-control system set up under the atoms-for-peace agreement then is not that this system is foolproof; it obviously is not. Rather it is that in establishing the system at all, the great powers were willing to take a step based largely upon faith and, before abandoning the search for a mutually acceptable inspection-control system, to test whether one based chiefly upon voluntary compliance and self-interest can be made to work.

"Atoms for Peace" and the Future

With headquarters established in Vienna, the International Atomic Energy Agency began functioning on October 1, 1957, utilizing an initial contribution of five and one-half tons of uranium–235 by the United States, a significantly smaller contribution from the

Soviet Union, and even lesser contributions from other advanced nations.[74] Thereafter, in a variety of ways, IAEA actively promoted the dissemination of knowledge and technology about the peaceful applications of nuclear energy. Specific activities included scientific conferences, such as the one held in Geneva in 1958, at which more than 2000 scientific papers, by experts from some 46 countries, were presented on various aspects of nuclear science; intimate collaboration with the UN Scientific Committee on the Effects of Atomic Radiation, established to study the dangers of radioactive fallout; selection of outstanding students for advanced training in peacetime nuclear technology; operation of a nuclear research reactor in Vienna; sponsorship of research contracts and supply of uranium to member states; promotion of studies relating to the application of nuclear technology in such fields as medicine, industry, and agriculture; and intensive study of problems associated with safe disposal of nuclear waste materials.[75]

As the years passed, it was apparent that some of the luster had worn off the atoms-for-peace plan. If it was still widely supported, particularly by economically backward countries that had not developed their own sources of nuclear power, widespread realization nevertheless existed that nuclear power was not likely to prove a panacea for nations committed to rapid industrialization. Events since the turn of the nuclear age indicated rather conclusively that extensive industrial use of atomic power was usually a case of "to him that hath shall be given. . . ." For many decades to come, industrialized nations of the West (including the Soviet Union) were likely to forge ahead most rapidly in applications of this new source of energy and, except in rare cases, to be the principal beneficiaries of it. The massive utilization of atomic energy for civilian purposes demanded the prior existence of an advanced "infrastructure" or high level of industrial development and technology. Nations lacking these requirements were not likely to possess either the resources or the know-how, perhaps for many years not even the demand, that would rapidly usher in the age of nuclear plenty and make it an era of accelerating industrial progress. Nuclear power, after all, was but a stage in the long evolutionary process beginning in the West with the Industrial Revolution. It might be regarded as the climax of that movement.

Understandably therefore, nations were not likely to jump from economic backwardness, in which the principal enterprise was often primitive agriculture, into an atomic utopia. Among the more serious inhibiting factors also in the rapid growth of peacetime nuclear power is the *cost* of such programs. As a generalization, nuclear power is not competitive with conventional fuels such as coal, oil and natural gas. This means that industrialized and developing countries alike are most prone to rely heavily upon nuclear fuels only when they lack traditional ones or when reliance upon the latter presents unusual financial problems.*

The logical inference to be drawn from these data is that the most rapid progress in the application of peacetime nuclear energy was likely to come in the already industrialized West, including the USSR and its European satellites. Experience in the late 1950s and early 1960s confirmed this expectation. Thus by 1962, the use or planned construction of nuclear power plants was confined almost exclusively to the United States, Western Europe, Eastern Europe, the Soviet Union, and Israel (whose economic system was much more comparable to Western countries than to its Arab neighbors).[76] The most intensive efforts to apply peacetime nuclear energy in a variety of fields was made by the nations of Western Europe. On January 1, 1958, six nations—France, Western Germany, Italy, Belgium, the Netherlands, and Luxembourg—joined in establishing the European Atomic Energy Community, popularly called Euratom. Euratom was designed to promote the peaceful uses of nuclear power for its members. Unlike the American Atomic Energy Commission, it has no interest in the development of atomic weapons, leaving it to individual countries—the principal one in Europe being France—to develop their own nuclear military technology.**

* See, for example, the views of Senator Clinton P. Anderson (Democrat of New Mexico), chairman of the congressional Atomic Energy Committee, who in 1960 called atoms for peace a "failure to date." His verdict was based upon a lengthy report on the program submitted to the committee. *The New York Herald-Tribune*, October 10, 1960.

** From the beginning, the United States supported Euratom as a regional cooperative enterprise in Europe—partially in the hope, according to Beloff, that a supranational organization of this kind would prevent the "proliferation" of nuclear weapons. This his been a consistent goal of American foreign policy since 1945. From the inception of Euratom, however, France demanded that nuclear weapons be excluded from the organization's jurisdiction. This in-

In common with many other institutions of postwar Europe, Euratom is essentially a body for promoting voluntary collaboration by its members in the solution of common problems. It is based upon mutual self-interest. Ben T. Moore has called it a "first attempt to enact community legislation on nuclear problems."[77]

Euratom sponsors research and development among its members, facilitates the exchange of technology, develops a "common market" for fissionable products, sponsors studies and regulations to assure safety and good health, facilitates investment in the nuclear energy field, and is the focal point of relations between its members and outside countries involving nuclear problems. Among the more specific goals of Euratom is reducing Western Europe's dependence upon Middle East oil supplies, a dependence that was painfully demonstrated when these supplies were jeopardized during the Suez Crisis of 1956.[78]

With nations belonging to Euratom, as with all other countries interested in the peacetime application of nuclear power, the atomic age has witnessed impressive progress in breaking down nationalistic barriers to the exchange of scientific information. At frequent intervals, international scientific conferences have been convened for the exchange of information about nuclear processes, such as the one in 1958 that predicted that atomic power would become competitive with existing methods of power generation for Europe during the 1960s and in "higher cost" areas such as the United States during the 1970s. Widespread utilization of nuclear-generated power in economically backward countries would likely require several decades.[79]

Science has proved that the atom can be made to yield vast riches for the human race. Plans have been made, and projects are well under way, for sharing the fruits of nuclear technology among all nations. How far mankind will ultimately benefit from those steps will depend, of course, upon the degree to which progress is achieved in dispelling the ever-present specter of nuclear war, waged with weapons capable of returning twentieth-century civilization to the Stone Age.

NOTES

1. James T. Shotwell and Marina Salvin, *Lessons on Security and Disarmament from the History of the League of Nations* (New York: King's Crown Press, 1949), p. 10. Provides valuable historical insight into experience with disarmament negotiations.
2. *The New York Times*, September 26, 1961.
3. Andrew Martin, *Collective Security* (Paris: UNESCO, 1952), p. 10. A review and analysis of collective security efforts under the League and the UN.
4. F. P. Walters, A *History of the League of Nations*, 1 (New York: Oxford University Press, 1952), 48–49. An authoritative study of the League's efforts in disarmament.
5. Senate Foreign Relations Committee, *Disarmament and Security: A Collection of Documents, 1919–1955*, 84th Congress, 2nd Session (Washington, D.C.: 1956), pp. 76–77. Documentary materials dealing with the period of the League and the UN.
6. H. G. Nicholas, *The United Nations as a Political Institution* (New York: Oxford University Press, 1962), p. 27.
7. House Foreign Affairs Committee, *Report on the Twelfth Session of the General Assembly of the United Nations*, 85th Congress, 2nd Session (Washington, D.C.: 1958), pp. 24–28.
8. Julius W. Pratt, A *History of United States Foreign Policy* (Englewood Cliffs, N.J.: Prentice-Hall, 1955), p. 556. Provides an introduction to the American approach to disarmament problems in recent history.
9. *Ibid.*, pp. 143–145.
10. Martin, *op. cit.*, pp. 28–29.
11. Senate Foreign Relations Committee, *Disarmament and Security, op. cit.*, pp. 170–171.
12. Martin, *op. cit.*, p. 30.
13. *Ibid.*, pp. 30–31.
14. *Ibid.*, pp. 31–32.
15. *Ibid.*, pp. 33–34.
16. Pratt, *op. cit.*, pp. 555–556.
17. *Ibid.*, pp. 538–539.
18. *Ibid.*, pp. 556–557.
19. Inis L. Claude, Jr., *Swords into Plowshares* (New York: Random House, 1956), p. 303. A perceptive analysis of disarmament,

---

dicated that de Gaulle's insistence upon a French nuclear *force de frappe* reflects a basic demand of the French society and is not merely his own personal eccentricity. Euratom has thus failed to prevent France from forging ahead with its own nuclear arsenal; yet it is certainly conceivable that in the absence of Euratom, other NATO countries might have embarked upon the same course. The problem is discussed more fully in Max Beloff, *The United States and the Unity of Europe* (New York: Random House, 1963), pp. 126–127; and George Lichtheim, *The New Europe: Today—and Tomorrow* (New York: Praeger, 1963), pp. 62–63.

within the broad context of promoting global security within the recent period.

20. Senate Foreign Relations Committee, *A Decade of American Foreign Policy, 1940–49*, 81st Congress, 1st Session (Washington, D.C.: 1950), pp. 1076–1077.
21. *Ibid.*, pp. 1079–1087.
22. *Ibid.*, pp. 1090–1091.
23. *Ibid.*, pp. 1093–1102.
24. See the text of President Kennedy's speech to the nation, in *The New York Times,* July 27, 1963.
25. Department of State, *American Foreign Policy, 1950–1955*, Publication No. 6446, "General Foreign Policy Series" 117, **II** (Washington, D.C.: 1957), 2874. Volume II contains documentary materials on American disarmament policy.
26. Text in *The New York Times,* July 27, 1963.
27. Lawrence W. Martin, "Disarmament: An Agency in Search of a Policy," *The Reporter,* **29** (July 4, 1963), 26.
28. *The New York Times,* September 26, 1961.
29. Department of State, *American Foreign Policy, 1950–1955,* **II,** *op. cit.,* 2850.
30. *Ibid.,* p. 1935.
31. *The New York Times,* September 26, 1961.
32. *The New York Times,* July 27, 1963.
33. *The New York Times,* August 14, 1963.
34. *The New York Times,* September 26, 1961.
35. Senate Foreign Relations Committee, *Control and Reduction of Armaments: A Decade of Negotiations, 1946–1956*, Staff Study No. 3, 84th Congress, 2nd Session (Washington, D.C.: 1956), p. 21.
36. Senate Foreign Relations Committee, *The Control and Reduction of Armaments,* Hearings, 84th Congress, 2nd Session (Washington, D.C.: 1956), Part 4, p. 165.
37. See the text of President Kennedy's speech in *The New York Times,* September 26, 1961.
38. "Disarmament: Proposals and Negotiations, 1946–1955," *World Today,* **11** (August, 1955), 337.
39. *Documents on American Foreign Relations: 1962* (New York: Harper & Row, 1963), p. 117.
40. Senate Foreign Relations Committee, *Control and Reduction of Armaments: Attitude of Soviet Leaders Toward Disarmament,* Staff Study No. 8, 85th Congress, 1st Session (Washington, D.C.: 1957).
41. Senate Foreign Relations Committee, *Control and Reduction of Armaments: A Decade of Negotiations, op. cit.,* pp. 5–7.
42. *Ibid.,* pp. 6–7.
43. *Ibid.,* pp. 8–9.
44. *Ibid.,* pp. 19–20.
45. Senate Foreign Relations Committee, *The Control and Reduction of Armaments, op. cit.,* Part 4, p. 163.
46. Dwight D. Eisenhower, *Mandate for Change: 1953–1956* (Garden City, N.Y.: Doubleday, 1963), pp. 520–522; Lincoln P. Bloomfield, *The United Nations and U.S. Foreign Policy* (Boston: Little, Brown, 1960), p. 94.
47. See the exchange of correspondence between President Kennedy and Premier Khrushchev, in *Documents on American Foreign Relations: 1962, op. cit.,* pp. 193–199.
48. *Ibid.,* pp. 116–117.
49. *The New York Times,* September 20, 1959.
50. *The New York Times,* December 25, 1963.
51. *The New York Times,* July 27, 1963.
52. *The New York Times,* May 4, 1958.
53. For American proposals and counterproposals, see Department of State, *U.S. Participation in the UN, 1956*, Publication No. 6577, "International Organization and Conference Series" III (Washington, D.C.: 1957), pp. 21–22. This annual series provides up-to-date information on disarmament proceedings.
54. See the text of President Kennedy's speech, in *The New York Times,* July 27, 1963.
55. *The New York Times,* November 10, 1963, dispatch by Thomas J. Hamilton.
56. *Idem.*
57. During the Belgrade Conference, the USSR resumed nuclear testing, unilaterally breaking a great-power moratorium on further testing. American officials were obviously distressed at the failure of the "neutralist" nations to condemn this act as vigorously as they were prone to condemn Western "colonialism" or racial discrimination—a fact that led the Washington correspondent for an influential Indian journal to conclude on the basis of "the highest authority" that for American officials this failure "confirms the worst fears harboured here" about neutralism, *Times of India,* September 6, 1961. A predominant American view was expressed by *Time* magazine, that "big bad Russia had in fact cowed them [the neutralist states] into appeasement." Other neutralist sources referred to impending moves by the Kennedy Administration to cut foreign aid to the more influential neutralist countries. See "Fall-Out from Belgrade," *The Eastern Economist,* October 22, 1961, pp. 541–

542; *Straits Times* of Singapore, September 9, 1961; *Times of India*, September 7, 1961.

58. *Documents on American Foreign Relations: 1962, op. cit.*, p. 80.
59. *Ibid.*, pp. 80–81.
60. *The New York Times*, November 10, 1963, dispatch by Thomas J. Hamilton.
61. Eisenhower, *op. cit.*, pp. 511–512. For Stassen's efforts to negotiate an arms control agreement—and his conflicts with Secretary of State Dulles in doing so—see Sherman Adams, *First-Hand Report: The Story of the Eisenhower Administration* (New York: Harper & Row, 1961), pp. 317–329.
62. Martin, "Disarmament: An Agency in Search of a Policy," *op. cit.*, p. 23.
63. *Ibid.*, p. 25.
64. *The New York Times*, December 22, 1963.
65. Eisenhower, *op. cit.*, pp. 252, 254.
66. Department of State, *American Foreign Policy, 1950–1955*, **II**, *op. cit.*, 2798–2805.
67. John Lear, "Ike and the Peaceful Atom," *The Reporter*, **14** (January 12, 1956), 16–17. This article describes the origins and early stages of the atoms-for-peace proposal.
68. *Ibid.*, *pp.* 16–18; Bloomfield, *op. cit.*, p. 226.

69. Senate Foreign Relations Committee, *Statute of the International Atomic Energy Agency*, 85th Congress, 1st Session (Washington, D.C.: 1957), p. 2. Traces out the atoms-for-peace proposal, culminating in IAEA.
70. *Ibid.*, pp. 4–5.
71. *Ibid.*, p. 6.
72. *Ibid.*, pp. 7–8.
73. Lear, *op. cit.*, p. 10.
74. David Cushman Coyle, *The United Nations and How It Works* (New York: Mentor Books, 1962), p. 148.
75. *Ibid.*, pp. 148–149.
76. See the map of global nuclear power installations in *The New York Times*, November 25, 1962.
77. Ben T. Moore, *Euratom: The American Interest in the European Atomic Energy Community* (New York: Twentieth Century Fund, 1958), pp. 1–4. Discusses the evolution of Euratom and its implications for American foreign policy.
78. *Ibid.*; Max Beloff, *The United States and the Unity of Europe* (New York: Random House, 1963), pp. 127–128.
79. *The New York Times*, September 7, 1958, dispatch by John W. Finney.

18 → THE GUIDING PRINCIPLES OF AMERICAN FOREIGN POLICY →

After reflecting upon the course of international affairs since World War I, a penetrating observer of Western society, Walter Lippmann, concluded that: ". . . There is a deep disorder in our society which comes not from the machinations of our enemies and from the adversities of the human condition but from within ourselves." He found symptoms of this "deep disorder" in the people's "incapacity to cope with reality, to govern their affairs, to defend their vital interests and, it might be, to insure their survival as free and democratic states. . . ." In his judgment "there was nothing to show that the Western democratic governments were in control of their affairs and capable of making the necessary decisions. They were reacting to events and they were not governing them."[1]

Among competent students of international affairs a conviction has been growing that conduct in the sphere of foreign relations is substantially determined by the philosophical frame of reference within which a society operates in evaluating developments on the world scene and out of which the nation's responses to these developments are derived. Judgments at any given time in history about how a country's foreign policy *is* being conducted and what *is* being accomplished, necessarily presuppose a prior conception of how foreign policy *ought* to be conducted and what it ideally *ought* to accomplish. Otherwise, foreign policy degenerates into a series of irrational, episodic responses to problems in the outside world. If a society fails to evolve some conception of what is *normative* in its approach to external issues, or fails to adhere to this conception, then its policies toward specific issues and problems are bound to reflect this neglect.

The question of the fundamental guiding principles of American foreign policy has engaged the attention of a host of commentators in recent years. For it has been most especially in this realm—failure to evolve and adhere to a reasonably consistent "philosophy of foreign relations"—that some of the greatest deficiencies in American foreign policy in the modern period have been most glaringly revealed. Americans are unphilosophical and unspeculative by nature. They are far more interested in devising plans for *carrying out* some project in foreign affairs designed to meet a specific challenge than they are in asking themselves *why* the challenge ought to be met in the first place, *why* some policies would meet it better than others, and above all, what the cumulative impact of a series of pragmatic decisions taken over an extended period of time in foreign relations is likely to be in terms of establishing a *discernible pattern* in the nation's approach to the outside world. The nation's diplomatic fortunes might greatly benefit from widespread, sober consideration by the citizenry of the basic principles which *ought* to animate the nation's diplomacy. This is the subject to which we direct our attention in this final chapter.

THE POSTWAR RE-EXAMINATION OF AMERICAN POLICY

The Need for Re-examination

More than any previous age in American history, the period since World War II has witnessed a continuing and searching re-examination of the underlying tenets of the nation's foreign policy. This re-examination has been spearheaded by a group of self-styled "realists," whose viewpoints are represented most pointedly in the writings of Professor Hans J. Morgenthau of the University of Chicago; George F. Kennan, former State Department official and recognized authority on the Soviet Union; and to a lesser extent by Walter Lippmann, one of the nation's leading journalists and commentators on American society; Hanson W. Baldwin, military analyst for *The New York Times*; and Professor Robert Strausz-Hupé of the University of Pennsylvania.

The "realist" approach has been sharply challenged by another school of writers who, for want of a better term, might be somewhat inaccurately characterized as "idealists." By and large, these writers have tended to reiterate traditional foreign policy principles, especially as they were expressed by President Woodrow Wilson, Secretary of State Cordell Hull, and President Franklin D. Roosevelt. Because these principles have been discussed extensively in earlier chapters of our study, in this chapter we shall concentrate primarily upon the "realist" challenge. Leading proponents of the "idealist" position have been Frank Tannenbaum, an authority on Latin America; former American Ambassador to India, Chester Bowles; the leading theologian Reinhold Niebuhr; Thomas I. Cook and Malcolm Moos of the Johns Hopkins University; and the well-known diplomatic historian, Dexter Perkins.*

While there are admitted differences among the "realists" concerning selected aspects of American foreign relations, most of them have placed strong emphasis on the frequent disparity between what the United States has *tried* to accomplish in foreign relations and what it has actually accomplished. They have found the gap between high hopes and disappointing results to be a recurrent, almost an ingrained, feature of America's relationships with the outside world. Closely associated with this problem is a second: the pendulumlike oscillations in American public opinion between energetic, passionate attempts to remake the world, and periods of cynicism and disillusionment toward events in the external realm. "Realists" have endeavored both to explain this phenomenon and to emphasize its consequences for national security.

Third, the "realists" have been particularly conscious of the *relationship between ends and means in foreign affairs*. This has led them to emphasize and re-emphasize what is surely the key concept of politics—*power*. They have cited instance after instance in which America, whose citizens remain curiously indifferent to the centrality of power, had what Walter Lippmann describes as a "bankrupt" foreign policy. American statesmen lacked or were unwilling to use the power necessary to protect diplomatic commitments and safeguard American security. "Realists" have found in this imbalance between the goals of foreign policy and the means necessary to achieve them another problem which appears well-nigh inherent in the American approach to foreign relations.

Fourth, the "realists" have emphasized what may well be in some respects the parent problem of all those alluded to above: sharp differences between the way Americans visualize events in the outside world and the actualities of international politics. It is widely conceded by well-informed students of American foreign policy that the wholesale existence of stereotypes, sacred cows, utopian images, vast

---

* Fuller acquaintance with the viewpoints of each school may be gained by consulting the following: Hanson W. Baldwin, *Great Mistakes of the War* (New York: Harper & Row, 1950); Chester Bowles, *Ambassador's Report* (New York: Harper & Row, 1954) and *Africa's Challenge to America* (Berkeley: University of California Press, 1956); D. W. Brogan, "Illusion of American Omnipotence," *Harper's Magazine*, **205** (December, 1952), 21–28; Thomas I. Cook and Malcolm Moos, *The Realism of Idealism as a Basis for Foreign Policy* (Baltimore: Johns Hopkins University Press, 1954); George F. Kennan, *American Diplomacy, 1900–1950* (New York: New American Library, 1952); Reinhold Niebuhr, *The*

Children of Light and the Children of Darkness (New York: Scribner's, 1944) and *Christian Realism and Political Problems* (New York: Scribner's, 1953); Dexter Perkins, *The American Approach to Foreign Policy* (Cambridge, Mass.: Harvard University Press, 1952); Robert Strausz-Hupé, "U.S. Foreign Policy and the Balance of Power," *Review of Politics*, **10** (January, 1948), 76–83; Frank Tannenbaum, *The American Tradition in Foreign Policy* (Norman, Okla.: University of Oklahoma Press, 1955); Ernest Lefever, *Ethics and United States Foreign Policy* (New York: Meridian, 1957).

areas of ignorance, and substantial apathy in the public mind seriously interferes with the formulation and execution of sound foreign policy decisions.

In brief, the re-examiners have summoned the nation to take a critical look at itself and its propensities in the realm of foreign relations. They have sought to lead the nation back to first principles, to help it develop a clear sense of purpose, to evolve guiding principles which will enable it to meet challenges in the external environment by something more than a pattern of expediential responses to outside pressures. In seeking to surmount what is often a *de facto* approach based upon "one problem at a time," the re-examiners are rendering an invaluable service to national, and ultimately perhaps to international, security.

To lend as much concreteness as possible to our consideration of the viewpoints of the re-examinists, let us concentrate primarily on the writings of Professor Hans J. Morgenthau and secondarily on the writings of other leading figures in this movement.

"National Interest"—The Pole Star of Diplomacy

No task is more urgently needed to assure success in the foreign policy field, according to Professor Morgenthau, than to "relearn the great principles of statecraft which guided the path of the republic in the first decade and—in moralistic disguise—in the first century of its existence." Among these principles highest priority must be given to a realization that the United States has acted "on the international scene, as all nations must, in power-political terms; we have tended to conceive of our actions in nonpolitical, moralistic terms." However much it may have been concealed by heavy encrustations of moralism and legalism, the underlying reality behind America's historic policies toward Europe, Asia, and Latin America down to World War I was maintenance of the balance of power. In the Western Hemisphere specifically, American policy, as epitomized by its most famous foreign policy principle, the Monroe Doctrine and its numerous corollaries, was aimed primarily at preserving "the unique position of the United States as a predominant power without rival." American policy toward Europe sought to prevent "the development of conditions . . . which would be conducive to a European nation's interference in the affairs of the Western Hemisphere or to a direct

attack upon the United States." A threat to American security would arise "if a European nation had gained such predominance that it could afford to look across the sea for conquest without fear of being menaced at the center of its power, that is, in Europe itself." America's historic diplomatic goals toward Asia were never so explicitly delineated and understood; moreover, they were subjected to moralistic influences in a measure from which the European and hemispheric policies were largely free. Yet principles, like the Open Door policy, which have been present in America's historic relations with Asia at least suggested the nation's concern with the balance-of-power concept.[2]

From about 1900 onward, however, this fundamental objective of policy—preserving the balance of power—came to be neglected by the United States. Instead, foreign policy, in Morgenthau's words, became "either improvisation in the face of an urgent problem . . . or —and especially in our century—the invocation of some abstract moral principle in the image of which the world was to be made over." George Kennan has made essentially the same point: " . . . I see the most serious fault of our past policy formulation to lie in something that I might call the legalistic-moralistic approach to international problems. This approach runs like a red skein through our foreign policy of the last fifty years." Woodrow Wilson personified the new approach to foreign relations; it was epitomized by such World War I slogans as "the war to end wars" and "the war to make the world safe for democracy" and by resounding principles such as "self-determination," "freedom of the seas," "collective security," and "nonintervention-ism." Concurrently, the legalistic-moralistic approach dictated renewed diplomatic activities in areas such as arbitration, disarmament, pacts to outlaw war, and pious declarations like the "Stimson Doctrine" (1932) withholding American "recognition" of territorial changes brought about in the Orient by military force. Permeating these activities, George Kennan has stated, was a firm belief "that it should be possible to suppress the chaotic and dangerous aspirations of governments in the international field by the acceptance of some system of legal rules and restraints."[3]

Wilson's cardinal error—and, in the judgment of the "realists" it was a cardinal one in terms of shaping the direction American policy was to take in the future—was his unwillingness to accept the centrality of power in international affairs, his naïve belief that power both could be, and would be, eliminated. On the level of operating policy, Wilson's fatal blunder was, in Morgenthau's words, that he did not seek "restoration of the European balance of power, traditional guarantor of American security." Instead, he substituted for "the concrete national interest of the United States the general postulate of a brave new world where the national interest of the United States, as that of all other nations, would disappear in a community of interests comprising mankind." This kind of thinking colored the American approach to foreign relations throughout subsequent decades and was in large measure responsible for the nearly disastrous neglect of national security during the 1930s.[4]

As the United States was drawn into the vortex of World War II, basically the same error was committed that had been made during and after World War I: the nation's diplomatic goals were expressed in resounding declarations of idealistic principles, typified by such documents as the Atlantic Charter proclaiming the "Four Freedoms"* and the UN Charter, which also expressed exalted goals toward which it was believed the international order was moving. The wartime demand for "unconditional surrender" was one of the most glaring examples of foreign policy being shaped in response to emotional-moralistic pressures, without any regard for the long-range politico-strategic interests of the nation. "The people wanted to be told," asserts Walter Lippmann, "that when this particular enemy had been forced to unconditional surrender, they would re-enter the golden age. This unique war would end all wars. This last war would make the world safe for democracy. This crusade would make the whole world a democracy." Hanson W. Baldwin has listed "unconditional surrender" among "the seven great mistakes of World War II."[5] No action could have been more antithetical to the balance-of-power principle because, as events after the war confirmed, the total elimination of Germany and Japan and, to a lesser extent, Italy from the ranks of the great powers inevitably created

* For the text of the Atlantic Charter and other wartime documents in the same vein, see Senate Foreign Relations Committee, *A Decade of American Foreign Policy, 1941–49*, 81st Congress, 1st Session (Washington, D.C.: 1950), pp. 1–32. The four freedoms enunciated in the Charter were: freedom from want, freedom from fear, freedom of speech, and freedom of religion.

a power vacuum in Europe and Asia. The existence of this vacuum was an open invitation to Soviet expansionism into these areas. And it was this expansionism primarily which triggered the cold war between the free world and the Communist world.

For nearly half a century, American foreign policy has been predominantly actuated by impulses arising out of Wilsonian idealism, whose basic goals were to usher in a new order of international society by abolishing power conflicts among hostile nation states. It required more than a century after 1789 for legalism-moralism "to drown out the older notion that international politics is an unending struggle for power in which the interests of individual nations must necessarily be defined in terms of power." Once this transformation occurred, a basic confusion—founded upon the romantic premise that power conflicts could be eliminated from the international scene—entered into American foreign policy. What Strausz-Hupé calls "pernicious abstractions" took hold of the American mind. A statesman who said he did not believe in power and the necessity for a balance of power, Morgenthau has written, was "like a scientist not believing in the law of gravity. . . ." The alternative to power is not a "higher morality," as Wilsonians would have it, but it is "moral deterioration through either political failure or the fanaticism of political crusades. . . ."[6]

Acceptance of the concept of "national interest" as the pole star of foreign policy, Morgenthau contends, would lead to an admission that throughout most of American history (until the era of Wilsonian idealism) the nation's foreign policy was "hard-headed and practical and at times ruthless." The American society's treatment of the Indians is cited as an example. If we are honest and realistic:

We know that this is the way all nations act when their interests are at stake—so cruel, so faithless, so cunning. We know that the United States has refrained from seeking dominions beyond the seas not because it was more virtuous than other nations, but because it had the better part of a continent to colonize.

To the oft-repeated charge that the concept of national interest is elusive and almost indefinable, the "realist" replies that it is comparable to other ideas, including such moralistic-legalistic concepts as "general welfare," "justice," and "freedom," whose precise content must be determined in the light of history and circumstances. In its most fundamental sense, national interest means self-preservation —the meaning which emerges most forcefully in time of war—and, even more specifically, the protection of the nation's territory. In peacetime, its exact connotations are admittedly more elusive; such forces as dominant personalities, public opinion, economic, sectional and minority interest groups, and the like, converge upon it and obscure its meaning. The realists' concept of national interest rests upon the assumption that there will be "continuous conflict and threat of war" among nations and that this must "be minimized through the continuous adjustment of conflicting interests by diplomatic action."[7]

For the "realist" there is, and can be, no conflict between moral values on the one hand and national interest—what we might call "political morality"—on the other. Quite the contrary, Morgenthau asserts, "the antithesis between moral principles and the national interest is not only intellectually mistaken but also morally pernicious. A foreign policy derived from the national interest is in fact morally superior to a foreign policy inspired by universal moral principles."* "Realists" condemn the "moralizing approach to foreign policy" because "it is derived from a false antithesis between morality and power politics, thus arrogating to itself all moral values and

* Policies based upon national interest, according to Morgenthau, are morally superior to those based upon supposedly universal moral principle because the latter derive from the former. Morgenthau finds a "profound and neglected truth" in observations of the seventeenth-century British philosopher Thomas Hobbes that, in Morgenthau's words, "the state creates morality as well as law and that there is neither morality nor law outside the state. Universal moral principles, such as justice or equality, are capable of guiding political action only to the extent that they have been given concrete content and have been related to political situations *by society*." See Morgenthau, *In Defense of the National Interest* (New York: Knopf, 1951), p. 34 (italics added). We shall evaluate the assumptions underlying "realism" later in the chapter. At this stage, however, it is worthwhile to point out that in deriving morality from the *nation state*, Morgenthau confuses two very basic ideas: the difference between the *nation state*—one of several possible political units—and *society itself*. It may be agreed, as Morgenthau contends, that morality is derived "by society"; this does not prove, however, that it is derived by society as it is organized along *national* lines. It could be, and before the dawn of the nation state was, derived from different political units. Morality, therefore, could continue to be derived "by society" and yet be identified with *supranational* political organizations just as much as with national ones.

placing the stigma of immorality upon the theory and practice of power politics."[8] As formulated by another advocate of the concept of "political morality," if power is defined as *"the capacity to effect results,"* then conflicts between different moral systems and values ("consciences-in-conflict") can "find no resolution save in compromise of power-claims." George Kennan has made essentially the same point by saying that a great deficiency in the American approach to foreign relations has been "the carrying-over into the affairs of states of the concept of right and wrong, the assumption that state behavior is a fit subject for moral judgment."[9]

Whether in domestic or foreign relations, according to the "realistic" conception, true morality consists of bringing rival national claims based on power into equilibrium, of achieving a "balance of power" which will hold these competing forces in check. Such a policy, in the words of T. V. Smith, makes possible the "progressive enlargement of compromise-areas."[10] Or, as Robert Strausz-Hupé has phrased it more concretely as a diplomatic goal, "The problem of U.S. foreign policy is the restoration of the balance of power in Europe and Asia."[11] Such, in brief, are the significant elements in the "realistic" position concerning the guiding principles which ought to activate American foreign policy.

The Uses of "National Interest"

Advocates of a "realistic" approach to foreign policy problems have made a number of immensely valuable contributions to a more intelligent understanding of America's relations with the outside world and have identified numerous weak spots in the armor of the nation's diplomacy. They have shown great skill in diagnosis, and, because correct diagnosis is usually the prerequisite to improvement in any sphere, have prepared the way for needed changes in the pattern of America's relationships with the outside world. Their contributions have been notably significant in the following specific ways.

First, the "realists" have directed their attack against one of the most conspicuous weaknesses of the American approach to foreign relations in the last half-century: the tendency to equate a resounding declaration of policy intentions with the actual realization of these intentions. As George Kennan wrote about the Open Door policy toward China:

Neither the obvious lack of practical results, nor the disillusionment of [Secretary of State John] Hay and the other persons involved, nor our unwillingness to bolster the policy in any forceful way, nor our subsequent departure from it ourselves—none of these things succeeded in shaking in any way the established opinion of the American public that here, in this episode of the Open Door notes, a tremendous blow had been struck for the triumph of American principles in international society—an American blow for an American idea.[12]

Basically the same observations might be made about Wilson's Fourteen Points, the Kellogg-Briand Pact outlawing war, official denunciations of aggressive dictators during the 1930s, the Atlantic Charter, the Charter of the United Nations, enunciation of the doctrine of containment in 1947, announcement of the Point Four program in 1949, proclamation of Dulles's doctrine of "massive retaliation" and veiled proposals suggesting the "liberation" of Eastern Europe under the Eisenhower Administration. In each instance, there was a greater or lesser tendency on the part of public opinion to believe that official proclamation of a stated goal was tantamount to achieving it.

Utopian expectations surrounding these steps have sooner or later bred a disillusionist reaction, conspicuous features of which were cynicism and indifference—translated in most cases into isolationism—toward events in the outside world. Within a comparatively brief time, Wilson's conception of a strife-free world had crumbled; the popular ecstasy which had supported the "war to end wars" gave way to a feeling of national disgust and bewilderment, translated into a willingness to "let Europe stew in its own juice." Similarly, after World War II, when the massive injection of American power into the conflict, coupled with enunciation and reiteration of idealistic goals such as the "Four Freedoms" failed to assure a better life for countless millions in Asia or guarantee a stable international order, America demobilized and reduced its diplomatic commitments to a minimum. In this instance, the retreat into isolationism was short-lived. In response to progressively more ominous threats to national security, American diplomacy entered a new era which soon began to exhibit many of the earmarks of World War I and II periods. Out of their growing recognition of the menace posed by

international communism and their stiffening determination to resist it, Americans came dangerously close to attributing all their vexatious problems in foreign affairs to the machinations of the Kremlin, just as they had attributed them to the Kaiser or Hitler or Tojo in earlier eras, and to believing that if only this root-source of their problems could somehow be "dealt with," then all their annoyances and challenges in the external realm would disappear.

The American society, as was emphasized in Chapter 2, is by nature optimistic, youthful, and supremely confident of its ability to solve human problems. Progress remains its watchword today as much as ever. Americans have almost limitless faith in their ability to bring forces in the internal and external environment into a socially beneficial equilibrium, much as a mechanic adjusts the engine of an automobile to achieve a smooth synchronization of all its parts. They have tended to believe—and this has been strikingly characteristic of their domestic "reform movements"—that righteous zeal is the universal solvent for society's problems; if problems are not dissolved by this solvent, than the answer is *more* righteous zeal, passionately applied! And, with all the evangelistic fervor characteristic of old-fashioned Gospel meetings, this is the way they have been inclined to attack thorny diplomatic problems. As a society which, on the whole, has experienced remarkably little difficulty in evolving and maintaining a national consensus upon its guiding principles, America has projected its own experience onto the international scene. Its citizens have believed that, once reasonable men were in general agreement about what ought to be done, and most especially after they had solemnly committed their agreement to paper, the process of advancing rapidly to a concrete solution was merely a matter of detail. Americans have exhibited very little psychological capacity to cope with a world in which other societies sometimes share neither America's *desire* for radical change nor its belief that such change is possible.

The "realist" position therefore provides a check against rampant utopianism in foreign affairs, against highly romanticized expectations regarding what America's active involvement in global issues can reasonably be expected to accomplish. Impressive as it is, American power is nonetheless *finite*. It cannot "make the world safe for democracy" or guarantee that vast multitudes throughout the world possess "freedom from want" as a kind of natural right. America's good intentions may know no bounds. Its *power* to effectuate these intentions however is often severely limited. In some instances it is virtually nil. Recognition of this fact, as the "realists" properly insist, will go far toward preventing the emergence of utopian hopes, followed by the disillusionment which inevitably sets in when these hopes are largely unfulfilled.

Closely related to this contribution is another for which students of foreign policy are indebted to the "realist" school of thought. This is the renewed focus on the all-important concept of power, as perhaps the key issue in politics, domestic and foreign. Political scientists are in wide agreement that power is the pivotal concept in the study of group relationships, both within states and among states. Power is ubiquitous and inescapable—save perhaps in the cemetery. It is therefore the omnipresent raw material of politics. In this sense, the term "power politics" is a tautology. Politics is by definition concerned with power —its nature, its control and regulation, its distribution and utilization by competing groups and states.

The "realists" are correct in insisting that an intelligent approach to international affairs can never overlook the centrality of power. In the two preceding chapters, on international organization and disarmament, it was emphasized how great nations have repeatedly approached questions in these fields on the basis of how their power positions are likely to be affected by contemplated decisions. Every nation admits the theoretical necessity for disarmament; practically, no nation is willing to take the steps required to achieve it, largely out of fear that its own power position will thereby be jeopardized.

Americans have not been reluctant to acknowledge the centrality of power considerations in the foreign policies of *other* nations. They have been much slower to recognize its importance in the foreign policy of their *own* country. They have been prone to conceive of power as an "Old World" concept which has no relevance for diplomatic conduct by the "New World." They have tended to believe that somehow they have transcended "power politics" and that their conduct is on a more altruistic-humanitarian plane than the conduct exhibited by other countries. The "realists" therefore offer a needed admonition against

cant and hypocrisy by the United States in dealing with other nations. And their arguments caution that, in periods when Americans thought they were "rising above" power considerations, they were more often than not entering a diplomatic fantasyland, only to have power considerations ultimately thrust themselves upon the nation in a form which threatened its very existence.

In the third place, in their analysis of American foreign policy the "realists" have laid the foundations for the kind of diplomatic conduct which is indispensable to national security in the nuclear age: continuous, soberly considered involvement in world affairs, as distinct from episodic involvement, characterized by alternating cycles of violent interventionism and sulky isolationism. The lesson which has been driven home painfully in the postwar period is that the vital interests of the nation require thoughtful assessment and protection at all times. The steady and rational application of moderate doses of American power can be expected to yield richer diplomatic dividends than dissipation of that power in ill-defined, emotionally satisfying crusades.

Fourth, the "realists" have called attention to the connection between ends and means in foreign policy. Neglect of this relationship easily qualifies as one of the most serious deficiencies in American foreign policy since 1900. In critical instances, Americans have evinced minimum awareness that an approximate balance must be struck between the goals of foreign policy and the means available for reaching them. They have tended to err in one of two directions. As we have already observed, sometimes they have become preoccupied with goals to the almost total exclusion of the means required for their realization. At other times, America has confused what are essentially the *means* of foreign policy with *ends* of policy.

One example of the former tendency is acquisition of the Philippine Islands and other Pacific possessions before and after the Spanish-American War. These territorial acquisitions entailed new diplomatic commitments. Yet as time passed, Americans manifested no significant awareness that their own security was involved in Asian affairs as never before or that diplomatic astuteness demanded a corresponding reallocation of national resources to protect these commitments. These observations also apply to the Open Door policy, which, in Kennan's words, "was not a policy that in general had a future. . . . It was not a policy that we Americans cared enough about to support in any determined way or for the results of which, if implemented, we were prepared to accept any particular responsibility."[13] An example from more recent experience is the policy of containment, the dominant goal of American foreign policy since 1947 toward the Communist bloc. This policy—surely the most ambitious ever undertaken in peacetime throughout American history—has demanded, and will continue to demand, prodigious national efforts, vast sums of money, and unceasing diplomatic vigilance for its successful implementation. Yet it may be questioned whether the average American is even now fully cognizant of the price that must be paid in the years ahead to carry out a goal which enjoys overwhelming popular support.

Taking the means of policy for policy itself has been evident during and immediately after each major war in which the United States has been involved since 1900. The "realists" insist upon the validity of Clausewitz's famous dictum that war is but the continuation of policy by other means. War is not an end in itself; it solves no political problems. War is always undertaken in behalf of *political* goals and is resorted to when nonviolent methods for protecting the diplomatic interests of nations have failed to accomplish this result. Victory in war can do nothing more than create the conditions within which diplomatic goals can be achieved. For this to occur, nations must possess a reasonably clear conception of their diplomatic goals and how they are to be realized by resort to war.

Neither in World War I, nor in World War II, nor in the Korean War could it be said that the American people possessed a clear understanding of why the nation was at war, the political aims it hoped to accomplish by fighting, and the methods by which it hoped to accomplish them. For instance, much of the public agitation within the United States surrounding issues accompanying the Korean War stemmed from a deep-seated confusion in the public and even in the official mind over the precise "war aims" of the United States. Were they to unify Korea politically? To eliminate communism from the Korean peninsula and perhaps from the mainland of China itself? To "repel aggression" by driving the Communist forces north of the 38th Parallel? Or were the nation's war aims some combination of these goals, or possibly some other goals? These questions were never answered explicitly so that no clear public consensus existed about them. The "realist" insists that, difficult as it may be, attempts to answer such questions are vital to diplomatic success. Diplomatic action undertaken in behalf of cloudy, ambivalent, and poorly thought-out goals can never be expected to produce satisfying results in the foreign policy field.

The most valuable contribution made by the "realists" to public thinking about global issues may well be their insistence that, in a world of power politics, differences among nations must be accommodated, harmonized, and compromised by the techniques of diplomacy. "Realists" warn against the belief that tensions among powerful states can be finally and forever "eliminated." No nation can expect to get its way on every issue dividing the world. Indiscriminate injection of "moral principle" into international disputes is likely to engender almost insoluble problems for the world community, because nations, especially *democratic* ones, find it well-nigh impossible "to compromise with principle." And where compromise is ruled out, the only method remaining for safeguarding diplomatic interests is war or perhaps cold war.

These admonitions are especially apt for the United States, which in the postwar period has come dangerously close to equating compromise with "appeasement." The very process of holding negotiations with the Russians, it was often believed, is not only a waste of time but a sacrifice of vital principles. So militantly opposed are Americans to the main tenets of communist ideology that they have tended to reason that there exists no basis for accommodation with demands growing out of Russia's needs *as a state*. Yet if Russia, in common with all other countries, is actuated primarily by power considerations, this at least holds out the possibility that there does exist a common denominator upon which mutually satisfactory agreement might be achieved. This point possesses special pertinence in connection with the widely prevailing assumption that the Russians cannot be counted on to keep diplomatic agreements. George Kennan has replied by saying:

They have their own interests, and I do not think that they practice deceit for the sake of practicing it. If you make an agreement with them which is in their interests, as they see it, and then see to it that it remains in their interest to observe, it will sometimes be observed.[14]

James P. Warburg makes essentially the same point when he declares:

> I submit that nations do not make agreements relying upon each other's good faith. They rely upon each other's intelligent pursuit of self-interest. History shows that the international agreements most likely to be broken are precisely those which are negotiated by one side or the other from a "position of strength"—that is, under some degree of duress. On the other hand, the agreements most likely to be kept are those negotiated on a give-and-take basis from a position of mutually recognized equality.
>
> The agreements which endure are those freely entered into because they serve the self-interest of both parties and thus become self-enforcing. That is the sort of agreement we must seek.[15]

Basically the same point was made by Secretary of State Dean Rusk, when he declared early in 1964 that all members of the United Nations, "despite their deep differences, share a common interest in survival—and therefore a common interest in preventing resort to force anywhere in the world." Enhancing the peacekeeping ability of the United Nations thus had to be regarded as "an indispensable service potentially in the national interest of all members—in the common interest of even rival states."[16]

TOWARD A PHILOSOPHY OF FOREIGN AFFAIRS

Valuable as they are in supplying correctives for widely acknowledged weaknesses in the American approach to foreign relations in the modern period, the arguments of the "realists" must be subjected to careful scrutiny before they are adopted *in toto* as the guiding principles of the nation's foreign policy. Their greatest poignancy derives from their description of *how nations actually behave* in the international community; their greatest weaknesses are manifested when they purport to explain either *how nations must or ought to behave*. At the level of value judgment and moral principle, "realist" arguments lose much of their appeal.

"National Interest" in the Mainstream of History

The starting point for a critical evaluation of the "realistic" philosophy of foreign relations is recognition that there is nothing intrinsically new or startling in the proposals made by

writers such as Hans J. Morgenthau, George F. Kennan, or Robert Strausz-Hupé. The "realism" advocated by such writers is a form of philosophical atavism. Clear antecedents can be discerned in the writings of Niccolò Machiavelli (1469–1527), Francis Bacon (1561–1626), Thomas Hobbes (1588–1679), Johann Fichte (1762–1814), Georg W. Hegel (1770–1831), Heinrich von Treitschke (1834–1896), Friedrich W. Nietzsche (1844–1900), Karl Marx (1818–1883), Nikolai Lenin (1870–1924), and their twentieth-century disciples. Obviously, it would be impossible in limited space to trace out the philosophical stream which has culminated in the "realistic" philosophy of today. So as to at least indicate something of the nature of this continuum, as well as to lay the basis for an evaluation of the "realistic" position, let us look briefly at the writings of one of the most famous and influential philosophers who ever lived: the Renaissance Florentine, Niccolò Machiavelli.* One

---

* Students who wish to carry an evaluation of the "realistic" position further could do no better than to study this position in the light of classical political philosophy. Such a study would suggest numerous parallels and would indicate many of the difficulties besetting the realistic position in a much fuller way than is possible here. It ought to be emphasized that much of present-day "realism" is a reinterpretation of Machiavelli's thought in the light of writings by later philosophers, particularly Thomas Hobbes.

Cf. the following Hobbesian passages: ". . . I put for a general inclination of all mankind, a perpetual and restless desire of power after power, that ceaseth only in death. . . . kings, whose power is greatest, turn their endeavours to the assuring it at home by laws, or abroad by wars. . . . Competition of riches, honour, command, or other power, inclineth to contention, enmity, and war. . . . To this war of every man, against every man . . . nothing can be unjust. The notions of right and wrong, justice and injustice have there no place." And "so in states, and commonwealths [nations] not dependent on one another, every commonwealth . . . has an absolute liberty, to do what it shall judge . . . most conducing to their [sic] benefit. But withal, they live in the condition of a perpetual war. . . ." Michael Oakeshott, ed., *The Leviathian* by Thomas Hobbes (New York: Macmillan, 1947), pp. 63, 83, 140.

Cook and Moos associate the philosophical roots of present day "realism" with ideas current in Europe in the nineteenth century. Hegel "made the evolution of the state the growth of reason and the progressive achievement of God on earth. The state was the very embodiment of right." A Swiss philosopher, Johann Casper Bluntschli, equated the state with a living organism; humans were its cells! Heinrich von Treitschke emphasized the necessity for the state to be strong, to dominate other states, to hold no scruples against imposition of its will by

reason for our selection of Machiavelli is that, in Hutchison's words, "the truth in Machiavelli is more apparent in 1950 than it was in 1850 or even 1900 to most Western readers."[17]

The problem engaging Machiavelli's attention within Italy was basically the same problem which has prevailed within the international community in modern history. This was how to create a system of law and order out of conditions of anarchy and political turmoil. With the decline of the two central authorities capable of maintaining order throughout Italy—the Holy Roman Empire and the Medieval Church—Machiavelli could foresee nothing but continued barbarism, bloodshed, and turbulence, as self-seeking groups pursued their own interests. And it was to this problem that Machiavelli addressed himself in his immortal classic, *The Prince*. His book was a plea for a powerful ruler to bring stability to the strife-torn Italian peninsula and a handbook telling him how it might be done.

Force, fraud, violence, duplicity, faithlessness, hypocrisy—none of these was excluded as methods to be employed by the prince. The prince ought to *appear* to act morally, but he could never afford the luxury of being animated predominantly by morality. Any methods were therefore legitimate for the prince so long as they achieved their intended result. From Machiavelli's pen the world received the most explicit formulation of the idea of *raison d'état*. Put in its simplest form, *raison d'état* meant that the actions of the state were exempt from the ordinary moral and ethical strictures applicable to the actions of individuals and groups *within* the state. In Ebenstein's words, Machiavelli "thus separates power from morality, ethics, religion, and metaphysics, and sets up the *state* as an *autonomous system of values* independent of any other source."[18]

In Machiavellian thought the actions of the states could not properly be categorized as

"moral" or "immoral." The state's actions were *amoral* in that they could not be judged by the canons of a moral-ethical code. Morality was any action that enabled the prince to establish and perpetuate his power; his actions were morally condemnable to the degree that they failed to achieve this end.

Machiavelli is generally acknowledged as the first "scientific" philosopher known to history. The ideas expressed in *The Prince* and his other writing grew out of careful observation of human behavior. His reflections upon human conduct and his assessment of human nature—in which Machiavelli's cynicism and pessimism were only surpassed by his overriding desire to see political stability restored to his native land—stemmed from his own immersion in Italian life during the infamous age of Cesare and Lucrezia Borgia. Accordingly, his "scientific" characterization of the nature of mankind in general, on the basis of behavior he observed all around him, achieved a pinnacle in "realism." Writes Ebenstein: "If Machiavelli had painted, in medieval fashion, the devils who inhabit hell, his impact would have been much less intense on his contemporaries and on posterity. What Machiavelli did, however, was to portray something worse, real human beings. . . ."[19] And it was to provide insight for the ruler, who had to impose his authority over self-willed, power-seeking individuals, that Machiavelli wrote *The Prince*.

The Relevance of Philosophic Insight

The contemporary student of American foreign relations has but to make appropriate substitutions in the thought of writers such as Machiavelli and many of his philosophical descendants to arrive at essentially the theory of political realism expounded today. If one substitutes the idea of "national interest" in its most elementary sense—self-preservation—for Machiavelli's goal of strong political authority in Italy, and projects Machiavelli's observations about power-motivated human behavior *within* states to the realm of *interstate* relations, if one elevates the concept of *raison d'état* into the impulse which motivates nation states in their relationships with each other, then Machiavelli's thought becomes practically indistinguishable from the philosophy of present-day "realists."

Accordingly, weaknesses inherent in Machiavelli's thought are also present in the thought of his contemporary imitators. Foremost among these perhaps is the assumption that value

---

force. "National interest" was its watchword. "Other purposes were subordinate and instrumental, and the welfare of the nation's citizens was incidental. Politics was a matter of competition between nations. Their purpose was to maintain and increase their own power. . . . The relations of nation-states were a Hobbesian war of all against all. . . ."

Hutchison emphasizes the "secularization" of philosophy from the eighteenth century onward as a major tributary giving rise to present-day "realism." See, Cook and Moos, *op. cit.*, pp. 114–115; John A. Hutchison, *The Two Cities* (Garden City, N.Y.: Doubleday, 1957), pp. 92–96.

judgments about how human society *ought* to conduct itself can be derived from a study of empirical data showing how it has conducted itself throughout history. From observations of human conduct, present-day Machiavellians purport to have discovered scientific laws of statecraft, based upon the supposedly inherent nature of states. No one has attacked this view more cogently than Reinhold Niebuhr. According to one commentator, "Niebuhr's heaviest blow is his claim that the fatal sin to which realism is constantly tempted is to make that which is universal in human behavior normative as well."[20] Professor Morgenthau, for example, categorically asserts that all nations act "in power-political terms"; that "politics is an unending struggle for power in which the interests of individual nations must necessarily be defined in terms of power"; that a statesman who says he does not believe in the "balance of power" is comparable to "a scientist who says he does not believe in the law of gravity"; and that "the national interest is . . . the last word in world politics."[21]

Now, such conclusions may be accepted as "scientific" insofar as evidence can be adduced for showing that they accurately describe the *actual* conduct of states. They are patently unscientific, however, in the very area in which they lay claim to the greatest scientific objectivity: as they purport to derive principles governing (1) what states *must* do and (2) what states *ought* to do, from empirical data. For it is in the area in which the highest scientific validity is asserted that conclusions are least amenable to scientific verifications. "Realists" maintain that states *ought* to do what they *must* do, because of their inherent domination by power impulses. Such a conception completely ignores any explicit consideration of the *ends* for which states exist and the goals they may legitimately pursue in their relationship with each other. It postulates the survival of the states as an end in itself and makes that end the highest goal of statecraft. It neither raises nor answers the question of *why* the survival of the state itself is a desirable goal; much less does it discuss the value of this end in relation to other ends for which human society might strive. But in classical political thought, as typified especially by writers in the Judaeo-Christian tradition, it is precisely this question—how the state contributes to the ends of human society—which has been one of the most fundamental questions of political thought through the ages. Actually, under the

guise of a "scientific" approach to the study of foreign policy, the operating assumption of the "realists"—the conception that pervades their entire philosophy—is that the power-seeking nation state in its twentieth-century manifestations represents the apex of political achievement and morality which man is capable of attaining.* *Assuming* this to be true—and the assumption is a cornerstone of the philosophical structure erected by "realists"—any action taken by a nation to maintain and perpetuate its power is not only permissible but becomes the quintessence of virtue and morality.[22]

Now, the shortcomings of such a philosophy ought to be as apparent as they are far-reaching. The grave defect in such reasoning is that it involves a logical contradiction. If "realists" are correct that it is an unalterable quality of mankind's nature—a kind of political law of gravity—to elevate power to the top of the hierarchy among possible goals, then there is no intrinsic reason why present-day civilization —including one of its most characteristic institutions, the nation state itself—is to be pre-

* To be sure, Morgenthau and other "realists" acknowledge the theoretical possibility that other viable political units might evolve in history to take over at least some of the functions of the nation state, as suggested in the idea that "above the national societies there exists no international society so integrated as to be able to define for them the concrete meaning of justice or equality, as national societies do for their individual members." This being so, "In the absence of an integrated international society, the attainment of a modicum of order and realization of a minimum of moral values are predicated upon the existence of *national* communities capable of preserving order and realizing moral values within the limits of their power." Morgenthau, *In Defense of the National Interest, op. cit.*, pp. 34, 38 (italics added).

"Realists" therefore may acknowledge the possibility that political organizations above the nation state could emerge. But this admission has no significant place in their philosophy, as reflected in: (1) their identification of true morality with pursuit of the *national* interest, (2) their deeply entrenched pessimism about the likelihood of any international organization emerging to supersede the nation state or fundamentally modify its powers, and (3) the almost total absence in their philosophy of emphasis upon the means—not to speak of the need—for evolving supranational institutions that would set limits to the power-seeking propensities of heavily armed nations. "Realists" are far more (one might even say, exclusively) concerned with what foreign policy *is* than what it is capable of becoming, as reflected in Morgenthau's viewpoint that "Foreign policy, like all politics, is in its essence a struggle for power, waged by sovereign *nations* for *national* advantage." *Ibid.*, p. 92 (italics added).

ferred over past or future eras of history, with their characteristic institutions. "Realists" contend that institutions and policies are "good" or "bad" depending upon the degree to which they contribute to the acquisition and maintenance of power. The political unit that we call the nation state, the *raison d'être* of which is pursuit of power, thus possesses no superiority of its own; it is merely a convenient mechanism evolved by society in a certain historical era for channeling and directing the search for power. Conceivably, other mechanisms—including supranational authorities—can be, and in history have been, *more* convenient than the nation state for realizing power objectives. Acknowledging this to be true, we arrive at the paradox that the pursuit of power can lead statesmen to subordinate and limit the power of individual countries to that of mankind as a whole, as expressed in supranational institutions resting upon a broad consensus in the international community. The continued pursuit of power thus can erode the principle of national interest, just as in earlier eras it eroded the concepts of "city-state interests" or "feudal interests."

"Realists" cannot have it both ways. They cannot rationalize anything a nation might do to further its "national interest," by claiming that such steps are legitimate in the quest for power, and then contend on the other hand that the pursuit of power *requires* a state to pursue national interest. They cannot apply purely expediential criteria to the conduct of *all* states and *all* political phenomena, and then maintain that there is any inherent and paramount virtue in perpetuating only one particular species of political organization known to history—the nation state. Quite obviously there are times when limits upon the conduct of nation states are most conducive to achieving and maintaining power. According to a philosopher who epitomized *Realpolitik*, Thomas Hobbes, man left a state of nature—where life was "nasty, brutish, and short"—precisely because of his conviction that the untrammeled quest for power among unrestrained individuals endangered the security of society itself; self-preservation demanded that limits upon human conduct be imposed. It is not necessary to be Hobbesian to see the application of this idea to twentieth-century international relations. Unfettered addiction to power goals by heavily armed nation states can jeopardize the continued existence of the human race, thereby inevitably threatening the

existence of individual nations that are a part of it. Attachment to a narrowly conceived, egocentric "national interest," therefore, is one of the ways best calculated to endanger the ultimate security—the *continued* capacity to pursue power—of every nation, including those most animated by national interest. Conversely, a national interest that realizes the interdependence of nations, that concedes the common stake of all in mitigating power conflicts and eliminating certain kinds altogether, and that conceives policies reflecting this realization constitutes a far greater "realism" than is manifested by twentieth-century advocates of *Realpolitik*.

The philosophy of present-day "realism" manifests the same contradiction that stands at the heart of Marxist-Leninist-Stalinist thought. Marxist thought derisively rejects any "natural law" precepts or inviolable moral-ethical principles. Marxists claim—by arguments remarkably parallel both to those of Machiavelli and his latter-day imitators—that the strictures imposed upon human society by legal codes, norms, moral-ethical values, and the individual conscience, are nothing more than attempts by the bourgeoisie to rationalize its dominant power position, to perpetuate its control over the proletariat. But if it is inherent in the nature of the bourgeoisie to do these things —if strictures upon human conduct represent *merely* rationalizations of the power-seeking propensities of the dominant class in any historical era—then the bourgeoisie cannot logically be condemned for doing them. There is nothing ethically "wrong" with oppression of the proletariat, since Marxist philosophy tells us that there can exist no absolute concept of "right" and "wrong," that these concepts are themselves products of the "class struggle." Presumably, the bourgeoisie is free to eliminate the proletariat outright (superseding it someday perhaps with computers), since this would only be condemnable if it *failed* to enhance the bourgeoisie's power position. The extent to which this action injured the proletariat would be irrelevant in determining its legitimacy.

As a matter of fact, we know that Marxists do *not* reason this way. They condemn the bourgeoisie precisely because its behavior injures the proletariat's welfare. Now the only possible ground for such inexcusable "value judgments" is the assumed existence of some kind of "proletarian ethic," which by Marxism's own dogma is "unscientific" because it postulates a standard of human conduct which has never existed, since the proletariat has not been in a position to dictate moral and ethical codes, laws, and other precepts of human conduct. The adherents of "scientific socialism" are thus the true utopians, in holding forth the image of a future society in which humans successfully abjure the ancient pattern of pursuing power, a pattern supposedly inherent in their nature. Ironically, it is this ultimate promise held out to mankind—that the human race in some communist Promised Land will behave as it has never behaved in the past—that imparts to Marxist thought much of its appeal as a global ideology.

A similar defect lies at the heart of Professor Morgenthau's elevation of the "national interest" into the guiding principle of statecraft and his equation of it with consummate political virtue. If states are inescapably propelled by power goals, if they "can't help" pursuing them above all other goals, then upon what basis does *American* national interest, or that of any other country, become preferable to all other competing national interests? Except as it *fails* to enhance American power, why should American domination of weaker allies be condemned as a policy? Or why, with the same exception, should Soviet hegemony over Eastern Europe—or possibly even the world—be denounced? Upon what basis should other countries choose to side with America or Russia or other great powers, except upon a fine calculation of which is the most powerful? In short, what grounds exist for questioning the belief that the national interest of one country could perhaps best be achieved by totally subordinating the interests of all other countries to its control? When looked at in purely tactical terms, diplomatic experience amply confirms the fact that America has promoted its own national interest to the degree that it convinced other countries there *was* some relationship between America's well-being and theirs; and its diplomatic interests have been impaired on many occasions when other countries became convinced that exclusive pursuit of national interest by the United States resulted in policies that were inimical to *their* national interests.

Yet "realists" do not as a rule draw the extreme conclusion that unswerving pursuit of national interest by any one state can legitimately result in damage to the national interest of other states, perhaps to the point of calling into jeopardy their continued existence

as nations. Instead, they cite the "balance-of-power" principle, which will presumably hold competing national interests in some kind of an equilibrium. Professor Morgenthau equates the balance-of-power concept with the law of gravity. States pursue power, just as matter obeys the law of gravity. But this analogy is faulty in several particulars. First, if nations have no more choice in obeying political "laws" than matter has in obeying physical laws, then the debate over whether the United States *ought* to follow national interest or the balance-of-power principle is entirely academic: it *does* follow the principle inexorably. It cannot help doing so, any more than a weight can help falling to the ground when it is dropped. It would be entirely superfluous to admonish statesmen to obey a "law" which they cannot avoid obeying and which they obey all the time! And if this is true, then the question may legitimately be asked: Why is it necessary for "realists" to call for a *return* to principles of statecraft that the nation has never left and by its nature is incapable of leaving? How did it happen that President Wilson, for example, led the nation into a diplomatic quagmire by refusing to pursue balance of power, when Wilson and all other leaders of nation states are presumably motivated by forces over which they have no control? And if they have no choice, then how can they be condemned for doing what they were irresistibly driven to do?

An escape from this *reductio ad absurdum* is to admit that statesmen *do* have a choice about whether to elevate concepts like national interest and balance of power into dominant foreign policy goals. Once this admission is made then, of course, there is no real analogy with the law of gravity, for it is conceded that man is not merely physical matter that responds automatically to "laws" beyond his control. The inquiry that follows next is: *Why* should statesmen choose national interest or balance of power over other possible goals? What are the criteria for selection? Assuming that choices in foreign affairs are made rationally (an assumption of course that is not always valid) there must exist, implicitly or explicitly, some standard for discriminating among competing goals. What are these standards and how are they derived? Discussion of this point necessarily involves us in a problem to which "realists" devote insufficient attention; and yet it is inextricably related to the question of why certain objectives in foreign affairs are to be preferred over others. This is the question of the *ends* for which political power is utilized and the relationship of means to the achievement of these ends. We shall have more to say about this question at a later stage. It must suffice to note here that "realists," no less than their philosophical adversaries, the "idealists," make certain assumptions about the ends to which political power is to be directed. More often than not, these assumptions are implicit in their thought, rather than explicitly elaborated. They are no less present, and no less crucial in shaping ultimate conclusions, because "realists" assert that the student of international politics can approach this subject matter on an "assumptionless" basis.

One final objection to the "realist" equation of diplomatic principles with laws in the physical realm may be noted briefly. Man realizes many of his fullest potentialities to the very degree that he discovers ways of freeing himself from limitations imposed by natural phenomena such as the law of gravity. The air and space age would not have become possible if the law of gravity had been accepted as the last word in natural science or in technology based upon science. At this point, Huchison's remarks about man's nature seem apropos:

> We note . . . in morality and ethics a primary difference between man and the animals. The ends or aims of animal life appear to be given by nature. . . . Thus if my dog satisfies his needs for activity, food, sex, etc., he appears to have a good life. Man possesses a great many such needs. . . . But of any such aim or desire man may ask the question: *Ought* I to satisfy this need? Is it right or wrong? Such questions mark off and open up the field of morality.[23]

As regards foreign affairs, all that observations resting upon empirical data can tell statesmen is what nations *have* done in the past and how alternative courses of action can contribute to the realization of ends whose legitimacy must, in the last analysis, be tested by reference to something other than studies of how mankind has behaved in earlier eras. Machiavelli differed in this respect from many of his contemporary imitators: he possessed a compelling vision of a better life for his native Italy, a conception of what "might be" in his native land, which he could not possibly have taken from the pattern of internecine strife he saw all around him. Power was *instrumental* for the realization of ends whose legitimacy Machiavelli took for granted.

But this conception is totally lacking in the supposedly "realistic" approach to the study of international affairs widely advocated today. There is no recognition that human society, imperfect as it is, retains the capacity to discriminate between the ideal and the actual, between what man is and does and what he is capable of being and becoming. Difficult as it may be sometimes for students of interstate relations to see tangible evidences of it, mankind does possess at least a vision of a more desirable international order; and occasionally, if far too infrequently, man demonstrates an ability to transcend his own self-centeredness. Machiavellians are right when they emphasize and re-emphasize that moral considerations *are* often totally absent from political affairs and that, on the basis of an objective study of political behavior, there is often very little ground for optimism that this condition is likely to change spectacularly. To that extent, admonitions against efforts to remake the international order by evangelical crusades and pious exhortations in foreign affairs are well founded and timely.

But Machiavellians betray a massive unrealism of their own when they postulate the pattern of interstate relations in nineteenth- and early twentieth-century Europe—in which the balance of power presumably operated with maximum efficacy—as normative. Under the *Pax Britannica*, the balance of power may have worked moderately well, so well in fact that moral-ethical ends may have been better served under a British-regulated balance of power than in most other historical eras.[24] Yet a strong case can be made for saying that its inherent instability led to World War I, which in turn gave rise to conditions largely rendering the traditional balance of power inoperative in today's world. In the nuclear missile age, conflicts engendered by hostile, increasingly powerful countries motivated by "national interest" imperil the future of civilization. To assert that mankind can do no better than continue to conduct its relationships upon the basis of national interest and balance of power, to declare that this is true because history teaches that it has been true, and to allege that this kind of conduct, far from being both morally reprehensible and potentially disastrous, represents the highest type of "morality," constitutes the ultimate in subjective judgments about what are essentially metaphysical questions relating to the nature and destiny of mankind on earth and in the universe.

One final point about the philosophical shortcomings of Machiavellian thought in both its earlier and more recent manifestations requires emphasis. This has to do with the interaction between the ends and means of policy. Machiavelli had little or nothing to say about the legitimacy of the ends for which the prince was to use his virtually unlimited power. He simply took it for granted that these ends—restoring law and order to Italy—were legitimate. To Machiavelli, many of the more traditional goals enunciated for the state in earlier philosophic thought, such as peace, justice, a well-ordered society, prosperity, and happiness, were predicated upon imposing a strong political authority upon an internally divided Italy.

Events in Italy and in many other European countries over the course of time revealed that once sheer expediency and opportunism (*raison d'état*) become the accepted means, these things more often than not become the ends for which the state exists and is perpetuated. It is therefore no surprise that the age of "Absolute Monarchy" and the "Divine Right of Kings" followed the spread of Machiavellian thought within Europe, and that political philosophers in later periods, like Jean Bodin, John Locke, Hugo Grotius, Jean Jacques Rousseau, Edmund Burke, and Thomas Jefferson, were primarily concerned with defining the limits upon what had become almost limitless governmental authority and with redefining the ends for which that authority might legitimately be utilized. In the modern period, a philosophy of "realism" might be looked upon as merely a statement of the "Divine Right of Nations."

These philosophical principles have importance for America's relationship with the outside world. It is one thing to acknowledge that the United States, in common with all other countries, sometimes fails to live up to its professed ideals. There are episodes in American foreign policy which typify a diplomacy based exclusively upon *Realpolitik*. Examples might include America's treatment of the Indians, the Mexican War, the Spanish-American War, the acquisition of the Panama Canal, numerous chapters in the history of America's relations with Latin America, and retention of the Japanese-owned Pacific islands at the end of World War II. In the postwar period, some commentators might cite American intervention in the Chinese civil war, widespread support for dictatorial regimes throughout the world, the revocation of the offer to assist with the Aswan Dam project in Egypt in 1956 and other cases of interventionism in Arab affairs, hesitation to take an unequivocal stand on colonial issues affecting the nation's allies, and continuing efforts to harass and perhaps overthrow Castro's regime in Cuba. Yet it may be less important to acknowledge that such episodes have taken place than to admit that they were aberrations and that, in many cases, later efforts were made to bring America's professions and its conduct more into harmony. Inauguration of the "Good Neighbor" policy in the early 1930s is an example of what this recognition meant in terms of reorienting the nation's Latin American policy as a result of this admission. Indispensable to changes of this kind, however, is recognition that the nation's earlier diplomacy was not consonant with its highest conception of moral-ethical conduct.

The Relationship of Ends and Means in Diplomacy

The relationship between ends and means in foreign policies is inordinately complex and baffling. Perhaps the means utilized to achieve stated goals are never, and in a human society cannot be, as morally commendable and as perfectly consonant with the ends as might be desired. As "the art of the possible," politics often demands compromises with moral principles, unless political processes are to lose touch altogether with the affairs of fallible man. Yet this is not to say that *any* legitimate end justifies any means for its realization. As Crane Brinton has put it:

> . . . men's ethical ideas and ideals, even though they do not stand in a simple causal relationship to men's deeds, stand in *some* relation to men's deeds. . . . Machiavelli makes the mistake still made by some of our deliberately hard-boiled writers on politics and morals; he writes off men's profession of good just because they do not wholly live up to them.[25]

Examination of the interaction between the ends and means of foreign policy is no merely academic, philosophically hairsplitting speculation. For it is precisely this problem upon which the outcome of the cold war today may very well hinge. For example, nations in the Afro-Asian bloc are much more apt to judge America's policies toward colonialism by what the United States *does* in dealing with colonial issues than by abstract pronouncements from the State Department about what it *believes* on the subject. The means actually utilized (or not utilized) to carry out the announced end are likely to be pivotal in shaping certain aspects of the nation's relationships with the outside world. The attachment of the United States to the goal of peace is judged by the same criteria. Endless reiteration of the nation's dedication to the goal of peace are far less persuasive in creating favorable viewpoints about the United States than what the nation actually does to make peace a reality. And if, as has happened repeatedly in the postwar era, other countries think, by looking at the *means* of American policy, that the United States is half-hearted and lethargic in working toward the goal, then properly or improperly these countries will decide that America does not really believe in peace, despite its ceaseless affirmations that this is a cardinal goal of American statecraft.

The USSR has confronted the same dilemma growing out of the relationship between the ends and means of policy. By "realistic" criteria, no moral condemnation attaches to Russia's domination of Eastern Europe, save perhaps as its policies have failed to enhance Russia's power position. The ruthless suppression of the Hungarian Revolt in 1956 is only condemnable to the degree it could be shown such conduct in the long-run weakened Soviet power. If this did not happen, then Russian policies are, by "realistic" canons, the quintessence of "political morality."

Now this reasoning may be perfectly consistent according to "realistic" terms of reference. We know from recent events, however, that it is unacceptable to an ever-growing circle of nations, who are becoming progressively disenchanted with the foreign policies of Russia and Communist China, as these policies are revealed in the deeds of the Communist world. As a high-ranking American official wrote concerning Soviet suppression of the Hungarian revolt:

> The Soviet leaders have been pinned under the spotlight of the moral judgment of the world. The dilemma they face is for them a hard one. They must respond to this moral judgment in increasing degree or forfeit the influence they covet to exert in much of the world.[26]

And another American official has written that, if for no other reason than in its own self-interest, the United States must do everything possible in global affairs to prevent other nations from conceiving the cold war "as a battle of the we's against the they's in which the only important consideration is that the we's win."[27] It is the *means* of policy by which the legitimacy of the ends are judged, rather than verbal attachment to abstract ideological goals. This is the reason why other countries regard Russia or Communist China or, in some instances the United States, as a menace to their existence.

Leaving out any question of whether immoral means ought to be used to achieve legitimate ends, it is clear that on the much lower level of operating policy, power (applied overtly or covertly, as expediency dictates) cannot for long achieve the goal which "realists" postulate for states in the international community: national security. Reinhold Niebuhr has called attention to the paradox in the elevation of security to the pinnacle of diplomatic goals:

> . . . the more man establishes himself in power and glory, the greater is the fear of tumbling from his eminence. . . . The will-to-power is thus an expression of insecurity even when it has achieved ends which . . . would seem to guarantee complete security. . . . There is no level of greatness and power in which the lash of fear is not at least one strand in the whip of ambition.[28]

There is in other words, as the USSR appears in some measure to have discovered, a law of diminishing returns governing the extent to which even the limited goal of national security can be achieved by a policy dictated solely by *raison d'état*. The unending pursuit of power ultimately results in insecurity, not only for the international community, but for any nation state that is a member of that community. This is the point well understood by Secretary of State William H. Seward, who once said that: "If one state has a right to intervene in any other . . . then every state has the same right to intervene in the affairs of every other nation. . . . The principle of intervention, thus practically carried out, would seem to render all sovereignty and independence, and even all international peace and amity, uncertain and fallacious."[29] And as Gauss has said of Machiavelli's thought: "hypocrisy works only because the majority of men are not hypocrites and are therefore not suspicious. When all princes practice deceit it soon fails to get results for any of them."[30]

"National Interest" as a Guide to Statecraft

Having examined some of the more glaring weaknesses in the "realistic" philosophy, there is another level on which this philosophy must be subjected to careful scrutiny. This is the plane of *operating* policy. Just how useful are the concepts of "national interest" and "balance of power" in the formulation and conduct of American foreign policy? Admittedly, as we have already suggested earlier in the chapter, the concepts have value as antidotes, as correctives against tendencies that have interfered with successful foreign policy in the past. They caution specifically against two dangers. The first is confusion of the concrete interests of groups within the state with the interest of the state itself. Thus emphasis upon the "national interest" goes far toward assuring that policy will be something more than a mere summation of powerful group interests. The second danger is believing that groups within states and states themselves can transcend attachment to their "interests" altogether and can submerge them in a quest for something called loosely "the good of mankind" or "the welfare of all nations." Nations do have interests that can never be ignored by statesmen. Pretending that interests do not exist—and that they do not sometimes clash fundamentally—is the ultimate in unreality and is an almost certain road to diplomatic ineptitude.

Yet in recognizing that ideas like "national interest" are valuable because they caution against unfortunate tendencies, we must at the same time recognize many limitations in the concept of "national interest" that prevent it from becoming the sole guide for diplomatic conduct. Speaking generally, it is clear that the concept of "national interest" raises more questions than it answers. In specific situations, adherence to the concept of national interest may tell us a good deal about what statesmen ought *not* to do; but it tells us little or nothing about what they *ought* to do. Indeed, it would be no exaggeration to say that *determination of the national interest in a never-ending series of problems confronting the nation is the continuing challenge facing foreign policy officials.* "Realists" imply that all that is needed is for American officials to proclam their attachment to the principle of "national interest" to assure diplomatic success. But every official in the government—from the State Department and other executive agencies to Congress—is convinced that his ideas about American foreign policy are identical with the national interest. The overriding problem therefore—and it is a problem to which "realists" give little or no attention—is how the national interest is to be determined and whose determination of it is to be binding upon the government. An experienced American diplomat has written concerning the selection of alternative lines of policy:

> I know of no case . . . in which the settlement of an issue of our national policy . . . would have been facilitated by injecting the question: Shall we or shall we not try to serve the national interest?
> The question . . . is not whether, but *how*, to serve the national interest. That involves the question of what is the national interest in a particular situation.
> . . . there are many national interests, not just one. The difficulties arise in the conflict of one interest with another; for example, in the clash of the interest in peace with the interest in preserving national institutions. . . .[31]

This diplomat emphasizes "the inconclusiveness of the national interest as a guide in any particular policy problem" and holds that it is "inadequate and misleading even as a broad concept upon which to found a policy."[32]

Stated differently, we may freely acknowledge that recognizing that national states have interests, and that these sometimes collide, is the beginning of wisdom in statecraft. But it is the *beginning* only—not the end, as realists frequently seem to suggest. Ironically, in their criticisms of movements such as Wilsonian idealism, realists stand in great danger of fostering a utopianism of their own by emphasis upon the concept of the "national interest," as though this were a formula or universal solvent that dissolves problems in the foreign policy field and eliminates the necessity for choices. In the writings of advocates of the concept such as Hans Morgenthau, the "national interest" almost becomes an incantation which, repeated sufficiently, gives officials insight into the course the United States ought to pursue in dealing with General de Gaulle, with Nasser's Egypt, or with Castro's Cuba.

The plain fact is, as the quotation cited above suggests, that in most difficult foreign policy decisions, officials are nearly always required to evolve a policy out of diverse, but often quite legitimate, conceptions of the national interest. They must continually balance the value of achieving one interest against another, of gaining this and losing that, of applying the limited power at their disposal to one situation in full knowledge that doing so will dilute the power available for dealing with other situations. More concretely, they are aware that if they assist Israel to use the waters of the Jordan river to promote its economic advancement, a legitimate interest of the United States, they may well alienate the Arab world, whose continued friendship is also a legitimate interest of the United States. Or, if they promise greatly expanded funds to assist in the economic development of backward countries, a goal that clearly accords with America's interests, they may create insurmountable legislative opposition to foreign aid *per se*, which would be highly detrimental to the nation's foreign policy goals. Or again, if they inject American power massively into conflicts such as those raging during the mid-1960s in South Vietnam, they may well impair the ability of the United States to influence opinion throughout the neutralist zone or prejudice the ability of the West to preserve European security. In short, insisting upon pursuit of the "national interest" tells us nothing about: (1) how it is to be defined, (2) who, or what agency of government, shall define it, (3) what policy-makers are to do when they must choose among legitimate interests of the United States in world affairs, or (4) the scale of priorities that policy-makers ought to apply in preferring one diplomatic interest of the United States over another.

Concepts like national interest and balance of power must also be viewed skeptically as adequate guides to diplomacy on the ground that they cannot indefinitely assure the well-being of the American people. At the outset, it may be observed that any analogy between the pursuit of power by groups and individuals *within* a state and the same objective *by* states themselves is faulty in at least one important particular. Pluralism within a state—the balancing of one competing interest against another —can result in a tolerable kind of power equilibrium among self-seeking groups precisely because this power struggle takes place within the context of dominant governmental authority. The existence of law within the state, and the monopoly of force which the state possesses to assure compliance with it, makes this constant pushing and pulling among power-seeking individuals and groups within the state endurable, without calling into jeopardy the continued existence of the state itself. Quite obviously, this is profoundly different from the situation obtaining within international relations. There the unending struggle for power among hostile states *does* imperil the

continued existence of the participants and, increasingly, the nonparticipants.

This is but another way of saying that in reality there is no "balance of power" *within* states between the governmental authority and lesser groups. The power of the government vis-à-vis other groups is supreme; the state itself brooks no rivals among lesser groups to its legal strictures. It is prepared to compel obedience by force if necessary. This is the only condition within which a struggle for power can go on endlessly among competing groups without jeopardizing the very basis of society itself.

Our knowledge of the nature of power also cautions us against acceptance of "national interest" and "balance of power" as the ultimate goals of foreign policy. Many of the most basic ingredients of national power—national character, civilian and military morale, the leadership potential of the nation, the nation's ability to "bounce back" from initial military reverses —are statistically immeasurable. Comparisons between the power differentials of two rival states must, therefore, be exceedingly crude. The only ultimate test is the very test from which "balance of power" is supposed to save us: a military showdown. Naturally, this is an undesirable, potentially, a suicidal, way of measuring power differentials among nations. Other criteria, inexact as they are, must be applied on a day-by-day basis in foreign policy to measure the power potentials of nations.

Recognition that the measurement of national power is highly inaccurate is of vital significance in evaluating the feasibility of balance of power as a goal of foreign policy. For this means that if there ever exists an equilibrium of power among hostile nations, it is an equilibrium which is largely accidental and outside direct control by statesmen. This is so because the elements of national power are: (1) by and large immeasurable and (2) undergoing a constant state of change. Many of the elements which enter into the determination of American power—morale, scientific-technological know-how, prevailing political leadership, and diplomatic astuteness—often are not amenable to deliberate calculation and control, even by the United States, except over very long periods of time. And certainly it would be impossible for the United States to calculate and control these same elements within the USSR. This means that, in the light of such forces as education, expanding scientific knowledge, and industrial technology, the balance of power is becoming more and more inherently unstable as a mechanism for preserving world peace or for safeguarding American security.

These considerations largely explain why the term "balance of power" itself is used by "realists" and others in at least two contradictory senses. It may mean that America ought to strive for an *equilibrium* of power between itself and possible enemies such as Soviet Russia or, more broadly, between nations in the free world and the Communist bloc. Or, it may mean that America ought to seek a *preponderance* of power—the kind of "balance" Morgenthau suggests was sought by America under the Monroe Doctrine—for the free world against the Communist world. Whatever may be the theoretical meaning of the term "balance of power," in the vast majority of cases it is the latter meaning which actually emerges as the operating goal of diplomacy. Preponderance may be the embraced and announced goal, as in the case of Nazi Germany; or it may simply occur because of the nature of national power itself which, being largely incalculable, is not amenable to being brought into an equilibrium in world affairs. Even the United States must eventually seek a preponderance of power, because it can accurately gauge neither its own power nor the power of its rivals. It must therefore allow a wide "margin of error" by overestimating its own defense requirements so as to "play safe" against the danger of being too weak in a military showdown. Even if, accidentally, it did achieve an absolute parity with the Soviet Union at any time, the United States could not be certain this parity would remain for any significant period. In spite of the best of intentions on both sides, it is almost a certainty that it would not be preserved, owing to the dynamic nature of power itself.

If American officials must "play safe" by overestimating their power needs in comparison with Russia, Soviet officials must do likewise. Even though ideally they too might desire an equilibrium of power with the United States, they dare not risk the eventuality that their country will be too weak to protect itself if war comes. They must consequently allow an additional increment as a kind of insurance, so as to tilt the scales in their favor if a conflict comes. It is out of this situation that runaway arms races begin and that they are perpetuated, even though no nation may be deliberately attempting to "upset" the balance of power and to provoke war. Given the best of intentions all around, national policies derived from the balance-of-power principle can have no other result in the long run than to keep the world in a constant state of tension and apprehension, to generate forces like armaments races, to foster the belief that "war is inevitable," to create an international atmosphere which makes the resolution of tensions extremely difficult, and, in the last analysis, to imperil the very goal—national security—which the statesman who starts out seeking balance of power is trying to achieve.

The American Approach to Foreign Relations

Our lengthy appraisal of contemporary "realist" thought has indicated the main elements of what must be the American approach to foreign relations. It remains merely to make explicit, and to summarize briefly, what has been implicit in preceding pages.

First, credit must be given to the "realists" for restoring an imbalance in the American approach to external affairs in recent years by cautioning against the dangers of sentimentality and starry-eyed utopianism, which seek forthwith to "grasp this sorry scheme of things entire" and "remould it nearer to the heart's desire" by grandiose plans which, however commendable their intentions, make no concessions to the frailties and the finiteness of man. Uncritical advocacy of such plans inevitably breeds disillusionment and sidetracks nations from a steady, realistic approach to the formidable problems of human existence in a world of sovereign states. Perhaps the most significant contribution of the "realists" is their insistence that noble ends must always be realized with *imperfect* means. The translation of these ends into policies and programs therefore can never completely satisfy the idealists. Failure to recognize this fact can lead idealistic movements into a blind alley of despair and impotence when they eventually confront the realities of human behavior.

In the second place, however much the "realists" have rendered a service by focusing attention upon the facts of national behavior, the American approach to foreign relations must preserve inviolate the distinction between what nations *do* and what they *ought* to do. Such an approach must reject any pseudoscientific conception of man's destiny as nothing more than a perpetual struggle for power, a struggle which is equated with incarnate virtue. This conception is antithetical to the mainstream of Western humanistic philosophy and the Judaeo-Christian tradition.

Instead, a proper philosophy of foreign relations must continue to preserve the duality which has been a conspicuous feature of Western thought for well over two millennia. It is the duality present in Augustine's *City of God*, which stands in contrast with the city of man. It is the duality present in the "Two Powers" philosophy of the Middle Ages, which postulated one kind of behavior for the Church and another for the state. In more recent philosophy, this duality is suggested in the titles of two of Reinhold Niebuhr's books, *Moral Man in Immoral Society* and *The Children of Light and the Children of Darkness*. This duality refers to the tension, always present in human society, between what man is and does, on the one hand, and what he wants to do and is capable of becoming, on the other. It was most succinctly expressed in St. Paul's lament: "The Law is spiritual; we know that. But then I am a creature of the flesh, in the thralldom of sin. I cannot understand my own actions; I do not act as I desire to act; on the contrary, I do what I detest. . . . The wish is there, but not the power of doing what is right. I cannot be good as I desire to be, and I do wrong against my wishes" (Romans 7:15–20, Moffat's translation). In his book *Christianity and World Issues*, T. B. Maston has described what this tension between man as he is and man as he ought to be means for the church and, more broadly, for any movement aimed at human betterment:

> . . . that tension should not become so great that the church will lose all opportunity to minister to the world. If we think of that tension as a rubber band . . . the speed with which the world is lifted toward the Christian ideal will be determined by the tautness of the rubber band. On the other hand, if the tension becomes too great the rubber band may break. If such happens the church has isolated itself from the world . . . the individual Christian or group that ministers most effectively to the world must start where the world is and progressively lift the world toward the Christian ideal for the world. This means that the Christian ideal, for the world as for the individual, is fleeting. As we move toward it, it moves ahead of us.[33]

Third, if what is must be the starting point for achieving what might be, a necessary corollary is that America can never relinquish the ultimate vision of greater perfectability of the political order. That vision cannot be abandoned because, as the "realists" properly insist, its attainment in any historical era can never be anything more than approximate. If "idealists" are always in danger of erring on the side of imparting to man a greater capacity for rapid self-improvement than man's history justifies, the "realists" commit what is a far more grievous error. In rejecting the view that there can be a heaven on earth because of man's inherent egoism—in theological terms, his sinfulness—"realists" go to the extreme of saying in effect that man's vices are his virtues, that man is forever predestined to act as though he were in hell and that this hell is in reality his heaven!

However freely it may be admitted that mankind strives for power, this propensity must be recognized for what it is: a trait which derives from man's own pride and his deliberate attachment to self-interest. It follows both that "all have sinned and come short of the glory of God" and that mankind comprises a community knit together by the trait of self-centeredness and the capacity for transcendence over self. The Judaeo-Christian tradition avers that man is not God, but that he is "made in the image of God," that he is "a little lower than the angels." This means, in Hutchison's words, that man possesses "transcendent and creative freedom. . . . The divine image is man's capacity in imagination to stand clear of himself and his world. . . . Because he can stand clear of himself and see himself, man possesses (always within limits) the capacity for self-determination. He can determine his own ends, and remake his own self; and for better and/or worse he is continuously doing so."[34]

Applying these ideas to the specific realm of foreign policy, we must accept what Cook and Moos have called the "realism of idealism." American "national interest" cannot be conceived as something rigid and immutable—and certainly not something which, by the nature of things, stands in opposition to the national interests of all other states. There is no such thing as a "national interest" divorced from broad human goals, such as progress toward the good life, in which the highest development of human personality is the universal goal. This is the true "national interest" of every state—perceived as never before in the nuclear age, when "one world" has become a fact because of unprecedented strides in scientific knowledge and technology. Moreover, the nuclear missile age has driven home as never before that the quintessence of utopianism is to imagine that any powerful nation can enjoy its security while remaining indifferent to the needs and aspirations of humanity at large, of which it is a part. Recognition of this fact, along with awareness that political action based upon it can never accomplish perfect results, is the beginning of political wisdom.

A satisfactory philosophy of American foreign policy must therefore reject that brand of contemporary "realism" which is a corruption of Renaissance humanistic thought, with engraftings from nineteenth-century German romanticism and Marxism. It accepts Hutchison's view that in any human world "there will be egotism, and this egotism will express itself in the will to dominate. Power impulses and the consequent clash or conflict of such power impulses are pervasive and perennial human facts. Wherever they occur it will be necessary to balance them in some sort of tolerable order."[35] But a true conception of the "national interest" of the United States does not stop there. It goes on to assert that the United States, in concert with every nation in the world community, must endeavor to create the conditions in international affairs that prevail in domestic affairs and that are the *sine qua non* of security for individuals within states: a system of world law, together with adequate powers of enforcement, that will permit competition among rival interests to go on *within carefully prescribed limits*, without calling into question the continued existence of organized society, perhaps even of the human race itself.

"Realists" are fully correct in asserting that this is a formidable challenge, that the path is filled with obstacles, and that progress will sometimes be dishearteningly slow. They are incorrect in asserting that the goal is totally unattainable and that mankind is chained to an increasingly devastating cycle of war and peace. A sincere dedication to the goals of self-preservation, national interest, security, and other national objectives requires them to join with "idealists" in discovering ways to achieve the framework of world law and order that is the only ultimate guarantor of security for the United States or any other nation on the world scene.

NOTES

1. Walter Lippman, *The Public Philosophy* (Boston: Little, Brown, 1955), pp. 5, 6, 4.

2. Hans J. Morgenthau, "The Mainspring of American Foreign Policy," *American Political Science Review*, 44 (December, 1950), 833, 836, 844, 835, and 834–835, respectively.

3. *Ibid.*, pp. 833–834; George F. Kennan, *American Diplomacy, 1900–1950* (New York: New American Library, 1952), pp. 93–94.

4. Morgenthau, *op. cit.*, p. 849.

5. Lippmann, *op. cit.*, p. 21; Hanson W. Baldwin, *Great Mistakes of the War* (New York: Harper & Row, 1950).

6. Morgenthau, *op. cit.*, pp. 840, 853–854; Robert Strausz-Hupé and Stefan Possony, *International Relations* (New York: McGraw-Hill, 1954), pp. 637–682, *passim*.

7. Hans J. Morgenthau, "Another 'Great Debate': The National Interest of the United States," *American Political Science Review*, 46 (December, 1952), 970–971, 972–973, 973–974, 978.

8. Hans J. Morgenthau, *In Defense of The National Interest* (New York: Knopf, 1951), pp. 34, 38–39.

9. T. V. Smith, "Power: Its Ubiquity and Legitimacy," *American Political Science Review*, 45 (September, 1951), 693, 695 (italics in original); Kennan, *op. cit.*, p. 98.

10. Smith, *op. cit.*, p. 695.

11. Robert Strausz-Hupé, "U.S. Foreign Policy and the Balance of Power," *Review of Politics*, 10 (January, 1948), p. 77.

12. Kennan, *op. cit.*, p. 41.

13. *Ibid.*, pp. 9–25, 40.

14. Senate Foreign Relations Committee, *The Control and Reduction of Armaments*, Hearings, 85th Congress, 1st Session (Washington, D.C.: 1957), Part II, p. 1008.

15. Senate Foreign Relations Committee, *Review of Foreign Policy*, Hearings, 85th Congress, 2nd Session (Washington, D.C.: 1958), Part IV, p. 762.

16. See the text of Rusk's speech in *The New York Times*, January 11, 1964.

17. John A. Hutchison, *The Two Cities* (Garden City, N.Y.: Doubleday, 1957), p. 86.

18. William Ebenstein, *Great Political Thinkers* (New York: Rinehart, Holt & Winston, 1956), p. 280 (italics in original).

19. *Idem.*

20. Quoted in Charles W. Kegley and Robert W. Bretall, *Reinhold Niebuhr: His Religious, Social, and Political Thought* (New York: Macmillan, 1956), pp. 172–173.

21. Morgenthau, "The Mainspring of American Foreign Policy," *op. cit.*, pp. 836, 853; and "Another 'Great Debate'," *op. cit.*, p. 972.

22. Frank Tannenbaum, *The American Tradition in Foreign Policy* (Norman, Okla.: University of Oklahoma Press, 1955), pp. 161–165.

23. Hutchison, *op. cit.*, p. 32 (italics in original).

24. Thomas I. Cook and Malcolm Moos, *The Realism of Idealism as a Basis for Foreign Policy* (Baltimore: Johns Hopkins University Press, 1954), pp. 106–111.

25. Crane Brinton, *Ideas and Men* (Englewood Cliffs, N.J.: Prentice-Hall, 1950), p. 360.

26. Livingston Merchant, "The Moral Element in Foreign Policy," *Department of State Bulletin,* 37 (September 2, 1957), 374–379.

27. Walter S. Robertson, "Report to the Founders on Foreign Affairs," *Department of State Bulletin,* 36 (April 29, 1957), 682–687.

28. Kegley and Bretall, *op. cit.*, p. 166.

29. Quoted in Tannenbaum, *op. cit.*, p. 61.

30. Christian Gauss, ed., *The Prince,* by Machiavelli (New York: New American Library, 1952), p. 32.

31. Charles B. Marshall, "The National Interest," in Robert A. Goldwin *et al.*, eds., *Readings in American Foreign Policy* (New York: Oxford University Press, 1959), pp. 665–666 (italics added).

32. *Ibid.*, p. 666.

33. T. B. Maston, *Christianity and World Issues* (New York: Macmillan, 1957), p. 353.

34. Hutchison, *op. cit.*, p. 24.

35. *Ibid.*, p. 155.

BIBLIOGRAPHY ➡

This bibliography is designed to supplement the list of references appearing at the end of each chapter. Normally, titles listed there have not been repeated. Instead, studies have been included here that relate various aspects of American foreign policy to the broad international environment that forms the context within which America must shape its response to the outside world. For convenience and ease in utilizing both the list of references at the end of chapters and this bibliography, references have been arranged here in the same order as the subject matter of the book. A list of bibliographies and general references precedes the topical reading lists.

Bibliographies

American Political Science Review. The quarterly issues of this journal contain comprehensive bibliographies on American foreign policy and closely related subjects.

Beers, H. P., *Bibliographies in American History* (New York: H. W. Wilson, 1942).

Bemis, Samuel F., and Grace G. Griffin, *Guide to the Diplomatic History of the United States, 1775–1921* (Washington, D.C.: Government Printing Office, 1935).

Council on Foreign Relations, *Foreign Affairs Bibliography, 1919–1932* (New York: Harper & Row, 1933).

Council on Foreign Relations, *Foreign Affairs Bibliography, 1932–1942* (New York: Harper & Row, 1945).

Council on Foreign Relations, *Foreign Affairs Bibliography, 1942–1952* (New York: Harper & Row, 1955).

Handlin, Oscar, *et al.*, *Harvard Guide to American History* (Cambridge, Mass.: Belknap Press, 1954).

Library of Congress, General Reference and Bibliography Division, *American History and Civilization: A List of Guides and Annotated or Selective Bibliographies* (Washington, D.C.: 1951).

Rips, Rae E., ed., *United States Government Publications*, 3rd rev. ed. (New York: H. W. Wilson, 1949).

United Nations, Headquarters Library, *Bibliographical Series.* Titles listed in this series include *Latin America, 1939–1949* (1952); *A Bibliography of the Charter of the United Nations* (1955); and *Industrialization in Underdeveloped Countries* (1956).

United Nations, Headquarters Library, *Ten Years of United Nations Publications, 1945–1955.* Provides a convenient source for locating UN publications on a variety of subjects.

United Nations, Headquarters Library, *United Nations Documents Index.* This publication is indispensable in using documentary sources relating to the UN.

United States Government, *U. S. Government Publications—Monthly Catalogue* (Washington, D.C.) An invaluable guide to the use of materials published by all branches of the American government.

General References

Carnegie Endowment for International Peace, *Institutes of International Affairs* (New York: 1953). Describes organizations within the United States and abroad interested in international relations.

Council on Foreign Relations, *The United States in World Affairs* (New York: Harper & Row, 1931 to date). This annual volume provides a readable secondary treatment of the main trends in American foreign policy.

Department of State. The Department of State publishes a number of continuing series devoted to selected aspects of American foreign relations. The following would perhaps be of greatest interest to the student:

Commercial Policy
Conference
Department and Foreign Service
Documents and State Papers
European and British Commonwealth
Far Eastern
General Foreign Policy

471

Inter-American
International Organization
Near and Middle Eastern
United States and the United Nations

London Institute of World Affairs, *The Year Book of World Affairs* (London: Stevens and Sons, Ltd., 1946 to date). This series contains articles on aspects of international affairs.

Periodicals. The following are scholarly periodicals dealing directly or indirectly with American foreign policy:

American Political Science Review, 1907–.
Annals of the American Academy of Political and Social Science, 1890–.
Current History, 1941–.
Department of State Bulletin, 1939–.
Foreign Affairs, 1922–.
International Affairs, London, 1922–.
International Conciliation, 1907–.
International Journal, Toronto, 1946–.
International Organization, 1947–.
Journal of International Affairs, 1947–.
Journal of Politics, 1945–.
Middle East Journal, 1947–.
Middle Eastern Affairs, 1950–.
Pacific Affairs, 1928–.
Political Science Quarterly, 1886–.
United Nations Review, 1954–.
Virginia Quarterly Review, 1925–.
Western Political Quarterly, 1948–.
World Affairs, 1901–.
World Politics, 1948–.
Yale Review, 1911–.

Royal Institute of International Affairs, *Documents on International Affairs* (London: Oxford University Press, 1928 to date).

Savord, Ruth, and Donald Wasson, *American Agencies Interested in International Affairs* (New York: Council on Foreign Relations, 1955). Describes the activities of agencies and groups within the United States active in the sphere of foreign relations.

United Nations, *Yearbook of the United Nations* (New York: Columbia University Press). A valuable summary of proceedings in the UN, providing a guide for further exploration in documentary sources.

World Peace Foundation, *Documents on American Foreign Relations* (Boston: 1939 to date). A convenient documentary source.

1. Foundations of Foreign Policy

Abshire, David M., and Richard V. Allen, eds., *National Security* (New York: Praeger, 1963).

Bidwell, Percy W., *Raw Materials: A Study of American Policy* (New York: Harper & Row, 1958).

Carlson, Lucile, *Geography and World Politics* (Englewood Cliffs, N.J.: Prentice-Hall, 1958).

Davis, Kingsley, "The Political Impact of New Population Trends," *Foreign Affairs,* **36** (January, 1958), 293–301.

Dugan, Arthur B., "MacKinder and His Critics Reconsidered," *Journal of Politics,* **24** (May, 1962), 241–258.

Haskins, C. P., "Technology, Science and American Foreign Policy," *Foreign Affairs,* **40** (January, 1962), 224–243.

Hauser, Philip M., ed., *Population and World Politics* (New York: Free Press of Glencoe, 1958).

Kendrick, J. W., *Productivity Trends in the United States* (Princeton, N.J.: Princeton University Press, 1961).

Schlesinger, James R., *The Political Economy of National Security: A Study of the Economic Aspects of the Contemporary Power Struggle* (New York: Praeger, 1960).

Schurr, Sam H., and Bruce C. Netschert, *Energy in the American Economy, 1850–1975: An Economic Study of its History and Prospects* (Baltimore: Johns Hopkins University Press, 1960).

2. National Character

Adler, Selig, *The Isolationist Impulse: Its Twentieth Century Reaction* (New York: Abelard-Schuman, 1957).

Aldridge, John W., *After the Lost Generation* (New York: McGraw-Hill, 1951). A critical study of writings on World Wars I and II.

Boorstin, D. J., *The Image: Or What Happened to the American Dream?* (New York: Atheneum, 1962). (Also published by Harper & Row, April, 1964.)

Buehrig, Edward H., *Wilson's Foreign Policy in Perspective* (Bloomington, Ind.: University of Indiana Press, 1957).

Chambers, C. A., "Belief in Progress in Twentieth-Century America," *Journal of the History of Ideas,* **19** (August, 1958), 633–639.

Gilbert, Felix, *To the Farewell Address: Ideas of Early American Foreign Policy* (Princeton, N.J.: Princeton University Press, 1961).

Kaplan, Lawrence S., "NATO and the Language of Isolationism," *South Atlantic Quarterly,* **57** (Spring, 1958), 204–215.

Lane, R. E., *Political Ideology: Why the American Common Man Believes What He Does* (New York: Free Press of Glencoe, 1962).

Morgenthau, Hans J., "Lessons of World War II's Mistakes," *Commentary,* **14** (October, 1952), 326–333.

Perkins, Dexter, *The American Approach to Foreign Policy* (Cambridge, Mass.: Harvard University Press, 1962, rev. ed.).

Pratt, Julius W., *America's Colonial Experiment* (Englewood Cliffs, N.J.: Prentice-Hall, 1950).

Pratt, Julius W., *Expansionists of 1812* (New York: Macmillan, 1925).

Pratt, Julius W., *Expansionists of 1898* (Baltimore: Johns Hopkins University Press, 1936).

Spiller, Robert E., and Eric Larrabee, eds., *American Perspectives* (Cambridge, Mass.: Harvard University Press, 1961).

Strausz-Hupé, Robert, and Harry W. Hazard, *The Idea of Colonialism* (New York: Praeger, 1958).

Strout, Cushing, *The American Image of the Old World* (New York: Harper & Row, 1963).

Weinberg, A. K., *Manifest Destiny* (Baltimore: Johns Hopkins University Press, 1935).

3. The President and Department of State

Ageton, Arthur A., "The American Ambassador and the Country Team," *World Affairs*, 123 (Summer, 1960), 40–44. On new duties of ambassadors and embassies abroad.

Bowie, Robert R., *Shaping the Future: Foreign Policy in an Age of Transition* (New York: Columbia University Press, 1964).

De Conde, Alexander, *The American Secretary of State: An Interpretation* (New York: Praeger, 1962).

Driggs, Don W., "The President as Chief Educator on Foreign Affairs," *Western Political Quarterly*, 11 (December, 1958), 813–820.

Elder, Robert Ellsworth, *The Policy Machine* (Syracuse, N.Y.: Syracuse University Press, 1961).

George, Alexander L., "American Policy-Making and North Korean Aggression," *World Politics*, 7 (January, 1955), 228–232.

Hamilton, William C., "Some Problems of Decision-Making in Foreign Affairs," *Department of State Bulletin*, 37 (September 9, 1957), 432–436.

Ilchman, Warren F., *Professional Diplomacy in the United States* (Chicago: University of Chicago Press, 1961). Traces out the evolution of the concept of professional diplomacy in America.

Koenig, Louis William, *The Invisible Presidency* (New York: Holt, Rinehart & Winston, 1960).

Kraft, Joseph, "The Comeback of the State Department," *Harper's Magazine*, 223 (November, 1961), 43–50.

McCamy, James L., *Conduct of the New Diplomacy* (New York: Harper & Row, 1964).

May, E. R., ed., *The Ultimate Decision: The President as Commander in Chief* (New York: Braziller, 1960).

Miller, E. P., "The Role of the Department of State in Educational and Cultural Affairs," *Department of State Bulletin*, 45 (November 13, 1961), 811–815.

Murphy, Robert, *Diplomat Among Warriors* (Garden City, N.Y.: Doubleday, 1964).

Neustadt, R. E., *Presidential Power* (New York: Wiley, 1960).

Plischke, Elmer, *The Conduct of American Diplomacy* (Princeton, N.J.: Van Nostrand, 1950).

Rosenau, James N., *National Leadership and Foreign Policy* (Princeton, N.J.: Princeton University Press, 1964).

Sorensen, T. C., *Decision-Making in the White House* (New York: Columbia University Press, 1963).

Wriston, Henry M., *Diplomacy in a Democracy* (New York: Harper & Row, 1956).

Wriston, Henry M., "The Secretary of State Abroad," *Foreign Affairs*, 34 (July, 1956), 523–541.

4. Military and Other Executive Departments

Gilpin, Robert, *American Scientists and Nuclear Weapons Policy* (Princeton, N.J.: Princeton University Press, 1962).

Ginsburgh, Col. Robert N., "The Challenge to Military Professionalism," *Foreign Affairs*, 42 (January, 1964), 255–268.

Goldwin, Robert A., *America Armed: Essays on United States Military Policy* (Chicago: Rand McNally, 1963). A collection of essays on military power in the United States.

Halperin, Morton A., *Limited War in the Nuclear Age* (New York: Wiley, 1963). An appraisal of the concept of limited war and its implications.

Howard, Michael, "Civil-Military Relations in Great Britain and the United States, 1945–1958," *Political Science Quarterly*, 75 (March, 1960), 35–46.

Kelly, George A., "The Global Civil-Military Dilemma," *Review of Politics*, 25 (July, 1963), 291–308.

Knorr, Klaus, "Failures in National Intelligence Estimates: The Case of the Cuban Missiles," *World Politics*, 16 (April, 1964), 455–467.

Lichterman, Martin, *The March to the Yalu: Case Study of Civil-Military Relations as They Affect Decision-Making* (New York: Twentieth Century Fund, 1958).

Masland, John W., *Soldiers and Scholars: Military Education and National Policy* (Princeton, N.J.: Princeton University Press, 1957).

Millis, Walter, *Arms and the State* (New York: Twentieth Century Fund, 1958).

Ransom, H. H., *Central Intelligence and National Security* (Cambridge, Mass.: Harvard University Press, 1958).

Raymond, Jack, *Power at the Pentagon* (New York: Harper & Row, 1964). A wide-ranging analysis, by a well-informed journalist, of American military power.

Schilling, Warner R., "Scientists, Foreign Policy, and Politics," *American Political Science Review*, 54 (June, 1962), 287–301.

Snyder, G. H., *Deterrence and Defense: Toward a Theory of National Security* (Princeton, N.J.: Princeton University Press, 1961).

Tristam, Coffin, *The Passion of the Hawks: Militarism in Modern America* (New York: Macmillan, 1964). A critical appraisal of the contemporary influence of militarism in American life.

Tully, Andrew, *CIA: The Inside Story* (New York: Morrow, 1962).

Van Wagenen, R. W., "American Defense Officials' Views on the United Nations," *Western Political Quarterly*, 14 (March, 1961), 104–119.

Warren, Unna, "CIA: Who Watches the Watchmen?" *Harper's Magazine*, 216 (April, 1958), 46–54.

Williams, T. H., *Americans at War: The Development of the American Military System* (Baton Rouge: Louisiana State University Press, 1960).

Wise, David, and Thomas B. Ross, *The U-2 Affair* (New York: Random House, 1962).

5. Congress

Carroll, H. N., *The House of Representatives and Foreign Affairs* (Pittsburgh: University of Pittsburgh Press, 1958).

Dahl, Robert A., *Congress and Foreign Policy* (New York: Norton, 1964). A major revision of a significant evaluation of Congress's foreign policy role.

Dawson, Raymond H., "Congressional Innovation and Intervention," *American Political Science Review*, 54 (March, 1962), 42–58.

Dulles, John Foster, "The Making of Treaties and Executive Agreements," *Department of State Bulletin*, 28 (April 20, 1953), 591–595.

Farnsworth, David N., "A Comparison of the Senate and Its Foreign Relations Committee on Selected Roll-Call Votes," *Western Political Quarterly*, 14 (March, 1961), 168–175.

Farnsworth, David N., *The Senate Committee on Foreign Relations* (Urbana, Ill.: University of Illinois Press, 1961).

Fenno, Richard F., Jr., "The House Appropriations Committee," *American Political Science Review*, 54 (June, 1962), 310–325.

Gordon, Bernard K., "The Military Budget: Congressional Phase," *Journal of Politics*, 23 (November, 1961), 689–711.

Hickey, John, "The Role of the Congress in Foreign Policy: The Cuban Disaster," *Inter-American Economic Affairs*, 14 (Spring, 1961), 67–91.

Jewell, Malcolm E., *Senatorial Politics and Foreign Policy* (Lexington, Ky.: University of Kentucky Press, 1962). An analysis of Senate attitudes on foreign policy on the basis of selected roll-call votes.

Kesselman, Mark, "Presidential Leadership in Congress on Foreign Policy," *Midwest Journal of Political Science*, 5 (August, 1961), 284–289.

Kalodziej, E. A., "Congressional Responsibility for the Common Defense: The Money Problem," *Western Political Quarterly*, 16 (March, 1963), 149–160.

McConaughy, James L., "Congressmen and the Pentagon," *Fortune*, 57 (April, 1958), 156–160.

Nelson, Randall H., "Legislative Participation in the Treaty and Agreement Making Process," *Western Political Quarterly*, 13 (March, 1960), 154–171.

Robinson, J. A., *Congress and Foreign Policy-Making: A Study in Legislative Influence and Initiative* (Homewood, Ill.: Dorsey, 1962).

Young, Roland, *The American Congress* (New York: Harper & Row, 1958).

6. Bipartisanship and Executive–Legislative Relations

Acheson, Dean G., "Legislative-Executive Relations," *Yale Review*, 45 (June, 1956), 481–495.

Binkley, W. E., *President and Congress*, 3rd rev. ed. (New York: Vintage Books, 1962).

Cohen, B. C., *The Political Process and Foreign Policy: The Making of the Japanese Peace Settlement* (Princeton, N.J.: Princeton University Press, 1957).

Crabb, Cecil V., Jr., "An End to Bipartisanship," *The Nation*, 188 (February 21, 1959), 155–159, 167.

Freeman, J. L., *The Political Process: Executive Bureau-Legislative Committee Relations* (Garden City, N.Y.: Doubleday, 1955).

Hillsman, Roger, "Congressional-Executive Relations and the Foreign Policy Process," *American Political Science Review*, 52 (September, 1958), 725–745.

Westerfield, H. Bradford, *Foreign Policy and Party Politics: Pearl Harbor to Korea* (New Haven: Yale University Press, 1955).

7. Public Opinion

Baker, R., *The American Legion and Foreign Policy* (New York: Bookman Associates, 1954).

Beloff, Max, *Foreign Policy and the Democratic Process* (Baltimore: Johns Hopkins University Press, 1955).

Burdick, Eugene, ed., *American Voting Behavior* (New York: Free Press of Glencoe, 1959).

Cohen, Bernard C., *The Press and Foreign Policy* (Princeton, N.J.: Princeton University Press, 1964).

Elder, Robert E., "The Public Studies Division of the Department of State," *Western Political Quarterly*, 10 (December, 1957), 783–792.

Foster, Schuyler, "The Role of the Public in U.S. Foreign Relations," *Department of State Bulletin*, 43 (November 28, 1960), 823–831.

Fuchs, Lawrence H., "Minority Groups and Foreign Policy," *Political Science Quarterly*, 74 (June, 1959), 161–176.

Graebner, Norman A., *The New Isolation: A Study of Politics and Foreign Policy Since 1950* (New York: Ronald, 1956).

Halperin, Samuel, *The Political World of American Zionism* (Detroit: Wayne State University Press, 1962).

Howard, Norman, "The Balfour Declaration in American Foreign Policy," *Middle East Forum*, 38 (December, 1962), 25–32.

International Political Science Association, *Interest Groups on Four Continents* (Pittsburgh: University of Pittsburgh Press, 1958).

Irish, Marian D., "Public Opinion and American Foreign Policy: The Quemoy Crisis of 1958," *Political Quarterly*, 31 (April–June, 1960), 151–163.

Karson, Marc, *American Labor Unions and Politics* (Carbondale, Ill.: Southern Illinois University Press, 1958).

Key, V. O., *Public Opinion and American Democracy* (New York: Random House, 1964).

Lippmann, Walter, *Public Opinion and Foreign Policy in the United States* (London: G. Allen, 1952).

McLellan, D. S., and C. E. Woodhouse, "Business Elite and Foreign Policy," *Western Political Quarterly*, 13 (March, 1960), 172–190.

McPhee, W. N., and William A. Glaser, eds., *Public Opinion and Congressional Elections* (New York: Free Press of Glencoe, 1962).

Milbrath, L. W., *The Washington Lobbyists* (Chicago: Rand McNally, 1963).

Oder, Irwin, "The United States in Search of a Policy: Franklin D. Roosevelt and Palestine," *Review of Politics*, 24 (July, 1962), 320–342.

Rosenau, J. N., *National Leadership and Foreign Policy: A Case Study in the Mobilization of Public Support* (Princeton, N.J.: Princeton University Press, 1963).

Smith, P. A., "Opinions, Publics, and World Affairs in the United States," *Western Political Quarterly*, 14 (September, 1961), 698–714.

8 and 9. The Cold War

Bergson, Abram, *The Real National Income of Soviet Russia Since 1928* (Cambridge, Mass.: Harvard University Press, 1962).

Bornstein, Morris, and Daniel R. Fusfeld, eds., *The Soviet Economy: A Book of Readings* (Homewood, Ill.: Irwin, 1962).

Bouscaren, A. T., *Soviet Foreign Policy: A Pattern of Persistence* (New York: Fordham University Press, 1962).

Brumberg, Abraham, ed., *Russia Under Khrushchev: An Anthology from Problems of Communism* (New York: Praeger, 1962).

Brezezinski, Z. K., *Ideology and Power in Soviet Politics* (New York: Praeger, 1962).

Cressey, G. B., *Soviet Potentials: A Geographic Appraisal* (Syracuse, N.Y.: Syracuse University Press, 1962).

Dallin, Alexander, et al., eds., *Diversity in International Communism. A Documentary Record: 1961–1962* (New York: Columbia University Press, 1963).

Erickson, John, "The 'Military Factor' in Soviet Policy," *International Affairs*, 39 (April, 1963), 214–226.

Herman, Leon M., "The Limits of Forced Economic Growth in the USSR," *World Politics*, 16 (April, 1964), 407–417.

Historicus, "Stalin on Revolution," *Foreign Affairs*, 27 (January, 1949), 175–215.

Holt, Robert T., and John E. Turner, eds., *Soviet Union: Paradox and Change* (New York: Holt, Rinehart & Winston, 1962). A symposium on various aspects of the Soviet regime in the recent period.

Holtzman, F. D., ed., *Readings on the Soviet Economy* (Chicago: Rand McNally, 1962).

Horelick, Arnold L., "The Cuban Missile Crisis: An Analysis of Soviet Calculations and Behavior," *World Politics*, 16 (April, 1964), 363–389.

Hunt, R. N. Carew, *A Guide to Communist Jargon* (New York: Macmillan, 1957).

Jasny, Naum, *Essays on the Soviet Economy* (New York: Praeger, 1962).

Kennan, George F., *Soviet-American Relations, 1917–20* (Princeton, N.J.: Princeton University Press, 1958).

Kohn, Hans, *The Mind of Modern Russia* (New Brunswick, N.J.: Rutgers University Press, 1955).

Kovner, Milton, *The Challenge of Coexistence* (Washington, D.C.: Public Affairs Press, 1961).

Lowenthal, Richard, "The Rise and Decline of International Communism," *Problems of Communism,* **12** (March–April, 1963), 19–31.

Mackintosh, J. M., *Strategy and Tactics of Soviet Foreign Policy* (New York: Oxford University Press, 1962).

Nove, Alec, "Revamping the Economy," *Problems of Communism,* **12** (January–February, 1963), 10–16.

Petersen, William, *The Realities of World Communism* (Englewood Cliffs, N.J.: Prentice-Hall, 1964).

Reshetar, John S., Jr., *A Concise History of the Communist Party of the Soviet Union* (New York: Praeger, 1960). A succinct history of the evolution of the Communist regime in the USSR.

Schapiro, Leonard, *The U.S.S.R. and the Future: An Analysis of the New Program of the CPSU* (New York: Praeger, 1963). An appraisal of the Communist program in the Khrushchev era.

Staar, Richard F. "How Strong Is the Soviet Bloc?", *Current History,* **45** (October, 1963), 209–215.

Swearer, Howard R., and Richard P. Longaker, *Contemporary Communism: Theory and Practice* (Belmont, Calif.: Wadsworth, 1963). A valuable compendium of primary and secondary source materials on foreign and domestic policies of the USSR.

Tillett, Lowell R., "Soviet Second Thoughts on Tsarist Colonialism," *Foreign Affairs,* **42** (January, 1964), 309–319.

Ulam, Adam B., "Soviet Ideology and Soviet Foreign Policy," *World Politics,* **11** (January, 1959), 153–173. A provocative treatment of the role played by ideology in the Kremlin's foreign relations.

Werth, Alexander, *Russia Under Khrushchev* (New York: Hill & Wang, 1962).

Wolfe, Bertram D., "Communist Ideology and Soviet Foreign Policy," *Foreign Affairs,* **41** (October, 1962), 152–170.

Zyzniewski, Stanley J., "Soviet Foreign Economic Policy," *Political Science Quarterly,* **73** (June, 1958), 206–234.

10. Western Europe

"A New Europe?" *Daedalus,* **93** (Winter, 1964), 1–567.

Beloff, Nora, *The General Says No* (Baltimore: Penguin, 1963). A succinct account of French opposition to British membership in EEC.

Buchan, Alastair, and Philip Windsor, *Arms and Stability in Europe* (New York: Praeger, 1964).

Burgess, W. Randolph, "The Economic and Political Consequences of General de Gaulle," *Political Science Quarterly,* **78** (December, 1963), 537–547.

Chester, E. W., *Europe Views America* (Washington, D.C.: Public Affairs Press, 1962).

Cottrell, Alvin J., and James E. Dougherty, *The Politics of the Atlantic Alliance* (New York: Praeger, 1964).

Council of Europe, *European Yearbook* (Strasbourg, France: 1955–). Relates important yearly developments in European integration.

Crossman, R. H. S., "British Labor Looks at Europe," *Foreign Affairs,* **41** (July, 1963), 732–743.

Deutsch, Karl, *et al., Political Community and the North Atlantic Area* (Princeton, N.J.: Princeton University Press, 1957).

Etzioni, Amitai, "European Unification: A Strategy of Change," *World Politics,* **14** (October, 1963), 32–51.

Grosser, Alfred, "General de Gaulle and the Foreign Policy of the Fifth Republic," *International Affairs,* **39** (April, 1963), 198–213.

Hallstein, Walter, "The European Economic Community," *Political Science Quarterly,* **78** (June, 1963), 161–178.

Humphrey, D. D., *The United States and the Common Market: A Background Study* (New York: Praeger, 1962).

Kennan, George F., "Disengagement Revisited," *Foreign Affairs,* **37** (January, 1959), 187–211.

Kleiman, Robert, *Atlantic Crisis: American Diplomacy Confronts a Resurgent Europe* (New York: Norton, 1964). Analyzes problems and prospects for relations among the North Atlantic community.

Krause, Lawence, ed., *The Common Market: Progress and Controversy* (Englewood Cliffs, N.J.: Prentice-Hall, 1964).

McQuade, Lawrence C., "NATO's Non-Nuclear Needs," *International Affairs,* **40** (January, 1964), 11–21.

Nieburg, H. L., "EURATOM: A Study in Coalition Politics," *World Politics,* **15** (July, 1963), 597–622.

Northedge, F. S., *British Foreign Policy: The Process of Readjustment, 1945–1961* (New York: Praeger, 1962).

Pinder, John, *Europe Against de Gaulle* (New York: Praeger, 1964).

Schmitt, H. A., *The Path to European Union: From the Marshall Plan to the Common Market* (Baton Rouge, La.: Louisiana State University Press, 1962).

Steel, Ronald, *The End of Alliance: America and the Future of Europe* (New York: Viking, 1964).

Strausz-Hupé, Robert, James E. Dougherty, and William R. Kintner, *Building the Atlantic World* (New York: Harper & Row, 1963).

Verrier, Anthony, "British Defense Policy Under Labor," *Foreign Affairs*, 42 (January, 1964), 282–292.

Watt, D. C., "The American Impact on Europe," *Political Quarterly*, 34 (October–December, 1963), 327–338.

Woodhouse, C. M., "Attitudes of the NATO Countries Toward the United States," *World Politics*, 10 (January, 1958), 202–219.

11. The Middle East and Africa

Allon, Yigal, "The Arab-Israel Conflict—Some Suggested Solutions," *International Affairs*, 40 (April, 1964), 205–218.

Baulin, Jacques, *The Arab Role in Africa* (Baltimore: Penguin, 1962). Explores a little-known aspect of Arab interests in foreign affairs.

Berger, Morroe, *The Arab World Today* (Garden City, N.Y.: Doubleday, 1962). A sociological analysis that makes a valuable supplement to political approaches to the Arab world.

Brown, William R., "The Yemeni Dilemma," *Middle East Journal*, 17 (Autumn, 1963), 349–367.

Brzezinski, Zbigniew, *Africa and the Communist World* (Stanford, Calif.: Stanford University Press, 1963).

Burke, Fred G., *Africa's Quest for Order* (Englewood Cliffs, N.J.: Prentice-Hall, 1964).

Campbell, John C., *Defense of the Middle East: Problems of American Policy* (New York: Harper & Row, 1958).

Castleberry, H. P., "Arab's View of Postwar American Foreign Policy," *Western Political Quarterly*, 12 (March, 1959), 9–36.

Cone, L. Winston, "Ghana's African and World Relations," *India Quarterly*, 17 (July–September, 1961), 258–277.

Cremeans, Charles D., *The Arabs and the World* (New York: Praeger, 1963). A perceptive and illuminating treatment of Arab approaches and attitudes in foreign affairs.

Dia, Mamadou, *The African Nations and World Solidarity*, translated from the French by Mercer Cook (New York: Praeger, 1961).

Duffy, James, and Robert A. Manners, eds., *Africa Speaks* (Princeton, N.J.: Princeton University Press, 1961).

Emerson, Rupert, "American Policy in Africa," *Foreign Affairs*, 40 (January, 1962), 303–315.

Gallagher, Charles F., *The United States and North Africa* (Cambridge, Mass.: Harvard University Press, 1964).

Haim, S. G., ed., *Arab Nationalism: An Anthology* (Berkeley, Calif.: University of California Press, 1962).

Halpern, Manfred, *The Politics of Social Change in the Middle East and North Africa* (Princeton, N.J.: Princeton University Press, 1964).

Hoskins, Halford L., "Arab Socialism in the UAR," *Current History*, 44 (January, 1963), 8–12.

Hourani, Albert, "The Decline of the West in the Middle East," *International Affairs*, 29 (January, 1953), 22–43 and (April, 1953), 156–184.

Issawi, Charles, *Egypt in Revolution: An Economic Analysis* (New York: Oxford University Press, 1963).

Jackson, Barbara Ward, "Free Africa and the Common Market," *Foreign Affairs*, 40 (April, 1962), 419–431.

Loya, A., "Radio Propaganda of the United Arab Republic—An Analysis," *Middle Eastern Affairs*, 13 (April, 1962), 98–110.

Mboya, Tom J., "The Party System and Democracy in Africa," *Foreign Affairs*, 41 (July, 1963), 650–658.

Mehdi, Mohammed T., *A Nation of Lions . . . Chained: An Arab Looks at America* (San Francisco: New World Press, 1962). A candid appraisal of Arab attitudes toward the United States.

Penfield, James K., "African Nationalism and United States Foreign Policy," *Department of State Bulletin*, 43 (December 26, 1960), 951–958. Traces out evolution of U.S. policies toward Africa.

Peretz, Don, *The Middle East Today* (New York: Holt, Rinehart & Winston, 1963). A well-informed authority discusses the political evolution of the Arab nations and their contemporary problems.

Pistrak, Lazar, "Soviet Views on Africa," *Problems of Communism*, 11 (March–April, 1962), 24–31.

Quigg, Philip W., ed., *Africa* (New York: Praeger, 1964). A collection of articles from *Foreign Affairs* centering upon internal and external problems of Africa.

Rivkin, Arnold, *The African Presence in World Affairs: National Development and Its Role in Foreign Policy* (New York: Free Press of Glencoe, 1964).

Safran, Nadav, *Egypt in Search of Political Community—An Analysis of the Intellectual and Political Evolution of Egypt 1804–1952* (Cambridge, Mass.: Harvard University Press, 1961).

Sanger, Clyde, "Toward Unity in Africa," *Foreign Affairs*, 42 (January, 1964), 269–281.

Schiff, Ze'ev, "Israel-African Co-operation and Aid," *New Outlook*, 6 (November–December, 1963), 73–78.

Selim, Sam E., "A Return to Arab-American Friendship," *Middle East Forum*, 38 (June, 1962), 15–22.

Senghor, Léopold Sedar, *On African Socialism* (New York: Praeger, 1964).

Siegman, Henry, "Arab Unity and Disunity," *Middle East Journal*, 16 (Winter, 1962), 48–60.

Slawecki, Leon M. S., "The Two Chinas in Africa," *Foreign Affairs*, 41 (January, 1963), 398–409.

Spector, Ivar, *The Soviet Union and the Muslim World, 1917–1958* (Seattle: University of Washington Press, 1959).

Stevens, Georgiana G., *The United States and the Middle East* (Englewood Cliffs, N.J.: Prentice-Hall, 1964). A series of succinct essays, prepared by leading authorities for the American Assembly.

Yakobson, Sergius, "The Soviet Union and Ethiopia: A Case of Traditional Behavior," *Review of Politics*, 25 (July, 1963), 329–342.

Yu, George T., "Peking Versus Taipei in the World Arena: Chinese Competition in Africa," *Asian Survey*, 3 (September, 1963), 439–453.

12. Latin America and Canada

Berle, Adolf A., *Latin America: Diplomacy and Reality* (New York: Harper & Row, 1962).

Burks, David, "The Future of Castroism," *Current History*, 44 (February, 1963), 78–83.

Burr, Robert N., ed., *Documents on Inter-American Cooperation* (Philadelphia: University of Pennsylvania Press, 1955).

Dreier, John C., "The Organization of American States and United States Policy," *International Organization*, 17 (Winter, 1963), 36–53.

Gordon, Lincoln, *A New Deal for Latin America* (Cambridge, Mass.: Harvard University Press, 1963).

Harbron, John D., "Cuba: Bibliography of a Revolution," *International Journal*, 18 (Spring, 1963), 215–223.

Holmes, J. W., "Canadian External Policies Since 1945," *International Journal*, 18 (Spring, 1963), 137–147.

Johnson, H. G., "Canada in a Changing World," *International Journal*, 18 (Winter, 1962–63), 17–28.

McClellan, G. S., ed., *U.S. Policy in Latin America* (New York: H. W. Wilson, 1963).

Madariaga, Salvador De, *Latin America Between the Eagle and the Bear* (New York: Praeger, 1962).

Matthews, Herbert, *The Cuban Story* (New York: Braziller, 1961). A provocative, if also often subjective, analysis of the Cuban revolution.

May, Ernest R., "The Alliance for Progress in Historical Perspective," *Foreign Affairs*, 41 (July 1963), 757–774.

Mecham, J. Lloyd, *The United States and Inter-American Security 1889–1960* (Austin, Tex.: University of Texas Press, 1961).

Padilla, Ezequel, "The Meaning of Pan-Americanism," *Foreign Affairs*, 32 (January, 1954), 270–82.

Palmer, Thomas W., *Search for a Latin American Policy* (Gainesville, Fla.: University of Florida Press, 1957).

Perkins, Dexter, *The United States and Latin America* (Baton Rouge, La.: Louisiana State University Press, 1961).

Pike, F. B., *Chile and the United States, 1880–1962* (Notre Dame, Ind.: University of Notre Dame Press, 1963).

Porter, Charles O., and Robert J. Alexander, *The Struggle for Democracy in America* (New York: Macmillan, 1961).

Rivero, Nicholas, *Castro's Cuba: An American Dilemma* (Washington, D.C.: Luce, 1962).

Rodrigues, José Honório, "The Foundations of Brazil's Foreign Policy," *International Affairs*, 38 (July, 1962), 324–339.

Schmitt, Karl M., and David D. Burks, *Evolution or Chaos: Dynamics of Latin American Government and Politics* (London: Pall Mall, 1963).

Schneider, Ronald M., "Five Years of Cuban Revolution," *Current History*, 46 (January, 1962), 26–33.

Schurz, William L., *This New World: The Civilization of Latin America* (New York: Dutton, 1964). A highly useful discussion of major forces and influences molding Latin American civilization.

Seers, Dudley, "Latin America and U.S. Foreign Policy," *Political Quarterly*, 34 (April–June, 1963), 200–210.

Thomas, David Y., *One Hundred Years of the Monroe Doctrine, 1823–1923* (New York: Macmillan, 1923).

Whitaker, Arthur P., *The United States and Argentina* (Cambridge, Mass.: Harvard University Press, 1954).

Whitaker, Arthur P., *The United States and South America: the Northern Republics* (Cambridge, Mass.: Harvard University Press, 1948).

13. Asia and the Pacific

Barnett, A. Doak, *Communist Strategies in Asia* (New York: Praeger, 1963). Tactics and policies of Communist parties in major Asian countries.

Bobrow, Davis B., "Peking's Military Calculus," *World Politics*, 16 (January, 1964), 287–301.

Brown, W. Norman, *The United States and India and Pakistan* (Cambridge, Mass.: Harvard University Press, 1963).

Brzezinski, Zbigniew, "Threat and Opportunity in the Communist Schism," *Foreign Affairs*, 41 (April, 1963), 513–525.

Clubb, O. E., *The United States and the Sino-Soviet Bloc in Southeast Asia* (Washington, D.C.: Brookings Institute, 1962).

Ebon, Martin, "Indonesian Communism: From Failure to Success," *Review of Politics*, 25 (January, 1963), 91–109.

Fifield, Russell H., *Southeast Asia in United States Policy* (New York: Praeger, 1963).

Fisher, M. W., *et al.*, *Himalayan Battleground: Sino-Indian Rivalry in Ladakh* (New York: Praeger, 1963).

FitzGerald, C. P., "A Fresh Look at the Chinese Revolution," *Pacific Affairs*, 36 (Spring, 1963), 47–53.

Gordon, Bernard K., "Problems of Regional Cooperation in Southeast Asia," *World Politics*, 16 (January, 1964), 222–253.

Hindley, Donald, "Foreign Aid to Indonesia and Its Political Implications," *Pacific Affairs*, 36 (Summer, 1963), 107–119.

Isaacs, Harold R., *Scratches on Our Minds: American Images of China and India* (New York: John Day, 1958).

Jordan, A. A., *Foreign Aid and the Defense of Southeast Asia* (New York: Praeger, 1962).

Khan, Mohammed Ayub, "The Pakistan-American Alliance: Stresses and Strains," *Foreign Affairs*, 42 (January, 1964), 195–209.

Lamb, Beatrice Pitney, *India: A World in Transition* (New York: Praeger, 1963). An appraisal of contemporary domestic and foreign policy of the Indian government.

Lewis, J. P., *Quiet Crisis in India: Economic Development and American Policy* (Washington, D.C.: Brookings Institute, 1962).

London, Kurt, ed., *Unity and Contradiction: Major Aspects of Sino-Soviet Relations* (New York: Praeger, 1962).

Medzini, Merom, "Chinese Penetration in the Middle East," *New Outlook*, 6 (Nov.–Dec., 1963), 16–28.

North, R. C., *Moscow and Chinese Communists*, 2nd ed. (Stanford, Calif.: Stanford University Press, 1962).

Quigley, H. S., *China's Politics in Perspective* (Minneapolis, Minn.: University of Minnesota Press, 1962).

Romein, J. M., *The Asian Century: A History of Modern Nationalism in Asia* (Berkeley, Calif.: University of California Press, 1962).

Scalapino, Robert A., "Moscow, Peking, and the Communist Parties of Asia," *Foreign Affairs*, 41 (January, 1963), 323–343.

Schram, Stuart R., *The Political Thought of Mao Tse-tung* (New York: Praeger, 1963). A series of excerpts from Mao's speeches and writings, giving the essentials of his political philosophy.

Scigliano, Robert, *South Vietnam: Nation Under Stress* (Boston: Houghton Mifflin, 1963). Discusses internal and external problems of South Vietnam in the contemporary era.

Smith, Roger M. "Laos in Perspective," *Asian Survey*, 3 (January, 1963), 61–68.

Szczesniak, Boleslaw, "The Western World and the Far East: Conflicting Relationships," *Review of Politics*, 26 (January, 1964), 91–99.

Taylor, C., "Indonesian Views of China," *Asian Survey*, 3 (March, 1963), 165–172.

Thornton, Thomas Perry, "Foreign Relations of the Asian Communist Satellites," *Pacific Affairs*, 35 (Winter, 1962–63), 341–352.

Torres, José Arsenio, "The Political Ideology of Guided Democracy," *Review of Politics*, 25 (January, 1963), 34–63.

14. Propaganda and Psychological Warfare

Barghoorn, F. C., *The Soviet Cultural Offensive* (Princeton, N.J.: Princeton University Press, 1960).

Benton, William, *The Voice of America* (New York: Harper & Row, 1961).

Blum, Robert, ed., *Cultural Affairs and Foreign Relations* (Englewood Cliffs, N.J.: Prentice Hall, 1963).

Childers, J. S., *The Nation on the Flying Trapeze: The United States as the People of the East See Us* (New York: McKay, 1960).

Dizard, W. P., *The Strategy of Truth: The Story of the U.S. Information Service* (Washington: Public Affairs Press, 1961).

Dyer, Murray, *The Weapon on the Wall: Rethinking Psychological Warfare* (Baltimore, Md.: Johns Hopkins University Press, 1959).

Evans, Frank B., ed., *Worldwide Communist Propaganda Activities* (New York: Macmillan, 1955).

Harter, Donald L., *Propaganda Handbook* (Philadelphia: Twentieth Century Publishing Co., 1953).

Holt, Robert T., *Radio Free Europe* (Minneapolis, Minn.: University of Minnesota Press, 1958).

Katz, Daniel, *et al.*, eds., *Public Opinion and Propaganda: A Book of Readings* (New York: Holt, Rinehart & Winston, 1954).

Laves, Walter H. C., and C. A. Thomson, *Cultural Relations and U.S. Foreign Policy* (Bloomington, Ind.: Indiana University Press, 1963).

Lerner, Daniel, ed., *Propaganda in War and Crisis* (South Norwalk, Conn.: Stewart, 1951).

Levine, Harold, *War Propaganda and the United States* (New Haven: Yale University Press, 1940).

Martin, Leslie J., *International Propaganda: Its Legal and Diplomatic Control* (Minneapolis, Minn.: University of Minnesota Press, 1958).

Stephens, Oren, *Facts to a Candid World* (Stanford, Calif.: Stanford University Press, 1955).

15. Foreign Trade and Aid

Angell, James W., "The United States International Payments Deficit: Dilemmas and Solutions," *Political Science Quarterly*, 79 (March, 1964), 1–24.

Berliner, Joseph S., *Soviet Economic Aid: A New Policy of Aid and Trade in Underdeveloped Countries* (New York: Praeger, 1958).

Buchanan, Norman S., and Howard S. Ellis, *Approaches to Economic Development* (New York: Twentieth Century Fund, 1955).

Butler, William, "Trade and the Less Developed Areas," *Foreign Affairs*, 41 (January, 1963), 372–383.

Clayton, William L., "GATT, The Marshall Plan, and OECD," *Political Science Quarterly*, 78 (December, 1963), 493–503.

Diebold, William, Jr., "The New Situation of International Trade Policy," *International Journal*, 18 (Autumn, 1963), 425–441.

Erasmus, C. J., *Man Takes Control: Cultural Development and American Aid* (Minneapolis, Minn.: University of Minnesota Press, 1961).

Harris, Seymour E., ed., *The Dollar in Crisis* (New York: Harcourt, Brace & World, 1962).

Jackson, Barbara Ward, "Foreign Aid: Strategy or Stop Gap?" *Foreign Affairs*, 41 (October, 1962), 90–104.

Kenen, Peter B., *Giant Among Nations: Problems in United States Foreign Economic Policy* (Chicago: Rand McNally, 1963). Essays on various aspects of American international economic problems.

Lary, H. B., *Problems of the United States as World Trader and Banker* (New York: National Bureau of Economic Research, 1963).

Morgenthau, Hans, "A Political Theory of Foreign Aid," *American Political Science Review*, 54 (June, 1962), 301–310.

Nove, A., "The Soviet Model and Under-Developed Countries," *International Affairs*, 37 (January, 1961), pp. 29–39.

Pincus, John A., "What Policy for Commodities?" *Foreign Affairs*, 42 (January, 1964), 227–241.

Pryor, Frederic L., *The Communist Foreign Trade System* (Cambridge, Mass.: MIT Press, 1963).

"Report of the Clay Committee on Foreign Aid: A Symposium," *Political Science Quarterly*, 78 (September, 1963), 321–361.

Shannon, Lyle W., ed., *Underdeveloped Areas: A Book of Readings and Research* (New York: Harper & Row, 1957).

Shonfield, Andrew, *The Attack on World Poverty* (New York: Random House, 1960).

Steel, Ronald, ed., *U.S. Foreign Trade Policy* (New York: H. W. Wilson, 1962).

Wiggins, J. W., and Helmut Schoeck, eds., *Foreign Aid Reexamined—A Critical Appraisal* (Washington, D.C.: Public Affairs Press, 1958).

16. International Organization

Claude, Inis L., Jr., *Swords into Plowshares* (New York: Random House, 1964).

Claude, Inis L., Jr., "The Management of Power in the Changing United Nations," *International Organization*, 15 (Spring, 1961), 219–236.

Claude, Inis L., Jr., "The Political Framework of the UN's Financial Problems," *International Organization*, 17 (Autumn, 1963), 831–859.

Claude, Inis L., Jr., *The United Nations and the Use of Force* (New York: Carnegie Endowment for International Peace, 1961).

Cohen, B. V., *The United Nations: Constitutional Developments, Growth, and Possibilities* (Cambridge, Mass.: Harvard University Press, 1961).

Cohen, Sir Andrew, "The New Africa and the United Nations," *International Affairs*, **36** (October, 1960), 476–489.

Dallin, Alexander, *The Soviet Union at the United Nations: an Inquiry into Soviet Motives and Objectives* (New York: Praeger, 1962).

Dallin, Alexander, "The Soviet View of the United Nations," *International Organization*, **14** (Winter, 1962), 20–37.

Frank, Isaiah, "Issues Before the U.N. Conference," *Foreign Affairs*, **42** (January, 1964), 210–226.

Green, James F., *The United Nations and Human Rights* (Washington, D.C.: Brookings Institution, 1956).

Henkin, Louis, "The United Nations and Its Supporters: A Self-Examination," *Political Science Quarterly*, **78** (December, 1963), 504–536.

Higgins, B. H., *United Nations and U.S. Foreign Economic Policy* (Homewood, Ill.: Irwin, 1962).

Hovet, Thomas, *Africa in the United Nations* (Evanston, Ill.: Northwestern University Press, 1963).

Jacobson, Harold K., "The United Nations and Colonialism: A Tentative Appraisal," *International Organization*, **16** (Winter, 1962), 37–57.

Kertesz, Stephen, "The United Nations: A Hope and Its Prospects," *Review of Politics*, **25** (October, 1963), 523–550.

Moor, Carol C., and Waldo Chamberlain, *How To Use United Nations Documents* (New York: New York University Press, 1952).

Padelford, Norman J., "Financial Crisis and the Future of the United Nations," *World Politics*, **15** (July, 1963), 531–568.

Padelford, Norman J., and Rupert Emerson, eds., "Africa and International Organization," *International Organization*, **14** (Spring, 1962), 275–404. Symposium containing several articles on this theme.

Riggs, Robert E., *Politics in the United Nations: A Study of United States Influence in the General Assembly* (Urbana, Ill.: University of Illinois Press, 1958).

Scott, W. A., and Stephen B. Withey, *The United States and the United Nations: The Public View, 1945–55* (New York: Manhattan Publishing Co., 1958).

Spencer, John H., "Africa at the U.N.: Some Observations," *International Organization*, **16** (Spring, 1962), 375–386.

Stromberg, R. N., *Collective Security and American Foreign Policy: From the League of Nations to NATO* (New York: Praeger, 1963).

Swift, Richard N., "The United Nations and Its Public," *International Organization*, **14** (Winter, 1960), 60–92.

Theobald, Robert, ed., *The UN and Its Future* (New York: H. W. Wilson, 1963).

Triska, Jan, and Howard E. Kock, Jr., "The Asian-African Nations and International Organization," *Review of Politics*, **21** (April, 1959), 417–457.

Wilcox, Francis O., and H. Field Haviland, *The United States and the United Nations* (Baltimore: Johns Hopkins University Press, 1961).

17. Disarmament and Nuclear Energy

Bechhoefer, Bernard G., *Postwar Negotiations for Arms Control* (Washington, D.C.: Brookings Institute, 1961).

Bechhoefer, Bernard G. "The Soviet Attitude Toward Disarmament," *Current History*, **45** (October, 1963), 193–199.

Benoit, Émile, and Kenneth E. Boulding, *Disarmament and the Economy* (New York: Harper & Row, 1963).

Bloomfield, Lincoln P., "Arms Control and World Government," *World Politics*, **14** (July, 1962), 633–646.

Brennan, D. G., ed., *Arms Control, Disarmament, and National Security* (New York: Braziller, 1961).

Finkelstein, Lawrence S., "Arms Inspection," *International Conciliation*, **540** (November, 1962), 1–89.

Finkelstein, Lawrence S., "The United Nations and Organizations for the Control of Armaments," *International Organization*, **16** (Winter, 1962), 1–20.

Frisch, D. H., ed., *Arms Reduction: Program and Issues* (New York: Twentieth Century Fund, 1961).

Hodgetts, J. E., *Administering the Atom for Peace* (New York: Atherton, 1964).

Luard, Evan, "Conventional Disarmament," *World Politics*, **16** (January, 1964), 189–204.

Melman, Seymour, ed., *Disarmament: Its Politics and Economics* (Boston: American Academy of Arts and Sciences, 1962).

Mullenbach, Phillip, *Civilian Nuclear Power* (New York: Twentieth Century Fund, 1963).

Nogee, Joseph L., *Soviet Policy Toward International Control of Atomic Energy* (Notre Dame, Ind.: University of Notre Dame Press, 1961).

Nogee, Joseph L., "The Diplomacy of Disarmament," *International Conciliation*, **526** (January, 1960), 235–303.

Spanier, J. W., and Joseph L. Nogee, *The Politics of Disarmament: A Study in Soviet-American Gamesmanship* (New York: Praeger, 1962).

18. Guiding Principles of American Foreign Policy

Acheson, Dean G., *Power and Diplomacy* (Cambridge, Mass.: Harvard University Press, 1958).

Buehrig, Edward H., *Woodrow Wilson and the Balance of Power* (Bloomington, Ind.: Indiana University Press, 1955).

Kennan, George F., *Realities of American Foreign Policy* (Princeton, N.J.: Princeton University Press, 1954).

Merchant, Livingston T., "The Moral Element in Foreign Policy," *Department of State Bulletin,* **37** (September 2, 1957), 374–379.

Miller, Lynn H., "The Contemporary Significance of the Doctrine of Just War," *World Politics,* **16** (January, 1964), 254–286.

Minar, David W., "Ideology and Political Behavior," *Midwest Journal of Political Science,* **5** (November, 1961), 317–331.

Modelski, G. A., *A Theory of Foreign Policy* (New York: Praeger, 1962).

Morgenthau, Hans J., *Dilemmas of Politics* (Chicago: University of Chicago Press, 1958).

Osgood, Robert E., *Ideals and Self-Interest in America's Foreign Relations* (Chicago: University of Chicago Press, 1953).

Perlmutter, O. William, "The 'Neo-Realism' of Dean Acheson," *Review of Politics,* **26** (January, 1964), 100–123.

Stevenson, Adlai E., *Call to Greatness* (New York: Harper & Row, 1954).

"The Idea of National Interest," *American Perspective,* **4** (Fall, 1950), 335–401.

Thompson, Kenneth W., *American Diplomacy and Emergent Patterns* (New York: New York University Press, 1962).

Thompson, Kenneth W., *Christian Ethics and the Dilemmas of Foreign Policy* (Durham, N.C.: Duke University Press, 1959).

Thompson, Kenneth W., *Political Realism and the Crisis of World Politics* (Princeton, N.J.: Princeton University Press, 1960).

Tucker, Robert W., "Force and Foreign Policy," *Yale Review,* **47** (March, 1958), pp. 374–392.

Weber, Theodore R., "Morality and National Power in International Politics," *Review of Politics,* **26** (January, 1964), 20–44.

INDEX ➡

Acheson, Dean G., 1, 53, 61, 63, 118, 124–125, 178, 210
Adams, John Quincy, 267
Adams, Sherman, 94–95, 104
Africa, agriculture in, 246–247
  anti-Westernism in, 249
  "Balkanization" of, 252
  colonialism in, 252–254
  diseases in, 246
  economic data, 245–247
  emergence of, 245
  European aid to, 249–272
  independence movements in, 245
  illiteracy in, 245
  languages, 245
  legislative criticisms of, 108
  political turbulence in, 245
  population of, 16, 245
  regional groups in, 256
  relations with U.S., 245–259
  resources, 245–247
  socialism in, 251–252
  State Department interest in, 57
  transportation, 245
  U.S. aid for, 247–251
  U.S. investments in, 248
  unity movements in, 256
  views of U.S. policy, 408–409
  Western aid for, 372
"African socialism," 251–252
Afro-Asian countries, and colonialism, 407–409
  in UN, 402–404
    See also Nonalignment
Agency for International Development, relation to State Department, 54, 85, 373–374
    See also Foreign aid
Agitprop, 343
    See also Propaganda; Union of Socialist Republics
Agricultural commodities, "chicken war," 365
  U.S. exports, 365
  and world trade, 362
Agricultural surpluses, 84
Agriculture, in Africa, 246–247
  Department of, 84
  interest groups in, 139
  production in U.S., 14–15
  in USSR, 185–186
  and U.S. foreign aid, 374–376
"Aid India Club," 384

Aiken, George D., 281, 417
Airpower, vulnerability of U.S., 9–10
Alexander I, 154–155
Alexander II, 159
Algeria, Republic of, 364
"Alliance for Progress," 281–286
    See also Latin America
Ambassadors, appointment of, 59–60
  career officers as, 60
  head of "country team," 57, 61
  President's power to receive, 47–48
American Farm Bureau Federation, 139
American Federation of Labor, 139
American Legion, 139
Anglo-American Committee of Inquiry (1946), 229
Anglo-Canadian-American declaration on nuclear weapon (1945), 428
Angola, 252
ANZUS, 328–329
"Appeasement," 28, 456
Appointments, President's power over, 46–47
  Senate confirmation, 94
Appropriations, congressional, and foreign policy, 94–100
Arab-Israeli conflict, 227–232
  border disputes, 231
  congressional attitudes toward, 104
  continuing problems, 230–232
  future of, 244
  refugee issue, 230–231
  U.S. policy toward, 230–232
  water dispute, 231
    See also Israel; Palestine
Arab nationalism, and Baghdad Pact, 236
  and communism, 242–243
  nature of, 236–238
  and nonalignment, 238–239
"Arab socialism," 238
Arab world, 227–244
  animosity toward U.S., 232
  and Baghdad Pact, 233–234
  and communism, 241–243
  nationalism in, 236–238
  relations with U.S., 244
  traditionalism in, 244
  views of NATO, 232
    See also Middle East
Arbenz, Jacobo, 289–290
Arbitration, 33, 394

Arctic, strategic importance, 265
"Arctic Inspection Zone" (1958), 438
Arévalo, Juan J., 289
Argentina, 274, 276
Armas, Castillo, 290–291
Arms Control and Disarmament Agency, 54, 441
"Arsenal of democracy," 15
Asia, Chinese goals in, 308–310
  colonialism in, 301, 327–328
  communism in, 327–328
  democracy in, 315
  defense system in, 328–330
  instability in, 327–328
  nationalism in, 314–315, 327–328
  nonalignment in, 314–326
  political elites in, 328
  political trends in, 315
  population of, 16
  Russian goals in, 309
  Sino-Soviet conflict in, 307–314, 323
  strategic importance, 327–330
  U.S. policy toward, 299–335
  western impact on, 328
  and Wilsonian idealism, 328
    See also India; Nonalignment; Southeast Asia
        Treaty Organization; Vietnam, Re-
        public of South
Aswan High Dam, 240
Atlantic Charter (1940), 452
"Atlantic partnership," 223–224
    See also European Economic Community
Atomic Energy Commission, and disarmament, 441
  expenditures of, 14
  and foreign policy, 84
"Atoms for Peace," 443–446
Australia, defense treaty, 328–329
Austria and E.E.C., 209
Axis peace treaties, 93, 398
Axis Powers and U.S., 29, 133–134
al-Azm Khalid, 242

Baghdad Pact, 233–236
    See also Central Treaty Organization
Bakunin, Michael, 157
Balance-of-payments, defined, 385–386
  and foreign aid, 379, 388
  of U.S., 364, 385–390
  and U.S. exports, 389
"Balance of power," 196
  ambiguity of concept, 467
  as goal of U.S. policy, 453
  instability of, 462
  as "law" of politics, 459
  and national security, 467
  within states, 466
  Wilson's views of, 451–452
  in World War II, 452
"Balance of terror" and NATO, 215–216
Baldwin, Hanson W., 69, 191, 333, 450, 452
Balewa, Abubakar, 253–254, 259
Baltic Sea, 188
Bandung Conference (1955), 304
Barker, Sir Ernest, 21
"Baruch Plan" (1946), 428–430
Batista, Fulgencio, 273, 291–292
"Battle Act," 369
    See also East-West trade

"Bay of Pigs" invasion (1961), 50–51, 117, 293,
    410–411
Beard, Charles A., 35
Belgrade Conference (1961), 318
    See also Nonalignment
Bell, David E., 73–74, 373, 379
Beloff, Max, 203
Bemis, Samuel F., 24
"Benelux union," 202
Berdyaev, Nicholas, 157
Billington, Ray A., 38
Bipartisanship, "advisers" to State Department, 123–
    124
  barriers to, 118–127
  and "Bay of Pigs" crisis, 117
  and Congress, 120–122
  consultations in, 114–116, 122–125
  and criticism of policy, 116–117
  and Cuban missile crisis, 114, 118
  definition of, 114
  and disarmament, 119–120
  and domestic issues, 123
  and Eisenhower Doctrine, 115
  Eisenhower's conception of, 124
  and elections, 118
  and executive disunity, 119–120
  and executive-legislative conflict, 118–119
  failure of, 117–118
  and foreign aid, 115
  goals of, 127
  and League of Nations, 113–114
  and legislative powers, 118–119
  majority party in, 126–127
  and Marshall Plan, 114
  minority party in, 126–127
  need for, 113–114
  and negotiations, 116
  and nuclear treaty, 116
  obligations under, 123
  and party system, 117, 120–121
  political assumptions of, 126–127
  and political campaigns, 125–127
  and presidential leadership, 118–119
  procedures of, 122–125
  role of individuals in, 122–123
  role of State Department in, 56, 115
  success of, 117
  techniques of, 114–118
  and "tripartisanship," 119
  and the UN, 114
  in U.S. policy, 112–127
  and Vietnam crisis, 120
  and wheat for India, 120–122
Birth control, 17, 72
Blaine, James G., 269
Bloomfield, Lincoln P., 411
Boggs, S. W., 9
Bogotá conference (1948), 270
Bolivia, conditions in, 288
Bowles, Chester, 246, 301, 316, 450
Boxer Rebellion (1900), 31
Bradley, Omar N., 66–67, 100
Brazil, economic progress in, 282–286
"Brazzaville group," 256
Brest-Litovsk, Treaty of (1918), 161 n.
Brinton, Crane, 463
Brogan, D. W., 30, 35, 37, 39

Brookings Institution, 62, 87
Brussels Treaty (1948), 209–210
    See also North Atlantic Treaty Organization
Bryan, William J., 394
Bryce, Viscount James, 37
Buddhism, 319
Budget, Bureau of, 74, 83–84
    and foreign policy, 73–75, 96–97
Burns, James M., 136
Business groups and foreign policy, 139
Byrd, Harry F., 97
Byrnes, James, 116

Cabinet and foreign policy, 82–83
Cabot, John M., 277
Calvinism, 138
Cambodia, 330, 332
"Campaign of Truth," 347
    See also Propaganda; United States Informa-
        tion Agency
Canada, Fenian invasion, 142
    "unguarded frontier" with U.S., 425
    U.S. investments in, 376
    U.S. relations with, 265
Capitalism, African views of, 252
    conflict with communism, 167–169
    and war, 168–169
"Caracas Declaration" (1954), 290
"Casablanca group," 256
Castro, Fidel, 292–296
    See also Cuba
Central Intelligence Agency, functions, 85–86
    and Guatemala, 291
Central Treaty Organization (CENTO), 211, 235
    See also Baghdad Pact
Chamberlain, Lawrence H., 50
Chapaltepec, Act of (1945), 270
Chiang Kai-shek, 302
    See also China, Nationalist
Chiari, Roberto, 271–272
"Chicken war," 365
China, Communist, admission to UN, 312
    and Afro-Asian states, 304
    aid to Morocco, 364
    alliance with USSR, 304–307
    American views of, 29
    anti-Americanism in, 303
    army of, 187
    and Bandung Conference, 304
    border accord with Pakistan, 322
    border claims of, 309–310
    commune system, 307
    congressional resolutions on, 107
    de Gaulle's policies, 314
    dispute with USSR, 170–171
    economic boycott of, 303
    and Formosa, 51, 303–304
    French recognition, 312
    ideology of, 306–308
    and India, 320–327
    "isolation" of, 313
    and Korean War, 414–415
    and Laos, 304, 334
    legislative views of, 95
    national goals, 308–310
    and nonalignment, 322–323
    and nuclear test-ban, 310

China, Communist (Continued)
    and nuclear war, 308
    "overseas Chinese," 312
    and Pakistan, 326
    population pressures in, 309–310
    recognition of, 48
    reexamination of U.S. policy, 314
    and South Vietnam, 330–335
    Soviet aid to, 323
    Soviet views of, 170
    trade embargo of, 369
    and the UN, 29
    and U.S., 302–314
    views of Khrushchev, 311
    Western relations with, 314
China, Nationalist, civil war in, 313–314
    defeat of, 302
    lobbying activities by, 144
    Open Door policy, 300–301
    and U.S., 299–301
Chou En-lai, 304
Churchill, Winston, 6, 21, 156
Civil and Defense Mobilization, Office of, 83
Civil-military relations, 67–80
    See also Military establishment
Civil rights and foreign policy, 348, 353–354
Civil War, American, 52, 159
"Clark Memorandum," 269
    See also Monroe Doctrine
"Class struggle," 167
    See also Communism
Climate of U.S., 8
Claude, Inis, 427
Clausewitz, Karl von, 25, 67, 456
"Clay Report" (1963), 373, 380
Coal supplies in U.S., 13
Cold War, in Africa, 255–258
    "balance of terror" in, 190–192
    economic aspects of, 182–186
    geopolitical aspects of, 178–182
    ideological aspects of, 166–178
    and the UN, 413–417
Colonialism, in Africa, 252–254
    in Asia, 327–328
    and China, 300–301
    neutralist views of communist, 318
    and the UN, 398–399, 407–409
    and U.S., 301, 355
"Common Market," see European Economic Com-
    munity
Commerce, Department of, 84
Commission for Conventional Armaments, 435
Committees, interdepartmental, and foreign policy,
    87–88
Commonwealth of Nations and E.E.C., 207–208
Communism, and Africa, 249, 251–252, 258–259
    American views of, 26, 454
    Arab opposition to, 241–243
    in Asia, 327–328
    challenge to NATO, 214–216
    in China, 302–314
    codification of belief, 175
    colonialism of, 318
    in Cuba, 293
    "different paths to," 306
    diversity of, 313–314
    "dogmatism" in, 173

Communism (*Continued*)
  as dynamic creed, 175
  economic goals of, 182–183
  flexibility of, 173–174
  geopolitical threat from, 179–180
  in Greece and Italy, 217
  ideological aspects of, 166–178
  in Laos, 333–334
  in Latin America, 274–275, 287–296
  means used by, 177–178
  in Middle East, 235–236
  morality of, 169–170
  neutralist views of, 355
  and "peaceful coexistence," 174
  propaganda activities, 338
  and "reformism," 167
  "reinterpretations" of, 173–174
  "revisionism" in, 177–178
  and Russian Messianism, 157–158
  and Russian nationalism, 170–171
  and South Vietnam, 330–335
  and Soviet foreign policy, 172–178
  strategy and tactics of, 169–170
  "tactical" shifts of, 177–178, 344
  U.S. views, 160
  varieties of, 166 n.
  views of foreign intervention, 161
  and war, 168–169
  and "world revolution," 167–169, 177–178
Communist bloc, creation of, 179–180
  economic power of, 182–183
  military power of, 187–192
  size of, 182
Communist Party, 342–343
  See also Communism
Communist Revolution of 1917, 160–161
"Community Ambassador" program, 351–352
Compromise, American attitudes on, 30
Conferences, international, American views of, 28–29
  growth in, 57
Conflict, American attitudes toward, 26, 30
Congo, Republic of, 144
Congo crisis, 402, 415
Congress, and aid to Latin America, 280–281
  and appropriations, 94–100
  and Arab-Israeli dispute, 104
  and armed forces, 100
  and bipartisanship, 118–122
  and Bureau of Budget, 83–84
  Committee on the Conduct of the War, 105
  committees of, 108
  control over executive information, 48–49
  and defense expenditures, 100–102
  and dismissal of Gen. MacArthur, 106
  and East-West trade, 369
  and European unity, 201
  expanded influence of, 91
  and expenditures, 95
  foreign affairs sub-committee system, 115
  and foreign aid, 95, 379–380
  foreign lobbying before, 143–144
  and Foreign Service Academy, 59 n.
  and "Formosa resolution," 51, 304
  general legislative authority, 103–104
  and Greek-Turkish aid, 198
  and India, 104
  investigation of Gen. MacArthur's dismissal, 125
  investigations by, 105–106

Congress (*Continued*)
  liaison among committees, 101
  liaison with State Department, 115
  and Marshall Plan, 97
  and military establishment, 77, 100
  and military reorganization, 79–80
  and neutralist governments, 104
  and "neutrality" legislation, 133
  and nuclear energy, 14
  Nye Committee, 105
  party discipline in, 120–121
  power of committees, 98
  power to "declare war," 45, 102–103
  power over military, 45–46
  proliferation of committees, 120
  and propaganda activities, 347
  and public opinion, 148
  resolutions by, 106–107
  role in foreign policy, 91–109
  role in recognition power, 47–48
  speeches in, 107
  standing committees of, 96
  and State Department, 56
  and Trade Expansion Act, 364–366
  travel by legislators, 108–109
  Truman Committee, 105
  UN financial crisis, 417–419
  and USIA, 353
  views toward party platform, 50
Connally, Tom, 93, 107–108
Constitution, American, and foreign policy, 42–48
  and military power, 45–46, 75–76
  provisions on appointments, 46–47
Consultations, bipartisan, 114–116
"Containment," origins of, 197–198
  as problem in U.S. policy, 456
    See also Greek-Turkish Aid Program
"Continentalism," 35
"Conventional weapons," defined, 430–431
  and disarmament, 430–431, 435–436
    See also "Limited war"
Cook, Thomas I., 450
Cooper, John S., 124
Corwin, Edward S., 51–52
Council of Economic Advisers, 83
Council of Europe, 220–221
"Counterpart funds," 109
"Country team," 57, 61
Cuba, under Batista, 291–292
  "Bay of Pigs" invasion, 293
  crisis with U.S., 291–296
  U.S. policies toward Batista, 273
"Cuban missile crisis," 33, 72–73, 412
Cultural affairs and State Department, 56
Cultural exchange, 351
Cutler, Robert A., 71
Czechoslovakia, arms agreement with Egypt, 240
  and Munich Conference, 163

Dahl, Robert, 103
Dana, Francis, 158
Davis, John W., 52
Defense, Department of, and budgetary process, 73–75
  and Congress, 100–102
  creation of, 69
  and disarmament, 441
  "functional organization" of, 78

Defense, Department of (*Continued*)
liaison with State Department, 73
"new look" in, 74
Office of International Security Affairs, 73
reorganization of, 70
Strategic Air Command, 70
Strike Command, 70
unified agencies in, 70
Defense, Secretary of, powers of, 69
See also Defense, Department of
Defense Mobilization, Office of, 83
Defense of U.S., 18
de Gaulle, Charles, and Anglo-Saxons, 208–209
and "Atlantic partnership," 224
and European political union, 222–224
force de frappe, 217–219
and "neutralization" of South Vietnam, 330–331
nuclear test ban, 219
opposes British membership in E.E.C., 207
proposals for Southeast Asia, 218
proposes NATO "directorate," 217
recognizes Red China, 218, 312
supports NATO, 217–218
and U.S. commitment to NATO, 216–217
views of European unity, 208–209
Democracy, in Asia, 315
contrasted with communism, 166
and foreign policy, 2–3, 112–113
and propaganda, 353–354
public information in, 49
public opinion in, 129
Democratic Party, 124
"Destroyer deal" (1940), 44, 134
Development Loan Fund, 281
See also Foreign aid
"Dialectical materialism," 167
See also Communism
Diplomacy, American views of, 28–30, 33–34
"democratization" of, 412–413
Diplomatic relations, President's powers, 46–48
Diplomatic relations, severance of, 46
Diplomats in U.S., 46
Disarmament, achievements in postwar era, 441–443
"aerial inspection," 437
Anglo-Canadian-American declaration (1945), 428
armed force "ceilings," 436
"Atoms for Peace," 443–446
Baruch Plan, 428–430
basic concepts, 422–425
"black box" proposal, 437
budgetary considerations in, 424
and "conventional weapons," 435–436
and defense industries, 441
enforcement proceedings, 436–437
French views of, 442–443
gains from, 423–424
Geneva Conference (1927), 427
Geneva Disarmament Conference (postwar), 440–441
Hague Conferences, 425–426
inspection and control, 436–438
and League of Nations, 422–423, 426–427
London Conference (1930), 427
neutralist role in, 440–441
nuclear test-ban, 438–439
"Open Skies" proposal, 437

Disarmament (*Continued*)
and outer space, 441–442
and political issues, 432–433
postwar negotiations, 428–443
propaganda aspects of, 424
and Red China, 443
and related problems, 422–424
scope of proposals, 431–432
and security, 422–425
Soviet nuclear proposals, 428–430
"staging" as problem in, 431, 434–435
and surprise attack, 437
and "tactical" nuclear weapons, 430 n.
"test zone" proposals, 438
and the UN, 435–436
U.S. organization for, 441
U.S. policies in interwar era, 426–427
U.S. policies in postwar period, 422–443
and war, 423–424
Washington Naval Armaments Conference, 426–427
Disengagement in Asia, 325
Djilas, Milovan, 176–177
"Dollar gap," 359
See also Balance of payments; International trade
Domestic affairs and foreign policy, 34–35
Dominican Republic, 274–275
Dulles, John F., 405
as adviser to State Department, 124
and Aswan High Dam, 240–241
and Atoms for Peace, 444
and bipartisanship, 117, 124, 126
criticisms of, 118
and Eisenhower Doctrine, 235
and European Defense Community, 221
and European unity, 201
on goals of U.S. policy, 1
and Guatemala, 289–290
and Japanese peace treaty, 93
and neutralism, 256, 322
powers of, 53
on President's powers over military, 46
and Suez crisis, 240–241
views on NATO, 211
Dunbarton Oaks Conference (1944), 396

East-West trade, European views of, 369–370
Japanese views of, 370
Eberstadt, Ferdinand, 68
Economic aspects of U.S. power, 10–15
Economic growth in U.S., 15
Economic problems of U.S. policy, 358–390
See also Balance of payments; Foreign aid; International trade
Eden, Sir Anthony, 28 n.
Education levels in U.S., 19
Educational exchange programs, 247
Egypt, and Aswan High Dam, 240
and communism, 242
See also Arab world
Eichelberger, Clark M., 401
Eisenhower, Dwight D., and appropriations, 94–95
Arctic Inspection proposals, 438
Atoms for Peace, 443
and bipartisanship, 115, 117
and the Cabinet, 82
and Communist China, 95

Eisenhower, Dwight D. (*Continued*)
  and criticism in foreign affairs, 124
  criticizes planning in State Department, 61
  foreign aid request for 1959, 96
  and Formosa, 51, 304
  and John Foster Dulles, 53
  and Lebanese crisis, 235
  letter to Charles E. Wilson, 49
  and "missile gap," 100
  and National Security Council, 71
  "Open Skies" proposal, 437
  President's war powers, 45
  and public opinion, 147
  and USIA, 347
  use of Vice-President, 49–50
  views on bureaucracy, 88
  views on military influence, 76
Eisenhower, Milton S., 273, 277, 279, 287
"Eisenhower Doctrine" (1957), 46, 235–236
Ellender, Allen J., 108
"Emergency powers" of President, 51–53
Emerson, Ralph Waldo, 36
Energy, sources in U.S., 13–14
"Enlightenment" philosophy and U.S., 38
"Equidistance," 317
    See also Nonalignment
Erhard, Ludwig, 222
"Estrada Doctrine," 275–276
Ethiopia, and African Nationalism, 259
  and nonalignment, 254
  U.S. aid to, 248
Eurasia and U.S. security, 10
Euratom, 203–204, 445–446
Europe, Eastern, East-West dispute over, 171–172
  liberalization of Soviet control, 310
  Soviet expansionism in, 178–179
  Soviet goals in, 153
  Soviet policies in, 29
  and U.S., 180
  U.S. nonrecognition of, 47–48
  wartime agreements toward, 180
Europe, proximity to U.S., 9
  U.S. attitudes toward, 23–24, 35–36
Europe, Western, aid to Africa, 249 n.
  Benelux union, 202
  Coal and Steel Community, 203–204
  containment policy in, 197–198
  defense of, 209–220
  disarmament schemes in, 438
  economic growth of, 183–184
  economic unification of, 201–209
  Euratom, 203–204
  and European Defense Community, 221
  European Economic Community, 204–205
  foreign aid by, 372
  Free Trade Area, 205–207
  historic American goals toward, 451
  19th century conflicts in, 196
  and nuclear energy, 445–446
  political unification in, 208, 220–224
  population growth in, 16–17
  prosperity in, 204–205
  "sector" schemes in, 203–204
  U.S. economic aid to, 200
  U.S. investments in, 376
  U.S. relations with (postwar), 194–224
  U.S. troops in, 45–46, 216–217
  Western European Union, 221–222

European Coal and Steel Community, 203–204
European Defense Community, 221
European Economic Community, African views of, 252, 255
  aid to Africa, 249 n.
  and British membership in, 207–209
  decision-making in, 205
  economic growth of, 184, 204–205
  establishment of, 204
  organization of, 205
  political goals of, 205, 208, 222–224
  prosperity in, 365
  trade data for, 204–205
  and U.S. trade, 362–363
European Free Trade Area, 205–207
  and E.E.C., 207
  goals of, 205–206
  trade by, 207
European Recovery Program, achievements of, 199
  bipartisanship toward, 114
  and Communist bloc, 199
  congressional study of, 97
  and European union, 202–203
  and O.E.E.C., 199
  origins of, 198–199
  U.S. appointments under, 94
Executive agencies, committees of, 87–88
  and foreign policy, 80–88
  growing role in foreign policy, 60–61
  overseas operations of, 57
    See also President
Executive agreements, 44
Executive branch, and bipartisanship, 119–120
  disunity in, 119–120
    See also Defense, Department of; President;
        State, Department of
Executive-Legislative relations and foreign policy, 112–127
  in treaty-making, 43–44
  after World War II, 93
    See also Bipartisanship
Expansionism, American attitudes toward, 31–32
  by the U.S., 27–28

Far East, see Asia
Fedayeen, 230
Feis, Herbert, 32
Ferguson, Homer, 50
Fidelismo, 295–296
    See also Castro, Fidel; Latin America
Fleming, D.F., 116
"Food for Peace" program, 374–376
Force and foreign policy, 5–6
    See also Power
Force de frappe, 217–219
    See also de Gaulle, Charles; North Atlantic
        Treaty Organization
Ford Foundation, 351
Foreign Agents Registration Act, 143
Foreign aid, achievements of, 382–383
  administrative reforms in, 373–374
  and Africa, 372
  African views of communist, 258–259
  agencies engaged in, 84–85
  "Aid India Club," 384
  American aid to Ghana, 258
  and balance-of-payments, 379
  beneficiaries of U.S., 372

Foreign aid (*Continued*)
 budget for 1959, 96
 categories of U.S., 374
 changes in direction of U.S., 200
 Clay Report, 380
 communist programs in Africa, 248
 curtailment of Egyptian, 104
 and domestic politics, 380
 and European countries, 200, 383–384
 failures of, 382
 "Food for Peace" program, 374–376
 future of, 384
 goals of, 381–382
 by international organizations, 384–385, 405–406
 in interwar period, 371
 legislative opposition, 95
 loans in, 372–374
 and national security, 3
 by OECD, 384
 opposition to, 379–381
 as percentage of GNP, 381
 principles of U.S., 373–374
 private activities in, 376–377
 public views on, 381
 results of, 16–17
 and trade expansion, 379
 trends in U.S., 371–374
 by U.S., 371–376
 U.S. and Africa, 247–251
 U.S. economic, 374
 and U.S. economy, 377–379
 U.S. and Europe, 200
 U.S. and India, 324
 U.S. and Latin America, 279–287
 U.S. military, 374
 U.S. for 1963-1964-1965, 374
 by U.S. since World War II, 16–17
 by U.S.S.R., 323, 360
Foreign policy, bipartisanship in, 112–127
 and budgetary process, 73–74
 Congress' role in, 91–109
 coordination of, 87–88
 disunity in U.S., 112–113
 and domestic policy, 360
 economic agencies in, 83–84
 economic aspects, 358–390
 ends and means in, 455–456, 463–464
 executive agencies in, 80–88
 and foreign aid, 84–85
 means of, 5–6
Foreign Service, growth of, 57–58
 reorganization of, 57–59
Foreign Service Academy, 59 n.
Foreign Service Act (1946), 58
Foreign Service Institute, 58–59
Foreign Service Reserve, 57
Foreign Service Staff, 57
Formosa, 144
 communist goals toward, 303–304
 U.S. protection of, 46
 See also China, Nationalist
"Formosa resolution" (1955), 51, 103 n., 304
France, blocks British membership in E.E.C., 207
 and E.D.C., 221
 and E.E.C., 208–209
 and European political unity, 222–224
 force de frappe, 217–219, 440
 and Indochina, 329

France (*Continued*)
 intervention in West Africa, 256
 and Suez crisis, 240
 and "multinational" NATO force, 219
 and NATO, 217–218
 See also de Gaulle, Charles
Franks, Sir Oliver, 203, 381
Frontier, influence on U.S. attitudes, 38
"Fullbright exchange program," 56
Fulbright, William J., 60, 115, 143, 177

Gabon, 255–256
Galbraith, John K., 325
Gas, natural, in U.S., 13–14
Gates, Thomas S., 73
Gavin, James M., 78
General Agreements on Tariff and Trade (GATT), 362
Geneva Conference (1954), 330, 334 n.
 See also Cambodia; Laos; Vietnam, Republic of South
Geneva Disarmament Conference (1927), 427
Geneva Disarmament Conference (postwar), *see* Disarmament
"Genocide," 416
Geography and U.S. power, 7–10
"Geopolitics," 8, 178–182
George, Walter F., 121
German-Americans, 141
Germany, American views toward, 26–27, 29
 and "nuclear parity," 219
 propaganda in U.S., 46
 rearmament, 221–222
Ghana, U.S. aid to, 248, 258
Gluck, Maxwell H., 59–60
Goals of foreign policy, 1–5
 of U.S. in war, 30–31
"Good Neighbor policy," 269
 See also Latin America
Gorer, Geoffrey, 38
Great Britain, economic decline of, 359
 and E.E.C., 207–209
 and E.F.T.A., 205–207
 and Greek crisis, 198
 intervention in Tanganyika, 256
 and Irish-Americans, 141–142
 and Monroe Doctrine, 196–197, 266–267
 and partition of Palestine, 228–229
 and "partnership" with U.S., 217
 rapprochement with U.S., 160
 "special relationship" with U.S., 208–209
 and Suez crisis, 240
 and Western European Union, 221–222
Greece, communist threat to, 197
Greek-Turkish Aid Program (1947), 197–198
 legislative approval of, 51
 U.S. appointments for, 94
Greenland and U.S., 47
Gross National Product of U.S., 14
"Guatemala crisis" (1954), 288–291
Guevara, Ernesto, 292
Guinea, 250, 254

Hague Conferences, 394, 425–426
Hague conventions, 33
Halle, Louis J., 176
Hallstein, Walter, 203
Hammarskjöld, Dag, 412

Harriman, Averell, 74, 287, 322
Hay, John, 300
Hay-Pauncefote Treaties (1900–1901), 160
Heilbroner, Robert L., 17 n.
"Hemispheric solidarity," 8–9
Herter, Christian, 63, 73
Hilsman, Roger, 63
"Himalayan crisis," see Sino-Indian crisis
Hinduism, 319
Ho Chi Minh, 330
    See also Vietnam, Republic of South
Hobbes, Thomas, 457 n.
Holy Alliance, 155, 194, 265, 393
Hoopes, Townsend, 62
Hoover, Herbert, 417
Hoover Commission, 54, 115
Hopkins, Harry, 47
House, Edward M., 47
House Foreign Affairs Committee, expanded activities of, 91–92
    and military aid to Europe, 104
House of Representatives, and appropriations, 101–102
    See also Congress
Hughes, Charles E., 267
Hull, Cordell, 66, 133–134, 269, 361
Human rights, 406–407
Hungarian revolt (1956), 240, 400, 464
Hutchinson, John A., 462
Huzar, Elias, 76, 100–101

"Idealism," philosophy of, 457–469
Ideology, and American society, 23–24
    and Cold War, 166–178
    and Soviet foreign policy, 172–178
Immigrants, American attitudes toward, 36
    in the U.S., 140–141
Immigration to U.S. (postwar), 107
Imperialism, and American policy, 31–32
    Arab fears of, 244
    in Middle East, 236–237
    See also Neocolonialism
Imports, U.S. of petroleum, 13–14
    U.S. of strategic metals, 11–12
    See also International Trade
Income, U.S. national, 14
Independence as goal of foreign policy, 1–2
India, Republic of, African views of, 318
    anti-Westernism in, 320
    conflict with Red China, 320–327
    congressional attitudes toward, 104
    defense expenditures of, 324
    domestic problems, 319
    foreign aid to, 384
    and Goa, 318
    and Kashmir, 326
    mediatory role of, 318–319
    and "neutrality," 317–318
    and nonalignment, 315–326
    political forces in, 319–320
    and Sino-Soviet dispute, 325
    U.S. aid, 321, 324
    U.S. opinion toward, 136
    U.S. wheat for, 120 n.
Indians, American, 31
"Indirect aggression," 235
"Indirect lobbying," 144
    See also Lobbying; Pressure Groups

Indochina, French defeat in, 329
    settlement of 1954, 25
    See also Vietnam, Republic of South
Industry in U.S., 14–15
Information and foreign policy, 48–49
Informational activities of foreign policy, 85
    See also Propaganda
Intelligence and foreign policy, 85–86
Inter-American System, 270–271
    See also Latin America; Organization of American States
Interest groups and foreign policy, 137–143
    See also Lobbying; Public opinion
"Interim appointments" by President, 47, 94
International Atomic Energy Agency, 443–444
International Cooperation Administration, 200
    See also Foreign aid
International Labor Organization, 395
International law, 393–394
    See also United Nations
International organization, see Disarmament; United Nations
International trade, East-West trade, 368–370
    and European Common Market, 363–366
    expansion of U.S., 389–390
    general agreement on tariffs and trade, 362
    in interwar period, 359
    liquidity in, 371
    principles of, 366–367
    "protectionism" vs. free trade, 366–367
    strategic imports of U.S., 359
    U.S. balance-of-payments, 364, 385–390
    and U.S. policy, 358–390
    U.S. tariff policies, 360–366
    and underdeveloped countries, 364, 406
"Interventionism," goals of, 26
    and isolationism, 35 n.
Investigations, legislative, 105–106
"Investment Guaranty" program, 377
Investments,
    guaranty program, 377
    in Latin America, 286
    U.S. in Africa, 248
    U.S. in Latin America, 264
    U.S. private overseas, 376–377
"Investment Survey" program, 377
Iraq, communism in, 242–243
    coup by Kassim, 235
    defects from Baghdad Pact, 235
Irish-Americans, 141–142
Iron Curtain, 156–157
Iron ore reserves in U.S., 11
Islam, and African socialism, 251–252
    and Arab nationalism, 236–237
    and Arab socialism, 238
    and communism, 242
Isolationism, decline of U.S., 37
    geographic roots of, 8–10
    and immigrant groups, 141
    in interwar period, 24–25
    in 1930s, 132–134
    prerequisites of, 194–197
    sources of American, 34–36
Israel, and Baghdad Pact, 233
    borders of, 231
    and conflict with Arabs, 227–232
    invades Sinai, 240
    lobbying in behalf of, 145

Israel (*Continued*)
  Zionist support for, 142
      See also Arab-Israeli dispute; Palestine
Italian-Americans, 141
Ivory Coast, 253 n.

Jackson, Henry M., 82, 108, 417
James, William, 32
Japan, American attitudes toward, 32
  American conflict with, 24, 160
  and European economic cooperation, 202–203
  "Gentleman's agreement" with, 44
  and Open Door policy, 301
  opening of, 67, 299
  peace treaty with, 93, 328
  productivity in, 389–390
  Russian relations with, 159
  Senate views toward, 107
  trade with China, 370
  and U.S., 299
Japanese Peace Conference (1951), 56
Japanese-Americans in World War II, 51
Jay Treaty (1794), 94
Jefferson, Thomas, 26, 36, 194
Jenner, William, 67
Jessup, Philip, 94
Jewish Agency, 145
      See also Zionism; Israel
Jewish groups and Israel, 142
Jiménez, Marcos P., 274
Johnson, Lyndon B., and Alliance for Progress, 283–284
  and Arab-Israeli dispute, 232
  foreign aid budget, 374
  and U.S. aid to Europe, 200
  views on Latin America, 287
Joint Chiefs of Staff, continuing problems, 78
  duties of, 69
      See also Defense, Department of; National Security Council
Jordan and U.S., 244
Jordan river waters, 231

Kashmir dispute, 104, 326
Kassim, Karim, 238
      See also Iraq
Kellogg-Briand Pact (1928), 39, 427
Kennan, George F., 36, 72–73, 87, 104, 112, 159, 170
  and containment policy, 197
  and re-examination of U.S. policy, 449–457
  views on legalism-moralism, 451
  views on national security, 2
  views on negotiations with Communists, 456
  views on Open Door policy, 453–455
  views on state behavior, 453
Kennedy, John F., and advisers, 71
  and aid by European countries, 200
  and Alliance for Progress, 282–283
  and "Atlantic partnership," 224
  and balance-of-payments, 389
  and "Bay of Pigs" invasion, 50–51, 293, 410–411
  and bipartisanship, 115
  and budgetary process, 75
  and career ambassadors, 60
  and civil rights, 348
  and colonialism, 409

Kennedy, John F. (*Continued*)
  and communism in Cuba, 292–295
  and coordination of executive policy, 80–82
  and "country team," 61
  and Cuban missile crisis, 118 n.
  decision-making by, 72–73
  and disarmament, 422, 434
  and foreign aid, 379, 381
  and goals of U.S. policy, 1
  and Himalayan crisis, 326
  and legislative opposition, 95
  and military power, 66
  and military reorganization, 79
  and national unity, 116
  and nonalignment, 259
  and nuclear test treaty, 116
  and "realities" of power, 39
  and Secretary of State, 53
  and Trade Expansion Act, 364–366
  and UN "Decade of Development," 406
  and UN financial crisis, 418–419
  and U.S. commitment to NATO, 216
  views of Chinese communism, 310
  views on Cuba, 283
  views on disarmament, 433
  views on Dominican Republic, 274–275
  views on interest-groups, 140
  views on Latin America, 282
  views on NATO, 211
  views on nuclear test-ban, 431
  views on underdeveloped countries, 381
  views on the UN, 418
  and wheat sale to USSR, 127 n.
Key, V. O., Jr., 130, 146
Khrushchev, Nikita, and East-West trade, 368
  and Mao Tse-tung, 306–314
  views on Arab nationalism, 243
  views on capitalism, 168
  views on disarmament, 437
      See also Communism; "Peaceful coexistence"; Sino-Soviet dispute
Kinter, William H., 87
Knowland, William F., 108
Kohn, Hans, 36
Korea, Republic of South, defense treaty, 329
Korean War, Chinese intervention, 303
  Indian role in, 318–319
  public opinion toward, 135
  and the UN, 414–415
  U.S. goals in, 456
  U.S. intervention in, 102
Kurds, 242
Kuwait, oil in, 233

Labor unions, 139, 389
LaFollette, Robert, 95
Lansing, Robert, 44, 267
Laos, Asian views of, 334
  and Communist China, 304
  crisis in, 333–334
  neutralization of, 330
Latin America, Alliance for Progress, 281–286
  British interests in, 196–197
  communism in, 287–296
  Cuban missile crisis, 291–296
  dictatorships in, 273–279
  economic growth, 264, 283–284
  economic problems of, 358

Latin America (*Continued*)
European intervention in, 194–195
and *Fidelismo*, 295–296
"good neighbor" policy, 269
Guatemalan crisis, 288–291
illiteracy in, 282
income in, 282
Inter-American System, 270–271
investments in, 264, 283, 286, 376–377
military influence in, 277–279
and Monroe Doctrine, 265–268
Nixon tour of, 358
Panama crisis, 271–273
Pan-American movement, 269–270
political trends in, 277–279
population in, 264
population growth in, 282
population of, 16–17
remoteness from U.S., 9
revolution in, 274
strategic importance of, 264–265, 287–288
trade with U.S., 264
U.S. aid to, 279–287
U.S. "interventionism" in, 268
U.S. policy toward, 264–296
League of Nations, and disarmament, 422–423, 426–427
economic and social activities, 395
establishment, 394
organs, 394–395
and U.S., 33, 113
weaknesses, 394–395
Lebanon, U.S. intervention in, 235
Legislation, *see* Congress
Legislation, President's role in, 50
Leites, Nathan, 153 n., 174–175
Lenin, Nikolai, 168, 344
Lerche, Charles, 146
Lerner, Max, 35 n.
Levi, Werner, 300
Liberia and U.S., 245
Lie, Trygve, 412
Life expectancy, in non-Western societies, 17–18
in U.S., 17–18
"Limited war," 191–192
in South Vietnam, 332–333
and U.S., 70, 79
Lincoln, Abraham, 45, 52
Lippmann, Walter, 23, 24, 25, 163, 450–457
Litvinov, Maxim, 162, 431
Lobbying, by foreign interests, 143–145
and foreign policy, 137–143
"indirect," 143–144
by Jewish groups, 145
regulation of, 145
See *also* Pressure groups; Public opinion
Lodge, Henry C., Jr., 410
Lodge, Henry Cabot, 113
"Lodge corollary," 268
London Disarmament Conference (1930), 427
Longfellow, Henry Wadsworth, 36
Lovett, Robert, 67, 75, 78, 87
Lowell, James Russell, 35
Lumumba, Patrice, 255

MacArthur, Douglas, 32, 67, 106, 125
McCamy, James, 137

McCarran, Pat, 107
McCarthy, Joseph, 48–49
McCloy, John J., 310
Machiavelli, Niccolò, 457–459
Mackinder, Sir Halford, 10, 179
McKinley, William, 94, 116
McNamara, Robert, 75, 125, 188–190, 433
Malaysia, and Indonesia, 322
Mali, 254
Malthus, Thomas, 16
Manchuria, Russian goals in, 155
"Manifest Destiny," 27–28
Mansfield, Mike, 332, 418
Mao Tse-Tung, 306–314
Marshall, George C., 102, 198
Marshall Plan, *see* European Recovery Program
Marshall, Samuel L. A., 187
Matson, T. B., 468
Marx, Karl, 153–154
See *also* Communism
"Massive retaliation," 215–216
See *also* North Atlantic Treaty Organization
Mba, Leon, 256
Means of foreign policy, 5–6
Meany, George, 389
Metals, strategic reserves in U.S., 11–12
"Metropolitan areas" in U.S., 18
Mercator map projection, 8
Merrow, Chester E., 91
Mexican War, 28
Mexico, U.S. policy toward, 275
Middle East, and communism, 235–236
defense of, 233–236
defined, 227 n.
oil in, 232–233
"power vacuum" in, 239
Russian goals in, 155–156
strategic importance, 232–236
unrest in, 236
See *also* Arab world; Arab-Israeli dispute
Mikoyan, Anastas, 292
Militarism and capitalism, 168
Military establishment, and American society, 75–78
American views of, 32
and budgetary process, 73–75
and Congress, 100–102
constitutional restrictions, 75–76
demobilization after World War II, 32
and foreign policy, 66–80
and "limited war," 70
"missile gap," 79
and political questions, 77
President's power over, 45–46
reorganization of, 67–70
unification of, 67–70, 78–79
See *also* Defense, Department of
"Military mind," 76–77
Military power, communist use of, 174
of East and West, 187–192
and foreign policy, 5–7
intangibles of, 189
of U.S., 11–12
Military vulnerability of U.S., 18
Morgenthau, Hans J., 449–469
Morocco and U.S., 241
Moscow Conference (1943), 396
Munich Conference (1938), 163
Murrow, Edward R., 346, 353

Mutual Defense Assistance Control Act (1951), 369
Mutual Security Program, 200
    See also Foreign aid
Minority groups and foreign policy, 137–138
Missiles, strength of East and West, 188
    threat to U.S. security, 9–10
"Missile gap," 100
Mitchell, Billy, 68
Monroe, James, 34, 265
Monroe Doctrine, 194–195
    corollaries of, 267–268
    evolution of, 265–268
    goals of, 451
    meaning, 266–267
    philosophy of, 24
    proclaimed unilaterally, 36–37
"Monrovia group," 256
    See also Africa, unification
Montevideo Conference (1933), 270
Montgomery, Viscount, 190
Moore, Barrington, Jr., 176
Moore, Ben T., 446
Moos, Malcolm, 450
"Moral equivalent for War," 32–34
Moralism, and morality, 27
    roots of in U.S., 29–30
    in U.S. policy, 27–30, 451–452
Morality, communist views of, 169–170
    and diplomatic conduct, 467–469
    and Machiavellian thought, 458
    and national interest, 452–453
    and U.S. policy, 30–34, 452–453
    and world law, 468–469

Nasser, Gamal Abdel, and Arab socialism, 238
    arms agreement with communists, 240
    and communism, 242
    congressional attitudes toward, 104
    and defense of Middle East, 239
    nationalizes Suez Canal, 240
    views on communism, 243
    views on nonalignment, 238–239
National Association of Manufacturers, 139
National character, importance of, 21–24
    limitations in study of, 22–23
    and U.S. policies, 21–40
National Farmers Union, 139
National Grange, 139
"National interest," 451–457
    concept evaluated, 464–466
    determination of, 452–453
    and morality, 452–453
    and other policy goals, 465–466
    philosophical roots of, 457–459
    role of concept in statecraft, 453–457
    value of concept, 464–466
    weaknesses of concept, 458–463
    See also Realism
National Security Act (1947), 68
    See also Defense, Department of
National Security Council, criticisms of, 87–88
    decision-making by, 71
    and Defense Department, 69
    establishment, 70
    and intelligence activities, 86
    members, 70
    problems of, 72–73
    purposes, 70–71

National Security Council (*Continued*)
    responsibility to President, 48
Nationalism, in Arab world, 236–238
    in Asia, 227–228, 314–315
    and neutralism, 314–319
    in Panama, 271–272
Nazi-Soviet Pact (1939), 163, 176
Neagle, *In re* (1890), 52
Near East, *see* Middle East
Negotiations, President's powers of, 43–44
"Negritude," 251
Nehru, Jawaharlal, and democracy, 322–323
    influence in Asia, 316
    and nonalignment, 315–326
    and Sino-Indian crisis, 320–327
    and Western defense planning, 325–326
    See also India, Republic of
"Neo-colonialism," 252
    See also Colonialism
Neutralism, in Africa, 254–258
    American views of, 256–257
    in Arab world, 238–239
    congressional attitudes toward, 104
    and NATO, 219–220
    U.S. attitudes to, 30
    See also Neutrality; Nonalignment
Neutralist countries, and E.E.C., 207 n.
    and the UN, 399
Neutrality, in interwar period, 132–134
    and "nonalignment," 239, 254, 317–318
"Neutralization" of Southeast Asia, 333–334
New Zealand and U.S., 328–329
Ngo Dinh Diem, 330
Niebuhr, Reinhold, 450, 459, 464
Nigeria, 259
Nitze, Paul, 326
Nixon, Richard M., 326
    and foreign policy in elections, 125
    tour of Latin America, 358
    as Vice-President, 49–50
    views on Aswan Dam, 240 n.
Nkrumah, Kwame, 408
    and nonalignment, 254–255
    views on communism, 258
    views on neo-colonialism, 252
    views on socialism, 251
Nonalignment, African versions of, 254–258
    American views of, 241, 321
    Arab conception, 238–239
    in Asia, 314–326
    changing U.S. views of, 256–259
    and communism, 318
    and disarmament, 440–441
    diverse conceptions of, 255, 316
    and domestic political forces, 319–320
    and "equidistance," 317
    as force in UN, 411–412
    and foreign aid, 324
    growth of, 315–316
    in India, 315–326
    "levels" of, 322, 326–327
    meaning of, 239, 316–318
    neutralist views of communism, 355
    and "neutrality," 239, 254, 317–318
    political forces sustaining, 319–320
    positive goals of, 320
    psychological roots, 316–317
    and Red China, 322–323

Nonalignment (*Continued*)
  security considerations in, 321
  and Sino-Indian crisis, 320–327
  sources of, 319–320
  Soviet views of, 323
  State Department views of, 243
  and the UN, 399
  U.S. policies toward, 239–243
  varieties of, 239 n., 318–319
Nonpartisanship, *see* Bipartisanship
"North Atlantic Quarter-Sphere," 10
North Atlantic Treaty Organization, and Africa, 253
  Arab views of, 232
  and colonialism, 408
  "credibility" of, 215–216
  defense strategy of, 215–216
  and East-West trade, 369–370
  force de frappe, 217–219
  "forward strategy" of, 216
  "integrated" forces, 212
  "limited war" by, 215–216
  and Middle East, 233
  military power of, 187 n., 214–216
  "multinational force" in, 219
  and neutralism, 219–220
  nuclear "sharing" in, 217–219
  organization of, 209–220
  origins of, 209–210
  and Portugal, 318
  problems of, 214–220
  strategic implications of, 211–212
  U.S. commitment under, 210–212, 216–217
  "Vandenberg resolution," 93
"Nuclear balance of terror," 190–192
Nuclear energy, "Atoms-for-Peace," 443–446
  cost of, 14
  development in U.S., 14
  in Europe, 203–204
  expansion of, 446–448
  global development, 14
Nuclear "fallout," 439 n.
"Nuclear sharing" by U.S. and Britain, 217
Nuclear tests in Africa, 254
Nuclear test-ban agreement (1963), 310, 438–439
Nuclear war and communism, 168
Nuclear weapons, development in World War II, 102
  effect on power balance, 6–7
  proliferation of, 439
  and Sino-Indian dispute, 323–324
  strength of East and West, 188
Nyasaland, 259
Nye Committee, 105, 132
Nyerere, Julius, 251–252

Office of War Information, 347
Oil, Middle East reserves, 232–233
  Soviet "dumping," 243
  in Venezuela, 288
  U.S. holdings in Middle East, 232–233
Olney, Richard, 268
"Open Door Policy," 299–301, 453–454
"Open Skies" proposal (1955), 437
  See also Disarmament
Organization of African Unity, 256
Organization of American States and Cuban Crisis, 293–296

Organization of American States (*Continued*)
  foreign aid by, 281
  and Guatemala, 289–290
  and Panama crisis, 272–273
Organization for European Economic Cooperation (OEEC), 199, 202–203
  Development Assistance Committee of, 384
  economic problems of, 203
  foreign aid activities, 200
  U.S. support of, 203
Oum, Boun, 334
"Overseas Chinese," 312

Pact of Paris (1928), 427
Pakistan, *détente* with China, 322
  and SEATO, 326 n.
Palestine, partition of, 228–229
  refugees in, 230–231
  truce in, 230
  war in, 229–230
  See also Arab-Israeli dispute
Panama Canal, *see* Panama crisis, 1964
Panama crisis (1964), 271–273
Pan-American movement, 269–270
Pan-American Union, 269–271
  See also Organization of American States
Pan-Arabism, 237
  See also Arab nationalism; Arab unity
Pan-Slavists, 157
Pâres, Bernard, 156
Partisanship, in foreign policy, *see* Bipartisanship
Passman, Otto E., 98 n.
Pathet Lao, 333–334
  See also Laos
Pax Americana, 3, 197
Pax Britannica, 159, 196, 462
Peace Corps, 54, 351
"Peaceful co-existence," 167–168, 174
  See also Communism
Peffer, Nathaniel, 328
People-to-People program, 351
Perkins, Dexter, 30–31, 131, 279
Perkins, Dr. James, 78
Permanent Court of Arbitration, 394
Perón, Juan, 274, 276
"Personal representatives" in foreign affairs, 47
Peter the Great, 154
Petroleum, 13–14
  See also Middle East; Oil
Philippines, Republic of, defense treaty with, 329
  as problem in U.S. policy, 455–456
  U.S. acquisition of, 24, 160, 301
Phillips, Cabell, 119
Philosophy of foreign affairs, 449–469
Philotheus, 157
Phouma, Souvanna, 333–334
Policy Planning Council, 61–62
"Political questions" and Supreme Court, 42
Political system, U.S., and Palestine, 229
  President's role in, 50
  and war, 25
  See also Bipartisanship
Polk, James K., 268
"Polycentricity," 310
  See also Communism; Nonalignment
Poole, DeWitt, 159
Population, "aging" of U.S., 18
  character of U.S., 17–19

Population (*Continued*)
  children in U.S., 18–19
  Chinese, 309–310
  as determinant of power, 15–19
  education of U.S., 19
  growth in U.S., 15–17
  health of U.S., 18–19
  rural-urban distribution in U.S., 18
  size of various countries, 15–17
  suburbs in U.S., 18
  trends in Latin America, 264
  world growth rates, 16–17
Population problems, and international relations, 17
  in underdeveloped countries, 16–17
Portugal, colonialism in Africa, 253
  U.S. views on, 253, 409
"Positive neutralism," *see* Neutralism; Nonalignment
Potsdam Agreement (1945), 171
Power, national, American attitudes toward, 5, 25–26
  as central concept in international relations, 450
  definition of, 5
  and disarmament, 423
  economic elements of, 15
  economic elements of U.S., 10–15
  and foreign policy, 67–68
  and geography, 7–10
  importance of concept, 454–455
  instrumental use of, 462–463
  intangibles of, 7
  limits of American, 454
  measurement of, 466–467
  military aspects of U.S. and USSR, 187–192
  and morality, 453
  as "Old World" concept, 455
  population as element in, 15–19
  "potential" and "in being," 6
  relativity of, 6–7
  varieties of, 6–7
Pragmatism in U.S. power, 39–40, 450
President, and advisers, 71
  and attack on NATO area, 216–217
  and bipartisanship, 118–119
  and budgetary process, 73–75, 100
  and coordination of executive policy, 80–82
  and East-West trade, 369
  and Eisenhower Doctrine, 235
  "emergency powers" of, 51–53
  and "First Secretary" of Cabinet, 63
  historical powers of, 48–51
  as legislative leader, 50, 95
  and National Security Council, 70–71
  as political leader, 50, 121
  power to commit nation, 50–51
  powers in foreign affairs, 43–53
  powers in war, 102–103
  and public opinion, 49–50, 133–135
  recognition power, 46–48
  and Secretary of State, 53, 62–63
  and trade agreements, 361–362
  and Trade Expansion Act, 364–366
  use of Foreign Service, 57
Press conferences, 49
Press and State Department, 56
Pressure groups, and foreign interests, 143–145
  and Palestine, 229
  and Trade Expansion Act, 365–366
Principles in U.S. policy, 23–29

Private enterprise and U.S. aid, 104
The Prize Cases, 45
Progress and hope in American society, 37–40
Propaganda, American activities in, 346–351
  American attitudes toward, 352–356
  and civil rights, 353–354
  Communist activities, 340–341
  cultural aspects of, 352
  definitions of, 339
  and disarmament, 424
  evaluation of, 348–351
  and force, 339
  and foreign policy, 338–356
  goals of, 339
  and pressure groups, 354
  private activities in, 351–352
  techniques of, 339–340
  U.S. agencies engaged in, 85
  in World War I, 339
Psychological warfare, 338–356
    See also Propaganda
Public opinion, agricultural groups, 139
  American views of war, 25
  apathy of, 136–137
  and Axis threat, 25
  business groups, 139
  "cross-pressures" in, 140
  cycles in, 135–136
  definitions of, 129
  determination of, 148
  diversity of, 130
  elements of, 130
  and foreign aid, 381
  and foreign interests, 143–145
  and foreign policy, 129–149
  formulation of, 131–132
  groups in, 137–143
  importance of, 129
  labor groups, 139
  minority groups, 137–138
  moods in, 26
  naive views of, 26–27
  nature of "opinions," 131
  "neutrality era," 132–134
  President's control over, 49–50
  process of, 130–132
  "publics" in, 130–131
  racial minorities, 140–143
  religious groups, 139–140
  sectionalism, 145–146
  State Department studies of, 56, 146–148
  and the UN, 412–413, 418–419
  Utopian views of, 26
  views toward other societies, 26–27
  views toward power, 25–26
  voter apathy in, 131
Public opinion polls, 131, 133–134
"Punta del Este" conference (1962), 293

Racial conflicts, 353–354
Radio Free Europe, 351
Radio Liberation, 351
Raw materials, consumption in U.S., 11–12
  in Latin America, 265–266
"Realism," philosophy of, 450–469
  assessment of philosophy, 458–469
  contributions of, 453–457

Realism (*Continued*)
and Marxism, 460–461
philosophical roots of, 457–459
Reciprocal trade, *see* Trade Agreements Act; Trade Expansion Act
Recognition, Congress' role in, 47–48
President's powers of, 46–48
U.S. of communist China, 303
U.S. of Israel, 230
U.S. policy on, 275–276
U.S. of USSR, 162
"Regional" organizations and State Department, 57
"Regionalism" in U.S., 145–146
Renner, George T., 8
Republican Party, "advisers" to State Department, 124
and wheat sale to USSR, 127 n.
Reston, James, 78
"Revisionism" in American history, 25, 132–133
Rhodesia, Northern, 252
Ridgway, Matthew B., 67, 74, 77
Rio Treaty of Reciprocal Assistance (1947), 270
Rockefeller Foundation, 351
Rogers Act (1924), 58
Rome-Berlin-Tokyo Axis, 163
See also Axis Powers
Roosevelt, Franklin D., "destroyer deal" with Britain, 44
and "good neighbor" policy, 269
and Harry Hopkins, 47
and Japan, 32
and "neutrality" era, 132–134
and Palestine, 229
powers in World War II, 51
and public opinion, 49
"Quarantine speech," 133
and reciprocal trade, 361
Roosevelt, Theodore, 44, 153, 159–160, 268
"Roosevelt Corollary," 268
Rooney, John J., 98–100
Root-Takahira agreement (1908), 160
Rossiter, Clinton, 53
Rush-Bagot Agreement (1817), 425
Rusk, Dean, and foreign aid, 374, 382
views on communism in Middle East, 241
views on European unity, 223
views on global conflicts, 457
views on India, 323
views on nonalignment, 243
views on Red China, 310
views on Secretary of State, 62
views on UN financial crisis, 419
views on USSR, 310
Russell, Richard, 106
Russia, communist, *see* Union of Soviet Socialist Republics
Russia, tsarist, and American north-west, 195, 265
Asian goals of, 155
economic goals of, 154–155
expansionism of, 153–155
foreign policy goals of, 152–158
"historic mission," 155
imperialism in China, 300
Messianism in, 157–158
security needs of, 156–157
views of U.S., 158
and warm water ports, 155–156

Russian, tsarist (*Continued*)
and World War I, 154
xenophobia in, 156–157
Russian-Americans in U.S., 141
Russo-Japanese War, 155, 159–160

Sahara desert, oil in, 233
Salisbury, Harrison, 182
San Francisco Conference (1945), 397
Santos, Eduardo, 281
Schumann, Maurice, 208 n.
"Schumann Plan," 223
Secretary of Foreign Affairs, 62–63
Secretary of State, evaluation of office, 62–63
as "First Secretary," 62–63
and President, 53
role of, 53
subordinates of, 54–56
See also State, Department of
Sectionalism in U.S., 145–146
Security, American viewpoints on, 3, 24–25
concept of, 1–3
differing conceptions of, 2–3
See also National interest; Power
Security Council of the UN, 403
See also United Nations
Senate, of the U.S., and appointments, 46–47, 94
and appropriations, 101–102
and Axis peace treaties, 93
disunity in, 122
and North Atlantic Treaty, 210
role in treaty-making, 43–44, 92–94
and Treaty of Versailles, 93, 113
and the UN, 94
See also Congress
Senate Foreign Relations Committee, investigation of foreign lobbying, 143–145
and NATO, 93
Senghor, Leopold, 251
Separation of powers and foreign policy, 42–43
See also Bipartisanship
Seward, William H., 464
Sino-Indian crisis, cease-fire in, 321
Chinese goals in, 325
"escalation" of, 323–324
evolution of, 320–327
foreign aid after, 324
impact on India, 320–321
neutralist views of, 325
and nonalignment, 320–327
and SEATO, 324
Soviet views on, 311
U.S. intervention in, 324
Western aid to India, 321
Sino-Soviet conflict, 307–314
and India, 325
sources of, 307–310
U.S. assessment of, 310–311
Slavophils, 157
Smith, T. V., 453
Smith, Wilfred C., 237
Smoot-Hawley Tariff, 361
Socialism, in Africa, 251
in the USSR, 167 n.
See also Communism
Somalia, U.S. aid to, 248
Souers, Sidney W., 67, 74

South, changing views of U.S., 146
Southeast Asia Treaty Organization, Asian views of, 331–332
  and communism, 329–330
  defense obligations under, 329–330
  and NATO, 211, 329
  and Pakistan, 326 n.
  and Sino-Indian crisis, 324
  and South Vietnam, 330–335
  and subversion, 329–330
Soviet Union, *see* Union of Soviet Socialist Republics
Spykman, Nicholas, 7, 12
Stalin, Joseph, and capitalism, 172
  Chinese views of, 307
  and conflicts with capitalism, 169
  and "creative Marxism," 173
  death of, 61
  and pact with Hitler, 163
State, Department of, and Africa, 247
  appointment of ambassadors, 59–60
  Bureau of Educational and Cultural Affairs, 56
  Bureau of Intelligence Research, 56
    See also Central Intelligence Agency
  Bureau of International Organization Affairs, 57
  Bureau of Public Affairs, 56
  Bureau of Security and Consular Affairs, 56
  and Congress, 98–100
  control over information, 48–49
  Counselor of, 56
  "country desks," 54
  employees in, 53–54
  and foreign aid, 84–85
  Foreign Service, 57–59
  functions of, 53–54, 56
  geographical bureaus in, 56–57
  growth of, 53–54
  "joint career service" in, 73
  and legislative travel, 108–109
  liaison with Defense Department, 73
  mission to the UN, 409–410
  new responsibilities of, 53–54
  Office of Congressional Relations, 56, 115
  Office of International Organization Affairs, 409–410
  organization of, 53–59
  overseas responsibilities of, 57
  Policy Planning Council, 56, 61–62
  political responsibilities of, 56–57
  propaganda activities by, 346–347
  and public opinion, 146–148
  reorganization of, 58–59
  Secretary of State's role in, 62–63
  "Wriston report" on, 58–59
Stassen, Harold, 441
Steel production in U.S., 11
"Steel seizure case," 52–53
Stevenson, Adlai, as adviser to State Department, 124
  and "Bay of Pigs" invasion, 410–411
  views of Afro-Asian states, 403–404
  views of the UN, 418
"Stimson Doctrine" (1932), 451
Strategic Air Command, 188, 190–191
Strausz-Hupé, Robert, 450, 452
Strike Command, 192
Submarines, strength of East and West in, 188
  and U.S. security, 9–10

Suez crisis (1956), 235, 240–241
  See also Aswan High Dam; Egypt
"Sugar quota," Cuban, 292
Summit conferences, U.S. views of, 33–34
"SUNFED," 405
  See also Foreign aid; United Nations
Supreme Court, powers in foreign policy, 42
  and President's "emergency powers," 51–53
  views on President's control of information, 48
Switzerland and E.E.C., 209
Syria and communism, 242

Taber, John, 97
Taft, Robert A., 117, 124
Taft, William H., 394
Tanganyika, British intervention in, 256
Tannenbaum, Frank, 274, 450
Tariff Commission of U.S., 84
Tariffs, evolution of U.S., 360–361
  "protectionism" in U.S., 361
  protectionist arguments for, 366–367
Taylor, Maxwell D., 78
Tehran Conference (1943), 396
Thant, U., 294, 404, 412
Third International, 162
  See also Communism; USSR
"Third Rome" idea, 157
Tilsit, Treaty of (1807), 154
Tocqueville, Alexis de, 112
Touré, Sékou, 354
  and African socialism, 251
  and communism, 250
  and nonalignment, 254
  views on colonialism, 252
Toynbee, Arnold, 3
Trade, by European Economic Community, 204–205
  by European nations, 199
  and national security, 3
  U.S. with Latin America, 264
    See also International trade
Trade Agreements Act, 361–362
Trade Expansion Act of 1962, 204
  and domestic industries, 367
  and European Economic Community, 364–366
  interest groups, 138–139
  provisions of, 364–366
Treasury, Department of, and foreign policy, 74, 83
Treaty-making power, 43–44, 92–94
Treaty of Portsmouth (1905), 159–160
"Troops-to-Europe" debate, 45–46
Truman, Harry S., and Air Force budget, 100
  appointments by, 94
  and bipartisanship, 116
  dismisses Gen. MacArthur, 32, 106
  "emergency powers" of, 51–52
  and Greek-Turkish Aid Program, 51, 198
  and immigration bill, 107
  and Korean War, 45, 414–415
  and military reorganization, 68
  and Palestine, 229
  and the press, 49
  and propaganda activities, 347
  seizes steel mills, 52–53
  and Zionists, 142
Truman Committee, 105

Tucker, Robert C., 169
"Tunisian crisis" (1961), 242
Turkey, communist threat to, 197
Turner, Frederick J., 38

Underdeveloped countries, 16–17
    capital requirements, 377
    and nuclear power, 445
    population problems of, 16–17
    and trade with West, 364
    U.S. investments in, 376–377
        See also Foreign aid; International trade
Union des patries, 223
Union of Soviet Socialist Republics, agricultural
        problems in, 185–186
    air-missile power of, 188
    alliance with Red China, 304–307
    Allied "interventions" in, 161
    anti-Semitism in, 355 n.
    and Arab world, 241–243
    and Atoms-for-Peace, 444–445
    and "Baruch Plan," 428–430
    civil war in, 161
    collectivization in, 185–186
    and colonialism, 408–409
    communism in, 161, 167 n.
        See also Communism
    and "conventional" weapons, 436
    and Cuba, 292–296
    disarmament proposals, 424
    and Eastern Europe, 29, 47–48, 180–182
    economic problems in, 183–187
    and Egypt, 243
    empire of, 178–179
    and European Recovery program, 199
    First Five Year Plan, 162, 183
    and foreign aid by, 323, 360, 364
    geopolitical base of, 178–182
    goals of, 152–158
    ground forces of, 187–188
    and Guatemala, 288–291
    and Guinea, 250
    and Hungarian Revolt, 464
    ideological goals of, 172–178
    and India, 323–324
    industry in, 182–183
    and Kurds, 242
    labor shortage in, 184–185
    and Laos, 333–334
    and "limited war," 191–192
    military threat of, 179–180, 187–192
    missile strength of, 9–10
    Nazi-Soviet Pact, 163
    negotiations with, 456
    and nuclear weapons, 188, 308, 430
    oil "dumping" by, 243
    population of, 16–17
    propaganda activities, 338, 344–346
    recognition by U.S., 44
    security interests of, 180–181
    Seven Year Plan, 183, 185
    and Sino-Soviet conflict, 170–171, 307–314
    socialism in, 167 n.
    space technology, 343
    trade policies, 359–360, 368–370
    transportation system, 185
    and Tunisian crisis, 242

Union of Soviet Socialist Republics (Continued)
    and the UN, 400, 419
    and U.S. (interwar), 158–164
    wartime destruction in, 183
    wheat purchases in U.S., 127 n.
    and world communism, 170–171
United Nations, accomplishments, 399–400, 418
    Afro-Asian influence, 399, 402–404
    American views of, 415–416, 418–419
    antecedents in 19th century, 393–394
    Atomic Energy Commission, 435
    and Axis peace treaty, 398
    and "Bay of Pigs" crisis, 410–411
    bipartisanship toward, 114
    and cold war, 413–417
    and colonial conflicts, 398–399, 407–409
    communist Chinese admission, 48, 312
    Conference on Trade and Development (1964),
        406
    Congo crisis, 402
    and Cuban missile crisis, 294–295, 412
    "Decade of Development," 406
    Disarmament Commission, 435–436
    Economic and Social Council, 403–405
    Emergency Force, 402
    establishment of, 396
    expanded membership, 402
    Expanded Program for Technical Assistance, 385,
        405
    financial crisis in, 417–419
    foreign aid activities, 385, 405–406
    General Assembly, 400–404
    and genocide, 416
    and great powers, 396, 398
    and Guatemala, 290–291
    and human rights, 406–407
    "interim assembly" plan, 401
    International Atomic Energy Agency, 443–444
    and Korean War, 414–415
    and League of Nations, 394–395
    legislative opposition to, 108
    and "open diplomacy," 412–413
    and Palestine, 229
    principles of, 397–399
    propaganda, 413
    and public opinion, 412–413
    San Francisco Conference, 397
    Secretary General, 412
    Security Council, 399–400
    and sovereignty, 397–398
    Soviet vetoes in, 400
    Special Fund, 385, 405
    specialized agencies, 397 n., 404
    and State Department, 57
    structure of, 396–397
    study of economic growth rates, 17
    and Suez crisis, 240, 402
    "Uniting for Peace Resolution," 401
    U.S. appointments to, 94
    and U.S. foreign policy, 393–419
    U.S. support of, 33
    veto in Security Council, 397, 400
    voting in, 396–397, 400–402
    wartime studies of, 396
    and world peace, 398
United Nations Participation Act, 44
United Nations Relief and Rehabilitation Adminis-
        tration, 198

United Nations Relief and Works Agency for Palestine Refugees, 230–231
United States, and Africa, 245–259
  and Afro-Asian countries in UN, 402–404
  agricultural exports, 365
  agricultural production in, 14–15, 185–186
  air-missile power of, 188
  and Alliance for Progress, 281–286
  American attitudes toward themselves, 38–39
  anticolonialism of, 355
  and Arab-Israeli conflict, 227–232
  and "Atlantic partnership," 223–224
  and Asia, 299–335
  and Aswan High Dam, 240
  and "Atoms-for-Peace," 443–446
  attitudes toward Europe, 23–24
  attitudes toward security, 24–25
  attitudes toward war, 23–27
  and Axis Powers, 29, 395
  balance-of-payments, 364, 385–390
  bankruptcy in foreign policy, 24–25
  belief in progress, 37–40
  and British power, 196–197
  and Canada, 265
  "classless society" in, 23–24
  colonial policies of, 31–32
  and colonialism, 228, 252–254, 407–409
  and communist China, 302–314
  communist view of, 169
  competitive position of, 389–390
  Constitution and foreign affairs, 42–48
  as creditor nation, 359
  and Cuban missile crisis, 291–296
  defense alliances of, 211–213
  and disarmament, 422–443
  disunity in foreign policy, 112–113
  domestic aspects of foreign policy, 360
  domestic concerns of, 34–35
  and East-West trade, 368–370
  and Eastern Europe, 180
  economic prospects in, 15, 183–187
  education in, 19
  and E.E.C., 201–209, 222–224, 363–366
  ends and means of foreign policy, 24–25
  expansionism of, 27–28, 31–32
  expediency in foreign policy, 39–40
  exports by, 389
  and foreign aid, 372–376
  foreign aid to Latin America, 279–287
  foreign attitudes toward, 352
  foreign economic policies of, 358–390
  and "foreign entanglements," 36–37
  and Formosa, 303–304
  geography of and foreign policy, 7–10
  Gross National Product, 14
  groups in, 137–143
  and General Agreement on Tariff and Trade, 362
  and Geneva accord (1954), 334 n.
  and Guatemala, 288–291
  and Guinea, 250
  health levels in, 18–19
  and human rights, 406–407
  immigrants in, 140–141
  industrial production in, 14–15
  intervention in USSR, 161
  investments overseas, 376–377
  isolation of, 8–9
  isolationism in, 34–37

United States (Continued)
  and Japan, 299, 370
  and Kellogg-Briand Pact, 427
  and Korean War, 414–415
  and Laos, 333–334
  and Latin America, 264–296
  and League of Nations, 395
  and Lebanese crisis, 235
  life expectancy in, 17–18
  and "limited war," 70, 191–192
  and the Middle East, 227–244
  militarism in, 32
  military power of, 187–192
  and Monroe Doctrine, 265–268
  moralism in foreign policy, 27–30
  morality in foreign policy, 30–34
  national character of, 21–40
  and Nationalist China, 299–301
  and NATO, 209–220
  naval strength of, 188–189
  and neutralist role in disarmament, 440–441
  and "neutralization" of Southeast Asia, 333–334
  as "new society," 35–36
  nuclear energy in, 14
  nuclear "sharing" by, 217–219
  and nuclear test-ban agreement, 438–439
  oil holdings in Middle East, 232–233
  optimism in, 39
  and Panama crisis, 271–273
  and partnership with Britain, 208–209
  "peaceful co-existence" with, 168
  philosophy of foreign affairs, 449–469
  population of, 15–19
  productivity in, 389–390
  propaganda activities, 338
  public opinion in, 26
  raw materials in, 11–13
  recognition policy of, 275
  re-examination of post-war policy, 449–457
  "reformist" impulses in, 454
  "revisionism" in, 25
  revolutionary tradition, 356
  and Russo-Japanese War, 159–160
  and SEATO, 329–330
  "second strike" capacity of, 190–191
  and Sino-Indian crisis, 320–327
  and Sino-Soviet conflict, 307–314
  social conflicts in, 23–24
  and South Vietnam, 330–335
  strategic imports of, 359
  and SUNFED, 405–406
  tariff policies, 360–362
  territorial acquisitions by, 31–32, 37
  trade with Latin America, 264
  and the UN, 33, 393–419
  and underdeveloped nations, 36
  as "universal nation," 36
  and USSR (interwar), 158–164
  views of communist Revolution, 160–161
  views of tsarist Russia, 158–159
  wartime political goals of, 456
  and Western Europe, 194–224
  and World Court, 395
United States Chamber of Commerce, 139
United States Information Agency, budget, 347–348, 353
  establishment, 85, 347
  evaluation of, 348–351

United States Information Agency (*Continued*)
  goals, 347
  overseas activities, 85, 347–348
  and public opinion, 352–353
  Voice of America, 348–350
Urrutia, Manuel, 292
Utopianism, and Marxism, 460–461
  and U.S. policy, 454

Vandenberg, Arthur H., 43, 93, 97, 114, 116, 121
"Vandenberg Resolution," 93, 210
  See also North Atlantic Treaty Organization
Venezuela, oil in, 288
  revolution in, 274
Versailles, Treaty of, 93–94, 113
Veterans organizations, 139
Vice-President and foreign policy, 49–50
Vinson, Carl, 80
"Vietcong," 330–335
  See also Vietnam, Republic of South
Viet Minh, 330
Vietnam, Republic of South, crisis in, 330–335
  disunity in U.S. policy, 80–82, 120
  "expansion" of war in, 332–333
  nationalism in, 333
  "neutralization" of, 330–331, 333–334
  political instability in, 330
  and SEATO, 331–332
  U.S. alternatives in, 332–335
  U.S. intervention in, 102
"Voice of America," 85, 348–350
  See also United States Information Agency
Volta River project, 258

Wallace, Henry A., 116, 119
War, American attitudes toward, 23–27
  American goals in, 30–31
  "declaration" of, 45, 102–103
  and diplomacy, 25
  "limited," 191–192
  "moral equivalent" for, 32–34
  participation by U.S. in, 30–31
  and political problems, 25, 456
  U.S. terms for enemies, 31
  viewed as "aberration," 25
"War powers" of President, 51–53
Warburg, James P., 457
Washington, George, 194

Washington Naval Armaments Conference (1921), 426–427
Weinberg, Albert K., 34
West, industrial levels in, 17
Western Europe, *see* Europe, Western
Western European Union, 221–222
Western hemisphere, distances in, 9
  U.S. policies in, 264–296
  See also Latin America
Wheat, U.S. sale to USSR, 127 n., 185–186
White, Henry, 93, 113, 116
White, William S., 106, 108, 121
Williams, G. Mennen, 249
Willkie, Wendell, 124
Wilson, Charles E., 48–49, 434, 436
Wilson, Woodrow, approach to foreign policy, 451–452
  idealism of, 452
  and Mexico, 275
  powers in World War I, 52
  and Treaty of Versailles, 93
World Bank, 384
World Court, 395
"World revolution," 168–169, 170, 177–178
  See also Communism
World War I, American disillusionment after, 454
  American views of, 29
  propaganda in, 339
  Russian goals in, 154
  Russian withdrawal from, 161
World War II, destruction in USSR, 183
  executive agreements in, 44
  legislative investigations during, 105
  political questions in, 66–67
  propaganda in, 347
  and Soviet expansionism, 178–179
  "unconditional surrender" in, 452
Wright, Quincy, 76
"Wriston Committee," 58–59

Yalta Conference (1945), 171, 180, 396
Yemen, crisis in, 244
  legislative attitudes toward, 104
Youngstown Company v. *Sawyer* (1952), 52–53
Yugoslavia and Congress, 104

Zionism, 142, 145, 228–229
  See also Arab-Israeli dispute; Palestine